FOURTH EDITION

CRIMINAL PROCEDURE
CONSTITUTION AND SOCIETY

MARVIN ZALMAN, J.D., PH.D.
WAYNE STATE UNIVERSITY

PEARSON
Prentice
Hall

Upper Saddle River, New Jersey 07458

Library of Congress Cataloging-in-Publication Data

Zalman, Marvin.
    Criminal procedure: constitution and society/Marvin Zalman.--4th ed.
      p. cm.
    Includes bibliographical references and index.
    ISBN 0-13-177708-4
     1. Criminal procedure--United States--Cases. 2. Criminal investigation--United
States--Cases. 3. Civil rights--United States--Cases. I. Title.

KF9618.Z35 2004
345.73'05--dc22

                                             2004053377

Executive Editor: Frank Mortimer, Jr.
Associate Editor: Sarah Holle
Production Editor: Heather Stratton Williams, The GTS Companies, Inc.
Production Liaison: Barbara Marttine Cappuccio
Director of Manufacturing and Production: Bruce Johnson
Managing Editor: Mary Carnis
Manufacturing Buyer: Cathleen Petersen
Creative Director: Cheryl Asherman
Cover Design Coordinator: Miguel Ortiz
Cover Designer: Anthony Inciong
Cover Image: James Leynse/Corbis
Marketing Manager: Tim Peyton
Formatting and Interior Design: The GTS Companies, Inc.
Printing and Binding: Courier Westford

Pearson Education Ltd.
Pearson Education Singapore Pte. Ltd.
Pearson Education Canada, Ltd.
Pearson Education—Japan
Pearson Education Australia Pty. Limited
Pearson Education North Asia Ltd.
Pearson Educación de Mexico, S.A. de C.V.
Pearson Education Malaysia Pte. Ltd.

10 9 8 7 6 5 4 3 2 1
ISBN 0-13-177708-4

To Greta

Contents

CHAPTER 11
THE TRIAL PROCESS 388

PREFACE

Criminal procedure is a dramatic subject. Each case tells a story of conflict that pits society's vital need for the communal peace and order that makes life livable, against the right of each individual to be free from unreasonable invasions of privacy and freedom by officers of the state. Criminal procedure is also a technical subject. It encompasses many legal rules and doctrines, not all of which are perfectly logical. The drama of criminal procedure may be conveyed by a book that explores one important case, such as *Gideon's Trumpet,* Anthony Lewis's classic story of Earl Clarence Gideon's fight for the right to counsel, that took his case to the United States Supreme Court. Simply studying dramatic cases, however, limits the student's exposure to many important topics.

The heart of American law lies in the cases of appellate courts. Textbooks about legal subjects present the subject matter either in a casebook format or in a textbook format. Each has its advantages. *Criminal Procedure: Constitution and Society* is an effort to present the best of both methods, with additional features that are uniquely tailored to social science students in criminal justice, criminology, sociology, and political science. The unique features of this text will make the study of criminal procedure a comprehensive educational experience.

This text is designed to do three things: (1) provide essential information about the law of constitutional criminal procedure for students of criminal justice; (2) present Supreme Court cases in a format that is sufficiently substantial so as to provide the benefits of the case-method, while adding study aids that make the cases more comprehensible to undergraduate students; and (3) provide materials that help the student to appreciate criminal procedure in its social, political, and historical contexts.

The basic text. The longest portion of this book presents and explains the core knowledge of constitutional criminal procedure. The topics covered are those of greatest interest to criminal justice students. Four chapters are devoted to the Fourth Amendment: the exclusionary rule (Chapter 2), the search warrant and essential Fourth Amendment doctrines such as plain view (Chapter 3), arrest and *Terry*-stops (Chapter 4), and warrantless searches (Chapter 5). The text is up to date, including discussions of cases decided in early 2004. The chapters are divided into coherent subtopics, giving instructors the flexibility to cover a general area but omit specific topics within it as they see fit.

Throughout the text I attempt to show that in most areas of criminal procedure there is an ongoing dialogue between justices adhering to the Due Process Model and those whose decisions better reflect the Crime Control Model. The late Professor Herbert Packer's great organizing paradigm provides a convenient way for students to grasp the overall subject matter and each case. Thus, both the text and the "Case & Comments" explicate these conflicting approaches.

The purpose of education, of course, is not the rote memorization of rules but *understanding*. To this end the text includes not just statements of rules, but describes the facts out of which the rules emerge and the often conflicting views of the justices. The relevant historic, social, and political factors that have influenced the decision are frequently provided. On occasion, where a subject is overly complex (e.g., the incorporation doctrine in Chapter 1 or the automobile search doctrine in Chapter 5), I help students thread their way through the maze by providing an overview of the subject in the form of a list. I have not, however, avoided presenting students with challenging theoretical materials in this text. For example, Chapter 2 includes materials on theories of the exclusionary rule that present students with recent philosophical discussions about the justification for the rule. Instructors who desire to challenge students are invited to cover this section, but it can be omitted without undermining a student's basic understanding of the topic.

The introductory chapter gives the student a broad picture of the context of constitutional criminal procedure. It presents basic information about law and courts that students may have studied in other courses. Chapter 1 helps a student to see that criminal procedure is not a narrow or technical subject, but a part of a liberal arts education. Criminal procedure can be a gateway to the study of history, politics, political theory, judicial biography, human rights, and important societal currents, for all of these influence criminal procedure.

An appendix to Chapter 1, on reading and briefing cases, is designed to sharpen the student's skills component of the course. Most students find that their reading comprehension and writing skills are improved with the study of law, better preparing them for professional careers in criminal justice.

The Challenge of 9/11/01. America was transformed in many ways on the morning of September 11, 2001. The terror attack on American soil and the two wars that followed in quick succession have had great repercussions for law enforcement and law. In this edition of *Criminal Procedure, Constitution and Society,* I have written entirely new sections for nine of the chapters exploring *order and liberty in a time of terror*. These materials can be helpful in generating class discussions and to sharpen the essential tension between order and liberty. By the time this book is used in classrooms, the legal aspects of the "war on terror" will be in sharper focus, for at the time this preface is written the United States Supreme Court has agreed to decide cases concerning the detention and the processing of American citizens taken into custody for their alleged roles in the terror campaign. The Court's decisions will be historic milestones in the story of liberty. This is a subject that simply has to be confronted by today's criminal justice students.

Case and Comments. A major feature of this book is the "Case & Comments." Reading Supreme Court cases is difficult for first-year law students, let alone undergraduates. The cases selected for the Case & Comments sections are the most important ones that criminal procedure instructors emphasize. They have been carefully edited to provide not just brief snippets of the cases, but a fair amount of the actual reasoning of the justices in their own words. To ensure complete understanding, in most of these cases relevant portions of the dissenting opinions have been added. This helps students to understand the law as a dialectical process.

To help students read and understand the cases, I have added comments identified by bracketed letters keyed to running comments. These critical tools help a student to read the case on his or her own. These comments achieve several goals. They: (1) point out the meaning or importance of technical legal words, (2) highlight disagreements between opposing justices, (3) point out logical weaknesses or clever arguments, (4) ask pointed questions of the students, (5) highlight underlying value judgments in an opinion, and (6) indicate how the case advances or violates the doctrine of *stare decisis*.

Law in Society Sections. These sections at the end of each chapter show the "law in action." Statements of legal rights often convey the idea that they are fully effective. Unfortunately, there is a gap between the ideals of law and the reality of its application. Some sections, such as the accounts of police perjury, racial profiling, and prosecutorial misconduct, show criminal justice personnel at their worst. The unmet promise of equal justice (Chapter 6) shows that our society is not willing to pay for justice for indigents. Of course, most police don't commit perjury, most lawyers and prosecutors competently do their jobs, most judges do not buckle under political pressure, and most persons found guilty of crimes *are* guilty. But this is not always the case. It is important for students to ponder the gap between constitutional ideals and the reality in the courthouse. Several Law in Society sections rely on social science research to indicate the complexity of the criminal process, and that simple statements or beliefs do not capture the full reality of the exclusionary rule, the use of mandatory arrest for domestic violence, or the belief that eyewitnesses who are positive are therefore accurate. In these sections we get to see that innocent people confess to crimes they did not commit despite having been read their *Miranda* warnings, and see the dark side of undercover policing. Information from news sources and from social science research expands our knowledge of the social reality of law and criminal justice.

Law in the States. This text stresses the provisions of the United States Constitution as interpreted by the United States Supreme Court. This is important because the Court took the lead in increasing the importance of criminal procedure via the incorporation of the Bill of Rights in the 1960s. Nevertheless, state courts have also shaped criminal procedure, most notably where they have departed from interpretations of the Supreme Court by granting state citizens greater individual protections. In this text I alerted students to these cross-currents with "Law in the States" boxes that indicate areas of significant divergence between state and federal law.

Supreme Court Justice Biographies. Beginning students often fail to appreciate the extent to which constitutional law is the product of the particular men and women who sit on the nation's highest court. Knowing the predilections of the justices helps students better understand the cases. The brief biographical sketches following each chapter highlight the contribution of the justices to criminal procedure and describes their general approach to the law. One reference is given for each justice so that an interested student can follow up to learn more about the life and work of that justice.

Appendix: Summary Information about Selected Supreme Court Justices. A one-line summary of the typical voting style of each justice is given. Many students have no knowledge about the justices and this "scorecard" information provides a valuable tip about the judge's orientation.

Legal Puzzles. At the conclusion of each chapter, recent cases from lower federal and state courts, covering some of the subjects presented in the chapter, are presented in the form of puzzles. They indicate how the courts apply Supreme Court rulings. The answers to the first puzzle in each chapter are given in the text. Additional answers are provided to instructors in the Instructor's Manual that is made available to them. Working through the puzzles is a very useful way to study and to understand this subject. They may also generate in-class discussions, in part because the solutions to the legal questions by some courts may be unexpected. The puzzles give students insight into the fact that the application of legal precedent is not mechanical, but requires lower courts to do a good deal of weighing and analysis to resolve issues.

Suggested Readings. A few books are listed at the end of each chapter. They allow students to explore the issues in the chapter in greater depth.

Key Terms and Phrases and Glossary. At the beginning of each chapter, students are alerted to key terms and phrases, which are bolded throughout the chapter. Each term is defined in a glossary, which can be used by the instructor as a pedagogic tool. A student who knows these terms will have a good grasp of the content of the text.

Excerpts of the United States Constitution. An appendix includes selected portions of the Constitution. This may be used by the student and instructor as a handy reference, and it may be used as a teaching tool, with certain provisions as required reading.

ACKNOWLEDGMENTS

The preparation of this book has been made much easier and greatly improved thanks to the helpful criticism of colleagues in many institutions, including Robert Lockwood, Portland State University, Portland, Oregon; James Frank, University of Cincinnati, Cincinnati, Ohio; Mathew Lipman, University of Illinois, Chicago, Illinois; and Kay Henriksen, Macmurry College, Springfield, Illinois.

I also owe a great debt to colleagues who reviewed the first and second editions of this text. They include: Andrew C. Blanar, John C. Conway, Jerry Dowling, Micheal Falvo, Zoltan Ferency (deceased), Robert A. Harvie, W. Richard Janikowski, Paul A. Mastriacovo, William Michalek, Andrew A. Mickle, Robert R. Reinertsen, Cliff Roberson, Cathryn Jo Rosen, Martha J. Sullivan, Donald H. Wallace, John T. Whitehead, Wayne L. Wolf, and Benjamin S. Wright. Also, several students were more than helpful in providing research assistance for earlier editions: Joyce Andries, Garth J. Milazzo, and Michael J. Vasich.

The staff at Pearson/Prentice-Hall has been fantastically supportive and helpful at every turn in making a large job move along very smoothly. Many thanks to Sarah Holle, Associate Editor; Heather Stratton Williams, Project Manager; Barbara Cappuccio, Senior Production Editor; Miguel Ortiz, Cover Design Coordinator.

Every writer feels some pangs of guilt for the idea, right or wrong, that time spent with the book meant less time with family. Greta and Amy and Seth should know that this book could not have been written without their sustaining love.

About The Author

Marvin Zalman began his career in criminal justice education in northern Nigeria. He and his wife Greta, then recent graduates of Brooklyn Law School, were inspired in their college years by President John F. Kennedy's challenge to young Americans: "ask not what your country can do for you, ask what you can do for your country." As Peace Corps volunteers from 1967 to 1969 they taught at the Faculty of Law at Ahmadu Bello University, in the city of Zaria. Zalman taught classes on criminal law and criminal procedure, beginning a lifetime of study of these subjects. He authored a casebook on Northern Nigerian criminal procedure and conducted a study of sentencing patterns in local criminal courts. Upon returning to the United States, he began formal studies in a then new field of scholarship, at the School of Criminal Justice at the State University of New York at Albany, from which he holds his Ph.D. degree. From 1971 to 1980 he taught at the School of Criminal Justice at Michigan State University and came to Wayne State University in Detroit, where he served as chair of the Criminal Justice Department from 1980 to 1987 and 2001 to 2003. From 1978 to 1980 Professor Zalman was the executive director of sentencing guideline development projects for the State of Michigan and in 1984 for the State of New York. He has published research and scholarship in the areas of criminal sentencing, criminal procedure, domestic violence, prisoners' rights, assisted suicide, and democracy and criminal justice. He teaches classes on criminal justice policy, criminal law, the judicial process, and criminal procedure. Marvin Zalman believes passionately that constitutional criminal procedure is the most important course that criminal justice students can take because it deals with individual liberty. His parents fled to the safety of America during World War II; he owes his life to the power and decency of the United States, embodied in its constitutional values. The message he wishes to convey is that every day, each police officer, defense lawyer, prosecutor, probation officer, and judge who does his or her job properly keeps the promise of liberty alive.

CHAPTER 1

THE MEANING OF CRIMINAL PROCEDURE

The Constitution of the United States was ordained, it is true, by descendants of Englishmen, who inherited the traditions of English law and history; but it was made for an undefined and expanding future, and for a people gathered and to be gathered from many nations and of many tongues.

—Justice Stanley Matthews, *Hurtado v. California,*
110 U.S. 516, 530–31 (1884)

CHAPTER OUTLINE

KEY TERMS AND PHRASES *(CONTINUES ON NEXT PAGE)*

Affirm

Brief

Burger Court

Case law

Certiorari, writ of

Checks and balances

Common law

Constitutionalism

Court of general jurisdiction

Court of limited jurisdiction

Crime Control Model

Dictum

Due process approach

Due Process Model

Ex post facto law

Federalism

Fundamental rights test

Habeas corpus, writ of

Hierarchy of constitutional rights

Holding

Human rights

Incorporation Doctrine

Incorporation plus

Judicial craftsmanship

Judicial restraint

Judicial review

Jurisdiction

Law

Legal reasoning

Liberty

Opinion

Order

Overrule

Precedent

Private law

Procedural law

Public law	Rule of Law	Stare decisis
Rehnquist Court	Rule application	Substantive law
Remand	Rule making	Supremacy Clause
Remedial law	Selective incorporation	Total incorporation
Reverse	"Shocks the conscience" test	Warren Court

ORDER AND LIBERTY

Criminal procedure is the branch of American constitutional law concerned with the power of the state to maintain an orderly society and the rights of citizens and residents to live in freedom from government interference with their liberty. Criminal procedure is based on the United States Constitution, which went into effect in 1789, and several Amendments to the Constitution. The most important Amendments for this subject are the Fourth, Fifth, Sixth, and Eighth amendments—all part of the Bill of Rights, ratified in 1791—and the Fourteenth Amendment ratified shortly after the Civil War in 1868. Equally important are the decisions of the United States Supreme Court interpreting the brief constitutional text. For the most part, the study of constitutional criminal procedure is the study of the Supreme Court's **opinions.**

Criminal procedure is one of the most important courses in the criminal justice curriculum because it deals directly with the necessary and difficult tension between **order** and **liberty** that is implicated in every area of criminal justice practice. The machinery of criminal justice—police forces, prosecution offices, courts, and correctional agencies—is the formal means by which order is maintained in our society. The system employs two million people and is authorized to use awesome powers against individuals and companies. These include the power to arrest and detain people; to break into homes and offices; to search purses, backpacks, and computer files; and to put people through a bewildering and expensive court process. If the process results in a criminal conviction, the state is authorized to execute, imprison, and fine defendants, and to control the lives of offenders placed on probation and parole in ways that are inconsistent with individual liberty.

The need for this system of monumental powers is obvious. Levels of crime are high in the United States.[1] Every year violent crime takes the lives and destroys the safety of tens of thousands, while property and white-collar crimes deprive millions of honest persons of their wealth and their sense of security. Without effective means of crime control, the lives of many more would be at risk, undermining the normal functioning of society. Widespread riots have become rare in the United States and real anarchy has never been a feature of American life. Recently, the persistent and widespread looting in Iraq that followed the U.S.-led invasion and overthrow of the Saddam Hussein regime in April 2003 has given Americans a glimpse into societal breakdown and the effects of virtually total lawlessness.[2] A society without order does not enjoy liberty—it endures license.

The obverse side of the coin is the repressive "order" of tyranny. The hideous dictatorship of Saddam Hussein's Iraq benefitted some classes of society at the expense of a brutal repression that "apparently killed its citizens on a huge scale, both systematically and indiscriminately. Human rights groups . . . estimate that nearly 300,000 Iraqis are missing and were probably executed. Tens of thousands more, according to Iraqi opposition groups, may have been imprisoned and tortured, their lives warped forever by what they saw and experienced."[3] Nothing close to this characterizes abuses that do, unfortunately, occur in the American criminal justice system. In every society, however, there is an ongoing need to curb the dangers of corruption, abuse of power, and the excessive use of force that inevitably arise when criminal justice powers are placed in the hands of human beings.

What is required, in short, is a *balance* between the order of legitimate state power and the liberty from state control that is the cherished right of all Americans. Nowhere is this balance more important and more difficult to achieve than in the criminal justice process. The law of criminal procedure is essential for maintaining ordered liberty.

The Two Models of Criminal Justice

A classic exposition of the tension between order and liberty in the context of constitutional criminal procedure is Herbert Packer's "two models of the criminal process."[4] Rather than using the terminology of political theory—"liberty" and "order"—Prof. Packer examined the competing values that underlie our constitutional order through two "models." A model is not itself reality, but an *abstraction* of reality that allows us to better understand the practices and rules of criminal procedure. Packer calls these the **Due Process Model** and the **Crime Control Model.** He warns that one is not "good" and the other "bad": both models embrace constitutional values that are necessary to the kind of society in which we wish to live.

It is important to note that people who lean toward one model or the other *share* many similar values. Police and prosecutors, who tend to favor the Crime Control Model, support many constitutional protections, including the rule that a person can only be prosecuted for a violation of a law that is "on the books." To allow the police to arrest someone for "bad" behavior that is not a violation of law, and then have the courts or legislature "create" a crime tailored to those "bad" acts—to prosecute a person for behavior that violated no law when committed—violates the prohibition against **ex post facto laws** that the Constitution places on both the state and federal governments (U.S. Const. art. I. §9, ¶3 and §10, ¶1). Police may be tempted to wish for the ability to arrest people for whatever they think is bad behavior, but they must realize that a state that gave them such powers would be a dictatorship in which they would not themselves be safe. Another norm shared by proponents of both models is that police and prosecutors have a duty to enforce the criminal law when they have notice of criminal violations. A third shared understanding "is the assumption that there are limits to the powers of government to investigate and apprehend persons suspected of committing crimes." Finally, there is a shared belief "that the alleged criminal is not merely an object to be acted upon, but an independent entity" who deserves his or her day in court and may demand a trial and other procedural safeguards. This last assumption of the adversary system is central to the Due Process Model and is de-emphasized but not entirely eliminated by the Crime Control Model.

The Crime Control Model emphasizes that "the *repression of criminal conduct* is by far the most important function to be performed by the criminal process" because public safety is essential to personal freedom. To be effective the criminal justice system must *efficiently* process those who have been lawfully apprehended. There is a premium on speed and finality. *Speed* "depends on informality and uniformity" (e.g., plea bargaining); "*finality* depends on minimizing the occasional challenge" (e.g., limiting the right to appeal). The administrative and routine functioning of criminal justice is stressed, almost viewing the system as a conveyor belt. An attitude (not a legal rule) of Crime Control Model supporters is a *"presumption of guilt"*—an assumption that police and prosecutors are accurate in their decisions to arrest and apprehend suspects. Because of this attitude of confidence that the investigative process has identified the right person, the remaining steps in the process (e.g., trial) can be relatively perfunctory, and any restrictions on the investigative stages are to be resisted.

"If the Crime Control Model resembles an assembly line, the Due Process Model looks very much like an obstacle course." Although it values the repression of crime, it does not assume that police fact-finding is accurate. Indeed, it assumes that the criminal justice system is *error-prone*. Because of this, there is an "insistence on *formal, adjudicative, adversary* fact-finding processes in which the factual case against the accused is publicly heard by an impartial tribunal and is evaluated only after the accused has had a full opportunity to discredit the case against him." Even after a full trial, the fear of an erroneous conviction generates a desire for many avenues of *appeal*. "The demand for finality is thus very low in the Due Process Model." This model demands the "prevention and *elimination of mistakes* to the extent possible; the Crime Control Model accepts the probability of mistakes up to the level at which they interfere with the goal of repressing crime." For the Due Process Model, the "aim of the process is at least as much to protect the factually innocent as it is to convict the factually guilty." The Due Process Model is highly suspicious of those who wield power and is ideologically driven by the "primacy of the individual and the complementary concept of *limitation on official power.* The Due Process Model insists on *legal guilt,* whereas the Crime Control Model stresses *factual*

guilt. The concept of legal guilt pervades the formal legal and trial process; no matter how "factually" guilty a person, there can be no conviction and punishment unless a court has **jurisdiction,** unless the prosecution occurs within the period of the statute of limitations, unless the offender is lawfully responsible (e.g., not insane). At this point, the "quixotic" *presumption of innocence* rises to the fore. The presumption is *not* the opposite of the "presumption of guilt," but is a normative principle that insists that the defendant be treated *as if* he or she were innocent, no matter how apparent the factual guilt. To this end, the prosecutor must prove a case beyond a *reasonable doubt* and the jury verdict must be unanimous. Important attributes of the Due Process Model include the emphasis on *equality of treatment* of all suspects and the strong belief that errors in the process invalidate convictions. The Crime Control Model strenuously disagrees with this last point, and it is over this point that many disputes arise in constitutional criminal procedure.

Order and Liberty in a Time of Terror

The September 11, 2001, suicide-terror attacks on New York's World Trade Center and the Pentagon took almost three thousand lives—more than were killed in the Japanese attack at Pearl Harbor in 1941. The United States and democratic nations were put on notice that a radical Islamist group with a worldwide network of supporters and operatives was determined to counter the reach of the global economy and the influence of Western culture and values. The 9/11 assault was preceded by a decade of attacks, including the 1993 World Trade Center bombing, the 1988 deadly bombings of American embassies in Kenya and Tanzania, and the killing of seventeen sailors aboard the destroyer U.S.S. *Cole* while moored in Yemen. The United States clearly faced the threat of sustained terror attacks, possibly with nuclear devices or other weapons of mass destruction.

The United States and its allies responded vigorously. A military campaign in Afghanistan wrested that country from Taliban control and suppressed the Al Qaeda movement and its leader, Osama bin Laden. In 2003 the United States led another war that ousted the Saddam Hussein regime in Iraq. These controversial and continuing campaigns are beyond the scope of this text. What is relevant is that the nation's criminal justice apparatus is in the forefront of the fight against terrorism. The United States and its allies are engaged in a full court press to investigate and break up terrorist cells. By the end of 2002, "nearly 3,000 suspected al Qaeda members and their supporters have been detained worldwide."[5] After an initial roundup of twelve hundred people in the United States, almost all of whom were entirely innocent of any connection to terrorism, the government has settled into a long-range strategy of monitoring suspected groups, deep intelligence gathering, and arrests of more dangerous terrorists.[6]

There is a danger that laws passed and acts taken in this vital struggle against terrorism threaten basic civil liberties. This risk, unfortunately, has many historical precedents.

- The undeclared naval war by Britain and France on the fledgling United States in the 1790s led President John Adams's Federalist-controlled Congress to pass the "Alien and Sedition Laws"—clear violations of the First Amendment. Prosecutions under the law, soon after repealed, were politically motivated.[7]

- President Lincoln suspended the writ of habeas corpus in thousands of cases during the Civil War. Although historians have granted the necessity and even the restraint of these acts, the Supreme Court repudiated this unilateral presidential power after the war ended.[8]

- A World War I sedition law criminalized criticism of the military draft. Prosecutions under the law stifled political speech. In reaction, the American Civil Liberties Union (ACLU) was formed and in a series of landmark cases, the Supreme Court strengthened First Amendment freedoms and limited attempts by all levels of government to stifle unpopular political expression. Fear of bolsheviks in the postwar turmoil, a deadly Wall Street bombing, and assassination threats in 1919 led to the "Palmer Raids"—roundups of thousands of people around the country, mostly leftist or pro-labor, organized by J. Edgar Hoover under the authority of Attorney General A. Mitchell Palmer.[9]

- A tragic overreaction to the Pearl Harbor attack led to the interning of more than a hundred thousand Japanese Americans for the duration of World War II, a move upheld by the Supreme Court.[10]

- President Roosevelt authorized national security wiretapping and eavesdropping on his authority, a necessary action that led to later abuses and controls. Roosevelt also established a military commission to try German saboteurs. This, too, was lawful but has created a dangerous precedent that was later curbed by the Foreign Intelligence Surveillance Act (FISA).[11]

- During the Korean War, President Truman nationalized the steel industry in order to break a strike that threatened war production. The Supreme Court swiftly ruled that this was an unconstitutional extension of the president's war powers.[12]

- The longest and most severe threat to civil liberty was the rise of the "national security state" for at least half of the twentieth century in an effort to thwart the real threat of communism. The threat of fascism, Naziism, and expansionist Soviet communism under Stalin was the supreme challenge to all Western democracies from the 1930s to the defeat of the fascist axis in 1945 and the ultimate fall of state communism in 1989. But in the long struggle to contain communist expansion around the globe, politics and justice in the United States became warped by political trials, the rise of loyalty oaths, the witch hunts of Sen. Joseph McCarthy (which missed real Soviet spies), blacklisting of artists, local police department "red squad" snooping on people, CIA spying on Americans within the country, wiretaps on Martin Luther King, Jr., and a climate of political fear that equated a belief in racial equality or other liberal opinions with communism by the FBI.[13]

After emergency periods passed, repressive laws have been repealed or declared unconstitutional, and curbs have been placed on excessive law enforcement behavior. Yet there exists concern that the lessons of past excesses will not be heeded in the present crisis, and fear that overreactions may find a permanent place in law and in criminal justice practice.

Will the present war on terrorism lead to similar violations of civil liberties? On the positive side, proactive criminal investigation in many countries have since resulted in many arrests of Al Qaeda operatives.[14] The normal process of prosecution and trial has led to several convictions of those who have plotted deadly and destabilizing attacks. President Bush, in the days after the 9/11 attacks, was outspoken in distinguishing between extremists and the mass of law-abiding Islamic people, and the courts have not been as submissive to the government's maneuvers as in past crises. Nevertheless, the federal government has expanded its authorized powers under the USA PATRIOT Act and the Justice Department has sought novel powers that pose real threats to the liberties of Americans, including prolonged detention without access to courts, undermining the ability of lawyers to represent clients, not allowing criminal defendants access to favorable witnesses, and a willingness to sidestep the courts by employing military tribunals.[15,16] These relevant and timely issues will be raised in the following chapters to allow students to ponder the greatest challenges of order and liberty confronting the United States today.

Thinking about criminal justice in a time of terror means confronting an entirely different paradigm from that on which the system of civilian justice rests. The "criminal model" that has emerged over the centuries is one of constitutional balance. Gone are the days when autocratic kings such as Henry VIII could compel the highest judges in the land to bring about any judgment of guilt he desired and the "legal execution" of those who opposed him. Painstakingly, after great struggle, our criminal justice system has learned that prosecutors can be mistaken, misguided, corrupt, or guided by political advancement; that judges can be partisans instead of neutral arbiters; and that the police can be used by the state for improper ends. As a result, a host of checks and balances have been built into an evolving system designed to ensure accuracy, fairness, and justice. The critical details of this system include trial by jury and all of the attendant jury rights guaranteed by the Sixth Amendment, bail, the assistance of counsel, judicial warrants, and the like. In the background lies a democratic government in which opposing views can be advanced without fear of reprisals by those in power, a free press to expose wrongs, and a citizenry that will act against threats to their liberties. The essence of the "criminal model" then, is that the people are trusted to go about their business without state interference, and their liberty is forfeited only after the state has good reason to believe a crime has been committed. The price of liberty undoubtedly is that it gives some people the space to engage in crime that an autocratic state, such as the late Soviet Union, was able to stifle.

When a country goes to war, all of this changes. The model is no longer the prosecution of past crimes. The essence of the "war model" is *prevention*.[17] Attorney General John Ashcroft's "new 'paradigm of prevention' has led prosecutors to use every tool at their disposal to investigate, observe and detain potential terrorists before they strike."[18] If the price of liberty is another 9/11 type of attack, the cost may be too high. In time of war, civil liberties are curtailed. The press is more circumspect; military censorship is necessary; certain areas are off limits; freedom of movement is curtailed; intelligence agencies are given a freer hand to probe into the secrets of anyone. Two risks to civil liberties arise out of war situations: first, that under the guise of emergency, powers concentrated into the hands of government agents are misused, and second, that when the emergency ends, liberties formerly enjoyed are permanently eroded. The Alien and Sedition Acts, clear violations of the First Amendment, were repealed after Jefferson and his party came to power in 1800, even as the threat of war hung over the nation for another dozen years. The grip of cold war surveillance and controls, in contrast, stayed in place, often warping domestic politics, until in the 1970s the Watergate affair exposed just how malignant these powers had become. The limits on intelligence operations established in the mid-1970s have perhaps not kept pace with the new threats to world order that emerged after the end of a bipolar balance of power. An invigorated effort to spy on, arrest, and prosecute would-be terrorists has occurred and is necessary. But as many have said, if this is done at the cost of fundamental rights and liberties, then the terrorists will have won.

In this text different aspects of the balance of civil liberties and effective law enforcement "in a time of terror" are briefly discussed in subsequent chapters. The sections are relevant to the subject matter of the chapter and are meant only to provide some basic information and raise questions. This is not the place for a systematic or exhaustive review of these questions. Nevertheless, the impact of the war on terror is the most critical issue confronting criminal justice today. It is a subject in which the rules of constitutional criminal procedure occupy a central place. It is something that we have to think about.

Sections on criminal justice in a time of terror are found in chapters 2 through 7, 10 and 11.

The Dangers of Injustice

Every case that reaches the Supreme Court involves not only questions of law, state power, and the political relationship between the individual and the state, but also questions of justice and injustice. The student should not forget, while grappling with concepts and cases, that each case involves a fight for justice. This is not to say that every defendant has a good case, and it would be unwise to romanticize defendants. As Justice Frankfurter said, "It is a fair summary of history to say that the safeguards of liberty have frequently been forged in controversies involving not very nice people."[19] On the other hand, defendants in several famous cases, like the "Scottsboro boys"

or Earl Clarence Gideon or Dr. Sam Sheppard, were innocent of the crimes for which they were convicted.[20] In any event, it is important to keep in mind that rights are fundamental and cannot be reserved for "actually innocent" defendants if not made available to all.

Every chapter details abuses of power and errors in the justice system. Many of the "Law in Society" sections focus on the negative—on errors, abuses, and even crimes committed by criminal justice officials. It should go without saying that for the most part police officers, prosecutors, defense attorneys, and judges act competently and professionally and often perform their work courageously or selflessly. Nevertheless, the burden of this branch of law is to unflinchingly confront the negligent and malignant aspects of criminal justice.

The text focuses heavily on the police practices portion of criminal procedure and so devotes a fair amount of space to police-generated injustices. The kinds of police abuse of concern in criminal procedure focus on abuses of power that undermine the constitutional rights of defendants. Thus, the significant problem of police brutality is not a significant concern. On the other hand, police perjury can destroy a defendant's reliance on Fourth Amendment rights and make a whole category of rights a nullity. When police play end-run games around the *Miranda* rules, they overrule the Supreme Court's rulings by their practices. Overzealous police, not intending to do so, have gulled some defendants into giving false confessions. Errors or falsehoods in the writing of search warrant affidavits undermine the privacy and security of citizens. Sloppy police work has made worse the underlying problems of mistaken eyewitness identification, leading to the conviction of innocent persons. The blue wall of silence makes it even more difficult to set criminal justice practice on a course of professionalism.

It is not just police misconduct that casts doubts on whether the criminal justice system lives up to its constitutional ideals. Prosecutorial misconduct occurs with regularity and can negate the very rationale of the adversary system. The same effect is produced by inadequate, poorly prepared, and overworked defense lawyers. The history of American justice is replete with trials that were mockeries, with judges unable or unwilling to conduct the proceedings to guarantee fairness.[21] It is not only famous or political trials, or trials of African American defendants in the Jim Crow era that have produced unfairness. Judges have to be continuously vigilant to ensure the evenhandedness of trials.

A counterpoint to this concern is the fact that our justice system is set up to correct injustices. This is done by appeals in criminal cases and by civil suits. Judges have total immunity against civil suits for acts performed in the course of their duty, and prosecutors have qualified immunity. Police are most likely to face the challenge of civil lawsuits. The existence of incompetence and injustices by a minority of criminal justice practitioners opens the door wider to appeals and civil lawsuits against all officers. In the last analysis, competent and honest police officers, lawyers, and judges should be as eager to eradicate instances of injustice as are defendants.

One lesson of the long struggle to ensure the **Rule of Law** and a civilized justice system is that it is vital that those who are ultimately proven to be guilty be treated fairly. An unfair system leads to the conviction of the innocent. The conviction of "actually innocent" persons has been a concern of the common law justice system since the Middle Ages as reflected in the ancient maxim, "better twenty guilty go free than one innocent convicted." The maxim finds concrete support in the high level of evidence needed to convict: proof beyond a reasonable doubt. The large number of wrongful convictions that have been announced with regularity since DNA testing became feasible in the early 1990s brings home the inadequacies of criminal procedure law to prevent injustice.

The Innocence Project has confirmed 131 wrongfully convicted persons as of August 2003.[22] The causes include mistaken eyewitnesses' identifications, police assuming that a first lead is the correct perpetrator, identification procedures that transfer the victims' memories of the criminals to innocent persons, interrogations that elicit false confessions, mass hysteria for convictions in high-profile cases, jailhouse snitches who lie to get favorable treatment, overzealous prosecutors, forensic investigators who are incompetent or who fabricate evidence, "junk science" like overreliance on hair evidence, incompetent defense lawyers, and legal and constitutional rules that act as roadblocks to getting to the truth.[23]

The world of criminal justice is just beginning to absorb the complex of problems that produce wrongful convictions. The issue is not simply one of cleaning up a few old, bad cases. The process of investigation, prosecution, and trial inevitably generates errors. "In 2002, Dwight E. Adams, director of the FBI Laboratory, disclosed that since his agency began using DNA testing in 1988, about 25 percent to 30 percent of the individuals suspected of committing crimes have been cleared through DNA technology."[24] The job for the next generation of leaders in criminal justice from police chiefs to the Chief Justice of the United States is to work to modify and improve the functioning and structure of criminal justice and where needed to change the rules of constitutional criminal procedure to promote a system that is more fair.

THE CONTEXT OF CRIMINAL PROCEDURE

Criminal procedure can be taught as a self-contained unit by studying only its primary legal sources, that is, relevant Supreme Court cases and statutes and court rules. The bulk of this text does focus on these primary sources. It is also true that the more a student knows about closely related subjects, the better that student's deeper understanding of criminal procedure will be. Most teachers of upper-division or graduate criminal procedure courses assume that students have taken courses in criminal justice and an introduction to American government. We assume that students have a basic understanding of American history, values, and society, including an appreciation of race relations. Knowledge of these factors help the student to understand why the cases are important and what impact they are likely to have on criminal justice practice

and American society. On the other hand, instructors cannot assume that students will have any academic grounding in English or American constitutional and legal history, advanced political theory, or human rights. Yet these areas of study also enhance an understanding of criminal procedure. This section briefly discusses these other areas of knowledge and, without going into great detail, explains why they are important to understanding criminal procedure. A few themes that are central to understanding criminal procedure are treated in greater detail in this chapter and are interlaced with cases in the body of the text.

The Criminal Justice System

The criminal justice system is mainly a part of government, although some private or quasi-private persons play important roles, including jurors, bail bondsmen, and private defense lawyers. The major agencies of criminal justice—police, prosecution, and corrections—are parts of the executive branch. The judicial branch of government, which adjudicates civil and criminal cases, plays a critical role in criminal justice. Although legislatures are not typically thought of as part of "the system," they play central roles in formulating the criminal law, prescribing sentences and sentencing structures, and in providing budgets for the primary agencies of criminal justice.

A solid understanding of criminal justice practices allows a better appreciation of the place of criminal procedure. For example, knowing that police officers have a good amount of discretion and often are not minutely supervised by superiors helps us to understand how some facts get into court. The sociology of police behavior during their law enforcement activity (e.g., arrest, automobile stops) is useful in understanding the limits of legal rules in shaping police behavior.

The law of criminal procedure covers six major areas of criminal justice practice that encompasses the work of police, prosecutor, trial judges, and appellate courts. These are (1) *Police* investigation, interrogation, search, and arrest; (2) *Pretrial process*, including the decision to grant bail, grand jury and preliminary examination screening of charges, and pretrial motions; (3) *Formal charging* by the prosecutor; (4) *Adjudication*, the determination of guilt or innocence by a jury or a bench trial or by the plea negotiation process; (5) *Sentencing*, imposing punishment on the convicted, a judicial decision in which probation officers, prosecutors, defense attorneys, and in some instances victims play roles; and (6) *Appellate review* by higher courts.[25] This book concentrates on the first stage of the criminal process—police activities that touch on individuals' rights and liberties—and also includes materials on the pretrial process, charging, and adjudication. Sentencing and correctional law, including prisoners' rights, are distinct areas of law not covered in this text. The last stage of the criminal process, appellate review, is where most of the constitutional rights of suspects are formed. This text excludes the kinds of technical appellate issues that are studied in law school and emphasizes the substance of Supreme Court cases that shape constitutional criminal procedure.

The Court System

In the American constitutional framework courts of law constitute a separate branch of government. They exist not only to decide legal disputes but also to provide **checks and balances** against the risks that the "political branches" of government—the executive and legislative branches—will violate the rights of individuals for improper political or corrupt purposes.

Courts are hierarchical, that is they are ranked by authority into trial and appellate courts. The basic function of trial courts is **rule application**—deciding individual cases in accord with the law. Trial courts do this by deciding issues of fact and resolving issues of law that apply to a case. Trial courts also foster civil settlements and pleas in criminal cases. In many states there are different levels of trial courts. Lower-tier courts are **courts of limited jurisdiction** (often called district or municipal courts) and decide misdemeanor cases and oversee the pretrial stages of felony cases. Felony cases are decided in trial **courts of general jurisdiction** (titled "superior courts" in most states, but also known as circuit or district courts). Trial judges can oversee juries, which decide issues of fact, under rules of law and evidence specified by the judge. Juries, incidentally, are not part of the judicial branch but are "the people." If a jury trial is waived, a judge sits as a trier of facts and law.

Appellate courts are "above" (or "superior to") trial courts in the court hierarchy. The basic function of appellate courts is **rule making**—making law (legal precedents) by a process of legal interpretation. Every state and the United States have supreme courts which are the final arbiters of issues of law that may be appealed by losing parties in civil lawsuits or criminal cases. Most states and the United States also have instituted intermediate courts of appeal, which became necessary as the volume of legal appeals grew too large to be handled by supreme courts. Issues of fact are not appealable. The major part of this text concentrates on constitutional rule making by the United States Supreme Court.

A basic understanding of the terminology and process of appeals courts is helpful for understanding criminal procedure. A party who loses a case in the trial court may have a right to appeal or may have to seek permission from the courts to appeal. In either case, the party has to initiate an appeal by asserting that his or her *legal* rights were violated during the trial. The violation may be based on the incorrect application or interpretation of the substantive law in the case; an error involving the law of evidence; or as is often the case in criminal procedure, a violation of rights based on errors committed by the police. Parties cannot (with rare exceptions) argue that the facts were incorrectly decided. Juries or trial judges who actually saw witnesses testify are in a better position than appellate judges to decide "what happened." Appellate courts assume that the facts decided during the trial are the facts of the case. Unlike trials, in which witnesses are sworn in and testify, appellate courts decide cases based only on legal arguments presented by lawyers. The arguments are always presented in formal written essays called **briefs** and may or may not also be presented in relatively short oral arguments before the court.

> The appeal begins when the party losing the case in the trial court, the "appellant," files a notice of appeal, usually a month or two after the trial court decision. Then within a few months the appellant files the trial court record in the appellate court. The record, often bulky, consists of the papers filed in the trial court along with a transcript of the trial testimony. Next the appellant and the opposing party, the "appellee," file briefs that argue for their respective positions. The briefs are usually followed by short oral presentations to the judge. Finally, the judges decide the case and issue a written opinion.[26]

Virtually all appeals to the United States Supreme Court are discretionary; that is, the Supreme Court only hears those cases that it wishes to decide. The appellate process in the Supreme Court is taken under a writ with a Latin title that goes back to English procedure: a **writ of certiorari.** Appellants in Supreme Court cases are known as "petitioners" and appellees are called "respondents."

Appellate courts issue very specific decisions in an appeal, in reference to the decision in the *last* court from which an appeal was taken. For example, before a case reaches the United States Supreme Court there may have been a trial verdict, an appeal in the state court of appeals, a decision of the state supreme court, a decision by a federal district court on a federal **writ of habeas corpus,** followed by a decision by a federal court of appeals. In such a case, the Supreme Court will **affirm** or **reverse** the decision of the federal court of appeals, "below." If there are several legals issues, the Supreme Court may affirm in part and reverse in part. The Supreme Court does not engage in applying its decision directly to the parties. Instead, it usually **remands,** or sends the case file back to the lower court, to handle the details of applying its decision. An appellate court can **overrule** its *own prior precedent* when it finds that one of its prior decisions was incorrect or unsound and replace it with a different ruling.

Although the Supreme Court decision (e.g., "judgment below affirmed") is exceedingly terse, the really important part of the case is the Court's *opinion*, which is often a lengthy essay, written for the benefit of lawyers and judges in a formal style, that purports to explain the reasons behind the Court's decision. We study these opinions to understand the reasoning process.

Law

A beginning student must grasp that there are several "sources," or types, of law and that these sources of law exist in a hierarchical order. A statute or a court's decision is typically referred to as "law," but is also called a "source" of law, to convey the idea that law is not only the words of the rule issued by the state, but the result of those words, or their effects that are *enforced* by the government. As commonly understood, **law** is a body of written rules issued by a legitimate government authority designed to guide and control the action of individuals and institutions. In the United States there are different forms of law, each of which are enforceable by the government. The most important forms of law are statutes or legislation and rules created by appellate courts, called "**case law**" or "**common law**." (This term will be further explained in the section on History). Both legislation and case law are legitimate sources of law and both are enforceable by governmental officers. A constitution, either of a state of the union or of the United States, is a special form of statute that has been ratified not by an ordinary session of the legislature, but by a special ratifying convention or process, so that it represents the will of the entire people. Other forms of law include the executive orders of the president or state governors, the regulations of administrative agencies, ordinances passed by local units of government, and court rules designed to guide the detailed procedures of the courts.

These sources of law stand in hierarchical relationship, and their relationship depends on the relative authority of the agency that issues the law. Let us begin with case law. Our system of law has inherited the English common law tradition that *courts* are part of the governing structure and the rules of **precedent** that constitute case law are rules of law binding on those subject to the authority of the state. This arose because earlier in England, judges were high officials of the king and spoke for him. However, America enjoys a republican form of government, in which the people, not a king, are sovereign. In our representative government, sovereign power of the people is delegated to elected representatives. Because of this, legislation, duly passed by a majority of the legislature under its established rules and signed by the president or a state governor, is a "higher" form of law than case law because it derives its legitimacy from a source that more directly represents the will of the sovereign people. In consequence, a legislature can pass a statute that modifies or abolishes a rule of common law. A common example is that many legislatures have passed no-fault insurance laws, to replace the common law rules that established liability for persons who caused injuries by negligence. In the United States virtually all states have replaced older "common law crimes" with crimes specifically defined by legislation.

An important qualification to the ability of a legislature to revise case law arises in constitutional law. The Constitution was ratified by "the people of the United States" and cannot be changed by ordinary legislation. The United States Constitution can be formally ratified only by procedures specified in Article V—by a proposed amendment passed by two-thirds of the House of Representatives and two-thirds of the Senate (or by a convention called by two-thirds of the state legislatures), and ratified by three-fourths of the state legislatures. Direct constitutional amendments are rare; only twenty-seven have been ratified. On the other hand, the meaning of a constitutional provision is fixed by a decision of the United States Supreme Court. Thousands of specific rules of constitutional law—created by the Supreme Court—are deemed to be parts of the Constitution and cannot be overruled by legislation. For example, in 1968 Congress passed a law supposedly overrul-

ing the mandatory effect of the famous ruling in *Miranda v. Arizona* (1966) that requires that persons be informed of their constitutional, Fifth Amendment right to silence, if any confessions they make under custodial interrogation can be admissible in a court. In 2000 the Supreme Court ruled that such a law was unconstitutional: "We hold that *Miranda*, being a constitutional decision of this Court, may not be in effect overruled by an Act of Congress, and we decline to overrule *Miranda* ourselves" (*Dickerson v. U.S.*, 2000). It is obvious, then, that the Supreme Court has enormous power to determine the meaning and content of constitutional law and thus to impose rules of conduct on police, prosecutors, judges, and other officials.

It is also helpful for the student to understand that law is classified in a variety of ways. For example, **private law** concerns private disputes and the rights of private individuals, groups, and corporations, while **public law** involves governmental power and disputes between governmental departments, or between private persons or groups and government agencies. Law is also classified by its specific *subject matter*. Private law includes such subjects as contracts, property, torts (the law of injuries), commercial law, copyright, civil procedure, and the like. Public law subject matter includes constitutional law, administrative law, and tax law, as well as substantive criminal law and criminal procedure. Law is also classified by three *functions*. **Substantive law** establishes and defines rights, powers, and obligations. Major areas of substantive law, for example, establish contractual obligations, property rights, and the freedom from being intentionally or negligently harmed. Substantive criminal law defines crimes such as homicide and theft and defenses such as insanity. **Procedural law** prescribes methods of enforcing substantive rights that are breached and includes rules of jurisdiction, the serving of legal process (e.g., a summons), and rules that guide the conduct of a trial. **Remedial law** determines the actual benefits or "remedies" obtained by a successful party to a lawsuit. *Civil remedies* include (i) *legal remedies*, or *money damages* to compensate loss and may also include punitive damages, and (ii) *equitable remedies*, i.e., *injunctions* or specific performance to remedy a violation of rights. Criminal law "remedies" are the lawful punishments that may be inflicted on convicted criminals.[27]

Let us now classify constitutional criminal procedure. It is, first, an important branch of public law because it regulates the relationship between the individual and the state. Its subject matter is that of constitutional law with a focus on such constitutional rules as the right to trial (U.S. Const. art. III; Sixth Amendment), arrest and search and seizure (U.S. Const. Fourth Amendment); and the privilege against self-incrimination (U.S. Const. Fifth Amendment). By its title, criminal procedure would appear to be procedural law. However, this is not so simple a matter. Many rules of criminal procedure, especially rules created by statute and court rules, are genuine procedural rules that help to *facilitate* the prosecution of a criminal investigation and prosecution. On the other hand, as the Supreme Court has come to rule that certain actions by police, prosecutors and judges have violated the rights of suspects, it has built up a body of rules that grant rights and protections to people who are subject to the state's authority in the enforcement of criminal law. In this way, then, criminal procedure can also be classified as an area of substantive law. If this is so, what remedies exist for violations of the rights of suspects and defendants? Under some circumstances, individuals can bring civil suits against state officers and win money damages for violations of their rights. An important attribute of criminal procedure has been the creation of *exclusionary rules* by the courts. Such rules disallow the use of illegally obtained evidence. The Fourth Amendment exclusionary rule is an important and controversial topic and an entire chapter is devoted to it (Chapter 2).

Federalism

A police officer makes a lawful arrest. Under which law does the officer operate? In a unitary nation (e.g., France, England) the answer is that the arrest is made under the laws of the nation. The United States, however, is a federated nation (as are, for example, Canada, Germany, and Mexico) with a *national* government (i.e., the government of the United States or the "federal government") and *state* governments. To answer the question, an officer making a lawful arrest in Augusta, Maine, or Des Moines, Iowa, must comply with the law of both Maine or Iowa, respectively, and applicable law of the United States.

This complicated arrangement is the result of **federalism,** which is the legal and power relationship between the national government on the one hand and the state governments on the other. Federalism is an important topic in criminal procedure because up until the mid–twentieth century, state and local criminal justice officials were guided exclusively by state law. In the twentieth century the Supreme Court began to apply provisions of the Bill of Rights to state officials, and this movement in a real sense created modern constitutional criminal procedure. The story of how this happened and its effects are detailed below in the section on the **Incorporation Doctrine.** This section provides a brief foundation for understanding incorporation.

The framers of the Constitution understood that some level of friction (as well as cooperation) would exist between two levels of governments, and between the states. They provided rules in the Constitution to create a nation in which the limited sovereignty of the states would be respected but in which the federal government would have certain exclusive powers. Foreign affairs and the war-making power are the most obvious examples of exclusive federal authority.[28] The Constitution also established numerous rules that would ensure a unified nation rather than competing states. These include a federally controlled postal system, federal oversight of interstate and foreign commerce, forbidding states from giving favorable treatment to their own citizens over the residents of other states, requiring one state to appropriately apply the laws or court judgments of another state ("full faith and credit"), requiring a state to extradite felons to the state from which the

person fled, federal control over territories, and the like.[29] Finally, the Constitution includes rules that require the governments of the United States and the states to adhere to a political philosophy of liberal republicanism. The preamble to the Constitution emphasizes that one of the six major purposes of American government is to "secure the Blessings of Liberty to ourselves and our Posterity." The national government guarantees to every state a "republican form of government"—in Abraham Lincoln's words, a "government of the people, by the people, for the people."[30] The states and the federal government are prohibited from passing ex post facto laws or bills of attainder that could undermine political liberty, or create "titles of Nobility" that could create a class of Americans other than citizens.[31]

To understand how federalism works in the criminal procedure context, we review a few basic facts and principles, followed by a focused review of jurisdiction, the supremacy clause, and the special role of the United States Supreme Court. Each state is a limited sovereign within the national framework. Each has a constitution that establishes a "republican form of government" and the structures of state governments are quite similar, including a chief executive or governor, a legislature, and a state court system with a supreme court and trial courts. With some variations, the legal systems of each state are comparable and parallel to the federal legal system. Each state legislature makes laws for the benefit of its people and each has its own bill of rights to guarantee the rights of its citizens and residents.

American federalism recognizes areas of exclusive federal control, areas of exclusive state action, and many areas where both federal and state laws and executive branch agencies can work together. In the enforcement of criminal law, for example, in the past forty years Congress has passed criminal laws that overlap substantially with state criminal laws, allowing either federal or state law enforcement agencies to investigate and either state or federal courts to try cases under their respective laws.[32]

JURISDICTION For our purposes, jurisdiction is the lawful authority of a government to exercise its powers and the authority of a court to decide cases brought before it. States are not administrative arms or subdivisions of the national government, but states do come under the Constitution in specific ways.[33] Every government officer, state and federal, swears to uphold the United States Constitution.[34] Despite this, the United States government, which was directly established by the Constitution, is in some ways a government of limited powers. In the legislative realm, state legislatures have *plenary*, or general, powers to pass laws for the good of their residents while the United States Congress can pass only laws that come under the provisions of Article I, Section 8.

Courts can decide cases only if they have lawful jurisdiction to do so. State courts derive their jurisdiction from state constitutions and statutes and federal court jurisdiction is conferred by the United States Constitution and by statutes of Congress. The Constitution and federal statutes grant jurisdiction to the Supreme Court and to any federal courts created by Congress *only* over *federal questions*: issues of law that arise under the United States Constitution, federal legislation, or treaties made by the United States and a foreign nation. As a result, the Supreme Court can review almost all decisions of lower federal courts.[35] On the other hand, the Supreme Court has *no* jurisdiction over matters of state law. Cases based *exclusively* on provisions of state constitutions, state legislation, or rules of state common law can be decided only by the courts of the state. In other words, the United States Supreme Court can review a case from the highest tribunal of a state *only* if it concerns a *federal* question.

In the area of constitutional criminal procedure, a federal question arises in a state court when a criminal suspect or defendant claims that an action taken by a local or state officer or court violated a right protected by the Fourteenth Amendment or Bill of Rights provisions that have been applied to the states. The Fourteenth Amendment states that "No *State* shall . . . deprive any person of life, liberty, or property, without due process of law." The section on the incorporation doctrine will explain how the interpretation of this provision has allowed federal courts to impose the Bill of Rights on local and state officers and courts in criminal appeals. There is another way in which federal issues that arise in state courts can be appealed to the United States Supreme Court. State residents can file *civil* suits in federal court against municipalities or local or state officers (but not against states) claiming that the local officers violated their constitutional rights. This is authorized by a civil rights law (42 United States Code §1983) passed in 1871 under the authority of the Fourteenth Amendment.

THE SUPREMACY CLAUSE   It should also be noted that a state judge can decide an issue under the U.S. Constitution when a defendant claims that his or her constitutional rights have been infringed upon by local officers. In other words, state as well as federal judges interpret and are guided by the United States Constitution. In such a case, the state judge's ruling can be appealed to a federal court. It is logical that the final determination of the meaning of the Constitution be vested in the Supreme Court. This understanding is confirmed by the **Supremacy Clause** of the Constitution.

Note that Article III of the U.S. Constitution (the "judicial article"), which confers jurisdiction on the Supreme Court, does not directly give that Court the jurisdiction to hear federal questions that arise in state courts. Nevertheless, this power was asserted by the Supreme Court in the early Republic and

is inherent in Article VI, Paragraph 2: the Supremacy Clause.[36] This clause says that where there is an issue of law that is applicable to both the federal and the state governments, federal law and the interpretation of the federal courts controls. The Supremacy Clause ensures that the United States will be a *united* nation, for if every state could decide the meaning of the U.S. Constitution in its own way, there would be no uniformity of constitutional doctrines.

SPECIAL ROLE OF THE SUPREME COURT   We are used to thinking of constitutional interpretation as "belonging" to the courts. Nevertheless, the president and Congress often justify their actions by citing the Constitution. The courts, however, have final say about the meaning of the Constitution. A state supreme court is the final authority on the meaning of a state constitution, and the United States Supreme Court has the last say on the meaning of the United States Constitution, giving it great power in shaping criminal procedure.

From the beginning of the Republic, the framers saw the courts as playing an essential role in protecting individual liberty. In a speech to the House of Representatives in 1789 proposing the Bill of Rights, James Madison said that if the rights were adopted "into the constitution, independent tribunals of justice will consider themselves in a peculiar manner the guardians of those rights; they will be an impenetrable bulwark against every assumption of power in the legislative or executive; they will be naturally led to resist every encroachment upon rights expressly stipulated for in the constitution by the declaration of rights."[37]

Political Theory

Law is not a self-referential, "closed system" of rules. To be fully understood and to be considered *legitimate*, law must rest on more fundamental beliefs among the people. For example criminal laws against murder, rape, robbery, and arson are uncontested because of the powerful underlying values that we place on life, personal autonomy, and the safe enjoyment of the home. On the other hand, controversy has trailed the legalizing or criminalizing of such acts as the recreational use of marijuana because of conflicts over underlying values and definitions, pitting fears of negative health effects and flouting the law against beliefs in personal autonomy in activity that does not cause direct harm to others.

In a similar vein the law of criminal procedure, and the specific rights it ensures, draws full meaning and importance

---

THE SUPREMACY CLAUSE

The Constitution, and the Laws of the United States which shall be made in Pursuance thereof; and all Treaties made, or which shall be made, under the Authority of the United States, shall be the Supreme Law of the Land; and the judges in every State shall be bound thereby, any Thing in the Constitution or Laws of any State to the Contrary notwithstanding.

Source: *United States Constitution*, Article VI, Paragraph 2.

from political values and underlying political philosophies. One of the most important philosophies is individual *liberty*.[38] Liberty is posited as an "unalienable right" by the Declaration of Independence (1776). The Preamble to the Constitution declares that one of the six basic purposes of government is to "secure the Blessings of Liberty to ourselves and our Posterity." To operate effectively, law enforcement officers have to deprive people of liberty. The framers' study of history taught them that rulers had used the state's forces of order to become tyrants by using their powers to unjustly deprive people of liberty. Indeed, "[p]olicing is a metaphor for state power; the capacity to use force is the defining characteristic of the police."[39]

Many rules of criminal procedure are designed to prevent this in order to ensure that the liberty of the individual will not be violated without good cause. Perhaps the most important is that the exercise of power by executive branch officers that interfere with liberty are subject to review by the judicial branch. Aside from authorized exceptions, searches have to be authorized by judicial warrants. Arrested persons have to be brought before a magistrate within forty-eight hours to ensure that there was probable cause for the arrest. Illegal detention may be questioned by a court under a writ of habeas corpus. Persons charged with crimes are presumed innocent and are for the most part entitled to bail.

The Fourth Amendment's warrant requirements also provide important supports for the value of personal *privacy*. An early Supreme Court decision that held that wiretapping does not violate Fourth Amendment rights was strongly criticized when first issued (*Olmstead v. United States*, 1928). The obvious invasion of privacy did not sit well with the American ethos. Since 1968, the law of electronic surveillance is more in accord with deeply held values. All forms of electronic eavesdropping are presumptively violations of Fourth Amendment rights, and are authorized only on the basis of a judicial warrant supported by probable cause and many other statutory requirements (*Katz v. United States*, 1968). In recent years Congress has passed many laws designed to ensure liberty of personal records, in bank records and the like, but exceptions have been created by the USA PATRIOT Act.[40] The balance of privacy and security is a critical issue.

Equality is another hard-won political value in American life that is supported by various rules of criminal procedure.[41] One of the most important is the requirement that a criminal trial (including a plea of guilty) is not valid if a defendant is not represented by a competent lawyer, and if a person is too poor to afford a lawyer, the state must provide one (*Gideon v. Wainwright*, 1963). Depending on the circumstances, the state may have to provide an expert witness (*Ake v. Oklahoma*, 1985). Of course, the basic requirements of the Sixth Amendment, requiring that the defendant be "confronted with the witnesses against him" and to be allowed to have favorable witnesses subpoenaed, were hard-fought rights won in England. At an early stage in English history, the deck was stacked against the defendant in cases where the Crown was directly concerned, as in the case of treason trials.

The operative political philosophy of the United States and all other Western democracies rests on two concepts that are inherently legal: **constitutionalism** and the Rule of Law. In its broadest definition a nation's constitution is its stable arrangements for the exercise of government power. *Constitutionalism* is essentially the ideal that government balances the interests of all its members and is not "captured" by and used for the benefit of one faction. It has roots in Roman ideals of a state's political structure:[42] "For more than two thousand years there has been a remarkably wide and stable consensus that government ought to be carried on within publicly known and enforceable restraints."[43] The modern concept of constitutionalism includes two ideas: limited government and the Rule of Law—"that governments exist only to serve specified ends and properly function only according to specified rules."[44] Constitutionalism implies balanced government and is antithetical to absolutism or tyranny.

The *Rule of Law* is neither *a* rule nor *a* law, but instead a concept of political and legal theory that holds that the government and its officers are not above the law and that the government conducts its business in accord with established legal norms and procedures. In enforcing law, the government does not exceed its legal authority. The Rule of Law stands in contrast to arbitrary rule and applies to all branches of government: a president may be subjected to a civil lawsuit while in office (*United States v. Nixon*, 1974; *Clinton v. Jones*, 1997); legislation is declared void by courts if found to be unconstitutional; judges' constitutional rulings can be reversed only by constitutional amendment or by a later Court that interprets the Constitution differently.[45]

Constitutional criminal procedure advances constitutionalism and the Rule of Law by preventing governmental abuses of power mainly through the operation of the courts. Every trial conducted under the rules of due process is an example of how the need for the government to attorn to the judicial branch before it can complete its exercise of power has become routine and reflexive in our society. Civil lawsuits against police officers also manifest the rule of law. In our democracy, abuses by law enforcement can also be checked by actions by the legislature and chief executives. A powerful example was an executive order by President Bush banning racial profiling in federal law enforcement, with certain exceptions for terrorism investigations.[46] The constitutional ban on ex post facto laws is a classic example of the rule of law that conviction under a retroactive law is conviction under no law at all. The same is the case for vague laws (*Papachristou v. Jacksonville*, 1972).[47]

The courts, as guardians of constitutional liberties, have a central role in maintaining the Rule of Law and constitutionalism. But the courts cannot maintain freedom if the people are not willing to fight for their rights. To a significant degree, the Rule of Law lies in "supporting institutions, procedures, and values."[48] Traditions of liberty, real political competition between the party in power and the "loyal opposition," a spirit of tolerance, the existence of interest groups who will fight vigorously in the political realm to enforce their rights, the absence of an oligarchy (an extremely lopsided distribution of wealth), a measure of political and economic stability, a vigorous political press, a literate and aware citizenry—all play a role in maintaining the Rule of Law. In this kind of society, courts can more effectively ensure that the Rule of Law continues.

History

At several points in the text, references are made to English and American legal, constitutional, and political history. Every subject can be better understood by knowing about its history, but legal history is not simply an aid to understanding constitutional law—it is an integral part of the reasoning process used by constitutional lawyers to argue cases and by judges to justify their opinions. For example, in *Printz v. United States* (1997) the Supreme Court decided that a provision of the federal Brady Handgun Violence Prevention Act, which requires local sheriffs and other law enforcement officers to participate in background checks of prospective handgun purchasers, was unconstitutional. Justice Antonin Scalia noted that the decision would turn in large part on the Court's exploration of legal history: "Because there is no constitutional text speaking to this precise question, the answer to the [Sheriff's] challenge must be sought in historical understanding and practice, in the structure of the Constitution, and in the jurisprudence of this Court."

It is not possible to provide a quick course in Anglo American constitutional history at this point. Where historical references are provided in the text, they are not included simply for ornamentation but are included because the points are essential to appreciating the Court's rulings on the question. At this point a few definitions and basic points are included to clarify the text. References are made in the text to "the common law." The term can be confusing because it is used as a synonym for "case law" or "judge-made law" and is also used to describe the long period in English history, from the twelfth to the eighteenth century, when the bulk of English law was developed by the courts rather than by statutes of Parliament. The term also refers to the body of law developed in this period.

The common law period of England is especially important to American criminal procedure. When the original thirteen states declared their independence, each adopted the common law of England as their law up to that point. Many of the great rights that are essential to the freedom of American citizens were developed in the common law era. The concept of *due process* has its roots in the provision of Magna Carta (1215) that no free man would be deprived of life, property, or liberty but according to the law of the land. The mode of *trial by jury* emerged at that time and became the hallmark of the common law system of justice. The *writ of habeas corpus*, which is protected by the Constitution, emerged in the fifteenth century. The *privilege against self-incrimination* became a standard of individual rights during the seventeenth century, a period of civil war that led to the victory of Parliament and the development of the constitutional monarchy. The use of *judicial warrants* to justify entry into homes to search

for stolen goods is an English practice that became solidified into a constitutional principle at the time of the American revolution. Various protections that make a jury trial fair had their roots in common law developments: the right to subpoena witnesses, to have notice of charges, the rule against double jeopardy, the right to be confronted with accusing witnesses, the right to an impartial and local jury, and the right to have trials open to the public. A critical component of individual liberty is that courts are independent. The Constitution gives federal judges life tenure and does not allow their pay to be cut, specifically in order to ensure that judges would not be subservient to the legislative or executive branches. This concept was first developed by English statute in 1702, after the autocratic monarchy had been replaced with a balanced, constitutional system of government. The one great right essential to liberty that was developed more in America than in England is the right to counsel in criminal trials. The story of the development of these rights in England, worthy of study in its own right, is beyond the scope of this text.[49]

The creation of the Constitution of 1789 and the Bill of Rights (1791) reflected the dominant concern of the governing class in the early Republic for the survival of the United States as a nation. The premise of those who framed, ratified, and implemented these foundational documents was that a united nation would only survive against external rivals and internal jealousies if it had a strong government. A strong government was created, but it was also restrained by deliberately fashioned checks and balances and constitutional guarantees of liberty to ensure that those who gained power by election would not misuse their powers. It is highly significant that many vital aspects of a balanced government involved limiting the state's criminal justice apparatus.

The Civil War (1861–1865) was as much a constitutional as a national crisis. In the period of Reconstruction following the capitulation of the rebellion, the Constitution was reframed, in Lincoln's words, to shape a "new nation" that was not only "conceived in Liberty," but also "dedicated to the proposition that all men are created equal."[50] The three "Reconstruction Amendments" did this by abolishing slavery, establishing national citizenship, and guaranteeing the vote to former slaves in the Thirteenth (1866), Fourteenth (1868), and Fifteenth (1870) amendments. Section 1 of the Fourteenth Amendment is referred to frequently in the text and is a foundation block of modern criminal procedure. It states that "All persons born or naturalized in the United States, and subject to the jurisdiction thereof, are citizens of the United States and of the State wherein they reside." This overruled the Supreme Court's decision of the *Dred Scott* case (1857) that ruled that persons of African ancestry could not be citizens of the United States because that was the original intent of the framers of the Constitution. The next sentence extended three rights to citizens enforceable against the states: the "privileges or immunities of citizens," due process, and "the equal protection of the laws." Over the period of a century, the due process clause of the Fourteenth Amendment became the vehicle by which the Supreme Court ensured that basic liberties were extended to *state* residents or citizens. Note the terms of the clause: ". . . nor shall any *State* deprive any person of life, liberty, or property, without due process of law." If a state deprives a person, who is a citizen or a resident of a state, of "due process," that person has recourse to the federal courts for protection. The process by which this occurred will be fleshed out in the section on the Incorporation Doctrine.

Recent history and politics has helped shape the contours of criminal procedure law.[51] At several points in the text these historic events will be spelled out.

Politics

Constitutional law cannot be entirely separated from politics. Politics is often defined as a contest for "who gets what." Political goals include not only political office and tangible benefits (e.g., appropriations, contracts, favorable tax laws), but symbolic and ideological "goods" as well. The most acrimonious debates in recent American history, over things like school prayer, abortion, gay rights, the war on drugs, and gun control, are concerned not with tangible gains but with complex symbols, which uphold a right way of life for many. There are examples in the text that link criminal procedure and politics, including information about the appointment of justices in their biographical sketches.

From the beginning of the Republic, political calculations have been intertwined with constitutional law and the Constitution. The constitutional convention in 1787 did not include a bill of rights in its draft and was soundly criticized for this by "antifederalists" who argued against the ratification of the Constitution in state ratifying conventions in 1787 and 1788. The antifederalists had a variety of motives for opposing the Constitution, but found it convenient to use the lack of a bill of rights as a rallying point.[52]

The Fourteenth Amendment (1868) is the essential foundation for the application of the Bill of Rights to the states under the Incorporation Doctrine. The post–Civil War Congress that framed that amendment was motivated both by high principles and by the intense and convoluted politics of Reconstruction.[53] The Supreme Court that grappled with the question of incorporation or "nationalizing" the Bill of Rights from the 1880s to the 1960s was not immune from considerations that the effect of such rulings would have on federalism, and the political outcry that would result from imposing federal limitations on the local administration of justice.[54]

The politics of racial justice has influenced the contours of constitutional criminal procedure throughout the twentieth century, an issue that will be discussed below.[55] Beginning with the 1964 presidential election campaign, crime and criminal justice have become major, national political issues. In the 1968 election campaign, candidate Richard Nixon politicized constitutional criminal procedure. He attacked the United States Supreme Court, and its famous 1966 *Miranda* ruling, as responsible for increasing crime rates and for the visible lawlessness of scores of inner-city riots by disaffected African Americans and hundreds of antiwar demonstrations on college campuses. He accused the Supreme Court of having "gone too far in weakening the peace forces as against the criminal forces in this country."[56]

As president, Mr. Nixon appointed justices who were expected to take a "hard line" on criminal justice issues. Since 1970, Republican presidents have appointed ten Supreme Court justices and Democratic presidents have appointed only two. These appointees have generally favored the Crime Control Model of criminal justice. Not every Supreme Court case raises major political issues, but this branch of constitutional law is often fraught with partisanship. It is impossible to entirely eliminate political considerations and influences from constitutional law. In this text, reference is frequently made to the general trend by which criminal procedure doctrines shifted from a "conservative," state-interests phase before 1960, to a "liberal" **Warren Court** (1953–1969) phase, then back to a more conservative phase after 1969 during the **Burger Court** (1969–1987) and **Rehnquist Court** (1987–) eras. Keep in mind that characterizing an era, a "Court" (e.g., "the Warren Court"), or a justice as "conservative" or "liberal" is always a matter of "more or less" and not an absolute. This overly simplified historic pattern (conservative to liberal to conservative) is traced in the development of search and seizure, the right to counsel, confessions, and lineup law in subsequent chapters. Keeping these historic shifts in mind will aid the student to understand the otherwise bewildering twists and turns in constitutional criminal procedure.

Race and Racism

The link between the long and troubled history and politics of the search for civil rights by African Americans and criminal procedure, subjects that seem unrelated, deserves special mention. The foundation of modern criminal procedure—the Fourteenth Amendment—was ratified in 1868 as part of the post–Civil War Reconstruction, to ensure that basic civil and political rights for freedmen would be guaranteed by the federal government.[57] The promise of equality faded and died in the late nineteenth century with the rise of "Jim Crow" segregation, economic oppression, and political exclusion of African Americans.[58] This oppression was enforced by the criminal justice system in the South, which tolerated vigilantism and Ku Klux Klan terrorism. The violent opposition to the civil rights movement made it apparent to the Supreme Court that the racial equality required by the Constitution, and epitomized by *Brown v. Board of Education* (1954), was threatened by a "lawless" criminal justice system.[59]

This understanding is what linked three of the great themes, or "agenda items," of the Warren Court. In a lecture delivered six years after he retired from the Supreme Court, Arthur J. Goldberg outlined these themes:

> To me, the major accomplishments of the Court during the fifteen years in which Earl Warren was Chief Justice were a translation of our society's proclaimed belief in racial equality into some measure of legal reality, the beginning of a profound change in the mechanics of our political democracy and the revolution in criminal justice, both state and federal.[60]

It is easy for a student reading criminal procedure cases to miss the link between racial segregation, the misapportionment of legislative districts, and the violation of defendants' rights in criminal cases. The cases themselves often avoid explicitly mentioning the fact that the defendant is African American (as it did in *Terry v. Ohio*, 1968), legal segregation is a relic of the past, and apportionment issues are more complex today.

The extension of formal rights has not ended the troubling mix of skewed criminal justice policies and racial inequality. In the decades since the civil rights revolution and the Warren Court era, advances for large numbers of African Americans and other minorities have been matched with the stubborn perpetuation of low employment, weak schools, inadequate social services, and substantial disenfranchisement of those left behind in concentrated zones of poverty in inner cities. Much has changed since the days that legal segregation, overt racism, and terroristic law enforcement kept minorities from the polls.[61] Nevertheless, sober arguments have been made that the "war on drugs" has been responsible for the incarceration of disproportionate numbers of minorities, and that this in turn has had the effect of critically undermining the voting power of black communities.[62] The intertwining of race, crime, and the law has been ably told by Professor Randall Kennedy, and is beyond the scope of this text.[63] Nevertheless, it forms an important historic and contemporary context of criminal procedure. At relevant points in the text, reference will be made to these matters.

Judicial Biography

This text includes brief biographical sketches of most of the Supreme Court justices who have served since the beginning of the twentieth century. They are included to make a critical point: *law is a human product.* Supreme Court decisions are not the mechanical application of preexisting legal rules to fact patterns. Every Supreme Court decision involves a case in which important issues of legal or constitutional policy are involved. Of necessity, these decisions also impact the policies and behaviors of the two million persons in the criminal justice system.

The reality of judicial policymaking can be quite complicated because Supreme Court justices carefully consider every case they decide to review, and their decisions are not perfectly predictable. On the other hand, most justices develop *patterns of decisions* that allow the justices to be classified. In criminal procedure some justices are associated with the *Crime Control Model* (described at the beginning of this chapter) and are called "conservative" justices. Others more in tune with the *Due Process Model* are labeled "liberal" justices. Justices whose decisions do not fall consistently on one side or the other are called moderate, or "swing," justices. This spectrum is filled out by identifying some justices as moderate conservatives or moderate liberals.[64] The Appendix to this text includes the table titled "Summary Information about Selected Supreme Court Justices" that provides the summary positions of individual justices.

As a general matter liberal justices tend to decide cases in favor of defendants and tend to support the individual's liberty over the power of the state. Conservative justices tend to decide cases in favor of the prosecution and thus lean toward the state's authority over individuals. Nevertheless, *all* of the justices appreciate the need to maintain an effective criminal justice system with proactive policing and vigorous prosecution. Likewise, *each* justice adheres to the values of individual liberties and rights specified in the Constitution. In short, the justices struggle with the tension between liberty and order that lies at the heart of constitutional criminal procedure. The fact that they often differ about the results of specific cases is a reflection on the tendency of human beings to differ.

Judicial biography is an important topic because the justices' predilections are the result of their total experiences: early socialization, educations, professional experiences, and the formations of their philosophies about public issues. It is worth adding that some justices are especially influential because of the quality of their judicial opinions. This is known as **judicial craftsmanship.** Opinions that display a wealth of legal scholarship, a depth of judicial wisdom, and an ability to live in the minds of readers by the use of powerful or memorable phrases are high in judicial craft. One aspect of judicial craftsmanship is whether Supreme Court opinions give clear guidance to judges, lawyers, government officers, and individuals who rely on the rulings. Well-crafted opinions have a greater potential to shape a body of law and to leave a lasting legal legacy.

Finally, justices have differed as to their views toward *judicial activism* or *judicial restraint.* Conservative justices opposed to the extension of the Bill of Rights to state officers in the 1960s accused the liberal justices of violating the tradition of simply deciding cases by "making law." Today many conservative decisions are quite "activist." In reality, the Supreme Court cannot help but "make law" whenever it decides a case.

Human Rights

American law is usually studied without reference to parallels in comparative law or international law, and indeed, this text focuses exclusively on United States law. However it is worth keeping in mind that the constitutional liberties guaranteed by criminal procedure are **human rights.** This branch of international law grew rapidly after the horrors of the Second World War and the revelations of the Nuremberg War Crimes Trials.[65] A landmark development in establishing human rights as an essential concern of legitimate governments was the adoption of the Universal Declaration of Human Rights (UDHR) in 1948 by the United Nations.[66]

Rights are claims created by law and enforced by courts. Human rights are a special class of rights held by a person simply by virtue of being human. They are moral rights of the highest order, grounded in the equal moral dignity of each person, that can and should be made legally binding in national, regional, or international law.[67] With this in mind, it is noteworthy that many of the rights of constitutional criminal procedure are specified as human rights under the UDHR.[68]

These include provisions of the Sixth Amendment, such as rights to a speedy and public trial, to subpoena and examine witnesses, and to a lawyer. Due process rights such as notice of charges, the presumption of innocence, and the right to be tried in one's presence are also counted as human rights. An independent and impartial judge is a human right, an element of justice enshrined in the lifetime tenure provision of Article III of the U.S. Constitution.

The Universal Declaration of Human Rights lists other criminal procedure rights that are human rights and are essential to a civilized society. For example, Article 5 states that "No one shall be subjected to *torture* or to cruel, inhuman or degrading treatment or punishment," which is borrowed from and elaborates on the Eighth Amendment prohibition on cruel and unusual punishment. Article 9 states that "no one shall be subjected to *arbitrary arrest,* detention or exile," a right that is in essence part of the Fourth Amendment. One right not included as a human right is the requirement of trial by jury, which is unique to the common law system and is not typically used in other civilized nations.[69]

It is gratifying to know that most provisions of the U.S. Constitution's Bill of Rights (1791) have been recognized as essential elements of human rights by the world community. This text is not the place to cover the movement to recognize human rights in various international charters, the development of regional and international courts of justice, or the difficulties in enforcing human rights around the globe.[70]

What is vital to know is that these rights appeal to a sense of justice and transcend local cultures. They are central to other rights because democratic politics and human dignity cannot exist when government has the power to crush all opposition. A criminal justice system that adheres to human rights principles of criminal procedure ensures a democratic form of government and a government bound by restraints of decency, which, in turn, helps ensure its legitimacy.[71]

Law and Society

These brief sections on the context of criminal procedure indicate that the subject can be studied as a "law and society" course, and suggest a variety of avenues for such an approach. There is good reason for focusing primarily on the content and analysis of the law in a first course on criminal procedure. Nevertheless, the judicious sprinkling of these contextual elements in the text gives the student a better understanding of the rules. Each subsequent chapter concludes with a *Law in Society* section that explores the relation between law and contemporary society. They may examine social forces that changed legal doctrines (e.g., concern over domestic violence), social science findings that illuminate weaknesses in legal doctrine (e.g., research on the exclusionary rule), or the fairness of the actual practice of criminal justice personnel in the light of the ideals of constitutional criminal procedure (e.g., racial profiling, prosecutorial misconduct, police

perjury). The sections that highlight abuses of constitutional rights do not mean that such abuses are the norm in America. The *Law in Society* sections are not intended to condemn the entire criminal justice system. The great majority of police, prosecutors, defense attorneys, and judges act professionally and perform their important duties competently and within the law. However, complacency is never a proper attitude when considering liberties, and abuses in the system must be studied if they are to be corrected. Lon Fuller, in his classic study of the Rule of Law, noted that the greatest way in which law fails is when there is a lack of congruence or fit between the law as written and the law in practice. It is too much to expect perfection; but too great a gap between professed constitutional liberties and actual practice will breed cynicism, demoralization, and the collapse of our system, as Justice Louis Brandeis warned in his 1928 dissent in *Olmstead v. United States.* (See the biographical sketch of Justice Brandeis for the quotation from this great opinion.)

THE INCORPORATION OF THE BILL OF RIGHTS

Overview

The incorporation doctrine holds that most of the rights contained in the Bill of Rights (First through Eighth Amendments) protect persons not only from actions of the *federal* government, but also against violations by *state* legislatures, courts, and executive branch officers, including *local* officers. (References to "state" officials includes state *and* local officers, as distinguished from federal officers.) The term "incorporation" indicates that the mechanism by which specific provisions of the Bill of Rights (e.g., the Fourth Amendment) apply to state officers is by application of the provision *through* the due process clause of the Fourteenth Amendment. To use an awkward metaphor, it is as if the due process clause were a "container" into which Bill of Rights provisions are poured.

Incorporation is a major issue because at the outset of the Republic, under the governing structure established by the Constitution, the Bill of Rights was held to *not* apply to the states. When the Fourteenth Amendment was ratified, some proponents in Congress said that establishing the "dual citizenship" of Americans (as state and United States citizens) meant that the Bill of Rights would apply to protect citizens against unconstitutional actions by local and state officials. This, however, did not occur and indeed was resisted by the Supreme Court for a century. When most of the criminal procedure provisions of the Bill of Rights were finally incorporated in the 1960s by the liberal Warren Court, its decisions generated an intense political debate. This debate, part of a larger contest over the meaning of the Constitution in such areas as abortion, affirmative action, flag burning and free speech, voting rights, property rights, and the like polarized constitutional law to a greater extent than had been the case since the days of the struggle over the constitutionality of President Roosevelt's New Deal legislation in the 1930s. After 1972 the composition of the Court became far more conservative. Although the Burger and Rehnquist courts have not dismantled incorporation, they have whittled down the extent to which provisions of the Bill of Rights protect individuals in a host of rulings that are the main subject of this text.

This section explores the process of legal history by which the Supreme Court resisted incorporation. The major reason for the resistance was the tug of *federalism*—the belief that the federal courts should not interfere in state matters. When incorporation occurred in the 1960s, it indicated that the nation had become more unified about the rights of its citizens, a result that was set in motion by the Civil War and its legal and constitutional outcome. It is worth noting that each of the elements of the context of criminal procedure, reviewed in the previous section, came into play in the process of incorporation.[72]

Before the Civil War

Before the Civil War the Supreme Court held that the Bill of Rights applied only to the federal government and not to the states, despite the fact that the Constitution does apply to the states. Article I, Section 10, for example, prohibits the states from many actions. Nevertheless in Chief Justice John Marshall's last constitutional opinion, *Barron v. Baltimore* (1833), the Supreme Court held that the Bill of Rights did not apply to the states. Barron's waterfront land was taken by Baltimore for public use. He felt Maryland did not pay him enough money and sued in *federal* court, arguing that the state violated his right to *just compensation* under the Fifth Amendment. The Supreme Court rejected his claim, saying that Barron simply had no case in the federal courts under the Bill of Rights. The primary reason was that the framers *intended* the Bill of Rights to restrict *only* the *federal* government, *not* state or local governments.

> The Constitution was ordained and established by the people of the United States for themselves, for their government, and not for the Government of the individual States. Each State established a Constitution for itself, and, in that Constitution, provided such limitations and restrictions on the powers of its particular government as its judgment dictated. (*Barron v. Baltimore,* 1833)

Despite the fact that not all Americans accepted the *Barron* ruling, this was the law of the land and there was no way to change it without amending the Constitution.[73]

The Growth of Federal Judicial Power

At the founding of the nation, most observers, including some who were appointed to the Supreme Court, felt that the Supreme Court would play a small role in the governing of the nation. Under the Court's third Chief Justice, John Marshall, the Court became a powerful institution. This point is not directly relevant to the development of the Incorporation Doctrine, but is relevant to the importance of constitutional criminal procedure. It is because the Court is

a powerful institution that its modern rulings on the right to counsel, confessions, search and seizure, and other topics are followed and help to shape a national policy on fundamental rights.

The Court's authority rests on three major powers that, while not explicitly conferred in the text of the Constitution, are implicit in constitutional history and were confirmed in authoritative decisions authored by Chief Justice Marshall. The first is the power of **judicial review:** the power to declare acts of Congress unconstitutional when they conflict with the Court's interpretation of the Constitution. This power was asserted in *Marbury v. Madison* (1803):

> Certainly all those who have framed written constitutions contemplate them as forming the fundamental and paramount law of the nation, and consequently the theory of every such government must be, that an act of the legislature, repugnant to the Constitution, is void. . . .
>
> It is emphatically the province and duty of the judicial department to say what the law is. Those who apply the rule to particular cases, must of necessity expound and interpret that rule. If two laws conflict with each other, the courts must decide on the operation of each. . . . (*Marbury v. Madison,* 1803)

Although controversy still surrounds the unusual circumstances of this case, there is no questioning this power of the United States Supreme Court.[74]

The Court's second great power is its ability to declare a *state* ruling, statute, or constitutional provision void because it conflicts with the United States Constitution. This may seem axiomatic under the Supremacy Clause (U.S. Const. art. VI, cl. 2). Nevertheless, the Court's power was directly challenged by the Supreme Court of Virginia at a time when the large states were very powerful and the reach of the authority of the United States government was not entirely spelled out. In *Fletcher v. Peck* (1810), the Court ruled a *state* law unconstitutional because it conflicted with the "Contract Clause" (U.S. Const. art. I, §10), which prohibits a state from "impairing the Obligation of Contracts." *Fletcher's* constitutional significance lay in Marshall's opinion, which:

> declared categorically that the states could not be viewed as a single, unconnected sovereign power, on whom no other restrictions are imposed than those found in its own constitution. On the contrary, it is a member of the Union, and "that Union has a constitution the supremacy of which all acknowledge, and which imposes limits to the legislatures of the several states, which none claim a right to pass."[75]

The third great power of the United States Supreme Court is to take jurisdiction over any state case that interprets *federal* law, including the Constitution, whether in a civil or in a criminal case, so as to have the final say. The Virginia Supreme Court again tried to shield its rulings over the application of federal laws in Virginia from federal Supreme Court review. In *Martin v. Hunter's Lessee* (1816) and *Cohens v. Virginia* (1821) the United States Supreme Court held that the Virginia Supreme Court could not hold United States civil and criminal statutes unconstitutional.

Together, these cases established the United States as a "real country" and not a loose federation of fully sovereign states. They confirmed the Supreme Court's authority as the final arbiter of cases arising under the Constitution. They made state governments and state courts responsible to act under the Constitution to uphold national law. The Court under Chief Justice Marshall became a legitimate wielder of power because "the Justices were able to elevate their decisions above the plane of partisan politics, to transform political issues into legal ones, and thereby to increase the political power of the Court."[76] This power, established in the early Republic, allowed the Court to play a central role in the fight to apply the Bill of Rights to the states a century and a half later.

The Dred Scott Case and the Fourteenth Amendment

The infamous "*Dred Scott*" case, *Scott v. Sandford* (1857), ruled that the "Missouri Compromise" of 1820, which drew an East-West line between free states to the north and slave states to the south, was unconstitutional. In the course of its ruling it also held that whether or not a state granted freedom and even state citizenship to Americans of African descent, such persons could not be United States citizens. This case inflamed political passions and probably hastened the Civil War. The ruling, part of the nation's constitutional law, could not be eradicated by simple legislation. The Thirteenth Amendment (1866), abolishing slavery, did not entirely clarify the civil status of ex-slaves; they were "free," but were they citizens invested with political as well as social and economic rights? The first sentence of the Fourteenth Amendment was designed to overrule *Scott v. Sandford*: "All persons born or naturalized in the United States and subject to the jurisdiction thereof, are citizens of the United States and of the State wherein they reside."

Having established national citizenship in all state citizens, the Fourteenth Amendment went on to confer three rights which national citizens could assert against the states: "the privileges or immunities of citizens of the United States," due process of law, and the equal protection of the laws. These were vague and open-ended provisions. Did the framers intend the Amendment to "incorporate" the Bill of Rights into the privileges of national citizenship and overrule *Barron v. Baltimore* (1833), as the first sentence of the Amendment overturned *Dred Scott* (1857)? Statements by the Amendment's leading proponents, Representative John A. Bingham and Senator Jacob M. Howard, made in the House and Senate during the debate concerning the Fourteenth Amendment, supported this intent. Nevertheless, for a century this interpretation was refused.[77] An early sign in the opposite direction, however, was *The Slaughter-House Cases* (1873). By declaring that common employment like butchering is *not* a privilege and immunity of federal citizenship, and thus beyond the protection of federal courts, the Supreme Court permanently made the Privileges or Immunities Clause a dead letter.[78] Could the Bill of Rights be applied to the states through the due process clause?

The Anti-Incorporation Cases, 1884–1908

The Slaughter-House Cases aborted the idea that the Privileges or Immunities Clause would be used to inaugurate **total incorporation** of the Bill of Rights. In a series of criminal appeals brought before the Supreme Court from state convictions, lawyers argued that specific provisions of the Bill of Rights of the U.S. Constitution should be held to apply to the states under the *due process clause* of the Fourteenth Amendment. The Supreme Court consistently refused to adopt this position in each of these cases from 1884 to 1908, with one exception.

In these cases Justice John M. Harlan was the lone voice who consistently argued for the application of the Bill of Rights to the states. Justice Harlan's great contribution to the debate was to drop the focus on the original intent of the framers. Instead, in his dissents, he focused on the idea that due process was a *fundamental right*, whose lineage went back to Magna Carta (1215). He argued that a state could not pretend to have a civilized system of government under constitutional requirements if it were allowed to violate the due process rights of its citizens.

Hurtado v. California (1884) was the first of these cases. A defendant convicted of murder argued that the use of a prosecutor's information to indict him rather than a grand jury indictment, as was required in federal prosecutions under the Fifth Amendment, was unconstitutional. The majority held that the use of an information to bring formal charges against a defendant did not violate the state defendant's Fourteenth Amendment due process rights. Harlan's dissenting opinion reviewed centuries of common law history to argue that common law institutions, including the grand jury, were essential to the *political* rights cherished by Americans. The majority opinion agreed with this concept as a general matter but concluded that the grand jury was *not* a guarantee of liberty and, therefore, not a component of due process. Note the language used by the majority:

> In the Fourteenth Amendment, by parity of reason, it refers to that law of the land in each State, which derives its authority from the inherent and reserved powers of the State, exerted *within the limits of those fundamental principles of liberty and justice which lie at the base of all our civil and political institutions.* . . . (*Hurtado* at 121, emphasis added).

This phrasing in effect adopted what came to be called the **fundamental rights test**—which became the ultimate criterion of incorporation, and gained clarity as it was applied in specific cases. It meant, in theory, that the Supreme Court would not uphold *any* state procedure of criminal justice. Laws or government practices that are blatantly arbitrary or discriminatory would be due process violations, even though established by the democratic process, for they would constitute the "despotism of the many, of the majority." To the *Hurtado* majority, information issued by an elected prosecutor was not unfair and did not undermine "fundamental principles of liberty and justice which lie at the base of all our civil and political institutions." In short, the grand jury is not a "fundamental" right. This is still the law.

Following *Hurtado,* the Court refused to incorporate a variety of other rights, finding that none of them were fundamental rights that were essential to the civil and political liberty of Americans. One case held that a state eight-person felony jury did not violate due process, although federal felony juries required by Article III and the Sixth Amendment were held to be composed of twelve, the traditional number at common law (*Maxwell v. Dow,* 1900). In another major non-incorporation case, the last of this era, *Twining v. New Jersey* (1908), the Court ruled that the Fifth Amendment privilege against self-incrimination was not incorporated into the Fourteenth Amendment. Specifically, the state trial judge informed the jury that they could take into consideration, when deciding guilt or innocence, a defendant's refusal to testify in his own behalf. In federal courts an instruction like this from a judge violated a defendant's Fifth Amendment absolute right to remain silent at trial. Any group of jurors are likely to ask themselves why the defendant did not take the stand. They will be instructed that the defendant has an absolute right to not testify under the Fifth Amendment. But if the judge adds that they can still take the defendant's silence into account, a jury will be prone to take the judge's statement as a green light to presume that the defendant has something to hide.

The only case that came close to an incorporation was *Chicago, Burlington and Quincy Railroad Company v. Chicago* (1897). The Court ruled that compensation paid by Illinois for some land taken from a railroad company for street improvements was inadequate and a violation of federal due process standards under the Fourteenth Amendment. This case did not mention or overrule *Barron v. Baltimore* (1833). By holding that the Due Process Clause required the states to grant just compensation, and that this right was guaranteed by federal courts, the Court seemed to "incorporate" the Fifth Amendment's Just Compensation Clause. A double standard clearly applied. *Property* rights were deemed so fundamental to the American polity that state violations of the Just Compensation Clause violated the constitutional rights of property owners. *Liberty* rights, however, were not offended by state rules of criminal procedure that afforded criminal defendants fewer protections than did federal rules under the Bill of Rights.

The underlying reason for the reluctance to apply the Bill of Rights to the states was *federalism.* The Court made it clear it was protecting states' rights, warning that if it decided that a state procedure violated the Fourteenth Amendment, "it diminishes the authority of the State, so necessary to the perpetuity of our dual form of government, and changes its relation to its people and to the Union" (*Twining,* p. 92). Perhaps the Court also feared that the federal judiciary, small in number and hampered by jurisdictional limits that were not lifted for several more decades by Congress, did not have the capacity to enforce civil rights on recalcitrant states. In the final analysis, it was just too big a change in the federal-state

relationship for the majority of the justices of the Supreme Court to accept.

Nevertheless, the language and reasoning of the cases denying incorporation opened the door to "selective" incorporation in the 1960s by accepting Justice Harlan's *fundamental* rights analysis. If a later Court viewed provisions of the Bill of Rights as fundamental, the state would be obligated to abide by them, and by the Supreme Court's interpretation of these rights.

The next two steps in the story of incorporation helped pave the way, although neither step directly involved incorporation. These steps were adoption of the **due process approach** and the incorporation of First Amendment rights.

Adopting the Due Process Approach

In this text the "due process approach" is defined as a ruling by the United States Supreme Court that an action of a state criminal justice officer violates the due process clause of the Fourteenth Amendment, but does not violate a specific provision of the Bill of Rights, even if there is a parallel between the action held unconstitutional under due process and the specific Bill of Rights provision.

In 1923 the Supreme Court held, for the first time in a criminal appeal from a state, that state court procedures violated a defendant's Fourteenth Amendment due process rights. Five African Americans were sentenced to death after a murder trial that, although perfect in form, was dominated by a bloodthirsty Arkansas lynch mob just outside the courthouse, screaming for death (*Moore v. Dempsey,* 1923).[79] A similar case had come before the Court in 1915, the notorious Leo Frank case in which an Atlanta mob's anti-Semitic chants and threats of lynching (later carried out) could be heard by the jury.[80] The Supreme Court in *Frank v. Mangum* (1915) held that a state prisoner could not use a federal writ of habeas corpus to challenge "mere errors" in his trial. Justice Holmes strenuously dissented in *Frank,* arguing that "Mob law does not become due process of law by securing the assent of a terrorized jury. We are not speaking of mere disorder, or more irregularities in procedure, but of a case where the processes of justice are actually subverted." Despite the hideous injustices surrounding Frank's trial, the majority of the Court could see no violation of due process.

In the next eight years, four members of the Court retired and were replaced, setting the stage for a different decision. Justice Holmes, now writing for the Court's majority, held that federal habeas corpus applied:

> It certainly is true that mere mistakes of law in the course of a trial are not to be corrected in that way. But if the case is that the whole proceeding is a mask—that counsel, jury and judge were swept to the fatal end by an irresistible wave of public passion, and that the State Courts failed to correct the wrong— neither perfection in the machinery for correction nor the possibility that the trial court and counsel saw no other way of avoiding an immediate outbreak of the mob can prevent this Court from securing to the petitioners their constitutional rights. (*Moore v. Dempsey,* p. 91)

The effect of *Moore v. Dempsey* was that a federal district judge could upset the verdict of a local jury, which had been upheld by the state supreme court, if the judge found the conviction to rest on a violation of the defendant's Fourteenth Amendment right to not be deprived of life, liberty, or property without due process of law. This was a revolutionary change in practice and in judicial attitudes, even if it fit the text and logic of the Fourteenth Amendment. *Moore v. Dempsey* breached the wall of federal judicial noninterference in state criminal justice. In the next fifteen years the Court would slowly begin to use this newfound authority to correct gross injustices in a handful of significant cases.

The first was *Powell v. Alabama* (1932)—the notorious "Scottsboro Case." The Court held that due process was violated because the defendants were not allowed time to prepare a defense and, under the circumstances, were not afforded lawyers. The Scottsboro defendants were retried, found guilty, and on further appeal, the Supreme Court held that their trial was unfair because African Americans were systematically excluded from Alabama grand juries (*Norris v. Alabama,* 1935). In 1936 the Court ruled that a confession obtained by torture violated due process (*Brown v. Mississippi,* 1936). This trickle of cases became a stream in the 1940s and a river by the 1950s. The Court had, by that time, made state criminal justice an "agenda" on its annual dockets. Without this growing attention to criminal cases on the Court's growing civil rights agenda, it is unlikely that it would have eventually incorporated the criminal provisions of the Bill of Rights.

The Incorporation of First Amendment Civil Liberties

Before the Court again considered incorporating criminal procedure provisions in the Bill of Rights, a momentous shift in American constitutional liberties occurred. By the 1930s, the Supreme Court, for the first time, struck down *state* laws that violated rights in the First Amendment by reading them into the Fourteenth Amendment, despite the Amendment's text that began, "*Congress* shall make no law. . . ." The free speech cases arose out of (1) state "criminal syndicalism" prosecutions for advocating violence against the government, designed to suppress left-wing political parties, and (2) World War I–era laws making it criminal to advocate resistance to the military draft.

In *dictum* in *Gitlow v. New York* (1925), Justice Edward T. Sanford assumed that "freedom of speech and of the press . . . are among the fundamental personal rights and 'liberties' protected by the Due Process Clause of the Fourteenth Amendment from impairment by the States." In *Fiske v. Kansas* (1927), the Court, in overturning a conviction of a person who simply carried a radical labor manifesto on his person, stated that the Kansas Criminal Syndicalism Law infringed on due process, without mentioning First Amendment free speech. Finally, *Stromberg v. California* (1931) overturned a California law making it a crime to display a red flag as an emblem of opposition to organized government. *Stromberg* held (7–2), in an

opinion by Chief Justice Charles Evans Hughes, that the state law violated First Amendment free speech, which was embraced by the liberty protected by the Fourteenth Amendment. This was followed by *Near v. Minnesota* (1931), in which the Court struck down a state law that allowed a judge, acting without a jury, to stop publication of a newspaper article deemed "malicious, scandalous, and defamatory." *Near* prohibited censorship and "prior restraint" of publications and explicitly stated that the freedom of press is included in Fourteenth Amendment due process and that prior restraint strikes at the core of the First Amendment. And in January 1937, a unanimous Court ruled in *DeJonge v. Oregon* that making it a crime to participate in a peaceful political rally violated the First Amendment right of peaceful assembly via the Due Process Clause. Together, these cases clearly "incorporated" First Amendment rights.

In the First Amendment cases the Court applied the fundamental rights test, which the Court had developed during the nonincorporation era. Thus, on the next occasion in which the Court faced challenges to a state criminal prosecution under the Fifth or Sixth amendments, the constitutional landscape was vastly different: the Court had incorporated several provisions of the First Amendment. Did the incorporation of First Amendment rights (with the free exercise of religion to soon follow) mean that the Court would be obliged to incorporate rights into the criminal procedure amendments as well?

Resistance to Incorporation and Growing Support, 1937–1959

The great weight of the anti-incorporation precedent in *criminal* cases still had a hold on the Court. In 1937 an important 8–1 decision by Justice Cardozo—*Palko v. Connecticut* (1937)—held that the double jeopardy clause of the Fifth Amendment was not a fundamental right and, therefore, was not incorporated into Fourteenth Amendment due process. The defendant had been convicted once for the murder of a police officer during a robbery and sentenced to life imprisonment. Under existing state law, the prosecution appealed on the ground of trial errors. On retrial, Palko was again found guilty and sentenced to death. He argued to the Supreme Court that a retrial after an appeal by the prosecutor violated double jeopardy. Because the first jury had implicitly acquitted him of first-degree murder, he argued that the retrial on that charge was double jeopardy.[81] The Court held that the Fifth Amendment double jeopardy guarantee did not apply against the states, despite the fact that a federal prosecution would violate double jeopardy on the facts of this case.

Why were First Amendment rights incorporated but not Fifth Amendment rights? Justice Cardozo drew a distinction between *fundamental rights* and *formal rights*. Freedoms of speech and press were "so rooted in the traditions and conscience of our people as to be ranked as *fundamental*" and thus included in due process liberty. Criminal procedure rights were merely "*formal*," and not a part of due process liberty. To be fundamental, a right had to be essential to justice and to the

American system of political liberty. The First Amendment cases blocked the operation of state laws out of the "belief that neither liberty nor justice would exist if [these rights] were sacrificed. . . . This is true, for illustration, of freedom of thought, and speech. Of that freedom one may say that it is the matrix, the indispensable condition, of nearly every other form of freedom." (*Palko v. Connecticut,* pp. 326–27).

First Amendment rights are fundamental, then, because political freedom rests on the free exchange of political ideas and the ability of citizens to address the government in protest. On the other hand, to Cardozo the criminal procedure provisions in the Bill of Rights were *not* "of the very essence of a scheme of ordered liberty." He indicated that many democracies had criminal procedure rules that did not afford procedures such as trial by jury, and that Palko's case was not the same as the state trying him many times to get a conviction. The *Palko* doctrine held sway for a quarter of a century before the Court began to incorporate most of the criminal procedure rights in the Bill of Rights into the Fourteenth Amendment Due Process Clause.

Justice Hugo Black's dissenting opinion in *Adamson v. California* (1947) marked a turning point that eventually led to incorporation. The case dealt with the same issue as *Twining v. New Jersey* (1908)—whether a judge's comment on a defendant's failure to testify violated his Fifth Amendment rights as incorporated under the Fourteenth Amendment Due Process Clause. Again the Court held that it did not. A defendant in Adamson's position, with a prior criminal record, faced a dilemma, for if he testified, the prosecutor could bring out the existence of the convictions to impeach his testimony. Otherwise the prosecutor could not introduce a defendant's prior convictions. If Adamson were tried in federal court, a judge would not have been allowed to comment. Applying the Bill of Rights to the states would make the administration of justice in the United States more uniform and afford greater constitutional protection to individuals.

The majority opinion essentially rested upon precedent. Justice Felix Frankfurter wrote a strong concurring opinion. He was a political liberal but also a judicial conservative and supporter of **judicial restraint;** his concurrence made him the champion of the Court's anti-incorporation faction. He challenged Justice Black's "total incorporation" idea by stressing that the Court could employ the "due process approach" to overturn atrocious state action.

What was special about Justice Black's opinion was that it was based on intense research into the framing of the Fourteenth Amendment that powerfully supported the position that the *original intent* of the framers included the application of the Bill of Rights to the states under the Fourteenth Amendment. This argument placed incorporation of the Bill of Rights on the "constitutional agenda," as three other liberal justices, Justices Douglas, Murphy, and Rutledge, agreed that the Bill of Rights should be incorporated. With four votes in favor, the chance that incorporation would become the law of the land was in reach of realization.

Justice Black was as much a "constitutional fundamentalist" as a liberal and argued for "total incorporation" in his *Adamson* dissent. There are at least two problems with the Supreme Court deciding in one case to apply all of the twenty-six provisions of the Bill of Rights to the states via the Fourteenth Amendment. The first is that no case can come before the Court raising such an issue. A defendant's case gets to the Court arguing that a *specific* right has been violated. Second, a case that incorporates a provision of the Bill of Rights involves an intense study of the history and jurisprudence of the right and of its impact on criminal justice practice. To do this for each of the twenty-six rights embedded in the first eight amendments is simply beyond the Court's capacity and would violate all norms of the judicial process.

Instead, the incorporation *process* that was proposed in these cases, and that would indeed occur in the 1960s, would be **selective incorporation,** the decision in a single case that a *specific* right in the Bill of Rights is included in the concept of Fourteenth Amendment due process "liberty" because the particular right is fundamental to the system of "ordered liberty." Any infringement by a state undermines "those fundamental principles of liberty and justice which lie at the base of all our civil and political institutions" (*Twining v. New Jersey,* 1908).

The next incorporation case demonstrated the cleavages between Justice Black and his more liberal colleagues. Police officers in *Wolf v. Colorado* (1949) entered a doctor's office without a warrant and seized patients' files. In a federal prosecution this blatant violation of the Fourth Amendment would have invoked the exclusionary rule, established in 1914 in *Weeks v. United States*, to exclude the use of these records at his trial. The issue was whether the exclusionary rule applied to the states. (This issue is covered in greater depth in Chapter 2).

The majority held, under the *Palko* standard, that it did not. In an adroit majority opinion, Justice Frankfurter held that the *substance* of the Fourth Amendment is a fundamental right and therefore incorporated into the Due Process Clause. However, the exclusionary rule was characterized as a remedy, and the Court declined to incorporate it. Justice Black, the champion of incorporation, concurred. As a "constitutional fundamentalist" he was stymied by the fact that the exclusionary rule was not included in the text of the Fourth Amendment and, therefore, could not be applied to the states as a constitutional rule. He felt that the exclusionary rule was appropriately applied to the federal courts under the Supreme Court's supervisory authority. The Court's liberals, Justices Murphy, Rutledge, and Douglas, dissented. They believed that exclusion was the only real "remedy" because the police virtually never lost civil suits brought against them in state courts: a right without a remedy is not a true right.

A further division between Justice Black and the rest of the Court was seen in his growing and partial opposition to the due process approach. The justices who opposed incorporation took the position that the *due process approach*, initiated with *Moore v. Dempsey* (1923), and which had been used more frequently in cases examining confessions taken by local police officers, was sufficient to protect the rights of Americans against the excesses of state and local criminal justice officers. The three liberal justices who followed Justice Black's lead

(Justices Douglas, Murphy, and Rutledge) nevertheless went beyond total incorporation to espouse "**incorporation plus**"—incorporation of the Bill of Rights plus the due process approach where appropriate. Justice Black opposed the due process approach because he saw the use of discretionary power by the justices as instances of judicial tyranny and a violation of the limited constitutional powers given to judges to decide cases. His position was designed not only to limit state and local government, but also to limit the discretion of federal judges. Justice Murphy, in a separate dissenting opinion in *Adamson*, stated that, "Occasions may arise where a proceeding falls so far short of conforming to fundamental standards of procedure as to warrant constitutional condemnation in terms of a lack of due process despite the absence of a specific provision in the Bill of Rights."

The Court next applied the due process approach in a case that erected the **"shocks the conscience" test.** In *Rochin v. California* (1952), police broke into the home of a suspected drug seller, invaded his bedroom, scuffled with him after seeing him swallow pills, and dragged him off to a hospital where he was forced to swallow an emetic to vomit up evidence. Justice Frankfurter, writing for the Court, threw out the evidence by relying on a subjective Fourteenth Amendment due process standard: "[T]he proceedings by which this conviction was obtained do more than offend some fastidious squeamishness or private sentimentalism about combating crime too energetically. This is action that shocks the conscience." These police activities "are methods too close to the rack and the screw to permit of constitutional differentiation." The phrase created a label for the Court's due process rule in search and seizure cases: the shocks the conscience test. Justice Black concurred, but argued instead that such acts compelled a defendant to be a witness against himself, suggesting that the Fifth Amendment prohibition against self-incrimination, which should be incorporated, applied to tangible as well as to testimonial evidence.

The *Rochin* test was criticized as too vague. What shocked the conscience of appellate judges was too capricious a standard to give guidance to police officers or trial judges. It gave the Court sweeping power to inject its likes and dislikes into the Constitution. This criticism was borne out by *Irvine v. California* (1954). Some justices were clearly shocked by FBI electronic eavesdropping of the bedroom of a married suspect for over a month. Justice Frankfurter characterized it as "repulsive." Still, the majority upheld the introduction of the wiretap evidence, did not incorporate the Fourth Amendment exclusionary rule, and limited *Rochin* to acts of physical violence.

The Court signaled its growing concern with civil liberties in search and seizure by overturning the "silver platter" doctrine in *Elkins v. United States* (1960). State police officers obtained evidence of crime by means of an illegal search and seizure of a defendant's home. The evidence was suppressed by a state court. Afterward, the state officers left the evidence (illegal telephone wiretapping equipment) in the safe-deposit box of a local bank, where federal agents obtained it and used the evidence as the basis of a federal prosecution. The Supreme Court held that the federal exclusionary rule applied even though the federal officers did not directly engage in the illegal search and seizure. This practice undermined state efforts to exclude illegally seized evidence by encouraging federal officers "tacitly to encourage state officers in the disregard of constitutionally protected freedom." Justice Stewart's majority opinion was quite favorable to the exclusionary rule, signaling the coming era of incorporation.

The Due Process Revolution

By 1962, the Supreme Court's membership had changed to include five pro-incorporation liberals: Justices Black and Douglas (Roosevelt appointees), Chief Justice Earl Warren and Justice William Brennan (Eisenhower appointees), and Justice Arthur Goldberg, appointed in 1962 by President John F. Kennedy. But even before this shift, the Court opened the floodgate of incorporation cases with *Mapp v. Ohio* (1961), which held that the Fourth Amendment exclusionary rule applied to eliminate illegally seized evidence from state as well as federal trials.

After *Mapp*, virtually every year during the 1960s brought the incorporation of an additional Bill of Rights provision into Fourteenth Amendment due process. (See Table 1-1.) The Eighth Amendment Cruel and Unusual Punishment Clause was applied to the states in 1962. A state law made narcotics *addiction* criminal. The Court viewed addiction as a disease and held in *Robinson v. California* that the conviction and punishment of a person for a *status* such as a disease was constitutionally forbidden cruel and unusual punishment. *Robinson* opened the door for the Supreme Court to consider *state* death penalty cases in *Furman v. Georgia* (1972) and *Gregg v. Georgia* (1976). In 1962, however, *Robinson* did not attract much popular attention.

The next incorporation case, *Gideon v. Wainwright* (1963), was widely publicized and quite popular. It incorporated the right to counsel in an opinion authored by Justice Black, who had argued for its incorporation in a dissent twenty-one years earlier. More than half the states provided counsel for indigent defendants by 1963. The decision appealed to the American sense of fair play: once a defendant is haled into court, he should have the same basic "equipment" to fight his fight as does the prosecutor. Congress acted to ensure that counsel would be available for indigents in federal cases, and many local bar associations and courts willingly developed systems to provide counsel. There were no dissents in *Gideon,* although some justices argued the decision should be based on the due process approach rather than incorporation.

The right against self-incrimination, the point of contention in *Twining v. New Jersey* (1908) and *Adamson v. California* (1947), was incorporated, and *Twining* was overruled in 1964 in *Malloy v. Hogan* and *Murphy v. Waterfront Commission of New York Harbor. Malloy* was a five-to-four decision bringing the Fifth Amendment right against self-incrimination into the Fourteenth Amendment by allowing a witness to refuse to answer questions before a state investigatory body under the Fifth Amendment. *Murphy* unanimously held that a state witness

TABLE 1–1 RIGHTS, ENUMERATED IN BILL OF RIGHTS (AMENDMENTS I–VIII)

RIGHTS ENUMERATED	SELECTIVE INCORPORATION	
	DATE	CASE
Amendment I		
Establishment of Religion	1947	*Everson v. Board of Education*
Free Exercise of Religion	1940	*Cantwell v. Connecticut*
Freedom of Speech	1925	*Gitlow v. New York*
	1927	*Fiske v. Kansas*
	1931	*Stromberg v. California*
Freedom of Press	1931	*Near v. Minnesota*
Freedom to Peaceably Assemble	1937	*DeJong v. Oregon*
Amendment II		
Militia/Right to Bear Arms	NI	[*Presser v. Illinois*, 1886]
Amendment III		
No Quartering Soldiers	NI	
Amendment IV		
No Unreasonable Search and Seizure	1949	*Wolf. v. Colorado* (basic right)
	1961	*Mapp v. Ohio* (exclusionary rule)
Amendment V		
Grand Jury	NI	[*Hurtado v. California*, 1884]
No Double Jeopardy	1969	*Benton v. Maryland*
Due Process	NI	
No Self-Incrimination	1964	*Malloy v. Hogan*
Just Compensation for Taking Private Property	1897	*Chicago, Burlington & Quincy RR v. Chicago*
Amendment VI		
Speedy Trial	1967	*Klopfer v. North Carolina*
Public Trial	1948	*In re Oliver*
Impartial Jury	1966	*Parker v. Gladden*
Jury Trial	1968	*Duncan v. Louisiana*
Vicinage and Venue	NI	[implied in due process]
Notice	NI	[implied in due process]
Confrontation	1965	*Pointer v. Texas*
Compulsory Process	1967	*Washington v. Texas*
Counsel	1963	*Gideon v. Wainwright*
Amendment VII		
Jury Trial in Civil Case	NI	[*Walker v. Sauvinet*, 1875]
Amendment VIII		
No Excessive Bail	[implied]	[*Schilb v. Kuebel*, 1971]
No Excessive Fine	NI	
No Cruel & Unusual Punishment	1962	*Robinson v. California*

NI, not incorporated.

was protected from self-incrimination in federal courts and a federal witness was protected from self-incrimination in state courts. The specific issue in *Adamson* (1947)—whether a judge could comment on a defendant's failure to testify in a state trial—was in effect overruled in *Griffin v. California* (1965).

Other cases incorporating Bill of Rights provisions came in quick succession: *Pointer v. Texas* (1965) (Sixth Amendment Confrontation Clause); *Parker v. Gladden* (1966) (Sixth Amendment right to an impartial jury); *Washington v. Texas* (1967) (Sixth Amendment right to subpoena witnesses under the Compulsory Process Clause); *Klopfer v. North Carolina* (1967) (Sixth Amendment right to a speedy trial); and *Benton v. Maryland* (1969) (Fifth Amendment protection against double jeopardy, overruling *Palko v. Connecticut,* 1937).

The Court incorporated the Sixth Amendment right to trial by jury in *Duncan v. Louisiana* (1968). Was a jury trial required for a crime carrying a maximum penalty of two years' imprisonment? To answer this, Justice Byron White analyzed the trend of the incorporation cases and concluded that the standard of what constituted a *fundamental right,* worthy of incorporation into the Due Process Clause and made applicable against the state, had shifted considerably since the 1937 *Palko* case:

> Earlier the Court can be seen as having asked, when inquiring into whether some particular procedural safeguard was required of a State, if a civilized system could be imagined that would not accord the particular protection. . . . The recent cases, on the other hand, have proceeded upon the valid assumption that state criminal processes are not imaginary and theoretical schemes but *actual systems bearing virtually every characteristic of the common-law system* that has been developing contemporaneously in England and this country. The question thus is whether given *this kind of system* a particular procedure is fundamental—whether, that is, a procedure is necessary to an Anglo-American regime of ordered liberty. (*Duncan v. Louisiana,* 1968, emphases added)

By the late 1960s, it appeared that the effect of incorporation rulings was to make state rules of constitutional criminal procedure identical to the federal rules. However, several important decisions made it clear that this was not always the case. The basic reason is that the Court did not hold that the Bill of Rights applied *directly* to the states.[82] To this extent *Barron v. Baltimore* (1833) still had a residual effect. Incorporation meant that a state procedure that came within the general scope of a Bill of Rights provision, but which did not afford rights that had been granted to federal defendants under the specific provision, were held to violate the Due Process Clause of the Fourteenth Amendment. The ruling then applied the interpretation that had been applied to federal defendants. But the intermediate step of incorporation—going through the Fourteenth Amendment—gave the Court some "wiggle room" in a few cases decided after 1970 to hold that the precise impact of the federal rule would not apply to the states.

The Sixth Amendment, for example, guarantees federal defendants a jury trial in *all* crimes. The Court, nevertheless, upheld state laws that eliminated jury trials for crimes punishable by six months or less of imprisonment, calling them "petty crimes." In *Baldwin v. New York* (1970), the Court drew the line of "petty crimes" at six months and struck down a New York law that allowed the crowded New York court system to deprive defendants of a jury trial for crimes carrying penalties of up to one year of imprisonment. In a case decided the same day, *Williams v. Florida* (1970), for the first time, *federal and state standards for rights diverged*. The Supreme Court held that the common law twelve-person jury was *not* constitutionally mandated by the Sixth Amendment, upholding a state felony conviction by a six-person jury.

Justice John M. Harlan II, who opposed the Incorporation Doctrine, noted that flexibility could have been introduced into constitutional criminal procedure by staying with the due process case-by-case approach of *Palko, Adamson,* and *Rochin.* Now, he argued, rights guaranteed to federal defendants were being diluted in order to impose Bill of Rights protections on the states. The Court was softening the clear meaning and requirements of the Bill of Rights in federal cases.

The Court has continued this trend. State felony convictions based on less-than-unanimous jury verdicts were upheld in *Johnson v. Louisiana* (1972) and *Apodaca v. Oregon* (1972), creating the risk that plurality juries would be far less deliberative than unanimous juries. The Court may have felt that it went far enough with these jury cases and in *Ballew v. Georgia* (1978), held that a five-person jury violated the constitutional guarantee of a jury.

At present, a few rights in the First through Eighth amendments have not been incorporated into the Fourteenth Amendment. These include indictment by grand jury, no excessive bail, jury trial in civil cases, the quartering of soldiers, and the right to bear arms as part of a militia. Reflecting on the rights excluded as a result of the selective incorporation approach, a leading commentator suggests that "perhaps it is just as well that they remain unincorporated."[83]

The due process revolution nationalized criminal justice by opening the door to federal court intervention of local and state agencies and courts, making criminal procedure somewhat more uniform. The due process revolution was in sync with the Warren Court's other major agenda items: eradicating legal racial segregation, providing "one-person-one-vote," and protecting First Amendment rights. All of these advances, together, were designed to ensure the equal participation of all citizens in the political life of the nation. The due process revolution and the other parts of the Court's agenda generated enormous antagonism toward the Supreme Court and its liberal chief justice, Earl Warren, by conservative politicians and many in law enforcement. Since 1970, the Supreme Court, with a more conservative membership under Chief Justices Burger and Rehnquist, has limited the expansion of pro-defendant criminal procedure rights but has not overruled incorporation. Most Americans, while wary of defendants' rights, nevertheless have come to accept the nationalization of the Bill of Rights.

The Counterrevolution

With historic regularity, revolutions produce counterrevolutions. The Warren Court had severe political critics (see the discussion following in this chapter), and a reaction to its rulings began in the early 1970s. Between 1969 and 1972, four justices retired and President Richard M. Nixon appointed conservative replacements. Between 1969 and 1996, twelve new justices were appointed to the Court, four by President Nixon, one by President Gerald R. Ford, three by President Ronald Reagan, two by President George H.W. Bush, and two by President Bill Clinton. The appointment of ten new justices by conservative Republicans and two by a "new," or middle-of-the-road, Democrat definitely swung the ideological makeup of the Court to the right. This section provides an overview of the shift from liberal to more-or-less conservative rulings in the period since the Due Process Revolution. This overview is a prelude to most of the cases analyzed in this text.

"THE COUNTERREVOLUTION THAT WASN'T": THE BURGER COURT 1969–1986   President Nixon's appointment of four justices led many to believe that the selective incorporation of the Bill of Rights would be overturned.[84] These fears were abetted by Chief Justice Burger's attack on the *Miranda* doctrine and the *Mapp* exclusionary rule in his early cases.[85] The Burger Court did not, however, execute a reactionary return to the preincorporation era. Instead, it held the line against the expansion of rights. "In place of the expected counterrevolution, the Burger Court waged a prolonged and rather bloody campaign of guerilla warfare. It typically left the facade of Warren Court decisions standing while it attacked these decisions from the sides and underneath."[86] For example, the *Miranda* rule stands after more than thirty years of conservative criticism, but a "public safety" exception allows prewarning questions (*New York v. Quarles,* 1984), and a defendant may be subsequently questioned after first having exercised *Miranda* rights by requesting the right to remain silent (*Michigan v. Mosley,* 1975). And although the *Mapp v. Ohio* (1961) exclusionary rule was not overruled, an exception was created that allowed the introduction of evidence based on a defective search warrant if the officer relied on it in "good faith" (*United States v. Leon,* 1984).

The Burger Court was not uniformly pro-prosecution and has extended defendants' rights on several occasions. It established, for example, a warrant requirement for entry of a house to make a felony arrest (*Payton v. New York,* 1980), and declared random automobile stops to check drivers' licenses to be a Fourth Amendment violation (*Delaware v. Prouse,* 1979).

One measure of the success of a Supreme Court's "agenda" over the period of a chief justice's tenure is whether or not the Court provides a coherent conceptual foundation for its decisions. In general, scholars have found the Burger Court to be lacking a coherent set of guiding principles by which decisions can be measured. Professor Charles Whitebread, examining the lack of doctrinal consistency, has suggested five ways in which the Burger Court approached criminal procedure cases that account for its generally conservative rulings, while not going to the point of rolling back the Warren Court's Bill of Rights incorporation revolution.

First, the Court emphasized the Crime Control Model of the criminal process and was "eager to accommodate what it perceived as legitimate needs of effective law enforcement."[87] Second, the Court established a **hierarchy of constitutional rights.** Those Sixth Amendment rights concerned with the integrity of the trial and the truth-finding process are protected more strictly than are Fifth Amendment self-incrimination issues, which in turn are given more protection than Fourth Amendment rights concerning search and seizure. Third, this hierarchy is connected with a *concern for the factual guilt or innocence* of the party whose case is before the Supreme Court. Whitebread believed that this concern distorted the Supreme Court's overriding duty to develop sound and principled general rules for the guidance of the entire court system.

A fourth aspect of the Court's approach was a "jurisprudential preference for *case-by-case analysis* rather than announcing its decisions in criminal cases in rules."[88] Whitebread saw this as the most dangerous characteristic of the Court's approach. This attribute fails to give lower courts and police clear-cut rules by which to guide their actions. Whitebread has predicted a spate of future cases generated by a need to determine how the narrow distinctions established by the Court are to be applied in specific instances. Fifth, the Court fostered the "new federalism" that partially closed the door to federal courts for state defendants, thus transferring significant power over criminal procedure to the state courts. For example, the Court applied a cost-benefit analysis in *Stone v. Powell* (1976) and ruled that Fourth Amendment claims, once raised and decided in state courts, could not be heard again on federal habeas corpus when the state provided a full and fair hearing. The narrowing of federal habeas corpus jurisdiction reversed a hallmark of the Warren Court, opening the door of the federal courts to state defendants in *Fay v. Noia* (1963). The reimposition of procedural barriers indicated an attitude of wishing to return to an era when federal protection of constitutional rights was minimal.

THE COUNTERREVOLUTION THAT WAS: THE REHNQUIST COURT 1986–PRESENT   It now seems clear that with a few exceptions, the Supreme Court from the mid-1980s to the present has taken a far more conservative stance than the Burger Court. Weddington and Janikowski write about the "counter-revolution that is."[89] The counterrevolution can be seen in search and seizure decisions. Although a few Rehnquist Court rulings have upheld traditional Fourth Amendment rights, these have had little practical effect on law enforcement. For example, the Court ruled that the common law "knock and announce" procedure is required by the Fourth Amendment. This ruling has little practical effect, for the "Amendment's flexible requirement of reasonableness should not be read to mandate a rigid rule of announcement that ignores countervailing law enforcement interests" (*Wilson v. Arkansas,* 1995). On the other hand, rulings that acknowledge drug courier profiles as a basis to stop individuals (*United States v. Sokolow,* 1989); that authorize drug "bus sweeps" (*Florida v. Bostick,* 1991); that allow searches based on anonymous telephone tips (*Alabama v. White* 1990); that uphold the "protective sweep" of homes during an arrest (*Maryland v. Buie,* 1990); that permit "plain feel" pat-downs (*Minnesota v. Dickerson,* 1993); that license electronic eavesdropping without minimization procedures (*United States v. Ojeda Rios,* 1990); that sanction arrests in violation of international law (*United States v. Alvarez-Machain,* 1992); that treat a police chase as not being a "search and seizure," (*California v. Hodari D.,* 1991); and that favor full searches of containers in automobiles without warrants (*California v. Acevedo,* 1991) have substantially unshackled police from serious Fourth Amendment limitations. Many see this diminution of rights as giving political support to an uncontrolled war on drugs and as condoning modern racism.

As for the highly controversial law of confessions, John Decker writes, "The Burger and Rehnquist Courts have more recently reflected a degree of apparent discomfort with the principles of *Miranda,* for the great majority of the opinions interpreting *Miranda* decided since the Warren Court period have not vigorously followed its lead."[90] For example, the use of undercover agents in a jail setting is allowed. While *Miranda* on its face prohibits *custodial interrogation* without Fifth Amendment warnings, the Court held that because a jailed suspect who speaks to an officer posing as a fellow inmate is *not compelled,* no warnings need be given (*Illinois v. Perkins,* 1990). The Court has also supported an aggressive campaign by federal prosecutors to disallow effective opposing defense attorneys (*Wheat v. United States,* 1988), claiming there would be a conflict of interest and has allowed money paid to defense attorneys by drug defendants to be forfeited (*United States v. Monsanto,* 1989; *Caplin & Drysdale v. United States,* 1989).

More telling than specific conservative rulings is the Rehnquist Court's tampering with underlying doctrines. In *Arizona v. Fulminante* (1991), a majority overturned a longstanding precedent and ruled that a coerced confession could be deemed "harmless error." Thus, if police coerce a confession and a court, in error, allows such a constitutionally invalid confession to be heard by a jury, a conviction based on the coerced confession can be upheld. The Court was explicit in directing that the central purpose of a trial is to decide questions of guilt or innocence; the introduction of unconstitutional evidence is of lesser importance. Perhaps the most dramatic example of the Rehnquist Court as an activist-conservative Court, interested more in achieving the "right" result than in upholding basic principles, is *Payne v. Tennessee* (1991), which allowed victim impact statements at death penalty hearings. What has shocked commentators is that *Payne* overruled two precedents that were only four years old and, in his opinion, Chief Justice Rehnquist openly stated that precedent is not important where earlier cases were decided by close votes (*Booth v. Maryland,* 1987; *South Carolina v. Gathers,* 1989). He believed "that **stare decisis** 'is not an inexorable command' but instead a 'principle of policy.' . . . *Stare decisis* principles are at their weakest point in 'constitutional cases,' he said, because correction through legislative initiative is virtu-

ally impossible."[91] He went on to say that precedent is more important in property and contract rights than in procedural and evidentiary cases. Justice Thurgood Marshall, dissenting, noted that under the majority's theory, the Court's rulings cannot be considered "impersonal reasoned judgements" and "[p]ower, not reason, is the new currency of this Court's decisionmaking." This was a polite way of saying that the majority opinion was lawless.

Finally, the Rehnquist Court has extended the work of the Burger Court in closing the door to federal and collateral appeals. *Brecht v. Abrahamson* (1993) made it more difficult for defendants to challenge errors on habeas corpus review of constitutional error than on direct appeal. Justice Rehnquist "explained that the beyond-reasonable-doubt standard had become too costly for the government."[92] These decisions display a Court that has become hostile to the claims of defendants. What is curious, and even brilliant, is that the Court has shifted virtually every rule and underlying doctrine in favor of the state while at the same time maintaining the facade of the essential right. Thus, the *Mapp* exclusionary rule exists and the *Miranda* warnings are still required, but these general rules are shot through with exceptions.

SUMMARY

Criminal procedure is a branch of constitutional law that pits public safety against guaranteeing liberty. This tension is resolved by the United States Supreme Court, which balances the need for liberty and order. The poles of the tension between order and liberty are also described as the "Crime Control Model," which stresses finality, or to the "Due Process Model," which stresses the overriding need to avoid miscarriages of justice; these orientations influence the direction of decisions in the Court.

Knowledge of the context of criminal procedure provides a better understanding of the subject than can be gleaned only by reading Supreme Court decisions. The context includes the criminal justice system. The Supreme Court, along with legislatures, helps to make rules for the criminal justice system, but criminal justice includes the people who enforce the rules. As a human process, the way criminal justice works in practice does not always accord with the dictates of the law.

The context of criminal procedure includes an understanding of the law and legal rules, as the creation of different bodies and people, including legislatures, courts, and chief executives, who are organized hierarchically according to legitimate legal and constitutional authority. Statutes or actions of executive officers are illegal if they conflict with rules of constitutional law. Substantive law creates rights and obligations; procedural law directs officers, lawyers, and judges as to how to proceed in carrying out their functions; and remedial law determines what benefits or remedies can be won by parties who prevail in lawsuits. Criminal procedure is procedural law in that it guides the conduct of criminal justice personnel but at the same time constitutional criminal procedure is substantive law because it creates constitutional rights of suspects and defendants.

The jurisdiction and hierarchy of the courts are a central aspect of criminal procedure. Appellate courts resolve issues of law; they do not retry the facts of a case. The United States Supreme Court decides only federal issues, but when it does, its rulings under the Constitution are superior to federal legislation and to state law (including state constitutions). State high courts can decide criminal procedure issues exclusively under their own state constitutions. When they base decisions on adequate and independent state grounds, state supreme courts can grant parties a greater level of individual rights than granted by the United States Supreme Court under the United States Constitution.

Other contextual aspects of criminal procedure that are found in the text include history, politics, judicial biography, and human rights. The context of political theory indicates that underlying ideas like liberty and equality give meaning to the rules of criminal procedure. They are reflected in the everyday working of criminal procedure.

The Incorporation Doctrine is the idea that the Bill of Rights applies as a limitation on state law and state and local officers. Before the Civil War, the Supreme Court ruled that the Bill of Rights applied only to the federal government. Under the Due Process Clause of the Fourteenth Amendment, a state cannot infringe upon the rights of each person, who is both a state and a federal citizen, of due process and equal protection. Congress and the federal courts have power to enforce the Fourteenth Amendment. Over the course of a century after 1868 the argument was made that specific provisions of the Bill of Rights are also guarantees of due process. The Court accepted this concept in the 1960s and in that decade incorporated most of the criminal procedure rights in the Bill of Rights so as to require that states abide by those rights.

The federal courts, in addition to finding that a state law or practice violated a right inherent in the Bill of Rights, may also find that a state practice violated Fourteenth Amendment due process if such a practice were fundamentally unfair, as determined by examining all of the facts and circumstances of the case.

Since the due process revolution of the 1960s, the Supreme Court has become quite conservative in its criminal procedure rulings. The Burger Court (1969–1986), in accord with the temper of the times that combined political conservatism with individualism, maintained the incorporation of rights but limited the expansion of most rights and created several exceptions. The Rehnquist Court (1986–present) has accelerated this trend.

FURTHER READING

CONTEXT

Charles Rembar, *The Law of the Land: The Evolution of Our Legal System* (New York: Touchstone, 1981).

Benjamin N. Cardozo, *The Nature of the Judicial Process* (New Haven, Conn.: Yale University Press, 1921).

Bernard Schwartz, *A History of the Supreme Court* (New York: Oxford University Press, 1993).

INCORPORATION:

Leonard W. Levy, *Original Intent and the Framers' Constitution* (New York: Macmillan, 1988).

Michael Kent Curtis, *No State Shall Abridge: The Fourteenth Amendment and the Bill of Rights* (Durham: University of North Carolina Press, 1986).

Akhil Reed Amar, *The Constitution and Criminal Procedure: First Principles* (New Haven: Yale University Press, 1997).

ENDNOTES

1. U.S. Bureau of Justice Statistics, "Criminal Victimization, Summary Findings," http://www.ojp.usdoj.gov/bjs/cvictgen.htm (accessed July 19, 2003). In 2001, U.S. residents age twelve or older experienced approximately 24.2 million crimes, according to findings from the National Crime Victimization Survey: 18.3 million were property crimes; 5.7 million were crimes of violence.

2. John F. Burns, "Baghdad Residents Begin a Long Climb to an Ordered City," *New York Times*, April 14, 2003; Patrick E. Tyler, "After the War: Disorder; Across Iraq, the Dark Shadow of Hussein Still Looms Large," *New York Times*, June 22, 2003.

3. Susan Sachs, "After the War: Mass Executions; A Grim Graveyard Window on Hussein's Iraq," *New York Times*, June 1, 2003.

4. Herbert L. Packer, "Two Models of the Criminal Process," *University of Pennsylvania Law Review* 113: (1964) 1–68; Herbert L. Packer, *The Limits of the Criminal Sanction* (Stanford, Cal.: Stanford University Press, 1968).

5. Dana Priest and Barton Gellman, "U.S. Decries Abuse but Defends Interrogations; 'Stress and Duress' Tactics Used on Terrorism Suspects Held in Secret Overseas Facilities," *Washington Post*, December 26, 2002.

6. Don Van Natta, Jr., "Six Groups Said to Be Monitored in U.S. for Possible Qaeda Links," *New York Times*, August 23, 2003; Eric Lichtblau with William Glaberson, "Millions Raised for Qaeda in Brooklyn, U.S. Says," *New York Times*, March 5, 2003.

7. David McCullough, *John Adams* (New York: Simon & Schuster, 2001); James F. Simon, *What Kind of Nation: Thomas Jefferson, John Marshall, and the Epic Struggle to Create a United States* (New York: Simon & Schuster, 2002).

8. Mark E. Neely, Jr., *The Fate of Liberty: Abraham Lincoln and Civil Liberties* (New York: Oxford University Press, 1991).

9. Roberta Strauss Feuerlicht, *America's Reign of Terror: World War I, the Red Scare, and the Palmer Raids* (New York: Random House, 1971).

10. *Korematsu v. United States* (1944).

11. Peter H. Irons, *Justice at War* (New York: Oxford University Press, 1983); Victor S. Navasky, *Kennedy Justice* (New York: Atheneum, 1971).

12. Alan F. Westin, *The Anatomy of a Constitutional Law Case: Youngstown Sheet and Tube Co. v. Sawyer; the Steel Seizure Decision* (New York: Macmillan, 1958).

13. Stanley I. Kutler, *The American Inquisition: Justice and Injustice in the Cold War* (New York: Hill and Wang, 1982); Frank Donner, *Protectors of Privilege: Red Squads and Police Repression in Urban America* (Berkeley: University of California Press, 1990); David Wise, *The American Police State* (New York: Random House, 1976); James MacGregor Burns and Stewart Burns, *A People's Charter: The Pursuit of Rights in America* (New York: Alfred Knopf, 1991).

14. David Johnston with Raymond Bonner, "Suspect in Indonesia Bombings Is Captured in Asia," *New York Times*, August 15, 2003; AP, "France Arrests Two in 9/11 Investigation," *New York Times*, June 6, 2003; Erik Eckholm, "Pakistanis Arrest Qaeda Figure Seen as Planner of 9/11," *New York Times*, March 2, 2003; Warren Hoge, "British Court Charges 4 Men as Terrorists; Arrests Spread," *New York Times*, January 14, 2003; John Tagliabue, "French Link 6 to 'Shoe Bomb' Attempt; 12 Other Militants Seized in Paris Raids," *New York Times*, November 27, 2002; Elaine Sciolino, "France Links Tunisian in Jail to Terror Cells in 5 Nations," *New York Times*, October 23, 2002; Desmond Butler, "The Netherlands; Sept. 11 Plotter Reportedly Sent Terror Funds Flowing Through Dutch Town," *New York Times,* September 22, 2002.

15. Uniting and Strengthening America by Providing Appropriate Tools Required to Intercept and Obstruct Terrorism Act of 2001 (USA PATRIOT Act), Pub. L. No. 107-56, 115 Stat. 272 (2001).

16. Stephen J. Schulhofer, *The Enemy Within: Intelligence Gathering, Law Enforcement, and Civil Liberties in the Wake of September 11* (New York: Century Foundation Press, 2000).

17. See John W. Whitehead and Steven H. Aden, "Forfeiting 'Enduring Freedom' for 'Homeland Security': A Constitutional Analysis of the USA PATRIOT Act and the Justice Department's Anti-terrorism Initiatives," *American University Law Review* 51 (2002): 1081–1133; George C. Harris, "Book Review: Terrorism and the Constitution: Sacrificing Civil Liberties in the Name of National Security," *Cornell International Law Journal* 36 (2003): 135–150 (Review of David Cole & James X. Dempsey, *Terrorism and the Constitution: Sacrificing Civil Liberties in the Name of National Security*, Second Edition (New York: The New Press, 2002)).

18. Mark Hamblett, "Terrorism Cases Put Judges Front and Center in Terror Cases," *New York Law Journal* (July 7, 2003): 1.

19. *United States v. Rabinowitz*, 339 U.S. 56, 69 (1950) (Frankfurter, J., dissenting).

20. Anthony Lewis, *Gideon's Trumpet* (New York: Vintage Books, 1964); James Goodman, *Stories of Scottsboro* (New York: Pantheon, 1994); James Neff, *The Wrong Man: The Final Verdict on the Dr. Sam Sheppard Murder Case* (New York: Random House, 2001).

21. Paul Averich, *The Haymarket Tragedy* (Princeton: Princeton University Press, 1984); Felix Frankfurter, *The Case of Sacco and Vanzetti* (Boston: Little, Brown, 1927).

22. The Innocence Project, description http://www.innocenceproject.org/ (accessed August 7, 2003).

23. Jim Dwyer, Barry Scheck, and Peter Neufeld, *Actual Innocence* (New York: Doubleday, 2000); Edward Humes, *Mean Justice* (New York: Simon & Schuster, 1999); *Arizona v. Youngblood* (1988).

24. *The Oklahoman,* November 2, 2002, quoted in The Innocence Project, "DNA News" http://www.innocenceproject.org/dnanews/index.php (accessed August 7, 2003).

25. Barton L. Ingraham, *The Structure of Criminal Procedure: Laws and Practice of France, the Soviet Union, China, and the United States* (New York: Greenwood Press, 1987), 22–25.

26. The Bureau of Justice Statistics, *The Growth of Appeals 1973–83 Trends* (Washington, D.C.: Department of Justice, 1985).

27. Stanley Kinyon, *Introduction to Law Study and Law Examination in a Nutshell* (St. Paul: West Publishing, 1971), 8–17.

28. Congress has power to make war (art. I., §8, cl. 8), raise army and maintain navy (art. I., §8, cl. 9 and 10), punish piracy on the high seas (art. I., §8, cl. 10), organize militias, allowing some state authority (art. I., §8, cl. 16); President is commander in chief of armed forces (art. II. Sec 2, cl. 1).

29. Postal (art. I., §8, cl. 7); Commerce (art. I., §8, cl. 3); equal privileges and immunities (art. IV, §2, cl. 1); full faith and credit (art. IV, §1); extradition (art. IV, §2, cl. 2); territories (art. IV, §3, cl. 2); no new state can be carved out of an existing state or by combining states without the consent of both state legislatures and Congress (art. IV, §3, cl. 1).

30. U.S. Const. art. IV, §4; Abraham Lincoln, "The Gettysburg Address" (1863) (Hay Draft), Library of Congress http://www.loc.gov/exhibits/gadd/gatr2.html (accessed August 3, 2003).

31. U.S. Const. art. I, §9, cl. 3 and art. 8; §10, cl. 1.

32. John S. Baker, Jr., "State Police Powers and the Federalization of Local Crime," *Temple Law Review* 72 (1999): 673–713.

33. The original thirteen states agreed to be bound by relevant portions of the Constitution and new states may be admitted to the Union only under art. IV, §3 and under laws passed under the authority of that section. In *Printz v. U.S.* (1997) the Supreme Court held that Congress could not require local sheriffs to enforce the background check portions of the Brady Handgun Violence Prevention Act and the portion of the Brady Bill requiring such action was unconstitutional.

34. U.S. Const. art. VI, cl. 3.

35. A federal court can hear issues of state law as a matter of its diversity jurisdiction (the parties reside in different states) or under "pendent jurisdiction" in which the court hears a case in which both federal and state issues are present. As a matter of judicial economy the federal court can decide the state law issue in accord with state precedents. The Supreme Court has no jurisdiction to decide a case based exclusively on state grounds, so a very small number of cases decided by federal courts cannot be appealed to the Supreme Court.

36. Bernard Schwartz, *A History of the Supreme Court* (New York: Oxford University Press, 1993), 43–45.

37. Helen E. Veit, Kenneth R. Bowling, and Charlene Bangs Bickford, eds., *Creating the Bill of Rights: The Documentary Record from the First Federal Congress* (Baltimore: Johns Hopkins University Press, 1991), 83–84.

38. Michael Kammen, *Spheres of Liberty: Changing Perceptions of Liberty in American Culture* (Madison: University of Wisconsin Press, 1986).

39. Candace McCoy, "The Cop's World: Modern Policing and the Difficulty of Legitimizing the Use of Force," *Human Rights Quarterly* 8 (1986): 270–293.

40. Patricia Mell, "Big Brother at the Door: Balancing National Security with Privacy Under the USA PATRIOT Act," *Denver University Law Review* 80 (2002): 374–427.

41. J. R. Pole, *The Pursuit of Equality in American History* (Berkeley: University of California Press, 1978).

42. For a readable account of Rome's greatest exponent of constitutionalism and the decline of that ideal, see Anthony Everitt, *Cicero: The Life and Times of Rome's Greatest Politician* (New York: Random House, 2003).

43. Glenn Tinder, *Political Thinking: The Perennial Questions, Fourth Edition* (Boston: Little, Brown, 1986), 117.

44. Gordon J. Schochet, "Constitutionalism, Liberalism, and the Study of Politics," in *Constitutionalism* by J. Roland Pennock and John W. Chapman, eds. (New York: New York University Press, 1979), 1.

45. Compare Raoul Berger, *Government by Judiciary* (Cambridge, Mass.: Harvard University Press, 1977), with R. Dworkin, "Political Judges and the Rule of Law," in *A Matter of Principle* by Dworkin (Cambridge, Mass.: Harvard University Press, 1985), 9–32.

46. Eric Lichtblau, "Bush Issues Racial Profiling Ban but Exempts Security Inquiries," *New York Times*, June 18, 2003.

47. Marvin Zalman, John Strate, Denis Hunter, and James Sellars, "Michigan's Assisted Suicide Three Ring Circus," *Ohio Northern University Law Review* 23 (1997): 863–968.

48. Jerome Hall, *General Principles of Criminal Law, Second Edition* (Indianapolis: Bobs-Merrill, 1961), 27.

49. Charles Rembar, *The Law of the Land: The Evolution of Our Legal System* (New York: Touchstone, 1981).

50. Abraham Lincoln, "The Gettysburg Address" (Hay Draft), Library of Congress http://www.loc.gov/exhibits/gadd/gatr2.html (accessed August 3, 2003).

51. See Samuel Walker, *Popular Justice: A History of American Criminal Justice, Second Edition* (New York: Oxford University Press, 1998), 180–193.

52. Leonard W. Levy, *Original Intent and the Framers' Constitution* (New York: Macmillan, 1988), 137–173.

53. Eric Foner, *Reconstruction: America's Unfinished Revolution, 1863–1877* (New York: Harper & Row, 1988), 251–261.

54. Michael Kent Curtis, *No State Shall Abridge: The Fourteenth Amendment and the Bill of Rights* (Durham, N.C.: Duke University Press, 1986).

55. See Robert A. Burt, *The Constitution in Conflict* (Cambridge, Mass.: Harvard University Press, 1992).

56. Fred P. Graham, *The Due Process Revolution: The Warren Court's Impact on Criminal Law* (New York: Hayden Book Co., 1970), 15; see Louis M. Kohlmeier, Jr., *"God Save This Honorable Court!"* (New York: Charles Scribner's Sons, 1972), 79; Willard M. Oliver, *The Law & Order Presidency* (Upper Saddle River, N.J.: Prentice-Hall, 2003), 70–76.

57. Earl M. Maltz, *Civil Rights, The Constitution, and Congress, 1863–1869* (Lawrence: University of Kansas Press, 1990); William E. Nelson, *The Fourteenth Amendment: From Political Principle to Judicial Doctrine* (Cambridge, Mass.: Harvard University Press, 1998).

58. August Meier and Elliott Rudwick, *From Plantation to Ghetto, Third Edition* (New York: Hill & Wang, 1976).

59. Richard Kluger, *Simple Justice* (New York: Andre Deutsch, 1977), 748–778.

60. Arthur J. Goldberg, *Equal Justice: The Warren Era of the Supreme Court* (New York: Farrar, Straus, & Giroux, 1971), 5–6.

61. Richard C. Cortner, *A Mob Intent on Death: The NAACP and the Arkansas Riot Case* (Middletown, Conn.: Wesleyan University Press, 1988); James Goodman, *Stories of Scottsboro* (New York: Pantheon Books, 1994).

62. Michael Tonry, *Malign Neglect—Race, Crime, and Punishment in America* (New York: Oxford University Press, 1995); Jamie Fellner and Marc Mauer, *Losing the Vote: The Impact of Felony Disenfranchisement Laws in the United States* (Sentencing Project; Human Rights Watch) (1998).

63. Randall Kennedy, *Race, Crime, and the Law* (New York: Pantheon, 1997).

64. Marvin Zalman and Elsa Shartsis, "A Roadblock Too Far? Justice O'Connor's Left Turn on the Fourth," *Journal of Contemporary Criminal Justice* 19 (2003): 182–204.

65. Ann Tusa and John Tusa, *The Nuremberg Trial* (New York: McGraw-Hill, 1983); Telford Taylor, *The Anatomy of the Nuremberg Trials* (Boston: Little, Brown, 1992).

66. Mary Ann Glendon, *A World Made New: Eleanor Roosevelt and the Universal Declaration of Human Rights* (New York: Random House, 2001).

67. Jack Donnelly, *Universal Human Rights in Theory and Practice* (Ithaca, NY: Cornell University Press, 1989), 9–14; John Humphrey, *No Distant Millennium: The International Law of Human Rights* (Paris: UNESCO, 1989), 20–21.

68. Michael J. Perry, *The Constitution, The Courts, and Human Rights* (New Haven: Yale University Press, 1982). One author on constitutional interpretation simply uses "human rights" as a term for constitutional rights.

69. See Richard J. Terrill, *World Criminal Justice Systems: A Survey, Fifth Edition* (Cincinnati: Anderson, 2003); Bron McKillop, "Anatomy of a French Murder Case," *American Journal of Comparative Law* 45 (1997): 527–583. Some nations use juries, but they do not have the same power as juries in the United States to render verdicts without the direct supervision and vote of judges. For recent exceptions, see Stephen C. Thaman, "Europe's New Jury Systems: The Cases of Spain and Russia," *Law and Contemporary Problems* 62 (1999): 233–259.

70. See M. Cherif Bassiouni, ed., *The Protection of Human Rights in the Administration of Criminal Justice: A Compendium of United Nations Norms and Standards* (Irvington-on-Hudson, N.Y.: Transnational Publishers, 1994). Reports such as Amnesty International, "Amnesty International Report 1995," (1995) provide pictures of the status of human rights at given points in time.

71. "Of course, procedural justice must contribute to the common goal of all governments, which is to further the freedom of each member of society and to secure the liberty of all. . . . Thus, criminal investigations and proceedings full of blind revenge and abhorrent to the spirit of the law are detested in western democratic societies." Wilfried Bottke, "'Rule of Law' or 'Due Process' as a Common Feature of Criminal Process in Western Democratic Societies," *University of Pittsburgh Law Review* 51 (1990): 419–461.

72. For a readable review of the scholarship on incorporation see Henry J. Abraham, *Freedom and the Court: Civil Rights and Civil Liberties in the United States,* 4th ed. (New York: Oxford University Press, 1982), 28–91.

73. Akhil Reed Amar, *The Bill of Rights: Creation and Reconstruction* (New Haven: Yale University Press, 1998), 145–162 (discussing the existence of "contrarians" who believed that the Bill of Rights should apply to state and local government).

74. See Robert Lowry Clinton, Marbury v. Madison *and Judicial Review* (Lawrence: University Press of Kansas, 1989); Wallace Mendelson, *Supreme Court Statecraft: The Rule of Law and Men* (Ames: Iowa State University Press, 1985), 207–262; Raoul Berger, *Congress v. The Supreme Court* (New York: Bantam Books, 1969).

75. Bernard Schwartz, *A History of the Supreme Court* (New York: Oxford University Press, 1993), 43, citing *Fletcher v. Peck* at p. 136.

76. G. Edward White, *The Marshall Court and Cultural Change,* abridged ed. (New York: Oxford University Press, 1991), 197.

77. Michael Kent Curtis, *No State Shall Abridge: The Fourteenth Amendment and the Bill of Rights* (Durham: Duke University Press, 1986), 129: the "weight of the evidence from the Thirty-ninth Congress supports the conclusion that the Fourteenth Amendment was designed to require the states to respect all guarantees of the Bill of Rights." See also Amar, *Bill of Rights.*

78. David A. J. Richards, *Conscience and the Constitution: History, Theory, and Law of the Reconstruction Amendments* (Princeton: Princeton University Press, 1993), makes a convincing argument for the idea of total incorporation based on the Privileges or Immunities Clause.

79. For an excellent history of the case, see Richard C. Cortner, *A Mob Intent on Death: The NAACP and the Arkansas Riot Case* (Middletown, Conn.: Wesleyan Press, 1988).

80. Leonard Dinnerstein, *The Leo Frank Case* (Athens: University of Georgia Press, 1987); Liva Baker, *The Justice from Beacon Hill* (New York: HarperCollins, 1991), 467–71.

81. Richard C. Cortner, *The Supreme Court and the Second Bill of Rights: The Fourteenth Amendment and the Nationalization of Civil Liberties* (Madison: University of Wisconsin Press, 1980), 126–139.

82. For an argument that such a theory is feasible, see Amar, *Bill of Rights.*

83. Abraham, *Freedom and the Court,* 90.

84. See, for example, Leonard Levy, *Against the Law: The Nixon Court and Criminal Justice* (New York: Harper Torchbooks, 1974).

85. *Bivens v. Six Unknown Named Agents* (1971); *Harris v. New York* (1971); see M. Braswell and J. Scheb II, "Conservative Pragmatism Versus Liberal Principles: Warren E. Burger on the Suppression of Evidence, 1956–86," *Creighton Law Review* 20 (1987): 789–831.

86. Albert Alschuler, "Failed Pragmatism: Reflections on the Burger Court," *Harvard Law Review* 100 (1987): 1436–1456.

87. C. Whitebread, "The Burger Court's Counter-Revolution in Criminal Procedure: The Recent Criminal Decisions of the United States Supreme Court," *Washburn Law Journal* 24 (1985): 471–498.

88. Ibid., 472.

89. Mary Margaret Weddington and W. Richard Janikowski, "The Rehnquist Court: The Counter-Revolution That Wasn't. Part II: The Counter-Revolution That Is," *Criminal Justice Review* 21 (2) (1997): 231–250.

90. John F. Decker, *Revolution to the Right: Criminal Procedure Jurisprudence During the Burger-Rehnquist Court Era* (New York: Garland Publishing, 1992), 65.

91. Ibid., 112.

92. Weddington and Janikowski, "Counter-Revolution That Is."

How to Read and Brief Cases

Although much of this book is straight text, every chapter includes long excerpts of Supreme Court cases. Reading and understanding opinions of Supreme Court decisions is an important part of a criminal procedure course. The cases are not written in hypertechnical language and so can be understood with a bit of practice. The challenge for beginning students (including first-term students in law schools) is to grasp the highly formal and polished usage of Supreme Court opinions, to sort out the major components of the opinion, and to understand the decision, and more importantly, the reasoning process by which the Court arrived at its decision.

In this book, the cases (Case & Comments) are accompanied by side comments that act like color commentary in a sports broadcast. The comments are designed to help the reader by defining technical terms, highlighting conflicts between the justices, noting interesting reasoning strategies, and asking questions about values inherent in the case.

In order to understand a Supreme Court opinion (a case is likely to include concurring and dissenting opinions as well as the Court's majority opinion), the reader should be forewarned that the decision and opinion involves **legal reasoning** embedded in a system of precedent. Before offering several mechanical hints about briefing a case, a few words on precedent are necessary.

Notes on Precedent

An appellate decision is *precedent*—a rule of case law (the holding) that *binds* lower courts within the court's jurisdiction (e.g., a state for a state supreme court, or a circuit for a federal Court of Appeals, or the nation for the United States Supreme Court). A lower court decision that does not follow precedent can be reversed on appeal. Precedent is also called "authority." A supreme court will generally follow its own precedent, but because American law is dynamic, in many cases prior precedent is overruled. For example, in the chapter on the right to counsel, the landmark case of *Gideon v. Wainwright* (1963), which held that a defendant has a right to counsel in all state felony trials, at state expense if necessary, overruled the prior precedent of *Betts v. Brady* (1942) that had stood for two decades. The process of overruling prior precedent is infrequent and tends to produce straightforward policy discussions in the Court's opinions.

A more subtle process of modifying earlier case decisions is known as *distinguishing* the earlier precedent. To understand the process of distinguishing prior precedent requires appreciating the difference between a court's **holding** and its *decision*. A decision is the simplest rule issued by the Court. It includes the ruling as to whether the decision of the court below is "affirmed" or "reversed." This indicates which party has "won." The decision is the judgment of the court. The Court's *holding* has a somewhat more technical meaning. The holding is the essential legal principle that is derived from a full reading of the court's opinion. The holding is linked to the critical facts that are essential to the court's decision.

The result of every case can be reduced to an abstract statement of a legal principle. Unfortunately, the usage to describe this is not precise and it is called the rule, or the principle, or the decision, or the holding of a case. But for purposes of briefing a case, the holding is the principle attached to the facts of the case.

A point to remember is that the court deciding a case and writing an opinion does not fix the meaning of its rule for all time. A *later* case can widen or narrow the impact of a prior precedent by the way in which it follows or distinguishes the prior case. An example is useful here. As noted in this chapter the Supreme Court decided in *Rochin v. California* (1952) that the use of evidence obtained by the police from Rochin, by entering his home without a warrant and by taking him to a hospital where he was subjected to "stomach-pumping" that forced him to vomit up swallowed drugs, "shocked the conscience" and therefore violated due process. Two years later in *Irvine v. California* (1954) the Court held that evidence of conversations obtained by placing a listening device in the bedroom of a married couple for twenty days did not "shock the conscience." The evidence was admitted. *Irvine* did not follow the *Rochin* decision, i.e., was not bound by *Rochin*, because it distinguished that case on its facts. The Court in *Irvine* excoriated the police action: "Few police measures have come to our attention that more flagrantly, deliberately, and persistently violated the fundamental principle declared by the Fourth Amendment as a restriction on the Federal Government." Nevertheless, the exclusionary rule did not apply at that time, for the rule of *Wolf v. Colorado* (1949) was in effect. Irvine, relying on the reasoning of *Rochin,* argued that what the police did shocked the conscience and should be excluded under the due process clause. Indeed,

Justice Frankfurter, the author of the *Rochin* opinion, agreed. The majority of the Court, however, distinguished the earlier case.

> An effort is made, however, to bring this case under the sway of *Rochin v. California.* That case involved, among other things, an illegal search of the defendant's person. But it also presented an element totally lacking here—coercion . . . , applied by a physical assault upon his person to compel submission to the use of a stomach pump. This was the feature which led to a result in *Rochin* contrary to that in *Wolf.* Although *Rochin* raised the search-and-seizure question, this Court studiously avoided it and never once mentioned the *Wolf* case. Obviously, it thought that illegal search and seizure alone did not call for reversal. However obnoxious are the facts in the case before us, they do not involve coercion, violence or brutality to the person, but rather a trespass to property, plus eavesdropping. (*Irvine v. California*, at 138 (1954), Jackson, J. for the majority)

The Court could have expanded the rule of *Rochin* to include, in the category of searches that shocked the conscience, those not involving physical coercion that undermined intimate privacy, but it did not.

A lower court can also distinguish precedent. A supreme court that modifies its earlier precedent might do so because its composition has changed and the new judges have different policy perspectives. This has clearly been the case in the realm of constitutional criminal procedure, as the Supreme Court's policy orientation shifted from conservative before the 1960s, to liberal in that decade, and back again in the following years. The process of distinguishing precedent requires great legal skill and how well it is done is a mark of a judge's craftsmanship.

The Components of an Opinion

Turn to *Mapp v. Ohio,* found in this text in Chapter 2, on page 48. The top line gives the title of the case. The "v." stands for "versus": the appeal is an adversary contest between two parties—a fight that each side is trying to win. The battle is conducted with words and with legal ideas. *Mapp* is the "petitioner"—the party who lost the case in the court from which the case was appealed. The State of *Ohio* is the "respondent"—the party who is responding to the petitioner. In state cases the terms "appellant" and "appellee" may be used.

The next line is the citation, telling readers where they can find the original printed source of the case which is excerpted here: volume 367 of the United States Reports (the official reporter published by the United States Government Printing Office), beginning at page 643; volume 81 of the Supreme Court Reports at page 1684 (published by the West Group, St. Paul); or volume 6 of the United States Reports, Lawyer's Edition, Second Series, beginning at page 1081 (published by the Lexis Corporation). Next, the name of the justice who wrote the majority opinion appears. This opinion is usually the majority opinion, but on rare occasions where a clear majority cannot be mustered, it is the plurality opinion. Not every opinion is authored. *Per curiam* opinions are issued by the Court without indicating an author. Most *per curiam* opinions are brief, straightforward opinions in relatively minor cases. This is followed by the body of the majority opinion, followed by concurring and dissenting opinions, listed in order of the seniority of the justices. The majority opinion ends with a line indicating the decision, e.g., "Reversed and Remanded."

The appellate court's holding is contained in an essay called the "opinion" of the court. The opinion includes the reasons given by the court for its decision. The reasoning process of an opinion may be complex or simple, eloquent or plain, convincing or vapid, based on narrow legal precedent or on grand principles. Some opinions of Supreme Court justices are classics of American political rhetoric. A majority opinion is not the lone effort of the author, but has been agreed to by the justices who "sign on" to it. Often the opinion's reasoning is a matter of compromise, as each of the justices who votes for it makes suggestions as to the proper legal basis for the decision. A statement in the opinion that is not necessary for the decision or the holding is called **dictum** (or obiter dictum). Dicta, which can be several paragraphs in length, therefore do not have weight as precedent.

An appellate case may include more than the Court's opinion. In addition, some judges may author "concurring" opinions, in which they join the decision or "judgment" of the court, but do so for different reasons. A justice who disagrees with the decision "dissents." A dissenting judge need not explain the dissent in a separate opinion, but it is now typical for Supreme Court justices who dissent to do so. Dissenting justices write not just to express their views. Throughout American constitutional history, many doctrines of constitutional law have been overruled by later courts. When this has happened, the later Court often looks to a dissenting opinion in an earlier case. Thus, a dissenting justice writes for the future, in the hope that in a later era his dissenting view will be adopted.

Briefing a Case

An appellate court opinion includes some or all of the following elements:

- The prior history of the case in the lower courts.
- The facts of the case.
- The legal/constitutional issue or issues that the court is called on to decide.
- The statute or administrative rule that is relevant to the case.
- Prior precedent.
- The "holding," or legal rule, in the case as applied to the case facts.
- The reasoning that is essential to the resolution of the case.
- Other nonessential information, known as *obiter dictum*.
- The decision or judgment (e.g., reversed, affirmed, remanded—who won the case?).

Justices need not write these parts of the opinion in any particular order or fashion, although they are usually presented in the order listed.

Students should make notes (a "brief") of each case. They should read the entire case once, without taking notes (underlining or highlighting may be helpful). After this first reading, they should write the title, page number in the text, the year of decision, the justice who authored the opinion, and enough of the prior history of the case so it is clear how the case got to the Court. This mechanical information is not the essence of the case, so it should be kept short.

There is no one way to **brief a case**—the method that works best should be used. Students should use abbreviations and short phrases, as long as they can understand them when they use the brief to study for a test. Students should then write out—*in their own words*—the most important parts of the case: those facts that are essential for the holding, the legal or constitutional issue, the essence of the reasoning used to resolve the issues, and the holding of the case and its decision. In constitutional law cases the court sometimes explicitly states the issue(s); at other times one has to read the entire case carefully to understand the actual issue. Since the student has read the case through one time, he or she will know which party won the case and have an idea of the issue and how it was resolved.

Stating the legal issue or issues in the case with precision is the key to fully comprehending the Court's reasoning. The Court often announces the issue, but at times it is only a formal issue and not the real issue. In a sense, you have to understand the entire case to accurately ascertain the issue. If you think the Court's statement of the issue is accurate, do not copy it, but restate it in your own words.

The Court's reasoning, which it uses to resolve the issue, may include an analysis of relevant statutes or prior decisions (precedent), and appeals to history, logic, and social policy. For example, in some criminal procedure cases, the justices will, to some degree, argue that the convenience of the police in enforcing the law is a factor in the decision. In cases arising from state courts, the Court will often raise the matter of federalism. It is often difficult to determine which parts of the opinion contain essential reasoning and which contain statements that are not essential.

The *holding* of the case is a concise statement of the decision and the facts on which the decision is based. The holding is different from an abstract rule of law and from the decision. The holding is especially important because the precedent of a case is based on the holding rather than on an abstract statement of the law. The concept of the holding is related to the role of courts, for it prevents appellate courts from usurping the legislative function. A court's primary function is to decide cases, and legal rules are formulated in the context of the case's specific facts. Since only the holding is precedent, courts cannot (or should not) issue broad rules that go beyond the facts of the case. In this way, case law builds incrementally, one case after another, based on unfolding experience. A legal *doctrine* is ascertained by following a "line" of case holdings on an issue. Learning how to trace the development of case law into doctrines is an important legal skill. Appellate courts often try to clarify a ruling by explicitly stating in a case, "We hold. . . ." Look for this when reading cases. The holding is more comprehensive than the decision of a case, but it is important to know who won. At times, students get so involved in the reasoning of the Court that they forget the outcome. It is useful to indicate "who won" the case in the brief.

A student's brief is a practical thing. It should probably be not longer than a page or two. It is a more efficient use of the student's time in preparing for tests to write a brief once, that is the product of thinking about and understanding the case, than it is to reread a case multiple times.

JUSTICES OF THE SUPREME COURT

THE PRECURSOR JUSTICES
HARLAN I–HOLMES–BRANDEIS–CARDOZO

The "precursor" justices of the United States Supreme Court include some of the greatest who have sat on the Court. They occupied seats on the Court from 1877 (Harlan I) to 1939 (Brandeis) and for the most part decided cases in areas other than criminal procedure. Each made an important contribution to constitutional criminal procedure, especially in framing positions concerning the incorporation of the criminal justice provisions of the Bill of Rights into the Due Process Clause of the Fourteenth Amendment.

John Marshall Harlan forcefully advocated the total incorporation of the Bill of Rights into the Fourteenth Amendment, thereby anticipating the revival of this doctrine by Justice Hugo Black and its eventual adoption, albeit in its "selective" form, during the 1960s. Justices Oliver Wendell Holmes and Louis Brandeis contributed to incorporation indirectly. First, they championed First Amendment freedom of speech as fundamental to American democracy. At first dissenting against the violation of free speech by state laws, they ultimately convinced the other justices that state laws that violate free speech are unconstitutional. This amounted to the incorporation of key provisions of the First Amendment and so "breached the wall" of the nonincorporation position. This foundation for incorporation was blocked by Justice Cardozo, who built an intellectually strong argument against incorporation in the Palko *(1938) case. That is, he defined First Amendment rights as fundamental and, therefore, as a part of due process. Fourth, Fifth, and Sixth amendment rights, however, were defined as "formal" and not worthy of incorporation.*

A profound principle of federalism, with enormous practical implications, was at play. Incorporation would undoubtedly bring the federal courts into the running of state criminal justice, and from the creation of the Republic criminal justice had been left entirely to the states. On this point, incorporation was also assisted by an important ruling, Moore v. Dempsey *(1923) championed by Justice Holmes. It held that a fundamentally unfair state trial violated the Due Process Clause of the Fourteenth Amendment, which prohibits any state from depriving a person of life, liberty, or property without due process of law. Thus, well before the Incorporation Doctrine became a matter of constitutional law in the 1960s, the door to federal court interference into state criminal justice had been opened.*

JOHN M. HARLAN, I

Kentucky 1833–1911

Republican

Appointed by
Rutherford B. Hayes

Years of Service:
1877–1911

Collection of the Supreme Court of the United States. Photographer: Mathew Bradey

LIFE AND CAREER   Harlan was the son of a prominent Kentucky attorney and of a slaveholding family. An 1850 graduate of Centre College, he studied law in his father's office. After admission to the bar in 1853, he practiced law and was politically active. During the Civil War he fought on the Union side. In 1864 he was elected attorney general of Kentucky as a Democrat, and opposed the Thirteenth Amendment. He later underwent an extreme change of views, becoming a radical Republican and an ardent supporter of African American civil rights.

Harlan ran unsuccessfully for Kentucky governor in 1871 and 1875. At the 1876 Republican nominating convention, he swung the Kentucky delegation to Rutherford B. Hayes and was rewarded with a nomination to the Supreme Court the following year.

CONTRIBUTION TO CRIMINAL PROCEDURE   Harlan's great contribution to criminal procedure was to champion the incorporation of the Bill of Rights into the Fourteenth Amendment, in order to make the federally guaranteed rights apply against state and local officers. He never succeeded in convincing the Court to incorporate any right except for the just compensation clause of the Fifth Amendment, but his efforts paved the way for the Due Process Revolution of the 1960s.

The importance of Harlan's dissents in *Hurtado v. California* (1884), *Twining v. New Jersey* (1908), and other cases concerning the rights of state criminal defendants under the Fifth, Sixth, and Eighth amendments, was not simply that he championed incorporation. As a "great dissenter" his forceful opinions required the majority to formulate reasoned arguments in response to his position that the post–Civil War Reconstruction amendments fundamentally changed the nature of American federalism. To his mind, these rights were essen-

(Continued)

tial to citizenship. The majority opinions in these cases were forced to agree that if a state were to violate the fundamental rights of a citizen, this would violate due process. Although the Court at that time did not view the criminal procedure rights as fundamental, a later Supreme Court used the fundamental rights formulation to selectively incorporate most of the Bill of Rights.

SIGNATURE OPINION   Dissenting opinion in *Hurtado v. California* (1884). He argued that the grand jury provision of the Fifth Amendment was violated by charging a person with a felony by a prosecutor's information rather than a grand jury indictment.

ASSESSMENT   In economic matters, Harlan opposed state economic regulations and favored laissez-faire procapitalist doctrines; on the other hand, he was a nationalist and so supported federal regulation, such as the Sherman Anti-Trust Act against great economic concentration. He is best known for his lone dissent in *Plessy v. Ferguson* (1896), arguing against the "separate but equal" interpretation of the Equal Protection Clause that upheld the state segregation laws. Harlan, arguing that the very intent of the law was to perpetuate inequality, castigated the majority for joining Louisiana in a charade. He wrote that "there is in this country no superior, dominant, ruling class of citizens. There is no caste here. Our Constitution is color-blind, and neither knows nor tolerates classes among citizens. . . . The destinies of the two races, in this country, are indissolubly linked together, and the interests of both require that the common government of all shall not permit the seeds of race hate to be planted under the sanction of the law. . . ." The "Great Dissenter" discerned more with accuracy than his brethren, the true nature of the American polity and its ideals.

FURTHER READING

Tinsley E. Yarbrough, *Judicial Enigma: The First Harlan* (New York: Oxford University Press, 1995).

OLIVER WENDELL HOLMES, JR.

Massachusetts 1841–1935

Republican

Appointed by Theodore Roosevelt

Years of Service: 1902–1932

Collection of the Supreme Court of the United States. Photographer: Harris and Ewing

LIFE AND CAREER   Holmes was born in Boston to an established "Boston Brahmin" family but not one of great wealth. His father was a professor of medicine at Harvard and a famous essayist. Holmes attended Harvard College in 1857. His family was devoted to the Union cause, and Holmes entered military service soon after the Civil War broke out. He was seriously wounded three times during his three years of service. He rose to the rank of captain and mustered out in the summer of 1864. His war experiences led him to see life as a struggle.

His great ambition was to become famous through his philosophical writings, but he entered the law in order to make a living. Nevertheless, while practicing law he pursued legal scholarship, editing the *American Law Review* and studying the old English cases of the common law. This resulted in a series of lectures and a book, *The Common Law* (1881), which is recognized as a seminal work of legal scholarship and which did indeed make him famous. The book delved into the tangled web of old cases and demonstrated that there were coherent utilitarian reasons for seemingly irrational rules of law. The magisterial opening phrase of *The Common Law* sounded the theme of the path-breaking philosophy of legal realism: "The life of the law has not been logic; it has been experience. The felt necessities of the time, the prevalent moral and political theories, intuitions of public policy, avowed or unconscious, even the prejudices which judges share with their fellow men, have a good deal more to do than the syllogism in determining the rules by which men should be governed."

After a brief appointment to the Harvard law faculty, he accepted an appointment to the Massachusetts Supreme Judicial Court (1883–1902), on which he served with distinction before his appointment to the United States Supreme Court.

CONTRIBUTION TO CRIMINAL PROCEDURE   The Supreme Court heard few criminal procedure cases in his era, and so Holmes had little opportunity to write extensively on these issues. He took a conservative stance in an early Eighth Amendment case, viewing the "cruel or unusual punishment" clause as static; he advanced modern Fourth Amendment law in the *Weeks* (1914) and *Silverthorne* (1920) cases by voting for and writing in favor of the exclusionary rule. His adherence to the Rule of Law was displayed in his dissent in the *Olmstead* (1928) wiretap case. Although not as eloquent as Brandeis's dissent in that case, he stated bluntly that the government should not be above the law, even at some cost to public safety. "We have to choose, and for my part I think it is a less evil that some criminals should escape than that the government should play an ignoble part."

SIGNATURE OPINION   *Moore v. Dempsey* (1923). This was a monumentally important case. Holmes had failed to convince the Court in *Frank v. Mangum* (1915) that a sham trial violates due process. When the Court's composition changed, Holmes's views became law. The importance of *Moore* was that the Supreme Court for the first time reversed a state criminal decision as a violation of due process. This opened the door to federal court intrusion into state criminal procedure, making criminal justice more civilized and uniform throughout the nation.

ASSESSMENT   Holmes was one of the great Supreme Court justices, perhaps second only to Chief Justice John Marshall (1801–1835). He also stands as one of the greatest shapers of the English and American common law in its eight-hundred-year history.

Holmes's accomplishments on the Supreme Court include (along with Brandeis) the creation of modern First Amendment law, enshrining free speech as a foundation of democracy, for free government is not possible unless all ideas be allowed to compete in the "marketplace of ideas."

FURTHER READING

Liva Baker, *The Justice from Beacon Hill: The Life and Times of Oliver Wendell Holmes* (New York: HarperCollins, 1991).

LOUIS DEMBITZ BRANDEIS

Massachusetts 1856–1941

Republican

Appointed by Woodrow Wilson

Years of Service: 1916–1939

Collection of the Supreme Court of the United States. Photographer: Harris and Ewing

LIFE AND CAREER   Brandeis was born in Louisville, Kentucky, to a German Jewish family that sided with the Union during the Civil War. He entered Harvard Law School shortly before his nineteenth birthday, supported himself as a tutor, earned the highest grades, and spent a third year at Harvard as an instructor and graduate student. Attracted by Boston's liberal and intellectual atmosphere, he entered law practice with his classmate, Samuel Warren. They built a thriving practice representing mid-sized businesses. Brandeis developed a tremendous reputation as a thorough attorney whose success was built on a deep study of the law.

Brandeis became wealthy practicing law, but gave it up to represent the interests of laborers struggling for economic security and protection of health and safety on the job. As an unpaid mediator and attorney in labor disputes, he became a renowned defender of workers' rights in early-twentieth-century America. In his victory before the conservative Supreme Court

in *Muller v. Oregon* (1908), upholding a state law limiting the working hours of female laundry employees, Brandeis used an innovative written argument (or "brief") filled with ninety-six pages of social, economic, and health facts about the damaging effects of long working hours, and only ten pages with the usual legal arguments. Since that time, this form of presentation has been known as a "Brandeis Brief."

As a leading progressive who opposed monopolies, he drew the animosity of the propertied classes but also became a key advisor to President Woodrow Wilson, who nominated him to the Supreme Court. He was appointed after a long and acrimonious confirmation debate in the Senate based mainly on his "radicalism," but also supported to some degree by anti-Semitism.

CONTRIBUTION TO CRIMINAL PROCEDURE   He supported the federal exclusionary rule and the extension of federal due process against the states in important cases like *Moore v. Dempsey* (1923), *Powell v. Alabama* (1932) (counsel), and *Brown v. Mississippi* (1936) (confessions).

SIGNATURE OPINION   Dissent in *Olmstead v. United States* (1928). Federal agents violated a state criminal law against wiretapping. The issue was whether this was a search and seizure and, if so, whether as illegally seized evidence the wiretap evidence should be excluded. Brandeis's dissent is a classic statement of the Rule of Law:

> Decency, security, and liberty alike demand that government officials shall be subjected to the same rules of conduct that are commands to the citizen. In a government of laws, existence of the government will be imperiled if it fails to observe the law scrupulously. Our government is the potent, the omnipresent teacher. For good or for ill, it teaches the whole people by its example. Crime is contagious. If the government becomes a lawbreaker, it breeds contempt for law; it invites every man to become a law unto himself; it invites anarchy. To declare that in the administration of the criminal law the end justifies the means—to declare that the government may commit crimes in order to secure the conviction of a private criminal—would bring terrible retribution. Against that pernicious doctrine this court should resolutely set its face.

ASSESSMENT   The dissents of Brandeis and Holmes in First Amendment cases ultimately persuaded the Court to hold that free speech and free press rights were so fundamental that the states could not abridge them. This incorporation of First Amendment rights helped open the door to the later incorporation of criminal procedure rights. His work in this and many other areas rank him as one of the greatest justices.

FURTHER READING

Philippa Strum, *Louis D. Brandeis: Justice for the People* (New York: Schocken Books, 1984).

BENJAMIN NATHAN CARDOZO

New York 1870–1938

Democrat

Appointed by
Herbert Hoover

Years of Service:
1932–1938

Collection of the Supreme Court of the United States. Photographer: Harris and Ewing

LIFE AND CAREER Cardozo, born into a distinguished New York family of Sephardic Jews who immigrated to America in the mid–eighteenth century, was a brilliant student and a noted lawyer, in practice with his older brother for twenty years. Despite his personality, described as gentle, courteous, lonely, ascetic, and saintly, and his apparent lack of political involvement, his reputation as a practitioner led to a judicial appointment to New York's highest court, the Court of Appeals, on which he served from 1913 to 1932.

Cardozo's outstanding reputation as a person and a judge led to an unparalleled national clamor for his appointment as the most worthy replacement for Justice Holmes. Thus, despite the facts that he was nominally of the wrong political party, that two justices from New York (Stone and Hughes) already sat on the Court, and that a Jewish justice (Brandeis) occupied another seat, President Hoover named Cardozo to the Court.

CONTRIBUTION TO CRIMINAL PROCEDURE Cardozo was a conservative judge in criminal matters and had opposed the exclusionary rule as a judge on the New York Court of Appeals.

SIGNATURE OPINION *Palko v. Connecticut* (1938). The Supreme Court had from 1925 to 1933 incorporated several First Amendment rights; it seemed likely that the Court would next incorporate criminal procedure rights. Palko, found guilty of murder and sentenced to prison, was retried after the prosecutor appealed under state law, again found guilty, and sentenced to death. He argued that this violated the Fifth Amendment Double Jeopardy Clause and should apply to the states via due process. Cardozo's majority opinion held that the Connecticut law did not violate due process or incorporate the Double Jeopardy Clause. This was achieved by distinguishing between "funda-

mental" First Amendment rights and "formal" Fifth Amendment rights:

> The line of division may seem to be wavering and broken if there is a hasty catalogue of the cases on the one side and the other. Reflection and analysis will induce a different view. There emerges the perception of a rationalizing principle which gives to discrete instances a proper order and coherence. The right to trial by jury and the immunity from prosecution except as the result of an indictment may have value and importance. Even so, they are not of the very essence of a scheme of ordered liberty. To abolish them is not to violate a "principle of justice so rooted in the traditions and conscience of our people as to be ranked as fundamental." . . .
>
> We reach a different plane of social and moral values when we pass to the privileges and immunities that have been taken over from the earlier articles of the Federal Bill of Rights and brought within the Fourteenth Amendment by a process of absorption. These in their origin were effective against the federal government alone. If the Fourteenth Amendment has absorbed them, the process of absorption has had its source in the belief that neither liberty nor justice would exist if they were sacrificed. . . . This is true, for illustration, of freedom of thought and speech. Of that freedom one may say that it is the matrix, the indispensable condition, of nearly every form of freedom.

The conservative *Palko* rationale retarded the advance of the incorporation doctrine for another quarter century.

ASSESSMENT Cardozo's reputation as a great common law judge is based mainly on his work on the New York Court of Appeals. His opinions were masterpieces of judicial craft that precisely analyzed basic principles of law; his decisions were neither immobilized by precedent nor excessively experimental. His fame was enhanced by his lectures and books (especially *The Nature of the Judicial Function,* 1921), which dissected the work of the appellate judge with such penetrating candor as to add a new chapter to the philosophy of judicial realism. His Supreme Court opinions were marked by total mastery over the subject matter at hand, a graceful and fluid writing style, and a penetrating intelligence. On the Court for only five and one-half terms, he mainly supported the New Deal in economic cases and had a mixed record in civil rights cases.

FURTHER READING

Andrew L. Kaufman, *Cardozo* (Cambridge: Harvard University Press, 1998).

CHAPTER 2

THE FOURTH AMENDMENT AND THE EXCLUSIONARY RULE

This guarantee of protection against unreasonable searches and seizures extends to the innocent and guilty alike. It marks the right of privacy as one of the unique values of our civilization and, with few exceptions, stays the hands of the police unless they have a search warrant issued by a magistrate on probable cause supported by oath or affirmation.

—Justice William O. Douglas, *McDonald v. United States,*
335 U.S. 451, 453 (1948)

CHAPTER OUTLINE

THE COMMON LAW BACKGROUND
THE STRUCTURE OF THE FOURTH
   AMENDMENT
DEVELOPMENT OF THE EXCLUSIONARY
   RULE, 1886–1921
   State Action Doctrine
   Fruits of the Poisonous Tree Doctrine
THE FEDERALIZATION OF THE
   EXCLUSIONARY RULE,
   1949–1963
   The Movement to Incorporate
   Incorporating the Exclusionary Rule
   Case & Comments: *Mapp v. Ohio*
UNDERMINING THE EXCLUSIONARY
   RULE
   Good Faith Exceptions

Case & Comments:
   United States v. Leon
   Standing
ARGUMENTS AGAINST THE
   EXCLUSIONARY RULE
ALTERNATIVE REMEDIES
   Civil Lawsuits for Damages
   Injunctions
   Criminal Prosecution
   Administrative Remedies
THEORIES OF THE EXCLUSIONARY
   RULE
SEARCHES IN A TIME OF TERROR
LAW IN SOCIETY: COSTS AND BENEFITS
   OF THE EXCLUSIONARY RULE

The Deterrent Effect of the Exclusionary
   Rule
The Educative Effect of the Exclusionary
   Rule
Costs of the Exclusionary
   Rule
The Effectiveness of Tort Remedies
SUMMARY
LEGAL PUZZLES
FURTHER READING
ENDNOTES
JUSTICES OF THE SUPREME COURT—
   The Adversaries
   Hugo Lafayette Black
   Felix Frankfurter

KEY TERMS AND PHRASES

Attenuation rule

Balancing test

Bivens suit

Contempt of court

Contraband

Damages

Derivative evidence

Disgorgement

Exclusionary rule

Expectation of privacy

Fruits of the poisonous tree doctrine

General-reasonableness construction

General warrant

Inevitable discovery rule

Independent source rule

Injunction

Pattern and practice suit

Property theory

Particularity requirement

Reasonableness clause

Reparation

Section 1983 lawsuit

Silver-platter doctrine

Standing

Target theory

Tort

Trespass

Warrant clause

Warrant-preference construction

Writ of assistance

In *Marbury v. Madison,* Chief Justice Marshall wrote, "The government of the United States has been emphatically termed a government of laws, and not of men. It will certainly cease to deserve this high appellation, if the laws furnish no remedy for the violation of a vested legal right" (*Marbury v. Madison* at 163, 1803). The greatest controversy to surround the Fourth Amendment has concerned the "remedy" of the **exclusionary rule**—the rule that evidence illegally seized by government officers cannot be introduced by the prosecution in a criminal trial to prove the guilt of the defendant. The exclusionary rule is not found in the text of the Fourth Amendment. It became a firm part of constitutional law in 1914 via the Court's interpretation of the Fourth Amendment (*Weeks v. United States*) but applied only to federal courts and law enforcement because of the effect of the nonincorporation doctrine in effect at that time (see Chapter 1).

This chapter details the history of the exclusionary rule and the controversy that has surrounded it. The issue has tremendous importance to constitutional theory and to everyday police and court actions in search and seizure cases. The reason lies in the politics that have surrounded the exclusionary rule. There was little controversy surrounding the rule until the Court applied it to the states (*Mapp v. Ohio,* 1961). The rule then became an affront to proponents of the Crime Control Model (see Chapter 1) and became a part of the domestic strategy by conservative presidents to denigrate any liberal decisions of the Supreme Court. When the balance of ideological control on the Supreme Court tipped to the conservative side in 1972, the Court began a campaign that eroded the essential meaning of the exclusionary rule as a constitutional rule. The rule still exists, but has been shot through with legal exceptions. A relentless series of Supreme Court cases has given police such powers to stop, question, and search persons outside the home as to overturn the basic understanding that a citizen cannot be stopped by an officer without just cause.[1] At the same time, local courts condone widespread police perjury that effectively undermines attempts to assert Fourth Amendment rights (*Law in Society* section, Chapter 3).

The Court's treatment of the exclusionary rule is a weather vane as to its attitudes about the privacy rights of citizens and residents under the Fourth Amendment. Shortly prior to the terror attack of September 11, 2001, the Court showed some sign of restraining government agents in their intrusive attacks on the right to be free from unreasonable search and seizure.[2] In the aftermath of that attack, it is unlikely that the Court will be willing to further ease the search powers of the police.

This chapter is the first of four that explores the law of search and seizure under the Fourth Amendment. Search and seizure law is the product of several historic developments. It begins with the common law ideal of the privacy of the home solidifying into a British legal rule protecting that privacy against *government* invasion shortly before the framing of the Constitution (1787). Next, the framers guaranteed this right in the Bill of Rights (1791). Then, about a century after the framing, the Supreme Court developed a remedial rule, the exclusionary rule, to ensure that evidence seized in violation of the Fourth Amendment's requirements would not be used in federal court to convict a person. The next major historic development in Fourth Amendment doctrine was the extension of the federal exclusionary rule to the states via the process of incorporation in *Mapp v. Ohio* (1961). Another doctrinal change of historic proportions occurred in the 1960s when the Court sought to replace the property-rights theory of Fourth Amendment protections with the **expectation of privacy** doctrine announced in *Katz v. United States* (1967) (see Chapter 3). During the Burger Court era, the exclusionary rule was "demoted" in status from a constitutional rule to a rule designed to deter police illegality. The shifts in doctrine discussed in this chapter are a case study of incorporation and the tug of federalism, display the importance of history and politics in the development of doctrines, show the tension between liberal and conservative understandings of the law, demonstrate the power of the justices to mold rules to fit their view of proper policy, and show that constitutional law cannot be understood apart from its role in society.

THE COMMON LAW BACKGROUND

The old English saying that a "man's home is his castle" expresses a universal desire for privacy. Historian William Cuddihy asserts that until the year 1600 English law protected against *private* but not *governmental* intrusion. "By 1760, however, public opinion had inverted the relative importance that it assigned to these considerations. Promiscuous searches by the *government* were now recognized as more onerous than undesired visits by private persons."[3] This change was rooted in altered social conditions and political thought, especially the emergence of a constitutional monarchy in England in the eighteenth century.

This new thinking was reflected in two important legal cases of the 1760s that influenced the development of the Fourth Amendment. The first, known as *Paxton's Case* or the **Writs of Assistance Case**, arose in colonial Massachusetts and was decided in 1761. The second set of cases, the **Wilkes** cases, was a series of civil lawsuits arising out of the political persecution of John Wilkes, a critic of King George III. These cases confirmed the hatred of "general warrants" in the colonies and the new Republic and led to the Fourth Amendment prohibition on "unreasonable searches and seizures."

Up to 1760, most English search warrants were general warrants. A **general warrant** could be issued by a judicial or a nonjudicial governmental official who did not personally have to be aware of probable cause for a search. "Promiscuously broad warrants allowed officers to search wherever they wanted and to seize whatever they wanted, with few exceptions."[4] General warrants were described as "a sort of legal pass key to all doors that places everyone's privacy at the capricious mercy of its holder."[5] Criticism of general warrants began in the mid–seventeenth century and public opinion came to favor specific warrants specifying the place to be searched and the items to be seized.[6] Nevertheless, most British warrants continued to be of the general kind.

A **writ of assistance** was a type of general warrant that authorized a crown official "to command the assistance" of a peace officer or a nearby person to execute the writ. The writ allowed a search for a specific purpose and was executed in the daytime. Writs of assistance were used in the colonies by British officers to enforce unpopular customs laws and were enormously unpopular. Customs officers with writs of assistance could enter warehouses and even homes to search for goods that were imported without paying the customs taxes and to collect unpaid duties. Crown impressment gangs used writs of assistance to invade private homes and public places like taverns "to kidnap able bodied men for service in the royal navy."[7] Once issued, the writ lasted for the life of the sovereign, plus six months.

After the death of George II, a customs officer in Massachusetts petitioned for a new writ of assistance. In February 1761 sixty-three leading Boston merchants challenged the legality of the application, presenting their case in the colony's high court. James Otis, a leading attorney, represented the merchants and offered a learned and passionate argument: The law authorizing the writs of assistance "is against the fundamental principles of English law" and is, therefore, unconstitutional and void. John Adams, a young attorney and future president of the United States, was present and was deeply impressed by Otis's argument. In 1776, as a delegate to the Continental Congress and as a signer of the Declaration of Independence, he reflected that the movement for American independence began with the writs of assistance dispute. The Boston merchants lost their case; nevertheless, the writs continued to be unpopular and were not well-enforced because of hostile attacks on revenue collectors. To generate revenue, England passed the Townshend Act (1767), authorizing high courts in each colony to issue writs of assistance to customs officers. The local Massachusetts grievance became a major source of friction between the colonies and the mother country.[8]

The Wilkes cases, argued in England, were a resounding political defeat of general warrants. They arose after John Wilkes (1725–1797), a British agitator, journalist, and member of Parliament, published the *North Briton*, Number 45, in 1763, a newsletter sharply critical of George III and his government. The king and Parliament tried to stifle his political attacks by charging him with seditious libel, a serious political crime. An English secretary of state issued a general warrant to officers to search for the newsletter and other writings. "Crown agents enforcing the warrants had unfettered discretion to search, seize, and arrest anyone as they pleased. They ransacked printers' shops and houses, and arrested forty-nine persons, including Wilkes, his printer, publisher, and bookseller. The officers seized his private papers for incriminating evidence after a thorough search; thousands of pages and scores of books belonging to persons associated with him were also seized."[9]

The case became a major political controversy on both sides of the Atlantic Ocean. "In the colonies, 'Wilkes and Liberty' became a slogan that patriot leaders exploited in the service of American causes."[10] Wilkes and his colleagues fought back in the courts in a series of civil lawsuits charging that the general searches were *illegal*. The courts upheld Wilkes and his allies. In general, the cases found that the searches were not authorized by law, were excessive, and that officers of the crown could be sued. "[T]he government paid a total of about 100,000 pounds in costs and judgments," an enormous sum at the time.[11]

In the most important of these cases, **Entick v. Carrington** (1765), Lord Camden, chief justice of the Court of Common Pleas, demolished every argument put forth by the government to support the legality of the warrants.[12] He ruled that general warrants were not authorized by act of Parliament or case law; that general warrants to search for papers were not like specific search warrants for stolen goods; and although the government had issued such warrants since the Glorious Revolution of 1688, that fact did not make the warrants legal "simply through long usage" or the previous silence of the courts. The court firmly rejected the blatantly political argument that the needs of the state took precedence over individual rights: "Political policy is not an argument in a court of law."[13] Lord Camden stressed that the case was of *constitutional* importance because it upheld the liberal political theory of the "social contract" by stressing that a main function of government is to protect the property of individuals.

Thus, just prior to the period of American state and federal constitution building (1776–1791), the common law had evolved to a point where general warrants were so disfavored as to be declared illegal in some cases. A person who had been arrested under a general warrant and whose home and other property had been invaded and searched by government agents could sue executive officers who authorized general search warrants and agents who executed the warrants and recover substantial **damages** if the arrests and searches were illegal.

In sum, the common law rule—which was to have enormous influence on the development of the exclusionary rule in the United States—was that searches of private property by government officers without a warrant or based on defective warrants (such as general warrants) were *illegal*. The only remedy known to the common law to redress such illegality was a civil lawsuit for money damages against the officers who took part. There was no common law rule excluding the use of illegally seized evidence from a criminal trial.

THE STRUCTURE OF THE FOURTH AMENDMENT

Prior to the drafting of the U.S. Constitution, most of the new states included prohibitions against general warrants in their new states' constitutions and bills of rights passed after 1776.[14] When Representative James Madison drafted a Bill of Rights as amendments to the new U.S. Constitution, he included such a provision. His draft drew heavily on the Massachusetts provision, written by John Adams, which used the novel phrase "unreasonable search and seizure."

The provision that became the Fourth Amendment was ratified in 1791:

> The right of the people to be secure in their persons, houses, papers, and effects, against unreasonable searches and seizures, shall not be violated, and no Warrants shall issue, but upon probable cause, supported by Oath or affirmation, and particularly describing the place to be searched, and the persons or things to be seized.

Unlike the states' bills of rights, the Fourth Amendment did not outlaw "general warrants" in specific terms. The modern interpretation of the amendment, stated in many cases, is that it contains two clauses: the **reasonableness clause** and the **warrant clause**. Under this construction, the ultimate test of constitutionality of any search and seizure is whether it is *reasonable*. Not all searches have to be authorized by a judicial warrant. *If* a search or arrest warrant is required, then it must meet the **particularity requirements** stated in the warrant clause.

Strong disagreement exists between conservative and liberal justices and scholars about the relative importance of the warrant clause. More conservative jurists, applying a **general-reasonableness construction**, have established a **balancing test** to determine if searches and seizures are proper without a warrant and have come very close to saying that search warrants are not actually required by the Fourth Amendment. This understanding of the Fourth Amendment has been gaining ground in recent decades. This construction allows the Court to give the police greater leeway to perform searches and seizures without judicial interference.

The more traditional construction, favored by liberal jurists, is the **warrant-preference construction**: warrantless searches and seizures are presumptively unreasonable. There is a narrow group of search warrant exceptions that were known as common law: entries in *hot pursuit,* the search of mobile *vehicles,* and "*search incident to arrest*"—the search of a person who has just been arrested. All modern legal thinkers, nevertheless, whether favoring the "general-reasonableness" or the "warrant-preference" approaches, agree on the two-clause understanding of the Fourth Amendment.[15] Indeed, until the very recent findings of historians, it was generally believed that this two-clause construction was intended by the framers.[16] However, the most penetrating studies lead to the conclusion that the original intent of the framers and the ratifiers of the Fourth Amendment was to ban Congress from authorizing general warrants and to ban judges from issuing them—nothing more.[17] This interpretation threatens the more conservative view, but is unlikely to overthrow the established two-clause interpretation.

A word about this seemingly arcane historical debate offers a strong lesson on how the realities of the day, forgotten centuries later, influenced constitutional interpretation. The two-clause wording of the Fourth Amendment seems obvious from its text. The needs of modern law enforcement to allow a wide variety of warrantless arrests and searches are so pressing, that modern commentators have "read back" the modern two-clause understanding of the Fourth Amendment into their perceptions of the intent of the framers. It seems inconceivable today that the framers were not concerned with warrantless searches of police officers. Yet, as Professor Thomas Y. Davies notes, there were *no police officers in 1791,* at least not in the modern sense. Constables were few and were viewed as untrustworthy.[18] In the late colonial era and at the time of the framing, there was *no* discretion used in constables' decisions to make arrests or searches upon probable cause. Like any citizen, a constable could lawfully arrest or search only if the person to be arrested did in fact *commit* the crime, or if **contraband** *actually* was found; if the constable acted on suspicion or probable cause and was wrong, the constable could be sued for false imprisonment or **trespass**. Further, misconduct by an officer was, paradoxically, seen not as official misconduct, but as *personal* misconduct. As a result, the government never committed a wrongful arrest or search, and the few officers who made arrests or conducted searches almost always did so under the authorization of a warrant. "[F]raming-era common law never permitted a warrantless officer to justify an arrest or search according to any standard as loose or flexible as 'reasonableness.'"[19] There was, consequently, no proactive policing at this period.

Given the needs of modern society, this original understanding, with its extremely tight rein on official discretion, soon began to erode. In the late nineteenth and early twentieth centuries, the Supreme Court began to erect modern Fourth Amendment law with the exclusionary rule at its center. Organized police departments were so actively involved in performing warrantless arrests, stops, and searches, that any Court that took Fourth Amendment values seriously would inevitably attempt to provide reasonable controls. Virtually none of the hundreds of Supreme Court Fourth Amendment cases deal with issues of general warrants. Indeed, the Supreme Court seems to have authorized, even required, general warrants for administrative searches (e.g., *Camara v. Municipal Court,* 1967).

The historical debate is relevant because the Supreme Court (or at least some of its justices) purports to base its jurisdiction and the legitimacy of its decisions on being true to the "intent of the framers." If the justices are mistaken regarding the intent of the Fourth Amendment, then the body of law they have created may be in question. Worse still, if the framers intended constables to have absolutely no authority to act "reasonably" when interfering with a person's liberty or privacy, and instead must be strictly controlled by judicial warrant, then the entire edifice of modern law enforcement could be deemed unconstitutional.

Much depends on the philosophy of judging held by members of the Court. Activist judges are not likely to be distracted by the recent historical interpretation of the Fourth Amendment, as they justify decisions in part on their understanding of history, however inconsistent it has been. Justices Antonin Scalia and Clarence Thomas claim their decisions are guided by the original intent of the framers and, therefore, are most likely to be swayed by Professor Davies' "authentic" reading of the Fourth Amendment, although this would conflict with their conservative, Crime Control, policy orientation.

Two points are important for the student. First, some changes to Fourth Amendment doctrines may occur if the "authentic" understanding of the amendment is accepted, making it important to understand the underlying reasons for doctrines, rather than simply memorizing the rules. Second, the large body of constitutional law is kept fairly stable by the operation of stare decisis, and it is unlikely that there will be a wholesale revolution in Fourth Amendment law.[20] For that reason, the text presents the standard understanding of Fourth Amendment law, based primarily on the decisions and analyses of the Supreme Court.

DEVELOPMENT OF THE EXCLUSIONARY RULE, 1886–1921

There was no exclusionary rule at common law and the text of the Fourth Amendment does not explicitly state that illegally seized evidence be excluded. This section explains the cases that established the rule. The few Fourth Amendment cases decided by the Supreme Court in the nineteenth and early twentieth centuries displayed a sensitivity to the civil liberties values inherent in the Fourth Amendment. For example, *Ex Parte Jackson* (1878) stated, in dictum, that sealed letters sent through the mails could not be opened by postal authorities without a warrant. Because the defendant did not challenge the opening of the package in which illegal lottery tickets were mailed, the issue of exclusion did not arise. In the major case of *Boyd v. United States* (1886), however, the Supreme Court *did suppress* the use of evidence obtained illegally by federal customs authorities, but did not establish a clear Fourth Amendment exclusionary rule.

Boyd v. United States was an odd case. To begin with, there was no actual search and seizure; instead, a subpoena was issued to E. A. Boyd & Co. to turn over an invoice on cases of imported glass to determine whether customs taxes had been paid. Boyd challenged the law, which created a presumption that import duties had not been paid if the invoice was not presented. The Supreme Court agreed with Boyd, holding that the order to produce the invoice and the law that authorized the order were unconstitutional and void under *both* Fourth and Fifth amendment rights. The opinion, infused with the history of the Revolutionary War era, created an expansive definition of a search and seizure, favorable to the individual:

> The principles laid down in *[Entick v. Carrington]* affect the very essence of constitutional liberty and security. They reach farther than the concrete form of the case then before the court, with its adventitious circumstances; they apply to all invasions on the part of the government and its employés of the sanctity of a man's home and the privacies of life. It is not the breaking of his doors, and the rummaging of his drawers, that constitutes the essence of the offence; but it is the invasion of his indefeasible right of personal security, personal liberty and private property, where that right has never been forfeited by his conviction of some public offence,—it is the invasion of this sacred right which underlies and constitutes the essence of Lord Camden's judgment. Breaking into a house and opening boxes and drawers are circumstances of aggravation; but any forcible and compulsory extortion of a man's own testimony or of his

private papers to be used as evidence to convict him of crime or to forfeit his goods, is within the condemnation of that judgment. In this regard the Fourth and Fifth Amendments run almost into each other. (*Boyd v. United States,* 1886, p. 630)

By ruling that a subpoena was the equivalent of a search and conflating the Fourth Amendment with the Fifth Amendment's right against self-incrimination, the Court avoided establishing a clear-cut exclusionary rule that applied to searches and seizures generally. Virtually none of *Boyd*'s expansive Fifth Amendment rules are operative today (e.g., a subpoena is not a search[21]). *Boyd* remains an important case as the precursor to the Fourth Amendment exclusionary rule.

The Supreme Court moved hesitantly toward this rule. It affirmed the traditional rule in *Adams v. New York* (1904), saying that "courts do not stop to inquire as to the means by which the evidence was obtained." This holding, that illegally seized evidence may be admitted as evidence in a criminal trial, while maintaining that the exclusionary ruling in *Boyd* was good law apparently, meant that the Court still felt that exclusion should be limited to cases in which some element of self-incrimination was present.

This changed radically in *Weeks v. United States* (1914), which adopted a straightforward Fourth Amendment exclusionary rule, not tied to the Fifth Amendment privilege against self-incrimination. Fremont Weeks was arrested by local police without a warrant at his place of work; at the same time, a United States marshal entered Weeks's home without a warrant and "carried away certain letters and envelopes found in the drawer of a chiffonier." Weeks's demand for the return of incriminating papers before trial was denied, and he was convicted in federal court for using the mails to transport lottery tickets. The Supreme Court held that all evidence seized without warrant was in violation of the Fourth Amendment and had to be returned; it could not be used against the defendant to prove his guilt. Its language was expansive and protective of individual privacy:

> The effect of the Fourth Amendment is to put the courts of the United States and Federal officials, in the exercise of their power and authority, under limitations and restraints as to the exercise of such power and authority, and to forever secure the people, their persons, houses, papers and effects against all unreasonable searches and seizures under the guise of law. This protection reaches all alike, whether accused of crime or not, and the duty of giving to it force and effect is obligatory upon all entrusted under our Federal system with the enforcement of the laws. The tendency of those who execute the criminal laws of the country to obtain conviction by means of unlawful seizures and enforced confessions, . . . should find no sanction in the judgments of the courts which are charged at all times with the support of the Constitution and to which people of all conditions have a right to appeal for the maintenance of such fundamental rights. (*Weeks v. United States,* 1914, pp. 391–92)

The rule was limited to federal cases and was held not to require a warrant for a search incident to arrest. In the opinion, the remedy of exclusion was inextricably tied to the constitutional right, in effect making the exclusionary rule a part of the

Constitution. A deterrence rationale was also hinted at: "If letters and private documents can . . . be seized and held and used in evidence against a citizen accused of an offense [as in this case], the protection of the Fourth Amendment declaring his right to be secure against such searches and seizures is of no value, and, so far as those thus placed are concerned, might as well be stricken from the Constitution."

The constitutional basis of the exclusionary rule was confirmed and strengthened in Justice Oliver Wendell Holmes's opinion in *Silverthorne Lumber Co. v. United States* (1920). Frederick W. Silverthorne and his father were indicted for a federal crime and arrested at home, while federal agents entered their business offices without a warrant and took business documents. The district court agreed with the defendants' contention that their Fourth Amendment rights were violated and, on their demand, ordered the documents returned. However, the government photographed the documents and these copies were the basis of a subpoena for the original documents. Silverthorne refused to comply with the subpoena. The district court, although having found that the documents were originally procured by an unconstitutional seizure, nevertheless ordered compliance with the subpoena. On refusal, the company was fined and Silverthorne was ordered jailed until he turned over the original documents.

The Supreme Court reversed the lower court's judgment. In Holmes's words, to allow the government to seize evidence in violation of the Fourth Amendment, and then use the knowledge gained by that wrong to obtain the evidence "legally," "reduces the Fourth Amendment to a form of words." Therefore, "[t]he essence of a provision forbidding the acquisition of evidence in a certain way is that not merely evidence so acquired shall not be used before the Court but that it shall not be used at all." This is the crux of one exclusionary rule theory that will be addressed later in this text: The government cannot profit from its illegal action. As Professor William Heffernan notes, this "no use" rule was fully rights-based and went further than the present scope of the exclusionary rule, which allows illegally obtained evidence to be used to impeach a lying witness, in civil deportation cases, as a basis for framing grand jury questions, and in other areas.[22]

Holmes added one important exception to the exclusionary rule: "Of course this does not mean that the facts thus obtained become sacred and inaccessible. If knowledge of them is gained from an independent source they may be proved like any others, but the knowledge gained by the Government's own wrong cannot be used by it in the way proposed." These rules later became known as the **fruits of the poisonous tree doctrine** and the independent source exception. The rationale is that government violation of a defendant's Fourth Amendment rights does not lead to a windfall in the guise of a dismissal of the case. The government can use other evidence to convict, if that evidence is obtained by a legal route.

Gouled v. United States (1921) filled out the law on the development of the exclusionary rule. It first held that the Fourth Amendment is as much violated by a "fraudulent" entry into a home or business office as by a forcible entry. In this case, a government investigator who happened to know Gouled, a fraud suspect, pretended to make a friendly call on Gouled at his business office. While Gouled was out of the room, the investigator surreptitiously took incriminating papers. The Court ruled that the *admission* of these papers violated the Fifth Amendment privilege against self-incrimination, thus continuing to conflate the Fourth and Fifth amendments when communicative papers were in question.

In this case, search warrants were issued to seize papers that were not the direct fruits of crime but were only evidence of Gouled's fraudulent conspiracy. The Court made a common law rule, known as the "mere evidence" rule, part of the Fourth Amendment exclusionary rule by holding that these papers could not be admitted into evidence. The theory was that property that was not itself a part of the crime (e.g., stolen goods, the document on which a fraud was based, or weapons or burglar's tools used to commit the crime) could not be seized. This rule shows that the Court saw the rights protected by the Fourth Amendment as essentially resting on *property*. The Court eventually dropped this rule in *Warden v. Hayden* (1967), one of a series of cases that shifted the conceptual basis of the Fourth Amendment from a property to a functional basis.

State Action Doctrine

The exclusionary rule applies only to evidence illegally seized by the *government* and not to evidence seized by private parties whether they committed a civil trespass or a burglary to obtain the incriminating evidence. The reason is that the purpose of the Bill of Rights and constitutional protections is to guard individuals against the excessive, arbitrary, and abusive power of the *state*. When a private party turns over illegally seized evidence to a prosecutor, courts adhere to the common law rule that they will not inquire into the source of relevant evidence (*Burdeau v. McDowell*, 1921).

On the other hand, if a private person acts as a *proxy* for the police or at their command, then state action exists and evidence seized by the private person is not admissible. The Court has provided guidelines to guide police action when a private party turns suspicious evidence over to the police. The rule is that when private individuals turn over suspicious items to police agents, the police may subject the items to *only minimal investigation* before requesting a search warrant. In one such case, the FBI, after being given pornographic films from an innocent, mistaken recipient, proceeded without a warrant to screen the films in order to determine their content. This screening was held to be state action because it went beyond what the private parties saw before turning over the evidence and was determined inadmissible (*Walter v. United States*, 1980). On the other hand, in *United States v. Jacobsen* (1984), white powder discovered by Federal Express employees was chemically "field tested" and found to be cocaine by federal drug agents (DEA). The warrantless examination by DEA agents was proper because it was *not a significant expansion* of the earlier private search; thus, this evidence was admissible.

The state action doctrine means that searches conducted by *any* government officer, not just by police officers acting for law enforcement purposes, fall under the protections of the Fourth Amendment. Searches by public school teachers, public hospital supervisors, probation officers, municipal building inspectors, Occupational Safety and Health Administration (OSHA) inspectors, federal mine-safety investigators, municipal fire department investigators, and customs agents must adhere to Fourth Amendment rules. Illegal searches by these personnel require the exclusion of evidence. This branch of search and seizure law, under which lesser standards for a valid search have been created for government personnel other than law enforcement officers, will be reviewed under the "special needs doctrine" later in the text.

PRIVATE SECURITY PERSONNEL   The question of whether the actions of private police personnel against individuals constitute state action often arises in the course of civil lawsuits, especially actions in federal court under 42 U.S.C. §1983 alleging that the security personnel acted "under color of state law." The Supreme Court has specifically left this question open (*Flagg Bros. v. Brooks*, 1978, p. 164 n. 14). Lower federal courts have held that private police have been held liable as state actors "when the state delegates a public function to a private entity."[23] This was so in a criminal case against privately employed railroad policemen who brutally beat vagrant trespassers. These railroad police officers were granted all of the same powers and duties as regular Chicago city police officers by relevant authorizing legislation.[24] Cases in the federal Seventh Circuit "have held that private hospital security guards and university policemen also can be state actors.* * * On the other hand, this court has held that a private mall security force was not a state actor, because the guards exercised no 'police powers.' "[25] Security personnel at a Chicago hospital were held to have come under state action in detaining a plaintiff. Their duties and powers as "special police officers" were specified in a Chicago ordinance that required licensing by the city, background checks, the wearing of a "suitable badge" issued by the superintendent of police, and conformance to rules and regulations governing city police officers. The ordinance stated that they "shall possess the powers of the regular police patrol at the places for which they are respectively appointed or in the line of duty for which they are engaged."[26] In a case where a private security guard hired by Chicago public housing shot a person in the groin, the court held the guard was not a state actor. The Chicago housing authority had a private police force, but the guard was a contract person, not part of the private police. The guard, although in uniform and armed with a sidearm, was assigned specifically to guard lobbies and had no authority to act outside the lobby of the assigned building.

A grandmother was arrested by security guards in a Detroit casino for taking a token worth five cents from the tray of an abandoned slot machine. She was excluded from the casino and not allowed to physically contact her friends with whom she was spending the day. The federal district court held that the security personnel acted under state authority. Under Michigan law, an employer may maintain private security *guards* in order to protect its property, or however, it may also employ private security *police*. A licensed private security police officer has the same authority to arrest a person without a warrant as a municipal or state police officer, when that private security police officer is on his employer's property. A private police officer must comply with state training requirements. The casino's security officers were private police. Private *guards* would not come under state action because they would have the same right as a private business owner to protect his or her property, and could thus detain an individual if the business owner suspected an individual of theft.[27] From the cases, a private security official may be seen to exercise state authority and be subject to constitutional rules if state authority is specifically conferred by law and if the functions exercised by the security personnel are as expansive, within spatial limits, as those exercised by police officers. Despite these cases extending state action to some security officers, in light of the enormous growth of the private security industry, some commentators have questioned the general rule that arrests and searches by private security agents do not amount to government action.[28]

Fruits of the Poisonous Tree Doctrine

Silverthorne v. United States (1920) added a necessary corollary to the exclusionary rule: evidence derived from knowledge obtained by an illegal search and seizure is not admissible. Were such **derivative evidence** admissible, police officers could violate Fourth Amendment rights with impunity, and then, after the original evidence is excluded, use information gained from the illegality to get a "legal" search warrant.

The derivative evidence rule reflects the axiom that, under the Fourth Amendment, justification for searches must be provided *prior to* the search. *Retroactive justification* turns the Amendment into a sham. An example is the per curiam decision of *Smith v. Ohio* (1990).[29] Two plainclothes police officers, without a warrant and without probable cause or reasonable suspicion, stopped Smith exiting a convenience store carrying a brown paper grocery bag marked with the store's logo. When the officers identified themselves, Smith put the sack he was carrying on the hood of his car. Smith did not answer a question about the content of the bag and tried to push one of the officer's hand away as he opened the bag. Drug paraphernalia were found and became the basis of an arrest and conviction. The Supreme Court reversed the conviction. The search was not justified on any Fourth Amendment ground. There was no basis for a self-protective stop under *Terry v. Ohio* (1967), the property was not abandoned, and there was no search incident to arrest—indeed, in *Smith,* the arrest occurred *after* the search. The obvious point, that the police simply cannot search whatever strikes their fancy and then make a "legal" arrest or seizure *if* their hunch or baseless action turns up contraband, prevents the undermining of the exclusionary rule.

The "fruit of the poisonous tree" metaphor for the derivative evidence rule was penned by Justice Frankfurter in *Nardone v. United States* (1939): What is excluded is not only the illegally seized evidence (the "poisonous tree"), but also different evidence *derived from* the illegally seized evidence (the "fruits"). Allowing the use of derivative evidence would create a rule "inconsistent with ethical standards and destructive of personal liberty." The Court in *Nardone* excluded not only the exact words overheard in a wiretap that violated a federal statute, but any information derived from the overheard conversations.

Silverthorne and *Nardone* recognize that the exclusionary rule, including the exclusion of derivative evidence, is not a windfall to the defendant—it does not lead to automatic dismissal of charges or to an amnesty on the use of other *properly obtained* evidence. The Supreme Court has recognized three exceptions to the derivative evidence exclusion: (1) evidence obtained from an **independent source**, (2) **inevitable discovery**, and (3) **attenuation**. One case noted that the inevitable discovery exception is an extrapolation of the independent source exception (*Murray v. United States*, 1988).

INDEPENDENT SOURCE   The Supreme Court has allowed illegally seized evidence when the evidence was obtained in a constitutional manner that was entirely unconnected to the illegality—from an independent source. In **Segura v. United States** (1984), a group of police illegally entered Segura's apartment. A search warrant was later obtained based on information developed before the illegal entry took place. The Supreme Court excluded evidence in plain view during the illegal search but allowed use of evidence obtained under the search warrant—it was independent of the illegal entry. In **Murray v. United States** (1988), police illegally entered a warehouse and saw suspicious bales believed to contain marijuana. This illegal entry was not mentioned in an affidavit for a search warrant. Nevertheless, the Court allowed the use of evidence obtained by executing the warrant because it was lawfully issued on the basis of other competent evidence.

INEVITABLE DISCOVERY   Illegally seized evidence is admissible if it was inevitably discovered independently of the unconstitutional action. *Brewer v. Williams* (1977) (*Williams I*) held that evidence of a murdered girl's body was excluded because it was discovered based on an unconstitutional interrogation (a so-called Christian Burial Speech, see Chapter 7). The Supreme Court, in **Nix v. Williams** (1984) (*Williams II*), held that this evidence was properly introduced at a retrial because a search party was within two-and-a-half miles of the body when it was found. Members of the search party were instructed to look into culverts (where the body was placed) and would have covered the area where the body was located. Thus, it inevitably would have been found, whether or not the defendant divulged its location to the police. The motivations of the police who improperly took the confession were irrelevant.

ATTENUATION   Evidence derived from an illegal or unconstitutional source is allowed into evidence where, for some reason, the *link* between the initial illegality and the evidence sought to be introduced has become so *weak* or *tenuous* that

the "fruit" has become "untainted." In *Nardone,* Justice Frankfurter wrote: "Sophisticated argument may prove a causal connection between information obtained through illicit wiretapping and the Government's proof. As a matter of good sense, however, such connection may have become so attenuated as to dissipate the taint."

Wong Sun v. United States (1963) explicates the attenuation doctrine. Six or seven narcotics officers illegally entered the San Francisco apartment of James Wah Toy behind his laundry shop at 6:00 A.M. looking for drugs. They rousted the inhabitants and questioned Toy. No drugs were found, but Toy named some people whom the agents questioned about drug dealing. The Supreme Court excluded from evidence an incriminating statement made by Toy as well as confessions and drugs obtained from a person questioned immediately after the raid on Toy's apartment because this evidence was the "tainted" fruit of the illegal entry into Toy's apartment. Wong Sun, one of the men arrested, was released after his arrest and he returned voluntarily several days later to make an incriminating statement. The Court held that this voluntary statement was admissible because the connection between the arrest and the statement had "become so attenuated as to dissipate the taint" (p. 491). The test for determining whether attenuation exists is: "whether, granting establishment of the primary illegality, the evidence to which instant objection is made has been come at by exploitation of that illegality or instead by means sufficiently distinguishable to be purged of the primary taint."

Attenuation issues arise when a "proper" confession is made after an illegal arrest. The fact that *Miranda* warnings are given does not automatically break the link between an illegal arrest and a confession, nor does the passage of two hours between the illegal arrest and the confession attenuate the illegality (*Brown v. Illinois,* 1975). To make *Miranda* warnings a "cure-all" for illegal police action would encourage illegal arrests and dilute the effectiveness of the *Miranda* exclusionary rule. Likewise, a six-hour delay between an illegal arrest and a confession, followed by a ten-minute meeting between the defendant and friends, did not attenuate the initial illegality despite three *Miranda* warnings (*Taylor v. Alabama,* 1982).

On the contrary, a confession was allowed into evidence in **New York v. Harris** (1990). Police illegally arrested Harris at his home without a warrant, read *Miranda* rights, and obtained a confession in the house. Taken to the police station, Harris again was read his rights, signed a waiver form, and confessed. The first confession was suppressed as the fruit of an illegal police action: entry into the home without a warrant when no exigency existed (*Payton v. New York,* 1980). But the Court held the station house confession to be admissible. The Court ruled that Harris was legally in custody because an illegal arrest does not deprive the court of jurisdiction to try the suspect. Therefore, "the statement, while *the product* of an arrest and being in custody, was *not the fruit* of the fact that the arrest was made in the house rather than somewhere else" (*New York v. Harris,* p. 20, emphasis added). The Court did not apply attenuation analysis but rather saw the case as a straightforward example of evidence not being the "fruit" or actual result of a prior illegal police action. The 5–4 decision in *Harris* may be explained by the hostility of the majority toward the exclusionary rule. The majority, however, distinguished the facts of *Harris* from those of *Brown* and *Taylor* because in *Harris* the police had probable cause to arrest the defendant, unlike the earlier cases. The opinion said that excluding the *first* confession vindicated the rule that made in-home arrests without a warrant unconstitutional and, thus, as for allowing in the second confession, "it does not follow from the emphasis on the exclusionary rule's deterrent value that 'anything which deters illegal searches is thereby commanded by the Fourth Amendment.'" (*New York v. Harris,* p. 20)

Determining whether the original illegality has become attenuated is not found by applying mechanical rules, but depends on whether, considering the totality of the circumstances, the second piece of evidence in the case would have been discovered had the original violation not taken place. If the subsequent evidence is considered to be independent of the original "tainted" search and seizure, then it can be used against the defendant in a court of law. Thus, attenuation depends on specific case facts. In **United States v. Ceccolini** (1978), a police officer, without any special design to investigate gambling, discovered betting slips in the defendant's flower shop by improperly looking into an envelope with cash sticking out located behind the customer counter. Ceccolini denied that gambling occurred in his place of business before a federal grand jury, but he was convicted of perjury after an employee testified about illegal gambling at his shop. The Court of Appeals ruled that the employee's statement was the fruit of the officer's original unconstitutional search and excluded the testimony. The Supreme Court reversed, finding that the link between the search and the witness's testimony had become so attenuated that the testimony could no longer be considered to be *caused* by the officer's unconstitutional act. The Court relied on a variety of facts: federal officials previously had the shop under suspicion and observation; several months passed between the officer telling the FBI about the slips and the initial questioning of the employee; the witness was in no way coerced or induced to testify, but did so for honorable motives; and the betting slips were not used in the questioning of the witness; the officer had no intent to investigate gambling. In this case, the Court also felt that the deterrent effect on police misconduct, of excluding the evidence, would be very limited.

THE FEDERALIZATION OF THE EXCLUSIONARY RULE, 1949–1963

The Movement to Incorporate

Shortly after *Adamson v. California* (1947), defense lawyers sought to have the Court incorporate the Fourth Amendment and its exclusionary rule into the Fourteenth Amendment, making them applicable to the states (see Chapter 1). The issue was raised in **Wolf v. Colorado** (1949). Sheriffs' deputies in Denver, under instructions of the district attorney's office, had "definite information" concerning an abortion performed by Dr. Wolf. They "went to the office of Wolf without a warrant and took him into custody and there they took possession of . . . his day books of 1944 and 1943 up to the time of the arrest. They were records of patients who consulted him professionally." These records were introduced in evidence and used to convict Dr. Wolf, who received a twelve- to eighteen-month prison sentence. The Colorado Supreme Court held the evidence admissible, although the search was illegal.[30] Had this been a federal search, it would have violated the Fourth Amendment and the evidence would have been ruled inadmissible under the *Weeks* exclusionary rule. The Fourth Amendment, however, did not bind local or state police and courts at that time. The United States Supreme Court held, in an opinion by Justice Frankfurter, that (1) the Fourth Amendment *is* "incorporated," but (2) the exclusionary rule is *not* "incorporated." That is, "in a prosecution in a State court for a State crime the Fourteenth Amendment does not forbid the admission of evidence obtained by an unreasonable search and seizure" (*Wolf v. Colorado,* p. 33). As to the first holding, Justice Frankfurter dismissed the idea of "total incorporation" as one that had consistently been rejected by the Supreme Court in many cases. Turning to "selective incorporation" under the Due Process Clause, he wrote:

> Due process of law thus conveys neither formal nor fixed nor narrow requirements. It is the compendious expression for all those rights which the courts must enforce because they are basic to our free society. But basic rights do not become petrified as of any one time, even though, as a matter of human experience, some may not too rhetorically be called eternal verities. It is of the very nature of a free society to advance in its standards of what is deemed reasonable and right. Representing as it does a living principle, due process is not confined within a permanent catalogue of what may at a given time be deemed the limits or the essentials of fundamental rights.
>
> The security of one's privacy against arbitrary intrusion by the police—which is at the core of the Fourth Amendment—is basic to a free society. It is therefore implicit in "the concept of ordered liberty" and as such enforceable against the States through the Due Process Clause. The knock at the door, whether by day or by night, as a prelude to a search, without authority of law but solely on the authority of the police, did not need the commentary of recent history to be condemned as inconsistent with the conception of human rights enshrined in the history and the basic constitutional documents of English-speaking peoples.
>
> Accordingly, we have no hesitation in saying that were a State affirmatively to sanction such police incursion into privacy it would run counter to the guaranty of the Fourteenth Amendment. (*Wolf v. Colorado,* pp. 27–28)

This elegant language, interspersed among paragraphs that disparage the incorporation doctrine, incorporates the substance of the Fourth Amendment, i.e., forbids the states from creating rules that violate the Fourth Amendment. However, the Court's majority refused to impose the exclusionary rule on the states via incorporation:

> But the ways of enforcing such a basic right raise questions of a different order. How such arbitrary conduct should be checked, what remedies against it should be afforded, the means by which the right should be made effective, are all questions that are not to be so dogmatically answered as to preclude the varying solutions which spring from an allowable range of judgment on issues not susceptible of quantitative solution.
>
> In *Weeks v. United States,* this Court held that in a federal prosecution the Fourth Amendment barred the use of evidence secured through an illegal search and seizure. This ruling was made for the first time in 1914. It was not derived from the explicit requirements of the Fourth Amendment; it was not based on legislation expressing Congressional policy in the enforcement of the Constitution. The decision was a matter of judicial implication. Since then it has been frequently applied and we stoutly adhere to it. But the immediate question is whether the basic right to protection against arbitrary intrusion by the police demands the exclusion of logically relevant evidence obtained by an unreasonable search and seizure because, in a federal prosecution for a federal crime, it would be excluded. As a matter of inherent reason, one would suppose this to be an issue as to which men with complete devotion to the protection of the right of privacy might give different answers. When we find that in fact most of the English-speaking world does not regard as vital to such protection the exclusion of evidence thus obtained, we must hesitate to treat this remedy as an essential ingredient of the right. The contrariety of views of the States is particularly impressive in view of the careful reconsideration which they have given the problem in the light of the *Weeks* decision. (*Wolf v. Colorado,* pp. 28–29)

Justice Frankfurter emphasized that the *basic* Fourth Amendment right, now applicable against state as well as federal encroachment, was protected by the "remedies" of civil lawsuits in all states whether or not they had adopted their own exclusionary rules. As of 1949, sixteen states had adopted the *Weeks* exclusionary doctrine as a matter of local law, while thirty-one had rejected it.

Justice Black, the leading proponent of incorporation, nevertheless joined the majority because he felt that "the federal exclusionary rule is not a command of the Fourth Amendment but is a judicially created rule of evidence which Congress might negate," i.e., is not a constitutional *requirement*. He managed to combine judicial activism with originalism (following the original intent of the framers)—a seemingly incongruous combination. He believed that the Fourteenth Amendment incorporated the Fourth Amendment and supported the *Weeks* exclusionary rule as it applied to federal law enforcement. Because the text of the Fourth Amendment did not include an exclusionary rule, he saw it as not extending to the states. This seemed inconsistent, and his position in *Wolf* would create an anomaly in the *Mapp v. Ohio* (1961) decision.

Three liberal justices, Douglas, Murphy, and Rutledge, dissented in *Wolf,* arguing in favor of incorporating the exclusionary rule. They argued that civil lawsuits and criminal prosecutions against police and prosecutors are virtually never successful, especially if the person alleging an unconstitutional search had a criminal record. This reality meant that, for all practical purposes, the Fourth Amendment was a right without a remedy. Justice Frank Murphy noted that in states that followed the *Weeks* doctrine, police are carefully trained in the law of search and seizure; whereas the subject was virtually ignored in states without the exclusionary rule. "The conclusion is inescapable that but one remedy exists to deter violations of the search and seizure clause. That is the rule which excludes illegally obtained evidence" (*Wolf v. Colorado,* p. 44).

Three years after *Wolf,* the Supreme Court in **Rochin v. California** (1952) did suppress evidence obtained in a state search and seizure, not via *Weeks*'s Fourth Amendment exclusionary rule, but under the more flexible due process rule of the Fourteenth Amendment. Los Angeles police officers, believing that Rochin was dealing drugs, invaded his home without a warrant, went up the stairs, and forced open a door to his bedroom. "Inside they found [Rochin] sitting partly dressed on the side of the bed, upon which his wife was lying. On a 'night stand' beside the bed the deputies spied two capsules. When asked 'Whose stuff is this?' Rochin seized the capsules and put them in his mouth. A struggle ensued, in the course of which the three officers 'jumped upon him' and attempted to extract the capsules. The force they applied proved unavailing against Rochin's resistance. He was handcuffed and taken to a hospital. At the direction of one of the officers a doctor forced an emetic solution through a tube into Rochin's stomach against his will. This 'stomach pumping' produced vomiting. In the vomited matter were found two capsules which proved to contain morphine."

In light of this outrageous police action, the justices, for different reasons, unanimously agreed that the evidence should not be admissible. Justice Frankfurter's majority opinion did not apply the *Weeks* rule of automatic exclusion, but instead excluded the evidence where the totality of circumstances "shocked the conscience" of the appellate court. Justice Frankfurter believed the shocks-the-conscience test was an objective standard that would guide lower courts. Justice Douglas, concurring in the decision, disagreed strongly with the shocks-the-conscience test. As with any due process test that rests on the "totality of the circumstances," the application of the rule could differ from one judge to another. As he saw it, unlike the "unequivocal, definite and workable rule of evidence" of the *Weeks* exclusionary rule, the rule fashioned in *Rochin* "turn[s] not on the Constitution but on the idiosyncrasies of the judges who sit here" (*Rochin v. California,* p. 179).

Justice Douglas's criticism was proven true in *Irvine v. California* (1954). Local police, suspecting Irvine of illegal bookmaking, secretly entered his home and, without a judicial search warrant, wired the house for sound, including the bedroom. The police listened in on the private conversations of Irvine and his wife for *weeks,* and testified to what they heard at Irvine's trial. The evidence was used to convict Irvine. Justice Robert Jackson's majority opinion stated: "Few police measures have come to our attention that more flagrantly, deliberately, and persistently violated the fundamental principle declared by the Fourth Amendment . . ." (*Irvine v. California,* p. 132). The Supreme Court, nevertheless, held that the evidence should *not* be excluded. The *Weeks* exclusionary rule did not apply to the states, and the majority refused to apply the *Rochin* shocks-the-conscience test because the facts of *Rochin* included the element of *coercion* not found in the *Irvine* case. This was too much for Justice Frankfurter, who dissented on the grounds that *Rochin* did apply. "The holding of the case is that a State cannot resort to methods that offend civilized standards of decency and fairness" (*Irvine v. California,* p. 144). The subjectivity of the shocks-the-conscience test was exposed when the majority in *Irvine* did not find such a flagrant violation of Fourth Ammendment privacy to "shock the conscience." In a spirited dissent, Justice Douglas called again for the incorporation of the exclusionary rule, saying, "The search and seizure conducted in this case smack of the police state, not the free America the Bill of Rights envisaged" (*Irvine v. California,* p. 149).

As the 1950s wore on, more states adopted the exclusionary rule by court action, most notably the California Supreme Court.[31] The tide in favor of reversing *Weeks* was "halting but seemingly inexorable."[32] A harbinger was **Elkins v. United States** (1960). Soon after *Weeks* (1914), the "**silver-platter**" **doctrine** arose—an end-run around the exclusionary rule. If state or local police seized evidence of a federal crime by an illegal search and seizure, the evidence was admissible in a federal trial as long as the federal officers did not participate in the illegal search. This, of course, put a premium on "pious perjury," or winking at the truth.

The Supreme Court signaled its unhappiness with this in **Rea v. United States** (1956). The Court exercised its supervisory authority to enjoin a federal narcotics agent, who had illegally seized marijuana that was excluded from a federal prosecution by a district judge, from testifying about the marijuana in a state prosecution. This eliminated a federal-to-state "silver platter" delivery of tainted evidence.

In *Elkins v. United States,* the Supreme Court put an end to the state-to-federal transfer of illegally seized evidence. Justice Stewart, writing for the majority in a 5–4 decision, noted that the basis of the silver-platter doctrine was eroded once *Wolf v. Colorado* (1949) held that *substantive* Fourth Amendment rights applied against the states. Four dissenting justices complained that the Court was interfering with states' rights. In reply, Justice Stewart wrote, "The very essence of a healthy federalism depends upon the avoidance of needless conflict between federal and state courts." Thus, in states with state exclusionary rules, the silver-platter doctrine undermined *state* policy. *Elkins* was decided not on constitutional grounds, but on "the Court's supervisory power over the administration of criminal justice in the federal courts" (p. 216). Justice Stewart's strong defense of the exclusionary rule foreshadowed the decision in *Mapp v. Ohio* (1961).

Incorporating the Exclusionary Rule

The due process revolution of the 1960s was initiated by *Mapp v. Ohio* (1961). The movement is associated with a five-justice

majority of the Warren Court in the 1960s. It is worth noting that Justice Tom Clark, who wrote the opinion of the Court, more often than not voted for the state.

— *Mapp v. Ohio* Case & Comments —

Two years after *Mapp,* in **Ker v. California** (1963), the Court fully "federalized" the exclusionary rule, saying that the "standard of reasonableness is the same under the Fourth and Fourteenth Amendments." Essentially, state courts would have to abide by the United States Supreme Court's exclusionary rule interpretations. The Court noted that it had no supervisory authority over the states, only the jurisdiction to interpret the Constitution. The majority opinion said that *Mapp* "implied no total obliteration of state laws relating to arrests and searches in favor of federal law. *Mapp* sounded no death knell for our federalism." On the other hand, "Findings of reasonableness, of course, are respected only insofar as consistent with federal constitutional guarantees." In practice this meant that state search and seizure law had to conform to Supreme Court–determined *minimum* constitutional standards; but under the adequate and independent state grounds concept, a state could expand a suspect's rights in a search and seizure case (see Chapter 1).

In 1965 the Supreme Court held, in **Linkletter v. Walker,** that the exclusionary rule was *not retroactive* to state cases decided prior to *Mapp;* its effect was prospective only. Applying the Court's pragmatic approach to determining if a constitutional rule should be applied retroactively, the 7–2 majority opinion stated that "*Mapp* had as its prime purpose the enforcement of the Fourth Amendment through the inclusion of the exclusionary rule within its rights. This, it was found, was the *only effective deterrent to lawless police action.* Indeed, all of the cases since *Wolf* requiring the exclusion of illegal evidence have been based on the necessity for an effective *deterrent* to illegal police action. . . . We cannot say that this purpose would be advanced by making the rule retrospective" (*Linkletter v. Walker,* pp. 636–37, emphasis added). At the time of this decision, the majority probably felt that the exclusionary rule was relatively secure. But these words in the *Linkletter* case became highly significant in the 1970s, when the *theory* of the exclusionary rule was reconsidered by a more conservative Court, with a view to eliminating or emasculating the rule.

The Warren Court's positive approach to the exclusionary rule was underscored by its application of the rule to a *civil* forfeiture of an automobile, which state liquor control officers stopped and searched because it was "low in the rear, quite low." Upon inspection, the officers found thirty-one cases of liquor. The Court in **One 1958 Plymouth Sedan v. Pennsylvania** (1965) agreed with the state trial judge, who found that the stop was made without probable cause. In applying the exclusionary rule, the Court noted that forfeitures are quasi-criminal procedures in which the penalty is often more onerous than a criminal sentence.

The exclusionary rule was subjected to judicial and political criticism during the remaining years of the Warren Court (to 1969). In fact, liberal Warren Court decisions regarding criminal suspects became a major issue in the 1968 presidential campaign. After his election, President Nixon sought to

• CASE & COMMENTS •

Mapp v. Ohio
367 U.S. 643, 81 S.Ct. 1684, 6 L.Ed.2d 1081 (1961)

MR. JUSTICE CLARK delivered the opinion of the Court.

[Cleveland police officers went to Mrs. Mapp's home on a tip that a suspected gambler involved in a bombing was residing there. She refused to let them enter without a warrant. The police broke in after a three-hour wait. There was a scuffle for a piece of paper that the police waved, but no warrant was ever produced. Mrs. Mapp and her daughter were handcuffed and confined to a bedroom while the police ransacked the house (looking into all rooms and into her personal papers and photograph albums). The police found obscene books in a trunk in the basement belonging to a roomer who was no longer living in the house. At trial, the alleged warrant was never produced. Mrs. Mapp was convicted for possession of obscene books seized during a search of her home. [a] The Ohio courts acknowledged that the books and pictures were "unlawfully seized during an unlawful search of [her] home, * * *" but still allowed the evidence to be used, relying on *Wolf v. Colorado*]

I.

Seventy-five years ago, in *Boyd v. United States* 1886, considering the Fourth and Fifth Amendments as running "almost into each other," on the facts before it, this Court held that the doctrines of those Amendments [b]

> "apply to all invasions on the part of the government and its employees of the sanctity of a man's home and the privacies of life. * * *"

The Court noted that

> "constitutional provisions for the security of person and property should be liberally construed. . . . It is the duty of courts to be watchful for the constitutional rights of the citizen, and against any stealthy encroachments thereon."

* * * Concluding, the Court specifically referred to the use of the evidence there seized as "unconstitutional."

> Less than 30 years after *Boyd,* this Court, in *Weeks v. United States* (1914), stated that "the Fourth Amendment . . . put the courts of the United States and Federal officials, in the exercise of their power and authority, under limitations and restraints. * * *

Specifically dealing with the use of the evidence unconstitutionally seized, the Court concluded:

> "If letters and private documents can thus be seized and held and used in evidence against a citizen accused of an offense, the protection of the Fourth Amendment declaring his right to be secure against such searches and seizures is of no value, and, so far as those thus placed are concerned, might as well be stricken from the Constitution. * * *

Finally, the Court in that case clearly stated that use of the seized evidence involved "a denial of the constitutional rights of the accused." . . . Thus, in the year 1914, in the *Weeks* case, this Court "for the first time" held that "in a federal prosecution the Fourth Amendment barred the use of evidence secured through an illegal search and seizure." * * *

There are in the cases of this Court some passing references to the *Weeks* rule as being one of evidence. But the plain and unequivocal language of *Weeks*—and its later paraphrase in *Wolf*—to the effect that the *Weeks* rule is of constitutional origin, remains entirely undisturbed. * * * [c]

II.

[In *Wolf v. Colorado* (1949), the Court first considered the applicability of the Fourth Amendment against the states, and] after declaring that the "security of one's privacy against arbitrary intrusion by the police" is "implicit in 'the concept of ordered liberty' and as such enforceable against the States through the Due Process Clause," * * * and announcing that it "stoutly adhere[d]" to the *Weeks* decision, [nevertheless] the Court decided that the *Weeks* exclusionary rule would not then be imposed upon the States as "an essential ingredient of the right." * * *

[Since 1949, a majority of the states have adopted the exclusionary rule and federal courts no longer allow into evidence items that were illegally seized by state officers.]

It, therefore, plainly appears that the factual considerations supporting the failure of the *Wolf* Court to include the *Weeks* exclusionary rule when it recognized the enforceability of the right to privacy

[a] This case was appealed to the Supreme Court primarily on First Amendment (free speech) grounds. The Fourth Amendment issue was added perfunctorily. The dissent accused the majority of "reaching out" to settle an issue that was not fully briefed.

[b] Justice Clark begins by quoting the *Boyd* view that exclusion depends on the Fourth and Fifth amendments operating together, rather than on the idea that *Weeks* created an exclusionary rule based exclusively on the Fourth Amendment. This seems odd, but in fact is a necessary tactic to gain a majority for the decision. Can you determine his motive for this reasoning?

[c] This states unequivocally that the exclusionary rule is a constitutional rule. The Supreme Court no longer accepts this theory of the exclusionary rule. The change involves changes of national politics and judicial policy. The change is traced in the next section.

• CASE & COMMENTS •

against the States in 1949, while not basically relevant to the constitutional consideration, could not, in any analysis, now be deemed controlling.

III.

* * * Today we once again examine *Wolf*'s constitutional documentation of the right to privacy free from unreasonable state intrusion, and, after its dozen years on our books, are led by it to close the only courtroom door remaining open to evidence secured by official lawlessness in flagrant abuse of that basic right, reserved to all persons as a specific guarantee against that very same unlawful conduct. We hold that all evidence obtained by searches and seizures in violation of the Constitution is, by that same authority, inadmissible in a state court.

IV.

Since the Fourth Amendment's right of privacy has been declared enforceable against the States through the Due Process Clause of the Fourteenth, it is enforceable against them by the same sanction of exclusion as is used against the Federal Government. * * * **[d]** In short, the admission of the new constitutional right by *Wolf* could not consistently tolerate denial of its most important constitutional privilege, namely, the exclusion of the evidence which an accused had been forced to give by reason of the unlawful seizure. To hold otherwise is to grant the right but in reality to withhold its privilege and enjoyment. * * *

V.

Moreover, our holding that the exclusionary rule is an essential part of both the Fourth and Fourteenth Amendments is not only the logical dictate of prior cases, but it also makes very good sense. There is no war between the Constitution and common sense. Presently, a federal prosecutor may make no use of evidence illegally seized, but a State's attorney across the street may, although he supposedly is operating under the enforceable prohibitions of the same Amendment. **[e]** Thus the State, by admitting evidence unlawfully seized, serves to encourage disobedience to the Federal Constitution which it is bound to uphold. * * * "[The] very essence of a healthy federalism depends upon the avoidance of needless conflict between state and federal courts." * * * **[f]**

Federal-state cooperation in the solution of crime under constitutional standards will be promoted, if only by recognition of their now mutual obligation to respect the same fundamental criteria in their approaches. "However much in a particular case insistence upon such rules may appear as a technicality that inures to the benefit of a guilty person, the history of the criminal law proves that tolerance of shortcut methods in law enforcement impairs its enduring effectiveness." * * * Denying shortcuts to only one of two cooperating law enforcement agencies tends naturally to breed legitimate suspicion of "working arrangements" whose results are equally tainted. * * *

There are those who say, as did JUSTICE (then Judge) CARDOZO, that under our constitutional exclusionary doctrine "[the] criminal is to go free because the constable has blundered." * * * In some cases this will undoubtedly be the result. **[g]** But, * * * "there is another consideration—the imperative of judicial integrity." The criminal goes free, if he must, but it is the law that sets him free. Nothing can destroy a government more quickly than its failure to observe its own laws, or worse, its disregard of the charter of its own existence. * * *

The ignoble shortcut to conviction left open to the State tends to destroy the entire system of constitutional restraints on which the liberties of the people rest. * * * [W]e can no longer permit that right to remain an empty promise. * * *
Reversed and remanded.

MR. JUSTICE BLACK, concurring.
[JUSTICE BLACK noted that in *Wolf*, he stated that "the federal exclusionary rule is not a command of the Fourth Amendment but is a judicially created rule of evidence which Congress might negate."]

* * *

I am still not persuaded that the Fourth Amendment, standing alone, would be enough to bar the introduction into evidence against an accused of papers and effects seized from him in violation of its commands. **[h]** For the Fourth Amendment does not itself contain any provision expressly precluding the use of such evidence, and I am extremely doubtful that such a provision could properly be inferred from nothing more than the basic command against unreasonable searches and seizures. Reflection on the problem, however, in the light of cases coming before the Court since *Wolf*, has led me to conclude

[d] The "same sanction" phrase is critically important to the entire Incorporation Doctrine. It means that the United States Constitution must be interpreted identically for the states as well as for the federal government. Since the Constitution is the "supreme law of the land," the practical effect of incorporation is that the Supreme Court makes specific rules for state courts and law enforcement.

[e] This refers not to the silver-platter doctrine, eliminated in *Elkins v. United States* (1960), but to the incongruity of uneven enforcement of constitutional rights.

[f] It appears that even with the elimination of the silver-platter doctrine, Justice Clark feared that allowing different search and seizure rules would cause tension between state and federal officers.

[g] The arguments in favor of and opposed to the exclusionary rule, and the various theories of the exclusionary rule, are considered in a later section.

[h] Justice Black's vote in favor of the exclusionary rule is the crucial fifth majority vote. His rationale makes it clear why Justice Clark's argument included *Boyd*'s theory that the Fourth and Fifth amendments operate in conjunction to exclude evidence. It is worth noting that the Fifth Amendment basis of the exclusionary rule, while still alluded to, had become obsolete by the 1960s, as the search and seizure exclusionary rule was treated exclusively as a Fourth Amendment issue.

that when the Fourth Amendment's ban against unreasonable searches and seizures is considered together with the Fifth Amendment's ban against compelled self-incrimination, a constitutional basis emerges which not only justifies but actually requires the exclusionary rule. * * *

[JUSTICE DOUGLAS concurred, expanding on the facts of the case and emphasizing the inability of any method other than exclusion to deter police illegalities.]

[JUSTICE STEWART expressed no opinion on the search and seizure issue; he would have reversed the conviction on First Amendment grounds.]

MR. JUSTICE HARLAN, whom MR. JUSTICE FRANKFURTER and MR. JUSTICE WHITTAKER join, dissenting.

In overruling the *Wolf* case the Court, in my opinion, has forgotten the sense of judicial restraint which, with due regard for *stare decisis,* is one element that should enter into deciding whether a past decision of this Court should be overruled. **[i]** Apart from that I also believe that the *Wolf* rule represents sounder Constitutional doctrine than the new rule which now replaces it. * * *

II

Essential to the majority's argument against *Wolf* is the proposition that the [exclusionary] rule of *Weeks* * * * derives not from the "supervisory power" of this Court over the federal judicial system, but from Constitutional requirement. This is so because no one, I suppose, would suggest that this Court possesses any general supervisory power over the state courts. **[j]** Although I entertain considerable doubt as to the soundness of this foundational proposition * * * I shall assume, for present purposes, that the *Weeks* rule "is of constitutional origin."

At the heart of the majority's opinion in this case is the following syllogism: (1) the rule excluding in federal criminal trials evidence which is the product of an illegal search and seizure is "part and parcel" of the Fourth Amendment; (2) *Wolf* held that the "privacy" assured against federal action by the Fourth Amendment is also protected against state action by the Fourteenth Amendment; and (3) it is therefore "logically and constitutionally necessary" that the *Weeks* exclusionary rule should also be enforced against the States.

This reasoning ultimately rests on the unsound premise that because *Wolf* carried into the States, as part of "the concept of ordered liberty" embodied in the Fourteenth Amendment, the principle of "privacy" underlying the *Fourth Amendment,* * * * it must follow that whatever configurations of the Fourth Amendment have been developed in the particularizing federal precedents are likewise to be deemed a part of "ordered liberty," and as such are enforceable against the States. For me, this does not follow at all. **[k]**

It cannot be too much emphasized that what was recognized in *Wolf* was not that the Fourth Amendment *as such* is enforceable against the States as a facet of due process, * * * but the principle of privacy "which is at the core of the Fourth Amendment." * * * It would not be proper to expect or impose any precise equivalence, either as regards the scope of the right or the means of its implementation, between the requirements of the Fourth and Fourteenth Amendments. For the Fourth, unlike what was said in *Wolf* of the Fourteenth, does not state a general principle only; it is a particular command, having its setting in a pre-existing legal context on which both interpreting decisions and enabling statutes must at least build.

* * * Since there is not the slightest suggestion that Ohio's policy is "affirmatively to sanction * * * police incursion into privacy" * * * what the Court is now doing is to impose upon the States not only federal substantive standards of "search and seizure" but also the basic federal remedy for violation of those standards. For I think it entirely clear that the *Weeks* exclusionary rule is but a remedy which, by penalizing past official misconduct, is aimed at deterring such conduct in the future. **[l]**

I would not impose upon the States this federal exclusionary remedy. The reasons given by the majority for now suddenly turning its back on *Wolf* seem to me notably unconvincing.

[JUSTICE HARLAN then gave several reasons for not extending the exclusionary rule to the states: (1) that many states have voluntarily adopted the exclusionary rule does not determine a constitutional question; (2) "the preservation of a proper balance between state and federal responsibility in the administration of criminal justice" *constitutionally* forbids the federal courts from developing solutions for perceived problems of state law enforcement; (3) procedural symmetry between the federal system and the states is not required by the Constitution; and (4) the purported analogy between the exclusion of involuntary confessions under the Fourteenth Amendment and search and seizure cases is spurious.]

[i] Justices differ in their adherence to precedent or *stare decisis.* Justice Harlan was a strong believer in restraint, or a reluctance to change established rules. Judicial restraint was seen as an attribute of judicial "conservatism." However, many justices who today advance a conservative policy agenda are "activist" in changing the law to suit their policy views.

[j] Look up "supervisory authority" in the Glossary. Why does the Supreme Court *not* have supervisory authority over state courts and state law enforcement?

[k] What follows is the nonincorporation view that had been part of Fourteenth Amendment jurisprudence since *Hurtado v. California* (1884). Justice Harlan's strenuous dissent is indeed a cry for stare decisis, for the majority decision in *Mapp* was genuinely revolutionary, by overturning the theory of the relationship between the Bill of Rights and the Fourteenth Amendment.

[l] A dissent always is a call to the future. As the personnel of the Supreme Court changed and the Court adopted a more activist-conservative stance, Justice Harlan's view of the nature of the exclusionary rule has become the accepted view of the Court. This will be discussed below in the section on the theories of the exclusionary rule.

nominate justices who would reverse these decisions (see Chapter 1). Within a decade of *Mapp,* a "counterattack" to erode the exclusionary rule was begun by a Supreme Court that had become far more conservative.

UNDERMINING THE EXCLUSIONARY RULE

After 1972, the Court's new conservative majority had a guarded, if not outrightly hostile, attitude toward the exclusionary rule. Chief Justice Burger, for example, called for its total overruling in a dissent in *Bivens v. Six Unknown Agents* (1971), stating that the *only* foundation for the rule was the *deterrence of police illegality.* The Court has never overruled the exclusionary rule, but since 1974, it has limited its application. The move to limit the rule was first applied in the breakthrough case of **United States v. Calandra** (1974). A majority of six justices held that a grand jury question could be based on information obtained from an unconstitutional search and seizure. Justice Lewis Powell's majority opinion specified reasons that would thereafter be the foundation for the Court's exclusionary rule decisions. These reasons completely upended the constitutional foundation of the exclusionary rule that had been established by the Warren Court in *Mapp* and its other Fourth Amendment cases.

1. In determining whether to apply the exclusionary rule to a proceeding, the Court must *balance* the cost to the law enforcement process (e.g., grand jury proceedings) against the benefits of the rule.
2. The *use* of illegally seized evidence against a suspect does not violate his Fourth Amendment rights. The Fourth Amendment violation "is *fully accomplished*" when the illegal search and seizure occurs. As a result, the introduction into evidence of illegally seized evidence is not itself a violation of a person's constitutional rights. This means that the exclusionary rule is not constitutionally required and decisions as to how far to apply the rule may be based on pragmatic considerations.
3. The "purpose of the exclusionary rule is not to redress the injury to the privacy of the search victim."
4. The "rule's prime purpose is to *deter future unlawful police conduct* and thereby effectuate the guarantee of the Fourth Amendment against unreasonable searches and seizures."
5. "In sum, the rule is a judicially created remedy designed to safeguard Fourth Amendment rights generally through its deterrent effect, rather than a personal constitutional right of the party aggrieved."

Justice Brennan, joined by Justices Douglas and Marshall, dissented vigorously at this "downgrading" of the exclusionary rule, but to no avail.

Stone v. Powell (1976) further indicates the Supreme Court's lower opinion of the exclusionary rule by limiting the scope for federal habeas corpus challenges to illegal searches. *Stone* held that if a person convicted in a state court already had a *full and fair opportunity* to litigate a Fourth Amendment claim in the state courts, he or she has no right to reopen the

issue in federal habeas corpus proceedings. Justice Powell noted that the rule was a judicially created means of enforcing Fourth Amendment rights, rather than a right itself and that it rests primarily on the theory of deterrence of police misconduct rather than "the imperative of judicial integrity." Further criticizing the rule, he noted that it "deflects the truthfinding process and often frees the guilty." The Court, significantly, has not limited federal habeas corpus review as to any other constitutional guarantee, indicating that the Burger and Rehnquist Courts have created a hierarchy among constitutional rights, with Fourth Amendment rights held in lower esteem than Fifth or Sixth amendment rights.

Chief Justice Burger, who had called for overruling the exclusionary rule in *Bivens v. Six Unknown Named Agents,* later agreed to accepting the continued existence of the rule, but in its weakened form. He stated that "the exclusionary rule has been operative long enough to demonstrate its flaws. The time has come to modify its reach, even if it is retained for a small and limited category of cases." This may reflect that a majority of the Court felt constrained by *stare decisis* and uneasy with dismantling an important protection for a fundamental constitutional right. Chief Justice Burger thus shifted ground to favor limitation of the exclusionary rule rather than its elimination.[33]

Calandra and *Stone v. Powell* set the foundation of constitutional reasoning on which the Court began to weaken the exclusionary rule. It did this by holding, in a series of cases, that the exclusionary rule does not apply to various procedures. These include an Internal Revenue Service civil tax proceedings (**United States v. Janis,** 1976) or INS deportation hearings (**I.N.S v. Lopez-Mendoza,** 1984). These rulings undercut the viability of *One 1958 Plymouth Sedan,* although that decision was never overruled. More recently, the Court declined to apply the exclusionary rule to parole revocation in **Pennsylvania Board of Probation and Parole v. Scott** (1998). Parole officers, without a warrant, entered the home of a parolee whom they believed possessed weapons in violation of parole conditions. The state courts ruled that the warrantless search of a parolee's home violated the Fourth Amendment because "illegal searches would be undeterred when officers know that the subjects of their searches are parolees and that illegally obtained evidence can be introduced at parole hearings." The exclusionary rule was referred to by Justice Thomas as a "grudgingly taken medicant."[34] He reviewed the Court's approach to the exclusionary rule in cases since *Calandra* and noted that the rule now applies only in criminal trials, and even there with some exceptions. Justice John Paul Stevens, writing for four dissenting justices in *Scott,* endorsed the view made by Justice Potter Stewart in a journal article that the "rule *is* constitutionally required, not as a 'right' explicitly incorporated in the fourth amendment's prohibitions, but as a remedy necessary to ensure that those prohibitions are observed in fact."[35] Justice David Souter, in dissent, noted that parole revocation proceedings often serve the same function as criminal trials.

The Supreme Court also held that illegally obtained evidence also can be used to *impeach the credibility* of a defendant who testifies, to show that her testimony is contradicted by the illegally seized evidence. This ruling of **Harris v. New York** (1971) effectively overruled an earlier case that did not allow such usage (*Agnello v. United States,* 1925), although it did build on a precedent that allowed the impeachment use of illegally seized evidence to rebut a defendant's statement about an issue tangential to guilt or innocence. In **United States v. Havens** (1980) a T-shirt with a pocket especially sewn in to hold drugs was illegally seized at an airport. Havens, tried for importing drugs on the testimony of his fellow traveler, denied drug activity on direct examination and denied any connection with the T-shirt. To rebut his testimony, the T-shirt was introduced on cross-examination. The Supreme Court held this use of the illegal evidence proper because the government did not "smuggle in" the evidence. Instead the cross-examination was reasonably suggested by Haven's direct examination. In his majority opinion, Justice White emphasized the importance of arriving at the truth in criminal trials and the dangers of allowing a constitutional shield to be "perverted into a license to use perjury." He also said that the use of illegally seized evidence for impeachment purposes would not undermine the deterrent effect of the exclusionary rule. The Court later limited this use of illegally seized evidence to impeach only the defendant and not other witnesses, out of concern that expanded impeachment use would create a premium to obtain evidence in violation of the Constitution and weaken its deterrent effect (*James v. Illinois,* 1990).

The effect of a line of cases that weaken a primary rule is a familiar phenomenon in constitutional law. The Court often speaks of a rule having been *eroded* by a series of inconsistent cases, and this often foretells the overruling of the major rule. Although this has not happened and probably will not happen with the *Mapp* exclusionary rule, as the law now stands, the effect of the exclusionary rule has been permanently weakened, as seen in the next two sections on the "good faith exception" and the cases on standing.

Good Faith Exceptions

The most powerful attack on the exclusionary rule has been the allowance of illegally seized evidence to be introduced in the trial to *prove* the defendant's *guilt*. Unlike *Calandra* and similar cases, where tainted evidence was used in peripheral proceedings, in the so-called "good faith exception cases," the Court has reasoned that the introduction of such evidence in the "case-in-chief" would not undermine the exclusionary rule's deterrent effect. These cases confirm the Court's present view, which modifies the original theory of the exclusionary rule: it is not a constitutional rule but is a judicially created remedy designed to deter police from violating Fourth Amendment rights.

The good faith exception was first adopted in principle in **Michigan v. DeFillippo** (1979). Detroit Police stopped DeFillippo on suspicion and arrested him for violating a 1976 ordinance that required stopped persons to give their identities to the police. A search incident to the arrest disclosed illegal drugs on his person. Michigan appellate courts later declared

the ordinance unconstitutionally vague and suppressed the evidence. The United States Supreme Court, in an opinion by Chief Justice Burger, held that the evidence could be introduced because the ordinance, although unconstitutional, did not undermine the probable cause requirement and because the police followed a then-valid ordinance in good faith. The stage was set for a major reassessment and limitation of the exclusionary rule in *United States v. Leon* (1984).

— *United States v. Leon* Case & Comments —

Leon was followed by **Illinois v. Krull** (1987), which held that the exclusionary rule does not apply where the police violate a person's rights in good faith reliance on a statute. Chicago police officers, under an Illinois regulatory statute, searched cars and records of an automobile wrecking yard without a search warrant. The statute was declared unconstitutional by a federal court. On appeal, the Supreme Court, applying the reasoning of *Leon,* found that because similar regulatory search schemes had been held constitutional in the past, the officers relied on the law in good faith. *Krull* differs from the *DeFillippo* case. In *DeFillippo,* the statute was voided because its vague wording violated the Fourteenth Amendment Due Process Clause, while in *Krull,* the purported constitutional infirmity was a violation of the Fourth Amendment. For this reason, the decision was closer in *Krull* (5–4), with Justice Sandra Day O'Connor writing the dissent, joined by Justices Brennan, Marshall, and Stevens. Justice O'Connor noted that the Fourth Amendment was originally designed to constrain the legislature. She minced no words: "[l]egislatures have, upon occasion, failed to adhere to the requirements of the Fourth Amendment." She also disagreed with the majority as to whether a legislature could be deterred by the application of the exclusionary rule in a case such as this one. "Providing legislatures a grace period during which the police may freely perform unreasonable searches in order to convict those who might otherwise escape provides a positive incentive to promulgate unconstitutional laws." Justice O'Connor's experience as a leader of the Arizona Senate seems to have provided the insight that, for political gain, legislators at times have decided to intentionally pass laws that violate individual rights.

Two instructive cases display instances in which the good faith exception makes sense and instances in which it does not. In **Massachusetts v. Sheppard** (1984), a companion case to *Leon,* a police officer filed a homicide search warrant affidavit on a form to search for controlled substances. Because it was Sunday, the courts were closed and the officer could not find the proper form. The officer and the magistrate modified the form, but, still, the search warrant erroneously authorized a search for controlled substances yet did not incorporate the affidavit. The warrant was executed and the detective along with other officers searched Sheppard's residence for items listed in the affidavit. They discovered several incriminating pieces of evidence and entered them into evidence. The Court held that in this case, the police objectively relied in good faith on a defective warrant. This is an instance in which a good faith reliance exception avoids a patently absurd conclusion. It is

• CASE & COMMENTS •

United States v. Leon
468 U.S. 897, 104 S.Ct. 3405, 82 L.Ed.2d 677 (1984)

JUSTICE WHITE delivered the opinion of the Court.

This case presents the question whether the Fourth Amendment exclusionary rule should be modified so as not to bar the use in the prosecution's case in chief of evidence obtained by officers acting in reasonable reliance on a search warrant issued by a detached and neutral magistrate but ultimately found to be unsupported by probable cause. **[a]** To resolve this question, we must consider once again the tension between the sometimes competing goals of, on the one hand, deterring official misconduct and removing inducements to unreasonable invasions of privacy and, on the other, establishing procedures under which criminal defendants are "acquitted or convicted on the basis of all the evidence which exposes the truth." * * *

I

[Local police obtained a "facially valid" search warrant from a state judge based on information from a confidential informant "of unproven reliability." A stakeout revealed suspected drug dealing at a house, and a car parked outside belonged to Leon, a previously convicted drug dealer. A search warrant affidavit was prepared by an experienced drug enforcement officer and reviewed by several assistant prosecutors. A warrant was issued by a state judge. The warrant was executed and drugs were found. On this evidence, Leon and others were indicted in a federal District Court for drug dealing. They moved to suppress evidence and challenged the constitutionality of the search warrant. The federal judge overturned the warrant—the informant's reliability was not established and probable cause of drug sales was not independently established. [This rule is covered in Chapter 3 under Probable Cause.] The court stated that the case was a close one and that the officers acted upon the warrant in the good faith belief that it was based upon probable cause, even though probable cause was not established. The federal Court of Appeals upheld the District Court. The case is decided on the understanding that the search warrant was not valid under the Fourth Amendment and in effect that the search violated Leon's Fourth Amendment rights.]

We have concluded that, in the Fourth Amendment context, the exclusionary rule can be modified somewhat without jeopardizing its ability to perform its intended functions. **[b]** Accordingly, we reverse the judgment of the Court of Appeals.

II

Language in opinions of this Court * * * has sometimes implied that the exclusionary rule is a necessary corollary of the Fourth Amendment, * * * [or] the conjunction of the Fourth and Fifth Amendments. [*Mapp v. Ohio*] **[c]** * * * These implications need not detain us long. The Fifth Amendment theory has not withstood critical analysis or the test of time, * * * and the Fourth Amendment "has never been interpreted to proscribe the introduction of illegally seized evidence in all proceedings or against all persons." * * *

A

The Fourth Amendment contains no provision expressly precluding the use of evidence obtained in violation of its commands, and * * * the use of [unlawfully seized evidence] "work[s] no new Fourth Amendment wrong." * * * The wrong condemned by the Amendment is "fully accomplished" by the unlawful search or seizure itself, * * * and the exclusionary rule is neither intended nor able to "cure the invasion of the defendant's rights which he has already suffered." The rule thus operates as "a judicially created remedy designed to safeguard Fourth Amendment rights generally through its deterrent effect, rather than a personal constitutional right of the party aggrieved." * * *

Whether the exclusionary sanction is appropriately imposed in a particular case is "an issue separate from the question whether the Fourth Amendment rights of the party seeking to invoke the rule were violated by police conduct." * * * **[d]** Only the former question is currently before us, and it must be resolved by weighing the costs and benefits of preventing the use in the prosecution's case-in-chief of inherently trustworthy tangible evidence obtained in reliance on a search warrant issued by a detached and neutral magistrate that ultimately is found to be defective.

The substantial social costs exacted by the exclusionary rule for the vindication of Fourth Amendment rights have long been a source of concern. **[e]** * * * "[U]nbending application of the exclusionary sanction to enforce ideals of governmental rectitude would impede unacceptably the

---

[a] Justice White states the issue *and* establishes a "judicial methodology"— the "balancing test"— to resolve the issue. The choice assists in producing the desired outcome. Is anything left out of the "competing goals"?

[b] This conclusion is analogous to a structural engineer deciding to construct a bridge without using materials that maximize safety. Does this kind of cost/benefit analysis have a place in civil rights law?

[c] Justice White dismisses the *Mapp* holding that the exclusionary rule is a *constitutional* rule—by his phrasing. The Fifth Amendment theory, used in *Mapp* to gain Justice Black's vote, linked the Fourth Amendment to a clear-cut exclusionary rule in the Fifth Amendment. By relying on post-*Mapp* cases, Justice White, a long-standing critic of *Mapp*, is now able to use precedents he helped create to weaken its effect.

[d] In criminal law a crime definition is incomplete without the penalty provision—the public's remedy is part of the right. Is the Fourth Amendment a true right without a remedy? Is the exclusionary rule a true remedy? See Theories of the Exclusionary Rule section.

[e] The exclusionary rule is "put on the defensive," stressing its costs, limits, and status as a "mere" remedy. The social cost of the exclusionary rule is still open to debate. Note how the "imperative of judicial integrity" of liberal justices becomes the "ideal of governmental rectitude" to conservative justices; the phrases convey different meanings.

truth-finding functions of judge and jury." * * * Particularly when law enforcement officers have acted in objective good faith or their transgressions have been minor, the magnitude of the benefit conferred on such guilty defendants offends basic concepts of the criminal justice system. * * * Indiscriminate application of the exclusionary rule, therefore, may well "generat[e] disrespect for the law and administration of justice." * * * Accordingly, "[a]s with any remedial device, the application of the rule has been restricted to those areas where its remedial objectives are thought most efficaciously served." * * *

B

[This section reviews cases in which the Court has "demoted" the exclusionary rule, including *Stone v. Powell* (1976); *United States v. Calandra,* (1974); and *United States v. Janis,* (1976), the attenuation cases, the impeachment cases, and the retroactivity cases.] **[f]**

[f] The text has reviewed these cases, showing the exclusionary rule's erosion. Precedent is "ammunition" used by the justice to get the desired result.

III

A

* * *

* * * To the extent that proponents of exclusion rely on its behavioral effects on judges and magistrates, * * * their reliance is misplaced. **[g]** First, the exclusionary rule is designed to deter police misconduct rather than to punish the errors of judges and magistrates. Second, there exists no evidence suggesting that judges and magistrates are inclined to ignore or subvert the Fourth Amendment or that lawlessness among these actors requires application of the extreme sanction of exclusion.

* * *

[M]ost important, we discern no basis, and are offered none, for believing that exclusion of evidence seized pursuant to a warrant will have a significant deterrent effect on the issuing judge or magistrate. **[h]** * * * [A]s neutral judicial officers, they have no stake in the outcome of particular criminal prosecutions. * * * Imposition of the exclusionary sanction is not necessary meaningfully to inform judicial officers of their errors. * * *

B

If exclusion of evidence obtained pursuant to a subsequently invalidated warrant is to have any deterrent effect, therefore, it must alter the behavior of individual law enforcement officers or the policies of their departments. One could argue that applying the exclusionary rule in cases where the police failed to demonstrate probable cause in the warrant application deters future inadequate presentations or "magistrate shopping" and thus promotes the ends of the Fourth Amendment. Suppressing evidence obtained pursuant to a technically defective warrant supported by probable cause also might encourage officers to scrutinize more closely the form of the warrant and to point out suspected judicial errors. **[i]** We find such arguments speculative and conclude that suppression of evidence obtained pursuant to a warrant should be ordered only on a case-by-case basis and only in those unusual cases in which exclusion will further the purposes of the exclusionary rule.

We have frequently questioned whether the exclusionary rule can have any deterrent effect when the offending officers acted in the objectively reasonable belief that their conduct did not violate the Fourth Amendment. "No empirical researcher, proponent or opponent of the rule, has yet been able to establish with any assurance whether the rule has a deterrent effect. * * *" But even assuming that the rule effectively deters some police misconduct and provides incentives for the law enforcement profession as a whole to conduct itself in accord with the Fourth Amendment, it cannot be expected, and should not be applied, to deter objectively reasonable law enforcement activity.

* * *

This is particularly true, we believe, when an officer acting with objective good faith has obtained a search warrant from a judge or magistrate and acted within its scope. In most such cases, there is no police illegality and thus nothing to deter. * * * **[j]**

[g] The Bill of Rights protects individual rights against violations by all branches of government. Excluding judges from the exclusionary rule means that it is not viewed as a constitutional right.

[h] Judges have immunity from lawsuit for errors made on the bench but are subject to reversal on appeal to correct their errors and deter them from not following precedent. Are not magistrates concerned if their warrants are overturned as illegal?

[i] Does Justice White select his assumptions? He brushes aside the educative function of the law—the idea that over time the exclusionary rule will educate police officers to follow the Amendment. See the *Law in Society* section on the effects of the Exclusionary Rule.

[j] What does Justice White imply by "no police illegality"? Leon's Fourth Amendment rights *have* been violated. If the officer is not civilly liable and there is no exclusion, what is the value of Leon's rights?

• CASE & COMMENTS •

C

* * *

Suppression * * * remains an appropriate remedy if the magistrate or judge in issuing a warrant was misled by information in an affidavit that the affiant knew was false or would have known was false except for his reckless disregard of the truth. * * * The exception we recognize today will also not apply in cases where the issuing magistrate wholly abandoned his judicial role. * * * Nor would an officer manifest objective good faith in relying on a warrant based on an affidavit "so lacking in indicia of probable cause as to render official belief in its existence entirely unreasonable." * * * Finally, depending on the circumstances of the particular case, a warrant may be so facially deficient—*i.e.,* in failing to particularize the place to be searched or the things to be seized—that the executing officers cannot reasonably presume it to be valid. * * * **[k]**

* * *

JUSTICE BLACKMUN, concurring.

* * *

* * * [T]he Court has narrowed the scope of the exclusionary rule because of an empirical judgment that the rule has little appreciable effect in cases where officers act in objectively reasonable reliance on search warrants. * * * **[l]**

What must be stressed, however, is that any empirical judgment about the effect of the exclusionary rule in a particular class of cases necessarily is a provisional one. By their very nature, the assumptions on which we proceed today cannot be cast in stone. To the contrary, they now will be tested in the real world of state and federal law enforcement, and this Court will attend to the results. If it should emerge from experience that, contrary to our expectations, the good-faith exception to the exclusionary rule results in a material change in police compliance with the Fourth Amendment, we shall have to reconsider what we have undertaken here. The logic of a decision that rests on untested predictions about police conduct demands no less.

* * *

JUSTICE BRENNAN, with whom JUSTICE MARSHALL joins, dissenting.

Ten years ago in *United States v. Calandra,* 414 U.S. 338 (1974), I expressed the fear that the Court's decision "may signal that a majority of my colleagues have positioned themselves to reopen the door [to evidence secured by official lawlessness] still further and abandon altogether the exclusionary rule in search-and-seizure cases" (dissenting opinion). **[m]** Since then, in case after case, I have witnessed the Court's gradual but determined strangulation of the rule. It now appears that the Court's victory over the Fourth Amendment is complete. * * *

* * *

The majority ignores the fundamental constitutional importance of what is at stake here. * * * [W]hat the Framers understood [in 1791] remains true today—that the task of combating crime and convicting the guilty will in every era seem of such critical and pressing concern that we may be lured by the temptations of expediency into forsaking our commitment to protecting individual liberty and privacy. It was for that very reason that the Framers of the Bill of Rights insisted that law enforcement efforts be permanently and unambiguously restricted in order to preserve personal freedoms. * * * **[n]** [T]he sometimes unpopular task of ensuring that the government's enforcement efforts remain within the strict boundaries fixed by the Fourth Amendment was entrusted to the courts. * * * If those independent tribunals lose their resolve, however, as the Court has done today, and give way to the seductive call of expediency, the vital guarantees of the Fourth Amendment are reduced to nothing more than a "form of words." * * *

I

* * *

A

[JUSTICE BRENNAN restated the majority argument here: the exclusionary rule is a mere judicial remedy designed to deter police illegality; the constitutional wrong is complete when the police invade

[k] The good faith reliance-on-the-warrant exception is not a blank check to the police. Four exceptions to the exception are set out where the exclusionary rule applies. This cautions police to get warrants where possible. Would it not be simpler for the Court to issue a bright line rule requiring warrants?

[l] Justice Blackmun's concurrence says that the Court may reverse its rule in *Leon* if the police misuse it with pretext searches. Does this seem odd to you? Isn't the Court supposed to establish firm rules of law? Is he just being honest about the flexibility of constitutional law?

[m] This strong language may be discounted as a tactic. But it *is* a way of reaching beyond the majority to stir a wider audience and future generations in the hope that a different Court might overturn this decision.

[n] Justice Brennan accuses the majority of "selling out" the Constitutional rights of citizens because fear of crime was a popular political issue to the presidents who appointed them. Do you agree?

a person's constitutionally protected privacy; and thus there is no constitutional violation if unconstitutionally seized evidence is admitted into evidence.]

Such a reading appears plausible, because, * * * the Fourth Amendment makes no express provision for the exclusion of evidence secured in violation of its commands. * * * [M]any of the Constitution's most vital imperatives are stated in general terms and the task of giving meaning to these precepts is therefore left to subsequent judicial decisionmaking in the context of concrete cases. **[o]** The nature of our Constitution, as CHIEF JUSTICE MARSHALL long ago explained, "requires that only its great outlines should be marked, its important objects designated, and the minor ingredients which compose those objects be deduced from the nature of the objects themselves." * * *

A more direct answer may be supplied by recognizing that the Amendment, like other provisions of the Bill of Rights, restrains the power of the government as a whole; it does not specify only a particular agency and exempt all others. The judiciary is responsible, no less than the executive, for ensuring that constitutional rights are respected.

* * * Once that connection between the evidence-gathering role of the police and the evidence-admitting function of the courts is acknowledged, the plausibility of the Court's interpretation becomes more suspect. * * * The Amendment therefore must be read to condemn not only the initial unconstitutional invasion of privacy—which is done, after all, for the purpose of securing evidence—but also the subsequent use of any evidence so obtained.

The Court evades this principle by drawing an artificial line between the constitutional rights and responsibilities that are engaged by actions of the police and those that are engaged when a defendant appears before the courts. **[p]** According to the Court, the substantive protections of the Fourth Amendment are wholly exhausted at the moment when police unlawfully invade an individual's privacy and thus no substantive force remains to those protections at the time of trial when the government seeks to use evidence obtained by the police.

I submit that such a crabbed reading of the Fourth Amendment * * * rests ultimately on an impoverished understanding of judicial responsibility in our constitutional scheme. For my part, "[t]he right of the people to be secure in their persons, houses, papers, and effects, against unreasonable searches and seizures" comprises a personal right to exclude all evidence secured by means of unreasonable searches and seizures. The right to be free from the initial invasion of privacy and the right of exclusion are coordinate components of the central embracing right to be free from unreasonable searches and seizures.

* * *

B

* * *

* * * [T]he Court since *Calandra* has gradually pressed the deterrence rationale for the rule back to center stage. * * * [JUSTICE BRENNAN then reviewed the cost-benefit analysis utilized by the majority.] * * *

* * * To the extent empirical data are available regarding the general costs and benefits of the exclusionary rule, it has shown, on the one hand, as the Court acknowledges today, that the costs are not as substantial as critics have asserted in the past, * * * and, on the other hand, that while the exclusionary rule may well have certain deterrent effects, it is extremely difficult to determine with any degree of precision whether the incidence of unlawful conduct by police is now lower than it was prior to *Mapp*. * * * The Court has sought to turn this uncertainty to its advantage by casting the burden of proof upon proponents of the rule. * * *

* * * [B]y basing the rule solely on the deterrence rationale, the Court has robbed the rule of legitimacy. A doctrine that is explained as if it were an empirical proposition but for which there is only limited empirical support is both inherently unstable and an easy mark for critics. **[q]** The extent of this Court's fidelity to Fourth Amendment requirements, however, should not turn on such statistical uncertainties. * * * Rather than seeking to give effect to the liberties secured by the Fourth Amendment through guesswork about deterrence, the Court should restore to its proper place the principle framed 70 years ago in *Weeks* that an individual whose privacy has been invaded in violation of the Fourth Amendment has a right grounded in that Amendment to prevent the government from subsequently making use of any evidence so obtained.

* * *

[o] This point might better apply to a more open textured right such as "due process" than to the more narrowly focused Fourth Amendment.

[p] Do you agree that the line between Fourth Amendment rights and the exclusionary rule is artificial, i.e., that the two should be inseparable? All legal doctrine involves line drawing. Do you think Justice Brennan provides a better rationale for the exclusionary rule as a constitutional right?

[q] This is a strong point. Should basic rights depend on measured effectiveness? If so, could a tyrant fail to uphold rights and then demand that they be abolished because they don't "work"? Does this critique properly apply to a "remedy"?

LEON IN THE STATES

According to Professor Latzer, the following states have approved of the *Leon* rule by court action or statute: Arkansas, California, Indiana, Kansas, Kentucky, Louisiana, Missouri, Ohio, South Dakota, Texas, Utah, Virginia, and Wyoming. "The courts of several states have cast doubt upon the good faith concept without actually rejecting *Leon*": Arizona, Florida, Georgia, Illinois, Minnesota, Mississippi, North Carolina, Washington, and Wisconsin. States which have repudiated *Leon* include: Connecticut, Idaho, Michigan, New Jersey, New Mexico, New York, Pennsylvania, and Vermont.

Barry Latzer, State Constitutional Criminal Law, §2.11–14.

In *Connecticut v. Marsala*, the Connecticut Supreme Court, rejecting the application of the *Leon* good faith reliance on a warrant rule under the state constitution, suggested that *Leon* exaggerated the "costs" of the exclusionary rule and held that they were not so substantial as to overcome the benefits of the exclusionary rule. More critically, the Connecticut court rejected the idea that the Fourth Amendment is separate from the exclusionary rule. "The exclusionary rule places no limitations on the actions of the police. The fourth amendment does."[36]

---

worth noting that Justice Stevens, concurring in the decision, felt that the warrant and affidavit were in fact quite specific and that the magistrate and the police officers were fully aware of their contents. Thus, he believed there simply was no Fourth Amendment defect and that the majority manufactured one in order to make new law.

A more disturbing case is ***Arizona v. Evans*** (1995). Evans was stopped by a Phoenix police officer for driving the wrong way on a one-way street. A computer check indicated an outstanding misdemeanor warrant; he was arrested, and marijuana was discovered. However, the arrest warrant against Evans had, in actuality, been quashed seventeen days prior to his arrest. An error in the *court* clerk's office resulted in the information not being conveyed to the sheriff's office to remove the arrest notation from the law enforcement computer database. The Arizona Supreme Court excluded the evidence because there was no basis for the arrest and the "application of the exclusionary rule would 'hopefully serve to improve the efficiency of those who keep records in our criminal justice system.'" On appeal by the state, the United States Supreme Court reversed. Chief Justice Rehnquist, writing for the Court, believed that Evans had no complaint because the wrong condemned by the Fourth Amendment is fully accomplished by the unlawful seizure itself, and the use of the "fruits" of a past unlawful search or seizure does not introduce a new Fourth Amendment violation. The Court noted that the exclusionary rule is designed to deter unconstitutional *police* activity, and not errors made by judges or personnel in judicial bureaucracies. It reasoned that there is no reason to believe that the exclusionary rule will deter errors by court clerks. Unlike police who are "zealous" in their desire to "get" suspects, court clerks "have no stake in the outcome of particular criminal prosecutions."

This reasoning seems as wrongheaded as the application of the exclusionary rule in a case like *Sheppard*. This seems to have been recognized in Justice O'Connor's concurring opinion, expressing some concern that widespread computer errors might undermine individual rights. Justice Stevens dissented on the grounds that the text and the history of the Fourth Amendment indicates a more majestic goal of protecting individual privacy and liberty from encroachment from *any* part of the government. *Arizona v. Evans* (1995), perhaps a limited ruling, shows that rights can be lost from the negligent maintenance of modern technology as they can from more direct state action.

It is critical to note that there is no free-floating "good faith exception" that allows police officers to enter homes or other areas in which people have an expectation of privacy because they reasonably feel they have probable cause. The Supreme Court has not approved an exclusionary rule exception for using illegally obtained evidence based on a police officer's good faith observations leading to a warrantless stop, arrest, or search. Each good faith exception is tied to the officer's *reliance* on the decision of a magistrate, a law, or official records. According to Professors Whitebread and Slobogin, the Court has deliberately avoided the issue of a general good faith exception.[41] There may indeed be instances when police arrest or search without probable cause, but do so in subjective good faith. Nevertheless, the inherent human subjectivity that tends to make every person a "biased judge" about his or her own actions would make such an exception a more risky proposition for individual rights than allowing the use of unconstitutional evidence obtained by the officer's good faith reliance on the judgment of the legislature or a judge. It seems that allowing officers to dispense with warrants on their own evaluation would tend to weaken if not destroy the Warrant Clause and seriously damage Fourth Amendment protections.

The Supreme Court has reminded police officers that they are personally liable in lawsuits to persons whose houses they enter if they rely on obviously defective search warrants. ***Groh v. Ramirez*** (2004) held, in a 5–4 decision, that a search warrant that did not list *any* of the items to be seized is plainly unconstitutional. Joseph Ramirez was not prosecuted and he sued agent Jeff Groh, a special agent for the Bureau of Alcohol, Tobacco, and Firearms (ATF), for violating his Fourth Amendment rights. The Supreme Court ruled that Agent Groh could not claim qualified immunity from the lawsuit because it would be clear to a reasonably competent officer that his conduct was unreasonable. The Court, in *Groh*, quoted *Leon*: "depending on the circumstances of the particular case, a warrant may be so facially deficient—*i.e.*, in failing to particularize the place to be searched or the things to be seized—that the executing officers cannot reasonably presume it to be valid." A law enforcement officer is not absolved from personal responsibility to read a warrant carefully and be sure it is constitutional on its face before executing it, merely because a magistrate has issued the warrant.

Standing

Standing is another rule that diminishes the exclusionary rule. Having "standing to sue" means that a person must have a sufficient *stake in a legal controversy* in order to obtain a judicial resolution. Standing, in constitutional cases, is predicated on Article III of the Constitution, which confers jurisdiction on the Supreme Court and federal courts only in "cases or controversies." A person must have a *real, legal claim* to begin with in order to be allowed to pursue a case or an issue in a court.

The Supreme Court has held that simply because evidence is introduced in a trial against a person does not give that person a Fourth Amendment right to challenge the constitutionality of the search and seizure. The search and seizure standing doctrine grew out of the older concept that Fourth Amendment rights are based on *property interests* and that one had to have some level of property interest to assert a personal claim against an alleged illegal search and seizure, i.e., to have standing. At first, this limited standing to owners or renters or persons who had some kind of legal connection to a place, such as a hotel guest. But guests in a house did not have standing. Also, a person who is charged with a crime of possession (e.g., drugs) or charged with a crime for which the possession of an item tends to prove guilt (e.g., burglar's tools, weapons used in the crime) can claim possession of the thing and have standing to challenge its seizure, but to do so is an admission of guilt.

The Supreme Court eased standing rules in *Jones v. United States* (1960). It held that a person charged with possession of drugs, after police entered an apartment with a warrant and discovered drugs inside, could establish standing based on a connection to the place. Jones did not rent the apartment, but was given a key to the place by the owner, was allowed to sleep there, and had some clothing in the place. The Court rejected technical property law classifications as the basis of standing and instead held that a defendant had standing to make a Fourth Amendment challenge when he was "legitimately on the premises." Therefore, Jones did not have to assert ownership of the drugs to make a claim that the search warrant was unconstitutional.

This language in *Jones* was so broad as to suggest that anyone against whom evidence obtained in a search and seizure was used (except burglars or trespassers) could challenge the legality of its seizure. This is known as the **target theory.** The Court, however, rejected this approach in *Alderman v. United States* (1969, p. 174) on the theory "that Fourth Amendment rights are personal rights which, like some other constitutional rights, may not be vicariously asserted." Thus, the Court retained the standing requirement. In *Alderman,* the incriminating evidence was conversations made by codefendants, to which Alderman was not a party, that were picked up by electronic eavesdropping. The Court ruled that his Fourth Amendment right to privacy was not violated by the eavesdropping on the conversations of others.

Since that time, the Court has continued to uphold standing while also continuing to follow the specific rule of *Jones.* In cases involving persons found in apartments, the Court ruled that having a key is not essential. In *Minnesota v. Olson* (1990), the Court affirmed the state court, which held that a defendant had standing to challenge the introduction of evidence taken from an apartment in which he was an overnight guest. Olson had indefinite permission to stay and had the right to allow or deny visitors entry. "To hold that an overnight guest has a legitimate expectation of privacy in his host's home merely recognizes the everyday expectations of privacy that we all share. . . . From the overnight guest's perspective, he seeks shelter precisely because it provides him with privacy, a place where he and his possessions will not be disturbed by anyone but his host and those his host allows inside" (*Minnesota v. Olson,* 1990).

Business occupants of an apartment, however, do not have standing. In *Minnesota v. Carter* (1998), police entered an apartment on a tip that illicit drug business was being conducted there and found two men bagging cocaine. They were from out of town and "had come to the apartment for the sole purpose of packaging the cocaine. [They] had never been to the apartment before and were only in the apartment for approximately 2 1/2 hours. In return for the use of the apartment, [they] had given [the renter] one-eighth of an ounce of the cocaine." On these facts the Court held that the defendants had no standing to challenge the constitutionality of the police search. The majority noted that the apartment was not the home of the drug dealers, and that they had less connection to the apartment than an employee has in his or her private office.

> If we regard the overnight guest in *Minnesota v. Olson* as typifying those who may claim the protection of the Fourth Amendment in the home of another, and one merely "legitimately on the premises" as typifying those who may not do so, the present case is obviously somewhere in between. But the purely commercial nature of the transaction engaged in here, the relatively short period of time on the premises, and the lack of any previous connection between respondents and the householder, all lead us to conclude that respondents' situation is closer to that of one simply permitted on the premises. We therefore hold that any search which may have occurred did not violate their Fourth Amendment rights. (*Minnesota v. Carter,* pp. 90–91)

Justice Ruth Bader Ginsburg dissented, arguing that the decision undermines the security of short-term guests and anyone that a home owner or renter invites "into her home to share in a common endeavor, whether it be for conversation, to engage in leisure activities, or for business purposes licit or illicit, that guest should share his host's shelter against unreasonable searches and seizures."

These holdings reflect the impact of *Katz v. United States,* which created the "expectation of privacy doctrine" in 1967 (see Chapter 3). This created another basis for standing—that a person has a subjective and objective expectation of privacy in a premises where a search took place. *Katz* logically would tend to expand Fourth Amendment standing, but the Supreme Court has not applied *Katz* consistently, as seen in **Rakas v. Illinois** (1978). In this case, police stopped a car on suspicion of it having been involved in a recent robbery. The driver was a woman who owned the car. Frank Rakas, another man, and a woman were passengers. Police officers searched the car and found a sawed-off rifle and rifle shells. This evidence was introduced into evidence to convict Rakas of robbery. The state courts ruled that Rakas, a passenger in the car who did not claim ownership or possession of the guns and shells, had no standing to challenge the constitutionality of the automobile search.

The Supreme Court agreed and refused to expand the rule of *Jones*. Indeed, it narrowed the rule. Essentially, Rakas argued that he had standing because he was legitimately in the car. Justice Rehnquist, writing for a five-justice majority, noted that the concept of standing added little to the analysis of the case. The real issue was whether the search violated the personal Fourth Amendment rights of the defendant, and that has to be determined by examining the facts of the case. The majority in *Rakas* stated that the phrase—"legitimately on the premises"—is too broad and would extend standing too far. Instead, a court must examine the defendant's *connection* with the premises. A casual visitor to an apartment, for example, has no standing to challenge a search, while an overnight guest does have standing. Likewise, the Court ruled that a passenger in a car did not have enough of a connection to challenge the seizure of a weapon that he claimed not to own.

Justice White, dissenting, felt that the *Katz* expectation of privacy doctrine clarified that the focus of Fourth Amendment analysis should be on the defendant's privacy right, uncoupled from ownership. To the dissenters, Rakas was legitimately in the car and had as much a privacy interest against an improper police search as did the driver. Justice White stated that the flaw in the majority opinion was that, "[t]he distinctions the Court would draw are based on relationships between private parties, but the Fourth Amendment is concerned with the relationship of one of those parties to the government." Finally, the dissent noted that "the ruling today undercuts the force of the exclusionary rule in the one area in which its use is most certainly justified—the deterrence of bad-faith violations of the Fourth Amendment." The *Rakas* holding tempts police to engage in questionable automobile searches in which there is a passenger, in the hope that the passenger would not have standing to challenge an illegal search.

The *Rakas* approach, limiting standing and, thus, limiting the exclusionary rule, was followed in *Rawlings v. Kentucky* (1980). The Court held that Rawlings had no standing to challenge a search of a companion's purse, even though Rawlings claimed that the illegal drugs in the bag belonged to him. In *Jones* the Supreme Court held that possession of the object of a possessory crime conferred standing. In *Rawlings* and a companion case, *United States v. Salvucci* (1980), this rule of automatic standing in possession cases was explicitly over-

ruled. One reason for the *Jones* rule, that a defendant who claimed standing had to assert possession of contraband, has been reversed in order to preserve a defendant's Fifth Amendment interests, thus providing a reason to overrule the automatic standing rule.

Professor William Heffernan has pointed out that the Supreme Court's restrictive standing rule is in conflict with its theory that the only purpose of the exclusionary rule is to deter police illegality. If the Court were more serious about deterrence, it would allow a broader scope for challenging possibly illegal searches.[37] What seems unmistakable is that the Burger and Rehnquist Courts' restrictive standing rule is tied to its distaste for the exclusionary rule.

ARGUMENTS AGAINST THE EXCLUSIONARY RULE

This section summarizes arguments that critics have leveled against the exclusionary rule, and is closely connected to the following sections on alternate remedies and theories that support the exclusionary rule.

1. A *civil lawsuit* against offending police officers for a Fourth Amendment violation is a *true remedy*. It is a traditional legal remedy for injuries and acts directly against the offending party. In contrast, the exclusion of evidence is not a liability that is necessarily felt by the officer who violated the defendant's rights. It causes a loss to a third party (the people, who lose an opportunity to truthfully adjudicate a criminal case), may give the victimized person a windfall in the guise of not being convicted, and still does not directly compensate the person whose rights were violated.

2. The exclusionary rule *suppresses relevant evidence* that tends to prove the defendant's guilt. Enforcing the Fourth Amendment via exclusion means, in the classic adage of Justice (then Judge) Cardozo, that "The criminal is to go free because the constable has blundered. . . ."[38] The cost to society is a weakening of the truth-finding attributes of the criminal trial, a crime goes unavenged, and a criminal is set free, perhaps to reoffend. This is in contrast to Fifth and Sixth amendment exclusionary rules that suppress confessions or lead to dismissals for lack of effective counsel where those errors might lead to the conviction of *innocent* defendants.

3. The exclusionary rule has *no deterrent effect* on Fourth Amendment violations *where nothing is seized*. In such cases, only the alternative remedies of civil lawsuits or criminal prosecution will vindicate the person whose rights were violated.

4. The actual *deterrent effect of the exclusionary rule will never be known* (see *Law in Society* section, this chapter). However, there are logical reasons the exclusionary rule is not well suited to be an effective deterrent: (a) the impact of exclusion is directly felt by the prosecutor rather than the officer, (b) police know and count on the fact that the rule is rarely applied, (c) judges are reluctant to find a Fourth

Amendment violation when they know that evidence points to guilt (hindsight biasing).[39]

5. Although the "cost" of the exclusionary rule is worth paying in excluding evidence from the "case-in-chief" where it is likely to have the greatest effect, it *need not be imposed where it will have limited effect,* e.g., impeachment, grand jury questions, civil cases, deportation, and parole revocation. It can be disregarded even in the trial to prove guilt where the officer reasonably and in good faith relied on the Fourth Amendment judgment of another official, such as a magistrate or the legislature because it will have limited deterrent effect.[40]

6. The exclusionary rule encourages *police perjury.* Very few rogue police officers manufacture or plant evidence on innocent suspects, but many officers "shade the truth" when testifying in court, especially in possession cases. (See *Law in Society* section, Chapter 3). Not only is this a negative consequence for a sense of fairness in the courts, but police know that they can reduce the effectiveness of the exclusionary rule by their own success in undermining it.[41]

7. Any police sanctioning that occurs as a result of the exclusion of evidence, occurs *indirectly* when the prosecutor complains to police administrators, who relay such complaints down the chain of command; and such sanctioning tends to be offset by the praise and recognition that officers receive for making good arrests that are not outrageous.[42]

8. The doctrinal attacks on the exclusionary rule made by Justice Frankfurter in *Wolf v. Colorado* (1949) and by Justice Harlan dissenting in *Mapp v. Ohio* (1961), were triggered by federalism concerns. The Court's post-*Calandra* jurisprudence shows more respect to states' rights.

Before concluding the chapter with a discussion of theories that support the exclusionary rule, the question of alternatives to the exclusionary rule are explored. These materials are important in their own right and also provide background for considering the ultimate question of whether the rule must be retained as a constitutional matter.

ALTERNATIVE REMEDIES

This section has a pragmatic and a theoretical orientation. From a pragmatic perspective, all law is designed to produce goals. Constitutional criminal procedure law is designed to ensure that the government's law enforcers stay within the law. A major argument in favor of incorporating the exclusionary rule in *Wolf* (1949) and *Mapp* (1961) is that other means of gaining police compliance were not effective. Because of changed legal and social conditions in the last half-century it appears that civil lawsuits and administrative measures have some better chance of modifying police behavior.

Aside from these pragmatic considerations, the furious legal debate over the exclusionary rule exposes important theoretical perspectives. These are explored in the previous section on arguments against the exclusionary rule and the next section on theories of the exclusionary rule. Opponents of the rule argue that it is not a legal remedy at all. In answer to the critics and as a prelude to the concluding sections, consider the following points, drawn from the analysis of Prof. William Heffernan.

Unlike most commentators who discuss remedies as a unitary concept, Prof. Heffernan demonstrates that there are three types and goals of remedies. *First-party remedies* aim at **reparation**, to restore the *injured party* to the position he occupied before the injury occurred. *Second-party* remedies have the goal of **disgorgement**, to place the *wrongdoer* in no better position than the one he occupied prior to his wrongful conduct. *Third-party* remedies aim at *deterrence* of future wrongdoing, to the benefit of the *general public,* i.e., "plac[ing] the public in a better position than it would be in if deterrence were not undertaken."[43] In practice, these types and goals of remedies may overlap in a single case, and may be mutually supportive or at odds with one another. All three rationales have been used by the Supreme Court to support the exclusionary rule.

To see this point, observe that the Fourth Amendment protects three distinct rights: *liberty, property*, and *privacy—not* just privacy alone. It is true, as conservative justices have said, that once the *privacy* rights of a suspect have been breached by a wrongful search and seizure, it is irreversible. (Once one's privacy has been violated by an illegal search and seizure, it "is fully accomplished by the original search," Justice Powell, *United States v. Calandra,* 1974, p. 354). The only true remedy for a completed violation of privacy rights is reparation, or a civil lawsuit for money damages. However, if the state exploits the privacy violation by also violating a defendant's property or liberty interests, these are *ongoing violations* that can be repaired by a return of the property or freeing the defendant.

Additionally, the reparation remedy of damages does not undermine the legitimacy of the remedial goals of disgorgement and deterrence. In civil lawsuits for **injunctions** or specific performance, disgorgement may be ordered where possible to prevent the violator of a person's rights from getting the benefit of a wrong. Furthermore, punitive damages may be paid to an injured party above what is needed to compensate for actual losses, specifically to deter the wrongdoer from doing the acts in the future, i.e., to protect the public.

At this point, various alternative remedies than the exclusionary rule are described. The text returns to the theoretical perspectives in the following sections.

The King's officers who invaded the homes of John Wilkes and his associates in the 1760s were sued in English common law courts, found liable for trespass, and assessed considerable money damages for violating the rights of British subjects. The Bostonians who challenged writs of assistance were, in effect, seeking injunctions to prevent the Crown from issuing general search warrants. When the Bill of Rights was ratified, it is likely that the framers assumed that any such violations of privacy by the government would lead to lawsuits, which in turn would embarrass the government into reversing and preventing abuses. As dissenting justices in *Wolf v. Colorado* and the majority in *Mapp v. Ohio* noted, however, police officers were almost never held responsible for violating individuals' Fourth Amendment rights. *Mapp* was predicated in part on the belief that *Weeks*'s exclusionary rule was the best way of deterring police breach of rights. More recently, exclusionary rule critics have argued that alternate remedies are preferable. This section briefly reviews the alternative or parallel remedies to exclusion, which fall into four general categories:

1. Civil lawsuits (federal and state)
2. Injunctions against police action
3. Criminal prosecution of police officers
4. Administrative measures

Remedies are central to the law and to the legitimacy of government's promise to do justice. The foundation of federal judicial power, *Marbury v. Madison* (1803), stated that:

> The very essence of civil liberty certainly consists in the right of every individual to claim the protection of the laws, whenever he receives an injury.
>
> * * *
>
> The government of the United States has been emphatically termed a government of laws, and not of men. It will certainly cease to deserve this high appellation if the laws furnish no remedy for the violation of a vested right.[44]

As Professor Cornelia Pillard stated, "According to *Marbury*'s ideal, legal rights are not mere precatory or aspirational statements, but remediable claims, redressable in courts, for violations of law."[45] In blunt terms, constitutional rights become meaningless platitudes unless officers and the state are held accountable and made to pay if and when their acts trample on the rights of individuals.

Civil Lawsuits for Damages

SECTION 1983: THE CIVIL RIGHTS ACT: STATE OFFICERS IN FEDERAL COURTS   Most civil rights lawsuits against municipal police officers are conducted in federal court under the Civil Rights Act of 1871, which is found in Title 42 *United States Code*, section 1983, and are commonly known as **Section 1983 lawsuits**. This right of action in federal courts against state and local officers was created by Congress after the Civil War, under the authority of the Fourteenth Amendment in order to counteract Ku Klux Klan terrorism against African Americans. Such a lawsuit is based on a violation of a person's federal statutory or constitutional rights by persons "acting under the color of state law" or custom. The law was not much used for a century. After the Supreme Court held that a Fourth Amendment violation stated a Section 1983 claim in *Monroe v. Pape* (1961), thousands of Section 1983 suits proliferated. In *Monroe*, Chicago police officers without a warrant entered the plaintiff's home at night, rousted his family, and arrested and detained the plaintiff for ten hours without probable cause before his release. The history and wording of Section 1983 prevents lawsuits against state governments. In 1978 the Court, on reexamining the history of the statute, extended Section 1983

lawsuits to cases against municipal governments, making such suits more attractive to plaintiffs; however, such suits are limited to situations in which the officer acted pursuant to a municipal policy.[46] A study by Scarborough and Hemmens of 734 Section 1983 appeals decided between 1989 and 1993 found that 58 percent were for excessive force, false arrest, and illegal search and seizure. Plaintiffs suing the police won 24 percent of the illegal search and seizure cases, the police prevailed in 44 percent of these cases, and in 32 percent the case was remanded for further findings. This study indicates that this form of civil lawsuit is not rare, that persons who sue law enforcement for rights violations have an opportunity to gain redress, but that a strong legal and factual case is needed to prevail.[47]

BIVENS SUITS: FEDERAL OFFICERS IN FEDERAL COURTS   The Supreme Court in *Bivens v. Six Unknown Named Agents* (1971) held for the first time that there is a federal constitutional **tort** remedy for violations of constitutional rights by federal agents. Prior to that time, a person whose only remedy was a civil suit had to pursue a doubly anomalous suit against such officers under state common law torts. The Civil Rights Act of 1871 (creating Section 1983 suits) applied only against local officers. The facts in *Bivens* demonstrate that the only remedy for the wrongs done to him was a civil lawsuit for money damages. Webster Bivens was arrested at home by federal narcotics agents who searched his Brooklyn apartment "from stem to stern" and was strip-searched at booking. He was never prosecuted, so exclusion of evidence was a meaningless remedy. Because it was unlikely that he would again be arrested, an injunction suit made no sense. His suit for damages, based on an illegal arrest and search and seizure, was thrown out of federal court because no such cause of action existed in federal law. If Bivens sued in state court, the federal government might have tried to remove the case to federal court where it would be dismissed on jurisdictional grounds. So, Bivens appealed to the Supreme Court, urging the creation of a federal tort remedy. The Supreme Court agreed with Bivens, in effect finding that the fundamental rule of a legal remedy for every legal wrong outweighed the doctrine of sovereign immunity that had previously blocked a federal constitutional tort. The Court noted that the underlying interests in a federal suit were more serious than a trespass suit under state law, and that after the creation of the expectation of privacy doctrine in *Katz v. United States* (1967), Fourth Amendment violations are deemed to be based on *constitutional* interests, and not simply on *property* rights that undergird one's right to be free of a civil trespass. The lawsuit by rancher Joseph Ramirez that was brought against ATF Agent Jeff Groh (see section on Good Faith Exceptions, earlier in this chapter), was brought under the jurisdiction created by *Bivens* (*Groh v. Ramirez*, 2004).

STATE COMMON LAW TORT SUITS   A person alleging that an arrest or a search occurred without probable cause can sue the offending police officer for an intentional tort such as false imprisonment or trespass. Private lawsuits against government units or agents were at one time blocked by the common law doctrine of "sovereign immunity" that was inherited from

England. States have lifted sovereign immunity in part, but actual rules differ in different states. In a Florida case, for example, a sheriff's deputy gratuitously beat a suspect in handcuffs during a booking procedure and the injured person sued the deputy and the Volusia County Sheriff's Department. Under Florida law, the deputy could be held liable for a civil battery if he acted within the scope of his employment. The department could be liable only if the deputy's acts exceeded the scope of his employment. Florida law was structured so that either the agency could be held liable, or the deputy, but not both.[48]

STATE CONSTITUTIONAL TORTS: STATE OFFICERS IN STATE COURT In addition to shoe-horning a constitutional violation into the shape of a common-law tort, some states' courts, following the federal example, have established distinct state constitutional torts: a direct cause of action for damages for violation of a constitutional right against a government or individual defendants. Unlike a state common-law tort, which is designed to vindicate personal interests, a constitutional tort "reinforces the moral accountability of the state and vindicates the reliance interest of the people; . . . [it] holds the government responsible as an agent of the people."[49] At the present time, nine states have recognized civil damages suits under their constitutions (a few with special conditions), nine state appellate courts have suggested that such lawsuits are proper under certain circumstances, and seven have rejected the idea.[50] For example, the New York Court of Appeals, that state's highest court, established a right to sue for a constitutional tort based on a violation of the search and seizure clause of the New York constitution. In that case, state police and local law enforcement officials embarked on a five-day "street sweep" in which every nonwhite male found in and around the City of Oneonta was stopped and interrogated for a reported crime.[51]

In addition to these standard avenues of redress, lawyers may seek other remedies that exist in state or federal common law. A startling example was a ruling by a Reagan-appointed federal trial judge that allowed the Los Angeles Police Department to be sued in August 2000, under the Racketeer Influenced and Corrupt Organizations (RICO) Act in the notorious Rampart Division scandal. The scandal involved anywhere from a dozen to seventy officers systematically arresting at least one hundred innocent people, planting incriminating evidence on them, giving perjured testimony, improperly using Immigration officials in making arrests, and physically assaulting people without cause. The RICO law was first established to attack organized crime families, but has been extended to other organizations that use illegal means to further their goals and interfere with interstate commerce. The benefit to the plaintiffs in the suit is that the RICO statute of limitations is ten years and it allows triple damages. The potential damages to Los Angeles were put at $100 million.[52]

Injunctions

Injunctions are not common remedies for Fourth Amendment violations. An injunction is a judicial order that either (1) commands a defendant to perform a particular act, (2) prohibits specified activity, or (3) orders a defendant to cease wrongful activity from continuing. Injunctions may be granted by a court where plaintiffs can prove that rights violations are *persistent* and repeated and that an injunction is the *only effective remedy*. Injunctions are enforced by the judicial power of **contempt of court,** which can include fines or jail for disobedience.

The Supreme Court has been reluctant to uphold federal injunctions against local police departments. It struck down an injunction against the Los Angeles Police Department that prohibited the use of chokeholds in **Los Angeles v. Lyons** (1983), which were not specifically prohibited or authorized by departmental regulations. "At the time *Lyons* was decided, the chokehold had caused the deaths of over a dozen persons; by 1991, twenty-seven people had died as a result of this restraint technique. The Court dismissed the suit, holding that in order to have standing to sue for an injunction, the plaintiff must show that he is likely to be a future victim of that same technique."[53] In **Rizzo v. Goode** (1976), the Court reversed a federal injunction against the Philadelphia Police Department's cumbersome procedural process for investigating citizens' complaints about the use of excessive force. The Court reasoned that complainants had failed to demonstrate that the existing policy resulted in *routine and persistent* patterns of excessive force and civil rights violations. These cases demonstrate that the Supreme Court believes it is unwise for federal courts to become involved in close judicial supervision of police departments' administration. It is deemed more judicious in such cases for the administrative and political process to bring about policy changes in police departments.

A prohibitory injunction was issued by a lower federal court and upheld on appeal by the Fourth Circuit in *Lankford v. Gelston* (1966) against a local police department that had been conducting a "dragnet" type search. Police officers searching for the killers of fellow police officers had, over a three-week period, entered three hundred houses based on anonymous tips and without legal justification. Because there were no arrests, the exclusionary rule could not be used to deter the officers, and the police activity was flagrant and persistent. Under these circumstances, the injunction was justified.[54]

Criminal Prosecution

STATE PROSECUTIONS Criminal prosecutions of police officers for acts committed in the line of duty are rare and limited to egregious cases, typically involving the death of a suspect.[55] It is difficult to obtain such a conviction if the defense attorney convinces the jury that the officers acted reasonably to enforce the law or if the victim suffered little or no personal injury. A notable example was the acquittal, in February 2000, of four New York City Street Crime Unit police officers of the murder of Amadou Diallo, an African immigrant, who was shot nineteen times as he reached for his wallet. Professor James Fyfe, an expert who more often testifies against police, testified that the facts showed that the officers believed Diallo had a gun and acted properly. A juror said the prosecution had not proved that the officers acted criminally.[56]

The past decade has been rife with notorious prosecutions of police officers, including the trial and first acquittal of Los Angeles police officers for beating Rodney King, a speeding motorist, which was videotaped and played to a national audience.[57] In Detroit, police officers were convicted and imprisoned for the beating death of Malice Green.[58] Three white suburban Pittsburgh police officers were acquitted of manslaughter in the asphyxiation death of an African American motorist, Jonny Gammage.[59] These sporadic prosecutions are a proper response to the specific cases, but they have an impact on systemic errors or abuse only if they spark reforms. In the aftermath of the Louima case (next section), for example, New York City bowed to pressure and agreed to federal monitoring of the way in which officers accused of abuse are investigated and disciplined.[60]

FEDERAL PROSECUTIONS OF LOCAL POLICE OFFICERS
A federal civil rights law originally enacted in 1866 authorizes federal prosecution of local officers who, acting under color of local law or custom, deprive a person of rights under the Constitution (18 U.S.C. §242). The Supreme Court has held that a conviction requires a purpose to deprive a person of a specific constitutional right.[61] In recent decades, federal prosecutors have become more active in investigating and prosecuting crimes by local police. Federal civil rights prosecutions have included several high-profile cases, e.g., the second trial of the police officers involved in the Rodney King beating and the trial of officers in the sexual brutalization of Haitian immigrant Abner Louima by New York City police officers. If the sexual torture inflicted on Louima was perpetrated by a private person, all persons would justly be horrified. But the additional concern in a civil rights violation was captured by the words of the federal judge who sentenced the police officer to thirty years imprisonment: "Short of intentional murder, one cannot imagine a more barbarous *misuse of power* than Volpe's."[62] Misuse of power undermines trust in the government, makes people—especially the poor and dispossessed—skeptical of protection by the criminal justice system, and makes people believe that honest police officers are actual or potential rights-violators.

Administrative Remedies

Ideally, violations of constitutional rights should rarely, if ever, occur. External legal sanction, such as the exclusionary rule or civil suits, may control police behavior to some extent, but they are *reactions to past violations*—they encourage future compliance through punishment, which has had limited effectiveness (see *Law in Society* section of this chapter). Nonjudicial and administrative methods, therefore, are essential to encourage police to adhere to the Rule of Law. Methods for making police more understanding of the people they police and more mindful of rights include community policing, civil-

ian review boards,[63] a police ombudsman,[64] accreditation of police departments,[65] civilianizing many roles in police departments,[66] tightening rules on the use of lethal force,[67] cultural diversity and sensitivity training,[68] higher standards for police recruits,[69] training in Asian martial arts,[70] and similar improvements. Better academy and in-service training in constitutional law is important. Jerome Skolnick and James Fyfe, leading police scholars, urge that the conditions under which there is a *duty* to use legitimate force be rethought and made more clear, to emphasize that *"The primary job of the police is to protect life."*[71]

If constitutional mandates like the Fourth Amendment are to be regularly obeyed by police officers, the impetus must come more from within police departments. For example, William Bratton, the innovative former New York City police commissioner, made obedience to the Constitution a key goal for the NYPD.[72] Policies that reward police with raises, promotions, and other advances if they follow constitutional guidelines are likely to guarantee stronger compliance with constitutional norms than external penalties. Police departments' internal review units clearly have a vital role to play.

Professor Christopher Slobogin, a leading criminal procedure scholar, has proposed that the exclusionary rule be abolished in favor of a legal-administrative program with the following features:

> An administrative agency would be responsible for bringing and assessing Fourth Amendment claims. The claims would be heard by a judge in proceedings that are streamlined in much the way most administrative proceedings are. Plaintiffs who prevail would receive liquidated damages amounting to a percentage of the typical field officer's salary (say, somewhere between one percent and five percent). The individual officer would be personally liable for the damages unless he or she acted in good faith, in which case the police department would be financially responsible. Variants of the damages remedy, such as class actions and injunctions, would also be available through the court. Appeals could be taken to the normal appellate court.[73]

Regardless of whether or not a state would adopt such a system, it indicates that many are searching for workable alternatives. In fact, one promising alternative approach has been passed by Congress.

PATTERN AND PRACTICE REVIEW   A federal law passed as part of the Violent Crime Control and Law Enforcement Act of 1994 has brought the weight of the Department of Justice (DOJ) to bear on finding nonjudicial solutions to police violations of constitutional rights. Title 42 U.S.C. §14141 prohibits *governmental authorities* from engaging in a "pattern or practice of conduct by law enforcement officials" that deprives persons of constitutional rights. When the Attorney General has reasonable cause to believe that a violation has occurred, the Justice Department is authorized to sue for equitable and declaratory relief "to eliminate the pattern or practice." DOJ monitoring is not triggered by isolated incidents of unlawful acts but by conditions where unlawful acts have virtually become "standard operating procedure." The law is an attempt to find a better way to respond to situations like the Rodney King beating than to civil and criminal cases aimed at specific officers.

By 1999 two police departments, Pittsburgh, Pennsylvania, and Steubenville, Ohio, had entered **pattern and practice** consent decrees for excessive force, improper searches and seizures, and false arrests. Since that beginning, several other major departments, including Cincinnati, Detroit, Los Angeles, and the New Jersey State Police, were investigated and have entered into monitoring processes designed to improve critical police performance.[74] The principal provisions of consent decrees under §14141 impose requirements in the areas of police "training, the receipt and investigation of referrals and complaints concerning improper police behavior; and the development and maintenance of an early warning system." Although enforcement of Section 14141 is in its earliest stages, this "new remedy for police misconduct" seems to offer a substantial improvement over traditional tort remedies.[75]

THEORIES OF THE EXCLUSIONARY RULE

Is the exclusionary rule constitutionally required? This chapter has shown that the Supreme Court developed the exclusionary rule by reasoning from case to case in response to lawyers' arguments and in accord with political and ideological pressures. There was no theoretically coherent plan. Different reasons, therefore, have been offered to justify the rule, leading to confusion and the hazard that the current theory is constitutionally suspect. This section describes several of the theories used to justify the exclusionary rule. These justifications are intertwined with arguments in favor of and opposed to the existence of the rule. No theory for (or against) the exclusionary rule is entirely coherent. The present state of the law is paradoxical, which can be seen in a brief overview of the rule's development:

1. From 1914 to 1974, the Court justified the rule as one required by the Constitution and applicable to federal and (later) state legislatures, executive agencies (i.e., the police), and courts in cases like *Weeks* (1914), *Elkins* (1960), and *Mapp* (1961).
2. Since 1974, in cases like *Calandra* (1974) and *Leon* (1984), the Court has ruled that the exclusionary rule is *not* a Constitutional rule, but is a judicially created remedy designed to deter Fourth Amendment violations by police only. (A minority of justices before 1974 argued that the rule was not constitutionally required, and a minority of justices after 1974 believe that it is.)
3. If the exclusionary rule is not a constitutional rule, then the Court's jurisdiction to create it in *Weeks* rested on supervisory authority, which applied *only* to federal cases. This idea casts doubt on the legitimacy of *Mapp* and the application of the rule to state courts. (This argument does not threaten *Rochin* (1952), which was based explicitly on the Fourteenth Amendment Due Process Clause.)

4. Were the existence of the exclusionary rule to come squarely before the Court, a variety of theoretical arguments could support its continued existence.

   a. For example, the Court could modify the incorporation theory, going back to Justice Harlan's dissent in *Mapp*, and assert that only the *core* of the Fourth Amendment rule is applied to the states through the more flexible Fourteenth Amendment rule, allowing different rules for federal and state cases. This would require overruling *Ker v. California* (1963) and would revive the problematic silver-platter doctrine.
   b. Or, the Court could dispose of a direct challenge to *Mapp* as it did with a direct challenge to *Miranda* in *Dickerson v. United States* (2000), by stating that however the present Court would have decided *Mapp* in 1961, principles of *stare decisis* (precedent) require that a rule that has been heavily relied on be upheld if its core meaning has not been eroded.
   c. Finally, the Court could return to a renewed *Weeks-Mapp* understanding that the exclusionary rule is required by the logic of the Fourth Amendment, if one agrees with Professor William Heffernan that "[W]ithout an exclusionary principle, the Amendment collapses on itself."[76] Such a return would undermine much of the conservative search and seizure jurisprudence erected by the Burger and Rehnquist Courts.

The discussion in this section borrows heavily from articles by Professor Heffernan, who supports the exclusionary rule, and Professor Slobogin, who believes it should be abolished.

DETERRENCE THEORY   This is the theory currently adhered to by the Court's majority. It was first erected in *Calandra* (1974) and was firmly established by *Leon* (1984). All punitive and remedial systems have some general deterrent effect; thus, even if the exclusionary rule is based on nonconsequentialist (ethical) reasons, it would still likely deter some misconduct by police and magistrates. Nevertheless, since *Calandra*, the Supreme Court has made deterrence the sole rationale for the exclusionary rule, and since *Leon* has applied it only to police misconduct. As a result, where deterrence is thought minimal, the rule does not apply.[77] Because deterrence is a utilitarian rationale, its legitimacy turns primarily on whether it is effective. This has been the subject of a huge debate and is the focus of this chapter's *Law in Society* section. The theories that follow are based on nonconsequential ideas and principles.

FIFTH AMENDMENT THEORY   *Boyd* (1886) excluded evidence from an invoice based on the idea that the "Fourth and Fifth Amendments run almost into each other." Both amendments concern privacy rights, and most critically, the Fifth Amendment was seen to explicitly require exclusion by its words ("No person . . . shall be compelled in any criminal case to be a witness against himself. . . ."), whereas the words of the Fourth Amendment do not explicitly command exclusion. Although *Weeks* explicitly rested on the Fourth Amendment, several cases thereafter relied on the *Boyd* Fourth + Fifth formula (*Gouled,* 1921). Justice Black's crucial fifth vote in *Mapp* was based on this theory. It may have made sense because, in many of the early exclusionary rule cases, including *Weeks,* the items taken were letters or other documents. Nevertheless, the Court discarded the theory in *Andresen v. Maryland* (1976), which held that business records could be seized with a warrant, and this was confirmed by Justice White's comment in *Leon:* "The Fifth Amendment theory has not withstood critical analysis or the test of time."[78] The idea that a search *compels* the disclosure of evidence would make searches impossible, because "the Fifth Amendment excludes all compelled testimony, whether or not it was obtained by police who had probable cause."[79] This could not have been contemplated by the framers of the Fourth Amendment.

PROPERTY THEORY *Weeks* (1914) and *Silverthorne* (1920), among other cases, seem to rest on the idea that a defendant rather than the state has a greater *property* right over evidence illegally seized by the state. There are some inconsistencies with this theory. If the successful defendant requests the return of contraband, the request will be denied even if the evidence is suppressed.[80] The mere evidence rule of *Gouled* (1921) indicates that the government has a possessory interest superior to the defendant-owner in contraband, fruits of crime, and instrumentalities. Under existing forfeiture laws, all sorts of "innocent" items used in the commission of crime may be forfeited. The Court has undermined *Boyd* and has allowed the seizure of papers. All these examples undermine a strong property basis for the exclusionary rule. The final straw is the "expectation of privacy" doctrine of *Katz v. United States* (1967), which attempted, and partially succeeded, to recast the foundation of Fourth Amendment jurisprudence. By making intangible information "seized" by electronic eavesdropping the subject of the Fourth Amendment, property was displaced, if not eliminated, as a theoretical basis of the exclusionary rule. The *Katz* philosophy was confirmed and strengthened by the abolition of the mere evidence rule in *Warden v. Hayden* (1967), under which Fourth Amendment principles (balancing law enforcement needs against individual privacy) outweigh property interests in determining whether the government may seize evidence.

STATUS QUO ANTE THEORY The exclusionary rule returns the parties to where they would have been had the Constitution been followed. This is a strong commonsense and ethical rationale. It also explains the inevitable discovery exception to the fruits of the poisonous tree doctrine: Because the police would have legally obtained the evidence in any event, they should not be placed in a difficult position because an unconstitutional search did happen. Professor Slobogin claims that the theory has holes because it does not result in the return of contraband and it cannot restore the "ruptured privacy" of the person subjected to an illegal search and seizure. His idea that the rule is not logically applied because it does not allow the introduction of evidence where the police *could have* lawfully obtained the evidence seems specious, and does not meet the

deeper objections posed by Professor Heffernan. The status quo ante theory blends into the last—and the most normative—ethical consideration: the imperative of judicial integrity. A conclusion as to the last theory will determine whether or not the exclusionary rule should be considered a necessary, constitutional rule.

THE IMPERATIVE OF JUDICIAL INTEGRITY/ RULE OF LAW No case rests entirely on this theory. In *Elkins v. United States* (1960) (which banned the silver-platter doctrine), Justice Potter Stewart reasoned that the effect of *Wolf v. Colorado* (1949), which unequivocally ruled that illegal searches and seizures by state officers violate the Constitution, was to undermine the other rule of *Wolf,* which did not apply the exclusionary rule to the states. One rationale for exclusion was to deter police illegality. "But there is another consideration—the imperative of judicial integrity" (*Elkins,* 1960, p. 222). The courts undermine the Rule of Law if they allow illegally seized evidence to be introduced. This strongly implies that the Constitution should offer no choice about the use of such evidence. This ethical theory, however, has not been fully worked out or explained in the cases, although its logic was intuited by Justice Holmes.[81]

The basic issue is whether the exclusionary rule is constitutionally required. The *Calandra-Leon* thesis is "no," because (a) the rule is not explicit in the language of the amendment; (b) the purpose of the Fourth Amendment is to prevent unreasonable government intrusions into the *privacy* of one's person, house, papers, or effects; (c) the invasion of privacy is *fully accomplished* by the original search without probable cause; and (d) the *use* of evidence illegally seized works no new Fourth Amendment wrong but is only a derivative use of the product of past unlawful search and seizure. Because the exclusionary rule, which has been created by the Supreme Court to deter police illegality, reaches only the derivative use of the evidence and not the Fourth Amendment wrong, it is not constitutionally required.

To this, Professor Slobogin adds that the Supreme Court, under some circumstances, allowed the use of illegally seized evidence for impeachment during the era when the rule was viewed as a constitutional requirement; therefore, it could not have been seen as a nullity (*Walder v. United States,* 1954). Also, *Mapp* was held not to be retroactive, implying that it is not an absolute constitutional right.[82] He concludes that none of the theories in support of the exclusionary rule "provide grounds for concluding that it is appropriate as a remedy in the typical case."

Justice Brennan, dissenting in *Calandra,* provided the answers to these arguments: (a) the justices who established the exclusionary rule made no mention of deterrence as a rationale but fashioned an enforceable remedy to give content and meaning to the Fourth Amendment's guarantees; (b) because judges have no direct power over the police, a remedy has to be feasible; (c) one goal of the exclusionary rule is to ensure that the courts will not be tainted by partnership in official lawlessness; (d) another goal of the exclusionary rule is to assure the people that the government would not profit from its lawless behavior; (e) the exclusionary rule is consistent with the Rule of Law; (f) *Linkletter v. Walker* (1965), the nonretroactivity case, can be explained pragmatically as taking into account state reliance on the precedent of *Wolf v. Colorado* (1949), and the possible "wholesale release of innumerable convicted prisoners" (*United States v. Calandra,* 1974, pp. 355–61).

Professor Heffernan's thorough analysis and criticism of the *Calandra-Leon* thesis, and his support of the constitutionality of the exclusionary rule takes into account the structure and functions of remedies in light of the multiplicity of interests protected by the Fourth Amendment. As noted above, remedies have the goals of reparation, disgorgement, and deterrence, and operate to protect privacy, property, and liberty interests inherent in the Fourth Amendment. Having reviewed other remedies, arguments against the exclusionary rule, and various theories of the rule, this chapter concludes with a sketch of Heffernan's justification.

Prof. Heffernan poses a hypothetical example in which a search and seizure occurs that does not entirely destroy a person's privacy interest. Suppose police entered a home illegally and seized encrypted computer discs suspected of containing criminal information. At this point there has been a violation of the householder's property rights in the discs, but no violation to the privacy of the information contained in them. If the person makes a legal claim for a return of the discs—his property—the government would have to return them. But what if the government tries to break the encryption code while the hearing proceeds? Should the government be allowed to hold the discs in order to break the code if the owner sues for their return? This would only compound the original wrong of the unconstitutional entry. Professor Heffernan suggests that this attempt to cause irreparable harm to the suspect's privacy interest requires their return, because the justification for using this evidence requires justification of the initial wrongful entry and seizure. This is essentially the same thing as officers searching randomly and without probable cause, and justifying any search that turns up incriminating evidence retrospectively, which the Supreme Court found unconstitutional in *Smith v. Ohio* (1990) (discussed in the section on the "fruits of the poisonous tree" doctrine). Without the exclusionary rule, the courts would have to admit evidence obtained in this way.

This leads to the conclusion that the internal logic of the Fourth Amendment against retroactive justification requires the "remedy" of exclusion even if the framers did not consider exclusion, because without the exclusionary rule the Amendment "collapses on itself."[83] The government cannot insist on holding on to illegally seized evidence in order to determine if it discloses incriminating information, for that would allow seizures before probable cause is obtained. "Absent exclusion, all personal property is held on a probationary basis: government agents can seize personal property at will, inspect it, and return it only if it is found not to provide evidence of a crime."[84] The internal logic of the Fourth Amendment cannot allow this kind of *retroactive legitimation*. If the exclusionary rule were totally eliminated, police could choose to violate

Fourth Amendment rights in specific cases they deem important and be willing to pay the price in a tort action if it came to that. Thus, Heffernan believes that Justice Holmes and the Court had it right in *Silverthorne* (1920). Whatever the framers thought about exclusion as a remedy, the Court in *Weeks* and *Silverthorne* intuited that the exclusionary principle "emerges from an analysis of the internal logic of the Amendment itself."[85] This is so even if exclusion does not repair the violation of first-party privacy interests and extracts a heavy cost to the public, whose third-party interest in deterrence is offset by an interest in convicting the guilty. Nevertheless, the liberty-protecting function of the Constitution coalesces with and is required by the second-party remedy of disgorgement via exclusion that is required by the logic of the Fourth Amendment.

SEARCHES IN A TIME OF TERROR

The USA PATRIOT Act has weakened the Fourth Amendment protections of all citizens, and not just suspected terrorists, by authorizing "sneak and peek" warrants (section 218) and delayed notification (section 213). These two sections of the act have to be read together to understand their import.

When search warrants are executed, the normal procedure is for officers to leave a copy of the warrant if the premises are unoccupied, and to file an inventory and return with the court issuing the warrant. This is an essential safeguard to ensure that the police are complying with the warrant. Section 213 of the Act allows agents to delay notification of the execution of a search warrant or

> some forms of electronic communications if the government can show that giving immediate notice will (1) endanger an individual's physical safety; (2) cause someone to flee prosecution; (3) cause evidence to be tampered with; (4) create potential for witness intimidation; or (5) jeopardize the investigation or unduly delay trial. This type of warrant authorizes officers to secretly enter (physically or electronically), conduct a search, observe, copy documents, download or transmit computer files without taking any tangible evidence or leaving notice of their presence.[86]

A rule similar to this existed under the Foreign Intelligence Surveillance Act (FISA). For such an order, however, senior FBI officials had to apply for a court order and certify that "the purpose of the surveillance is to obtain foreign intelligence information" to access various records. A regular search warrant had to be obtained for investigations leading to prosecutions.

> Section 218 of the Act amends FISA to permit the FBI to conduct secret physical searches and surveillances to obtain evidence of a crime without a prior determination of probable cause. Rather than requiring a showing that the purpose of the surveillance is to obtain foreign intelligence, as was required under FISA, section 218 instead requires certification that foreign intelligence gathering is for a "significant purpose." As a result, this section allows law enforcement agencies to circumvent the Fourth Amendment so long as they are able to establish that the gathering of foreign intelligence constitutes "a

significant purpose." This runs contrary to the court decision in United States v. United States District Court for the Eastern District of Michigan n16 where the U.S. Supreme Court rejected President Nixon's proposal for the unchecked executive power to conduct warrantless wiretaps when investigating national security threats posed by domestic groups with no foreign ties.[87]

Early news reports regarding the application of these provisions indicate real abuses. The *Dallas Morning News* reported in September 2003 that FBI agents "have used 'sneak-and-peek' warrants, wiretaps, Internet surveillance and other Patriot tools in pursuit of thieves, computer hackers, drug dealers and money launderers. And they're exploring how the law can be used in other realms."[88] The chief author of the USA PATRIOT Act acknowledged that this use was possible under the act and was not at all apologetic: "'A lot of these tools can be used in ordinary crimes,' former Assistant Attorney General Viet Dinh acknowledged during a recent debate over the Patriot Act on CNN, 'But heck, if we happen to catch a murderer, excuse me for not apologizing.'"[89] This cavalier attitude seems oblivious to the fact that the law allows federal agents to entirely circumvent established warrant procedures, raising the specter of a permanent impairment of the constitutional balance achieved under the Fourth Amendment. It seems that the Justice Department is contemplating and has been acting on such an expansion:

> In a May 2002 bulletin to the nation's 94 U.S. attorneys, a staffer in Justice's Computer Crimes and Intellectual Property Section wrote enthusiastically about the Patriot Act's reach beyond terrorism cases. "Indeed, investigations of all manner of criminal conduct with a nexus to the Internet have benefitted from these amendments," the trial attorney wrote.[90]

Such actions have sparked a reaction to curb the excesses built into some provisions of the PATRIOT Act. Both Democrats and Republicans in Congress have proposed bills to limit these powers to genuine terrorist or foreign power investigations. The House of Representatives voted 309–118 to repeal the Act's covert "sneak and peek" provisions in the summer of 2003. By the Fall of 2003 more than 150 towns and cities had passed resolutions condemning the Act's excesses.[91] The Oregon state Senate passed a resolution imploring Congress to correct the Act "and oppose any future federal legislation to the extent that it infringes on United States residents' civil rights and liberties."[92] In response to this criticism, Attorney General Ashcroft went on a publicity tour to defend the PATRIOT Act. Despite many valuable provisions, the concerns raised by a broad spectrum of public opinion ought to alert the administration that the law has flaws that, by creating unbalanced search and seizure rules, threaten the civil liberties of all Americans. The PATRIOT Act has a sunset provision. It remains to be seen if its excessive provisions are repealed—as were the Alien and Sedition laws of 1798—as the nation and its allies get a grip on the fight against foreign terrorists. If not, the issues raised would be sure to come before the Supreme Court for a constitutional showdown.

LAW IN SOCIETY

COSTS AND BENEFITS OF THE EXCLUSIONARY RULE

Since 1974, the Supreme Court has confronted two empirical issues concerning the exclusionary rule: its deterrent effect and its costs in lost convictions. Both issues have been used in arguments for and against the rule, so that studies and findings have been examined with partisan intensity. In the course of examining these empirical questions, the Supreme Court has used and, on occasion, misused social science data. This section reviews some of the findings on these sensitive issues.

In order to understand human behavior, social scientists first attempt to accurately measure behavior systematically and with quantitative precision to the greatest extent possible. Statistical tests are applied to data to determine the extent to which the collected data (a sample) reflects actual behavior (the universe). These rigorous attempts to quantify knowledge contrast with the human tendency to generalize: to make overly broad conclusions about human behavior based on a small number of personal experiences or on the basis of a few stories heard from others or from external sources.

THE DETERRENT EFFECT OF THE EXCLUSIONARY RULE

Calandra v. United States (1974) "adopted the view that the primary rationale for the federal exclusionary rule is the factual premise that suppression of illegally seized evidence will deter the police from conducting illegal searches."[93] Only a few studies of the exclusionary rule had been published by 1974. The most prominent, by Dallin Oaks, appeared to show that the exclusionary rule had no effect on police behavior in several cities.[94] Oaks's *data* did *not* conclusively show whether the exclusionary rule deterred police misconduct. Rather, his stated *personal opinion* was that the rule failed to deter and should be abolished. According to Thomas Davies, "the Oaks study has probably established something of a record for being widely cited as empirical support for a finding it did not really claim to make."[95]

Proponents of the exclusionary rule were fearful that the Supreme Court would use a finding of no deterrence to abolish the rule. For example, in his *Bivens* dissent, Chief Justice Burger stated: "If an effective alternative remedy is available, concern for official observance of the law does not require adherence to the exclusionary rule." This would be especially troublesome if the Court made constitutional law based on flawed research. Indeed, Oaks's research conclusion, if not his data, was flawed in that he believed the exclusionary rule failed simply because Fourth Amendment violations continued to occur after the *Mapp* decision. This was a conceptual failure: The more appropriate question was whether the number and rates of such violations increased, decreased, or remained level after *Mapp*. Oaks failed to make these comparisons.[96]

In *United States v. Janis* (1976), a careful and exhaustive review of the deterrence research in Justice Harry Blackmun's majority opinion finally put to bed the deterrence issue. The issue in *Janis* was whether the exclusionary rule would be extended to federal IRS civil tax assessment hearings to exclude illegally seized evidence. A strong finding about the deterrent effect could sway the Court to extend the rule or to abolish it. Justice Blackmun's honest review of the research literature concluded that there is *no conclusive evidence that the rule has or does not have a deterrent effect:* "The final conclusion is clear. No empirical researcher, proponent or opponent of the rule, has yet been able to establish with any assurance whether the rule has a deterrent effect even in the situations in which it is now applied" (*Janis,* fn. 22). The way in which the Court applied this equivocal and correct empirical conclusion is interesting. Justice Blackmun said that even if the exclusionary rule has a strong deterrent effect "the additional marginal deterrence provided" by extending the rule to federal civil tax proceedings "surely does not outweigh the *cost to society* of extending the rule to that situation" (*Janis,* pp. 453–54, emphasis added). The majority in *Janis* clearly did not want to extend the exclusionary rule and so its analysis had a "heads I win, tails you lose" quality, by switching the focus of inquiry from deterrence to the costs of the exclusionary rule.

Nevertheless, the Court's conclusion in *Janis* in regard to the empirical research is supported by Professor Davies' thorough review of the issue.[97] The problem is not so much that of poor research designs, but of the special difficulty of defining and studying legal deterrence. According to Davies, "it is quite unlikely that there will be any rigorous measurement of the rule's specific deterrent effect in terms of how often illegal searches have been prevented."[98] This problem arose partly because the research community paid little attention to the exclusionary rule when criminal justice research made it clear that the rule was a minor factor in the total disposition of cases. Thus, studies on the effectiveness of deterrence and on its "costs" were left to policy-relevant studies that framed the issue narrowly.[99]

THE EDUCATIVE EFFECT OF THE EXCLUSIONARY RULE

Another empirical question is whether the exclusionary rule has had a broad educative effect. Proponents have not been able to establish this by rigorous empirical research, but there is a widespread understanding that because of the rule, police are now trained in the law, police and prosecutors seriously discuss search and seizure rules, and the police community generally takes the Fourth Amendment more seriously than it did before *Mapp.*[100] A study comparing drug, weapons, and gambling arrests in nineteen cities before and after *Mapp* appears to indicate that *Mapp* had a decided effect in six cities, no effect in ten cities, and an intermediate effect in three.[101] This suggests "that *Mapp's* impact largely has been mediated by differentials in attitudes and styles among police and civic leaders. . . . [T]he police are likely to behave differently in a city where the chief almost openly encourages evasion of a Supreme Court decision than in one where the chief insists on obedience."[102]

This is supported by the observational study of police by law professor Richard Uviller, who noted that honest police officers bring to their work an "innate sense of limits" that prevails "over the broad license allowed by law" in many situations.[103] Too often the "legal focus" portrays police as overly aggressive, overly zealous, and filled only with a "crime control" mentality. Uviller's closely observed police officers display a good deal of common sense, decency, and a real desire to operate within the limits of the law, even if they are not always precisely correct about the operative rules. This perspective is one that suggests that, over the long run, police behavior actually will become more law abiding. One may also speculate that as Burger and Rehnquist Courts decisions are more favorable to the police, it is easier for police to obey rules of constitutional criminal procedure. A more cynical possibility may be that successful evasion of the exclusionary rule is a factor in police acquiescence to the rule. All these factors may be at play simultaneously. In any event, to bring police behavior into line with constitutional norms requires practical training for police officers. Where the law does place limits on what the police may do, departments are well advised to include some training into the reasons for these limits.

COSTS OF THE EXCLUSIONARY RULE

The Court, in its anti-exclusionary rule mood, tended to emphasize the costs of lost convictions in broad terms. Justice White's concurrence in *Illinois v. Gates* (1983) is an example of poorly reviewing social science studies, in contrast to Justice Blackmun's more precise review of the deterrence studies. For example, his broad conclusion—"We will never know how many guilty defendants go free as a result of the rule's operation"[104]—is wrong. To make matters worse, he quoted a misleading National Institute of Justice (NIJ) study that reported: "prosecutors rejected approximately 30 percent of all felony drug arrests because of search and seizure problems."[105] As we shall see, this was a gross exaggeration of the costs of the exclusionary rule.

Unlike deterrence, which is inherently difficult to measure, lost cases can be more precisely measured. Because the total number of arrests and the number of cases dismissed owing to search and seizure errors can be obtained from prosecution and court records, the proportion of "lost cases" can be calculated. Several research studies are in general agreement that the "costs" of the exclusionary rule are not great. In almost all instances, the percentage of cases dropped because of search and seizure problems is *less than 1 percent:*

1. *Forst, Lucianovic, and Cox* (1974)—arrests in Washington, D.C.: prosecutors rejected 168 out of 17,534 arrests (1 percent) for all kinds of due process problems, including but not limited to, search and seizure violations.[106]
2. *Brosi* (1977)—prosecutors declined to issue complaints for all types of due process errors in 1 percent of the cases in Washington, D.C.; 2 percent in Cobb County, Georgia; 2 percent in Salt Lake City; 4 percent in Los Angeles; and 9 percent in New Orleans.[107]

3. *Forst et al.* (1977 and 1978)—due process violations led to dismissals in less than 1 percent of arrests in six cities, 2 percent in Los Angeles, and 6 percent in New Orleans.[108]
4. *General Accounting Office* (1979)—case attrition in federal prosecutions: prosecutors declined to accept 46 percent of all cases; 6.6 percent of the declined cases were rejected for legal violations. Overall, 0.4 percent of all cases were declined because of illegal searches.[109]
5. *Nardulli* (1983)—reviewed 7,500 cases in nine counties in three states; motions to suppress physical evidence were filed in fewer than 5 percent of the cases and were successful in 0.69 percent of the cases; motions to suppress illegal confessions or identifications were filed in 2 percent of the cases and successful in 4 percent of these; some defendants were convicted even after the evidence was suppressed; in the entire sample, 46 out of 7,500 cases were lost (less than 0.6 percent) because of the three exclusionary rules combined.[110]
6. *Feeney et al.* (1983)—nine out of 885 nonconvictions (1 percent) were lost due to illegal searches; since about half of the arrests resulted in nonconvictions, 0.5 percent of the cases in Jacksonville and San Diego were lost because of the exclusionary rule.[111]
7. *Uchida and Bynum* (1991)—seven cities: 1.4 percent of all defendants (19 out of 1,355) in cases based on search warrants were granted motions to suppress.[112]

Despite the virtually unanimous conclusion that about 1 percent or less of cases are lost because of the rule, Justice White claimed in *Gates* that 30 percent of the cases were lost due to excluded evidence. He based this on a federal study of California case processing, and repeated the figure put forward in the solicitor general's brief. Davies notes that the NIJ study was seriously flawed and that the 30 percent figure was grossly misleading. First, the NIJ study showed that 4.8 percent of *all rejected* felony cases are lost because of search and seizure problems. This in no way indicates the cost of the exclusionary rule—it does not show what proportion of cases are lost due to the rule; it instead shows that *among those cases that prosecutors rejected*, 4.8 percent were lost due to the exclusionary rule. This is meaningless because the percentage calculated in this way can change dramatically depending on changes in the other reasons for dismissals. When the NIJ data of lost cases are calculated against a *base figure of total arrests*, those lost due to the exclusionary rule drop to about 0.8 percent, more in line with the other studies. As for the 30 percent figure, it was drawn from a sample of 150 drug cases from two local prosecutors' offices in Los Angeles, which was not at all representative, for, as Davies indicates, between 1978 and 1982 statewide, California prosecutors rejected 2.4 percent of felony drug arrests because of illegal searches.

Further, the studies show that the number of cases rejected on Fourth Amendment grounds in *serious violent felonies* is lower, about 0.2 percent of all arrests, and somewhat higher for drug offenses. Davies makes the point that many such rejected arrests in drug cases may not be those of carefully planned

raids, but rather are arrests on suspicion where drugs are found and the probable cause basis is very weak to begin with. Thus, unlike the inconclusive result of the exclusionary rule's deterrent effect, research findings of its costs firmly show that fewer than one percent of arrests are lost because of the exclusionary rule. In half of these lost cases, *convictions are still obtained* because of other evidence.

Do these findings mean that the costs are low? This is a normative issue. The figures show that the exclusionary rule is not subverting law enforcement efforts. Yet, its effect may still be unacceptably high to some. "Indeed, some critics have taken the position that *even one lost arrest* is an excessive cost."[113] Thus, when Justice White had to confront this new evidence, he stated that "the small percentages with which [the researchers] deal mask a large absolute number of felons who are released because the cases against them were based in part on illegal searches or seizures" (*United States v. Leon*, 1984, fn. 6). Of course, in a country with a population of 260 million, virtually any small percentage will generate large numbers. I would tend to agree with Uchida and Bynum, quoting Van Duizend and colleagues, "that the exclusionary rule, though seldom invoked, serves as an incentive for many police officers to follow the limits imposed by the Fourth Amendment as defined in their jurisdictions."[114] Thus, the exclusionary rule debate presents an interesting case history of the use and misuse of social science data in the judicial decision-making process.

THE EFFECTIVENESS OF TORT REMEDIES

Another aspect of the exclusionary rule debate is the effectiveness of tort suits against the police. The evidence is generally that they do not provide strong control over police misbehavior, including police brutality. Empirical studies of *Bivens* suits, for example, disclose that they virtually never lead to findings of police officer liability.

Government figures reflect that, out of approximately twelve thousand *Bivens* claims filed between 1971 and 1985, *Bivens* plaintiffs actually obtained a judgment that was not reversed on appeal in only four cases. While similar figures have not been systematically kept since 1985, recoveries from both settlements and litigated judgments continue to be extraordinarily rare. According to one estimate, plaintiffs obtain a judgment awarding them damages in a fraction of 1 percent of *Bivens* cases and obtain a monetary settlement in less than 1 percent of such cases. The low rate of successful claims indicates that, notwithstanding *Bivens*, federal constitutional violations are almost never remedied by damages. The low success rate of these claims also reflects that the courts are processing a tremendous amount of *Bivens* litigation. When analyzed by traditional measures of a claim's "success"— whether damages were obtained through settlement or court order—*Bivens* litigation is fruitless and wasteful, because it does not provide the remedies contemplated by the decision, and it burdens litigants and the judicial system.[115]

While recovery in other kinds of tort cases against the police may not be quite so nonexistent, they are hard to obtain and monetary claims are low. In a study based on telephone interviews with civil rights attorneys in southern California, a variety of reasons were given for the lack of success:[116]

- Civil rights attorneys are unwilling to take weak cases.
- Witnesses with past criminal records are not credible to jurors.
- Police have a qualified immunity defense for acts taken in good faith.
- Municipalities provide the costs of defense and pay for any settlement in cases won by plaintiffs.
- It is more difficult for plaintiffs to discover facts in the hands of defendants in these cases compared to other civil litigation.
- Defendants can tie up plaintiffs, who tend to have limited resources, with interlocutory appeals in §1983 suits.
- The "blue curtain" of silence makes police witnesses very reluctant to testify.
- Police perjury is rampant (see *Law in Society* section in Chapter 3).
- Jurors almost always believe the police.

As a result, the likely deterrent effect of lawsuits on police *brutality* is very low. Commissions on police brutality report that many cases of abuse are committed by officers who are repeat offenders, indicating that departments do a poor job of sanctioning officers with a history of excessive violence. Many cities in the past decade have paid out multiples of millions of dollars in tort damages for police brutality, and the numbers do not appear to have substantially diminished. Although there seems to be a slight, growing public interest in police brutality in the early twenty-first century, there is virtually no political pressure for police departments to abide by the Constitution.[117] As Professor Canon noted in his study of police departments that follow warrant procedure, much depends on the attitudes of the police chief. "The chief and higher-ranking supervisors establish the tone and culture within a police department. If the upper ranks do not enforce violations of department policy, there will be no curb on officers' misconduct out on the street." Chiefs who are concerned with the legal conduct of their officers can affect policy and action by the selection of field training officers, by their own disciplinary decisions, by the emphasis given to legal issues in academy and in-service training, and by having records of tort cases become part of an officer's file and be taken into account in promotions.[118] All such measures should not lead to demoralization of police officers or overdeterrence so that police shy away from performing their difficult jobs effectively. But there are examples, such as William Bratton's tenure as New York City police commissioner, that, to paraphrase Justice Tom Clark, there is no war between effective policing and law-abiding policing.

SUMMARY

The structure and content of search and seizure law is the product of history. English common law came to protect the privacy of one's home against *government* invasion shortly be-

fore the framing of the Constitution (1787) in the *Writs of Assistance* case and the *Wilkes* cases. They held that general warrants are illegal and that a victim of a general warrant could sue the government for damages.

The Fourth Amendment was intended to eliminate the government's use of general search warrants. In the founding era, police had no power to conduct warrantless arrests or searches based on probable cause; a warrant was required. Nevertheless, modern constitutional interpretation authorizes warrantless arrests and searches upon probable cause under the general-reasonableness construction of the Fourth Amendment. The warrant-preference construction holds that warrants are required except in hot pursuit, vehicle searches, and searches incident to arrest.

The Fourth Amendment exclusionary rule states that illegally seized evidence may not be introduced into evidence in a trial. It was established in *Weeks v. United States* (1914) and *Silverthorne Lumber Co. v. United States* (1920). The rule was based on the Constitution and stated that illegally seized evidence shall not be used at all. The rule applies only to government officers, not to illegal searches by private individuals. Evidence derived from illegally seized evidence cannot be introduced into evidence (fruits of the poisonous tree doctrine), despite an illegal search. However, evidence of the crime may be introduced if it is obtained from an independent source, by inevitable discovery, or because the link between the primary illegality and the evidence seized has become attenuated, where there has been an illegal search and seizure.

The Supreme Court incorporated the exclusionary rule (extended it to the states) in *Mapp v. Ohio* (1961), after having refused to do so in *Wolf v. Colorado* (1949) and *Rochin v. California* (1952). In the latter case, the Court excluded evidence that was seized by methods that "shocked the conscience." This was a due process, "totality of the circumstances" test, and criticism of its subjectivity was a factor in the *Mapp* decision. The basis of *Mapp* was that the exclusionary rule is required by the Fourth Amendment and that exclusion is the best deterrent of police misbehavior.

After *Mapp,* a more conservative Supreme Court eroded the exclusionary rule. It upheld the use of illegally seized evidence as a basis of a grand jury question in *United States v. Calandra* (1974), which modified the theoretical basis of the exclusionary rule. It became viewed as a judicially created remedy designed to safeguard Fourth Amendment rights generally through its deterrent effect on future unlawful police conduct, rather than a personal constitutional right of the party aggrieved. This concept was expanded by *United States v. Leon* (1984), which allowed the introduction of illegally seized evidence for the proof of guilt where the evidence was obtained by police officers in the "good faith" reliance on a statute or search warrant. It also held that the exclusionary rule does not apply to unconstitutional acts committed by the judiciary.

In order to challenge evidence taken in violation of the Fourth Amendment, a party must have standing, that is, the party must have suffered a personal invasion of privacy rights rather than suffered actual harm because of the invasion of the privacy rights of another person. In *Rakas v. Illinois* (1978), the Court held that a passenger of an automobile does not have such a personal right. A personal interest to raise a Fourth Amendment challenge does not depend on the defendant's strict property right but in his level of interest in a place; thus, overnight guests in an apartment have standing, but persons invited into an apartment for business purposes do not have standing.

Aside from the exclusionary rule, individuals whose Fourth Amendment rights have been violated have other potential sources of relief. These include lawsuits against the police officer or the department. Different types of tort lawsuits include: state common law tort suits, state constitutional torts wherein state officers are sued in state courts, Section 1983—civil rights suits against state and local officers and municipalities (but not state governments) in federal courts, and *Bivens* suits against federal officers in federal courts. For violations that are likely to persist against specific individuals, injunctions that prohibit the illegal police activity from recurring are available, but the Supreme Court generally disfavors injunctions. Federal and state criminal prosecutions are also brought against police officers, but are typically reserved for the most egregious violations involving unnecessary violence. Police departments can improve their record of abiding by the law by adopting better recruitment, training, and supervision procedures and by other administrative measures. Congress passed Title 42 U.S.C. §14141 in 1994, allowing the Department of Justice to bring suits against police departments to correct violations by means such as improved hiring, training, and complaint procedures where a pattern or practice of conduct by law enforcement officials that deprives persons of constitutional rights has been proven.

The exclusionary rule remains controversial. Arguments against it include: it is not a true remedy against the offending officer; it suppresses relevant evidence of crime and thus thwarts the truth-finding goal of the criminal trial; it has little or no deterrent effect; it leads to police perjury; and it undermines the authority of the states to fashion their own rules of criminal procedure.

Fourth Amendment law has been confused because there are overlapping and conflicting theories of the exclusionary rule. These include the idea that the rule is required by the Constitution; that it is only a judicially created rule designed to deter police from violating individuals' rights; that it is based on the Fifth Amendment privilege against self-incrimination; that it is based on property rights; that it is based on returning the parties to their original position; that once breached, privacy rights can never be repaired; and that violations of privacy interests involve property or liberty violations that should be repaired under a theory of disgorgement. Each of these theories has at least one weakness. Thus, there is some level of policy choice open to jurists in deciding how to justify the exclusionary rule. The most philosophically coherent view is that the exclusionary rule is a Fourth Amendment requirement; otherwise the government could justify illegal searches retroactively, subject only to tort remedies, which causes the amendment to collapse.

LEGAL PUZZLES

HOW HAVE COURTS DECIDED THESE CASES?

STATE ACTION

2–1. Nancy Regan did not "say no to drugs." This Casper, Wyoming, resident was involved in methamphetamine dealing. She lived in a house with and cared for Alvin Bauerlein, who was terminally ill with cancer; Alvin's wife, Patty Harris Bauerlein, who married Alvin shortly before his death; and Alvin's daughter Judith. Carlton Humphrey, a friend of Regan who also was involved in drug dealing, stayed at the house at times and was a frequent visitor. Regan was appointed fourteen-year-old Judith's guardian after Alvin's death. Patty contacted a Sheriff's investigator to put a stop to the drug dealing because Humphrey and Regan were involving Judith. Humphrey was arrested based on a tip supplied by Patty. Patty later gave the investigator a purse belonging to Nancy Regan that contained records of drug transactions. These records were admitted at trial.

Was Patty's act of stealing Nancy Regan's purse the act of a private person (making the contents of the purse admissible), or was this an illegal search and seizure by Patty acting as a government agent?

HELD: Private person—evidence admissible on this ground.

The district judge determined that Patty Bauerlein was not acting as a government agent. Patty had a "working relationship" with the Sheriff's investigator, but this alone did not make her a government agent. Although the court did not flesh out its support for the district court's ruling, the facts make it clear that Patty acted on her own initiative. It was she who decided to take Nancy Regan's purse and turn it over to the police. The investigator did not insist that Patty keep searching for more incriminating evidence. *United States v. Humphrey,* 208 F.3d 1190 (10th Cir. 2000).

STANDING

2–2. Plaintiffs are users of two computer networks seized by defendants, who are members of the Hamilton County (Ohio) Sheriff's Department Regional Electronic Computer Intelligence Task Force (RECI). Plaintiffs allege violations of their First Amendment and Fourth Amendment rights. A complaint about online obscenity led to a RECI investigation. RECI officers assumed undercover identities and downloaded obscene images that were used to obtain search warrants. Two computer bulletin board systems were seized at the homes of their operators: (1) CCC BBS, operated by Robert Emerson, which had thousands of subscribers, who could, with a password, send e-mail; participate in chat room conversations, online games, and conferences; post or read messages on many topics; and download files such as computer programs and pictures and (2) SI BBS, a smaller bulletin board system run by a teenager on his father's home computer; only one user could log on at a time, and SI BBS included a posted disclaimer on privacy notifying users that "there are NO provisions for private messages on this board."

Do the plaintiffs have standing to challenge violations of their Fourth Amendment rights?

Holding available from instructor

GOOD FAITH EXCEPTION

2–3. Spring Valley, New York, is a village located within the town of Ramapo. Each entity has a police department. Anthony Santa was arrested by a Ramapo police officer in connection with a theft. The Spring Valley Village Court issued an arrest warrant that was entered in the New York State Police Information Network (NYSPIN) a statewide law enforcement computer database. Two weeks later the Village Court issued a request to vacate (vacatur) the warrant, but misdirected the request to the Spring Valley rather than the Ramapo Police Department.

Typically, when the Spring Valley PD receives a vacatur, it promptly removes the warrant from NYSPIN and its internal station house computer, if it was the complaining agency. If it receives a mistaken request to vacate a warrant belonging to another police department, it returns the request to the Village Court where it can be directed to the complaining agency. The Village Court and the Spring Valley Police Department are located across the hall from each other in the same building, and vacatur requests are typically hand-delivered. The Village Court never sent its request to vacate Santa's warrant to the Ramapo Police Department. Santa wrote to the Ramapo Justice Court and received a letter indicating that the charges had been dismissed.

Two years later a Spring Valley police officer ran a "wanted person check" on Santa and learned that Santa was wanted by the Ramapo Town Police on an outstanding arrest warrant—the warrant that should have been removed from NYSPIN. Santa was arrested on the basis of the outstanding warrant and during the search incident to arrest, thirty bags of crack cocaine were found on his person. The arresting officer was not aware that the earlier warrant had been vacated by a court.

(1) Was the error in the record caused by the Spring Valley PD or by the Spring Valley Village Court?
(2) Are the drugs admissible?

Holding available from instructor

INEVITABLE DISCOVERY

2–4. Maria Vasquez De Reyes was convicted for marriage fraud. Immigration (INS) agents operating in the Virgin Islands received an informant's tip that three female illegal aliens would be in Maxi's Bar in Christiansted on the island of St. Croix of the United States Virgin Islands to sell fraudulent numbers for permanent residency cards (or "green cards"). The three women were described with minimal characteristics as follows: one had red hair, another was short and "hefty"

with brown hair, and the third was named Carmen. The INS officers, with no other details about the women, went to the bar and encountered Ms. De Reyes, a native of the Dominican Republic. She proceeded to walk away from the agents. They then subjected her to a *Terry* stop, found to be illegal because there was insufficient cause.

Ms. De Reyes was detained and held overnight. She admitted to Dominican Republic citizenship and produced papers showing that she was married to Escolastico De Reyes, a Virgin Islands resident. Further investigation showed that Escolastico De Reyes did not live with his wife, and Escolastico then confessed that the marriage was a fraud that had been established to enable Ms. De Reyes to obtain a green card. She pled guilty. On appeal, she moved to suppress all incriminating statements, arguing that the investigation was predicated on an unconstitutional stop.

The prosecution argues that even if acquired illegally, the evidence would have been inevitably acquired through the lawful means of a thorough INS investigation that occurs after an I-485 form (an adjustment of status form) is filed by a person on American soil. There is no time limit within which an applicant must file the I-485 form.

Does the inevitable discovery doctrine operate here?

Holding available from instructor

FURTHER READING

J. David Hirschel, *Fourth Amendment Rights* (Lexington, Mass.: Lexington Books, 1979).

Richard C. Cortner, *The Supreme Court and the Second Bill of Rights: The Fourteenth Amendment and the Nationalization of Civil Liberties* (Madison: University of Wisconsin Press, 1981).

H. Richard Uviller, *The Tilted Playing Field: Is Criminal Justice Unfair?* (New Haven: Yale University Press, 1999).

ENDNOTES

1. Marvin Zalman, "Fleeing from the Fourth Amendment," *Criminal Law Bulletin* 36 (2) (2000): 129–47.
2. Marvin Zalman and Elsa Shartsis, "A Roadblock Too Far? Justice O'Connor's Left Turn on the Fourth," *Journal of Contemporary Criminal Justice* 19 (2003): 182–204.
3. William J. Cuddihy, *The Fourth Amendment: Origins and Meaning, 602–1791* (Doctoral Dissertation), c.
4. Leonard W. Levy, *Original Intent and the Framers' Constitution* (New York: Macmillan Publishing Co., 1988), 224.
5. Cuddihy, *Fourth Amendment*, cii.
6. Ibid., 200 et seq.
7. Levy, *Original Intent*, 226.
8. Ibid., 222–29; Catherine Drinker Bowen, *John Adams and the American Revolution* (New York: Grosset & Dunlap, 1950), 208–19. See also Cuddihy, *Fourth Amendment*, 757–825; M. H. Smith, *The Writs of Assistance Case* (Berkeley: University of California Press, 1978).

9. Levy, *Original Intent*, 229.

10. Ibid., 230.

11. Ibid., 231.

12. 95 Eng. Rep. 807; C. Stephenson and F. Marcham, *Sources of English Constitutional History* (New York: Harper, 1937) 705–10.

13. C. R. Lovell, *English Constitutional and Legal History* (New York: Oxford University Press, 1962), 454.

14. Cuddihy, *Fourth Amendment*, 1231–1358; Thomas Y. Davies, "Recovering the Original Fourth Amendment," *Michigan Law Review* 98 (3) (1999): 547–750.

15. Davies, "Original Fourth Amendment," 557–60.

16. Akhil Reed Amar, *The Constitution and Criminal Procedure: First Principles* (New Haven: Yale University Press, 1997), 1–45. Professor Amar's scholarship is refuted in detail by Professor Davies, "Original Fourth Amendment."

17. Gerard V. Bradley, "The Constitutional Theory of the Fourth Amendment," *DePaul Law Review* 38 (4) (1989): 817–872; Davies, "Original Fourth Amendment."

18. Davies, "Original Fourth Amendment," 577.

19. Davies, "Original Fourth Amendment," 578, 620–29, 632–34, 660–64.

20. *Planned Parenthood v. Casey* (1992); *Dickerson v. U.S.* (2000).

21. *Hale v. Henkel* (1906); *Fisher v. U.S.* (1976); *Andresen v. Maryland* (1976); *U.S. v. Jacobsen* (1984), 113.

22. William C. Heffernan, "Foreword: The Fourth Amendment Exclusionary Rule as a Constitutional Remedy," *Georgetown Law Journal* 88 (5) (2000): 799–878.

23. *Payton v. Rush*, 184 F.3d 623, 628 (7th Cir. 1999).

24. *United States v. Hoffman*, 498 F.2d 879, 881–82 (7th Cir. 1974).

25. *Payton v. Rush*, 184 F.3d at 628, citing district court cases.

26. *Payton v. Rush*, 184 F.3d at 624.

27. *Romanski v. Detroit Entertainment, L.L.C.*, 265 F. Supp.2d 835 (E.D. Mich. 2003).

28. John M. Burkoff, "Not So Private Searches and the Constitution," *Cornell Law Review* 66 (1981): 627; Lynn M. Gagel, "Comment: Stealthy Encroachments upon the Fourth Amendment: Constitutional Constraints and Their Applicability to the Long Arm of Ohio's Private Security Forces," *University of Cincinnati Law Review* 63 (1995): 1807.

29. The case was brought to my attention by William C. Heffernan, Foreword, 838–40.

30. *Wolf v. People*, 117 Colo. 279; 187 P.2d 926 (1947), *Irvine v. California* (1952), 133.

31. *People v. Cahan*, 44 Cal. 2d 434, 282 P. 2d 905 (1955).

32. *Elkins v. United States* (1960), 218.

33. Justice Burger's thinking is examined in M. Braswell and J. Scheb II, "Conservative Pragmatism versus Liberal Principles: Warren E. Burger on the Suppression of Evidence, 1956–86," *Creighton Law Review* 20 (1987): 789–831.

34. Justice Thomas in *Pennsylvania Board of Probation v. Scott*, 369.

35. Potter Stewart, "The Road to *Mapp v. Ohio* and Beyond: The Origins, Development and Future of the Exclusionary Rule in Search-and-Seizure Cases," *Columbia Law Review* 83 (1983): 1365–1404.

36. 216 Conn. 150, 165; 579 A.2d 58, 65, citing Potter Stewart, "The Road to *Mapp v. Ohio* and Beyond: The Origins, Development and Future of the Exclusionary Rule in Search-and-Seizure Cases," *Columbia Law Review* 83 (1983): 1365, 1392–93.

37. William C. Heffernan, Foreword, 859.

38. *People v. Defore*, 242 N.Y. 13, 21, 150 N.E. 585, 587 (1926).

39. Christopher Slobogin, "Why Liberals Should Chuck the Exclusionary Rule," *University of Illinois Law Review* (1999): 363–446.

40. Heffernan, Foreword, 826.

41. Slobogin, "Why Liberals," 376, n. 40.

42. Ibid., 378–79.

43. Heffernan, Foreword, 806.

44. *Marbury v. Madison* (1803), 137, 163.

45. Cornelia T.L. Pillard, "Taking Fiction Seriously: The Strange Results of Public Officials' Individual Liability Under *Bivens*," *Georgetown Law Journal* 88 (1999): 65–105.

46. *Monell v. Department of Social Services* (1978); cities have "deeper pockets" than individual officers.

47. Kathryn Scarborough and Craig Hemmens, "Section 1983 Suits Against Law Enforcement in the Circuit Courts of Appeal," *Thomas Jefferson Law Review* 21 (1999): 1–21.

48. *McGhee v. Volusia County*, 679 So.2d 729 (Fla. 1996).

49. T. Hunter Jefferson, "Note: Constitutional Wrongs and Common Law Principles: The Case for the Recognition of State Constitutional Tort Actions against State Governments," *Vanderbilt Law Review* 50 (1997): 1525–76.

50. Jefferson, "Constitutional Wrongs," 1534.

51. *Brown v. New York*, 89 N.Y.2d 172, 674 N.E.2d 1129, 652 N.Y.S.2d 223, 75 A.L.R. 5th 769 (1996).

52. Henry Weinstein, "Judge Oks Use of Racketeering Law in Rampart Suits; Scandal: LAPD Can Be Sued as a Criminal Enterprise, He Rules. The Decision Could Triple the City's Financial Liability for Mistreatment of Citizens, Experts Say," *Los Angeles Times*, August 29, 2000; David Rosenzweig, "L.A. Seeks to Appeal Racketeering Ruling; Rampart: the City Asks Judge's Permission to Challenge His Decision That the LAPD Can Be Sued under RICO Law," *Los Angeles Times*, August 31, 2000.

53. Alison L. Patton, "Note: The Endless Cycle of Abuse: Why *42 U.S.C. §1983* Is Ineffective in Deterring Police Brutality," *Hastings Law Journal* 44 (1993): 753–808.

54. *Lankford v. Gelston*, 364 F.2d 197 (4th Cir. 1966).

55. P. Applebome and R. Suro, "Texas Slaying: A Tale of Two Counties," *New York Times*, May 11, 1990. In 1990 a local jury in Tyler, Texas, convicted three white police officers of the killing of Loyal Garner, Jr., an African American man with no prior criminal history, while he was held in jail for alleged drunk driving.

56. Jan Hoffman, "Police Reformer Draws on His Experience," *New York Times*, February 24, 2000; Somini Sengupta, "The Diallo Case: The Jurors; 2 Jurors Defend Diallo Acquittal," *New York Times*, February 27, 2000; Winnie Hu, "The Diallo Case: The Deliberations; When Case Was Weighed, Prosecution Was Wanting, Juror Says," *New York Times*, February 28, 2000.

57. M. Zalman and M. Gates, "Rethinking Venue in Light of the 'Rodney King' Case: An Interest Analysis," *Cleveland State Law Review* 41 (2) (1993): 215–277.

58. J. Wilson, "Ex-Cops Get Prison, Budzyn, Nevers Are Remorseful over Death," *Detroit Free Press,* October 13, 1993.

59. Robyn Meredith, "Jurors Acquit White Officer in the Death of Black Driver," *New York Times,* November 14, 1996.

60. William K. Rashbaum, "A Reversal on Oversight of the Police," *New York Times,* July 7, 2000.

61. *United States v. Screws* (1945).

62. Joseph P. Fried, "Volpe Sentenced to a 30-year Term in Louima Torture," *New York Times,* December 14, 1999.

63. Edward Littlejohn, "The Civilian Police Commission: A Deterrent of Police Misconduct," *Detroit Journal of Urban Law* 59 (1981): 5.

64. Suggested in Whitebread and Slobogin, 65.

65. J. H. Skolnick and J. J. Fyfe, *Above the Law: Police and the Excessive Use of Force* (New York: Free Press, 1993), 243–45.

66. Skolnick and Fyfe, *Above the Law,* 255–57.

67. D. Johnston, "Reno Tightening Rules on Use of Lethal Force by Federal Agents," *New York Times,* October 18, 1995.

68. M. Newman, "Training for Trust; a Course for Police Recruits Examines How They Judge and Are Judged," *Pittsburgh Post-Gazette,* April 10, 1996.

69. Editorial, "Higher Standards for Police Recruits," *New York Times,* November 28, 1995, (nat. ed.).

70. J. McKinnon, "Police Add Japanese Martial Art to Skills," *Pittsburgh Post-Gazette,* January 23, 1996.

71. Skolnick and Fyfe, *Above the Law,* 239–245.

72. William Bratton and Peter Knobler, *Turnaround: How America's Top Cop Reversed the Crime Epidemic* (New York: Random House, 1998), 241–44.

73. Christopher Slobogin, "Why Liberals Should Chuck the Exclusionary Rule," *University of Illinois Law Review* (1999): 363–446.

74. M.L. Elrick and Ben Schmitt, "U.S. Plans to Oversee Detroit Cops; Costly Changes May Be Required," *Detroit Free Press,* June 11, 2003; David Shepardson and Darren A. Nichols, "Detroit Cop Reform Launched; Federal Watchdog Takes over Today, Says Five-year Oversight Plan Will Top $6 Million," *Detroit News,* July 23, 2003; Eugene Kim, "Note: Vindicating Civil Rights Under 42 U.S.C. 14141: Guidance from Procedures in Complex Litigation," *Hastings Constitutional Law Quarterly* 29 (2002): 767–805.

75. Debra Livingston, "Police Reform and the Department of Justice: An Essay on Accountability," *Buffalo Criminal Law Review* 2 (1999): 815–857.

76. Heffernan, Foreword, 840.

77. Slobogin, 424, citing *U.S. v. Havens* (1980), *U.S. v. Janis* (1976).

78. Ibid., 425–27.

79. Ibid., 427.

80. Fed. Rules of Criminal Procedure 41(e). Heffernan, Foreword, p. 813, notes that several lower courts in the 1920s did return contraband, and that the issue never reached the Supreme Court.

81. *Elkins* at 222–23: "For those who agree with me," said Mr. Justice Holmes, "no distinction can be taken between the Government as prosecutor and the Government as judge." *277 U.S., at 470.* (Dissenting opinion in *Olmstead*). In *Silverthorne* (1920), Justice Holmes wrote, concerning the use of illegally seized evidence by the government: "In our opinion such is not the law. It reduces the Fourth Amendment to a form of words. The essence of a provision forbidding the acquisition of evidence in a certain way is that not merely evidence so acquired shall not be used before the Court but that it shall not be used at all." (p. 392).

82. Slobogin, 435–36.

83. Heffernan, 832–40, 848–60, quote at 840.

84. Ibid., 837.

85. Ibid., 838.

86. Rita Shulman, "Note: USA Patriot Act: Granting the U.S. Government the Unprecedented Power to Circumvent American Civil Liberties in the Name of National Security," *University of Detroit Mercy Law Review* 80 (2003): 427–444.

87. Ibid., 430–31.

88. Michelle Mittelstadt, "Patriot Act Available Against Many Types of Criminals," *Dallas Morning News,* September 8, 2003.

89. Ibid.

90. Ibid.

91. Bill Rankin, "Sept. 11: Unfinished Business: Civil Liberties: Towns Raise Eyebrows, Voices over Patriot Act," *Atlanta Journal and Constitution,* September 7, 2003.

92. David Sarasohn, "State Senate's Thunderous Patriotic Act," *The Oregonian,* September 3, 2003.

93. Thomas Davies, "A Hard Look at What We Know (and Still Need to Learn) about the 'Costs' of the Exclusionary Rule: The NIJ Study and Other Studies of 'Lost' Arrests," *American Bar Foundation Research Journal* (1983): 611–90.

94. Dallin Oaks, "Studying the Exclusionary Rule in Search and Seizure," *University of Chicago Law Review* 37 (1970): 665.

95. Davies, "A Hard Look," 628.

96. This criticism is raised by Donald Horowitz, who is generally not an advocate of an activist judiciary. See D. Horowitz, *The Courts and Social Policy* (Washington, D.C.: Brookings Institution, 1977), 224–25.

97. Davies, "A Hard Look."

98. Ibid., p. 619.

99. For example, D. Oaks, "Studying the Exclusionary Rule in Search and Seizure," *University of Chicago Law Review* 37 (1970): 665; J. Spiotto, "Search and Seizure: An Empirical Study of the Exclusionary Rule and Its Alternatives," *Journal of Legal Studies* 2 (1973): 243. These were sharply criticized by Davies, "A Hard Look," 627–28.

100. Davies, "A Hard Look," 630.

101. Bradley C. Canon, "Testing the Effectiveness of Civil Liberties Policies at the State and Federal Levels: The Case of the Exclusionary Rule," *American Politics Quarterly* 5 (1) (1977): 57–82.

102. Ibid., p. 71.

103. H.R. Uviller, *Tempered Zeal* (Chicago: Contemporary Books, 1988), 131.

104. *Illinois v. Gates,* 257.

105. National Institute of Justice, *The Effects of the Exclusionary Rule: A Study in California* (Washington, D.C.: U.S. Dept. of Justice, 1982).

106. B. Forst, J. Lucianovic, and S. Cox, *What Happens After Arrest: A Court Perspective of Police Operations in the District of Columbia* (Washington, D.C.: U.S. Dept. of Justice, Law Enforcement Assistance Administration, 1978).

107. K. Brosi, *A Cross City Comparison of Felony Case Processing* (Washington, D.C.: U.S. Dept. of Justice, Law Enforcement Assistance Administration, 1979).

108. B. Forst, et al., *Arrest Convictability as a Measure of Police Performance* (Washington, D.C.: U.S. Dept. of Justice, National Institute of Justice, 1982).

109. Report of the Comptroller General of the United States, *Impact of the Exclusionary Rule on Federal Criminal Prosecutions* (Washington, D.C.: U.S. General Accounting Office, 1979).

110. P. Nardulli, "The Societal Cost of the Exclusionary Rule: An Empirical Assessment," *American Bar Foundation Research Journal* (1983): 585–609.

111. F. Feeney, F. Dill, and A. Weir, *Arrests without Conviction: How Often They Occur and Why* (Washington, D.C.: U.S. Dept. of Justice, National Institute of Justice, 1983).

112. Craig D. Uchida and Timothy S. Bynum, "Search Warrants, Motions to Suppress and 'Lost Cases': The Effects of the Exclusionary Rule in Seven Jurisdictions," *Journal of Criminal Law and Criminology* 81 (4) (1991): 1034–66.

113. Davies, "A Hard Look," 679.

114. R. Van Duizend, L. Sutton, and C. Carter, *The Search Warrant Process: Preconceptions, Perceptions, and Practices* (1986), 106, quoted in Uchida and Bynum, 1065.

115. Cornelia T.L. Pillard, "Taking Fiction Seriously: The Strange Results of Public Officials' Individual Liability Under *Bivens*," *Georgetown Law Journal* 88 (1999): 65–105 (footnotes excluded).

116. Alison L. Patton, "Note: The Endless Cycle of Abuse: Why *42 U.S.C. §1983* Is Ineffective in Deterring Police Brutality," *Hastings Law Journal* 44 (1993): 753–808. See John L. Burris, *Black vs. Blue* (New York: St. Martin's Press, 1999).

117. Patton, "Endless Cycle," 767–779.

118. Patton, "Endless Cycle," 780–90, drawing heavily on the Christopher Commission Report, issued after the Los Angeles riots following the Rodney King beating case.

JUSTICES OF THE SUPREME COURT

THE ADVERSARIES
BLACK—FRANKFURTER

It is ironic that two New Deal liberals appointed by President Franklin Roosevelt came to be bitter foes on the Supreme Court. For many years, Justices Hugo Black and Felix Frankfurter clashed over vital issues, including the incorporation of the Bill of Rights, the extent to which speech could be regulated by the government, and whether the Supreme Court should intervene to equalize the voting representation of electoral districts. In the 1940s and 1950s Frankfurter usually had the upper hand as the intellectual leader of the conservative wing of the Court. But over time Black's dogged pursuit of a more liberal agenda bore fruit, depriving Frankfurter of imposing his views on the entire Court.

Both justices championed democracy, yet each took a different approach to modern government and the Court's role in it. Their disagreements, based on deeply held philosophies of judging, became a matter of personal antagonism.

On the question of incorporation, Black was motivated by a strong belief that the Supreme Court must adhere as closely as possible to the strict meaning of the Constitution and should not use the Due Process Clause to insert its notion of what is "reasonable" into constitutional law. He recalled that a conservative Supreme Court had done this very thing prior to the New Deal and understood that unfettered power allowed courts to be as unjust as the legislative or executive branches. Out of this emerged the idea that the Supreme Court had to apply the Bill of Rights totally and literally to the states. Frankfurter, although a great proponent of the philosophy of judicial restraint, came to opposite conclusions. He not only believed that the justices ought to fill out the contours of the Due Process Clause in order to achieve fundamental fairness in criminal procedure, but also believed that the Fourteenth Amendment was not intended to incorporate the Bill of Rights.

HUGO L. BLACK

Alabama 1886–1971

Democrat

Appointed by
Franklin Delano Roosevelt

Years of Service:
1937–1971

Collection of the Supreme Court of the United States. Photographer: Harris and Ewing

LIFE AND CAREER   The son of a country storekeeper, Hugo Black received a law degree from the University of Alabama. He practiced law in Birmingham, representing poor people, white and black, in civil cases against large corporations and in criminal matters. He also served terms as a district attorney and as a city judge, where he tried to mitigate the harsh treatment of poor people. Active in politics, he was elected to the U.S. Senate in 1926 as a populist. He was a key supporter of President Roosevelt's New Deal program, backed the "court packing" legislation to increase the size of the Supreme Court, and was Roosevelt's first choice to fill a vacancy on the Court.

CONTRIBUTION TO CRIMINAL PROCEDURE   Justice Black was the chief architect of modern constitutional criminal procedure. His foremost contribution was to champion the Incorporation Doctrine, picking up the mantle of the first Justice

Harlan, and ultimately getting the Court to agree in the 1960s that the criminal provisions of the Bill of Rights should apply to the states as a matter of Fourteenth Amendment due process. He also wrote powerful opinions against coerced confessions and took the lead in formulating the doctrine that an attorney was an absolute requirement in all criminal cases.

SIGNATURE OPINION   *Gideon v. Wainwright* (1963). In 1942 Black dissented in *Betts v. Brady,* which held that a state felony trial in which an indigent had to defend himself or herself was fair under the Due Process Clause. He strongly believed that a fair trial is impossible without a defense attorney, and if a person cannot afford a lawyer, one must be provided by the government without cost. Prior to *Betts* he wrote the majority opinion in *Johnson v. Zerbst* (1938), which held that in a federal felony prosecution, the assistance of counsel is essential unless the defendant knowingly and intelligently waives counsel. His persistence in pursuing this goal succeeded in *Gideon,* where the Court incorporated the Sixth Amendment right to counsel into the Fourteenth Amendment, thus requiring the states to provide counsel for indigent defendants.

ASSESSMENT   Justice Black is widely recognized as one of the greatest justices, an intellectual leader of the Warren Court, and the single greatest influence on the development of modern constitutional criminal procedure. In other constitutional areas, he led the Court, along with Justice Douglas, toward an "absolutist" vision of First Amendment free speech, and he spearheaded the move to require states to reapportion voting districts to equalize the voting power of voters in different districts.

Although many of the positions he supported defined a "liberal" policy agenda, he was not so much a liberal in judicial philosophy as were other Roosevelt appointees such as Douglas, Murphy, or Rutledge. Rather, his judicial philosophy may be better described as "strict constructionist" or "constitutional fundamentalism." He believed that the Court should strictly adhere to the terms of the Constitution, which he tended to define in fairly narrow terms.

Thus, even in the incorporation area, he maintained an independent stance. He did not vote for the incorporation of the Fourth Amendment exclusionary rule in *Wolf v. Colorado* (1949) because the rule was not stated explicitly in the Constitution. He later developed the perspective that the exclusionary rule could be incorporated only if it were seen as also protecting Fifth Amendment values against self-incrimination.

FURTHER READING

Gerald T. Dunne, *Hugo Black and the Judicial Revolution* (New York: Simon and Schuster, 1977).

FELIX FRANKFURTER

Massachusetts 1882–1965

Independent

Appointed by
Franklin Delano Roosevelt

Years of Service:
1939–1962

Collection of the Supreme Court of the United States. Photographer: Pach Brothers Studio

LIFE AND CAREER Frankfurter emigrated to America with his family from Vienna at the age of twelve and grew up in the Lower East Side Jewish ghetto in New York City. He graduated from the City College of New York and attended Harvard Law School, becoming editor of the *Harvard Law Review* on the basis of his top grades. After graduating in 1906, he worked in a large law firm for a while, but soon chose a public service career. As a protégé of Henry L. Stimson, a leading Progressive, he went to Washington in 1911 when Stimson became secretary of war, forming an intellectual circle of young lawyers who befriended Justice Holmes.

In 1914 Frankfurter was appointed to the Harvard Law School faculty, a position he held until his appointment to the Court. During his tenure, he became a nationally known liberal activist who served as a labor mediator during World War I, attended the Paris Peace Conference in 1919, represented Zionist interests, cofounded the American Civil Liberties Union,

contributed to *The New Republic* magazine, spoke out for the convicted anarchists Sacco and Vanzetti, and provided free counsel for the National Consumers' League. His coauthored book, *The Labor Injunction,* attacked the federal courts for stifling the labor movement. He was the codirector in 1921 of the ground-breaking Cleveland Crime Survey, a multidisciplinary social scientific study of the administration of justice. He appeared frequently before the Supreme Court on behalf of unions and other progressive causes.

As a Harvard professor, he developed a following among his students resulting from a combined passion for academic excellence and a zeal for public service. He had a close rapport with several Supreme Court justices and selected law clerks from among his students for Holmes and Brandeis. During the New Deal, he became an important advisor to President Roosevelt and placed many of his former students in important administrative and policy-shaping positions, thus enhancing his influence.

CONTRIBUTION TO CRIMINAL PROCEDURE Frankfurter's liberal policy temperament clashed with his philosophy of judicial restraint. As a result, his positions in criminal procedure were inconsistent, but must generally be counted as conservative. On this side, he staunchly opposed the total incorporation of the Bill of Rights championed by Hugo Black and favored by the liberal wing of the Court; he voted for the rule that a judge's comment on a defendant's silence does not undermine the privilege against self-incrimination; he opposed the extension of the right to counsel to all defendants in state cases; and he characterized the Fourth Amendment exclusionary rule as a mere remedy and not a constitutional rule. Nevertheless, he was sharply critical of abuses of power by the police and when interpreting the flexible Due Process Clause, ruled in favor of defendants in cases involving coerced confessions and search and seizures that "shocked the conscience." In the entrapment area he favored the objective test.

SIGNATURE OPINION *Rochin v. California* (1952). The "stomach pump" case perfectly expressed Frankfurter's judicial philosophy of restraint and respect for the authority of the states, except where the actions of local police or state courts have so grossly violated a person's right to fair treatment that a judge could exercise judgment to deem the actions as violations of due process. In these instances Frankfurter's standard was that due process is violated where police action "shocks the conscience." He trusted the wisdom of courts to determine what shocks the conscience and somehow believed that such judgment would be objective and not simply private notions of what is acceptable. Justices Black and Douglas dissented in *Rochin,* arguing that this vague standard gave judges too much power.

ASSESSMENT Frankfurter was a giant of American constitutional law, as a scholar, a public servant, and justice. He was

(Continued)

expected to be a leading liberal on the Court, but his judicial philosophy of restraint overcame his liberal instincts. As the Court's agenda swung from economic issues to civil liberties, he failed to sense the direction of the country and the Court's special role as a guardian of liberty. Thus, he adopted cramped positions in many free speech cases and ruled against finding that seriously imbalanced state electoral districts violated the Equal Protection Clause. In supporting the school desegregation case, Frankfurter played a leading liberal role, but thereafter he took a more cautious approach than did other justices.

His conservative views were generally repudiated by the liberal Warren Court, although some of his rulings, including the "shocks the conscience" test, have been relied on by today's far more conservative Court.

FURTHER READING

Melvin I. Urofsky, *Felix Frankfurter: Judicial Restraint and Individual Liberties* (Boston: Twayne, 1991).

CHAPTER
3

ESSENTIAL FOURTH AMENDMENT DOCTRINES

These [Fourth Amendment rights], I protest, are not mere second-class rights but belong in the catalog of indispensable freedoms. Among deprivations of rights, none is so effective in cowing a population, crushing the spirit of the individual and putting terror in every heart. Uncontrolled search and seizure is one of the first and most effective weapons in the arsenal of every arbitrary government. And one need only briefly to have dwelt and worked among a people possessed of many admirable qualities but deprived of these rights to know that the human personality deteriorates and dignity and self-reliance disappear where homes, persons and possessions are subject at any hour to unheralded search and seizure by the police.

—Justice Robert Jackson, dissenting in *Bringar v. United States*,
338 U.S. 160, 180–81 (1949)

CHAPTER OUTLINE

KEY TERMS AND PHRASES *(CONTINUES ON NEXT PAGE)*

Anticipatory warrant

Balancing of interests

Beeper

Consent search

Constitutionally protected area

Controlled delivery

Curtilage

Enhancement device

Exigency

Ex parte	Neutral and detached magistrate	Probable cause
Expectation of privacy	No-knock warrant	Secret informant
Industrial curtilage	Open fields	Telephonic warrant
Inventory and return	"Plain feel" rule	Thermal imaging
Knock and announce rule	Plain view	Two-pronged test
Magistrate	Plurality opinion	Undercover agent
Media ride-along		

INTRODUCTION

This chapter presents five basic areas of Fourth Amendment law: (1) the search warrant, (2) the expectation of privacy doctrine, (3) probable cause, (4) the plain view doctrine, and (5) consent searches. Fourth Amendment analysis has an interlocking quality—that is, several issues are often considered simultaneously in the same case. This makes it difficult for a beginning student to follow a Fourth Amendment case because one has to know *all* the law before understanding *any* of it! To add to the complexity, Fourth Amendment doctrines have developed chronologically in a case-by-case fashion, and have at times been fully or partially reversed as the justices have focused on specific issues or have advanced preset agendas. Finally, as seen in Chapter 2, competing theories are at work in this area, and different justices may use different theories in the same case. In any event, these five doctrinal areas are presented here as isolated topics for ease of study.

THE SEARCH WARRANT

Search Warrant Values: A Neutral and Detached Magistrate

A grand function of the Constitution is to protect the liberty and rights of residents from the illegal and harmful acts of government agents, especially from those granted law enforcement powers by the state. Requiring executive branch officers to get permission from judicial officers, via search warrants, is one of the principal methods of keeping the constitutional balance true. This has always been recognized by the Supreme Court.

> The presence of a search warrant serves a high function. Absent some grave emergency, the Fourth Amendment has interposed a magistrate between the citizen and the police. This was done not to shield criminals nor to make the home a safe haven for illegal activities. It was done so that an objective mind might weigh the need to invade that privacy in order to enforce the law. The right of privacy was deemed too precious to entrust to the discretion of those whose job is the detection of crime and the arrest of criminals. (*McDonald v. United States,* 1948, pp. 455–56)

These values are embodied in the traditional "warrant-preference construction" of the Fourth Amendment (see Chapter 2), which holds that search and seizures are presumed *unreasonable* unless authorized by a judicial warrant except for a few well-established exceptions.

Under this construction, the Court has frequently expressed a *preference for the search warrant.* To ensure that officers apply to magistrates for warrants, the Court has at times eased the strict requirements of probable cause. In *United States v. Ventresca* (1965), for example, the issue was whether hearsay was sufficient to establish probable cause and support a warrant to search a house for an illegal liquor distillery. The Court made it clear that in a close case, if the search was conducted under a warrant, the Court would lean in favor of upholding the search: "A grudging or negative attitude by reviewing courts toward warrants will tend to discourage police officers from submitting their evidence to a judicial officer before acting." Of course, this does not mean that a magistrate must automatically grant a warrant simply on request (*Ventresca,* pp. 108–09). A search occurring without a warrant has been a reason given by the Supreme Court to find the search illegal.

This preference for a search warrant is based on three factors: the long history of warrant use, the Fourth Amendment's text, and the policy and values that underlie the amendment. The values sought to be protected are highly prized by Americans: personal autonomy, privacy, security, and freedom. The policy of the Amendment is to protect these values by establishing procedures that place the decision in the hands of the courts whether to invade a person's liberties for law enforcement purposes and to do so as infrequently as possible. The rationale was best expressed by Justice Robert Jackson:

> The point of the Fourth Amendment, which often is not grasped by zealous officers, is not that it denies law enforcement the support of the usual inferences which reasonable men draw from evidence. Its protection consists in requiring that those inferences be drawn by a **neutral and detached magistrate** instead of being judged by the officer engaged in the often competitive enterprise of ferreting out crime. Any assumption that evidence sufficient to support a magistrate's disinterested determination to issue a search warrant will justify the officers in making a search without a warrant would reduce the Amendment to a nullity and leave the people's homes secure only in the discretion of police officers. (***Johnson v. United States,*** 1948, pp. 13–14)

In *Johnson* an experienced federal narcotics officer standing in a hotel corridor smelled burning opium coming from a closed hotel room in Seattle, Washington. He demanded entry and found one person in the room in possession of opium. The Court noted: "At the time entry was demanded the officers were possessed of evidence which a magistrate might have found to be probable cause for issuing a search warrant." The evidence was nevertheless excluded because the officer invaded Anne Johnson's room without first submitting his evidence to the judgment of a judicial officer.

In giving priority in ascertaining probable cause to judges, the Supreme Court does not place the judge above the police officer because of any belief that the judge is more intelligent or more expert than the officer, or simply because of the traditional use of warrants. The policy is wrapped up in Justice Jackson's memorable phrase "a neutral and detached magistrate." This conveys that the **magistrate** is part of the judicial branch, *detached* from "the government" (i.e., the executive branch) and, therefore, not part of the apparatus that seeks to prosecute the suspect. Further, the judge is *neutral* in the case. The officer is a *partisan* who is "engaged in the often competitive enterprise of ferreting out crime." Because the officer is a partisan, he or she is likely to judge a case in his or her own favor and find that probable cause exists. This does not suggest that the officer is dishonest; but human nature is such that a partisan virtually always sees things his or her way. The judge is formally neutral—an arbiter between the police and prosecution on the one side, and the defendant on the other. It is because the magistrate is neutral that he or she is more likely to exercise balanced judgment.

The Supreme Court has decided several revealing cases to determine whether the actions of a magistrate or another governmental officer rose to the standards of a "neutral and detached magistrate." In *Coolidge v. New Hampshire* (1971), the state *attorney general*, an executive branch officer, personally took charge of a murder investigation. An archaic statute made him a justice of the peace and, as such, he issued a search warrant to himself! Over the dissents of three justices, who viewed this action as "harmless error," the Supreme Court ruled that it violated the fundamental Fourth Amendment premise that warrants must issue from a neutral and detached magistrate. What was important was not that the statute *called* the Attorney General a "justice of the peace," but that *in fact* he was not a "detached" judicial officer; he was the chief investigator and prosecutor in the case.

Shadwick v. City of Tampa (1972) also shows that formal title is less important than the actual situation of the officer issuing a warrant. Here, the Supreme Court upheld a law and practice that allowed a *municipal court clerk* to issue arrest warrants for *municipal ordinance* violations. The clerk met two tests: (1) he was capable of determining whether probable cause existed as to ordinance violations, such as impaired driving or breach of the peace, and (2) he was neutral and detached in that he was not under the authority of the prosecutor or police but worked in the judicial branch, subject to the supervision of the municipal court judge. Thus, under limited circumstances, a valid warrant can be issued by a person who is not a lawyer or a judge.

The Supreme Court has ruled that a magistrate is not neutral or detached if he receives not a salary but rather gets a *fee*, even a small one, for each warrant that is issued. In *Connally*

v. Georgia (1977), the magistrate received five dollars for each search warrant issued but nothing if a warrant was denied. The *possibility* of personal, financial gain is sufficient to violate the due process and Fourth Amendment rights of suspects, whatever the actual disposition of the magistrate. In addition, the magistrate's actions can cause him or her to lose the element of neutrality in a specific case. This was held to occur in *Lo-Ji Sales, Inc. v. New York* (1979). An overly helpful town justice, rather than simply issuing a search warrant for the seizure of films from an adult bookstore, also joined police officers and prosecutors on a six-hour raid of the premises, determining at the scene whether there was probable cause to seize various materials. In determining that the warrant was improper, a unanimous Court said, "The Town Justice did not manifest that neutrality and detachment demanded of a judicial officer when presented with a warrant application for a search and seizure." This loss of "detachment" was not, according to the Court, a matter of subjective intent but was inferred from the objective fact that the town justice "allowed himself to *become a member, if not the leader, of the search party* which was essentially a police operation." Yet despite the objective nature of the rule, it is easy to imagine that a judge who works too closely with the prosecutors will come to see himself as a member of the "prosecution team" rather than a neutral and detached magistrate in a subjective sense.

The neutral and detached magistrate principle led the Supreme Court to invalidate a portion of the 1968 electronic eavesdropping law that allowed the president of the United States to authorize electronic eavesdropping for a "national security" purpose without a warrant (*United States v. United States District Court,* 1972). The Court ruled that even if the president were exempt from particular procedural requirements of the rest of the electronic eavesdropping statute, he was still required to seek "judicial approval prior to initiation of a search or surveillance" under the Fourth Amendment. The Court reasoned that dangers to free speech and political liberty are too great in national security cases to entrust electronic eavesdropping exclusively to the executive branch, and that national security would not be compromised by requiring the president to seek prior judicial approval for national security eavesdropping. Since 1978, under the Foreign Intelligence Surveillance Act, warrants for electronic eavesdropping for national security purposes are issued by a special court drawn for each case from among sitting federal judges.[1] This formerly obscure function has moved to center stage since the 9/11 terror attack and is discussed below.

There are costs to the warrant process. Obtaining a search warrant from a judge is *less efficient* than allowing police to make a decision to enter a home on their own assessment of probable cause. This adds a cost to public safety—a cost that the Framers felt was necessary to maintain liberty, exhibiting a consciousness of the Due Process Model. Skeptics question whether the warrant practice, in fact, adds that much protection. In high-publicity cases public pressure can cause a magistrate to blunder. This was the case when Judge Kathleen Kennedy-Powell ruled that Los Angeles Police detectives

Mark Fuhrman and Philip Vannatter were justified in vaulting over the wall of O.J. Simpson's estate in the early morning hours of June 13, 1994, without a search warrant because they claimed that they feared for his safety.[2] This was a patently weak reason because ex-husbands are typically prime suspects in spouse killings and Fuhrman had been called to the Simpson residence earlier to investigate a wife-beating. As lawyer-novelist Scott Turow noted, "If veteran police detectives did not arrive at the gate of Mr. Simpson's home thinking he might have committed these murders, then they should have been fired."[3] Ironically, Judge Kennedy-Powell's case-saving ruling backfired. When Fuhrman's perjurious, racist statements later came out, the jury might have also questioned his truthfulness about the entry and search of Simpson's home and grounds.

To add to the skepticism, there is some concern that magistrates tend to rubber-stamp warrant requests. Despite all this, law professor Richard Uviller, after observing police for a year, reflects on the value of search warrants.

> It's easy to say that the whole routine is a sham: magistrates are not actually neutral or detached but just as closely associated with the prosecution as the cops; they don't really read the affidavits, many of those exercising the authority would not know the difference between probable cause and potato chips, much less the complexities of the law regarding the reliability of third-party informants who supply the hearsay on which the cop's belief may be founded.
>
> However much truth there may be in such assertions, it has always seemed to me that the real values of the search warrant procedure are: (1) It makes the officer pause in his pursuit and reflect on whether he has a good reason to go into someone's private space; (2) it requires him to make a record of his reasons, recording what he knows about the case before he makes the move; and (3) his recorded reasons stand immutably for review by a knowledgeable judge after the fact, at trial, and again on appeal, if the search is challenged. In the enforced hesitation, recorded articulation, and prospect of true review, the objectives of the Fourth Amendment are well served.[4]

Prof. Uviller's comments remind us that the warrant procedure does not absolve police and prosecutors from fairly evaluating the facts and making *their own* probable cause decisions before applying for a warrant (*Groh v. Ramirez*, 2004).

Obtaining a Search Warrant

The Fourth Amendment requires that "no Warrant shall issue but upon probable cause supported by Oath or affirmation. . . ." In order to obtain a search warrant, law enforcement officers must: (1) present a *written affidavit* to a magistrate, which requests that a warrant be issued; (2) *swear under oath* that the information in the affidavit is truthful; and (3) convince the magistrate that the information sworn to *establishes probable cause* to believe that a search warrant is justified. The magistrate should question the officer requesting the warrant about the circumstances of the case and must be personally satisfied that the evidence constitutes probable cause. The oath signifies that the officer takes responsibility for the facts alleged.[5]

The affidavit, or sworn statement, is presented to the court at an *ex parte* hearing, i.e., a hearing with only one party present. Such a procedure normally would violate due process but is allowed out of necessity and is hemmed in with other safeguards, such as the return on the warrant, which requires the officer to report on the execution of the warrant. The magistrate usually questions only the affiant but may require additional witnesses to testify before being satisfied that there is sufficient evidence. The law enforcement agency applying for a warrant should keep all evidence and records of its application; if the warrant is challenged, the loss of such information would weigh heavily against the agency. Also, if a jurisdiction allows the agency to make a new warrant application to a different magistrate if an initial request is turned down, then the evidence submitted in the first application must be submitted in the second application.

The *classes of evidence* that may be searched and seized under a warrant are spelled out in the Federal Rules of Criminal Procedure: "A warrant may be issued under this rule to search for and seize any (1) property that constitutes *evidence* of the commission of a criminal offense; or (2) *contraband,* the fruits of crime, or things otherwise criminally possessed; or (3) property designed or intended for use or which is or has been used as a *means* of committing a criminal offense; or (4) *person* for whose arrest there is probable cause, or who is unlawfully restrained" (F.R.C.P. Rule 41(b), emphasis added).

The typical affidavit and warrant for a search need not be lengthy; they are often only one or two pages long. What is important is that the affidavit state sufficient evidence to establish *probable cause* and that the warrant give clear directions to the executing officers. In some jurisdictions, a warrant is issued without attaching the affidavit; in others the warrant incorporates the affidavit. This is the practice in Detroit, Michigan, from which a warrant and affidavit are included (with names and identifying information changed) as an example of what is required to establish probable cause.

TELEPHONIC WARRANTS   Modern technology makes it possible to reduce the time between requesting a search warrant and receiving authorization if large distances between the police officers and the court make the normal affidavit process cumbersome. In 1970 California enacted legislation to allow **telephonic warrants** and, according to Professor Geoffrey Alpert, another eight states and the federal government have followed suit.[6] Under F.R.C.P. Rule 41(c)(2), a federal magistrate may issue a warrant on oral testimony given over a telephone "[i]f the circumstances make it reasonable to dispense, in whole or in part, with a written affidavit." The magistrate must record the "duplicate original warrant" prepared by the officer or have a stenographic or longhand verbatim record made. In either case, the caller is immediately placed under oath by the magistrate.

Professor Alpert suggests that the advent of telephonic warrants may cast doubt on the validity of certain warrantless arrests as it becomes easier for police to get judicial permission to conduct searches when distance or time would

STATE OF MICHIGAN

SS   **SEARCH WARRANT AND AFFIDAVIT**
County of Wayne

TO THE SHERIFF OR ANY PEACE OFFICER OF SAID COUNTY: Wayne; Police Officer Phillip Melon.

Affiant, having subscribed and sworn to an affidavit for a Search Warrant, and I having under oath examined affiant, am satisfied that probable cause exists.

THEREFORE, IN THE NAME OF THE PEOPLE OF THE STATE OF MICHIGAN, I command that you search the following described please:

18793 Colorado, a one story brick building, bearing the name O'Grady's Collision, located in the City of Detroit, County of Wayne, State of Michigan, and to seize, secure, tabulate and make return according to law the following property and things:

1. A 1-1984 Chevrolet Nova, Blue, VIN#1FABPO758EW236587, bearing license plate #241-LUS
2. Any stolen vehicles or parts of stolen vehicles
3. Any and all other vehicles belonging to Stephen Switzerland and Warren Switzerland
4. Any repair orders, estimates or other paperwork relating to the repair of vehicles.

The following facts are sworn to by affiant in support of the issuance of this Warrant:

Affiant is a member of the Detroit Police Department, assigned to the Commercial Auto Theft Section. Affiant on January 19, 1988 and January 20, 1988 executed search warrants on this location and seized a stolen vehicle, a 1984 Chevrolet, 241-LUS. Affiant while conducting an investigation in regard to this stolen vehicle discovered that the vehicle had been falsely reported stolen in order to collect the insurance monies from Mackinac Insurance Company. On March 24, 1988, a warrant for Attempted OMUFP O/100 (Obtaining Money under False Pretenses over $100) were obtained against Irwin Schmidlopp (Owner of the 1984 Chevrolet Nova) and for Stephen Switzerland (Owner of O'Grady's Collision). During the investigation it was discovered that persons would obtain insurance through the Mackinac Agency for vehicles that they did not own and then a claim would be submitted to the insurance company and an adjuster would arrive at O'Grady's Collision (an unlicensed motor vehicle repair facility). The insurance company would then issue a check to O'Grady's Collision and the insured party for the repair of this vehicle. One vehicle, a 1985 Oldsmobile, was repaired at least three times by O'Grady's listing three different owners when, in fact, none of these alleged owners ever owned the vehicle or got into an accident with this 1985 Oldsmobile. All three checks were co-issued to O'Grady's Collision and all three checks, totaling about $15,000.00, were cashed by Stephen Switzerland through his account at First of America. Affiant on March 29, 1988, observed the 1984 Chevrolet, belonging to defendant, Irwin Schmidlopp, still inside this location. Affiant believes that estimates and bills and receipts will be found inside this location to show further schemes and frauds committed by these suspects to defraud the insurance companies.

Phillip Melon
Affiant

Subscribed and sworn to before me and issued under my hand this **30**th day of **March**, 19**88**

Approved:
John Carter

Assistant Prosecuting Attorney

P91234

Jane Ellis

Judge of 36th District Court,
Wayne County, Michigan, and a Magistrate

---

otherwise impede them. For such an ideal situation to occur, which simultaneously ensures effective law enforcement while protecting individual liberty, officers must be aware of the procedure and courts must be structured to accept warrants. This would require that police routinely have recording devices available to record their oral requests.[7] Most important, it requires police to have knowledge of the procedure and their willingness to use it; however, both may be lacking. For example, in the O. J. Simpson murder trial, Detective Mark Fuhrman was asked on cross-examination "why the detectives did not try to secure a warrant by telephone."[8] A commentator noted that "while judges are available by phone, many police detectives simply don't use that procedure; Detective Mark Fuhrman testified in the preliminary hearings that he has never used telephonic warrants."[9] Another commentator

noted that in Colorado, telephonic warrants are obtained in an hour and a half.[10]

Particularity

The Fourth Amendment requires that a warrant "*particularly* describ[e] the place to be searched, and the persons or things to be seized." This rule is substantive and not formal. Thus, an officer making an affidavit must investigate to ensure that the place is accurately described. In addition to a street number, it is wise to add a description of the premises in case a mistake might render a search illegal. For example, police planned a drug raid at a house located at the corner of Short and Adkinson Streets. The warrant incorrectly listed the place to be searched as "325 Atkinson Street" when in fact it was 325

Short Street. The affidavit also described the house as a single residence with silver siding and red trim on the south side of the street. Despite the street number error, the search was held valid—the description met the particularity requirement—because the "test for determining the sufficiency of the description of the place to be searched is whether [it] is described with sufficient particularity as to enable the executing officer to locate and identify the premises with reasonable effort, and whether there is any reasonable probability that another premise might be mistakenly searched."[11]

The Supreme Court confirmed that mistakes in a warrant do not violate the Fourth Amendment if they are "reasonable." In **Maryland v. Garrison** (1987), police obtained "a warrant to search the person of Lawrence McWebb and 'the premises known as 2036 Park Avenue third floor apartment.'" Diligent police investigation did not reveal that there was another apartment on the third floor. When executing the warrant, police officers encountered McWebb downstairs and required him to walk up to the third floor. He opened the only apartment door, which led to a vestibule. Garrison was standing there and doors to both Garrison's and McWebb's apartments were open; the police did not, at that time, know that there were two apartments. They entered Garrison's apartment and seized drugs in **plain view**. As soon as they were told that it was not McWebb's apartment, they left. The Supreme Court ruled that the police did not know and could not reasonably have known that there were two apartments on the third floor. Consequently, their mistake did not invalidate an otherwise valid warrant and the seizure of drugs in Garrison's apartment. "[S]ufficient probability, not certainty, is the touchstone of reasonableness under the Fourth Amendment. . . ."

The goal of the "things to be seized" particularity requirement is that "nothing is left to the discretion of the officer executing the warrant" (*Marron v. United States,* 1927). Nonetheless, reasonable latitude is allowed. If police investigation shows that heroin is being sold from a particular location, the warrant can specify that police search for and seize "a quantity of drugs." It is important that the police investigate the situation to the greatest extent feasible and make a good faith effort to know in advance what is likely to be discovered in the place to be searched. The plain view doctrine (discussed later in this chapter) necessarily creates an expansion of what items the police may lawfully seize from a premises. Executing a valid search warrant is one of the ways in which police are legitimately in a premises; once legitimately in a place, they may seize all contraband in plain view, even if it is unrelated to the object of the search warrant.

In **Groh v. Ramirez** (2004) "a concerned citizen informed [ATF Agent Groh] that on a number of visits to [the Ramirez] ranch the visitor had seen a large stock of weaponry, including an automatic rifle, grenades, a grenade launcher, and a rocket launcher." Agent Groh prepared and signed a warrant application to search for "any automatic firearms or parts to automatic weapons, destructive devices to include but not limited to grenades, grenade launchers, rocket launchers, and any and all receipts pertaining to the purchase or manufacture of automatic

weapons or explosive devices or launchers." The application was supported by a detailed affidavit and a warrant form that Agent Groh filled out. A federal magistrate signed the warrant. The warrant completely "failed to identify any of the items that [Groh] intended to seize." In the place on the form "that called for a description of the 'person or property' to be seized, [Groh] typed a description of respondents' two-story blue house rather than the alleged stockpile of firearms." When he executed the warrant, only Mrs. Ramirez was home. Agent Groh apparently told her that he was looking for "an explosive device in a box."

The Supreme Court ruled that the warrant violated the Fourth Amendment because it failed to particularly describe the things to be seized. Despite the absence of any description of the things to be seized, the warrant would have been found constitutional if a detailed affidavit were attached or if it cross-referenced a supporting application or affidavit that accompanied the warrant. The fact that the magistrate believed there was probable cause to support the warrant does not cure this defect. Groh argued that the search itself was reasonable, and because of this, the warrant's defect should be overlooked. The Court rejected this: "Even though [Groh] acted with restraint in conducting the search, 'the inescapable fact is that this restraint was imposed by the agents themselves, not by a judicial officer.'" (*Groh v. Ramirez,* 2004, 124 S.Ct. 1292, citing *Katz v. United States,* 1967: 356). Groh also argued that he "orally described" what he was searching for to Mrs. Ramirez, thus giving her actual notice. But the Supreme Court ruled that her version, that the agents were looking for explosives in a box, had to be believed. The problem with police giving verbal descriptions of what they are authorized to take from a person whose house is being entered, is that the descriptions will tend to become open ended, and the householder will have no basis to argue that a search may be going too far. Searches based on verbal descriptions in effect become general searches.

Searches that tread on *First Amendment* free speech are closely scrutinized. In **Stanford v. Texas** (1965) a warrant authorized police to search Stanford's San Antonio home to seize "books, records, pamphlets, cards, receipts, lists, memoranda, pictures, recordings and other written instruments concerning the . . . operations of the Communist Party of Texas. . . ." In actions eerily reminiscent of *Entick v. Carrington* (1765), officers spent almost five hours in Stanford's home, taking more than a thousand books from his small business and his personal library. Books seized included some by alleged radical authors such as "Karl Marx, Jean Paul Sartre, Theodore Draper, Fidel Castro, Earl Browder, Pope John XXIII, and MR. JUSTICE HUGO L. BLACK." Many of Stanford's private documents and papers, "including his marriage certificate, his personal insurance policies, his household bills and receipts, and files of his personal correspondence," were seized. Ironically, no "records of the Communist Party" or any "party lists and dues payments" were found. The Court held that this was a *general warrant* that violated the Fourth and Fourteenth amendments, and added that when the things to be seized are books "and the basis of their seizure is the ideas which they contain," this implicates the First Amendment, and particularity must "be accorded the most scrupulous exactitude." Noting the historic continuity between this case and the earliest days of the American republic, Justice Stewart concluded by stating that "the Fourth and Fourteenth amendments guarantee to John Stanford that no official of the State shall ransack his home and seize his books and papers under the unbridled authority of a general warrant—no less than the law 200 years ago shielded John Entick from the messengers of the King."

Anticipatory Warrants

The United States Supreme Court has not ruled on **anticipatory warrants**, but such warrants have been authorized by F.R.C.P. Rule 41(a) since 1991 and are a useful law enforcement tool.[12] In a typical warrant, police have probable cause to believe that contraband is *already* in a specified place when the warrant application is made. In an ongoing investigation, however, police may have good reason to believe that contraband or seizable evidence *will be* found in a specified place on the condition that another event, usually a delivery, occurs. A search warrant issued on such a basis *anticipates* the existence of facts that will make a search and seizure lawful. Allowing anticipatory warrants encourages the use of search warrants over warrantless searches based on exigent circumstances, especially in drug-related crimes.[13]

Under the federal rule, anticipatory warrants can be issued (1) where the suspect or contraband is anticipated to be in the district in the future, and (2) where the suspect or contraband is currently in the district but may move out before the warrant is executed.[14] If the warrant is issued by a federal magistrate, federal law enforcement officers may execute it anywhere in the United States.

The rule facilitates **controlled deliveries**. If law enforcement becomes aware that illicit drugs or other contraband are in transit, they may *delay* the movement of the goods long enough to obtain a warrant, and then follow the delivery of the package to its destination. The basis of probable cause in a controlled delivery is often established by a reasonable seizure made by customs or mail officials who establish that goods are contraband drugs or child pornography. At that point, law enforcement agents will have probable cause to arrest the recipient of the package and to search the package.

Without more evidence, however, this situation does not give agents probable cause to search the *place* to which the suspected package was delivered.[15] Therefore, the *scope of the search* following the controlled delivery depends on the extent of the information that the police have *before* they initiate the search. To be sure that officers do not write affidavits for anticipatory searches that are subterfuges for officers to enter and to "create" plain view, "affidavits in support of such warrants should demonstrate probable cause to believe additional evidence is on the premises and should specify the nature of that additional evidence."[16]

The goal of controlled deliveries is to identify the persons engaged in the criminal transaction and to view a completed crime in order to establish a basis for prosecution. For this to occur, the goods must be delivered to their "final" destination. In a controlled delivery scenario, a magistrate can be certain of the actual delivery. An affidavit should also include corroborating information to support an observed but uncontrolled delivery. Where probable cause is based on information supplied by an informant, the informant's reliability should be well established. Professor James Adams argues that "exercise of the officer's discretion will have to be objectively reasonable under all the circumstances" and that the "good faith" exception should *not* apply to such situations.[17]

When the final destination of the contraband is not previously known, it may be impossible to meet the Fourth Amendment requirement that the place to be searched be particularly described. A search under this condition must be based either on (1) an anticipatory warrant that authorizes police to search the "ultimate location," (2) an application for a telephone warrant or a telephone call to the magistrate with information before entering the premises, or (3) entrance of the premises under exigent circumstances. If an **exigency** does not exist, or if it is impractical to telephone the magistrate, the first option is the only one that makes controlled deliveries worth the effort. In that case, several courts have stated that the police should have as little discretion in determining the place, or the "ultimate location," as possible.[18]

Controlled deliveries create extra hazards of unconstitutional searches. Therefore, when police or prosecutors request, and magistrates issue, anticipatory warrants, they have to be especially careful about: (1) the basis for probable cause, (2) the degree of certainty that a seizable item will be delivered to a specified location, (3) the specificity of the place to be searched, and (4) the appropriate scope of the warrant.[19]

Challenging a Search Warrant Affidavit

Police officers who lie on search warrant affidavits, or glide around the truth, subvert the integrity of the warrant system. Despite this obvious risk, the established rule was that a defendant could not directly challenge the officer-affiant's veracity. The Supreme Court changed this in *Franks v. Delaware* (1978), a 7–2 decision holding that if a defendant can show that police injected lies into an affidavit, the defendant is entitled to a hearing to present evidence to void the warrant. The older rule, reflecting the Crime Control Model (see Chapter 1) was more efficient in that bad warrants based on lies could be exposed at pretrial probable cause hearings, at trial, or on appeal. The *Franks* rule upholds the values espoused by the Due Process Model.

In *Franks* two detectives swore in an affidavit that they contacted Jerome Franks's coworkers about relevant evidence of an alleged rape and "did have personal conversation with both these people." After the warrant was executed, the defense attorney requested a hearing in order to call Franks's coworkers to testify that they never spoke personally to the detectives and that "although they might have talked to another police officer, any information given by them to that officer was 'somewhat different' from what was recited in the affidavit." The Delaware courts denied the hearing and the United States Supreme Court reversed.

Franks v. Delaware requires that a defendant make a *substantial* preliminary showing that the police made a false statement on the search warrant affidavit, either knowingly and intentionally, or with reckless disregard for the truth. If this can be shown, the Fourth Amendment requires a hearing. The defendant's challenge to the truthfulness of factual statements made in the affidavit must be established by a *preponderance* of the evidence. If the defendant prevails, the magistrate then sets aside the false statements and decides whether probable cause still exists to support the warrant. If not, the warrant is voided and the fruits of the search are excluded to the same extent as if probable cause was lacking on the face of the affidavit. This exacting standard precludes frequent challenge to affidavits.

In finding for Franks, Justice Blackmun reviewed the *competing values* that were involved in the case. The arguments *against ever* allowing a hearing to challenge an affidavit included (1) that it magnifies the use of the exclusionary rule, which is only a judicially created remedy and not a personal right; (2) that swearing to the affidavit sufficiently protects privacy, as do perjury prosecutions for a tiny number of falsified affidavits; (3) the magistrate can ferret out the truth at the warrant application; (4) allowing a post-affidavit hearing undermines the magistrate's authority; (5) the issue of an affidavit's truthfulness is collateral to the question of the defendant's guilt; (6) the truth of statements in an affidavit are often beyond the complete control of the officer since the affidavit may include hearsay; and (7) a hearing undermines the value of *finality,* that legal proceedings must come to an end at some point and should not be dragged on.

Against these objections, Justice Blackmun raised the following points: (1) "[A] flat ban on impeachment of veracity could denude the probable-cause requirement of all real meaning"; (2) A one-sided *ex parte* hearing is not entirely sufficient to block the introduction of perjury; (3) Alternative sanctions such as a perjury prosecution, administrative discipline, contempt, or a civil suit are relatively weak threats and thus not adequate to deter an officer bent on lying; (4) "[A]llowing an evidentiary hearing, after a suitable preliminary proffer of material falsity, would not diminish the importance and solemnity of the warrant-issuing process"; (5) A hearing to determine if an affidavit is truthful in no way interferes with the truth-finding aspects of the criminal case; (6) Given the requirements on the defendant to obtain a hearing, the right to challenge an affidavit will be infrequent and will not waste judicial resources; and (7) The exclusionary rule should be applied to evidence obtained by means of police perjury.

Execution of the Search Warrant

Search warrants can become *stale.* They must be executed as quickly as possible because the criminal evidence may be moved or destroyed or lose its character as contraband. F.R.C.P. Rule 41(c)(1) authorizes the magistrate to specify the time period within which the search must be carried out,

within an outer limit of ten days. Similar rules exist in every state. Because nighttime searches create a greater intrusion on privacy and raise the risk of greater violence born of confusion, the federal rules specify: "The warrant shall be served in the daytime, unless the issuing authority, by appropriate provision in the warrant, and for reasonable cause shown, authorizes its execution at times other than daytime."[20] Not every state requires that a magistrate authorize a nighttime entry, leaving it up to the discretion of law enforcement officers.

The common law rule that officers must *announce their presence* before entering and state that they have a warrant— the **knock and announce rule**—is designed to (1) reduce the potential for violent confrontations, (2) protect individual privacy by minimizing the chance of forced entry into the dwelling of the wrong person, and (3) prevent a physical invasion of privacy by giving the occupant time to voluntarily admit the officers.[21] However, when officers have reason to believe, *based on specific facts,* that announcing their entry would produce immediate violence or an attempt to destroy all the evidence, they may dispense with the announcement.[22] This is a well-litigated area, and if it is proved that the police were unreasonable in failing to announce their entry, then the evidence will be excluded. It may seem odd that the constitutionality of the "knock and announce" requirement was not resolved until fairly recently. The issue has been addressed by four Supreme Court cases.

In *Ker v. California* (1963) police had sufficient probable cause to believe that Ker possessed marijuana in his apartment but did not get a search warrant. They went to the building manager, obtained a passkey to Ker's apartment, and, knowing that Ker was inside, entered without knocking. The United States Supreme Court upheld the search and seizure on the grounds that the police entered for the purpose of arresting Ker and not to search. Four justices urged that the arrest be held unconstitutional because of the unannounced entry, a position later adopted in *Payton v. New York* (1979) (see Chapter 5). The constitutionality of the knock and announce rule, however, remained unsettled.

That opportunity to settle the question finally arose in *Wilson v. Arkansas* (1995). Petitioner Sharlene Wilson made a series of narcotics sales to a police informant at the home that Wilson shared with Bryson Jacobs. At one sale, Wilson produced a semiautomatic pistol and waved it in the informant's face, threatening to kill her if she turned out to be working for the police. Based on information supplied by the informant, police obtained a warrant to search the house and to arrest Wilson and Jacobs. The affidavits stated that Jacobs had previously been convicted of arson and firebombing. The warrant did not authorize an unannounced entry.

> The search was conducted later that afternoon. Police officers found the main door to petitioner's home open. While opening an unlocked screen door and entering the residence, they identified themselves as police officers and stated that they had a warrant. Once inside the home, the officers seized marijuana, methamphetamine, valium, narcotics paraphernalia, a gun, and ammunition. They also found petitioner in the bathroom,

flushing marijuana down the toilet. Petitioner and Jacobs were arrested and charged with delivery of marijuana, delivery of methamphetamine, possession of drug paraphernalia, and possession of marijuana. (*Wilson v. Arkansas*, 1995)

The Arkansas Supreme Court upheld the search and seizure and specifically found that the Fourth Amendment does not include a rule that police must knock and announce. A unanimous United States Supreme Court reversed that decision.

Because the Fourth Amendment's text does not specify a knock and announce rule, it can be argued that the rule is not part of the amendment. The opinion by Justice Clarence Thomas, who along with Justice Scalia is an "originalist" justice, took a different tack. "In evaluating the scope of this right, we have looked to the traditional protections against unreasonable searches and seizures afforded by the common law at the time of the framing." That is, the Court will engraft a rule onto the Fourth Amendment so long as the rule existed in the common law of England prior to the adoption of the Constitution. The justification is that the basic Fourth Amendment requirement is that searches be *reasonable* (the "general-reasonableness construction"), and what was reasonable to the Framers can be determined by knowing late-eighteenth-century common law rules. Also significant was the fact that most new states, shortly after July 4, 1776, passed "reception" statutes making the English common law the law of the state up until independence. Justice Thomas cited a noted seventeenth-century case, *Semayne's Case* (1603), and several prominent English commentators, to establish that "At the time of the framing, the common law of search and seizure recognized a law enforcement officer's authority to break open the doors of a dwelling, but generally indicated that he first ought to announce his presence and authority." Furthermore, the "common-law knock-and-announce principle was woven quickly into the fabric of early American law." In all, the Court's opinion surmised that the Framers thought that the "knock and announce" rule was part of the "reasonableness" analysis of the Fourth Amendment.

The Court did not pass on the constitutionality of the actual search in this case. It did note that *exceptions* to the "knock and announce" rule existed under various circumstances:

- A threat of physical violence.
- A suspect escapes from an officer and retreats to his dwelling.
- A demand to open the door was refused.
- Reason to believe that evidence would likely be destroyed if advance notice were given. The case was remanded to the Arkansas courts to determine if any exception permitted the search and seizure in this case.

It appears that *Wilson v. Arkansas* does not create an impediment to unannounced entry when it can be justified by the exceptions. The Supreme Court has made it clear, nevertheless, that the circumstances allowing a constitutional unannounced search must be justified in each case. In *Richards v. Wisconsin* (1997) police executed a search warrant that required knock and entry to enter a hotel room of a man suspected of deal-

ing drugs. The trial court nevertheless allowed the introduction of the evidence under the specific facts of the case, and emphasized that the easily disposable nature of the drugs further justified their decision to identify themselves as they crossed the threshold instead of announcing their presence before seeking entry. The Wisconsin Supreme Court, in affirming, held that when police officers execute a warrant to search for drugs, the circumstances *automatically* raise exigent circumstances. In other words, the Wisconsin Court held that police *never* have to knock and announce in a drug case. The United States Supreme Court unanimously reversed. It found that a blanket no-knock exception had two flaws: (1) some drug search warrants might be executed at a house where the occupants, at the time of the search, were not involved in the drug trade; and (2) such an exception would soon negate the rule because it would be extended to all other crimes. The Court in *Richards* also specified the *evidentiary standard* to support an *exception*—a **no-knock warrant**: "a reasonable suspicion that knocking and announcing their presence, under the particular circumstances, would be dangerous or futile, or that it would inhibit the effective investigation of the crime by, for example, allowing the destruction of evidence." (*Richards v. Wisconsin*, p. 394)

The rules concerning the execution of no-knock searches were further refined in **United States v. Ramirez** (1998). The Court unanimously held that police officers are not held to a higher standard than "*reasonable suspicion*" when the execution of a no-knock warrant results in damage to property. A reliable confidential informant told federal agents that a dangerous prisoner, who escaped from a county jail in Oregon, where he had been sent to testify in a case, was hiding in the home of Hernan Ramirez. A no-knock warrant was obtained to search Ramirez's home for the prisoner.

> In the early morning of November 5, approximately 45 officers gathered to execute the warrant. The officers set up a portable loud speaker system and began announcing that they had a search warrant. Simultaneously, they broke a single window in the garage and pointed a gun through the opening, hoping thereby to dissuade any of the occupants from rushing to the weapons the officers believed might be in the garage.

Ramirez, awakened by this, thought his house was being burglarized and took his pistol and fired it into the ceiling of his garage. He dropped the gun when he realized the besiegers were police officers. Ramirez was indicted for being a felon in possession of firearms. The federal district court granted his motion to suppress evidence regarding the weapon possession; it found that the Fourth Amendment had been violated because there were "insufficient exigent circumstances" to justify the police officer's destruction of property in their execution of the warrant. The Ninth Circuit Court of Appeals affirmed, holding that property destruction accompanying a no-knock entry required more than a "mild" exigency. The Supreme Court unanimously reversed. It held that there is not a higher standard for a no-knock entry when property damage occurs as part of the entry. While noting that excessive property damage created during an entry could amount to a Fourth Amendment violation, the breaking of a single pane of glass, in this case, was reasonable.

In *United States v. Banks* (2003) the Supreme Court unanimously confirmed that the rule governing the "knock and announce" rule in the execution of a search warrant is whether the entry is reasonable under all of the facts and circumstances of the case. In this case the police were executing a warrant to search for cocaine during the daytime when people are up and about. They loudly announced their presence. Under these circumstances the Court unanimously ruled that it was reasonable to force open the door after waiting for 15 to 20 seconds with no answer. A "prudent dealer" was likely to keep cocaine "near a commode or kitchen sink" and so would have had the opportunity to get rid of the illegal drugs within a short period of time. "Police seeking a stolen piano may be able to spend more time to make sure they really need the battering ram" (*United States v. Banks*, 2003).

Inventory and Return

After a search is executed, statutes or rules require the officers to promptly complete a written **inventory and return** of any property taken (F.R.C.P. Rule 41(d)). The inventory must be made in the presence of a "credible person other than the applicant for the warrant or the person from whose possession or premises the property was taken." This practice ensures the regularity of the search and seizure process, provides notice to suspects that the state intruded on their privacy, and protects police officers from charges of theft.

The detail of an inventory and return can be seen in this excerpt from an FBI Agent's Affidavit and Inventory of the 1996 search of the cabin of Theodore J. Kaczynski, the notorious Unabomber whose seventeen-year bombing campaign led to three deaths.

> Your affiant, Special Agent (S.A.) Donald J. Sachtleben, Federal Bureau of Investigation, states as follows: 1. I, S.A. Donald J. Sachtleben, have been a Special Agent for 12 years. I graduated from the F.B.I. Hazardous Devices School and the F.B.I. Post Blast School. I have investigated bombing cases for 10 years and taught classes on the investigation of improvised explosive devices (I.E.D.). I have participated in the on scene investigation of bombing cases. * * *
>
> 5. In order to construct a pipe bomb, one needs either a commercially manufactured explosive or an improvised explosive, a casing, a device to detonate the explosive, and a power source for the detonating device. During the search I observed materials from which all of these could be made. In particular, during the search I observed the following:
>
>   1. Ten three-ring binders. . . .
>   2. Pipes that appear to be galvanized metal, copper and plastic. Four of the copper pipes had plates affixed to one end, which is one of the first steps in the construction of a pipe bomb. . . .
>   3. Containers containing powders labeled as "KClO3" (potassium chlorate), "NaClO3" (sodium chlorate), "Sugar",

> "Zinc", "Aluminum", "Lead", and "Silver Oxide." Necessary ingredients in the preparation of explosives include an oxidizer and a fuel. Sugar, zinc, aluminum, lead and silver oxide all can serve as fuels, and potassium chlorate can be oxidizers. . . .
>
>   4. Solid cast ingots, one of which is labeled aluminum. . . . Aluminum can be used as an additional fuel and a catalyst in an explosive mixture.
>   5. C cell batteries and electrical wire. . . . * * *

The importance of police *honesty and accuracy* in the search warrant process cannot be overstated. The *Law in Society* section in this chapter deals with police perjury. On September 29, 1999, four Denver SWAT officers were sent to execute a no-knock warrant at 3738 High Street, a two-story home—it was the *wrong* house. Instead of executing the warrant, the officers who broke in executed forty-five-year-old Mexican migrant laborer Ismael Mena, father of nine, when he raised a gun as the police entered his bedroom. The SWAT officers were exonerated after a close examination of their responses. But the officer who swore out the affidavit, Joseph Bini, was charged with perjury and faces a six-year term if convicted. He was charged with "'unlawfully and knowingly' lying on a search warrant affidavit." He claimed in the affidavit that "he personally observed an informant make his or her way on foot to the house" at 3738 High Street. Based on his affidavit, an assistant district attorney reviewed and signed the warrant and a county judge read and signed the warrant. But, in fact, the drug deal took place at 3742 High Street, a single-story home. Bini dropped the informant off four blocks from the house. The district attorney believed "[The informant] attempted to determine the address by counting the houses down the alley and up the front on this particular block. He apparently miscounted the houses and wrote the address down wrong." As a result, a man died, Denver paid Mena's family $400,000 to settle legal claims, and the police chief was fired. On recommendations from a panel, Denver police will have only three days instead of ten days to serve no-knock warrants, more training will be provided, and experienced police supervisors will evaluate and approve no-knock raids. Denver's mayor said he thinks "the public can expect to see a decrease in the number of no-knock raids" as a result of the tighter guidelines. But it took an unnecessary death to achieve that result.[23]

REVOLUTIONIZING THE FOURTH AMENDMENT

For many years, Fourth Amendment law was tied to *property* concepts, especially the idea that a search and seizure involved a *physical trespass* onto a person's **"constitutionally protected area."** This concept was based on traditional practice and on the words of the Fourth Amendment, protecting "persons, houses, papers and effects" from unreasonable search and seizure. Yet this thinking created problems when the Supreme Court in *Olmstead v. United States* (1928) held that wiretapping did *not* constitute a search and seizure. This withdrew constitutional protection from a vital area of privacy and caused many to realize that the Fourth Amendment should protect vital *interests* rather than property alone. It was not until 1967 that the Court revisited and overruled *Olmstead,* but to do so it had to establish an entirely new doctrine, because protecting intangible privacy interests was broader than the "constitutionally protected area" doctrine.

Modernizing Search and Seizure Law

In 1967 and 1968, the Supreme Court "revolutionized" Fourth Amendment law in four cases that upset established doctrines and opened the door for a freewheeling mode of search and seizure interpretation. The first of these cases, *Katz v. United States* (1967) was the centerpiece of this revolution. It broke the law of search and seizure away from its traditional mooring in property law. In its stead, issues were now to be decided more explicitly on a **balancing of interests** deemed central to the Fourth Amendment: These interests were the need for effective law enforcement versus the protection of privacy and liberty based on the notion of the **"expectation of privacy."**

Katz was followed by **Warden v. Hayden** (1967), the second case in this series, which abolished the "mere evidence" rule of *Gouled v. United States* (1921) (see Chapter 2). *Gouled* held that only the fruits of a crime, contraband, or the instrumentality used to commit the crime could be seized by police. So-called "mere evidence" which did not fit these categories could not be seized by police to be used in evidence. In *Warden v. Hayden* police seized clothing that could be used to identify an alleged robber during a lawful search of Hayden's house. The Supreme Court held that the clothing could be seized by the police, and held by the state for the duration of the prosecution to be used as evidence that a man wearing similar clothing was the perpetrator. The old rule (1) did not serve a defendant's legitimate privacy interest, (2) was based on outmoded property concepts, and (3) hampered the legitimate law enforcement interests of the state. The new rule better balanced the competing interests.

Next came **Camara v. Municipal Court** (1967) and its companion case *See v. City of Seattle* (1967), which appeared to expand Fourth Amendment rights of individuals by requiring a warrant for administrative searches that did not directly enforce the criminal law. Under a 1959 case, *Frank v. Maryland,* the Supreme Court held that a search of a premises, whether a house or a business place, conducted by an administrative officer for the purpose of enforcing administrative regulations rather than the state's penal code, was simply not a search protected by the Fourth Amendment. In *Camara* the Court was constrained to rule that the text of the Fourth Amendment applied to the intrusion by *any* government officer into "areas" protected by the expectation of privacy. Entry by health, fire, or housing inspectors, for purposes of enforcing regulations, were now covered by the Fourth Amendment.

This, however, created a dilemma. Most administrative inspection programs are based not on particularized probable cause of a safety hazard in a particular home or business, but on administrative assessments that houses or businesses in an *entire neighborhood* should be entered and inspected. If a municipality had to get particularized probable cause for each house in the neighborhood, the inspection program would fail. The Court solved the problem by ruling that less specific administrative *warrants* could be issued based on general area inspections that provided information about such general conditions as the age of buildings in a specific subdivision or statistical information about the number of fires in a neighborhood. Probable cause was "defined down." This solution, however, created a new way of thinking about the Fourth Amendment that is more flexible. In a real sense, *Camara* opened the door to the general reasonableness construction of the amendment (see Chapter 2). The Court based its holding on the fact that the text of the Fourth Amendment does not absolutely require search warrants, but at minimum requires that all search and seizures be *reasonable.* Under this newer, flexible reasoning, the Supreme Court found that warrants that are general, the very thing that the generation of 1776 found abominable, were constitutional. This relaxed mode of interpretation was later used to allow greater government intrusion into areas of privacy by non–law enforcement officers under the "special needs" doctrine (see Chapter 5).

The last case in this series, *Terry v. Ohio* (1968), for the first time in American constitutional history, upheld temporary but forcible stops of persons even though the police officer did not have probable cause to believe that the person committed a crime. A state deprivation of liberty could now be based on a lesser standard of evidence that came to be known as "reasonable suspicion." (*Terry* is discussed in Chapter 4). The decision in *Terry* depended on the new mode of Fourth Amendment reasoning: balancing of interests between the state and the individual, flexibility, and reliance on the "reasonableness clause."

These four revolutionary decisions were not inherently liberal or conservative—two of them explicitly expanded the powers of the state (*Warden* and *Terry*) while the other two (*Katz* and *Camara*) formally expanded the rights of individuals. In their larger effects, the cases were "liberal" in that they brought a larger measure of police work within constitutional oversight, but "conservative" in permitting a flexible approach that made it easier for the Court to water down traditional Fourth Amendment standards. It is ironic that the liberal Warren Court laid a foundation of flexible interpretation—an approach that was resisted by relatively "conservative" justices like John M. Harlan II—that was adapted by the politically conservative Burger and Rehnquist Courts to expand the powers of the state against the individual.

Creating the Expectation of Privacy Doctrine

This section takes a closer look at the decision and reasoning in **Katz v. United States** (1967). Modern conditions generate problems that require novel legal thinking. Electronic communication by telegraph, telephone, and by wireless communication—unknown to the Framers in 1791—led to invasions of privacy by police that did not have the appearance of a traditional search and seizure, with the police pounding at the door and physically searching a place. In 1928 the Supreme Court thus ruled in *Olmstead v. United States*, by a 5–4 majority, that wiretapping did *not* constitute a search because there was no *physical trespass* into the house and no tangible evidence was taken. This ruling was deeply disturbing because wiretapping and electronic eavesdropping by the government is an obvious intrusion into the lives and privacy of individuals, values that are at the core of the Fourth Amendment. Indeed, the decision produced a powerful dissent by Justice Brandeis (see Brandeis' biographical sketch), was not popular with the public, and a federal statute soon placed some controls on telephone wiretapping.[24] The federal law, incidentally, did not cover "bugging"—electronic eavesdropping by means of a wireless listening device—which was not as well known and not then seen as within the purview of the Federal government's jurisdiction over interstate communications.[25]

Over the next few years, the Court grappled with the question of electronic eavesdropping. The application of traditional, property-based Fourth Amendment concepts produced weirdly inconsistent results. *Goldman v. United States* (1942), for example, held that placing an electronic listening device *against* a wall of a house was not a trespass, and therefore, under *Olmstead,* was not a Fourth Amendment search and seizure. Evidence so obtained could be used against the defendant. Dissatisfied with the notion of leaving individuals open to government spying, the Court in *Silverman v. United States* (1961) held that when a microphone was *tacked into* a wall, rather than placed up against it, there was a *physical* trespass and thus a search and seizure subject to the rules of the Fourth Amendment. In this case the evidence seized by the eavesdropping was not admissible. These contradictory decisions were inherently unstable. The Supreme Court, nevertheless, was not eager to clear up this doctrinal mess.

The Court's chief concern was that a case squarely holding that electronic eavesdropping was a search and seizure within the purview of the Fourth Amendment could entirely outlaw bugging and wiretapping. The reason is that a bug or wiretap is an inherently general search that picks up all conversations, of the suspect as well as of nonsuspected persons who happen to call or be in the place being bugged. It was difficult to comprehend how a warrant for the placement of an electronic eavesdropping device could ever square with the particularity requirement of the Fourth Amendment. The justices in the 1940s and the 1950s included former senators and Attorneys-General who were familiar with the workings of government. They knew that electronic eavesdropping was a powerful law enforcement tool and that it was often impossible to obtain evidence of such areas of criminality as organized crime, white-collar crime, and government fraud and bribery without bugs and taps. On the other hand, they were well versed in the dangers of unchecked electronic spying by the government. As was later made known to the general public, the FBI under its long-time director J. Edgar Hoover, and with the compliance of presidents, spied on members of Congress and a sig-

nificant number of citizens. At least one Supreme Court justice believed that he was the subject of FBI taps.[26] The dilemma confronting the Court, seemingly insoluble until the late 1960s, was how to allow but to tame electronic eavesdropping.

A potential answer to this dilemma began to emerge in 1966. Under established doctrine, there is no violation of statutory or Fourth Amendment rights or to the expectation of privacy when a person's voice is recorded in a conversation made *voluntarily* with the interceptor. A person who says things in a conversation to another lives with the risk that the false friend will reveal any confidences to others, including the authorities (*Hoffa v. United States*, 1966; *Lewis v. United States*, 1966). The Court has ruled that this is the case even if the false friend is speaking on a telephone and a police officer is listening on an extension line (*Rathbun v. United States,* 1957), or secretly wearing a listening device (*On Lee v. United States*, 1952; *Lopez v. United States,* 1963). In short, a law enforcement officer or agent need not obtain a judicial warrant to "wear a wire." Despite this firm rule, to be on the safe side government investigators in *Osborn v. United States* (1966) had Vick, a private cooperating undercover agent, make a written statement under oath that Vick was hired by Osborn, an attorney, to bribe a juror in a prosecution of national labor leader James R. Hoffa. The statement was taken to two federal district judges who authorized Vick to wear an electronic recorder while next speaking to Osborn about the bribery. This practice was upheld by the Court in *Osborn* although not made mandatory. The following year, the Supreme Court, in *Katz,* praised the practice of seeking a warrant for a narrow and precise search. Here was a case of capturing a conversation that would not overhear innocent speakers.

Shortly before deciding *Katz,* the Supreme Court struck down New York's electronic eavesdropping law as too broad in *Berger v. New York* (1967). Objectionable features of the New York law included the fact that it "lays down no requirement for particularity in the warrant as to what specific crime has been or is being committed;" that a warrant is granted for sixty days of uninterrupted listening; that the statute failed to describe the conversations sought with specific particularity; that once incriminating conversations were recorded, the eavesdropping did not have to cease; that extensions of the initial sixty-day listening period could be obtained without new reasons; and that no return was required, so that a person who was tapped or bugged would not know of it. *Osborn* and *Berger* were the extreme ends of electronic eavesdropping—one extremely precise and narrow and the other overly broad.

The facts in *Katz* were simple. Federal agents suspected that Charles Katz, a "bookie" was transmitting betting information across state lines in violation of a federal law by doing so over the telephone. Katz was observed making calls from the same telephone booth at about the same time every day in Los Angeles. For the period of a week, FBI agents placed a microphone on the top of the telephone booth and activated it only when Katz used the booth to make calls. Incriminating conversations were recorded in this way. Katz appealed his conviction on the ground that the electronic eavesdropping violated his Fourth Amendment rights. The government argued that this case was the same as *Goldman,* in that there was no physical intrusion into a constitutionally protected area and so no Fourth Amendment violation.

The Supreme Court overruled *Olmstead* and *Goldman* and replaced the concept that the Fourth Amendment applies in "constitutionally protected areas" with a memorable phrase in Justice Potter Stewart's majority opinion:

> For the Fourth Amendment protects people, not places. What a person knowingly exposes to the public, even in his own home or office, is not a subject of Fourth Amendment protection. But what he seeks to preserve as private, even in an area accessible to the public, may be constitutionally protected. (*Katz v. United States,* 1967, p. 351).

It did not matter that Katz was visible to the eye in the phone booth.

> But what he sought to exclude when he entered the booth was not the intruding eye—it was the uninvited ear. He did not shed his right to do so simply because he made his calls from a place where he might be seen. * * * One who occupies it, shuts the door behind him, and pays the toll that permits him to place a call is surely entitled to assume that the words he utters into the mouthpiece will not be broadcast to the world. To read the Constitution more narrowly is to ignore the vital role that the public telephone has come to play in private communication. (*Katz,* 1967, p. 352).

The Court made it clear that property interests do not determine the scope of Fourth Amendment protections. It held that "The Government's activities in electronically listening to and recording the petitioner's words violated the privacy upon which he justifiably relied while using the telephone booth and thus constituted a "search and seizure" within the meaning of the Fourth Amendment" (*Katz,* 1967, p. 353).

The Court then decided that the government's search and seizure violated the Fourth Amendment because agents did not seek a warrant. The Court took special pains to note that the search was very narrow in that it seemed to be based on probable cause and was conducted in such a way as to obtain only Katz's words at a time and place that were likely to involve his suspected criminal activity. The Court noted that a magistrate probably could have issued a warrant. Nevertheless, drawing on the great importance of the warrant, the search was held unconstitutional because the agents did not obtain a search warrant.

The *Katz* doctrine is a product not simply of the majority opinion, but of that decision plus the heart of Justice Harlan's concurrence.

> My understanding of the rule that has emerged from prior decisions is that there is a twofold requirement, first that a person have exhibited an actual (subjective) expectation of privacy and, second, that the expectation be one that society is prepared to recognize as "reasonable" (*Katz v. United States,* 1967, p. 361, Harlan, J. Concurring).

This **two-pronged test** means that there is a subjective (personal) and an objective (societal) component of what constitutes an "expectation of privacy." The objective component prevents defendants from making outlandish or unacceptable claims of Fourth Amendment privacy, and this will be detailed in the following section. Justice Hugo Black was the lone dissenter. He argued that although electronics were unknown in 1791, eavesdropping was a familiar practice and the framers could have protected private conversations if they so wished. He instead adhered to the notion of *Olmstead* that the Fourth Amendment indeed did refer to and protect the seizure of tangible items. By this narrow adherence to the words of the Fourth Amendment, Justice Black solidified his standing as a "constitutional fundamentalist" rather than a "judicial liberal."

Application of the Expectation of Privacy Doctrine

Katz has substantially changed the way in which the Court analyzes Fourth Amendment issues. Nevertheless, although the Supreme Court has decided some cases based on the analysis that a government intrusion amounts to an invasion of a subjective and objective expectation of privacy, in other cases the Court has seemed to adhere to the "constitutionally protected area" idea, affording greater protection to the home than other places. In certain Fourth Amendment standing cases, the Court has resisted the logic of the *Katz* ruling. The dissent in *Rakas v. Illinois* (1978), for example, noted that

> The Court today holds that the Fourth Amendment protects property, not people, and specifically that a legitimate occupant of an automobile may not invoke the exclusionary rule and challenge a search of that vehicle unless he happens to own or have a possessory interest in it. * * * The majority's conclusion has no support in the Court's controlling decisions, in the logic of the Fourth Amendment, or in common sense.

It appears in such cases that a conservative Court is motivated more by limiting the rights of suspects than by creating a coherent body of Fourth Amendment law. One may almost say that the *Katz* doctrine is used by the Court to resolve Fourth Amendment issues except when the Court rules otherwise.

EXPECTATION OF PRIVACY IN ONE'S BODY   Obtaining physical evidence from within a person's body raises Fourth Amendment questions which have been answered by closely examining the severity of the intrusion and the law enforcement interests. Factors include the risk to safety or health in the procedure, the extent of control used on the person's body, and the effect on the suspect's personal dignity. Thus, on the one hand forced *surgery* to remove a bullet lodged in a robbery suspect was held to violate his Fourth Amendment rights because the expectation of privacy in one's bodily integrity is great (*Winston v. Lee,* 1985). On the other hand, taking *blood* in a medical setting to determine a driver's blood alcohol level after a fatal accident has been upheld as constitutional—it presents virtually no health risk and is so routine as to involve a minimal interference with Fourth Amendment dignity interests (*Schmerber v. California,* 1966). Lower courts have also perceived a greater privacy interest in bodily integrity in cases involving body cavity searches and strip searches.[27]

A person's observable physical characteristics, such as one's facial description, voice, or handwriting are not "seized" if someone testifies to them at a trial or if a person's description is taken by police in an investigation (*Holt v. United States,* 1910; *United States v. Dionisio,* 1973; *United States v. Mara,* 1973). Requiring a person to participate in a lineup does not violate one's Fourth or Fifth amendment rights (*United States v. Wade,* 1967).

The Supreme Court has held that *urine collection and testing* to ascertain the presence of drugs in a person's body intrudes upon expectations of privacy that society has long recognized as reasonable. "There are few activities in our society more personal or private than the passing of urine. Most people describe it by euphemisms if they talk about it at all. It is a function traditionally performed without public observation; indeed, its performance in public is generally prohibited by law as well as social custom." The Court noted that the expectation of privacy is not only rooted in the traditional dictates of modesty, but also in the fact that the chemical analysis of urine, like that of blood, can reveal a host of medical facts about a person. Although urine testing by state agencies in order to detect drugs or alcohol is protected by the Fourth Amendment, the collection is allowed under certain conditions (*Skinner v. Railway Labor Executives' Association,* 1989) (see Chapter 5). In contrast, private business is not restricted in this practice by the Fourth Amendment because there is no state action.

MAINTAINING PROPERTY INTERESTS AFTER KATZ

The Court made it clear that the Fourth Amendment continues to protect property interests. In **Soldal v. Cook County** (1992) a mobile home park evicted Soldal and his mobile home from its property and utilities. The mobile home park owner had the Sheriff's department send deputies to stand by in the event that the eviction might lead to violence. The employees of the park pushed Soldal's trailer into a road, causing major property damage. The park did not act in accordance with local statutes. There was no invasion of Soldal's *privacy,* as the employees never entered Soldal's trailer, but his *property* was damaged. Although the officers did not physically assist in the eviction, the Supreme Court held that their presence established state action (see Chapter 2). Soldal sued the Sheriff's department under 42 U.S.C. §1983, claiming that his Fourth Amendment rights were violated. The government argued that without a *Katz*-like violation to *privacy* rights, there was no Fourth Amendment wrong. This argument was firmly rejected: *Katz* protects *both* privacy and property rights. According to Justice White, although there was *no search,* there was a *seizure*—a "meaningful interference with an individual's possessory interests in that property." Because "[w]hat matters is the intrusion on the people's security from governmental interference," this case fell within the Fourth Amendment, allowing Soldal's lawsuit to go forward.

EXPECTATION OF PRIVACY IN DWELLINGS

"At the risk of belaboring the obvious, private residences are places in which the individual normally expects privacy free of governmental intrusion not authorized by a warrant, and that expectation is plainly one that society is prepared to recognize as justifiable." (*United States v. Karo,* 1984, p. 714).

At times, the Supreme Court has leaned in favor of a defendant's rights for this reason. For example, in *Payton v. New York* (1979) (see Chapter 4), the Court ruled that an arrest warrant must be obtained in order to forcibly enter a home to arrest a person. The "physical entry of the home is the chief evil against which the wording of the Fourth Amendment is directed."[28] The protection of the home applies to apartments, offices, garages, and temporary dwellings, such as hotel rooms. This has been confirmed in cases where the Court has denied landlords and hotel keepers the right to consent to police searches of the rooms of tenants (*Chapman v. California,* 1961; *Stoner v. California,* 1964). The protection of home privacy was a key reason for the Court's modification of the hot pursuit doctrine to disallow warrantless home entry for relatively minor offenses. (*Welsh v. Wisconsin,* 1984) (see Chapter 5).

When the core area of the home is involved, even a relatively conservative Court has scrupulously protected Fourth Amendment rights by maintaining the warrant and probable cause requirements. A person has no expectation of privacy in his or her public movements and, thus, no warrant was required when police placed an electronic **beeper** in a drum containing chloroform to monitor a suspected drug manufacturer driving along public streets (*United States v. Knotts,* 1983). On the other hand, a suspect's Fourth Amendment rights were violated when, without a warrant, agents traced a drum with a beeper attached into the home of a suspect and noted its movement there. "The beeper tells the agent that a particular article is actually located at a particular time in the private residence and is in the possession of the person or persons whose residence is being watched. Even if visual surveillance has revealed that the article to which the beeper is attached has entered the house, the later monitoring not only verifies the officers' observations but also establishes that the article remains on the premises." (*United States v. Karo,* 1984).

There is no Fourth Amendment protection of real estate as such, called "**open fields**" in the cases (*Hester v. United States,* 1924; *Oliver v. United States,* 1984). The Supreme Court has taken the common-law concept of the **curtilage**—the area immediately surrounding a house—and given it constitutional protection (*United States v. Dunn,* 1987; *Oliver v. United States,* 1984). Still, the Court has strained to not apply the curtilage idea to police observations of backyards from low-flying fixed-wing airplanes and helicopters. (*California v. Ciraolo,* 1986; *Florida v. Riley,* 1989)

PERSONS UNDER CORRECTIONAL JURISDICTION

Certain dwellings are not clothed with Fourth Amendment protection. No matter how closely attached a prisoner becomes to his or her *prison cell*, "a prison shares none of the attributes of privacy of a home." Although prisoners retain certain constitutional rights, such as freedom of religion, freedom from cruel and unusual punishment, and due process, "society is not prepared to recognize as legitimate any subjective expectation of privacy that a prisoner might have in his prison cell; . . . the

Fourth Amendment proscription against unreasonable searches and seizures does not apply within the confines of the prison cell." The practical consequence of this is that prison authorities are allowed under the Constitution to make random shakedown searches of prisoners' cells. There may be some limits to the practice if it is intended only to harass the prisoner (*Hudson v. Palmer,* 1984).

Similarly, the Court, over a strong dissent, allowed a probation officer to enter a *probationer's home* without a warrant and on less than probable cause (*Griffin v. Wisconsin,* 1987). The Court said that a "probationer's home, like anyone else's, is protected by the Fourth Amendment's requirement that searches be 'reasonable.'" On the other hand, in Wisconsin all probationers came under a regulation that permits any probation officer to search a probationer's home without a warrant as long as his supervisor approves and as long as there are "reasonable grounds" to believe the presence of contraband. The Supreme Court upheld the regulation on the ground that probation supervision is a "special need beyond the normal need for law enforcement"—a Fourth Amendment doctrine that permits warrantless searches on less than probable cause. Thus, while a probationer is not as devoid as a prisoner of an expectation of privacy in his or her dwelling, *Griffin* implied that a probationer's criminal status imposes a lower expectation of privacy at home than unconvicted persons.

The home privacy rights of probationers were further diminished in *United States v. Knights* (2001). A California probationer signed a probation order acknowledging as a condition of probation that he would "submit his . . . person, property, place of residence, vehicle, personal effects, to search at anytime, with or without a search warrant, warrant of arrest or reasonable cause by any probation officer or law enforcement officer." Knights's apartment was searched by a police officer who had investigated an arson and had reasonable suspicion but not probable cause that evidence of the crime was in the apartment. The officer did not obtain a search warrant because he knew of Knights's probation condition. Incriminating evidence was found and was used to convict Knights of a new crime. Knights argued that a warrantless search was permissible only for the special needs purpose of enforcing probation regulations, and not for the investigation of new crimes. In rejecting this position, the Court noted that "'the very assumption of the institution of probation' is that the probationer 'is more likely than the ordinary citizen to violate the law'" (*United States v. Knights,* 2001: 120, citing *Griffin v. Wisconsin,* 1987: 880).

The major difference between the privacy expectation of a prison cell and a probationer's home is that the latter cannot be entered at will by probation or police officers; entry under current conditions requires some level of cause. The only Supreme Court case involving the warrantless entry of the home of a parolee, *Pennsylvania Board of Probation and Parole v. Scott* (1998), held that the exclusionary rule does not apply to an illegal entry of the home of a parolee. This clearly implies that a parolee has a lesser expectation of privacy in a home than a free citizen, although the Supreme Court did not analyze the case under *Katz.*

MEDIA RIDE-ALONG   In *Wilson v. Layne* (1999) the Court held it "a violation of the Fourth Amendment for police to bring members of the media or other third parties into a home during the execution of a warrant when the presence of the third parties in the home was not in aid of the execution of the warrant." A proper arrest warrant, supported by probable cause, was issued to United States Marshals to enter a home in Rockville, Maryland, to arrest Dominic Wilson, a dangerous fugitive. Unbeknownst to the police, it was the home of the fugitive's parents. The arrest warrant was executed at 6:45 A.M., much to the surprise of the parents. After discovering that Dominic was not at the house, the arrest team departed. The team "was accompanied by a reporter and a photographer from the *Washington Post,* who had been invited by the Marshals to accompany them on their mission as part of a Marshal's service ride-along policy." The reporter took numerous photographs but none were published. The reporter was in the living room and observed a scuffle and the handcuffing of Mr. Wilson, who was wearing briefs. The reporters did not assist in executing the warrant. The Wilsons brought a civil lawsuit for money damages against the Marshal's service for violating their Fourth Amendment right of privacy by bringing reporters into their home.

The government tried to justify the **media ride-along** by arguing that (1) media presence promotes accurate reporting and crime fighting, (2) the presence of third parties minimizes police abuses and protects the suspects, and (3) the police should be allowed to determine if these law enforcement interests are advanced by the ride-along. The Court found these reasons unpersuasive. These factors, even if reasonable, promote *general* interests and are not sufficient to overcome the *specific* constitutional right held by the Wilsons.

The Court did not refer to *Katz* or the expectation of privacy in *Wilson;* instead it emphasized the "the importance of the right of residential privacy at the core of the Fourth Amendment," a "centuries-old principle of respect for the privacy of the home." Beyond this, the Court did not reason except to say that, "Were such generalized 'law enforcement objectives' themselves sufficient to trump the Fourth Amendment, the protections guaranteed by that Amendment's text would be significantly watered down." *Wilson* shows a trend of the modern Court to emphasize the expectation of privacy in the home but not to apply the *Katz* doctrine to the fullest extent in other areas of law enforcement practice.

EXPECTATION OF PRIVACY IN AUTOMOBILES   There is a lesser expectation of privacy in an automobile than in a home (*California v. Carney,* 1985). The Supreme Court has found that at common law mobile vehicles could be stopped without a warrant and has generally extended this exception into the Fourth Amendment "automobile exception" (*Carroll v. United States,* 1925). Yet, the Court has applied the expectation of privacy doctrine to the stopping of automobiles by United States Border Patrol Officers, and later to all police agencies, and has found that the stopping of an automobile is a seizure, and that it can cause annoyance or fright. Therefore, a warrantless stop of a vehicle must be justified by reasonable suspicion or probable cause of a traffic violation or crime (*United States v. Brignoni-Ponce*, 1975; *Delaware v. Prouse*, 1979). On the other hand, because a stop at a fixed checkpoint does not produce the same anxiety as that associated with being stopped by a roving patrol, the expectation of privacy is less and the stop need not be justified by particularized suspicion. (*United States v. Martinez-Fuerte*, 1976; *Mich. Dep. of State Police v. Sitz*, 1990)

EXPECTATION OF PRIVACY IN PROPERTY AND EFFECTS
The Supreme Court has held that a *footlocker* is protected by a subjective and objective expectation of privacy. Police had probable cause to believe that a footlocker contained marijuana, had arrested its possessor, and had the luggage in custody. Opening the footlocker violated Chadwick's Fourth Amendment rights and the evidence was suppressed. The police should have sought a search warrant from a magistrate (*United States v. Chadwick*, 1977). The Court has further extended the expectation of privacy to soft baggage that was squeezed by a Border Patrol agent. A bus traveling from California to Arkansas stopped at a Border Patrol checkpoint in Texas, and the agent boarded the bus to check the immigration status of its passengers. After reaching the back of the bus, having satisfied himself that the passengers were lawfully in the United States, the agent began walking toward the front. Along the way, he squeezed the soft luggage that passengers had placed in the overhead storage space above the seats. He squeezed a green canvas bag belonging to passenger Steven Dewayne Bond and noticed that it contained a "brick-like" object later identified as methamphetamine. The Supreme Court held that this physical examination was a search. Bond exhibited an actual expectation of privacy by using an opaque bag and placing that bag directly above his seat. The agent's manipulation of the bag went beyond that tolerated by society:

> When a bus passenger places a bag in an overhead bin, he expects that other passengers or bus employees may move it for one reason or another. Thus, a bus passenger clearly expects that his bag may be handled. He does not expect that other passengers or bus employees will, as a matter of course, feel the bag in an exploratory manner. But this is exactly what the agent did here. We therefore hold that the agent's physical manipulation of petitioner's bag violated the Fourth Amendment. (**Bond v. United States**, 2000)

On the other hand, the Court has come close to stating that a person has no expectation of privacy in the *odor of drugs* emanating from a piece of luggage in a public area if detected by a trained drug-sniffing canine (*United States v. Place*, 1983). There is no expectation of privacy in *abandoned property* such as *trash* left in opaque plastic bags at curbside. It may be seized and searched without a warrant. The general public does not believe that a person expects trash to be kept private because the bags can be opened by children playing, by animals, or by scavengers (***California v. Greenwood,*** 1988). The same result occurs under the older property theory: once people abandon property, they lose all control over it.

EXPECTATION OF PRIVACY IN BUSINESS RECORDS AND COMMERCIAL PROPERTY   The Court has held that by depositing money in banks, people expose financial information in *bank records* to strangers such as bank employees and thus lose an expectation of privacy. As a result, Congress may require that large cash or other transactions be reported to federal agencies without showing particularized suspicion. One's banking records can be subpoenaed by the government under the Bank Secrecy Act (*California Bankers Association v. Schultz*, 1974; *United States v. Miller*, 1976).

The Court has held that *business records* are not protected by the Fifth Amendment privilege against compelled self-incrimination, and thus are subject to seizure under the Fourth Amendment with a proper search warrant (*Andresen v. Maryland*, 1976). *Business premises* are protected by the Fourth Amendment (*Hale v. Henkel*, 1906; *See v. City of Seattle*, 1967). If commercial property is open to the public, such as a retail store, a police agent may enter the premises and observe or purchase suspected items, and such an entry and purchase is not a search and seizure (*Maryland v. Macon*, 1985). Although warrants are required for commercial health or safety inspections under the *Camara–See* doctrine, they require a lesser standard of evidence than the traditional probable cause standard (*Marshall v. Barlow's, Inc.*, 1978). Some commercial properties are subject to warrantless inspections, although retaining expectations of privacy, because of the nature of the business or the special risks that the business creates (e.g., mining) (*Donovan v. Dewey*, 1981).

Undercover Agents and the Fourth Amendment

In *Gouled v. United States* (1921) Army investigators sent a "secret agent" into Gouled's office, not by means of a trespass or burglary, but by false pretenses. The Court held that a physical seizure of papers in these circumstances violated Gouled's Fourth Amendment rights. The question not answered was whether gaining entry by false pretenses invalidated the use of statements made in confidence by the suspect to the **undercover agent**. The Supreme Court resolved the issue in two cases decided on the same day in 1966. There is no Fourth Amendment right of privacy against "inviting" a person who is a secret government agent into the home.

Lewis v. United States (1966) dealt with the common situation of a narcotics agent being invited into a home to conclude an illicit drug transaction after having misrepresented his intentions. The Fourth Amendment was not violated because Lewis had converted his home "into a commercial center to which outsiders are invited for purposes of transacting unlawful business." Whether one applies the older property theory or the *Katz* expectation of privacy concept of Fourth Amendment rights, there is no constitutional violation in this scenario. The Court warned that entry gained by invitation did not give the undercover investigator the right to conduct a general search of the premises. In *Lewis* the Court also expressed its concern for the practical needs of law enforcement:

Were we to hold the deceptions of the agent in this case constitutionally prohibited, we would come near to a rule that the use of undercover agents in any manner is virtually unconstitutional *per se*. Such a rule would, for example, severely hamper the Government in ferreting out those organized criminal activities that are characterized by covert dealings with victims who either cannot or do not protest. A prime example is provided by the narcotics traffic. (*Lewis v. United States*, p. 210, footnote omitted)

In *Hoffa v. United States* (1966) national Teamster Union president James Hoffa was convicted of bribing jurors in an earlier trial. Evidence of the jury tampering was offered by Edward Partin, a teamster union official who was in trouble with the law, and who was present in Hoffa's hotel apartment during the earlier trial. He had assisted Hoffa while simultaneously reporting on the jury tampering to federal agents. Partin went to Hoffa's apartment as a government agent; in return for his spying, state and federal criminal charges against him were dropped and Partin's wife was paid $1,200 out of government funds. Hoffa argued that Partin's entry into the apartment violated his Fourth Amendment right to privacy and was an illegal "search" for verbal evidence. The Court agreed that Hoffa had a Fourth Amendment right to privacy in the hotel apartment, and that entry could have been made both by a trespass and, as in *Gouled*, by trickery. What Hoffa relied on was the protection offered by the place. Thus, if Partin had opened a desk drawer or a filing cabinet and stolen incriminating evidence, this would have intruded into Hoffa's constitutionally protected area. The same result would occur by applying the *Katz* expectation of privacy analysis. However,

> It is obvious that [Hoffa] was not relying on the security of his hotel suite when he made the incriminating statements to Partin or in Partin's presence. Partin did not enter the suite by force or by stealth. He was not a surreptitious eavesdropper. Partin was in the suite by invitation, and every conversation which he heard was either directed to him or knowingly carried on in his presence. The petitioner, in a word, was not relying on the security of the hotel room; he was relying upon his misplaced confidence that Partin would not reveal his wrongdoing. . . .
>
> Neither this Court nor any member of it has ever expressed the view that the Fourth Amendment protects a wrongdoer's misplaced belief that a person to whom he voluntarily confides his wrongdoing will not reveal it. (*Hoffa v. United States*, p. 302)

The Fourth Amendment does not protect a person against false friends.

A related question is whether there is any Fourth Amendment protection when a "false friend" wears a concealed microphone on his body to transmit and/or record incriminating conversations. The Supreme Court has consistently ruled that this practice is not prohibited by the Fourth Amendment. When a person "invites" an undercover agent to speak with him voluntarily, the effect of the recording device is to improve the accuracy of the agent's testimony against the defendant. The Court has so held, both before and after *Katz,* and the federal electronic eavesdropping law has confirmed this rule as a matter of federal law.[29]

SURVEILLANCE AND ELECTRONIC EAVESDROPPING IN A TIME OF TERROR

In 1968 Congress legitimized electronic eavesdropping in Title III of the Crime Control Act of 1968. The Act built on the lessons of the *Burger* and *Katz* cases by requiring extensive probable cause for an eavesdropping warrant. A warrant application had to specify the persons whose conversations were sought, what information the conversations were expected to reveal, and prior attempts to get information. Eavesdropping had to be kept to a minimum and the government could keep a listening device in place for a maximum of thirty days. Title III allowed the president to authorize foreign intelligence eavesdropping without a warrant. The United States Supreme Court declared this presidential power unconstitutional in *United States v. United States District Court* (1972). After the Watergate crisis, a Senate report criticized the use of national security eavesdropping by the Nixon Administration to spy on the activities of its political opponents. This led to the passage of the Foreign Intelligence Surveillance Act (FISA) in 1978, setting up a special court (FISC), consisting of seven sitting federal judges. They review applications for a court order approving the use of electronic surveillance to obtain foreign intelligence information. The act applied to electronic eavesdropping and in 1994 was expanded to cover physical searches. "Between 1979 and 2001, there were 14,036 applications for FISA surveillances or searches. During that time period, all but one of these requests were granted."[30] Only four applications were modified before being issued.

The USA PATRIOT Act expanded the number of judges on the FISC to eleven and, with "two little words," made a major change in the law. Under the original act, FISA applications were only properly granted when foreign intelligence, from a foreign power or its agent, was "*the purpose*" of the investigation. Under the 2001 amendment, the government must certify "that *a significant* purpose of the surveillance is to obtain foreign intelligence information." The definition of a "foreign power" includes "a group engaged in international terrorism or activities in preparation therefor."[31]

The significance of the change from "the purpose" to "a significant purpose" was to eliminate a practice known as "the wall" between the justice department and intelligence agencies, especially the CIA, to allow greater cooperation between the FBI and the CIA. After the misuse of foreign intelligence eavesdropping by President Nixon, there was a concern that eavesdropping warrants obtained under the more lenient FISA standards not be used for prosecuting criminals. In the aftermath of 9/11, it came to light that FBI field agents had sought help from the CIA to investigate Zacarias Moussaoui, believed to be the twentieth 9/11 hijacker. FBI officials at headquarters saw this as a breach of protocol, and before September 11, 2001, rejected a request from the Minneapolis field office to seek a warrant to search Moussaoui's computer.[32] In light of the FBI's demonstrated weaknesses in antiterrorism, greater cooperation was certainly called for. Whether it *should* include using FISA warrants *only* for preventive purposes in the war on terrorism, and not for prosecution, was answered not only by Congress, but also by the courts.

In a first-ever appeal taken from a decision of the FISC to the Foreign Intelligence Surveillance Court of Review, the FISC had issued a warrant but added a special condition that "law enforcement officials shall not make recommendations to intelligence officials concerning the initiation, operation, continuation or expansion of FISA searches or surveillances." The Court of Review reversed the special condition, noting that the FISC "apparently believes it can approve applications for electronic surveillance only if the government's objective is *not* primarily directed toward criminal prosecution of the foreign agents for their foreign intelligence activity."[33] This, however, was not supported by text of the FISA or the USA PATRIOT Act. The FISC relied on "minimization procedures" in the law to justify its special condition. The Court of Review struck this down as not being in the language or legislative history of the act. It pointed out that

> the definition of foreign intelligence information includes evidence of crimes such as espionage, sabotage or terrorism. Indeed, it is virtually impossible to read the 1978 FISA to exclude from its purpose the prosecution of foreign intelligence crimes, most importantly because, as we have noted, the definition of an agent of a foreign power—if he or she is a U.S. person—is grounded on criminal conduct.[34]

Further, the Court of Review agreed with the government that "arresting and prosecuting terrorist agents of, or spies for, a foreign power may well be the best technique to prevent them from successfully continuing their terrorist or espionage activity."[35]

The attempt by the FISC to preserve the "wall" between the intelligence and the law enforcement/prosecutorial branches of the executive were in part stimulated by the fact that in at least seventy-five cases it was misled by the FBI, which misstated or omitted material facts and sought to allow intelligence material to be shared freely with criminal investigators.[36] It is true that the older, clear distinction between foreign intelligence threats and terrorism, which is defined largely by crimes of violence, has broken down. Perhaps the use of FISA warrants in terrorism cases that result in criminal prosecution will improve necessary cooperation between intelligence agencies and the FBI. Several commentators, however, have argued that the PATRIOT Act Amendment to FISA is unconstitutional and raises serious risks of misuse.[37] The dangers are real that investigators will try to avoid the more stringent requirements of Title III, which often require applications of a hundred pages, and take the easier FISA warrant route, which allows for ninety days of surveillance for U.S. persons (citizens and legal aliens) as opposed to thirty days for Title III warrants. One commentator fears that the "result is an open season for law enforcement officials to conduct illegitimate and indiscriminate wiretapping on individuals without the threshold requirements mandated by the Fourth Amendment."[38]

PROBABLE CAUSE AND THE FOURTH AMENDMENT

The Fourth Amendment states that warrants must be issued on **probable cause,** and this standard has been used as the touchstone of all Fourth Amendment action, including arrests, warrantless searches, and both search and arrest warrants. Until *Terry v. Ohio* (1967), a forcible police interference with liberty, property, or privacy on less than probable cause violated the Fourth Amendment. *Terry*'s flexible interpretation, first applied to field interrogation, introduced the lower evidentiary standard of reasonable suspicion. This section explores the meaning and contours of probable cause.

The Concept of Evidence Sufficiency

Liberty is a fundamental precept of American political life. This means that a person's liberty interests—freedom of movement, privacy, or property—must not be stopped or interfered with by the government unless the government can first show a need to interfere that is justified by law. In Fourth Amendment terms, a police officer must have *evidence* to support a stop, arrest, or search *before* the search takes place. The best way for a police agent to do this is to obtain a warrant. If a warrantless stop, arrest, or search is challenged, the officer must convince a court that he or she had a sufficient level of evidence to lawfully interfere with the defendant's liberty interests. In other areas where the criminal justice or legal process interferes with liberty, other levels of evidence sufficiency are required. This is illustrated in Table 3-1. The concept of evidence sufficiency is therefore a latent part of due process and helps to ensure fundamental fairness.

Defining Probable Cause

Probable cause is defined as *known facts that could lead a reasonably prudent person to draw conclusions about unknown facts,* and is a standard of *evidence* that triggers and justifies government interference with liberty. It is also referred to as *reasonable cause.* Because the evidence standard for stops under *Terry v. Ohio* is commonly known as "*reasonable suspicion,*" it is important to use these terms precisely as technical terms. Evidence is any kind of proof offered to establish the existence of a fact. Evidence may be (1) the *testimony* of a witness as to what was heard, seen, smelled, tasted, or felt: or (2) *physical items* such as documents, drugs, or weapons. Physical evidence is sometimes called *real evidence.*

Probable cause is one of several standards of evidence that trigger and justify intrusive governmental action. Table 3-1 displays a hierarchy of evidentiary standards. These standards pertain to the *sufficiency* or *weight* of evidence rather than to its admissibility. In general, the greater the impact of a legal action on an individual, the more stringent is the evidentiary standard.

Probable cause is the evidentiary standard for a wide variety of police and legal decisions in the pretrial criminal process: Arrest, search and seizure, a magistrate authorizing a

TABLE 3–1 STANDARDS OF EVIDENCE SUFFICIENCY

STANDARD	MEANING	LEGAL CONSEQUENCE
Proof beyond a reasonable doubt	No actual and substantial doubt must be present; not a vague apprehension or imaginary doubt; not absolute certainty	Conviction of guilt in a criminal trial
Clear and convincing evidence	Higher than a preponderance of evidence; need not be conclusive	Hold a person without bail under preventive detention; involuntary civil commitment; establish civil fraud; prove a gift
Preponderance of the evidence	Evidence reasonably tending to prove the essential facts in a case; the greater weight of the evidence	Verdict for the plaintiff in a civil litigation
Prima facie case	Evidence good and sufficient on its face to prove a fact or group of facts	Evidence that makes out the plaintiff's or prosecutor's case at trial and is strong enough to prevent a directed verdict for the defendant; in some jurisdictions, a prima facie case is required as the basis for indictment instead of probable cause
Substantial evidence on the whole record	Such evidence that a reasonable mind might accept as adequate to support a conclusion	Judicial review upholding administrative agency action
Probable cause	Known facts that would lead a reasonably prudent person to draw a conclusion about unknown facts	Lawful arrest; reasonable search and seizure; judicial determination to hold a suspect after an initial inquiry; bindover by magistrate after preliminary examination; prosecutor's information; indictment after grand jury deliberations
Reasonable suspicion	Facts that would lead an experienced police officer to believe that a crime has been, is being, or is about to be committed	Stop, pat-down search of outer clothing, and brief questioning of a person
None or "mere" suspicion	Whimsy; randomness; mere suspicion	Observation and surveillance of person by police or government agent that does not amount to harassment or otherwise unduly interfere with the reasonable expectation of privacy

charge after an initial hearing, a magistrate's bindover decision after a preliminary hearing, and the formal charging of a criminal defendant by a prosecutor's information or by an indictment by a grand jury voting a "true bill" against a suspect. (In some states, the grand jury or bindover decision might be subjected to the slightly more rigorous "prima facie case" standard.) Probable cause to *arrest* a person consists of facts that would lead a prudent person to believe that a crime has been committed and that the suspect has committed it. Probable cause to *search* a place and seize evidence consists of facts that would lead a prudent person to believe that "seizable" items (i.e., contraband, the fruits of a crime, instrumentalities used to commit a crime, or evidence of criminality) are or soon will be located at a particular place.

The line between probable cause and the lesser reasonable suspicion standard is a fine one. *Terry* (1967) did not use the term "reasonable suspicion" but upheld a temporary "stop"—a lesser intrusion than an arrest—where an officer believed that "criminal activity is afoot" based on *articulable facts,* taken together with logical inferences from those facts. A mere

hunch does not support reasonable suspicion. Reasonable suspicion will be explored at greater length in Chapter 4.

Probable cause is not only a lower "weight" of evidence than that needed for civil or criminal verdicts, but it also relies on less stringent rules guiding the admissibility of evidence. Thus, probable cause may be established on the basis of *hearsay evidence;* it is up to the magistrate to weigh the hearsay to determine whether it is plausible and genuine on the one hand, or farfetched or even fabricated on the other.

Probable Cause Based on Informers' Tips

An officer/affiant seeking a search warrant swears to the magistrate that the information presented is true. Where the officer affirms that he or she saw things or smelled odors (common in drug cases) that would lead a prudent person to believe that contraband is located at a specific place, the magistrate can directly question the officer to be sure of the accuracy of the evidence. Likewise, information given to an officer or magistrate by a victim of a crime is usually considered to be honest and accurate.

However, much criminal activity—including bribery by government officials, white-collar crime, organized crime, and illicit drug trading—is conducted in secret. Officers or blameless victims cannot get access to the criminal behavior. Often, the only way for law enforcement agencies to detect and prosecute such crimes is by using undercover agents to infiltrate the worlds of drug trafficking, organized crime, and white-collar crime. These **secret informants** are themselves often involved in criminal activity. Professors Robert Reinertsen and Robert Bronson state, "Informants are generally unsavory types, engaged in marginal activities that involve betrayal of others. Nonetheless, despite their negative image, informants play such a large and important role in law enforcement efforts that they cannot be ignored."[39] The common terms—snitch, fink, stool pigeon—attests to the negative image and reality of informants. They rarely aid the police out of altruistic motives. More likely, they are being paid, given a promise of prosecutorial leniency, or even rewarded with illicit drugs.

Law enforcement agencies are caught in a dilemma. Knowing the risk of receiving unreliable information when using criminal informants, agencies establish policies regarding informants' recruitment, control, and payment. The proper use of informants depends in large measure on the honesty and mature judgment of the law enforcement officers who control them and good management practices.[40]

Despite internal law enforcement controls, informants have an incentive to lie, and have in numerous cases sent innocent persons to prison.[41] The question facing the judicial system is whether it can take steps to ensure that the threat to justice from lying informants is minimized. One solution would be to have the police bring informers before the magistrate so that instead of presenting hearsay, the magistrate can examine the informant personally. The Supreme Court refused to take this path. In *Rovario v. United States* (1957) the Court held that the identity of an informant must be made available at the trial, but prior to trial, law enforcement agencies are allowed to keep the identity of informants secret (see judicial biography of Justice Harold Burton, Chapter 4). There is a legitimate fear that bringing the informant to the courthouse, and having the identity made known to judges and other court personnel, would undermine the integrity and success of investigations. It is also not the role of the judicial branch to exercise administrative oversight of the executive branch.

Still, magistrates play an important role in screening out fabrications by informants. When magistrates receive affidavits for search warrants based on information supplied by unnamed informants, they have good reason to be cautious and to examine the affidavit with special care. The Court has, indeed, confirmed this notion by establishing an *exclusionary rule*—evidence seized on the basis of a search warrant or a warrant affidavit that does not adequately state the facts that constitute probable cause and explain the source of its information violates the probable cause requirement of the Fourth Amendment and is inadmissible.

In *Nathanson v. United States* (1933) the Court excluded liquor seized from a private home based on a warrant that "went upon a mere affirmation of suspicion and belief without any statement of adequate supporting facts." A magistrate could not "properly issue a warrant to search a private dwelling unless he can find probable cause therefor from facts or circumstances presented to him under oath or affirmation. Mere affirmance of belief or suspicion is not enough." Another way of stating the rule of *Nathanson* is that a magistrate cannot issue a warrant on the mere say-so of the officer or on a hunch about the suspect's behavior or reputation.

Nathanson was supported in *Aguilar v. Texas* (1964). The search warrant application from police officers simply stated that "Affiants have received reliable information from a credible person and do believe" that drugs are located in Aguilar's home. Here, the hearsay basis of the officers' suspicions was more clearly stated than in *Nathanson*. The Court reaffirmed that "an affidavit may be based on hearsay information and need not reflect the direct personal observations of the affiant." Nevertheless, "the magistrate must be informed of some of the *underlying circumstances* from which the informant concluded that the narcotics were where he claimed they were, and some of the underlying circumstances from which the officer concluded that the informant, whose identity need not be disclosed, was '*credible*' or his information '*reliable*'" (*Aguilar v. Texas,* emphasis added). Again, the Supreme Court ruled that a magistrate's warrant is fatally flawed under the Fourth Amendment if the magistrate simply takes the police officer's word that an informant was reliable or credible, and that the contraband is where the officer says it is. This rule is a necessary corollary to the "detached and neutral magistrate" doctrine. If a warrant is issued simply on an officer's say-so, the magistrate becomes a rubber stamp for the executive branch and fails to uphold his or her duty under the Constitution. Justice John Harlan, a conservative jurist, concurred in *Aguilar*. Justice Clark's dissent, joined by Justices Black and Stewart, argued that the officers' statement that they "received reliable information from a credible person" was sufficient to provide probable cause.

The rule of *Aguilar* was confirmed and strengthened in *Spinelli v. United States* (1969). William Spinelli was being investigated by the FBI for bookmaking in St. Louis. A search warrant was obtained to enter an apartment for evidence of an illegal gambling establishment. The affidavit, when reduced to its essential information, contained four facts: (1) that for four of the five days he was followed, Spinelli crossed into Missouri from Illinois at about noon, went to the same apartment house about 4:00 P.M., and was seen to enter a particular apartment; (2) that there were two telephones in the apartment listed under another's name; (3) that Spinelli had a reputation as a bookmaker and gambler among law enforcement agents, including the affiant; and (4) that a "confidential reliable informant" told the FBI agent that Spinelli was operating a gambling operation with the telephones in the apartment. Evidence seized in the apartment was used to convict Spinelli of interstate travel in aid of racketeering, specifically, of illegal bookmaking.

Justice Harlan wrote the majority opinion holding that this affidavit did not provide probable cause and the evidence seized had to be excluded. He quickly tossed out the first three items in the affidavit as essentially not supportive of probable cause. There is simply no reason why traveling from one city to another every day would lead anyone to suspect the traveler of being a bookie. The existence of two telephones in the apartment, described as a "petty luxury" was also deemed not at all suspicious.

The third item, Spinelli's *reputation,* was dismissed: "the allegation that Spinelli was 'known' to the affiant and to other federal and local law enforcement officers as a gambler is but a bald and unilluminating assertion of suspicion that is entitled to no weight in appraising the magistrate's decision." Justice Harlan cited *Nathanson* for this point. Reputation evidence is hearsay and hearsay is proper evidence in a search warrant affidavit. It would appear that the Court, almost instinctively, understood that hearsay about an individual can be entirely baseless and scurrilous, and indeed, could even be manufactured by the government. Although it may be useful as a starting point for investigation, the reliance on a person's reputation as a matter of Fourth Amendment law could lead to gross injustices.

This, then, left the statement about the "confidential reliable informant" as the sole basis for the warrant. The prosecution argued that the innocent facts in the affidavit corroborated the informant's tip "thereby entitling it to more weight." The Court disagreed, saying that "the *totality of circumstances*' approach . . . paints with too broad a brush." Instead of a "totality" approach, Justice Harlan, refining the elements of the *Aguilar* case, provided "a more precise analysis" by which the affidavit's statements regarding a secret informant had to stand on its own. He stated the rules of *Aguilar* that could be reduced to two tests:

[W]e first consider the weight to be given the informer's tip when it is considered apart from the rest of the affidavit. It is clear that a Commissioner could not credit it without abdicating his constitutional function. Though the affiant swore that his confidant was "reliable," he offered the magistrate no reason in support of this conclusion. Perhaps even more important is the fact that *Aguilar*'s other test has not been satisfied. The tip does not contain a sufficient statement of the underlying circumstances from which the informer concluded that Spinelli was running a bookmaking operation. We are not told how the FBI's source received his information—it is not alleged that the informant personally observed Spinelli at work or that he had ever placed a bet with him. Moreover, if the informant came by the information indirectly, he did not explain why his sources were reliable. . . . In the absence of a statement detailing the manner in which the information was gathered, it is especially important that the tip describe the accused's criminal activity in sufficient detail that the magistrate may know that he is relying on something more substantial than a casual rumor circulating in the underworld or an accusation based merely on an individual's general reputation. (*Spinelli v. United States,* p. 416)

The *Aguilar-Spinelli* "two-pronged test" to obtaining a warrant based on an informer's hearsay includes: (1) a *veracity,* or truthfulness, prong—showing that the informant is truthful because he was used successfully in the past or because the tip is so strong, or so well corroborated, that it is inherently believable; and (2) a *basis-of-knowledge* prong— showing that the facts were obtained by the informant in a manner that is sufficiently reliable to establish probable cause. The facts that support the prongs must be strong enough to convince the magistrate making an *independent determination* that the informant had a real basis for knowing about the criminal activity. The facts would also give the magistrate a basis for ascertaining whether they support probable cause.

The dissenters in *Spinelli,* Justices Black, Fortas, and Stewart, felt that the four elements found wanting by the majority constituted probable cause. Justice Fortas referred to the length of the affidavit to indicate that it was not simply conclusory. But he did not adequately respond to Justice Harlan's analysis that cut through the lengthy verbiage of the affidavit to reduce it to its essential elements. Justice White concurred in the holding of *Spinelli,* but he expressed concern that *Spinelli*'s holding did not fully comport with that of *Draper v. United States* (1959), on which the Court relied.

Justice Harlan, in *Spinelli,* demonstrated how a magistrate should critically evaluate information presented in an affidavit by drawing on the 1959 case of **Draper v. United States.** In that case, a paid informer named Hereford told Bureau of Narcotics agents that Draper would travel from Chicago to Denver on a train on one of two days with three ounces of heroin. Hereford precisely described what Draper looked like, and told the agents that Draper would be carrying "a tan zipper bag," that he habitually "walked real fast," and would be wearing a light-colored raincoat, brown slacks, and black shoes. Agents waited at the incoming trains from Chicago in the Denver station and saw a man fitting the exact description given by Hereford. The man was arrested and turned out to be Draper, carrying heroin. The Supreme Court held that the agents had probable cause to arrest and search Draper, based on the hearsay description of the informant, Hereford. Significantly, Hereford did not provide information to show how he obtained his information about Draper: the "basis of knowledge" prong of the *Aguilar-Spinelli* rule was absent. The Supreme Court upheld the seizure and search in Draper because the highly detailed facts were verified by the agent (except for the possession of heroin) before making the arrest. Draper, therefore, stands for the proposition that any weaknesses in the information provided by the informant can be strengthened by the police gathering *corroborating* information.

Conservative Revisions

A task of the Supreme Court, to lay down clear rules for the guidance of lower court judges and government officers, seems to have been fulfilled in *Spinelli* when the Court clarified a line of informers' tip decisions, beginning with *Nathanson v. United States* (1933), with relatively clear procedural guides for resolving probable cause issues. *Spinelli* exemplified the Warren Court's penchant for establishing structured rules. This changed with the advent of the Burger Court as conservative activism replaced liberal activism.

Professor Charles Whitebread described the five elements of the Burger Court's criminal procedure jurisprudence (see Chapter 1):[42]

- A crime control orientation.
- A constitutional hierarchy that values Sixth Amendment trial rights above Fourth Amendment rights.
- A preference for case-by-case analysis rather than establishing general rules.
- A tendency to uphold the prosecution if the Court believes the defendant is factually guilty.
- The denial of federal jurisdiction from state cases.

These tendencies were clearly at work in *Illinois v. Gates,* which upset the *Aguilar-Spinelli* rule after fourteen years during which there was little criticism of the two-pronged test.

—*Illinois v. Gates* Case & Comments—

It is interesting that the nine justices came up with four different analyses of whether the facts established probable cause:

1. The majority (Chief Justice Burger and Justices Rehnquist, Blackmun, Powell, and O'Connor) found probable cause to exist under the new totality-of-the-circumstances test.
2. Justice White, concurring, found that probable cause existed under the *Aguilar-Spinelli* two-pronged test.
3. Justices Brennan and Marshall, dissenting, found that the anonymous letter plus the corroboration did not amount to probable cause under either test.
4. Justice Stevens, dissenting, found no probable cause because at the time the magistrate issued the warrant, he did *not* know that the Gateses' had driven twenty-two hours nonstop from West Palm Beach to Bloomingdale, a suspicious activity in light of the anonymous letter. The anonymous letter predicted that Sue would fly back to Illinois while Lance drove. This discrepancy undermined probable cause because it indicated (1) the Gateses' willingness to leave their house unattended implied it did not contain drugs, and (2) that their activity was not as unusual as if they had left separately.

Gates is a constitutionally important decision that significantly shifted the criminal procedure balance in favor of the state, a result that has been criticized by some legal commentators.[43] An interesting study published in 2000, examining the practices of six Atlanta-area police academies, shows that the departments train their officers in the *Aguilar-Spinelli* two-pronged test rather than the open-ended *Gates* totality test. Two reasons were given by the training officers: (1) they felt that prosecutors and courts were likely to demand adherence to the two-pronged or a similar test, and (2) "almost all of the instructors stated that they did not believe a majority of their recruits could master the intricacies of an open-ended standard such as the *Gates* standard."[44] This is contrary to the main reason given by Justice Rehnquist for the majority opinion. This

would not be the first time that police practice did not agree with legal speculation.

PLAIN VIEW AND RELATED DOCTRINES

Plain view is a useful doctrine for police officers. It allows *seizures* of evidence without a warrant when the police are *already* lawfully in a place or have made a *lawful search*. This section also examines the related "open fields" doctrine and the use of enhancement devices.

Plain View

The simple idea that a police officer can seize contraband lying about in a public place is so obvious that it has rarely been litigated. In **Cardwell v. Lewis** (1974) the Court articulated the principle that there is no Fourth Amendment privacy interest in material or possessions that are exposed to public scrutiny. In this case, a car owned by a murder suspect was in a public parking lot; the police scraped a bit of paint from a fender to be used as evidence. The court found no constitutional violation: "where probable cause exists, a warrantless examination of the exterior of a car is not unreasonable under the Fourth and Fourteenth Amendments."

It is a different matter for police to seize material from inside a place that is protected by the Fourth Amendment. Professors Whitebread and Slobogin assert, correctly, that a police officer who saw marijuana through a house window while standing on a sidewalk could not enter and seize the evidence, although in a factual sense it was in "plain view."[47] As the Supreme Court stated in *Agnello v. United States* (1925): "Belief, however well-founded, that an article sought is concealed in a dwelling house furnishes no justification for a search of that place without a warrant." In such a case, the officer would have to obtain a warrant to enter lawfully.

PRIOR JUSTIFIED SEARCH   The basic rules of plain view were established in **Coolidge v. New Hampshire** (1971). In that case, Justice Stewart, writing for a plurality, made clear the ancillary or "piggyback," nature of the doctrine:

> What the "plain view" cases have in common is that the police officer in each of them had a *prior justification* for an intrusion. . . . The doctrine serves to supplement the prior justification— whether it be a warrant for another object, hot pursuit, search incident to lawful arrest, or some other legitimate reason for being present unconnected with a search directed against the accused—and permits the warrantless seizure. (*Coolidge v. New Hampshire,* p. 466, emphasis added)

Under *Katz,* a plain view seizure of property is justified on the ground that there is no reasonable expectation of privacy in items that are contraband or the clear evidence of crime; police have a legitimate interest, not blocked by the Fourth Amendment, to take such items.

Nevertheless, it must be stressed that the *first rule* of plain view is that there must be a *lawful intrusion*. In *Coolidge,* Justice Stewart noted:

Illinois v. Gates
462 U.S. 213, 103 S.Ct. 2317, 76 L.Ed.2d 527 (1983)

JUSTICE REHNQUIST delivered the opinion of the Court.

Respondents Lance and Susan Gates were indicted for violation of state drug laws after police officers, executing a search warrant, discovered marihuana and other contraband in their automobile and home. * * * The Illinois Supreme Court * * * held that the affidavit submitted in support of the State's application for a warrant to search the Gateses' property was inadequate under this Court's decisions in *Aguilar v. Texas,* 378 U.S. 108 (1964) and *Spinelli v. United States* (1969).

We granted certiorari to consider the application of the Fourth Amendment to a magistrate's issuance of a search warrant on the basis of a partially corroborated anonymous informant's tip. * * *

* * *

II

* * * On May 3, 1978, the Bloomingdale Police Department received by mail an anonymous handwritten letter which read as follows: **[a]**

> "This letter is to inform you that you have a couple in your town who strictly make their living on selling drugs. They are Sue and Lance Gates, they live on Greenway, off Bloomingdale Rd. in the condominiums. Most of their buys are done in Florida. Sue his wife drives their car to Florida, where she leaves it to be loaded up with drugs, then Lance flys down and drives it back. Sue flys back after she drops the car off in Florida. May 3 she is driving down there again and Lance will be flying down in a few days to drive it back. At the time Lance drives the car back he has the trunk loaded with over $100,000.00 in drugs. Presently they have over $100,000.00 worth of drugs in their basement.
>
> "They brag about the fact they never have to work, and make their entire living on pushers.
>
> I guarantee if you watch them carefully you will make a big catch. They are friends with some big drugs dealers, who visit their house often.
> "Lance & Susan Gates
> "Greenway
> "in Condominiums"

The letter was referred by the Chief of Police * * * to Detective Mader, who decided to pursue the tip. Mader learned * * * that an Illinois driver's license had been issued to one Lance Gates, residing at a stated address in Bloomingdale. He contacted a confidential informant, whose examination of certain financial records revealed a more recent address for the Gateses, and he also learned from a police officer assigned to O'Hare Airport that "L. Gates" had made a reservation on Eastern Airlines Flight 245 to West Palm Beach, Fla., scheduled to depart from Chicago on May 5 at 4:15 P.M.

Mader then made arrangements with an agent of the Drug Enforcement Administration for surveillance of the May 5 Eastern Airlines flight. The agent later reported to Mader that Gates had boarded the flight, and that federal agents in Florida had observed him arrive in West Palm Beach and take a taxi to the nearby Holiday Inn. They also reported that Gates went to a room registered to one Susan Gates and that, at 7 o'clock A.M. the next morning, Gates and an unidentified woman left the motel in a Mercury bearing Illinois license plates and drove northbound on an interstate highway frequently used by travelers to the Chicago area. In addition, the DEA agent informed Mader that the license plate number on the Mercury was registered to a Hornet station wagon owned by Gates. The agent also advised Mader that the driving time between West Palm Beach and Bloomingdale was approximately 22 to 24 hours. **[b]**

Mader signed an affidavit setting forth the foregoing facts, and submitted it to a judge of the Circuit Court of Du Page County, together with a copy of the anonymous letter. The judge of that court thereupon issued a search warrant for the Gateses' residence and for their automobile. The judge, in deciding to issue the warrant, could have determined that the *modus operandi* of the Gateses had been substantially corroborated. As the anonymous letter predicted, Lance Gates had flown from Chicago to West Palm Beach late in the afternoon of May 5th, had checked into a hotel room registered in the name of his wife, and, at 7 o'clock A.M. the following morning, had headed north, accompanied by an unidentified woman, out of West Palm Beach on an interstate highway used by travelers from South Florida to Chicago in an automobile bearing a license plate issued to him. **[c]**

At 5:15 A.M. on March 7, only 36 hours after he had flown out of Chicago, Lance Gates, and his wife, returned to their home in Bloomingdale, driving the car in which they had left West Palm Beach some 22 hours earlier. The Bloomingdale police were awaiting them, searched the trunk of the

[a] What motivates such an anonymous letter? Motives like envy or revenge could enhance its reliability; on the other hand, a false, incriminating letter could be written as a prank or as a means to harass someone. The police and the magistrate did not rely exclusively on the letter to initiate the search.

[b] Can you think of any *legitimate* explanations for this travel plan; are the Gateses' travels consistent only with a criminal conspiracy? If there is a legitimate explanation, does it negate probable cause to search?

[c] Is the level and type of specificity in the letter similar to, or different from, that given by Hereford in *Draper?* Although the travel plans

Mercury, and uncovered approximately 350 pounds of marihuana. A search of the Gateses' home revealed marihuana, weapons, and other contraband. * * *

The Illinois Supreme Court concluded—and we are inclined to agree—that, standing alone, the anonymous letter * * * would not provide the basis for a magistrate's determination that there was probable cause to believe contraband would be found in the Gateses' car and home. **[d]** The letter provides virtually nothing from which one might conclude that its author is either honest or his information reliable; likewise, the letter gives absolutely no indication of the basis for the writer's predictions regarding the Gateses' criminal activities. Something more was required.

* * *

[The evidence was suppressed by the Illinois courts. Each lower court held that probable cause was not made out under the *Aguilar-Spinelli* test.]

* * * The Illinois Supreme Court, like some others, apparently understood *Spinelli* as requiring that the anonymous letter satisfy each of two independent requirements before it could be relied on. * * * According to this view, the letter, as supplemented by Mader's affidavit, first had to adequately reveal the "basis of knowledge" of the letterwriter—the particular means by which he came by the information given in his report. Second, it had to provide facts sufficiently establishing either the "veracity" of the affiant's informant, or, alternatively, the "reliability" of the informant's report in this particular case.

The Illinois court, * * * found that the test had not been satisfied. First, the "veracity" prong was not satisfied because, "[t]here was simply no basis [for] conclud[ing] that the anonymous person [who wrote the letter to the Bloomingdale Police Department] was credible." * * * The court indicated that corroboration by police of details contained in the letter might never satisfy the "veracity" prong, and in any event, could not do so if, as in the present case, only "innocent" details are corroborated. * * * **[e]** In addition, the letter gave no indication of the basis of its writer's knowledge of the Gateses' activities: [it] * * * failed to provide sufficient detail to permit such an inference. Thus, it concluded that no showing of probable cause had been made.

We agree with the Illinois Supreme Court that an informant's "veracity," "reliability," and "basis of knowledge" are all highly relevant in determining the value of his report. We do not agree, however, that these elements should be understood as entirely separate and independent requirements to be rigidly exacted in every case, which the opinion of the Supreme Court of Illinois would imply. Rather, as detailed below, they should be understood simply as closely intertwined issues that may usefully illuminate the commonsense, practical question whether there is "probable cause" to believe that contraband or evidence is located in a particular place.

III

This totality-of-the-circumstances approach is far more consistent with our prior treatment of probable cause than is any rigid demand that specific "tests" be satisfied by every informant's tip. **[f]** Perhaps the central teaching of our decisions bearing on the probable-cause standard is that it is a "practical, nontechnical conception." * * * "In dealing with probable cause, * * * as the very name implies, we deal with probabilities. These are not technical; they are the factual and practical considerations of everyday life on which reasonable and prudent men, not legal technicians, act." * * *

* * * [P]robable cause is a fluid concept—turning on the assessment of probabilities in particular factual contexts—not readily, or even usefully, reduced to a neat set of legal rules. * * * "Informants' tips, like all other clues and evidence coming to a policeman on the scene, may vary greatly in their value and reliability." Rigid legal rules are ill-suited to an area of such diversity. "One simple rule will not cover every situation." * * *

Moreover, the "two-pronged test" directs analysis into two largely independent channels—the informant's "veracity" or "reliability" and his "basis of knowledge." **[g]** There are persuasive arguments against according these two elements such independent status. Instead, they are better understood as relevant considerations in the totality-of-the-circumstances analysis that traditionally has guided probable-cause determinations: a deficiency in one may be compensated for, in determining the overall reliability of a tip, by a strong showing as to the other, or by some other indicia of reliability. * * *

[Justice Rehnquist suggests that an unusually reliable informant should be believed when on occasion he fails to state the basis of knowledge regarding a prediction of crime.] * * *

* * *

We also have recognized that affidavits "are normally drafted by nonlawyers in the midst and haste of a criminal investigation. Technical requirements of elaborate specificity once exacted under common law pleadings have no proper place in this area." * * * Likewise, search and arrest warrants long have

stated in the letter were mostly corroborated, does that dissolve doubts about the fact that Officer Mader had no idea who wrote the letter?

[d] The Court is wary of information from anonymous tips—yet it does not close the door on the use of such information.

[e] Did the close match between the Gateses' travels and the letter establish the veracity of the anonymous letter writer? If so, was it veracity regarding the Gateses' travel patterns or veracity as to their drug dealing?

[f] "Totality of the circumstances" was proposed to the Court by the government in *Spinelli* but rejected by the Court at that time. What factors caused the Court to shift gears?

[g] Justice Harlan, a noted conservative, said in *Spinelli* that a weakness in one prong should not be made up in another: even a "reliable" informant may, at times, obtain information from a weak hearsay source.

• CASE & COMMENTS •

been issued by persons who are neither lawyers nor judges, and who certainly do not remain abreast of each judicial refinement of the nature of "probable cause." * * * **[h]** The rigorous inquiry into the *Spinelli* prongs and the complex superstructure of evidentiary and analytical rules that some have seen implicit in our *Spinelli* decision, cannot be reconciled with the fact that many warrants are—quite properly,—issued on the basis of nontechnical, common-sense judgments of laymen applying a standard less demanding than those used in more formal legal proceedings. Likewise, given the informal, often hurried context in which it must be applied, the "built-in subtleties," * * * of the "two-pronged test" are particularly unlikely to assist magistrates in determining probable cause.

               * * *

[Justice Rehnquist urged that courts not review the facts of magistrates' probable cause decisions, but pay them great deference. He also argued that if courts continue to scrutinize affidavits according to the two-pronged test, police will stop using warrants and will turn more to warrantless searches.]

Finally, the direction taken by decisions following *Spinelli* poorly serves "[t]he most basic function of any government": "to provide for the security of the individual and of his property." * * * **[i]** If, as the Illinois Supreme Court apparently thought, that test must be rigorously applied in every case, anonymous tips would be of greatly diminished value in police work. * * *

* * * [W]e conclude that it is wiser to abandon the "two-pronged test" established by our decisions in *Aguilar* and *Spinelli*. In its place we reaffirm the totality-of-the-circumstances analysis that traditionally has informed probable-cause determinations. * * *

               * * *

JUSTICE BRENNAN's dissent also suggests that "[w]ords such as 'practical,' 'nontechnical,' and 'common sense,' as used in the Court's opinion, are but code words for an overly permissive attitude towards police practices in derogation of the rights secured by the Fourth Amendment." * * * **[j]** [N]o one doubts that "under our Constitution only measures consistent with the Fourth Amendment may be employed by government to cure [the horrors of drug trafficking];" * * * but this agreement does not advance the inquiry as to which measures are, and which measures are not, consistent with the Fourth Amendment. "Fidelity" to the commands of the Constitution suggests balanced judgment rather than exhortation. The highest "fidelity" is not achieved by the judge who instinctively goes furthest in upholding even the most bizarre claim of individual constitutional rights, any more than it is achieved by a judge who instinctively goes furthest in accepting the most restrictive claims of governmental authorities. The task of this Court, as of other courts, is to "hold the balance true," and we think we have done that in this case.

IV

Our decisions applying the totality-of-the-circumstances analysis outlined above have consistently recognized the value of corroboration of details of an informant's tip by independent police work. * * *

               * * *

The showing of probable cause in the present case was * * * compelling. * * * **[k]** Even standing alone, the facts obtained through the independent investigation of Mader and the DEA at least suggested that the Gateses were involved in drug trafficking. In addition to being a popular vacation site, Florida is well known as a source of narcotics and other illegal drugs. * * * Lance Gates' flight to Palm Beach, his brief, overnight stay in a motel, and apparent immediate return north to Chicago in the family car, conveniently awaiting him in West Palm Beach, is as suggestive of a prearranged drug run, as it is of an ordinary vacation trip.

In addition, the judge could rely on the anonymous letter, which had been corroborated in major part by Mader's efforts. * * *

Finally, the anonymous letter contained a range of details relating not just to easily obtained facts and conditions existing at the time of the tip, but to future actions of third parties ordinarily not easily predicted. The letterwriter's accurate information as to the travel plans of each of the Gateses was of a character likely obtained only from the Gateses themselves, or from someone familiar with their not entirely ordinary travel plans. If the informant had access to accurate information of this type a magistrate could properly conclude that it was not unlikely that he also had access to reliable information of the Gateses' alleged illegal activities. Of course, the Gateses' travel plans might have been learned from a talkative neighbor or travel agent; under the "two-pronged test" developed from *Spinelli*, the character of the details in the anonymous letter might well not permit a sufficiently clear inference regarding the letterwriter's "basis of knowledge." But, as discussed previously, * * * probable cause does not demand the certainty we associate with formal trials. It is enough that there was a fair probability that the writer of the anonymous letter had obtained his entire story either from the Gateses or someone they

[h] This analysis is belied by a recent article that shows that police agencies prefer the two-prong rule reviewed at the conclusion of this case. Is Justice Rehnquist setting his sights too low regarding the mental capabilities of lay magistrates and police officers?

[i] Is this a "constitutional" reason or a "policy" reason? Can such a division be neatly made? Does this seem result-oriented?

[j] Justice Brennan, a result-oriented liberal, argues in his dissent that Justice Rehnquist's opinion is result-oriented. In reply, Justice Rehnquist makes the valid point that different justices (and different people) genuinely view constitutional rules differently.

[k] Do you agree with Justice Rehnquist that this evidence is "compelling"? Or is it a close call? When deciding to intrude into a person's home and car, should magistrates lean toward restraint? If the warrant were not issued in this case, how much additional investigation would the Bloomingdale Police Department have to do after the Gateses' return to make a stronger case for probable cause? Given the Court's allowance of a corroborated anonymous letter as the basis of probable cause, does this create a risk that a dishonest police officer will be tempted to have an "anonymous" letter submitted in a hard-to-crack case?

trusted. And corroboration of major portions of the letter's predictions provides just this probability. It is apparent, therefore, that the judge issuing the warrant had a "substantial basis for * * * conclud[ing]" that probable cause to search the Gateses' home and car existed. The judgment of the Supreme Court of Illinois therefore must be

Reversed.

JUSTICE BRENNAN, with whom JUSTICE MARSHALL joins, dissenting.

* * *

I

* * *

Until today the Court has never squarely addressed the application of the *Aguilar* and *Spinelli* standards to tips from anonymous informants. Both *Aguilar* and *Spinelli* dealt with tips from informants known at least to the police. * * * And surely there is even more reason to subject anonymous informants' tips to the tests established by *Aguilar* and *Spinelli*. By definition nothing is known about an anonymous informant's identity, honesty, or reliability. * * *

To suggest that anonymous informants' tips are subject to the tests established by *Aguilar* and *Spinelli* is not to suggest that they can never provide a basis for a finding of probable cause. **[l]** It is conceivable that police corroboration of the details of the tip might establish the reliability of the informant under *Aguilar*'s veracity prong, as refined in *Spinelli,* and that the details in the tip might be sufficient to qualify under the "self-verifying detail" test established by *Spinelli* as a means of satisfying *Aguilar*'s basis of knowledge prong. The *Aguilar* and *Spinelli* tests must be applied to anonymous informants' tips, however, if we are to continue to ensure that findings of probable cause, and attendant intrusions, are based on information provided by an honest or credible person who has acquired the information in a reliable way. * * *

II

* * *

* * * But of particular concern to all Americans must be that the Court gives virtually no consideration to the value of insuring that findings of probable cause are based on information that a magistrate can reasonably say has been obtained in a reliable way by an honest or credible person. I share JUSTICE WHITE's fear that the Court's rejection of *Aguilar* and *Spinelli* and its adoption of a new totality-of-the-circumstances test, * * * "may foretell an evisceration of the probable-cause standard. * * *" * * *

[l] What sort of fact would verify the basis of knowledge in an anonymous tip? Perhaps a verifiable reference to criminal activity that would not be known to an average person? If it would be impossible for a magistrate to rely on an anonymous tip, would the proper law enforcement response be to get additional corroboration in order to establish independent probable cause?

But it is important to keep in mind that, in the vast majority of cases, *any* evidence seized by the police will be in plain view, at least at the moment of seizure. The problem with the "plain view" doctrine has been to identify the circumstances in which plain view has legal significance rather than being simply the normal concomitant of any search, legal or illegal. (*Coolidge v. New Hampshire,* p. 466, emphasis in original)

Police cannot "create" plain view by taking advantage of an illegal search. Justice Stewart put it this way: "[P]lain view alone is never enough to justify the warrantless seizure of evidence." It would destroy Fourth Amendment protections to allow the police to search at will, or without a warrant where a warrant is otherwise required, and to rationalize a seizure because an unearthed item is seen to be contraband or evidence of criminality.

IMMEDIATELY APPARENT *Coolidge* established a *second rule* of plain view—the "immediately apparent" rule. The police

in Coolidge conducted a warrantless search of an automobile suspected to contain fiber evidence and sought to justify it because the car itself was "in plain view." The cars were obviously in plain view, but vacuumed microscopic particles certainly were not. Justice Stewart said, "Of course, the extension of the original justification is legitimate only when it is *immediately apparent* to the police that they have evidence before them; the "plain view" doctrine may not be used to extend a general exploratory search from one object to another until something incriminating at last emerges." The rule that the evidence in plain view must be immediately apparent as contraband is another way of saying that *probable cause* must exist to secure the evidence at the moment of seizure.

As with all probable cause decisions, absolute certainty is not required. For example, in *Texas v. Brown* (1983) a police officer looked into an automobile at night with a flashlight at a routine traffic license checkpoint and saw an opaque, green party balloon knotted about one-half inch from the tip. The

GATES IN THE STATES

According to Professor Latzer, the "Gates rule has been widely approved on state constitutional grounds"—citing cases of twenty-six states that have applied the totality of circumstances analysis. Several states have rejected *Gates* in favor of retaining the *Aguilar-Spinelli* rule.

The New York Court of Appeals (that state's highest court) in *People v. Griminger* (1988) held that evidence introduced into state courts, obtained as a result of search warrants based on the hearsay of confidential informants (whether issued by federal or state magistrates), must make a minimal showing of the informant's reliability. In explicitly requiring that the *Aguilar-Spinelli* two-pronged test be used, the Court rejected several of the arguments put forth in *Illinois v. Gates*. The New York Court disagreed with the idea that police would be less likely to apply for warrants merely because the state continued to apply the *Aguilar-Spinelli* test. The Court of Appeals disagreed with the idea that the two-pronged test was hypertechnical. Instead, the more structured "bright line" *Aguilar-Spinelli* test better serves the highly desirable "aims of predictability and precision in judicial review of search and seizure cases," and . . . "the protection of the individual rights of our citizens are best promoted by applying State constitutional standards."[45]

The facts in *Griminger* demonstrate the need for caution in accepting hearsay warrants. Federal Secret Service agents arrested a counterfeiting informant, who, while under arrest, accused Griminger of keeping large quantities of drugs in his home. An agent prepared a federal affidavit stating that "a confidential informant known as source 'A' . . . observed 150 to 200 pounds of marijuana in defendant's bedroom and adjacent attic. . . ." Although the agent did not personally know the counterfeiting suspect, his affidavit said that the undisclosed informant was "a person known to your deponent." The agent also omitted the fact that the informant was under arrest when he provided this information. On the basis of this affidavit, a federal magistrate issued a warrant and a subsequent search of Griminger's home turned up "10 ounces of marijuana, over $6,000 in cash and drug-related paraphernalia." The lower state courts found that the Secret Service agent had not established the reliability of the informant. These facts indicate the dangers in a rule that makes it easy for police to rely on any arrested person as an informant. They support New York's skepticism: "Our courts should not 'blithely accept as true the accusations of an informant unless some good reason for doing so has been established.'"[46]

Barry Latzer, *State Constitutional Criminal Law,* §3.13.

Supreme Court ruled that he had probable cause to believe that the balloon contained illegal drugs because it was known that this was a common way for drug dealers to carry their wares. The Court thus allows the police some leeway for making an inference in determining whether it was immediately apparent that drugs were in the car.

—*Arizona v. Hicks* Case & Comments—

PLAIN FEEL   Plain view is not limited to matters viewed by eyesight, but applies to evidence known to any of the senses. In **Minnesota v. Dickerson** (1993) police lawfully stopped Dickerson outside a known drug house when his overall behavior created a reasonable suspicion that he carried drugs. An officer, following the rule of *Terry* (1968), patted down the outside of Dickerson's jacket to check for weapons. He testified that "I felt a lump, a small lump, in the front pocket. I examined it with my fingers and it slid and it felt to be a lump of crack cocaine in cellophane." The officer then retrieved a small plastic bag with crack cocaine from Dickerson's pocket.

Dickerson raised two plain view issues. First, must the police *visually observe* an item for it to be in plain view? The Court answered that plain "view" applies to any seizable item apparent to *any of the senses*.

> To this Court there is no distinction as to which sensory perception the officer uses to conclude that the material is contraband. An experienced officer may rely upon his sense of smell in DWI stops or in recognizing the smell of burning marijuana in an automobile. The sound of a shotgun being racked would clearly support certain reactions by an officer. The sense of touch, grounded in experience and training, is as reliable as perceptions drawn from other senses. "Plain feel," therefore, is no different than plain view and will equally support the seizure here. (*Minnesota v. Dickerson* (1993), pp. 369–70, quoting trial judge)

Two arguments to the contrary were raised by the Minnesota Supreme Court to reject the so-called **"plain feel" rule:** (1) that the sense of touch is inherently less immediate and less reliable than the sense of sight, and (2) that the sense of touch is far more intrusive into personal privacy. The United States Supreme Court, noting that the facts in *Terry* (1968) allowed the sense of touch to be used for pat-down searches, disagreed.

The *Dickerson* case required the resolution of a second issue: whether what the officer felt was *immediately apparent* as crack cocaine. Justice White's close examination of the facts led to the conclusion that the officer "overstepped the bounds" of the limited search authorized by *Terry* because he *continued to explore* Dickerson's outer pocket after determining that it contained no weapon. The *Terry* rule overlapped with the immediacy/probable cause rule: "If . . . the police lack probable cause to believe that an object in plain view is contraband without conducting some further search of the object—*i.e.,* if "its incriminating character [is not] 'immediately apparent,' . . . the plain-view doctrine cannot

Arizona v. Hicks
480 U.S. 321, 107 S.Ct. 1149, 94 L.Ed.2d 347 (1987)

JUSTICE SCALIA delivered the opinion of the Court.

In *Coolidge v. New Hampshire* (1971), we said that in certain circumstances a warrantless seizure by police of an item that comes within plain view during their lawful search of a private area may be reasonable under the Fourth Amendment. * * * [The issue] in the present case [is] whether this "plain view" doctrine may be invoked when the police have less than probable cause to believe that the item in question is evidence of a crime or is contraband.

I

[Police entered an apartment without a warrant to search for a person who shot a bullet through the floor, injuring a man in the apartment below.] **[a]** They found and seized three weapons, including a sawed-off rifle. * * *

One of the policemen, Officer Nelson, noticed two sets of expensive stereo components, which seemed out of place in the squalid and otherwise ill-appointed four room apartment. Suspecting that they were stolen, he read and recorded their serial numbers—moving some of the components, including a Bang and Olufsen turn-table, in order to do so—which he then reported by phone to his headquarters. On being advised that the turntable had been taken in an armed robbery, he seized it immediately. It was later determined that some of the other serial numbers matched those on other stereo equipment taken in the same armed robbery, and a warrant was obtained and executed to seize that equipment as well. Respondent was subsequently indicted for the robbery.

[On a suppression motion, the state trial court and court of appeals held that the view of the serial numbers was an *additional search*, unrelated to the exigency of the search for the shooter. These holdings impliedly rejected the idea that the actions were justified by the plain view doctrine. The evidence was suppressed. The state appealed.]

II

* * * We agree that the mere recording of the serial numbers did not constitute a seizure. * * * In and of itself * * * it did not "meaningfully interfere" with respondent's possessory interest in either the serial number or the equipment, and therefore did not amount to a seizure. * * *

Officer Nelson's moving of the equipment, however, did constitute a "search" separate and apart from the search for the shooter, victims, and weapons that was the lawful objective of his entry into the apartment. Merely inspecting those parts of the turntable that came into view during the latter search would not have constituted an independent search, because it would have produced no additional invasion of respondent's privacy interest. **[b]** But taking action, unrelated to the objectives of the authorized intrusion, which exposed to view concealed portions of the apartment or its contents, did produce a new invasion of respondent's privacy unjustified by the exigent circumstance that validated the entry. This is why * * * the "distinction between 'looking' at a suspicious object in plain view and 'moving' it even a few inches" is much more than trivial for purposes of the Fourth Amendment. It matters not that the search uncovered nothing of any great personal value to the respondent— serial numbers rather than (what might conceivably have been hidden behind or under the equipment) letters or photographs. A search is a search, even if it happens to disclose nothing but the bottom of a turntable.

III

The remaining question is whether the search was "reasonable" under the Fourth Amendment.

* * * [W]e reject, at the outset, the * * * position * * * that because the officers' action directed to the stereo equipment was unrelated to the justification for their entry into respondent's apartment, it was *ipso facto* unreasonable. **[c]** That lack of relationship *always* exists with regard to action validated under the "plain view" doctrine; where action is taken for the purpose of justifying entry, invocation of the doctrine is superfluous. * * *

We turn, then, to application of the doctrine to the facts of this case. "It is well established that under certain circumstances the police may *seize* evidence in plain view without a warrant," *Coolidge v. New Hampshire* * * * (**plurality opinion**) (emphasis added). Those circumstances include situations "[w]here the initial intrusion that brings the police within plain view of such [evidence] is supported . . . by one of the recognized exceptions to the warrant requirement. * * * It would be absurd to

[a] The three standard exigency exceptions to the warrant requirement are hot pursuit, automobile search, and search incident to arrest. The fact that the Court upheld the entry in *Hicks* means that a general exigency category exists, based on reasonableness.

[b] This paragraph implies that the plain view rule simply recognizes commonsense reality. If Officer Nelson saw obvious contraband, e.g., drugs, sitting on a table in the apartment, it would be silly to hold that the officer could not act on that information. On the other hand, allowing Officer Nelson, lawfully in the apartment for the limited purpose of looking for the shooter, to expand that search into another, could provide incentives for pretext searches of homes.

[c] The defendant argued that the police could seize only items in plain view that related to the shooting; such an argument would destroy the practical value of the plain view doctrine and would not adhere to its logic. Note that both the defense and the prosecution make extreme arguments to the Court in this case.

say that an object could lawfully be seized and taken from the premises, but could not be moved for closer examination." It is clear, therefore, that the search here was valid if the "plain view" doctrine would have sustained a seizure of the equipment.

There is no doubt it would have done so if Officer Nelson had probable cause to believe that the equipment was stolen. **[d]** The State conceded, however, that he had only a "reasonable suspicion," by which it means something less than probable cause. * * *

We now hold that probable cause is required. To say otherwise would be to cut the "plain view" doctrine loose from its theoretical and practical moorings. The theory of that doctrine consists of extending to nonpublic places such as the home, where searches and seizures without a warrant are presumptively unreasonable, the police's longstanding authority to make warrantless seizures in public places of such objects as weapons and contraband. And the practical justification for that extension is the desirability of sparing police, whose viewing of the object in the course of a lawful search is as legitimate as it would have been in a public place, the inconvenience and the risk—to themselves or to preservation of the evidence—of going to obtain a warrant. **[e]** Dispensing with the need for a warrant is worlds apart from permitting a lesser standard of *cause* for the seizure than a warrant would require, *i.e.*, the standard of probable cause. No reason is apparent why an object should routinely be seizable on lesser grounds, during an unrelated search and seizure, than would have been needed to obtain a warrant for that same object if it had been known to be on the premises.

We do not say, of course, that a seizure can never be justified on less than probable cause. **[f]** We have held that it can—where, for example, the seizure is minimally intrusive and operational necessities render it the only practicable means of detecting certain types of crime. See, *e.g., United States v. Cortez (1981)* (investigative detention of vehicle suspected to be transporting illegal aliens);* * * *United States v. Place, (1983)* (dictum) (seizure of suspected drug dealer's luggage at airport to permit exposure to specially trained dog). No special operational necessities are relied on here, however—but rather the mere fact that the items in question came lawfully within the officer's plain view. That alone cannot supplant the requirement of probable cause.

The same considerations preclude us from holding that, even though probable cause would have been necessary for a *seizure*, the *search* of objects in plain view that occurred here could be sustained on lesser grounds. A dwelling-place search, no less than a dwelling-place seizure, requires probable cause, and there is no reason in theory or practicality why application of the "plain view" doctrine would supplant that requirement. * * * **[g]** [T]o treat searches more liberally would especially erode the plurality's warning in *Coolidge* that "the 'plain view' doctrine may not be used to extend a general exploratory search from one object to another until something incriminating at last emerges." * * * In short, whether legal authority to move the equipment could be found only as an inevitable concomitant of the authority to seize it, or also as a consequence of some independent power to search certain objects in plain view, probable cause to believe the equipment was stolen was required. **[h]**

* * *

For the reasons stated, the judgment of the Court of Appeals of Arizona is

Affirmed.

JUSTICE O'CONNOR, with whom THE CHIEF JUSTICE and JUSTICE POWELL join, dissenting.

The Court today gives the right answer to the wrong question. The Court asks whether the police must have probable cause before either seizing an object in plain view or conducting a full-blown search of that object, and concludes that they must. I agree. In my view, however, this case presents a different question: whether police must have probable cause before conducting a cursory inspection of an item in plain view. **[i]** Because I conclude that such an inspection is reasonable if the police are aware of facts or circumstances that justify a reasonable suspicion that the item is evidence of a crime, I would reverse the judgment of the Arizona Court of Appeals, and therefore dissent.

[A *Coolidge* requirement is that for evidence to be within the "plain view" exception,] it must be "immediately apparent" to the police that the items they observe may be evidence of a crime, contraband, or otherwise subject to seizure. * * *

The purpose of the "immediately apparent" requirement is to prevent "general exploratory rummaging in a person's belongings." If an officer could indiscriminately search every item in plain view, a search justified by a limited purpose—such as exigent circumstances—could be used to eviscerate the protections of the Fourth Amendment. * * *

[d] Why should the turntable be in "plain view" if Officer Nelson had probable cause to believe it was stolen but not if he had reasonable suspicion?

[c] The *practical* justification for the plain view rule is couched in terms of assisting police. The theoretical justification is not discussed in depth. Does the rule have practical justification that benefits the defendant?

[f] The examples in this paragraph are applications of the *Terry* "stop and frisk" doctrine. This simply does not apply to the facts of *Hicks*.

[g] To the dissent, lifting the stereo is not a search but rather a "cursory inspection." But the majority fears that to allow police to rummage in a home beyond their lawful purpose, to *create* plain view, opens a theoretic rift in the plain view doctrine that can have negative, practical consequences.

[h] Is Justice Scalia's opinion a "conservative" or "liberal" ruling?

[i] Justice O'Connor seeks to create a new rule: a "cursory inspection" plain view seizure.

---

* * *

* * * When a police officer makes a cursory inspection of a suspicious item in plain view in order to determine whether it is indeed evidence of a crime, there is no "exploratory rummaging." Only those items that the police officer "reasonably suspects" as evidence of a crime may be inspected, and perhaps more importantly, the scope of such an inspection is quite limited. **[j]** In short, if police officers have a reasonable, articulable suspicion that an object they come across during the course of a lawful search is evidence of crime, in my view they may make a cursory examination of the object to verify their suspicion. If the officers wish to go beyond such a cursory examination of the object, however, they must have probable cause. This distinction between a full-blown search and seizure of an item and a mere inspection of the item * * * [is] based on their relative intrusiveness. * * *

* * *

[j] Do you think that a "cursory examination" doctrine based on reasonable suspicion would prevent police from engaging in "exploratory rummaging"? If this rule existed, do you think that Officer Nelson would have limited his exploration only to moving the B&O turntable?

---

justify its seizure."[48] Here, because the officer had to slide the object in the pocket around, it was *not* immediately apparent as contraband and was not admissible as evidence in a trial.

INADVERTENCE *Coolidge* stated a *third* plain view rule, that the officer must come across incriminating evidence *inadvertently*. This rule, supported by a plurality of four justices and not a majority in *Coolidge,* was overturned by the Court in **Horton v. California** (1990). Justice Stewart, in *Coolidge,* thought that without the rule of inadvertence police could simply dispense with a search warrant whenever they had reason to believe that contraband was located in a premises. This, of course, is not the case. But *Horton*'s facts made it reasonable to dispense with the inadvertence rule.

Justice Stevens, writing for the majority in *Horton,* stated that the inadvertency requirement served no purpose in protecting individual rights and could frustrate legitimate searches. The police had probable cause to believe that Horton committed a robbery and that he had the stolen property (three specifically described rings) and weapons (an Uzi machine gun, a .38-caliber revolver, and a stun gun) in his home. The warrant affidavit mentioned both the robbery proceeds and the weapons, but the magistrate's warrant mentioned only the stolen property. When executing the warrant, an officer saw and seized the weapons but did not find the stolen property. Because the officer had prior knowledge of the weapons, they were not seized inadvertently. Horton argued that the evidence should be suppressed under the *Coolidge* plurality rule. The Supreme Court disagreed.

The majority concluded that the rule adds nothing to protect an individual's right to privacy. First, an officer's anticipation that evidence would be present does not harm the defendant's rights as long as the officer is legitimately on the premises. Second, the inadvertence requirement itself does not prevent a search from becoming a general search or prevent a particular warrant from becoming a general warrant. If the

police go beyond the terms of a valid warrant or exceed the limits of a warrantless search, the evidence will be inadmissible as a violation of the Fourth Amendment particularity requirement. A second protection is not needed. On the other hand, if a search is within the scope of a warrant, the Court reasoned that the individual's privacy has already been legitimately invaded and that no additional right against seizure is needed other than the "immediately apparent" requirement.

Justice Brennan, joined by Justice Marshall, dissented in *Horton.* He argued that an officer who fails to mention an item known to be in a place in an affidavit, and seizes it anyway, violates the Fourth Amendment. He was also concerned that the lack of an inadvertency requirement for plain view would lead to a larger number of *pretext searches.* He cited several state cases where this had happened, while admitting that the entry in *Horton* did not seem to be a pretext to seize the guns. Given the fact that the Court has since ruled that a pretextual auto stop is not unconstitutional as long as an officer has a valid basis to search or make an arrest, this argument takes on greater urgency.[49]

Curtilage and Open Fields

The Fourth Amendment protects the privacy, liberty, and property interests of "persons, houses, papers and effects against unreasonable searches and seizures." Does Fourth Amendment protection extend to landed property? The answer depends upon the location of the land in relation to a house. As a general rule, what is referred to as "open fields" in Fourth Amendment law does *not* come under the protection of the amendment, whereas areas close to the house—known as the curtilage—are protected. As a result, police do not need a warrant to go onto "open fields" and any contraband found there may be seized in plain view. In other words, a government intrusion upon an open field is not a "search" in the constitutional sense.

CURTILAGE   In *Oliver v. United States* (1984) the Supreme Court noted that "At common law, the curtilage is the area to which extends the intimate activity associated with the 'sanctity of a man's home and the privacies of life,' * * * and therefore has been considered part of the home itself for Fourth Amendment purposes. Thus, courts have extended Fourth Amendment protection to the curtilage; and they have defined the curtilage, as did the common law, by reference to the factors that determine whether an individual reasonably may expect that an area immediately adjacent to the home will remain private."

More precisely, the curtilage included the area under the eaves of the main house; small structures near the main house, such as a shed, smokehouse, or garage; and the area around a house. The yard of a typical suburban home is a curtilage; the wall around O.J. Simpson's Brentwood estate (the scene of the one of the most notorious police investigations of the twentieth century) described its curtilage, and before Detective Mark Fuhrman could enter, he should have had a search warrant or a valid warrant exception.

In *United States v. Dunn* (1987) DEA agents, without a warrant, went onto Dunn's land to see if they could detect evidence of illegal amphetamine manufacture. Dunn's house was a half mile from a public road on a 198-acre ranch, which was completely encircled by a perimeter fence. Two barns were located about fifty yards from the residence. The property contained several interior fences, constructed mainly of posts and multiple strands of barbed wire. The house and a small greenhouse were surrounded by a fence. One barn was enclosed by a wooden fence. The DEA agents crossed the perimeter fence and one interior fence. Standing approximately midway between the residence and the barns, they smelled what was believed to be the odor of phenylacetic acid coming from the direction of the barns. They then crossed another barbed wire fence and a wooden fence to get to the large barn. They walked under the barn's overhang and, using a flashlight, peered into the barn. "They observed what the DEA agent thought to be a phenylacetone laboratory. The officers did not enter the barn. At this point the officers departed from respondent's property." A warrant was issued on the basis of facts obtained by police observations of a barn. (*Dunn v. United States,* pp. 297–98)

The Court ruled that the barn was *not* within the curtilage, and the police officers violated no Fourth Amendment expectation of privacy when they went up to the barn and observed an illegal drug factory inside.

OPEN FIELDS   "Conversely, the common law implies, as we reaffirm today, that no expectation of privacy legitimately attaches to open fields" (*Oliver v. United States,* p. 180). The rule was first stated tersely by Justice Holmes in *Hester v. United States* (1924): The "special protection accorded by the Fourth Amendment to the people in their 'persons, houses, papers, and effects,' is not extended to the open fields. The distinction between the latter and the house is as old as the common law." After *Katz,* the question arose as to whether this distinction still stood under a modernized, nonproperty inter-

pretation of the Fourth Amendment, or whether expectation of privacy analysis would extend Fourth Amendment protection to so-called open fields.

Oliver v. United States (1984) was two consolidated cases. The essential facts were that police officers, without warrants or consent, went onto the lands owned by defendants and discovered marijuana patches. The privately owned fields were posted with "No Trespassing" signs. One site was highly secluded, more than a mile from the defendant's house, and a gate to the fields was locked. To reach the other site, officers had to walk a path between the defendant's house and a neighbor's house. In one case, the lower court upheld the search; in the other the evidence was suppressed.

Justice Powell's majority opinion provided several reasons for upholding the open fields rule. First, the explicit language of the Fourth Amendment "is not extended to the open fields." Second, open fields are not "effects" within the meaning of the Fourth Amendment. Significantly, a first draft of the Fourth Amendment included a protection of "other property" along with persons, houses, and papers. The change in wording confirms the idea that "effects" refers to personal property. Third, the majority felt there was no expectation of privacy in open fields that society is prepared to recognize as reasonable, i.e., *Katz* had not changed the open fields rule. Open land is put to uses, such as the cultivation of crops, which are not the kinds of intimate activities that occur in homes that have historically called for strong privacy protection.

Fourth, "as a practical matter these lands usually are accessible to the public and the police in ways that a home, an office, or commercial structure would not be." Rural land may be fenced and posted with "No Trespassing" signs, but these do not effectively keep hikers or hunters off the land. They certainly do not provide the same kind of psychological barrier that apartment and house doors and windows provide. Also, "the public and police lawfully may survey lands from the air." Fifth, the common law distinction between open fields and the curtilage supports the idea that the framers did not intend to extend Fourth Amendment protection to open fields. Sixth, a defendant's *property interest,* such as ownership or leaseholding, that is violated by police committing a trespass to land, no longer decides the case under *Katz.* "The existence of a property right is but one element in determining whether expectations of privacy are legitimate."

The Court also provided practical reasons for supporting the open fields doctrine. An argument was made that in each case where police trespass on real estate and discover contraband, the courts should conduct a factual inquiry to discover whether the land and its uses come within the open fields rule. The Court rejected this. Under a case-by-case approach, "police officers would have to guess before every search whether landowners had erected fences sufficiently high, posted a sufficient number of warning signs, or located contraband in an area sufficiently secluded to establish a right of privacy. The lawfulness of a search would turn on '[a] highly sophisticated set of rules, qualified by all sorts of ifs, ands, and buts and requiring the drawing of subtle nuances and hairline distinctions. . . .'"

A bright-line rule better serves law enforcement and ensures that constitutional rights will uniformly be enforced.

Justice Marshall, joined by Justices Brennan and Stevens, wrote a spirited dissent. He felt, first, that provisions that "identify a fundamental human liberty" should "be shielded forever from government intrusion" and so should be interpreted in an expansive manner "to lend them meanings that ensure that the liberties the Framers sought to protect are not undermined by the changing activities of government officials." Next, he argued that if, as the majority believed, the Fourth Amendment offered no protection to real property, then the protection extended to the curtilage is inconsistent. Again, the objective expectation of privacy is seen in laws that allow the prosecution of trespassers. Posting and fencing is a clear way in which owners announce their expectation of privacy and it is understood by all. Finally, the dissent disagreed with the majority that the uses to which property owners put lands are not the sort of activities that society deems worthy of privacy:

> The uses to which a place is put are highly relevant to the assessment of a privacy interest asserted therein. * * * If, in light of our shared sensibilities, those activities are of a kind in which people should be able to engage without fear of intrusion by private persons or government officials, we extend the protection of the Fourth Amendment to the space in question, even in the absence of any entitlement derived from positive law. * * *
>
> Privately owned woods and fields that are not exposed to public view regularly are employed in a variety of ways that society acknowledges deserve privacy. Many landowners like to take solitary walks on their property, confident that they will not be confronted in their rambles by strangers or policemen. Others conduct agricultural businesses on their property. Some landowners use their secluded spaces to meet lovers, others to gather together with fellow worshippers, still others to engage in sustained creative endeavor. Private land is sometimes used as a refuge for wildlife, where flora and fauna are protected from human intervention of any kind. Our respect for the freedom of landowners to use their posted "open fields" in ways such as these partially explains the seriousness with which the positive law regards deliberate invasions of such spaces, * * * and substantially reinforces the landowners' contention that their expectations of privacy are "reasonable." (*Oliver v. United States*, pp. 191–92)

The curtilage concept expands the Fourth Amendment definition of a house to a certain "reasonable" amount of land around a house. This gives the Fourth Amendment protections of home privacy some "breathing room" and prevents the open fields exception from allowing police to tightly surround a house or creep up to windows to peer in or eavesdrop.

Airspace

If the curtilage is open to view, police may observe it from a public vantage point such as a road. What they may not do is physically invade the curtilage itself to encroach on the *zone of privacy* that one expects to have around a dwelling. In several cases that the Framers surely could not have contemplated, the Supreme Court considered the extent to which the curtilage protection applied to airspace above premises.

The *Katz* doctrine provided no protection against the warrantless *aerial surveillance* by police of a backyard where marijuana was growing. The Court in *California v. Ciraolo* (1986) upheld the police action, saying that the defendant's expectation of privacy in his backyard was not one that society was prepared to honor. The owner had surrounded the backyard, which also contained a swimming pool, with a six-foot outer fence and a ten-foot inner fence. Police could not observe the backyard to confirm an anonymous tip that marijuana was growing in Ciraolo's backyard, so they hired a private airplane and buzzed the suburban backyard to gather visual evidence with the naked eye from about one thousand feet. The Court reasoned that the yard was *exposed to the public* because it was subject to the gaze of passengers in commercial airplane overflights. In effect, the search was held to be within the open fields category. Justice Powell, in a stinging dissent, accused the Court of failing to uphold its role as a guardian of rights by allowing a "stealthy encroachment" on rights by the remote intrusion of commercial overflights. He noted that the curtilage was entitled to similar protections as a home and that the use of a private airplane to peer down into Ciraolo's backyard, pool and all, was similar to the use of listening devices by law enforcement officers.

The Court, on the same day in *Dow Chemical v. United States* (1986) upheld an aerial search of two thousand acres of commercial property by an airplane equipped with a sophisticated camera that could magnify its pictures to detect pipes a half-inch thick from twelve hundred feet. Even if the government officers could not, under the Fourth Amendment, physically go onto the commercial complex, the warrantless overflight was held not to be a search and seizure. Thus, *Dow Chemical* upheld the concept of an **industrial curtilage** but, as in *Ciraolo,* held it did not protect property from aerial surveillance while using ordinary camera resolution.

The Court continued this approach in *Florida v. Riley* (1989). A four-justice plurality upheld the surveillance of a partially covered greenhouse in a residential backyard from a *helicopter* hovering four hundred feet above ground. Justice White reasoned that this flight did not violate any law or regulation, and any member of the public with a helicopter could have legally hovered above Riley's property and observed the contents of the greenhouse. This reasoning was not satisfactory to Justice O'Connor who concurred only in the judgment. She thought that the Court relied too heavily on police compliance with Federal Aviation Administration (FAA) regulations and suggested that if lower overflights were sufficiently rare, even if they were in FAA compliance, in such a case, the householder would have a reasonable expectation of privacy. Justice Brennan dissented (joined by Justices Marshall and Stevens), arguing that by not taking into account the difficulty and lengths to which the police must go in making an "open fields" aerial search, the Court was ignoring the "the very essence of *Katz.*"

In these cases, areas that are within the curtilage and nominally protected by the Fourth Amendment were, in fact,

OVERFLIGHT CASES IN THE STATES

Professor Latzer's treatise indicates that almost all the state courts that have considered the airplane or helicopter overflight issue under their state constitutions have agreed with the approach taken by the United States Supreme Court. These include Colorado, Hawaii, Kentucky, New York, Oregon, Tennessee, Washington, and possibly Florida. California has made an interesting distinction. The California Supreme Court held in 1985 that under the California constitution's search and seizure provision, a warrantless flight sixteen hundred feet over the defendant's backyard violates an owner's reasonable expectation of privacy in the home and curtilage. The court said that the reasonableness of an individual's expectation of privacy is not defined solely by technological progress (*People*

v. Cook, 1985).[50] On the other hand, in *People v. Mayhoff* (1986), the California Supreme Court did not apply this rule to airplane overflights of open fields looking for illegal cultivation of marijuana.[51] Three reasons to distinguish *Mayhoff* from *Cook* were offered: (1) the open fields doctrine provides an initial justification for the search; (2) unlike *Cook*, there is less chance that open fields overflights will pry on innocent activities occurring within a legitimate zone of privacy; and (3) law enforcement interests are stronger where aerial surveillance of remote areas may be the only feasible way of discovering illegal cultivation.

Barry Latzer, *State Constitutional Criminal Law*, §3.6.

---

opened up to warrantless police surveillance under reasoning that stretched the traditional categories of open fields and narrowed the protection of the curtilage. The fact that conservative justices such as Lewis Powell and Sandra Day O'Connor were bothered by the decisions shows the malleability of constitutional concepts, and suggests the extent to which the Court's decisions are influenced by result-oriented jurisprudence.

Enhancement Devices

Is an item in plain view if it is detected, or its contraband nature is disclosed, by the use of an **enhancement device?** Logically, if the police have to resort to technology to determine whether or not evidence is incriminating, then it is not *immediately apparent* as such. If so, a judicial warrant based on probable cause is required to use the technology. This logic seemed to be at work in *Coolidge v. New Hampshire* (1971), where evidence obtained by the warrantless vacuuming of a car for fiber evidence was deemed inadmissible. Similarly, in *Katz* and other surreptitious electronic eavesdropping cases, private conversations that are obtained via enhancement devices that amplify the aural sense are protected by the Fourth Amendment. Such information is within the individual's zone of constitutionally protected privacy.

The Supreme Court's cases on the use of "beepers," provide a baseline of analysis. Beepers are radio transmitters, usually battery-operated, that emit periodic signals. They allow agents to trace the movement of an object in which the beeper is surreptitiously placed. As noted previously, the Court ruled that there is no constitutional impediment to the government using beepers to enhance the senses (e.g., visual observation) if the device does not infringe an expectation of privacy. In **United States v. Knotts** (1983), agents placed a beeper in a five-gallon can of chloroform and tracked its movement in an automobile driven on public streets. A person has no reasonable expectation of privacy in his movements from one public place to another, and so the use of the beeper was held not to constitute a search. In **United States v. Karo** (1984), however, the Court ruled that detecting motion with the use of beepers *inside a person's house* equated to a search and required a prior warrant. The beeper was the equivalent of an agent secretly entering a house to verify that a drum of ether is inside, a clear Fourth Amendment violation. Justice White expressed the policy that: "Indiscriminate monitoring of property that has been withdrawn from public view would present far too serious a threat to privacy interests in the home to escape entirely some sort of Fourth Amendment oversight." For this kind of in-house tracking to be constitutional, a warrant must be obtained.

Some use of enhancement devices poses no constitutional problems. In *Texas v. Brown* (1983) the Court said that it was "beyond dispute" that an officer "shining his flashlight to illuminate the interior of [a] car trenched upon no right secured . . . by the Fourth Amendment." Citing *United States v. Lee* (1927), the Court also found no constitutional objection to "the use of a marine glass or a field glass. It is not prohibited by the Constitution." Flashlights and field glasses are in such common use that allowing their use may be explained by the fact that they are common devices used everyday in ordinary situations. However, the Court has also found no Fourth Amendment impediment to more high-tech devices. In *Dow Chemical* (1986) the Court upheld a warrantless aerial surveillance of a two-thousand-acre chemical manufacturing facility, heavily secured against entry on the ground but partially exposed to visual observation from the air, by the Environmental Protection Agency, to check emissions from the facility's power plant. The "EPA employed a commercial aerial photographer, using a standard floor-mounted, precision aerial-mapping camera, to take photographs of the facility from altitudes of 12,000, 3,000, and 1,200 feet." In upholding this level of surveillance as not protected by the Fourth Amendment, the Court noted that "The photographs at issue in this case are essentially like those commonly used in mapmaking. Any person with an airplane and an aerial camera could readily duplicate them." With the end of the Cold War, "spy satellites" are now commercially available and have been used by "mining companies, mapmakers, geologists, city planners, ecologists, farmers, hydrologists, road makers, journalists, land managers, disaster-relief officials and others seeking to monitor the planet's changing face. The global market in such imagery is expected to reach as high as $5 billion by 2004."[52] The implications are that there are virtually no limits to aerial surveillance by the police for law enforcement purposes.[53]

The Supreme Court has recently acted to exert some judicial control over the use of **thermal imaging**, and has attempted to establish rules to guide the use of advanced information-gathering technology.

—*Kyllo v. United States* Case & Comments—

CONSENT SEARCHES

The consent-based procedure is the bread and butter of the criminal justice system."[54] To an astonishing degree, criminal suspects plead guilty, confess to crime, allow police into their homes, and meekly submit to arrests rather than go to jury trial, stay mum, refuse to allow police entry without a warrant, and forcibly resist arrest. What is surprising about the first three scenarios is that suspects *give up* their constitutional rights to trial, against self-incrimination, and to privacy, which are guaranteed by the Sixth, Fifth, and Fourth amendments. Constitutional law has, for many years, allowed defendants to give up these rights under certain conditions. Not all rights can be voluntarily set aside. The law will not allow a person to give up his or her rights to due process under the Fifth and Fourteenth amendments or Eighth Amendment right to be free from cruel and unusual punishments under any conditions. No court would uphold a contract by which a person sold himself into slavery, which is prohibited by the Thirteenth Amendment.

Police favor **consent searches** and stops because it eliminates questions about a suspect's constitutional rights. A person may have an absolute constitutional right to refuse to stop, or to open the door to his or her home or automobile trunk when requested to do so by a police officer—but if the person consents, it is of no matter that the officer did not have reasonable suspicion to stop or a warrant to enter. Once voluntarily allowed in, the officer is lawfully in the premises; if contraband happens to be observed in plain view, it may be seized and the possessor arrested for possession. "[A] search authorized by consent is wholly valid."[55]

Voluntariness Requirement

The one absolute requirement of a valid consent to give up one's Fourth Amendment rights is that the consent must be voluntary. If any threat or force is used to obtain consent, it is invalid. An arrested person can never give valid consent to a search because the person is by definition forcibly detained and in the custody of the police—any lawful search incident to arrest is made forcibly.[56] To voluntarily give up one's rights, one must be free to do so, both physically and psychologically. The following cases help to define the voluntariness requirement by example.

In *Amos v. United States* (1921) two federal "revenuers" looking for untaxed whiskey came to Amos's house without a warrant. He was not there and his wife opened the door. They told her "that they were revenue officers and had come to search the premises 'for violations of the revenue law'; that thereupon the woman opened the store and the witnesses entered, and in a barrel of peas found a bottle containing not quite a half-pint of illicitly distilled whisky, which they called 'blockade whisky.'" A unanimous Court summarily dismissed the contention that the officers were let in voluntarily because they *demanded* entry under government authority. A similar case is *Bumper v. North Carolina* (1968). Bumper, a murder suspect not yet arrested, "lived with his grandmother, Mrs. Hattie Leath, a 66-year-old Negro widow, in a house located in a rural area at the end of an isolated mile-long dirt road." Four officers came to the house and told Mrs. Leath that they had a search warrant. In response, she allowed them to search the house and a weapon was discovered. It was later determined that there never was a search warrant. The Supreme Court held that Mrs. Leath, who did not appear from her testimony to have been at all intimidated, nevertheless did not give valid consent to the warrantless search:

> A search conducted in reliance upon a warrant cannot later be justified on the basis of consent if it turns out that the warrant was invalid. The result can be no different when it turns out that the State does not even attempt to rely upon the validity of the warrant, or fails to show that there was, in fact, any warrant at all.
>
> When a law enforcement officer claims authority to search a home under a warrant, he announces in effect that the occupant has no right to resist the search. The situation is instinct with coercion—albeit colorably lawful coercion. Where there is coercion there cannot be consent.
>
> We hold that Mrs. Leath did not consent to the search, and that it was constitutional error to admit the rifle in evidence against the petitioner. (*Bumper v. North Carolina*, pp. 549–50)

The coercion of law is not assumed simply from the fact that police officers ask a person if they may enter. However, if officers falsely claim to have a warrant or *demand* entry as the law required it, then they are acting under *color of law*, and this is coercive. But if a police officer *asks* a person in a nonthreatening manner if he or she may enter a home, or speak with a person, or view a briefcase or the trunk of a car, and the person agrees, then the person voluntarily relinquishes his or her Fourth Amendment right to privacy. It does not matter whether the officer views the person as a suspect.

A basic rule is that the *burden of proof* is on the government to prove consent:

> When a prosecutor seeks to rely upon consent to justify the lawfulness of a search, he has the burden of proving that the consent was, in fact, freely and voluntarily given. This burden cannot be discharged by showing no more than acquiescence to a claim of lawful authority. (*Bumper v. North Carolina*, pp. 548–49)

There is no formula by which a court can automatically determine if consent to search was voluntary. The only rule is that

• CASE & COMMENTS •

Kyllo v. United States
533 U.S. 27, 121 S. Ct. 2038, 150 L. Ed. 2d 94 (2001)

JUSTICE SCALIA delivered the opinion of the Court.

This case presents the question whether the use of a thermal-imaging device aimed at a private home from a public street to detect relative amounts of heat within the home constitutes a "search" within the meaning of the Fourth Amendment. **[a]**

I

[U.S. Department of Interior Agent Elliott suspected] that marijuana was being grown in the home belonging to * * * Danny Kyllo, part of a triplex * * * in Florence, Oregon. Indoor marijuana growth typically requires high-intensity lamps. In order to determine whether an amount of heat was emanating from petitioner's home consistent with the use of such lamps, at 3:20 A.M., * * * Agent Elliott and Dan Haas used an Agema Thermovision 210 thermal imager to scan the triplex. Thermal imagers detect infrared radiation, which virtually all objects emit but which is not visible to the naked eye. The imager converts radiation into images based on relative warmth—black is cool, white is hot, shades of gray connote relative differences; in that respect, it operates somewhat like a video camera showing heat images. The scan of Kyllo's home took only a few minutes and was performed from the passenger seat of Agent Elliott's vehicle across the street from the front of the house and also from the street in back of the house. The scan showed that the roof over the garage and a side wall of petitioner's home were relatively hot compared to the rest of the home and substantially warmer than neighboring homes in the triplex. Agent Elliott concluded that petitioner was using halide lights to grow marijuana in his house, which indeed he was. Based on tips from informants, utility bills, and the thermal imaging, a Federal Magistrate Judge issued a warrant authorizing a search of petitioner's home, and the agents found an indoor growing operation involving more than 100 plants. * * *

[Kyllo was indicted and pled conditionally guilty. On appeal, the Court of Appeals upheld the conviction: Kyllo had shown no subjective expectation of privacy because he had made no attempt to conceal the heat escaping from his home, and even if he had, there was no objectively reasonable expectation of privacy because the imager "did not expose any intimate details of Kyllo's life," only "amorphous 'hot spots' on the roof and exterior wall."]

II

* * * With few exceptions, the question whether a warrantless search of a home is reasonable and hence constitutional must be answered no. * * *

On the other hand, the antecedent question of whether or not a Fourth Amendment "search" has occurred is not so simple under our precedent. **[b]** The permissibility of ordinary visual surveillance of a home used to be clear because, well into the 20th century, our Fourth Amendment jurisprudence was tied to common-law trespass. * * * Visual surveillance was unquestionably lawful. . . . As we observed * * * "the Fourth Amendment protection of the home has never been extended to require law enforcement officers to shield their eyes when passing by a home on public thoroughfares." **[c]**

* * * [W]e have held that visual observation is no "search" at all. * * * In assessing when a search is not a search, we have applied somewhat in reverse the principle first enunciated in *Katz* (1967). * * *

The present case involves officers on a public street engaged in more than naked-eye surveillance of a home. We have previously reserved judgment as to how much technological enhancement of ordinary perception from such a vantage point, if any, is too much. While we upheld enhanced aerial photography of an industrial complex in *Dow Chemical,* we noted that we found "it important that this is *not* an area immediately adjacent to a private home, where privacy expectations are most heightened." * * *

III

It would be foolish to contend that the degree of privacy secured to citizens by the Fourth Amendment has been entirely unaffected by the advance of technology. For example, * * * the technology enabling human flight has exposed to public view (and hence, we have said, to official observation) uncovered portions of the house and its curtilage that once were private. * * * The question we confront today is what limits there are upon this power of technology to shrink the realm of guaranteed privacy.

* * * While it may be difficult to refine *Katz* when the search of areas such as telephone booths, automobiles, or even the curtilage and uncovered portions of residences are at issue, in the case of the search of the interior of homes—the prototypical and hence most commonly litigated area of protected

[a] After reading the entire case, does the case and its rule apply only to thermal-imaging technology or to all sense-enhancing technology?

[b] Does Agent Elliott's thermal scan fit your idea of a search? Do you think what constitutes a search can be determined by an "objective" test? Or should the definition of a search depend on the policy issues and values involved?

[c] Would it make sense to require a search warrant every time investigators "stake out" a house to see who enters and leaves?

• CASE & COMMENTS •

privacy—there is a ready criterion, with roots deep in the common law, of the minimal expectation of privacy that *exists,* and that is acknowledged to be *reasonable.* To withdraw protection of this minimum expectation would be to permit police technology to erode the privacy guaranteed by the Fourth Amendment. We think that obtaining by sense-enhancing technology any information regarding the interior of the home that could not otherwise have been obtained without physical "intrusion into a constitutionally protected area," * * * constitutes a search—at least where (as here) the technology in question is not in general public use. **[d]** This assures preservation of that degree of privacy against government that existed when the Fourth Amendment was adopted. **[e]** On the basis of this criterion, the information obtained by the thermal imager in this case was the product of a search.

The Government maintains, however, that the thermal imaging must be upheld because it detected "only heat radiating from the external surface of the house." * * * The dissent makes this its leading point, contending that there is a fundamental difference between what it calls "off-the-wall" observations and "through-the-wall surveillance." But just as a thermal imager captures only heat emanating from a house, so also a powerful directional microphone picks up only sound emanating from a house—and a satellite capable of scanning from many miles away would pick up only visible light emanating from a house. We rejected such a mechanical interpretation of the Fourth Amendment in *Katz,* where the eavesdropping device picked up only sound waves that reached the exterior of the phone booth. **[f]** Reversing that approach would leave the homeowner at the mercy of advancing technology—including imaging technology that could discern all human activity in the home. While the technology used in the present case was relatively crude, the rule we adopt must take account of more sophisticated systems that are already in use or in development. **[g]** The dissent's reliance on the distinction between "off-the-wall" and "through-the-wall" observation is entirely incompatible with the dissent's belief * * * that thermal-imaging observations of the intimate details of a home are impermissible. The most sophisticated thermal imaging devices continue to measure heat "off-the-wall" rather than "through-the-wall"; the dissent's disapproval of those more sophisticated thermal-imaging devices, * * * is an acknowledgment that there is no substance to this distinction. As for the dissent's extraordinary assertion that anything learned through "an inference" cannot be a search, * * * that would validate even the "through-the-wall" technologies that the dissent purports to disapprove. Surely the dissent does not believe that the through-the-wall radar or ultrasound technology produces an 8-by-10 Kodak glossy that needs no analysis (*i.e.,* the making of inferences). And, of course, the novel proposition that inference insulates a search is blatantly contrary to *United States v. Karo,* (1984), where the police "inferred" from the activation of a beeper that a certain can of ether was in the home. The police activity was held to be a search, and the search was held unlawful.

The Government also contends that the thermal imaging was constitutional because it did not "detect private activities occurring in private areas." * * * It points out that in *Dow Chemical* we observed that the enhanced aerial photography did not reveal any "intimate details." * * * *Dow Chemical,* however, involved enhanced aerial photography of an industrial complex, which does not share the Fourth Amendment sanctity of the home. The Fourth Amendment's protection of the home has never been tied to measurement of the quality or quantity of information obtained. In *Silverman,* for example, we made clear that any physical invasion of the structure of the home, "by even a fraction of an inch," was too much, * * * and there is certainly no exception to the warrant requirement for the officer who barely cracks open the front door and sees nothing but the nonintimate rug on the vestibule floor. **[h]** In the home, our cases show, *all* details are intimate details, because the entire area is held safe from prying government eyes. Thus, in *Karo,* the only thing detected was a can of ether in the home; and in *Arizona v. Hicks,* (1987), the only thing detected by a physical search that went beyond what officers lawfully present could observe in "plain view" was the registration number of a phonograph turntable. These were intimate details because they were details of the home, just as was the detail of how warm—or even how relatively warm—Kyllo was heating his residence.

[It would be extremely difficult, if not impossible, to determine what is an "intimate detail" and what is a "nonintimate detail" in a house. Even if a rule could make out this distinction, police would not know in advance if the search with a thermal imager or other high-tech device, would disclose an intimate or nonintimate detail.]

Where, as here, the Government uses a device that is not in general public use, to explore details of the home that would previously have been unknowable without physical intrusion, the surveillance is a "search" and is presumptively unreasonable without a warrant.

Since we hold the Thermovision imaging to have been an unlawful search, it will remain for the District Court to determine whether, without the evidence it provided, the search warrant issued in this case was supported by probable cause—and if not, whether there is any other basis for supporting admission of the evidence that the search pursuant to the warrant produced.

* * *

[d] Notice that the definition of a search has two parts. What are they? Also notice that the sentence preceding Justice Scalia's definition of a search is a statement of policy—a concern that a different definition could erode in-home protections.

[e] Notice this reference to the expectations of Congress and the states in 1791. As with Justice Thomas's *Wilson v. Arkansas* (1995) opinion, Justice Scalia, the other "originalist" on the Court, feels the legitimacy of a ruling depends on whether it squares with the purported intent of the Framers and their common law environment.

[f] This statement seems to answer the question raised in Comment [a]—the Court always deals in questions of constitutional policy, and has to consider the consequences of its decisions.

[g] One consequence, as Justice Scalia states, is to attempt to foresee a future when highly intrusive technology would allow easy observation into the privacy of houses and apartments. In a footnote, the opinion said that "The ability to 'see' through walls and other opaque barriers is a clear, and scientifically feasible, goal of law enforcement research and development."

[h] Is this distinction between a business premises and a home sound? What if a person operates a business out of a home office? For purposes of a search is this a home or a business? Is a fully mobile home such as a recreational vehicle a home or a vehicle?

• CASE & COMMENTS •

The judgment of the Court of Appeals is reversed; the case is remanded for further proceedings consistent with this opinion.

It is so ordered.

JUSTICE STEVENS, with whom THE CHIEF JUSTICE, JUSTICE O'CONNOR, and JUSTICE KENNEDY join, dissenting.

* * *

I

* * * [S]earches and seizures of property in plain view are presumptively reasonable. * * * Whether that property is residential or commercial, the basic principle is the same: "What a person knowingly exposes to the public, even in his own home or office, is not a subject of Fourth Amendment protection." That is the principle implicated here.

While the Court "takes the long view" and decides this case based largely on the potential of yet-to-be-developed technology that might allow "through-the-wall surveillance," * * * this case involves nothing more than off-the-wall surveillance by law enforcement officers to gather information exposed to the general public from the outside of petitioner's home. **[i]** All that the infrared camera did in this case was passively measure heat emitted from the exterior surfaces of petitioner's home; all that those measurements showed were relative differences in emission levels, vaguely indicating that some areas of the roof and outside walls were warmer than others. As still images from the infrared scans show, * * * no details regarding the interior of petitioner's home were revealed. Unlike an x-ray scan, or other possible "through-the-wall" techniques, the detection of infrared radiation emanating from the home did not accomplish "an unauthorized physical penetration into the premises," * * * nor did it "obtain information that it could not have obtained by observation from outside the curtilage of the house." * * *

Indeed, the ordinary use of the senses might enable a neighbor or passerby to notice the heat emanating from a building, particularly if it is vented, as was the case here. Additionally, any member of the public might notice that one part of a house is warmer than another part or a nearby building if, for example, rainwater evaporates or snow melts at different rates across its surfaces. * * * **[j]**

Thus, the notion that heat emissions from the outside of a dwelling is a private matter implicating the protections of the Fourth Amendment (the text of which guarantees the right of people "to be secure *in* their . . . houses" against unreasonable searches and seizures (emphasis added)) is not only unprecedented but also quite difficult to take seriously. Heat waves, like aromas that are generated in a kitchen, or in a laboratory or opium den, enter the public domain if and when they leave a building. A subjective expectation that they would remain private is not only implausible but also surely not "one that society is prepared to recognize as 'reasonable.'" * * *

* * * In my judgment, monitoring such emissions with "sense-enhancing technology," * * * and drawing useful conclusions from such monitoring, is an entirely reasonable public service.

On the other hand, the countervailing privacy interest is at best trivial. After all, homes generally are insulated to keep heat in, rather than to prevent the detection of heat going out, and it does not seem to me that society will suffer from a rule requiring the rare homeowner who both intends to engage in uncommon activities that produce extraordinary amounts of heat, and wishes to conceal that production from outsiders, to make sure that the surrounding area is well insulated. * * * The interest in concealing the heat escaping from one's house pales in significance to the "the chief evil against which the wording of the Fourth Amendment is directed," the "physical entry of the home," * * * and it is hard to believe that it is an interest the Framers sought to protect in our Constitution.

Since what was involved in this case was nothing more than drawing inferences from off-the-wall surveillance, rather than any "through-the-wall" surveillance, the officers' conduct did not amount to a search and was perfectly reasonable.

II

[The application of the Court's holding to technology that is "not in general public use" means that as intrusive technology becomes commonplace, it will allow searches of private areas to be held constitutional. The dissent noted that more than ten thousand thermal-sensing units had been manufactured and could be purchased by anyone. Another criticism is that the holding was limited to privacy only in the home; if new technology has the effect of getting information that otherwise could be obtained only by having an officer enter a place, under the expectation of privacy doctrine, it should apply to commercial places as well as to homes.]

* * *

I respectfully dissent.

[i] Was the heat emanating from Kyllo's house in *plain* view if it took a heat sensor to detect it?

[j] Is this the same as thermal imaging by a government agent?

"the Fourth and Fourteenth Amendments require that a consent not be coerced, by explicit or implicit means, by implied threat or covert force. For, no matter how subtly the coercion was applied, the resulting 'consent' would be no more than a pretext for the unjustified police intrusion against which the Fourth Amendment is directed" (*Schneckloth*, p. 228). In order to determine whether a consent to search was voluntary, a court delves into the facts of the case.

In Chapter 4 many cases are presented where the validity of a *personal search* turns on whether the person was arrested, temporarily stopped on the basis of reasonable suspicion, or gave consent. **United States v. Mendenhall** (1980) demonstrates the difficulty of determining consent. The defendant deplaned at the Detroit Metropolitan Airport. She was observed by two DEA agents who thought her conduct appeared to be "characteristic of persons unlawfully carrying narcotics." They approached Mendenhall, identified themselves as federal agents, and asked to see her identification and airline ticket. The name on her driver's license, Sylvia Mendenhall, and that on the ticket, Annette Ford, did not match. When asked why, she replied she "just felt like using that name." One agent then specifically identified himself as a narcotics agent and Mendenhall "became quite shaken, extremely nervous. She had a hard time speaking." She was then asked if she would accompany the agents to offices just fifty feet away. Once there, she was asked if she would allow a search of her person and handbag. She was told she had the right to decline if she desired. She responded: "Go ahead." A female police officer conducting the search asked Ms. Mendenhall if she consented to the search; she replied that she did. Heroin was found in her undergarments and she was arrested and convicted. The District Court concluded that Ms. Mendenhall had consented to the search.

Two justices, Stewart and Rehnquist, believed that Ms. Mendenhall had consented to the initial stop. Justice Stewart's plurality opinion reasoned that not every police-citizen encounter is a seizure of the person requiring reasonable suspicion or probable cause to be lawful. The test that distinguishes between a consent stop and a seizure is whether, in view of all the facts and circumstances, *a reasonable person would believe that he or she is not free to leave;* "a person is 'seized' only when, by means of physical force or show of authority, his freedom of movement is restrained." This plurality opinion concluded that Ms. Mendenhall could have walked away from the agents at any point. No grabbing or touching occurred. The agents were not in uniform and no weapons were displayed. The initial encounter occurred in public. They asked, but did not demand, to see her identification.

Three justices (Burger, Powell, and Blackmun) felt that the initial stop was a seizure, but was constitutional because the officers had reasonable suspicion to believe that Ms. Mendenhall was a drug courier. These five justices agreed that Ms. Mendenhall was lawfully stopped and searched, but for different reasons. They felt that there was no arrest until the heroin was found. Four dissenting justices (White, Brennan, Marshall, and Stevens) concluded, to the contrary, that Ms. Mendenhall was seized without reasonable suspicion, was subject to an unconstitutional arrest, and that the search was unconstitutional. Although the legality of airport drug stops has been clarified by the Court's acceptance of drug courier profiles as constituting reasonable suspicion, *Mendenhall* demonstrates the difficulty of sorting out the facts that constitute consent.

Knowledge of One's Rights

Sylvia Mendenhall was told that she had a right to not be searched. Is knowledge of one's Fourth Amendment rights a constitutional requirement for a consent search?

—*Schneckloth v. Bustamonte* Case & Comments—

In **Ohio v. Robinette** (1996) a police officer stopped a motorist for speeding and issued a warning. The officer then asked the driver if he, Robinette, was carrying any contraband. He answered that he was not. The officer then asked if he could search the car and Robinette gave consent. The officer did not tell him that he was "free to go." Contraband was found. The Court found that the search was constitutional and that the officer did not have to tell Robinette that he was free to go. The Court noted that in *Schneckloth* it "rejected a *per se* rule very similar to" the Ohio court's ruling that a driver had to be told that he is "free to go" before a valid consent to search the vehicle of a driver about to be released. It reiterated the rule that "voluntariness is a question of fact to be determined from all the circumstances."

Third-Party Consent

The general rule is when two or more persons share a room or common area, one person may voluntarily consent to a search of the *common area* by the police. If evidence is found that incriminates the other party, it may be admitted in evidence. The prosecution must show by a preponderance of the evidence that a person who gave consent had actual authority to consent.

In the leading case on third-party consent searches, **United States v. Matlock** (1974), police searched a house, including the bedroom, with the consent of Mrs. Graff, who was living with Matlock. Evidence of a robbery was found and admitted to prove guilt. The fact that the couple was not married was irrelevant for Fourth Amendment purposes to negate consent. The authority of a third party to consent to the search depends not on property law concepts or on rules of evidence that apply in a trial, "[b]ut rests rather on mutual use of the property by persons generally having *joint access or control* for most purposes, so that it is reasonable to recognize that any of the coinhabitants has the right to permit the inspection in his own right and that the others have assumed the risk that one of their number might permit the common area to be searched" (*United States v. Matlock*). Similarly, a roommate who shares a duffel bag may consent to its search. (*Frazier v. Cupp*, 1969)

In contrast to *Matlock,* the Court held in **Stoner v. California** (1964) that a hotel clerk did not have authority to consent to a police search of a guest's room. The Court said, "It is important to bear in mind that it was the petitioner's constitutional right which was at stake here, and not the night clerk's

• CASE & COMMENTS •

Schneckloth v. Bustamonte
412 U.S. 218, 93 S.Ct. 2041, 36 L.Ed.2d 854 (1973)

MR. JUSTICE STEWART delivered the opinion of the Court.

It is well settled under the Fourth and Fourteenth Amendments that a search conducted without a warrant issued upon probable cause is "*per se* unreasonable . . . subject only to a few specifically established and well-delineated exceptions." It is equally well settled that one of the specifically established exceptions to the requirements of both a warrant and probable cause is a search that is conducted pursuant to consent. **[a]** The constitutional question in the present case concerns the definition of "consent" in this Fourth and Fourteenth Amendment context.

I

[Bustamonte was tried on] a charge of possessing a check with intent to defraud. * * * [At 2:40 A.M., Officer Rand stopped a car with a headlight and a license plate light burned out. Six men were in the car. The driver had no driver's license. Bustamonte and Joe Alcala were passengers. Only Alcala had a driver's license. He said the car belonged to his brother. At the officer's request, all the passengers exited the car. Two other officers arrived.] Officer Rand asked Alcala if he could search the car. Alcala replied, "Sure, go ahead." Prior to the search no one was threatened with arrest and, according to Officer Rand's uncontradicted testimony, it "was all very congenial at this time." Gonzales testified that Alcala actually helped in the search of the car, by opening the trunk and glove compartment. * * * [The police found stolen checks in the trunk that were used to convict Bustamonte of possessing a check with intent to defraud.]

[The evidence was held admissible by the California courts on the ground that the consent to search was voluntarily given. A federal District Court denied a writ of habeas corpus, but the federal Court of Appeals held that consent was a waiver of Fourth and Fourteenth amendment rights and that the state had to prove that respondent knew he had a right to refuse to have his vehicle searched. The Supreme Court took the case to determine whether knowledge of one's rights is required for a valid consent search].

II

* * * [A] search conducted pursuant to a valid consent is constitutionally permissible [and] is wholly valid. * * *

The precise question in this case, then, is what must the prosecution prove to demonstrate that a consent was "voluntarily" given. **[b]** And upon that question there is a square conflict of views. * * * [The Federal Court of Appeals] concluded that it is an essential part of the State's initial burden to prove that a person knows he has a right to refuse consent. The California courts have followed the rule that voluntariness is a question of fact to be determined from the totality of all the circumstances, and that the state of a defendant's knowledge is only one factor to be taken into account in assessing the voluntariness of a consent. * * *

B

* * * [We] agree with the courts of California that the question whether a consent to a search was in fact "voluntary" or was the product of duress or coercion, express or implied, is a question of fact to be determined from the totality of all the circumstances. **[c]** While knowledge of the right to refuse consent is one factor to be taken into account, the government need not establish such knowledge as the *sine qua non* of an effective consent. As with police questioning, two competing concerns must be accommodated in determining the meaning of a "voluntary" consent—the legitimate need for such searches and the equally important requirement of assuring the absence of coercion. In situations where the police have some evidence of illicit activity, but lack probable cause to arrest or search, a search authorized by a valid consent may be the only means of obtaining important and reliable evidence. * * * **[d]** [In] cases where there is probable cause to arrest or search, but where the police lack a warrant, a consent search may still be valuable. If the search is conducted and proves fruitless, that in itself may convince the police that an arrest with its possible stigma and embarrassment is unnecessary, or that a far more extensive search pursuant to a warrant is not justified. In short, a search pursuant to consent may result in considerably less inconvenience for the subject of the search, and, properly conducted, is a constitutionally permissible and wholly legitimate aspect of effective police activity.

[a] Justice Stewart authored the *Coolidge* opinion, a "liberal" warrant-preference construction of the Fourth Amendment. Will this predict his decision on the issue of whether knowledge of one's rights is an element of a consent search?

[b] Can the issue be stated in different ways? State the issue in your own words.

[c] The Court states its decision at the outset: Knowledge of the right to refuse to consent is not constitutionally required. The remainder of the opinion goes to justify the conclusion.

[d] Justice Stewart praises the practical benefits of consent both as a boon to police and as a way to protect the innocent. Does this prove that consent without knowledge of one's rights is constitutional?

· CASE & COMMENTS ·

But the Fourth and Fourteenth Amendments require that a consent not be coerced, by explicit or implicit means, by implied threat or covert force. **[e]** For, no matter how subtly the coercion were applied, the resulting "consent" would be no more than a pretext for the unjustified police intrusion against which the Fourth Amendment is directed. * * *

The approach of the Court of Appeals * * * would, in practice, create serious doubt whether consent searches could continue to be conducted. [Except for rare cases,] * * * where there was no evidence of any coercion, explicit or implicit, the prosecution would nevertheless be unable to demonstrate that the subject of the search in fact had known of his right to refuse consent. **[f]**

The very object of the inquiry—the nature of a person's subjective understanding—underlines the difficulty of the prosecution's burden under the rule applied by the Court of Appeals in this case. Any defendant who was the subject of a search authorized solely by his consent could effectively frustrate the introduction into evidence of the fruits of that search by simply failing to testify that he in fact knew he could refuse to consent. * * *

One alternative that would go far toward proving that the subject of a search did know he had a right to refuse consent would be to advise him of that right before eliciting his consent. That, however, is a suggestion that has been almost universally repudiated by both federal and state courts, and, we think, rightly so. **[g]** For it would be thoroughly impractical to impose on the normal consent search the detailed requirements of an effective warning. Consent searches are part of the standard investigatory techniques of law enforcement agencies. They normally occur on the highway, or in a person's home or office, and under informal and unstructured conditions. The circumstances that prompt the initial request to search may develop quickly or be a logical extension of investigative police questioning. The police may seek to investigate further suspicious circumstances or to follow up leads developed in questioning persons at the scene of a crime. These situations are a far cry from the structured atmosphere of a trial where, assisted by counsel if he chooses, a defendant is informed of his trial rights. **[h]** * * * And, while surely a closer question, these situations are still immeasurably far removed from "custodial interrogation" where, in *Miranda v. Arizona,* we found that the Constitution required certain now familiar warnings as a prerequisite to police interrogation. * * *

Consequently, we cannot accept the position of the Court of Appeals. * * *

* * *

In short, neither this Court's prior cases, nor the traditional definition of "voluntariness" requires proof of knowledge of a right to refuse as the *sine qua non* of an effective consent to a search.

* * *

C

[Bustamonte argues that a "consent" is a "waiver" of rights under the Fourth Amendment and should be treated the same as other waivers. Under *Johnson v. Zerbst,* a "waiver" of the Sixth Amendment right to counsel, and under *Miranda v. Arizona,* a waiver of the Fifth Amendment right to silence, requires the State to demonstrate "an intentional relinquishment or abandonment of a known right or privilege" on the part of the defendant. This requires that the suspect be informed of his rights and that a record be made.]

But these standards were enunciated in *Johnson* in the context of the safeguards of a fair criminal trial. Our cases do not reflect an uncritical demand for a knowing and intelligent waiver in every situation where a person has failed to invoke a constitutional protection. * * * **[i]**

* * *

And in *Miranda v. Arizona,* the Court * * * made it clear that the basis for decision was the need to protect the fairness of the trial itself [because of the inherently coercive atmosphere of police custody]. * * * **[j]**

There is a vast difference between those rights that protect a fair criminal trial and the rights guaranteed under the Fourth Amendment. Nothing, either in the purposes behind requiring a "knowing" and "intelligent" waiver of trial rights, or in the practical application of such a requirement suggests that it ought to be extended to the constitutional guarantee against unreasonable searches and seizures.

A strict standard of waiver has been applied to those rights guaranteed to a criminal defendant to ensure that he will be accorded the greatest possible opportunity to utilize every facet of the constitutional model of a fair criminal trial. Any trial conducted in derogation of that model leaves open the

[e] This reiterates the rule that a consent search must be voluntary. Can voluntariness be separated from knowledge of one's rights?

[f] Justice Stewart indicates a concern that the knowledge-of-rights requirement would end or seriously diminish the number of consent searches. Is this fear realistic? If so, is it too high a price to pay for requiring police to tell individuals what their rights are?

[g] Was it inconvenient for Officer Rand to say to Alcala, "May I open the trunk? You have a right to refuse."? If the officer had provided a written waiver form, would *that* have been impractical? Is the real concern that such statements would reduce the number of consent searches?

[h] How does questioning a suspect in custody differ from requesting consent to search?

[i] The Burger Court's "hierarchy of rights" places Fifth and Sixth Amendment rights above Fourth Amendment rights. Why?

[j] Having stated that the knowledge-of-rights requirement is essential to processes such as confessions and waivers of trial, the Court now goes on to explain why.

possibility that the trial reached an unfair result precisely because all the protections specified in the Constitution were not provided. A prime example is the right to counsel. For without that right, a wholly innocent accused faces the real and substantial danger that simply because of his lack of legal expertise he may be convicted. * * * **[k]**

The protections of the Fourth Amendment are of a wholly different order, and have nothing whatever to do with promoting the fair ascertainment of truth at a criminal trial. Rather, * * * the Fourth Amendment protects the "security of one's privacy against arbitrary intrusion by the police. . . ." * * *

Nor can it even be said that a search, as opposed to an eventual trial, is somehow "unfair" if a person consents to a search. While the Fourth and Fourteenth Amendments limit the circumstances under which the police can conduct a search, there is nothing constitutionally suspect in a person's voluntarily allowing a search. The actual conduct of the search may be precisely the same as if the police had obtained a warrant. And, unlike those constitutional guarantees that protect a defendant at trial, it cannot be said every reasonable presumption ought to be indulged against voluntary relinquishment. **[l]** We have only recently stated: "[It] is no part of the policy underlying the Fourth and Fourteenth Amendments to discourage citizens from aiding to the utmost of their ability in the apprehension of criminals." * * * Rather, the community has a real interest in encouraging consent, for the resulting search may yield necessary evidence for the solution and prosecution of crime, evidence that may ensure that a wholly innocent person is not wrongly charged with a criminal offense.

* * *

E

Our decision today is a narrow one. We hold only that when the subject of a search is not in custody and the State attempts to justify a search on the basis of his consent, the Fourth and Fourteenth Amendments require that it demonstrate that the consent was in fact voluntarily given, and not the result of duress or coercion, express or implied. Voluntariness is a question of fact to be determined from all the circumstances, and while the subject's knowledge of a right to refuse is a factor to be taken into account, the prosecution is not required to demonstrate such knowledge as a prerequisite to establishing a voluntary consent. * * *

MR. JUSTICE MARSHALL, dissenting. [Justices Douglas and Brennan also dissented]

* * * [T]oday the Court reaches the curious result that one can choose to relinquish a constitutional right—the right to be free of unreasonable searches—without knowing that he has the alternative of refusing to accede to a police request to search. I cannot agree, and therefore dissent.

I

B

* * * Freedom from coercion is a substantive right, guaranteed by the Fifth and Fourteenth Amendments. Consent, however, is a mechanism by which substantive requirements, otherwise applicable, are avoided. **[m]** [Unlike exigency exceptions to the warrant requirement, in consent searches] * * * the needs of law enforcement are significantly more attenuated, for probable cause to search may be lacking but a search permitted if the subject's consent has been obtained. **[n]** Thus, consent searches are permitted, not because such an exception to the requirements of probable cause and warrant is essential to proper law enforcement, but because we permit our citizens to choose whether or not they wish to exercise their constitutional rights. Our prior decisions simply do not support the view that a meaningful choice has been made solely because no coercion was brought to bear on the subject.

[The majority mistakenly rests its holding on the convenience of the police, a factor that is not relied on in the search incident to arrest or automobile search rationales. Furthermore, it is too easy for the police to demand entry to search without the overt use of force and for courts to uphold these as consent searches.] * * * I cannot believe that the protections of the Constitution mean so little.

II

My approach to the case is straightforward and, to me, obviously required by the notion of consent as a relinquishment of Fourth Amendment rights. I am at a loss to understand why consent "cannot be taken literally to mean a 'knowing' choice." In fact, I have difficulty in comprehending how a decision made without knowledge of available alternatives can be treated as a choice at all.

[k] The "unfair result" is the conviction of innocent persons. As in the exclusionary rule debate, the point is that Fourth Amendment errors may lead to the exclusion of evidence that proves that the suspect is guilty.

[l] Is Justice Stewart saying that it is fair for the police to take advantage of the ignorance of suspects? Can this be correct? Should standards of fairness be less refined in criminal justice than in other settings (like the proverbial used-car salesperson).

[m] Justice Marshall suggests that consent may be involuntary even when there is no coercion. Is the lack of knowledge of a right the equivalent of coercion?

[n] This is the crux of Justice Marshall's dissent. He views consent as a freedom—to give up a constitutional right—and as such should be narrowly construed. This disagrees sharply with Justice Stewart's view that consent is a law enforcement tool, that Courts should broadly construe and support.

---

* * * I would therefore hold, at a minimum, that the prosecution may not rely on a purported consent to search if the subject of the search did not know that he could refuse to give consent. * * *

* * *

I must conclude, with some reluctance, that when the Court speaks of practicality, what it really is talking of is the continued ability of the police to capitalize on the ignorance of citizens so as to accomplish by subterfuge what they could not achieve by relying only on the knowing relinquishment of constitutional rights. Of course it would be "practical" for the police to ignore the commands of the Fourth Amendment, if by practicality we mean that more criminals will be apprehended, even though the constitutional rights of innocent people also go by the board. But such a practical advantage is achieved only at the cost of permitting the police to disregard the limitations that the Constitution places on their behavior, a cost that a constitutional democracy cannot long absorb. * * *

---

or the hotel's." Although *Stoner* was decided before the "expectation of privacy" principle of *Katz* (1967) was enunciated, as a rule of thumb it seems that only persons with an expectation of privacy over an area may consent to a search. *Stoner* was preceded by *Chapman v. California* (1961), which held that a landlord may not give consent to a police search into a tenant's apartment or house, even though the landlord has a general right of entry for normal inspection purposes.

Matlock and *Stoner* were clarified, extended, and harmonized in **Illinois v. Rodriguez** (1990). Police were given consent to enter a house by a person who in reality did not possess common authority over the premises; however, the police *reasonably believed* that she had common authority and possession of the place. The Court held that the entry was reasonable under the Fourth Amendment. Gail Fisher complained to Chicago police that Edward Rodriguez had beaten her. The police accompanied Gail from her mother's apartment to the respondent's apartment, where she let them in with a key that she had. On the drive to Rodriguez's apartment, she referred to his apartment as "our" place. The officers did not know that she had moved out a month earlier, had removed her clothing, did not invite friends there, was never in the house when Rodriguez was not there, did not contribute to the rent, and did not have her name on the lease.

Instead of characterizing the case as one of a valid waiver of Fourth Amendment rights, the proper question is "whether the right to be free of *unreasonable* searches has been *violated*." The Court noted that in making probable cause decisions, police and magistrates do not violate Fourth Amendment rights if they make reasonable mistakes. By analogy, a reasonable mistake in a consent case does not violate the individual's Fourth Amendment rights. Thus, *Rodriguez* answers a question left open by *Matlock* and extends the authority of police to enter a place under third-party consent. The Court differentiated *Stoner,* which is still good law, by indicating that the case does not mean that apparent authority can never be the basis for a third-party search, only that the police must have a reasonable basis to believe that a third party has authority over a place. Ordinarily,

motel clerks do not have general authority to enter a guest's room outside of normal cleaning and maintenance functions. On the other hand, when a woman with a key to an apartment claims that her boyfriend beat her, there is no reason the police should not believe that she lives in the apartment. Justice Marshall dissented in *Rodriguez,* (joined by Justices Brennan and Stevens), urging the theory that because entry into a home without a warrant is presumptively unreasonable, police cannot dispense with the rights of a person where that person has not limited his expectation of privacy by sharing his home with another. Under this analysis, the reasonableness of the police officers' action is irrelevant. He stressed that the police should have obtained a warrant in this situation and that the warrant requirement should not be dropped to prevent inconvenience to police officers.

Scope of Consent

Dade County police officer, Frank Trujillo, overheard . . . Enio Jimeno, arranging what appeared to be a drug transaction over a public telephone. Believing that Jimeno might be involved in illegal drug trafficking, Officer Trujillo followed his car. The officer . . . pulled Jimeno over to the side of the road in order to issue him a traffic citation [for making an illegal turn]. Officer Trujillo told Jimeno that he had been stopped for committing a traffic infraction. The officer went on to say that he had reason to believe that Jimeno was carrying narcotics in his car, and asked permission to search the car. He explained that Jimeno did not have to consent to a search of the car. Jimeno stated that he had nothing to hide and gave Trujillo permission to search the automobile. After Jimeno's spouse, respondent Luz Jimeno, stepped out of the car, Officer Trujillo went to the passenger side, opened the door, and saw a folded, brown paper bag on the floorboard. The officer picked up the bag, opened it, and found a kilogram of cocaine inside.

The Jimenos were charged with possession with intent to distribute cocaine in violation of Florida law. (***Florida v. Jimeno,*** 1991, pp. 249–50)

The Florida Supreme Court ruled that the officer had to receive specific consent to open the container. The United

States Supreme Court reversed, holding that under the Fourth Amendment the scope of a consent search depends on whether the search was reasonable. In this case, the search was reasonable because, according to Chief Justice Rehnquist, the "scope of a search is generally defined by its expressed object." Jimeno "did not place any explicit limitation on the scope of the search," and a "reasonable person may be expected to know that narcotics are generally carried in some form of a container." He stressed that Jimeno could have limited the scope of the search, and concluded with the policy expressed in *Schneckloth,* that "The community has a real interest in encouraging consent, for the resulting search may yield necessary evidence for the solution and prosecution of crime. . . ."

Justice Marshall dissented, joined by Justice Stevens. He noted that under the Court's precedent, there is a lesser expectation of privacy in cars, but a heightened expectation of privacy in the content of closed containers. These "distinct privacy expectations . . . do not merge when the individual uses his car to transport the container." Also, the way in which "reasonableness" is used by the majority could lead to absurd or unacceptable results. After all, if "a reasonable person may be expected to know that drug couriers frequently store their contraband on their persons or in their body cavities" then consent to search a car could lead to a body-cavity search. He argued that Jimeno, in fact, did not consent to a search of the envelope and the Court should interpret rights expansively and interpret limitation of rights (such as consent) narrowly.

LAW IN SOCIETY

POLICE PERJURY AND THE FOURTH AMENDMENT

A decade ago, police perjury was the "the dirty little secret of our criminal justice system."[57] Now it is common knowledge, thanks in large part to the exposed perjury of Detective Mark Fuhrman in the O. J. Simpson murder trial.[58] A law professor reports that his students frequently interrupt classroom hypotheticals involving illegal police conduct with statements such as, "What if the police just lie about what happened?"[59] And this, indeed, is the critical point. People in all walks of life, from presidents of the United States on down, have been known to lie, and it is necessary for society to prosecute business fraud, for professional organizations to investigate and sanction falsehoods by its members, and so forth. "What distinguishes police officers is their unique power—to use force, to summarily deprive a citizen of freedom, to even use deadly force, if necessary—and their commensurately unique responsibilities—to be the living embodiment of the 'law' in our communities, as applied fairly to every member."[60] If police officers routinely commit perjury about the legality of arrests or searches and routinely get away with it, then the true result is not a personal benefit (a good arrest record) or even a misguided belief that this enhances public safety—it effectively destroys the basic constitutional rights of every person who is subject to such illegal action and threatens the rights of the rest of us (including cops) who have not yet been framed by police lies. This kind of perjury occurs most frequently in drug enforcement.

It is important to begin with Professor Morgan Cloud's observation that not "all police officers lie under oath, or that most officers lie, or that even some officers lie all the time."[61] An insightful article by Professor Andrew McClurg notes a profound paradox: (1) "Most police officers are honorable, moral persons," and (2) "Many of these same police officers lie in the course of their official duties." Any resolution of the problem of police perjury requires understanding the pressures that proliferate police perjury.

The kind of police perjury most likely to undermine Fourth Amendment rights occurs when (1) a police officer thinks that a defendant was in possession of contraband or incriminating evidence, (2) the officer obtained the evidence by an unconstitutional act, and (3) in a suppression hearing the officer "embellishes" the truth by testifying so as to make it appear as if the stop, arrest, or search was performed in a constitutional manner. "Routine" perjury is a greater threat to rights than more outrageous action, such as planting evidence on innocent persons or "booming" (illegally breaking into homes without a warrant or pretense of legality), because most cops, being honorable, draw the line at such "over-the-top" behavior.[62] But they will "shade" the truth, if they view constitutional rights as "mere technicalities"—as impediments to effective law enforcement. Professor Richard Uviller, who spent a year observing a New York Police Department street crimes unit, notes that like most people, "cops were raised with a strong sense of justice, and they naturally apply it when the occasion arises."[63]

Scholars who have studied this issue believe that routine perjury in regard to the seizure of incriminating evidence began as a result of the federalization of the exclusionary rule in *Mapp v. Ohio* (1961). A frequently cited 1971 article by Irving Younger, a former prosecutor and judge, noted that before *Mapp,* police easily testified to making illegal stops and finding contraband—"This had the ring of truth." After *Mapp,* judges suppressed evidence obtained in this way. Police officers then discovered "that if the defendant drops the narcotics on the ground, after which the policeman arrests him, then the search is reasonable and the evidence is admissible." After this, "dropsy" testimony increased enormously.[64] Younger's observations were substantiated by a before-after empirical study of police testimony in misdemeanor narcotics arrests showing that the percent of arrests where narcotics were "hidden on the body" dropped from about 25 percent of all arrests to about 5 percent, while "dropsy" cases, which accounted for about 10 percent to 15 percent of arrests before *Mapp,* increased to 41 percent for narcotics officers.[65]

"Routine" perjury is close to impossible for defense lawyers, prosecutors, or judges to detect because it is so simple:

Lying about search and seizure matters "was part of everyday police work" according to a former New York City police officer interviewed for an article announcing that cops in New

York must now go to school to learn to tell the truth. The Mollen Commission cataloged a "litany" of manufactured search and seizure tales uncovered by its investigation:

> For example, when officers unlawfully stop and search a vehicle because they believe it contains drugs or guns, officers will falsely claim in police reports and under oath that the car ran a red light (or committed some other traffic violation) and that they subsequently saw contraband in the car in plain view. To conceal an unlawful search of an individual who officers believe is carrying drugs or a gun, they will falsely assert that they saw a bulge in the person's pocket or saw drugs and money changing hands. To justify unlawfully entering an apartment where officers believe narcotics or cash can be found, they pretend to have information from an unidentified civilian informant or claim they saw the drugs in plain view after responding to the premises on a radio run. To arrest people they suspect are guilty of dealing drugs, they falsely assert that the defendants had drugs in their possession when, in fact, the drugs were found elsewhere where the officers had no lawful right to be.[66]

A Harvard Law School conference held shortly after the verdict in the O. J. Simpson case concluded: "There are no national studies or statistics on police perjury, and there is considerable disagreement on how widespread the problem is."[67] Nevertheless, a great deal of anecdotal evidence from police commissions and others indicate that police perjury is widespread.[68] A study of Chicago police asked them: "In your experience, do police officers ever shade the facts a little (or a lot) to establish probable cause when there may not have been probable cause in fact?"—sixteen officers responded "yes" and five responded "no."[69] Of course, the actual number is unknown because "[b]y their very nature, successful lies will remain undetected, and we would expect a perjurer to attempt to conceal his crime".[70] Former Kansas City and San Jose police chief and Hoover Institution research fellow, Joseph D. McNamara, estimated "that *hundreds of thousands* of law-enforcement officers commit felony perjury every year testifying about drug arrests." He based this estimate on the fact that about one million drug arrests a year are for possession, not selling; that hundreds of thousands of police swear under oath that the drugs were in *plain view* or that the defendant gave *consent* to a search; and that: "This may happen occasionally but it defies belief that so many drug users are careless enough to leave illegal drugs where the police can see them or so dumb as to give cops consent to search them when they possess drugs."[71]

"Routine" perjury has serious consequences. First, there is the danger that police fabrication will lead to the charging or conviction of innocent persons. In some cases, the police have convinced themselves, against the evidence, that the victim of their lies was guilty. Well-known cases include Richard Jewell, suspected of bombing Olympic Park at the 1996 Atlanta Olympics, and Rolando Cruz, who was on death row in Illinois—but there are many others.[72]

Second, the frequent commission of "pious perjury" creates an enabling atmosphere that allows a minority of "rogue cops" to go "over-the-top" by planting evidence on innocent people or booming. There is no way of knowing whether such abuses are widespread. Commission reports and the anecdotes of police and lawyers do *not* indicate that such practices are routine. Nevertheless, when such cases do occur, they are reported and quite a few have appeared in the last decade.

- Philadelphia's 39th District scandal where six "rogue cops" planted evidence on many innocent people, including a grandmother who pestered them with questions when they came looking for her grandson, and spent two years in prison for her verbal challenges; the city paid out at least seven million dollars and fourteen hundred cases were reviewed.[73]
- Perjury convictions of cops in the mid-1990's NYPD 30th Precinct scandal in which wrongful arrests and booming were connected to police participation in illegal drug sales.[74]
- Convictions of five New York State Troopers who faked fingerprint evidence in thirty cases by lifting fingerprints from *a corpse,* planning to plant it on anyone charged with the crime.[75]
- Perjury to cover up a police ring that systematically shook down drug dealers in Hartford, Connecticut.[76]
- The conviction of Eufrasio G. Cortez, a California narcotics Officer of the Year, who admitted that he stole a half-million dollars from drug busts, committed perjury thirty times, beat suspects on twenty occasions, and used false statements in search warrants one hundred times over a fifteen-and-a-half-year police career.[77]

Third, the practice cannot be kept hidden and eventually leads to a loss of public confidence in the police. As a result, jurors become skeptical of police testimony that undermines fair prosecutions, minorities become less willing to call the police for protection, and the public is less interested in law enforcement as a career.[78]

Fourth, the practice undermines the morale and diminishes the sense of pride felt by honest officers.[79] When police lie to cover their corruption, the professional self-esteem of honest cops is injured. Professor Uviller sensed in honest cops "a sense of betrayal by the corrupt members who have demeaned the Job and made it harder for the rest to convince the public of their probity."[80]

Fifth, the practice leads to corrupt police work, including the use of drugs by undercover officers who then lie to the jury about such practices. East Texas police officer and FBI undercover agent Kim Wozencraft finally told the truth about routinely planting evidence, using drugs with suspects, and lying about it in court. She was convicted of perjury, served time, and later resumed her life as a novelist and editor of *Prison Life* magazine.[81]

Sixth, perjury by police forces honest cops into the risky role of being "whistle-blowers" and suffering consequences, or joining the "blue wall of silence" and tolerating the corruption around them. Officer Michael McEvoy of the Arlington Heights, Illinois, Police Department "blew the whistle" on a case of police perjury and would have been fired by his chief, but the Arlington Heights Board of Fire and Police Commissioners reinstated McEvoy when his account was substantiated by a third officer.[82] It is not implausible to believe that a number of whistle-blowers were not as lucky as Officer McEvoy.

Seventh, the practice drives a wedge between judges who occasionally suppress evidence and police who become angry at judges who do not accept their lies. Judge Joseph Q. Koletsky of Hartford, Connecticut, threw out evidence of a crime after the testimony of arresting police was clearly contradicted by physical evidence. Detectives told a plausible story of stopping a suspect *next* to his truck. He was arrested because he reached behind himself, establishing the basis for an arrest and a search incident to arrest during which cocaine was supposedly found. However, spilled powder cocaine *in the cab* of the truck supported the defendant's testimony that the officers simply drew guns and arrested him, illegally, in his truck. After the evidence was suppressed, the detectives insisted that they did the right thing. "It's a bad decision, but what can you do?" Officer Murzin said. "Some people live in the real world and some people don't."[83] In the *real world,* people with power can lie and get away with it.

In a more famous case, federal judge Harold Baer suppressed evidence in a New York City drug bust. He had been a member of the Mollen Commission on Police Corruption and expressed skepticism of the police in his decision. After media coverage, it quickly became a national issue during the 1996 presidential campaign. In an unusual move, the judge ordered a second hearing, heard more testimony, and decided that the search and seizure was lawful.[84]

Finally, and most important, police perjury diminishes liberty and undermines the constitutional order. In addition to the growing subcultural belief that the Constitution is an impediment to be overcome, judicial acceptance of police perjury undermines the very rationale given for the exclusionary rule: deterrence of police illegality.

An important reason police perjury is pervasive is that it is in large measure condoned by the courts. According to Alan Dershowitz, "A judge in Detroit after listening on one day to more than a dozen 'dropsy' cases . . . chastised the police for not being more 'creative,' but nonetheless accepted their testimony."[85] Professor Cloud gives five reasons judges accept police perjury:

1. It can be difficult to determine if a witness is lying.
2. Judicial dislike of the exclusionary rule.
3. The cynical belief that "most defendants in the criminal justice system are guilty," and "even if they are innocent of these specific crimes, [they] are guilty of something." Therefore, "it is not too disturbing that evidence will not be suppressed."
4. They assume that criminal defendants will commit perjury and so distrust the testimony of suspects.
5. Tact. "Judges simply do not like to call other government officials liars—especially those who appear regularly in court. It is distasteful; it is indelicate; it is bad manners."[86]

To this list Professor McClurg adds that "judges do not want to generate adverse publicity that portrays them as being 'soft on crime;' especially, "elected judges are afraid of jeopardizing their chances of reelection."[87]

Numerous proposals have been made to deal with this issue. Many involve modifying legal rules and procedures, including:

- Eliminate the exclusionary rule.
- Eliminate the exclusionary rule for violent crimes but not for crimes like drug possession.
- Expand the use of judicial warrants to all nonexigent searches and seizures while narrowing the exigency exception.
- Admit polygraphs of witnesses in suppression hearings.
- Make probable cause more flexible to allow commonsense judgments.
- Permit impeachment of police testimony through proof of bias and motive to lie, and by allowing evidence of the prevalence of the blue wall of silence.
- Allow judges to order discovery and allow cross-examination where there is an initial showing of police perjury in a suppression hearing.[88]

Some of these proposals are implausible, but some may have a limited impact on police perjury. Institutional changes have been proposed. Skolnick and Fyfe propose major changes in police departments and a move toward community policing as a way to ameliorate the problem.[89] Professor McClurg believes that "[w]e cannot rely with confidence on external actors or institutions to control police lying," and that "[p]olice lying will be substantially reduced only when more police officers come to view it as an unacceptable practice."[90] He believes that police perjury is so pervasive because of the contradiction between the fact that most police officers are moral persons and that many will commit "routine" perjury, which causes cognitive dissonance, and to reduce the tension, the officers rationalize their behavior by coming to believe that lying is moral behavior.[91] To deal effectively with police perjury, he proposed a system of police academy training and on-the-street mentoring to show that the end-justifies-the-means reasoning that supports perjury is short-sighted and injurious, and to fortify the initial decency that rookies bring to the academy before it becomes hardened into cynicism.[92] The details of this interesting proposal are beyond the scope of this section. Clearly it can work only if the head of the law enforcement agency and the political leadership of the municipality support this.

To sum up, "routine" police perjury is pervasive and it seriously threatens the existence of Fourth Amendment rights. As noted in Chapter 1, the most important aspect of the Rule of Law is "congruence": "The practices of the government must be *congruent* with the law as written. The glorious promises of procedural justice enshrined in the Bill of Rights can quickly become hollow and breed a terrible cynicism against government and law if they are routinely ignored."

Such cynicism is widespread, and it is vital that judges, and more important, that the police, take rights seriously.

SUMMARY

The Supreme Court has expressed a preference for the search warrant over warrantless searches. The most important reason is that a warrant places the judgment of a detached and neutral judicial officer between the police and the citizen in deciding whether probable cause exists to effect a search. A judicial officer who receives fees from warrants issued or who becomes too closely attached to the police search effort is not a neutral and detached magistrate. To obtain a search warrant, an officer must present a written affidavit to a magistrate and swear to the truth of the facts in an *ex parte* hearing that purports to show probable cause. If authorized by statute, a warrant can be obtained by telephone. The place to be searched must be precisely described, but a reasonable mistake in describing the place will not make the search illegal. Search warrants for materials protected by the First Amendment must describe the materials exactly. Statutes allow anticipatory warrants that authorize police to seize evidence from places that do not contain the contraband at the time the warrant is issued, but reasonably expect the contraband to be delivered to the location. A defendant can obtain a hearing to challenge an executed search warrant in cases where he or she can make out a preliminary showing that the officer who made out the warrant intentionally lied about material facts or made statements in the warrant with reckless disregard for the truth. Search warrants must be executed within ten days of issuance. The Fourth Amendment requires that police officers knock and announce their presence when executing a warrant; the knock and announce element can be set aside by a magistrate in a no-knock warrant where potential danger to officers or loss of evidence is likely if the police knock and announce. However, a blanket no-knock policy violates the Fourth Amendment. After a warrant is executed, the officer must specify each item seized on an inventory and return, and a copy must be presented to the person whose premises were searched.

In the 1960s search and seizure law was modernized by creating the expectation of privacy doctrine under *Katz v. United States,* eliminating the mere evidence rule, and using the general-reasonableness construction of the Fourth Amendment to weaken the particularity requirement to support administrative search warrants and to authorize investigative stops on less than probable cause as in *Terry* (1968). Together these changes made Fourth Amendment interpretation more flexible. The expectation of privacy doctrine holds that the Fourth Amendment protects that which a person seeks to keep private and that which society is prepared to recognize as reasonable. The expectation of privacy doctrine brought electronic eavesdropping by the government within the parameters of the Fourth Amendment. Property interests are still protected by the Fourth Amendment, but the Court looks to the subjective and objective expectation of privacy balanced against the needs of effective law enforcement. The

expectations given the greatest weight are those of the privacy of the home and bodily integrity. Under *Camara v. Municipal Court* (1967) a nonpolice government employee who seeks to enter a home without the consent of the owner to enforce an administrative ordinance must have a judicial warrant; such a warrant, however, need not have all the characteristics of a criminal search warrant, and indeed, in some ways resembles a general warrant. The Fourth Amendment does not prohibit the use of undercover agents who are invited into homes and private areas under false pretense; such an agent cannot conduct a general search of the premises, but can testify as to any criminal activity that occurs in his presence.

Eavesdropping warrants are easier to obtain under the Foreign Intelligence Surveillance Act than under normal warrant procedures. A change of the law under the USA PATRIOT Act allows the CIA and FBI to trade information more easily, but also allows such warrants to be used for ordinary law enforcement purposes as well as against terrorism, raising threats to civil liberties.

Probable cause is defined as known facts that could lead a reasonably prudent person to draw conclusions about unknown facts. It is a standard of evidence sufficiency that allows a law enforcement official to arrest a person, obtain a warrant, or perform a warrantless search. Probable cause may be based on hearsay. When the hearsay is provided by a secret informant, the Supreme Court has required magistrates to examine the affidavits carefully. Under the older *Aguilar-Spinelli* two-pronged test, the magistrate had to be convinced that the officer's affidavit supplied credible information about the informant's veracity and his or her basis of knowledge. The Court in *Illinois v. Gates* (1983) replaced the two-pronged test with a totality-of-the-circumstances test, which it applied to an anonymous tip so that a deficiency in one prong can be compensated for by a strong showing as to the other, or by some other indicia of reliability in determining the overall reliability of a tip.

The plain view doctrine allows the seizure of contraband when a police officer who makes the seizure is lawfully in the place (by a warrant or by virtue of being in a public place) and the illegal nature of the thing seized is immediately apparent. The "immediately apparent" rule is, in effect, a rule of probable cause. A police officer cannot create plain view by illegally entering a premises or by manipulating evidence beyond that authorized by the purpose of the officer's mandate. A plain view seizure can be based on any of the senses, not only on sight. Open fields are not protected by the Fourth Amendment; evidence seized by officers who trespass on open land is admissible. The curtilage is the area and buildings immediately surrounding a house, and is protected by the Fourth Amendment to the extent that the expectation of privacy in the area is secured. Airplane and helicopter flyovers may lawfully obtain evidence of what is visible in a curtilage, even if fenced, because commercial overflights have eliminated the expectation of privacy from the air. Ordinary devices, such as flashlights and field glasses, that enhance the senses do not undermine the "immediately apparent" rule. The use of an enhancement device such as a beeper or a thermal imager, without a warrant, that detects movement within a home and suggests criminal activity, violates the Fourth Amendment. A warrant must be obtained for enhancement devices that are not in general public use.

A person may consent to relinquish his Fourth Amendment right to privacy to a law enforcement officer. An officer who seeks consent to search need have no reasonable suspicion or probable cause to do so. An officer need not inform a person, when requesting consent to search, that the person has a constitutional right to refuse. Facts and circumstances of a consent encounter must show that the consent was voluntary. The burden of proof is on the government to show voluntariness. Entry under the pretense of having a search warrant negates consent. A person who shares a common area with another may give consent to the police to search, as may a person who reasonably appears to share a place. Landlords or hotel keepers cannot give consent for a criminal search. Police may rely on consent given by a person who reasonably appears to have shared control over an area, even if, in fact, the person has no authority or control over an area. Consent to search an area, such as a car, gives police the right to open containers located in the area.

LEGAL PUZZLES

HOW HAVE COURTS DECIDED THESE CASES?

DETACHED AND NEUTRAL MAGISTRATE

3–1. Defendant was arrested during a controlled purchase of marijuana. A detective from the Kentucky State Police Department and the Commonwealth Attorney for Warren County went to the office of the Circuit Court Clerk to obtain the search warrant at issue. Several weeks prior to the issuance of the warrant, the Clerk was informed that all of the judges for Warren County would be absent from the county and that she would be responsible for signing all search warrants. She contacted the court's legal counsel to confirm that she possessed the authority to sign search warrants in this situation. She was advised that under Kentucky statutory law, she, as the Circuit Court Clerk, was authorized to sign search warrants when all of the judges were absent from Warren County.

The Clerk was presented with a search warrant, an affidavit in support thereof, and a certification that all judges were absent from the county. The Clerk read both the search warrant and the affidavit. She found that there was sufficient probable cause for the warrant to issue and she signed the warrant.

Defendant questions whether the Clerk was sufficiently neutral and detached from law enforcement, noting that she ran in a partisan race to be elected to her post, belongs to the same political party as the Commonwealth's Attorney, and that the two have attended some of the same fundraisers.

Kentucky's circuit court clerks are assigned to the judicial branch and are under the administrative control of the Chief Justice of the Kentucky Supreme Court.

Was the magistrate detached and neutral?

HELD: Yes

3-1. Circuit court clerks are associated with the judiciary, not with law enforcement. Thus, in accordance with *Shadwick,* there is no per se lack of neutrality and detachment with respect to Kentucky's circuit court clerks. A *statute* allows circuit court clerks to issue search warrants in the absence of all judges from the county. Unlike the situation in *Coolidge,* the clerk is not confronted with the dual and conflicting responsibility of both "ferreting out crime" and prosecuting crime. Unlike in *Lo-Ji,* the clerk did not participate in the execution of the warrant, accompany police officers to the scene, nor direct them as to which items should be seized. *United States v. Bennett,* 170 F.3d 632 (6th Cir. 1999).

SEARCH WARRANT: ANTICIPATORY

3–2. Responding to a Postal Inspection Service undercover operation advertisement placed in a sexually explicit magazine. Defendant wrote to an undercover agent indicating a willingness to trade tapes of child pornography. A call between Defendant and the agent was monitored. Defendant gave detailed descriptions of some of the tapes in his collection and told the agent that he could "put together" tapes for trading. He requested tapes of girls between the ages of eight and ten in a bathtub ("Bath Time"), and forwarded a name and mailing address at a post office box. The mail box and Defendant's name and home address were verified, and a tape was sent to the P.O. mail box.

On the same day, an application for an anticipatory search warrant for Defendant's residence was made, requesting authorization to seize evidence of child pornography. The evidence to be seized included videotapes depicting child pornography; video equipment for viewing, producing, and reproducing child pornography; and lists of individuals with whom Defendant traded. The application conditioned the search on Defendant accepting delivery of the "Bath Time" tape and returning to his residence with the tape in his possession. The anticipatory warrant was granted by a federal magistrate.

Defendant was observed picking up the tape at the post office box and returning with it to his home, where the warrant was executed. A tape depicting child pornography, fifteen computer disks containing child pornography, fifty videocassettes, several pornographic magazines, a VCR player and television set, as well as various letters describing Defendant's solicitation of child pornography and his offers to trade such materials were seized.

Was the anticipatory warrant supported by probable cause?

Holding available from instructor

EXPECTATION OF PRIVACY

3–3. John Doe sued Detective Broderick under 42 U.S.C. §1983 alleging that Det. Broderick (1) violated Doe's Fourth Amendment rights by entering the file room of a substance abuse treatment clinic and searching Doe's confidential treatment records along with numerous other patients' records; and (2) violated his rights under 42 U.S.C.A. §290dd-2, which prohibits the disclosure of treatment records of any patient in substance abuse education treatment.

A robbery from a jewelry store near a methadone clinic led Det. Broderick to speculate that the robber might be a patient, and that knowing the identities of the patients who had been receiving treatment at the clinic during or near the time of the grand larceny would aid the investigation. Det. Broderick prepared a search warrant affidavit requesting all patients' names, dates of birth, Social Security numbers, photographs, home addresses, and work locations if available, the opening of any file cabinets, desks, closets, locked safes, boxes, bags, compartments, or things in the nature thereof, found in or upon said premises to include any and all electronically stored computer data. The affidavit explained that narcotics addicts often resort to robbery. A magistrate issued a warrant. A clinic employee initially refused to allow officers into the file room but relented when threatened with obstruction of justice charges. Items seized and taken from the clinic include the clinic's log book, files with biographical information for seventy-nine male patients, their photographs, and a large number of dosage sheets that detailed how much methadone was being administered to a given patient. Doe's records included his urine screen history and confidences that Doe shared with his counselors at the clinic.

Does Doe have an expectation of privacy in his methadone clinic records?

Holding available from instructor

PLAIN VIEW

3–4. An experienced police officer made a valid automobile stop of a car driven by a lone male at 2:45 A.M.; the vehicle was registered in a woman's name; the vehicle was displaying an out-of-area license plate. The driver, Murphy, told the officer that he had no driver's license or other identification on him. Given these facts, the court held that the officer's pat-down search of the driver for weapons was valid under *Terry v. Ohio*. While conducting the pat-down search, the officer noticed a wallet in Mr. Murphy's back pants pocket. He asked Mr. Murphy about the wallet, and Mr. Murphy voluntarily showed it to him, stating that it contained only pictures and no document of identification. The officer discerned what looked like a driver's license or identification card protruding from the wallet, however, and he seized the wallet for a search and found a driver's license.

Was the nature of the driver's license immediately apparent and therefore in plain view?

Holding available from instructor

CONSENT

3–5. The Boston PD established a TIPS (Boston Police Taxi Inspection Program for Safety) program in response to numerous robberies and the murders of two taxi cab drivers. Taxi cab and fleet owners could opt to participate by affixing decals to each of the cab's rear side windows and a third in a conspicuous location in the rear passenger compartment. The decals stated in English and Spanish that "THIS VEHICLE MAY BE STOPPED AND VISUALLY INSPECTED BY THE BOSTON POLICE AT ANY TIME TO ENSURE DRIVER'S SAFETY." The police commissioner's order instructed uniformed and plainclothes personnel to make frequent stops of taxis that featured the decals to check on the operators' safety. Officers were told that stops were especially necessary during the evening and early morning hours and in isolated and high-crime areas. Taxi drivers were not to be detained longer than is necessary to check on the welfare of the operator. Passengers are to be given a brief explanation of the purpose of the stop, and a form had to be completed at the time of the stop.

Plainclothes officers in an unmarked police car stopped a taxi after midnight in a high-crime area shortly after receiving a radio call of a robbery in the vicinity indicating that foot patrol officers were following a suspect. The plainclothes officers saw a man enter the cab near the vicinity of the crime. The passenger looked at the officers and slouched down. The officers followed the cab, thought they saw indications of gun possession by the passenger by the way he moved his shoulders, and stopped the cab. The officers testified that they were aware of the TIPS decals, but their primary concern was the shooting investigation. The passenger reached into his left jacket pocket with his left hand, and was ordered out of the cab. When he did so a gun fell out of his pocket. He was arrested and convicted with being a felon in possession of a firearm. The cab was owned by a fleet owner.

Was the stop justified by consent to stop the cab?

Holding available from instructor

FURTHER READING

Fred P. Graham, *The Due Process Revolution: The Warren Court's Impact on the Criminal Law* (New York: Hayden Book Co., 1970).

Craig M. Bradley, *The Failure of the Criminal Procedure Revolution* (Philadelphia: University of Pennsylvania Press, 1993).

Barbara J. Shapiro, *"Beyond Reasonable Doubt" and "Probable Cause": Historical Perspectives on the Anglo-American Law of Evidence* (Berkeley: University of California Press, 1991).

ENDNOTES

1. Jim McGee and Brian Duffy, "Someone to Watch over Us," *Washington Post,* June 23, 1996.

2. B. Drummond Ayres Jr., "The Simpson Case: The Law; For Judge, a Case Where Circumstances Outweigh Safeguards," *New York Times,* July 8, 1994.

3. Scott Turow, "Policing the Police: The D.A.'s Job," in Jeffrey Abramson, ed. *Postmortem: The O.J. Simpson Case* (City Basic Books, 1996), 190.

4. H. R. Uviller, *Tempered Zeal* (Chicago: Contemporary Books, 1988), 125–26.

5. *United States ex rel., Pugh v. Pate,* 401 F.2d 6 (7th Cir. 1968), quoted in Commentary to *Federal Rules of Criminal Procedure,* 1987–88 Educational Edition (St. Paul: West Publishing Co., 1987), 129.

6. Geoffrey P. Alpert, "Telecommunications in the Courtroom: Telephonic Search Warrants," *University of Miami Law Review* 38 (1996): 625–35; the states are: Arizona, Montana, Nebraska, New York, Oregon, South Dakota, Utah, Washington, and Wisconsin.

7. Alpert, "Telecommunications," 630.

8. P. Pringle, "Officer Explains Search of Simpson's Property Police Say They Saw Blood, Feared a Life at Stake," *Dallas Morning News,* July 6, 1994.

9. S. Estrich, "Who's on Trial, O.J. or Cops?" *USA Today,* September 22, 1994.

10. Walter Gerash, "Next Two Days Critical for Simpson Hearing," *Rocky Mountain News,* July 6, 1994.

11. *Lyons v. Robinson,* 783 F.2d 737 (8th Cir. 1985), citing *U. S. v. Gitcho,* 601 F.2d 369, 371 (8th Cir. 1979).

12. James A. Adams, "Anticipatory Search Warrants: Constitutionality, Requirements, and Scope," *Kentucky Law Journal* 79 (1991): 681–733, 687, n. 19.

13. Ibid., 705–706, n. 67.

14. Ibid., 695–97.

15. Ibid., 698–99.

16. Ibid., 720–21.

17. Ibid., 715, 727–29.

18. Ibid., 715, 727–29.

19. Ibid., 709–10.

20. *Federal Rules of Criminal Procedure,* R. 41(C)(1).

21. *U.S. v. Ruminer,* 786 F.2d 381 (10th Cir. 1986).

22. *Ker v. California* (1963).

23. Information from the *Denver Post,* February 4, 2000; July 18, 2000; and the *Denver Rocky Mountain News,* February 5, 2000; February 6, 2000; March 14, 2000; June 28, 2000.

24. Federal Communications Act of 1934, §605.

25. Walter F. Murphy, *Wiretapping on Trial: A Case Study in the Judicial Process* (New York: Random House, 1965).

26. Bruce Allen Murphy, *Wild Bill: The Legend and Life of William O. Douglas* (New York: Random House, 2003).

27. See *Ward v. County of San Diego,* 791 F.2d 1329 (9th Cir. 1986); *Stewart v. Lubbock County,* 767 F.2d 153 (5th Cir. 1985).

28. *Payton,* 585–86, citing *United States v. United States District Court,* 313.

29. *On Lee v. United States* (1952); *Lopez v. United States* (1963); *United States v. White* (1971) (plurality opinion); 18 U.S.C. §2511(2)(c) & (d).

30. Michael P. O'Connor and Celia Rumann, "Emergency and Anti-Terrorist Power: Going, Going, Gone: Sealing the Fate of the Fourth Amendment," *Fordham International Law Journal* 26 (2003): 1234–1264.

31. 50 U.S.C. §§1801, 1804.

32. James Risen and David Johnston, "F.B.I. Report Found Agency Not Ready to Counter Terror," *New York Times,* June 1, 2002; David Johnston and Don Van Natta Jr., "Wary of Risk, Slow to Adapt, F.B.I. Stumbles in Terror War," *New York Times,* June 2, 2002.

33. In re: Sealed Case No. 02-001, 310 F.3d 717, 721 (U.S. FISCR 2002).

34. 310 F.3d at 723.

35. 310 F.3d at 724.

36. Philip Shenon, "Secret Court Says F.B.I. Aides Misled Judges in 75 Cases," *New York Times,* August 23, 2002.

37. O'Connor and Rumann; David Hardin, "Note: The Fuss over Two Small Words: The Unconstitutionality of the USA PATRIOT Act Amendments to FISA Under the Fourth Amendment," *George Washington Law Review* 71 (2003): 291–345.

38. Hardin, "The Fuss," 345.

39. Robert R. Reinertsen and Robert J. Bronson, "Informant Is a Dirty Word," in J.N. Gilbert, ed., *Criminal Investigation: Essays and Cases* (Columbus: Merrill Publishing Co.), 99–103.

40. Reinertsen and Bronson, "Informant," 99.

41. "Snitches" have been implicated in many cases of wrongful conviction: see Clifford Zimmerman, "From the Jailhouse to the Courthouse: The Role of Informants in Wrongful Convictions," in Saundra D. Westervelt and John A. Humphrey, eds. *Wrongly Convicted: Perspectives of Failed Justice* (New Brunswick, NJ: Rutgers University Press, 2001), 55–76.

42. C. Whitebread, "The Burger Court's Counter-Revolution in Criminal Procedure: The Recent Criminal Decisions of the United States Supreme Court," *Washburn Law Journal* 24 (1985): 471–98.

43. See Wayne R. LaFave, "Fourth Amendment Vagaries (of Improbable Cause, Imperceptible Plain View, Notorious Privacy, and Balancing Askew)," *Journal of Criminal Law and Criminology* 74 (1983): 1171–1224.

44. Corey Fleming Hirokawa, "Making the 'Law of the Land' the Law on the Street: How Police Academies Teach Evolving Fourth Amendment Law," *Emory Law Journal* 49 (1) (2000): 295–334.

45. *People v. Griminger,* 71 N.Y.2d 635, 640, 524 N.E.2d 409, 412, 529 N.Y.S.2d 55 (1988).

46. *Griminger,* 71 N.Y. at 639, citing *People v. Rodriguez,* 52 NY2d 483, at 489 (1981).

47. Charles H. Whitebread and Christopher Slobogin, *Criminal Procedure: An Analysis of Cases and Concepts, Fourth Edition* (New York: Foundation Press, 2000), 225.

48. *Dickerson v. Minnesota* (1993).

49. *Whren v. U.S.* (1996), see Chapter 4.

50. 41 Cal.3d 373, 21 Cal. Rptr. 499, 710 P.2d 299 (1985).

51. 42 Cal.3d 1302, 233 Cal. Rptr. 2, 729 P.2d 166 (1986).

52. William J. Broad, "Ideas & Trends; We're Ready for Our Close-Ups Now," *New York Times,* January 16, 2000.

53. The Joint Operations Command Center, operational in Washington, D.C., since 9/11, and shared by the Metropolitan Police Department, the F.B.I., the Secret Service, the State Department, and the Defense Intelligence Agency, quickly allowed an author to view on a screen lawn furniture and plantings in his backyard in a Washington, D.C., neighborhood. "Theoretically, with a

few clicks of the mouse the system could also link up with thousands of closed-circuit cameras in shopping malls, department stores and office buildings, and is programmed to handle live feeds from up to six helicopters simultaneously." Matthew Brzezinski, "Fortress America," *New York Times Magazine*, February 23, 2003, §6, 38.

54. F.J. Remington, D.J. Newman, E.L. Kimball, M. Melli and H. Goldstein, *Criminal Justice Administration, Materials and Cases*, (Indianapolis: Bobbs-Merrill, 1969), 32.

55. *Schneckloth v. Bustamonte* (1973), 222.

56. In *Davis v. U.S.* (1946) the Supreme Court upheld a conviction in which evidence was obtained from a locked room by an arrested person upon the demand of government agents. The evidence consisted of rationing stamps, which were public property and which the defendant-proprietor was required by law to keep. The opinion stressed that this decision would not apply to private property. This opinion seems anomalous with current law.

57. Morgan Cloud, "The Dirty Little Secret," *Emory Law Journal* 43 (1994): 1311–49.

58. Scott Turow, "Simpson Prosecutors Pay for Their Blunders," *New York Times,* October 4, 1995; *Larry King Live,* 9:00 PM ET, CNN, August 28, 1995, Transcript No. 1524–2, "Will O.J. Testify?" (Guests: Alan Dershowitz, Simpson Defense Attorney; Bill Hodes, Professor of Law, Indiana University); David Margolick, "Forget O.J.—The Question Becomes: Is Fuhrman the Question?" *New York Times,* September 10, 1995; Carl Rowan, "Fuhrman Tips the Scale at Simpson Trial," *Chicago Sun-Times,* September 10, 1995; Charles L. Lindner, "The Simpson Trial; When You Can't See the Forest for the Leaf," *Los Angeles Times,* September 3, 1995.

59. Andrew J. McClurg, "Good Cop, Bad Cop: Using Cognitive Dissonance Theory to Reduce Police Lying," *University of California at Davis Law Review* 32 (1999): 389–453.

60. David N. Dorfman, "Proving the Lie: Litigating Police Credibility," *American Journal of Criminal Law* 26 (1999): 462–503.

61. Cloud, "Secret," 1313, footnote omitted.

62. George James, "Officer Admits Illegal Apartment Entries," *New York Times,* January 10, 1996. He claimed the precinct's most senior officers raided and searched a building without first obtaining a warrant, and "[i]t was kind of implied that this was what they wanted." This account was hotly denied by Commissioner Bratton, who claimed that it was not corroborated: Barbara Ross and Wendell Jamieson, "Bratton Slams Dirty 30 Sgt.," *Daily News* (New York), January 12, 1996.

63. H. Richard Uviller, *Tempered Zeal* (Chicago: Contemporary Books, 1988), 158.

64. Irving Younger, "The Perjury Routine," *The Nation,* (1967) 596–97, cited in Cloud, "Secret," 1317; as a judge he noted the problem in *People v. McMurtry*, 314 N.Y.S.2d 194 (Crim. Ct. 1970).

65. Sarah Barlow, "Patterns of Arrests for Misdemeanor Narcotics Possession: Manhattan Police Practices 1960–62," *Criminal Law Bulletin* 4 (1968): 549–81. See Paul Chevigny, "Comment," *Criminal Law Bulletin* 4 (1968): 581.

66. McClurg, "Good Cop," 398–99, footnotes omitted.

67. Sarah Terry, "Experts Try to Pin Down Extent of Police Misconduct," *New York Times,* November 19, 1995.

68. See Joseph D. Grano, "A Dilemma for Defense Counsel: *Spinelli-Harris* Search Warrants and the Possibility of Police Perjury," *University of Illinois Law Forum* (1971): 405, 409, cited in Cloud, "Secret," 1312, n. 4. Other legal commentators cited in Cloud include: Alan Dershowitz, *The Best Defense,* (1982) xxi–xxii; Comment, "Police Perjury in Narcotics 'Dropsy' Cases: A New Credibility Gap," *Georgetown Law Journal* 60 (1971): 507. Professors Cloud, McClurg (396–404), and Dorfman (460–62) review all these materials, and they all believe that these kinds of practices are routine.

69. Myron W. Orfield, Jr., "The Exclusionary Rule and Deterrence: An Empirical Study of Chicago Narcotics Officers," *University of Chicago Law Review* 54 (1987): 1016–69.

70. Cloud, "Secret," 1313, footnote omitted.

71. Joseph D. McNamara, "Law Enforcement; Has the Drug War Created an Officer Liars' Club?" *Los Angeles Times,* February 11, 1996.

72. McClurg, "Good Cop," 417–419; Daniel Jeffreys, "Last Hope on Death Row: Call McCloskey; He Gave up a Lucrative Career in Business to Help People Wrongly Imprisoned. He Has Saved Four Lives: So Far." *The Independent,* January 3, 1996.

73. Don Terry, "Philadelphia Shaken by Criminal Police Officers," *New York Times,* August 28, 1995; Barbara Whitaker, "Philadelphia Still Reeling from Police Scandal Officials Review More than 1,400 Arrests Made by Six Officers Charged with Theft, Framing Suspects," *Dallas Morning News,* September 3, 1995.

74. "Officer Is Acquitted in Theft and Perjury," *New York Times,* January 26, 1996, (Officer Stephen Setteducato. Earlier, Officer John Arena was cleared by a federal jury in Manhattan), *New York Times,* January 5, 1996; Seth Faison, "In Plea Deal, Officer Agrees to Give Details of Corruption," *New York Times,* May 24, 1994; George James, "Officer Admits Illegal Apartment Entries," *New York Times,* January 10, 1996; see note 62.

75. "Ex-Trooper Admits a Plot to Falsify Fingerprints," *New York Times,* December 29, 1995; "Prosecutor Tries to Make Trooper Talk on Tampering," *New York Times,* January 4, 1996.

76. Lynne Tuohy, "Grand Juror Details Police Abuse of Power; 6 Arrests Made, More Expected; Police Corruption Probe Leads to Six Arrests in Hartford," *Hartford Courant,* December 2, 1993; "Police Arrested in Corruption Probe; State Trooper, Hartford Officer in Custody After 9-month Inquiry; State, Hartford Officer Taken into Custody," *Hartford Courant,* December 1, 1993.

77. Victor Merina, "Officers Marked Sobel for Death, Jury Told; Trial: Ex-deputy Says He and Colleagues Wanted to Eliminate the Sheriff's Sergeant When They Learned He Secretly Cooperated with Prosecutors," *Los Angeles Times,* March 21, 1992.

78. Joe Sexton, "Jurors Question Honesty of Police," *New York Times,* September 25, 1995; McClurg, "Good Cop," 419–23.

79. H. Richard Uviller, *Tempered Zeal* (Chicago: Contemporary Books, 1988), 115.

80. Ibid., 12–13.

81. Keith Kachtick, "Rush to Justice," *Texas Monthly,* January 1996.

82. Marco Buscaglia, "Board Clears Officer of Misconduct Charges," *Chicago Tribune,* January 5, 1996, (Metro Nwest).

83. Matthew Kauffman, "Judge Doubts City Officers' Account of Arrest," *Hartford Courant,* February 6, 1996 (Statewide Section).

84. Dorfman, "Proving," 471, n. 73; McClurg, "Good Cop," 406–11.

85. Alan Dershowitz, "Police Tampering: How Often, Where" *Buffalo News,* February 21, 1995.

86. Cloud, "Secret," 1321–24, footnotes omitted.

87. McClurg, "Good Cop," 405.

88. The many sources of these proposals are found in Dorfman. The last proposal is that of Prof. Dorfman.

89. Jerome K. Skolnick and James J. Fyfe, *Above the Law: Police and the Excessive Use of Force* (New York; Free Press, 1993).

90. McClurg, "Good Cop," 410.

91. Ibid., 412–15, 424–29.

92. Ibid., 412–13, 428–53.

JUSTICES OF THE SUPREME COURT

ROOSEVELT'S LIBERALS
DOUGLAS–MURPHY–JACKSON–RUTLEDGE

Franklin Roosevelt appointed no justices during his first term in office and yet ended up appointing more justices (nine) than any president except Washington, thanks in large part to his unprecedented four terms in office. Roosevelt's primary goal was to name individuals who would support New Deal legislation on economic and labor issues. For a half century, a conservative Supreme Court had, on behalf of the wealthy, more or less restricted the ability of the democratic branches of government to pass legislation to improve working conditions and on behalf of the interests of workers, farmers, and the lower middle class.

The ascendancy of the Roosevelt administration during the great economic crisis of the 1930s finally led to a liberalization of the bench. As the Supreme Court reduced its role in passing on the wisdom of economic legislation, a new wave of civil rights cases began to press forward for hearing. The civil liberties cases of the 1940s and 1950s included freedom of speech, freedom of the press, religious

freedom, freedom of conscience regarding loyalty issues, and criminal procedure. It was not a foregone conclusion that justices who were liberal on economic matters would also be liberal on civil rights and criminal procedure questions. Four of Roosevelt's appointees—Black, Douglas, Murphy, and Rutledge—were "liberal" in favoring the incorporation of the Bill of Rights into the Fourteenth Amendment. They tended to vote for criminal defendants and, when joined by Frankfurter and Jackson, placed limits on local police officers whose actions were found to have violated the Due Process Clause of the Fourteenth Amendment.

Justices Douglas, Rutledge, and Jackson have been ranked as "near great" and Justice Murphy as average by a poll of scholars, but Murphy's originality in criminal procedure stands as a real contribution to criminal jurisprudence, as it defined the actual position taken during the due process revolution of the 1960s.

WILLIAM O. DOUGLAS

Connecticut 1898–1980

Democrat

Appointed by
Franklin Delano Roosevelt

Years of Service:
1939–1975

*Collection of the Supreme Court
of the United States.
Photographer: Harris and Ewing*

LIFE AND CAREER Douglas grew up in relative poverty in Yakima, Washington; he was six years old when his father, a Presbyterian missionary, died. He entered Whitman College in 1916 and taught school for a few years before entering law school. He graduated second in his class at Columbia Law School, practiced briefly at a Wall Street law firm, and then taught at Columbia and Yale law schools, gaining recognition as an expert in financial law and as a proponent of the pragmatic jurisprudence of legal realism.

Douglas joined President Roosevelt's New Deal administration in 1934, to work on the Securities and Exchange Commission (SEC), a new watchdog agency designed to regulate the stock market. He became a member of the SEC in 1936 and its chairman in 1937. First known as antibusiness, Douglas

built bridges to the business world and tried to stimulate internal reform in the stock exchange to minimize governmental intrusion. He became an adviser to the president and was Roosevelt's fourth nominee to the Court at the young age of thirty-nine. Intensely ambitious, Douglas was seen as a potential presidential candidate before President Roosevelt ran for a third term, and was a leading candidate for the vice presidential post in 1940 and 1944, after he had been appointed to the Supreme Court.

A restless man and hard worker, he traveled to all parts of the world, authored thirty-two books (many were travelogues), was a frequent speaker on issues of foreign policy and was a staunch environmentalist long before it was a popular issue. When not traveling, he spent his summers hiking and camping in Washington state. He was thrice divorced and married four times, indicating a somewhat chaotic person life.

CONTRIBUTION TO CRIMINAL PROCEDURE Despite his enormous output of cases, he wrote relatively few criminal procedure opinions. In his early years on the Court, he was tentative in taking a consistent liberal position, and wrote a 1944 opinion holding that an arrest in a public place involving public property was not entitled to the same protection as a search of the home, a decision severely criticized by Justice Frankfurter. Nevertheless, he became a very liberal justice and consistently voted for the "incorporation plus" doctrine. His solid liberal vote on criminal issues under five chief justices was a critical element in the due process revolution.

(Continued)

SIGNATURE OPINION *Griffin v. California* (1965) Held: a state judge could not tell a jury that although a defendant had a right to remain silent, it could take his failure to deny or explain facts in the case into consideration in determining whether the facts are true. The Court held that the federal rule against such comment was based on the Fifth Amendment privilege against self-incrimination, and that it therefore applied to the states via the Due Process Clause of the Fourteenth Amendment. "For comment on the refusal to testify is a remnant of the 'inquisitorial system of criminal justice,' which the Fifth Amendment outlaws. It is a penalty imposed by courts for exercising a constitutional privilege."

ASSESSMENT Douglas served longer than any other justice: thirty-six years. He was steeped in the philosophy of Legal Realism, which held that a judge's policy preferences were the prime determiner of the judge's decisions. His outspoken activism made him one of the most controversial justices. He was extremely hard working, and wrote a large number of opinions (many on antitrust and economic issues), but wrote them very quickly. Despite his acknowledged brilliance, his opinions did not always spell out the doctrinal foundation of his decisions. His *Douglas v. California* (1963) opinion, holding that a defendant has a right to counsel on first appeal, did not clarify whether the decision rested on due process or equal protection.

In addition to his contributions to the law of business regulation, Douglas helped to advance an absolutist concept of free speech, with his dissent in *Dennis v. United States* (1951), arguing against the conviction of Communist Party leaders for advocating the violent overthrow of the government (his dissent became the law in the 1970s). He wrote, "Free speech has occupied an exalted position because of the high service it has given our society. Its protection is essential to the very existence of a democracy." His *Griswold v. Connecticut* (1965) contraception law opinion, established the right of privacy, based on values inherent in the First, Fourth, and Fifth Amendments. *Griswold* laid the foundation for the *Roe v. Wade* (1973) abortion rights ruling.

FURTHER READING

Bruce Allen Murphy, *Wild Bill: The Legend and Life of William O. Douglas* (New York: Random House, 2003).

FRANK MURPHY

Michigan 1890–1949

Democrat

Appointed by
Franklin Delano Roosevelt

Years of Service:
1940–1949

Collection of the Supreme Court of the United States. Photographer: Pach Brothers Studio

LIFE AND CAREER Frank Murphy, a native of Michigan, obtained his undergraduate and law degrees from the University of Michigan. He had an extensive public career prior to his appointment to the Court, serving as an Army officer in World War I; a federal assistant prosecutor; a judge of the Detroit Recorder's Court; mayor of Detroit from 1930 to 1933, when he gained national fame for innovative attempts to ease the burden of the Great Depression; governor general of the Philippines from 1933 to 1937, on a presidential appointment; governor of Michigan from 1937 to 1939, during which time he refused to order the violent suppression of automobile workers' sit-down strikes; and attorney general of the United States from 1939 to 1940, when he established the civil rights division. His vigor and compassion made him a leading political figure and even a potential presidential candidate, despite the fact that he was Catholic, a handicap at that time.

CONTRIBUTION TO CRIMINAL PROCEDURE In other criminal procedure cases, Murphy voted in favor of the defendant's right to counsel in every case; wrote a majority opinion that struck down the systematic exclusion of day-laborers from juries; and dissented in cases that allowed the government to wiretap and electronically eavesdrop without a warrant. With one exception, he sided with the defendant in coerced confessions cases.

SIGNATURE OPINION Dissent in *Adamson v. California* (1947). The majority held that the Fifth Amendment is not incorporated into the Fourteenth Amendment. Justice Black dissented, arguing for total incorporation. Justice Murphy's dissent best anticipated the due process revolution of the 1960s, by establishing the "incorporation plus" concept that supported both the incorporation of the Bill of Rights into the Fourteenth Amendment *and* the independent use of the Due Process Clause to strike down unfair governmental action. "Occasions may arise where a proceeding falls so far short of conforming to fundamental standards of procedure as to warrant constitutional condemnation in terms of a lack of due process despite the absence of a specific provision in the Bill of Rights."

(Continued)

ASSESSMENT Justice Murphy was, with Justices Douglas and Rutledge, the most liberal justice on the Court in the 1940s. He dissented in the case upholding the removal of Japanese Americans from their homes to relocation centers during World War II. He wrote many pro-worker opinions in the field of labor law. He consistently favored the expansion of First Amendment rights, opposed racial segregation, favored gender equality, and generally supported the underdog.

Murphy was not a great legal stylist or a profound legal thinker and has been rated an average justice by scholars. He probably delegated more drafting to his law clerks than other justices. He brought to the Court his extensive experience in public life and "a great heart attuned to the cries of the weak and suffering." His unwavering commitment to civil liberties strengthened the "solid minority" of criminal procedure liberals in the Stone and Vinson Courts and helped pave the way to the due process revolution.

FURTHER READING

J. Woodford Howard, Jr., *Mr. Justice Murphy*: *A Political Biography* (Princeton: Princeton University Press, 1968).

ROBERT H. JACKSON

New York 1892–1954

Democrat

Appointed by
Franklin Delano Roosevelt

Years of Service: 1941–1954

Collection of the Supreme Court of the United States. Photographer: Harris and Ewing

LIFE AND CAREER Robert Jackson developed a reputation as the most skillful government litigator in Washington, D.C., in the heady days of the New Deal. Yet his formal educational background consisted only of high school and a year at Albany Law School. He trained for the law as an apprentice in a law office and opened his own practice in Jamestown, New York, in 1913. Over the next twenty years, he developed a prosperous practice and became a respected attorney in his region.

Treasury Secretary Morgenthau persuaded Jackson to join the New Deal administration in 1934 as general counsel for the Bureau of Internal Revenue. His reputation soared by winning complex cases for the government. He was appointed assistant attorney general in charge of the Antitrust Division in 1936 and

argued ten cases for the government before the Supreme Court. He won the important case upholding the Social Security Act on broad grounds that made the laws easier to administer. He supported President Roosevelt's "court packing" plan. He became solicitor general in 1938, where he "showed a remarkable insight into both basic governmental policy and the tactics of advocacy." His service as attorney general from January 1940 to mid-1941 was marked more by careful legal advice than by administrative innovations. His most brilliant achievement was his Attorney General's Opinion justifying President Roosevelt's controversial "lend-lease" program in the dark days before America's entry into World War II, whereby fifty overage destroyers were transferred to the British navy in return for military bases in Bermuda.

CONTRIBUTION TO CRIMINAL PROCEDURE He generally joined Justice Frankfurter in opposing incorporation. His votes were mixed; in some Fourth Amendment cases he was quite critical of abusive police work, but he was not as consistently liberal as Justices Black, Douglas, Murphy, or Rutledge. He believed in judicial restraint and was a strong proponent of federalism. Thus, in state confessions cases he often voted to uphold the confession under the Due Process Clause, especially where a very serious crime was charged, unless the police action made it perfectly clear that the confession was obtained involuntarily.

SIGNATURE OPINION *Johnson v. United States* (1948). Police standing outside a hotel room smelled opium and entered without a warrant. In holding that this was a violation of the Fourth Amendment, Justice Jackson issued the classic statement about the value of a search warrant: "The point of the Fourth Amendment, which often is not grasped by zealous officers, is not that it denies law enforcement the support of the usual inferences which reasonable men draw from evidence. Its protection consists in requiring that those inferences be drawn by a neutral and detached magistrate instead of being judged by the officer engaged in the often competitive enterprise of ferreting out crime."

ASSESSMENT He generally was liberal on civil rights issues, writing the decisive compulsory flag salute opinion (holding that requiring school children to salute the flag violated First Amendment rights). In substantive criminal law, he wrote a ringing affirmation of the common law principle that the government cannot create a legislative definition of a serious crime, such as theft, without the element of criminal intent (*mens rea*).

He was a great stylist, and many of his opinions are filled with interesting and quotable passages. He was interested in the improvement of criminal justice and chaired the American Bar Association special committee on the administration of criminal justice. He interrupted his service as a justice for over a year after World War II to serve as the chief American prosecutor at the Nuremberg War Crimes Tribunal trials of the top Nazi leaders. In this role, he made an abiding contribution to international law and the development of human rights.

FURTHER READING

Glendon Schubert, ed. *Dispassionate Justice: A Synthesis of the Judicial Opinions of Robert H. Jackson* (Indianapolis: Bobbs-Merrill, 1969).

WILEY B. RUTLEDGE

Iowa 1894–1949

Democrat

Appointed by
Franklin Delano Roosevelt

Years of Service:
1943–1949

Collection of the Supreme Court of the United States. Photographer: Harris and Ewing

LIFE AND CAREER Rutledge was the son of a fundamentalist Baptist minister who preached in Kentucky, Tennessee, and North Carolina. A biographer notes that "although in later life he became a Unitarian, his father's fervor was reflected in his zeal for justice and right." He graduated from the University of Wisconsin in 1914, taught school for a few years, and nearly died from tuberculosis. He recovered and received his LL.B. degree from the University of Colorado in 1922. After two years of law practice in Boulder, he became a law professor, and then dean of the University of Iowa College of Law in the 1930s. He developed a reputation as an inspiring teacher and civic activist.

Moved by the plight of the poor and unemployed during the Great Depression, he spoke out publicly against the Supreme Court's rulings that struck down New Deal legislation. As one of the few academics to support President Roosevelt's "court packing" scheme in 1937—a stance that led several Iowa state legislators to threaten to withhold law school

salaries in reprisal—Rutledge came to the attention of the Roosevelt administration. He was appointed to the United States Court of Appeals for Washington, D.C., in 1939 and served for four years before his nomination to the Supreme Court.

CONTRIBUTION TO CRIMINAL PROCEDURE Rutledge joined Justice Black to be a member of the Court's liberal bloc in the 1940s in favor of incorporating the Bill of Rights in *Adamson* (1947), helping to make incorporation a respectable, if controversial, position. Indeed, he joined the more liberal "incorporation plus" position with Justices Murphy and Douglas.

SIGNATURE OPINION *Brinegar v. United States* (1949). Writing for the majority in upholding an automobile search of a bootlegger, Justice Rutledge stated the classical definition of probable cause that has been oft-repeated by the Court: "In dealing with probable cause, however, as the very name implies, we deal with probabilities. These are not technical; they are the factual and practical considerations of everyday life on which reasonable and prudent men, not legal technicians, act. . . . Requiring more would unduly hamper law enforcement. To allow less would be to leave law-abiding citizens at the mercy of the officers' whim or caprice."

ASSESSMENT Rutledge's tenure on the Court was marked by a fierce dedication to the principles of liberty. His most famous opinion, a dissent in the *Yamashita* (1946) case, acknowledged the authority of the United States to try the former Japanese commander of the Philippines accused of authorizing or allowing atrocities by his troops, but dissented bitterly that the proceeding was characterized by none of the hallmarks of due process. He agreed with the Court in another case that a naturalized citizen could not have his citizenship revoked merely because he had belonged to the Communist Party at the time of his naturalization.

FURTHER READING

Landon G. Rockwell, "Justice Rutledge on Civil Liberties," *Yale Law Journal* 59 (1949): 27.

CHAPTER
4

ARREST AND STOP UNDER THE FOURTH AMENDMENT

Because the strongest advocates of Fourth Amendment rights are frequently criminals, it is easy to forget that our interpretations of such rights apply to the innocent and the guilty alike.

—Justice Thurgood Marshall in *United States v. Sokolow,*
490 U.S. 1, 11 (1989)

CHAPTER OUTLINE

KEY TERMS AND PHRASES *(CONTINUES ON NEXT PAGE)*

Arrest

Arrest warrant

Body cavity search

Booking

Brevity requirement

Bright-line rule

Citizen's arrest

Companion case

Custodial arrest

Custody

De novo review

Drug courier profile

False arrest

Field interrogation

"Fleeing felon" rule

Frisk

Illegal arrest

In personam jurisdiction

In-presence rule

Internal passport

Inventory search

Investigative stop

Least intrusive means

Merchant's privilege

Mistaken arrest

Mixed question of law and facts

Police officer expertise

Pretext search	Search incident to arrest	Stop and frisk
Protective sweep	Seizure of the person	Strip search
Reasonable force	Sobriety checklane	Sui generis
Roadblock	Source city	*Terry* stop
Scope of a search incident to arrest	Stop	Vagrancy statute

ARREST IN A TIME OF TERROR

In the weeks and months following 9/11, federal agents rounded up twelve hundred persons, keeping their identity secret and detaining some for months. "Except for 93 individuals facing criminal charges, virtually none of the detainees has been identified publicly, and the locations where they are held also remain secret."[1] Most of the arrests were based on the alien or illegal alien status of detainees, so that the strict rules of arrest under probable cause did not apply. In June 2003 the Department of Justice Office of the Inspector General (OIG) issued a report critical of many of these arrests and the conditions of detention following them. For example, "The FBI in New York City made little attempt to distinguish between aliens who were subjects of the FBI terrorism investigation . . . and those encountered coincidentally. . . . [E]ven in the chaotic aftermath of the September 11 attacks, the FBI should have expended more effort attempting to distinguish between aliens who it actually suspected of having a connection to terrorism from those aliens who, while possibly guilty of violating federal immigration law, had no connection to terrorism but simply were encountered in connection with" a lead.[2] The DOJ admitted that it sought every legal way to detain suspects in the immediate aftermath of the attack. "But the inspector general's report found that some lawyers in the department raised concerns about the legality of the tactics, only to be overridden by senior officials."[3] As evidence that the DOJ cast "too wide a net," *none* of the 762 immigrants of the twelve hundred arrestees were charged as terrorists, although most were deported. A "communications blackout" and limits on phone calls to one per week kept families of the detainees in the dark about their whereabouts. Some were not notified of charges against them for over a month, although pre-9/11 Immigration and Naturalization Service (INS) rules required notice within twenty-four hours.[4]

Although aliens can be detained without probable cause, no good purpose is served by using law enforcement resources on flimsy cases. Some of the arrests were based on mere rumors. "Some illegal immigrants were picked up at random traffic stops, others because of anonymous tips that they were Muslims with erratic schedules, officials said. . . . A Muslim man, for instance, was arrested when an acquaintance wrote to officials that the man had made 'anti-American statements.' The statements 'were very general and did not involve threats of violence or suggest any direct connection to terrorism,' the report found, but the man had overstayed his visa and was held."[5] The arrests did not follow standard procedures for arrests of aliens before 9/11. On September 17, 2001, Chief INS Administrative Judge Michael Creppy issued an order closing all postarrest hearings of "special interest" cases to the public; deleting case identification from court calendars posted outside courtrooms where hearings were held; and restricting the means of contacting lawyers (the government does not provide counsel for INS deportation hearings). Professor Schulhofer has criticized these postarrest procedures for "the strict conditions of *secrecy* that surround the program, the *length* of detentions, and the absence of any *judicial review* at key stages."[6]

A detailed story was provided of the arrest of Dr. Al Bader al-Hazmi, a Saudi citizen, on September 12, 2001, in his San Antonio townhouse.[7] Dr. al-Hazmi, 31, "a wisp of a man with soulful eyes and an almost unsettling serenity," was living in the United States with his wife and young daughters while in a radiology residency at the University of Texas Health Science Center. FBI agents came to his home because the passenger list of the flight that crashed into the Pentagon included Nawaf and Salem Alhazmi (an alternate rendering of the name). Dr. al-Hazmi told the agents that "Al-Hazmi is common like the Smith name in Saudi Arabia." The doctor said he would not answer questions without seeing a lawyer. The agents searched his home for six hours, allowing al-Hazmi to make a call after five hours. He called a lawyer for Saudi Aramco, the oil company that was sponsoring his medical residency. Knowing of his good character, the lawyer told him not to worry. Nevertheless, al-Hazmi was arrested and taken from his home in his nightshirt, and no word was heard from him for about a week. He was not informed of any charges. There was no suspicious background evidence whatsoever against Dr. al-Hazmi. After a night in a holding cell with illegal aliens from Mexico, he spent a second night in solitary confinement in the county jail. The next day he was flown to New York, in a plane that stopped in Minneapolis to pick up the genuine 9/11 suspect, Zacarias Moussaoui. After seven days in custody in Manhattan, he was again transferred, shackled, to a prison in Brooklyn. He finally saw a court-appointed lawyer on his seventh day of confinement in New York. On the tenth day, he met with a lawyer hired by the Saudi consulate.

On his twelfth day of confinement, he was able to explain away a variety of facts that appeared suspicious to the investigators: that al-Hazmi is a common name; that it was common for Saudis to obtain American visas in Jiddah; that the $10,000 he wired from Saudi Arabia to another Saudi doctor in Texas was for him to buy furniture and a car when he moved to America; that recent trips to Boston and Washington were to attend medical courses; that five plane tickets to California that he had purchased on Travelocity for "people with Saudi names" were for him, his wife, and his three children to accompany him to a medical conference; and that two calls that he had received in the past couple of years from a bin Laden were from an Abdullah bin Laden who directed the Northern Virginia office of a world assembly of Muslim youth. An FBI spokesman said that this was not cleared up when the FBI agents first came to Dr. al-Hazmi's home because "as soon as he lawyered up, we couldn't ask him to clear up our questions, and then the system took over and he was off to New York." This is not entirely convincing, for were he allowed to have better access to a lawyer on the first day he was arrested, he and his family would have been spared a good deal of trauma and the United States would have not expended valuable investigation resources on an innocent party.

Most of the 9/11 "sweeps" were aimed at aliens, who have lesser rights against arrest for immigration purposes. The government has used the material witness law to arrest persons believed to have information about terrorists. This law applies to all persons—citizens and aliens alike.[8] At least one New York federal judge has dismissed a perjury indictment after a person was detained on the federal material witness act, finding that the government exceeded its authority because it did not detain the person for a criminal proceeding. Without going into the details of the material witness law, this case, *United States v. Awadallah*, raises serious concerns about the potential for misuse of the power to detain people in a time of terror.[9]

OVERVIEW OF THE LAW OF PERSONAL DETENTION

The physical detention of a person by a police officer is a drastic event even if it is a routine police activity. It is stressful to the person intercepted, whether justified or not; for some it may be psychologically traumatic. To a police officer, even the most routine act of detaining a person may quickly escalate into a life-threatening episode, although firearms are not used in 99.8 percent of all arrests and in only 5.1 percent of arrests are weapons of any type used, displayed, or threatened by police. Indeed, in 84 percent of all arrests, police use no tactics at all—persons simply submit to arrest.[10] Despite this, the law of detention considers all seizures to be forcible in the sense that they are not consensual encounters.

Arrests and Investigative Stops

A police detention of a person can be *lawful* or *illegal*. Because liberty has priority in American political theory and constitutional law, all detentions by government officers must be justified by legal standards. In the past, the only dividing line between lawful or unlawful detention was whether probable cause existed to make an **arrest**. In *Henry v. United States* (1959) two federal agents had some suspicion, but no clear indication, that two men they had observed in a neighborhood during daylight hours were involved in the interstate thefts of whiskey. The agents observed the men loading a few boxes into a car, followed them for a short period, and then stopped the car. "The agents searched the car, placed the cartons (which bore the name 'Admiral' and were addressed to an out-of-state company) in their car, took the merchandise and [the men] to their office and held them for about two hours when the agents learned that the cartons contained stolen radios. They then placed the men under formal arrest." The Supreme Court reversed the conviction and ruled that the arrest took place when the car was stopped. At that point, the two men were forcibly detained (although they offered no resistance), and the Court ruled that because the agents did not have probable cause to arrest, it was illegal.

Since *Terry v. Ohio* (1968), the older rule has been qualified. Now there is a lesser type of detention known simply as a **stop** (or **investigative stop**) that can be predicated on a lesser standard of evidence, which is typically called "reasonable suspicion." Under the Fourth Amendment, both arrests and stops are "seizures." Seizures are lawful if justified by probable cause *or* reasonable suspicion, but a detention or seizure is illegal if the police officer acts on a hunch or arbitrarily.

Another distinction compares seizures to police-citizen encounters that are not detentions at all (i.e., not a **seizure of the person** under the Fourth Amendment). The latter category falls into two groups: (1) consensual encounters, where a person voluntarily agrees to talk to officers or even allows a purse or piece of luggage to be searched, and (2) situations in which an officer observes a person in a public place without interacting with the person. Both situations "intrude[] upon no constitutionally protected interest" (*United States v. Mendenhall*, 1980, p. 552). A police officer need establish *no* level of evidence sufficiency to merely observe a person in public.

The cases that have shaped the law of detention arose in two ways. (1) A person sues the police in a *civil action* for money damages for a wrongful arrest or seizure, sometimes involving a wrongful death action. (2) More often, in a *criminal case* the legality of a seizure is challenged because a search following the detention produced incriminating evidence or contraband. The incentive for the challenge is that the evidence found in a search following an illegal seizure is the "fruit" of a "poisonous tree" and may be suppressed under the exclusionary rule.

This chapter reviews *arrests, stops,* and *consensual encounters* in detail. At the outset, a few brief distinctions and definitions provide useful guideposts:

- When *arrested*, a person is in the **custody** of the police and loses his or her freedom; the person will frequently be taken to a police station for booking and may be jailed during the pretrial process; the arrest is executed for the purpose of initiating a criminal prosecution. In contrast, a *stop* confers limited powers in the police to detain a person; it is temporary and not designed to initiate a criminal prosecution but to give an officer a brief time to question the person to determine if suspicious circumstances are, in fact, innocent.

- An arrested person may be thoroughly *searched* for weapons and for incriminating evidence. A person held briefly under a *Terry* **stop** may be subjected only to a brief *pat-down of outer clothing* to determine if he or she is armed.

- If a person is properly stopped based on *reasonable suspicion*, but the personal search becomes too intrusive or the person is held for too long a time, the officer has overstepped the bounds and has, unlawfully, turned the *stop* into an *arrest*. Likewise, a consensual encounter may escalate into an investigative stop or an arrest if the encounter becomes coercive. It then becomes a Fourth Amendment seizure, justified only by the requisite level of evidence.

Legal categories are, at times, *created* by the Supreme Court to fit the needs of an ordered society. In *Terry v. Ohio* (1968) the Court created a new legal category, the *investigative stop,* for the purpose of bringing police practice within the scope of judicial control. The Court believed that the investigative stop function was necessary to police work, and, when conducted properly, balanced the needs of law enforcement with individual liberty. In addition to the major categories of arrest and investigative stop, the Court has had to consider other kinds of detention, which only partially fit into the arrest and stop categories, and has, up to a point, made *special rules* to deal with them. Two examples are detentions for investigative purposes and detention while executing a search warrant.

Detention to Investigate

A person's *physical characteristics*—such as fingerprints, voiceprint (*United States v. Dionisio,* 1973), or a handwriting sample (*United States v. Mara,* 1973)—are not protected by the expectation of privacy and, therefore, may rightfully be obtained during an investigation when a defendant is lawfully in custody. A person in custody can be required to appear at a lineup and cannot hide his face during a trial—observing a defendant's face is not a seizure.

However, may police *detain* a person for investigation purposes absent probable cause or reasonable suspicion? In two cases the Supreme Court held that detentions to fingerprint suspects were unreasonable Fourth Amendment violations, but held open the possibility that a one-time detention for fingerprinting might be lawful in some circumstances. In *Davis v. Mississippi* (1969) police rounded up twenty-five African American teenagers to collect fingerprint samples, attempting to match those found at the scene of a crime. These mass arrests, justified only by a witness's statement that the offender was black, were not authorized by a judicial warrant. The detentions did not focus on a specific group of persons on whom some suspicion fell, and involved a second fingerprinting session and interrogations. This violated the Fourth Amendment. Yet the Court, in dictum, stated that brief detention for fingerprinting may be reasonable because (1) fingerprinting does not intrude into a person's thoughts or belongings, (2) fingerprints can be obtained briefly during normal business hours and need be taken only once, and (3) fingerprints are an inherently reliable means of identification. In *Hayes v. Florida* (1985) a majority of the Court, again in dictum, suggested that fingerprinting at the scene of a crime would be permissible. In this case, however, the Court found that fingerprinting at the station house was impermissible because the defendant was forcibly taken to the station house without probable cause.

The Court categorically stated that the police have no authority to detain persons at will and take them to the police station—without probable cause, reasonable suspicion, or consent—to investigate a crime. In *Dunaway v. New York* (1979) Rochester police were told by an informant that Dunaway was involved in a murder and robbery. Without gaining more evidence, the detective in charge ordered officers to "pick up" Dunaway and "bring him in" for questioning. At that point, there was not sufficient evidence to obtain an arrest warrant. The defendant was not told he was under arrest, but he would have been restrained if he had attempted to leave. During the subsequent interrogation, Dunaway made incriminating statements and was convicted of murder. The Court refused to extend the *Terry* principle; if police have reasonable suspicion against a person, they can briefly detain and question him where he is found but cannot take him into custody. Dunaway was unlawfully arrested without probable cause and statements made while in custody were suppressed.

Police suspected that Robert Kaupp, aged seventeen, was involved in a murder (*Kaupp v. Texas,* 2003). He had passed a polygraph examination and a magistrate refused to issue an arrest warrant. Detectives nevertheless went to his house at 3 A.M. on a January morning. Robert's father let them in. Robert was awakened by a detective with a flashlight and told "we need to go and talk." He said "OK." He was then handcuffed and, shoeless and dressed only in boxer shorts and a T-shirt, taken to the station house where he was read *Miranda* rights and interviewed. He made incriminating statements and was convicted for murder.

Kaupp was seized and arrested without probable cause. The Court's opinion noted "This evidence points to arrest even more starkly than the facts in *Dunaway v. New York,* (1979)." Because the arrest was illegal the confession was excluded as the *fruit of the poisonous tree.* The *Miranda* warnings did not dissipate the effect of the illegal seizure of Kaupp under *Brown v. Illinois* (see Chapter 2). Nor did Kaupp *consent* to the detention or the questioning. Under the facts of this case, "There is no reason to think Kaupp's answer ["OK"] was anything more than 'a mere submission to a claim of lawful authority'" (see Chapter 3).

Detention and Search During the Execution of a Search Warrant

In *Michigan v. Summers* (1981) Detroit police officers executed a valid search warrant of a house for narcotics. They encountered Summers, the owner, walking down the front steps and asked his assistance in entering the house. Summers was detained during the search. After discovering narcotics in the basement, the police arrested him. A search incident to the arrest revealed an envelope with heroin in Summers's pocket. Although the police did not have probable cause to believe that Summers was carrying drugs before the arrest, the seizure was nevertheless upheld. The Supreme Court concluded that there was reasonable suspicion for the initial stop; the arrest and search was justified by finding drugs in his house.

Summers is general authority for the rule that police may detain homeowners or others present in a place while executing a search warrant. The individual's significant right to liberty is outweighed by law enforcement needs. Giving police routine "command of the situation" minimizes the likelihood of harm to the police and the residents that may be caused by sudden violence or frantic efforts to conceal or destroy evidence. Detaining the resident facilitates the orderly completion of the search with minimal damage to property, because the owner can open locked doors and cabinets. Detention in the person's own home also avoids the public stigma and inconvenience of being taken to the police station. Further, there is a legitimate law enforcement interest in preventing the flight of a person if incriminating evidence is found. The length of the detention, however, is limited to the time it takes to search the house.

Summers did *not* create a rule that allows police to automatically search anyone present in a premises during the execution of a warrant. In *Ybarra v. Illinois* (1979) police had a valid warrant to search a bar and a bartender for drugs, but not the patrons. Police entered the bar and announced to a dozen patrons that they would all be frisked for weapons. Ybarra, a bar patron, was searched. A cigarette pack was retrieved from his pants pocket and heroin was found inside. The Supreme Court overturned Ybarra's conviction. There was no probable cause to search Ybarra or any patrons. Simply because Ybarra was a patron in a bar where drugs were sold was no indication that he participated in purchases. "[A] person's mere propinquity to others independently suspected of criminal activity does not, without more, give rise to probable cause to search that person." The patrons' passive behavior when the raid was announced gave rise to no facts amounting to a reasonable suspicion that they were armed and presently dangerous.

In *Illinois v. McArthur* (2001) the Supreme Court ruled that where reasonable, police can prevent a householder from entering his home while awaiting the arrival of a search warrant. Officers accompanied Tera McArthur to the trailer where she lived with her husband, Charles, to keep the peace while she removed her belongings. The police stayed outside. After Tera removed her belongings, she told the officers that "Chuck had dope in there" and that she had seen Chuck "slide some dope underneath the couch." McArthur refused to consent to a search the trailer. He was then prevented from reentering his home without an officer present for about two hours in the afternoon until one of the officers had obtained a search warrant. A search turned up marijuana and McArthur was charged with misdemeanors. The Illinois courts suppressed the evidence.

The Supreme Court reversed, and held that the police acted reasonably under the Fourth Amendment. The search and seizure, and the temporary removal of McArthur from his home, were constitutional. There was *probable cause* (the police positively assessed Tera's reliability) and an *exigency* (a good chance that if left alone, McArthur would destroy the marijuana). The Court reasoned that the police "made reasonable efforts to reconcile their law enforcement needs with the demands of personal privacy" and "imposed a significantly less restrictive restraint, preventing McArthur only from entering the trailer unaccompanied" rather than searching without a warrant. The restriction on McArthur's freedom to enter his home was for a limited and reasonable period of time. Justice Stevens, dissenting, argued that the balance should be struck in favor of liberty where the offense was a minor one, relying on

the rule of *Welsh v. Wisconsin* (see Chapter 5). "[S]ome offenses may be so minor as to make it unreasonable for police to undertake searches that would be constitutionally permissible if graver offenses were suspected."

ARREST

Consequences of Arrest

A person who is seized by police officers is in their custody. The lawful "purpose of an arrest at common law, in both criminal and civil cases, was '*only* to compel an appearance in court'" (*Albright v. Oliver* (1994), Justice Ginsburg, concurring, emphasis added). The judicial process will put the arrested person through various "screens" (initial appearance, preliminary hearing, grand jury) to determine whether to charge the person with a crime and, if charged, to adjudicate the person's guilt. Because of this goal, there is a belief that a "real" arrest does not occur until *administrative formalities* occur at the police station, including fingerprinting, identification, and a criminal history check. The colorful phrase—"**booking**" the suspect—requires forms to be filled out to begin court processing and entry of the arrest in computer files. In law these formalities are not the essence of arrest. Arrest occurs at the moment a police officer significantly interferes with a person's liberty and takes him or her into custody. The lawfulness of an arrest is determined by what happens at the moment of the seizure.

Once arrested, a suspect loses his or her freedom of movement and most rights of personal privacy. A major consequence of arrest is that the person is subject to a "*search incident to arrest*," which is discussed later in this chapter. The search incident to arrest is a major *exception* to the Fourth Amendment *warrant* requirement.

Arrested persons have no right to prevent police officers from observing their movements and activities. In *Washington v. Chrisman* (1982) the Court announced a clear rule: "[I]t is not 'unreasonable' for a police officer, as a matter of routine, to monitor the movements of an arrested person, as his judgment dictates, following an arrest. The officer's need to ensure his own safety—as well as the integrity of the arrest—is compelling." In this case, a campus police officer arrested an apparently underage student for possession of a bottle of gin. The student entered his dormitory room in order to retrieve identification and the officer followed. As the officer stood outside the door, he saw what appeared to be marijuana seeds and a pipe lying on a desk. The officer entered the room, confirmed that the seeds were marijuana, and determined that the pipe smelled of marijuana. The Court ruled that the officer had a right to follow the arrested student into the room—without a warrant—to maintain secure custody; any motivation the officer had for observing the room in addition to keeping the arrested person under custody was irrelevant. Because the contraband was in plain view, and the officer was lawfully in the room, the marijuana was lawfully seized.

The Supreme Court held that an officer can take a person into custody for an offense that is punishable only with a minor fine (*Atwater v. City of Lago Vista,* 2001). Gail Atwater, an established Lago Vista (pop. 2,486) resident was driving at about 15 mph in broad daylight with her two young children (ages three and five) in the front seat. None were wearing seatbelts. Driving without a seatbelt is a misdemeanor in Texas punishable with a fine of $25 and $50 for a second offense. She was pulled over by Officer Bart Turek. The children began to scream; Ms. Atwater asked Officer Turek to lower his voice because he was scaring the children. The officer jabbed his finger in her face and said, "You're going to jail." She asked if her children could be brought to a neighbor's house, but Turek told her that the children would also be brought to the police station. Neighborhood children saw these events, an adult neighbor was called, and Ms. Atwater had her neighbor take her children. "With the children gone, Officer Turek handcuffed Ms. Atwater with her hands behind her back, placed her in the police car, and drove her to the police station. Ironically, Turek did not secure Atwater in a seat belt for the drive." At "the local police station, . . . booking officers had her remove her shoes, jewelry, and eyeglasses, and empty her pockets. Officers took Atwater's 'mug shot' and placed her, alone, in a jail cell for about one hour, after which she was taken before a magistrate and released on $310 bond." She later pled no contest to the misdemeanor and paid the $50 fine.

A 5–4 decision by the Supreme Court in a §1983 suit against the police held this custody to be constitutional. The majority maintained a **bright-line rule** so that officers did not have to guess whether an offense was or was not jailable, which could generate lawsuits against the police, or have to decide whether or not the arrested person was subject to fleeing. Justice O'Connor, a conservative judge, wrote for the dissenters, arguing that the decision for a full-custody arrest imposes severe limitations on liberty. She noted that Atwater could have been detained for up to forty-eight hours before seeing a magistrate, jailed together with potentially violent offenders, and had a permanent record of arrest. An exception to a flat ban on arrests for nonjailable misdemeanors creates no problem because an officer who decides that an exception applies has immunity from civil liability for making erroneous judgment calls. She concluded that the decision violated basic Fourth Amendment principles and that the balance between liberty and security should have been struck in favor of liberty.

There is a distinction between a **mistaken arrest** and an **illegal arrest,** and each has different consequences. An *illegal* arrest occurs if a person is taken into custody by a government officer *without probable cause.* Cases of illegal arrests usually occur without any malicious intent on the part of the law enforcement officers. Nevertheless, having violated the Constitution, the arrest is illegal because the probable cause standard for arrest is *objective,* not subjective. The most important consequence of an illegal arrest is that any evidence seized as a result of the arrest is *inadmissible* under the exclusionary rule. This gives arrested defendants found with contraband an incentive to challenge the legality of the arrest. An officer can also be held civilly liable for an illegal arrest.

Another way in which an arrest can be illegal is if the arresting officer had *no jurisdiction* to make the arrest. This has

occurred in *Frisbie v. Collins* (1952), when police officers from southwest Michigan traveled to Chicago to arrest Collins for a murder, rather than seeking extradition or requesting that an arrest be made by a cooperating Illinois law enforcement agency. Collins argued that this illegal arrest, possibly a violation of the Federal Kidnapping Act, deprived the trial court of jurisdiction to try him and that his conviction was a nullity. The Supreme Court upheld the common law rule that a court does not lose jurisdiction to try the defendant if she is brought to the court by illegal means. Once a court has **in personam jurisdiction,** or physical custody over a criminal defendant, it does not inquire into the means by which the person is brought into court. The Supreme Court stood by this rule in a much-criticized case, *United States v. Alvarez-Machain* (1992), in which American agents had the defendant abducted in Mexico and transferred to the United States for trial.[11]

A *mistaken arrest* occurs when an officer makes an arrest *with* probable cause, but it turns out that in fact the wrong person was arrested. The only consequence is that the person arrested must be released if no evidence of criminality is discovered. An innocent person has no civil cause of action against the police because the officer acted in a reasonable manner. However, a search conducted pursuant to the mistaken arrest is valid insofar as it discovered any contraband. The rule reflects the idea that probable cause does not require certainty but only an assessment of facts that would lead a prudent person to believe that the suspect was involved in a crime. In **Hill v. California** (1971) the Supreme Court ruled that police had probable cause to arrest Hill. Two men, driving Hill's car, were arrested for a narcotics possession. A search of the car produced evidence of a robbery. The two men admitted to the robbery and implicated Hill. The police verified Hill's automobile ownership, his description, and his association with one of the men. Armed with this probable cause, the police went to Hill's motel room to arrest him. They knocked and the door was opened by Miller, who fit Hill's description. Miller was arrested despite the fact that he produced identification indicating he was Miller. Articles seized in plain view and incident to the search were used to convict Hill of robbery.

Miller's arrest was supported by probable cause; he could not satisfactorily explain why he was in Hill's room and his personal identification could have been fabricated. This probable cause was based upon reasonable facts and circumstances and not on the subjective good faith of the police. As a result, contraband seized during the arrest was admissible. Because it can be difficult to ascertain the true motives of police, the distinction between an illegal and a mistaken arrest turns on the objective reasonableness of the police behaviors, not on subjective motives.

Defining a Fourth Amendment Seizure and Arrest

The Supreme Court has offered two definitions for an arrest: the *Mendenhall* definition and the *Hodari D.* definition.

In *United States v. Mendenhall* (1980) the Court said: "*a person has been 'seized' within the meaning of the Fourth*

Amendment only if, in view of all of the circumstances surrounding the incident, a reasonable person would have believed that he was not free to leave." A person, therefore, can be arrested even though not physically held or even touched by an officer. Also, there are no specific words that have to be spoken to effect an arrest: Neither an announcement that a person is under arrest, nor a description of a crime for which a person is arrested, nor a reading of *Miranda* warnings (a popular misconception) is required. Examples of personal seizure offered by the Court in *Mendenhall* include: "the threatening presence of several officers, the display of a weapon by an officer, some physical touching of the person of the citizen, or the use of language or tone of voice indicating that compliance with the officer's request might be compelled" (*Mendenhall,* 1980: 554).

The *Mendenhall* definition, however, does not encompass every situation. The Court amended the *Mendenhall* definition in *California v. Hodari D.* (1991) to rule that a seizure (and hence an arrest) occurs *only* when an assertion and intent to arrest, on the part of an officer, is followed by *physical control* over or *submission* of the arrested party. The rationale for the *Hodari D.* definition, and the issues raised by the case, are explored later in this chapter.

A Fourth Amendment seizure can occur in a variety of ways. In *Tennessee v. Garner* (1985) the Court ruled that when a person who is *shot* by the police is arrested: "there can be no question that apprehension by the use of deadly force is a seizure subject to the reasonableness requirement of the Fourth Amendment." A **roadblock** set up intentionally to intercept a driver fleeing from the police becomes the instrument of an arrest if the driver plows into it (*Brower v. Inyo County,* 1989). This is an arrest because there has been an "intentional acquisition of physical control" over the person by the use of the roadblock. "[A] roadblock is not just a significant show of authority to induce a voluntary stop, but is designed to produce a stop by physical impact if voluntary compliance does not occur." Finally, a person who, after hearing that a warrant has been issued for his arrest, *voluntarily surrenders* to the police, is seized for purposes of the Fourth Amendment (*Albright v. Oliver,* 1994, Justice Ginsburg, concurring).

In each of these cases, there was an intent on the part of the police to gain custody of the suspect and actual custody. If either element is absent, there is no seizure. The intent element was clarified in *County of Sacramento v. Lewis* (1998), a civil lawsuit against an officer whose car hit and killed a motorcycle passenger. The officer was engaged in a high-speed pursuit of a speeding motorcycle. The passenger was thrown from the motorcycle and killed by the oncoming patrol car. Because a police pursuit is not a seizure, the Court found that the Fourteenth Amendment Due Process Clause applied to the case, and not the more specific Fourth Amendment. On the basis of *Brower v. Inyo County* the Court reasoned that a Fourth Amendment seizure does not result every time an officer terminates an individual's freedom of movement, but only where freedom of movement is terminated *"through means intentionally applied."* The officer's almost instinctive chase of a motorcyclist who sped away after an order to stop displayed no

deliberate or reckless indifference to life. The officer's acts therefore did not shock the conscience and did not violate the substantive due process rights of the deceased passenger.

Probable Cause to Make an Arrest

Probable cause to arrest can be determined by a magistrate issuing an arrest warrant. Most arrests, however, are made without warrants and in such cases the officer must make a probable cause determination.

> Whether that arrest was constitutionally valid depends in turn upon whether, at the moment the arrest was made, the officers had probable cause to make it—whether at that moment the *facts and circumstances within their knowledge and of which they had reasonably trustworthy information were sufficient to warrant a prudent man in believing that the petitioner had committed or was committing an offense.* (*Beck v. Ohio,* 1964, p. 91, emphasis added)

In *Beck v. Ohio* (1964) police officers in a squad car saw William Beck driving his car and stopped and arrested him without a warrant. One officer testified that he knew what Beck looked like and had heard only general reports that Beck had a criminal record and was involved in gambling. A search of Beck's person at the police station disclosed betting slips in his shoe. The Supreme Court ruled this arrest *illegal.* At the time the police stopped the car, the officers did not have a level of evidence that would have satisfied a magistrate that Beck was then transporting betting slips. Beck's appearance and prior record were not "inadmissible or entirely irrelevant upon the issue of probable cause. But to hold that knowledge of either or both of these facts constituted probable cause would be to hold that anyone with a previous criminal record could be arrested at will." Thus, hearsay can be lawfully used to support probable cause, but it must be more reliable than simple rumors.

Ultimately, a court will review whether probable cause existed to make a warrantless arrest, and courts must be given *facts* to make the decision, and cannot rely on the officer's good faith:

> We may assume that the officers acted in good faith in arresting the petitioner. But "good faith on the part of the arresting officers is not enough." If subjective good faith alone were the test, the protections of the Fourth Amendment would evaporate, and the people would be "secure in their persons, houses, papers, and effects," only in the discretion of the police. (*Beck v. Ohio,* p. 97)

Thus, the probable cause standard for arrest is *objective,* not subjective.

In a typical case, probable cause is established by the *officer's observation of a crime in progress* or by the *report of an eyewitness.* In *Peters v. New York* (1968), a companion case to *Terry v. Ohio* (1968), a police officer observed two men in his apartment building tip-toeing in the hallway. In the twelve years he had been living there, Officer Lasky had never seen these men. The men were still there when the officer had completed a phone call. When he approached them, they fled. He apprehended Peters, who gave no satisfactory reason for his actions. Lasky searched him and found burglar's tools. The Supreme Court ruled that "It is difficult to conceive of stronger grounds for an arrest, short of actual eyewitness observation of criminal activity." While Lasky did not actually see Peters trying to jimmy a lock, the other evidence supplied probable cause: facts that would lead a prudent person to believe that Peters was engaged in an attempt to break and enter.

In **Chambers v. Maroney** (1970) a light-blue compact station wagon carrying four men was stopped by police on a spring evening in North Braddock, Pennsylvania, about one hour after the robbery of a Gulf service station and about two miles from the station. Chambers, one of the men in the car, was wearing a green sweater, and there was a trench coat in the car:

> Two teen-agers, who had earlier noticed a blue compact station wagon circling the block in the vicinity of the Gulf station, then saw the station wagon speed away from a parking lot close to the Gulf station. About the same time, they learned that the Gulf station had been robbed. They reported to police, who arrived immediately, that four men were in the station wagon and one was wearing a green sweater. [The station attendant] told the police that one of the men who robbed him was wearing a green sweater and the other was wearing a trench coat. A description of the car and the two robbers was broadcast over the police radio.

This is a typical example of police obtaining probable cause from a reliable (and nonsecret) informant. It is hearsay, but it is fully reliable. Of course, such information should never be taken for absolute proof of a crime. In rare cases, the initial information may be given as a misguided prank or out of malice. In many cases, facts are garbled and eyewitness identification of key facts may be wrong, especially about the identity of an offender (see Chapter 8 on identification).

Probable cause must focus on a *specific individual.* In **Johnson v. United States** (1948) an officer standing outside an apartment smelled burning opium in the hallway, but was not sure who occupied the place. The officer knocked and announced his presence. Anne Johnson opened the door and the officer told her "to consider yourself under arrest." The Supreme Court held that the entry into the home without a warrant was a Fourth Amendment violation. Further, the arrest itself was illegal because "the arresting officer did not have probable cause to arrest [Johnson] until he had entered her room and found her to be the sole occupant." Another common problem confronting police is whether probable cause exists to arrest a person who is in close proximity to another person who is lawfully arrested.

Mere proximity to a person committing a crime does not create probable cause (*Ybarra v. Illinois,* 1979). For example, in **United States v. Di Re** (1948) an informer, Reed, told investigators that he was going to buy counterfeit ration coupons from one "Buttitta at a named place in the City of Buffalo, New York." Agents followed a car driven by Buttitta. Michael Di Re was the front-seat passenger and Reed sat in the back. Di Re was not known to the agents. The car was stopped and Buttitta and Di Re were arrested. Di Re was searched at the station house. After the arrest, counterfeit ration coupons were found in an envelope concealed between Di Re's shirt and underwear. The Supreme Court ruled that this evidence was seized illegally because the agents did not have probable cause to believe that Di Re was involved in the crime, invalidating the arrest. Reed had not named Di Re as a suspect. The police suspicion against Buttitta was based on the word of their informant, Reed. "But the officer had no such information as to Di Re. All they had was his presence, and if his presence was not enough to make a case for arrest for a misdemeanor, it is hard to see how it was enough for the felony of" possessing illegal coupons with knowledge that they were counterfeit. The Court also dismissed the argument that there was a conspiracy simply because Di Re was in the car.

In contrast to *Di Re* is **Ker v. California** (1963) (see Chapter 3). By their own observations and the word of an informer, police had probable cause to believe that George Ker was dealing marijuana from his house. The Court held that the police entered lawfully without a warrant. After entering, an agent saw George Ker sitting in the living room, Diane Ker emerge from the kitchen, and through the open doorway a small scale atop the kitchen sink, upon which lay a "brick-like—brick-shaped package containing the green leafy substance which he recognized as marijuana." The Court conceded that the police did not have probable cause to arrest Diane Ker when they entered the apartment. But it ruled that viewing the marijuana in plain view established probable cause to believe that she was involved in the illicit business with her husband. This was not simply guilt by association, but a rational inference. In *Di Re* the police could not infer, to the level of probable cause, that Di Re possessed counterfeit ration coupons. But Diane Ker had to know that there was marijuana in the kitchen, and given the probable cause that police had that George Ker was illegally dealing, it was a rational inference that she was "in joint possession with her husband." This amounted to probable cause to believe that she was "committing the offense of possession of marijuana in the presence of the officers."

Police, in **Maryland v. Pringle** (2004), stopped a car at 3:16 A.M. for speeding. Partlow was driving, Pringle sat in the front seat, and Smith was a back-seat passenger. When Partlow opened the glove compartment to retrieve the vehicle registration, the officer observed a large roll of cash. A consent search of the vehicle uncovered five plastic glassine baggies containing cocaine placed behind the upright rear seat armrest. None of the three men admitted to owning the drugs, and all three were arrested. Pringle later confessed to owning the drugs. The issue in the case was whether finding drugs in the rear seat gave police probable cause to arrest Pringle. This is not a case of guilt by association. Unlike the tavern patrons in *Ybarra v. Illinois* (1979), Pringle was in a small car with two men he knew, and car passengers will often be involved in a "common enterprise with the driver." Unlike *United States v. Di Re* (1948), this was not a case where the police had previous probable cause to suspect only the driver. The Supreme Court held that under the facts of the case there was probable cause to arrest Pringle. It was objectively reasonable for the officer on the scene to believe "that any or all three of the occupants had knowledge of, and exercised dominion and control over, the cocaine. Thus a reasonable officer could conclude that there was probable cause to believe Pringle committed the crime of possession of cocaine, either solely or jointly" (*Maryland v. Pringle*, 2004, slip op., p. 6).

JUDICIAL DETERMINATION OF PROBABLE CAUSE   If police arrest without a warrant, their probable cause determination must be reviewed by a judge or magistrate as soon as possible. A Florida law allowed a person to be arrested on a prosecutor's bill of information and held for a *month* before being brought before a magistrate. This was struck down as a Fourth Amendment violation in **Gerstein v. Pugh** (1975):

> [A] policeman's on-the-scene assessment of probable cause provides legal justification for arresting a person suspected of crime, and for a brief period of detention to take the administrative steps incident to arrest. Once the suspect is in custody, however, the reasons that justify dispensing with the magistrate's neutral judgment evaporate. There no longer is any danger that the suspect will escape or commit further crimes while the police submit their evidence to a magistrate. And, while the State's reasons for taking summary action subside, the suspect's need for a neutral determination of probable cause increases significantly. The consequences of prolonged detention may be more serious than the interference occasioned by arrest. Pretrial confinement may imperil the suspect's job, interrupt his source of income, and impair his family relationships. Even pretrial release may be accompanied by burdensome conditions that effect a significant restraint on liberty. When the stakes are this high, the detached judgment of a neutral magistrate is essential if the Fourth Amendment is to furnish meaningful protection from unfounded interference with liberty. Accordingly, we hold that the Fourth Amendment requires a judicial determination of probable cause as a prerequisite to extended restraint on liberty following arrest. (*Gerstein v. Pugh*, pp. 113–14)

The law in every state and for the federal government, based on common law practice, has long required police to bring arrested persons *promptly* before a magistrate for initial processing. The Florida rule was quite unusual. The Court in *Gerstein* did not define what constituted a prompt arraignment.

The Supreme Court clarified the time period for which a person can be held after arrest before being brought before a magistrate in **County of Riverside v. McLaughlin** (1991). The majority, in an opinion by Justice O'Connor, ruled that a jurisdiction must bring an arrested person before a magistrate for a probable cause hearing as soon as is reasonably feasible, but in no event later than *forty-eight hours* after arrest. Where an arrested person does not receive a probable cause determination within forty-eight hours, the burden of proof shifts to the government to demonstrate the existence of a bona fide emergency or other extraordinary circumstance, which cannot include intervening weekends. Under the county's rule, which excluded weekends, a "person arrested on Thursday may have to wait until the following Monday before they receive a probable cause determination" or up to seven days over a Thanksgiving holiday. The Court also suggested that holding off bringing a person before a magistrate in order to gather additional evidence was not a bona fide emergency.

There were two dissents—by liberal and by conservative/ originalist justices. The liberal position (*per* Justice Marshall)

was that the proper constitutional rule is that a person must be brought before a magistrate immediately upon *completion of the administrative steps* incident to arrest. Justice Scalia opted for a twenty-four-hour time period based on his "originalist" research that found that such a time period was common in the late eighteenth and early nineteenth centuries. In the past, lengthy postarrest detention without recourse to a magistrate was used to force confessions out of suspects. Such a practice tempts police to abuse their control over a suspect. The rules of *Gerstein* and *Riverside County* rightfully make constitutional what is now standard practice.

USE OF SECONDARY INFORMATION   A police officer may depend on a reliable informant to establish probable cause to arrest. An informant could be an impartial witness, a victim, or an "undercover" informant who works for the police or receives lenient treatment in return for information about crimes such as drug sales (*Draper v. United States*, 1959; *McCray v. Illinois*, 1967).

In this era of high mobility and instantaneous communications, it is necessary for police to rely on the *radio bulletins* or *computer notifications* from other police departments as a basis for probable cause to arrest. In **Whitely v. Warden** (1971) the Court ruled that police may rely on a radio bulletin from another police department informing them that an arrest warrant was issued. In *Whitely* the original arrest warrant was defective; the magistrate erred in finding probable cause. As a result, the arrest was illegal and the evidence seized in a search incident to the arrest was not admissible. The clear implication of *Whitely*, however, was that the officers who made the arrest reasonably relied upon the radio bulletin and should not be held civilly liable for the arrest. They acted reasonably even if there was no probable cause for the original arrest warrant.

In **Arizona v. Evans** (1995) (see Chapter 2) Evans was stopped for driving the wrong way on a one-way street. The *police* computer indicated, erroneously, that Evans had an outstanding warrant. He was arrested on the basis of the supposed outstanding warrant. Because the error was based on mistakes in the *court* clerk's office, the Supreme Court refused to suppress a marijuana cigarette discovered in the search, on the grounds that the exclusionary rule applied only to police errors. The merits of *Arizona v. Evans* (1995) aside, the case points to the need for accuracy in police records in order to prevent unconstitutional searches. Justice O'Connor, concurring, expressed some concerns that widespread computer errors might undermine individual rights.

THE FELONY/MISDEMEANOR RULE   The traditional, common law rules for felony and misdemeanor arrests by law enforcement officers differ. A police officer may arrest a person for a *felony* when he or she has probable cause to believe that a crime has been committed and that the arrestee is the perpetrator.[12] For a *misdemeanor* arrest to be lawful, however, the misdemeanor must have been committed in the officer's *presence*. The reason for this distinction is that public safety requires swift arrests for more serious crimes. Because petty crimes are often the result of squabbles between individuals, an arrest based on a complainant's say-so may result in instances of false arrest and legally sanctioned harassment. The victim of a misdemeanor had to obtain an arrest warrant from a judge via a formal complaint in order to initiate the criminal process. In recent years, the **in-presence rule** has come under severe criticism because it has prevented police from making arrests in cases of domestic violence. State legislatures have rethought the rule and virtually all have modified it to allow or require an officer to arrest in cases of domestic violence. (See *Law in Society* section, this chapter.) Statutes have also modified the misdemeanor arrest rule for traffic-related misdemeanors not observed directly by a police officer.[13]

CITIZEN'S ARRESTS   Private individuals have the right to arrest a felon. However, the personal consequences for a sworn law enforcement officer and a private person making a mistaken arrest differ. A police officer who makes a mistaken arrest (e.g., arrests the wrong person) that is based on *probable cause* cannot be held civilly liable for the tort of false arrest because the officer acted reasonably. A private person who effects a "**citizen's arrest**" is held *strictly accountable* to the arrested person for any errors made during the arrest. No matter how reasonable the citizen's arrest, if a mistake was made, the person making the arrest may be successfully sued for the tort of **false arrest.** The rule places a high premium on individual liberty to be free from unwarranted interference. The relaxation of the common law rule of strict liability for law enforcement officers is evidence of a policy that encourages officers to be less fearful of the consequences of their acts so that they will not shirk their duty. This recognizes the difficulties that confront law enforcement officers when hard decisions must be made with little time for reflection and under circumstances of heightened stress.

This common law rule has great effect on *security guards;* they cannot arrest a person for theft, for example, without the threat of liability unless they are actually correct. "Unless the owner has given consent, a security guard's search of private property will generally constitute a trespass. And arrests or detentions not authorized by state law generally will expose a security guard to civil and criminal liability for false imprisonment and, if force is involved, for assault."[14] On the other hand, "most states have codified a '**merchant's privilege**' that allows store investigators, and in some instances other categories of private security personnel, to conduct brief investigatory detentions that would be tortious or criminal if carried out by ordinary citizens."[15]

The Use of Force

"The criminal justice process rests basically on force, the authority of the state to use raw power, properly and appropriately applied, to apprehend, detain, try, and imprison. The basis of force pervades and colors the whole criminal justice system."[16] The system's force may be mute, as in prison walls, or symbolized by the judge's robe and the patrol officer's uniform. It may be mostly held in reserve, but when consent and compliance fail, the system, and especially the police, are required to use physical power to carry out its functions. The use of force is problematic because liberty is primary in the American constitutional scheme, but is justified by the goal of enforcing public law.

The application of force, however, must be appropriate and lawful. The common law of arrest provides a simple, but ambiguous, rule: the force used to effect an arrest must be *reasonable*; it must not be excessive. What is **reasonable force**? Few guidelines exist: One guideline is that the force must be commensurate with the resistance offered by a person whom the police try to arrest. If a person resists with nondeadly force, then the police may use nonlethal force to subdue him. If a person resists with deadly force, then the police can reply in kind.

THE "FLEEING FELON" RULE   Under the common law, a police officer could use deadly force to subdue and arrest a "fleeing felon" even though the felon had not used deadly force. Presumably because most common law felonies were punishable by death, their seriousness tended to increase the likelihood that felons were dangerous to the life of others. The "**fleeing felon**" **rule** served as a substitute for the executioner! In America the fleeing felon rule has been controversial and seriously criticized in the decades since 1960, as the use of the death penalty decreased and many felonies are no longer dangerous to life. By 1980, most states had modified the fleeing felon rule by statute, and many police departments altered their policies so that deadly force could be used only when a suspect presented clear evidence of violent intentions. These states felt that a blanket rule allowing police to shoot at any fleeing felon was excessive.

The issue came before the Supreme Court, giving it a rare opportunity to discuss the police use of force from a constitutional perspective in *Tennessee v. Garner* (1985). The Court modified the fleeing felon rule as a matter of Fourth Amendment law and held, in an opinion by Justice Byron White, that

> The use of deadly force to prevent the escape of all felony suspects, whatever the circumstances, is constitutionally unreasonable. It is not better that all felony suspects die than that they escape. Where the suspect poses no immediate threat to the officer and no threat to others, the harm resulting from failing to apprehend him does not justify the use of deadly force to do so. (*Tennessee v. Garner*, 1985, p. 11)

The fleeing felon rule violated the Fourth Amendment rather than the Due Process Clauses of the Fourteenth Amendments. This creates a flat rule: A statute that allows police to shoot-to-kill *any* fleeing felon is void. A due process rule would have subjected the issue to painstaking case-by-case analysis. Deadly force against a fleeing felon is still allowed where reasonable: "Where the officer has probable cause to believe that the suspect poses a threat of serious physical harm, either to the officer or to others, it is not constitutionally unreasonable to prevent escape by using deadly force." Thus, the Court in *Garner* upheld the common law framework: Determining the legality of the use of force by police is based on what was reasonable under all the facts and circumstances of a case; all the Court did was to announce that as a matter of the

Constitution, a flat use-of-deadly-force rule in all fleeing felon circumstances was unreasonable.

Justice O'Connor dissented, joined by Chief Justice Burger and Justice Rehnquist. A teenager of average height was shot and killed by a police officer while trying to get over a fence after running from a nonviolent house burglary. As the Circuit Court noted, "the officer fired at the upper part of the body, using a 38-calibre pistol loaded with hollow point bullets, as he was trained to do by his superiors at the Memphis Police Department. He shot because he believed the boy would elude capture in the dark once he was over the fence. The officer was taught that it was proper under Tennessee law to kill a fleeing felon rather than run the risk of allowing him to escape."[17] The youth died of the gunshot wound. On his person were ten dollars and jewelry he had taken from the house. Justice O'Connor pointed out that no matter how regrettable were the consequences of this case, it was not unreasonable for an officer to shoot at a fleeing burglar at night since it was not known whether the burglar was armed nor what had happened in the burglarized house. "With respect to a particular burglary, subsequent investigation simply cannot represent a substitute for immediate apprehension of the criminal suspect at the scene." The dissent is more willing to grant unreviewed discretion to the police than the majority.

The "real world" effects of legal rules are often unknown. *Tennessee v. Garner,* however, has positively stimulated police departments to modify policies and practices that have had life-saving effects, not only for suspects but also for police. Jerome Skolnick and James Fyfe, leading police scholars, write:

> When police have started their attempts to develop policy with the principle that good policing in any situation consists of the actions that best meet the primary police responsibility to protect life, the results have been remarkably successful. Deadly force policies that, in both philosophy and substance, emphasize the sanctity of life over the need to apprehend suspects have reduced killings by police—and the backlash that often follows—without negative effects on the safety of citizens or the safety and effectiveness of officers.[18]

Section 1983 cases dealing with excessive use of force by police offer some guidance on the legal meaning of excessive force.

In **Graham v. Connor** (1989) Officer Connor stopped Dethorne Graham a half-mile from a crowded convenience store in Charlotte, North Carolina, after seeing him hastily enter and then leave. Connor did not know that Graham, a diabetic, was driven to the store by a friend so he could buy orange juice to counteract an insulin reaction. Graham left the store because of a long line to go to a friend's house to get sugar. When stopped, Graham told Connor about the insulin reaction. Connor told him to wait until he returned to the store to discover what happened and to call for backup forces. Graham was handcuffed, his pleas for sugar were ignored by one officer who said, "I've seen a lot of people with sugar diabetes that never acted like this. Ain't nothing wrong with the M. F. but drunk. Lock the S. B. up." Graham passed out twice. He asked an officer to look into his wallet for a diabetic decal and was told to "shut up." A friend brought some orange juice to the patrol car for Graham but the officers refused to let him have it. After dis-

covering that nothing criminal occurred at the convenience store, the police drove Graham home and released him. Graham sustained a broken foot, cuts on the wrist, a bruised forehead, and an injured shoulder. The lower federal courts held that Officer Connor did not violate Graham's rights.

Did the police violate Graham's Fourth Amendment rights? Did they act reasonably? The Supreme Court ruled that a case in which an officer seizes a person, as occurred here, must be decided under the more specific Fourth Amendment rather than the more general rules of substantive due process under the Fourteenth Amendment. Therefore, the question of whether excessive force was used is to be decided by *objective factors*—the officer's *motive* is *irrelevant*. "An officer's evil intentions will not make a Fourth Amendment violation out of an objectively reasonable use of force; nor will an officer's good intentions make an objectively unreasonable use of force constitutional." (*Graham v. Connor,* p. 397). Next, the

> reasonableness of a particular use of force must be judged from the perspective of a *reasonable officer on the scene,* rather than with the 20/20 vision of hindsight. . . . The calculus of reasonableness must embody allowance for the fact that police officers are often forced to make split-second judgments—in circumstances that are tense, uncertain, and rapidly evolving—about the amount of force that is necessary in a particular situation. (*Graham v. Connor,* p. 396, emphasis added)

Under more open-ended substantive due process analysis that had been used by most courts prior to *Graham,* looking at the amount of force used under the circumstances, the extent of injuries and the motive of the officer, plaintiffs may have had greater leeway to prevail in section 1983 action. Nevertheless, the Court's decision was unanimous. The case was remanded for reconsideration by lower courts.

Brower v. Inyo County (1989) established that a roadblock can be an instrument of force that effects an arrest. Brower stole a car and eluded the police in a high-speed, twenty-mile chase. A police roadblock was set up consisting of an unilluminated eighteen-wheel tractor-trailer blocking both lanes of a road behind a curve, with a police car's headlights pointing at the oncoming traffic. Brower was killed when his car hit the roadblock. This constituted an arrest. The remaining question is whether excessive force was used. The Supreme Court indicated that this was a factual issue depending on the circumstances of the roadblock, and remanded the case for further proceedings.

THE ARREST WARRANT REQUIREMENT

The need to obtain an **arrest warrant** to effect an arrest and whether a search warrant is also required are determined by the circumstances and settings under which the suspect is to be taken into custody. This section reviews the law that pertains to arresting suspects (1) in public, (2) in their own homes, and (3) in the homes of third parties.

Arrest in Public

— *United States v. Watson* **Case & Comments** —

• CASE & COMMENTS •

United States v. Watson
423 U.S. 411, 96 S.Ct. 820, 46 L.Ed.2d 598 (1976)

MR. JUSTICE WHITE delivered the opinion of the Court.

This case presents questions under the Fourth Amendment as to the legality of a warrantless arrest. * * *

I.

[A reliable informant, Khoury, informed postal inspectors that Watson would furnish stolen credit cards. Acting under their instructions, Khoury arranged a meeting with Watson five days later in a restaurant.] Khoury had been instructed that if Watson had additional stolen credit cards, Khoury was to give a designated signal. The signal was given, the officers closed in, and Watson was forthwith arrested. [No stolen credit cards were found on Watson, but some were found in his automobile. The Court of Appeals ruled that the arrest was a violation of the Fourth Amendment because there was no arrest warrant and *no exigency;* consequently, evidence obtained from the search of Watson's automobile and seizure of the credit cards had to be excluded as the fruits of an illegal arrest.]

II.

* * *

Contrary to the Court of Appeals' view, Watson's arrest was not invalid because executed without a warrant. **[a]** Title 18 U.S.C. sec. 3061(a)(3) expressly empowers the * * * Postal Service to authorize Postal Service officers and employees "performing duties related to the inspection of postal matters" to

> "make arrests without warrant for felonies * * * if they have reasonable grounds to believe that the person to be arrested has committed or is committing such a felony."

* * * Because there was probable cause in this case to believe that Watson had violated [the law], the inspector and his subordinates, in arresting Watson, were acting strictly in accordance with the governing statute and regulations. **[b]** The effect of the judgment of the Court of Appeals was to invalidate the statute as applied in this case and as applied to all the situations where a court fails to find exigent circumstances justifying a warrantless arrest. We reverse that judgment.

Under the Fourth Amendment, the people are to be "secure in their persons, houses, papers, and effects, against unreasonable searches and seizures, * * * and no Warrants shall issue, but upon probable cause. * * *" **[c]** Section 3061 represents a judgment by Congress that it is not unreasonable under the Fourth Amendment for postal inspectors to arrest without a warrant provided they have probable cause to do so. This was not an isolated or quixotic judgment of the legislative branch. Other federal law enforcement officers have been expressly authorized by statute for many years to make felony arrests on probable cause but without a warrant. * * * **[d]**

* * * [T]here is nothing in the Court's prior cases indicating that under the Fourth Amendment a warrant is required to make a valid arrest for a felony. Indeed, the relevant prior decisions are uniformly to the contrary.

"The usual rule is that a police officer may arrest without warrant one believed by the officer upon reasonable cause to have been guilty of a felony. . . ." * * * **[e]** Just last Term, while recognizing that maximum protection of individual rights could be assured by requiring a magistrate's review of the factual justification prior to any arrest, we stated that "such a requirement would constitute an intolerable handicap for legitimate law enforcement" and noted that the Court "has never invalidated an arrest supported by probable cause solely because the officers failed to secure a warrant." *Gerstein v. Pugh.* * * *

The cases construing the Fourth Amendment thus reflect the ancient common-law rule that a peace officer was permitted to arrest without a warrant for a misdemeanor or felony committed in his presence as well as for a felony not committed in his presence if there was reasonable ground for making the arrest. * * * This has also been the prevailing rule under state constitutions and statutes. * * * **[f]**

The balance struck by the common law in generally authorizing felony arrests on probable cause, but without a warrant, has survived substantially intact. It appears in almost all of the States in the form of express statutory authorization. * * * [The American Law Institute's *Model Code of Pre-arraignment Procedure* in 1975 adopted] "the traditional and almost universal standard for arrest without a warrant."

* * * Congress has plainly decided against conditioning warrantless arrest power on proof of exigent circumstances. Law enforcement officers may find it wise to seek arrest warrants where practicable

[a] The Court states its decision at the outset. What follows are the reasons for this decision. The Court of Appeals invalidated the statute under its reading of the Fourth Amendment. Does the statute's authorization of warrantless arrests end the constitutional reasoning process?

[b] Would *you* nevertheless require the police to get a judicial arrest warrant in investigations where they have *plenty of time* to get one?

[c] Does the judgment of Congress violate the Fourth Amendment's plain words?

[d] *Entick v. Carrington* (1765) said that an illegal practice does not become legal simply because it has been practiced for a long time. Does this point weaken Justice White's argument?

[e] Is the need for law enforcement efficiency a *constitutional* reason? Could this reasoning lead to the total elimination of arrest warrants?

[f] This assumes that the Fourth Amendment absorbed common law practice. Another perspective is that the amendment changed common law practices to expand the protection of individual liberty.

• CASE & COMMENTS •

to do so, and their judgments about probable cause may be more readily accepted where backed by a warrant issued by a magistrate. * * * **[g]** But we decline to transform this judicial preference into a constitutional rule when the judgment of the Nation and Congress has for so long been to authorize warrantless public arrests on probable cause rather than to encumber criminal prosecutions with endless litigation with respect to the existence of exigent circumstances, whether it was practicable to get a warrant, whether the suspect was about to flee, and the like.

Watson's arrest did not violate the Fourth Amendment, and the Court of Appeals erred in holding to the contrary.

* * *

MR. JUSTICE POWELL, concurring.

* * * Today's decision is the first square holding that the Fourth Amendment permits a duly authorized law enforcement officer to make a warrantless arrest in a public place even though he had adequate opportunity to procure a warrant after developing probable cause for arrest. **[h]**

On its face, our decision today creates a certain anomaly. There is no more basic constitutional rule in the Fourth Amendment area than that which makes a warrantless search unreasonable except in a few "jealously and carefully drawn" exceptional circumstances. * * * On more than one occasion this Court has rejected an argument that a law enforcement officer's own probable cause to search a private place for contraband or evidence of crime should excuse his otherwise unexplained failure to procure a warrant beforehand. * * * **[i]**

Since the Fourth Amendment speaks equally to both searches and seizures, and since an arrest, the taking hold of one's person, is quintessentially a seizure, it would seem that the constitutional provision should impose the same limitations upon arrests that it does upon searches. Indeed, as an abstract matter an argument can be made that the restrictions upon arrest perhaps should be greater. **[j]** A search may cause only annoyance and temporary inconvenience to the law-abiding citizen, assuming more serious dimension only when it turns up evidence of criminality. An arrest, however, is a serious personal intrusion regardless of whether the person seized is guilty or innocent. Although an arrestee cannot be held for a significant period without some neutral determination that there are grounds to do so, * * * no decision that he should go free can come quickly enough to erase the invasion of his privacy that already will have occurred. * * * Logic therefore would seem to dictate that arrests be subject to the warrant requirement at least to the same extent as searches.

But logic sometimes must defer to history and experience. **[k]** [Justice Powell then goes on to argue that historical practice shows that the Fourth Amendment was not intended to require arrest warrants and that to adopt such a rule would severely hamper law enforcement].

* * *

MR. JUSTICE MARSHALL, with whom MR. JUSTICE BRENNAN joins, dissenting.

* * *

There is no doubt that by the reference to the seizure of persons, the Fourth Amendment was intended to apply to arrests. * * *

The Court next turns to history. It relies on the English common-law rule of arrest and the many state and federal statutes following it. There are two serious flaws in this approach. First, as a matter of factual analysis, the substance of the ancient common-law rule provides no support for the far-reaching modern rule that the Court fashions on its model. Second, as a matter of doctrine, the longstanding existence of a Government practice does not immunize the practice from scrutiny under the mandate of our Constitution.

The common-law rule was indeed as the Court states it. * * * To apply the rule blindly today, however, makes [little] sense * * * without understanding the meaning of * * * words in the context of their age. For the fact is that a felony at common law and a felony today bear only slight resemblance, with the result that the relevance of the common-law rule of arrest to the modern interpretation of our Constitution is minimal.

* * * Only the most serious crimes were felonies at common law, and many crimes now classified as felonies under federal or state law were treated as misdemeanors. * * * **[l]**

* * * To make an arrest for any of these crimes [misdemeanors] at common law, the police officer was required to obtain a warrant, unless the crime was committed in his presence. Since many of these same crimes are commonly classified as felonies today, however, under the Court's holding a warrant is no longer needed to make such arrests, a result in contravention of the common law.

[g] If this makes arrest warrants totally discretionary, of what use is the Fourth Amendment?

[h] It is interesting that a practice could exist for centuries before being challenged legally. There was greater acceptance of the legal status quo in the past.

[i] Justice Powell politely says that the majority opinion has skirted the main question.

[j] Does this argument undermine the Court's decision? How can the Court avoid the "logic" of the Fourth Amendment?

[k] Is this too easy an out? Does this mean that the Court need not follow the Constitution just because it has not been followed for a long time?

[l] Does Justice Marshall's analysis (requiring arrest warrants for non-life-threatening crimes) make more sense than the majority's? Would such a rule undermine effective law enforcement?

• **CASE & COMMENTS** •

Thus the lesson of the common law, and those courts in this country that have accepted its rule, is an ambiguous one. Applied in its original context, the common-law rule would allow the warrantless arrest of some, but not all, of those we call felons today. Accordingly, the Court is simply historically wrong when it tells us that "[t]he balance struck by the common law in generally authorizing felony arrests on probable cause, but without a warrant, has survived substantially intact." As a matter of substance, the balance struck by the common law in accommodating the public need for the most certain and immediate arrest of criminal suspects with the requirement of magisterial oversight to protect against mistaken insults to privacy decreed that only in the most serious of cases could the warrant be dispensed with. This balance is not recognized when the common-law rule is unthinkingly transposed to our present classifications of criminal offenses. Indeed, the only clear lesson of history is contrary to the one the Court draws: the common law considered the arrest warrant far more important than today's decision leaves it.

* * * [T]he Court's unblinking literalism cannot replace analysis of the constitutional interests involved. **[m]** While we can learn from the common law, the ancient rule does not provide a simple answer directly transferable to our system. Thus, in considering the applicability of the common-law rule to our present constitutional scheme, we must consider *both* of the rule's two opposing constructs: the presumption favoring warrants, as well as the exception allowing immediate arrests of the most dangerous criminals. The Court's failure to do so, indeed its failure to recognize any tension in the common-law rule at all, drains all validity from its historical analysis.

[m] Does Justice Marshall's analysis better comport with the "originalist" idea of adhering to the "intent of the framers"?

* * *

Watson upheld the authority of the police to arrest felons in public places without a warrant. It left several questions unresolved, the most important of which was whether an arrest warrant was necessary to enter a home in order to make an arrest. This question was answered four years later in *Payton v. New York* (1980).

Arrest in the Home

Payton v. New York (1980) held that absent an exigency, police were required to have an arrest warrant to enter a person's home to make an arrest. Police had probable cause to believe that Payton committed a murder and robbery. Around 7:30 A.M., six officers went to Payton's apartment without an arrest warrant, intending to arrest him. Lights were on and music was heard in the apartment, but there was no response to their knock on the metal door. About thirty minutes later, the police used crowbars to break open the door and enter the apartment. No one was there, but a .30-caliber shell casing in plain view was seized and admitted into evidence at Payton's murder trial. Payton moved to suppress the shell casing as the product of an illegal arrest.

The majority (*per* Justice Stevens) held that entering the home to make a routine felony arrest without a warrant violated the Fourth Amendment. The government argued that the Fourth Amendment was designed only to prevent "general warrants," and not to require warrants when the police had probable cause to arrest. The Court replied, "the evil the Amendment was designed to prevent was broader than the abuse of a general warrant. Unreasonable searches or seizures

conducted without any warrant at all are condemned by the plain language of the first clause of the Amendment."

Was this ruling consistent with *Watson,* which overlooked the literal words of the Amendment? The Court did not disturb the *Watson* rule but instead *distinguished* arrests made in the home from arrests made in public places: "[H]owever, . . . [a] greater burden is placed . . . on officials who enter a home or dwelling without consent. Freedom from intrusion into the home or dwelling is the archetype of the privacy protection secured by the Fourth Amendment." The "right of a man to retreat into his own home and there be free from unreasonable governmental intrusion" stands at the very core of the Fourth Amendment. *Payton* is one of several post-*Katz* cases that places a special emphasis on the privacy of the *home* rather than treating all "expectations of privacy" the same. The majority supported its position with common law history and trends among the states: a "long-standing, widespread practice is not immune from constitutional scrutiny. But neither is it to be lightly brushed aside." As for the concern by law enforcement that the rule would undermine public safety, the Court made it clear that the police may enter a home without a warrant when there is an exigency.

Justice White dissented, joined by Chief Justice Burger and Justice Rehnquist, giving four reasons to uphold the rule that had allowed police to enter a house without a warrant to make an arrest: (1) the rule was limited to felonies and did not apply to misdemeanors, (2) the privacy of the resident was protected by the "knock and announce" rule, (3) the arrest had to be made in the daytime, and (4) such arrest was lawful only if supported by "stringent probable cause." These are rather weak arguments since the dissent restates conditions that would exist in any event. If pushed to the extreme, such arguments could totally eliminate the requirement for arrest warrants for home arrests, just as *Watson* had, in effect, destroyed any constitutional underpinning for arrest warrants in public places.

The difference between the *Watson* and *Payton* decisions is, at one level, explained by the factual difference between an arrest in public and in one's home. Yet, there is enough similarity in these cases to illustrate how "middle-of-the-road" or "swing" justices influence Supreme Court decision making. In these cases, two consistently liberal justices, Brennan and Marshall, voted for a warrant in both *Watson* and *Payton*. Similarly, three more conservative justices—White, Rehnquist, and Burger—voted against the warrant in both cases. The different outcomes in the two cases may be explained by the thinking of the three "swing" justices—Stewart, Blackmun, and Powell—who voted against a warrant in *Watson* (1976) but in favor of a warrant in *Payton* (1980). The swing justices were joined by Justice Stevens, who was appointed to the Court between the two cases. Thus, the facts alone did not explain the different holdings in *Watson* and *Payton*. Rather, the *attitudes* of the justices who evaluated those facts were decisive. The preexisting leanings in favor of or against law enforcement of the "conservative" and "liberal" justices made their votes unresponsive to the differing facts of *Watson* and *Payton*. The justices with less ideological leanings concerning this issue were able to evaluate the cases differently. This "political" evaluation of the Supreme Court does not explain every case, but it does show that justices' personalities, temperaments, life experiences, and belief systems come into play in fashioning the rules and doctrines of constitutional law.

EXIGENT CIRCUMSTANCES *Payton* stated that police may enter the suspect's home to make an arrest without a warrant when exigent circumstances exist. The Supreme Court has been highly protective of the expectation of privacy in one's home and has narrowly viewed police claims that they have entered under an "exigency." For example, in *Welsh v. Wisconsin* (1984) (see Chapter 5), police entered a suspect's home without a warrant or consent in "hot pursuit" of a person suspected in a nonjailable, first-time, civil, driving-under-the-influence offense. The police tried to justify the entry on an exigency basis: that the blood alcohol level of a suspected drunk driver was decreasing over time. The Court found that this "exigency" simply did not outweigh the sanctity of the home.

In *Minnesota v. Olson* (1990) police made a warrantless entry into an apartment in which Olson was a guest and discovered incriminating evidence. The Court first held that under *Rakas v. Illinois*, Olson had a legitimate expectation of privacy (see Chapter 2). Did the police breach that privacy by entering without a warrant? In this case, the crime—a robbery and murder—was far more serious than in *Welsh*. The Minnesota Supreme Court applied a "totality of the circumstances approach" to find there was no exigency compelling the police to enter the home without a warrant. That court looked at the gravity of the crime, whether the suspect was reasonably believed to be armed, the strength of the probable cause against the defendant, and the likelihood of escape.[19] In this case, Olson was not clearly identified as the driver of a car involved in a robbery and murder. The only link was a few papers found in the car and identified by an unverifiable, anonymous tip. The police did not rush to arrest him when they learned of his identity and knew that he was in the apartment with women who called the police. They had sufficient time to obtain a warrant. There was no hot pursuit of a dangerous felon. The destruction of incriminating evidence was not imminent. The apparent danger of violence or escape was low in light of the police actions. The Minnesota courts found that no exigency existed and suppressed the incriminating evidence. The United States Supreme Court upheld this fact-based application of the lower court's suppression of the evidence and agreed that there was no exigency to override the *Payton* rule.

ARRESTS AND SEARCHES IN THE HOMES OF THIRD-PARTIES Is a *search warrant* needed to arrest a person who is in the home of a third party, or is an arrest warrant for the suspect sufficient? In *Steagald v. United States* (1981) police obtained an arrest warrant for Ricky Lyons. Two days later, they proceeded to Steagald's home, where they believed Lyons was hiding. Outside the premises, they stopped and frisked Gary Steagald and an acquaintance, and then entered the home to look for Lyons. Lyons was not present, but the police observed cocaine in plain sight. Based on that observation, a search warrant was obtained, and large quantities of cocaine were seized. The Supreme Court held that the initial intrusion into the home was unconstitutional. There was neither an exigency, a search warrant, nor consent to authorize or allow entry into the home of a third party to look for Lyons: An arrest warrant does not give officers the right to enter the home of a third party who knows the person named in the arrest warrant. Even if the officers had a reasonable belief that the suspect was in the house, that belief was not "subjected to the detached scrutiny of a judicial officer." The privacy interests of a homeowner superseded the authority of the police to enter under these circumstances.

SEARCH INCIDENT TO ARREST

The police have the authority to conduct a warrantless search of a person for *weapons* and *evidence* whenever a person is lawfully arrested upon probable cause for any crime. An arrest always creates an exigency—the risk of injury to the officer and the likelihood of destruction of evidence. Under the warrant-preference construction of the Fourth Amendment, the **search incident to arrest** is one of three well-accepted warrant exceptions; the other two are entries into homes in hot pursuit and automobile searches. Waiting for a magistrate's warrant to search a person just arrested would indeed undermine legitimate law enforcement interests.

Scope of the Search Incident to Arrest

The question of the **scope of a search incident to arrest** proceeds in two directions—toward and away from the arrested person. That is, how intrusive a search of the body and clothing of the arrested *person* is allowed, and how far away from the suspect can a search incident to arrest go to *areas under the arrestee's control*?

The first part of the "scope" rule was clarified in **United States v. Robinson** (1973). Officer Jenks of the Washington, D.C., Police Department saw Robinson driving an automobile and knew that Robinson's driver's license had been revoked four days earlier. Having reason to believe that Robinson was driving without a license, Jenks stopped Robinson and cited him for driving without a license. Under Washington, D.C., law, driving without a license was a crime for which a person could be *brought into custody* at a police station. According to police department procedures, Officer Jenks patted down Robinson's clothing. "He felt an object in the left breast pocket of the heavy coat" Robinson was wearing, could not tell what it was, and reached into the pocket and pulled out a "crumpled up cigarette package." The officer opened it and found fourteen gelatin capsules of heroin.

Writing for the Court, Justice Rehnquist distinguished between the search that may be made of the *person* and a search of the *area under his control* following a lawful arrest, the issue decided four years earlier in *Chimel v. California.* Unlike the area-of-control rule, which had varied over time, courts have consistently upheld the right of the police to *thoroughly search* a person incident to arrest in order to secure and preserve evidence of crime and "to disarm the suspect in order to take him into custody." These reasons are in force when a police officer has probable cause and makes a **custodial arrest.** When a person is taken into custody, a *Terry* pat-down does not offer the officer sufficient protection against weapons that may be concealed and could be used during the transport to a police station. The arrest was considered proper and the search was allowed under the Fourth Amendment, making the evidence admissible.

Four dissenting justices argued that an arrest for a traffic violation does not raise suspicion of drug possession and that the extent of the search must be limited by the nature of the crime. The majority, however, refused to limit the authority of the police in such a manner. "A police officer's determination as to how and where to search the person of a suspect whom he has arrested is necessarily a quick *ad hoc* judgment which the Fourth Amendment does not require to be broken down in each instance into an analysis of each step in the search. The authority to search the person incident to a lawful custodial arrest, while based upon the need to disarm and to discover evidence, does not depend on what a court may later decide was the probability in a particular

arrest situation that weapons or evidence would in fact be found upon the person of the suspect." The Court thus created a bright-line rule: Police do not have to weigh each arrest situation on the street to guess whether this particular crime justifies a particular level of search. The constitutional rule is that the police may conduct a thorough search of the person upon arrest, without having to account for whether the search was related to the crime or the circumstances of the arrest.

The rule of *Atwater v. City of Lago Vista* (2001) (above, this chapter), authorizing an officer to take a person into custody for a fine-only offense, means that there is no longer such a thing as a noncustodial arrest. There are two situations in which a personal search is not authorized after a person is seized by police. The first are temporary investigative stops made under the authority of *Terry v. Ohio* (1967), which authorize only a brief pat-down of the outer clothing for weapons. The second situation came into play in **Knowles v. Iowa** (1998). A police officer stopped an automobile driver for speeding, issued the driver a *citation* rather than arresting him and, with neither the driver's consent nor probable cause, conducted a full automobile search, yielding a bag of marijuana and a "pot pipe." Iowa statutes allow an officer either to arrest a person for a traffic offense and bring the person before a magistrate, or allow "the far more usual practice of issuing a citation in lieu of arrest or in lieu of continued custody after an initial arrest." The statutes also authorize officers to make a full custody search of a stopped car, even though a citation has been issued. The Supreme Court held that the search in this case violated the Fourth Amendment, even though authorized by state law. The two rationales for the *Robinson* search incident to arrest rule are not strongly supported here. "The threat to officer safety from issuing a traffic citation . . . is a good deal less than in the case of a custodial arrest." As for the second rationale: "Nor has Iowa shown the second justification for the authority to search incident to arrest—the need to discover and preserve evidence. Once Knowles was stopped for speeding and issued a citation, all the evidence necessary to prosecute that offense had been obtained. No further evidence of excessive speed was going to be found either on the person of the offender or in the passenger compartment of the car." The Court also rejected Iowa's contention that a full-blown search of the car might turn up evidence of another, undetected crime.

Chimel deals with the other "direction" of the scope of a search incident to arrest—how far *away* from the arrested individual may the search be conducted? Although the right to conduct a warrantless search incident to arrest has never been questioned, the Supreme Court had, over a half-century period from 1914 to 1969, issued an inconsistent string of rulings on the scope question. In *Chimel v. California* (1969) the Supreme Court sought to finally resolve the issue by handing down a clear statement concerning the proper extent of boundaries of warrantless searches around the person following an arrest.

— *Chimel v. California* **Case & Comments** —

Chimel v. California
395 U.S. 752, 89 S.Ct. 2034, 23 L.Ed.2d 685 (1969)

MR. JUSTICE STEWART delivered the opinion of the Court.

This case raises basic questions concerning the permissible scope under the Fourth Amendment of a search incident to a lawful arrest.

* * * Late [one] afternoon * * * three police officers arrived at the * * * home of the petitioner with a warrant authorizing his arrest for [a] burglary. * * * The officers knocked on the door, identified themselves to the petitioner's wife, and asked if they might come inside. She ushered them into the house, where they waited 10 or 15 minutes until the petitioner returned home from work. **[a]** When the petitioner entered the house, one of the officers handed him the arrest warrant and asked for permission to "look around." The petitioner objected, but was advised that "on the basis of the lawful arrest," the officers would nonetheless conduct a search. No search warrant had been issued.

Accompanied by the petitioner's wife, the officers then looked through the entire three-bedroom house, including the attic, the garage, and a small workshop. In some rooms the search was relatively cursory. In the master bedroom and sewing room, however, the officers directed the petitioner's wife to open drawers and "to physically move contents of the drawers from side to side so that [they] might view any items that would have come from [the] burglary." **[b]** After completing the search, they seized numerous items—primarily coins, but also several medals, tokens, and a few other objects. The entire search took between 45 minutes and an hour.

[Items seized during the search were admitted in evidence against Chimel at a criminal trial.] * * *

[The Court assumed that the arrest was valid.] This brings us directly to the question whether the warrantless search of the petitioner's entire house can be constitutionally justified as incident to that arrest. The decisions of this Court bearing upon that question have been far from consistent, as even the most cursory review makes evident.

[Dictum in *Weeks v. United States* (1914) referred in passing to a well-known exception to the warrant requirement: "to search the person of the accused when legally arrested."] That statement made no reference to any right to search the *place* where an arrest occurs. * * * Eleven years later the case of *Carroll v. United States* (1925) brought the following embellishment of the *Weeks* statement:

"When a man is legally arrested for an offense, whatever is found upon his person *or in his control* which it is unlawful for him to have and which may be used to prove the offense may be seized and held as evidence in the prosecution." * * * (Emphasis added.)

[Another 1925 case, *Agnello v. United States,* "still by way of dictum" said:] **[c]**

"The right without a search warrant contemporaneously to search persons lawfully arrested while committing crime and to search the place where the arrest is made in order to find and seize things connected with the crime as its fruits or as the means by which it was committed, as well as weapons and other things to effect an escape from custody, is not to be doubted." * * *

And in *Marron v. United States* (1927), two years later, the dictum of *Agnello* appeared to be the foundation of the Court's decision, [where agents with a search warrant to seize liquor and a still also seized a ledger. **[d]** The ledger was seized as incident to the arrest of the illicit producers at the still.] The Court upheld the seizure of the ledger by holding that since the agents had made a lawful arrest, "[t]hey had a right without a warrant contemporaneously to search the place in order to find and seize the things used to carry on the criminal enterprise." * * *

That the *Marron* opinion did not mean all that it seemed to say became evident, however, a few years later in *Go-Bart Importing Co. v. United States* (1931) and *United States v. Lefkowitz* (1932). * * * [In these cases the Supreme Court limited the *Marron* ruling to situations where the things seized incident to arrest "were visible and accessible and in the offender's immediate custody."] * * * [I]n *Lefkowitz,* * * * the Court held unlawful a search of desk drawers and a cabinet despite the fact that the search had accompanied a lawful arrest. * * * **[e]**

The limiting views expressed in *Go-Bart* and *Lefkowitz* were thrown to the winds, however, in *Harris v. United States,* decided in 1947. * * * [Harris] was arrested [on an arrest warrant] in the living room of his four-room apartment, and in an attempt to recover two canceled checks thought to have been used in effecting the forgery, the officers undertook a thorough search of the entire apartment. Inside a desk drawer they found a sealed envelope marked "George Harris, personal papers." The envelope, which was then torn open, was found to contain altered Selective Service documents, and those documents were used

[a] Why did the officers wait for Chimel to return home before searching the home? If Chimel's wife had refused them entry and they arrested Chimel outside his house, would a search of his house be just as reasonable? Justified? Could they have demanded entry under the arrest warrant?

[b] A magistrate specifies the things to be searched in a search warrant. By searching without a warrant or under an arrest warrant, does an officer potentially have a greater scope to search than if a search warrant had been obtained?

[c] The words "in his control" and "search the place" could *logically* apply to the actions of the police in Chimel's house.

[d] Does the *Marron* decision appear to authorize the search of an entire house where an arrest is made?

[e] If *Lefkowitz* or *Go-Bart* did not explicitly overrule *Marron*, does this inject uncertainty into the law? Or does the most recent case control?

• CASE & COMMENTS •

to secure Harris' conviction for violating the Selective Training and Service Act of 1940. The Court rejected Harris' Fourth Amendment claim, sustaining the search as "incident to arrest." * * *

Only a year after *Harris,* however, the pendulum swung again. In *Trupiano v. United States* [1948], [the Court invalidated the seizure of evidence at an illegal distillery made without a search warrant but pursuant to arrests.] The opinion stated:

* * *

"A search or seizure without a warrant as an incident to a lawful arrest has always been considered to be a strictly limited right. It grows out of the inherent necessities of the situation at the time of the arrest. But there must be something more in the way of necessity than merely a lawful arrest." * * *

In 1950, two years after *Trupiano,* came *United States v. Rabinowitz,* the decision upon which California primarily relies in the case now before us. **[f]** In *Rabinowitz,* federal authorities * * * [armed with an arrest warrant arrested the defendant] at his one-room business office. At the time of the arrest, the officers "searched the desk, safe, and file cabinets in the office for about an hour and a half," * * * and seized 573 stamps with forged overprints. * * * The Court held that the search in its entirety fell within the principle giving law enforcement authorities "[t]he right 'to search the place where the arrest is made in order to find and seize things connected with the crime * * *'" * * * The test, said the Court, "is not whether it is reasonable to procure a search warrant, but whether the search was reasonable." * * * **[g]**

* * * [The *Rabinowitz*] doctrine, however, at least in the broad sense in which it was applied by the California courts in this case, can withstand neither historical nor rational analysis.

* * *

[The Court then noted that the line of cases supporting the *Rabinowitz* rule was quite wavering. Furthermore, the historic background of the Fourth Amendment was the strongly felt abuses of general warrants, hated by the American colonists, implying that] * * * the general requirement that a search warrant be obtained is not lightly to be dispensed with, and "the burden is on those seeking [an] exemption [from the requirement] to show the need for it * * *" * * *

Only last Term in *Terry v. Ohio* (1968), we emphasized that "the police must, whenever practicable, obtain advance judicial approval of searches and seizures through the warrant procedure," * * * and that "[t]he scope of [a] search must be 'strictly tied to and justified by' the circumstances which rendered its initiation permissible." * * *

A similar analysis underlies the "search incident to arrest" principle, and marks its proper extent. When an arrest is made, it is reasonable for the arresting officer to search the person arrested in order to remove any weapons that the latter might seek to use in order to resist arrest or effect his escape. **[h]** Otherwise, the officer's safety might well be endangered, and the arrest itself frustrated. In addition, it is entirely reasonable for the arresting officer to search for and seize any evidence on the arrestee's person in order to prevent its concealment or destruction. And the area into which an arrestee might reach in order to grab a weapon or evidentiary items must, of course, be governed by a like rule. A gun on a table or in a drawer in front of one who is arrested can be as dangerous to the arresting officer as one concealed in the clothing of the person arrested. **[i]** There is ample justification, therefore, for a search of the arrestee's person and the area "within his immediate control"—construing that phrase to mean the area from within which he might gain possession of a weapon or destructible evidence.

There is no comparable justification, however, for routinely searching any room other than that in which an arrest occurs—or, for that matter, for searching through all the desk drawers or other closed or concealed areas in that room itself. Such searches, in the absence of well-recognized exceptions, may be made only under the authority of a search warrant. The "adherence to judicial processes" mandated by the Fourth Amendment requires no less.

* * *

It is argued in the present case that it is "reasonable" to search a man's house when he is arrested in it. But that argument is founded on little more than a subjective view regarding the acceptability of certain sorts of police conduct, and not on considerations relevant to Fourth Amendment interests. **[j]** Under such an unconfined analysis, Fourth Amendment protection in this area would approach the evaporation point. It is not easy to explain why, for instance, it is less subjectively "reasonable" to search a man's house when he is arrested on his front lawn—or just down the street—than it is when he happens to be in the house at the time of arrest. * * * Thus, although "[t]he recurring questions of the reasonableness of searches"

[f] Two of the most liberal justices, Frank Murphy and Wiley Rutledge, died in 1949 and were replaced by more conservative justices, Tom Clark and Sherman Minton.

[g] On a sheet of paper, trace the zigzag of the Court's rulings on the scope of the search incident to arrest.

[h] The dual purposes of the search incident to arrest of the person are extended to the search of the immediate area around the arrest. The Court here states the operative rule of *Chimel.*

[i] The search of a closed drawer is consistent with *Lefkowitz* (1932).

[j] The *Chimel* case is evaluated through the lens of the warrant-preference construction of the Fourth Amendment, rather than the general-reasonableness construction.

depend upon "the facts and circumstances—the total atmosphere of the case," * * * those facts and circumstances must be viewed in the light of established Fourth Amendment principles.

* * *

[The Court noted that the *Rabinowitz* rule creates the possibility for "pretext" arrests, where the police deliberately attempt to arrest a suspect at home so as to avoid the necessity to obtain a search warrant, especially where probable cause does not exist. Thus, in effect, police could operate as if they had general warrants.]

    Rabinowitz and *Harris* have been the subject of critical commentary for many years and have been relied upon less and less in our own decisions. **[k]** It is time, for the reasons we have stated, to hold that on their own facts, and insofar as the principles they stand for are inconsistent with those that we have endorsed today, they are no longer to be followed.

    Application of sound Fourth Amendment principles to the facts of this case produces a clear result. The search here went far beyond the petitioner's person and the area from within which he might have obtained either a weapon or something that could have been used as evidence against him. There was no constitutional justification, in the absence of a search warrant, for extending the search beyond that area. The scope of the search was, therefore, "unreasonable" under the Fourth and Fourteenth Amendments, and the petitioner's conviction cannot stand.

    Reversed.

    [Justice White dissented, joined by Justice Black. He argued that the broad search-incident-to-arrest rule of *Rabinowitz* was correct because the searches must adhere to a general rule of reasonableness. In this case, the search was reasonable because the arrest alerted Mrs. Chimel, and she would have been in a position to get rid of incriminating evidence after the police had left the house.]

[k] The Court here explicitly overrules cases that allowed a broad interpretation of the scope of a search incident to arrest. This clarifies the wavering line of prior cases and seeks to put a definite end to the Court's "pendulum swings."

In *New York v. Belton* (1981) the Supreme Court conflated the automobile search exception to the search warrant (see Chapter 5) and the search incident to arrest rationale in upholding a search. A lone New York state trooper stopped a speeding car on the New York Thruway, discovered that none of the four men in the car owned it, smelled burnt marijuana, and saw an envelope on the floor of the car characteristic of those containing marijuana. The trooper ordered the men out of the car, separated them, searched each, and then searched the passenger compartment of the car. He found that the envelope contained marijuana and placed the four men under arrest. The trooper then found a leather jacket belonging to Roger Belton, one of the occupants, unzipped one of the pockets, and discovered cocaine. The issue is whether the opening of the zippered jacket pocket was a constitutional search.

    The Court relied on the automobile search rule and the search incident rule to hold the search valid under the Fourth Amendment. "[W]e hold that when a policeman has made a lawful custodial arrest of the occupant of an automobile, he may, as a contemporaneous incident of that arrest, search the passenger compartment of that automobile." The rationale for the holding was that police needed a *bright-line rule* to guide them in postarrest searches of persons arrested in automobiles. Was *Chimel* stretched too far? The suspects were not near the interior of the car when the search was actually made. *Belton* was not an unjustifiable extension of *Chimel* because the officer was outnumbered by four arrestees and, even though he had secured them outside the car, he could not be certain that one of them would not bolt for the car and find a concealed

weapon. *Belton*'s bright-line holding, however, precludes the argument that under some circumstances a search incident to arrest at a vehicle is unreasonable, as, for example, when two police officers arrest a sole driver.

The Protective Sweep Exception

Maryland v. Buie (1990) established the **protective sweep** warrant exception under the Fourth Amendment. Justice White's majority opinion defined a protective sweep as "*a quick and limited search of a premises, incident to an arrest and conducted to protect the safety of police officers or others.* It is narrowly confined to *a cursory visual inspection of those places in which a person might be hiding.*" It can be thought of as a "**frisk**" of a house to search for persons other than the arrested person who might endanger the officers.

    In *Buie* two robbers, one wearing a red running suit, held up a pizza parlor and fled. An arrest warrant was obtained against Jerome Buie and his alleged accomplice, Lloyd Allen. Buie's house was placed under surveillance. Two days later, the arrest warrant was executed by seven officers who entered the house after verifying that Buie was home. They knew that the robbery had been committed by a pair of men and could not be sure that Buie was alone in the house. Upon entering, the officers "fanned out through the first and second floors." A corporal shouted down to the basement, and Buie, hiding there, surrendered and "emerged from the basement." He was arrested and handcuffed. A detective then entered the basement "in case there was someone else down there." He spotted the red running suit laying on a stack of clothes in plain view and seized it as evidence. If the detective's entry into the basement was an improper intrusion on Buie's expectation of privacy, the running suit would be inadmissible as the fruit of an illegal search.

The Court held the running suit *admissible* under the plain view doctrine: the officer was legitimately in the basement, although Buie had already been arrested. The majority justified the officer's going into another part of the house on the basis of police officer *safety*. When police enter a house under an arrest warrant, hot pursuit, or a valid exigency (as in *Arizona v. Hicks,* 1987), they can go throughout the house looking for the suspect in any likely places where the suspect might reasonably hide. It is true that once the person has been seized, the arrest warrant is executed and the exigency is at an end. At that point, the resident's underlying expectation of privacy in the home comes back into play.

However, Buie's expectation of privacy in his home, once he was arrested, did *not immunize* other rooms from entry after his arrest. The *balancing approach* of Fourth Amendment analysis of *Terry v. Ohio* shows a basic concern for officers' safety by allowing them to frisk potentially armed suspects. The protective sweep, similarly, is designed to protect the arresting officers by allowing them "to take steps to assure themselves that the house in which a suspect is being or had just been arrested is *not harboring other persons who are dangerous* and who could unexpectedly launch an attack" (*Buie,* emphasis added). The risk of danger in a home arrest is as great as, if not greater than, an on-the-street or roadside investigatory encounter.

> A frisk occurs before a police-citizen confrontation has escalated to the point of arrest. A protective sweep, in contrast, occurs as an adjunct to the serious step of taking a person into custody for the purpose of prosecuting him for a crime. Moreover, unlike an encounter on the street or along a highway, an in-home arrest puts the officer at the disadvantage of being on his adversary's "turf." An ambush in a confined setting of unknown configuration is more to be feared than it is in open, more familiar surroundings. (*Maryland v. Buie,* 1990, p. 333)

Once holding that a protective sweep was reasonable, the Court had to determine the *standard of evidence* needed by police to go beyond the room in which the person sought was arrested: (I) probable cause, (II) reasonable suspicion, or (III) no evidence at all? In *Buie* the prosecution argued for position III—that the police should be permitted to conduct a protective sweep whenever they make an in-home arrest for a violent crime. The Maryland courts and the United States Supreme Court disagreed. The Maryland courts had ruled that for officers to go beyond the place of arrest in a home, they were required to have *probable cause* (position I) to believe that other persons were present.

The Supreme Court instead created a two-part rule. First "that there must be articulable facts which, taken together with the rational inferences from those facts, would warrant a reasonably prudent officer in believing that the area to be swept harbors an individual posing a danger to those on the arrest

scene." A protective sweep of the *entire* house must be based on *reasonable suspicion*. But the Court also held "that as an incident to the arrest the officers could, as a precautionary matter and without probable cause or reasonable suspicion, look in closets and other spaces *immediately adjoining* the place of arrest from which an attack could be immediately launched." Thus, the "sweep" of the entire house is differentiated from an "adjoining space" search.

Justice White emphasized that the protective sweep of an entire house is *limited* only to protecting the safety of arresting officers if justified by the circumstances. It may extend only to a cursory inspection of those spaces where a person may be found, and is limited to that period necessary to dispel the reasonable suspicion of danger "and in any event no longer than it takes to complete the arrest and depart the premises."

Justice Brennan, joined by Justice Marshall, dissented. He said that the narrow *Terry* exception swallowed the general rule that searches are reasonable only if based on probable cause. He argued that the majority's characterization of a protective sweep as a "minimally intrusive" search akin to a *Terry* frisk "markedly undervalues the nature and scope of the privacy interests involved." As he saw it, a protective sweep was not far removed from a full-blown search that was not allowed in *Chimel v. California.*

> "A protective sweep would bring within police purview virtually all personal possessions within the house not hidden from view in a small enclosed space. Police officers searching for potential ambushers might enter every room including basements and attics; open up closets, lockers, chests, wardrobes, and cars; and peer under beds and behind furniture. The officers will view letters, documents and personal effects that are on tables or desks or are visible inside open drawers; books, records, tapes, and pictures on shelves; and clothing, medicines, toiletries and other paraphernalia not carefully stored in dresser drawers or bathroom cupboards. While perhaps not a 'full-blown' or 'top-to-bottom' search, a protective sweep is much closer to it than to a 'limited patdown for weapons.'"

Searching at the Station House

INVENTORY SEARCH When an arrested person is brought to a police lockup or a jail for booking, it is standard practice for officers to *inventory* every item of property that the person has on his or her person. In ***Illinois v. Lafayette*** (1983) Ralph Lafayette was arrested for disturbing the peace. He was taken to the Kankakee police station where, in the process of booking him, a warrantless search of his shoulder bag, made for the purpose of inventorying his possessions, turned up amphetamine pills. The Illinois Appellate Court ruled that the privacy interest in an item of personal luggage like a shoulder bag during an **inventory search** is greater than that in an automobile inventory search, and suppressed the evidence of the drugs. The United States Supreme Court reversed.

In the Court's opinion, Chief Justice Burger ruled that because an inventory search does *not* rest on probable cause, the lack of a warrant is immaterial. The inventory search constitutes a well-defined exception to the warrant requirement: It "is not an independent legal concept but rather an incidental *administrative* step following arrest and preceding incarceration" (emphasis added). An inventory search of a jailed person's backpack or similar items is justified by balancing privacy interests in the bag versus the government's interests. The Court found that the state's interests outweighed those of the individual—the routine inventorying of all items in a person's possession is therefore reasonable under the Fourth Amendment. The Illinois Supreme Court's ruling was reversed and the *plain view* seizure of the amphetamines upheld.

The governmental and the individual interests that support the conclusion that a station house inventory search is reasonable include:

- Protecting the arrestee's property from theft by police officers.
- Protecting police from false claims of theft by the arrested person ("A standardized procedure for making a list or inventory as soon as reasonable after reaching the station house not only deters false claims but also inhibits theft or careless handling of articles taken from the arrested person.").
- Accurately determining the identity of the arrested person.
- Ensuring the safety of all persons in jail ("Dangerous instrumentalities—such as razor blades, bombs, or weapons—can be concealed in innocent-looking articles taken from the arrestee's possession.").

Chief Justice Burger stated that "The governmental interests underlying a stationhouse search of the arrestee's person and possessions may in some circumstances be even greater than those supporting a search immediately following arrest." He dismissed the suggestion of the Illinois court that it was feasible in such situations to secure the property of arrestees in secure lockers and thus preserve their individual rights of privacy.

In dictum, the Chief Justice referred to whether or not a person can be ordered to undress at the station house: "Police conduct that would be impractical or unreasonable—or embarrassingly intrusive—on the street can more readily—and privately—be performed at the station. For example, the interests supporting a search incident to arrest would hardly justify disrobing an arrestee on the street, but the practical necessities of routine jail administration may even justify taking a prisoner's clothes before confining him, although that step would be rare."

WARRANTLESS STATION HOUSE SEARCH FOR EVIDENCE   A locked footlocker that police take into custody following an arrest, with probable cause to believe it contains drugs, cannot be opened by the police without having obtained a search warrant (***United States v. Chadwick,*** 1977). It constitutes an "effect" protected by the warrant clause of the Fourth Amendment.

To the contrary, station house investigative seizures are allowed where an exigency exists that the suspect can destroy evidence. In ***United States v. Edwards*** (1974) police had probable cause to believe that the clothing worn by Edwards, who was arrested and in a police lockup, contained evidence of a crime—paint chips from the scene of a burglary. The Court held that the police could, without a warrant, require him to exchange his clothing for other clothing, even ten hours after his jailing. The time delay was reasonable because the police waited until morning, when a substitute set of clothing could be purchased. *Edwards* fell within the search incident to arrest exception and made clear that when a person is in a police lockup or jail, the exigency that supports the search incident to arrest (i.e., destruction of evidence) may continue for considerable periods of time. The exchange of clothing could also be allowed at the time of an inventory.

A warrantless search was also upheld in ***Cupp v. Murphy*** (1973). The search and seizure consisted of police at a police

---

LAFAYETTE IN THE STATES

"Massachusetts permits inventory searches, but demands adherence to written guidelines explicit enough to guard against the possibility that police officers may exercise discretion in opening closed containers."

Thea Rostad was stopped while driving for speeding and swerving, and arrested for driving without a license by a Belchertown police officer. At the police station an "officer unzipped and opened the defendant's handbag and inventoried its contents, which included bags and packets containing drugs." This was done pursuant to a written policy that read, "the officer-in-charge or an officer designated by him shall search the arrestee and make an inventory of all items collected. The arrestee shall be asked to sign the inventory list." The Supreme Judicial Court of Massachusetts held this inventory search to violate Article 14 of the Massachusetts Declaration of Rights, which requires probable cause for all searches. An inventory exception is allowed for reasons given in federal cases, but any inventory must be conducted under specific written regulations. "[W]e do not agree that the written policy of the Belchertown police, . . . was specific or 'obvious' enough. More precisely, perhaps, we do not agree that the policy was explicit enough to guard against the possibility that police officers would exercise discretion with respect to whether to open closed wallets and handbags as part of their inventory search." *Commonwealth v. Rostad,* 410 Mass. 618, 574 N.E.2d 381 (1991)

Barry Latzer, *State Constitutional Criminal Law,* §3:22.

station taking dry blood scrapings from the finger of a man who voluntarily appeared at a police station after the strangulation death of his wife. When the police noticed the stain and the man held his hands behind his back, an exigency arose because he might have destroyed evidence. *Cupp* is problematic because at the time the blood was scraped from the individual's finger there was no formal custodial arrest. In that case, the police had at best only reasonable suspicion that the person murdered his wife, but their action was a very limited intrusion, and the evidence was the kind that could be readily destroyed. Under these circumstances, the search and seizure were held constitutional.

STRIP SEARCHES   The Supreme Court has not dealt with the issue of whether the **strip search** of a person held in jail on a *minor* offense is reasonable. In ***Bell v. Wolfish*** (1979) the Court ruled on the conditions of confinement of *pretrial detainees* in facilities that also housed convicted prisoners awaiting transportation or serving short sentences. Detainees who were held in a federal jail on *serious* federal charges were required to expose their body cavities for visual inspection as a part of a strip search conducted after every contact visit with a person from outside the institution. The practice was justified by correctional authorities "not only to discover but also to deter the smuggling of weapons, drugs, and other contraband into the institution." The Supreme Court applied the general reasonableness construction of the Fourth Amendment in upholding this practice as reasonable. "A detention facility is a unique place fraught with serious security dangers. Smuggling of money, drugs, weapons, and other contraband is all too common an occurrence."

On the other hand, lower federal and state courts have held blanket strip search, or **body cavity search,** regulations and practices unreasonable for minor crimes. The Seventh Circuit Court of Appeals, in *Mary Beth G. v. City of Chicago* (1983), described strip searches as "demeaning, dehumanizing, undignified, humiliating, terrifying, unpleasant, embarrassing, repulsive, signifying degradation and submission."[20] A City of Chicago policy in force from 1952 to 1980 required all females who were detained to be subjected to a strip search regardless of the charges while all males were patted down. In four consolidated cases, women had been subjected to strip searches after arrests for having outstanding parking tickets, failing to produce a driver's license, and disorderly conduct. The Court of Appeals for the Seventh Circuit found these searches to be within the search incident to arrest exception to the warrant requirement and relied on the *Bell v. Wolfish* balancing test to determine whether these strip searches were reasonable. The government's primary justification for the strip searches was to prevent the women from bringing weapons or contraband into the jail. The specific holding of *Wolfish* did *not* apply to the Chicago cases because the essential facts differed. In *Mary Beth G.* the plaintiffs "are minor offenders who were not inherently dangerous and who were being detained only briefly while awaiting bond." Further, *Wolfish* "does not validate strip searches in detention settings *per se*." After carefully weighing the competing interests, the Seventh Circuit held that

the strip searches in Chicago bore an insubstantial relationship to security needs and, when balanced against the plaintiff's privacy interests, could not be considered reasonable.[21] Despite such rulings, municipal police departments in many places have continued to use strip and body cavity searches in inappropriate situations and have lost substantial lawsuits as a result. Some departments have instituted regulations to utilize these searches when reasonable. "Two states, New Jersey and Tennessee, have passed statutes requiring a search warrant or consent in order to perform a visual body cavity search." In neither state have police departments complained that these laws made their lockups unsafe.[22]

STOP AND FRISK

This section explores the second major category of personal seizure: the investigative stop, otherwise called field interrogation.

Establishing the Constitutional Authority to Stop

Arrest law is rooted in common law cases going back hundreds of years. Virtually no law existed regarding the temporary stopping of individuals by the police in order to obtain information. Organized police forces, however, exercised this power as a matter of custom since their inception in the nineteenth century. In the 1960s state statutes and cases began to define the so-called "**stop and frisk**" power. These laws generated constitutional challenges that soon landed on the Supreme Court's doorstep. The basic rules were formulated in *Terry v. Ohio* (1968).

Terry was handed down during an explosive moment in American history—an extended period of intense racial conflict that boiled over into hundreds of inner-city riots that lasted from 1964 to 1972, reaching its highest pitch in the summers of 1967 and 1968. The immediate catalyst of these riots often were episodes between largely all-white police forces and mostly young, male African Americans who felt that the promises of the civil rights movement were not being fulfilled.[23] Given the overheated political climate of 1968, some commentators suggest that the liberal Warren Court justices voted to extend the powers of the police in part as a way of mollifying the bitter attacks on the Court by the police establishment and many conservatives in Congress following the 1966 decision in *Miranda v. Arizona*.[24] Journalist Fred Graham, in this skeptical vein, noted that "[t]he Supreme Court has never conceded that it intentionally compensates for a tough decision on one point by handing down a soft ruling on another, but its actions occasionally give that impression. . . ."[25] Thus, within two years after *Miranda,* the Court upheld the use of informers and electronic eavesdropping, dropped the mere evidence restriction on searches, and authorized stop and frisk on less than probable cause. This does not prove that the Court acted from narrow political motives, but does fuel speculation that the Supreme Court's decisions are not entirely divorced from major national events.

— *Terry v. Ohio* **Case & Comments** —

• CASE & COMMENTS •

Terry v. Ohio
392 U.S. 1, 88 S.Ct. 1868, 20 L.Ed.2d 889 (1968)

MR. CHIEF JUSTICE WARREN delivered the opinion of the Court.

This case presents serious questions concerning the role of the Fourth Amendment in the confrontation on the street between the citizen and the policeman investigating suspicious circumstances.

Petitioner Terry was convicted of carrying a concealed weapon. * * * Officer McFadden testified that while he was patrolling in plain clothes in downtown Cleveland [one] afternoon * * * his attention was attracted by two men, Chilton and Terry, standing on the corner of Huron Road and Euclid Avenue. * * * [H]e was unable to say precisely what first drew his eye to them. However, he testified that he had been a policeman for thirty-nine years. * * * [H]e had developed routine habits of observation over the years[;] * * * he would "stand and watch people or walk and watch people at many intervals of the day." **[a]** He added: "Now, in this case when I looked over they didn't look right to me at the time."

* * * [Officer McFadden saw them pace up and down the block five or six times each, pausing frequently to look into the window of a jewelry store and to confer.] After this had gone on for 10 to 12 minutes, the two men walked off together [following a third]. * * *

* * * He testified that * * * he suspected the two men of "casing a job, a stick-up," and that he considered it his duty as a police officer to investigate further. He added that he feared "they may have a gun." **[b]** * * * Deciding that the situation was ripe for direct action, Officer McFadden approached the three men, identified himself as a police officer and asked for their names. At this point his knowledge was confined to what he had observed. * * * When the men "mumbled something" in response to his inquiries, Officer McFadden grabbed petitioner Terry, spun him around * * * and patted down the outside of his clothing. In the left breast pocket of Terry's overcoat Officer McFadden felt a pistol. * * * At this point, * * * the officer ordered all three men to enter Zucker's store. As they went in, he removed Terry's overcoat completely [and] removed a .38-caliber revolver from the pocket. * * * [Pat-downs of Chilton and Katz produced a gun on Chilton but not on Katz.] The officer testified that he only patted the men down to see whether they had weapons, and that he did not put his hands beneath the outer garments of either Terry or Chilton until he felt their guns. * * *

I.

* * * Unquestionably petitioner was entitled to the protection of the Fourth Amendment as he walked down the street in Cleveland. * * * The question is whether in all the circumstances of this on-the-street encounter, his right to personal security was violated by an unreasonable search and seizure.

* * * [T]his question thrusts to the fore difficult and troublesome issues regarding a sensitive area of police activity[:] * * * the power of the police to "stop and frisk"—as it is sometimes euphemistically termed—suspicious persons. * * *

[The police claim they need authority to deal with street encounters and that the brief detention of a "stop and frisk" not amounting to arrest should not be governed by the Fourth Amendment. It is a petty indignity. **[c]** The defendant argues that unless the police have probable cause to arrest, they have no power under the Fourth Amendment to forcibly detain a person temporarily or to frisk them.]

In this context we approach the issues in this case mindful of the limitations of the judicial function in controlling the myriad daily situations in which policemen and citizens confront each other on the street. * * *

* * * [I]n some contexts the [exclusionary] rule is ineffective as a deterrent [to police misconduct]. Street encounters between citizens and police officers are incredibly rich in diversity. They range from wholly friendly exchanges of pleasantries or mutually useful information to hostile confrontations of armed men involving arrests, or injuries, or loss of life. Moreover, hostile confrontations are not all of a piece. Some of them begin in a friendly enough manner, only to take a different turn upon the injection of some unexpected element into the conversation. Encounters are initiated by the police for a wide variety of purposes, some of which are wholly unrelated to a desire to prosecute for crime. **[d]** Doubtless some police "**field interrogation**" conduct violates the Fourth Amendment. But a stern refusal by this Court to condone such activity does not necessarily render it responsive to the exclusionary rule. Regardless of how effective the rule may be where obtaining convictions is an important objective of the police, it is powerless to deter invasions of constitutionally guaranteed rights where the police either have no interest in prosecuting or are willing to forgo successful prosecution in the interest of serving some other goal.

* * * The wholesale harassment by certain elements of the police community, of which minority groups, particularly Negroes, frequently complain, will not be stopped by the exclusion of any evidence

[a] The case does not indicate that Terry and Chilton were African Americans and the third who joined them, Katz, was a white male. Should this be suspicious?

[b] Is Officer McFadden's suspicion based on facts? Are they reasonable? Does probable cause exist to arrest these men on the basis of what he saw? For what crime?

[c] The police wish to forcibly stop persons without any legal basis. Does this sound right?

[d] The Court admits that bringing the stop and frisk power within the Constitution will not enable courts to supervise instances of police misconduct where the stop does not result in an arrest and the person is simply let go.

from any criminal trial. * * * **[e]** Nothing we say today is to be taken as indicating approval of police conduct outside the legitimate investigative sphere. Under our decision, courts still retain their traditional responsibility to guard against police conduct which is overbearing or harassing, or which trenches upon personal security without the objective evidentiary justification which the Constitution requires. When such conduct is identified, it must be condemned by the judiciary and its fruits must be excluded from evidence in criminal trials. * * *

* * * [W]e turn our attention to the quite narrow question posed by the facts before us: whether it is always unreasonable for a policeman to seize a person and subject him to a limited search for weapons unless there is probable cause for an arrest. * * *

II.

Our first task is to establish at what point in this encounter the Fourth Amendment becomes relevant. That is, we must decide whether and when Officer McFadden "seized" Terry and whether and when he conducted a "search." * * * It must be recognized that whenever a police officer accosts an individual and restrains his freedom to walk away, he has "seized" that person. And it is nothing less than sheer torture of the English language to suggest that a careful exploration of the outer surfaces of a person's clothing all over his or her body in an attempt to find weapons is not a "search." * * * It is a serious intrusion upon the sanctity of the person. * * * **[f]**

* * * This Court has held in the past that a search which is reasonable at its inception may violate the Fourth Amendment by virtue of its intolerable intensity and scope. * * * The scope of the search must be "strictly tied to and justified by" the circumstances which render its initiation permissible. * * *

* * * We therefore reject the notions that the Fourth Amendment does not come into play at all as a limitation upon police conduct if the officers stop short of something called a "technical arrest" or a "full-blown search."

[The next question is whether this seizure and search were unreasonable, that is, whether the officer's action was justified at its inception and whether it was reasonably related in scope to the circumstances that justified the interference in the first place.]

III.

* * * [W]e deal here with an entire rubric of police conduct—necessarily swift action predicated upon the on-the-spot observations of the officer on the beat—which historically has not been, and as a practical matter could not be, subjected to the warrant procedure. **[g]** Instead, the conduct involved in this case must be tested by the Fourth Amendment's general proscription against unreasonable searches and seizures.

Nonetheless, the notions which underlie both the warrant procedure and the requirement of probable cause remain fully relevant in this context. * * * **[h]** [I]n justifying the particular intrusion the police officer must be able to point to specific and articulable facts which, taken together with rational inferences from those facts, reasonably warrant that intrusion. The scheme of the Fourth Amendment becomes meaningful only when it is assured that at some point the conduct of those charged with enforcing the laws can be subjected to the more detached, neutral scrutiny of a judge who must evaluate the reasonableness of a particular search or seizure in light of the particular circumstances. **[i]** And in making that assessment it is imperative that the facts be judged against an objective standard: would the facts available to the officer at the moment of the seizure or the search "warrant a man of reasonable caution in the belief" that the action taken was appropriate? * * * Anything less would invite intrusions upon constitutionally guaranteed rights based on nothing more substantial than inarticulate hunches, a result this Court has consistently refused to sanction. * * * And simple " 'good faith on the part of the arresting officer is not enough.' * * * If subjective good faith alone were the test, the protections of the Fourth Amendment would evaporate, and the people would be 'secure in their persons, houses, papers, and effects,' only in the discretion of the police." * * *

[The Court noted that the police have an interest to prevent and detect crime that necessitates temporary stops of individuals to inquire into suspicious circumstances.]

The crux of this case, however, is not the propriety of Officer McFadden's taking steps to investigate petitioner's suspicious behavior, but rather, whether there was justification for McFadden's invasion of Terry's personal security by searching him for weapons in the course of that investigation. **[j]** * * * Certainly it would be unreasonable to require that police officers take unnecessary risks in the performance of their duties. American criminals have a long tradition of armed violence, and every year in this country many law enforcement officers are killed in the line of duty. * * *

[e] The Court signals its awareness and condemnation of widespread police misconduct and racism, which was rampant in that era.

[f] Thus, by stopping and frisking Terry, Officer McFadden seized and searched him. Note that the frisk is defined as a limited search for one purpose only.

[g] *Terry* here solidifies the "general reasonableness" construction of the Fourth Amendment.

[h] What is an "articulable fact"? It seems to be *any* reason other than a hunch. This suggests a *lower* standard than probable cause, which is defined as facts that would lead a prudent person to conclude that a crime is occurring or has occurred.

[i] Here, the Court provides a standard closer to traditional probable cause. Note that this paragraph does not use the words "reasonable suspicion," although later cases concluded that this lower standard is the rule.

[j] The Court turns its attention to the frisk, and devotes more attention to this subject than to the stop.

• CASE & COMMENTS •

In view of these facts, we cannot blind ourselves to the need for law enforcement officers to protect themselves and other prospective victims of violence in situations where they may lack probable cause for an arrest. * * *

We must still consider, however, the nature and quality of the intrusion on individual rights which must be accepted if police officers are to be conceded the right to search for weapons in situations where probable cause to arrest for crime is lacking. Even a limited search of the outer clothing for weapons constitutes a severe, though brief, intrusion upon cherished personal security, and it must surely be an annoying, frightening, and perhaps humiliating experience. **[k]** Petitioner contends that such an intrusion is permissible only incident to a lawful arrest, either for a crime involving the possession of weapons or for a crime the commission of which led the officer to investigate in the first place. However, this argument must be closely examined.

* * * [Terry] says it is unreasonable for the policeman to [disarm a suspect] until such time as the situation evolves to a point where there is probable cause to make an arrest. When that point has been reached, petitioner would concede the officer's right to conduct a search of the suspect for weapons, fruits or instrumentalities of the crime, or "mere" evidence, incident to the arrest.

There are two weaknesses in this line of reasoning, however. First, it fails to take account of traditional limitations upon the scope of searches, and thus recognizes no distinction in purpose, character, and extent between a search incident to an arrest and a limited search for weapons. **[l]** The former, although justified in part by the acknowledged necessity to protect the arresting officer from assault with a concealed weapon, * * * is also justified on other grounds, and can therefore involve a relatively extensive exploration of the person. A search for weapons in the absence of probable cause to arrest, however, must, like any other search, be strictly circumscribed by the exigencies which justify its initiation. * * * Thus it must be limited to that which is necessary for the discovery of weapons which might be used to harm the officer or others nearby, and may realistically be characterized as something less than a "full" search. * * *

* * * [Second,] [a]n arrest is a wholly different kind of intrusion upon individual freedom from a limited search for weapons, and the interests each is designed to serve are likewise quite different. An arrest is the initial stage of a criminal prosecution. It is intended to vindicate society's interest in having its laws obeyed, and it is inevitably accompanied by future interference with the individual's freedom of movement, whether or not trial or conviction ultimately follows. **[m]** The protective search for weapons, on the other hand, constitutes a brief, though far from inconsiderable, intrusion upon the sanctity of the person. It does not follow that because an officer may lawfully arrest a person only when he is apprised of facts sufficient to warrant a belief that the person has committed or is committing a crime, the officer is equally unjustified, absent that kind of evidence, in making any intrusions short of an arrest. Moreover, a perfectly reasonable apprehension of danger may arise long before the officer is possessed of adequate information to justify taking a person into custody for the purpose of prosecuting him for a crime. * * *

IV.

* * * We think * * * a reasonably prudent man would have been warranted in believing petitioner was armed and thus presented a threat to the officer's safety while he was investigating his suspicious behavior. * * * **[n]** We cannot say [Officer McFadden's] decision at that point to seize Terry and pat his clothing for weapons was the product of a volatile or inventive imagination, or was undertaken simply as an act of harassment; the record evidences the tempered act of a policeman who in the course of an investigation had to make a quick decision as to how to protect himself and others from possible danger, and took limited steps to do so. * * *

* * * **[o]** The sole justification of the search in the present situation is the protection of the police officer and others nearby, and it must therefore be confined in scope to an intrusion reasonably designed to discover guns, knives, clubs, or other hidden instruments for the assault of the police officer.

* * *

V.

* * * **[p]** We merely hold today that where a police officer observes unusual conduct which leads him reasonably to conclude in light of his experience that criminal activity may be afoot and that the persons with whom he is dealing may be armed and presently dangerous, where in the course of investigating this behavior he identifies himself as a policeman and makes reasonable inquiries, and where nothing in the initial stages of the encounter serves to dispel his reasonable fear for his own or others'

[k] In this case Officer McFadden placed his hands on Terry's coat (the frisk) simultaneously with the stop. He did not have probable cause to believe Terry was armed. Terry was arrested *after* the frisk disclosed a gun. Thus, the case facts do not fit the rules of a "search incident to arrest."

[l] The Court draws a fairly clear distinction between a full search after arrest and a limited frisk (pat down) after or accompanying a stop.

[m] The Court slips back to explaining and justifying a stop and compares it to a full custody arrest. This analysis of the stop is interleaved with that of the frisk, making it difficult to untangle the two issues.

[n] The general rules laid down in the case are applied to the specific facts. The Court concludes that Terry's seizure was based on more than a hunch.

[o] The Court reemphasizes the limited scope of the frisk.

[p] This paragraph summarizes the case.

safety, he is entitled for the protection of himself and others in the area to conduct a carefully limited search of the outer clothing of such persons in an attempt to discover weapons which might be used to assault him. Such a search is a reasonable search under the Fourth Amendment, and any weapons seized may properly be introduced in evidence against the person from whom they were taken.

Affirmed.

MR. JUSTICE HARLAN, concurring.

* * *

* * * [I]f the frisk is justified in order to protect the officer during an encounter with a citizen, the officer must first have constitutional grounds to insist on an encounter, to make a *forcible* stop. * * * I would make it perfectly clear that the right to frisk in this case depends upon the reasonableness of a forcible stop to investigate a suspected crime. **[q]**

Where such a stop is reasonable, however, the right to frisk must be immediate and automatic if the reason for the stop is, as here, an articulable suspicion of a crime of violence. Just as a full search incident to a lawful arrest requires no additional justification, a limited frisk incident to a lawful stop must often be rapid and routine. There is no reason why an officer, rightfully but forcibly confronting a person suspected of a serious crime, should have to ask one question and take the risk that the answer might be a bullet. * * *

* * *

MR. JUSTICE DOUGLAS, dissenting.

I agree that petitioner was "seized" within the meaning of the Fourth Amendment. I also agree that frisking petitioner and his companions for guns was a "search." But it is a mystery how that "search" and that "seizure" can be constitutional by Fourth Amendment standards, unless there was "probable cause" to believe that (1) a crime had been committed or (2) a crime was in the process of being committed or (3) a crime was about to be committed. **[r]**

* * * If loitering were in issue and that was the offense charged, there would be "probable cause" shown. But the crime here is carrying concealed weapons; and there is no basis for concluding that the officer had "probable cause" for believing that that crime was being committed. * * * [A] magistrate would, therefore, have been unauthorized to issue [a warrant], for he can act only if there is a showing of "probable cause." We hold today that the police have greater authority to make a "seizure" and conduct a "search" than a judge has to authorize such action. **[s]** We have said precisely the opposite over and over again.

* * *

To give the police greater power than a magistrate is to take a long step down the totalitarian path. Perhaps such a step is desirable to cope with modern forms of lawlessness. But if it is taken, it should be the deliberate choice of the people through a constitutional amendment. * * *

* * *

[q] Justice Harlan's point is that officers need have no additional reasonable suspicion to believe that the person stopped is armed; a legal frisk is justified solely by the legality of the stop. As with his concurrence in *Katz,* Justice Harlan's point came to be accepted as part of the *Terry* rule.

[r] Justice Douglas, perhaps the most liberal member of the Warren Court, here combines a liberal policy result with a nonactivist position of adhering to established rules of law.

[s] By changing the rules that guide police on the street detention, the Court imposed on magistrates the duty to uphold police stops short of traditional arrests.

TERRY AND VAGRANCY LAWS: CLOSING A LEGAL LOOPHOLE   While *Terry* can be viewed as a conservative turn for the decidedly liberal Warren Court, several years later, in ***Papachristou v. City of Jacksonville*** (1972), the more conservative Burger Court took a "liberal" stance in *restricting* the use of overly broad or vague **vagrancy statutes.** These laws had for centuries given police in England and the United States a "cover" to stop and question individuals who merely appeared suspicious but against whom no probable cause to arrest existed.[26] Vagrancy laws were used not only to question persons suspected of crime, but to control and harass social deviants and poor people as well. A destructive aspect of these laws was their use as "cover" charges: a police officer ensured against a lawsuit for false arrest by charging a person stopped with "vagrancy." The Supreme Court, by openly recognizing the field-interrogation power of the police in *Terry,* and by shutting down the abusive

extremes of overbroad vagrancy laws in *Papachristou,* eliminated a source of hypocrisy in police work and, in theory, brought this area of police activity under judicial scrutiny.

After *Papachristou,* the states could continue to rely on loitering laws but tended to narrowly tailor them to specifically target disruptive behavior such as prowling around homes, streetwalking prostitution, and on-the-street drug sales. These laws provided very detailed definitions of loitering. The change worked by *Papachristou* was that now citizens could turn to the courts to determine if such specifically targeted laws met due process criteria.

* * *

The Supreme Court has applied the stop-and-frisk doctrine in a variety of cases in the years following *Terry.* While some cases have limited the power of police officers to stop, most have expanded the investigative stop doctrine beyond a strict reading of

Terry. Most commentators believe that a rough balance between pro-police rights and individual rights established in the Burger Court years has given way to a legal regime that decidedly favors police in the Rehnquist Court. The mostly Republican-appointed Court has been charged with creating a "drug exception" to the Fourth Amendment linked to the nation's "war on drugs."[27]

In the cases that follow, the Court often has had to determine whether police action constituted an arrest, a *Terry* stop, or a consensual encounter, and if a seizure, if the seizure was justified by probable cause or reasonable suspicion. Instead of organizing the cases in a purely chronological fashion, they are presented, somewhat artificially, by the source of reasonable suspicion and the place in which the stop occurs.

The Sources of Reasonable Suspicion

HEARSAY   At first it seemed that the novel *Terry* rule, allowing a Fourth Amendment seizure on *less* than probable cause (on "reasonable suspicion") had to be based on the *personal observations of an experienced police officer. Terry* stated: "in determining whether the officer acted reasonably in such circumstances, due weight must be given, not to his inchoate and unparticularized suspicion or 'hunch,' but to the specific reasonable inferences which he is entitled to draw from the facts in light of his experience." Nevertheless, the Court soon established that reasonable suspicion can be based upon reliable hearsay.

In *Adams v. Williams* (1972) a person known to Police Sgt. Connolly approached him at 2:15 A.M. in a high-crime area and told him that an individual in a nearby car was carrying narcotics and had a gun at his waist. Sgt. Connolly approached the car, tapped on the driver's window, and asked the occupant to open the door. Williams, who was alone in the car, rolled down the window instead, and the officer reached in and seized a loaded gun from Williams's waistband. Based on the discovery of the gun, Connolly arrested Williams for illegal possession of a weapon, searched him, and discovered drugs that were admitted into evidence. Unlike Officer McFadden in *Terry,* who personally saw suspicious behavior, Sgt. Connolly did not personally see the gun or corroborate this fact before simultaneously stopping and frisking (i.e., searching and seizing). The Court expressly ruled that *reliable hearsay* may be the basis of an officer's investigative stop, which occurred when Sgt. Connolly tapped on the window and demanded that the occupant step out.

Adams v. Williams also extended the *Terry* ruling in several other ways. It extended the stop-and-frisk authority to *crimes of possession.* Some felt *Terry* should be limited to violent crimes or thefts. This extension has made stop and frisk a potent tool in the "war on drugs" and has also been at the center of the bitter controversy over racial profiling (see *Law in Society* section, Chapter 5). *Adams* is not a perfect precedent for the proposition that a frisk does not need to be supported by independent reasonable suspicion, but if an officer has reasonable suspicion that a person stopped is armed, the officer may frisk before asking any questions.

ANONYMOUS TIPS   The Court in *Adams* noted that "[t]his is a stronger case than obtains in the case of an anonymous telephone tip." Such a situation was resolved by the Court in *Alabama v. White* (1990). At 3:00 P.M., Montgomery police received "a telephone call from an anonymous person, stating that Vanessa White would be leaving 235-C Lynwood Terrace Apartments at a particular time in a brown Plymouth station wagon with the right tail-light lens broken and that she would be going to Dobey's Motel and would be in possession of about an ounce of cocaine inside a brown attaché case." The police did not know Vanessa White or what she looked like, but they corroborated the facts (except that White was not carrying an attaché case) and stopped White in her car shortly before she reached Dobey's Motel. The officers told her she was stopped because she was suspected of carrying cocaine; they obtained consent to look into her locked, brown attaché case that was in the car. They found drugs in the attaché case.

The Supreme Court held (6–3) that "the tip, as corroborated by independent police work, exhibited sufficient indicia of reliability to provide reasonable suspicion to make the investigatory stop." The decision was assisted to some extent by the ruling of *Illinois v. Gates* (see Chapter 3) in which the Court approved a "totality of circumstances" approach to determining whether an anonymous informant who supplied probable cause for a search warrant was reliable, truthful, and had a basis of knowledge. In *White* the Court applied this approach to find that the totality of circumstances apparently indicated that the informant was so familiar with Vanessa White's movements as to be reliable and truthful and have a basis of knowledge. In the course of its opinion, the Court made an important distinction between probable cause and reasonable suspicion. Reasonable suspicion not only is a lesser quantum of proof, but it is also *less reliable.* "[R]easonable suspicion can arise from information that is less reliable than that required to show probable cause." This language gives police greater leeway to *stop* individuals without great concern that the information supplied is unreliable than to search those individuals.

Justice Stevens, dissenting, saw these facts differently. "An anonymous neighbor's prediction about somebody's time of departure and probable destination is anything but a reliable basis for assuming that the commuter is in possession of an illegal substance." He suggested that White may have been a room clerk at the motel and offered a much more troubling suggestion—that in cases like this, the tipster could be another police officer who has a "hunch" about a person. This is not mere surmise, but it is a technique used by corrupt police, as noted in a book on the subject:

> There happened to be money missing on a job they went on, and the guy who lost the money came into the precinct bitching. It was a set-up job. It wasn't a real radio run. They [police] had *dropped a dime* on the guy. They had called 911 themselves and then responded to the bogus call to get inside the building. . . .[28]

The Supreme Court has recently limited the acceptability of anonymous information that presented only *general information.* In *Florida v. J. L.* (2000), a unanimous decision, an anonymous caller reported to the Miami-Dade Police that a young black male standing at a particular bus stop and wearing a plaid shirt was carrying a gun. Officers went to the bus stop and saw three black males, one of whom, respondent J. L., was wearing a plaid shirt. Apart from the tip, the officers had no reason to suspect any of the three of illegal conduct. The officers did not see a firearm or observe any unusual movements. One of the officers frisked J. L. and seized a gun from his pocket. J. L., who was then almost sixteen years of age, was charged under state law with carrying a concealed firearm without a license and possessing a firearm while under the age of eighteen. The Court distinguished *Alabama v. White* by noting that although the tip itself in *White* did not amount to reasonable suspicion, once "police observation showed that the informant had accurately predicted the woman's movements, . . . it become reasonable to think the tipster had inside knowledge about the suspect and therefore to credit his assertion about the cocaine" (*Florida v. J. L.*). Justice Ginsburg, in her opinion, called *White* a "borderline" decision.

> The tip in the instant case lacked the moderate indicia of reliability present in *White* and essential to the Court's decision in that case. The anonymous call concerning J. L. provided no predictive information and therefore left the police without means to test the informant's knowledge or credibility. That the allegation about the gun turned out to be correct does not suggest that the officers, prior to the frisks, had a reasonable basis for suspecting J. L. of engaging in unlawful conduct. The reasonableness of official suspicion must be measured by what the officers knew before they conducted their search. All the police had to go on in this case was the bare report of an unknown, unaccountable informant who neither explained how he knew about the gun nor supplied any basis for believing he had inside information about J. L. If *White* was a close case on the reliability of anonymous tips, this one surely falls on the other side of the line. (*Florida v. J. L.*)

POLICE BULLETIN The *Terry* basis of reasonable suspicion was also expanded in **United States v. Hensley** (1985). *Hensley* ruled that police may stop a suspect based on information contained in a flyer or bulletin they receive from another law enforcement department. If the flyer has been issued on the basis of articulable facts supporting a reasonable suspicion that the wanted person has committed an offense (rather than probable cause), then it justifies a stop to check identification, to pose questions to the person, or to detain the person briefly while attempting to obtain further information. *Hensley,* therefore, held that stops not only may be made to prevent a *future* crime or stop *ongoing* offenses, as was the case in *Terry,* but also can be used to inquire about *past* criminal acts. Justice O'Connor maintained that although the crime prevention rationale and the exigency present in *Terry* did not exist in *Hensley,* the ability to stop a suspect for questions based on reasonable suspicion promotes the government interest of solving crime and prevents the chance that a suspect might flee.

Terry on the Streets

The Court found, in several post-*Terry* cases, that police stopped individuals without reasonable suspicion, violating their liberty rights. **Sibron v. New York** (1968), was a **companion case** to *Terry*. An NYPD patrol officer noticed Sibron "hanging around" a street corner for many hours in the late afternoon and evening where drug sales were believed to occur. He was seen talking to known drug addicts. Sibron went into a diner and, as he was eating pie and drinking coffee, was ordered outside by the officer. The officer had seen no evidence of a drug sale but approached Sibron, said "You know what I am after," reached into Sibron's pocket, and found a packet of heroin. The Court held that this seizure was not based on reasonable suspicion and, therefore, was an unreasonable and unconstitutional stop. There were no articulable objective facts to establish drug dealing or possession. It was also clear that the officer was not "frisking" Sibron for a weapon but simply searching for drugs. The drugs were suppressed as the product of an illegal search and seizure. This case illustrates the line between legal and illegal stops.

IDENTIFICATION AND LOITERING LAWS The following cases involve statutes that authorize police to ask for identification and seek to control loitering.

The Supreme Court has held that the police do *not* have a generalized power to obtain *personal identification* from a person in the context of a statute that empowered police to obtain the identification of a person abroad on the street. In **Brown v. Texas** (1979) officers saw Brown and a man in an alley in El Paso, in a high-crime area, at midday. The officer testified that the situation "looked suspicious, but he was unable to point to any facts supporting that conclusion. There is no indication in the record that it was unusual for people to be in the alley." When *asked for identification*, Brown angrily refused to give it. He was arrested, jailed, and upon conviction, fined twenty dollars for violating a Texas statute that made it a crime for a person to intentionally refuse to report his name and address to a police officer who has *lawfully stopped* the person and requested such information. The Court ruled that the application of the statute violated the Fourth Amendment because the police had no grounds for stopping Brown in the first place. The mere fact that the area was frequented by drug users was not reasonable suspicion to stop Brown. This leaves open the question of whether a person who refuses to answer a question as to his identity on a valid *Terry* stop can be convicted for failure to talk.

The Court went a step beyond *Brown v. Texas* in favor of individual liberty in **Kolender v. Lawson** (1983), a case decided on the grounds that a California statute violated *due process*. The California statute required persons who loiter or wander on the streets to identify themselves and to account for their presence when a peace officer requests information. Edward Lawson was detained or arrested under this statute, while walking on the streets of San Diego, California, on approximately fifteen occasions between March 1975 and January 1977. He was prosecuted twice and convicted once. He brought a civil suit to have the law declared unconstitutional. The California courts limited the application of the statute only to instances where a police officer "has reasonable suspicion of criminal activity sufficient to justify a *Terry* detention." The Supreme Court ruled, that even as so construed, the statute still violated the Fourteenth Amendment in that it was *"void-for-vagueness."*

This doctrine states that a law violates due process if it is not sufficiently definite, so that ordinary people are unable to understand what conduct is prohibited. The essential fault with such a law is that it gives police authority in such an open-ended fashion, without standards, that it encourages arbitrary and discriminatory enforcement of the law. The California statute left police with virtually complete discretion to determine whether the suspect offered "credible and reliable" identification. Because the law contained no such standards, it raised the possibility of arbitrary enforcement, a violation of due process of law. This may be discerned from the facts: An African American man, a business consultant in his mid-thirties who wore his hair in dread locks, was arrested fifteen times within two years for simply walking about (see *Law in Society* section, Chapter 5). Justice O'Connor, writing for the majority, commented on the values that underpin these rules: "Our Constitution is designed to maximize individual freedoms within a framework of ordered liberty."

Justice Brennan, concurring in the decision, disagreed with the majority's due process reasoning. He argued that even if the defect in the California law were cured to define which kinds of identification were acceptable, *any* law requiring citizens to identify themselves in the absence of a criminal act is in violation of the Fourth Amendment: "Merely to facilitate the general law enforcement objectives of investigating and preventing unspecified crimes, States may not authorize the arrest and criminal prosecution of an individual for failing to produce identification or further information by a police officer." Justices White and Rehnquist dissented on the ground that a person who is given actual notice of the application of the statute cannot challenge it on the grounds of vagueness because he is apprised of the impact of the law.

A distinguishing hallmark of American life is that there is no general requirement that citizens carry official identification at all times, unlike many democratic nations that require its citizens to carry "**internal passports.**" However reasonable the general requirement that Americans carry identification at all times, it has been resisted because of the powerful cultural norms of individuality and freedom that mark the American character. The American aversion to an internal passport system helps to explain a specific ruling like *Kolender v. Lawson*. However, after 9/11 some have called for a national identification card or a system that links drivers' licenses to a national registry.[29]

The Court again confronted a loitering statute in **City of Chicago v. Morales** (1999). Chicago enacted a "gang congregation" ordinance, with criminal penalties, that prohibited loitering together in any public place by two or more people if at least one individual was a "criminal street gang member." The ordinance defined "loitering" as remaining in any one place with no apparent purpose. A police officer who observed what she reasonably believed was loitering was required to order persons to disperse. A failure to disperse incurred criminal penalties. The Chicago PD promulgated guidelines to prevent arbitrary or discriminatory enforcement of the ordinance. These allowed only designated gang squad officers to use the ordinance, established detailed criteria for determining street gangs and membership, and limited enforcement only to areas with high gang activity

(but not disclosed to the public). The Court struck down the ordinance on due process vagueness grounds.

The ordinance had been vigorously enforced: forty-two thousand people had been arrested for loitering over a three-year period. Justice Stevens, a Chicago native, wrote for the majority. He noted that the reason for the ordinance, that gang violence imperils safety and disrupts normal street life, was not in dispute. As *Papachristou v. City of Jacksonville* (1972) made clear, however, a person has a right to "loiter"—i.e., "to remove from one place to another according to inclination." Such "loitering" is "an attribute of personal liberty" protected by the Constitution. The Court held that the ordinance specifically violated the Due Process Clause by not clearly defining terms like "disperse" and leaving the "locality." What exactly would purported gang members have to do to "disperse"? How quickly did they have to move? How far would they have to go? Also, the ordinance did not adequately define "loitering" with the specificity seen in ordinances that targeted on-the-street drug dealing or prostitution. It therefore "necessarily entrusts lawmaking to the moment-to-moment judgment of the policeman on his beat." Finally, the ordinance could apply to essentially peaceful activity and not to underlying activities that are dangerous. In sum, the ordinance violated the Due Process Clause.

FLEEING FROM THE POLICE   Among the most hotly contested post-*Terry* cases have been those concerning scenarios in which a police officer follows or chases a person. **Michigan v. Chesternut** (1988) held that police "intrusion" did not amount to an illegal detention and search. Chesternut, standing on a Detroit street corner, began to run when he saw a police car drive near. The patrol car turned the corner and followed to see where he was going. The car quickly caught up with him and drove alongside for a short distance. The officers noticed Chesternut discard packets from his right-hand pocket which they retrieved, and found pills that one officer who was trained as a paramedic identified as codeine. Chesternut was arrested and searched, and drugs were found on his person. The Michigan courts held the police were engaged in an "investigatory pursuit" that amounted to a seizure under *Terry*.

A unanimous Supreme Court reversed, holding that the police conduct of driving alongside the defendant did not constitute a stop or a Fourth Amendment seizure. The police used no flashers or siren, drew no weapons, nor ordered the defendant to stop. The car was not operated in an aggressive way to block Chesternut's course or otherwise control his speed or movement. "While the very presence of a police car driving parallel to a running pedestrian could be somewhat intimidating, this kind of police presence does not, standing alone, constitute a seizure. . . . The police therefore were not required to have 'a particularized and objective basis for suspecting [Chesternut] of criminal activity,' in order to pursue him." *Chesternut* is an example of the rule that police need no evidentiary basis for observing on-the-street behavior, even if the observation becomes obvious.

In *California v. Hodari D.* the police did not simply follow, but clearly *chased*, a person on foot.

— *California v. Hodari D.* **Case & Comments —**

• CASE & COMMENTS •

California v. Hodari D.
499 U.S. 621, 111 S. Ct. 1547, 113 L.Ed.2d 690 (1991)

JUSTICE SCALIA delivered the opinion of the Court.

Late one evening in April 1988, Officers Brian McColgin and Jerry Pertoso were on patrol in a high-crime area of Oakland, California. They were dressed in street clothes but wearing jackets with "Police" embossed on both front and back. Their unmarked car proceeded west on Foothill Boulevard, and turned south onto 63rd Avenue. As they rounded the corner, they saw four or five youths huddled around a small red car parked at the curb. **[a]** When the youths [including Hodari D.] saw the officers' car approaching they apparently panicked, and took flight. * * *

The officers were suspicious and gave chase. **[b]** McColgin remained in the car * * *; Pertoso left the car [and chased on foot]. Hodari [emerged from an alley and did not see] Pertoso until the officer was almost upon him, whereupon he tossed away what appeared to be a small rock. A moment later, Pertoso tackled Hodari, handcuffed him, and radioed for assistance. Hodari was found to be carrying $130 in cash and a pager; and the rock he had discarded was found to be crack cocaine.

In the juvenile proceeding brought against him, Hodari moved to suppress the evidence relating to the cocaine. The court denied the motion without opinion. The California Court of Appeal reversed, holding that Hodari had been "seized" when he saw Officer Pertoso running towards him, that this seizure was unreasonable under the Fourth Amendment, and that the evidence of cocaine had to be suppressed as the fruit of that illegal seizure. The California Supreme Court denied the State's application for review. We granted certiorari. * * *

As this case comes to us, the only issue presented is whether, at the time he dropped the drugs, Hodari had been "seized" within the meaning of the Fourth Amendment. **[c]** If so, respondent argues, the drugs were the fruit of that seizure and the evidence concerning them was properly excluded. If not, the drugs were abandoned by Hodari and lawfully recovered by the police, and the evidence should have been admitted. (In addition, of course, Pertoso's seeing the rock of cocaine, at least if he recognized it as such, would provide reasonable suspicion for the unquestioned seizure that occurred when he tackled Hodari. * * *).

We have long understood that the Fourth Amendment's protection against "unreasonable . . . seizures" includes seizure of the person. * * * From the time of the founding to the present, the word "seizure" has meant a "taking possession," * * * For most purposes at common law, the word connoted not merely grasping, or applying physical force to, the animate or inanimate object in question, but actually bringing it within physical control. A ship still fleeing, even though under attack, would not be considered to have been seized as a war prize. **[d]** * * * To constitute an arrest, however—the quintessential "seizure of the person" under our Fourth Amendment jurisprudence—the mere grasping or application of physical force with lawful authority, whether or not it succeeded in subduing the arrestee, was sufficient. * * *

To say that an arrest is effected by the slightest application of physical force, despite the arrestee's escape, is not to say that for Fourth Amendment purposes there is a *continuing* arrest during the period of fugitivity. If, for example, Pertoso had laid his hands upon Hodari to arrest him, but Hodari had broken away and had *then* cast away the cocaine, it would hardly be realistic to say that that disclosure had been made during the course of an arrest. * * * The present case, however, is even one step further removed. It does not involve the application of any physical force; Hodari was untouched by Officer Pertoso at the time he discarded the cocaine. His defense relies instead upon the proposition that a seizure occurs "when the officer, by means of physical force *or show of authority*, has in some way restrained the liberty of a citizen." *Terry v. Ohio* (emphasis added). Hodari contends (and we accept as true for purposes of this decision) that Pertoso's pursuit qualified as a "show of authority" calling upon Hodari to halt. The narrow question before us is whether, with respect to a show of authority as with respect to application of physical force, a seizure occurs even though the subject does not yield. We hold that it does not.

The language of the Fourth Amendment, of course, cannot sustain respondent's contention. The word "seizure" readily bears the meaning of a laying on of hands or application of physical force to restrain movement, even when it is ultimately unsuccessful. ("She seized the purse-snatcher, but he broke out of her grasp.") It does not remotely apply, however, to the prospect of a policeman yelling "Stop, in the name of the law!" at a fleeing form that continues to flee. That is no seizure. **[e]** Nor can the result respondent wishes to achieve be produced—indirectly, as it were—by suggesting that Pertoso's uncomplied-with show of authority was a common-law arrest, and then appealing to the principle that all common-law arrests are seizures. An arrest requires *either* physical force (as described above) *or*, where that is absent, *submission* to the assertion of authority. * * *

[a] Does a group of huddled teenagers provide grounds to arrest them? To forcibly stop them under *Terry*?

[b] Do you think that a teen who runs from the sight of a cop should be chased? If caught, should he be arrested? Subjected to field interrogation?

[c] California conceded that the flight of the youths upon seeing the police was not in itself reasonable suspicion for a *Terry* stop. Although Justice Scalia thought the point was arguable, he was bound by this concession. The issue was left open for a later case.

[d] Is the chase of a sailing ship on the high seas a good analogy for a police officer chasing a youth through a city neighborhood?

[e] As *U.S. v. Watson* (1976) demonstrated, a strict reading of the language of the Constitution does not always bind the Court. Is it *reasonable* to view a chase as a seizure if the police officer is close to the person running and is likely to capture him?

• CASE & COMMENTS •

We do not think it desirable, even as a policy matter, to stretch the Fourth Amendment beyond its words and beyond the meaning of arrest, as respondent urges. Street pursuits always place the public at some risk, and compliance with police orders to stop should therefore be encouraged. * * *

Respondent contends that his position is sustained by the so-called *Mendenhall* test, . . . "A person has been 'seized' within the meaning of the Fourth Amendment only if, in view of all the circumstances surrounding the incident, a reasonable person would have believed that he was not free to leave." * * * **[f]** In seeking to rely upon that test here, respondent fails to read it carefully. It says that a person has been seized "only if," not that he has been seized "whenever"; it states a *necessary,* but not a *sufficient* condition for seizure—or, more precisely, for seizure effected through a "show of authority." *Mendenhall* establishes that the test for existence of a "show of authority" is an objective one: not whether the citizen perceived that he was being ordered to restrict his movement, but whether the officer's words and actions would have conveyed that to a reasonable person. * * *

[This case is like the chase in *Brower v. Inyo County* (1989): There was no arrest until Brower crashed into the roadblock.]

In sum, assuming that Pertoso's pursuit in the present case constituted a "show of authority" enjoining Hodari to halt, since Hodari did not comply with that injunction he was not seized until he was tackled. The cocaine abandoned while he was running was in this case not the fruit of a seizure, and his motion to exclude evidence of it was properly denied. We reverse the decision of the California Court of Appeal, and remand for further proceedings not inconsistent with this opinion.

JUSTICE STEVENS, with whom JUSTICE MARSHALL joins, dissenting.

The Court's narrow construction of the word "seizure" represents a significant, and in my view, unfortunate, departure from prior case law construing the Fourth Amendment. * * * [T]he Court now adopts a definition of "seizure" that is unfaithful to a long line of Fourth Amendment cases. Even if the Court were defining seizure for the first time, which it is not, the definition that it chooses today is profoundly unwise. In its decision, the Court assumes, without acknowledging, that a police officer may now fire his weapon at an innocent citizen and not implicate the Fourth Amendment—as long as he misses his target. **[g]**

For the purposes of decision, the following propositions are not in dispute. First, when Officer Pertoso began his pursuit of respondent, the officer did not have a lawful basis for either stopping or arresting respondent. * * * Second, the officer's chase amounted to a "show of force" as soon as respondent saw the officer nearly upon him. * * * Third, the act of discarding the rock of cocaine was the direct consequence of the show of force. * * * Fourth, as the Court correctly demonstrates, no common-law arrest occurred until the officer tackled respondent. * * * Thus, the Court is quite right in concluding that the abandonment of the rock was not the fruit of a common-law arrest.

It is equally clear, however, that if the officer had succeeded in touching respondent before he dropped the rock—even if he did not subdue him—an arrest would have occurred. **[h]** * * * In that event (assuming the touching precipitated the abandonment), the evidence would have been the fruit of an unlawful common-law arrest. The distinction between the actual case and the hypothetical case is the same as the distinction between the common-law torts of assault and battery—a touching converts the former into the latter. Although the distinction between assault and battery was important for pleading purposes, * * * the distinction should not take on constitutional dimensions. The Court mistakenly allows this common-law distinction to define its interpretation of the Fourth Amendment.

At the same time, the Court fails to recognize the existence of another, more telling, common-law distinction—the distinction between an arrest and an attempted arrest. As the Court teaches us, the distinction between battery and assault was critical to a correct understanding of the common law of arrest. * * * ("An arrest requires either physical force . . . *or,* where that is absent, *submission* to the assertion of authority"). However, the facts of this case do not describe an actual arrest, but rather, an unlawful *attempt* to take a presumptively innocent person into custody. Such an attempt was unlawful at common law. **[i]** Thus, if the Court wants to define the scope of the Fourth Amendment based on the common law, it should look, not to the common law of arrest, but to the common law of attempted arrest, according to the facts of this case.

* * *

[The dissent goes on to criticize the majority for taking a narrow view of seizure that goes against the policy purposes of *Katz* that broadened the range of behaviors that came within the scope of Fourth Amendment seizures, such as the "stop and frisk" in *Terry v. Ohio. Terry* said that a Fourth Amendment

[f] Would it not seem to a reasonable person, from the officer's actions, that Hodari D. believed he was not free to leave? Does this conclusion help Hodari D.'s argument?

[g] If a police officer, without probable cause or reasonable suspicion, fired a gun at you and missed, should you be able to claim a violation of your Fourth Amendment rights in a civil suit against the officer? If so, this example undermines Justice Scalia's argument.

[h] A touching would manifest the officer's intent to arrest and would make the person liable for resisting arrest. Should constitutional rights turn on whether the officer "tagged" the fleeing youth?

[i] This challenges the accuracy and completeness of Justice Scalia's common law analysis—an especially sharp attack because Justice Scalia, as an originalist, relies heavily on the common law.

• CASE & COMMENTS •

seizure occurs when an officer, by means of physical force or show of authority, has *in some way* restrained a citizen's liberty. Such an interference with liberty occurred in this case, and so the majority's common law reasoning fails to comport with the constitutional dimensions of Fourth Amendment law after *Terry*.] Even though momentary, a seizure occurs whenever an objective evaluation of a police officer's show of force conveys the message that the citizen is not entirely free to leave—in other words, that his or her liberty is being restrained in a significant way. * * *

* * *

A commentator saw *Hodari D.* as the "culmination of a struggle between two factions of the Supreme Court," and a victory by the group led by conservative Justices Kennedy and Scalia. If the *Mendenhall* Court meant what it said when it proposed that a seizure is to be measured by the reasonable understanding of the individual, then the majority in *Hodari D.* created a new rule when it added a "physical restraint" element to Fourth Amendment seizures.[30] A year before *Hodari D.*, a leading scholar accepted as an established rule that "[w]hen a cop accosts a citizen on the street, the constitutional standard for measuring whether a seizure occurs is whether—in light of the totality of the circumstances—a reasonable person would feel free to leave the scene."[31] Professor Maclin saw this as a matter of commonsense reality: "In the typical street encounter, few persons, if any, feel free to ignore or leave the presence of a police officer who has approached and questioned them. . . . [T]he average individual who is approached by a police officer does not feel free to leave."[32] The implication of a pure *Mendenhall* rule plus "what everyone knows about being approached by the police" was that a police officer who "rushes" an individual without reasonable suspicion has seized that person; and if the person flees and tosses away contraband, its seizure is the product of an illegal search and seizure. The *Hodari D.* modification allows the tossed contraband to be taken and used as "abandoned" property.

The unresolved issue in *Hodari D.*, whether mere flight from the sight of a police officer alone established reasonable suspicion for an officer to give chase, was settled in favor of the police in ***Illinois v. Wardlow*** (2000). A four-car police caravan was cruising through a "high crime neighborhood" looking for on-the-street drug deals. Sam Wardlow was standing alone and holding an opaque bag; he made eye contact with an officer in the last car and "fled." Two officers in the car watched Wardlow run through a gangway and an alley and eventually cornered him on the street. One officer exited his car, stopped Wardlow, "and immediately conducted a protective pat-down search for weapons because in his experience it

HODARI D. IN THE STATES

"As for the Hodari D. test for seizures—actual submission to authority, or application of physical force—some state high courts swiftly repudiated it." States rejecting the *Hodari D.* test include Connecticut, Hawaii, Louisiana, Minnesota, New Hampshire, New Jersey, New York, Pennsylvania, and West Virginia. States that have adopted the *Hodari D.* test for a seizure are Florida, Idaho, Illinois, Maryland, Nebraska, Texas, and Washington.

Shreveport and Louisiana State Police conducted a drug sweep of an area code-named "Operation Thor." Its objective was to reclaim certain high-crime areas from drug trafficking and gang-related activities. The sweep began at around 10:30 P.M., when approximately ten to twelve marked police vehicles carrying twenty to thirty officers converged on Roby's Arcade. As officers approached, they observed Tucker and another man standing huddled together by a parked car outside the arcade. When the two men noticed the approaching police cars, they quickly broke apart and began to leave the scene. As they did, Officer Wilson stopped his car and began to get out while simultaneously ordering the two men to "halt" and "prone out." One of the men laid down immediately. Tucker, however, moved several steps toward the rear of the arcade and tossed away a plastic bag. He then obeyed the police command and lay down. The bag was retrieved and found to contain forty-seven rolled marijuana cigarettes.

Was Tucker seized when ordered to "prone out" or did he abandon the property without being seized? Under Article 1, Section 5 of the Louisiana Constitution, that state's high court held that Tucker was seized: It "is only when the citizen is *actually stopped* without reasonable cause or when a stop without reasonable cause is *imminent* that the 'right to be left alone' is violated, thereby rendering unlawful any resultant seizure of abandoned property. *State v. Tucker,* 626 So.2d 707, 710–11 (La. 1993)"

Barry Latzer, *State Constitutional Criminal Law,* §3:23.

was common for there to be weapons in the near vicinity of narcotics transactions. During the frisk, Officer Nolan squeezed the bag respondent was carrying and felt a heavy, hard object similar to the shape of a gun. The officer then opened the bag and discovered a .38-caliber handgun with five live rounds of ammunition. The officers arrested Wardlow."

The Court emphasized the rule of *Brown v. Texas* (1979)—the simple presence of a person in a high-crime area does not give officers reasonable suspicion to stop a person. On the other hand, the Court ruled that unprovoked flight from the police, as a "commonsense judgment[] and inferences about human behavior," and in the totality of circumstances, constitutes reasonable suspicion. The Court did not say that flight is a *per se* factor that always established reasonable suspicion. While simple, unprovoked flight tends to be a basis of reasonable suspicion, under this view, the officer may also take into account other factors, such as the belief that a neighborhood is a high-crime area. Four justices in *Wardlow*—Stevens, Souter, Ginsburg, and Breyer—concurred in part and dissented in part. The concurring opinion kept alive the idea that under some conditions, flight will not be viewed as reasonable suspicion for a stop.

The ruling creates some tension with another rule of *Terry*: that a person against whom the police do not have reasonable suspicion may refuse to talk to the officer and, citing *Bostick*, "any 'refusal to cooperate, without more, does not furnish the minimal level of objective justification needed for a detention or seizure.'" If a police officer, with no reasonable suspicion, approaches a person on the street to ask if the person will consent to talk to the officer and the person "flees," this could invoke reasonable suspicion. Much would depend on the facts of such a scenario. *Wardlow* does not fully define what is meant by flight. Thus, it is unclear whether, under the facts of *Wardlow*, flight occurs if the person, after looking at an officer, slowly walked away, got on a bicycle and rode away, or entered a taxi and drove off, or entered the building he was standing in front of.[33] Resolution of such issues will be decided in future cases. *Wardlow* clearly expands the actual authority of police to control the streets.

Terry on the Road

Many auxiliary rules for interpreting the "stop and frisk" authority have arisen in automobile stop situations. Apart from this, the scope of a warrantless automobile search based on probable cause is dealt with in Chapter 5.

SCOPE OF A *TERRY* STOP AND FRISK Most *Terry* cases involve a "frisk" of the *person*. **Michigan v. Long** (1983) held that when police stop a driver without arresting him, they may make a quick and cursory examination of the car's interior—a frisk of the car, so to speak. Sheriff's deputies stopped a speeding and erratically driven car. The driver pulled into a ditch and exited the car. The door was left open. The driver, David Long, did not produce identification when so requested. Long began to walk back to the car but was stopped and frisked. No weapons were found. The deputies saw a hunting knife on the

floorboard of the driver's side of the car. One deputy peered into the car with a flashlight and saw something protruding from under the armrest on the front seat. He knelt in the vehicle and lifted the armrest, saw an open pouch on the front seat, and upon flashing his light on the pouch, determined that it contained what appeared to be marijuana. Long was arrested and a search of the car's trunk revealed seventy-five pounds of marijuana.

The Court held the search constitutional under the principles of *Terry*. One reason is that "investigative detentions involving suspects in vehicles are especially fraught with danger to police officers." Thus, to protect their safety, police officers who stop cars may engage in a cursory examination of the passenger areas of the vehicle *to look for weapons* in those areas in which a weapon may be placed or hidden when they have a reasonable belief based on articulable facts that the suspect poses a danger and may gain immediate control of the weapons.

INFERENTIAL REASONING AND REASONABLE SUSPICION *Terry* defines reasonable suspicion, which justifies a stop, as "specific and articulable facts which, taken together with *rational inferences from those facts,* reasonably warrant that intrusion" (*Terry*, p. 29, emphasis added). This important part of the *Terry* doctrine was clarified and extended in **United States v. Cortez** (1981). U.S. Border Patrol officers, alerted by distinctive footprints and tire tracks in a sparsely settled area of desert thirty miles north of the Mexican border, deduced that a truck capable of holding eight to twenty persons would approach from the east and stop between 2 A.M. and 6 A.M. near milepost 122 on Highway 86. As the officers surveyed the road on a particularly bright moonlit night, a camper passed traveling west and then returned approaching from the east at about the time it would take to return from milepost 122. Agents stopped the camper and illegal aliens were found on board. The Court unanimously held that this stop was based on reasonable suspicion. Chief Justice Burger established a structure for reasonable suspicion analysis:

> Courts have used a variety of terms to capture the elusive concept of what cause is sufficient to authorize police to stop a person. Terms like "articulable reasons" and "founded suspicion" are not self-defining; they fall short of providing clear guidance dispositive of the myriad factual situations that arise. But the essence of all that has been written is that the totality of the circumstances—the whole picture—must be taken into account. . . .
>
> The idea that an assessment of the whole picture must yield a particularized suspicion contains two elements, each of which must be present before a stop is permissible. First, the assessment must be based upon all the circumstances. The analysis proceeds with various objective observations, information from police reports, if such are available, and consideration of the modes or patterns of operation of certain kinds of lawbreakers. From these data, a trained officer draws inferences and makes deductions—inferences and deductions that might well elude an untrained person.
>
> The process does not deal with hard certainties, but with probabilities. . . .
>
> The second element contained in the idea that an assessment of the whole picture must yield a particularized

suspicion is the concept that the process just described must raise a suspicion that the particular individual being stopped is engaged in wrongdoing. (*United States v. Cortez,* pp. 417–18)

Cortez supports the concept of **police officer expertise** that was a basis of finding reasonable suspicion in the *Terry* case.

Inferences were key to the decision in **United States v. Arvizu** (2002). Arvizu was driving a minivan with his wife and children on an unpaved road in a remote area in the Coronado National Forest of southeastern Arizona known for drug trafficking. Border patrol checkpoints are staffed intermittently and roving patrols are used to apprehend smugglers trying to circumvent the checkpoints. Magnetic sensors facilitate agents' efforts in patrolling these areas. A sensor was triggered around 2:15 P.M. This timing coincided with the time when agents begin heading back to the checkpoint for a shift change, leaving the area unpatrolled. Alien smugglers do extensive scouting and seem to be most active when agents are returning to the checkpoint. An agent told Agent Stoddard that the same sensor had gone off several weeks before, leading to the apprehension of a drug-carrying minivan using the same route.

Stoddard proceeded to the area and observed the minivan passing. As it approached, it slowed dramatically, from about 50–55 to 25–30 miles per hour. He saw five occupants inside: two adults in the front seat and three children in the back. The driver appeared stiff and his posture very rigid. He did not look at Stoddard and seemed to be trying to pretend that Stoddard was not there. Stoddard thought this suspicious because in his experience on patrol most persons look over and see what is going on, and in that area most drivers give border patrol agents a friendly wave. Stoddard noticed that the knees of the two children sitting in the very back seat were unusually high, as if their feet were propped up on some cargo on the floor. As Stoddard followed the minivan, all of the children, still facing forward, put their hands up at the same time and began to wave at Stoddard in an abnormal pattern. It looked to Stoddard as if the children were being instructed. Their odd waving continued on and off for about four to five minutes. A registration check disclosed that the minivan was registered to an address in Douglas, Arizona, four blocks north of the border in an area notorious for alien and narcotics smuggling. Stoddard stopped the van, asked if he could search, and Arvizu agreed. A duffel bag containing 128.85 pounds of marijuana was found.

The Court of Appeals struck down the stop, by isolating the factors and noting that each was innocent. For example, that court noted that slowing down after seeing an officer is common. It dismissed entirely the children's waving, saying, "If every odd act engaged in by one's children . . . could contribute to a finding of reasonable suspicion, the vast majority of American parents might be stopped regularly within a block of their homes." The Supreme Court reversed and unanimously upheld the stop. It emphasized that the *totality of the circumstances* must be considered. "This process allows officers to draw on their own experience and specialized training to make inferences from and deductions about the cumulative information available to them that 'might well elude an untrained person.'" The Court noted that it has deliberately avoided reducing reasonable suspicion to "a neat set of legal rules." Giving due weight to the factual inferences drawn by Stoddard and the District Court judge, the Court ruled that the agent had reasonable suspicion to believe that Arvizu was engaged in illegal activity.

BREVITY REQUIREMENT   Another automobile stop-and-frisk case clarified an important *Terry* rule: A legal detention must be reasonably *brief.* In **United States v. Sharpe** (1985) a United States Drug Enforcement Agency (DEA) agent patrolling a road under surveillance for suspected drug trafficking noticed an overloaded pickup truck with an attached trailer being followed closely by a Pontiac. After following the two vehicles for twenty miles, the officer decided to make an investigatory stop and radioed the South Carolina Highway Patrol for assistance. When the DEA agent and the state police officer indicated that the two vehicles were to pull over, the Pontiac did so but the truck continued along the road in an attempt to evade the state police. The driver of the Pontiac was detained for twenty minutes while the DEA agent followed the truck, approached it after it was stopped, smelled marijuana in it, and returned to the detained Pontiac. While the Court found that the officer had reasonable suspicion to make the initial stop, at issue was whether a twenty-minute detention was too long under the *Terry* doctrine because it violated the **brevity requirement** for stops. The Supreme Court held that whether a stop is too long (and thus becomes an arrest) depends not only on the length of time of the stop but also on the *surrounding circumstances.* The question is whether the length of time employed was *reasonable.* In *Sharpe* the delay occurred because of the evasive action of the driver of the truck. The Court found that because the police acted diligently to ascertain the facts without creating unnecessary delays, *Terry* was not violated. Note that a twenty-minute stop was sufficiently long so that a special reason had to be supplied to justify it. *Terry* stops are supposed to be just long enough for an officer to ask questions to determine, based on objective factors, whether there is probable cause to arrest or no basis for further detention.

AUTHORITY TO STOP AN AUTOMOBILE   A patrol officer in **Delaware v. Prouse** (1979) made a "routine" stop of the car, explaining, "I saw the car in the area and wasn't answering any complaints, so I decided to pull them off." Prior to the vehicle stop, he did not observe any traffic or equipment violations nor any suspicious activity. He made the stop merely to check the driver's license and registration. The officer did not act pursuant to any standards, guidelines, or procedures pertaining to document spot checks as defined by his department or the state attorney general. During the stop the officer smelled marijuana and made an arrest and seizure.

Lower courts had split on whether this kind of vehicle stop, without reasonable suspicion or probable cause, violated the Fourth Amendment. The Supreme Court, holding this kind of stop and seizure unconstitutional, was not writing on a blank slate. Four years earlier it decided in **United States v. Brignoni-Ponce** (1975) that Border Patrol agents conducting

there is probable cause to search the automobile, with the *Atwater* rule that authorizes the custodial seizure for any arrest, an officer's control over a stopped automobile is complete.[35]

Terry in Tight Places

The nature of a stop was explored in ***Immigration and Naturalization Service v. Delgado*** (1984). United States Immigration and Naturalization Service (INS) officers looking for illegal immigrants walked through a factory with the owner's consent. They briefly questioned workers at their work stations and, if reasonable, asked to see immigration papers. Agents were posted at the factory exits. The Supreme Court held that the illegal workers were *not seized* within the meaning of the Fourth Amendment, reasoning that "police questioning, by itself, is unlikely to result in a Fourth Amendment violation." The factory workers were not free to leave, but the "detention" was caused not by the police but by the workers' normal employment requirements. The Court held that the agents were simply questioning people and that these encounters were consensual. Justices Brennan and Marshall dissented, arguing instead that the *show of authority* by the immigration officials was sufficiently substantial to "overbear the will of any reasonable person." Based on this show of authority, reasoned the dissenters, the factory workers were forcibly stopped within the meaning of *Terry*.

The use of drug courier profiles at airports (discussed below) spawned similar practices at bus and train stations. In ***Florida v. Bostick*** (1991), decided shortly after *Hodari D.*, the Supreme Court confirmed its sharp swing toward supporting the police in investigatory stops.

> Two [Broward County Sheriff's] officers, complete with badges, insignia and one of them holding a recognizable zipper pouch, containing a pistol, boarded a bus bound from Miami to Atlanta during a stopover in Fort Lauderdale. Eyeing the passengers, the officers admittedly without articulable suspicion, picked out the defendant passenger and asked to inspect his ticket and identification. The ticket, from Miami to Atlanta, matched the defendant's identification and both were immediately returned to him as unremarkable. However, the two police officers persisted and explained their presence as narcotics agents on the lookout for illegal drugs. In pursuit of that aim, they then requested the defendant's consent to search his luggage. (*Florida v. Bostick*, pp. 431–32)

Cocaine was found in the bag. Before they began this encounter, the officers had no reasonable suspicion or probable cause to believe that Terrance Bostick was carrying drugs.

The issue was whether Bostick consented to the search or whether he was seized. Justice O'Connor's majority opinion held that Bostick *consented*: "Our cases make it clear that a seizure does not occur simply because a police officer approaches an individual and asks a few questions. So long as a reasonable person would feel free to disregard the police and go about his business, . . . the encounter is consensual and no reasonable suspicion is required" (*Florida v. Bostick*, internal quotation marks eliminated). It is curious that the Court cited *Hodari D.* for this proposition rather than relying exclusively on *Mendenhall*. The Court's

majority in these cases appears to have selected a different theory in each case to ensure the decision would favor law enforcement: under *Hodari D.*, one who flees is not seized; under *Mendenhall-Bostick* one who relents, consents. This seems to create a "heads I win, tails you lose" rule, with the police holding the coin.

Justice Marshall dissented, joined by Justices Blackmun and Stevens. He harshly castigated this form of investigation: "These sweeps are conducted in 'dragnet' style," noting that this high-volume practice (sweeps of three thousand buses in a nine-month period) inconveniences a large number of innocent persons (one case found that sweeps of one hundred buses resulted in seven arrests). The heart of the dissent was that the police questioning is inherently coercive, undermining consent:

> To put it mildly, these sweeps "are inconvenient, intrusive, and intimidating." They occur within cramped confines, with officers typically placing themselves in between the passenger selected for an interview and the exit of the bus. Because the bus is only temporarily stationed at a point short of its destination, the passengers are in no position to leave as a means of evading the officers' questioning. (*Florida v. Bostick*, Marshall, J. dissenting)

The majority pointed out, to the contrary, that:

> The present case is analytically indistinguishable from *Delgado*. Like the workers in that case, Bostick's freedom of movement was restricted by a factor independent of police conduct—i.e., by his being a passenger on a bus. Accordingly, the "free to leave" analysis on which Bostick relies is inapplicable. In such a situation, the appropriate inquiry is whether a reasonable person would feel free to decline the officers' requests or otherwise terminate the encounter. (*Florida v. Bostick*, p. 436)

Indeed, Bostick was told he had a right to refuse, the pouched gun was never removed nor did the officers ever point it at Bostick or use it in a threatening manner, and Bostick agreed to open his bag. These factors, according to the majority, negated coercion and supported the conclusion that Bostick volunteered to open his bag.

The Supreme Court held in ***United States v. Drayton*** (2002), a bus-sweep case with facts very similar to *Bostick*, that the police need not inform a bus rider that he has a right to refuse to consent to a search of his baggage, relying on *Ohio v. Robinette* and *Schneckloth v. Bustamonte*. Justice Souter dissented, joined by Justices Stevens and Ginsburg. He argued that if three officers approached a person on the street, hemmed him in very closely and asked if they could search any luggage, this would be intimidation that undermines consent. The same is the case in the close quarters of a bus with an aisle fifteen inches wide, cramped seats, the police in apparent control of the bus, and officers saying that they were "conducting a bus interdiction" and "wanted cooperation."

Most scholarly commentators agree with the dissent in *Bostick* and refer to the decisions in this case and *Hodari D.* as the "no seizure" rule. Professor Gerald Ashdown, for example, writes: "Hardly anyone who is confronted and questioned by armed officers, asked for identification and permission to search, believes he is free to do much of anything, certainly not to refuse to answer or to walk away. Anyone with a lick of sense knows that doing these things will only aggravate the situation and cause him more trouble."[36]

AUTOMOBILE CHECKLANES   In *Delaware v. Prouse* (1979), discussed above, the Court held that a car cannot be stopped while proceeding in traffic unless an officer has specific suspicion to believe that it was engaged in a traffic violation or criminal act. *Prouse* distinguished on-the-road stops from stops at roadblocks or fixed checkpoints, contending that motorists do not feel the same anxiety because they observe other motorists going through the same drill. The Supreme Court specifically upheld sobriety checklanes in **Michigan Dept. of State Police v. Sitz** (1990). These stops are not Fourth Amendment seizures.

In deciding that **sobriety checklanes** are not a violation of a person's reasonable expectation of privacy, the Court relied on border search–fixed checkpoint cases: *United States v. Ortiz* (1975) and *United States v. Martinez-Fuerte* (1976). Those cases compared the subjective and psychological level of intrusion of fixed checkpoints on the highway as compared to stops made by roving patrols. Since at the fixed checkpoint the motorist sees other vehicles being briefly detained and sees the visible indicia of the police officers' authority, "he is much less likely to be frightened or annoyed by the intrusion" (*Ortiz*, quoted in *Martinez-Fuerte*). These findings were applied to the Michigan sobriety checklane situation: "Here, checkpoints are selected pursuant to the guidelines, and uniformed police officers stop every approaching vehicle. The intrusion resulting from the brief stop at the sobriety checkpoint is for constitutional purposes indistinguishable from the checkpoint stops we upheld in *Martinez-Fuerte*" (*Michigan Dept. of State Police v. Sitz*). Chief Justice Rehnquist's majority opinion also pointed out that drunk driving is a serious national problem resulting in approximately twenty-five thousand deaths annually. This idea of the checklane as a regulatory device played some role in the decision.

In *Sitz* the Court also considered whether the *effectiveness* of checklanes in combating drunk driving was a factor of Fourth Amendment balancing. Sitz argued that other methods were more effective. The Court ruled that the choice of enforcement modalities was up to the legislature and the executive branches—politically accountable officials—rather than courts to determine which law enforcement techniques to employ to deal with a serious public danger among reasonable alternatives.

Justice Stevens, dissenting, disagreed with the Court's finding that sobriety checklanes are essentially the same as border checklanes. Sobriety checklanes, for example, occur at night, are not at fixed checkpoints but are set up quickly to effect the element of surprise, and are less standardized than a review of registration papers, for the officer must visually assess the sobriety of the driver.

An important ruling, **City of Indianapolis v. Edmond** (2000) limited the *Sitz* ruling to sobriety checklanes. The Court decided (6–3) that a roadblock whose *primary purpose* was general law enforcement and the detection of ordinary criminal wrongdoing, and not traffic safety, violated the Fourth Amendment. Indianapolis police set up roadblocks identified as *narcotics checkpoints*, detained drivers for about two to three minutes, examined drivers' licenses and registrations, and had a narcotics-detection dog walk around each vehicle. In finding this practice unconstitutional, the Court distinguished the reasoning of pretext stops (*Whren*), of brief checkpoint stops for purposes of detecting alcohol-impaired drivers or illegal aliens (*Sitz*; *Martinez-Fuerte*), and special needs (*Von Raab*). The City argued that all other checkpoint stops upheld by the Court employed arrests and criminal prosecutions in pursuit of other goals that were essentially not the enforcement of the criminal law. In a statement that captured the deep policy concerns of the Court, Justice O'Connor, in her majority opinion, replied:

IN THE STATES: *SITZ* ON REMAND

When the *Sitz* case was returned to the Michigan courts for retrial, they held that sobriety checklanes violated the Michigan Constitution and that state's supreme court agreed: "Because there is no support in the constitutional history of Michigan for the proposition that the police may engage in warrantless and suspicionless seizures of automobiles for the purpose of enforcing the criminal law, we hold that sobriety checklanes violate art 1, §11 of the Michigan Constitution." The opinion recalled that Michigan had been one of the first states to adopt the exclusionary rule. It noted that the Michigan search and seizure provision should be read as similar to federal law unless there is a compelling reason to deviate, but the compelling reason standard is not "a conclusive presumption artificially linking state constitutional interpretation to federal law." Turning to the specific issue, the court concluded, quite contrary to the reasoning of the United States Supreme Court, that it retained the right to determine what constituted reasonable searches under state law:

> This Court has never recognized the right of the state, without any level of suspicion whatsoever, to detain members of the population at large for criminal investigatory purposes. Nor has Michigan completely acquiesced to the judgment of "politically accountable officials" when determining reasonableness in such a context. In these circumstances, the Michigan Constitution offers more protection than the United States Supreme Court's interpretation of the Fourth Amendment.

Sitz v. Michigan Dept. of State Police, 443 Mich. 744, 506 N.W.2d 209 (1993).

If we were to rest the case at this high level of generality, there would be little check on the ability of the authorities to construct roadblocks for almost any conceivable law enforcement purpose. Without drawing the line at roadblocks designed primarily to serve the general interest in crime control, the Fourth Amendment would do little to prevent such intrusions from becoming a routine part of American life. (*City of Indianapolis v. Edmond*, 2000)

After a raft of cases that expanded the ability of police to stop virtually any car, control the passengers, and examine all containers, the Court was faced with a line, which if crossed, might have made the total surveillance of anyone walking abroad subject to inspection. The Court was informed, in a brief by the National League of Cities, that many cities were prepared to initiate narcotics checkpoints depending on the outcome of *Edmond*. What was left unsaid was that a ruling favorable to the government in *Edmond* could have opened the door to virtually unrestricted on-the-street surveillance with drug-sniffing dogs and with highly intrusive electronic and thermal-sensing devices that penetrated the clothing of individuals. It is noteworthy that the three most conservative justices—Rehnquist, Scalia, and Thomas—dissented, but that swing justices—O'Connor and Kennedy—voted to declare such practices unconstitutional.

Edmond was held not to prevent *informational roadblocks*. In *Illinois v. Lidster* (2004) police in Lombard, Illinois, partially blocked a highway to force cars into a single lane. At the checkpoint an officer asked the occupants whether they had seen anything happen there the previous weekend. Each driver was handed a flyer that said "ALERT . . . FATAL HIT & RUN ACCIDENT." It requested "assistance in identifying the vehicle and driver in this accident which killed a 70-year-old bicyclist." Each stop lasted about ten to fifteen seconds. As Lidster approached the roadblock he swerved, nearly hit an officer, and was arrested and convicted for driving under the influence of alcohol. He challenged the constitutionality of the roadblock stop. The Supreme Court held that a roadblock of this type is constitutional as long as it is reasonably tailored to the particular circumstances of the case and to a legitimate law enforcement function. The stop in this case was constitutional for a variety of reasons. The primary purpose of the stop was not to investigate the occupants for criminal activity, but to obtain information about an unsolved fatal hit-and-run accident that had occurred in the same area a few days before. Such stops are brief and not likely to produce anxiety. Police are not likely to ask incriminating questions, any more than would police questioning pedestrians in the vicinity of a crime as to whether they had seen anything suspicious. Voluntary requests for information "play a vital role in police investigatory work." The traffic delays that result "should prove no more onerous than many that typically accompany normal traffic congestion." The crime being investigated was serious, and the informational checkpoint in this case was narrowly tailored to getting specific information about it. The law enforcement needs and the reasonableness of the intrusion outweighed the minimal interference with liberty in this case.

Terry at the Airport: Drug Stops and Drug Courier Profiles

The typical scenario of the cases in this section (previously described in *United States v. Mendenhall* (1980), see Chapter 3), is for narcotics agents to ask to speak with a person at an airport. The officers regularly scan airports and other transportation hubs for people who may be transporting illegal drugs. These cases differ from those in which agents have been tipped off by informants that a specific courier is arriving at an airport. Instead, the officers approach a person on a *hunch* that he or she looks like the sort of person who carries drugs (often young people of college age) or based on a person fitting a "profile" of variables that seem to be characteristic of people who carry drugs. The cases in this section ask whether the facts amount to a voluntary consent encounter, a *Terry* stop and search, or an arrest. They also describe the path of the Court's cases that eventually accepted the "drug courier profile" as a constitutional basis for an investigative stop.

The drug courier profile was developed in the early 1970s by DEA agent Paul Markonni, working out of the Detroit Metropolitan Airport. He borrowed the idea from an airplane hijacker profile developed in the late 1960s. The use of the drug courier profile spread to airports throughout the nation.[37] "Because even local police officers now receive high quality training by the DEA, street level drug interdiction programs have resulted in surprisingly few complaints of individual police officer misconduct, such as unjustified, armed threats or arbitrary harassment."[38] Stephen Hall briefly describes how they are used:

> One or more DEA agents (or other law enforcement officers) observe individuals at an airport for characteristics that match the profile. Agents single out an individual as a match, approach the suspect, and identify themselves as law enforcement officers. They then ask the suspect's name and destination. If the agents are still suspicious, they usually ask the suspect to accompany them to another location for further questioning. At this point, agents ask the suspect to consent to a search of his person, luggage or both.[39]

In *Mendenhall* (1980) the young woman who deplaned was politely approached by DEA agents and asked to accompany them to a room (see Chapter 3, section on consent). After some discussion, she agreed to be searched by a female officer in private and drugs were found on her person. *Mendenhall* can be read for three purposes. First, given the varied opinions of the justices in this case it demonstrates the difficulty of sorting out the facts to determine whether they amounted to a consent encounter or a personal seizure. Second, it shows a concern with drug courier profiles. Third, it established the test for a seizure: *a person reasonably believing that she was not free to leave in view of all of the circumstances surrounding the incident*. Although the *Mendenhall* test was modified to fit the contours of the chase in *Hodari D.*, it was, and still is, the standard that is applied in airport scenarios.

The stop of Ms. Mendenhall at the Detroit Metropolitan Airport was triggered by her supposedly fitting the characteristics of such a drug courier profile. Justice Powell spoke favorably of this device. He referred to "highly skilled agents" carrying out a "highly specialized law enforcement operation" being assigned to the Detroit airport "as part of a nationwide program to intercept drug couriers transporting narcotics between major drug sources and distribution centers in the United States." He noted, "During the first 18 months of the program, agents watching the Detroit Airport searched 141 persons in 96 encounters. They found controlled substances in 77 of the encounters and arrested 122 persons" (*United States v. Mendenhall* (1980), p. 562, Powell, J., concurring). Despite this endorsement, neither the lead opinion nor the concurrence in *Mendenhall* was based on a blank acceptance of the profile. The tone of Justice White's dissent was less enthusiastic: "[T]he Government sought to justify the stop by arguing that Ms. Mendenhall's behavior had given rise to reasonable suspicion because it was consistent with portions of the so-called 'drug courier profile,' an informal amalgam of characteristics thought to be associated with persons carrying illegal drugs" (*United States v. Mendenhall* (1980), pp. 567–68, White, J., dissenting). Although the majority in *Mendenhall* held that the encounter did not violate the Fourth Amendment, it did so on the basis of consent. *Mendenhall* did not constitutionalize the drug courier profile.

The Supreme Court expressed skepticism of profiles and found no basis of reasonable suspicion in **Reid v. Georgia** (1980, *per curiam*). The mere fact that a man got off a plane in Atlanta from Fort Lauderdale, Florida (a "principal place of origin of cocaine sold elsewhere in the country"), and, exiting in a single-file line, occasionally looked back in the direction of another man carrying a similar shoulder bag, who caught up with Reid and exchanged a few words with him—is hardly the kind of fact that creates a drug courier profile or establishes reasonable suspicion to support an investigative stop.

In **Florida v. Royer** (1983) the Supreme Court held that a seizure at the airport violated Mark Royer's Fourth Amendment rights, but the justices could not agree on a reason. Royer was approached by two county narcotics officers at the Miami International Airport because he purportedly fit a drug courier profile: He had purchased a one-way ticket to New York City, was carrying two American Tourister suitcases that appeared to be heavy, was casually dressed, appeared pale and nervous, paid for his ticket in cash with a large number of bills, and wrote only a name on the airline identification tag. The officers identified themselves and asked Royer if he had a "moment" to speak with them. He said yes. Without oral consent, he produced his ticket and a driver's license upon request. He explained a discrepancy between his name and the name "Holt" written on the baggage tag by saying that a friend named Holt had made the reservations. The officers did not return the ticket or license but asked Royer to accompany them to a room forty feet away. In the small office, Royer was told that he was suspected of transporting narcotics and was asked if he would consent to a search of the suitcases. Without orally responding, Royer

produced a key, opened the baggage, and marijuana was found. These events took about fifteen minutes.

The Court's five-justice majority found that by holding on to Royer's ticket and driver's license, the officers had, in effect, *arrested* him without probable cause. When police officers retain these important documents, a reasonable person could not believe that he is free to leave. Thus, when Royer went along with the police to the room, he did not consent but had to follow or give up his ticket and license! Holding these documents was the equivalent of a show of force.

Four of the majority justices (White, Powell, Marshall, and Stevens) also believed, however, that facts in *Royer* established reasonable suspicion that would have supported a temporary stop and questioning of Royer to confirm or dispel the suspicion. Because a majority did not share this view, the *Royer* case did not establish the constitutionality of drug courier profiles. It did indicate that a number of justices were leaning in that direction. Nevertheless, the majority felt that the police action of obtaining the key to Royer's luggage went beyond that justified by a *Terry* stop. This was not a frisk for weapons but a search for evidence. Justice Brennan, concurring, thought the majority was wrong to comment on its belief that reasonable suspicion existed. Four dissenting justices (Burger, Blackmun, Rehnquist, and O'Connor) believed that the acts of the police officers were reasonable and would have upheld the encounter as based on consent.

The next airport search case, **United States v. Place** (1983), held the stop unconstitutional because the *brevity requirement* of *Terry* was violated. Raymond Place aroused the suspicions of DEA agents at the Miami International Airport. They briefly detained him for questioning. He agreed to a search of his luggage, but because his airplane was departing, the search was postponed. The agents called ahead to LaGuardia Airport in New York City, where another team of DEA agents observed Place when he arrived. Their suspicions also aroused, they detained him and told Place that they believed he was carrying narcotics. Place did *not consent* to a search of his luggage. The agents seized the bags, giving Place information as to where they could be retrieved. The bags were then sent to Kennedy Airport, unopened, where a trained narcotics-detection dog indicated the presence of drugs. This process took ninety minutes. After the positive identification, as it was Friday afternoon, the bags were held until Monday, when a search warrant was obtained and drugs were found in the bags.

Because Place was detained, not on probable cause but at best on reasonable suspicion, the extent of the detention must be "minimally intrusive of the individual's Fourth Amendment interests." By holding a person's luggage, the person is *detained* by the police although the person is technically free to go. "[S]uch a seizure can effectively restrain the person since he is subjected to the possible disruption of his travel plans in order to remain with his luggage or to arrange for its return." Thus, the seizure of luggage at the airport effectively "seizes" a person. Indeed, the *Terry* brevity principle was violated simply by the length of the detention of Place's luggage. Justice O'Connor noted:

Although the 90-minute detention of respondent's luggage is sufficient to render the seizure unreasonable, the violation was exacerbated by the failure of the agents to accurately inform respondent of the place to which they were transporting his luggage, of the length of time he might be dispossessed, and of what arrangements would be made for return of the luggage if the investigation dispelled the suspicion. In short, we hold that the detention of respondent's luggage in this case went beyond the narrow authority possessed by police to detain briefly luggage reasonably suspected to contain narcotics.

The Court commented favorably on the *canine sniff* as an important investigative technique. As a general matter, it appears that when police have reasonable suspicion of drug possession they can *briefly* detain luggage to ascertain whether drugs are present by use of a trained dog.

A "canine sniff" by a well-trained narcotics detection dog, . . . does not require opening the luggage. It does not expose noncontraband items that otherwise would remain hidden from public view, as does, for example, an officer's rummaging through the contents of the luggage. Thus, the manner in which information is obtained through this investigative technique is much less intrusive than a typical search. Moreover, the sniff discloses only the presence or absence of narcotics, a contraband item. Thus, despite the fact that the sniff tells the authorities something about the contents of the luggage, the information obtained is limited. This limited disclosure also ensures that the owner of the property is not subjected to the embarrassment and inconvenience entailed in less discriminate and more intrusive investigative methods. In these respects, the canine sniff is **sui generis.** We are aware of no other investigative procedure that is so limited both in the manner in which the information is obtained and in the content of the information revealed by the procedure. Therefore, we conclude that the particular course of investigation that the agents intended to pursue here—exposure of respondent's luggage, which was located in a public place, to a trained canine—did not constitute a "search" within the meaning of the Fourth Amendment.

This does not resolve all constitutional questions about the use of trained dogs in drug detection, but it indicates that the Court views the technique with favor.

The constitutionality of drug courier profiles was finally upheld in **United States v. Sokolow** (1989). Andrew Sokolow was forcibly stopped by DEA agents at the Honolulu airport because he fit the following profile elements: he paid $2,100 for two airplane tickets from a roll of $20 bills; he traveled under a name that did not match the name under which his telephone number was listed; his original destination was Miami, a **source city** for illicit drugs; he stayed in Miami for only forty-eight hours even though a round-trip flight from Honolulu to Miami takes twenty hours; he appeared nervous during his trip; and he checked none of his luggage. He wore the same black jumpsuit with gold jewelry on both his outgoing and returning trips. At this point Sokolow and a travelling companion were forcibly stopped. They were taken to a DEA office at the airport where a canine sniff indicated the presence of drugs. Sokolow was arrested, warrants were obtained to search his luggage, and more than a thousand grams of cocaine were found.

The Supreme Court held that a suspect fitting a drug courier profile raises the mere suspicion of the agent to the level of reasonable suspicion that allows a *Terry* stop. The majority held that the profile elements in this case amounted to reasonable suspicion. Although each of the facts separately are not indicative of criminality, *taken together* they were out of the ordinary and amounted to reasonable suspicion. Justice Rehnquist wrote, "While a trip from Honolulu to Miami, standing alone, is not a cause for any sort of suspicion, here there was more: surely few residents of Honolulu travel from that city for 20 hours to spend 48 hours in Miami during the month of July." Second, the Court ruled explicitly that reasonable suspicion may be established even though each articulable element of suspicion is innocent. It is not necessary that there also be evidence of ongoing criminal activity to establish reasonable suspicion, as the lower court had held. Finally, the majority also ruled that it was not necessary for the officers to use the "**least intrusive means** available to verify or dispel their suspicions that he was smuggling narcotics," for example, by approaching the suspect and speaking with him, rather than forcibly detaining him. The "least intrusive" rule "would unduly hamper the police's ability to make swift on-the-spot decisions—here, respondent was about to get into a taxicab—and it would require courts to indulge in unrealistic second-guessing" (*Sokolow*, internal quotation marks eliminated).

Justice Marshall offered a spirited attack on the drug courier profile in *Sokolow* but failed to convince a majority that profiles are flawed. He noted that many cases applying *Terry* required evidence of *ongoing criminality*—such as taking evasive action, "casing" a store, using an alibi, or the word of an informant—to trigger the reasonable suspicion standard. No such indicator of criminality existed in this case. Next, he warned that the mechanistic application of a profile would "dull the officer's ability and determination to make sensitive and fact-specific inferences 'in light of his experience.'" Most telling, he observed that what constituted profile factors seemed to shift from case to case. Citing specific cases, previously decided by lower courts, he pointed out that the profile has been held to be established by the fact that the suspect:

• Was the first to deplane, *or* the last to deplane, *or* got off in the middle.
• Purchased a one-way ticket *or* a round-trip ticket.
• Took a nonstop flight *or* changed planes.
• Had one shoulder bag *or* had a new suitcase.
• Was traveling alone *or* was traveling with a companion.
• Acted too nervously *or* acted too calmly.

Justice Marshall thus demonstrated that the cases undermined the majority's belief that drug courier profiles are stable and reliable. Indeed, elements of the profile shift from case to case to uphold convictions.

There is little research on the effectiveness of these profiles, but a sampling of records by a reporter at the New York

Miami, and Houston airports indicates "a success rate of about fifty–fifty." A DEA spokesperson conceded that innocent persons are stopped as often as guilty ones, adding, "It's not a science, . . . [i]t's a technique." The story noted that those stopped under a profile are often handcuffed and held for several hours, including being taken to a hospital for X-rays, before being released. The story also suggested that African Americans and Hispanics are stopped more frequently, although the DEA does not keep records of airport stops that can confirm these observations. Finally, it was also noted that drug courier profiles are used on highways, in train stations, and on interstate buses, although less frequently than in airports.[40]

Most scholarly commentators are skeptical or critical of these profiles. A primary reason is given by Justice Marshall: "no uniform drug courier profile exists throughout the nation. Instead, agents create their own individual profiles based on their own professional experiences and observations."[41] A trial court noted that the profile consists of "anything that arouses the agent's suspicion."[42] Professors Janikowski and Giacopassi point out that unlike the FAA "skyjacker profile," which was formulated and tested by psychologists and was tested on 500,000 passengers yielding 1,406 stops and sixteen arrests, "there is some concern as to whether a profile truly exists or whether the profile is, in reality, a loose and malleable compilation of characteristics based on experiential knowledge of the drug trade and the exigencies of the situation."[43] A highly detailed analysis of the use of the profiles by Prof. Morgan Cloud, predating *Sokolow,* confirms Justice Marshall's analysis that the profiles are not predictive. By relying on the profiles, the courts are abdicating their constitutional responsibilities.[44]

LAW IN SOCIETY

ARREST AND DOMESTIC VIOLENCE

A significant policy debate concerns the rules for arresting wife batterers. Domestic violence is a serious problem: "[S]urveys in 1995 and 1996 estimated that anywhere between one million and four million women a year experience violence at the hands of their partners."[45] About half of all women who are murdered "were killed by either a husband, ex-husband, common law husband, or boyfriend."[46] Studies that sort out instances of female self-defensive violence estimate that women are the perpetrators of domestic violence in only 4 to 10 percent of all cases.[47] Aside from individual physical and psychological injury, a lax criminal justice system strengthens cultural norms that tolerate these assaults, which in turn perpetuates the social and political subjugation of women.[48] The criminal justice response to domestic violence is therefore a weather vane of gender equality, and arrest policies are a critical component of the criminal justice response. The key issues are:

- What role is played by police discretion in responding to domestic violence?
- How did the misdemeanor arrest rule contribute to lax domestic violence enforcement?

- Does arrest deter domestic violence?
- Is the proper police response to domestic violence mandatory or discretionary arrest?
- What are the strengths and limits of arrest as a response to domestic violence?

CHANGING NORMS AND LAWS ABOUT DOMESTIC VIOLENCE

From the early 1970s to the mid-1980s, forty-nine states and the District of Columbia had enacted legislation to provide legal remedies to the victims of domestic violence. These included judicial protection orders, shelters for battered women, and diversion programs for offenders subjected to prosecution.[49] The police community shifted from a policy of separating couples and nonarrest in domestic fights in the late 1960s, to a law enforcement approach by the mid-1970s.[50,51] In 1984, the United States Attorney General's *Task Force on Family Violence* said, "Family violence should be recognized and responded to as a criminal activity."[52] Women's and the victims' rights groups "were particularly vocal in their support of a more punitive approach. . . ."[53] These changes were caused primarily by "the rise of the new feminist movement, gathering force from about 1970 and affecting virtually every aspect of American life and thought, including the law. . . . [T]he ideological basis of the new feminism, in general, has been gender equality in most spheres of life. As a legal and political phenomenon, feminism has without doubt 'empowered' women. As an empowered group, women forced society at large to shake off the selective social vision that formerly took little notice of the physical abuse of spouses."[54]

The early models for dealing with domestic violence, such as protection orders, were not fully effective but did "increase police responsiveness to the requests of battered women for assistance."[55,56] In the 1970s the first mandatory arrest laws were resisted by police officers who were reluctant to arrest spouse beaters.[57] In order to push police into enforcing these laws, several successful civil lawsuits were won against police departments. *Nearing v. Weaver* (1983) held that by failing to enforce the Oregon mandatory arrest statute, police violated the specific legal duty they owed to Nearing to arrest her estranged husband after repeated incidents of threats, harassment, and beatings, and numerous calls by Nearing to the police to enforce a restraining order.[58,59] Another early case, *Thurman v. City of Torrington,* was the first case in which a federal court held that police handling of domestic violence cases differently from other assaults is gender-based discrimination and violates the Fourteenth Amendment Equal Protection Clause.[60,61]

IMPEDIMENT TO CHANGE: POLICE DISCRETION AND DOMESTIC VIOLENCE

Legal rules define probable cause, the use of force, the scope of a search incident to arrest, and when a warrant is required for an arrest. Yet, no common law or constitutional doctrine guides the vital question of discretion: When is it proper for a law enforcement officer to arrest or not arrest a suspect? Total enforcement of criminal law is impossible.[62] Police discretion in making arrest decisions is inevitable for several reasons: some laws (e.g., disorderly conduct) are vague or open-ended; police departments are understaffed; and enforcing every minor offense to the maximum extent may be excessively rigid and unfair.[63] Police discretion typically is exercised by the lowest-ranking officers, with minimal guidance from supervisors—a "low visibility" practice that often undermines the equal application of the law. Ideally, police use discretion to arrest all serious offenders and to mitigate the harshness of the crime according to "common sense," but it does not always work so nicely.[64] Discretion can also breed unfairness if it is shaped by inappropriate "common sense" values.[65] Thus, a response to a domestic call—whether arrest, avoidance, lecturing, clinical-type counseling, or judgmental intervention—was not a matter of deliberate policy, but depended on the individual police officer's beliefs about the rightness of wife beating.[66] In this, the police reflected the larger society that traditionally condoned wife beating to such an extent that it was not considered a criminal act by many.[67] Yet the crimes committed by a wife beater "include assault and/or battery, aggravated assault, intent to assault or to commit murder, and, in cases where the woman is coerced sexually, rape."[68] The combination of traditional views and police discretion has thus discouraged the arrest of batterers. Even mandatory arrest laws may not result in more arrests—a point borne out in a study by Professor Kathleen Ferraro, observing arrest patterns by Phoenix police officers in domestic cases under a mandatory arrest law. She found that police discretion shaped how officers assessed the existence of probable cause, leading to questionable no-probable-cause decisions. Police discretion remains and is influenced by legal, ideological, practical, and political factors, even when a department adopts a mandatory arrest policy.[69] As a result, for there to be any change in police behavior, there must be changes in fundamental social thinking on the part of police officers, and more attention to control of discretion by high-ranking supervisors.

IMPEDIMENT TO CHANGE: WARRANTLESS MISDEMEANOR ARRESTS

The common law rule is that an officer cannot make a misdemeanor arrest unless it occurs in his presence. This rule prevented officers from making domestic violence arrests in "the largest category of calls received by police each year."[70] Two-thirds of domestic violence cases are classified as misdemeanors. A battering victim would have had to file a complaint and get a judicial warrant to have the beater arrested, a situation that virtually never occurred.[71] When this problem became apparent in the wave of feminist criticism in the 1970s, the states quickly responded and dropped the in-presence requirement for misdemeanor arrests in domestic violence cases. "Statutes in 47 states and the District of Columbia now authorize or mandate warrantless, probable cause arrest for crimes involving domestic violence. This is a significant departure from the common law."[72] Officers could now arrest if probable cause

exists to believe (1) that the suspect has committed a misdemeanor involving domestic violence, or (2) that the suspect has committed a misdemeanor and there is reason to believe that the suspect presents a continuing danger if not immediately arrested.[73] This legal change is especially important because 42 percent of the victims of "simple assaults" suffered physical injury, compared to 36 percent of women who reported felony crimes in domestic violence. This may be because the display of a weapon without any physical injury raises the crime to a felony.[74]

THE MINNEAPOLIS EXPERIMENT AND THE REPLICATION EXPERIMENTS

In 1984 a report of a Minneapolis police experiment conducted by Professors Lawrence Sherman and Richard Berk showed that arresting a batterer produced lower levels of official reports of domestic violence than giving the parties on-the-spot mediation or simply separating the couple. The report, suggesting that arrest alone deterred spousal abuse, caused a sensation. Among criminologists it raised questions because it went against substantial research evidence that specific programs generally do not measurably deter crime.[75] The report had a tremendous impact on police policies for two reasons. First, one of the authors publicized the research in the news media otherwise broadcasting the findings to the general public and police chiefs.[76] Second, these publications fit the temper of the time; they likely accelerated a trend toward the arrest of batterers that was already under way.[77]

Because of the controversial nature of the findings, and the importance of the policy issue, the National Institute of Justice funded several replications of the Minneapolis experiment in the late 1980s in Charlotte, Colorado Springs, Miami, Milwaukee, and Omaha. The results of these experiments unleashed a new barrage of controversy. The most important result is that there was no simple deterrent effect of arrest on domestic violence recidivism. Sherman summarized the paradoxical and contradictory findings in four "policy dilemmas":

1. Arrest reduces domestic violence in some cities but increases it in others.
2. Arrest reduces domestic violence among employed people but increases it among unemployed people.
3. Arrest reduces domestic violence in the short run but can increase it in the long run.
4. Police can predict which couples are most likely to suffer future violence, but our society values privacy too highly to encourage preventive action.[78]

It would be incoherent and unconstitutional to fine tune an arrest policy that mandates arrests of employed batterers but not those without a job! What Professor Sherman proposed was to repeal mandatory arrest laws but allow warrantless misdemeanor arrests, and encourage police departments to develop local policies. He also recommended the creation of special units and policies to focus on chronically violent couples.[79]

A RESPONSE TO THE REPLICATION STUDIES

Joan Zorza, in an article critical of the replication studies, supports mandatory arrest of batterers while pointing out the limitations of relying on arrest alone to deal with a deep-seated behavioral problem. She notes that the arrest studies were conducted in isolation of what arrest could accomplish as part of a coordinated response.[80] The National Council of Juvenile and Family Court Judges, for example, has proposed a detailed and coordinated effort to deal with domestic violence.[81] Zorza also suggests that batterers should not be released sooner than others charged with assault and that police should arrest when they have probable cause (or obtain arrest warrants for absent abusers). If findings show that unemployed batterers are least deterred by arrest, then court programs should seek employment for them, but not at the expense of services and employment opportunities for victims of violent crime. Zorza concludes by saying that the "real implication of the police replication studies are that a coordinated community response is what is needed to best eliminate domestic violence."[82] But even with coordinated policies, the policy debate over mandatory arrest laws continues.

MANDATORY ARREST LAWS AND POLICIES

AGAINST MANDATORY ARREST   First, the deterrent effect of a mandatory arrest policy is far from proven; any effect seems to be temporary. Mandatory arrest ignores the wide range of behavior that falls within the definition of domestic violence and may amount to overkill. If the arrested partner is acquitted, the abused spouse will feel let down and the incident might spark further violence. Even the goal of immediate protection may be short-lived, as an arrested partner is likely to be released shortly on bond or recognizance. Again, this may place the victim in a worse situation. Mandatory arrest increases the probability of abuse of the process by police officers or by a vindictive spouse. Some advocates for battered women oppose mandatory arrest on the belief that it "further erodes victims' self-esteem and contributes to their sense of helplessness by usurping their control." Others are concerned that women will lose economic support.[83]

There is no guarantee that an arrest would lead to a close prosecutor-victim interaction that will increase the determination and awareness of the victim. Finally, a mandatory arrest policy assumes that relationships are always power relationships, where the woman is essentially powerless and requires strong external intervention.[84] Instead, Carol Wright proposes a wide range of options, including discretionary arrest, victim assistance techniques, mediation programs, shelters and other social programs, a comprehensive legislative framework, and publicity to give domestic abuse victims a better awareness of all their options.[85]

FOR MANDATORY ARREST[86]   Rates of arrest in domestic violence are so low, often because police fail to find probable cause and thus discourage victims from pressing charges, that mandatory arrest laws are needed to counteract police bias and send a message that arrest is the appropriate response to bat-

tering. Further, mandatory arrest laws do not strip police officers of all discretion. Mandatory arrest relieves police officers of the inappropriate role of family counselors. It also removes the decision to arrest from the victim's control, where the victim's fear and a power imbalance in the relationship are likely to cause the victim to not opt for arrest. Thus, mandatory arrest laws may empower victims by giving them the courage to call the police in the first place. Studies that show increased violence after arrest may be flawed.

Marion Wanless notes that as of 1996, sixteen states and the District of Columbia have adopted mandatory arrest laws. States with such laws have seen a sharp increase in arrests for domestic violence. This shows that "In states with the laws, police take domestic violence seriously."[87] In a close examination of these laws, she notes that not all mandatory arrest laws are the same. By their terms, they pose three levels of arrest threshold: low, moderate, and high. In high-threshold states, mandatory arrest is required only when a condition such as injury occurs, unless the officer believes that the victim will be protected from further injury. This undermines the mandatory arrest rule. Wanless recommends laws with moderate thresholds: Arrest is mandatory where injury has occurred, there is a risk for continued danger, or a dangerous weapon was used.[88]

Still, even this strong proponent of mandatory arrest laws concludes that "Mandatory arrest, without more, may also be insufficient to protect victims."[89] Even in a system with vigorous prosecution of batterers and a full array of sentencing and social intervention options, the police play a critical role as gatekeepers, shunting domestic violence cases to the criminal justice system or the social service system, or leaving them as private matters.

CONCLUSION

This section has explored the powerful tradition of arrest discretion and discussed how in an area of particular concern to the public, domestic violence, it has come under legal attack. Because old habits die hard, we see there are several legal avenues that women have used to remind the criminal justice system that its obligations to protect the personal safety of people do not end at the doorstep of the home. Arrest of batterers has been subject to social science inquiry, yielding complex results. Policy must be developed without final evidence of what arrest can achieve. In any event, using arrest without prosecution as a method of social control raises due process questions. Thus, a policy of mandatory, or at least preferred, arrest, followed by vigorous prosecution and well-thought-out court and probation programs seems to be the best approach to dealing with the distressing issue of domestic abuse.

SUMMARY

In the aftermath of the 9/11 attacks, federal agents rounded up twelve hundred persons, mostly aliens. The government has not released all the information about this initial wave of detainees, but it appears that almost none were in any way involved in terrorism. This overreaction in the aftermath of the horrific attacks of 9/11 is understandable, but is evidence of unpreparedness and unprofessionalism. It reflects the awesome power that federal and local law enforcement agencies can amass when called for and adds a caution for the need for legal restraints.

The personal detention of a person by a police officer may be legal or illegal. Legal detentions or seizures under the Fourth Amendment fall into two categories: arrests supported by probable cause or investigative stops supported by reasonable suspicion. In addition, a person may consent to engage in an encounter with a law enforcement agent, for which the officer requires no level of evidence. Police have no right to detain persons at will to investigate without a level of suspicion. A lawful arrest authorizes an officer to take a person into custody to begin a process of prosecution. An officer who has only reasonable suspicion may temporarily detain a person for brief questioning to confirm or dispel the suspicion. A person in a premises may be detained during the time a search warrant is executed. An arrested person may be subjected to a thorough search for evidence of crime or weapons. A person briefly detained for an investigatory stop may only be subjected to a "frisk": a brief pat-down of outer clothing to detect the presence of a weapon.

Two definitions of an arrest issued by the Supreme Court are: (1) an arrest occurs when a person believes he or she is not free to leave (*Mendenhall*), and (2) when physically stopped (*Hodari D.*). A person who is fleeing from a police officer intent on stopping him is not seized until the instant the person is physically stopped. An arrested person loses his right to privacy and may be kept in view of police at all times. An officer must have probable cause *before* making an arrest. Probable cause is an objective standard supported by facts, and not based on the good faith of an officer. Proximity to a crime alone does not establish probable cause. Every warrantless arrest is subjected to a probable cause determination by a judicial officer soon after an arrest, typically within forty-eight hours. Probable cause can also be based on direct observation of an officer, hearsay, or reports from other police departments. Misdemeanor arrests can be made only for offenses committed in the officer's presence; except that in most states, by statute, misdemeanor arrests can be made on probable cause in domestic violence cases. A court does not lose jurisdiction of a case if an officer makes an illegal arrest. Evidence seized during an illegal arrest is inadmissible; but evidence obtained during an arrest based on probable cause that was in fact mistaken is admissible. A "citizen's arrest" may be made on probable cause but if mistaken, the person making the arrest is strictly liable for the tort of false arrest. Police may use reasonable force to effect an arrest and deadly force where it is reasonable. The common law rule allowing an officer to shoot to kill a fleeing felon even without evidence that the felon is armed and dangerous violates the Fourth Amendment because it is excessive and unreasonable.

The Fourth Amendment does not require an arrest warrant for a lawful arrest that is made in a public place, even if the police have had time to obtain the warrant. On the other hand, police must have an arrest warrant to enter a person's home to arrest the person unless the entry is justified by an exigency. An exigency is not created merely because the crime for which the arrest is made was a serious crime. Police cannot rely on an arrest warrant to enter the home of a third party to arrest a person—such an entry has to be justified with a search warrant.

A person arrested for a crime that authorizes the officer to take the person into custody may be thoroughly searched for weapons and for evidence. The evidence from a search incident to arrest need not pertain to the crime for which a person was arrested. A police officer who stops a speeding car and issues a citation rather than making an arrest has no justification to search the car. When a person is arrested, the police may search the area within the person's immediate control for weapons or evidence but may not go beyond to search a house or other premises. When police enter a premises and arrest a person, they may look into the adjoining room, without any evidentiary basis, to look for another person who could injure the officers. However, for them to conduct a protective sweep of the entire premises to look for a confederate of the arrested person, they must have reasonable suspicion to believe that another person is in the house. Police may conduct an inventory of all an arrested person's belongings at a police lockup or jail; this is not a Fourth Amendment search for evidence but an administrative procedure designed to promote safety and deter theft and false claims of theft of the prisoner's goods. A search incident to arrest may be made at the police station. Pretrial detainees held in a jail may be subjected to strip and body cavity searches but only when reasonable.

The Court has recognized the law enforcement power to briefly detain suspects who are reasonably believed to be involved in criminal activity in order to question them about their suspicious activity and to frisk them for weapons. The standard of evidence for such a "stop and frisk" is "reasonable suspicion," a lesser standard than probable cause to believe that a crime has been committed and that the suspect committed it. Reasonable suspicion can be based on an officer's expertise in drawing inferences from observed facts, on an informant's hearsay, from a verified and reliable anonymous call, or from a police bulletin. Reasonable suspicion is based on a totality of the circumstances, including inferences from facts. An investigatory stop must be brief and nonintrusive.

A person cannot be stopped on the street simply for identification under an indefinite vagrancy statute or because he or she is standing in a high-crime neighborhood. A gang loitering ordinance that makes it a crime for gang members to simply "loiter" and not "disperse" when so ordered violates the void-for-vagueness doctrine of the Fourteenth Amendment. A person who is chased by a police officer is not seized until the person is physically caught, and any property that the person throws away before being caught has been abandoned and is not protected by the Fourth Amendment expectation of privacy. A person who flees from a police officer without provocation in a high-crime area establishes reasonable suspicion for an investigatory stop.

Automobile drivers cannot be stopped at random on the highway by police for a registration and license check without probable cause or reasonable suspicion of a crime or a motor vehicle violation. When a person is stopped in a car for an investigatory stop, officers may visually scan the interior of the car for weapons. There is no Fourth Amendment violation if an officer who stops a car for an existing traffic offense did so for the purpose of searching for drugs—a pretext search is constitutional. A drug courier profile can be the basis for making a stop of a person in an automobile. The standard for appellate review of a reasonable suspicion or probable cause determination is *de novo* review that independently evaluates the facts and not deference to the magistrate's decision. Once a car is stopped, the officer may, for his own safety, order the driver and passengers to exit the automobile.

When police officers accost a person in a nonthreatening manner in a space where the person would not ordinarily be free to move about, such as at a factory workstation or in an intercity bus, that fact alone does not turn a consensual encounter into a seizure. A person stopped for an open automobile sobriety checklane is not seized for Fourth Amendment purposes. Police who accost a person at an airport and ask to speak to him or her about drug transportation do not seize such a person unless they detain the passenger's ticket or luggage for more than a few moments. A sniff of luggage by a trained-for-narcotics dog is not a Fourth Amendment search. A person who gets off an airplane from Florida on an early morning flight and looks behind him for a companion does not fit a drug courier profile. A drug courier profile may be based on a series of innocent facts that, when taken together, allow an officer to draw a reasonable conclusion that the person is a drug courier. Police have reasonable suspicion to stop a person who fits a drug courier profile.

LEGAL PUZZLES

HOW HAVE COURTS DECIDED THESE CASES?

PROBABLE CAUSE TO ARREST: POLICE OFFICER'S OBSERVATIONS

4–1. At 2:30 on a July afternoon a DEA agent driving past a park in Puerto Rico noticed eight or nine men grouped around a concrete bench near one of the park's basketball courts. Seven or eight vehicles were parked in a row alongside the group of men. One was talking on a cellular phone and another had a cellular phone attached to his waist. The men were not dressed to play basketball and did not appear to have coolers, sodas, or alcoholic beverages. The agent did not know any of the men by name; he had occasionally seen one near a drug distribution spot in a local housing project. The agent observed the men from an adjacent parking lot with binoculars.

About ten minutes later, a black Nissan Pathfinder drove up. The passenger exited the vehicle and conversed with four of the men. The passenger then removed a large handbag from

the rear of the black Pathfinder and placed it between a white GMC van and a gray Mercury Cougar parked side-by-side next to the basketball court. The passenger removed a second handbag from the black Pathfinder and placed it next to the first. The agent then drove through the parking lot to get a closer look. As he passed by, he saw the four men and the passenger gathered around the handbags. The passenger was handling square-shaped packages that appeared to contain cocaine.

The agent called for backup. Another transaction like the one involving the passenger of the Pathfinder occurred. DEA agents arrested fourteen men and seized a large quantity of illegal drugs.

Was probable cause to arrest established?

HELD: Yes Although the men were in a park near a basketball court, they were neither dressed to play nor visibly equipped for a social gathering. A cellular phone is a known tool of the drug trade. While these facts might not be enough alone to constitute probable cause, they do weigh in the evaluation of the "totality of the circumstances." When these facts are combined with the transactions by which a vehicle arrived and the passenger removed two handbags from the vehicle and placed them between two previously parked vehicles where the men were congregating, and the men all gathered around as the passenger handled what appeared to be packages of cocaine—these facts would lead a prudent person to believe that a large-scale cocaine transaction was transpiring and that the men were involved. *United States v. Martinez-Molina*, 64 F.3d 719 (1st Cir. 1995)

SEARCH INCIDENT TO ARREST

4–2. Lisa A. and her husband, a prison guard, lived in a townhouse. Her young children sometimes played music in the townhouse too loudly, causing neighbors to complain. On an August day, Officer Stephen Hargrave of the Dumfries, Virginia, Police Department responded to a complaint from a neighbor about the loud music coming from Lisa's townhouse. Hargrave instructed her to turn down the music, and she did so. At that time, Hargrave told Lisa that he would not arrest her unless he received another complaint about the noise level. Believing that Hargrave was unnecessarily impolite in his handling of the matter, Lisa A. called the County Police Department and complained about Hargrave's conduct. Hargrave discovered that Lisa had registered a complaint against him later that afternoon and two days later, without any further complaints about the noise level, secured an arrest warrant charging Lisa for the two-day-old violation of the town misdemeanor noise ordinance.

After nine o'clock that night, Officer Pfluger took his trainee, West, and other officers to the townhouse to execute the arrest warrant. When Pfluger and West knocked on the door, a nude Lisa A. was in her bathroom preparing for bed. She covered herself with a house dress and followed her husband downstairs. (This was West's first arrest of a woman. He resigned from the police force approximately six months later.)

When Lisa A. answered the door with her husband, Pfluger told her she was under arrest. Lisa A. fully cooperated during the arrest, but when told that she was to be handcuffed, she pointed out to the officers that she was completely naked under the dress and requested permission to get dressed because she would no longer be able to hold her dress closed once handcuffed. This request was denied, and Lisa's hands were secured behind her back, causing her dress to fall open below her chest.

Pfluger then turned to West, who was at the door with Pfluger, and told him to complete Lisa's processing. West escorted Lisa A. to the police car in her semiclad state, walking past several officers on the way to the car. Lisa A. proceeded to enter the back door of the car, which West had opened. West stopped her and told her that he would have to search her before she entered the car. Lisa A. protested that she was not wearing any underwear, and West said, "I still have to search you." West then stood in front of Lisa, squeezed her hips and, inside her opened dress, "swiped" one ungloved hand, palm up, across her bare vagina, at which time the tip of his finger slightly penetrated her genitals. Lisa A. jumped back, still in handcuffs, and exclaimed, "I told you I don't have on any underwear." West did not respond and proceeded to put his hand "up into [her] butt cheeks," kneading them. West then allowed Lisa A. to enter the car. This search took place directly in front of the townhouse, where the other police officers, Lisa's husband, her five children, and all of her neighbors had the opportunity to observe.

Was this a constitutional search incident to arrest?

Holding available from instructor

REASONABLE SUSPICION

4–3. Officer Scism lawfully stopped April Lebrun while driving for a traffic violation. He detained her car until a drug-sniffing dog could be brought to the scene. At the time of the traffic stop, Ms. Lebrun and another individual were passengers in a vehicle that Ms. Lebrun had rented; Steven Krebbs was the driver. While Officer Scism conducted the traffic stop and prepared a warning citation to Mr. Krebbs, he asked all three of the occupants of the vehicle some routine questions about their travel plans and the purpose of their trip, and received vague and confused answers from them. Officer Scism also noticed that they were all unusually nervous: Mr. Krebbs was sweating profusely even though the temperature was cold, Ms. Lebrun fidgeted and kept moving around in her seat, and the other passenger would not make eye contact with the officer and her hands trembled excessively. Last, Officer Scism saw that there were drink containers, food wrappers, a cellular telephone, a road atlas, pillows, and blankets in the vehicle.

The drug-sniffing dog arrived in twenty minutes.

1. Did these facts constitute reasonable suspicion to detain the car long enough for a drug-sniffing dog to be brought?
2. Was the detention too long for a *Terry* stop?

REASONABLE SUSPICION

4–4. A United States Postal Inspection Officer intercepted and detained an Express Mail package sent by appellant from the Los Angeles International Airport. The package fit the characteristics of an Express Mail/Narcotics Profile developed to detect the use of Express Mail service for drug trafficking: the return and destination labels were hand-written, the package was mailed from one individual (appellant) to another individual at the same address, the package was mailed from a narcotics "source" state (California), and the return address ZIP code was different from the accepting ZIP code. The inspector did not testify at the suppression hearing, and his affidavit stated that he had eight years of experience as a postal inspector along with some training courses, and that the package in question met the Express Mail/Narcotics Profile.

Do these facts amount to reasonable suspicion to intercept and detain the package to be presented to a drug-sniffing dog?

Holding available from instructor

FURTHER READING

Lawrence P. Tiffany, Donald M. McIntyre, Jr., and Daniel L. Rotenberg, *Detection of Crime* (Boston: Little Brown & Company, 1967).

William Ker Muir, Jr., *Police: Streetcorner Politicians* (Chicago: University of Chicago Press, 1977).

Human Rights Watch, *Shielded from Justice: Police Brutality and Accountability in the United States* (New York: Human Rights Watch, 1998).

ENDNOTES

1. Stephen J. Schulhofer, *The Enemy Within: Intelligence Gathering, Law Enforcement, and Civil Liberties in the Wake of September 11* (New York: Century Foundation Press, 2002), 11.
2. Office of the Inspector General, DOJ, "The September 11 Detainees: A Review of the Treatment of Aliens Held on Immigration Charges in Connection with the Investigation of the September 11 Attacks," news release, June 2003, http://www.usdoj.gov/oig/special/03-06/press.htm.
3. Eric Lichtblau, "U.S. Report Faults the Roundup of Illegal Immigrants After 9/11," *New York Times*, June 3, 2003.
4. Ibid.
5. Ibid.
6. Schulhofer, *Enemy Within,* 12 (emphasis in original).
7. Deborah Sontag, "'Who Is This Kafka That People Keep Mentioning?'" *New York Times Magazine*, October 21, 2001.
8. Siobhan Roth, "Material Support Law: Weapon in War on Terror; the United States Has Charged More than 30 People with Aiding Terrorists; a Roundup of Where the Cases Stand," *Legal Times*, May 5, 2003.
9. 202 F. Supp. 2d 55 (S.D.N.Y. 2002). See Stacey M. Studnicki and John P. Apol, "Witness Detention and Intimidation: The History and Future of Material Witness Law," *St. John's Law Review* 76 (2002): 483–533.

10. Kenneth Adams, et al., *Use of Force by Police: Overview of National and Local Data* (Washington: National Institute of Justice and Bureau of Justice Statistics, October 1999).

11. Michael J. Glennon, "International Kidnapping: State-sponsored Abduction: A Comment on *United States v. Alvarez-Machain,*" *American Society of International Law Newsletter* 86 (October 1992): 746.

12. These rules may not, as is commonly believed, be traceable to the old English common law but may be relatively modern developments of the late eighteenth and the nineteenth centuries. See Thomas Y. Davies, "Recovering the Original Fourth Amendment," *Michigan Law Review* 98 (3)(1999): 547–750.

13. See J. Bradley Ortins, "District of Columbia Survey: Warrantless Misdemeanor Arrest for Drunk Driving Found Invalid in *Schram v. District of Columbia,*" *Catholic University Law Review* 34 (1985): 1241–54.

14. David A. Sklansky, "The Private Police," *UCLA Law Review* 46 (1999):1165–1287.

15. Ibid, 1184.

16. F. J. Remington, D. J. Newman, E. L. Kimball, M. Melli, and H. Goldstein, *Criminal Justice Administration, Materials and Cases* (Indianapolis: Bobbs–Merrill, 1969), 20.

17. *Garner v. Memphis Police Department,* 710 F.2d 240 (6th Cir. 1983).

18. Jerome H. Skolnick and James J. Fyfe, *Above the Law: Police and the Excessive Use of Force* (New York: Free Press, 1993), 246.

19. *Dorman v. United States,* 435 F.2d 385, 392–93 (D.C. Cir. 1970).

20. 723 F.2d 1263 (7th Cir. 1983).

21. Robin Lee Fenton, "Comment: the Constitutionality of Policies Requiring Strip Searches of All Misdemeanants and Minor Traffic Offenders," *University of Cincinnati Law Review* 54 (1985): 175–89.

22. William J. Simonitsch, "Comment: Visual Body Cavity Searches Incident to Arrest: Validity Under the Fourth Amendment," *University of Miami Law Review* 54 (2000): 665–88.

23. D. Caute, *The Year of the Barricades: A Journey Through 1968* (New York: Harper & Row, 1988).

24. However, one biographer read *Terry* at face value as a balancing of law enforcement needs against privacy rights; G. Edward White, *Earl Warren: A Public Life* (New York: Oxford University Press, 1982), 276–78.

25. F. Graham, *The Due Process Revolution: The Warren Court's Impact on Criminal Law* (New York: Hayden Book Co., 1970), 22–23.

26. P. Chevigny, *Police Power: Police Abuses in New York City* (New York: Pantheon, 1969).

27. M. Lippman, "The Drug War and the Vanishing Fourth Amendment," *Criminal Justice Journal* 14 (1992): 229–308.

28. M. McAlary, *Buddy Boys: When Good Cops Turn Bad* (New York: Putnam's, 1987), 87.

29. Jennifer Lee, "Upgraded Driver's Licenses Are Urged as National ID's," *New York Times,* January 8, 2002.

30. T. J. Devetski, "Fourth Amendment—Protection Against Unreasonable Seizure of the Person: The New (?) Common Law Arrest Test for Seizure," *Journal of Criminal Law & Criminology* 82 (1992): 747–72.

31. Tracey Maclin, "Book Review: Seeing the Constitution from the Backseat of a Police Squad Car," *Boston University Law Review* 70 (1990): 543–91 (emphasis added).

32. Maclin, "Book Review," 550.

33. Marvin Zalman, "Fleeing from the Fourth Amendment," *Criminal Law Bulletin* 36 (2)(2000): 129–47.

34. George C. Thomas, III, "*Terry v. Ohio* in the Trenches: A Glimpse at How Courts Apply 'Reasonable Suspicion,'" *St. John's Law Review* 72 (1998): 1025–41.

35. David Moran, "The New Fourth Amendment Vehicle Doctrine: Stop and Search Any Car at Any Time," *Villanova Law Review* 47 (2002): 815–838.

36. G. G. Ashdown, "Drugs, Ideology, and the Deconstitutionalization of Criminal Procedure," *West Virginia Law Review* 95 (1992): 1–54 (paragraph breaks ignored).

37. M. Cloud, "Search and Seizures by the Numbers: The Drug Courier Profile and Judicial Review of Investigative Formulas," *Boston University Law Review* 65 (1985): 843–921; S. E. Hall, "A Balancing Approach to the Constitutionality of Drug Courier Profiles," *University of Illinois Law Review* 1993: 1007–1036.

38. S. Guerra, "Domestic Drug Interdiction Operations: Finding the Balance," *Journal of Criminal Law & Criminology* 82 (1992): 1109–61.

39. Hall, "A Balancing Approach," 1010.

40. Lisa Belkin, "Airport Anti-Drug Nets Snare Many People Fitting 'Profiles,'" *New York Times,* March 20, 1990.

41. Hall, "A Balancing Approach," 1010–11.

42. Cases cited in Hall, "A Balancing Approach," 1011, n. 35.

43. W. R. Janikowski and D. J. Giacopassi, "Pyrrhic Images, Dancing Shadows, and Flights of Fancy: The Drug Courier Profile as Legal Fiction," *Journal of Contemporary Criminal Justice* 9 (1993): 60–69.

44. Cloud, "Search and Seizures," n. 32.

45. Betsy Tsai, "Note: The Trend Toward Specialized Domestic Violence Courts: Improvements on an Effective Innovation," *Fordham Law Review* 68 (2000): 1285, 1292, citing The Commission on Domestic Violence, Statistics. http://www.abanet.org/domviol/stats.html (accessed October 15, 1999).

46. E. S. Buzawa and C. G. Buzawa, *Domestic Violence: The Criminal Justice Response* (Newbury Park, CA: Sage, 1990), 20.

47. J. Zorza, "Must We Stop Arresting Batterers?: Analysis and Policy Implications of New Police Domestic Violence Studies," *New England Law Review* 28 (1994): 929–90.

48. Buzawa and Buzawa, *Domestic Violence,* 20.

49. Lisa G. Lerman, "Statute: A Model State Act: Remedies for Domestic Abuse," *Harvard Journal on Legislation* 21 (1984).

50. Richard J. Gelles and Murray A. Straus, *Intimate Violence* (New York: Touchstone, 1989), 114. The earlier training manual is International Association of Chiefs of Police, *Training Key 16: Handling Disturbance Calls* (Gaithersburg, MD: International Association of Chiefs of Police, 1967).

51. International Association of Chiefs of Police, *Training Key 245: Wife Beating* (Gaithersburg, MD: International Association of Chiefs of Police, 1976). "The officer who starts legal action may give the wife the courage she needs to realistically face and correct her situation."

52. Gelles and Straus, *Intimate Violence,* 166; U.S. Attorney-General's Task Force on Family Violence, *Report* (Washington, D.C.: U.S. Department of Justice, 1984).

53. A. Binder and J. Meeker, "The Development of Social Attitudes Toward Spousal Abuse," in *Domestic Violence: The Changing Criminal Justice Response,* E. S. Buzawa and C.G. Buzawa, eds. (Westport, CT: Auburn House, 1992), 3–19, 82. See generally, F. J. Weed, *Certainty of Justice: Reform in the Criminal Justice Movement* (New York: Aldine de Gruyter, 1995).

54. M. Zalman, "The Courts' Response to Police Intervention in Domestic Violence," in *Domestic Violence: The Changing Criminal Justice Response,* E. S. Buzawa and C. G. Buzawa, eds. (Westport, CT: Auburn House, 1992), 79–110.

55. Lerman, "Statute," 76–120; see comment in Gary Brown, Karin A. Keitel, and Sandra E. Lundy, "Starting a TRO Project: Student Representation of Battered Women," *Yale Law Journal* 96 (1987): 1985–2020. They are also known as restraining orders, protective orders, or temporary restraining orders.

56. B. Hart, "State Codes on Domestic Violence: Analysis, Commentary and Recommendations," *Juvenile and Family Court Journal* 43 (1992): 24 (footnotes omitted).

57. Ruth Gundle, "Civil Liability for Police Failure to Arrest: *Nearing v. Weaver,*" *Women's Rights Law Reporter* 9 (3 and 4) (1986): 259–265. Injunction suits were brought: *Bruno v. Codd,* 90 Misc.2d 1047, 396 N.Y.S.2d 974 (Sup Ct. Special Term 1977), *rev'd in part, appeal dismissed in part,* 64 A.D.2d 582, 407 N.Y.S.2d 165 (1978), *aff'd,* 47 N.Y.2d 582, 393 N.E.2d 976, 419 N.Y.S.2d 901 (1979) (class action; consent decree entered to enforce protection orders); *Scott v. Hart,* No. C–76–2395 (N.D., Cal. filed November 24, 1976); *Raguz v. Chandler,* No. C–74–1064 (N.D. Ohio, filed November 20, 1974). These cases are discussed in Gundle, "Civil Liability," 261–262; Case Comment, Carolyne R. Hathaway, "Gender Based Discrimination in Police Reluctance to Respond to Domestic Assault Complaints," *Georgetown Law Review* 75 (1986): 667–91. Their effectiveness is limited to a single individual or municipality.

58. 295 Or. 702, 670 P.2d 137 (1983).

59. *DeShaney v. Winnebago County* (1989).

60. 595 F. Supp. 1521 (D. Conn 1984).

61. Case Comment in Hathaway, "Gender Based Discrimination," 669.

62. American Bar Association, *Standards Relating to the Urban Police Function* (1972), 116; J. Goldstein, "Police Discretion Not to Invoke the Criminal Process: Low-Visibility Decisions in the Administration of Justice," in *Criminal Justice: Law and Politics,* 5th ed., by G. Cole (Pacific Grove, CA: Brooks/Cole, 1988), 83–102, from *Yale Law Journal* 69 (1960): 543–94; William Ker Muir, Jr., *Police: Streetcorner Politicians* (Chicago: University of Chicago Press, 1977).

63. See M. Zalman, "Mandatory Sentencing Legislation: Myth and Reality," in *Implementing Criminal Justice Policies,* by M. Morash (Beverly Hills, CA: Sage, 1982), 61–69. Indeed, legislatures at times assume that laws they pass will not be strictly enforced by the police.

64. Muir, *Police,* 101–25; Goldstein, "Police Discretion," 94–97.

65. K. C. Davis, *Discretionary Justice: A Preliminary Inquiry* (Baton Rouge: Louisiana State University Press, 1969), 3, 5.

66. Muir, *Police,* 57, 82–100.

67. Lloyd Ohlin and Michael Tonry, "Family Violence in Perspective," in *Family Violence* (Chicago: University of Chicago Press, 1989), 1–18. Irene H. Frieze and Angela Browne, "Violence in Marriage," in *Family Violence,* Ohlin and Tonry, eds., 165. A 1970 survey found that 25 percent of the male respondents and 17 percent of the females approved of a husband slapping his wife under certain circumstances.

68. Del Martin, *Battered Wives, Revised, Updated* (San Francisco: Volcano Press, 1981), 87–88.

69. K. J. Ferraro, "Policing Women Battering," *Social Problems* 36 (1) (1989): 61–74.

70. J. Zorza, "The Criminal Law of Misdemeanor Domestic Violence," *Journal of Criminal Law and Criminology* 83 (1992): 46–72.

71. Patrick A. Langan and Christopher A. Innes, *Bureau of Justice Statistics Special Report: Preventing Domestic Violence Against Women* (Washington, D.C.: U.S. Department of Justice, 1986). A national victimization survey found that one-third of battered spouses were victims of the felonies of rape, robbery, or aggravated assault, while two-thirds were victimized by misdemeanor simple assaults.

72. Hart, State Codes, 1–81.

73. Lerman, "Statute," 61–143. Illinois has adopted such a provision.

74. Langan and Innes, *Bureau of Justice Statistics Special Report;* Lisa G. Lerman, "Expansion of Arrest Power: A Key to Effective Intervention," *Vermont Law Review* 7 (1982): 59–70.

75. The research involved an experimental design and the type of intervention was determined randomly and before the police entered the house so that there would be no exercise of discretion; the sample was quite small. It was conducted by Lawrence W. Sherman and Richard A. Berk and published in the *Police Foundation Reports* (1984). A scholarly journal article was also published: L. Sherman and R. Berk, "The Specific Deterrent Effects of Arrest for Domestic Violence," *American Sociological Review* 49 (2) (1984): 261–72. The authors were cautious in drawing policy conclusions, but despite such cautions, the findings were widely publicized and "caught fire" with the relevant public of police administrators and state legislators. The Minneapolis report, L. Sherman's replication report, and a general analysis of these issues is found in L. Sherman, *Policing Domestic Violence: Experiments and Dilemmas* (New York: Free Press, 1992).

76. R. Lempert, "Humility Is a Virtue: On the Publicization of Policy-Relevant Research," *Law & Society Review* 23 (1989): 146–161.

77. Zorza, "Arresting Batterers," 935–36.

78. Sherman, *Policing,* 19.

79. Sherman *Policing,* 22–24.

80. Zorza, "Arresting Batterers," 985.

81. S. Herrell and M. Hofford, *Family Violence: Improving Court Practice* (Reno: National Council of Juvenile and Family Court Judges, 1990).

82. Zorza, "Arresting Batterers," 985 (emphasis added).

83. Marion Wanless, "Notes: Mandatory Arrest: A Step Toward Eradicating Domestic Violence, but Is It Enough?" *University of Illinois Law Review* 1996 (1996): 533–75.

84. Carol Wright "Comment: Immediate Arrest in Domestic Violence Situations: Mandate or Alternative," *Capital University Law Review* 14 (1985): 243–68.

85. Ibid., 261–267.

86. See Wanless, "Mandatory Arrest."

87. Ibid., 559.

88. Ibid., 558.

89. Ibid., 562.

JUSTICES OF THE SUPREME COURT

STALWART CONSERVATIVES, 1938–1962
REED–VINSON–BURTON–MINTON–WHITTAKER

These five justices, appointees of Presidents Franklin D. Roosevelt, Harry S. Truman, and Dwight D. Eisenhower, were instrumental in delaying the implementation of the due process "incorporation" revolution of the 1960s. They were largely conservative in their criminal procedure rulings, both in denying the validity of the incorporation argument and in construing the due process clause narrowly. For the most part, legal commentators rank these justices as not especially distinguished: Their visions of the Court's role tended to be cramped, and they failed to explain their positions with intellectual force. They typically followed the lead of justices with more manifest abilities, especially Felix Frankfurter and John Harlan II. These justices displayed basic legal competence but little independence in their decisions, and their opinions were not written with the high craft that is critical to shaping the law.

This group of justices, with Justice Clark, formed a majority of the Court from 1949 to 1953 (excluding Justice Whittaker, who sat from 1957 to 1962). From 1953 to 1962, a combination of centrist and less dyed-in-the-wool conservatives kept the Court from breaching the Palko *doctrine until Justice Clark's decision in* Mapp. *With Justice Frankfurter's retirement and replacement by Justice Arthur Goldberg in 1962, the Court took a decidedly liberal turn that marked the Warren Court of the 1960s.*

STANLEY F. REED

Kentucky 1884–1980

Democrat

Appointed by
Franklin Delano Roosevelt

Years of Service:
1938–1957

Collection of the Supreme Court of the United States. Photographer: Harris and Ewing

LIFE AND CAREER Justice Reed held B.A. degrees from Kentucky Wesleyan College and Yale University and studied law at the Sorbonne, Columbia University, and the University of Virginia without graduating. He completed legal studies by reading law in a Kentucky lawyer's office and practiced from 1910 to the 1920s. He entered government service under President Hoover but remained in the attorney general's office as a faithful New Dealer under President Roosevelt. As solicitor general from 1935, he argued some of the key New Deal cases before the Supreme Court and developed a high reputation for legal craftsmanship. He was President Roosevelt's second appointment to the Supreme Court.

CONTRIBUTION TO CRIMINAL PROCEDURE He was a stalwart supporter of Justice Frankfurter and helped to block the movement toward incorporation, applying the criminal provisions of the Bill of Rights to the states.

SIGNATURE OPINION *Adamson v. California* (1947). Reed's majority opinion in *Adamson* kept the Court's anti-incorporation position intact. Adamson was tried for murder; he did not take the stand in his own defense, knowing that if he did so, prior convictions for burglary, larceny, and robbery would have been introduced into evidence to impeach him. California law allowed the judge to comment on the defendant's silence to the jury. Writing for the majority, Reed relied on a long train of cases, including *Twining v. New Jersey* (1908), for the proposition that the Self-Incrimination Clause was not a fundamental right incorporated into the Due Process Clause of the Fourteenth Amendment. He relied on the *Palko* case, noting that this ruling allowed the states to pursue their own criminal procedure policies unfettered by rules under the Bill of Rights, which had limited the federal government. "It accords with the constitutional doctrine of federalism by leaving to the states the responsibility of dealing with the privileges and immunities of their citizens except those inherent in national citizenship."

In addition, Justice Reed made it clear that he did not entirely disapprove of the practical impact of a judge telling a jury that they could take the defendant's refusal to testify into account in weighing the evidence, even though by 1947 a majority of the states had abolished the practice by statute or state constitutional rule. Adamson argued that this placed a penalty on his right to silence under the California constitution and shifted the burden of proof from the government to himself. Justice Reed, to the contrary, noted: "[W]e see no reason why comment should not be made upon his silence. It seems quite natural that when a defendant has opportunity to deny or explain facts and determines not to do so, the prosecution should bring out the strength of the evidence by commenting upon defendant's failure to explain or deny it. The prosecution

(Continued)

evidence may be of facts that may be beyond the knowledge of the accused. If so, his failure to testify would have little if any weight. But the facts may be such as are necessarily in the knowledge of the accused. In that case a failure to explain would point to an inability to explain."

ASSESSMENT Justice Reed's record was "liberal" in regard to New Deal economic issues. He was a strong believer in judicial restraint, and feared what he called "krytocracy" or government by judges. He was a judicial conservative vote in many civil liberties areas and voted consistently with Justice Frankfurter's bloc. On the question of school desegregation, he had consistently voted against segregated facilities under the "separate but equal" doctrine but was at first reluctant to overturn the doctrine in *Brown v. Board of Education* (1954). After Chief Justice Vinson died during deliberations, Chief Justice Earl Warren persuaded Reed to join a unanimous Court in overruling *Plessy v. Ferguson* (1896).

FURTHER READING

John D. Fassett, *New Deal Justice: The Life of Stanley Reed of Kentucky* (New York: Vantage, 1994).

FRED M. VINSON

Kentucky 1890–1953

Democrat

Appointed Chief Justice by Harry S. Truman

Years of Service: 1946–1953

Collection of the Supreme Court of the United States. Photographer: Harris and Ewing

LIFE AND CAREER Vinson, born in Kentucky, was educated at Kentucky Normal School and Centre College, where he excelled in athletics and received a law degree. Vinson practiced law from 1911 to 1931. Elected to the House of Representatives in 1924, he rose to a position of power on the Ways and Means Committee and, as loyal ally to Roosevelt, was instrumental in developing New Deal tax and coal programs. He was appointed to the United States Circuit Court for the District of Columbia in 1938, but resigned during World War II to become director of economic stabilization and later director of war mobilization. He developed a strong friendship with President Truman who appointed him secretary of the treasury.

Vinson's public philosophy, including his theory of the Supreme Court's role, was shaped by these momentous events. He believed the federal government needed the power to solve the enormous problems threatening the nation. He was pragmatic and, while serving in all three branches, had participated in the process of big government winning the greatest war in history and taming the worst political-economic crisis in the life of the United States. He had faith born of experience that American political institutions and the American public had the judgment to successfully resolve competing interests for the public good.

CONTRIBUTION TO CRIMINAL PROCEDURE In 1946 a liberal bloc of four justices (Black, Douglas, Murphy, and Rutledge) came close to inaugurating the incorporation of the Bill of Rights. Vinson opposed this action, and during his tenure, the number of justices opposed to incorporation increased as Murphy and Rutledge were replaced by Clark and Minton. Also, Justices Frankfurter and Jackson, while of a more liberal temperament and more willing to find for defendants under the Due Process Clause, were opposed to the incorporation doctrine.

SIGNATURE OPINION Although Vinson voted in favor of the federal government in its heavy-handed repression of American communists in loyalty cases during the Cold War, he drew a line at the use of the courts to stifle traditional rights. The right to bail came up in *Stack v. Boyle* (1951). Pretrial bail was set at fifty-thousand dollars each for leaders of the American Communist Party on trial for the theoretical advocacy of the violent overthrow of the government. Writing for the Court, Vinson held that the bail was excessive because it was set at a figure higher than reasonably calculated to giving adequate assurance that the defendant would return to stand trial and submit to sentence. He wrote: "This traditional right to freedom before conviction permits the unhampered preparation of a defense, and serves to prevent the infliction of punishment prior to conviction. Unless this right to bail before trial is preserved, the presumption of innocence, secured only after centuries of struggle, would lose its meaning."

ASSESSMENT Vinson believed in judicial restraint. Having seen a conservative Supreme Court subvert the political will at the beginning of the New Deal, Vinson consistently voted to uphold the power of government in civil liberties (in loyalty oath and Communist conspiracy cases), in economic affairs, and in criminal law. He was appointed Chief Justice in part to calm several personal antagonisms that had developed among more brilliant justices, but his lack of constitutional vision and craft made him an ineffective chief justice.

FURTHER READING

Melvin I. Urofsky, *Division and Discord: The Supreme Court Under Stone and Vinson, 1941–1953* (Columbia: University of South Carolina Press, 1997).

HAROLD BURTON

Ohio 1888–1965

Republican

Appointed by
Harry S. Truman

Years of Service:
1945–1958

Collection of the Supreme Court of the United States. Photographer: Harris and Ewing

LIFE AND CAREER   Harold Burton was born in Jamaica Plain, Massachusetts; educated at Bowdoin College and Harvard Law School; and practiced law in the West before settling in Cleveland. His political career included service in the Ohio House of Representatives from 1929, election to mayor of Cleveland in 1935—serving two terms, and election to the Senate in 1941. Although a Republican mayor, he cooperated with the national government, a position taken by few midwestern Republicans. Although sometimes critical of the Democratic administration, Burton was supportive of the economic and social policies of the New Deal and was supportive of the entry of the United States into the United Nations. These positions made Burton an acceptable Republican nominee by a Democratic president. Again, as with all of Truman's nominees, the president and Senator Burton were friends; Burton had been a member of Truman's committee to investigate wartime fraud.

CONTRIBUTION TO CRIMINAL PROCEDURE   Burton was a stalwart conservative in opposing the incorporation doctrine. In confessions cases, he was unwilling to use the Due Process Clause to exclude confessions that the Court's majority found coercive. On the other hand, he was in the minority in a case that held that a person who was electrocuted and lived could be executed a second time without violating any constitutional provision, including the fundamental fairness aspect of due process.

SIGNATURE OPINION   *Rovario v. United States* (1957). Writing for a 6–1 majority, Justice Burton held that the identity of a secret undercover informant must be made known to the defendant during a trial for heroin possession where the informer had taken a material part in bringing about Rovario's possession of the drugs, had been present with Rovario while the crime occurred, and might have been a material witness as to whether Rovario knowingly transported the drugs. He ruled that the so-called "informer's privilege" is in reality the government's privilege to withhold from disclosure the identity of persons who furnish information of violations of law to officers charged with enforcement of that law. This "privilege" as-

sists effective law enforcement by encouraging people to inform about crime, but where it conflicts with fundamental fairness, it must give way to the defendant's right to a fair trial. In effect, where a conviction depends upon the disclosure of the identity of a secret informant, the government must either divulge the informant's identity or dismiss the prosecution. *Rovario* indicates that the stalwart conservatives in criminal procedure, while tending to favor the prosecution, adhered to fundamental standards of a fair trial.

ASSESSMENT   On the Court, Burton's conservative positions on civil liberties were close to those of Justice Reed. As Chief Justice Vinson, Sherman Minton, and Tom Clark were appointed, they joined to form what seemed to be a voting bloc that upheld the government's loyalty oath programs.

FURTHER READING

Mary Frances Berry, *Stability, Security, and Continuity: Mr. Justice Burton and Decision-Making in the Supreme Court, 1945–1958* (Westport, Conn.: Greenwood Press, 1978).

SHERMAN MINTON

Indiana 1890–1965

Democrat

Appointed by
Harry S. Truman

Years of Service:
1949–1956

Collection of the Supreme Court of the United States. Photographer: Harris and Ewing

LIFE AND CAREER   Sherman Minton was born in Indiana, graduated at the head of his class at Indiana University, studied law at Yale University, and returned home to practice law while engaging in local politics. In 1933 he was appointed counselor to that state's Public Service Commission. He played a significant role in developing a state version of the New Deal and was elected in 1934 to the Senate, where he was a staunch supporter of the Roosevelt Administration. His legal knowledge and militant manner in debate led to his rise to a Senate leadership role in which he supported Roosevelt's "court packing" plan. He was an internationalist, a position that was not too popular in the Midwest, and lost his Senate seat in 1940. He worked as a presidential assistant for the next year and was appointed to the United States Court of Appeals

(Continued)

for the Seventh Circuit (Indiana, Illinois, and Wisconsin) in 1941. It was Minton's good fortune to be seated next to another freshman senator, Harry Truman, in 1934. They became and remained good friends, which was a key element in each of Truman's appointments to the Supreme Court.

CONTRIBUTION TO CRIMINAL PROCEDURE As a stalwart conservative on criminal matters, Minton joined the Frankfurter-led bloc to halt any advance toward incorporation.

SIGNATURE OPINION He wrote the majority opinion in *United States v. Rabinowitz* (1950), which established the rule that a search incident to arrest could justify the search of the entire premises—a rule that stood until overturned by the *Chimel* decision in 1969. He wrote: "What is a reasonable search is not to be determined by any fixed formula. The Constitution does not define what are 'unreasonable' searches and, regrettably, in our discipline we have no ready litmus-paper test. The recurring questions of the reasonableness of searches must find resolution in the facts and circumstances of each case." In *Rabinowitz* Justice Minton viewed the search as reasonable because the search and seizure were incident to a valid arrest; the place of the search was a business room to which the public was invited; the room was small and under the immediate and complete control of respondent; the search did not extend beyond the room used for unlawful purposes; and the possession of the forged stamps was a crime. The Court was clearly influenced by the Crime Control Model of criminal justice: "A rule of thumb requiring that a search warrant always be procured whenever practicable may be appealing from the vantage point of easy administration. But we cannot agree that this requirement should be crystallized into a *sine qua non* to the reasonableness of a search. . . . The judgment of the officers as to when to close the trap on a criminal committing a crime in their presence or who they have reasonable cause to believe is committing a felony is not determined solely upon whether there was time to procure a search warrant. Some flexibility will be accorded law officers engaged in daily battle with criminals for whose restraint criminal laws are essential."

ASSESSMENT Minton replaced liberal Justice Rutledge and was thought by most observers at the time to be in the liberal mold. However, he fit very closely into the Vinson-Reed-Burton camp; as a New Dealer, he acquiesced to Congress in economic matters, but in civil rights issues, he had the most conservative record, voting for the government even more than Chief Justice Vinson. As a judicial conservative, he strongly maintained that the Court had no special obligation to support civil rights and that the Court had no power to legislate.

FURTHER READING

Harry L. Wallace, "Mr. Justice Minton: Hoosier Justice on the Supreme Court," *Indiana Law Journal* 34 (1959): 145–205.

CHARLES E. WHITTAKER

Missouri 1901–1973

Republican

Appointed by
Dwight D. Eisenhower

Years of Service:
1957–1962

Collection of the Supreme Court of the United States. Photographer: Abdon Daoud Ackad

LIFE AND CAREER Charles Whittaker was born and raised on a modest Kansas farm, where he trapped small animals and tracked game to supplement his family's income. He attended the University of Kansas City Law School at night while working as a clerk in a law firm, graduating in 1924. From then until 1954 (as partner from 1930), he practiced law in the same firm, which represented many large corporations doing business in Missouri, first as a litigator and later as an advisor to the firm's large business clients. He was active in bar association activities and became president of the Missouri State Bar Association. In 1954 he was appointed by President Eisenhower as a federal district judge and in 1956 as a judge to the United States Court of Appeals for the Eighth Circuit. He was known for his hard work and efficiency as a judge and established conservative credentials in ruling that a tenured professor in a private university could be dismissed for refusing to answer questions asked by a congressional committee and the University's Board of Trustees about possible Communist Party affiliations. He was selected to replace Justice Reed, as President Eisenhower was seeking a conservative Republican judge.

CONTRIBUTION TO CRIMINAL PROCEDURE Justice Whittaker strove to put aside ideological considerations and decide cases on their merits alone. This led to a somewhat inconsistent position. While he voted for the defendant in a number of cases, he also opposed the incorporation of the Fourth Amendment exclusionary rule in *Mapp v. Ohio* (1961).

SIGNATURE OPINION *Draper v. United States* (1959). Writing for a 6–1 majority, Whittaker ruled that probable cause existed to arrest Draper based on evidence given by a known, reliable informant. An officer was told that Draper, a known drug peddler in Denver, would return by train from Chicago with a supply of heroin. The informant told the officer the clothing that Draper would be wearing (a light-colored raincoat, brown slacks, and black shoes). The Court held that probable cause existed because the officer, having corroborated every factual element about Draper, except the possession of drugs when he detrained, "had 'reasonable grounds' to believe that the remaining unverified bit of [the informant's] information—that Draper would have the heroin with him—was likewise true."

ASSESSMENT On the Court, Justice Whittaker aligned himself with such conservative justices as Frankfurter, Harlan, Clark, Burton, and Stewart to maintain a slim majority in several civil liberties and criminal procedure cases. Unlike these conservative justices, he never was able to articulate a coherent philosophy of judging by which to guide his opinions. Thus, when he did rule in favor of defendants, his votes appeared to be based more on emotional factors of sympathy than on a firm understanding of the role of the federal judiciary. It would appear that he did not outgrow his position as a district court judge who could achieve success in applying the law; as a Supreme Court justice, it is necessary to expound the contours of the Constitution in novel and difficult cases. It is possible that Justice Whittaker's abilities were overtaxed, for he apparently put in an enormous number of hours and worried substantially about the cases. He fell ill in March 1962, apparently exhausted from his work. He resigned from the Court that year and accepted a position as a legal advisor to the General Motors Corporation.

FURTHER READING

Barbara B. Christensen, "Mister Justice Whittaker: The Man on the Right," *Santa Clara Law Review* 19 (1979): 1039–1062.

CHAPTER
5

Warrantless Searches

[T]he most basic constitutional rule in this area is that "searches conducted outside the judicial process, without prior approval by judge or magistrate, are per se *unreasonable under the Fourth Amendment—subject only to a few specifically established and well-delineated exceptions." . . . In times of unrest, whether caused by crime or racial conflict or fear of internal subversion, this basic law and the values that it represents may appear unrealistic or "extravagant" to some. But the values were those of the authors of our fundamental constitutional concepts.*

—Justice Potter Stewart in *Coolidge v. New Hampshire*,
403 U.S. 443, 455 (1971)

CHAPTER OUTLINE

KEY TERMS AND PHRASES

Administrative search

Automobile search

Border

Border search

Crime scene investigation exception

Exigency exception

Extraterritoriality

Fixed checkpoint

Hot pursuit

Impound

In loco parentis

Inventory search

Pervasively regulated industry

Roving patrol

"Special needs" doctrine

Warrantless search

INTRODUCTION

Warrantless searches are of enormous practical importance to police work. Despite the Supreme Court's preference for a search warrant, warrantless searches are far more common. Every warrantless search is conducted without prior judicial review but is subject to judicial review after the fact. Nevertheless, a search based on an officer's assessment of probable cause is more likely to be arbitrary than one subjected to the warrant process.

This text has already discussed several kinds of warrantless searches: plain view, consent, search incident to arrest, and the *Terry* "stop and frisk." Each is based on a different rationale and is held to different legal standards. An item seized in plain view, for example, involves no Fourth Amendment interest or expectation of privacy because the officer is in a public or other lawful place when the "plain view" occurs. The Fourth Amendment is not burdened by a consent search because the person has voluntarily given up the right of privacy. An officer can seek consent without having probable cause or reasonable suspicion to believe that a person is carrying contraband, and can even exploit the person's ignorance of the right to refuse. The Fourth Amendment, however, imposes one absolute standard on all warrantless searches—they must be *reasonable*. Thus, for example, consent must be truly voluntary, and an item in "plain view" must be immediately apparent as contraband.

In contrast to consent or inventory searches, which do not directly interfere with Fourth Amendment rights, a group of warrantless searches are valid even though they directly interfere with a person's rights under the search and seizure amendment. These warrantless searches impinge on a person's expectation of privacy, but are deemed reasonable because each occurs under emergency conditions. These **exigency exceptions** include (1) home entries under a condition of **hot pursuit**, (2) the "automobile exception," (3) search incident to arrest (see Chapter 4). The Supreme Court has also allowed forcible warrantless searches for evidence in a few miscellaneous cases that Profs. Whitebread and Slobogin have labeled "evanescent evidence." That is, when evidence may be destroyed or may disappear, police can forcibly restrain a suspect and take the evidence, as long as the methods are not brutal.[1] This includes taking blood from a vehicular homicide suspect (*Schmerber v. California*, 1966, see Chapter 3) or scrapings of dried blood from the finger of a homicide suspect (*Cupp v. Murphy*, 1973, see Chapter 4). In addition warrantless entries into premises are allowed for exigencies, as the home entry in *Arizona v. Hicks* (1987) (Chapter 3) and firefighters entering a burning building (this chapter).

For an exigency search to be lawful, an officer must have *probable cause* to believe that contraband is in the place or vehicle being entered, or to arrest the person being searched incident to arrest. These exigency exceptions are compatible with the warrant-preference construction of the Fourth Amendment (see Chapter 2, Structure of the Fourth Amendment section):

Thus the most basic constitutional rule in this area is that "searches conducted outside the judicial process, without prior approval by judge or magistrate, are *per se* unreasonable under the Fourth Amendment—subject only to a few specifically established and well-delineated exceptions." The exceptions are "jealously and carefully drawn," and there must be "a showing by those who seek exemption . . . that the exigencies of the situation made that course imperative." (*Coolidge v. New Hampshire*, pp. 454–55)

The exigency exceptions existed under common law and because of their obvious necessity, do not undermine the warrant requirement. The warrant-preference construction warns against creating new categories of exceptions. Recently, however, the Court has indeed weakened the warrant-preference policy of the Fourth Amendment by extending the scope of **automobile searches** and creating a class of warrantless searches justified by "special needs beyond the normal need for law enforcement." This chapter also reviews other kinds of nonexigency warrantless searches: **inventory searches, administrative searches,** and **border searches.**

To reiterate, the basic rule that justifies all warrantless searches under the Fourth Amendment is *reasonableness*. Beyond this basic requirement, the exigency exceptions require the prior existence of probable cause. Some warrantless searches dispense with probable cause and rely on reasonable suspicion (e.g., *Terry* stops, searches of public school students' bags by teachers). Other warrantless searches require no probable cause or reasonable suspicion (e.g., automobile inventory searches). And still others dispense with particularized suspicion against a specific person (e.g., automobile sobriety checklanes).

HOT PURSUIT AND OTHER EXIGENCY SEARCHES

Hot pursuit occurs when a dangerous criminal suspect is being chased by police and enters a place that is protected by the Fourth Amendment expectation of privacy, such as the suspect's home. The suspect presents a *danger* to society; he may flee or harm someone, or may destroy evidence. Police officers need to enter the premises immediately to make an arrest and search for weapons and contraband. The immediacy of a hot pursuit makes it absurd to "stop the action" to obtain a search warrant to enter. A greater danger to the public and to the police might develop if police cordoned off a house; it gives the suspect an opportunity to destroy evidence and to fortify the residence. As a result, the hot pursuit exception allows the police to enter immediately, without an arrest or search warrant, to make an arrest. If evidence of a crime is observed in *plain view* during the "hot pursuit" entry for purposes of arrest, it may be seized and is admissible in criminal trials.

In *Warden v. Hayden* (1967) cab drivers followed Hayden to a house after he had robbed the taxi company office. They transmitted the information to the taxi dispatcher, who in turn relayed the information to the police. Police officers arrived at Hayden's home "within minutes" of receiving the call, knocked on his door, and entered when the door was opened by his wife. They searched through the house, looking for the suspect, and found incriminating evidence (clothing similar to that worn by the robber). This evidence was admissible only if the initial entry was lawful. The Supreme Court, holding the entry and search constitutional, explained the basis of the hot pursuit exception to the warrant requirement:

> The Fourth Amendment does not require police officers to delay in the course of an investigation if to do so would gravely endanger their lives or the lives of others. Speed here was essential, and only a thorough search of the house for persons and weapons could have ensured that Hayden was the only man present and that the police had control of all weapons which could be used against them or to effect an escape. (*Warden v. Hayden*, pp. 298–99)

Several legal principles of the hot pursuit exception can be derived from this case. First, the hot pursuit warrant exception, as an exigency exception, must be based on *probable cause* to believe that the persons who have just entered the premises have committed a felony or are dangerous to the safety of others. Second, hot pursuit may be based either on the officer's personal observations or on reliable *hearsay*. Third, the pursuit need not be immediate; there may be *a short time lapse* between the suspect's entry into the house and the arrival of the police. The fourth rule concerns the *scope* of the search pursuant to the hot pursuit entry. "The permissible scope of search must, . . . at the least, be as broad as may reasonably be necessary to prevent the dangers that the suspect at large in the house may resist or escape" (*Warden v. Hayden*, p. 299). In other words, until the offender is found, the police may *search the entire premises* for the suspect, weapons, and evidence of the crime. However, once the offender is apprehended, the police may not search beyond the limits of a search incident to an arrest.

Most hot pursuits proceed from public property onto private property. *United States v. Santana* (1976) established a fifth rule: The pursuit may begin on *private* property. Officers had reliable information that the suspect was in possession of marked money from a heroin buy. As the police approached her house, Ms. Santana was standing in the doorway holding a paper bag. She retreated to a vestibule, where the police seized her. In a brief struggle, heroin packets fell from the bag and were lawfully seized by the police. Here, although the pursuit technically began on private property, the Court held that for Fourth Amendment purposes, it was a public place. The *Santana* ruling, however, does not allow the police to enter a house where there is no exigency and thereby "create" one.

The sixth rule, established by **Welsh v. Wisconsin** (1984), concerns the *gravity of the offense*: Police may enter a premises without a warrant in hot pursuit only for *serious crimes*. A minor offense does not create an exigency that overrides the Fourth Amendment rule that police must obtain an arrest warrant in order to arrest a suspect in his or her home (*Payton v. New York*, 1980). The offense in this case was a civil infraction of driving while intoxicated (DWI). Welsh's erratic driving resulted in his car careening off a road and into a ditch on a rainy night. A witness saw the apparently intoxicated driver walk off

into the night and called the police, who arrived at Welsh's nearby home within the hour. They entered the house without a warrant or the consent of Welsh's stepdaughter, found Welsh in bed, arrested him, and took him to the police station, where he refused to submit to a breath analysis test. His refusal could result in a license revocation only if the arrest was legal, and this, in turn, depended on the legality of the forcible, warrantless home entry. The state's only rationale for a constitutional entry was hot pursuit.

The Wisconsin Supreme Court upheld the warrantless entry because of the need to prevent harm to the offender and the public resulting from drunk driving, and to prevent the "destruction" of the blood alcohol evidence by its dissipation before testing could be completed. The United States Supreme Court reversed. It discounted the weak public safety reasoning because the offender was in bed and thus no longer a threat to anyone. Preservation of evidence is a basis of the hot pursuit exigency, but the Court held "that an important factor to be considered when determining whether any exigency exists is the gravity of the underlying offense for which the arrest is being made." Under Wisconsin law, the underlying offense in this case—first offense DWI—was a noncriminal violation subject to a $200 fine. Justice Brennan, writing for the majority, noted that a warrantless entry into a home is *presumptively unreasonable* and the *burden of proof* is on the government to show that an exigency makes a warrantless entry *reasonable*. The Court felt that a hot pursuit entry for a minor crime is presumptively unreasonable and difficult for the government to rebut.

The entry and search in this case violated the Fourth Amendment because: (1) "there was no immediate or continuous pursuit of the petitioner from the scene of a crime;" (2) Welsh had arrived home and abandoned his car, so there was little remaining threat to the public safety; and (3) the exigency of ascertaining Welsh's blood-alcohol level was outweighed by the fact that first-offense DWI was classified as a civil offense. The majority believed that this would be "unreasonable police behavior that the principles of the Fourth Amendment will not sanction."

Justice White's dissent noted that a warrantless entry into a home is as serious a Fourth Amendment intrusion for a person wanted for a serious felony as for a minor crime. He disagreed with the majority's assessment of gravity because of the danger to highway safety by drunk drivers. The warrantless intrusion into Welsh's bedroom promoted the "valid and substantial state interests" of prosecuting drunk driving. He also suggested that police are better served by bright-line rules so that what constitutes a serious offense—justifying hot pursuit—is not open to interpretation. The dissent also urged the Court to defer to the State's judgment as to the seriousness of the offense.

Welsh does not indicate what constitutes a nonserious crime, outside of the civil offense of first-time DWI punishable by a fine. Justice Brennan implied that a simple bright-line division between felonies and misdemeanors is not the proper line between serious and nonserious offenses. Even if the *Welsh* rule does not apply only to civil offenses punishable by a fine, the case itself does not establish the serious-nonserious criterion. Perhaps, then, it is the penalty, such as imprisonment for thirty days or six months. Possibly, hot pursuit is not proper for some nonviolent felonies, but is for some violent misdemeanors. Another uncertainty left by *Welsh* is whether the hot pursuit exception for minor crimes applies in premises other than the home.

The Supreme Court held in **Minnesota v. Olson** (1990) that being wanted for a serious felony does not in itself create an exigency. Police suspected that Olson, a murder suspect, was in a house, and they entered without a warrant. Their attempt to justify the warrantless entry on the basis of hot pursuit was undercut by several factors:

- The suspect was thought to be the driver of a getaway car and not the shooter.
- The police had already recovered the murder weapon.
- There was no suggestion of danger to persons with the suspect.
- The entry occurred a day after the murder-robbery.
- Three or four police squads surrounded the house, which was secured.

Minnesota v. Olson demonstrates that the finding of an exigency is a factual determination made by a court assessing all of the circumstances of the case.

OTHER EXIGENCIES   The hot pursuit warrant exception is an example of a general rule that police may enter a premises or conduct a search without a warrant when exigent circumstances justify the search or intrusion. The exigent circumstance may be an imminent threat to the life or safety of people that no police officer should ignore. In *Arizona v. Hicks* (1987) (see Chapter 4) the officer properly entered an apartment to search for a man who had shot a bullet through the floor into another apartment, injuring a person, and creating an obvious and continuing threat to life and safety. In *Hicks* there was probable cause to believe that a person had committed a felony. There was no hot pursuit as such, but the entry met all the reasonableness criterion of an exigency exception.

Warrantless entry into homes by government agents who are not police officers enforcing the criminal law must also be supported by a real exigency: firefighting is a prime example (*Michigan v. Tyler*, 1978; *Michigan v. Clifford*, 1984). Where probable cause exists to believe a suspect committed a crime and an immediate search is essential to prevent the destruction of evidence of the crime, the search is constitutional if it is reasonable and the intrusion on privacy interests are minimal. An example is *Schmerber v. California* (1966). A driver was arrested at a hospital while being treated for injuries suffered in an accident involving the automobile that he had been driving. The police directed a physician to draw a blood sample, and a blood alcohol test was admitted in evidence to convict Schmerber of driving while intoxicated. The critical evidence would quickly be lost if the blood were not drawn promptly. The Court upheld this warrantless search for blood alcohol, noting that taking blood by medical workers in this case is not

dangerous, is routine, is not very invasive or humiliating, and is likely to produce highly accurate evidence.

Other cases have upheld warrantless searches as reasonable because of the exigency that evidence might be destroyed. In these cases, privacy rights were minimal and the cases did not precisely fit the search incident to arrest warrant exception. *United States v. Edwards* (1974) involved taking potentially incriminating paint chips from the clothing of a police lockup inmate who was ordered to exchange his clothing for jail issue. *Cupp v. Murphy* (1973) (discussed in Chapter 4), upheld the removal of what was apparently dried blood from the finger of a potential murder suspect, who had not been arrested, at a police station.

REJECTING THE HOMICIDE CRIME SCENE INVESTIGATION EXCEPTION   The Supreme Court rejected a **crime scene investigation exception** to the warrant requirement in *Mincey v. Arizona* (1978). A police officer was killed in a drug raid in the Tucson, Arizona, apartment of Rufus Mincey, who was apparently shot by the slain officer. Backup officers entered the apartment, located other persons, called for emergency assistance, and refrained from further investigation. Ten minutes later homicide investigators arrived, arranged for the removal of the fatally injured officer and the suspects, and secured the apartment. They then proceeded to gather evidence.

> Their search lasted four days, during which period the entire apartment was searched, photographed, and diagrammed. The officers opened drawers, closets, and cupboards, and inspected their contents; they emptied clothing pockets; they dug bullet fragments out of the walls and floors; they pulled up sections of the carpet and removed them for examination. Every item in the apartment was closely examined and inventoried, and 200 to 300 objects were seized. In short, Mincey's apartment was subjected to an exhaustive and intrusive search. No warrant was ever obtained. (*Mincey v. Arizona*, 1978, p. 389)

Evidence was obtained and was introduced at trial to convict Mincey of homicide and drug possession. The Arizona Supreme Court upheld the warrantless search as reasonable when conducted to investigate "the scene of a homicide—or of a serious personal injury with likelihood of death where there is reason to suspect foul play" as long as "the purpose [is] limited to determining the circumstances of death and the scope [does] not exceed that purpose. The search must also begin within a reasonable period following the time when the officials first learn of the murder (or potential murder)."

The Supreme Court unanimously reversed, holding that this warrantless search violated the Fourth Amendment. Although Mincey was a suspect, he retained some reasonable expectation of privacy in his home. To strip a suspect of all rights of privacy in the home "would impermissibly convict the suspect even before the evidence against him was gathered." The fact that Mincey was arrested and in custody does not lessen "his right to privacy in his entire house" (*Mincey v. Arizona*, p. 391). An exigency after the violent crime authorized the initial entry into Mincey's apartment, the protective sweep, the securing of the apartment, and the seizure of contraband items in plain view. But "a four-day search that included opening dresser drawers and ripping up carpets can hardly be rationalized in terms of the legitimate concerns that justify an emergency search" (*Mincey v. Arizona*, p. 392). The Court also rejected the idea that special promptness was required to search the scene of a homicide, suggesting that an exception for that crime would lead to a blanket crime scene warrant exception and the argument that dispensing with a warrant would be more efficient. There was no suggestion that a search warrant could not have been easily and conveniently obtained. The Supreme Court later held that a warrantless, thorough, *sixteen-hour* homicide investigation of a cabin violates Fourth Amendment rights under the *Mincey* ruling (*Flippo v. West Virginia*, 1999).

THE AUTOMOBILE EXCEPTION
An Overview of Vehicle Search Rules

The stop and search of a mobile vehicle by police raises a variety of constitutional issues, some of which are discussed in Chapters 3, 4, and 7.

1. *Stopping I:* Probable cause or reasonable suspicion is required to stop a mobile vehicle. (*Delaware v. Prouse*, 1979; Chapter 4).
2. *Stopping II:* Innocent behavior can be the basis for stopping an automobile (*United States v. Arvizu*, 2002; Chapter 4).
3. *Pretext Stops:* An officer may stop a car with objective reasonable suspicion or probable cause of a traffic violation even though the real (subjective) reason for the stop is to search for drugs, and there is no legal basis to stop the car for drugs. (*Whren v. United States*, 1996; Chapter 4).
4. *Stop and Frisk:* An officer may enter an automobile to frisk a suspect or inspect the interior (See *Adams v. Williams*, 1972; *Michigan v. Long*, 1983; Chapter 4).
5. *Control of Driver and Passengers:* An officer may order the driver and passengers to remain in or exit the vehicle (*Pennsylvania v. Mimms*, 1977; *Maryland v. Wilson*, 1997; Chapter 4).
6. *Knowledge and Consent:* An officer need not inform a driver that he or she is free to go before obtaining consent to search a vehicle (*Schneckloth v. Bustamonte*, 1973; *Ohio v. Robinette*, 1996; Chapter 3).
7. *Scope of Consent:* Consent to search a car includes consent to search a container in the car (*Florida v. Jimeno*, 1991; Chapter 4).
8. *Questioning:* An officer need not read *Miranda* warnings for a routine stop or for most aspects of a stop for drunk driving (*Berkemer v. McCarty*, 1984; *Pennsylvania v. Muniz*, 1990; Chapter 7).
9. *Checklanes:* Mobile vehicles may be stopped at checklanes to examine drivers for sobriety or to gather information, but not for illegal drug possession (*Michigan Department of State Police v. Sitz*, 1990; *Illinois v. Lidster*, 2004; *City of Indianapolis v. Edmond*, 2000; Chapter 4).
10. *Automobile Exception: Search of Vehicle:* What is the scope of an officer's authority to search a stopped mobile vehicle without a warrant? (See *United States v. Ross*, 1982; this chapter.)
11. *Automobile Exception: Search of Containers:* What is the scope of an officer's authority to look into or to search closed areas or closed containers in a stopped mobile vehicle without a warrant? (See *California v. Acevedo*, 1991; this chapter.)
12. *Impounded Vehicles:* What rules guide the *inventory search* of impounded vehicles? (See *Florida v. Wells*, 1990; this chapter.)

Clearly, an "automobile search" is a complex legal area. The development of various auto search rules over the past three decades has been one of the most confusing and contentious areas of criminal procedure. Most legal scholars have criticized the Supreme Court automobile search rulings that cut into the Fourth Amendment, accusing the Court of twisting principles to ensure that police officers can search automobiles almost at will. One scholar states: "Although the Court has described warrantless searches as presumptively invalid, more than twenty seemingly haphazard exceptions to the warrant clause in fact have swallowed the warrant requirement."[2] The relentless pressure by police to search cars is driven by the "war on drugs" and by the fact that police departments can augment their budgets by the forfeiture of automobiles found to be transporting illegal drugs.[3] The constitutional debate has recently become an explosive law enforcement and political issue as the practice of racial profiling has been exposed (*Law in Society*, this chapter).

Professor David Steinberg has classified the constitutional law of automobile searches into three broad categories: (1) the automobile, or mobile vehicle, exception to the warrant clause; (2) cases concerning whether a warrant is required before police can open a closed container found in an automobile; and (3) groups of cases in which the police "do not rely on the automobile exception at all." This third category includes search incident to arrest (see *New York v. Belton*, 1981; Chapter 4), inventory search, plain view search (see *Texas v. Brown*, 1983; Chapter 3), consent, and fixed checkpoint searches. The discussion of the "automobile exception," narrowly defined, usually focuses on the first two categories. However, in the "real world" of policing, the totality of rules and exceptions come together to produce a powerful regime of rules that makes it possible for a police officer to search virtually any car that he or she has a mind to stop. Driving is a pervasive activity in America, and it is nearly impossible for anyone to drive without violating some motor vehicle law, including speeding, driving over a line, changing lanes without signaling, inoperative taillight, headlights not on one-half hour after sunset to one-half hour before sunrise "and at such other times as atmospheric conditions render visibility as low as or lower than is ordinarily the case during that period," and an excessively loud muffler.[4] Therefore, a police officer following a vehicle is likely to spot a violation at some point, and upon stopping that car, can utilize one of the various automobile search rules to engage in some level of lawful search. This potential—and reality—of pervasive stopping of black and Hispanic drivers in large numbers on pretextual grounds has led Professor David Harris to claim that, "Indeed, it is no exaggeration to say that in cases involving cars, the Fourth Amendment is all but dead."[5] Professor David Moran indicates that this trend culminated in *United States v. Arvizu* (2002), which found reasonable suspicion based on a family driving in a camper and "scrupulously obeying all traffic laws. . . . The Court's new vehicle doctrine is now complete: The police may lawfully stop any car at any time and virtually always search the car."[6] The following section demonstrates how a major component of the Court's automobile search doctrine was fashioned.

The Automobile Exception

The Supreme Court has upheld warrantless searches of automobiles for two reasons:

> Our first cases establishing the automobile exception to the Fourth Amendment's warrant requirement were based on the automobile's "ready mobility," an exigency sufficient to excuse failure to obtain a search warrant once probable cause to conduct the search is clear. . . . *Carroll v. United States* (1925). More recent cases provide a further justification: the individual's reduced expectation of privacy in an automobile, owing to its pervasive regulation. (*Pennsylvania v. Labron*, 1996)

Early on, the Supreme Court applied the "automobile" exception to a boat, and lower courts have applied the rule to searches of such mobile vehicles as train roomettes, airplanes, ferries, and houseboats (*United States v. Lee*, 1927).[7]

Carroll v. United States (1925) is the foundation case for the automobile exigency exception. Chief Justice William Howard Taft wrote:

> The guaranty of freedom from unreasonable searches and seizures by the Fourth Amendment has been construed, practically since the beginning of the government, as recognizing a difference between a search of a store, dwelling house or other structure in respect of which a proper official search warrant readily may be obtained, and a search of a ship, motor boat, wagon or automobile for contraband goods, where it is not practicable to secure a warrant, because the vehicle can be quickly moved out of the locality or jurisdiction in which the warrant must be sought. (*Carroll v. United States*, p. 153)

The *Carroll* rule requires that (1) police have probable cause to believe the vehicle contains contraband, and (2) there is a "mobility exigency"—the vehicle will be driven off if it is not immediately seized. It is absurd for the police to leave a suspected vehicle to obtain a warrant. In *Carroll* the officers had probable cause to believe that bootleggers were transporting illegally imported liquor in violation of the Prohibition laws when they spotted the "Carroll boys" driving toward Grand Rapids, Michigan. The officers felt the back seat, noticed that it was hard, and proceeded to rip and destroy the seat in order to get to the bottles of whiskey. The Court did not comment on this, indicating that the authority to search for contraband may reasonably include the destruction of some property necessary to get to the evidence.

The second rationale for a warrantless automobile search, a *lesser expectation of privacy* than exists in homes or in luggage, was explained in *California v. Carney:*

> Even in cases where an automobile was not immediately mobile, the lesser expectation of privacy resulting from its use as a readily mobile vehicle justified application of the vehicular exception. In some cases, the configuration of the vehicle contributed to the lower expectation of privacy; for example we held in *Cardwell v. Lewis* (1974) that, because the passenger compartment of a standard automobile is relatively open to plain view, there are lesser expectations of privacy. But even when enclosed "repository" areas have been involved, we have concluded that the lesser expectations of privacy warrant application of the exception. We have applied the exception in the context of a locked car trunk, a sealed package in a car trunk, a closed compartment under the dashboard, the interior of a vehicle's upholstery, or sealed packages inside a covered pickup truck.
>
> These reduced expectations of privacy derive not from the fact that the area to be searched is in plain view, but from the pervasive regulation of vehicles capable of traveling on the public highways (*California v. Carney*, p. 391).

The pervasive regulation includes periodic inspection and licensing requirements, and ticketing for driving with expired license plates or inspection stickers or for such violations as exhaust fumes or excessive noise. Furthermore, all members of the public are fully aware of these regulations and know that they can be stopped while driving for such errors.

The mobility rationale—a traditional, common law, and exigency exception to the warrant requirement—easily fits into the warrant-preference construction of the Fourth Amendment. It is a commonsense explanation for dispensing with a

---

THE AUTOMOBILE WARRANT EXCEPTION IN THE STATES

"A substantial majority of the states have approved the automobile exception as a matter of state constitutional law." Approximately twenty-nine states were identified as having automobile search warrant rules that closely matched the United States Supreme Court's interpretation of the Fourth Amendment in regard to automobile searches.

Nine states were identified as having automobile search rules that, in some respect, tended to favor the individual: Connecticut, Hawaii, Indiana, New Hampshire, New Mexico, Pennsylvania, Utah, Vermont, and Washington.

Barry Latzer, *State Constitutional Criminal Law*, §3:28.

warrant. Professor Steinberg states that the lesser expectation of privacy rationale, however, "makes no sense. Under this line of reasoning, a state could eviscerate Fourth Amendment protections simply by heavy regulation of an activity or location." Also, although houses are "regulated extensively by building codes," police cannot search them without a warrant.[8] It suggests a policy preference on the part of the Supreme Court's majority to simply give police a free hand when searching in and around an automobile. This conclusion is drawn by Professor Harris who believes the Court is motivated by "the desire that the police have wide latitude to investigate and the safety of the officers while they carry out these duties."[9]

THE MOBILITY FACTOR   In **Coolidge v. New Hampshire** (1971) a plurality of the Court ruled that the exception does not apply to *immobilized* vehicles. The defendant was arrested and detained for murder. Two days later, his car was impounded by police and searched pursuant to a search warrant which was later found to be defective. The state argued that the search was nevertheless constitutional under the automobile search exception. The Court rejected this argument, holding that the exception does not apply simply because an automobile was searched:

> The word "automobile" is not a talisman in whose presence the Fourth Amendment fades away and disappears. And surely there is nothing in this case to invoke the meaning and purpose of the rule of *Carroll v. United States*—no alerted criminal bent on flight, no fleeting opportunity on an open highway after a hazardous chase, no contraband or stolen goods or weapons, no confederates waiting to move the evidence, not even the inconvenience of a special police detail to guard the immobilized automobile. In short, by no possible stretch of the legal imagination can this be made into a case where "it is not practicable to secure a warrant," . . . and the "automobile exception," despite its label, is simply irrelevant. (*Coolidge v. New Hampshire*, pp. 461–62)

The Court, unfortunately, has not strictly held to this aspect of *Coolidge*. It has in numerous cases invoked the automobile exception to uphold the search of a *parked* automobile where mobility was not a factor. *Coolidge* appeared to say that the mobility exigency was based on *actual mobility*—the immediate, or almost immediate, possibility that the car would be driven away by the suspect. More recently, the Court has diluted this rationale by leaning toward the *potential mobility* of the vehicle. Thus, in **Pennsylvania v. Labron** (1996) the Court upheld the search of a car belonging to a suspect who had been arrested for a drug transaction. There was no confederate to take the car away and a warrant could have been obtained. The Pennsylvania Supreme Court ruled that a warrant was required. The United States Supreme Court reversed, stating: "If a car is *readily* mobile and probable cause exists to believe it contains contraband, the Fourth Amendment thus permits police to search the vehicle without more" (*Pennsylvania v. Labron*, p. 940, emphasis added). The rights of drivers have also been weakened in cases dealing with the time frame of the exigency, both before and after the search.

TIME FRAME OF THE EXIGENCY   In *Coolidge* the automobile was searched two-and-a-half weeks after the police obtained probable cause, far after the time that any real exigency might have existed. The Court, however, has *expanded* the time frame within which an exigency is said to exist in ways that do not seem reasonable. The foundation for this approach was laid in a Prohibition Era case of the same vintage as *Carroll*—**Husty v. United States** (1927). A reliable informant told a prohibition officer that Husty, a previously convicted bootlegger, had "had two loads of liquor in automobiles of a particular make and description, parked in particular places on named streets." The agent proceeded to the car, although he had sufficient time to obtain a warrant. He saw Husty and two other men get into the car. At that point, the agent approached, and the two other men fled. The car was searched and contraband found. In response to the argument that the agents had sufficient time to obtain a warrant, Justice Harlan Fiske Stone reasoned the agent "could not know when Husty would come to the car or how soon it would be removed. In such circumstances we do not think the officers should be required to speculate upon the chances of successfully carrying out the search, after the delay and withdrawal from the scene of one or more officers which would have been necessary to procure a warrant" (*Husty v. United States*, p. 701). Under these circumstances an actual exigency existed.

Four decades later, the Supreme Court moved the time frame from the actual to the *potential* exigency and beyond. When an automobile is stopped by police with probable cause to believe it contains contraband, the police can search on the spot or perhaps uphold a strict reading of the Fourth Amendment by securing the vehicle until a warrant has been obtained. The Supreme Court properly rejected the argument that a warrant had to be obtained in **Chambers v. Maroney** (1970): "For constitutional purposes, we see no difference between on the one hand seizing and holding a car before presenting the probable cause issue to a magistrate and on the other hand carrying out an immediate search without a warrant. Given probable cause to search, either course is reasonable under the Fourth Amendment." Although the Court has stated a preference for a search warrant, holding a person at roadside until a warrant can be obtained is a severe intrusion of liberty. Justice Harlan, dissenting, preferred the latter course; he thought that the warrantless search was more intrusive because it could lead to a criminal conviction. He believed that a person with nothing to hide would give police consent to search the car. Despite this reasoning, requiring police to obtain a warrant to search a stopped vehicle can create unnecessary risks and burdens on law enforcement.

In *Chambers* the police stopped a car at night because the car and its four passengers fit the description of a car recently involved in a gas station robbery. Under these circumstances, it was neither practical nor safe for the officers to conduct the search on the roadside; consequently, the car was searched at the police station after the suspects were detained. No warrant was obtained to search the car. The Supreme Court held the search to be constitutional as an automobile search. This was

CHAMBERS V. MARONEY IN THE STATES

"In *State v. Miller*, the Connecticut Supreme Court rejected on state constitutional grounds the *Chambers* tow-and-search rule.[10] Miller was taken into custody as he exited an automobile that matched the vehicle described by a witness to a supermarket robbery. After he was transported to the police station, defendant's car was towed to a police department garage, where the police secured it and conducted a warrantless search which revealed a .357 Smith and Wesson revolver in the trunk. Miller was convicted of criminal possession of a weapon.

"The issue . . . was 'whether the state constitution prohibits a warrantless automobile search supported by probable cause but conducted while the automobile is impounded at a police station.' The court first noted a strong state constitutional policy in favor of warrants. . . . It then rejected 'the fiction that the legitimate safety concern that may necessitate towing an automobile from the site of its seizure to the police station also provides justification for the warrantless search of that automobile at the station.' Next, the court rebuffed the state's contention that privacy interests in an automobile are invaded to the same extent by a warrantless search at the scene of its seizure as by a warrantless search at the police station.

> "We tolerate the warrantless-on-the-scene automobile search only because obtaining a warrant would be impracticable in light of the inherent mobility of automobiles and the latent exigency that that mobility creates. . . . If the impracticability of obtaining a warrant no longer exists, however, our state constitutional preference for warrants regains its dominant place in that balance, and a warrant is required."

Barry Latzer, *State Constitutional Criminal Law*, §3:28.

---

a difficult decision because the time of the exigency had ended. Perhaps it was possible for a confederate or a stranger to enter the automobile and destroy evidence, but this reasoning stretches belief. The *Chambers* decision demonstrates that the Court ignored the mobility rationale of *Carroll*, even before establishing the lesser expectation of privacy rationale for automobile searches. In more recent years, as a practical matter, the *ad hoc* custody of the automobile practiced in *Chambers* has been replaced by more routine police practices of impounding all seized vehicles and subjecting them to a detailed inventory search.

Chambers may be explained in part by the Court's desire to protect police officers' safety (discussed later in this chapter). This made it reasonable for the officer to take the car to the station house instead of searching it on the road at night; there was a real exigency when the car was *first* seized. But in **Texas v. White** (1975) the Court allowed the search of a vehicle at the station house, although there was, at best, a potential exigency when the car was seized. White was arrested at 1:30 P.M. while attempting to pass fraudulent checks at a drive-in window of a bank, after police had a report of a similar incident at another bank earlier that day by a person matching White's description. He was ordered to park his car and was observed by a bank employee and an officer attempting to stuff something between the seats. White was driven to the station house while another officer drove his car there. After thirty to forty-five minutes of questioning, White refused to consent to a search of his car, but the officers proceeded to search it anyway. During the search, four wrinkled checks corresponding to those White had attempted to pass at the first bank were discovered. The Court, in a brief *per curiam* opinion, upheld the search on this reading of *Chambers:* "police officers with probable cause to search an automobile on the scene where it was stopped could constitutionally do so later at the station house without first obtaining a warrant." Justice Thurgood Marshall, joined by Justice Brennan, dissented. He took the majority to task for misreading the holding of *Chambers*. The facts in *Chambers* included a nighttime stop of a car with four suspected armed robbers, a clearly perilous scenario. "*Chambers* simply held [the station house search] to be the rule when it is *reasonable* to take the car to the station house in the first place" (*Texas v. White*, p. 69, emphasis added). By ignoring these facts, the Court created a *per se* rule that allows a car seized with probable cause to be searched, even if the car's mobility was at an end.

The decisions in *Chambers* and *Texas v. White* stretch the time frame of an "exigency" to mythic proportions. A commonsense understanding of an exigency indicates that no true exigency was present when the police searched the cars in these two cases. It is useful to note that these cases occurred prior to the Supreme Court validating the routine inventory search (discussed below). A routine inventory search is not an exigency search and serves other constitutional interests than those of a probable cause search. Nevertheless, as a functional matter, if not as a matter of constitutional law, routine inventory searches in effect allow the seizure of all contraband found in a car that is searched well after an arrested person has been taken into custody. In any event, the creation of the lesser expectation of privacy rationale and the "stretching" of the time frame for an exigency were vital elements in the Court's expansion of the power of police to search cars. The next step was the Court's willingness to authorize warrantless automobile searches of parked cars.

WHAT IS AN AUTOMOBILE? *California v. Carney* (1985) gave a precise definition of an "automobile" for Fourth Amendment purposes. Carney lived in a fully mobile motor home. Police, suspicious that he was trading drugs for sex, had his motor home under surveillance while it was parked in a downtown San Diego public parking lot not far from the courthouse. They observed a youth enter the vehicle and stay there for an hour and a quarter. The youth emerged, was stopped by the police, and he told them that he received marijuana in return for allowing Carney sexual contact. The police and the youth went to the motor home, knocked, and after Carney stepped out, entered it without a warrant and seized illegal drugs.

Carney argued that because this vehicle was also his home, it had to be given the same Fourth Amendment protection as a stationary home, that is, the police could not search it without obtaining a warrant. The Supreme Court disagreed, holding that such a van is a mobile vehicle, subject to similar licensing and regulation requirements as an automobile; therefore, the reasonable (i.e., objective) expectation of privacy in a van is equivalent to what one expects in an automobile, not a home. These factors brought the van under the exigency exception to the warrant requirement: "Our application of the vehicle exception has never turned on the other uses to which a vehicle might be put."

Justice Stevens dissented in *Carney* on the grounds that there was no exigency. He urged the Court to rule that the automobile exception should not apply to a *parked vehicle where there is time to obtain a warrant*, but only to vehicles in motion along the highway. The majority refused to adopt this restriction. However, in *Coolidge v. New Hampshire* (1971) there was time to obtain a warrant and the search was held to violate the Fourth Amendment. The Court in *Carney* distinguished *Coolidge* on its facts. The seizure in *Coolidge* was preceded by a two-week investigation and the vehicle was in full police control, while in *Carney* the surveillance of the van lasted for a little over an hour. The police had ample time to plan their action in *Coolidge,* while the police in *Carney* acted with less preparation or planning, although they apparently had the ability to obtain a warrant. In *Coolidge* the car was taken to the police station, while in *Carney* the mobile home was in a public parking lot. In *Coolidge* neither the defendant nor anyone associated with him had access to the car, while *Carney* was in his vehicle and could have driven it away if he were not arrested. The Court stated in *Carney,* "[T]he respondent's motor home was readily mobile. Absent the prompt search and seizure, it could readily have been moved beyond the reach of the police."

The Supreme Court is clearly reluctant to add any qualification or addition to the automobile exigency rule that benefits defendants. In **Maryland v. Dyson** (1999) police had advance warning, amounting to probable cause, that a specific vehicle would come into the jurisdiction with illegal drugs. An intermediate Maryland appellate court ruled that because the police had time to obtain a warrant, there was no exigency and a search warrant was required. The Court, in a *per curiam* opinion, reversed. "[U]nder our established precedent, the 'automobile exception' has no separate exigency requirement." Nevertheless, the *Dyson* decision does not seem consistent with the principle, if not the precise facts, of *Coolidge v. New Hampshire* (1971).

THE VIN RULE   The Supreme Court demonstrated its creativity in upholding the legality of a warrantless police entry into a vehicle in **New York v. Class** (1986) by fabricating a limited right of intrusion into a car without probable cause in order to view a vehicle identification number (VIN) not viewable from outside the car. Police stopped a car for speeding. The driver produced a registration certificate and proof of insurance but no driver's license. The officer could not see the VIN on the dashboard so he "reached into the interior of the car to move some papers obscuring the area of the dashboard where the VIN is located in all post-1969 models. In doing so, the officer saw the handle of a gun, and respondent was promptly arrested." As a valid VIN entry, the gun was in plain view and thus admissible. The Court reasoned that the VIN is needed to protect safety and property and is required by federal regulations to be in a place that can be easily read by someone standing outside the automobile. Combining the special requirements of the VIN with the lesser expectation of privacy in an automobile, the Court felt justified in creating a warrant exception authorizing such an entry without probable cause to believe there was contraband in the car. *Class* created a limited police power, because police cannot enter a vehicle if the VIN is observable from the car's exterior, and newer model cars are designed to make it impossible to cover the VIN. The case illustrates the Court's creativity in engineering a rule in a particular situation that favors the police.

SEIZURE OF A CAR SUBJECT TO FORFEITURE   In **Florida v. White** (1999) officers observed Tyvessel Tyvorus White make cocaine deliveries in his car in July and August 1993 but did not arrest him. Under the Florida Contraband Forfeiture Act, his car was subject to forfeiture. Several months later, White was arrested at his workplace on charges unrelated to the cocaine delivery. Police officers went to the employer's parking lot where White's car was parked and seized it without a warrant. A subsequent inventory search disclosed cocaine. The Florida Supreme Court ruled the warrantless seizure unconstitutional. The United States Supreme Court reversed and offered two reasons for upholding the warrantless seizure. First, although the police had no probable cause to believe the car contained contraband, "they certainly had probable cause to believe that the vehicle *itself* was contraband under Florida law," and the mobility rationale applies to the warrantless seizure of contraband in a mobile vehicle and the mobile vehicle itself. Second, "our Fourth Amendment jurisprudence has consistently accorded law enforcement officials greater latitude in exercising their duties in public places." The Court treated the owner's private property as a public place for Fourth Amendment purposes and concluded that "the Fourth Amendment did not require a warrant to seize respondent's automobile . . ." (*Florida v. White*, pp. 565–66).

Justice Stevens dissented in *White,* joined by Justice Ginsburg. Under *Soldal v. Cook County* (1992), the Fourth Amendment protects property as well as privacy interests. There was no exigency here. White had been arrested and there was sufficient time to obtain a search warrant. The car is not inherent contraband, such as drugs or firearms, so its seizure is not required to preserve public safety. A "warrant application interjects the judgment of a neutral decisionmaker, one with no pecuniary interest in the matter." Justice Stevens found it "particularly troubling . . . not that the State provides a weak excuse for failing to obtain a warrant either before or after White's arrest, but that it offers us no reason at all" and concluded that "the officers who seized White's car simply preferred to avoid the hassle of seeking approval from a judicial officer." The simple convenience of officers was thought too feeble a reason to override Fourth Amendment rights. Although the majority paid lip service to the warrant requirement, "its decision suggests that the exceptions have all but swallowed the general rule."

Searches of Containers in Mobile Vehicles

In the 1970s and 1980s, the most hotly contested issue in automobile search cases was the *scope* of a search of closed areas and containers found in mobile vehicles. The "container" cases demonstrate that visions of constitutional interpretation are shaped by judges' ideologies. On the one side stood liberal-moderate justices Brennan, Marshall, and Stevens. They urged the Court to require warrants to search mobile containers that had been secured by police. This position supported the warrant-preference construction of the Fourth Amendment and reflected the Due Process Model of criminal justice. On the other side stood a growing conservative majority on the Court. They found the Crime Control Model of criminal justice more congenial. Despite some doctrinal difficulties, they ultimately ruled that under the general-reasonableness construction of the Fourth Amendment, warrants are *not* needed to open closed areas and containers in automobiles if there is probable cause to believe that the containers contain contraband.

SEARCH OF CONTAINERS NOT IN AUTOMOBILES In *Carroll v. United States* (1925) the Supreme Court held that when the automobile exception comes into play, officers could search *any part of the car in which the contraband could reasonably be found*. The officer's determination of what to search was coextensive with that of a magistrate. In *Carroll* an agent determined that the backseat of the roadster was hard and began to tear up the seat cushion. Thus, the *destruction* of parts of the car within which contraband was stored was allowed, if reasonably necessary to find the contraband.

In contrast to this aspect of the *Carroll* case, **United States v. Chadwick** (1977) held that a person's "effects" are given full constitutional protection. A container, out of the context of the automobile exception, cannot lawfully be opened by an officer unless the officer has a warrant, even if the officer has probable cause to believe that the container contains contraband. *Chadwick* involved a *controlled delivery* of the kind upheld in *United States v. Van Leeuwen* (1970), where police temporarily seized a suspicious package without a warrant in order to give them time to continue investigating, to corroborate their suspicion and to obtain a warrant to search the package. In

Chadwick Amtrak officials in San Diego became suspicious when two persons, one of whom fit the profile of a drug trafficker, loaded a footlocker that was unusually heavy for its size and leaking talcum powder (used to mask the odor of marijuana) on a Boston-bound train. Federal narcotics agents in Boston were on hand two days later when the footlocker arrived. They had no arrest or search warrant, but a trained dog signaled the presence of a controlled substance inside the trunk. Three persons took possession of the footlocker and loaded it into the trunk of a car. At that moment, the agents arrested the three men and seized the footlocker, which was taken to the federal building. An hour and a half later, the agents obtained the key to the footlocker, opened it, and found large amounts of marijuana.

The Supreme Court, in a 7–2 opinion authored by Chief Justice Burger, held that this warrantless search violated the Fourth Amendment. Although the agents had probable cause to believe that the footlocker contained illicit drugs, it was protected by the warrant clause, which "makes a significant contribution to [the] protection" against unreasonable searches and seizures. As early as 1878, the Supreme Court had said that "[l]etters and sealed packages . . . are as fully guarded from examination and inspection, except as to their outward form and weight, as if they were retained by the parties forwarding them in their own domiciles" (*Ex Parte Jackson*, 1878). Important privacy interests are at stake when a person sends a locked trunk to another place, both subjective and reasonable (socially objective). There is a constitutional expectation of privacy in such a container. The Court ruled brief contact of the footlocker with a car did not turn this into an automobile search case. The Court also found that under the facts of the case, a warrantless search of the footlocker could not be justified as a search incident to arrest. The *Chadwick* Court distinguished a footlocker (an "effect") from an automobile. Although a footlocker is mobile, it is afforded *greater* Fourth Amendment protection because it is not subjected to the pervasive government regulation of an automobile. Furthermore, once the footlocker's general mobility was ended and it was secured in the Boston federal building under the exclusive control of the police, there was no exigency that required an on-the-spot search without a warrant. "With the footlocker safely immobilized, it was unreasonable to undertake the additional and greater intrusion of a search without a warrant" (*United States v. Chadwick*, 1977).

THE SEARCH OF MOBILE CONTAINERS IN AUTOMOBILES If *Chadwick* is to be logically followed, when police search an automobile under the automobile exigency exception, and they discover a container that does not immediately indicate that it holds contraband (the hardness of the back seat of the roadster in *Carroll* indicated bottles of whiskey), they should seize the container and apply to a magistrate for a search warrant. The court followed this mode of analysis in **Arkansas v. Sanders** (1979). The police had probable cause, supplied by a reliable informant's tip, that Sanders would arrive at an airport with drugs. They followed Sanders, who carried a suitcase and entered a taxi cab. The police followed the cab for several blocks and pulled it over. Without asking permission, they took the suitcase from the cab, opened it, and found over nine pounds of marijuana. The Supreme Court held that although the police had probable cause to believe the suitcase contained drugs, and although they were justified in stopping the taxi and *seizing* the suitcase, the suitcase could not be *opened and searched* without a search warrant because the mobility exigency regarding the suitcase had ended. The *Sanders* decision was a straightforward application of Chadwick:

> [W]e hold that the warrant requirement of the Fourth Amendment applies to personal luggage taken from an automobile to the same degree it applies to such luggage in other locations. Thus, insofar as the police are entitled to search such luggage without a warrant, their actions must be justified under some exception to the warrant requirement other than that applicable to automobiles stopped on the highway. (*Arkansas v. Sanders*, p. 766)

The *Sanders* rule, however, proved to be unstable and short-lived. The five justices in the majority included liberal and moderate justices (Justice Powell authored the opinion, joined by Brennan, Stewart, White, and Marshall). Justices Blackmun and Rehnquist dissented on the grounds that *Chadwick* was not correctly decided, and even if it were, a container that police had probable cause to believe held contraband in a mobile vehicle should be subject to the rules of *Carroll* (1925) and *Chambers v. Maroney* (1970); i.e., the police should be able to open it on the spot without a warrant. The dissent stressed the "untoward costs on the criminal justice system of this country in terms of added delay and uncertainty" caused by the *Chadwick-Sanders* rule. Quite significantly, two concurring justices (Chief Justice Burger and Justice Stevens) argued that the situation in *Sanders* was *not* an automobile exigency search, thus clouding an understanding of the scope of a search of containers found in a mobile vehicle.

Sanders was followed by ***New York v. Belton*** (1981), which held that a police officer who had probable cause to *arrest* a suspect after stopping his automobile acquired the right to search the interior compartment of the automobile (see Chapter 4). In *Belton* a New York State Trooper stopped a speeding car on the New York Thruway, ordered the driver and three passengers out, found that none had a vehicle registration, and smelled marijuana in the vehicle. He arrested all four occupants, secured them with handcuffs, searched them individually, and returned to the car to pick up an envelope marked "Supergold." He unzipped a pocket of a black leather jacket which was laying on the back seat of the car and found that it contained cocaine. The admissibility of the cocaine into evidence was contested. The Supreme Court held that "when a policeman has made a lawful custodial arrest of the occupant of an automobile, he may, as a contemporaneous incident of that arrest, search the *passenger compartment* of that automobile." And, as an extension of that rule, the Court stated that "the police may also examine the *contents of any containers* found within

the passenger compartment, for if the passenger compartment is within reach of the arrestee, so also will containers be within his reach" (emphasis added). This language was inconsistent with the *Chadwick-Sanders* rule.

The apparent inconsistency between *Belton* and *Chadwick-Sanders* can be explained by *Belton*'s specific facts, and the *search incident to arrest* rationale for the search. One police officer arresting four men at the side of a limited-access highway could reasonably be in danger that one of them would run to the car to seize a weapon or evidence in the passenger compartment. This is factually distinguishable from several officers arresting individuals in possession of a locked footlocker, where there is no ready chance that they could overwhelm the officers and flee. The Supreme Court, however, preferred not to establish a rule that tracked the precise extent of the exigency, but rather established a "*bright-line*" rule to give better guidance to police officers in fast-moving street situations. As a result, *Belton* proved to be a confusing precedent, because its absolute language in support of a container search in a car was undercut by its facts. While it did not clarify the authority of officers to search closed containers in a motor vehicle, it seemed to be at odds with *Chadwick-Sanders*.

The issue was further confused by the Court's fractured decision in ***Robbins v. California*** (1981). Police stopped a station wagon traveling erratically. An officer smelled marijuana smoke when Robbins emerged, searched him and found a vial of liquid. The officer then searched the interior of the car and found marijuana. Police officers then opened the tailgate of the station wagon and raised the cover of a recessed luggage compartment, in which they found two packages wrapped in green opaque plastic. The police unwrapped the packages and discovered a large amount of marijuana in each. The issue was whether the opening of the two packages violated the Fourth Amendment. The Supreme Court, in a *plurality opinion* by Justice Stewart, held this an unreasonable search and seizure on the authority of *Chadwick* and *Sanders*: (1) the outward appearance of the package did not undermine Robbins' expectation of privacy, and (2) there was no constitutional difference between a footlocker (a "worthy" container) and a plastic bag or package (an "unworthy" container). Concurring Justices Powell and Chief Justice Burger, however, expressed reservations about the decision and suggested a line of reasoning that would soon undermine the *Chadwick-Sanders* rule, namely that "when the police have probable cause to search an automobile, rather than only to search a particular container that fortuitously is located in it, the exigencies that allow the police to search the entire automobile without a warrant support the warrantless search of every container found therein."

BRIGHT-LINE RULES FOR THE SCOPE OF AUTOMOBILE EXCEPTION SEARCHES   The reasoning of *Robbins* undermined its strength as a precedent. In the following year, Justice Stewart retired and was replaced by the more conservative Justice O'Connor. This allowed reconsideration of the doubts raised in *Robbins*. Indeed, the Court overturned *Robbins* the next year in **United States v. Ross** (1982). In *Ross* and *California v. Acevedo* (1991), a conservative tide on the Court swept away the *Chadwick-Sanders* rule in two waves, finally establishing the bright-line rule that allowed police to search automobiles and *any* closed compartments or containers in them without a search warrant whenever probable cause existed to believe that contraband was in the car generally *or* in a specific container. Their rules are simple. *Ross* holds that when police have probable cause to believe that contraband is located somewhere in an automobile, they may, under the automobile exception, open any closed container in the car that may logically hold the contraband; this overrules *Robbins*. *Acevedo* holds that when an officer has probable cause to believe that a *specific container* located in a car contains contraband, the officer may, upon lawfully stopping the car and gaining access to its interior, open the container. This overrules *Sanders* but not *Chadwick*, because *Chadwick* was not treated as an automobile exception case.

The facts in *Ross* were that a known reliable informant telephoned a police detective and told him that an individual known as "Bandit" was selling narcotics kept in the trunk of a "purplish maroon" Chevrolet Malibu parked at a specific street location. The informant had just observed "Bandit" complete a sale, and said that "Bandit" told him that additional narcotics were in the trunk. A police car drove to the street address, saw a maroon Malibu parked there. The officers completed a computer check and discovered that the car was registered to Albert Ross, who fit the informant's description and who used the alias "Bandit." The officers drove through the neighborhood twice but did not observe anyone matching Ross's description. They returned five minutes later and saw the maroon Malibu being driven off by a man matching the description. The officers stopped the car and ordered Ross out of the car. Officers observed a bullet on the front seat, so they searched the interior of the car and found a pistol in the glove compartment, whereupon they arrested and handcuffed Ross. A detective took Ross's keys, opened the trunk, and found a closed brown paper bag. When opened, the bag was found to contain a number of glassine bags containing a white powder that was later determined to be heroin. At the station house, the car trunk was searched without a warrant and a zippered red leather pouch found and opened. It contained thirty-two hundred dollars in cash. Did the officers have constitutional authority to open the bags in the trunk of Ross's automobile?

Ross squarely presented the issue of the *scope* of an automobile search wherein police had probable cause to believe that contraband was located *somewhere in the car or the trunk*, but not in a specific bag or container. On the one hand, the *Carroll* case allowed police, without a warrant, to rip open the upholstery of a car stopped at the side of the road to get at the contraband. On the other hand, *Chadwick* ruled that the container can be seized and held (but not opened) until a search warrant was obtained. The Court opted for the *Carroll*

approach. The details of *Ross* were not the same as the facts of *Sanders*, where police had probable cause to believe that there was contraband in a specific container located in a moving car, but no probable cause to believe that there was contraband elsewhere in the car. For the time being, *Chadwick* controlled *Sanders*-type situations.

The Court advanced several reasons for its decision. It noted that from the *Carroll* case in 1925 up to *Chadwick* (1977), decisions of lower courts and the Supreme Court never questioned the right of police to open bags of suspected contraband found in lawfully stopped cars. The practical benefits of the *Carroll* rule would be largely nullified by not allowing police to open closed containers reasonably suspected of housing contraband because illegal materials are usually secured to be kept out of sight. Also, *Carroll* did not increase the scope of a lawful search, but instead "merely relaxed the requirements for a warrant on grounds of practicability" (*Henry v. United States*, 1959, p. 104). Thus, a search warrant allowing a search for contraband implies that officers may open containers in the premises that could logically hold the kind of contraband sought.

> When a legitimate search is under way, and when its purpose and its limits have been precisely defined, nice distinctions between closets, drawers, and containers, in the case of a home, or between glove compartments, upholstered seats, trunks, and wrapped packages, in the case of a vehicle, must give way to the interest in the prompt and efficient completion of the task at hand. (*United States v. Ross*, p. 821)

This rule applies to all containers; the Court upheld the concept of *Robbins* that a constitutional distinction between "worthy" and "unworthy" containers was improper, as long as the container shielded its contents from plain view. Finally, because a search under the automobile exception was as valid as a search incident to arrest or a search under a warrant, the suspect loses the expectation of privacy to the same extent as in these cases, which allow the opening of "some containers." In conclusion, the "scope of a warrantless search of an automobile . . . is not defined by the nature of the container in which the contraband is secreted [but] by the object of the search and the places in which there is probable cause to believe that it may be found" (*United States v. Ross*, p. 824). Significantly, the majority rejected the holding of *Robbins*, but upheld the specific holding in *Sanders*, although it rejected some of its reasoning, thus requiring police to seize but not search containers where police had probable cause to believe that the specific container contained contraband.

Justice Marshall dissented, joined by Justices Brennan and White, harshly accusing the Court of "repeal[ing] the Fourth Amendment warrant requirement itself" and "utterly disregard[ing] the value of a neutral and detached magistrate." He reiterated the value of a search warrant and the positive effect of the warrant process on officers who had to write affidavits to justify searches. He noted that in many automobile warrant exception cases there was an *actual exigency* that justified police searching without a warrant. To the contrary, however, Fourth Amendment principles are undermined when the automobile exigency exception is applied to *every* search of an automobile, even when the suspect is arrested and there is no likelihood that another person will get to the car. Ignoring this difference is a sleight-of-hand move on the part of the majority. A decision based on Fourth Amendment principles must apply the *Chadwick* rule to a search of an automobile when the exigency is over. Finally, the majority's ruling in *Ross* is inconsistent with the rule of *Sanders*. Prophetically, Justice Marshall stated that "This case will have profound implications for the privacy of citizens traveling in automobiles."

A decade later, the Court dropped the other shoe and, in ***California v. Acevedo*** (1991), overruled *Arkansas v. Sanders* (1979). Between 1982 and 1991, the composition of the Court had become considerably more conservative, with Justice Rehnquist becoming Chief Justice upon the retirement of Chief Justice Burger; the addition of Justices Scalia, Kennedy, and Souter to the Court; and the retirement of Justices Powell and Brennan. Justice Blackmun, who had dissented in *Sanders*, now had the opportunity to bury that decision in his majority opinion, and was joined by Chief Justice Rehnquist, and Justices O'Connor, Kennedy, and Souter. Justice Scalia concurred with the majority. Justices White, Stevens, and Marshall dissented.

In *Acevedo* marijuana lawfully seized by the DEA in Hawaii was shipped to Officer Coleman of the Santa Ana, California, Police Department. He set up a controlled delivery to one Jamie Daza, who picked up the package from a Federal Express office at 10:30 A.M. Daza, package in hand, was followed to his apartment. At 11:45 A.M., Daza left the apartment and dropped the marijuana container's wrapping into a trash bin. Officer Coleman left the scene to get a search warrant. At 12:30 P.M. respondent Charles Steven Acevedo arrived. He entered Daza's apartment, stayed for about ten minutes, and emerged carrying a brown paper bag that appeared full. Other officers observing the scene noticed that the bag was the size of one of the wrapped marijuana packages sent from Hawaii. Acevedo walked to a silver Honda in the parking lot, placed the bag in the trunk of the car, and started to drive away. Fearing the loss of evidence, officers in a marked police car stopped him. They opened the trunk and the bag, and found marijuana. The California Court of Appeals suppressed the marijuana on the basis of *Chadwick* (instead of *Ross*) because the officers had probable cause to believe that the *paper bag* contained drugs but lacked probable cause to suspect that Acevedo's *car* itself otherwise contained contraband.

The reasons given for allowing a warrantless search of a closed container in an operative vehicle, which had become immobilized and the driver taken into custody, began with an observation on *Ross*: Where police have probable cause to believe that contraband is located in a car but have not pinpointed a specific container, "the time and expense of the warrant process would be misdirected if the police could

search every cubic inch of an automobile until they discovered a paper sack, at which point the Fourth Amendment required them to take the sack to a magistrate for permission to look inside." The majority forthrightly noted:

> that a container found after a general search of the automobile and a container found in a car after a limited search for the container are equally easy for the police to store and for the suspect to hide or destroy. In fact, we see no principled distinction in terms of either the privacy expectation or the exigent circumstances between the paper bag found by the police in *Ross* and the paper bag found by the police here. Furthermore, by attempting to distinguish between a container for which the police are specifically searching and a container which they come across in a car, we have provided only minimal protection for privacy and have impeded effective law enforcement. (*California v. Acevedo*, p. 574)

Put this way, it seems clear that the fine line between *Chadwick-Sanders* (specific probable cause) cases and *Carroll-Ross* (general probable cause) cases is a thin one—that it would be better for the cases to be decided consistently—either all containers can be opened by the police or all containers should be held until a magistrate has ruled on the police officer's assessment of probable cause.

Which way was best? The path chosen by the majority was based, first, on its stated assumption that the *Ross* rule provided "minimal protection for privacy" because in the *Chadwick-Sanders* situation the suspicious package is seized and held for a warrant in any event. Next, the Court noted that the clear theoretical distinction is not always clear to a police officer in the field searching a car. If some doubt exists about *locus* of probable cause in an automobile search case, a defendant would inevitably argue that the probable cause applied to the container and not the entire vehicle, to get the protection of *Chadwick-Sanders,* causing unneeded litigation. Also, police might try to circumvent the *Chadwick-Sanders* rule by needlessly searching an entire car to make it seem as if the *Ross* rule operates when they really had probable cause to believe that the contraband is located in a specific container. Further, the opening of a container is less physically intrusive than a full search of an automobile: "If destroying the interior of an automobile is not unreasonable, we cannot conclude that looking inside a closed container is." Justice Blackmun's majority opinion argued that the dichotomy between the two automobile search rules has created confusion in the lower courts and impeded effective law enforcement. "The *Chadwick-Sanders* rule is the antithesis of a 'clear and unequivocal' guideline." The Supreme Court thus overruled *Arkansas v. Sanders* (1979) and stated that it had returned all automobile search cases to the basic rule of *Carroll.*

Justice Stevens's dissent was unusually blunt in specifically referred to the Court relying "on arguments that *conservative judges* have repeatedly rejected in past cases" (emphasis added). Justices are aware of their and their colleagues' ideological leanings, but rarely state this so forthrightly in an opinion. Because a dissent is the justice's personal statement, it is often more freewheeling or idiosyncratic than a majority opinion, which reflects the judgment of each justice who joins the opinion. By stating that conservative justices in the past supported the *Sanders* rule, Justice Stevens suggested that the *Acevedo* majority are extremists. His opinion began with an exposition on constitutional policy favoring the use of warrants and reminding that "[t]he Fourth Amendment is a restraint on Executive power." The burdens of obtaining warrants "are outweighed by the individual interest in privacy that is protected by advance judicial approval." He then argued that *Ross* and *Chadwick-Sanders* were not inconsistent; *Ross* applied to the scope of an *automobile* search, whereas *Sanders* applied to the search of *all closed containers*, whether found in automobiles or not. He also noted, as did Justice Marshall, dissenting in *Ross*, that the *Chadwick-Sanders* rule allows for exigency exceptions.

Justice Stevens challenged three specific points made in Justice Blackmun's majority opinion. First, the majority claimed that the existence of the *Chadwick-Sanders* rule and the *Ross* rule was confusing and anomalous. Justice Stevens recited cases that seemed to have no difficulty in distinguishing between the two, and so disagreed as to the confusion. If there was an anomaly in the law, it was created by the majority, "For, surely it is anomalous to prohibit a search of a briefcase while the owner is carrying it exposed on a public street yet to permit a search once the owner has placed the briefcase in the locked trunk of his car" (*California v. Acevedo*, p. 598). Justice Stevens thought that making the automobile search rules the same by *eliminating* the warrant requirement in both was the worse solution because the person had the same expectation of privacy in the container, whether found in or out of a car.

Second, he disagreed that the *Chadwick-Sanders* rule does not protect any significant interest in privacy. "Every citizen clearly has an interest in the privacy of the contents of his or her luggage, briefcase, handbag or any other container that conceals private papers and effects from public scrutiny. . . .

Under the Court's holding today, the privacy interest that protects the contents of a suitcase or a briefcase from a warrantless search when it is in public view simply vanishes when its owner climbs into a taxicab. Unquestionably the rejection of the *Sanders* line of cases by today's decision will result in a significant loss of individual privacy."

The majority's third argument was that the older rules impede effective law enforcement. Justice Stevens noted that the Court cited no authority for this contention. Even if true, it was "in any event, an insufficient reason for creating a new exception to the warrant requirement." This last point, of course, is an expected statement for one who leans toward the Due Process Approach; a proponent of the Crime Control Model of criminal justice would disagree.

Ross and *Acevedo* are significant cases because, by creating bright-line rules, they resolved the tangled legal threads on the scope of automobile and sealed container searches. To the dissenting justices, these cases seriously undermine Fourth Amendment rights and give the police carte blanche to search cars. Each majority opinion, however, mandates that there must be a clear connection between probable cause and the scope of a search. Doctrinally, *Ross* and *Acevedo* do not grant police unbridled searching power; for example, police cannot search the locked trunk of a car if its driver is arrested for driving under the influence of alcohol or a controlled substance. However, the real fear is that lenient rules will be applied by the police as license to use their discretion to search, guided only by their common sense and innate sense of decency, and that when police step over the legal line, lower court judges will excuse such behavior. Indeed, as suggested at the beginning of this section, it appears that the totality of automobile search rules provides very little restraint on auto searches.

The *Ross* rule was extended to *automobile passengers* in *Wyoming v. Houghton*.

— *Wyoming v. Houghton* **Case & Comments** —

• CASE & COMMENTS •

Wyoming v. Houghton
526 U.S. 295, 119 S.Ct. 1297, 143 L. Ed. 2d 408 (1999)

JUSTICE SCALIA delivered the opinion of the Court.

This case presents the question whether police officers violate the Fourth Amendment when they search a passenger's personal belongings inside an automobile that they have probable cause to believe contains contraband.

In the early morning hours * * * a Wyoming Highway Patrol officer stopped an automobile for speeding and driving with a faulty brake light. There were three passengers in the front seat of the car: David Young (the driver), his girlfriend, and respondent. While questioning Young, the officer noticed a hypodermic syringe in Young's shirt pocket. He left the occupants under the supervision of two backup officers as he went to get gloves from his patrol car. Upon his return, he instructed Young to step out of the car and place the syringe on the hood. The officer then asked Young why he had a syringe; with refreshing candor, Young replied that he used it to take drugs. **[a]**

[The two female passengers were ordered out of the car. Asked for identification, Houghton falsely identified herself as "Sandra James." In light of Young's admission, the officer searched the passenger compartment of the car for contraband, and found a purse on the backseat, which Houghton claimed as hers. He removed her wallet containing her driver's license. When the officer asked her why she had lied about her name, she replied: "In case things went bad." The officer then removed a brown pouch and a black wallet-type container. Houghton denied that the pouch was hers, and claimed ignorance of how it came to be there. It contained drug paraphernalia and a syringe with 60 ccs of methamphetamine. The officer also found fresh needle-track marks on Houghton's arms. He placed her under arrest. The trial court denied Houghton's motion to suppress evidence obtained from the purse as the fruit of a Fourth Amendment violation. She was convicted of felony possession of methamphetamine. The trial court held that the officer had probable cause to search the car for contraband, and, by extension, any containers therein that could hold such contraband.

The Wyoming Supreme Court, reversing the conviction, ruled that where an officer has probable cause to believe that contraband is somewhere in a lawfully stopped car, the officer may search all containers in the car *except* containers that the officer knows or should know are personal effects of a passenger who is not suspected of criminal activity, "*unless* someone had the opportunity to conceal the contraband within the personal effect to avoid detection."]

II.

* * *

* * * [I]n the present case [] the police officers had probable cause to believe there were illegal drugs in the car. **[b]** *Carroll v. United States* (1925) * * * held that "contraband goods concealed and illegally transported in an automobile or other vehicle may be searched for without a warrant" where probable cause exists.

We have furthermore read the historical evidence to show that the Framers would have regarded as reasonable (if there was probable cause) the warrantless search of containers *within* an automobile. **[c]** In *Ross* we upheld as reasonable the warrantless search of a paper bag and leather pouch found in the trunk of the defendant's car by officers who had probable cause to believe that the trunk contained drugs. * * *

Ross summarized its holding as follows: "If probable cause justifies the search of a lawfully stopped vehicle, it justifies the search of *every part of the vehicle and its contents* that may conceal the object of the search." (emphasis added). **[d]** And our later cases describing *Ross* have characterized it as applying broadly to *all* containers within a car, without qualification as to ownership.* * *

* * *

In sum, neither *Ross* itself nor the historical evidence it relied upon admits of a distinction among packages or containers based on ownership. When there is probable cause to search for contraband in a car, it is reasonable for police officers—like customs officials in the Founding era—to examine packages and containers without a showing of individualized probable cause for each one. **[e]** A passenger's personal belongings, just like the driver's belongings or containers attached to the car like a glove compartment, are "in" the car, and the officer has probable cause to search for contraband *in* the car.

Even if the historical evidence, as described by *Ross*, were thought to be equivocal, we would find that the balancing of the relative interests weighs decidedly in favor of allowing searches of a passenger's belongings. Passengers, no less than drivers, possess a reduced expectation of privacy with regard to the property that they transport in cars, which "travel public thoroughfares." * * *

In this regard—the degree of intrusiveness upon personal privacy and indeed even personal dignity—the two cases the Wyoming Supreme Court found dispositive differ substantially from the package search at issue here. **[f]** *United States v. Di Re* (1948), held that probable cause to search a car did not justify a body search of a passenger. And *Ybarra v. Illinois*, (1979), held that a search warrant for a tavern and its bartender did not permit body searches of all the bar's patrons. These cases turned on the unique, significantly heightened protection afforded against searches of one's person. * * *

Whereas the passenger's privacy expectations are, as we have described, considerably diminished, the governmental interests at stake are substantial. **[g]** Effective law enforcement would be appreciably impaired without the ability to search a passenger's personal belongings when there is reason to believe contraband or evidence of criminal wrongdoing is hidden in the car. As in all car-search cases, the

[a] Suppose you are driven to classes by a friend and the car is stopped for speeding. The officer orders your friend out of the car and notices a single marijuana cigarette on the floor. Should the officer be able to search *your* backpack, which is sitting on the backseat? Should it matter if you claim the backpack as your property?

[b] Notice that the exigency reasoning of *Carroll* is not mentioned.

[c] As an "originalist," Justice Scalia justifies Fourth Amendment rulings by "finding" what he thinks the framers would have ruled in 1791.

[d] This logically includes Houghton's purse.

[e] *Ross* did not involve passengers, and so does not establish direct precedent for a rule that allows an officer to open a passenger's purse.

[f] *Di Re* is central to Justice Steven's dissent. The majority does not overrule *Di Re* but instead distinguishes it, so that the rule of *Di Re* still exists, but so too does the rule of *Houghton*.

[g] Given the control that the police had over the car (the driver arrested, the car subject to impoundment), are references to "ready mobility" a smokescreen that simply allow police to search a car and all its contents simply because it is a car?

"ready mobility" of an automobile creates a risk that the evidence or contraband will be permanently lost while a warrant is obtained. In addition, a car passenger—unlike the unwitting tavern patron in *Ybarra*—will often be engaged in a common enterprise with the driver, and have the same interest in concealing the fruits or the evidence of their wrongdoing. **[h]** A criminal might be able to hide contraband in a passenger's belongings as readily as in other containers in the car,—perhaps even surreptitiously, without the passenger's knowledge or permission. * * *

To be sure, these factors favoring a search will not always be present, but the balancing of interests must be conducted with an eye to the generality of cases. To require that the investigating officer have positive reason to believe that the passenger and driver were engaged in a common enterprise, or positive reason to believe that the driver had time and occasion to conceal the item in the passenger's belongings, surreptitiously or with friendly permission, is to impose requirements so seldom met that a "passenger's property" rule would dramatically reduce the ability to find and seize contraband and evidence of crime. [Litigation would increase over the issue of whether the police officer should have believed a passenger's claim of ownership.] We think they militate in favor of the needs of law enforcement, and against a personal-privacy interest that is ordinarily weak.

* * *

We hold that police officers with probable cause to search a car may inspect passengers' belongings found in the car that are capable of concealing the object of the search. The judgment of the Wyoming Supreme Court is reversed.

[Justice Breyer concurred.]

JUSTICE STEVENS, with whom JUSTICE SOUTER and JUSTICE GINSBURG join, dissenting.

* * *

* * * In the only automobile case confronting the search of a passenger defendant—*United States v. Di Re*, (1948)—**[i]** the Court held that the exception to the warrant requirement did not apply (addressing searches of the passenger's pockets and the space between his shirt and underwear, both of which uncovered counterfeit fuel rations). In *Di Re*, as here, the information prompting the search directly implicated the driver, not the passenger. Today, instead of adhering to the settled distinction between drivers and passengers, the Court fashions a new rule that is based on a distinction between property contained in clothing worn by a passenger and property contained in a passenger's briefcase or purse. **[j]** In cases on both sides of the Court's newly minted test, the property is in a "container" (whether a pocket or a pouch) located in the vehicle. Moreover, unlike the Court, I think it quite plain that the search of a passenger's purse or briefcase involves an intrusion on privacy that may be just as serious as was the intrusion in *Di Re*.

Even apart from *Di Re*, the Court's rights-restrictive approach is not dictated by precedent. **[k]** For example, in *United States v. Ross* (1982), we were concerned with the interest of the driver in the integrity of "his automobile," and we categorically rejected the notion that the scope of a warrantless search of a vehicle might be "defined by the nature of the container in which the contraband is secreted," . . . "Rather, it is defined by the object of the search and the places in which there is probable cause to believe that it may be found." We thus disapproved of a possible container-based distinction between a man's pocket and a woman's pocketbook. * * *

Nor am I persuaded that the mere spatial association between a passenger and a driver provides an acceptable basis for presuming that they are partners in crime or for ignoring privacy interests in a purse. Whether or not the Fourth Amendment required a warrant to search Houghton's purse, at the very least the trooper in this case had to have probable cause to believe that her purse contained contraband. The Wyoming Supreme Court concluded that he did not.

Finally, in my view, the State's legitimate interest in effective law enforcement does not outweigh the privacy concerns at issue. I am as confident in a police officer's ability to apply a rule requiring a warrant or individualized probable cause to search belongings that are—as in this case—obviously owned by and in the custody of a passenger as is the Court in a "passenger-confederate[']s" ability to circumvent the rule. Certainly the ostensible clarity of the Court's rule is attractive. But that virtue is insufficient justification for its adoption. Moreover, a rule requiring a warrant or individualized probable cause to search passenger belongings is every bit as simple as the Court's rule; it simply protects more privacy.

* * *

[h] The real difference between the majority and the dissenters is that the majority imposes a *per se*, bright-line rule allowing no *Ross* exception for the belongings of a passenger. The dissent allows a search of a passenger's bag if an officer has probable cause that it held contraband. Justice Scalia suggests that such a rule would lessen the number of seizures from automobiles and enmesh police in fine-tuned adjudications of probable cause.

[i] See *Di Re* in Chapter 4. In that case an informer was riding in the car and would have seen the driver pass contraband to Di Re.

[j] If *Di Re* is still good law and the search of Houghton's purse is constitutional, could an officer lawfully open a "fanny pack" worn by a passenger on a belt?

[k] Although *Ross* is not direct precedent for the search of a passenger's bag, the "object" of the search in *Ross* was drugs located somewhere in the car, not in a specific container, making the extension of *Ross* to a passenger's belongings logical. Justice Stevens, the author of the *Ross* opinion, did not mention a pocket or pocketbook in that opinion. The *Ross* case made no reference to *Di Re*. Does Justice Stevens regret the Ross decision? Or simply believe that the majority is going too far?

As of August 2000, six states have followed *Wyoming v. Houghton*: Arkansas, Georgia, Nebraska, Ohio, South Dakota, and Wisconsin. *Houghton* has been rejected by Washington, in *State v. Parker* (1999) on the basis of Article I, Section 7 of the state constitution, and not under the Fourth Amendment. In three consolidated cases, police stopped a car and arrested the driver; in each the personal effects of nonarrested passengers were searched and police knew the items searched belonged to the passengers. The Washington Supreme Court held that the search of the purses and jackets of the respondents violated the state constitution. "[V]ehicle passengers hold an independent, constitutionally protected privacy interest. This interest is not diminished merely upon stepping into an automobile with others."[11] The Washington court specifically adopted the reasoning of the Wyoming Supreme Court in *Houghton v. State*, that had been reversed by the United States Supreme Court, on Fourth Amendment grounds, in *Wyoming v. Houghton* (1999).[12]

AUTOMOBILE INVENTORY SEARCHES

Statutes and local ordinances provide reasons to **impound** vehicles:

- To remove vehicles involved in accidents to permit the flow of traffic and preserve evidence.
- To remove damaged vehicles from the highways.
- To tow away automobiles that violate parking ordinances.
- To remove cars after the driver has been arrested.
- To impound automobiles subject to forfeiture.

Of course, a vehicle seized after the driver's felony arrest may also be impounded and subjected to an inventory search. Unlike these numerous *administrative* reasons for vehicle impoundment, an inventory of an arrested person's property at a police lockup or a jail is legal only if the underlying arrest is legal (see Chapter 4). Impounded vehicles have been placed in the unsecured private lot of a local garage (*Cady v. Dombrowski*, 1973) (rural area, lot seven miles from the police station), or in an impoundment lot operated by a municipality (*South Dakota v. Opperman*, 1976).

An inventory search of an impounded motor vehicle by law enforcement officers is an *administrative search*, deemed reasonable under the Fourth Amendment, and designed to perform a *caretaking* function. An inventory is a list of *all* items found in an impounded car. A vehicle inventory search is *not* a search for evidence that requires a warrant and probable cause. Any contraband disclosed in an inventory is in plain view and, consequently, is admissible in a criminal prosecution.

Consequently, inventory searches do *not* come under the automobile exigency warrant exception of *United States v. Carroll*. Neither a judicial warrant, probable cause, nor reasonable suspicion is needed to justify an inventory search. Indeed, an inventory search is the *opposite* of an exigency search—it must be conducted under *standardized rules and regulations* so that each inventory search is as much like another as possible. The Supreme Court has ruled that the inventory's administrative "interests outweighed the individual's Fourth Amendment interests" (*Colorado v. Bertine*, p. 372). In *Cady v. Dombrowski* (1973) Justice Rehnquist explained that "Local police officers . . . frequently investigate vehicle accidents in which there is no claim of criminal liability and engage in what, for want of a better term, may be described as community caretaking functions, totally divorced from the detection, investigation, or acquisition of evidence relating to the violation of a criminal statute."

REASONS FOR THE INVENTORY SEARCH   The purposes of automobile inventory and the inventory of a person taken into custody are similar. First, the routine listing of the contents of the vehicle protects the owner's property against theft or careless handling by the police while it remains in police custody. Second, the inventory protects the police against false claims or disputes over lost or stolen property by the owner. Third, it protects the police from potential danger. Additionally, the inventory helps determine whether a vehicle has been stolen (*South Dakota v. Opperman*, 1976). A prime reason to inventory persons taken into custody in police lockups—to prevent them from injuring themselves or others with weapons or dangerous instruments—is rarely the case in vehicle inventories. In unusual cases, however, explosives or weapons may be present, which if stolen from an impounded vehicle, can pose a threat to the public. Also, opening a vehicle containing explosives can risk the lives of officers.[13]

SCOPE OF AN INVENTORY SEARCH   The cases show that an inventory search can be extremely thorough. In *South Dakota v. Opperman* (1976) the Supreme Court upheld the inventory of items in the unlocked glove compartment of an automobile. In *Michigan v. Thomas* (1982) the Court upheld the inventory search of a car's locked trunk, the space under the front seat and under the dashboard, and the opening of air vents under the dashboard where a loaded revolver was found. The Court rejected the argument that the search of the air vents was improper because that is not a place where personal items are normally stored. In *Florida v. Meyers* (1984) the Court, in a *per curiam* opinion, upheld, without explanation, a second inventory search of an automobile made eight hours after the car was first searched and impounded. In *Illinois v. Lafayette* (1983), a police lockup inventory case (see Chapter 4), the police searched a purse-type shoulder bag belonging to a person taken into custody; the Supreme Court held that the police were under no obligation to place it in a secure box or locker even if this was less intrusive than the inventory search. "The reasonableness of any particular governmental activity does not necessarily or invariably turn on the existence of alternative 'less intrusive' means" (*Illinois v. Lafayette*, p. 647).

The issue of the *scope* of an inventory was revisited in **Colorado v. Bertine** (1987) to determine if *United States v. Chadwick* (1977)—holding warrantless searches of closed trunks and suitcases to violate the Fourth Amendment—modified the rule for vehicle inventory searches. *Bertine* reaffirmed the *Opperman* decision. A van was impounded after the driver was arrested for driving under the influence of alcohol. The van's contents were subjected to a detailed inspection and inventory in accordance with local police procedures. An officer then opened a closed backpack and found drugs. The Supreme Court found that the search was legal and the drugs admissible in evidence. Chief Justice Rehnquist, for the majority, said that an inventory search is made for regulatory reasons and is not a search for criminal evidence. There was no proof that the police acted in bad faith for the sole purpose of investigation, and the police department's regulations mandated the opening of closed containers and the listing of their contents. Justice Marshall, dissenting, argued that, in fact, the procedures were not standardized, thereby making the action a criminal search rather than an inventory. He wrote that the search was conducted in a "slipshod" manner that undermined the purposes of an inventory procedure, and that the rule of *Chadwick* should apply to a backpack.

THE NECESSITY OF STANDARDIZED RULES The Supreme Court's motor vehicle inventory doctrine has evolved from allowing an ad hoc inventory when made for inventory purposes (*Cady v. Dombrowski*, 1973) to a rule that requires that a police department have in place *standardized inventory rules and procedures* in order for an inventory search to be constitutional (*Florida v. Wells*, 1990).

In *Colorado v. Bertine* (1987) the Court has emphasized the importance of written, standardized procedures to guide the inventory search. No such procedures apparently existed in **Cady v. Dombrowski** (1973), which involved the warrantless search of a car for the express purpose of finding the weapon in the private vehicle of a drunk driver who was a police officer. The inventory search was upheld because it was clearly performed for administrative purposes and not as a search for criminal evidence. A driver involved in a serious single-car accident was taken into custody one evening for drunk driving in a rural Wisconsin town. He stated that he was a Chicago police officer. The Wisconsin officers believed that Chicago police officers were required by regulation to carry their service revolvers at all times. They were concerned that someone could steal a weapon from the car, which was placed in an unsecured lot. As a result, they looked into the passenger compartment and glove box but found no service revolver. A tow truck arrived and removed the disabled car to a garage seven miles from the police station, where it was left unguarded. Dombrowski, the driver, was hospitalized after lapsing into a coma. Hours later, after midnight, an officer went to the car to search for

Dombrowski's police weapon. The officer testified that the effort to find the revolver was "standard procedure in our department." He opened the trunk of Dombrowski's car and did not find a gun but did find his police uniform, a Chicago police baton with his name imprinted on it, and fresh blood that was introduced into evidence to convict Dombrowski of first-degree murder. Under these circumstances, the Court treated this search as a valid administrative search and not as a search for criminal evidence. "Where, as here, the trunk of an automobile, which the officer reasonably believed to contain a gun, was vulnerable to intrusion by vandals, we hold that the search was not 'unreasonable' within the meaning of the Fourth and Fourteenth Amendments" (*Cady v. Dombrowski*, p. 448).

From the somewhat loose procedure upheld in *Dombrowski*, the Court has moved to a position that for an inventory search to be constitutionally reasonable it must be authorized by (1) departmental policy and regulations that establish standard procedures, or (2) established routine. The rationale is that one inventory search should be conducted like another, and that the procedure should actually produce an inventory—a list. The goal is to limit the discretion of the officer as to the manner in which the inventory is to be conducted. "The individual police officer must not be allowed so much latitude that inventory searches are turned into 'a purposeful and general means of discovering evidence of crime'" (*Florida v. Wells*, 1990, citing *Colorado v. Bertine*, 1987).

Florida v. Wells (1990) is an example of an officer turning a routine inventory into a search for evidence because he overstepped administrative regulations. Wells was stopped for speeding and arrested for DUI after an officer smelled alcohol on his breath. An inventory search of the car revealed two marijuana cigarette butts in an ashtray and a locked suitcase in the trunk. There was *no* departmental inventory policy. The officer used his discretion to order the suitcase forced open. Large quantities of marijuana in a plastic bag were found. The United States Supreme Court agreed with the Florida Supreme Court that the evidence should be suppressed as a Fourth Amendment violation because the police department had no inventory policy at all. In the course of his majority opinion, Chief Justice Rehnquist said:

> A police officer may be allowed sufficient latitude to determine whether a particular container should or should not be opened in light of the nature of the search and characteristics of the container itself. Thus, while policies of opening all containers or of opening no containers are unquestionably permissible, it would be equally permissible, for example, to allow the opening of closed containers whose contents officers determine they are unable to ascertain from examining the containers' exteriors. The allowance of the exercise of judgment based on concerns related to the purposes of an inventory search does not violate the Fourth Amendment. (*Florida v. Wells*, p. 4)

This quote was treated as dictum by four justices who disagreed with it. Thus, the question of whether an officer has discretion to open some containers has not been finally resolved. The concurring justices felt that the officer should not have such discretion, i.e., that an inventory policy should order an officer to open all containers or none. Justice Brennan expressed concern that "police may use the excuse of an 'inventory search' as a pretext for broad searches of vehicles and their contents."

Border Searches

Every sovereign nation has a right to control its **borders** to determine who or what shall come into or exit the country, to collect customs, and to control smuggling. To enforce this plenary power, a country may search entering persons and luggage. As a general rule, the Fourth Amendment does not apply to searches and seizures at the border of the United States. As Justice Rehnquist noted:

> Since the founding of our Republic, Congress has granted the Executive plenary authority to conduct routine searches and seizures at the border, without probable cause or a warrant, in order to regulate the collection of duties and to prevent the introduction of contraband into this country. . . . This Court has long recognized Congress' power to police entrants at the border. (*United States v. Montoya de Hernandez*, 1985)[14]

United States v. Ramsey (1977) described border searches as "reasonable" simply because a person or item enters into the country from outside, without any regard to the existence of probable cause or recourse to a judicial warrant. In practice, any automobile or passenger entering the United States at the Canadian or Mexican border, or any international traveler entering at an international seaport or airport, may be searched at random by customs officers. Such a practice, of course, would be intolerable and blatantly unconstitutional if it were conducted by law enforcement officers within the United States.

In recent decades, as the United States has dealt with mounting problems of drug importation, illegal aliens, and foreign terrorists, issues concerning border searches have proliferated. Along with thorny political and law enforcement issues, the constitutional law of border searches has become complex because the Supreme Court has had to resolve issues arising from variations on the location of the "border" search and specific kinds of intrusions. The cases deal with five types of border searches:

1. At the actual border.
2. At a **fixed checkpoint** miles from the border.
3. **Roving patrols** by the Border Patrol up to one hundred miles from the border.
4. Search of international mail.
5. Boarding ships in open waters.

SEARCHES AT THE ACTUAL BORDER For *routine searches* by customs officers, the general rule is alive and well—any person seeking entry may be stopped and searched without probable cause or reasonable suspicion. In 1999 a customs officer stopped an Algerian national at the small Port Angeles, Washington, checkpoint on the United States–Canadian border on a *hunch*. She discovered explosives in the wheel well of the Algerian's car. As it turned out, the suspect, Ahmed

Ressam, was then thought to have ties to Osama bin Laden.[15] After the 9/11 attacks, Ressam, who was awaiting sentencing for plotting to bomb the Los Angeles International Airport during the 2000 millennium celebrations, provided federal authorities with new information about people involved in Al Qaeda–related terrorist cells.[16]

For *nonroutine border searches,* the Fourth Amendment requires that officials have *reasonable suspicion* of a crime to justify search and detention. In **United States v. Montoya de Hernandez** (1985) Rosa Elvira Montoya de Hernandez arrived in Los Angeles on a flight from Bogota, Colombia. An experienced customs agent thought she was smuggling drugs by having swallowed drug-filled balloons. An airline refused to return her to Colombia because she did not have a proper visa. As a result, she was held without a warrant in a locked room for sixteen hours, during which she "refused all offers of food and drink, and refused to use the toilet facilities." She "exhibited symptoms of discomfort consistent with 'heroic efforts to resist the usual calls of nature.'" Ultimately, a court order was obtained and a medical examination determined the existence of a foreign substance in her rectal canal. Subsequently, she "passed 88 balloons containing a total of 528 grams of 80 percent pure cocaine hydrochloride."

The Supreme Court found that the customs officer had reasonable suspicion to believe she was smuggling drugs and this was sufficient grounds for the court order and the body cavity search. She said she came to Los Angeles to purchase merchandise for her husband's store. However, because she arrived from a "source city" for drugs, could not speak English, and did not have family or friends in the United States, her explanation was questionable. She had not scheduled appointments with merchandise vendors nor made hotel reservations. Even though she carried $5,000 in cash (mostly $50 bills), she did not have a billfold nor did she possess checks, waybills, credit cards, or letters of credit, and, she did not recall how her ticket was purchased. She told an implausible story that she "planned to ride around Los Angeles in taxicabs visiting retail stores such as J. C. Penney and K-Mart in order to buy goods for her husband's store with the $5,000." These articulable facts "clearly supported a reasonable suspicion that respondent was an alimentary canal smuggler."

Was the sixteen-hour detention without a warrant and the delay in summoning medical personnel "reasonably related in scope to the circumstances which justified it initially?" The Court rejected a hard-and-fast time limit as to what is reasonable. In this case, Ms. Montoya refused to be X-rayed, falsely claiming to be pregnant. The alternatives were to hold her for observation or allow her into the interior of the country.

Justice Brennan dissented, joined by Justice Marshall. He felt that more intrusive border detentions and searches are constitutionally reasonable only if authorized by a judicial officer upon *probable cause* of criminality. There was no exigency in this case and a warrant could have been obtained at the outset. The majority replied that "not only is the expectation of privacy less at the border than in the interior, . . . [but] the Fourth Amendment balance between the interests of the Government and the privacy right of the individual is also struck much more favorably to the Government at the border."

STOPS AND SEARCHES AT FIXED CHECKPOINTS

Permanent or fixed checkpoints may be located up to one hundred miles from the United States boundary and the Supreme Court has applied standard Fourth Amendment reasoning to fixed checkpoint searches, employing the concepts of administrative searches, stop and frisk, and arrest. The rule is that *no level of evidence sufficiency is needed to *stop* a vehicle at a fixed checkpoint, but that *probable cause* is required to *search* a car that has been stopped.

A well-marked checkpoint at San Clemente, California, warned motorists a mile in advance they would have to slow down or stop. At the checkpoint a "point" agent visually screened all northbound traffic. Standing between two lanes of traffic, the agent directed some cars to a secondary inspection area where the driver and passengers were questioned for three to five minutes. If the stop produced proof that the passengers were illegal aliens, they were arrested and returned to Mexico. In **United States v. Martinez-Fuerte** (1976) a detected illegal alien challenged his conviction on the basis that the stop at the San Clemente checkpoint was without reasonable suspicion, probable cause, or a warrant and, therefore, violated the Fourth Amendment.

The Court agreed "that checkpoint stops are 'seizures' within the meaning of the Fourth Amendment," but they are a reasonable and valid governmental response to a serious problem. A requirement that the stops be based on reasonable suspicion "would be too impractical because the flow of traffic tends to be too heavy to allow the particularized study of a given car that would enable it to be identified as a possible carrier of illegal aliens." The intrusion of these stops "is quite limited" and involves only a brief detention during which a few questions must be answered. "Neither the vehicle nor its occupants are searched, and visual inspection of the vehicle is limited to what can be seen without a search." Unlike a roving patrol, checkpoint stops involve less discretion, and notice of the checkpoint is clearly given to those approaching it; checkpoints do not create the same concern or fear that may be generated during a stop along a road by a patrol car. As a result, no evidentiary requirement is necessary for a fixed checkpoint stop.

The Supreme Court held unanimously in **United States v. Ortiz** (1975) that the trunk of a car cannot be opened (i.e., searched) during a checkpoint stop, unless the officers have *probable cause* to believe that contraband or illegal aliens are present in the closed area. The Court reasoned that Fourth Amendment considerations come to the fore when the brief stop at the checkpoint, miles from the border, moves beyond a brief visual inspection and the asking of a few questions, which is a *seizure,* to a more intrusive *search* by customs officials. The Court noted that many factors could be taken into account by the Border Patrol officers to determine probable cause, including "the number of persons in a vehicle, the appearance and behavior of the driver and passengers, their inability to speak English, the responses they give to officers' questions, the nature of the vehicle, and indications that it may be heavily loaded." No such factors were apparent in *Ortiz*, and the Court found the search to be unconstitutional.

STOPS AND SEARCHES BY ROVING CUSTOMS PATROLS

Because of the difficulties involved in enforcing customs and immigration rules along our extensive borders, Congress authorized the Border Patrol to conduct roving patrols along the roads and in off-road areas within one hundred air miles of the border. Roving patrol *stops* by the Border Patrol are more intrusive than checkpoint stops and therefore, **United States v. Brignoni-Ponce** (1975) held they must be justified with *reasonable suspicion*. An officer must be "aware of specific articulable facts, together with rational inferences from those facts, that reasonably warrant suspicion" that a vehicle contains illegal aliens. Four years later, the reasoning in *Brignoni-Ponce* led the Court to extend the same right to drivers throughout the United States in *Delaware v. Prouse* (1979). Earlier, **Almeida-Sanchez v. United States** (1973) held that the *search* of an automobile stopped by Border Patrol officers is a great intrusion on personal privacy mandating the need for *probable cause* for the search to be constitutional. The majority was concerned that allowing roving patrol searches up to one hundred miles from the border would destroy the Fourth Amendment rights of local residents.

INSPECTIONS AND INVESTIGATION OF INTERNATIONAL MAIL

United States v. Ramsey (1977) held that customs officials may inspect incoming mail from outside the United States if they have *reasonable suspicion* to believe the mail contains contraband. While examining a sack of international mail from Thailand, a customs inspector noticed eight bulky envelopes bound for four different locations in the Washington, D.C., area. The addresses apparently had been typed on the same typewriter. He felt and weighed the envelopes and determined that they contained items other than paper. He opened the envelopes and in each found plastic bags containing heroin placed between cardboard. A warrant was then obtained and the presence of heroin reconfirmed. The packages were resealed and delivered, which ultimately led to the arrest of the defendant.

The Supreme Court held that the more exacting probable cause standard was not required to justify opening the mail under the Fourth Amendment because (1) the federal statute that guided this action imposes a less stringent requirement than that of "probable cause" required for the issuance of warrants, and (2) mail inspection is justified by the greater authority that the government has to make stops at the border. Justice Stevens dissented in *Ramsey*, joined by Justices Brennan and Marshall. He argued that the 1866 statute that authorized mail stops was intended to apply to large packages and that until 1971, the post office opened mail only in the presence of the addressee or under the authority of a court order supported by probable cause.

CONTROLLED DELIVERIES In *Illinois v. Andreas* (1983) the Supreme Court ruled that an initial inspection of international shipments that discloses contraband may lead to a "controlled delivery" to suspects in the interior of the country. Persons to whom contraband-laden packages are delivered may be arrested and the packages searched without a warrant when they take possession of the delivered contraband. In *Andreas* customs agents found marijuana in a table shipped from India, repackaged it, and had police officers posing as delivery men convey it. The defendant accepted the package and was arrested less than an hour later as he exited his house. The warrantless arrest and search was justified by the initial customs inspection, which found contraband, thus creating a lesser expectation of privacy for Andreas. Resealing the package does not function to revive or restore the lawfully invaded privacy rights. After the first inspection, the contraband was, in effect, in plain view. The lapse of time during which the police could not see the defendant did not reinstate his privacy rights. The Court noted that perfect controlled deliveries are not always possible, and the arrest and search was not unreasonable because there was a "substantial likelihood" that the illegal contents of the container were not changed.

BOARDING AND SEARCHING SEAGOING VESSELS Under federal law in force continuously since 1790, Coast Guard and customs officers may, without a warrant or reasonable articulable suspicion of criminal activity, hail, stop, and board any vessel located in waters that provide ready access to the open sea. The purpose is to inspect the ship's manifest and other documents. In contrast, automobiles may not be stopped without probable cause or reasonable suspicion of a traffic violation or crime (*United States v. Brignoni-Ponce*, 1975; *Delaware v. Prouse*, 1979). This rule for ships was held to be reasonable in *United States v. Villamonte-Marquez* (1983) because at sea it is impossible to establish the equivalent of border checkpoints or roadblocks. Although checkpoints could be established in ports, smugglers could easily avoid ports by anchoring at obscure points along the shore or by transferring cargo to other vessels. Also, the documentation requirements for vessels are different and more complex than automobile licensure, and information about the ship's registry and travel manifests cannot be known without boarding to inspect documents, as the identity of ships involved in smuggling may be falsified.[17] The intrusion on a ship's Fourth Amendment interests by the Coast Guard boarding is limited, constituting "a brief detention while officials come on board, visit public areas of the vessel, and inspect documents." In *Villamonte-Marquez* a forty-foot sailboat named the *Henry Morgan II* was packed with tons of marijuana and the odor gave customs officials plain view authority to search. Justice Brennan, joined by Justice Marshall, dissented in *Villamonte-Marquez*, arguing that as a practical matter, ships in a channel can be funneled into a checkpoint area that allows the uniform checking of documents of all ships.

EXTRATERRITORIAL LAW ENFORCEMENT IN A TIME OF TERROR

Roberto Iraola, an FBI Senior Legal Advisor, noted after 9/11 that "as a result of the globalization of crime and the emergence of international terrorism, the apprehension of those who violate American criminal laws will often have to take place abroad."[18] Indeed, for more than a decade before 9/11 the FBI had established permanent offices in dozens of cities overseas to fight organized crime and terrorism.[19] The Supreme Court had also issued rulings on whether the Constitution "follows the flag"—whether the constitutional limitations on government power apply to the activities of United States civilian law enforcement personnel in other countries.

This section reviews three issues concerning the extraterritorial reach of the Constitution: whether an illegal arrest deprives a court of jurisdiction to try a defendant, whether the Fourth Amendment exclusionary rule applies to searches conducted overseas, and whether the Fifth Amendment and the *Miranda* rule apply to overseas interrogation by United States personnel.

Kidnapping and Illegal Arrests

As noted in Chapter 4, the Supreme Court has ruled that the illegal arrest or even kidnapping of a defendant does not divest a court of the jurisdiction to try the defendant (*Frisbie v. Collins*, 1952). This rule applies even if a defendant was seized in another country (*United States v. Alvarez-Machain*, 1992). The *Alvarez* case began in 1985 when an American Drug Enforcement Agency (DEA) agent, Enrique Camarena Salazar, was kidnapped, tortured, and killed by Mexican drug dealers, a major event that strained relations between the United States and Mexico. The United States indicted nineteen Mexicans, including high-level government persons, for the torture-killing of "Kiki" Camarena. One of those charged was Dr. Humberto Alvarez-Machain, a gynecologist practicing in Guadalajara, Mexico.[20] In 1990 the DEA hired Mexican bounty hunters to kidnap Dr. Alvarez and bring him to the United States, where he was arrested and put on trial for Agent Camarena's murder. "The arrest of Alvarez took place without an extradition request by the United States, without the involvement of the Mexican judiciary or law enforcement, and under protest by Mexico."[21] Prior to his trial, the question of whether the United States had jurisdiction to try him was decided by the Supreme Court.

In a 6–3 decision, the Supreme Court held that the United States had jurisdiction to try Dr. Alvarez. Although an extradition treaty existed between Mexico and the United States, the treaty did not specifically address the question of forcible abductions. Therefore, according to Chief Justice Rehnquist's majority opinion, the treaty and its procedural history did not prohibit forcible abductions. The treaty, in this view, did not specify the *only* way that one country could gain custody over the citizen of the other country. The Supreme Court refused to interpret the treaty beyond its terms, even if the actions of the DEA agents were "shocking" and "in violation of general international law principles." Justice Stevens, dissenting for himself and Justices Blackmun and O'Connor, argued that the majority's interpretation in effect nullified the extradition treaty, breaking faith with Mexico. Justice Stevens showed that the trial of Dr. Alvarez violated the rules of customary international law concerning jurisdiction. The world would view the majority's decision as "monstrous" and the ruling weakens America's quest to strengthen the Rule of Law in the international arena by demonstrating that the United States did not live up to international law.

The case ended badly for the United States. Dr. Alvarez-Machain was acquitted of murder and torture in the Los Angeles Federal District Court in December 1992. The trial judge threw out the case, calling the prosecution's case the "wildest speculation" after discovering that the wrong doctor was kidnapped. Others were convicted for the murder. The incident caused much resentment of the United States in Mexico. As a result of the incident, the Clinton Administration promised Mexico that the United States will not engage in any cross-border kidnapping of Mexican citizens pending a revised extradition treaty. International opinion and international law scholars roundly criticized the United States. Dr. Alvarez-Machain sued federal law enforcement officials for $20 million in damages for kidnapping, torture, and false imprisonment. In mid-2003, after a decade of litigation, an en banc decision of the Court of Appeals for the Ninth Circuit decided that Dr. Alvarez has a right to sue the United States under the Alien Tort Claims Act and the Federal Tort Claims Act.[22]

The 1992 *Alvarez-Machain* Supreme Court ruling, though it ignores international law and has been soundly criticized, is still the law. The fact that Dr. Alvarez may nevertheless bring a civil lawsuit alleging that the United States violated international law may not have much effect on seizures by U.S. military or law enforcement personnel acting under antiterrorism authority. The Ninth Circuit was careful to note the limits of its ruling that Dr. Alvarez could sue the United States:

> Our holding . . . is a limited one. It does not speak to the authority of other enforcement agencies or the military, nor to the capacity of the Executive to detain terrorists or other fugitives under circumstances that may implicate our national security interests. The Fourth Circuit recently underscored this distinction when it recognized, in approving the detention of an American citizen captured abroad and designated as an "enemy combatant," that it was "not . . . dealing with a defendant who has been indicted on criminal charges in the exercise of the executive's law enforcement powers" but rather "with the executive's assertion of its power to detain under the war powers of Article II." *Hamdi v. Rumsfeld*, 316 F.3d 450, 473 (4th Cir. 2003). We, by contrast, are dealing with the former, not the latter.[23]

Extraterritorial Application of the Fourth Amendment

The Supreme Court held in *United States v. Verdugo-Urquidez* (1990) that the Fourth Amendment has no effect when United States officers search the premises of an alien in a foreign country. This is so even if the alien is arrested, in federal custody on American soil at the time of the search, and the purpose of the search is to obtain evidence for the conviction of the alien of a federal crime in a United States court.

Verdugo-Urquidez, a reputed drug dealer, was arrested in Mexico by Mexican officers at the request of American authorities and charged in federal court for the kidnapping and murder of DEA special agent Enrique Camarena Salazar. A raid of Verdugo's home in Mexico was carried out by a joint Mexican Police–DEA task force and the evidence obtained was used exclusively by the DEA to prosecute Verdugo. No approval or warrant was sought from United States Attorneys or magistrates for the raid. The Ninth Circuit Court of Appeals held that a warrant was required for such a search. Although the warrant would be of no legal validity in Mexico, it would "define the scope of the search" for American authorities. In rejecting this argument, Chief Justice Rehnquist, writing for the majority, noted that the Fourth Amendment had never been extended to protect aliens on foreign soil. The fact that Verdugo was in custody on American soil at the time of the raid is a "fortuitous circumstance" that should not dictate the outcome of the case.

Foreign relations activities may have influenced the *Verdugo-Urquidez* decision. While the case was being considered, the United States invaded Panama to rid that country of its military dictator, Manuel Noriega, who was under federal indictment for drug dealing. Noriega surrendered to United States forces and was transported to the United States for trial.[24] Chief Justice Rehnquist noted that the United States had employed its armed forces more than two hundred times on foreign soil. "Application of the Fourth Amendment to those circumstances could significantly disrupt the ability of the political branches to respond to foreign situations involving our national interest." The Court clearly thought it would be bad policy to impose the burden or concern on the president and members of Congress "as to what might be reasonable in the way of searches and seizures conducted abroad" before authorizing such military actions.

Justice Brennan, dissenting, noted that in recent years the extraterritorial reach of American criminal law against foreign nationals has been increasing under United States drug, antitrust, securities, antiterrorist, and piracy statutes. If the United States can extend its criminal law overseas, then the Fourth Amendment should "travel with" American agents who go abroad to exercise criminal jurisdiction. It is unlikely that the Supreme Court will adopt such a rule in the context of what will probably be a very long war on terrorism worldwide.[25]

Extraterritorial Application of the Fifth Amendment and *Miranda*

The Supreme Court has not ruled on this area, but federal courts have held that there are Fifth Amendment limitations on the admissibility of confessions in court based on violations of Fifth Amendment principles. Unlike the Fourth Amendment, which is applied at the place where a search occurs, the Fifth Amendment rule against self-incrimination is an exclusionary rule that takes effect not when a confession is taken but in the courtroom when the effects of a confession are sought to be introduced into evidence.

Federal courts have excluded the introduction of involuntary confessions obtained by foreign police forces overseas against American citizens. "Recently, in the prosecution of several foreign nationals charged with the bombing of the American Embassies in Nairobi, Kenya and Dar es Salaam, Tanzania, Judge Leonard B. Sand ruled in *United States v. Bin Laden* that they were entitled to the same Fifth Amendment rights against self-incrimination as suspects questioned in the United States."[26] The holding is not based on the extraterritorial reach of the Fifth Amendment. "This is because any violation of the privilege against self-incrimination occurs, not at the moment law enforcement officials coerce statements through custodial interrogation, but when a defendant's involuntary statements are actually used against him at an American criminal proceeding."[27] This underlying principle was confirmed by the Supreme Court in a nonforeign context in 2003 in *Chavez v. Martinez* (see Chapter 7). Indeed, the government in the bin Laden prosecution acted as if the defendants were protected by various Fifth Amendment provisions.[28]

In summary, the war on terrorism means that American law enforcement and criminal procedure will regularly involve questions of **extraterritoriality** in a variety of settings. The rulings in *Alvarez-Machain* and *Verdugo-Urquidez* reduce the need of government agents to process extraterritorial enforcement through the courts in ways required by the Constitution in domestic law enforcement. These rules may come under increasing criticism by friendly governments, and the pressure to modify them may be the price of greater international police cooperation. To the contrary, the exigency of fighting terror might strengthen the resolve of the Supreme Court to limit the extent to which the Fourth Amendment follows the flag. The Second Circuit ruling in *Bin Laden*—requiring that confessions obtained by American agents be preceded by *Miranda* warnings to be admissible—is likely to force United States agencies to make a clear option between the war model or the criminal model when questioning suspects. If the primary goal of interrogation is to gather information about terrorist organizations or impending attacks, agents may forgo *Miranda* warnings and select methods that probably would be deemed coercive under the Due Process Clause (see Chapter 7, section on "Interrogation in a Time of Terror"). If the goal of interrogation is to bring terrorists to justice, as was the case in the 1993 WTC bombing or the embassy bombings, United States agents will have to abide by Fifth Amendment law.

Many other issues, beyond the scope of this section, will have to be resolved in the context of extraterritorial law enforcement. Such issues include whether prosecutors will have to abide by discovery rules in such cases, and whether terror suspects can be held indefinitely, under what status, and whether they have to be tried in civilian courts or in special military tribunals.

THE SPECIAL NEEDS DOCTRINE AND REGULATORY SEARCHES

Origins of the Doctrine and Administrative Searches

In *New Jersey v. T.L.O.* (1985) the Supreme Court ruled that a public school student in a high school has a Fourth Amendment expectation of privacy in her purse. Nevertheless, the Court ruled that when the circumstances made it reasonable, a public school official could inspect the content of the student's purse, looking for materials that could subject the student to criminal prosecution, without first obtaining a warrant and even without probable cause to believe that the purse contained illegal contraband. This case set off a chain of rulings that have collectively come under a rule known as the **"special needs" doctrine**. It is not clear that the Court intended to create a "doctrine," for the cases that have relied on the reasoning of "special needs *beyond the need for normal law enforcement*" involve different factual settings and even allow searches with different evidentiary foundations. In some cases, a government official must have reasonable suspicion of wrongdoing before searching without a warrant while under other factual circumstances there need be no individualized suspicion for a search to take place. What the cases have in common is that in each case the search is conducted by a government officer who is *not* a police officer engaged in the enforcement of criminal law.

The special needs cases are closely related to *administrative searches*—a type of search that the Supreme Court brought under the aegis of the Fourth Amendment in 1967. The section in Chapter 3 on "Revolutionizing the Fourth Amendment" notes that in the 1960s the *Katz* expectation of privacy doctrine, which replaced the idea that privacy protection depended on property rights, *expanded* Fourth Amendment protection. In addition, the Supreme Court modified search and seizure jurisprudence by making it more *flexible. Terry v. Ohio* (1968) thus allowed police, for the first time in common law history, to stop a person on *less* than probable cause, and *Warden v. Hayden* (1967) held that police could seize and possess a defendant's "mere property" for the duration of a prosecution if it could be used to prove guilt.

The fourth "revolutionary" case, ***Camara v. Municipal Court*** (1967), ruled that the Fourth Amendment applied even to home entry by administrative officers enforcing municipal safety, health, or occupancy ordinances, and not investigating crimes. *Camara* overruled an earlier case that held that the Fourth Amendment did not apply at all to these kinds of essentially noncriminal searches.[29] The Court in *Camara* recognized that the Fourth Amendment protected against *all* official intrusions into the privacy of a home, whether by police officers or by government regulatory inspectors looking for unsanitary conditions and the like. The *Camara* decision to extend the Fourth Amendment to administrative searches created a dilemma because it allowed a householder to refuse entry to an inspector without a warrant. But it was close to impossible for an inspector to obtain probable cause to believe that *this* particular householder, for example, kept oily rags next to her furnace. The warrant requirement threatened to undermine the effectiveness of inspection programs, which relied on the inspections of *all* the houses in a neighborhood to be effective. The Supreme Court got around this sticking point by holding that administrative search warrants could be obtained by proving to a court that the conditions in *an area* made inspections necessary. Without quite saying so, the Supreme Court indicated that the particularity requirement in the amendment's warrant clause could be modified, as long as the warrant was *reasonable*. In effect, the Supreme Court authorized *general warrants*, so hated by the framers of the Constitution.

The Supreme Court applied the administrative search doctrine, with its "area warrants," to inspections of commercial establishments (*See v. Seattle*, 1967). Indeed, the Court soon held that even area warrants could be dispensed with when inspectors entered a "**pervasively regulated industry**," such as liquor stores or gun dealerships, as long as they did so during normal business hours and did not use force. Dealers who refused inspections, however, could lose their licenses (*Colonnade Catering v. United States*, 1970; *United States v. Biswell*, 1972). Under the administrative search rules, unannounced safety inspections of mines without a warrant was permissible under the Mine Safety and Health Act because the law was known to all mine owners and provides a *constitutionally adequate substitute for a warrant* (*Donovan v. Dewey*, 1981). The Supreme Court did require area warrants for worker safety inspections under OSHA. It ruled that simply requiring safety and health regulations does not transform monitored industries into "pervasively regulated industries" (*Marshall v. Barlow's, Inc.*, 1978).

The flexible interpretation of the Fourth Amendment established by the administrative search cases then made the Court receptive to relying on the reasonableness clause of the Fourth Amendment to uphold a variety of warrantless searches under the "special needs" rubric.

Early Special Needs Cases: The Creation of a Doctrine

The "special needs" doctrine originated in *New Jersey v. T.L.O.* (1985). Keep in mind that no "special needs" doctrine existed prior to this case. In the course of deciding a case that did not fit easily into a preexisting category, the Court laid a conceptual foundation that later cases recognized as a basis for decisions applied to dissimilar facts.

A teacher discovered a fourteen-year-old public high school freshman smoking in a lavatory in violation of a school rule. She was brought to the principal's office and questioned by an assistant vice principal. Ms. T.L.O. denied that she had been smoking and claimed that she did not smoke at all. The assistant vice principal then demanded to see her purse, opened the purse, found a pack of cigarettes, and, upon removing the cigarettes, noticed a pack of cigarette rolling papers. Rolling papers are closely associated with the use of marijuana. The assistant vice principal proceeded to search the purse thoroughly and found a small amount of marijuana, a pipe, a number of empty plastic bags, a substantial quantity of money in one-dollar bills, an index card containing a list of those students who owed the student money, and two letters that implicated the student in marijuana dealing. This led to T.L.O.'s adjudication as a delinquent and a one-year probation sentence.

Was the vice principal's search of T.L.O.'s purse a constitutional violation? State action existed in this search and seizure case because public schools are established by units of government. Its administrators and teachers exercise legitimate control over students by virtue of their positions. Justice White's majority explored the question of whether T.L.O. had a Fourth Amendment privacy interest in her purse at some length. The Court's unanimous decision on this point rested on a close analysis of the actualities of school life in the 1980s:

> Students at a minimum must bring to school not only the supplies needed for their studies, but also keys, money, and the necessaries of personal hygiene and grooming. In addition, students may carry on their persons or in purses or wallets such nondisruptive yet highly personal items as photographs, letters, and diaries. Finally, students may have perfectly legitimate reasons to carry with them articles of property needed in connection with extracurricular or recreational activities. In short, school children may find it necessary to carry with them a variety of legitimate, noncontraband items, and there is no reason to conclude that they have necessarily waived all rights to privacy in such items merely by bringing them onto school grounds. (*New Jersey v. T.L.O.*, p. 339)

The state argued that public school students had *no* reasonable expectation of privacy in school. If this were the rule, school authorities could search the belongings of high school students at will. The Court rejected the idea that teachers stood **in loco parentis**—in the place of parents. The old-fashioned idea that a parent transfers personal authority to teachers does not fit the reality that modern schools are in many ways large bureaucracies.

Having decided that public school students, at least those in high school, enjoy an expectation of privacy, the next issue was whether the vice principal's search violated this right. This involved two further issues: Was a warrant necessary, and if not, what was the proper standard of evidence for a lawful warrantless search in a school setting? The Court stated that schools have an interest in maintaining order by enforcing such school rules as the ban on smoking. To further this goal, all the justices agreed that the "warrant requirement, in particular, is unsuited to the school environment: requiring a teacher to obtain a warrant before searching a child suspected of an infraction of school rules (or of the criminal law) would unduly interfere with the maintenance of the swift and informal disciplinary procedures needed in the schools."

The final question was whether the balance between the student's expectation of privacy in her purse and the school's need to enforce rules was properly met by the search in this case. Having denied smoking after being caught, it was reasonable for the vice principal to determine if T.L.O. carried cigarettes, as that would help to resolve a dispute between the teacher and the student. When the vice principal saw the rolling papers, he had some suspicion that T.L.O. might be in possession of marijuana. On the other hand, some student might use the paper to roll tobacco. It was also possible that she was carrying the rolling paper for another student or another person. In short, the observation of the papers did not establish probable cause but did provide the vice principal with reasonable suspicion that she had marijuana in her purse.

The Court rejected the probable cause standard, saying it is not an irreducible requirement of a valid search. The decision to uphold the constitutionality of the search based on reasonable suspicion of marijuana possession was based on application of the general-reasonableness construction of the Fourth Amendment to the specific facts of this a school search.

Justice Brennan, dissenting, noted that an exception to Fourth Amendment requirements had been allowed in past cases only where there was some pressing emergency. He and Justices Marshall and Stevens did not find that the facts in this case rose to such a level of seriousness as to cause the constitutional balance to tip in favor of the school's interests when measured against the right to privacy. The suspected infraction, smoking, was not a crime. "Considerations of the deepest significance for the freedom of our citizens counsel strict adherence to the principle that no search may be conducted where the official is not in possession of probable cause" (T.L.O., p. 361, Brennan, J. dissenting). Justice Stevens, also dissenting, stated that the kind of search engaged in, in this case would be justified if there were an allegation involving in-school violence.

This case is an example of how legal doctrines evolve. In a footnote Justice White wrote that "the special needs of the school environment require assessment of the legality of such searches against a standard less exacting than that of probable cause." Justice Blackmun, in a concurring opinion, wrote that "Only in those exceptional circumstances in which special needs, beyond the normal need for law enforcement, make the warrant and probable-cause requirement impracticable, is a court entitled to substitute its balancing of interests for that of the Framers" (New Jersey v. T.L.O., p. 351). The use of the term "special needs" was probably not seen as the creation of a doctrine but was simply a phrase used to explain the basis of the Court's ruling.

Two years after T.L.O., however, the Supreme Court decided three cases that relied on T.L.O. as precedent and used the "special needs" language as justification for the decisions. These cases established the idea that the ruling of New Jersey v. T.L.O. established a new doctrine. None of the cases involved public school searches.

The first, **O'Connor v. Ortega** (1987), was a civil suit in which a supervisor thoroughly searched the office, desk, and filing cabinet of a psychiatrist employed by a state hospital. He was suspected of improprieties in the acquisition of a computer and charges were brought against him for sexual harassment of female hospital employees and inappropriate disciplinary action against a resident. Because the search was ordered by the executive director of a *state* hospital, it constituted state action. The Court found that Dr. Ortega had a reasonable expectation of privacy in his office but also stated that an expectation of privacy can be overcome if a governmental interest outweighs an individual's privacy interests. The Supreme Court held the search to be justified. In her majority opinion justifying the search, Justice O'Connor relied heavily on the incipient rule in Justice Blackmun's *T.L.O.* concurrence, and quoted his special needs formulation (i.e., "special needs, beyond the normal need for law enforcement") as a reason for upholding the search of a a public employee's office on less than probable cause. Both Justice O'Connor and Justice Scalia referred to these words, but both omitted the opening words in Justice Blackmun's sentence in *T.L.O.*, recognizing a "special needs" exception only in "exceptional circumstances." If *T.L.O.* were known as the "exceptional circumstances" doctrine, perhaps it would have been less frequently employed as precedent.

In the next special needs case, the Court combined that doctrine with the pervasively regulated industry warrant exception to administrative search warrants. **New York v. Burger** (1987) held that evidence found in plain view during a *police* inspection of automobile junk shops could be admitted in a criminal case. A state statute required vehicle dismantlers to maintain records of cars in their junkyards and to allow police or motor vehicle inspectors to examine their records during working hours. Failure to produce records was a misdemeanor. NYPD officers, who were part of a team that conducted five to ten junk shop inspections daily, identified stolen vehicles by their VINs during such an inspection.

The Court upheld this search and seizure even though the police had no warrant or any suspicion of wrongdoing. It relied on several reasons: (1) junkyards are a pervasively regulated industry, providing a reduced expectation of privacy; (2) warrantless inspections are necessary to make the inspection system work and are of limited scope; and (3) the statute is not a pretext for criminal searches without a warrant. As to the last point, the Court said that a state can address a major social problem both through the administrative system and penal sanctions. In this regard, the police officers were treated simply as regulatory agents. This last point is rather weak, as the major "social problem" aimed at by the New York law was the dismantling of stolen cars. If this logic were pushed to its extreme, every crime could be declared a social problem and the application of constitutional protections eliminated.

The third special needs case of 1987, **Griffin v. Wisconsin**, ruled that a probationer's home could be entered and searched without a warrant by probation officers, as long as there were reasonable grounds to believe contraband was present, as was required by state law. Justice Scalia offered this justification: "The search of Griffin's home satisfied the demands of the Fourth Amendment because it was carried out pursuant to a regulation that itself satisfies the Fourth Amendment's reasonableness requirement under well-established principles. . . ."

> A probationer's home, like anyone else's, is protected by the Fourth Amendment's requirement that searches be "reasonable." Although we usually require that a search be undertaken only pursuant to a warrant (and thus supported by probable cause, as the Constitution says warrants must be), . . . we have permitted exceptions when "special needs, beyond the normal need for law enforcement, make the warrant and probable-cause requirement impracticable." (*Griffin v. Wisconsin*, 1987)

In support Justice Scalia cited *New Jersey v. T.L.O.*, *O'Connor v. Ortega*, and the administrative search cases. The creation of a new doctrine requires a certain amount of maneuvering. Strictly speaking, neither *T.L.O.* nor *O'Connor v. Ortega* applied to a home. Justice Scalia also cited *Payton v. New York* (1980), which held that an arrest warrant is necessary for entry into a home to make a felony arrest. But instead of characterizing the search of a probationer's home as a home search, the Court instead lumped the search in with a part of operating a probation system "like [the] operation of a school, government office or prison, or . . . supervision of a regulated industry." As a form of punishment, the probationer is under correctional supervision and enjoys only conditional liberty. This diminishes her expectation of privacy, even in the home.

These initial "special needs" cases demonstrate how new legal doctrines are formed. First, a case was decided that did not precisely fit earlier precedent. In its opinion, the Court provides *a phrase* that helps to explain the decision. Subsequent cases apply the phrase as a basis for decisions to cases that are not precisely the same as the first. The phrase is now becoming a doctrine—a legal category that can be used as a framework to decide future cases. This produces the appearance that the system of common law reasoning is more inductive than deductive.[30] By organizing the cases under a doctrine, the Court attempts to offer a consistent and satisfactory explanation to lower court judges and police officers who must decide novel cases.

The creation of a doctrine is not simply a neutral process of logic. In the example of the "special needs" doctrine, the new category allowed a conservative Court to advance a theory that relied on the reasonableness clause and the general-reasonableness construction of the Fourth Amendment (see Chapter 2, section on "The Structure of the Fourth Amendment"). This made it feasible to get around the obstacles of the warrant clause and the probable cause requirement to uphold action by government officers that intruded on the Fourth Amendment privacy in different situations. Liberal justices saw the special needs cases as an assault on fundamental rights. As Justice Thurgood Marshall wrote, "In the four years since this Court, in *T.L.O.*, first began recognizing 'special needs' exceptions to the Fourth Amendment, the clarity of Fourth Amendment doctrine has been badly distorted, as the

Court has eclipsed the probable-cause requirement in a patchwork quilt of settings" (*Skinner v. Railway Labor Executives' Association*, 1989, p. 639).

Before returning to the expansion of the "special needs" doctrine in the area of drug testing, we examine the rules regarding the search of premises for inspecting the causes of fires under the Fourth Amendment. These rules combine the basic law of criminal searches with those of administrative searches.

Fire Inspections

Determining the cause of a blaze involves a postfire inspection, which is conducted for both administrative and criminal investigation purposes. Rules for these kinds of searches were established in *Michigan v. Tyler* (1978) and *Michigan v. Clifford* (1984) and provide a mix of administrative search and criminal search rules:

Rule 1. "A burning building creates an exigency that justifies a warrantless entry by fire officials to fight the blaze."

Rule 2. "Moreover, . . . once in the building, officials need no warrant to *remain* for 'a reasonable time to investigate the cause of a blaze after it has been extinguished.'"

Rule 3. "Where, however, reasonable expectations of privacy remain in the fire-damaged property, additional investigations begun after the fire has been extinguished and fire and police officials have left the scene, generally must be made pursuant to a warrant or the identification of some new exigency."

Rule 4. "If the primary object [of a renewed search] is to determine the cause and origin of a recent fire, an administrative warrant will suffice. To obtain such a warrant, fire officials need show only that a fire of undetermined origin has occurred on the premises, that the scope of the proposed search is reasonable and will not intrude unnecessarily on the fire victim's privacy, and that the search will be executed at a reasonable and convenient time."

Rule 5. "If the primary object of the [renewed] search is to gather evidence of criminal activity, a criminal search warrant may be obtained only on a showing of probable cause to believe that relevant evidence will be found in the place to be searched."

Rule 6. "If evidence of criminal activity is discovered during the course of a valid administrative search [or during the initial firefighting], it may be seized under the 'plain view' doctrine. . . . This evidence then may be used to establish probable cause to obtain a criminal search warrant."

In *Michigan v. Tyler* a fire broke out in a furniture store at midnight. At 2:00 A.M., just as the firefighters were "watering down smoldering embers," fire inspectors arrived to determine the cause, and they seized two plastic containers of flammable liquid. A police detective arrived at 3:30 A.M. and took photographs of the suspected arson. Shortly thereafter, the police investigator abandoned the investigation because the smoke and darkness made careful observation of the crime scene impossible. The fire inspectors returned briefly at 8:00 A.M., after the fire had been fully extinguished and the building was empty. They left and returned with the police investigator at 9:30 A.M. During this search, they discovered more evidence of arson: pieces of tape on a stairway with burn marks and pieces of carpet suggesting a fuse trail. The investigators left to obtain tools, returned, and seized the incriminating evidence. Three weeks later, an investigator with the state police arson section returned to take pictures. All the entries were made without consent or warrants.

The Court held that the Fourth Amendment applied to post-fire searches, noting that a magistrate must not be a "rubber stamp" when issuing an administrative search warrant: The magistrate must ensure that the investigation does not stray beyond reasonable limits. The magistrate's role is to prevent undue harassment of property owners and to keep the inspection to a minimum.

Applying the postfire search rules to the facts of *Tyler,* the Court held that the warrantless entry and search immediately after the fire were proper (Rules 1 and 2). The search at 9:30 the next morning was construed by the Court as a *continuation of the search* begun a few hours before. That search was cut off owing to the smoke and darkness and "[l]ittle purpose would have been served by their remaining in the building, except to remove any doubt about the legality of the warrantless search and seizure later that same morning." The photographs taken by the state police investigator, however, were not admissible without a warrant: Too much time had elapsed and suspicion accrued.

Michigan v. Clifford involved an early-morning house fire. Firefighters arrived on the scene at 5:40 A.M., extinguished the blaze, and left the scene shortly after 7:00 A.M. One hour later, a police fire investigator received an order to investigate. Because he was working on other cases, he did not arrive on the scene until 1:00 P.M. When he arrived, a work crew hired by the owner was boarding up the house and pumping water out of the basement. Clifford was out of town on a vacation and was communicating about the situation through a neighbor and Clifford's insurance agent. After the work crew departed, the investigators entered the basement of the house without obtaining consent or an administrative warrant and quickly found evidence of arson (a strong odor of fuel and a Crock-Pot attached to a timer set for 3:45 A.M. which stopped at 4:00 A.M.). This evidence was seized and marked. The officer proceeded through the remainder of the house, much of which was still intact, and seized other suspicious evidence.

The Supreme Court held this seizure to be a Fourth Amendment violation. The owner, by hiring a crew to board up and pump out his house clearly maintained an expectation of privacy in his home. Therefore, before entry, the officer should have obtained an *administrative* search warrant; the time lapse meant there was no longer an exigent circumstance. Once the officer found incriminating items in the basement, it was necessary to halt the search and take the evidence to a magistrate to seek a *criminal* search warrant. Thus, all the evidence was inadmissible.

In sum, fire officials have the right to enter burned premises immediately after a fire in an attempt to determine the cause of a fire. Owners or residents, however, do not lose their right to privacy; more extensive, long-term investigations and searches must be accompanied by a warrant.

Drug Testing

Increased awareness of the personal and social costs of alcohol and illicit-drug abuse has made them prime domestic issues. Governmental agencies and private employers, including major league sports franchises, have turned to random or mandatory drug testing as a way to deter drug use and identify users. The pervasiveness and visibility of drug testing has assured court challenges. Drug testing by *private* businesses is not a Fourth Amendment concern, just as searches in *private* schools do not infringe on a *constitutional* right of privacy; drug testing by *government* agencies, on the other hand, comes under the Fourth Amendment. The Supreme Court has decided six special needs cases arising from drug testing by government authorities. In two of the cases the Court found that there were no special needs justifying intrusions on privacy and the testing programs were held to be unconstitutional.

EARLY CASES   The first two cases were decided in favor of the government-mandated testing programs in 1989. One upheld the mandatory testing of every crew member after any major rail accident (*Skinner v. Railway Labor Executives' Association*, 1989). The other allowed the U.S. Customs Service to drug test virtually all of its agents at some point in their careers (*National Treasury Employees Union v. Von Raab*, 1989).

An initial issue in both cases was whether taking and testing blood and urine samples intruded on reasonable expectations of privacy. As noted in Chapter 3, under the doctrine of *Katz v. United States* (1967), the Court held in *Skinner* that *urine collection and testing* to ascertain the presence of drugs in a person's body intrudes upon expectations of privacy that society has long recognized as reasonable. "There are few activities in our society more personal or private than the passing of urine. Most people describe it by euphemisms if they talk about it at all. It is a function traditionally performed without public observation; indeed, its performance in public is generally prohibited by law as well as social custom." The Court noted that the expectation of privacy is not only rooted in the traditional dictates of modesty, but also in the fact that the chemical analysis of urine, like that of blood, can reveal a host of medical facts about a person. Although urine testing by state agencies in order to detect drugs or alcohol is protected by the Fourth Amendment, the collection is allowed under certain conditions (*Skinner v. Railway Labor Executives' Association*, 1989).

The second issue in both cases was what standards were needed to ascertain the constitutionality of drug testing? In each case, the Court applied the "special needs" doctrine to find these drug-testing programs *reasonable* under the Fourth Amendment, even though no warrant was required and *no level of individualized suspicion* was needed to trigger drug testing. Each case was decided on the particular facts of the respective testing program. The linchpin of the holdings in *Skinner* and *Von Raab* was that the purposes of these laws were essentially administrative, although the discovery of the presence of drugs could lead to criminal prosecution.

The Court in ***Skinner v. Railway Labor Executives' Association*** (1989) upheld a federal law that mandated drug testing of all on-site employees after a major train accident, whether the employees worked for a private railroad company or a line run by the government. State action was based on the facts that the program was mandated by law for the public safety. The Court's decision that mandatory testing was *reasonable* and constitutional was based on several points: (1) preserving the life and safety of train passengers is of great importance; (2) the employees subjected to the testing program are involved in safety-sensitive tasks; (3) the absolute prohibition of alcohol and drug use while on the job is a reasonable requirement; and (4) the usual sanction for on-the-job intoxication is dismissal and not criminal prosecution. The warrant requirement would add little to further the aims of the drug-testing program because the tests were standardized. The fact that blood alcohol levels drop at a constant rate requires swift testing and creates an exigency. Waiting to get a warrant before testing would effectively undermine the usefulness of the testing.

The railway union argued in *Skinner* that there must be a *particularized suspicion* against specific railroad employees after an accident before they could be tested. The Court disagreed and concluded that mandatory and comprehensive testing was constitutional for the following reasons:

- Although blood and urine testing are Fourth Amendment searches, they are *relatively limited encroachments* on the expectations of privacy of the railway employees because they are job- and safety-related requirements in a pervasively regulated industry.

- The testing is relatively *limited in time*, intrusiveness, and ancillary risk.

- The *government's interest* in testing without individualized suspicion is *compelling* because it is not easy for supervisors to spot individuals who have used a drug and are still under its influence.

- A mandatory testing and dismissal rule has a *greater deterrent effect* than a weaker mandatory testing policy.

- An *accident scene is chaotic* and it may be extremely difficult for supervisors to sort out who is to be tested and who is not to be tested on the basis of individualized suspicion.

- The fact that drug tests are not, in themselves, conclusive proof of impairment does not solely render the program unconstitutional because the statistical evidence obtained from mandatory, across-the-board testing is very useful to the railway industry in *assessing the causes* of accidents.

The balance of interests in ***National Treasury Employees Union v. Von Raab*** (1989) differed in several respects. The challenged rule of the U.S. Customs Service required the automatic drug testing of all officers who (1) are directly involved in drug interdiction or the enforcement of drug laws, (2) are required to carry firearms, or (3) handle classified material that would be useful to drug smugglers and could be relinquished through the bribery or blackmail of drug-dependent employees. This testing program was not triggered by a particular negative incident but was required for *hiring* or *promotion* into sensitive posts. The governmental interest was not proposed to prevent on-the-job impairment as a direct result of alcohol or drug use. Instead, the interest was to ensure that customs officers in drug enforcement positions who carried firearms would *lead drug-free lives*. The government argued that drug-addicted customs agents are targets for bribery and cannot carry out their functions in a positive way (i.e., they may be sympathetic to the goals of drug traffickers). Furthermore, government employees in sensitive jobs (i.e., employees of the United States Mint, military or intelligence officers, or customs officers) "have a diminished expectation of privacy in respect to the intrusions occasioned by" their positions.

Justice Kennedy, writing for the majority, held as he did in *Skinner* that neither a warrant nor individualized suspicion would serve a useful purpose in such a program. The majority agreed with the first two rationales presented by the Customs service, holding the program of drug testing for those agents directly involved in drug law enforcement and for those who carried firearms. It could not agree on the reasonableness of the third rationale, preventing the compromise of agents handling classified information, and remanded the case for further fact finding.

Justice Marshall, joined by Justice Brennan, dissented in both *Skinner* and *Von Raab* on the grounds that their "special needs" analyses were flawed. They did not find that the goals and methods of the two programs provided a reasonable basis to dispense with the Fourth Amendment's requirement that individualized suspicion is the basis of interfering with a person's constitutional rights. Justice Marshall did not believe that the need for individualized suspicion would undermine these programs. He accused the majority of submitting to popular pressure generated by public hysteria over the drug problem and giving away precious rights.

Justices Scalia and Stevens concurred in *Skinner* but dissented in *Von Raab*. Justice Scalia's dissent noted that the factual predicate for the two cases differed. In *Skinner* the government gave evidence to show that a substantial number of train accidents were caused by intoxicated railroad employees. In *Von Raab*, on the other hand, "neither the frequency of use nor connection to harm is demonstrated or even likely. In my view the Customs Service rules are a kind of immolation of privacy and human dignity in symbolic opposition to drug use." Justice Scalia noted that the government did not supply even *one* example in which the purported state interest of preventing bribe-taking, poor intentions, unsympathetic law enforcement, or the compromise of classified information was endangered by drug use. Some of the government's arguments were weak. For example, the fact that an agent used drugs does not necessarily mean the officer would be hostile or indifferent to drug enforcement. Calling the Customs Service reasons "feeble," Justice Scalia noted that its commissioner said that the drug-testing program would "set an important example in our country's struggle with this most serious threat to our national health and security." In effect, Justice Scalia agreed with Justice Marshall's point, that the testing of customs officers was an unnecessary sacrifice of constitutional freedoms as a result of public and political pressure.

DRUG TESTING OF POLITICAL CANDIDATES The Supreme Court finally drew the line at mandatory drug testing in *Chandler v. Miller* (1997). A Georgia law required every candidate for state office to be drug tested. Two libertarian candidates for statewide offices challenged the law as an infringement of their Fourth Amendment rights. The Supreme Court, in an 8–1 opinion authored by Justice Ginsburg, agreed. Drug testing under the law was not based on individualized suspicion against the candidate. Indeed, the program was "relatively noninvasive" because it permitted a candidate to provide a urine specimen in the office of his or her private physician. The results are given to the candidate, who controls further dissemination of the report. The core issue was whether the *certification of drug testing* required before a person's name could be placed on a ballot was a "special need" that overrides the basic requirements of the Fourth Amendment.

> Nothing in the record hints that the hazards respondents broadly describe [i.e., drug-addicted candidates] are real and not simply hypothetical for Georgia's polity. The statute was not enacted, as counsel for respondents readily acknowledged at oral argument, in response to any fear or suspicion of drug use by state officials. (*Chandler v. Miller*, p. 319)

The testing program was simply too weak to identify or to deter candidates who violate antidrug laws. In contrast other drug testing programs designed to deal with the real dangers of illicit drug use, Justice Ginsburg wrote that the real purpose of the law was simply to project an "image" of being tough on drugs. "By requiring candidates for public office to submit to drug testing, Georgia displays its commitment to the struggle against drug abuse. The suspicionless tests, according to respondents, signify that candidates, if elected, will be fit to serve their constituents free from the influence of illegal drugs" (*Chandler v. Miller*, p. 321). A law that is merely *symbolic* does not create the "special need" that allows an individual's right to privacy to be overridden without a warrant and individualized suspicion.

Chief Justice Rehnquist, the lone dissenter, found no infringement on a personal right and, displaying his pro-state philosophy, wrote, "Nothing in the Fourth Amendment or in any other part of the Constitution prevents a State from enacting a statute whose principal vice is that it may seem misguided or even silly to the members of this Court" (*Chandler v. Miller,* p. 328).

DRUG TESTING PREGNANT WOMEN The Supreme Court again drew a line against the special needs justification for drug testing pregnant women enrolled in a public prenatal care program in *Ferguson v. City of Charleston* (2001). Staff members at a Charleston public hospital in 1988 were concerned that patients who were receiving prenatal treatment were using cocaine. A policy was established to identify and test pregnant patients suspected of drug use. Women who tested positive were referred to the county substance abuse commission for counseling and treatment. The program did not reduce the incidence of cocaine use among patients.

A task force then developed a policy, in conjunction with the local prosecutor and police, to perform drug screens on all women in the program who met one of nine criteria, including "late prenatal care after 24 weeks gestation," " incomplete prenatal care," "abruptio placentae," "IUGR [intrauterine growth retardation] 'of no obvious cause,'" "previously known drug or alcohol abuse," or "unexplained congenital anomalies." The new policy had a treatment component, but also required that information about drug use be forwarded to police authorities for prosecution. The policy also prescribed in detail the precise offenses with which a woman could be charged, depending on the stage of her pregnancy, from simple possession to possession and distribution to a person under the age of eighteen, and unlawful neglect of a child. Although women in the prenatal care program signed consent forms, it was not clear that they were informed of the possibility of prosecution for receiving health care. The Court assumed that the women did not know they were being tested for drugs and that the results were forwarded to law enforcement officials for prosecution.

The Supreme Court decided the case on the issue of whether there were special needs beyond the normal need for law enforcement that justified the drug testing of these women without a search warrant or any individualized suspicion. In reaching its conclusion that the testing program was unconstitutional, the Court concluded that the nine criteria used to initiate testing did not amount to probable cause or even reasonable suspicion that a woman had ingested cocaine. Justice Stevens's majority opinion noted that there was no "evidence in the record indicating that any of the nine search criteria was more apt to be caused by cocaine use than by some other factor, such as malnutrition, illness, or indigency." The Circuit Court's decision upholding the testing program rested "on the premise that the policy would be valid even if the tests were conducted randomly." (*Ferguson,* p. 77, n. 10).

The key factor that distinguished *Ferguson* from the earlier drug-testing special needs cases is that in the earlier cases there was some administrative rationale and the consequences involved such action as dismissal from a position or discipline for substance use. In *Ferguson,* on the other hand, although a goal of the program was to prevent cocaine use by pregnant women, "In this case, however, the central and indispensable feature of the policy from its inception was the use of law enforcement to coerce the patients into substance abuse treatment" (*Ferguson,* p. 80). However beneficent the ultimate goal of the policy, as in *Indianapolis v. Edmond* (2000) "the purpose actually served by the [hospital's] searches 'is ultimately indistinguishable from the general interest in crime control.'" (*Ferguson,* p. 81). The fact is that Charleston police and prosecutors "were extensively involved in the day-to-day administration of the policy" (*Ferguson*, p. 82). This close involvement had the effect of making the hospital staff so closely involved in law enforcement that they had "a special obligation to make sure that the patients are fully informed about their constitutional rights, as standards of knowing waiver require" (*Ferguson*, p. 85).

Justice Scalia dissented, joined by Chief Justice Rehnquist and Justice Thomas. He argued that drug *testing* is not a search, but at most "a 'derivative use of the product of a past unlawful search,' which 'works no new Fourth Amendment wrong' and 'presents a question, not of rights, but of remedies'" (*Ferguson*, p. 92, Scalia, J., dissenting). Thus, the dissenters were attempting to have the case decided as a matter of the applicability of the exclusionary rule.

Writing in 1999, Lynn Paltrow, Program Director of the National Advocates for Pregnant Women (NAPW), noted that "In the name of fetal rights, over 200 pregnant women or new mothers in approximately twenty states have been arrested. Most of the women arrested have been low-income women of color with untreated drug addictions. Thus, the arrests focus on those people and issues that are hardest to defend in the court of public opinion. Wrongly prejudged as irresponsible and uncaring, the public has expressed little support for them."[31] She viewed these prosecution programs as an assault on the reproductive rights of women. Some justification for this is that "[m]any more children are harmed every year from prenatal alcohol use than by cocaine or marijuana. Yet fetal alcohol syndrome, which is characterized by retardation, is not prosecuted under such laws, because alcohol, like other possible detriments to a healthy baby, is legal."[32] Recent studies have shown that the impairment of fetuses from alcohol use is far worse than that resulting from cocaine and that impairment previously attributed to cocaine use was the result of alcohol ingestion.[33]

DRUG TESTING OF HIGH SCHOOL STUDENTS In two cases, the Supreme Court has upheld the mandatory testing of all high school students who are involved in athletics and extracurricular activities. In the first case, **Vernonia School District 47J v. Acton** (1995), the Court upheld a policy of *mandatory* drug testing of *all* students involved in interscholastic athletic programs. As in *Skinner* (1989) and *Von Raab* (1989), it upheld intrusions on Fourth Amendment privacy by searches conducted without a warrant or any level of individualized suspicion. *Vernonia* went beyond *T.L.O.*, in which the search of a student's belongings was based on *individualized* suspicion of wrongdoing and a violation of a school rule.

Justice Scalia's majority opinion gave several reasons for supporting the blanket searches, not based on individual suspicion, to be reasonable:

- Drug use had become evident in the school system and was believed to be widespread. The school district was concerned, among other things, that student athletes using drugs were prone to injury.
- Urine testing constitutes a Fourth Amendment search.

- The actual privacy interests of student athletes, however, are "negligible." Public schools have "custodial and tutelary responsibility for children"; students are subject to physical examinations and vaccinations for health purposes; and "school sports are not for the bashful," as the athletes bathe in communal showers.
- The intrusion is limited. The school personnel who collect the urine samples do not directly observe the function; all student athletes are subject to testing; laboratories reveal only the presence of illicit drugs and not other health information; the results are known only by a limited group of school personnel; and results are not turned over to police.
- The state's interest is very important because drug use is especially harmful to youngsters.

As a result, the district need not base its testing on individualized suspicion. The state is not required to select the "least intrusive" method of search—it can balance the practicalities and select this method. The Court noted that focusing on "troublesome" students for testing could lead to arbitrary testing decisions.

Justice Ginsburg, concurring, noted that the decision does not determine whether routine testing of all public school students in a school or a district, not just those enrolled in interscholastic athletics, is allowable.

A spirited dissent in *Vernonia* was written by Justice O'Connor, joined by Justices Stevens and Souter. She focused on the *lack of individualized suspicion*. The Court's decision means that millions of student athletes, the "overwhelming majority" who have given school officials "no reason whatsoever to suspect they use drugs at school, are open to an intrusive bodily search." The Framers of the Constitution were concerned with general *searches* as well as with general warrants. "[M]ass, suspicionless searches" are unreasonable in the criminal law enforcement context, and each "special needs" case that dispenses with individualized suspicion has to advance a "sound reason[] why such a regime would likely be ineffectual under the usual circumstances. . . ." Furthermore, her careful review of the facts discounted the costs of not drug testing. The failure to drug test school athletes simply did not put the lives and safety of many people at risk. Therefore, the district cannot simply decide to discard individualized suspicion; without specific and compelling reasons to show that eliminating individualized suspicion is reasonable, the requirement is constitutionally necessary.

We cannot know the deeper reasons two conservative justices split in this case. This author speculates that the *Vernonia* opinions offer glimpses into the justices' constitutional norms, their views of political theory, and even their personal backgrounds. Justice O'Connor gave the following reason for her dissent:

> Searches based on individualized suspicion also afford potential targets considerable control over whether they will, in fact, be searched because a person can avoid such a search by not acting in an objectively suspicious way. And given that the surest way

to avoid acting suspiciously is to avoid the underlying wrongdoing, the costs of such a regime, one would think, are minimal. (*Vernonia School District v. Acton,* p. 667)

This logical, deterrence-based argument connects the Fourth Amendment's individualized suspicion requirement to a political philosophy of *individualism*. The Constitution balances public safety against individual liberty. The Framers have commanded later generations of Americans to take risks in regard to public safety by trusting its citizens to make their own personal decisions to be law abiding. Perhaps this strong leaning toward individualism can be explained, in part, by Justice O'Connor's upbringing. She "spent her early years on the Lazy B ranch doing the chores expected of a child growing up on a ranch—driving tractors, fixing fences, branding cattle. Sandra learned to be independent at an early age."[34]

In contrast, Justice Scalia's majority opinion can be seen as *statist*. The Vernonia District formulated a school policy that emphasizes public control of all students, under the pain of penalty, rather than individual self-control. Justice Scalia's opinion refers positively to the fact that teachers in private schools "stand *in loco parentis* over the children entrusted to them." This had no direct bearing on a case involving public schools, but it offers insight into his authority-based reasoning in this and later cases. We can speculate that Justice Scalia's comfort with an authoritarian regime of drug testing is not entirely unrelated to the fact that he attended high school at a Catholic military academy.[35] Finally, to return to Justice O'Connor's dissent, she writes: "Blanket searches, because they can involve 'thousands or millions' of searches, 'pose a greater threat to liberty' than do suspicion-based ones, which 'affect one person at a time,'" citing her dissent in *Illinois v. Krull* (1987). As suggested in Chapter 2, this concern by a conservative justice may have been generated by her experience as a state legislator.

In *Board of Education of Independent School District No. 92 of Pottawatomie County v. Earls* (2002) the Court, in a 5–4 decision, extended the rule of *Vernonia v. Acton* to high school students engaged in extracurricular activities. The basis for the majority ruling in *Earls* was much weaker than in *Vernonia*. For example, there was no evidence of a widespread drug problem in the Tecumseh, Oklahoma, schools. Justice Thomas's majority opinion suggests that the national problem of teen drug use had grown worse since 1995. As for Tecumseh, the rural school district's basis for concern was the testimony of two teachers that one student once appeared to be under the influence of drugs and another was overheard talking about drugs, marijuana cigarettes were once detected by a drug-sniffing dog near the school's parking lot, and that "Police officers once found drugs or drug paraphernalia in a car driven by a Future Farmers of America member" (*Earls*, p. 835).

In *Vernonia,* as Justice Ginsburg's dissent (joined by Justices Stevens, O'Connor, and Souter) pointed out, there were two good reasons for the decision—that drug use could be physically harmful for athletes and that athletes were leaders of an aggressive drug cult. Neither reason applies to all extracurricular

activities. It borders on the comical to be concerned for injury to members of the band lifting heavy instruments, Future Farmers guiding livestock, and Future Homemakers of America risking injury from sharp cutlery. It appears then, that the majority based the special needs allowing drug testing of all students engaged in extracurricular activity on a generalized concern about drug use among teens. In support of the decision, Justice Thomas noted that "the test results are not turned over to any law enforcement authority" (*Earls*, p. 833). This is so, although the majority characterized the urine collection and testing as "minimally intrusive" and concluded that "the invasion of students' privacy is not significant" (*Earls*, p. 834).

The dissent noted that although extracurricular activities are nominally voluntary, a large proportion of students engage in them. "Participation in such activities is a key component of school life, essential in reality for students applying to college, and, for all participants, a significant contributor to the breadth and quality of the educational experience." (*Earls*, p. 845, Ginsburg, J., dissenting). Ironically, a study cited indicated that students enrolled in extracurricular activities are less likely to develop substance abuse problems. It seems, then, that the majority decision is close to allowing schools to require mandatory drug testing for all students. The dissent viewed the school policy as closer to the symbolic program adopted in *Chandler v. Miller* (1997).

Although *Earls* allows school districts to adopt drug-testing programs, a recent study of school administrators in one suburban district found that the level of support for drug testing was mixed and that the *Earls* case itself did not lead to the adoption of random testing in schools without such policies.[36] Thus, the case may have limited practical effect. In this vein, a large study of seventy-six thousand high school students nationwide found that drug use was no different in schools with or without random drug-testing programs. A newspaper article reporting the study noted that "[m]ost schools have shied away from drug testing" and that "only 18 percent of the nation's schools did any kind of screening from 1998 to 2001."[37]

***

The "special needs" doctrine has garnered scholarly criticism. Robert D. Dodson, citing eight critical law review articles, notes that "[c]onsiderable doubt exists over whether the Court should have ever adopted the special needs doctrine."[38] As Justice Thurgood Marshall noted, there is no textual support for this doctrine in the Fourth Amendment, that weakens civil liberties. Dodson notes that the "Court has never adequately defined what it means by special need."[39] Dodson proposed that the "special needs" doctrine be modified to ensure that warrantless searches would be allowed only if the program was one that affected the safety of large numbers of people, and if the courts could identify factors that made the policy truly special. He notes that evidence obtained under the "special needs" doctrine has indeed led to a large number of prosecutions, and recommends that an exclusionary rule apply to these instances to prevent the perversion of the doctrine into another tool of law enforcement.

LAW IN SOCIETY

RACIAL PROFILING AND CONSTITUTIONAL RIGHTS

No discussion of law enforcement and constitutional rights is complete without acknowledging the pernicious and continuing role played by race and racism. The scope of this topic spans the historic injustices of slavery and the Jim Crow Era, the effects of race on the judicial process, and all aspects of police brutality to the present time.[40] This section focuses on a narrower, but hardly inconsiderable, problem: racial profiling—unequal law enforcement based on skin color and the propensity of police officers to stop individuals who are black or Hispanic in circumstances under which a white person would not be stopped. Racial profiling is an old and pervasive practice, known and endured within minority communities, that has become a major political issue only since 1998. In the black community, the practice was half-jokingly referred to as DWB—Driving While Black—a phrase that has since become mainstream.[41] Analysis suggests that seemingly neutral constitutional doctrines have contributed to racial profiling.

Awareness of racial profiling in the larger community had previously been low. A computer search of newspapers for the terms "racial profiling" or "driving while black" resulted in twenty-one stories using these terms from 1990 to 1995. The number increased to 269 in 1998 and more than 1,000 in 1999.[42] Books on the topic have recently appeared including a 1999 volume by civil rights attorney, John L. Burris, and journalist Kenneth Meeks's *Driving While Black,* which relates specific incidents and gives readers practical advice about how to respond to profiling.[43] The issue has escalated, and in political science jargon, it has been placed on the political agenda.

THE PREVALENCE OF RACIAL PROFILING

Do police, in fact, violate the Fourth Amendment rights of racial minorities in greater proportion to whites when stopping, arresting, or searching them? Until recently, the evidence for racial profiling was largely anecdotal. The official statistics indicated a direct correlation between the rate of arrests for *serious crimes* and the rate of commission for both black and white suspects; i.e., that there was no systematic discrimination in arrest practices.[44] The higher rates of African Americans arrested reflected higher crime rates generated by poverty and repression; a phenomenon noted by the distinguished scholar W. E. B. DuBois as early as 1899.[45] But the lack of discrimination in major crime arrests failed to examine on-the-street police behavior where persons were stopped and released or arrested and cited for traffic offenses. In this sphere, anecdotes of racial profiling—large numbers of innocent minority men and women detained on streets, in airports, in bus terminals, and in train stations, and stopped in their cars—were plentiful.

Fifteen years before defending O. J. Simpson, Johnnie Cochran "was driving down Sunset Boulevard in his Rolls-Royce with two of his children in the back seat. Suddenly, he saw police lights flashing in the rear-view mirror, and pulled over. 'Get out

with your hands up,' a police officer commanded over a bullhorn. 'I knew not to make any quick moves, especially with my kids in the car,' Mr. Cochran recalled, 'and I got out of the car and I looked back and I saw the police officers had their guns out.' His children started to cry. Then, as Mr. Cochran watched incredulously, the police began searching the car. They soon found his badge from the District Attorney's office, where he was then the third-highest ranking official. Realizing they had made what could be a career-ending mistake, they muttered quick, embarrassed apologies and sped away."[46]

There is no official record of Cochran's stop. The incident lives on only in memory.

Newark Judge Claude Colman was arrested in a New Jersey Bloomingdale's while Christmas shopping because earlier in the day a black man who bore no resemblance to Judge Colman had tried to use a stolen credit card. Colman was handcuffed, led through the crowd, chained to a wall, and prevented from calling a lawyer.[47]

A black Los Angeles psychologist leaves his work identification badge on during his drive home from work—just in case he is pulled over by police, he wants the officer to see he is a professional, not a criminal.[48]

African American Don Jackson, a former police officer, was documenting police discrimination while driving in Long Beach, California. He was stopped by police and during questioning was pushed through a plate glass window. The incident was filmed by NBC News.[49]

Two former students of the author, both lawyers and African American men, have recounted being stopped in their cars by police for no reason—one was driving with his white wife in Los Angeles; the other was returning a video, with his child properly secured in a rear child seat, while driving from Detroit into Grosse Pointe, Michigan, a wealthy white suburb.

"Filemon B. Vela is a federal judge, but a Border Patrol agent recently mistook him for an illegal immigrant or a drug smuggler. Mr. Vela and three aides were driving on an isolated road when the agent pulled them over. Why? Because, the agent explained, there were too many people in the car."[50]

"Nearly every contemporary black writer tells similar stories. In *Parallel Time: Growing Up in Black and White* (1994), Brent Staples, a member of the editorial board of the *New York Times*, recounts numerous incidents of stereotyping that he encountered as a college graduate and since. . . . Harvard philosopher Cornel West writes in *Race Matters* (1993) of being stopped 'on false charges of trafficking in cocaine while driving to Williams College and of "being stopped three times in my first ten days in Princeton for driving too slowly on a residential street with a speed limit of twenty-five miles per hour."[51]

While a large number of anecdotes do provide powerful evidence, they cannot show that the stopping was disproportionate, and some African American men can claim they have never been subjected to racial profiling.[52] Until 1998, there was no statistical evidence to support this wealth of anecdotes indicating that blacks and Hispanics were stopped in far greater numbers than whites in comparable situations. Now quantitative evidence of systematic racial profiling exists. There are at least three sources of data, all discussed in a December 1999 article by Professor David Harris.[53] The first two sources extracted data from two lawsuits against state police in New Jersey and Maryland, which claimed racial profiling on the New Jersey Turnpike and on I-95. The third was conducted by Professor Harris using data from four Ohio cities.

The New Jersey and Maryland studies were conducted by Dr. John Lamberth of Temple University. In order to conclude that minorities were disproportionately stopped, he had to discover: (1) the rate at which blacks were being stopped, ticketed, and/or arrested on the relevant part of the highway, and (2) the percentage of blacks among travelers on that same stretch of road. The second question was answered by teams counting cars on the road and tabulating the apparent race of drivers and occupants. "The teams observed each car that they passed or that passed them, noted the race of the driver, and also noted whether or not the driver was exceeding the speed limit." Data were recorded on forty-two thousand cars for the New Jersey study. Arrest and stop data were supplied by the police agencies. The New Jersey study found (1) that black and white drivers violated the speed limits at almost exactly the same rate, (2) blacks were 73.2 percent of those arrested but constituted only 13.5 percent of all drivers, and (3) blacks were 35 percent of all drivers stopped while accounting for 13.5 percent of drivers or passengers. Dr. Lamberth concluded that the odds of these results occurring by chance was "substantially less than one in one billion" and that "it would appear that the race of the occupants and/or drivers of the cars is a decisive factor" for arrests and stops.

Similar findings surfaced in the Maryland I-95 study. Observations of six thousand cars showed that "the percentages of blacks and whites violating the traffic code were virtually indistinguishable." Blacks constituted 17.5 percent of the population violating the traffic code but more than 72 percent of those stopped and searched. "The disparity between 17.5 percent black and 72 percent stopped includes 34.6 standard deviations. Such statistical significance, Lamberth said, 'is literally off the charts.'" He concluded that "While no one can know the motivation of each individual trooper in conducting a traffic stop, the statistics presented herein, . . . show without question a racially discriminatory impact on blacks . . . from state police behavior along I-95. The disparities are sufficiently great that taken as a whole, they are consistent and strongly support the assertion that the state police targeted the community of black motorists for stop, detention, and investigation. . . ."[54]

Professor Harris obtained Municipal Court records from four Ohio counties in which the cities of Akron, Columbus, Dayton, and Toledo were located. This gave the races of persons arrested for traffic offenses. Any findings of racial disparity were conservative because these data did not include stops in which there was either no action taken or merely simple warnings given, and Hispanics were tabulated as white. Arrest figures were compared with census data on the percentage of whites and blacks of driving age in the four counties. The percentage for blacks was reduced by 21 percent to account for the fact that 21 percent of black households do not own a vehicle. A likelihood ratio was computed to determine whether blacks received tickets in numbers that are out of proportion to their presence in the estimated driving population. The "likelihood ratios for Akron, Dayton, Toledo, and Franklin County [Columbus], Ohio, all either approach or exceed 2.0. In other words, blacks are about twice as likely to be ticketed as nonblacks." Thus, for the first time, quantitative evidence exists to show that in six localities studied thus far, there is statistically significant evidence to show that drivers are being stopped on the highways because they are members of a racial minority.[55]

These findings have been confirmed by more recent evidence—ninety-one thousand pages of internal state records released by New Jersey on November 27, 2000—indicating that over a period of ten years, eight out of every ten automobile searches carried out by New Jersey state troopers involved cars driven by blacks and Hispanics, who constituted 13 percent of all drivers. Of all cars stopped, 30 percent yielded some kind of contraband, whereas 70 percent of those stopped were completely innocent. Furthermore, the records indicated that the New Jersey police were trained in on-the-road drug interdiction by the federal Drug Enforcement Agency and Department of Transportation in a program called Operate Pipeline, which has trained more than twenty-five thousand officers in forty-eight states. Despite claims by the DEA that it did not teach racial profiling, critics argue that the agency is in denial about what amounts to racial profiling.[56]

MOTIVATIONS FOR RACIAL PROFILING

In the past, motives for racial profiling surely included harassment for its own sake, as well as social and political repression. It is probably the case that these motives have entirely disappeared as official policy today and are relatively rare among individual police officers, although it would be foolish to entirely discount the existence of simple racism among some.

> A 1988 investigation of the Reynoldsburg, Ohio, police department established that a group of officers identified themselves as a "SNAT" team, standing for "strategic" or "special nigger arrest team." At best, SNAT was a crude and offensive joke. At worst, the interviews suggested that a number of Reynoldsburg police officers, referring to themselves as the SNAT team, intentionally discriminated against blacks.[57]

As for racially discriminatory police action, it is worth remembering that only since about 1970 has there begun to be a reasonable promise of equal treatment in American society. After centuries of slavery, legal segregation, and bitter resistance to the civil rights movement, it is small wonder that deep and indelible traces of discrimination remain in the mental reactions of white Americans.[58] Police action before 1970 occurred against a background of what Professor William Julius Wilson calls "historic discrimination." Things have changed, but instead of true equality, a more complex social situation has emerged, which Wilson characterizes as "contemporary discrimination."[59] Policing now occurs in a different social matrix. Economically, a substantial black middle class has emerged, but a substantial black underclass persists.[60] Political participation of African Americans has increased but has "not led to equality with whites commensurate to that achieved in civil status."[61] Residential segregation remains high.[62] And closer to our inquiry, "there has been a steady increase in support among white Americans for principles of racial equality, but substantially less support for policies intended to implement principles of racial equality."[63]

Against this backdrop of progress in race relations, the criminal justice picture is fraught with powerful negative examples, including the "demonization" of blacks as criminals by presidential candidate George H. W. Bush in 1988 in the notorious Willie Horton advertisement;[64] the mass hysteria in Boston when Charles Stuart, who murdered his wife and later committed suicide, falsely claimed that she had been killed by a black assailant, thereby unleashing mass stops of black men in Boston for weeks;[65] and in New York City in the late 1990s, the brutalization of Abner Louima by NYPD officer Justin Volpe and the nearly successful attempt to cover up the sordid incident;[66] the killing of Ahmadou Diallo by four members of the NYPD street crimes unit, even though legally justified;[67] and the killing of Patrick Dorismond, an unarmed African American man who was approached without cause by a sting officer trying to sell drugs.[68] These cases indicate that white America is too quick to jump on evidence of black criminality, real or fabricated, which is uncomfortably close to a "presumption of guilt" against all African Americans. This aura of black criminality, acting on the minds of many police officers, when combined with the police propensity to react negatively to real or perceived slights to their authority, and stimulated by the "war on drugs," creates a situation that increases the likelihood of racial profiling.

This complex reality helps to explain a paradox: the existence of racial profiling by police officers who see nothing wrong in what they are doing. The reason is understandable: White police officers (and perhaps some minority officers as well) seem to believe that race is a proxy for crime. Even though most of the people they stop in drug interdiction teams at airports and bus stations are innocent, and even though the vast majority of people who live in urban poverty areas are law abiding ("roughly 97.9 percent of the national population of blacks and 99.5 percent of the national population of whites in any given year will not be arrested for committing a crime"[69]), the fact that rates of serious crime are higher among African Americans has been used inaccurately to "criminalize blackness."[70] It seems that police are overgeneralizing, a problem noted by all who focus on the issue. Legal scholar-critics of racial profiling acknowledge that there are cases in which the police legitimately use a variety of factors that include the suspect elements of race and place, and do not suggest a blanket rule that ties the hands of the police.[71] This is miles away from scruffily dressed undercover agents who roughly stopped a vacationing African American school teacher, six months pregnant, at midday in the Baltimore, Maryland, Amtrak station.

The drug interdiction teams were supposed to be looking for "what they call the 'Yo girls,' young black women with long fingernails and hair weaves who carry Fendi bags."[72] The officers acted in a racially discriminatory way by not making fine discriminations in the factors of their supposed profile. Because they could get away with it, their drug interdiction profile had been reduced to the factor of skin color.

What is especially illogical about these policies is that while the crime rate for serious felonies is tragically higher among poor minority communities, there is little evidence that this is true for drug crimes. National statistics indicate that "The percentages of drug *users* who are black or white are roughly the same as the presence of those groups in the population as a whole."[73] This suggests that drug sellers are more proportionate to the racial mix of users, i.e., the racial mix of society, but insofar as police overly target minorities, their drug arrest statistics tend to reflect police policies and practices rather than drug-selling activity.

RACIAL PROFILING AND THE LAW

Racial profiling has been wrapped up with the Supreme Court's stop-and-frisk and automobile search cases since *Terry v. Ohio*. With a few exceptions, the cases have almost all tended to expand the discretion of police officers to a point where as a practical matter, police can target any car and legally stop it, and target most persons and get them to place themselves into the temporary custody of the officer. The totalitarian nightmare that police officers can stop anyone at any time for any reason does not exist for most white Americans, but is very close to a palpable reality for most African Americans and Hispanics. Police on the prowl for drugs and for the profits of drug asset forfeitures can and do stop cars the occupants of which often are completely innocent. A prominent Detroit attorney, Dennis Archer, then president of the Michigan Bar Association, was stopped by drug cops fifteen years ago, while driving a Cadillac Seville. This was before he was elected to the state Supreme Court and before he became mayor of Detroit. And it has happened several times in recent years to his son, Dennis Archer, Jr., also an attorney. He was stopped in the Detroit suburb of Royal Oak in a Jeep that matched the one used in a robbery. The initial stop was clearly supported by reasonable suspicion, but it took the white officers who handcuffed Archer and his female companion fifteen minutes to determine that she was an assistant county prosecutor, although she had asked them immediately to check her handbag.[74]

Under the automobile search cases, a car can be stopped on a pretext, the driver and passengers ordered out, and the interior carefully inspected; if any evidence of crime on the driver's part is uncovered, the passengers can be searched. All can be questioned without *Miranda* warnings. Police can ask stopped drivers for consent to search without ever indicating their rights, and the subjective sense of intimidation is legally irrelevant if no arrest has been made. Even if a driver refuses to consent, the car can be held until a drug-sniffing dog is brought onto the scene. And while the Supreme Court has limited the time of a stop, students tell of far longer waits on the side of the road. "The upshot is that officers are free to exercise a vast amount of discretion when they decide who to stop."[75] Even if one were to cling to the view that the Court's doctrine adequately protect one's reasonable expectation of privacy, Professor Tracey Maclin, examining the issue of racial profiling, agrees that a "huge gap exists between the law as theory and the law that gets applied to black males on the street."[76]

THE POLITICAL REACTION TO RACIAL PROFILING

To date, the legal response to racial profiling by lower courts has been disappointing, as courts have tended to uphold stops made on the basis of actions occurring in "high crime neighborhoods," rather than allowing closer inquiry into the motives and methods of police.[77] Recommendations for better police racial sensitivity training alone has also fallen short of the mark.[78] Racial profiling has had a great and harmful impact on society, on law enforcement, and on the criminal justice system. It has caused "deep cynicism among blacks about the fairness and legitimacy of law enforcement and courts." It has created a corrosive ends-justify-the-means mentality in law enforcement. It has generated skeptical jurors who disbelieve the testimony of police officers. It has fueled the skyrocketing imprisonment of black men for drug crimes, as serious felonies have steadily declined. It has distorted the way in which law-abiding minorities act and dress, made them wary of police, and has caused them to question such life-affirming programs as mandatory seat belt laws because such laws give police one more reason to stop a car. The distrust bred by racial profiling undermines efforts to establish and entrench community policing.[79]

After years of obscurity, the issue has burst onto the political scene. On August 26, 2000, a rally in front of the Lincoln Memorial on the thirty-seventh anniversary of Martin Luther King, Jr.'s march on Washington drew tens of thousands of demonstrators and national news coverage meant to focus on the issue of racial profiling. One participant said that "The exhaustive news coverage of the rally . . . accomplished much in educating the public to the problem of profiling and brutality."[80] The rally occurred at a time of unprecedented political action. Representative John Conyers of Michigan introduced a bill to require police departments to gather data on the races of persons stopped. The bill initially passed in the House but was killed in the Senate by the opposition of police groups; however, it is likely to be reintroduced.[81] Similar laws have been passed in North Carolina and Connecticut, and have been introduced in Arkansas, Rhode Island, Pennsylvania, Illinois, Virginia, Massachusetts, Ohio, New Jersey, Maryland, South Carolina, Oklahoma, and Florida.[82] A racial profiling information act was passed by both houses of the California legislature but was vetoed by Governor Gray Davis.[83]

Legal action in New Jersey and Maryland has required the collection of race data on stops by state troopers. The Michigan State Police decided to follow suit, as have the Washington State police and the Seattle Police Department.[84] But foot-dragging in the Seattle plan will not require officers to record their own race, an important factor in assessing the nature of racial profiling.[85] Numerous newspaper stories gathered in August 2000 show racial profiling to be a prominent issue in St. Louis; Greensboro, North Carolina; Arlington, Texas; Milwaukee; Los Angeles; Cleveland; and San Diego. Racial profiling was detected among the police force of Michigan State University.[86] It is too early to tell whether this activity will begin to reduce the practice of racial profiling, while Fourth Amendment law leaves so much power in the hands of police, but it is certainly a step in the right direction.

However, it would be a mistake to think that racial profiling has been generated simply by racial misperceptions and the lingering effects of racism. The prime generator of police stops of motorists and travelers has been the "war on drugs." If police perceptions are wrong about the greater propensity of minorities to carry drugs, then their profiling activity is failing to deter drug transportation. Steven Landsburg, commenting on an economic study of racial bias in automobile searches, notes that a study of stops on a stretch of I-95 in Maryland showed that both one-third of whites and blacks stopped were found to be carrying drugs, but that blacks were three and one-half times as likely as whites to be stopped.[87] He argued that if blacks are aware of racial profiling and still are discovered carrying drugs in equal proportion, they may be more likely to be carrying drugs in the first place. This seems to make racial profiling "rational." But the much larger number of white travelers means that a police focus on black drivers "makes it easier for white drug carriers to slip through the net." Continuing this economic analysis, Landsburg argues that if the police were motivated by racism, they would crack down further on black drivers to a point where very few would be caught with drugs. "Instead we see equal conviction rates, which suggests that the police concentrate on stopping blacks right up to the point where it helps them increase their conviction rates and no further." But this policy, while boosting police arrest rates, does not maximize deterrence because racial profiling "advertises to whites that they have little to fear from the police, which emboldens more whites to carry drugs. And because there are so many white people around, this effect can be quite large."[88] This analysis suggests that the "war on drugs" can be fought more effectively by eliminating racial profiling and training police, again to use the word correctly and ironically, to be more discriminating, i.e., to focus on the more likely drug dealers. The economic analysis fails to consider the cynical conclusion that legal but constitutionally dangerous policies that have undermined the actual expectation of privacy of African Americans will continue to be unleashed on the young and the poor, while effective treatments for the drug scourge may lie elsewhere.

SUMMARY

Warrantless searches are a routine and practically important part of police work, despite the Supreme Court's preference for a search warrant. Each type of warrantless search is based on a unique rationale. Every warrantless search must meet the minimum constitutional requirement for reasonableness. Exigency exceptions to the warrant requirement are lawful only if police have probable cause to believe that contraband is present; they include hot pursuit entries, the "automobile exception," search incident to arrest, and miscellaneous exigencies that impinge on Fourth Amendment interests. They are compatible with the warrant-preference construction of the Fourth Amendment.

Hot pursuit occurs when a dangerous criminal suspect is being chased by police and is seen entering a premises that is cloaked with Fourth Amendment protection. An exigency exists that allows the police to enter without a warrant. A constitutional hot pursuit entry must be based on probable cause, may be based on hearsay, may occur a few minutes after the suspect has entered a premises, may begin on private property outside the premises, authorizes the police to search an entire premises to find the suspect, and is limited to chases of suspects of serious crimes. Police must obtain search warrants to continue a crime scene investigation, after the initial exigency entrance to secure the premises ends.

Automobile searches constitute another exception to the search warrant requirement based on the exigency of mobility and on the lesser expectation of privacy accorded to people in cars. In addition to the automobile exigency exception, an automobile search involves several other warrantless search rules, including consent, plain view, stop and frisk, and pretext searches. The Supreme Court appears to allow warrantless automobile searches even when cars are immobilized and the suspect is in custody, as long as the car is potentially mobile. Any operative motor vehicle is an automobile for purposes of the exception, even if it is a person's home. The automobile exception applies even if police have time to obtain a warrant. A car subject to forfeiture may be seized from a public area without warrant.

A "container"—whether a footlocker or a closed paper bag—is an "effect" and thus protected by Fourth Amendment privacy rights. If police arrest a person and have probable cause to believe there is contraband in a closed container, a warrant must be obtained to open the container (unless it is subject to a search incident to arrest). However, after some case development, the Supreme Court has held that when police have probable cause to believe that contraband is located in a automobile, they may open any closed container, under the automobile exception, located in the car that may logically hold the contraband (*United States v. Ross,* 1982). When an officer has probable cause to believe that a specific container located in a car contains contraband, the officer may, upon lawfully stopping the car and gaining access to its interior, open the container (*California v. Acevedo*, 1991). *Ross* was extended to passengers: Police officers with probable cause to search a car may inspect passengers' belongings found in the car, which are capable of concealing the object of the search (*Wyoming v. Houghton*, 1999).

An automobile inventory search is a regulatory search based on a routine policy to make an inventory of items contained in all cars that are impounded by police for traffic or other violations. No probable cause is required. The main purposes for making an inventory are to protect the owner's property against theft or careless handling by the police, to protect the police against false claims or disputes over lost or stolen property, and to protect the police from potential danger. Inventory searches must be made routinely and under proper standards and procedures that limit the discretion of the officer. Officers conducting inventory searches may look into an unlocked glove compartment, a locked trunk, the space under the front seat and under the dashboard, and the opening of air vents under the dashboard, as well as the open area. Any contraband found in the course of an inventory search is seized in plain view and is admissible in evidence.

A border search is based on a nation's sovereign power to control entry and egress of people and goods, and requires no warrant or probable cause. In addition to a search at the actual border, this area of law covers roving patrols and fixed checkpoints. In general, there is a lesser expectation of privacy at the border, but both aliens and citizens retain some Fourth Amendment protections. At the border, or its functional equivalent, a person may be detained and searched at random, but the search must be reasonable. Reasonable suspicion must exist before border agents may subject a person to a body cavity search. Border agents operating fixed checkpoints or roving patrols must have probable cause to search parties who have been stopped under reasonable suspicion by roving patrols, or no suspicion at fixed checkpoints. Reasonable suspicion of contraband is required before international mail can be searched. Because of the well-established rules for ships, the complex nature of ships' documents, and the special difficulties of stopping sea-going vessels, government agents may stop and board vessels for document inspections without warrants or reasonable suspicion.

The Supreme Court has held that the Fourth Amendment does not apply to extraterritorial arrests or searches, i.e., searches and seizures that are conducted by United States officers in foreign countries. An arrest of a foreign national in a foreign country, conducted or directed by United States agents, does not divest a federal court of jurisdiction to try a prosecution against the suspect, even if the suspect had been kidnapped. Likewise, a search warrant issued by an American judge is not required to authorize a search on foreign territory conducted by U.S. officers; evidence seized in such a search is admissible. To the contrary, courts have held that confessions obtained by interrogation conducted by or at the request of United States agents are not admissible unless *Miranda* warnings are given. This is so because the Fifth Amendment privilege against self-incrimination operates as an exclusionary rule at the time evidence is introduced into a trial.

Searches by government employees infringe on Fourth Amendment interests but may be allowed without a warrant or probable cause if they are conducted for "special needs beyond the normal need for law enforcement." This has been applied to a public school teacher searching the bag of a student who is reasonably suspected of violating a school no-smoking rule, the search of the office of a physician hired by a state hospital and suspected of violating rules, the warrantless search of the home of a probationer for violating a condition of probation (no reasonable suspicion required), and a *police* inspection of automobile junk shops without a warrant under a regulatory law.

Special needs searches are closely related to administrative searches, and rely on the reasonableness clause of the Fourth Amendment. An administrative search warrant is based on conditions in an *area* rather than in a particular premises, and so is like a general warrant.

Firefighters who enter a premises to extinguish a fire intrude on an expectation of privacy but may do so because the fire creates an exigency. They may stay after the fire is extinguished to investigate the cause of a blaze. If the firefighters leave the site of a fire that retains an expectation of privacy, they must obtain an administrative warrant before returning to determine the cause of a recent fire and must obtain a criminal search warrant if they are suspicious of arson.

Drug testing by government agencies intrudes on a reasonable expectation of privacy but may be upheld if special needs beyond the normal need for law enforcement make it reasonable. The Supreme Court has upheld the drug testing of railway workers after a crash without individualized suspicion, the drug testing of Customs Service officers who were in drug enforcement positions and who carried firearms, and the testing of high school varsity athletes and high school students who are involved in extracurricular activities.

In two cases the Supreme Court held that special needs does not justify drug testing by public agencies. A law requiring the testing of candidates for statewide political offices was held unconstitutional because there were no indications that drug use had ever been a problem with political candidates; i.e., there were no special needs. The surreptitious drug testing of pregnant women enrolled in a public health program was deemed unconstitutional because the results were sent to law enforcement authorities for arrest and prosecution. This was not a special needs *beyond* the normal need for law enforcement but an intrusion of Fourth Amendment privacy for a law enforcement purpose.

LEGAL PUZZLES

How Have Courts Decided These Cases?

HOT PURSUIT

5–1. A taxi cab driver in Key West, Florida, reported to the police that Steve Brown was throwing full beer cans at passing cars at an intersection at 2:30 A.M. Officer Stinson arrived on the scene and found a full beer can. By that time Steve Brown went into the home of Richard and Kathleen Moody, where he and Ray Thorn were staying. The home was a short distance from the intersection. The taxi driver had followed Brown and Thorn to the Moody home and alerted the police officer that Brown had already gone inside the residence. Thorn had not thrown any beer cans. Officer Stinson entered the front yard. Thorn was outside and attempted to go inside the Moody home. According to Thorn, Officer Stinson stuck his foot in the front door. Thorn was thrown to the floor and arrested. Several officers entered the Moody home and a scuffle ensued. Richard

Moody and Ray Thorn were arrested. Steve Brown was arrested for throwing a beer can. The charges against Richard Moody were nolle prossed. Thorn entered a plea to reduced charges of simple battery and resisting arrest without violence.

This is a civil[§] 1983 action against the police. The police claim they had a right to enter the house as a hot pursuit.

Was there a proper hot pursuit of Steve Brown by Key West police officers?

HELD: No

5–1. The officers claim that they arrived promptly and that their entry of the home was authorized as being made in hot pursuit. The Florida Court of Appeals relied on *Welsh v. Wisconsin*: "On the facts of this case the claim of hot pursuit is unconvincing because there was no immediate or continuous pursuit of the petitioner from the scene of the crime." In this case, when the police arrived at the Moody residence, Brown was already inside. There was no immediate or continuous pursuit of Brown originating outside the house and continuing into the house. There has been no argument that there was any other emergency or exigent circumstance. *Moody v. City of Key West*, 805 So.2d 1018 (Ct. App. Fla. 3rd Dist., 2001)

AUTOMOBILE CONTAINER SEARCH

5–2. Police officers on routine patrol in the early evening hours stopped a red Pontiac Fiero driven by Kellen Lee Betz because its left headlight was extinguished. Mr. Betz quicky exited the car, closing the door behind him, and awaited the police officer. While asking Mr. Betz for his driver's license, the officer smelled a very strong odor of marijuana coming directly out of the rolled-down window of the Fiero. He also observed grey smoke in the vehicle. When he then noticed the marijuana odor emanating from Mr. Betz's shirt, the officer advised Mr. Betz that he was about to search the Fiero's trunk. Before doing so, the officer patted down Mr. Betz for weapons and contraband. He felt a long, cylindrical, hard object between four and six inches long which he could hear crinkling and rustling as he grabbed it. As the officer expected, the object, when seized, proved to be a plastic baggie containing some green plant matter that looked and smelled like marijuana. The officer placed Mr. Betz under arrest, searched the car and, ultimately, the trunk. Inside the trunk was a briefcase; inside the briefcase was a metal box; inside the metal box was a second bag of marijuana.

Was the search of the car's trunk, and of the containers in the trunk, constitutional?

Holding available from instructor

REGULATORY STOP

5–3. Alvester Fort's conviction for marijuana possession arose from the stop of his commercial truck by a Texas Department of Public Safety officer, Mike Scales, who stopped the truck to conduct a routine commercial safety inspection. A Texas regulatory statute allows officers to "detain" commercial vehicles for safety inspections. The truck was stopped while being driven on the highway, and there was no evidence that Officer Scales had probable cause to stop Fort's truck. Safety violations were detected. Officer Scales ran a license and wanted persons check on Mr. Fort, which revealed that Louisiana issued a warrant for Fort's arrest for a parole violation. The underlying offense for the Louisiana warrant was possession of marijuana with intent to deliver. Fort gave consent to the search of his truck. Approximately 561.2 pounds of marijuana was discovered.

Was the initial stop of the truck constitutional?

BORDER SEARCH

5–4. Ms. Dodd returned to the United States from a business trip in Malaysia, arriving at Detroit Metropolitan Airport. The initial search of Dodd involved an inquisition at the primary inspection podium, a detention at the luggage table, the search of her luggage, a pat-down prior to her entry to the search room, and a detention in the search room to the extent that it involved only questioning. Ms. Dodd was then subjected to a strip search and body cavity search. Dodd is suing Defendants, two female customs inspectors, for the violation of her constitutional rights as a result of these actions.

Ms. Dodd did not purchase her ticket immediately prior to her flight, did not pay in cash for her ticket, had plenty of luggage (to wit, two suitcases and a video camera), stayed in Malaysia for three weeks, and was traveling on business with three coworkers for a major company. The Defendants assert that Ms. Dodd had bloodshot eyes, trembling hands, and traveled from a source city (to wit, Amsterdam). Moreover, they contend that Dodd fidgeted and was nervous. Dodd claims that she offered the Defendants several options in an effort to verify her answers to questions, including contacting her three traveling companions, her employer, and her doctor to explain the trembling hands.

Did the Customs Officers violate Ms. Dodd's rights?

Holding available from instructor

SPECIAL NEEDS

5–5. Simons was an electronic engineer at a division of the CIA. He was provided an office, which he did not share with anyone, and a computer with Internet access. His unit instituted a policy that limited Internet usage by employees for official government business only. Accessing unlawful material was specifically prohibited. The policy explained that electronic audits would be conducted to insure compliance. During a check of the division's computer network firewall, a specialist discovered a large number of "hits" with the word "sex" emanating from Simon's computer. The specialist was instructed to view one of Simons's Web sites. The site contained pictures of nude women. Simons had downloaded more than one thousand such files. An inspection indicated that

some were pornographic. A list of the files was printed by the specialist. A criminal investigator with the CIA viewed selected files from the copy of Simons's hard drive; the pictures were of minors. A supervisor physically entered Simons's office, removed the original hard drive, replaced it with a copy, and gave the original to the CIA criminal investigator. An examination of the hard disk disclosed that many of the images contained child pornography. A warrant was then obtained to search Simons's office.

1. Did Simons have a legitimate expectation of privacy in his office?
2. Was the entry into his office to retrieve his computer hard disk without a warrant reasonable under the Fourth Amendment; i.e., Did the "special needs beyond normal need for law enforcement" doctrine apply?

Holding available from instructor

FURTHER READING

Randall Kennedy, *Race, Crime, and the Law* (New York: Pantheon Books, 1997).

Leonard W. Levy, *A License to Steal: The Forfeiture of Property* (Chapel Hill: The University of North Carolina Press, 1996).

James F. Simon, *The Center Holds: The Power Struggle Inside the Rehnquist Court* (New York: Simon & Schuster, 1995).

ENDNOTES

1. Charles Whitebread and Christopher Slobogin, *Criminal Procedure: An Analysis of Cases and Concepts, Fourth Edition* (New York: Foundation Press, 2000), pp. 216–23.
2. David E. Steinberg, "The Drive Toward Warrantless Auto Searches: Suggestions from a Back Seat Driver," *Boston University Law Review* 80 (2) (2000): 545–575.
3. Marvin Zalman, "Judges in Their Own Case: A Lockean Analysis of Drug Asset Forfeiture," *Criminal Justice Review*, 21 (2) (1996): 197–230; Eric Blumenson and Eva Nilsen, "Policing for Profit: The Drug War's Hidden Economic Agenda," *University of Chicago Law Review* 65 (1998): 35.
4. David Harris, "Car Wars: The Fourth Amendment's Death on the Highway," *George Washington Law Review* 66 (1998): 556–91.
5. Ibid., 556.
6. David Moran, "The New Fourth Amendment Vehicle Doctrine: Stop and Search Any Car at Any Time," *Villanova Law Review* 47 (2002): 815–838.
7. *United States v. Whitehead*, 849 F.2d 849 (4th Cir. 1988); *United States v. Nigro*, 727 F.2d 100 (6th Cir. 1984); *United States v. Boynes*, 149 F.3d 208 (3rd Cir. 1998); *United States v. Albers*, 136 F.3d 670 (9th Cir. 1998).
8. Steinberg, "Back Seat Driver," 549.
9. Harris, "Car Wars," 566–67.
10. 227 Conn. 363, 630 A.2d1315 (1993).
11. *State v. Parker*, 139 Wn.2d 486, 496, 987 P.2d 73, 79 (1999).
12. 956 P.2d 363 (Wyoming 1998).

13. Charles Whitebread and Christopher Slobogin, *Criminal Procedure: An Analysis of Cases and Concepts,* 4th ed. (New York: Foundation Press, 2000), 309.

14. See *Carroll v. United States* (1925); *United States v. 12 200-Foot Reels of Film* (1973).

15. Robin Wright, "Bin Laden Tie Seen in Border Arrest," *Los Angeles Times,* December 19, 1999.

16. Timothy Egan, "A Nation Challenged: The Convicted Terrorist; Man Caught in 2000 Plot Is Helping Investigators," *New York Times,* September 27, 2001.

17. See William Langewiesche, "Anarchy at Sea," *The Atlantic,* September 2003.

18. Roberto Iraola, "A Primer on Legal Issues Surrounding the Extraterritorial Apprehension of Criminals," *American Journal of Criminal Law* 29 (2001): 1–27.

19. "F.B.I. Plans to Open an Office in Poland," *New York Times,* July 2, 1994; David Johnston, "Fighting the Mob; The F.B.I. Makes Friends in (Of All Places) Moscow," *New York Times,* July 10, 1994; David Johnston, "Strength Is Seen in a U.S. Export: Law Enforcement," *New York Times,* April 17, 1995.

20. Richard L. Berke, "2 Ex-Mexican Aides Charged in Slaying of U.S. Drug Agent," *New York Times,* February 1, 1990.

21. *Alvarez-Machain v. U.S.,* 331 F.3d 604 (9th Cir. 2003).

22. Ibid., See Michael J. Glennon, "International Kidnapping: State-sponsored Abduction: A Comment on *United States v. Alvarez-Machain,*" *American Society of International Law Newsletter* 86 (October 1992): 746; Neil A. Lewis, "U.S. Tries to Quiet Storm Abroad over High Court's Right-to-Kidnap Ruling," *New York Times,* June 17, 1992; Seth Mydans, "Judge Clears Mexican in Agent's Killing," *New York Times,* December 15, 1992; Associated Press, "Judge Says U.S. Was Told It Held Wrong Doctor in Agent's Killing," *New York Times,* December 17, 1992; Steven A. Holmes, "U.S. Gives Mexico Abduction Pledge," *New York Times,* June 22, 1993.

23. 331 F.3d at 609. The case is currently before the Supreme Court.

24. Andrew Rosenthal, "Noriega Gives Himself up to U.S. Military; Is Flown to Florida to Face Drug Charges," *New York Times,* January 4, 1990.

25. See Robert A. Pape, "Dying to Kill Us," *New York Times,* September 22, 2003 (arguing on basis of research that number of suicide bombings is increasing and is due not to religion but to a secular and specific goal to compel liberal democracies to withdraw from territory terrorists consider their homelands).

26. Iraola, "Primer," 21.

27. *United States v. Usama Bin Laden,* 132 F. Supp.2d 168, 181–82 (E.D.N.Y. 2001).

28. 132 F. Supp.2d at 184 (grand jury indictment, no multiplicitous charges, privilege against compelled self-incrimination).

29. *Frank v. Maryland* (1959).

30. See Edward Levi, *An Introduction to Legal Reasoning* (Chicago: University of Chicago Press, 1949, 1961).

31. Lynn M. Paltrow, "Pregnant Drug Users, Fetal Persons, and the Threat to *Roe v. Wade,*" *Albany Law Review* 62 (1999): 999–1055.

32. Editorial, "Policing of Pregnancies Won't Protect Children," *New York Times,* August 4, 1996.

33. Linda Carroll, "Alcohol's Toll on Fetuses: Even Worse Than Thought," *New York Times,* November 4, 2002.

34. Nancy Maveety, "*Justice Sandra Day O'Connor: Strategist on the Supreme Court*" (Lanham: Rowman & Littlefield, 1996), 12–13. See Sandra Day O'Connor and H. Alan Day, *Lazy B: Growing Up on a Cattle Ranch in the American Southwest* (New York: Random House, 2002).

35. David A. Schultz and Christopher E. Smith, *The Jurisprudential Vision of Justice Antonin Scalia* (London: Rowman & Littlefield, 1996), xiii.

36. Cynthia Kelly Conlon, "Urineschool: A Study of the Impact of the *Earls* Decisions on High School Random Drug Testing Policies," *Journal of Law & Education* 32 (2003): 297–319.

37. Greg Winter, "Study Finds No Sign That Testing Deters Students' Drug Use," *New York Times,* May 17, 2003.

38. Robert D. Dodson, "Ten Years of Randomized Jurisprudence: Amending the Special Needs Doctrine," *South Carolina Law Review* 51 (2000): 258–289.

39. Ibid., 284

40. See generally, Randall Kennedy, *Race, Crime, and the Law* (New York: Pantheon Books, 1997).

41. Henry Louis Gates, Jr., "Thirteen Ways of Looking at a Black Man," *New Yorker,* October 23, 1995, cited in *Race, Crime,* by Kennedy, 151–52.

42. Lexis search in "newsgroup" news file; search: "racial profiling or driving while black and police and date = [year]."

43. John L. Burris (with Catherine Whitney), *Blue vs. Black: Let's End the Conflict Between Cops and Minorities* (New York: St. Martin's Press, 1999); Kenneth Meeks, *Driving While Black: Highways, Shopping Malls, Taxicabs, Sidewalks* (New York: Broadway Books, 2000).

44. M. Tonry, *Malign Neglect—Race, Crime, and Punishment in America* (New York: Oxford University Press, 1995), 70.

45. See Tonry, *Malign Neglect,* 52–56.

46. K. B. Noble, "A Showman in the Courtroom, for Whom Race is a Defining Issue," *New York Times,* January 20, 1995.

47. Cited in Tonry, *Malign Neglect,* 50–51.

48. A. Wallace and S. Chavez, "Understanding the Riots Six Months Later; Separate Lives/Dealing with Race in L.A.; Can We All Get Along?" *Los Angeles Times,* November 16, 1992.

49. T. Maclin, "'Black and Blue Encounters'—Some Preliminary Thoughts about Fourth Amendment Seizures: Should Race Matter?" *Valparaiso University Law Review* 26 (1991): 243–79.

50. Jim Yardley, "Some Texans Say Border Patrol Singles out Too Many Blameless Hispanics," *New York Times,* January 26, 2000.

51. Tonry, *Malign Neglect,* 51.

52. Bill Johnson, "The Answer to Driving While Black Is Not More Racial Profiling," *Detroit News,* July 30, 1999.

53. David A. Harris, "The Stories, the Statistics, and the Law: Why 'Driving While Black' Matters," *Minnesota Law Review* 84 (1999): 265–326.

54. Ibid., 277–81.

55. Ibid., 281–88.

56. David Kocieniewski and Robert Hanley, "'Racial Profiling was the Routine,' New Jersey Finds," *New York Times,* November 28, 2000; David Kocieniewski, "New Jersey Argues that the U.S. Wrote the Book on Race Profiling," *New York Times,* November 29, 2000.

57. *Murphy v. Reynoldsburg,* 1991 WL 150938 (Ohio Ct. App. 10th App. Dist. Franklin Co., 1991); *Murphy v. Reynoldsburg,* 65 Ohio St. 3d 356, 604 N.E.2d 138 (1992).

58. See H. Sitkoff, *The Struggle for Black Equality, 1954–1992*, rev. ed. (New York: Hill and Wang, 1993); P. Finkelman, "The Crime of Color," *Tulane Law Review* 67 (1993): 2063–2112; S. Walker, *Popular Justice* (New York: Oxford University Press, 1980); L. Friedman, *Crime and Punishment in American History* (New York: Basic Books, 1993); C. R. Mann, *Unequal Justice: A Matter of Color* (Bloomington: Indiana University Press, 1993).

59. W. J. Wilson, *The Truly Disadvantaged* (Chicago: University of Chicago Press, 1987).

60. G. J. Jaynes and R. M. Williams, Jr., *A Common Destiny: Blacks and American Society* (Washington, D.C.: National Academy Press, 1989), 6, 274.

61. Ibid., 258.

62. Ibid., 88–91.

63. Ibid., 117.

64. Tonry, *Malign Neglect*, 10–12; D. C. Anderson, *Crime and the Politics of Hysteria: How the Willie Horton Story Changed American Justice* (New York: Times Books, 1995).

65. Anderson, *Crime and the Politics*, 8–9.

66. David Barstow and Kevin Flynn, "Officer Who Broke the Code of Silence Defies Labels," *New York Times,* May 15, 1999.

67. Jodi Wilgoren and Ginger Thompson, "After Shooting, an Eroding Trust in the Police," *New York Times,* February 19, 1999.

68. Bob Herbert, "In America—The Mud-Slingers," *New York Times,* March 20, 2000.

69. Developments in the Law—"Race and the Criminal Process," *Harvard Law Review* 101 (1988): 1472–1641.

70. Harris, "The Stories," 291–94.

71. S. L. Johnson, "Race and the Decision to Detain a Suspect," *Yale Law Journal* 93 (1983): 218–219; R. Kennedy, *Race, Crime,* 153–63.

72. Meeks, *Driving While Black*, 63–67.

73. Harris, "The Stories," 296, emphasis added, citing 1997 United States Dept. of Health and Human Services data from the National Household Survey on Drug Abuse.

74. Robyn Meredith, "Near Detroit, a Familiar Sting in Being a Black Driver," *New York Times,* July 16, 1999.

75. Harris, "The Stories," 318, see 310–20.

76. Maclin, "Black and Blue Encounters," 252.

77. Johnson, "Decision to Detain," 214–58; Maclin, "Black and Blue Encounters," 268–79; Developments—"Criminal Process," 1519.

78. D. E. Georges Abeyie, "Symposium: Law Enforcement and Racial and Ethnic Bias," *Florida State University Law Review* 19 (1992): 717–26; R. A. Carter, "Point of View: Improving Minority Relations," *FBI Law Enforcement Bulletin* 64 (1995): 14–17.

79. Harris, "The Stories," 298–309.

80. Cindy Loose and Chris L. Jenkins, "Rallying to 'Redeem the Dream'; Rights' Leaders Target Racial Profiling," *Washington Post*, August 27, 2000.

81. Harris, "The Stories," 319–21.

82. Ibid., 321–22.

83. Miguel Bustillo and Carl Ingram, "Bill on Racial Profiling Scrapped," *Los Angeles Times*, August 25, 2000.

84. David Shepardson, "Police Track Race of Drivers: It's to Show Motorists Are Not Ticketed Based on Skin Color," *Detroit News*, July 26, 1999.

85. Susan Paynter, "Race-Profile Issue Means 'You Have to Have Faith,'" *Seattle Post-Intelligencer*, August 25, 2000; Kimberly A.C. Wilson, "New Dispute Erupts on Race Profiling Issue; Police Officers Won't Have to Record Own Ethnic Background," *Seattle Post-Intelligencer,* August 24, 2000.

86. Eric Lacy, "Michigan State U. Report Examines Racial Profiling," *The State News* via U-Wire, August 7, 2000.

87. The study is John Knowls, Nicola Persico, and Petra Todd, *Racial Bias in Motor Vehicle Searches: Theory and Evidence* (Cambridge, MA: National Bureau of Economic Research, 1999).

88. Steven E. Landsburg, "The Crazy Incentives of the Drug War," *Slate Magazine*, August 14, 2000.

JUSTICES OF THE SUPREME COURT

THOUGHTFUL CONSERVATIVES
CLARK—HARLAN II—STEWART—WHITE

Justices Tom Clark, John Marshall Harlan II, Potter Stewart, and Byron White were appointed by presidents (Truman, Eisenhower, and Kennedy) with differing political philosophies. Nevertheless, these four justices exhibited several similarities. On criminal procedure issues, all were conservative in that they generally opposed incorporation; they tended to find for the prosecution. On the other hand, all were receptive to the civil rights claims of African Americans. Clark, as a key architect of President Truman's anti-Communist loyalty oath program, was fiercely opposed to easing the application of these rules. Each of these justices were thorough and thoughtful in his review of cases, and each had at times ruled in support of criminal defendants in significant cases.

Among these justices, John Harlan ranks as the most acute legal thinker. Known as a lawyer's justice, he carefully crafted opinions without ambiguity to be applied by practic-

ing lawyers and trial judges. Potter Stewart was the most centrist of these justices in criminal procedure matters. He dissented in Miranda v. Arizona *(1966), but his opinions in such cases as* Chimel v. California *(1969) (reach-and-lunge rule) and* Coolidge v. New Hampshire *(1971) (warrant preference interpretation) were quite liberal. His opinion in* Katz v. United States *(1967) was the keystone in modernizing Fourth Amendment law.*

Justice White may have been a surprise; nominated by a liberal president, he quickly joined the conservative wing of the Court on many issues, especially criminal procedure. In this regard, he stands in sharp contrast to Kennedy's other appointee, Arthur Goldberg. Justice White's influence on the Court was enhanced by his lengthy tenure and his practice of at times shifting to the center of the Court so as to occupy the pivotal middle ground.

TOM C. CLARK

Texas 1899–1977

Democrat

Appointed by
Harry Truman

Years of Service:
1949–1967

Collection of the Supreme Court of the United States. Photographer: Harris and Ewing

LIFE AND CAREER   The son of a Dallas lawyer, Clark served in the United States Army during World War I, graduated from the University of Texas Law School, and practiced in his father's law firm from 1922 to 1927. Thereafter, he held appointed posts as civil district attorney and assistant (criminal) district attorney for Dallas. His involvement in politics led to his appointment to the U.S. Justice Department in 1937, where he worked on a variety of issues including war claims, antitrust, the evacuation of Japanese Americans from the West Coast to camps during World War II, and war frauds. In 1943 he was appointed assistant attorney general and headed the antitrust and the criminal divisions.

He supported Harry Truman for the vice-presidential nomination in 1944 and was appointed by Truman as attorney

general in 1945. Clark was a vigorous attorney general, instituting 160 antitrust cases, supporting civil rights actions designed to end racial segregation, and playing a key role in developing President Truman's anti-Communist loyalty oath program, generated by Cold War fears of internal subversion.

In 1967 Justice Clark resigned from the Court as a gesture of paternal love when his son, Ramsey Clark, was appointed by President Johnson as attorney general. That would have created a conflict of interest that would have arisen in every Supreme Court case involving the United States government. For the next decade of his life, he actively participated as a judge in the various federal circuits and contributed to numerous programs designed to enhance the quality of the American judiciary.

CONTRIBUTION TO CRIMINAL PROCEDURE   He more often than not voted in favor of the state in this area. For example, he dissented in *Miranda v. Arizona* (1966). He dissented in a case that held that probable cause could not be based on a person's general reputation (*Beck,* 1964); he dissented in a case that excluded evidence seized from a second person pursuant to an illegal arrest of a first person (*Wong Sun,* 1963); and he joined Justice Minton's decision in *Rabinowitz* (1950). Nevertheless, he wrote the majority opinion in the breakthrough incorporation decision of *Mapp v. Ohio*. On the other hand, he was a staunch supporter of fair trials, as seen in his opinions finding constitutional error because of excessive pretrial publicity.

SIGNATURE OPINION   *Mapp v. Ohio* (1961). Why did a generally conservative justice on criminal matters support the incorporation of the exclusionary rule? In a revealing interview

(Continued)

after retirement, Clark told a seminar of students that as a young lawyer, he defended his cook's son against a Prohibition charge (possessing liquor) after Dallas police simply entered the accused's room, ripped open a mattress, and gave the bottle of liquor they found to federal agents. Clark was shocked that police could do this. Thus, although as a justice he was loath to curb the legitimate power of police officers, the facts of *Mapp* were excessive. To Justice Clark, the exclusionary rule, applied to the states as well as the federal government, simply made sense, and as he wrote in *Mapp*, "there is no war between the Constitution and common sense."

ASSESSMENT Clark replaced the staunch liberal justice, Frank Murphy, in 1949, tilting the Vinson Court in a more conservative direction. Clark generally joined justices Reed, Frankfurter, Jackson, and Burton, although he was somewhat more liberal than Chief Justice Vinson. During the 1950s he supported the government in antitrust and loyalty cases, where his experiences as attorney general shaped his approaches, thus taking a liberal stance in the first area and a conservative stance in the latter. His positions on First Amendment, voting district reapportionment, and racial segregation issues were in sync with the liberal Warren Court.

FURTHER READING

Richard Kirkendall, "Tom C. Clark," in *The Justices of the United States Supreme Court, 1789–1969*, Leon Friedman and Fred L. Israel, eds., vol. 4, 2665–95 (New York: Chelsea House, 1969).

JOHN M. HARLAN II

New York 1899–1971

Republican

Appointed by
Dwight D. Eisenhower

Years of Service:
1955–1971

Collection of the Supreme Court of the United States. Photographer: Harris and Ewing

LIFE AND CAREER The grandson of a Supreme Court justice by the same name, John Harlan was viewed as a "progressive Republican" when appointed. He was born in Chicago, educated at private schools, and served briefly in World War I. He received his bachelor's degree from Princeton in 1920, was a Rhodes Scholar at Oxford, and completed his legal studies at New York Law School in 1924. He practiced law in New York with a prestigious Wall Street law firm up until his appoint-

ment to the Second Circuit Court of Appeals in early 1954. However, his background also included years of public service. He prosecuted a former United States attorney general for corruption when he was an assistant United States attorney in the 1920s, acted as a special prosecutor for New York State in a major investigation of municipal graft in the 1930s, directed a critical unit of experts advising the commanding general of the Eighth Air Force on bombing operations in Europe during World War II, and was chief counsel of an organized crime investigation for the state of New York in the early 1950s. After less than a year on the Second Circuit Court of Appeals, he was nominated by President Eisenhower to the Supreme Court.

CONTRIBUTION TO CRIMINAL PROCEDURE He opposed incorporation and dissented in *Mapp* and *Miranda*; he believed the federal government should be held to higher standards of procedural regularity under the Bill of Rights than states under the Fourteenth Amendment. He was generally conservative and voted for the state, but not slavishly so. Thus, he concurred on extending the right to counsel to all felony defendants (*Gideon*, 1963); he concurred in extending the right to counsel to juveniles (*In re Gault*, 1967) and in *Katz v. United States* (1967). He dissented in *United States v. White* (1971), arguing that police agents should not be able to wear body-mikes without a prior judicial warrant.

SIGNATURE OPINION *Spinelli v. United States* (1969). His opinion upheld the two-pronged test for determining when the hearsay evidence of a confidential informant can amount to probable cause for a search warrant. Harlan closely examined the facts put forth by the FBI and penetrated the affidavit's veneer of certainty to show that the agency was, in effect, asking for a blank check on its decision. The opinion highlights the vital importance of judicial scrutiny of police affidavit requests to the preservation of Fourth Amendment privacy and liberty.

ASSESSMENT Justice Harlan developed a close intellectual friendship with Justice Frankfurter; with Frankfurter's resignation in 1962, Harlan took on the mantle of the chief spokesperson for judicial restraint and traditional judicial conservatism. During the entire period of the due process revolution, Justice Harlan wrote the most exhaustive and penetrating dissents against the incorporation doctrine.

Justice Harlan was "a lawyer's judge"—he closely examined cases and often based decisions on fine factual distinctions rather than upon broad generalizations, and his opinions reflected a concern to give lawyers and judges clear guidance in applying the rules of the case. He had a profound respect for judicial precedent and felt the Court should interfere as little as possible into the political workings of both state and federal government. His incorporation dissents noted that "the American federal system is itself constitutionally ordained, that it embodies values profoundly making for lasting liberties in this country. . . ." He was skeptical about the ability of courts to ensure true liberty by their rulings, believing that liberty "can rise no higher or be made more secure than the spirit of a people to achieve and maintain

(Continued)

it." He also believed that federalism encouraged differences between the states and that it was not the role of the Supreme Court to eradicate these differences by applying the Bill of Rights as a steamroller over variations of state procedure.

FURTHER READING

Tinsley E. Yarbrough, *John Marshall Harlan: Great Dissenter of the Warren Court* (New York: Oxford University Press, 1992).

POTTER STEWART

Ohio 1915–1986

Republican

Appointed by
Dwight D. Eisenhower

Years of Service:
1958–1981

Collection of the Supreme Court of the United States. Photographer: Harris and Ewing

LIFE AND CAREER Born into a politically active Republican Ohio family with "a strong tradition of public service," Stewart was educated at the Hotchkiss School, Yale University (where he was a Phi Beta Kappa), and Yale Law School, where he generally supported the New Deal. He served as a deck officer on an oil tanker during World War II, which put him in contact with men of a different background than he would meet at Yale or in corporate law practice. He practiced law in his hometown of Cincinnati from 1946 to 1954. His political activity (he was twice elected to the Cincinnati City Council) and his support for Dwight Eisenhower for the Republican presidential nomination in 1952 against Ohio Senator Robert Taft led President Eisenhower to name him to the Sixth Circuit Court of Appeals in 1954 at the young age of thirty-nine. His reputation as an excellent judge led to his nomination to the Supreme Court in 1958.

CONTRIBUTION TO CRIMINAL PROCEDURE Although known as a middle-of-the-road justice who did not automatically side with either liberal or conservative justices, Justice Stewart wrote a large number of Fourth Amendment opinions for the Supreme Court that often tended to expand defendants' rights. On the

"liberal or pro-defendant" side were *Vale v. Louisiana* (1970) (a doorstep arrest does not authorize a general search of a premises) and *Coolidge v. New Hampshire* (1971) (supporting the warrant preference construction of the Fourth Amendment). On the pro-prosecution side, Stewart opposed incorporation, dissented in *Miranda v. Arizona*, and wrote the majority opinion in *Schneckloth v. Bustamonte* (1973), holding that the police need not warn suspects of their Fourth Amendment rights before requesting consent to search.

Justice Stewart had a talent for turning a pithy phrase that encapsulates a rule, and wrote logical, well-organized opinions. This was seen in his most important Fourth Amendment opinion, *Katz v. United States* (1967), where his emblematic statement—"For the Fourth Amendment protects people, not places"—nicely summed up the major shift in Fourth Amendment jurisprudence from its foundations in property law to its new basis on an expectation of privacy.

SIGNATURE OPINION His majority opinion in *Chimel v. California* (1969) ended the long zigzag course of opinions on the scope of a search incident to arrest; it confirmed that while officers may reasonably search the area within the immediate control of an arrested suspect to seize weapons and contraband, they may not use the arrest as an excuse to search a premises without a warrant.

ASSESSMENT His approach to constitutional law was cautious and restrained. His middle-of-the-road votes made him a "swing justice" in many areas. His judicial philosophy appeared to be that a judge should first defer to legislative and executive branch authority, but not hesitate to exercise judicial review in order to maintain essential procedural safeguards and prevent abuses of power. Justice Stewart favored narrow rulings and preferred that cases be resolved on the specific facts when necessary. He was a lone dissenter in the case that held school prayer to violate the First Amendment but voted for free speech in censorship cases. On the death penalty, he held it to be unconstitutional as applied in 1972, but voted to uphold revised death penalty laws in 1976 that incorporated the element of guided discretion. He decided a very large number of criminal procedure cases. Ultimately, it was not possible to classify Justice Stewart simply as a liberal or conservative or as an activist or passivist judge.

FURTHER READING

Tinsley E. Yarbrough, "Justice Potter Stewart: Decisional Patterns in Search of Doctrinal Moorings," in *The Burger Court: Political and Judicial Profiles*, Charles M. Lamb and Stephen C. Halpern, eds., 375–406 (Urbana: University of Illinois Press, 1991).

BYRON R. WHITE

Colorado 1917–2002

Democrat

Appointed by
John F. Kennedy

Years of Service:
1962–1993

*Collection of the Supreme
Court of the United States.
Photographer: Joseph Bailey*

LIFE AND CAREER Byron White's youth was filled with hard work in the beet fields of rural Colorado and on railroad section crews. He was an excellent student and outstanding athlete in high school and at the University of Colorado, where he was elected to Phi Beta Kappa, graduated first in his class in 1938, and attracted national attention as a star tailback (nicknamed "Whizzer") on Colorado's unbeaten football team. He also won varsity letters in basketball and baseball. Between 1938 and 1942, White spent a year at Oxford University as a Rhodes Scholar (where he met Ambassador Joseph Kennedy's son, John), was the highest-paid professional football player in America, and began law school. While serving as a naval intelligence officer in the South Pacific during World War II, he again met John Fitzgerald Kennedy. White completed his law degree at Yale after the war, clerked for Chief Justice Fred Vinson (1946–1947), and while in Washington, had numerous opportunities to meet with freshman Congressman John Kennedy of Massachusetts. In 1947 he returned to Colorado and the private practice of law.

In 1959 White led the Colorado organization on behalf of Kennedy's efforts to gain the Democratic presidential nomination. He was appointed deputy United States attorney general in 1961 and won recognition as an able administrator, effectively acting as "chief of staff" of the Justice Department. During the tense days in May 1961, when Attorney General Robert Kennedy dispatched four hundred federal marshals to Alabama to protect freedom riders, White calmly and competently supervised the marshals and deputies. In this position, he ably screened candidates for federal judgeships.

CONTRIBUTION TO CRIMINAL PROCEDURE White was generally conservative on criminal procedure issues; he dissented strongly in *Escobedo* (1964) and *Miranda* (1966) and was clearly opposed to the incorporation of the Fourth Amendment exclusionary rule. On occasion, he could decide in favor of the defendant. In *Duncan v. Louisiana* (1968), however, he effectively ended the *Palko* (1937) approach to fundamental rights and wrote that if a Bill of Rights procedure is fundamental to the *American* system of justice, it ought to be incorporated.

His pro-government rulings include the late-1980s ruling that a helicopter overflight of a backyard at four hundred feet is not a search; there is no expectation of privacy in abandoned trash; an indicted defendant may waive his right to counsel and be interrogated without his attorney present; and government forfeiture of funds to prevent paying an attorney does not violate the right to counsel. On the other hand, in *Arizona v. Fulminante* (1991) he led a liberal coalition in holding that a confession was coerced, and dissenting against a new rule that a coerced confession can be harmless error.

SIGNATURE OPINION His most significant Fourth Amendment opinion was *United States v. Leon* (1984), which held admissible evidence obtained without probable cause by a police officer relying in good faith on a faulty judicial warrant. *Leon* was the first clear exception to the *Mapp v. Ohio* (1961) exclusionary rule and a significant victory for conservative justices opposed to the expansion of the rights of criminal suspects. *Leon's* reasoning relied heavily on a balancing analysis and to some extent on shaky empirical research.

ASSESSMENT He was generally a middle-of-the-road or swing justice. In the 1960s he supported governmental authority over individual liberty in cases involving the investigation of Communists and other groups. On the other hand, his votes on the civil rights of minorities usually favored integration, school busing, and affirmative action. White has puzzled commentators because of his apparent lack of a clear judicial philosophy. Thus, despite his generally strong support for civil rights and "one man one vote," he has on occasion ruled inconsistently. Some inconsistent decisions can be explained by his concern with the specific factual and procedural contours of each case.

FURTHER READING

Dennis J. Hutchinson, *The Man Who Once Was Whizzer White: A Portrait of Byron R. White* (New York: Free Press, 1998).

CHAPTER 6

THE RIGHT TO COUNSEL

It is a fair summary of history to say that the safeguards of liberty have frequently been forged in controversies involving not very nice people.

—Justice Felix Frankfurter, dissenting in *United States v. Rabinowitz,*
339 U.S. 56, 69 (1950)

CHAPTER OUTLINE

KEY TERMS AND PHRASES

Actual imprisonment rule
Appointed counsel
Asset forfeiture
Assigned counsel
Authorized imprisonment rule
Conflict of interest
Continuance
Critical stage

Deficient performance
Formal charge rule
Indigent
Multiple representation
Parallel right
Prejudice prong
Pro bono publico
Pro se defense

Public defender
Recoupment
Retained counsel
Right to counsel
Self-representation
Special circumstances rule
Standby counsel
Waiver of counsel

INTRODUCTION

A defense lawyer stands next to her criminal client in court. Both face judge and jury while awaiting verdict. The defendant will suffer the penalty for a guilty verdict, but their standing together is a powerful reminder that the attorney is the defendant's surrogate—the lawyer "stands in the defendant's shoes." The attorney owes the client an undivided duty of representation, within the law, marked by "warm zeal." The attorney is cloaked with the attorney-client privilege that preserves a criminal client's right against self-incrimination and without which adequate representation and a fair trial are impossible.

Although a fair trial now seems inseparable from a defendant having access to a competent lawyer, it was not always so in the English common law trial by jury. From the origins of trial by jury in the middle ages and well into the modern age, defendants in English criminal trials defended themselves. At the same time, except in major treason trials, public prosecutors did not exist. An English criminal trial was a "long argument" between the defendant and a private accuser.[1] It was only in 1695 that English law allowed a defendant the right to have legal representation in a treason trial. Lawyers began to advise felony defendants shortly after that date, but by law were barred from speaking in the trial. This rule was seen as unjust and was at times breached in practice.[2] Nevertheless, it was not until 1836 that English defendants gained the ability to be represented by a paid lawyer in a felony trial.

In contrast to England, colonial America embraced the use of attorneys in criminal trials. John Adams, later the second president of the United States, defended many criminal cases. In the celebrated Boston Massacre case, Adams, although a member of the pro-liberty party, vigorously defended and won acquittals for the British soldiers who fired in self-defense on a large, stone-throwing mob of zealous patriots.[3] Many state constitutions included guarantees of counsel in criminal cases.[4] Despite the **right to counsel** guarantee in the federal and state bills of rights, most **indigent** defendants represented themselves. The right to counsel existed only for those who could afford a lawyer. When poor defendants tried their own cases, ideally, the judge took special care to provide some advice to ensure that they did not completely ruin their defense. In death penalty cases, judges often ordered a lawyer to donate services free of charge as a professional obligation.

The framers clearly viewed the right to counsel favorably, even if not intending to provide free lawyers for indigent defendants. The primary source of the right to counsel is found in the Sixth Amendment: "In all criminal prosecutions the accused shall enjoy the right . . . to have the assistance of counsel for his defence."[5] Because the Sixth Amendment right is limited to criminal prosecutions, in certain proceedings a right to counsel is based on the fairness concept of the Due Process Clauses (Fifth and Fourteenth amendments). This includes counsel in the correctional process, e.g., at a probation revocation hearing. The right to counsel at a custodial interrogation made famous by *Miranda* warnings is a right that derives from the Fifth Amendment privilege against self-incrimination. The Equal Protection Clause of the Fourteenth Amendment has also been used by the Court to guarantee equitable treatment in the trial process by ensuring that an indigent defendant need not pay filing fees or be denied transcripts if they are important for the defense. The combined force of due process and equal protection was held to guarantee a lawyer for a convicted defendant's first appeal as of right.

Prior to the incorporation of the Sixth Amendment right to counsel into the Due Process Clause in 1963 by *Gideon v. Wainwright*, the Due Process Clause of the Fourteenth Amendment was an important vehicle for guaranteeing the provision of counsel in certain state proceedings.

Before the mid-twentieth century, the Sixth Amendment right to counsel meant that a court or statute could not abolish a defendant's right to be represented in court by a paid, licensed lawyer of his or her choosing. At first the right did not mean that the state had to pay for a defense lawyer—until the early twentieth century it was constitutionally acceptable for a poor person to defend himself without a lawyer in a felony trial—and with whatever help the judge was disposed to grant. In complex or death penalty cases, judges used to order local lawyers to represent indigent defendants for no charge, **pro bono publico,** but the practice was not uniform. The development of the right to counsel in the twentieth century has centered on the practical issue of whether the state has to pay for a lawyer for a person who is too poor to pay.

Lawyers play a key role in ensuring *fair* criminal trials. In the common law trial by jury, the truth is seen to emerge from the clash of evidence provided by prosecution and defense. The trial is a technical and intimidating process. Criminal attorneys are trained in the rapidly changing and intricate substantive criminal law, have to know all the rules of local criminal procedure, must have the rules of evidence at their fingertips, and have developed the practical skills to bring these rules to life in the conduct of trials. In addition to trial advocacy, an attorney directs pretrial investigations (for evidence of innocence; for such defenses as insanity), and protects the defendant's rights in legally complex pretrial hearings. Motions for bail, discovery, suppression of illegally obtained evidence, change of venue in notorious cases, and the conduct of plea negotiations require experienced attorneys. Plea bargaining, contrary to common belief, is quite adversarial. Attorneys who prepare negotiated cases as if they were going to trial learn strengths and weaknesses of the case and are in a position to back up their negotiating position with a resort to trial if needed. The adversarial nature of American trials pervades the entire adjudication process and makes even routine cases dependent on the abilities of trained, professional advocates. A defendant without a lawyer is at a severe disadvantage.

The benefits of a defense attorney were once available only to those who could afford one. The critical issue that ran through all of the cases that came before the Supreme Court was whether the state had to provide counsel for indigents—those who were too poor to pay for a lawyer.

THE DEVELOPMENT OF THE RIGHT TO COUNSEL TO 1961

The twentieth century growth of urban populations and bureaucratic, multijudge courts required that ad hoc methods of providing lawyers for indigents had to be replaced with more formal legal aid and defender systems. Some cities and states had begun to do this in the early twentieth century. But under the U.S. Constitution, there was no obligation in federal or state criminal trials that the government, which was prosecuting the defendant, had any obligation to ensure a fair trial by providing defense counsel. In 1932 the Supreme Court began to define the right to counsel. Thirty years later it applied the Sixth Amendment right to the states by incorporating that right into the Fourteenth Amendment Due Process Clause. The constitutional journey began with one of the most celebrated trials in American history, the infamous "Scottsboro" case. In *Powell v. Alabama* (1932) the Court found that under certain circumstances state courts had to provide criminal defendants with free counsel.

Powell v. Alabama: The Scottsboro Case

Nine African American teens, arrested after a fistfight with several white boys on a freight train rolling through Alabama in 1931, were falsely accused of rape by two white women passengers. The teens were tried for a capital crime in Scottsboro, Alabama. Thus began one of the great trial sagas in American history. It did not end until the last of the defendants was released from prison decades later.[6] The "Scottsboro boys" were tried three times in a climate dripping with racism; sentenced to death; gained national notoriety; grew to maturity in prison; were saved by appeals, stays of execution, and commutations; and twice saw their cases go before the United States Supreme Court.[7]

The first trials were one-day affairs held on successive days. Eight of the teens were sentenced to death. The Alabama Supreme Court affirmed seven of the capital sentences. The United States Supreme Court accepted the case and reversed the convictions in November 1932. Justice George Sutherland's majority opinion in *Powell v. Alabama* (1932) held that the defendants' due process rights were violated.

The issue in *Powell* was whether the defendants' due process rights were violated by the denial of the right to counsel, "with the accustomed incidents of consultation and opportunity of preparation for trial." Prior to 1932, the Supreme Court had not incorporated any of the criminal procedure rights in the Bill of Rights, which included the guarantee of the assistance of counsel. The Supreme Court, however, had ruled less than a decade before that a state prosecution obtained through the pressure of a lynch mob infringed a *state* defendant's constitutional rights under the Fourteenth Amendment Due Process Clause (*Moore v. Dempsey,* 1923; Chapter 1). "Mob justice" was not the precise basis of the *Powell* decision, although Justice Sutherland did note that the atmosphere surrounding the trials was one of "tense, hostile and excited public sentiment."

How were the defendants represented in the Scottsboro case? The transcript indicated that lawyers for the defendants examined and cross-examined witnesses and made arguments. On this basis, the Alabama Supreme Court ruled that Ozie Powell and the other youths were represented by counsel and not denied due process. Why did the United States Supreme Court conclude otherwise? Justice Sutherland noted that the defendants, who were young and poor strangers in Scottsboro, were not asked if they had access to lawyers. They were not given much time to contact their families in other states to arrange for counsel:

> It is hardly necessary to say that, the right to counsel being conceded, a defendant should be afforded a fair opportunity to secure counsel of his own choice. Not only was that not done here, but such designation of counsel as was attempted was either so indefinite or so close upon the trial as to amount to a denial of effective and substantial aid in that regard. (*Powell v. Alabama,* p. 53)

Indeed, the trial transcript disclosed that in fact none of the lawyers was willing to definitely be a lawyer for a specific defendant. Steven Roddy, a Tennessee lawyer, was asked by the court whether he intended to appear for the defendants. Roddy replied that he was not really hired although he "would like to appear along with counsel that the court might appoint."[8] Ultimately, no single lawyer was appointed for all the defendants, nor was each defendant appointed individual counsel. Instead, the trial judge "appointed *all* the members of the bar for the purpose of arraigning the defendants" and continued that arrangement for the trial when neither Roddy nor any of the local lawyers would stand up to be *the* attorney of record.[9] The white lawyers were obviously unwilling to vigorously defend poor African American teens and drifters accused of the rape of two white women in the segregated South. In the critical time period before trial, when a lawyer could have organized an investigation into the facts and marshaled legal arguments, no one focused on this task. This lack of resolution and focus clearly offended Justice Sutherland:[10]

> It is not enough to assume that counsel thus precipitated into the case thought there was no defense, and exercised their best judgment in proceeding to trial without preparation. Neither they nor the court could say what a prompt and thoroughgoing investigation might disclose as to the facts. No attempt was made to investigate. No opportunity to do so was given. Defendants were immediately hurried to trial. . . . Under the circumstances disclosed, we hold that defendants were not accorded the right of counsel in any substantial sense. To decide otherwise, would simply be to ignore actualities. (*Powell v. Alabama,* p. 58)

Did Justice Sutherland's holding—that the defendants were not accorded the right to counsel in any substantial sense—incorporate the Sixth Amendment, i.e., directly apply the Sixth Amendment assistance of counsel right to the state courts in all felony trials? Although his bare words can give that impression, Justice Sutherland based his decision on the Due Process Clause alone. He first reviewed the history of the right to counsel in the original states: twelve established the right to counsel when no such right existed in England, showing its importance. In death penalty cases, some *colonies* required the appointment of defense counsel as was the law in Alabama in 1931.

Justice Sutherland then addressed the incorporation issue. The right to counsel is in the Bill of Rights, but *Hurtado v. California* (1884), standing alone, held that the federal courts could not incorporate a Bill of Rights provision into the Fourteenth Amendment Due Process Clause, making it a state requirement. But *Hurtado* did not stand alone. *Chicago, Burlington & Quincy R. Co. v. Chicago* (1897) held that the states, as a matter of Fourteenth Amendment due process, had to grant just compensation when the state took private property for public use, even though a Just Compensation Clause existed in the Fifth Amendment. Furthermore, "freedom of speech and of the press are rights protected by the Due Process Clause of the Fourteenth Amendment, although in the First Amendment, Congress is prohibited in specific terms from abridging the right."[11] Therefore, a right found in the Bill of Rights as a proscription on the federal government, could also exist as a **parallel right,** within the scope of due process. This "parallel right" approach is clearly not the "total incorporation" under the Privileges or Immunities Clause (desired by the first Justice Harlan or Hugo Black), nor is it the modern approach of "selective incorporation." Yet, it seems clear that Sutherland was influenced by the "fundamental rights" reasoning of *Twining v. New Jersey* (1908) (see Chapter 1).

Although Justice Sutherland and the Court did not cleanly incorporate the Sixth Amendment right to counsel, his opinion came rather close to calling it a fundamental right. The philosopher Hadley Arkes suggests that Justice Sutherland was concerned with basic principles: "To begin at the root, the purpose of a trial was to do justice, to punish the guilty and vindicate the innocent. The central task was to make reasoned discriminations between the innocent and the guilty and arrive at verdicts that were substantially just."[12] At minimum, due process requires notice, a fair hearing, and a competent tribunal. Justice Sutherland then wrote the classic passage explaining the vital importance of a fully committed defense attorney in a criminal case to fulfilling the ideal of a fair trial.

> What, then, does a hearing include? Historically and in practice, in our own country at least, it has always included the right to the aid of counsel when desired and provided by the party asserting the right. The right to be heard would be, in many cases, of little avail if it did not comprehend the right to be heard by counsel. Even the intelligent and educated layman has small and sometimes no skill in the science of law. If charged with crime, he is incapable, generally, of determining for himself whether the indictment is good or bad. He is unfamiliar with the rules of evidence. Left without the aid of counsel he may be put on trial without a proper charge, and convicted upon incompetent evidence, or evidence irrelevant to the issue or otherwise inadmissible. He lacks both the skill and knowledge adequately to prepare his defense, even though he had a perfect one. He requires the guiding hand of counsel at every step in

the proceedings against him. Without it, though he be not guilty, he faces the danger of conviction because he does not know how to establish his innocence. If that be true of men of intelligence, how much more true is it of the ignorant and illiterate, or those of feeble intellect. If in any case, civil or criminal, a state or federal court were arbitrarily to refuse to hear a party by counsel, employed by and appearing for him, it reasonably may not be doubted that such a refusal would be a denial of a hearing, and, therefore, of due process in the constitutional sense. (*Powell v. Alabama,* pp. 68–69)

With this, the Court easily ruled that the Fourteenth Amendment due process rights of the Scottsboro defendants were violated, and a new trial was required.

Note, however, that *Powell v. Alabama* did not rule that the states had to provide a lawyer for every indigent defendant in every felony trial. The scope of its application was narrower. The decision was based on its facts and circumstances.

> All that it is necessary now to decide, as we do decide, is that in a capital case, where the defendant is unable to employ counsel, and is incapable adequately of making his own defense because of ignorance, feeble mindedness, illiteracy, or the like, it is the duty of the court, whether requested or not, to assign counsel for him as a necessary requisite of due process of law. . . . (*Powell v. Alabama,* p. 71)

As a Due Process Clause precedent, *Powell* became known as the **special circumstances rule:** i.e., due process requires counsel in cases where "special circumstances" exist.

After *Powell:* Toward Incorporation

Six years after *Powell,* Justice Hugo Black's majority opinion in **Johnson v. Zerbst** (1938) forcefully made the assistance of counsel in a *federal* case—*directly* applying the Sixth Amendment, uncluttered by states' rights or special circumstances considerations—an *absolute* right. Two soldiers, on leave in South Carolina, were convicted of passing counterfeit currency in a federal prosecution. They were tried without the assistance of counsel. This case shows why a lawyer is necessary. The defendants presented a defense that was inartful at best and one that a jury could read as an evasion of guilt. Johnson misused his time by attempting to answer minor, possibly prejudicial, statements by the prosecutor (e.g., that he was a "hoodlum from New York"). Johnson also failed to challenge the evidence and neglected to raise legal challenges that could have mitigated the crime or won an acquittal.

Justice Black's majority opinion secured two important constitutional rules. First, it held for the first time that a federal felony trial conducted without a defense lawyer, unless properly waived, is a *jurisdictional violation.* It is not a mere technical mistake, but an infringement of the Sixth Amendment that deprives the court of "the power and authority to deprive an accused of his life or liberty" (*Johnson,* p. 463).

> This is [a] safeguard[] . . . deemed necessary to ensure fundamental human rights of life and liberty. [It is an] essential barrier[] against arbitrary or unjust deprivation of human rights. The Sixth Amendment stands as a constant admonition that if

the constitutional safeguards it provides be lost, justice will not 'still be done.'" (*Johnson v. Zerbst,* p. 462)

Second, the case specified the rules for **waiver of counsel.** There is a *presumption against the waiver* of such a fundamental right. Even if the defendant silently goes along with the conduct of a trial without complaining about the lack of counsel, his or her silence does not amount to a waiver. A waiver is defined as "an *intelligent relinquishment or abandonment of a known right or privilege.*" For a waiver to be constitutional, the defendant must *know* that he or she has a right to counsel and *voluntarily* give it up, knowing that the right to claim it exists. The Supreme Court later required trial judges to carefully investigate waivers of counsel and make a *written record* of any waivers (*Von Moltke v. Gillies,* 1948). "Presuming waiver from a silent record is impermissible. The record must show . . . that an accused was offered counsel but intelligently and understandably rejected the offer" (*Carnley v. Cochran,* 1962). These rules became the standard for all Fifth and Sixth Amendment waivers, including waivers of the right to remain silent after having been read one's *Miranda* warnings.

Betts v. Brady (1942), decided a decade after *Powell,* was a setback to the incorporation of the Sixth Amendment. *Betts* confirmed the *special circumstances* rule of *Powell.* Betts, a farm hand, was indicted for noncapital robbery. Not having the money to hire a lawyer, he asked the judge for **appointed counsel** at his arraignment. The judge refused, saying that the Carroll County court appointed counsel for indigent defendants only in prosecutions for murder and rape. Betts pleaded not guilty and defended himself in a nonjury trial before the judge.

> At his request witnesses were summoned in his behalf. He cross-examined the State's witnesses and examined his own. The latter gave testimony tending to establish an alibi. Although afforded the opportunity, he did not take the witness stand. The judge found him guilty and imposed a sentence of eight years. (*Betts v. Brady,* p. 457)

The issue before the Supreme Court, sharpened by Betts's explicit request for a lawyer, was (as in *Powell*) whether a *state* felony trial conducted without defense counsel was a deprivation of Fourteenth Amendment due process liberty. The majority, in an opinion by Justice Owen Roberts, clearly rejected "incorporation"—the "Sixth Amendment of the national Constitution applies only to trials in federal courts." Relying on *Palko v. Connecticut* (1938), it refused to apply the rule of *Johnson* to state cases. The Court found that the *Sixth Amendment* right to counsel is not *in* the Due Process Clause. Instead, the contours of the Due Process Clause, insofar as the clause required the appointment of a lawyer for an indigent in a state case, were set out in *Powell.* The Court dealt with Betts's petition as a "pure" due process issue, which must decide, on an "appraisal of the totality of facts in a given case," whether a trial without defense counsel is "a denial of fundamental fairness, shocking to the universal sense of justice" (*Betts v. Brady,* p. 462).

Applying *Powell,* Justice Roberts concluded that *special circumstances* did not exist in Betts's case. Therefore, due process did not require the state to appoint counsel. The case was not complicated: Did Betts commit a robbery? He put alibi witnesses on the stand and the issue for the judge was a simple matter of witness credibility. Unlike the defendants in *Powell,* Betts was "not helpless, but was a man forty-three years old, of ordinary intelligence, and [able] to take care of his own interests on the trial of that narrow issue. He had once before been in a criminal court, pleaded guilty to larceny and served a sentence and was not wholly unfamiliar with criminal procedure" (*Betts v. Brady,* p. 472). None of the racism and lynch-mob atmosphere of *Powell* surrounded this run-of-the-mill case. In affirming Betts's uncounseled conviction of a noncapital felony, the majority was satisfied that its conclusion did not violate "natural, inherent, and fundamental principles of fairness." First, uncounseled defense was a common practice to "those who have lived under the Anglo-American system of law." Most states then provided an attorney at no charge to the defendant in noncapital cases only at the discretion of the court, and not as a mandatory right. At that time, the provision of counsel was seen as a legislative or political issue, not as a fundamental right. Furthermore, Maryland law required the appointment of counsel if special circumstances existed. The Supreme Court worried that a flat rule would burden states with the cost of providing counsel even in "small crimes tried before justices of the peace" and in "trials in the Traffic Court."

Justice Black's spirited dissent, joined by Justices Douglas and Murphy, urged incorporation of the Sixth Amendment right to counsel into the Fourteenth Amendment. Failing that, he argued that Justice Sutherland's logic in *Powell*—that it is difficult for any layperson to adequately defend oneself in a criminal trial—means that a felony trial conducted without defense counsel is *always* unfair and a due process violation. Justice Black sought to extend *Johnson v. Zerbst* to state cases. Black, a former populist Senator, emphasized the greater risks of unjust conviction to *poor people.* "A practice cannot be reconciled with 'common and fundamental ideas of fairness and right,' which subjects innocent men to increased dangers of conviction merely because of their poverty. . . . Denial to the poor of the request for counsel in proceedings based on charges of serious crime has long been regarded as shocking to the 'universal sense of justice' throughout this country" (*Betts v. Brady,* p. 476, paragraph break disregarded).

Justice Black was later vindicated in *Gideon v. Wainwright* (1963). In the two decades following *Betts,* the Court undermined the special circumstances test by finding that special circumstances existed in many instances. The Court held that counsel was required by due process in all death penalty trials (*Bute v. Illinois,* 1948); in all capital case arraignments (*Hamilton v. Alabama,* 1961); and in cases involving an unsworn defendant who wishes to make a statement (*Ferguson v. Georgia,* 1961). Justice Stanley Reed revealed that the Court was divided as to noncapital cases but that several justices felt "the Due Process Clause . . . requires counsel for all persons charged with serious crimes . . ." (*Uveges v. Pennsylvania*, 1948). These cases paved the way to *Gideon.*

The Equal Protection Approach

Griffin v. Illinois (1956) opened the door to a new theory on which to base rights connected to the right to counsel. The Court held that under the Fourteenth Amendment *Equal Protection Clause* indigent defendants are entitled to a *trial transcript* in order to facilitate appeals. Under Illinois procedure then in effect, to obtain a full appeal of a criminal conviction a defendant had to furnish the appellate court with a bill of exceptions specifying the legal grounds for the appeal, certified by the trial judge. The state agreed that "it is sometimes impossible to prepare such bills of exceptions . . . without a stenographic transcript of the trial proceedings." Stenographic transcripts are quite expensive and free transcripts were provided at county expense only to indigent defendants sentenced to death. "In all other criminal cases defendants needing a transcript, whether indigent or not, must themselves buy it." In this case the Court held that a free transcript must be provided. Justice Black's opinion did not rule that trial transcripts had to be provided to indigent defendants in *every* case: only where the effect of not having a transcript effectively denied indigents a right to appeal because of their poverty. The opinion noted that although the Constitution did not mandate appellate courts, once a state established them, appellate review could not be administered in a manner that discriminated against the poor.

Justice Burton's dissent (joined by Justices Minton, Reed, and Harlan), expressed a concern for *federalism.* A free transcript was a fine thing, but it should be provided by the states as they saw fit, and not required by federal constitutional law. They expressed concern that an equal protection ruling saying that rich and poor had to be treated equally would lead to "lev-

eling," by abolishing all laws that had *any* disparate economic impact on the rich and the poor (e.g., disallowing fixed taxes like a sales tax).

Justice Black's opinion in *Griffin* was probably designed to undermine the *Betts* special circumstances rule, replacing it with a flat requirement that the state had to provide counsel to indigents. He wrote: "There can be no equal justice where the kind of *trial* a man gets depends on the amount of money he has" (emphasis added). This seems to be a logical derivation from *Griffin*'s principle: that the state should eliminate the differences between the rich and the poor so as to ensure *equal justice*. If people with the means had an absolute right to counsel, and if counsel is essential to a fair trial, should not a lawyer be provided for indigents? As it turned out, however, the Equal Protection Clause was *not* the platform for the rule requiring trial counsel.

Cases under the *Griffin* equality principle did benefit indigent persons by eliminating filing fees in criminal appeals and state postconviction/habeas corpus hearings. It also ensured the right on appeal to free transcripts of preliminary hearing records, lower court habeas corpus hearings, and local ordinance violation trials.[13,14] By 1970, it appeared to be an absolute rule requiring that an indigent who was involved in the criminal process be given any benefit that a wealthier person could afford. Still, the more conservative Burger Court limited the expansion of the equal justice doctrine when it came to providing counsel on discretionary appeals, discussed below.

GIDEON V. WAINWRIGHT AND ITS AFTERMATH

In *Gideon v. Wainwright* the Supreme Court guaranteed the right to counsel to all *state* felony defendants by incorporating the Sixth Amendment into Fourteenth Amendment due process.

— *Gideon v. Wainwright* **Case & Comments** —

• **CASE & COMMENTS** •

Gideon v. Wainwright
372 U.S. 335, 83 S.Ct. 792, 9 L.Ed.2d 799 (1963)

MR. JUSTICE BLACK delivered the opinion of the Court. **[a]**

[Gideon, charged with breaking into a pool hall, a felony, demanded (because of his indigency) and was refused appointed counsel. He conducted his own defense.] He made an opening statement to the jury, cross-examined the State's witnesses, presented witnesses in his own defense, declined to testify himself, and made a short argument "emphasizing his innocence to the charge contained in the Information filed in this case." The jury returned a verdict of guilty, and petitioner was sentenced to serve five years in the state prison. [The Court characterized the facts as similar to *Betts v. Brady* (this text) and set the case for review to reconsider the *Betts* rule because of the "continuing source of controversy and litigation in both state and federal courts" that the *Betts* rule presented.]

* * * Upon full reconsideration we conclude that *Betts v. Brady* should be overruled.

We have construed [the Sixth Amendment] to mean that in federal courts counsel must be provided for defendants unable to employ counsel unless the right is competently and intelligently waived. [JUSTICE BLACK reviewed *Betts v. Brady,* noting that it held the Sixth Amendment right of

[a] Justice Black had the pleasure of writing the opinion in a landmark decision overruling a case in which he strenuously dissented two decades before.

• CASE & COMMENTS •

counsel not fundamental, and thus not incorporated into the Due Process Clause of the Fourteenth Amendment.] **[b]**

We accept *Betts v. Brady*'s assumption, based as it was on our prior cases, that a provision of the Bill of Rights which is "fundamental and essential to a fair trial" is made obligatory upon the States by the Fourteenth Amendment. We think the Court in *Betts* was wrong, however, in concluding that the Sixth Amendment's guarantee of counsel is not one of these fundamental rights. Ten years before *Betts v. Brady,* this Court, after full consideration of all the historical data examined in *Betts,* had unequivocally declared that "the right to the aid of counsel is of this fundamental character." *Powell v. Alabama.* * * * While the Court at the close of its *Powell* opinion did by its language, as this Court frequently does, limit its holding to the particular facts and circumstances of that case, its conclusions about the fundamental nature of the right to counsel are unmistakable. * * *

* * * The fact is that in deciding as it did—that "appointment of counsel is not a fundamental right, essential to a fair trial"—the Court in *Betts v. Brady* made an abrupt break with its own well-considered precedents. In returning to these old precedents, sounder we believe than the new, we but restore constitutional principles established to achieve a fair system of justice. **[c]** Not only these precedents but also reason and reflection require us to recognize that in our adversary system of criminal justice, any person haled into court, who is too poor to hire a lawyer, cannot be assured a fair trial unless counsel is provided for him. This seems to us to be an obvious truth. Governments, both state and federal, quite properly spend vast sums of money to establish machinery to try defendants accused of crime. Lawyers to prosecute are everywhere deemed essential to protect the public's interest in an orderly society. Similarly, there are few defendants charged with crime, few indeed, who fail to hire the best lawyers they can get to prepare and present their defenses. That government hires lawyers to prosecute and defendants who have the money hire lawyers to defend are the strongest indications of the widespread belief that lawyers in criminal courts are necessities, not luxuries. The right of one charged with crime to counsel may not be deemed fundamental and essential to fair trials in some countries, but it is in ours. From the very beginning, our state and national constitutions and laws have laid great emphasis on procedural and substantive safeguards designed to assure fair trials before impartial tribunals in which every defendant stands equal before the law. This noble ideal cannot be realized if the poor man charged with crime has to face his accusers without a lawyer to assist him. * * *

The judgment is reversed. * * * **[d]**

[JUSTICES DOUGLAS and CLARK concurred in separate opinions].

MR. JUSTICE HARLAN, concurring.

I agree that *Betts v. Brady* should be overruled, but consider it entitled to a more respectful burial than has been accorded, at least on the part of those of us who were not on the Court when that case was decided.

I cannot subscribe to the view that *Betts v. Brady* represented "an abrupt break with its own well-considered precedents." * * * In 1932, in *Powell v. Alabama,* * * * a capital case, this Court declared that under the particular facts there presented—"the ignorance and illiteracy of the defendants, their youth, the circumstances of public hostility * * * and above all that they stood in deadly peril of their lives" * * *—the state court had a duty to assign counsel for the trial as a necessary requisite of due process of law. It is evident that these limiting facts were not added to the opinion as an afterthought; they were repeatedly emphasized, * * * and were clearly regarded as important to the result.

Thus when this Court, a decade later, decided *Betts v. Brady,* it did no more than to admit of the possible existence of special circumstances in noncapital as well as capital trials, while at the same time insisting that such circumstances be shown in order to establish a denial of due process. The right to appointed counsel had been recognized as being considerably broader in federal prosecutions [*Johnson v. Zerbst*], but to have imposed these requirements on the States would indeed have been "an abrupt break" with the almost immediate past. The declaration that the right to appointed counsel in state prosecutions, as established in *Powell v. Alabama,* was not limited to capital cases was in truth not a departure from, but an extension of, existing precedent.

The principles declared in *Powell* and in *Betts,* however, have had a troubled journey throughout the years. * * * **[e]**

[More and more capital and noncapital cases found "special circumstances," even in doubtful instances.] The Court has come to recognize, in other words, that the mere existence of a serious criminal charge constituted in itself special circumstances requiring the services of counsel at trial. In truth the *Betts v. Brady* rule is no longer a reality.

[b] This was the Supreme Court's third criminal procedure "incorporation" case of the 1960s. As in other incorporation cases, the federal rule interpreting a Bill of Rights provision was more favorable to the defendant's rights than the state rule.

[c] Justice Black seems to be stretching a fair reading of the "older precedent" of *Powell v. Alabama* by viewing it as having guaranteed the right of counsel to indigents in *all* felony cases. Compare this reading of precedent to that made in the concurrence by Justice Harlan.

[d] The case was remanded and Earl Clarence Gideon was tried again in Panama City, Florida, this time represented by counsel. Anthony Lewis's celebrated book, *Gideon's Trumpet,* recounts the second trial. Gideon's lawyer, Fred Turner, prepared the case carefully by thoroughly reviewing the facts and observing the pool hall. His skillful cross-examination of the lead prosecution witness raised the real possibility that the teen who had identified Gideon as the criminal was himself the burglar. Gideon was acquitted.

[e] Justice Harlan correctly points out that in the twenty years between *Betts* and *Gideon,* many narrow decisions began to shift toward granting the right to counsel in more and more cases. He posits a less absolutist view of constitutional rights and constitutional change than does Justice Black. In Justice Harlan's view, the meaning of constitutional provisions can change gradually over time to take into account new social realities. This was anathema to Justice Black, who strenuously rejected what he saw as judicial lawmaking.

• CASE & COMMENTS •

This evolution, however, appears not to have been fully recognized by many state courts, in this instance charged with the front-line responsibility for the enforcement of constitutional rights. To continue a rule which is honored by this Court only with lip service is not a healthy thing and in the long run will do disservice to the federal system.

The special circumstances rule has been formally abandoned in capital cases, and the time has now come when it should be similarly abandoned in noncapital cases, at least as to offenses which, as the one involved here, carry the possibility of a substantial prison sentence. (Whether the rule should extend to *all* criminal cases need not now be decided.) This indeed does no more than to make explicit something that has long since been foreshadowed in our decisions.

[JUSTICE HARLAN then stated his disagreement with the majority over the incorporation question, stating that in his opinion, the *Gideon* decision falls under the Fourteenth Amendment only, and not the Sixth.]

On these premises I join in the judgment of the Court.

Does *Gideon* Apply to Misdemeanor Trials?

In *Argersinger v. Hamlin* (1972) the Supreme Court found no constitutional basis for distinguishing between a misdemeanor and a felony for purposes of **assigned counsel** for indigents. It held that counsel was required by the Sixth Amendment in misdemeanor cases where a defendant is actually sentenced to imprisonment. The Court reserved the issue of whether counsel is constitutionally required in cases involving *imprisonment as an authorized punishment,* but the defendant does not actually lose liberty.

Justice Powell, dissenting in *Argersinger,* urged the Court to choose a due process special circumstances rule rather than the majority's approach of requiring counsel if a defendant was to spend even one day in jail. An example of a special circumstance would be whether there were complex legal issues; in such case the trial court could appoint an attorney in its discretion. Justice Powell was concerned with requiring the states to shoulder the costs of providing counsel in each and every case, no matter how straightforward and simple the issues.

The issue reserved in *Argersinger* was decided in a case concerning a shoplifter, who was convicted without the assistance of a lawyer and fined fifty dollars, although the law authorized a jail term. In *Scott v. Illinois* (1979) the Court ruled that *Argersinger* meant that actual imprisonment differs from a penalty of a fine or a threat of jailing. Therefore, "the Sixth and Fourteenth Amendments to the United States Constitution require only that no indigent criminal defendant be sentenced to a term of imprisonment unless the State has afforded him the right to assistance of appointed counsel in his defense." The mere fact that one is being tried under a statute that *authorizes* incarceration does not automatically guarantee counsel. Justice Brennan, dissenting, argued that *Argersinger* required appointment of counsel if there is actual incarceration *or* if the crime charged is punishable by more than six months in prison. He thus urged the Court to adopt an **"authorized imprisonment" rule** rather than an **"actual imprisonment" rule.**

Scott injects an illogical element into the Sixth Amendment: a person charged with a felony must have a lawyer, even if not sentenced to prison, but this is not so for a misdemeanor defendant in the same circumstance. Justice Powell, concurring, expressed some concern that the "actual imprisonment" rule would lead judges to guess in advance of the trial what the likely outcome would be and thus distort the judicial process. He concurred because he thought the Court should substitute the flexible due process rule rather than the rigid Sixth Amendment requirement to misdemeanor trials.

When Does the Right to Counsel Attach? Pretrial: The Critical Stage and Formal Charge Rules

Gideon did not resolve all issues concerning the right to counsel. The Sixth Amendment, now applicable to state as well as federal felony trials, applies to "all criminal prosecutions."

ARGERSINGER IN THE STATES

"California, in *Mills v. Municipal Court,* criticized the *Argersinger* rule for requiring a trial judge to attempt to predict at the outset of a criminal prosecution whether or not imprisonment may be an appropriate sanction without access to the most relevant sentencing material, such as the defendant's prior record.[15] *Mills* thought the better approach was to offer counsel to all, and permit on-the-record waivers by any defendant."

Barry Latzer, *State Constitutional Criminal Law,* §5.4.

What proceedings are included in a Sixth Amendment *criminal prosecution?* The answer is found in the **critical stage** doctrine developed by the Court. Counsel is required at a pretrial proceeding if it is one in which factual determinations can be made that could determine the outcome of the case and in which a lawyer plays a significant role.

ARRAIGNMENT   The critical stage doctrine was developed prior to *Gideon.* A unanimous Court in **Hamilton v. Alabama** (1961) ruled that, under Alabama law, an arraignment in a *capital case* was a critical stage because it was the only point in the criminal process at which a defendant could raise an insanity defense without the approval of the trial judge. Other important motions, such as a challenge to the systematic exclusion of one race from the grand jury had to be made at arraignment. "Available defenses may be as irretrievably lost, if not then and there asserted, as they are when an accused represented by counsel waives a right for strategic purposes" (*Hamilton,* p. 54). If an arraignment is a simple formality where no important decision is made (such as arranging for bail), then the lack of counsel is not a due process or Sixth Amendment violation. Otherwise, a defendant must be represented by an attorney.

PRELIMINARY EXAMINATION   In *Coleman v. Alabama* (1970) the Supreme Court ruled that a preliminary examination is a critical stage requiring assistance of counsel. Under Alabama law, the defendant was not required to raise a defense, but if he was without counsel to cross-examine prosecution witnesses, any testimony taken was inadmissible at trial. The Alabama courts saw this as a fair rule that prevented the lack of counsel from causing prejudice to the defendant's case. Yet, Justice Brennan's majority opinion noted that: (1) a lawyer's skilled cross-examination of witnesses can expose fatal weaknesses in the prosecution case that will lead a magistrate to dismiss; (2) cross-examination of witnesses may establish a basis for impeaching witnesses at the trial; (3) trained counsel can use the hearing as a way of discovering prosecution information that can prove helpful in devising a defense strategy; and (4) counsel can be influential in making arguments for bail or for a psychiatric examination. "The inability of the indigent accused on his own to realize these advantages of a lawyer's assistance compels the conclusion that the Alabama preliminary hearing is a 'critical stage' of the State's criminal process at which the accused is 'as much entitled to such aid [of counsel] . . . as at the trial itself' " (*Coleman,* p. 10).

PLEA BARGAINING   The Supreme Court has made it clear that the assistance of counsel is as important in plea bargaining as it is in the felony trial. A decision rendered a month after *Gideon* held that an arraignment conducted without counsel was unconstitutional because "petitioner entered a plea before the magistrate and that plea was taken at a time when he had no counsel." When a lawyer is not present at a critical stage, the Court does "not stop to determine whether prejudice resulted: 'Only the presence of counsel could have enabled this accused to know all the defenses available to him and to plead intelligently'" (*White v. Maryland,* 1963). "Since an intelligent assessment of the relative advantages of pleading guilty is frequently impossible without the assistance of an attorney, this Court has scrutinized with special care pleas of guilty entered by defendants without the assistance of counsel and without a valid waiver of the right to counsel. . . . Since *Gideon v. Wainwright* it has been clear that a guilty plea to a felony charge entered without counsel and without a waiver of counsel is invalid" (*Brady v. U.S.,* 1970, p. 748, n. 6).

POLICE INVESTIGATION   No court has ever held that a lawyer must accompany police in conducting interviews or in gathering physical evidence of a crime. A lawyer has no traditional role to play during investigation, and any problems with the evidence may be derived from discovery or cross-examination. Counsel is not required in investigative hearings, such as grand jury and legislative hearings, or when taking fingerprints, handwriting samples, or voice exemplars.[16]

CUSTODIAL INTERROGATION   In *Miranda v. Arizona* (1966) the Supreme Court ruled that police interrogation conducted while a suspect is in custody raises a sufficient level of compulsion to become a potential violation of the suspect's right against self-incrimination under the Fifth Amendment, requiring warnings that include a right to counsel. This right is included under the *Fifth Amendment* and is *not* part of Sixth Amendment critical stage analysis (see Chapter 7).

LINEUP IDENTIFICATION   The Supreme Court has held that a Sixth Amendment right to counsel applies to *postindictment* lineup identifications (*United States v. Wade,* 1967), but *not* to preindictment showups (*Kirby v. Illinois,* 1972). The basis for this distinction was that the laying of a formal charge, by indictment or information, brought the Sixth Amendment into play. The Court in *Kirby* said that the initiation of a prosecution is not a "mere formalism" for it is "then that a defendant finds himself faced with the prosecutorial forces of organized society, and immersed in the intricacies of substantive and procedural criminal law." Nevertheless, in *United States v. Ash* (1973) the Court held that counsel was *not* required under the Sixth Amendment during a postindictment *photographic display* because, since the defendant was not present, there is not the kind of confrontation that was contemplated in *Wade.* The dissent in *Ash* reasoned that the same suggestibility that can taint a lineup can taint a photographic identification, and an attorney can play the same role of preventing or observing the suggestive acts (see Chapter 8).

PRISON ADMINISTRATIVE DETENTION   Four prison inmates were suspected of murdering another prisoner. They were held in administrative detention for ninety days without counsel during the investigation and were indicted for the murder nineteen months after the crime. The federal court of appeals held that they were entitled to counsel during the period of detention. The Supreme Court reversed in *United States v. Gouveia* (1984), holding that the *formal charges* rule of *Kirby* applied to prison as well as to nonprison settings: There is no right to counsel until the accused has been formally charged.

The **"formal charge" rule** of *Kirby v. Illinois* and the cases and the "critical stage" rule of *Coleman v. Alabama* seem to conflict. *Kirby* involves formal line-drawing. *Coleman* provides a functional analysis as to whether in fact the lack of counsel could result in the conviction of an innocent person or deprive a defendant of a legitimate defense. *Kirby* can be explained in part by the effort of an ideologically conservative Court attempting to limit the right of counsel. It seems logical, for example, that if counsel plays an important role in preventing or observing suggestive behaviors during a postindictment lineup, the same role is played during a preindictment lineup or a photographic identification.

When Does the Right to Counsel Attach? Postconviction and Other Processes

Important criminal justice processes occur *after conviction* in the correctional system and in other proceedings that affect the rights of convicted persons. If a procedure is part of the Sixth Amendment criminal prosecution, *Gideon* applies and counsel is absolutely required. Otherwise, if counsel is required at all, it must be through the more flexible "facts and circumstances" approach of due process.

SENTENCING AND DEFERRED SENTENCING *Mempa v. Rhay* (1967) involved a sentencing hearing following a deferred sentence with probation. The Court held that counsel was required under the Sixth Amendment. Justice Marshall, for the majority, stated that the Sixth Amendment right to counsel applied to sentencing because it was part of the "criminal prosecution." Sentencing was held to include deferred sentencing that involved the revocation of conditional liberty. The Court announced a broad principle: "appointment of counsel for an indigent is required at every stage of a criminal proceeding where substantial rights of a criminal accused may be affected." But, in subsequent years, the Court has refused to extend this logic to probation and parole revocations and prison disciplinary hearings, which apply to convicted persons.

PROBATION AND PAROLE REVOCATION The Supreme Court ruled in *Gagnon v. Scarpelli* (1973) (probation) and *Morrissey v. Brewer* (1972) (parole) that "Probation revocation, like parole revocation, is not a stage of a criminal prosecution, but does result in a loss of liberty." (*Gagnon*, p. 782). As a result, neither probation nor parole could be revoked without a formal, due process hearing that required notice, disclosure of evidence, an opportunity to be heard, a neutral hearing body, and written statements of the fact finders. In neither case, however, was counsel required by the Sixth Amendment. Instead of holding that counsel be *required* as a matter of due process fundamental fairness, the Court established more flexible due process rules. The Court offered guidelines in *Gagnon*:

> Presumptively, . . . counsel should be provided in cases where, after being informed of his right to request counsel, the probationer or parolee makes such a request, based on a timely and colorable claim (i) that he has not committed the alleged

violation of the conditions upon which he is at liberty; or (ii) that, even if the violation is a matter of public record or is uncontested, there are substantial reasons which justified or mitigated the violation and make revocation inappropriate, and that the reasons are complex or otherwise difficult to develop or present. In passing on a request for the appointment of counsel, the responsible agency also should consider, especially in doubtful cases, whether the probationer appears to be capable of speaking effectively for himself. (*Gagnon v. Scarpelli*, pp. 790–91)

Gagnon in effect resurrected the *Betts v. Brady* special circumstances test for the requirement of counsel for indigent defendants at probation revocation hearings.

PRISON DISCIPLINARY HEARINGS Prisoners have even fewer procedural rights in disciplinary hearings than do probationers or parolees facing revocation, since they have much less freedom to lose than probationers or parolees. In *Wolff v. McDonnell* (1974) the Court required a due process hearing before an inmate could be subjected to major institutional forms of discipline involving losses of liberty, such as placement in solitary confinement or a loss of good time. But the dangerous reality of prisons, when combined with the lesser liberty interest of prisoners, led the Court to conclude that inmates had no absolute right to confront and cross-examine witnesses and were, therefore, at the mercy of the prison hearing officer's discretion. As for counsel, the Court, after reviewing its ruling in *Gagnon*, said, "At this stage of the development of these procedures we are not prepared to hold that inmates have a right to either *retained* or appointed counsel in disciplinary proceedings" (emphasis added). Thus, whereas a probationer facing revocation has a right to the assistance of **retained counsel**, a prisoner has no Fourteenth Amendment right to a paid lawyer's presence in an administrative prison disciplinary hearing. In the interests of inmate safety and prison security, a prison may legitimately bar all attorneys from disciplinary hearings.

PSYCHIATRIC EXPERT WITNESS The case-by-case approach was applied in *Ake v. Oklahoma* (1985), where the Court held that a psychiatrist must be provided for an indigent defendant whenever insanity is reasonably raised as an issue. The holding was based on a combination of equal protection and due process reasoning. According to Justice Marshall, "[m]eaningful access to justice has been the consistent theme of these cases. . . . [A] criminal trial is fundamentally unfair if the State proceeds against an individual defendant without making certain that he has access to the raw materials integral to the building of an effective defense."

SUMMARY COURT-MARTIAL *Middendorf v. Henry* (1976) held that a summary court-martial was not a criminal prosecution within the meaning of the Sixth Amendment. Under due process, a defendant is not constitutionally entitled to counsel in a summary court-martial where the maximum penalty could not exceed thirty days' confinement. In addition, analysis of the summary court-martial's function demonstrated that, unlike special and general courts-martial where counsel was provided, in summary proceedings the goal is to exercise justice promptly for purposes of discipline. The proceeding, informal and conducted by one officer, has none of the trappings of a courtroom. Justice Rehnquist noted that the potential of confinement was not a controlling factor in not labeling the proceeding a criminal prosecution because it occurred within the special context of the military community.

JUVENILE DELINQUENCY TRIALS The Court held in *In re Gault* (1967) that a juvenile delinquency adjudication is not a criminal trial within the contemplation of the Sixth Amendment. Yet, under the Due Process Clause, the Court held that an adjudication of juvenile delinquency, that may result in commitment to an institution, is so much like an adult criminal trial that the provision of counsel was essential. If the child or parents could not afford counsel, the state was required to appoint a lawyer to represent the child.

Limitations on the Right to Counsel

RIGHT TO CHOOSE RETAINED COUNSEL The right to retain one's own counsel for a criminal defense is not absolute. "Regardless of his persuasive powers, an advocate who is not a member of the bar may not represent clients (other than himself) in court. Similarly, a defendant may not insist on representation by an attorney he cannot afford or who for other reasons declines to represent the defendant. Nor may a defendant insist on the counsel of an attorney who has a previous or ongoing relationship with an opposing party, even when the opposing party is the government." (*Wheat v. United States,* 1988, p. 159). In *Wheat* the Court held that a trial court could deny a defendant the counsel of his choice if, according to the district court's opinion, the representation carried a substantial possibility of a **conflict of interest.** This ruling subordinates the right to counsel to that of a fair adversary trial. Here, the court was concerned that **multiple representation** of three drug-sale defendants in separate trials by the same lawyer would undermine the lawyer's ability to cross-examine his clients. Thus, even though the defendants were willing to waive their right to a trial free of conflict of interest, the Court refused to accept their waivers. Four dissenting justices agreed that the right to select a lawyer is not absolute, but they would recognize a presumption in favor of a defendant's counsel of choice. In a stinging dissent, Justice Stevens characterized the Court's rule in *Wheat* as paternalistic and said, "This is not the first case in which the Court has demonstrated 'its apparent unawareness of the function of the independent lawyer as a guardian of our freedom.'"

PAYMENT AND ASSET FORFEITURE Two 1989 decisions upheld congressional acts which allow prosecutors to freeze assets of suspected organized crime and drug dealers "before trial [and] without regard to whether the person will have enough money left to hire a lawyer."[17] The **asset forfeiture** law, used aggressively by federal prosecutors, was thought by many to undermine the Sixth Amendment right to adequate representation. *Caplin & Drysdale v. United States* (1989) was a suit by a law firm for its legal fees, which had been placed in escrow before trial, and which the government tried to seize after their client's conviction. In *United States v. Monsanto* (1989) pretrial freezing of assets forced the defendant to rely on a **public defender.** The Supreme Court, 5–4, found both practices to be constitutional.

The forfeiture law made assets that were proceeds of crime government property from the time of the commission of the crime. Since illegal assets were declared government property, a defendant's payment to her lawyer was, in effect, spending someone else's (i.e., the government's) money. Relying on *Wheat v. United States,* the Court said that "a defendant may not insist on representation by an attorney he cannot afford." The law created some exemptions to this rule (owners of stolen property and some innocent retailers), but none for attorneys' fees.

Four dissenting justices felt that the constitutional requirement of adequate representation required the Court to create an exemption for legal fees so that the alleged proceeds of a crime could be used for lawyers. They argued that pretrial asset freezing would "undermine the adversary system as we know it" because it gives the Government "an intolerable degree of power over any private attorney who takes on the task of representing a defendant in a forfeiture case." It allows prosecutors to

> use the forfeiture weapon against a defense attorney who is particularly talented or aggressive on the client's behalf—the attorney who is better than what, in the Government's view, the defendant deserves. The spectre of the Government's selectively excluding only the most talented defense counsel is a serious threat to the equality of forces necessary for the adversarial system to perform at its best. (*Caplin & Drysdale v. United States,* 1989)

MEANINGFUL ATTORNEY-CLIENT RELATIONSHIP *Morris v. Slappy* (1983) held that the Sixth Amendment does not guarantee a meaningful relationship between defendant and appointed counsel. A deputy public defender represented Slappy at a preliminary hearing and supervised an extensive investigation in his rape prosecution. Shortly before trial, the deputy public defender was hospitalized for emergency surgery and a senior trial attorney from the public defender's office was assigned to the case. Slappy claimed that the attorney did not have enough time to prepare the case and moved for a **continuance.** The newly assigned attorney stated that he was prepared and that a further delay would not benefit him in presenting the case. The trial court denied Slappy's motion, the trial continued, and Slappy was found guilty by a jury on three counts. During a second trial of counts left unresolved in the first trial, Slappy refused to cooperate with or even speak to his attorney. The jury returned a guilty verdict on the other counts. The federal appeals court, in a federal habeas corpus action, held that the Sixth Amendment includes the right to a meaningful attorney-client relationship.

The Supreme Court reversed, and held that under the circumstances of this case, there was no Sixth Amendment violation by the trial court refusing to grant a continuance when the attorney himself did not want one. The Court rejected the novel idea that an indigent defendant is guaranteed a "meaningful" relationship with assigned counsel; furthermore, an indigent defendant does not have an unqualified right to the appointment of counsel of his or her own choosing. Justice Brennan, while concurring in the decision, noted that lower federal courts have recognized the importance of a defendant's relationship with his attorney, so that a defendant with *retained* counsel was seen to have "a qualified right to continue that relationship." The qualified right is not the guarantee of "rapport" between client and attorney. Rather, according to Justice Brennan, where an attorney has put sufficient work into a case so that she has become knowledgeable of its intricacies, a court should take into account the length of delay before allowing another attorney to try the case.

RECOUPMENT OF COSTS The governmental unit that pays for indigent assigned counsel may constitutionally seek to recoup the costs of the defense whenever the defendant has the means to pay. According to *Fuller v. Oregon* (1974), a **recoupment** law does not violate the Equal Protection Clause providing it allows the indigent person to claim all the exemptions granted to other judgment debtors in the state's civil code and does not require payment if the defendant remains or again becomes indigent. The *exemption* of indigents who are *acquitted* was deemed a rational distinction in the law. Dissenting justices felt that recoupment would have a "chilling effect" on the right to counsel; an indigent defendant would decline to accept free counsel knowing that he or she may have to repay the costs of the defense. However, Justice Stewart thought this unlikely because of the protections in the statute ensuring that an indigent cannot be compelled to pay. The Court also noted that defendants whose financial status places them just above the poverty line may have to go into debt in order to pay the costs of a criminal defense. "We cannot say that the Constitution requires that those only slightly poorer must remain forever immune from any obligation to shoulder the expenses of their legal defense, even when they are able to pay without hardship."

The Right to Counsel on Appeal

"[E]very state and the federal system provide some means of review to defendants in criminal cases. However, according to a long line of Supreme Court opinions, there is no constitutional mandate that states provide any type of review process for defendants convicted in their criminal courts."[18] If so, does this mean that there is no right to counsel on appeal? The appellate process is not included within the wording of the Sixth Amendment's "criminal prosecution." The Supreme Court analyzed the question of the right to counsel on appeal in state courts under the Fourteenth Amendment and has applied a functional analysis. It has concluded that counsel is required

on first appeals as of right, but is not required for subsequent, discretionary appeals.

RIGHT TO COUNSEL ON FIRST, MANDATORY APPEAL *Douglas v. California* (1963) held that the Fourteenth Amendment guarantees a defendant the right to representation of counsel on a first, mandatory appeal. By 1963, every state granted a convicted criminal defendant the right to one mandatory appeal, but not every state guaranteed counsel for these appeals. In California the rule allowed a court after reviewing part of the trial record to appoint counsel for an indigent convicted person if in the court's discretion an attorney would serve any useful purpose. In contrast, counsel was always appointed for indigents on mandatory first appeals from convictions in federal court, whether or not the federal court thought that a lawyer was needed.

The United States Supreme Court held that the California procedure was invidious discrimination against persons too poor to hire a lawyer to assist them on appeal. It relied on *Griffin v. Illinois* and its "equality principle" in its opinion. The majority thought it unfair that a person with means will present his or her case to the appellate court with "the full benefit of written briefs and oral argument by counsel," while a person who cannot afford a lawyer has to rely on a judge to review the record without the benefit of partisan legal analysis and argument. A case often has hidden merit, and a neutral reviewer, rather than a partisan attorney, can miss it. Justice William O. Douglas's majority opinion was not a model of doctrinal clarity and his writing mixed up Due Process Clause fairness concerns with Equal Protection Clause equality concerns, a point that was challenged by the dissent. This decision did not apply to second, discretionary appeals, such as writs of habeas corpus or petitions for certiorari. The decision also acknowledged that some differences based on wealth can stand as long as the state does not draw pernicious lines between the rich and the poor. For example, an indigent granted counsel cannot insist on the most highly paid lawyer available.

Justice Harlan's dissenting opinion concluded that the Equal Protection Clause is *not* the proper basis for a holding. Rather the issue should be whether California's procedure violated the fair trial rule of the Due Process Clause. He felt that it did not. In his view there was no equal protection violation because the state does not deny appeals to indigents and the state cannot lift all disabilities flowing from economic differences. As for the due process issue, he noted that appellate review is not required by the Fourteenth Amendment, and therefore issues of fairness had to be decided in the context of the state providing a discretionary benefit. He felt that issues that arise on appeal are not as complex as factual issues at a trial, and so it was fair to allow state judges to review a case to see whether or not a lawyer was needed in a particular appeal.

RIGHT TO COUNSEL ON SECOND, DISCRETIONARY APPEALS A decade later, a more conservative Supreme Court refused to extend the guarantee of counsel to second, discretionary appeals. *Ross v. Moffitt* (1974) involved two convictions against Claude Moffitt for uttering forged instruments in two different North Carolina counties. In both cases Moffitt appealed as of right, represented by assigned counsel, and lost both appeals. He then sought the appointment of counsel to pursue a discretionary *habeas corpus* writ to the state supreme court. After a failure in the state appeal, he sought appointment of counsel to prepare petitions for a *writ of certiorari* to the United States Supreme Court. North Carolina opposed the granting of counsel as a matter of constitutional right. The U.S. Court of Appeals for the Fourth Circuit ruled that the principle of *Douglas v. California* applied even when a convicted person was taking a second appeal to a court that had discretion to deny the appeal. Many state supreme courts, like the United States Supreme Court, will decide to hear cases primarily because the issue raised is of significant public importance. They may deny appeals even if a particular case might have been wrongly decided against a petitioner's interest. Nevertheless, according to the Court of Appeals

> A defendant with adequate resources to engage counsel has a meaningful right to seek access to the state's highest court. An indigent should be afforded counsel to give him a comparably meaningful right. . . . Denied the assistance of a competent lawyer, the quality of justice for the indigent has been substantially impaired in comparison with the quality of justice afforded his more affluent brothers. (*Moffitt v. Ross*, 483 F.2d 650, 653 (4th Cir. 1973)

The Supreme Court reversed in an opinion by Justice Rehnquist, borrowing somewhat from Justice Harlan's dissent in *Douglas*. Justice Rehnquist first ruled that the Due Process Clause does not require a state to provide a convicted person—who has been represented by counsel at trial and by counsel at the one appeal as of right—with counsel on his discretionary appeal to the state Supreme Court. Relying on the fact that the Constitution does not mandate appeals, and that a defendant in Moffitt's position is seeking to overturn a conviction, he reasoned that there would be unfairness "only if indigents are singled out by the State and denied meaningful access to the appellate system because of their poverty." Viewing the issue as one better analyzed under equal protection, he turned to that clause.

The "Fourteenth Amendment 'does not require absolute equality or precisely equal advantages.' . . . It does require that the state appellate system be 'free of unreasoned distinctions.'" The majority noted that because the indigent person had already "received the benefit of counsel in examining the record of his trial" in the appeal as of right, there was no "unreasoned distinction" in allowing a wealthier person with a lawyer to pursue a writ while not providing counsel for an indigent petitioner. The high court will have the transcript and appellate papers prepared by counsel for the earlier appeal. This is especially so because the purpose of discretionary appeals "is not whether there has been 'a correct adjudication of guilt' in every individual case, . . . but rather whether 'the subject matter of the appeal has significant public interest,' [or] whether 'the cause involves legal principles of major significance to the jurisprudence of the State.'"

Justice William Douglas, at the twilight of his career, dissented in *Ross* on the equality and fairness grounds specified in *Douglas*. He quoted from *Douglas v. California* that the "same concepts of fairness and equality, which require counsel in a first appeal of right, require counsel in other and subsequent discretionary appeals." But that belief, so resonant to an older generation, failed to convince a newer generation of justices that the constitution required state and local governments to pay for counsel in the context of discretionary appeals.

THE RIGHT TO COUNSEL FOR DISCRETIONARY APPEAL BY INDIGENT DEATH-ROW INMATES *Murray v. Giarratano* (1989) held that under *Ross* indigent death-row inmates seeking postconviction review of their death sentences, after their first appeals, had no Fourteenth Amendment right to counsel at the expense of the state. The majority was unmoved by the petitioner's three arguments that were seen as valid by four dissenting justices: (1) death-row inmates are under *greater emotional stress* than other inmates and thus less able to write adequate legal briefs; (2) Virginia's law *postponed some issues* normally heard at first appeal to the postconviction proceedings, thus making these second appeals more like first appeals for death-row inmates; and (3) "*a grim deadline imposes a finite [time] limit* on the condemned person's capacity for useful research." In rejecting these arguments, the Court emphatically limited the right to counsel on Fourteenth Amendment equal protection and due process grounds in procedures other than the trial. While indigents retain the same basic rights as wealthier persons, there are limits to what the state must do to remedy the infirmities in the justice system caused by economic inequality.

THE RIGHT TO SELF-REPRESENTATION

The Sixth Amendment right to the assistance of counsel coexists with a defendant's seemingly contradictory right of self-representation. Before the Supreme Court constitutionalized the right of a defendant to proceed *pro se*—in one's own behalf—federal statutes and the laws of thirty-six states upheld such a right.[21] Data are not kept on the prevalence of *pro se* **defense;** one expert estimated that approximately fifty such trials occurred in 1997. A survey in one jurisdiction indicates that civil litigants are more likely to represent themselves than are criminal defendants and that the number of *pro se* defendants is rising.[22]

Self-Representation and the Waiver of Counsel

Self-representation reflects the American value of self-reliance and a distrust of lawyers. It also may conflict with the right to a fair trial. Some defend themselves in notorious, political trials, in order to publicize their point of view. Angela Davis, an African American Communist and philosophy instructor, was tried in California for abetting the murder of a judge in the Soledad Brothers case and won an acquittal in 1972. She represented herself, but had substantial assistance. Jack Kevorkian, the well-known proponent and practitioner of physician-assisted suicide, was acquitted three times when ably defended by counsel, but was convicted of murder when he sought to defend himself.[23] *Pro se* defense is more likely to occur when a defendant becomes frustrated with the actual or perceived incompetence of assigned counsel or a public defender, or when a defendant sharply disagrees with his lawyer's legal strategy. A defendant may also request self-representation with the underhanded intention of causing delay or a mistrial by asking for a lawyer once the trial has begun.

Several problems can result from self-representation. One is that a *pro se* defendant may cause a mockery of justice. A prime example is Colin Ferguson, who shot and killed six and wounded nineteen commuters on a Long Island Railroad car in 1993. He claimed to have acted out of a sense of "black rage." The Supreme Court had ruled in *Godinez v. Moran* (1993) that the standard of competency to waive counsel is the same as the standard to stand trial—a rational and factual understanding of the proceedings. Under this standard, Ferguson was allowed to dismiss his well-known "radical" lawyers, Ronald Kuby and the late William Kunstler, who wanted him to plead insanity and who correctly predicted that the trial would become a circus.[24] Against overwhelming evidence, Ferguson, speaking clearly but saying bizarre and fanciful things, claimed that an unknown white man did the shooting; asked to subpoena President Clinton; without any evidence, claimed that the jury he helped pick was biased; and blandly cross-examined surviving shooting victims who then testified that Ferguson shot them.[25,26] He told jurors that "There were 93 counts to that indictment, 93 counts only because it matches the year 1993. If it had it been 1925, it would have been a 25-count indict-

ment."[27] His standby counsel, Alton Rose, sitting while Ferguson made it impossible for an insanity defense to succeed, could "only watch in silence from the defense table, where he often slumps, clasping his head as if trying to prevent it from splitting apart in frustration."[28] A person who avidly watched the televised trial said, "I know it's the way the legal system works, but the way we let this guy carry on [made] buffoons out of all of us."[29]

A more recent example arose in the pretrial process of Zacarias Moussaoui, the alleged conspirator in the 9/11/01 attack. Federal judge Leonie M. Brinkema allowed him to represent himself in mid-2002, "a decision that his court-appointed lawyers warned could turn the courtroom into a circus."[30] By November 2003, that prediction proved to have been accurate, and the judge revoked Moussaoui's right of self-representation. In the seventeen months he had been in charge of his case, the judge said "he had repeatedly violated her orders by filing court papers that were 'frivolous, scandalous, disrespectful or repetitive.' " He flooded the docket with "rambling, sometimes incoherent and often anti-Semitic and racist filings that insulted Judge Brinkema and the court-appointed defense team he tried to fire." The judge noted he had used "contemptuous language that would never be tolerated from an attorney and will no longer be tolerated from this defendant." Moussaoui, who has acknowledged that he is loyal to Osama bin Laden, accused his attorneys "of conspiring with the government to ensure his execution, calling them the 'death team.' " In handwritten court filings, he said he wanted "anthrax for Jew sympathisers only," and referred to Judge Brinkema as "Leonie you Despotically Judge." In earlier filing, he requested that Attorney General Ashcroft "be sent to Alexandria jail so I can torture him. After all," he added, "torture is now part of the American way of life." Judge Brinkema said the court-appointed lawyers, who had continued to file motions on Mr. Moussaoui's behalf even without his cooperation, would now formally resume control of the case.[31]

Another problem with *pro se* defense is that it may require a judge to intervene and tell the defendant that he has made an error and instruct him as to how to proceed. This creates the appearance of bias to the jury and may make it difficult for the judge to be completely impartial in ruling on trial motions. In these instances, it falls to the trial judge, while inquiring into a waiver of the right to counsel, to discover whether the defendant has the legal knowledge to conduct a trial and whether his or her actions are likely to cause costly delays, a mistrial, and/or a subsequent appeal.

Faretta v. California

In *Faretta v. California* (1975) the Supreme Court decided, 6–3, that the Sixth Amendment established a right to self-representation and set down guidelines for *pro se defense.* Justice Stewart, writing for the majority, said that the issue "is whether a State may constitutionally hale a person into its criminal courts and there force a lawyer upon him, even when he insists that he wants to conduct his own defense" (*Faretta,*

p. 807). Faretta, charged with grand theft, had previously defended himself in court. He believed his assigned counsel in the Los Angeles Superior Court was too burdened with a high caseload to adequately assist him. The trial judge questioned Faretta about the hearsay rule and the law regarding challenges to potential jurors, and ruled that he had no constitutional right to self-representation. The trial was conducted with appointed counsel.

The core of the decision was the basic significance of the Sixth Amendment's text:

> The Sixth Amendment does not provide merely that a defense shall be made for the accused; it grants to the accused personally the right to make his defense. It is the accused, not counsel, who must be "informed of the nature and cause of the accusation," who must be "confronted with the witnesses against him," and who must be accorded "compulsory process for obtaining witnesses in his favor." Although not stated in the Amendment in so many words, the right to self-representation—to make one's own defense personally—is thus necessarily implied by the structure of the Amendment. The right to defend is given directly to the accused; for it is he who suffers the consequences if the defense fails.
>
> . . .
>
> The counsel provision supplements this design. It speaks of the "assistance" of counsel, and an assistant, however expert, is still an assistant. The language and spirit of the Sixth Amendment contemplate that counsel, like the other defense tools guaranteed by the Amendment, shall be an aid to a willing defendant—not an organ of the State interposed between an unwilling defendant and his right to defend himself personally. To thrust counsel upon the accused, against his considered wish, thus violates the logic of the Amendment. In such a case, counsel is not an assistant, but a master; and the right to make a defense is stripped of the personal character upon which the Amendment insists. It is true that when a defendant chooses to have a lawyer manage and present his case, law and tradition may allocate to the counsel the power to make binding decisions of trial strategy in many areas. . . . This allocation can only be justified, however, by the defendant's consent, at the outset, to accept counsel as his representative. An unwanted counsel "represents" the defendant only through a tenuous and unacceptable legal fiction. Unless the accused has acquiesced in such representation, the defense presented is not the defense guaranteed him by the Constitution, for, in a very real sense, it is not his defense. . . . (*Faretta*, pp. 819–21)

Therefore, the right to counsel announced in *Gideon v. Wainwright* was not inconsistent with the right to self-representation: "Personal liberties are not rooted in the law of averages. The right to defend is personal" (*Faretta*, p. 834).

On the other hand, self-representation is not a license. To accept a waiver of counsel, a judge has to be convinced that a defendant has the *minimal ability* to conduct the trial. "A defendant need not himself have the skill and experience of a lawyer in order to competently and intelligently choose self-representation" (*Faretta*, p. 835). A judge cannot deny self-representation to a defendant simply because the defendant does not have *expert knowledge* of criminal law and procedure. The record in the case showed "that Faretta was literate, competent, and understanding, and that he was voluntarily exercising his informed free will." The trial judge was in error in denying him the right to represent himself, even if he did not have expert knowledge of hearsay rules (*Faretta*, pp. 835–36).

Chief Justice Burger dissented in *Faretta* (pp. 836–46). He saw the basic right as the Sixth Amendment right to a *fair trial*. The entire justice system and the people at large have a stake in a fair and competent trial system. "That goal is ill-served, and the integrity of and public confidence in the system are undermined, when an easy conviction is obtained due to the defendant's ill-advised decision to waive counsel." Furthermore, the dissent saw the majority opinion as undermining the authority of the trial judge who should retain final discretion on this question, because the judge "is in the best position to determine whether the accused is capable of conducting his defense."

In sum, the waiver of counsel is an unusual and extreme step. When requested, a judge should personally inform the defendant who wishes to defend *pro se,* "of the many procedural complications of representing oneself, that he will be given no special treatment, and that waiving counsel is generally unwise."[32] In the colloquy with the defendant, the judge takes pains to ensure that the waiver is *voluntary,* that it is *unequivocal* and *expressed,* that it is *knowing* and *intelligent,* and that the defendant is *mentally able* to make the waiver. The verbal exchange between the judge and the defendant is placed on the *record.* If, after all this, the defendant meets the minimum standard of competency and continues to insist on self-representation, the judge has no right to deny self-representation.

Standby Counsel

The practice of the judge appointing **standby counsel** to assist a *pro se* defendant was upheld by the Supreme Court in **McKaskle v. Wiggins** (1984). Justice O'Connor ruled that a defendant's Sixth Amendment rights are not violated when standby counsel is appointed, even over the defendant's objection. To ensure that standby counsel does not overwhelm the defendant's personal right to make a defense, two rules guide the conduct of such counsel and determine when the attorney might have undermined the defendant's rights.

> First, the *pro se* defendant is entitled to preserve *actual control* over the case he chooses to present to the jury. . . . If standby counsel's participation over the defendant's objection effectively allows counsel to make or substantially interfere with any significant tactical decisions, or to control the questioning of witnesses, or to speak *instead* of the defendant on any matter of importance, the *Faretta* right is eroded.
>
> Second, participation by standby counsel without the defendant's consent should not be allowed to destroy the *jury's perception that the defendant is representing himself.* The defendant's appearance in the status of one conducting his own defense . . . exists to affirm the accused's individual dignity and autonomy. (*McKaskle v. Wiggins,* 1984, emphasis added).

Dissenting justices suggested that this two-pronged rule actually gives trial judges little guidance on how to restrain standby counsel from taking over the case from the self-represented defendant. Also, the dissenters sharply differed with the majority about whether the activity of standby counsel in this case (including more than fifty interventions in a three-day trial precipitating some disagreements that were observed by the jury) amounted to a violation of the *Faretta* self-representation right.

Four reasons support the regular appointment of standby counsel. (1) If a *pro se* defendant, purposely or out of confusion, decides during trial to ask for a lawyer, there will be no delay—standby counsel will be able to immediately continue the case. (2) Standby counsel, by providing expert advice, helps the *pro se* defendant "exercise his right of self-representation more effectively and begins to level the playing field in the courtroom."[33] (3) Standby counsel can assist "a defendant of questionable mental or emotional fortitude," who still meets the low appointment standard of *Godinez v. Moran* (1993) in making a meaningful defense and thus maintain the fairness of the judicial process.[34] (4) Standby counsel eliminates the need for a judge to give the appearance of bias by giving the defendant practice pointers during the trial.

Some problems, however, may occur from the use of standby counsel. As *McKaskle v. Wiggins* noted, when standby counsel interferes too strongly, the defendant may feel that his or her right to self-representation is infringed. Also, it is unwise for a court to appoint as standby counsel the lawyer whom the defendant dismissed. Finally, "hybrid representation," where both the defendant and standby counsel appear before the jury, should be disallowed. It causes confusion in the jury's mind and may prejudice the defendant's case. To correct this, Marie Williams suggests that (a) standby counsel be appointed in every *pro se* defense, (b) the jury be instructed as to the constitutionality and nature of standby counsel, and (c) that hybrid representation not be allowed except when the defendant is cross-examining the victim and when the defendant takes the stand to testify.[35]

COUNSEL IN A TIME OF TERROR

Confidentiality between a client and attorney is an essential element of the adversary system. The attorney-client privilege, however, can be waived or breached. A court order can be obtained to surreptitiously eavesdrop on conversations between an attorney and a prisoner, for example, if the authorities can show that the attorney is involved in furthering the prisoner's criminal activities, special limitations can be placed on communication by mail and visits.[36] On the day that the USA PATRIOT Act was signed into law, Attorney General Ashcroft quietly implemented a new prison regulation that

> permits the Department of Justice ("DOJ") unlimited and unreviewable discretion to eavesdrop on confidential attorney-client conversations of persons in custody, with no judicial oversight and no meaningful standards. It applies not just to inmates who have been convicted of a criminal offense, but also to all persons in the custody of the DOJ, including pretrial detainees, material witnesses and immigration detainees who have not been accused or convicted of any crime.[37]

This regulation replaced the detached and neutral judgement of a court, based on probable cause, with that of the Attorney General, based only on reasonable suspicion, that a prisoner *may* use communications with attorneys to further terrorism. This regulation provided that unless a court order is obtained, the attorneys and the client must be informed that their conversation will be monitored. If privileged attorney-client information is expressed, a "privilege team" of Department of Justice attorneys will separate those conversations and keep them from prosecutors, although there does not appear to be any way of ensuring that the "privilege team" does not leak the data.

The intention of the new rule was to prevent an inmate from passing "messages through the lawyer in order to further terrorist activity."[38] Aside from raising serious the threats to civil liberties, this rule seems entirely self-defeating, according to Professor Stephen Schulhofer. Persons detained for acts related to terrorism or as material witnesses "could have useful information about actual or suspected terrorist networks and operations."[39] They may not even understand the value of their information. Such persons are likely to be highly suspicious of their interrogators and unlikely to talk.

> Defense attorneys traditionally have served as essential intermediaries in alerting prosecutors that their clients have inside information and are willing to cooperate in return for assurances regarding the charge, the sentence, or the risk of deportation. Once warned that he is subject to monitoring, however, the inmate not only will be deterred from passing messages through his attorney to other terrorists but also will be deterred from telling the attorneys anything else he knows about terrorist organizations and plans. The attorney then will have no opportunity to advise his client whether to cooperate and reveal what he knows. As a result, the monitoring rule could well cause investigators to *lose* access to important information—information that could save lives, prevent further terrorist activity, and assist in identifying and apprehending important suspects.[40]

Such an ill-considered regulation raises the concern that it was passed more for the political goal of "doing something," or worse, to scare competent attorneys away from representing clients charged with terrorism. If the government were truly concerned with getting information of impending terrorist attacks, it could present probable cause to a judge that an interned person and his or her attorney are terrorist conspirators and get a Title III or FISA electronic eavesdropping warrant. This would be an effective way of obtaining information of terrorism. Prof. Marjorie Cohn indicates that the "Attorney General . . . provided no factual basis for his assertion that this extraordinary procedure is necessary to prevent violent crime or terrorism."[41]

The politicized nature of the Bush administration's posture on the right to counsel is revealed by its April 2002 indictment of attorney Lynne Stewart arising from alleged violations of these regulations in communications with her client, Sheik Abdel Rahman, a blind Islamic cleric. Ms. Stewart, 63, is an experienced criminal defense lawyer noted for defending highly unpopular suspects, including radicals and organized-crime figures. Sheik Rahman is serving a life-plus sixty-five-years sentence in federal prison for a 1995 conviction in a terrorist plot to blow up New York landmarks. He was a leading figure in "the Islamic Group," founded in Egypt and designated as a terrorist organization by the U.S. government. In addition to a charge of providing material support to a terrorist organization, Ms. Stewart was also "charged . . . with making false statements and conspiring to defraud the government, allegations stemming from what prosecutors say was her broken promise not to be a conduit for Mr. Abdel Rahman."[42] In order to represent the Sheik in prison, she signed an agreement to communicate with Rahman only concerning legal matters, through an interpreter, and not to "use my meetings, correspondence, or phone calls with Abdel Rahman to pass messages between third parties (including, but not limited to, the media) and Abdel Rahman." The indictment alleged that Stewart allowed an interpreter to read letters to Rahman regarding Islamic Group matters, and to conduct a discussion with Rahman regarding whether the Islamic Group should continue to comply with a cease-fire in Egypt.[43] More than a year later, a federal judge dismissed the charge of providing material assistance to a terrorist organization, calling the law too vague.[44] The remaining charges are pending.

A troubling aspect of this case is whether the true intent of the United States was to undermine effective legal representation of those charged with terrorism. Professor Deborah Rhode commented:

> When Attorney General John Ashcroft announced the indictment of Lynne Stewart, . . . the threat he exposed was less to national security than to individual liberty. The indictment raises serious concerns about defendants' access to counsel. . . . [S]uch felony indictments could affect lawyers' willingness to defend despised groups, like suspected terrorists, at all. . . .

Ms. Stewart's office was searched, and confidential records and computer files were seized. She faces up to 40 years in prison if convicted. . . .

Lawyers who defend terrorists already pay an enormous price. Hate mail, death threats, bomb scares and ostracism by other potential clients are routine costs of representing social pariahs. Now the government has added the risk that lawyers suspected of being conduits of client messages will face wholesale invasions of privacy and felony indictments.

In effect, the attorney general has asserted unchecked authority to determine who may have confidential conversations with attorneys and who may not. Such essentially lawless exercises of law-enforcement prerogatives lose sight of the liberties that we are fighting to preserve.[45]

Before the United States came into being, the ability of an American lawyer to defend the most politically hated persons was etched into the national character when John Adams unflinchingly and successfully defended "redcoats" against murder charges, even though he was politically opposed to the Crown. It is ironic and tragic that an administration is seeking to crush those who are acting to ensure that the law and the courts function as they are intended, to maintain the balance of security and liberty. Without a judicial check, the government, like all governments, will tend to act in ways that are secret, and secrecy by governments has always been a condition that breeds tyrannous action.

THE EFFECTIVE ASSISTANCE OF COUNSEL

In 1970 the Supreme Court ruled that the Sixth Amendment assistance of counsel guarantee in criminal cases means the *effective* assistance of retained and appointed counsel (*McMann v. Richardson*). The Court clarified the meaning of effective assistance in *Strickland v. Washington* (1984) and established rules for interpreting this standard in practice.

— *Strickland v. Washington* Case & Comments —

• CASE & COMMENTS •

Strickland v. Washington
466 U.S. 668, 104 S.Ct. 2052, 80 L.Ed.2d 674 (1984)

JUSTICE O'CONNOR delivered the opinion of the Court.

* * *

I

A

[Respondent, David Leroy Washington, was found guilty and sentenced to death in Florida for a crime spree that included three murders, torture, kidnapping, and theft. He confessed to the police. Against the advice of his experienced, assigned defense lawyer, Washington waived a jury trial and pleaded guilty, telling the judge that he accepted responsibility for his acts. Against counsel's advice, once again, Washington also waived an advisory jury on the death penalty issue.] **[a]**

[*Case history:* After his trial, conviction and death sentence, Washington appealed as of right to the Florida Supreme Court, which upheld his conviction and sentence. A collateral state appeal on ineffective assistance of counsel grounds resulted in a ruling, upheld by the Florida Supreme Court, that

[a] For purposes of effective assistance of counsel, a criminal trial and the death penalty phase of a capital case are treated the same, because a jury decides one of two sentences, death or life. This parallels a criminal verdict of guilty or not guilty.

Washington's lawyer was competent. Washington then filed a petition for a writ of habeas corpus in federal district court; an evidentiary hearing resulted in finding the lawyer competent. An *en banc* decision of the federal Circuit Court ultimately reversed and remanded. Florida petitioned the United States Supreme Court, which reversed the Court of Appeals, finding that the federal district court was correct in denying the writ of habeas corpus.]

* * *

In preparing for the sentencing hearing, counsel spoke with respondent about his background. He also spoke on the telephone with respondent's wife and mother, though he did not follow up on the one unsuccessful effort to meet with them. He did not otherwise seek out character witnesses for respondent. **[b]** * * * Nor did he request a psychiatric examination, since his conversations with his client gave no indication that respondent had psychological problems. * * *

Counsel decided not to present and hence not to look further for evidence concerning respondent's character and emotional state. That decision reflected trial counsel's sense of hopelessness about overcoming the evidentiary effect of respondent's confessions to the gruesome crimes. * * * It also reflected the judgment that it was advisable to rely on the plea colloquy for evidence about respondent's background and about his claim of emotional stress: the plea colloquy communicated sufficient information about these subjects, and by foregoing the opportunity to present new evidence on these subjects, counsel prevented the State from cross examining respondent on his claim and from putting on psychiatric evidence of its own.

Counsel also excluded from the sentencing hearing other evidence he thought was potentially damaging. He successfully moved to exclude respondent's "rap sheet." **[c]** * * * Because he judged that a presentence report might prove more detrimental than helpful, as it would have included respondent's criminal history and thereby undermined the claim of no significant history of criminal activity, he did not request that one be prepared. * * *

At the sentencing hearing, counsel's strategy [stressed Washington's remorse, his acceptance of responsibility, the stress that he claimed he was under at the time of the crime spree, and his apparently clean prior criminal record.] The State put on evidence and witnesses largely for the purpose of describing the details of the crimes. Counsel did not cross-examine the medical experts who testified about the manner of death of respondent's victims.

[The trial judge found that the aggravating circumstances outweighed the mitigating circumstances and sentenced Washington to death.]

* * *

B

* * * Respondent challenged counsel's assistance in six respects. He asserted that counsel was ineffective because he failed to move for a continuance to prepare for sentencing, to request a psychiatric report, to investigate and present character witnesses, to seek a presentence investigation report, to present meaningful arguments to the sentencing judge, and to investigate the medical examiner's reports or cross-examine the medical experts. **[d]** In support of the claim, respondent submitted 14 affidavits from friends, neighbors, and relatives stating that they would have testified if asked to do so. He also submitted one psychiatric report and one psychological report stating that respondent, though not under the influence of extreme mental or emotional disturbance, was "chronically frustrated and depressed because of his economic dilemma" at the time of his crimes.

[Florida courts found Washington's six claims to be groundless: (1) there was no legal basis for seeking a continuance; (2) state psychiatric examinations of Washington disclosed no mental abnormalities; (3) character witnesses would not have rebutted aggravating circumstances and would have added no mitigating circumstances; (4) a presentence report would have brought out the respondent's prior criminal record, which was otherwise kept out of the proceedings; (5) counsel presented an "admirable" argument for the respondent in light of the overwhelming nature of the aggravating circumstances; and (6) cross-examination of the state's psychiatric witnesses could have led the prosecution, on rebuttal, to undermine Washington's claim that he was under stress when he went on his crime spree.]

* * * [T]he trial court concluded * * * "there is not even the remotest chance that the outcome would have been any different. The plain fact is that the aggravating circumstances proved in this case were completely *overwhelming*. * * *"

[b] Character witnesses testify only about a defendant's general reputation and rarely make negative statements. Judges are less likely to be impressed by character witnesses than are juries.

[c] Washington's lawyer seems to be doing little to present mitigating factors and some positive and human side of his client, but he also keeps damaging information out of consideration by this strategy.

[d] This information was gathered by Washington's appellate lawyers, who seek to reverse the death penalty by showing it resulted from the ineffectiveness of his trial attorney.

• CASE & COMMENTS •

II

* * * The right to counsel plays a crucial role in the adversarial system embodied in the Sixth Amendment, since access to counsel's skill and knowledge is necessary to accord defendants the "ample opportunity to meet the case of the prosecution" to which they are entitled. * * * **[e]**

* * * That a person who happens to be a lawyer is present at trial alongside the accused, however, is not enough to satisfy the constitutional command. The Sixth Amendment recognizes the right to the assistance of counsel because it envisions counsel's playing a role that is critical to the ability of the adversarial system to produce just results. An accused is entitled to be assisted by an attorney, whether retained or appointed, who plays the role necessary to ensure that the trial is fair.

For that reason, the Court has recognized that "the right to counsel is the right to the effective assistance of counsel." * * *

* * * The benchmark for judging any claim of ineffectiveness must be whether counsel's conduct so undermined the proper functioning of the adversarial process that the trial cannot be relied on as having produced a just result. **[f]**

[e] The right to counsel is placed in the context of the right to a fair trial; thus it serves the interests of society while benefitting the individual defendant.

[f] Justice O'Connor's "benchmark" means that some errors by counsel can be overlooked if the overall result of the trial was just.

III

A convicted defendant's claim that counsel's assistance was so defective as to require reversal of a conviction or death sentence has two components. **[g]** First, the defendant must show that counsel's performance was deficient. This requires showing that counsel made errors so serious that counsel was not functioning as the "counsel" guaranteed the defendant by the Sixth Amendment. Second, the defendant must show that the deficient performance prejudiced the defense. This requires showing that counsel's errors were so serious as to deprive the defendant of a fair trial, a trial whose result is reliable. Unless a defendant makes both showings, it cannot be said that the conviction or death sentence resulted from a breakdown in the adversary process that renders the result unreliable.

[g] The Court establishes a "two-pronged" test for the effective assistance of counsel. The "performance" prong is discussed in III.A. and the "prejudice" prong in III.B.

A

[T]he proper standard for attorney performance is that of reasonably effective assistance. * * * When a convicted defendant complains of the ineffectiveness of counsel's assistance, the defendant must show that counsel's representation fell below an objective standard of reasonableness. **[h]**

More specific guidelines are not appropriate. The Sixth Amendment * * * relies instead on the legal profession's maintenance of standards sufficient to justify the law's presumption that counsel will fulfill the role in the adversary process that the Amendment envisions. * * * The proper measure of attorney performance remains simply reasonableness under prevailing professional norms.

* * * Counsel's function is to assist the defendant, and hence counsel owes the client a duty of loyalty, a duty to avoid conflicts of interest. * * * From counsel's function as assistant to the defendant derive the overarching duty to advocate the defendant's cause and the more particular duties to consult with the defendant on important decisions and to keep the defendant informed of important developments in the course of the prosecution. **[i]** Counsel also has a duty to bring to bear such skill and knowledge as will render the trial a reliable adversarial testing process. * * *

These basic duties neither exhaustively define the obligations of counsel nor form a checklist for judicial evaluation of attorney performance. In any case presenting an ineffectiveness claim, the performance inquiry must be whether counsel's assistance was reasonable considering all the circumstances. Prevailing norms of practice as reflected in American Bar Association standards and the like * * * are guides to determining what is reasonable, but they are only guides. No particular set of detailed rules for counsel's conduct can satisfactorily take account of the variety of circumstances faced by defense counsel or the range of legitimate decisions regarding how best to represent a criminal defendant. Any such set of rules would interfere with the constitutionally protected independence of counsel and restrict the wide latitude counsel must have in making tactical decisions. * * *

Judicial scrutiny of counsel's performance must be highly deferential. **[j]** It is all too tempting for a defendant to second-guess counsel's assistance after conviction or adverse sentence, and it is all too easy for a court, examining counsel's defense after it has proved unsuccessful, to conclude that a particular act or omission of counsel was unreasonable. * * * [A] court must indulge a strong presumption that counsel's conduct falls within the wide range of reasonable professional assistance. * * * There are countless ways to provide effective assistance in any given case. Even the best criminal defense attorneys would not defend a particular client in the same way. * * *

[h] The burden of proof is on the convicted defendant to prove that her lawyer was ineffective.

[i] The "objective" measure is the performance of other lawyers. Only general guidelines of effective (or deficient) performance by a criminal defense lawyer are provided here. Thus, **deficient performance** must be determined from case-by-case decisions of the courts.

[j] Deferential review means that the benefit of doubt is resolved in favor of finding a lawyer's performance competent.

• CASE & COMMENTS •

[Intense scrutiny of lawyers' performances by appellate courts would produce a flood of ineffectiveness challenges that would make lawyers less willing to represent criminal defendants and undermine trust between attorney and client.]

* * * A convicted defendant making a claim of ineffective assistance must identify the acts or omissions of counsel that are alleged not to have been the result of reasonable professional judgment. The court must then determine whether, in light of all the circumstances, the identified acts or omissions were outside the wide range of professionally competent assistance.

* * *

B

An error by counsel, even if professionally unreasonable, does not warrant setting aside the judgment of a criminal proceeding if the error had no effect on the judgment. * * * The purpose of the Sixth Amendment guarantee of counsel is to ensure that a defendant has the assistance necessary to justify reliance on the outcome of the proceeding. **[k]** Accordingly, any deficiencies in counsel's performance must be prejudicial to the defense in order to constitute ineffective assistance under the Constitution.

In certain Sixth Amendment contexts, prejudice is presumed. Actual or constructive denial of the assistance of counsel altogether is legally presumed to result in prejudice. * * * Prejudice in these circumstances is so likely that case-by-case inquiry into prejudice is not worth the cost. * * *

One type of actual ineffectiveness claim warrants a similar, though more limited, presumption of prejudice. In *Cuyler v. Sullivan* (1980), the Court held that prejudice is presumed when counsel is burdened by an actual conflict of interest. In those circumstances, counsel breaches the duty of loyalty, perhaps the most basic of counsel's duties. * * * Prejudice is presumed only if the defendant demonstrates that counsel "actively represented conflicting interests" and that "an actual conflict of interest adversely affected his lawyer's performance." * * * **[l]**

Conflict of interest claims aside, actual ineffectiveness claims alleging a deficiency in attorney performance are subject to a general requirement that the defendant affirmatively prove prejudice. * * * Attorney errors come in an infinite variety and are as likely to be utterly harmless in a particular case as they are to be prejudicial. They cannot be classified according to likelihood of causing prejudice. Nor can they be defined with sufficient precision to inform defense attorneys correctly just what conduct to avoid. Representation is an art, and an act or omission that is unprofessional in one case may be sound or even brilliant in another. Even if a defendant shows that particular errors of counsel were unreasonable, therefore, the defendant must show that they actually had an adverse effect on the defense.

* * *

[The defendant cannot argue that his or her conviction would likely not have occurred because the jury would have nullified the law. The **prejudice prong** must be assessed on the basis of assuming that a conscientious jury would have applied legal standards impartially.]

* * * When a defendant challenges a conviction, the question is whether there is a reasonable probability that, absent the errors, the factfinder would have had a reasonable doubt respecting guilt. **[m]** When a defendant challenges a death sentence such as the one at issue in this case, the question is whether there is a reasonable probability that, absent the errors, the sentencer * * * would have concluded that the balance of aggravating and mitigating circumstances did not warrant death.

In making this determination, a court hearing an ineffectiveness claim must consider the totality of the evidence before the judge or jury. Some of the factual findings will have been unaffected by the errors, and factual findings that were affected will have been affected in different ways. Some errors will have had a pervasive effect on the inferences to be drawn from the evidence, altering the entire evidentiary picture, and some will have had an isolated, trivial effect. Moreover, a verdict or conclusion only weakly supported by the record is more likely to have been affected by errors than one with overwhelming record support. **[n]** Taking the unaffected findings as a given, and taking due account of the effect of the errors on the remaining findings, a court making the prejudice inquiry must ask if the defendant has met the burden of showing that the decision reached would reasonably likely have been different absent the errors.

[In Part V, the Court applied the standards announced in Parts II and III to the facts of the case. The majority concluded that the conduct of Washington's lawyer was adequate and was not the cause of the death penalty sentence.]

JUSTICE MARSHALL, dissenting.

* * *

[k] The *prejudice* prong asks whether counsel's performance substantially contributed to the guilty verdict or sentence of death. It does not mean "discrimination" in this context.

[l] Two kinds of "automatic prejudice" eliminate the defendant's need to prove prejudice: (1) no assistance of counsel, and (2) conflict of interest. In other cases, prejudice must be proven beyond a reasonable doubt on the facts.

[m] The appellate court must decide whether the outcome would likely have differed if the attorney had not made the errors that established deficient performance under the first prong.

[n] A "facts and circumstances" or "totality of the evidence" standard is open-ended; it is the antithesis of a "bright-line" rule. As with the "deficient performance" prong, standards will develop incrementally as the courts decide specific cases.

I

A

My objection to the performance standard adopted by the Court is that it is so malleable that, in practice, it will either have no grip at all or will yield excessive variation in the manner in which the Sixth Amendment is interpreted and applied by different courts. To tell lawyers and the lower courts that counsel for a criminal defendant must behave "reasonably" and must act like "a reasonably competent attorney," is to tell them almost nothing. In essence, the majority has instructed judges called upon to assess claims of ineffective assistance of counsel to advert to their own intuitions regarding what constitutes "professional" representation, and has discouraged them from trying to develop more detailed standards governing the performance of defense counsel. **[o]** In my view, the Court has thereby not only abdicated its own responsibility to interpret the Constitution, but also impaired the ability of the lower courts to exercise theirs. * * *

[o] If Justice Marshall is correct, is it possible to specify good lawyering? Should Washington's lawyer have performed each of the six acts not done?

B

I object to the prejudice standard adopted by the Court for two independent reasons. First, it is often very difficult to tell whether a defendant convicted after a trial in which he was ineffectively represented would have fared better if his lawyer had been competent. Seemingly impregnable cases can sometimes be dismantled by good defense counsel. On the basis of a cold record, it may be impossible for a reviewing court confidently to ascertain how the government's evidence and arguments would have stood up against rebuttal and cross-examination by a shrewd, well-prepared lawyer. The difficulties of estimating prejudice after the fact are exacerbated by the possibility that evidence of injury to the defendant may be missing from the record precisely because of the incompetence of defense counsel. **[p]** In view of all these impediments to a fair evaluation of the probability that the outcome of a trial was affected by ineffectiveness of counsel, it seems to me senseless to impose on a defendant whose lawyer has been shown to have been incompetent the burden of demonstrating prejudice.

[p] In other words, Justice Marshall would eliminate the prejudice prong entirely. Would this make it very difficult to uphold convictions on appeal?

Second and more fundamentally, the assumption on which the Court's holding rests is that the only purpose of the constitutional guarantee of effective assistance of counsel is to reduce the chance that innocent persons will be convicted. In my view, the guarantee also functions to ensure that convictions are obtained only through fundamentally fair procedures. The majority contends that the Sixth Amendment is not violated when a manifestly guilty defendant is convicted after a trial in which he was represented by a manifestly ineffective attorney. **[q]** I cannot agree. Every defendant is entitled to a trial in which his interests are vigorously and conscientiously advocated by an able lawyer. A proceeding in which the defendant does not receive meaningful assistance in meeting the forces of the State does not, in my opinion, constitute due process.

[q] Justice Marshall was the most experienced trial attorney sitting on the Court. As an African American lawyer challenging racial segregation in Southern courts in the 1930s, 1940s, and 1950s, he often worked under extremely hostile circumstances. Should his experience give his views special weight?

* * *

Applying the *Strickland* Test

Strickland's rules apply not only to felony trials and death penalty sentencing proceedings, but also at plea bargaining (*Hill v. Lockhart,* 1985). In **Glover v. United States** (2001) the Supreme Court held that an attorney's failure to argue a point under the federal sentencing guidelines that might have resulted in an increase in the defendant's sentence by six months imprisonment was a sufficiently large loss to raise an effective assistance of counsel argument. For purposes of the *Strickland v. Washington* rule, a defendant establishes prejudice where a trial court made a wrong guidelines determination, the attorney failed to argue against the error, and as a result of such error the defendant's sentence was increased. It is not clear whether the rule of *Glover* applies to state sentencing processes that are entirely indeterminate, discretionary, and unstructured. These proceedings may be informal and involve standardless discretion. As such, it may be impossible to establish criteria of effective assistance. Capital sentencing and guideline sentencing, however, have elements of an adversary trial so that the standards of the *Strickland* two-pronged test can be applied.

STRICKLAND V. WASHINGTON IN THE STATES

"With few exceptions, state constitutional case law nearly always utilizes the *Strickland* test or a close approximation. . . . Three states—Hawaii, Massachusetts and Maine—offer state constitutional tests that differ from *Strickland*'s, especially in the language of the prejudice prong."

Barry Latzer, *State Constitutional Criminal Law*, § 5:9.

The test given by the Hawaii Supreme Court is: "The defendant has the burden of establishing ineffective assistance of counsel and must meet the following two-part test: 1) that there were specific errors or omissions reflecting counsel's lack of skill, judgment, or diligence; and 2) that such errors or omissions resulted in either the withdrawal or substantial impairment of a potentially meritorious defense." [*State v. Aplaca*, 837 P.2d 1298 (1992)] *Aplaca* ruled that "the decision not to conduct a pretrial investigation of prospective defense witnesses cannot be classified as a tactical decision or trial strategy." Thus, a lawyer must almost always conduct a pretrial investigation of the facts. The Massachusetts Supreme Judicial Court applied the ineffective assistance of counsel rule to ordinary (i.e., noncapital) sentencing, and held that a defendant who was deprived of effective assistance of counsel at sentencing is entitled to a new sentencing hearing. (*Commonwealth v. Lycus*, 406 Mass. 135; 546 N.E.2d 159 (1989))

PROOF OF INEFFECTIVE ASSISTANCE   *United States v. Cronic* (1984) ruled that ineffective assistance of counsel must be affirmatively proven and is not to be inferred. A defendant convicted of mail fraud claimed ineffective assistance of counsel because: (1) the lawyer was inexperienced; (2) the charge was serious; (3) the facts were complex; (4) the time to investigate was limited to thirty days; and (5) some witnesses were inaccessible. The *Strickland* standard puts the *burden of proof* on the convicted complainant to prove that his lawyer's assistance was ineffective. Cronic raised a set of relevant factors, but could not point to any *specific action* by his lawyer that showed deficient performance. If Cronic's position were accepted, the Court could find ineffective assistance even though the lawyer's performance was flawless. None of the factors in the case, alone or in combination, deprived Cronic of a fair trial: relevant evidence was supplied and the government's evidence cross-examined. The Court also noted in *Cronic* that the test of adequate performance did not require that the lawyer perform flawlessly in a trial. "When a true adversarial criminal trial has been conducted—even if defense counsel may have made demonstrable errors—the kind of testing envisioned by the Sixth Amendment has occurred."

A death penalty was appealed on the grounds of ineffective assistance of counsel in *Bell v. Cone* (2002). After conviction for a brutal murder, at which the insanity defense was rejected, the prosecutor established aggravating factors warranting the death penalty at the death penalty phase of the trial. After the junior prosecutor gave a low-key closing, defense counsel waived final argument, which prevented the lead prosecutor, by all accounts an extremely effective advocate, from arguing in rebuttal. The defense counsel cross-examined prosecution witnesses, but called no witnesses. He called the jury's attention to the mitigating evidence presented at trial, relating to Gary Cone's substance abuse and post-traumatic stress disorders resulting from his Vietnam military service; the jury was reminded that his mother testified that Cone returned from Vietnam a changed person. The jury found four aggravating factors and no mitigating circumstances, which required the imposition of the death penalty.

The United States Supreme Court upheld the state appellate court's finding that the performance of Cone's counsel was within the permissible range of competency under the attorney-performance standard of *Strickland v. Washington*. The Supreme Court noted that the state court's application of *Strickland* was reasonable, especially in light of the guideline that "judicial scrutiny of a counsel's performance must be highly deferential" and that "every effort [must] be made to eliminate the distorting effects of hindsight, to reconstruct the circumstances of counsel's challenged conduct, and to evaluate the conduct from counsel's perspective at the time." (*Bell v. Cone*, p. 698, citing *Strickland*). In this light, the defense attorney's decision to not make a closing statement so as to preclude an effective close by an experienced prosecutor, plus his cross-examination and bringing out mitigating factors, can reasonably be considered sound trial strategy.

EXAMPLES OF INEFFECTIVE ASSISTANCE   An example of deficient performance is found in *Kimmelman v. Morrison* (1986). The defense lawyer in a rape prosecution failed to object to the introduction of illegally seized evidence, filed a late motion for the suppression of evidence, and did not ask for discovery of police reports that would have indicated that the seizure of evidence was arguably unconstitutional. The attorney's excuse was that he believed it was the state's responsibility to turn over all relevant evidence. Since there is no such general obligation, the Supreme Court ruled that the lawyer's failure to take normal and routine steps before trial to obtain relevant evidence was inexcusable negligence, amounting to deficient performance. The Court remanded to determine if the deficient performance prejudiced the outcome of the case.

In *Williams v. Taylor* (2000) the Supreme Court reinstated a trial court's finding that counsel were ineffective at the death penalty phase of a trial, over the ruling of the Virginia Supreme Court that the performance was reasonable. In this robbery and capital murder case, the trial judge held that defense counsel had not presented and explained the significance of all the available mitigating factors. If they had, the cumulative mitigation evidence would have raised a reasonable probability that the result of the sentencing proceeding would have been different. Defense counsel began to prepare for the capital sentencing only a week before the trial and failed to conduct an investigation that would have uncovered extensive records of mitigation, not because of any strategic calculation, but because they incorrectly thought that state law barred access to such records. The mitigating factors would have included Terry Williams's borderline mental retardation; his parents' conviction for neglect; his severe and repeated beating by his father; his stay in an abusive foster home; his return to his abusive parents after their release from prison; prison records indicating that Williams received commendations for helping to crack a prison drug ring and for returning a guard's missing wallet; and testimony of prison officials who described Williams as among the inmates least likely to act in a violent, dangerous, or provocative way.

EFFECTIVE ASSISTANCE AND TRUTH   The attorney's obligation to maintain the integrity of the trial process and to elicit the truth can appear to conflict with the specific obligation to provide the best defense. It is fundamental to the adjudication process that evidence cannot be fabricated. A lawyer has no obligation to support a defendant with false testimony. In **Nix v. Whiteside** (1986) a defendant charged with murder claimed self-defense. He told his lawyer that he did not actually see a gun in his assailant's hand, but believed it was there. He wanted to testify that he saw "something metallic" because a jury would be more likely to believe the assailant had a gun. Counsel told Whiteside that as a matter of law, it was not necessary for the defendant to see a gun to prove self-defense, and made it clear that if Whiteside perjured himself, the lawyer would indicate this to the judge. Whiteside was convicted and argued that the lawyer's advice was ineffective assistance. The Supreme Court ruled that there is no right, constitutional or otherwise, to testify falsely. Therefore, the lawyer's assistance was not deficient.

Conflict of Interest

Multiple representation occurs when a retained or assigned attorney represents two or more codefendants. In **Cuyler v. Sullivan** (1980) two attorneys, DiBona and Peruto, represented three defendants. DiBona was primarily responsible for Sullivan's trial, while Peruto, responsible for the trial of Sullivan's codefendants, advised DiBona in the Sullivan trial. The Supreme Court held that this constituted multiple representation, but the multiple representation did *not,* in itself, violate an attorney's obligations to adequately defend and to give full and complete attention to the client's defense. Multiple representation, therefore, is not automatically a *conflict of interest.* This rule takes economic realities of providing counsel into consideration. As Justice Stevens said in *Burger v. Kemp* (1987), "Particularly in smaller communities where the supply of qualified lawyers willing to accept the demanding and unrewarding work of representing capital prisoners is extremely limited, the de-

fendants may actually benefit from the joint efforts of two partners who supplement one another in their preparation. Moreover, we generally presume that the lawyer is fully conscious of the overarching duty of complete loyalty to his or her client."

A *conflict of interest* arises when, in the circumstance of multiple representation, an attorney renders *less effective assistance to one client out of consideration for the interests of the other client.* It is a long-standing rule that where a conflict of interest is shown to exist, the defendant has established ineffective assistance of counsel *per se* and need not show that the conflict of interest prejudiced the case (*Glasser v. United States,* 1942). A trial judge is not obligated to hold a hearing into the possibility of a conflict of interest in every case of multiple representation (*Cuyler v. Sullivan,* 1980). However, should an assigned attorney raise a *timely objection* to multiple representation on the grounds that it constitutes a conflict of interest, the trial judge is required to hold a hearing to make certain that there is no genuine conflict before the trial can proceed (*Holloway v. Arkansas,* 1978).

A conflict of interest can be difficult to prove, as the defendant "must demonstrate that an actual conflict of interest adversely affected his lawyer's performance." (*Cuyler v. Sullivan,* 1980). **Burger v. Kemp** (1987) is an example where the *possibility* of a conflict of interest does not amount to the ineffective assistance of counsel under *Strickland.* Burger first argued that his lawyer, in an appellate brief, failed to raise as a death penalty mitigation that Burger was less culpable for the killing than a codefendant. The Supreme Court rejected this contention because (1) the lesser culpability defense was raised and rejected at trial; (2) Burger actually killed the victim; (3) the Georgia Supreme Court found his acts to be "inhuman"; and (4) lower courts found that it was not deficient performance by the attorney to forgo this avenue on appeal. Burger next claimed that the lawyer failed to obtain a plea bargain resulting in a life sentence. However, the facts indicated that the defense lawyer attempted to obtain a plea, but the prosecutor simply refused to agree to a plea bargain. Finally, Burger claimed that the lawyer failed to bring out mitigating circumstances at the death penalty sentencing hearing. The omission of some mitigating information was deemed a tactical decision by the lawyer, designed to keep the defendant off the stand and thereby keep aggravating information from the court. Over the vigorous dissent of four justices, the Supreme Court held in this case that there was no deficient performance or conflict of interest.

LAW IN SOCIETY

The Unmet Promise of Equal Justice

Gideon v. Wainwright, Argersinger v. Hamlin, and *Strickland v. Washington* guarantee a competent attorney for every defendant facing a serious criminal charge—even if the defendant is too poor to pay for legal services. A legal guarantee "on the books" is only as good as its enforcement. The promise of equal justice is meaningless if the lawyers, courts, county commissions, state legislators, and governors—and ultimately the American people—fail to implement it substantially. Have the legal community and responsible government units responded to the guarantee of equal justice?

It is true that the nation established several methods to providing lawyers for indigent defendants in criminal cases.[46] Different cities, counties, and states either assign lawyers, fund legal aid and defenders' agencies, or establish contract systems by which bar associations of private firms agree to provide indigent defense for a set fee. As a result, a lawyer always represents an indigent client at public expense. Nevertheless, fees are usually capped and quite low for assigned counsel and public defenders often have unrealistically high caseloads. It is a struggle to obtain adequate investigators or expert witnesses. The lack of funding for indigent defense undermines the ability even of competent attorneys to provide adequate defense. Proper criminal defense work is an expensive, labor-intensive, expert undertaking. Sadly, America's people and its governmental servants have grown increasingly insensitive in the past few decades to the promise for equal justice.

THE EXPENSE OF PRIVATE CRIMINAL DEFENSE

The cost of retaining a private defense lawyer can be enormous. A 1996 survey by journalists of indigent cases in Houston, Texas, found that retained lawyers "often can earn $25,000 to $75,000 to defend a felony case, depending on the complexity of the case and the probability that it will go to trial. Several top criminal defense attorneys acknowledged that fees for complex, high-profile cases can run into the hundreds of thousands of dollars."[47]

- A car service dispatcher in Queens, New York, who was charged with felonious assault in 1995, claimed self-defense. A seasoned attorney charged $15,000 and hired an investigator at $50 an hour to find witnesses. The dispatcher was found guilty of a lesser charge "and probably avoided prison time." His father mistakenly believed that the money would be returned if his son was found not guilty.[48]

- In the notorious Wenatchee, Washington, witch hunt, police officer Robert Perez accused Pentecostal Minister Robert Roberson, his wife Connie, and more than forty parishioners of conducting orgies with children. The case ultimately collapsed after several poor and mentally retarded parishioners were imprisoned. Attorney Robert Van Siclen, who volunteered to defend Mr. Roberson, estimated the case cost his firm $100,000. He planned to sue the county in an effort to recoup the cost of defending the six-week trial.[49]

- Karen and Jeffrey Wilson, a paralegal and a high school teacher respectively, were charged with child abuse when their seven-month-old son, Brock, was treated for a head injury. They spent $60,000 in legal fees to regain custody of Brock, who was taken from them by the social service department. Charges were dismissed by the family court.[50]

- Between January and March 2000, Representative Earl Hilliard spent $37,500 in legal fees, out of the $40,000 that he raised for his reelection campaign, to defend himself against an ethics investigation into his previous race.[51]

- An injured trucker, accused of perpetrating criminal workers' compensation fraud, spent more than $100,000 in attorneys' fees fighting criminal allegations. The trucker was vindicated.[52]

- In late 1999 seven big vitamin companies pleaded guilty to price fixing and agreed to pay $1.05 billion in damages. The attorneys' fees were estimated at $122 million.[53]

- Linda Tripp, whose Maryland charges for wiretapping in the Whitewater/Lewinsky scandal were ultimately dismissed, ran up legal bills of about $750,000. A defense fund has been set up to help her pay these charges.[54]

- Monica Lewinsky, the White House intern and a central figure in the scandal that led to the impeachment trial of President Clinton, was represented by top lawyers Plato Cacheris and Jacob Stein, who charge hourly billing rates in the range of $400. At the time she hired this team it was predicted that, "she'll likely owe more than $300,000 to her first legal team, led by William Ginsburg," whom she dismissed.[55]

- President Clinton's bill for legal services in the impeachment and the trial on the impeachment exceeded $10 million. To pay these bills, President Clinton created a legal defense fund to receive private donations.[56]

- Murder cases are in a special league. "'In a murder case, practically every defendant is indigent,' says Larry Hammond, a criminal lawyer in Phoenix, Arizona. 'They may not have started that way, but for anyone other than the super-rich, they will be indigent before the case is over.'" Dale Bertsch, an anesthesiologist accused of murdering his ex-wife, in a case with no physical evidence against him, was quoted fees in the $250,000 range. Hammond took the case for the sum total of Bertsch's liquidated assets, which came to about $160,000. He could not pay for an evidentiary hearing, which would have required $50,000, or a mock jury for $30,000. Dr. Bertsch was convicted.[57]

- As for the "super-rich," O. J. Simpson, whose net worth before his trial was said to be $10 million, took out a $3 million credit line on his Brentwood home, spent $100,000 for a jury consultant, paid a fee of $100,000 a month for twelve months to Robert Shapiro, and paid Johnnie Cochran, Jr., "a large flat fee," to mention only the lead attorneys.[58]

- Multimillionaire Robert Durst, acquitted of murdering a neighbor, having dismembered the corpse, while living in obscurity in a run-down Galveston neighborhood, was taped in a jail conversation with his wife mentioning $1.2 million as the cost of his defense, but defense attorneys declined to say what Durst paid for their successful representation.[59]

FUNDING FOR INDIGENT DEFENSE

The underfunding of indigent criminal defense makes a mockery of the constitutional ideal of equal justice. The "largely hospitable funding environment" for indigent defense of the 1960s has given way to "public outcry over the neglect of . . .

crime victims" and a steering of "resources toward law enforcement and away from indigent defense."[60] The late chief judge David Bazelon, of the Washington, D.C., United States Court of Appeals, wrote in 1984 that the "battle for equal justice is being lost in the trenches of the criminal courts," as the poor, uneducated, and unemployed are being represented all too often by "walking violations of the sixth amendment."[61]

In all jurisdictions, the amounts paid to assigned counsel are significantly below what retained counsel charge. As of May 2000, New York State had not raised assigned attorney fees in fourteen years.[62] In 1999 the federal Criminal Justice Act, which since 1964 has provided funding for assigned counsel in federal cases, set a *maximum* fee of $60 per hour for in-court time and $40 per hour for out-of-court time, far below going rates for retained lawyers.[63] Virginia places a cap of $845 on the amount an attorney can receive for representing a defendant on a murder charge, but its General Assembly has approved a 24 percent increase in fees, effective July 1, 2001. "That level of funding will keep Virginia at or near the bottom of the rankings for payment of court-appointed attorneys' fees."[64]

As for public defender's offices, in most places, the caseloads of public defenders are so high, because of underfunding, as to diminish the ability of defenders to perform at the best of their abilities. There is no survey that assesses the total picture in the United States, but there is substantial evidence of real underfunding of indigent defense.

Across the nation, the bulk of criminal justice funds go to the police, prosecutors and jails. Only *2.3 percent* of the seventy-four billion dollars spent on the justice system in 1990 went to pay for attorneys *for indigent defendants* while *7.4 percent went to the prosecution.* However, the number of defendants unable to afford an attorney had risen dramatically, from 48 percent in 1982 to *80 percent* today. *Public defenders handle more than 11 million of the 13 million cases* which are tried annually. Yet, as of 1990, the United States Department of Justice found that nationally, public defenders are receiving less than one-third of the resources provided to the prosecution. *Prosecutors' offices received $5.5 billion* from federal, state, local, county, and municipal governments as opposed to the *$1.7 billion provided for public defense* by the same government sources. Moreover, defense lawyers are further overwhelmed by additional resources provided to prosecutors, including a great deal of investigatory work by law enforcement which are officially classified as "police expenditures."[65]

- An assistant public defender in the western United States admitted to doing an inadequate job in open court. She testified that she had collapsed in court and her health was seriously threatened by a caseload of two thousand cases per year. She resigned from the public defender's office, saying that she was "actually doing the defendants more harm by just presenting a live body than if they had no representation at all."[66]

- A New Orleans public defender, representing 418 clients in the first seven months of 1991 and with seventy cases pending trial, obtained a court ruling that his excessive caseload precluded effective representation to the clients. "Not even a lawyer with an 'S' on his chest," the judge ruled, "could handle this docket."[67]

- In 1992 New Jersey eliminated $2.9 million budgeted to the Department of the Public Advocate to pay for counsel in cases where a conflict of interest barred the public defender. This left indigent defendants jailed without an attorney to represent them. The public advocate resigned "in disgust" to protest the budget reductions.[68]

- A late 1980s survey showed an annual starting salary of $24,259 for public defenders and an average salary of $34,787 for a defender with five years' experience. This may not have improved by the late 1990s, as the legal profession had become "saturated."[69]

THE CRISIS IN DEATH PENALTY CASES

The most acute problem is that the most serious cases, involving capital punishment, are among the most severely affected by underfunding and incompetent attorneys.

- George Alec Robinson, charged with capital murder in Virginia, was vigorously defended by two appointed attorneys who worked a combined total of six hundred hours. Robinson was found guilty, but was spared death by the electric chair. The attorneys submitted a bill of approximately $55,000 at prevailing rates for private clients. During this trial, the attorneys neglected their private practices and even their personal lives under the pressure of having the responsibility for a man's life. The State of Virginia paid them $573—each. "The two lawyers subsequently removed their names from the list of attorneys willing to accept appointments. They joined an increasing number of experienced attorneys nationwide who are no longer willing to provide their services at such great personal and financial sacrifice."[70]

- Calvin Jerold Burdine was released by a federal court from a Texas prison after spending sixteen years on death row. His lawyer had no co-counsel and slept through substantial portions of his trial. The Texas Court of Criminal Appeals did not think that this constituted ineffective assistance of counsel. Burdine's case was one of several of Texas prisoners on death row whose lawyers slept during their trials. Then Governor George Bush of Texas vetoed a bill in 1999 to improve the quality of legal representation of poor defendants, expressing satisfaction with the Texas justice system.[71]

- Frederico Martinez-Macias, a common laborer convicted of a double murder, was defended by a court-appointed attorney who was paid $11.84 an hour but did no legal research to correct his erroneous view about key evidence and failed to call an alibi witness who would have placed Martinez-Macias miles away from the crime. After being sentenced to death, a Washington firm took his case pro bono. Full investigation established his innocence.[72] The pro bono lawyers invested about $1 million of billable hours, spent $11,599 for psychological testimony, and found eyewitnesses who did not identify Martinez-Macias at the murder scene.[73] Other cases like this exist.[74]

• Attorney Mike Williams, a small town Alabama lawyer, was assigned a capital murder case of James Wyman Smith. Williams was given no money for an investigator and estimated that he received $4.98 per hour to prepare for the defense. Another Alabama solo practitioner, Wilson Meyers, submitted an itemized bill for $13,399 to the trial court, which reduced the amount to $4,128. The court agreed that Mr. Meyers had put in the time, but called the fees too excessive. After paying his investigator and paralegal, Mr. Meyers netted $5.05 an hour on this case. As a result, earnest lawyers like Mike Williams, who learn the ropes of doing three or four death cases, drop out because of the financial burden, leaving inexperienced or incompetent lawyers to take such cases.[75]

• Some lawyers are forced to take assigned capital cases or face contempt of court. They may put in about fifty hours on death penalty cases when, according to experts, adequate preparation requires 500 to 1,000 hours.[76]

CAUSES OF INEFFECTIVE COUNSEL

What is the cause for the diminished funding for indigent defense?

• Tough-on-crime attitudes: "Providing free attorneys to accused criminals is probably one of the government's least popular functions. In recent years, 'victim's rights' movements have become increasingly popular. Many politicians, being sensitive to public opinion, are concerned with appearing to be 'tough on crime.' Citizens and politicians alike often have little understanding of or sympathy for the needs of the adversary system, at least insofar as it requires a strong defense advocate. Defense attorneys are often seen as obstacles to justice. . . ."[77]

• Rising caseloads: From 1982 to 1984, there was a 40 percent increase in caseloads for the nation's indigent defense systems. A 1990 study, commissioned by Chief Justice Rehnquist, concluded that the most pressing problem for federal courts was the unprecedented number of federal drug prosecutions. In 1964 federal courts made sixteen thousand compensated appointments of counsel under the Criminal Justice Act of 1964. By 1993, that number rose to eighty-nine thousand indigent appointments in federal courts.[78]

• Diminishing governmental resources: "Recently, many local governments, the primary locus of funding of defense services, have seen their resources dwindle, as tax-cutting measures are passed by the electorate and federal funds for local programs are cut."[79]

• Greater demands on defense attorneys: Prosecutors have either limited or eliminated plea bargaining for certain crimes, have increased the number of charges filed against defendants, and have charged more serious crimes. All of this requires greater defense efforts. New crimes and harsher penalties passed by legislatures require defense attorneys to spend time learning the law, developing appellate challenges to the new provisions, and offering a more dogged defense against higher penalties.[80]

SOLVING THE PROBLEM OF INEFFECTIVE COUNSEL

Several steps can be taken to solve the problem of the ineffective assistance of counsel, including:

• Modify the rule of *Strickland v. Washington* to make it easier for courts to find ineffective assistance of counsel.

• Improve the efficiency of public defenders' offices by the widespread use of advanced technology for managing information in complex cases, in case tracking, and for information exchange.[81]

• Reengineer the role of chief public defenders from that of narrow and defensive managers to be spokespersons for the need for adequate funding for indigent defense. This may include developing better relations with legislators, prosecutors, police, corrections, the media, and community groups in an effort to advocate the need for indigent defense and to sponsor community crime-prevention programs.[82]

• Tie the expenditure of indigent defense (all systems) to a percentage of funding of public prosecution, at a suggested rate of 75 percent.[83]

• Public defenders' offices negotiate reasonable caseload limits with courts and funding agencies.

• Require minimum experience before assigning major cases.[84]

• Eliminate the practice of judges compelling attorneys to take major cases on a pro bono basis.[85]

• Finance indigent defense in part with a portion of court fees.

• Reduce the enforcement component of the "war on drugs," with its draconian punishments for low level crimes, and replace this with more treatment options.

Until such practical solutions are implemented, the promise of the Constitution—equal justice under law—will go unfulfilled.

SUMMARY

The right to the assistance of counsel in a criminal prosecution is guaranteed by the Sixth Amendment. It is fundamental to the proper conduct of criminal trials and the adversary system of justice. In other proceedings, a right to counsel has been guaranteed by the Due Process and Equal Protection Clauses of the Fourteenth Amendment as well as the Fifth Amendment right against self-incrimination. Defense counsel is more important in common law trials than in trials under the European civil law system. The actual use of lawyers in trials was a late common law development.

Prior to its incorporation into the Fourteenth Amendment in *Gideon v. Wainwright* (1963), the Sixth Amendment right applied only to federal prosecutions. Under federal law, a defendant had to be represented and could waive counsel only if it specifically appeared on the record that the defendant did so knowingly and voluntarily (*Johnson v. Zerbst,* 1938). In state cases, lack of counsel violated a defendant's Fourteenth Amendment due process right to a fair trial only when special circumstances existed: e.g., death penalty, defendant's immaturity or ignorance, complex issues, or an atmosphere of prejudice (*Powell v. Alabama*, 1932). *Griffin v. Illinois* (1956) held that under the Fourteenth Amendment Equal Protection Clause, in which the state allows certain legal benefits to those who can afford it, the state must provide at no cost benefits, such as transcripts for appeals, to indigent defendants.

Gideon v. Wainwright (1963) incorporated the Sixth Amendment right to counsel into the Fourteenth Amendment Due Process Clause. The right to counsel was later applied to all misdemeanor cases in which the defendant was actually imprisoned. The Sixth Amendment right to counsel extends to all critical stages (preliminary examination, capital arraignment, sentencing), but not to postconviction correctional processes (probation revocation, parole revocation, or prison disciplinary hearings). The Sixth Amendment requires appointment of a psychiatric expert where necessary to decide an insanity issue.

In proceedings that are not Sixth Amendment prosecutions, counsel is authorized by the Due Process Clause in some proceedings (probation and parole revocations, juvenile delinquency adjudication) but not in others (prison discipline, summary court-martial). In probation revocation hearings, courts have discretion to appoint counsel to indigents where special circumstances exist; but in juvenile adjudication, counsel must be provided.

Courts can prevent persons who are not licensed in the practice of law from serving as counsel and can bar an attorney from representing a person where the court believes there will be a conflict of interest. A federal forfeiture statute that allows the confiscation of attorneys' fees before trial does not violate the Sixth Amendment right to counsel. The Sixth Amendment does not guarantee a meaningful relationship between a defendant and assigned counsel. When counsel is provided without cost to an indigent defendant, the state has a right to seek compensation at a later time when the defendant has obtained the money to repay the costs.

Counsel is guaranteed on a first appeal under the Due Process and Equal Protection Clauses (*Douglas v. California*, 1963). The Court limited the extension of this rule in *Ross v. Moffitt* (1974) so that counsel is not constitutionally required for indigent litigants pursuing discretionary second appeals or habeas corpus proceedings, as long as the state allows indigent prisoners to pursue such appeals.

The right to representation at a criminal trial is personal, and a defendant has a right to waive the assistance of counsel and conduct a defense *pro se* (*Faretta v. California*, 1975). A waiver requires the trial judge to closely examine the defendant to be sure he or she understands the benefits of counsel and waives appointed counsel voluntarily, and to be sure that the defendant has the minimum skills needed to conduct a reasonable defense. The court cannot disqualify a *pro se* defense because the defendant does not have expert knowledge of the law or of the trial process. In instances of *pro se* defense, the court may appoint standby counsel over the defendant's objection.

A federal regulation allowed a judge to authorize eavesdropping on conversations between lawyers and clients in federal jail or prison where there was cause to believe the attorney was involved in furthering criminal activity. In the aftermath of 9/11, the federal government quietly replaced the judicial warrant requirement, allowing agents to listen in on attorney-client conversations with the approval of the attorney general based on only reasonable suspicion that a prisoner *may* use communications with attorneys to further terrorism. This rule, plus the partially failed attack on defense attorney Lynne Stewart, suggests that in the name of fighting terrorism, the government has used measures that are unduly broad and actually ineffective, perhaps for political advantage, imperiling basic liberties.

The Sixth Amendment requires that the assistance afforded to a defendant be effective. The basic rules of effective assistance are, first, that the attorney's conduct must be reasonable, or not deficient, according to the prevailing standards of practicing attorneys in the locality and, second, that if the attorney's performance was deficient, this must have prejudiced the defendant's case so that the conviction was a result of the deficient performance. The complaining defendant has the burden of proving ineffective assistance. Ineffective assistance will not be presumed. It is not deficient performance to refuse to assist a client in committing perjury. In cases involving a real conflict of interest, ineffective assistance is presumed, but the mere fact that an attorney represented two clients is not in itself a conflict of interest. If an attorney raises a reasonable possibility of a conflict of interest, a trial judge must hold a hearing to inquire into the matter.

LEGAL PUZZLES

HOW HAVE COURTS DECIDED THESE CASES?

RIGHT TO COUNSEL

6–1. Ronford Styron, was convicted of the capital murder of his eleven-month-old son, Lee, and sentenced to death. Medical evidence indicated that Lee died as a result of subdural hemorrhaging caused by trauma to the head, consistent with repeated episodes of shaken-baby trauma. Styron testified that he punched Lee in the head one time and offered no explanation as to how the boy received multiple bruises on his head.

Styron was indicted by the grand jury of the 75th District Court of Liberty County, Texas, with intentionally causing the death of Lee. Counsel was appointed to represent him. At the request of the State, without notice to Styron or his attorney and without a hearing, the case was transferred by the 75th District Court to the 253rd District Court of Liberty County about two months after the indictment. Styron contends that the government manipulated the transfer to secure a more favorable forum in which to prosecute the action. The prosecution contends that the district court clerk assigns indictments to the court in which the prosecutor handling the case was assigned. The District Attorney's office randomly assigned cases to prosecutors. In this case, Styron's prosecutor was assigned to the 253rd District Court, and the clerk then transferred the case to the 253rd District Court without a hearing and without notice to either Styron or his attorney to accommodate the trial prosecutor.

Did the transfer of the case from one trial court to another trial court, without a hearing and without informing Styron or his counsel, constitute the denial of counsel because it was a procedure at which counsel attached?

HELD: No

6–1. The transfer was made pursuant to prosecutorial discretion. Styron failed to prove that the discretion had been abused. There was no due process violation because Styron did not show that he was in any way prejudiced by the lack of hearing and notice of the transfer. (The trial court hearing on the motion and the appellate and state writ process afforded Styron a full and fair hearing on this matter.) The district court also found no violation of the right to counsel because an administrative act transferring the case was not a criminal proceeding in which the rights of Styron might be affected because the act of transfer was not a "critical stage" in the prosecution.

The right to counsel attaches "at or after the initiation of adversary judicial proceedings against the defendant" (*United States v. Gouveia*, 1984). This right extends to critical pretrial proceedings as "the accused is guaranteed that he need not stand alone against the State at any stage of the prosecution, formal or informal, in court or out, where counsel's absence might derogate from the accused's right to a fair trial" (*United States v. Wade*, 1967). The court must "analyze whether potential substantial prejudice to defendant's rights inheres in the particular confrontation and the ability of counsel to help avoid that prejudice." In *Gouveia* the Supreme Court characterized the situations where the right extends as instances where "the results of the confrontation 'might well settle the accused's fate and reduce the trial itself to a mere formality.'" Thus, the Court has found a violation of the right to counsel where counsel was not notified or allowed to confer with his client prior to a pretrial psychiatric interview later used at the sentencing phase. *Estelle v. Smith* (1981); see also *Mempa v. Rhay* (1967) (holding that counsel must be appointed at a proceeding where certain legal rights like appeal may be lost). *Styron v. Johnson*, 262 F.3d 438 (5th Cir. 2001)

RIGHT TO COUNSEL—WAIVER

6–2. Frank Akins pled guilty to a fourth-degree assault against his girlfriend. He signed a written waiver of trial and pled to the misdemeanor without representation by counsel. The waiver form stated that a person pleading guilty gives up some trial rights but did not mention anything about the right to counsel. Akins was sentenced to ninety days in jail and eighty-eight days were suspended. There is no indication on the record that he had been advised by a judge of the value of being represented by a lawyer. Akins was later indicted for possession of a firearm by a person previously convicted of a misdemeanor crime of domestic violence. He argues that the

misdemeanor conviction cannot be considered because the plea was obtained without a voluntary and intelligent waiver of the assistance of counsel.

Should a plea to a misdemeanor be made void if the defendant waived representation by counsel without being informed of the benefits of counsel?

Holding available from instructor

SELF-REPRESENTATION/RIGHT TO COUNSEL

6–3. Richard LaBare seeks to exclude a prior conviction for terrorizing with a weapon from consideration for sentencing because he claims that the trial leading to the prior conviction involved a violation to his right to counsel and, therefore, cannot be used in the present sentencing.

At the earlier trial LaBare had been assigned counsel (Joanne Kroll) to represent him. Partway through the trial, he asked the trial judge for a continuance to obtain new counsel because of a disagreement with Kroll. The trial judge made an effort to obtain substitute counsel without delaying the trial, but when this failed, the trial judge gave LaBare the choice between proceeding *pro se* or continuing with Kroll, whom the court found to be providing proper assistance.

LaBare, insisting that he wanted new counsel, refused Kroll's further representation (she became his standby counsel) and began to represent himself—despite the trial judge's warning to LaBare "that even a lawyer has a fool for a client if he chooses to represent himself." After some time, LaBare declared that he was not qualified and did not want to represent himself. The trial judge asked Kroll if she was willing to resume full representation, but she declined; the judge thereupon told LaBare that he was to continue representing himself, using Kroll as standby counsel if he wanted advice.

Prior to this trial, LaBare, a thirty-seven-year-old man, had been convicted of serious crimes on three separate occasions.

1. Regarding the decision to proceed *pro se*, was LaBare's decision voluntary and properly informed?
2. Regarding the judge's order to LaBare to represent himself after Kroll declined to again represent LaBare, was this a denial of the assistance of counsel?

Holding available from instructor

INEFFECTIVE ASSISTANCE OF COUNSEL

6–4. Charles Elliott was convicted in New Mexico state court for criminal sexual penetration and kidnapping of his then ex-wife, Toni Elliott. Elliott challenges the constitutionality of his state court convictions on the ground that he was denied effective assistance of counsel at trial when his attorney failed not only to present an opening or closing statement to the jury, but declined entirely to present any defense after the prosecution rested.

This is an appeal to a federal circuit court. The New Mexico Court of Appeals determined counsel's decisions not to present opening or closing arguments were "questions of trial tactics and strategy" not to be "second-guessed" on appeal, and speculated that trial counsel "may have believed the State's case so weak or incredible that no further argument was needed." This conclusion of the New Mexico court was not based on a review of the facts of the case.

The defense attorney cross-examined Toni, who indicated on cross-examination that she did not believe she was the victim of a kidnapping or rape, in contradiction to pretrial statements. Further, the prosecution introduced a confession by Elliott, which he claims was made while he was under the influence of heroin.

1. Was the defense attorney's failure to make opening and closing statements, and failure to develop a defense case, deficient performance?
2. Did this case result in the ineffective assistance of counsel?

Holding available from instructor

FURTHER READING

James Goodman, *Stories of Scottsboro* (New York: Pantheon Books, 1994).

Anthony Lewis, *Gideon's Trumpet* (New York: Vintage Books, 1964).

David J. Bodenhamer, *Fair Trial: Rights of the Accused in American History* (New York: Oxford University Press, 1992).

ENDNOTES

1. *Faretta v. California* (1975), quoting Holdsworth, *History of English Law;* C. Rembar, *The Law of the Land* (New York: Simon and Schuster, 1980), 181; L. Levy, *Origins of the Fifth Amendment* (New York: Oxford University Press, 1968), 19.

2. William Blackstone, *Commentaries on the Laws of England, Volume 4—Of Public Wrongs* (Chicago: University of Chicago Press, 1979, facsimile of First Edition, 1769), 349–50.

3. Hiller B. Zobel, *The Boston Massacre* (New York: W.W. Norton, 1970).

4. *Powell v. Alabama* (1932), citing the right to counsel in the first constitutions of Maryland, Massachusetts, New Hampshire, New York, Pennsylvania, Delaware, New Jersey, and Connecticut (not adopted until 1818) and statutes of North Carolina and South Carolina and later constitutions of Georgia and Rhode Island.

5. In England and Canada, and in colonial and early Republican United States, the word was spelled "defence." The modern American spelling is "defense."

6. Two excellent histories of the Scottsboro case are D. T. Carter, *Scottsboro: A Tragedy of the American South,* rev. ed. (Baton Rouge: Louisiana State University Press, 1979) and J. Goodman, *Stories of Scottsboro* (New York: Pantheon Books, 1994). The narrative of the case is taken from these sources.

7. The second appeal to the United States Supreme Court, *Norris v. Alabama* (1934) held that the exclusion of African Americans from juries violated the defendants' right to equal protection under the Fourteenth Amendment.

8. H. Arkes, *The Return of George Sutherland: Restoring a Jurisprudence of Natural Rights* (Princeton: Princeton University Press, 1994), 264–65.

9. Ibid.

10. Ibid, 265.

11. He cited *Gitlow v. New York* (1925), *Stromberg v. California* (1931), and *Near v. Minnesota* (1931).

12. Arkes, *Return of George Sutherland,* 268.

13. *Smith v. Bennett* (1961); *Burns v. Ohio* (1959).

14. *Roberts v. Lavallee* (1967); *Gardner v. California* (1969); *Mayer v. Chicago* (1971).

15. *Mills v. Municipal Court for San Diego Judicial District* (1973) 10 Cal 3d 288, 110 Cal Rptr 329, 515 P2d 273.

16. *In re Groban* (1957) (dictum); *Davis v. Mississippi* (1969); *Gilbert v. California* (1967); *United States v. Dionisio* (1973).

17. Linda Greenhouse, "High Court Backs Seizure of Assets in Criminal Cases," *New York Times,* June 22, 1989.

18. David Rossman, "'Were There No Appeal': The History of Review in American Criminal Courts," *Journal of Criminal Law and Criminology,* 81 (3) (1990): 518–566.

19. *People v. Valdez,* (1990, Colo) 789 P2d 406.

20. Ibid, 408.

21. Marie Higgins Williams, "Comment: The Pro Se Criminal Defendant, Standby Counsel, and the Judge: A Proposal for Better Defined Roles," *University of Colorado Law Review,* 71 (2000): 789–818.

22. Williams, "Pro Se Criminal Defendant," 793, n. 28, citing a past president of the National Association of Criminal Defense Lawyers.

23. Ron Christenson, ed., *Political Trials in History* (New Brunswick: Transaction Publishers, 1991), 91–93; Williams, "Pro Se Criminal Defendant," 789–90.

24. J. T. McQuiston, "Suspect in L.I.R.R. Killings Ruled Competent for Trial," *New York Times,* December 10, 1994; J. T. McQuiston, "Adviser to L.I.R.R. Suspect Threatens to Quit," *New York Times,* February 7, 1995. They became standby counsel, but later resigned when Ferguson's antics became intolerably bizarre.

25. J. T. McQuiston, "L.I.R.R. Defendant Helps Pick Jury, Then Says It Is Biased," *New York Times,* January 24, 1995.

26. J. T. McQuiston, "In the Bizarre L.I.R.R. Trial, Equally Bizarre Confrontations," *New York Times,* February 5, 1995.

27. D. Van Biema, "A Fool for a Client; Accused L.I.R.R. Killer Colin Ferguson Is Defending Himself, and That May Be Something of a Crime," *Time,* February 6, 1995.

28. J. Hoffman, "Hapless Lawyer, Thankless Job; Colin Ferguson's Adviser Sees Reputation and Practice Suffer," *New York Times,* February 14, 1995.

29. P. Marks, "Relief That the Book Is Closed on a Looking-Glass Trial," *New York Times,* February 19, 1995.

30. Philip Shenon, "Judge Lets Man Accused in Sept. 11 Plot Defend Himself," *New York Times,* June 14, 2002.

31. Philip Shenon, "Judge Bars 9/11 Suspect from Being Own Lawyer," *New York Times,* November 15, 2003.

32. Williams, "Pro Se Criminal Defendant," 801.

33. Ibid., 805.

34. Ibid.

35. Ibid., 809–815.

36. Rules and Regulations, Bureau of Prisons, U.S. Dep't. of Justice, 28 C.F.R. §§540.18, 540.19, 540.48.

37. Marjorie Cohn, "Looking Backward: The Evisceration of the Attorney-Client Privilege in the Wake of September 11, 2001,"

Fordham Law Review 2003 (2003): 1233–1255; Rules and Regulations, Bureau of Prisons, U.S. Dep't. of Justice, 28 C.F.R. 500, 501 (2002); Prevention of Acts of Violence and Terrorism, 66 *Fed. Reg.* 55062, (October. 31, 2001).

38. Stephen J. Schulhofer, *The Enemy Within: Intelligence Gathering, Law Enforcement, and Civil Liberties in the Wake of September 11* (New York: Century Foundation Press, 2000), 23.

39. Ibid., 25.

40. Ibid., 25–6.

41. Cohn, "Looking Backward," 1244.

42. Benjamin Weiser and Robert F. Worth, "Indictment Says Lawyer Helped a Terror Group," *New York Times*, April 10, 2002.

43. Cohn, "Looking Backward," 1249–1250.

44. Michael Wilson, "Judge Dismisses Terror Charges Against Lawyer," *New York Times*, July 23, 2003.

45. Deborah L. Rhode, "Terrorists and Their Lawyers," *New York Times*, April 16, 2002, A27.

46. See the Spangenberg Group, *Indigent Defense and Technology: A Progress Report* (Bureau of Justice Assistance, NCJ 179003, November 1999).

47. Bob Sablatura, "Study Confirms Money Counts in County's Courts; Those Using Appointed Lawyers Are Twice as Likely to Serve Time," *Houston Chronicle*, October 17, 1999.

48. "I Think You Get All the Justice You Can Afford," *Time*, June 19, 1995, pp. 46–47.

49. Gregg Herrington, "Sex Ring Attorney Looks to Civil Trial," *The Columbian*, December 15, 1995; T. Egan, "Pastor and Wife Are Acquitted on All Charges in Sex-Abuse Case," *New York Times*, December 12, 1995; D. Nathan, "Justice in Wenatchee," *New York Times*, December 19, 1995; See Dorothy Rabinowitz, *No Crueler Tyrannies* (New York: A Wall Street Journal Book, 2003).

50. D. West, "Cleared of Child Abuse, but the Anguish Lingers," *New York Times*, October 19, 1995.

51. Bulletin Broadfaxing Network, The Bulletin's Frontrunner, April 26, 2000: "Legal Fees Reduce Hilliard's Warchest to $149; Blames Racism for His Problem."

52. "CHSWC Okays New Study on Drug Costs," *Workers' Comp Executive*, 9 (22) (1999).

53. David Lawsky, "$1 Billion Settlement Reported in Vitamin Suit," *Toronto Star*, November 4, 1999.

54. Del Quentin Wilber (*Baltimore Sun*), "Tripp Seeks Help Paying Lawyers," *Des Moines Register*, November 18, 1999.

55. Jill Abramson, "The Nation: The Price of Being Lewinsky; Dream Team, Nightmare Tab," *New York Times*, June 7, 1998.

56. Don Van Natta, Jr., "Fewer Donations Coming in for Clinton Defense Fund," *New York Times*, August 13, 1999.

57. "I Think You Get," 46–47.

58. E. Gleick, "Rich Justice, Poor Justice," *Time*, June 19, 1995.

59. Kevin Moran, "Durst Told Wife He Would Be Acquitted," *Houston Chronicle*, November 13, 2003.

60. Kim Taylor-Thompson, "Effective Assistance: Reconceiving the Role of the Chief Public Defender," *Journal of the Institute for the Study of Legal Ethics* 2 (1999): 199–220.

61. David Bazelon, quoted in R. Klein, "The Emperor *Gideon* Has No Clothes: The Empty Promise of the Constitutional Right to Effective Assistance of Counsel," *Hastings Constitutional Law Quarterly* 13 (1986): 625–93.

62. Editorial, "Judicial Reforms in Albany," *New York Times*, May 26, 2000.

63. Martha K. Harrison, "Note: Claims for Compensation: The Implications of Getting Paid When Appointed under the Criminal Justice Act," *Boston University Law Review* 79 (1999): 553–76, p. 555, n. 15.

64. Alan Cooper, "Appointed Lawyer's Low Fee Ruled No Bar to Fair Trial," *Richmond Times Dispatch*, May 5, 2000.

65. R. Marcus, "Racism in Our Courts: The Underfunding of Public Defenders and Its Disproportionate Impact upon Racial Minorities," *Hastings Constitutional Law Quarterly* 22 (1994): 219–67 (footnotes omitted, emphasis added).

66. S. Mounts, "The Right to Counsel and the Indigent Defense System," *New York University Review of Law & Social Change* 14 (1986): 221–41, citing *Cooper v. Fitzharris*, 551 F.2d 1162, at 1163, n.1 (9th Cir. 1977).

67. R. L. Spangenberg and T. J. Schwartz, "The Indigent Defense Crisis Is Chronic," *Criminal Justice* (Summer 1994), 13, citing *State v. Peart*, 621 So. 2d 780 (La. 1993).

68. Spangenberg and Schwartz, "Indigent Defense" citing *National Law Journal* (August 20, 1992).

69. R. L. Spangenberg, "We Are Still Not Defending the Poor Properly," *Criminal Justice*, 11–131 (Fall 1989).

70. S. E. Mounts and R. J. Wilson, "Systems for Providing Indigent Defense: An Introduction," *New York University Review of Law & Social Change*, 14 (1986): 193–201, citing *Washington Post*, June 25, 1984.

71. Ross E. Milloy, "Judge Frees Texas Inmate Whose Lawyer Slept at Trial," *New York Times*, March 2, 2000; Paul Duggan, "George W. Bush: The Record in Texas; Attorneys' Ineptitude Doesn't Halt Executions," *Washington Post*, May 12, 2000.

72. S. Bright, "Counsel for the Poor: The Death Sentence Not for the Worst Crime but for the Worst Lawyer," *Yale Law Journal* 103(1994):1835–83, pp. 1838–39.

73. A. Cohen, "The Difference a Million Makes," *Time*, June 19, 1993, 53.

74. "Another Wrongly Convicted Man," *Indianapolis Star*, February 10, 2000; Bright, "Counsel for the Poor."

75. Sara Rimer, "Questions of Death Row Justice for Poor People in Alabama," *New York Times*, March 1, 2000.

76. Ibid.

77. Mounts and Wilson, "Providing Indigent Defense," 200–201.

78. Spangenberg and Schwartz, "Indigent Defense," 14; J. J. Cleary, "Federal Defender Services: Serving the System or the Client?" *Law and Contemporary Problems* 58 (1995): 65–80.

79. Mounts and Wilson, "Providing Indigent Defense," 200–201.

80. Spangenberg and Schwartz, "Indigent Defense."

81. Spangenberg Group, *Indigent Defense*.

82. Taylor-Thompson, "Effective Assistance."

83. Ibid., 207–08.

84. Jo Becker, "Rules Set for Death Row Lawyers," *St. Petersburg (FL) Times*, October 30, 1999.

85. Stafford Henderson Byers, "Delivering Indigents' Right to Counsel While Respecting Lawyers' Right to Their Profession: A System "Between a Rock and a Hard Place"," *St. John's Journal of Legal Commentary* 13 (1999): 491–526.

JUSTICES OF THE SUPREME COURT

WARREN COURT LIBERALS
WARREN—GOLDBERG—FORTAS

The liberal reputation of the Warren Court (1954–1969) rests primarily on its work in four major areas: destroying legalized racial segregation, mandating equal voting power through the apportionment of voting districts so that each voter's vote was of approximately equal weight, expanding First Amendment rights, and incorporating most of the criminal procedure provisions of the Bill of Rights. The last achievement, in fact, began in 1961 with Mapp v. Ohio, *and gathered momentum only with the appointment of Justice Goldberg upon the retirement of Justice Frankfurter. The incorporation cases often, but not invariably, hinged on the votes of a slim majority—Warren, Black, Douglas, Brennan, and Goldberg (and Fortas after him). This is not sur-*

prising to constitutional scholars, because important constitutional innovations often embody one side of a large conflict of ideals of the society. The competing ideals of liberty and security are both essential, so the law of criminal procedure is bound to exhibit some tension and shift. The adoption of a competing ideal in a particular case is less a matter of "right and wrong" in a factual sense than a value choice between the approaches and a response to differing perceived needs of the nation at a given time. This may explain why American electoral politics, policy choices, and constitutional doctrines are subject to broad swings over the decades; there may be no other way to maintain peaceful continuity in a nation so vast and so varied.

EARL WARREN

California 1891–1974

Republican

Appointed Chief Justice by Dwight D. Eisenhower

Years of Service: 1953–1969

Collection of the Supreme Court of the United States. Photographer: Abdon Daoud Ackad

LIFE AND CAREER   The son of a Norwegian immigrant railroad car inspector, Warren received his undergraduate and law degrees from the University of California, Berkeley. After army service in World War I, he entered public service and became district attorney (prosecutor) of Alameda County (Oakland, California) in 1925. His vigorous prosecution of corrupt politicians and organized crime helped to elevate him to California's attorney general in 1938. In that role, he backed the relocation of Japanese Americans from their homes to internment camps for the duration of World War II. He was elected Governor of California in 1943, and he ran for vice president of the United States in 1948 on the losing Republican ticket with Thomas Dewey of New York. (His support of a rule that allowed Dwight Eisenhower to win the nomination of the Republican party led to his appointment as Chief Justice in 1953.)

CONTRIBUTION TO CRIMINAL PROCEDURE   After his first two terms on the Court, Warren became a critical liberal vote, and

with the appointment of Goldberg to replace Frankfurter in 1962, the way was clear to accomplish the "due process revolution" by which most of the criminal provisions of the Bill of Rights were incorporated. His important majority opinions include *Terry v. Ohio* (1967) (stop and frisk), *Sherman v. United States* (1958) (entrapment), and *Klopfer v. North Carolina* (1967) (incorporating the Sixth Amendment right to a speedy trial). Earl Warren, a tough prosecutor, knew well how such public servants could abuse their great powers of office to overwhelm the will of the individual.

SIGNATURE OPINION   *Miranda v. Arizona* (1966) is the case that revolutionized the law of confessions. Warren characteristically devoted relatively little space to the discussion of the precedents that would ordinarily be critical to justify a decision and instead devoted the lion's share of the opinion to documenting the numerous ways that law enforcement officers "subjugated the individual to the will of his examiner." The decision in *Miranda* spelled out practical rules and their application for police and prosecutors, an approach that has been derided by critics as judicial legislation. *Miranda* was characteristic of his activism and liberalism, and his willingness to ignite controversy if he believed his position was the fair course to take.

ASSESSMENT   Warren is ranked a great chief justice, not because he had a brilliant legal mind or because of his judicial craft in writing opinions, but for his leadership. He was a progressive with strong streaks of moralism and populism, and a superb administrator who knew how to motivate people and get things done. He is most remembered for his masterful ability to take a divided Court on the monumental issue of school segregation and steer it to a unanimous opinion in *Brown v. Board of Education* (1954), a feat considered to be the hallmark

(Continued)

of judicial statesmanship. During an oral argument, he often cut through technical presentations to ask lawyers if the position they were supporting was fair, a question some saw as unsophisticated. However, this approach provided the framework for rulings that transformed American politics, law enforcement, and society. Under Warren, the Supreme Court was marked by activism, liberalism, and populism. It outlawed racial segregation, ended unrepresentative voting districts in the states, extended First Amendment rights, and vigorously upheld antitrust laws.

FURTHER READING

Bernard Schwartz, *Super Chief: Earl Warren and His Supreme Court—A Judicial Biography,* unabridged (New York: New York University Press, 1983).

ARTHUR J. GOLDBERG

Illinois 1908–1990

Democrat

Appointed by
John F. Kennedy

Years of Service:
1962–1965

Collection of the Supreme Court of the United States. Photographer: Abdon Daoud Ackad

LIFE AND CAREER The youngest of eleven children of Russian immigrants, Goldberg was educated in Chicago public schools and received his bachelor's and law degrees from Northwestern University, graduating first in his law school class. He practiced law in Chicago until World War II and in 1938 began to practice labor law. During the war, he served in the Office of Strategic Services in charge of labor espionage behind enemy lines.

After the war, he became a leading labor lawyer and in 1948 became general counsel for the United Steelworkers Union. He played a central role in the merger of the American Federation of Labor and the Congress of Industrial Organizations (AFL-CIO), becoming the group's general counsel. In 1957 he led the fight to expel the crime-ridden Teamster's Union from the labor body. Through this work and his excellent reputation as a negotiator, Goldberg gained national prominence. He became an adviser to Senator John F. Kennedy in his 1960 bid for the presidency and was selected

by President Kennedy to be Secretary of Labor, where he played an active role in settling several major strikes. In 1962 he was nominated by Kennedy to replace Justice Frankfurter.

In 1965 President Lyndon Johnson persuaded Justice Goldberg to resign his seat to become Ambassador to the United Nations in the hope that his negotiating skills would help in bringing a speedy end to the Vietnam War.

CONTRIBUTION TO CRIMINAL PROCEDURE Despite his short period of service on the Court, Goldberg's appointment created a liberal majority on the Court and thus inaugurated the due process revolution of applying the Bill of Rights to the states in criminal procedure.

SIGNATURE OPINION *Escobedo v. Illinois* (1964), the confessions case that held that police refusal of a lawyer's request to see a client violated the right to counsel; a confession obtained under those conditions was inadmissible in court. *Escobedo,* a breakthrough case, paved the way to *Miranda v. Arizona* (1966).

ASSESSMENT Goldberg was a liberal who believed that the Court has a legitimate problem-solving role and an important role in democracy by imposing constitutional-majoritarian restraints to protect minority rights. He was a creative justice and established himself as the leading liberal spokesperson on a wide variety of explosive civil rights issues. In *Griswold v. Connecticut* (1965), the "contraceptive" case that established a framework for abortion rights, Goldberg concurred on the intellectually daring position that the rarely used Ninth Amendment should be the basis for removing criminal penalties against physicians who dispense, and married persons who seek, contraception advice. He argued that the Court should look to the "traditions and [collective] conscience of our people" to discover which rights are fundamental and beyond the reach of the legislature. He also opposed the death penalty, arguing in 1963 that the Court should decide its constitutionality, an issue that the Court did not confront until the 1970s. He took a bold approach to civil rights, urging the Court to go beyond declaring discriminatory laws unconstitutional, and requiring the states to act affirmatively to guarantee civil rights, a position shared by only two other justices.

FURTHER READING

Stephen J. Friedman, "Arthur Goldberg," in *The Justices of the United States Supreme Court, 1789–1969,* Leon Friedman and Fred L. Israel, eds., vol. 4, 2977–2990 (New York: Chelsea House, 1969).

ABE FORTAS

Tennessee 1910–1982

Democrat

Appointed by
Lyndon Johnson

Years of Service:
1965–1969

Collection of the Supreme Court of the United States. Photographer: Harris and Ewing

LIFE AND CAREER   A native of Memphis and the son of a poor tailor, Fortas graduated from Southwest College and Yale Law School. At Yale, he came to the attention of Professor William O. Douglas, who brought Fortas to Washington during the New Deal. Fortas was a tough and brilliant government lawyer; at the age of thirty-two, as under-secretary of the interior, he argued unsuccessfully against the removal of Japanese Americans from the West Coast.

After World War II he went into private law practice in Washington, D.C. The firm of Arnold, Porter, and Fortas developed a reputation for effectively representing large corporations and for courageously defending the civil liberties of persons hounded by the government during the anti-communist hysteria of the late 1940s and early 1950s. Fortas skillfully represented Texas Congressman Lyndon Johnson, under charges of election fraud, in a notorious 1948 Senate primary election vote recount that secured Johnson a Senate seat. Fortas, thereafter, became a close advisor to Johnson.

As a private lawyer, Fortas took several *pro bono* cases that significantly changed criminal law and procedure. *Durham v. United States* (District of Columbia Court of Appeals (1954) later reversed) made a major change in the insanity defense in Washington, D.C. He argued for the defendant in *Gideon v. Wainwright* (1963), playing an important role in advancing the incorporation doctrine and expanding the right to counsel.

Fortas was nominated by President Johnson to be chief justice after Earl Warren announced his *prospective* retirement in 1968. Johnson did not seek a new term because of the intense politics surrounding the Vietnam War. As a result, Re-

publicans in the Senate blocked Fortas's appointment, and he eventually withdrew it. During the nomination process, the press discovered that Fortas was a major presidential advisor while sitting on the bench and that he was receiving an annual payment of $20,000 from a family foundation of a businessman who had gone to prison for stock manipulation. Again, under intense public scrutiny and abetted by inside pressure from President Nixon's Attorney General John Mitchell, Fortas resigned in 1969, although he had done nothing illegal.

CONTRIBUTION TO CRIMINAL PROCEDURE   As a Warren Court liberal, Fortas voted for the incorporation doctrine and for the expansion of suspects' and defendants' procedural rights in several important cases, providing the crucial fifth majority vote in *Miranda v. Arizona* (1966). He had a special interest in the rights of juvenile delinquents, a novel area for the Court, and his majority opinion in *Kent v. United States* (1966) held that a juvenile is entitled to a hearing under the Due Process Clause before a delinquency case can be transferred from juvenile court into the adult criminal system.

SIGNATURE OPINION   *In re Gault* (1967) made major changes in the way that juvenile court proceedings would henceforth be conducted. Before being adjudged delinquent, juveniles were entitled to many of the same procedural guarantees afforded to adults, including counsel, notice, the confrontation of witnesses, cross-examination, a written transcript, and appellate review. Fortas's opinion was powerful because it recognized that a benevolent governmental purpose can mask oppression in practice, and emphasized that the procedural rights of the Constitution are critical to the legitimacy of American courts, even special courts designed to help juveniles and not merely to punish. No matter how noble the goal of the state, the Due Process Clause applies whenever a person, including a minor, is stripped of life, liberty, or property.

ASSESSMENT   Fortas was a solid liberal in all civil rights areas, but unlike most liberal justices, in antitrust matters he was not opposed to big business and usually did not vote against corporate mergers. His resignation allowed an additional appointment by President Nixon, thus shifting the center of gravity of the Court from a liberal to a moderate-conservative stance in the area of criminal procedure.

FURTHER READING

Laura Kalman, *Abe Fortas: A Biography* (New Haven, CT: Yale University Press, 1990).

CHAPTER
7

INTERROGATION AND THE LAW OF CONFESSIONS

The Constitution of the United States stands as a bar against the conviction of any individual in an American court by means of a coerced confession. There have been, and are now, certain foreign nations with governments dedicated to an opposite policy: governments which convict individuals with testimony obtained by police organizations possessed of an unrestrained power to seize persons suspected of crimes against the state, hold them in secret custody, and wring from them confessions by physical or mental torture. So long as the Constitution remains the basic law of our Republic, America will not have that kind of government.

—Justice Hugo Black, *Ashcraft v. Tennessee,*
322 U.S. 143, 155 (1944)

CHAPTER OUTLINE

KEY TERMS AND PHRASES

Admission
Bright-line rule
Compulsion
Confession
Cruel trilemma
De minimis
Dying declaration

Exculpatory
Immunity from prosecution
Inculpatory
Interrogation
Involuntary confession
Material witness
Privilege

Real evidence
Self-incrimination
Supervisory authority
Testimonial evidence
Third Degree
Voluntariness test

INTRODUCTION

Interviewing witnesses and interrogating suspects are essential police investigation techniques.[1] Interviewing is the most useful method for police to develop an understanding of what occurred at a crime scene. Following an arrest, police will interrogate the suspect to obtain **admissions** or **confessions** of guilt that can be used in court to convict. Historically, **interrogation** has been accompanied by abuses, chiefly, torture and forcing innocent persons to confess. Although torture is now rare in the United States, instances of excessive force do occur and the potential for police brutality is a constant that must be guarded against.[2] Furthermore, recent research shows that contemporary practice of "psychological interrogation" is producing too many cases of false confessions by innocent persons.[3]

Three constitutional rights have been applied by the courts to check abusive interrogation. Before a suspect in a criminal case has hired or been assigned an attorney, rules developed under the Fifth and Fourteenth amendment *Due Process* Clauses and the Fifth Amendment *Self-Incrimination* Clause (applicable to the states via the Fourteenth Amendment) declare confessions obtained by abusive interrogation to be inadmissible. Since 1966 the major focus of interrogation law has been *Miranda v. Arizona* (1966), which interprets the Self-Incrimination Clause, and the interpretive cases following *Miranda*. Finally, under the *right to counsel* clause of the Sixth Amendment, a person who has been formally charged with a crime cannot be questioned, openly or surreptitiously, without the presence of her lawyer, a rule announced in *Massiah v. United States* (1964).

In a nutshell, there are three points. (1) The due process prohibits the introduction of **involuntary confessions**. (2) The *Miranda* case holds that police interrogation that takes place while a suspect is in custody is inherently coercive, and any confession or admission is presumed to be the product of **compulsion** unless a suspect is informed of his rights and voluntarily waives his right of silence under the **privilege** against **self-incrimination**. (3) The right to counsel is a flat prohibition on contacts between a criminal defendant and the police designed to elicit incriminating statements without the defendant's lawyer being present.

The Privilege against Self-Incrimination

The Self-Incrimination Clause appears to focus on testimony in a criminal trial: "No person . . . shall be compelled in any criminal case to be a witness against himself. . . ." The meaning of this famous rule, as to confessions, is even now not fully settled. The state of confessions law has been in flux since *Miranda v. Arizona* (1966) was decided. Recent cases have not determined the consequences of police failures to properly administer *Miranda* warnings.[4] The Supreme Court has granted certiorari in two cases, to be decided in 2004, that ought to clarify these issues.[5] This matter, discussed below, requires a basic understanding of contemporary self-incrimination law.

The privilege against self-incrimination clearly allows a defendant to remain silent in a criminal trial and have a defense conducted by counsel entirely by cross-examination. The defendant cannot be forced to testify, no matter how relevant his testimony may be. A prosecutor or judge who mentions a defendant's silence, except at the behest of the defendant or under limited circumstances, violates her right against self-incrimination (*Griffin v. California*, 1965; *Lakeside v. Oregon,* 1978). Jurors may believe that a defendant who does not take the stand has something to hide, but a hint by a judge or prosecutor so unbalances the scales of justice in the state's favor as to undermine a fair adversary trial. Prosecutorial or judicial comment also puts pressure (compulsion) on the defendant to give up the right to silence.

CLAIMING THE PRIVILEGE In order to ensure that the right is not destroyed before a criminal prosecution begins, a person may claim the right of silence under the Fifth Amendment in a variety of proceedings where he is called as a witness. These include criminal and civil cases (*United States v. Monia*, 1943; *McCarthy v. Arndstein,* 1924); administrative proceedings (*Malloy v. Hogan*, 1964); congressional investigations (*Watkins v. United States,* 1957); and grand juries (*Counselman v. Hitchcock,* 1892). If witnesses in these proceedings were forced to testify, their preserved testimony, if incriminating, could later be introduced against them in a criminal trial.

To understand why the privilege has to be actively invoked in these proceedings, it is helpful to understand that the privilege against self-incrimination is an *exception* to the general rule that individuals have an obligation to assist the state in prosecuting crimes and gathering information for legitimate purposes. Anterior to any formal proceedings, state officers may request information, as when a police officer asks residents for information about a criminal incident. At this stage, the officer cannot compel a person to provide information. Given Americans' well-honed sense of privacy, many may to refuse to "get involved." Nevertheless, as Chief Justice Warren stated, "It is an act of responsible citizenship for individuals to give whatever information they may have to aid in law enforcement" (*Miranda v. Arizona,* pp. 478–9). If a person not in custody does respond to a police officer, she has an obligation to answer questions truthfully, and may be charged criminally for lying (*Brogan v. United States,* 1998). If the prosecution believes that a person has information material to the prosecution of a pending criminal charge or grand jury investigation, the person may be arrested and confined as a **material witness** if a judge believes the person will flee, or may be subpoenaed to testify before the grand jury.[6]

In sum, persons formally subpoenaed by judicial, executive, or legislative bodies, or by a grand jury, or held as material witnesses must give testimony *unless* they have a legal privilege or right to refuse to testify. Failure to testify will lead to a finding of contempt that can be punished with fines or even jail. The law recognizes several privileges that exempt a person from providing information to lawful authority. These include the privileges of religious, medical, or legal practitioners not to divulge information given in professional confidence, and the marital privilege that protects the natural privacy of spouses.[7]

VALUES PROTECTED BY THE PRIVILEGE   The privilege against self-incrimination "is widely regarded as both fundamental to human liberty and venerable in the history of the development of civil rights."[8] It is related to modern notions of the right to privacy. As important, it is a mainstay of the adversary system of justice. It supports the requirement that the *burden of proof* of guilt rests on the prosecution, and that guilt must be proven beyond a *reasonable doubt.*

The privilege against self-incrimination stands in contrast to brutal legal measures in ancient Rome and medieval continental Europe that allowed the use of torture to obtain evidence of serious crime.[9] It also contrasts with far more civilized European criminal justice systems today that many view as more effective in getting at the truth.[10] As the Supreme Court has stated, the privilege

> reflects many of our fundamental values and most noble aspirations: our unwillingness to subject those suspected of crime to the **cruel trilemma** of self-accusation, perjury or contempt; our preference for an accusatorial rather than an inquisitorial system of criminal justice; our fear that self-incriminating statements will be elicited by inhumane treatment and abuses; our sense of fair play which dictates a fair state-individual balance by requiring the government to leave the individual alone until good cause is shown for disturbing him and by requiring the government in its contest with the individual to shoulder the entire load; our respect for the inviolability of the human personality and of the right of each individual to a private enclave where he may lead a private life; our distrust of self-deprecatory statements; and our realization that the privilege, while sometimes a shelter to the guilty, is often a protection to the innocent. (*Murphy v. Waterfront Commission of New York Harbor,* 1964, p. 55, internal references and quotation marks omitted)

Prior to 1964, the privilege applied only to the federal government. In *Malloy v. Hogan* (1964) it was incorporated into the Fourteenth Amendment Due Process Clause and held to "secure[] against state invasion the same privilege that the Fifth Amendment guarantees against federal infringement— the right of a person to remain silent unless he chooses to speak in the unfettered exercise of his own will, and to suffer no penalty . . . for such silence."

The privilege applies only to *natural persons.* It cannot be claimed on behalf of corporations or other business entities by their officers, even sole proprietorships—they are deemed "artificial persons" for self-incrimination purposes (*Wilson v. United States,* 1911; *Bellis v. United States,* 1974; *United States v. Doe,* 1984). Tax records created by an individual and delivered to her attorney are not immune from subpoena power (*Fisher v. United States,* 1976).

APPLICATION OF THE PRIVILEGE   The privilege applies only to **testimonial evidence**—evidence given by a live witness (or in personal writings like a diary) that is of a "communicative nature." Testimony conveys information based on what the witness knows or believes he knows. A testimonial "communication must itself, explicitly or implicitly, relate a factual assertion, or disclose information" that expresses "the contents of an individual's mind" (*Doe v. United States,* 1988). This is important because even if testimony is not directly self-incriminating, a witness who speaks reveals something about his or her mental process to the listener. This opens up the witness's mind and psychological process to the listener's scrutiny. A witness who testifies opens the possibility that his statements will lead the listener to infer that the witness has admitted to a fact that is incriminating, even if no explicit confession is made.

The privilege against self-incrimination does not apply to *physical evidence,* also called **real evidence,** no matter how incriminating, because it is not testimonial. Justice Holmes ruled that a suspect has no right to prevent the court, jury, or witnesses from viewing the suspect's face and person (*Holt v. United States,* 1910). The government can "compel a person to reenact a crime; shave his beard or mustache; try on clothing; dye her hair; demonstrate speech or other physical characteristics; furnish handwriting samples, hair samples, or fingerprints; have her gums examined; or take a blood-alcohol, breathalyser, or urine test."[11] A suspect can be photographed or measured, have tattoos and scars examined, and be required to stand in a lineup. Police can require a person to provide blood samples taken by medical personnel where blood alcohol levels are relevant evidence (*Schmerber v. California,* 1966). A driver stopped for DUI who refuses to take a breathalyzer test may have his driver's license revoked, and the fact of refusal can be used against him at a subsequent criminal trial even if the police did not inform the driver of that fact (*South Dakota v. Neville,* 1983). Blood taking is distinguished from a "lie detector" session, which not only gathers physiological attributes, but also may elicit testimonial responses. Police departments uniformly give *Miranda* warnings before administering polygraph examinations.

COMPULSION   Compulsion is an aspect of the right against self-incrimination. A purely voluntary admission of guilt to a friend or to an undercover agent is not made under compulsion— the listener can later testify to what was said. An ordinary witness in a trial or grand jury hearing, although subpoenaed and sworn to testify, is not deemed to be under such compulsion that she cannot invoke her Fifth Amendment privilege. Therefore, ordinary witnesses need not be warned of their Fifth Amendment rights (*United States v. Monia,* 1943). In other words, the privilege against self-incrimination is *not self-executing* and must be claimed by the witness or it will be lost.

The Fifth Amendment does not absolutely prohibit prosecutorial compulsion against a suspect or against a witness who claims the privilege. The state can achieve its legitimate goal to gather information in an inquiry or to further prosecution, by granting the witness **immunity from prosecution.** Immunity is granted when the prosecutor believes that an individual who claims the privilege has relevant information. If immunity from prosecution is granted and the witness continues to refuse to testify, the courts have power "to compel testimony . . . by use of civil contempt and coerced imprisonment. *Shillitani v. United States* (1966)" (*Lefkowitz v. Turley,* 1973).

An important consequence of granting immunity—for understanding the most recent controversy regarding confessions law—is that once immunity is granted, the statement made cannot be used against the witness in *any* way. "Testimony given in response to a grant of legislative immunity is the *essence of coerced testimony.* In such cases there is no question whether physical or psychological pressures overrode the defendant's will; the witness is told to talk or face the government's coercive sanctions, notably, a conviction for contempt" (***New Jersey v. Portash,*** 1979). Therefore, grand jury testimony compelled by a grant of immunity could not be used later in a trial to impeach the witness's credibility. As of 2004, the rule is different under *Miranda* law.

The ability of the government to compel testimony, for purposes other than criminal prosecution, also is seen in the so-called "penalty cases." The Supreme Court has held that when police officers were required to testify to an administrative body about corruption or forfeit their jobs, the testimony could not later be admitted in a criminal case (*Garrity v. New Jersey,* 1967). Also, an officer who refused to testify *or to waive immunity* could not be fired because it was based on his "refusal to waive a constitutional right" (*Gardner v. Broderick,* 1968). In *Spevack v. Klein* (1987) an attorney under judicial investigation for misconduct "asserted the privilege and refused to comply with a subpoena duces tecum demanding testimony and documents, despite facing disciplinary action for his refusal. When he appealed his resulting disbarment, a plurality of the Court determined that the threat of disbarment constituted compulsion under the Fifth Amendment and held that the state could not impose the penalty for an assertion of the privilege."[12]

Although these cases seem to confirm the notion that the state could not compel the officers to testify, the Court later made it clear that the state can indeed require officers to testify on pain of losing their jobs, or require contractors to testify on pain of losing contracts, as long as they were granted immunity from criminal prosecution (*Lefkowitz v. Turley,* 1973). The result of these cases is to treat penalties (e.g., loss of jobs or contacts, disbarment) as compulsion, but to allow the compulsion as long as the witnesses are immunized from the use of their testimony in later criminal prosecutions.

The simple fact that a police officer asks a person questions is not Fifth Amendment compulsion. *Miranda v. Arizona* (1966), however, has held that police compulsion exists during custodial interrogation of a suspect. In this instance, the privilege is "self-executing" and the police must inform the suspect of his rights by reading several warnings. (Cases distinguishing between police interviewing and interrogation are reviewed later in this chapter.)

INCRIMINATION   A person cannot lawfully refuse to testify to protect another, to avoid trouble with private parties, or for any reason under the privilege except to avoid being prosecuted for a crime. The Supreme Court ruled that this includes prosecution for juvenile delinquency, as the penalties for a delinquency adjudication are essentially penal in nature (*In re Gault,* 1967). Similarly, when a defendant speaks with a state psychiatrist in a pretrial hearing to determine competence to stand trial, any incriminating statements cannot be introduced in the defendant's sentencing hearing, unless the defendant waived his right against self-incrimination at the hearing, following *Miranda* warnings (*Estelle v. Smith,* 1981).

To the contrary, the Court has not extended self-incrimination protection to proceedings under sexual offender statutes that lead to incarceration or additional penalties. These programs are declared civil, and not penal, in nature. Allen was charged with a sexual assault (***Allen v. Illinois,*** 1986). Criminal charges were dropped and the state proceeded against him under the Sexually Dangerous Persons Act. Examining psychiatrists for the state testified at the bench trial on the petition. Allen objected that they had elicited information from him in violation of his self-incrimination privilege. Based on that testimony, as well as that of the victim of the sexual assault, the court found Allen to be a sexually dangerous person under the act, authorizing potentially indefinite commitment to the "sex deviate facility" located in the Wisconsin State Prison. The state proved that Allen had a mental disorder for more than one year and a propensity to commit sexual assaults. The Supreme Court held (5–4) that the program was one of civil commitment, despite the fact that the act provides some safeguards applicable in criminal trials (counsel, jury trial, confrontation and cross-examination of witnesses, prove dangerousness beyond a reasonable doubt) or that a person adjudged sexually dangerous is committed to a maximum-security institution that also houses convicts needing psychiatric care.

In ***McKune v. Lile*** (2002) a prison inmate convicted of rape was ordered into a treatment program a few years before his scheduled release. To participate, Robert Lile had to answer questions that would disclose criminal activity. No immunity was granted for any incriminating disclosures. Lile refused to participate. As a result, his prison privileges would be reduced, resulting in the automatic curtailment of his visitation rights, earnings, work opportunities, ability to send money to family, canteen expenditures, access to a personal television, and other privileges. He also would be transferred to a potentially more dangerous maximum-security unit. The Supreme Court held (5–4) that the requirement to disclose criminal information did not violate the Self-Incrimination Clause. In a plurality opinion, Justice Kennedy reasoned that although prisoners have Fifth Amendment rights, the program does not compel prisoners to testify because the lost privileges and transfer to a maximum-security unit "are not [consequences] that compel a prisoner to speak about his past crimes despite a desire to remain silent." The adverse consequences that Lile suffered were, furthermore, related to the objectives of a program that had legitimate penological goals. There was no self-incrimination violation as long as the program objectives do not constitute atypical and significant hardships. Justice Stevens, dissenting, felt that the penalty imposed for not participating was severe. More fundamentally, a person was punished for exercising his rights under the Self-Incrimination Clause.

Allen was criticized because it "is insensitive to the reality of the commitment system" that makes it very much like an indefinite prison sentence.[13] The kinds of programs upheld in *Allen* and *McKune* are politically popular. They are an attempt to deal with some highly predatory criminals. Nevertheless, there is evidence that some offenders placed in these programs do not fit the profiles of mentally aberrant patients and the programs may be covert ways of imposing virtual life sentences. The evidence used to place prisoners in programs may consist more of their prior record than any medical information.[14]

The privilege protects only against incrimination in American courts. A Nazi camp guard, unprosecutable in the United States because the statute of limitations had run out, was subpoenaed to testify in deportation hearings. He claimed self-incrimination protection because his testimony could be used to prosecute him in other countries, including Lithuania or Germany. The Supreme Court held that the self-incrimination clause refers to American procedures, as do the other clauses of the Fifth Amendment (grand jury, double jeopardy, due process, and just compensation) (*United States v. Balsys,* 1998).

THE ACT OF PRODUCING EVIDENCE   Several federal appellate courts have held that although "the *contents* of voluntarily prepared papers are not protected by the Fifth Amendment, the *act of producing* such documents is protected . . . if the act itself is both testimonial and incriminating."[15] Production of subpoenaed evidence exposes the producer to four potentially incriminating facts in regard to the evidence: (1) its existence, (2) its authenticity, (3) possession, and (4) the belief that the documents match the terms of a subpoena (*Fisher v. United States,* 1976). The Supreme Court has not established a **bright-line rule** that immunizes compelled production of records from prosecution. Each case must be resolved on its own facts. Where a court determines that production itself is incriminating, the individual may still have to produce the records but may be granted immunity, although this is not automatic (*United States v. Doe,* 1984).

Certainly the oddest and most dramatic act-of-production case is **Baltimore Department of Social Services v. Bouknight** (1990). The Baltimore City Department of Social Services (BCDSS), fearing child abuse, removed an infant, Maurice, from his mother, Jacqueline Bouknight. He was returned to her a few months later, under various conditions. Eight months later, fearing for Maurice's safety, the juvenile court ordered his return to BCDSS custody. Jacqueline Bouknight refused to turn over the boy. A diligent search by police and relatives failed to produce him. Bouknight was held in contempt of court for failing to produce Maurice and was jailed. She challenged this in the United States Supreme Court on the ground that the compelled production of Maurice might tend to incriminate her.

The Supreme Court held that Bouknight had no Fifth Amendment claim because Maurice's physical condition was not testimonial evidence. She argued that "her implicit communication of control over Maurice at the moment of production might aid the State in prosecuting Bouknight." The Court ruled that even if the boy's production were testimonial, it still did not give her the right to refuse the order, "because she has assumed *custodial duties* related to production [of Maurice] and production is required as a part of a *noncriminal regulatory scheme*" (emphasis added). The Court did not answer the question whether the Fifth Amendment would protect Bouknight against prosecution if she complied with the order, produced Maurice, and was prosecuted for child abuse because of evidence obtained from her act of production.

Having lost her case, Jacqueline Bouknight remained in jail for contempt of court for seven and a half years, one of the longest terms for contempt in United States history. She was released in October 1995. The judge who ordered the release said that continued imprisonment was no longer an effective tool to force the information from her. Her lawyers called Bouknight a hero of civil disobedience, but the judge who had held her in contempt expressed fears that the child might be dead.[16]

Confessions Law before *Miranda*

English and American courts developed a common law "rule of evidence which precludes the use at trial of involuntary statements," from the mid–eighteenth to the mid–nineteenth centuries. Police could question suspects, and incriminating statements could be used in evidence against them as long as the statements were not "induced by force, threat of force, or promise of leniency from a person in authority, for if it has been so obtained, it is considered 'involuntary' and excluded."[17] In 1912 the English Courts advanced the protection offered to a suspect from coercive interrogation by establishing the so-called *Judges' Rules* for the guidance of police officers. The *Judges' Rules* stated that before asking a person about to be charged with a crime if he or she wished to say anything in answer to the charges, that person should be told "You are not obliged to say anything unless you wish to do so, but whatever you say will be taken down in writing and may be given in evidence."[18] A failure to give the warning would render a statement improper and it could be excluded from consideration at trial. While the *Judges' Rules*, of course, had no legal effect in American states, they were well-known to American jurists and established the idea that it is proper to inform a suspect of his basic right against self-incrimination.

The **voluntariness test** was established in each American state by the late nineteenth century. The Supreme Court, in **Bram v. United States** (1897), held that coerced confessions in *federal* cases were guided by the Fifth Amendment right against self-incrimination. The test of admissibility under *Bram,* however, was essentially the voluntariness test. In both state and federal law, therefore, coerced or involuntary confessions were excluded from evidence, although no warning requirement was yet established. In this era, the criminal justice amendments of the Bill of Rights had not yet been incorporated, and so, the self-incrimination rule of *Bram* did not apply to the states.

In practice, state courts were often reluctant to exclude confessions even when there was compelling evidence of coercion. As a result, defendants whose confessions were the product of coercion turned to the federal courts, claiming that coerced confessions violated the Fourteenth Amendment Due Process Clause. From 1936 until 1966, the Supreme Court decided more than thirty confessions cases from the states under the Due Process Clause. In 1964 the Fifth Amendment self-incrimination rule was incorporated, paving the way to *Miranda v. Arizona* (1966). A brief review of the due process voluntariness test helps us appreciate the significance of the "*Miranda* revolution."

In **Brown v. Mississippi** (1936), the first Supreme Court case to review a confession obtained by state or local officers, three African American men confessed to committing a murder after being subjected to torture during their interrogation by the local sheriff and others. Their treatment included being hung by a rope to a tree, being let down, and being hung again, and whipping "with a leather strap with buckles on it" that cut their backs to pieces. After resisting these tortures over three days, they were told that it would continue until they signed a confession dictated by a deputy. The Supreme Court held that confessions obtained by such physical torture was "not consistent" with Fourteenth Amendment due process of law, rendering the trial and conviction void because it "is a mere pretense where the state authorities have contrived a conviction resting solely upon confessions obtained by violence" (*Brown v. Mississippi*, 1936). The legal foundation of *Brown* was not a specific Bill of Rights provision but the "fair trial" idea of the Fourteenth Amendment Due Process Clause, first adopted by the Court in *Moore v. Dempsey* (1923) (see Chapter 1).

The due process approach toward involuntary confessions initiated by *Brown* was not limited to physical torture. The Court soon applied the voluntariness test to lesser forms of coercion. The basic question was whether, under the facts and circumstances of the case, a particular confession was *voluntary*. Was it made of the defendant's *free will*? Was it obtained by police interrogation tactics that *overcame the defendant's will*? In case after case, the Supreme Court moved inexorably toward *more refined* standards. In **Ashcraft v. Tennessee** (1944), for example, the police did not beat the defendant but questioned him "in relays" for *thirty-six hours* with no interruption until he confessed to murdering his wife. The Supreme Court held that the long period of straight questioning was itself sufficient coercion so that his statements were not voluntary but compelled. Justice Black cited the Wickersham Commission's report of 1930 that condemned this kind of police behavior, known as the **third degree**, "as a secret and illegal practice."[19] The "third degree," common in that era, ranged from severe questioning to police beatings of suspects to force confessions out of them. The Court, by deciding a stream of state confessions cases, was enforcing the

involuntary confession rule in order to cause police departments to adopt more civilized methods of investigation. "An opinion in a coerced confessions case, *Chambers v. Florida* (1940), clearly acknowledged that the federal government had a duty to guarantee fair trials in state as well as federal courts."[20]

Other practices held to undermine the defendant's will and induce involuntary confessions in violation of the Fourteenth Amendment included:

- Defendant moved to secret places so that family, lawyers, or friends could not contact him (*Chambers v. Florida,* 1940; *Ward v. Texas,* 1942).
- Defendant kept naked for several hours (*Malinski v. New York*, 1945).
- Defendant told by a state-employed psychiatrist that the doctor was there to help him and would provide medical assistance, thus gaining the defendant's confidence and incriminating information (*Leyra v. Denno*, 1954).
- Suspect, a young African American, told that he would be handed over to a lynch mob (*Payne v. Arkansas*, 1958).
- Defendant, in his cell, told by a police officer (a childhood friend of the defendant) over a period of time, that the officer would lose his job if he did not get a statement (*Spano v. New York*, 1959).
- Vigorous interrogation of a mentally defective or insane suspect (*Blackburn v. Alabama*, 1960; *Culombe v. Connecticut*, 1961).
- Using "truth serum" (*Townsend v. Sain*, 1963).
- Defendant told that her children's welfare assistance would be cut off and her children taken from her if she failed to cooperate with the police (*Lynumn v. Illinois*, 1963).

The justices were clearly appalled by these excessive and coercive methods. As a court of law, the Supreme Court could not directly require police to follow more civilized procedures. Through its due process jurisdiction, however, the Court could indirectly affect police practices by reversing convictions where police went too far. By progressively refining the standard of what constituted an involuntary confession, the Court sent signals to the police community to eliminate coercive methods of interrogation. The positive aspect of using due process as a vehicle to upgrade police interrogation was that it combined the community's "highest values with operating realities, to fashion a rule." The negative aspect was that it approached the problem of police coercion piecemeal.

PROBLEMS WITH THE VOLUNTARINESS RULE The due process approach injected a level of *subjectivity* into the law that was unsatisfactory to many in the legal community because it produced no clear guidance for lower courts and for police. Its piecemeal due process approach gave the police a list of examples of what to avoid but no clear-cut or bright-line rule stating how constitutional interrogation should be conducted. This growing dissatisfaction was a reason for the Court adopting a set of seemingly clear, rule-like guidelines in *Miranda*. Professor Richard Cortner commented:

> Adhering to the fair trial approach to the Due Process Clause, the Court followed a meandering and ofttimes puzzling course in state criminal cases during the 1950s. . . . [T]he Court's performance under the Due Process Clause was such as to involve it in unpredictable intrusions into the state criminal process on the basis of standards nowhere satisfactorily articulated—with the result that serious federal-state strains developed.[21]

This totality of the circumstances approach to coerced confessions made it seem that the Court was engaging in *ad hoc*, case-by-case decision making rather than following a firm constitutional policy.

Another problem was that in different cases the Court suggested different constitutional reasons for the due process voluntariness test: "(1) ensuring that convictions are based on *reliable evidence;* (2) *deterring improper police conduct;* or (3) assuring that a defendant's confession is the product of his *free and rational choice.*"[22] The Court shuttled between these rationales, leaving lawyers and trial judges in confusion. In early cases like *Brown* and *Ashcraft* all three elements coincided: excessive police conduct overpowered the suspect's will and raised real doubts about the accuracy of the confession. In some later cases, the Court seemed to focus primarily on the *reliability* or accuracy of confessions. *Lyons v. Oklahoma* (1944) ruled that a confession would be admissible if the state "employed a fair standard in adjudicating common law in voluntariness claims" as long as it appeared that the confession was *true*, a rationale that would have narrowed the scope of the voluntariness rule. But in other cases, the Court set aside convictions even where the confession's truthfulness was substantially corroborated, because the police misconduct was too great (*Watts v. Indiana*, 1949). A police misconduct rationale would broaden the Court's control over police behavior. Indeed, without signaling a clear intention to do so, the Court in the 1950s seemed to be shifting toward a *police conduct* test, concerned less with the accuracy of the confession or its actual voluntariness, and more with controlling egregious police conduct. In *Rogers v. Richmond* (1961), for example, the Court struck down a seemingly accurate and voluntary confession because the police tricked the suspect into thinking they were going to arrest his ailing wife for questioning. The Court did not, in fact, use the *Rogers* case as a vehicle to sharply limit police interrogation practices. It thus produced inconsistent results because it emphasized different purposes in different cases. The lack of clarity of the rules and the underlying purposes of its due process cases led the Court to search for bright-line confessions rules to give police firmer guidance.

THE FEDERAL "TIME TEST"   One attempt to create a bright-line exclusionary rule was established only for federal officers in *McNabb v. United States* (1943) and applied later in *Mallory v. United States* (1957). The rule excluded confessions if an arrested suspect was not brought before a magistrate without "unnecessary delay," as required by the Federal Rules of Criminal Procedure. *McNabb* stated that a goal of this rule was to lessen the opportunity for police coercion and the "third degree." This rationale was repeated in *Mallory*, which also said that an important function of the judge at the initial appearance was to inform a suspect of his or her rights.

The dangers inherent in the police holding suspects in custody without bringing them to a judge were highlighted shortly before *Miranda* in **Davis v. North Carolina** (1966). Elmer Davis, Jr., an African American with low mental functioning who had escaped from a prison camp, was held as a suspect in a rape-murder for *sixteen days* in a police lockup cell measuring six by ten feet and questioned every day in order to obtain a confession. A written stationhouse order instructed police not to allow anyone to have contact with Davis. Only after confessing was he taken before a magistrate, despite the state rule requiring that an arrested person be brought before a magistrate within a reasonable period of time. The Supreme Court ruled his confession to be involuntary.

The *McNabb-Mallory* rule only applied to *federal* law enforcement officers and agencies because it was not based on the Fourteenth Amendment due process doctrine of "fundamental fairness." It was instead based on the Supreme Court's inherent **supervisory authority** over lower *federal* courts and *federal* law enforcement. The "time test," although not applicable to the states, showed that the justices were displeased by heavy-handed police actions in obtaining confessions, a concern that would animate the *Miranda* decision.

RIGHT TO COUNSEL   The *secrecy* of police interrogation was a major concern. Without representation by counsel, the defendant is alone and vulnerable to improper police tactics. In two late 1950s cases, *Crooker v. California* (1958) and *Cicenia v. LaGay* (1958), dissenting justices argued that *voluntary* confessions should be excluded on the grounds that defendants' requests for attorneys were denied. The majority, however, held that a mere denial to see one's attorney was not in itself a due process violation. This position began to erode in *Spano v. New York* (1959), which held that overbearing police tactics led to an involuntary confession. Four concurring justices in *Spano* argued that the defendant had a right of access to counsel and noted that he had been formally charged by indictment before confessing. *Gideon v. Wainwright* (1963), decided four years later, incorporated the right to counsel at trial, and increased the pressure to view police interrogation as a *critical stage* in the prosecution. Furthermore, in 1964 the Court in *Massiah v. United States* (this chapter) held that *indicted* defendants who had already obtained counsel could not be secretly taped or questioned by the police without the consent of the defendant's lawyer.

The turning point in the move to replace the voluntariness test with a clearer rule came in **Escobedo v. Illinois** (1964), which held that a preindictment suspect had a Sixth Amendment right to counsel during police interrogation, but only if the lawyer had been hired before the interrogation began. The *Escobedo* case was, according to Fred Graham, "enigmatic" because its holding was based on a complicated set of facts, and it was not clear which of these facts would be crucial in extending the right to counsel during interrogation in later cases.[23] For example, in *Escobedo* a lawyer was hired by the family of a murder suspect; he made repeated attempts over a period of three or four hours to see his client at the police station; at one point, Escobedo and his lawyer made eye contact; the police refused to allow them to meet. The Court held that although his confession was made voluntarily, it was deemed unconstitutional because his Sixth Amendment right to counsel was violated. Was *Escobedo* another "special circumstances" case (like *Powell v. Alabama* and *Betts v. Brady* regarding the right to counsel), or was it a first step toward requiring attorneys during every police interrogation?

The Court's opinion muddied the Sixth Amendment basis for its holding by injecting Fifth Amendment concerns: "Without informing him of his *absolute right to remain silent* in the face of this accusation, the police urged him to make a statement." *Escobedo* was an important case, but it was clearly not the final word or a firm rule for the guidance of police interrogation. In addition to the fact-specific nature of the holding, basing a right to counsel at police interrogation on the Sixth Amendment was problematic because the Sixth Amendment applies to the "criminal prosecution," which does not commence until *formal charges* have been issued against a defendant. *Escobedo* left many questions unanswered, and the Supreme Court expected it would receive appeals, over a period of years, designed to clarify the ambiguities of the case. Instead of a trickle, it received a flood of cases, and within two years startled the legal community with its monumental *Miranda* decision. *Miranda* took a new turn and, "decid[ing] to answer all of the questions at once," placed state confessions law firmly on a Fifth Amendment foundation.[24]

THE *MIRANDA* DECISION

Miranda was not an "incorporation case," although the recently incorporated rights to counsel and against self-incrimination gave the Supreme Court the impetus to forge a new approach, to establish a definitive confessions rule in an area of law that had bedeviled it for three decades. As it turned out, the Fifth Amendment, not the Sixth Amendment, provided the constitutional foundation for the *Miranda* rule. *Miranda* was, for a time, one of the most severely criticized cases in the Court's history, referred to by some as a "self-inflicted wound." Many in the legal community were offended by the unprecedented and legislative-like style of the ruling, while police officials and conservative politicians denounced the Court for its pro-defendant ruling.[25]

Ernesto Miranda was retried for rape and convicted in 1967 on the testimony of his common law wife. He was later paroled but continued to get into trouble. Miranda was stabbed to death on January 31, 1976, in the restroom of a cheap bar in Phoenix, Arizona, after a fistfight. Police caught the man who had assailed Ernesto and read him his *Miranda* warnings.[26]

—*Miranda v. Arizona* Case & Comments—

• CASE & COMMENTS •

Miranda v. Arizona
384 U.S. 436, 86 S.Ct. 1602, 16 L.Ed.2d 694 (1966)

[In four consolidated cases none of the defendants were fully informed of their constitutional rights, although some were informed of their right to remain silent. **[a]** In *Miranda v. Arizona* Miranda confessed to a rape after being interrogated for only two hours at a police station. In *Vignera v. New York* a robbery suspect questioned by police made an oral admission in the afternoon and a written confession to a prosecutor that evening. In *Westover v. United States* local police arrested a defendant for a robbery and interrogated him that evening. The next day FBI agents began to interrogate Westover at 9 A.M. At noon he was read warnings and he confessed at 2:00 P.M. In *Stewart v. California* the defendant was interrogated nine times over five days by the police, and was held incommunicado until he confessed. He was then taken before an examining magistrate. There was no evidence of threats or violence in any of these cases. The majority opinion discussed the facts of the cases after fifty pages of constitutional analysis.]

MR. CHIEF JUSTICE WARREN delivered the opinion of the Court.

The cases before us raise questions which go to the roots of our concepts of American criminal jurisprudence: the restraints society must observe consistent with the Federal Constitution in prosecuting individuals for crime. More specifically, we deal with the admissibility of statements obtained from an individual who is subjected to custodial police interrogation and the necessity for procedures which assure that the individual is accorded his privilege under the Fifth Amendment to the Constitution not to be compelled to incriminate himself. **[b]**

* * *

We start here, as we did in *Escobedo,* with the premise that our holding is not an innovation in our jurisprudence, but is an application of principles long recognized and applied in other settings. **[c]** * * *

[a] The Supreme Court stated that these facts did not make the confessions unconstitutional under the due process voluntariness test. In Part V of the majority opinion, it applied the general rules of the decision and found that in each case the self-incrimination rights of the defendants were violated.

[b] The Court clearly specifies the factual predicate of these cases: *custodial police interrogation*; and the decision's constitutional basis: the *privilege against self-incrimination*.

[c] This is disingenuous. As the dissents state, this case was clearly a constitutional innovation.

• CASE & COMMENTS •

* * *

Our holding * * * briefly stated is this: the prosecution may not use statements, whether **exculpatory** or **inculpatory,** stemming from custodial interrogation of the defendant unless it demonstrates the use of procedural safeguards effective to secure the privilege against self-incrimination. By custodial interrogation, we mean questioning initiated by law enforcement officers after a person has been taken into custody or otherwise deprived of his freedom of action in any significant way.

I

* * * [All the cases here] share salient features—incommunicado interrogation of individuals in a police-dominated atmosphere, resulting in self-incriminating statements without full warning of constitutional rights. **[d]**

An understanding of the nature and setting of this in-custody interrogation is essential to our decisions today. The difficulty in depicting what transpires at such interrogations stems from the fact that in this country they have largely taken place incommunicado. From extensive factual studies undertaken in the early 1930s, including the famous Wickersham Report to Congress by a Presidential Commission, it is clear that police violence and the "third degree" flourished at that time. In a series of cases decided by this Court long after these studies, the police resorted to physical brutality—beatings, hanging, whipping— and to sustained and protracted questioning incommunicado in order to extort confessions. * * *

* * *

Again we stress that the modern practice of in-custody interrogation is psychologically rather than physically oriented. * * * ["T]his Court has recognized that coercion can be mental as well as physical, and that the blood of the accused is not the only hallmark of an unconstitutional inquisition." * * * **[e]** Interrogation still takes place in privacy. Privacy results in secrecy and this in turn results in a gap in our knowledge as to what in fact goes on in the interrogation rooms. A valuable source of information about present police practices, however, may be found in various police manuals and texts which document procedures employed with success in the past, and which recommend various other effective tactics. * * *

The officers are told by the manuals that the "principal psychological factor contributing to a successful interrogation is privacy—being alone with the person under interrogation." * * *

To highlight the isolation and unfamiliar surroundings, the manuals instruct the police to display an air of confidence in the suspect's guilt and from outward appearance to maintain only an interest in confirming certain details. **[f]** The guilt of the subject is to be posited as a fact. The interrogator should direct his comments toward the reasons why the subject committed the act, rather than court failure by asking the subject whether he did it. Like other men, perhaps the subject has had a bad family life, had an unhappy childhood, had too much to drink, had an unrequited desire for women. The officers are instructed to minimize the moral seriousness of the offense, to cast blame on the victim or on society. These tactics are designed to put the subject in a psychological state where his story is but an elaboration of what the police purport to know already—that he is guilty. Explanations to the contrary are dismissed and discouraged. * * *

* * *

When the techniques described above prove unavailing, the texts recommend they be alternated with a show of some hostility. One ploy often used has been termed the "friendly-unfriendly" or the "Mutt and Jeff" act. * * *

The interrogators sometimes are instructed to induce a confession out of trickery. **[g]** The technique here is quite effective in crimes which require identification or which run in series. In the identification situation, the interrogator may take a break in his questioning to place the subject among a group of men in a line-up [and to coach a witness to identify the suspect]. * * * A variation on this technique is called the "reverse line-up":

> "The accused is placed in a line-up, but this time he is identified by several fictitious witnesses or victims who associated him with different offenses. It is expected that the subject will become desperate and confess to the offense under investigation in order to escape from the false accusations."

* * *

From these representative samples of interrogation techniques, the setting prescribed by the manuals and observed in practice becomes clear. **[h]** In essence, it is this: To be alone with the subject is essential to

[d] The case is decided not on the specific facts in each of the four consolidated cases, but merely on the fact that in each there was police custodial interrogation and the defendant's rights were not explained to him. There was no distinct physical or psychological coercion in these cases. The review of interrogation techniques found in police manuals substitutes for a finding of specific case facts.

[e] Notice the negative attitude toward interrogation. Early findings of brutality or extreme psychological pressure are taken to be a risk in any police interrogation. Thus, every custodial interrogation, conducted in secrecy, establishes compulsion under the privilege against self-incrimination.

[f] Are these practices outrageous? Or simply like "high-pressure sales tactics" used to get the suspect to admit to the crime?

[g] Are tricks and lies ethical if it is the only way to get a "guilty" person to confess? What if the suspect is in fact not guilty? Should there be a limit to trickery?

[h] These examples from police manuals are not scientifically drawn random samples of police activity; nevertheless, there is no reason to believe that they are uncommon. In your opinion, are they *inherently* coercive?

prevent distraction and to deprive him of any outside support. The aura of confidence in his guilt undermines his will to resist. He merely confirms the preconceived story the police seek to have him describe. Patience and persistence, at times relentless questioning, are employed. To obtain a confession, the interrogator must "patiently maneuver himself or his quarry into a position from which the desired objective may be attained." When normal procedures fail to produce the needed result, the police may resort to deceptive stratagems such as giving false legal advice. It is important to keep the subject off balance, for example, by trading on his insecurity about himself or his surroundings. The police then persuade, trick, or cajole him out of exercising his constitutional rights.

* * *

In the cases before us today, given this background, we concern ourselves primarily with this interrogation atmosphere and the evils it can bring. * * *

In these cases, we might not find the defendants' statements to have been involuntary in traditional terms. **[i]** Our concern for adequate safeguards to protect precious Fifth Amendment rights is, of course, not lessened in the slightest. * * * The fact remains that in none of these cases did the officers undertake to afford appropriate safeguards at the outset of the interrogation to insure that the statements were truly the product of free choice.

It is obvious that such an interrogation environment is created for no purpose other than to subjugate the individual to the will of his examiner. This atmosphere carries its own badge of intimidation. To be sure, this is not physical intimidation, but it is equally destructive of human dignity. * * * Unless adequate protective devices are employed to dispel the compulsion inherent in custodial surroundings, no statement obtained from the defendant can truly be the product of his free choice.

* * *

[Part II of the opinion reviewed the history of the right against self-incrimination in English and American law, and its incorporation into the Fourteenth Amendment in *Malloy v. Hogan* (1964), which established the constitutional jurisdiction for the Court to apply the Fifth Amendment's privilege against self-incrimination to the states.]

III

Today, then, there can be no doubt that the Fifth Amendment privilege is available outside of criminal court proceedings and serves to protect persons in all settings in which their freedom of action is curtailed in any significant way from being compelled to incriminate themselves. We have concluded that without proper safeguards the process of in-custody interrogation of persons suspected or accused of crime contains inherently compelling pressures which work to undermine the individual's will to resist and to compel him to speak where he would not otherwise do so freely. In order to combat these pressures and to permit a full opportunity to exercise the privilege against self-incrimination, the accused must be adequately and effectively apprised of his rights and the exercise of those rights must be fully honored.

It is impossible for us to foresee the potential alternatives for protecting the privilege which might be devised by Congress or the States in the exercise of their creative rule-making capacities. **[j]** Therefore we cannot say that the Constitution necessarily requires adherence to any particular solution for the inherent compulsions of the interrogation process as it is presently conducted. Our decision in no way creates a constitutional straitjacket which will handicap sound efforts at reform, nor is it intended to have this effect. We encourage Congress and the States to continue their laudable search for increasingly effective ways of protecting the rights of the individual while promoting efficient enforcement of our criminal laws. However, unless we are shown other procedures which are at least as effective in apprising accused persons of their right of silence and in assuring a continuous opportunity to exercise it, the following safeguards must be observed.

At the outset, if a person in custody is to be subjected to interrogation, he must first be informed in clear and unequivocal terms that he has the right to remain silent. **[k]** For those unaware of the privilege, the warning is needed simply to make them aware of it—the threshold requirement for an intelligent decision as to its exercise. More important, such a warning is an absolute prerequisite in overcoming the inherent pressures of the interrogation atmosphere. * * *

The Fifth Amendment privilege is so fundamental to our system of constitutional rule and the expedient of giving an adequate warning as to the availability of the privilege so simple, we will not pause to inquire in individual cases whether the defendant was aware of his rights without a warning being given. * * *

[i] The Court puts the finishing touch on its argument: (1) the Self-Incrimination Clause forbids compelled testimony; (2) secret police interrogation is inherently compelling; therefore (3) safeguards are required in order to "dispel" compulsion.

[j] The suggestion that other protective techniques could replace the warnings became an extremely controversial point. A more conservative Court used this statement to argue that *Miranda* warnings are not rules required by the Constitution.

[k] The first warning. Are the reasons for it convincing?

• CASE & COMMENTS •

The warning of the right to remain silent must be accompanied by the explanation that anything said can and will be used against the individual in court. **[l]** This warning is needed in order to make him aware not only of the privilege, but also of the consequences of foregoing it. It is only through an awareness of these consequences that there can be any assurance of real understanding and intelligent exercise of the privilege. Moreover, this warning may serve to make the individual more acutely aware that he is faced with a phase of the adversary system—that he is not in the presence of persons acting solely in his interest.

[l] The second warning.

The circumstances surrounding in-custody interrogation can operate very quickly to overbear the will of one merely made aware of his privilege by his interrogators. Therefore, the right to have counsel present at the interrogation is indispensable to the protection of the Fifth Amendment privilege. **[m]** * * *

[m] The third warning. It is *not* based on the Sixth Amendment; it is required to protect Fifth Amendment rights.

* * *

In order fully to apprise a person interrogated of the extent of his rights under this system then, it is necessary to warn him not only that he has the right to consult with an attorney, but also that if he is indigent a lawyer will be appointed to represent him. **[n]** Without this additional warning, the admonition of the right to consult with counsel would often be understood as meaning only that he can consult with a lawyer if he has one or has the funds to obtain one. * * *

[n] The fourth warning.

Once warnings have been given, the subsequent procedure is clear. If the individual indicates in any manner, at any time prior to or during questioning, that he wishes to remain silent, the interrogation must cease. **[o]** At this point he has shown that he intends to exercise his Fifth Amendment privilege; any statement taken after the person invokes his privilege cannot be other than the product of compulsion, subtle or otherwise. Without the right to cut off questioning, the setting of in-custody interrogation operates on the individual to overcome free choice in producing a statement after the privilege has been once invoked. If the individual states that he wants an attorney, the interrogation must cease until an attorney is present. At that time, the individual must have an opportunity to confer with the attorney and to have him present during any subsequent questioning. If the individual cannot obtain an attorney and he indicates that he wants one before speaking to police, they must respect his decision to remain silent.

[o] Consequences of the warnings. A suspect can "just say no" when asked to talk by the police, even after answering some questions.

This does not mean, as some have suggested, that each police station must have a "station house lawyer" present at all times to advise prisoners. * * *

If the interrogation continues without the presence of an attorney and a statement is taken, a heavy burden rests on the government to demonstrate that the defendant knowingly and intelligently waived his privilege against self-incrimination and his right to retained or appointed counsel. **[p]** * * * Since the State is responsible for establishing the isolated circumstances under which the interrogation takes place and has the only means of making available corroborated evidence of warnings given during incommunicado interrogation, the burden is rightly on its shoulders.

[p] The burden of proof of a voluntary waiver is on the State; the State must produce some proof of a waiver.

An express statement that the individual is willing to make a statement and does not want an attorney followed closely by a statement could constitute a waiver. But a valid waiver will not be presumed simply from the silence of the accused after warnings are given or simply from the fact that a confession was in fact eventually obtained. * * *

* * *

The warnings required and the waiver necessary in accordance with our opinion today are, in the absence of a fully effective equivalent, prerequisites to the admissibility of any statement made by a defendant. **[q]** No distinction can be drawn between statements which are direct confessions and statements which amount to "admissions" of part or all of an offense. The privilege against self-incrimination protects the individual from being compelled to incriminate himself in any manner; it does not distinguish degrees of incrimination. Similarly, for precisely the same reason, no distinction may be drawn between inculpatory statements and statements alleged to be merely "exculpatory." If a statement made were in fact truly exculpatory it would, of course, never be used by the prosecution. In fact, statements merely intended to be exculpatory by the defendant are often used to impeach his testimony at trial or to demonstrate untruths in the statement given under interrogation and thus to prove guilt by implication. These statements are incriminating in any meaningful sense of the word and may not be used without the full warnings and effective waiver required for any other statement. In *Escobedo* itself, the defendant fully intended his accusation of another as the slayer to be exculpatory as to himself.

[q] This paragraph closes potential *Miranda* rules loopholes. A suspect might be led to say things he *thinks* will clear him (*exculpatory* statements) but which instead lead to independent evidence of guilt. These too are covered by the *Miranda* warnings.

The principles announced today deal with the protection which must be given to the privilege against self-incrimination when the individual is first subjected to police interrogation while in custody at the station or otherwise deprived of his freedom of action in any significant way. **[r]** It is at this point that our adversary system of criminal proceedings commences, distinguishing itself at the outset from the inquisitorial system recognized in some countries. * * *

Our decision is not intended to hamper the traditional function of police officers in investigating crime. * * *

* * *

In dealing with statements obtained through interrogation, we do not purport to find all confessions inadmissible. Confessions remain a proper element in law enforcement. Any statement given freely and voluntarily without any compelling influences is, of course, admissible in evidence. * * * There is no requirement that police stop a person who enters a police station and states that he wishes to confess to a crime, or a person who calls the police to offer a confession or any other statement he desires to make. **[s]** Volunteered statements of any kind are not barred by the Fifth Amendment and their admissibility is not affected by our holding today.

* * *

[Part IV presented policy arguments in favor of the warnings requirement, noting that warnings were required in England and many Commonwealth nations, and were routinely given by FBI agents and military police without any loss of effective law enforcement.]

[Justices Clark (concurring in *Stewart v. California*), Harlan, and White each wrote dissenting opinions.]

MR. JUSTICE WHITE, with whom MR. JUSTICE HARLAN and MR. JUSTICE STEWART join, dissenting. * * *

I

The proposition that the privilege against self-incrimination forbids in-custody interrogation without the warnings specified in the majority opinion * * * has no significant support in the history of the privilege or in the language of the Fifth Amendment. * * * The rule excluding coerced confessions matured about 100 years [after the privilege against self-incrimination did,] "but there is nothing in the reports to suggest that the theory has its roots in the privilege against self-incrimination. . . ." * * * **[t]**

* * *

* * * [T]he Fifth Amendment privilege was . . . extended to encompass the then well-established rule against coerced confessions * * * [in] *Bram v. United States*. * * *

* * *

Bram, however, itself rejected the proposition which the Court now espouses. The question in *Bram* was whether a confession, obtained during custodial interrogation, had been compelled. * * * [T]he Court declared that:

> "* * * the mere fact that the confession is made to a police officer, while the accused was under arrest in or out of prison, or was drawn out by his questions, does not necessarily render the confession involuntary; but, as one of the circumstances, such imprisonment or interrogation may be taken into account in determining whether or not the statements of the prisoner were voluntary" * * *

* * *

III

* * * Rather than asserting new knowledge, the Court concedes that it cannot truly know what occurs during custodial questioning, because of the innate secrecy of such proceedings. **[u]** It extrapolates a picture of what it conceives to be the norm from police investigatorial manuals, published in 1959 and 1962 or earlier, without any attempt to allow for adjustments in police practices that may have occurred in the wake of more recent decisions of state appellate tribunals or this Court. But even if the relentless application of the described procedures could lead to involuntary confessions, it most assuredly does not follow that each and every case will disclose this kind of interrogation or this kind of consequence. Insofar as appears from the Court's opinion, it has not examined a single transcript of any police interrogation, let alone the interrogation that took place in any one of these cases which it decides today. * * * [T]he factual basis for the Court's premise is patently inadequate.

[r] This makes a critical point. The Fifth Amendment privilege applies prior to formal charges during custodial police interrogation, and not only at judicial-like hearings as the dissenters argued.

[s] Some critics feared that the Supreme Court would make all extrajudicial confessions illegal. The Court tries to allay these fears.

[t] Recent scholarship casts some doubt on Justice White's historical argument.[27]

[u] Justice White accuses the majority of fabricating the constitutional element of coercion by assuming that the police manuals describe the reality of every interrogation, without proof of coercion in each specific case.

• CASE & COMMENTS •

* * *

* * * [E]ven if one assumed that there was an adequate factual basis for the conclusion that all confessions obtained during in-custody interrogation are the product of compulsion, the rule propounded by the Court would still be irrational, for, apparently, it is only if the accused is also warned of his right to counsel and waives both that right and the right against self-incrimination that the inherent compulsiveness of interrogation disappears. **[v]** But if the defendant may not answer without a warning a question such as "Where were you last night?" without having his answer be a compelled one, how can the Court ever accept his negative answer to the question of whether he wants to consult his retained counsel or counsel whom the court will appoint? * * * The Court apparently realizes its dilemma of foreclosing questioning without the necessary warnings but at the same time permitting the accused, sitting in the same chair in front of the same policemen, to waive his right to consult an attorney. * * *

* * * By considering any answers to any interrogation to be compelled regardless of the content and course of examination and by escalating the requirements to prove waiver, the Court not only prevents the use of compelled confessions but for all practical purposes forbids interrogation except in the presence of counsel. That is, instead of confining itself to protection of the right against compelled self-incrimination the Court has created a limited Fifth Amendment right to counsel—or, as the Court expresses it, a "need for counsel to protect the Fifth Amendment privilege." * * * The focus then is not on the will of the accused but on the will of counsel and how much influence he can have on the accused. Obviously there is no warrant in the Fifth Amendment for thus installing counsel as the arbiter of the privilege.

In sum, for all the Court's expounding on the menacing atmosphere of police interrogation procedures, it has failed to supply any foundation for the conclusions it draws or the measures it adopts.

IV

* * *

In some unknown number of cases the Court's rule will return a killer, a rapist or other criminal to the streets and to the environment which produced him, to repeat his crime whenever it pleases him. **[w]** As a consequence, there will not be a gain, but a loss, in human dignity. The real concern is not the unfortunate consequences of this new decision on the criminal law as an abstract, disembodied series of authoritative proscriptions, but the impact on those who rely on the public authority for protection and who without it can only engage in violent self-help with guns, knives and the help of their neighbors similarly inclined. * * *

Nor can this decision do other than have a corrosive effect on the criminal law as an effective device to prevent crime. A major component in its effectiveness in this regard is its swift and sure enforcement. The easier it is to get away with rape and murder, the less the deterrent effect on those who are inclined to attempt it. This is still good common sense. * * *

* * *

[v] Justice White sees a logical flaw in the opinion. If the stationhouse atmosphere is inherently coercive, is it logically impossible for suspects to voluntarily waive their rights in that atmosphere, after being informed of their rights? He assumes that in the future all interrogation will occur with defense counsel present. This has not been the case.

[w] There is always a trade-off between security and liberty in criminal procedure; Justice White sees little gain in civil liberties by limiting the power of the police in this area.

AN INTERPRETATION OF *MIRANDA* Although critics saw *Miranda* as a revolutionary break with the older due process voluntariness rule, it could be seen as an extension of that test for the constitutionality of confessions. The underlying rationale of the self-incrimination and due process clauses is the same: forbidding compelled testimony. The voluntariness test had itself evolved over time from outlawing torture to finding that certain psychological pressure tactics were unconstitutional. In this light, *Miranda* has continued the progressive civilizing approach of the confessions exclusionary rule, by attacking the source of undue compulsion.

If the Court, therefore, correctly assessed modern police interrogation as so highly manipulative as to amount to compulsion, *Miranda* can be seen as a conservative ruling in that it *preserved* police interrogation. A logical extension of the voluntariness test could have led the Court to rule that all secret interrogation is unconstitutional. The effect of such a rule would have been like the *Massiah* rule (discussed at the end of this chapter), forbidding all questioning of a suspect without a lawyer being present.

There is an irony about *Miranda*. The Court's desire—to replace numerous case-specific decisions under the "facts and circumstances" approach of the voluntariness test with one bright-line rule for determining the constitutionality of confessions—was not to be. After *Miranda*, the Court had to deal with a cascade of cases litigating its meaning. These cases are reviewed in subsequent sections.

Voluntariness after *Miranda*

Miranda v. Arizona did not eliminate the due process voluntariness test. Even if *Miranda* warnings are read to a suspect, police interrogation may still be coercive and overbear the suspect's will. In such a case, a confession is inadmissible under the Fifth or Fourteenth Amendment Due Process Clause because it is coerced. Additionally, a coerced confession cannot be used to impeach the defendant should he choose to testify at trial.

Mincey v. Arizona (1978) provides a blatant example of involuntariness. Rufus Mincey, shot and left semiconscious after a shoot-out with a police officer, was brought to a hospital intensive care unit in critical condition and was treated. That evening Detective Hust went to the intensive care unit, told Mincey he was under arrest for the murder of a police officer, gave him *Miranda* warnings, and proceeded to ask questions about the shoot-out. Mincey asked repeatedly that the interrogation stop until he could get a lawyer, but Hust continued to question him until almost midnight. Throughout, Mincey was heavily medicated by an intravenous device; tubes were inserted into his throat, to help him breathe, and through his nose into his stomach, to keep him from vomiting; and a catheter was inserted into his bladder. Mincey could not talk, so answers were written on pieces of paper.

When asked by Detective Hust, "Did you shoot anyone?" it seemed clear to the Court that Mincey's reply, "I can't say, I have to see a lawyer," was evidence of a clear desire not to speak. Yet he was pressed by the detective and made an incriminating statement. Justice Stewart wrote

> It is hard to imagine a situation less conducive to the exercise of "a rational intellect and a free will" than Mincey's. He had been seriously wounded just a few hours earlier, and had arrived at the hospital "depressed almost to the point of coma," according to his attending physician. Although he had received some treatment, his condition at the time of [Detective] Hust's interrogation was still sufficiently serious that he was in the intensive care unit. He complained to Hust that the pain in his leg was "unbearable." He was evidently confused and unable to think clearly about either the events of that afternoon or the circumstances of his interrogation, since some of his written answers were on their face not entirely coherent. Finally, while Mincey was being questioned he was lying on his back on a hospital bed, encumbered by tubes, needles, and breathing apparatus. He was, in short, "at the complete mercy" of Detective Hust, unable to escape or resist the thrust of Hust's interrogation. (*Mincey v. Arizona*, pp. 398–99)

Despite the fact that Mincey had made some coherent statements, the Court concluded:

> It is apparent from the record in this case that Mincey's statements were not "the product of his free and rational choice." . . . To the contrary, the undisputed evidence makes clear that Mincey wanted *not* to answer Detective Hust. But Mincey was weakened by pain and shock, isolated from family, friends, and legal counsel, and barely conscious, and his will was simply overborne. Due process of law requires that

> statements obtained as these were cannot be used in any way against a defendant at his trial. (*Mincey v. Arizona*, pp. 401–02)

Thus, the state could not use Mincey's statements for impeachment purposes.

The Supreme Court held (5–4) a confession to be involuntary in *Arizona v. Fulminante* (1991). Fulminante, in federal prison for a weapons offense, was suspected of having murdered his stepdaughter. He was befriended by another inmate, Anthony Sarivola, a former police officer who became a paid informant for the FBI. Masquerading as an organized crime figure, Sarivola promised to protect Fulminante against violence from other inmates if they discovered he had killed his stepdaughter, but only if he told Sarivola whether he committed the crime. Fulminante admitted the crime to Sarivola, who later testified at Fulminante's murder trial. The Supreme Court affirmed the Arizona Supreme Court's decision that "[T]he confession was obtained as a direct result of extreme coercion and was tendered in the belief that the defendant's life was in jeopardy if he did not confess. This is a true coerced confession in every sense of the word." Both courts drew on common knowledge of the fact that prisoners are known to assault and even murder child abusers and, thus, could conclude that Fulminante had spoken out of fear for his life.

Crane v. Kentucky (1986) held that when a defendant raises the issue of a coerced confession under the Due Process Clause at trial, he must be allowed to introduce evidence of "the physical and psychological environment in which the confession was obtained." Therefore, even if a court determines in a pretrial hearing that a confession is voluntary, a jury may disagree and find that the confession was involuntary, or decide not to give it great weight. Innocent suspects have been known to make voluntary confessions, which they later retract. It would be impossible for a defendant making such a claim to be able to prove it if evidence were excluded about the environment in which the confession was taken.

MIRANDA AS A CONSTITUTIONAL RULE

The Consequences of the *Miranda* Ruling: Attacking Its Constitutional Basis

THEORIES OF *MIRANDA*   A theoretical debate about the nature of *Miranda* warnings has divided the Court for decades. It is a debate with real-world consequences. The conservative justices appointed by President Nixon between 1969 and 1972 were generally hostile to the Warren Court's *Miranda* ruling.[28] There was some hope among conservative scholars that the new Court would overrule *Miranda*.[29] But instead of overruling *Miranda*, the justices reinterpreted it in several cases after 1971 to say that *Miranda* warnings were *not* themselves constitutional rules. As a result, although statements taken during custodial interrogation without any warnings being given, or after defective warnings were given, were inadmissible at trial to convict the defendant, they *could* be used for collateral purposes. The collateral or peripheral purposes included using the statements to *impeach* the defendant if he decided to testify at trial, and using the statement *to lead to additional incriminating evidence*. In contrast to *Miranda* violations, statements obtained by "pure" compulsion to testify under a grant of immunity, or involuntary confessions that are the product of egregious police behavior (violating the suspect's due process rights) *cannot* be used for these collateral purposes.

As a result of these cases, it was logical to believe that *Miranda* was not a constitutional ruling. A leading conservative scholar, Joseph Grano, argued that if that were the case then the Court had no legitimate authority to impose a non-constitutional rule on the states.[30] Nevertheless, the Court did not overrule *Miranda*. Rather, on numerous occasions it narrowed its interpretation of *Miranda* in decisions that favored the state and allowed the use of confessions. In fact, the Court became somewhat supportive of an attenuated *Miranda* rule, as noted by Chief Justice Burger's aside in a 1980 case: "The meaning of *Miranda* has become reasonably clear and law enforcement practices have adjusted to its strictures; I would neither overrule *Miranda*, disparage it, nor extend it at this late date" (*Rhode Island v. Innis*, 1980, concurring). The reasons for this position were (1) a concern that overruling *Miranda* "at this late date" might be misread by the police as a withdrawal of the Court's concern, thus tacitly condoning abusive police tactics; (2) a desire, for symbolic purposes, to not make it seem that the Court was retracting individual liberties; and perhaps most important, (3) a realization by 1980 that *Miranda* was not hampering police in obtaining confessions. Under this attenuated *Miranda* regime, a public safety exception was carved out of the rule (*New York v. Quarles*, 1984).

Then, in 2000, the Court seemed to shift direction in *Dickerson v. United States* (2000), holding that a statute purporting to overrule *Miranda* was void because *Miranda* was a constitutional rule. This seemed to forecast a possible change in the Court's ruling on the collateral use of statements taken in violation of *Miranda* to bring the *Miranda* rule in line with the ban on collateral use after pure compulsion or due process violations. The Court then seemed to backtrack in *Chavez v. Martinez* (2003), holding that the mere failure to read *Miranda* warnings to a suspect is not a violation of his right against self-incrimination, and the suspect could not bring a §1983 civil action for this failure. As of early 2004 it is uncertain how the Court will decide two cases before it concerning the collateral use of *Miranda*-violated statements.

This section now proceeds to explore this meandering and confusing path of cases in greater detail. To better understand the debate, note that a suspect in custody is protected by the self-incrimination clause when subject to interrogation. As we have seen, a witness can invoke the privilege in any official venue where she is subpoenaed to testify, whether at a criminal trial, civil trial, administrative hearing, grand jury proceeding, or a legislative inquiry. It makes sense to extend the privilege to a suspect in the station house. After all, it is impermissible for a court to order a suspect to talk to the police on pain of a contempt citation and then to use whatever is said against the defendant in a criminal trial. Such a hypothetical rule would entirely nullify the defendant's absolute right to silence at the trial.

Miranda, then, clearly established that suspects have a right to silence during custodial interrogation. It then built several protections to ensure that the right would not be nullified by what the police do to a person who is in custody. The theoretical debate, however, asks whether the *warnings* are themselves constitutional rules.

COLLATERAL USE OF *MIRANDA*-VIOLATED STATEMENTS   *Harris v. New York* (1971) held that a confession obtained without complete *Miranda* warnings could nevertheless be introduced into evidence, not to prove guilt, but to *impeach* the credibility of the defendant whose testimony contradicted his earlier confession. This suggested that *Miranda* was not a constitutional rule. Justice Brennan, in dissent, quoted a passage from *Miranda* that rebutted the position taken by the majority. *Miranda* explicitly stated that incriminating statements taken without the full warnings being given *cannot* be used to impeach the defendant's testimony at trial. Chief Justice Burger's majority opinion, however, declared that this statement in *Miranda* was mere *dictum* that "was not at all necessary to the Court's holding [in *Miranda*] and cannot be regarded as controlling." The *Harris* decision is the direct opposite of *New Jersey v. Portash* (1979), which held that grand jury testimony compelled by a grant of immunity could *not* be used to impeach the witness at a later trial because such use was a violation of the Self-Incrimination Clause. In this way, the Court in *Harris* began to chip away at the underlying theory of the *Miranda* warnings as constitutional rules.

The *Harris* ruling was confirmed by **Oregon v. Hass** (1975). A suspect, arrested for a theft and burglary, was read *Miranda* warnings. On the way to the police station, Hass said he wanted to call his attorney. The officer said that he could do so when they reached the station. Hass then made incriminating statements in the police car. At the trial, Hass claimed he was innocent, testifying that a friend impulsively stole a bicycle and threw it into Hass's truck. The victim then drove up to Hass's truck and took its license plate number. The police traced the number to Hass's home and arrested him. In rebuttal, the officer testified that Hass made incriminating statements in the patrol car after he asked for his attorney. The trial court advised the jury that the officer's testimony could not be used as proof of Hass's guilt, but only to evaluate the credibility of Hass as a witness, i.e., only for impeachment purposes.

The Supreme Court held that the rule of *Harris* applied. Continuing to interrogate Hass after he asked for a lawyer was a *Miranda* violation. However, the officer's statement could be introduced to impeach Hass's credibility as a witness. Justice Blackmun, for the majority, wrote that "the shield provided by *Miranda* is not to be perverted to a license to testify inconsistently, or even perjuriously, free from the risk of confrontation with prior inconsistent utterances" (*Oregon v. Hass*, p. 722). Justice Brennan, dissenting, repeated his point in *Harris* that "An incriminating statement is as incriminating when used to impeach credibility as it is when used as direct proof of guilt and no constitutional distinction can legitimately be drawn." He noted that once *Miranda* warnings were given, the state has no incentive to obey the rule, for by continuing to question the "police may obtain a statement which can be used for impeachment if the accused has the temerity to testify in his own defense."

Michigan v. Tucker (1974) continued to undermine *Miranda*. It went beyond *Harris* by providing the conceptual framework that has limited the *Miranda* ruling. *Miranda*-deficient warnings were given to Tucker before interrogation (he was not informed of the right to *appointed* counsel). Tucker gave police the name of a witness whose statements incriminated Tucker. Nothing that Tucker said was used against him, but evidence *derived* from his statement, i.e., the witness's statement, was used against him to prove his guilt of a rape.[31]

The importance of *Tucker* lay in Justice Rehnquist's reasoning. He declared that *Miranda* warnings are prophylactic rules developed to protect the underlying right of silence in the Self-Incrimination Clause, and not constitutional rules in their own right. The police failure to give warnings therefore did not violate Tucker's privilege against self-incrimination but only the *Miranda* protective rules. He suggested that this was the rule of the *Miranda* case by selectively reading it. He quoted the following passage from *Miranda* (p. 467): "We cannot say that the Constitution necessarily requires adherence to any particular solution for the inherent compulsions of the interrogation process as it is presently conducted." However, Justice Rehnquist failed to quote the following from the *Miranda* opinion, which appeared three sentences later: "However, unless we are shown other procedures which are at least as effective in apprising accused persons of their right of silence and in assuring a continuous opportunity to exercise it, the following safeguards must be observed." The mandatory nature of the warnings requirement, plus the statement that the Constitution requires the protections, makes it plausible that the Warren Court majority did not intend in *Miranda* to separate the Fifth Amendment privilege from the warnings.

Nevertheless, the *Tucker* majority interpreted these words as dictum, and not a rule. The majority in *Tucker* concluded that the police did not violate Tucker's right against compulsory self-incrimination "but rather failed to make available to him the full measure of procedural safeguards associated with that right since *Miranda*." Since a violation of the *Miranda* warnings was not a violation of the right against self-incrimination, it did not require the exclusion of derivative evidence. The majority added that no additional deterrence to police misconduct could be expected by the use of evidence derived from a good-faith failure to follow the *Miranda* rules.

Oregon v. Elstad (1985) provides another way in which a violation of *Miranda* rules did not prevent the use of the defendant's statements. Police arrested eighteen-year-old Michael Elstad in his home. Elstad was suspected of stealing $150,000 worth of art objects and furnishings from the home of his friend. Elstad made incriminating statements to the police upon being questioned about the burglary just after the arrest. He was not warned of his rights. At the Sheriff's offices later in the day, Elstad was again questioned, but this time *Miranda* warnings were read and he initialed a waiver form. He again made incriminating statements and these statements were admitted into evidence. The Court ruled that the fruit-of-the-poisonous-tree doctrine did not bar the second confession: It was not "tainted" as a result of the prior, unwarned, admission. Justice O'Connor believed that the police action did not in itself violate the self-incrimination privilege. She noted that "The *Miranda* exclusionary rule, however, serves the Fifth Amendment and sweeps more broadly than the Fifth Amendment itself. It may be triggered even in the absence of a Fifth Amendment violation" (*Oregon v. Elstad*, 1985). Therefore, a *Miranda* default does not necessarily carry other constitutional implications. The majority felt that if the first admission had been coerced under the voluntariness test, that might have invalidated a later confession.

Justice Brennan dissented strongly. He argued that the *Elstad* example was a classic ploy designed to break a suspect's will. The first question might have been asked of eighteen-year-old Michael Elstad to "soften him up" into a confessing mood. This made him more willing to waive his rights and talk at the police station, since the "cat was out of the bag." The majority and the dissenters clearly differed as to whether *Miranda* was a constitutional rule. Justice Brennan believed that "*Miranda* clearly emphasized that warnings and an informed waiver are essential to the Fifth Amendment privilege itself."

The Public Safety Exception

The doctrinal foundation laid in *Harris, Hass, Tucker,* and *Elstad* bore full fruit in ***New York v. Quarles*** (1984), a case that created a "public safety" exception to *Miranda*. By creating an explicit exception to *Miranda* based on a balancing test, the Court seemed to confirm its view that the *Miranda* warnings were not themselves constitutional requirements.

At 12:30 A.M. two police officers were approached by a woman who told them that she had just been raped by a black male. She described his jacket with the name "Big Ben" printed in yellow letters on the back and told the officers that the man had just entered a supermarket located nearby, carrying a gun. The officers spotted the man in the supermarket and arrested him after a brief chase through the aisles. When frisked, the man, Benjamin Quarles, was wearing an empty shoulder holster. After handcuffing him, Officer Kraft asked him where the gun was. Quarles nodded in the direction of some empty cartons and responded, "The gun is over there." Officer Kraft then retrieved a loaded .38-caliber revolver from a carton, formally placed Quarles under arrest, and read him his *Miranda* rights from a printed card. Quarles said that he would be willing to answer questions. When Officer Kraft asked him if he owned the gun and where he had purchased it, Quarles answered that he did own it and that he had purchased it in Miami.

THE PUBLIC SAFETY EXCEPTION IN THE STATES

Most states appear to have adopted the public safety exception. However, in its application, some courts have found that it does not always apply.

MINNESOTA   A police officer arrested Hazley and without reading *Miranda* warnings asked him who he was and who he was with. Hazley replied and the answer was incriminating because it connected him to a robber. The trial court admitted the statement under the public safety exception. The Minnesota Court of Appeals held that this did not come under the public safety exception even though the police had reason to believe that one of the robbers carried a gun. "Missing accomplices cannot be equated with missing guns in the absence of evidence that the accomplice presents a danger to the public 'requiring immediate action by the officers beyond the normal need expeditiously to solve a serious crime.'" *State v. Hazley* (Minn. App. 1988)[32]

The New York courts, at every level, excluded Quarles's initial statement and the gun from evidence in the trial because he had not been read *Miranda* warnings before the question was asked, and also excluded the statement about the ownership and purchase of the gun as being derived from an illegal interrogation. The Supreme Court agreed that the brief scenario in *Quarles* constituted custodial interrogation by police, a situation that calls for warning a suspect of his rights under *Miranda* for any statement to be admissible in evidence. Nevertheless, the Court (6–3) reversed the New York Court of Appeals, that state's highest court.

The basis of the Court's holding was that "this case presents a situation where concern for public safety must be paramount to adherence to the literal language of the prophylactic rules enunciated in *Miranda*." The Court thus injected something like the Fourth Amendment balancing test and an exigent-circumstances exception into a Fifth Amendment area. Were *Miranda* a constitutional rule, this would not be permissible for "the Fifth Amendment's strictures, unlike the Fourth's, are not removed by showing reasonableness" (*Quarles*, p. 653, n. 6); i.e., the Fifth Amendment privilege is absolute. Since *Quarles* creates an exception to the *Miranda* warnings requirement, the warnings cannot be the same as the privilege, because in theory an exception cannot be made for the privilege. The Court characterized the warnings as "'practical reinforcement' for the Fifth Amendment right" (*Quarles*, p. 654, citing *Michigan v. Tucker*). The likelihood of police committing "constitutionally impermissible practices" during interrogation is lessened by the administration of the warnings.

Justice Rehnquist, writing for the majority, held that:

on these facts there is a "public safety" exception to the requirement that *Miranda* warnings be given before a suspect's answers may be admitted into evidence, and that the availability of that exception does not depend upon the motivation of the individual officers involved. In a kaleidoscopic situation such as the one confronting these officers, where spontaneity rather than adherence to a police manual is necessarily the order of the day, the application of the exception which we recognize today should not be made to depend on . . . the subjective motivation of the arresting officer. Undoubtedly most police officers, if placed in Officer Kraft's position, would act out of a host of different, instinctive, and largely unverifiable motives—their

own safety, the safety of others, and perhaps as well the desire to obtain incriminating evidence from the suspect. (*New York v. Quarles,* pp. 655–56)

The holding was criticized by three dissenting justices. Justice Marshall wrote that because the "Court in *Miranda* determined that custodial interrogations are inherently coercive . . . [it] therefore created a *constitutional presumption* that statements made during custodial interrogations are compelled in violation of the Fifth Amendment and are thus inadmissible in criminal prosecutions" (*New York v. Quarles*, Marshall, J., dissenting, p. 683, emphasis added). He chided the majority for substituting its view that a threat to public safety existed, when the New York courts unanimously found no threat to public safety. The store was deserted in the middle of the night; there was no indication that Quarles had a confederate who might use the gun; the police were certain that the gun was in the immediate area of the arrest; Quarles was handcuffed; and "the arresting officers were sufficiently confident of their safety to put away their guns." Justice Marshall noted that if there was a genuine threat of violence, the officers could violate *Miranda* to get the weapons, but the statement should not be admissible.

The dissent noted that conservative justices often defer to state court evaluations of the facts in a case. Consequently, the majority's analysis of the facts seemed wrong and hypocritical. It is as if the majority wanted to create an exception and manipulated the facts of the case to ensure the "proper" outcome. Justice O'Connor concurred, raising a concern that the exception blurred *Miranda*'s bright-line rule.

Rehabilitating *Miranda*?

In *Dickerson v. United States* (2000) the Supreme Court finally confronted the issue of whether *Miranda* was a constitutional ruling. To the surprise of many, the Court held that it is. Charles Dickerson was indicted by a federal grand jury for bank robbery and related crimes. He moved to suppress a statement he had made to FBI agents during an interrogation on the ground that he had not received *Miranda* warnings. The district court granted the motion to suppress because of technical errors in warning Dickerson, and specifically ruled that the confession was otherwise *voluntary*. Federal prosecutors appealed this ruling to the Court of Appeals for the Fourth Circuit, reputed to be the most conservative federal court of appeals in the nation.[33] That court found that although the *Miranda* warnings were defective, the confession was admissible under 18 U.S.C. §3501, which says that in any federal prosecution a confession "shall be admissible in evidence if it is voluntarily given."

This federal statute was passed in 1968, shortly after the *Miranda* decision, expressing political outrage against the decision. Under the law, being advised of one's right to remain silent is not required for a confession to be admissible, but is only one factor to be taken into account to determine if the confession is voluntary. The law sought, in effect, to overrule *Miranda*. One commentator called it "the most sweeping attack on the Supreme Court since Franklin Roosevelt tried to expand its membership in 1937."[34] The law had not been used by federal prosecutors or the Justice Department prior to the *Dickerson* case because they did not want to create a constitutional clash between the Court and Congress. At this point, the Clinton Administration, through a letter from Attorney General Janet Reno to Congress, asserted that insofar as §3501 sought to overrule *Miranda*, it was unconstitutional.

The Court of Appeals nevertheless held (2–1) that "Congress, pursuant to its power to establish the rules of evidence and procedure in the federal courts, acted well within its authority in enacting §3501, [and] §3501, rather than *Miranda*, governs the admissibility of confessions in federal court." The stage was set for a showdown between the Supreme Court and Congress over *Miranda*. It is fundamental to American constitutionalism that Congress can by legislation modify or void a Court-made rule, but cannot overrule a Court-made doctrine of constitutional law. When the Supreme Court establishes a constitutional doctrine by its interpretation of a constitutional provision, the only way in which that can properly be modified is by the Court itself overruling its own rulings (e.g., *Gideon v. Wainwright* overruling *Betts v. Brady*) or by constitutional amendment (e.g., the first sentence of the Fourteenth Amendment "overruled" the *Dred Scott* case).

In a 7–2 opinion for the Court, Chief Justice Rehnquist, acknowledging that Congress had intended to overrule *Miranda*, wrote:

> We hold that *Miranda*, being a constitutional decision of this Court, may not be in effect overruled by an Act of Congress, and we decline to overrule *Miranda* ourselves. We therefore hold that *Miranda* and its progeny in this Court govern the admissibility of statements made during custodial interrogation in both state and federal courts. (*Dickerson v. United States*, 120 S. Ct. 2329–30)

The majority opinion in *Dickerson* declared the federal statute unconstitutional for a number of reasons.

- Chief Justice Rehnquist simply brushed away decades of calling *Miranda* a prophylactic rule: "[W]e concede that there is language in some of our opinions that supports the view" that *Miranda* is not a constitutional rule.

- He reasoned that *Miranda* was not based on the Court's supervisory power (which applies only to federal courts and agents) because it had applied the *Miranda* rule to the states from the very beginning.

- Further, the justices in the *Miranda* case, both the majority and the dissenters, understood its ruling as a constitutional rule. The *Miranda* case itself stated that it was giving "concrete *constitutional* guidelines" to law enforcement officers.

- Another reason adopted the argument of the dissenters in *Tucker*: The warnings required by *Miranda* have not been superseded by other methods of securing a suspect's right to remain silent in the coercive atmosphere of a police station.

- As for cases like *Quarles* and *Harris* that created exceptions to *Miranda* or allowed collateral use of *Miranda*, the answer was (1) that the Court had also broadened the scope of *Miranda* in a few cases, and (2) that a constitutional rule can have exceptions.

- Chief Justice Rehnquist relied heavily on the concept of *stare decisis*, or precedent.

> Whether or not we would agree with *Miranda*'s reasoning and its resulting rule, were we addressing the issue in the first instance, the principles of *stare decisis* weigh heavily against overruling it now. * * * While *stare decisis* is not an inexorable command, particularly when we are interpreting the Constitution, even in constitutional cases, the doctrine carries such persuasive force that we have always required a departure from precedent to be supported by some special justification.
>
> We do not think there is such justification for overruling *Miranda*. *Miranda* has become embedded in routine police practice to the point where the warnings have become part of our national culture. (*Dickerson v. United States*, p. 2336, internal citations and quotations omitted)

- A final reason was that the due process voluntariness test "is more difficult than *Miranda* for law enforcement officers to conform to, and for courts to apply in a consistent manner."

The two most conservative justices, Scalia and Thomas, dissented. Justice Scalia's opinion noted that "Justices whose votes are needed to compose today's majority are on record as believing that a violation of *Miranda* is *not* a violation of the Constitution." He noted that several of the justices, including Chief Justice Rehnquist, made an about-face. Justice Scalia's opinion also suggests that the majority did not fully establish the constitutionality of *Miranda* warnings. The Court used phrases like "*Miranda* is a constitutional decision," "*Miranda* is constitutionally based," and *Miranda* has "constitutional underpinnings," without saying "that custodial interrogation that is not preceded by *Miranda* warnings or their equivalent violates the Constitution of the United States" (*Dickerson*, pp. 2337–38). The dissent discerned a fundamental violation of constitutional principle. Chief Justice Rehnquist's adroit opinion, on the other hand, can be seen as a mature reflection of the fact that constitutional government can be based on understandings—constitutional norms—that develop over time. The decision also signals to Congress that it cannot tread on an area within the preserve of the Supreme Court's authority.

To the dismay of scholars the *Dickerson* majority seemed to continue the logical and constitutional inconsistency of pre-*Dickerson* law. Prof Susan Klein wrote:

> This opinion was, in a word, terrible. The Court, when squarely faced with the issue of whether the four *Miranda* warnings were required by the federal constitution, not only refused to answer coherently, but breached its duty to provide a justification for *Miranda* or *Dickerson* and squandered an opportunity to rationalize contradictory case law regarding *Miranda*'s exceptions.[35]

By refusing to repudiate the various exceptions that allowed the use of statements taken in violation of the *Miranda* rules, the Supreme Court continued what Prof. Stephen Schulhofer has called "Fifth Amendment exceptionalism."[36] While there can be no direct or collateral use made of statements taken in direct contravention of the privilege against self-incrimination or coerced confessions that violate due process, admissions taken in violation of *Miranda* can be put to collateral (e.g., impeachment, leads to new evidence) or direct (e.g., public safety exception, *Elstad* use of a "cured" statement) use. This issue continues to trouble the Court.

The decision in ***Chavez v. Martinez*** (2003) provides mixed signals on this point. Two police officers, Andrew Salinas and Maria Pena, were questioning a person outdoors about drug dealing in the area. Oliverio Martinez, a field worker, rode by on his bicycle. The officers told him to stop, dismount, spread his legs, and place his hands behind his head. Martinez complied. Officer Salinas frisked Martinez and felt a knife (used to cut strawberries) in a sheath tucked into his waistband. A scuffle ensued. During the altercation Salinas yelled "He's got my gun!" Backup officer Pena shot Martinez five times, leaving him blind and paralyzed. The officers then handcuffed Martinez. Moments later, Sgt. Ben Chavez arrived with paramedics, and proceeded to interrogate Martinez on the suspicion that he had attempted to murder the officers. He was concerned that Martinez might die before providing information or an admission. *Miranda* warnings were never administered. Sgt. Chavez questioned Martinez for about ten minutes during a forty-five-minute period while medical personnel worked to save his life. Martinez intermittently cried out in pain, begged for treatment, expressed fear of dying and answered Sgt. Chavez's questions inconsistently, at one point admitting to pointing officer Salinas's gun at him, after having denied it.

Martinez was never charged with a crime and his answers were never used against him in a trial. He sued Sgt. Chavez under §1983 for violating his rights under the Self-Incrimination Clause and under the Due Process Clause by interrogating him without reading *Miranda* warnings and for his abusive interrogation. The case produced six opinions and a fractured decision consisting of two holdings. One holding, decided by five justices, was to remand the *due process* issue to the lower courts to determine whether the questioning by Sgt. Chavez was behavior that either "shocked the conscience" or was action that would render a confession involuntary. Three of these justices (Stevens, Kennedy, and Ginsburg) believed that Sgt.

Chavez violated Martinez's substantive due process rights. Justice Scalia dissented on this point, arguing that Martinez had no substantive due process claim. On this point, Justice Kennedy offered a specific reason for believing that there was a due process violation that occurred during the interviewing. Recognizing that police interrogation can occur under the most difficult situations that might involve taking a **dying declaration** from a suspect, he wrote:

> There is no rule against interrogating suspects who are in anguish and pain. The police may have legitimate reasons, borne of exigency, to question a person who is suffering or in distress. Locating the victim of a kidnaping, ascertaining the whereabouts of a dangerous assailant or accomplice, or determining whether there is a rogue police officer at large are some examples. That a suspect is in fear of dying, furthermore, may not show compulsion but just the opposite. The fear may be a motivating factor to volunteer information. The words of a declarant who believes his death is imminent have a special status in the law of evidence. (*Chavez v. Martinez*, pp. 1012–13)

What distinguished this case, and created the due process violation, according to Justice Kennedy, was the "use of torture or its equivalent in an attempt to induce a statement." Specifically, the transcript indicated that at one point in the emergency room, when Martinez (who was blinded) was screaming for medical attention, Chavez gave the impression that Martinez would be treated only if he answered the questions. This was the equivalent of the police creating the injuries to Martinez in order to get him to talk.

There were differing opinions concerning the application of the Self-Incrimination Clause to this case. The first, agreed to by all nine justices, was that the simple failure of a police officer to read *Miranda* warnings to a suspect prior to custodial interrogation does not establish a violation of the suspect's privilege against self-incrimination. A plurality of four justices (Thomas, Rehnquist, O'Connor, and Scalia) posited that what happens during interrogation, even torture, could *never* be a violation of the Fifth Amendment privilege because the privilege against self-incrimination can only be violated by the introduction of tainted evidence into a criminal trial. If a person were tortured, he could seek redress under the due process "shocks the conscience" test. The plurality opinion authored by Justice Thomas based its holding on the text of the Fifth Amendment privilege, which they read as an exclusionary rule only, and by decisions of federal appellate courts that have rejected civil claims against officers. As Prof. Arnold Loewy put it, "the fifth amendment does not contain an exclusionary rule; it is itself an exclusionary rule."[37]

Justice Kennedy (joined by Stevens and Ginsburg) asserted a different theory in a dissent. He suggested that "the Self-Incrimination Clause is applicable at the time and place police use compulsion to extract a statement from a suspect." This position views the Self-Incrimination Clause as more than an exclusionary rule. He agrees that a simple failure to read *Miranda* warnings is not a violation of the suspect's privilege against self-incrimination. Nevertheless, in the view of the dissenters, "an actionable violation arose at once under the

Self-Incrimination Clause (applicable to the States through the Fourteenth Amendment) when the police, after failing to warn, used *severe compulsion* or *extraordinary pressure* in an attempt to elicit a statement or confession" (*Chavez v. Martinez*, p. 1008, emphasis added).

Chavez v. Martinez, despite the holding of *Dickerson*, leaves open the question of whether the *Miranda* warnings in and of themselves are constitutional rights. The plurality opinion of Justice Thomas continued to describe the warnings as "judicially crafted prophylactic rules" and did not once cite *Dickerson*. The Court's unanimous decision that the failure to warn a suspect is not actionable can be read in either of two ways. First, it can be seen as indicating that the warnings themselves are not a constitutional requirement. A different reading is that for a wrong to rise to the level of a constitutional violation, it must be more than a *de minimis* violation. The latter view seems to explain Justice Kennedy's minority opinion. Even if the warnings are not themselves constitutional rights, a significant concurrence by Justice Souter (joined by Breyer) may hold the key to the Court's future decisions. Justice Souter agreed with the plurality that the only *core* right under the Self-Incrimination Clause is to not have compelled statements admitted into evidence (i.e., not to be forced to be a witness against oneself). All other so-called Fifth Amendment rights are indeed peripheral. However, the Court may create protective rules "if clearly shown to be desirable means to protect the basic right against the invasive pressures of contemporary society" (*Chavez v. Martinez*, 2003, Souter, J. concurring). Under this interpretation, the Court could, if it felt it was justified, bring *Miranda* law into line with other self-incrimination rules. Specifically, it could find that all or some of the *Miranda* exceptions that have caused such controversy could be eliminated if they threaten the suspect's underlying right against self-incrimination. Whether or not the core right itself exists at the station house, the rules that guide custodial interrogation can so undermine the core right as to make them meaningless. If this is the case, then the Court might reconsider its decisions in *Harris, Tucker, Hass, Quarles,* and *Elstad* in the future.

These conflicting views about the constitutional stature of the *Miranda* warnings are important for the collateral use of *Miranda*-violated statements. The Supreme Court clearly understands this, because it has granted certiorari in two cases to be decided in the Court's 2003–2004 term, which will directly confront the continued existence of *Miranda* exceptionalism.[38] The decision in these cases will have a huge practical effect on police interrogation if they legitimate a practice known as "interrogation outside *Miranda*." This means that police interrogators deliberately or inadvertently *violate* the *Miranda* rules when it is in their benefit to do so. For example, if a suspect invokes the right to silence or asks for an attorney, according to *Miranda*, interrogation must cease. The interrogator may believe that it is worth it to violate the suspect's *Miranda* rights to obtain statements that can be used for collateral purposes. This is especially so after the ruling in *Chavez v. Martinez* that the simple failure to give warnings does not impose any civil liability on police officers.

This practice is not a hit-or-miss event, but had become policy in some California police departments in the mid-1990s, as noted by Prof. Charles Weisselberg. Police legal advisers and trainers produced training books and videos, and lectured on the practice. Their message was that the collateral use cases mean that "the warning and waiver components of Miranda were simply a court-created 'series of recommended "procedural safeguards" that were not themselves rights protected by the Constitution.'"[39] The manuals and training materials explicitly recommended that when a suspect invokes his right to silence or asks for a lawyer, that interrogating officers deliberately ignore the requests, even though this violates the strictures of *Miranda*. These manuals stated that police would not be sued for this, as long as interrogation was "benign," because *Miranda* "is not of constitutional dimension."[40] The training bulletins were acutely aware that the only consequence of violating the *Miranda* warning and waiver rules is that incriminating evidence is inadmissible in the case-in-chief. If a suspect invokes silence or asks for a lawyer, however, from the police perspective there is nothing to lose by continuing to interrogate. The benefits listed included obtaining statements that could be used to impeach the defendant at trial, or as a lead to other incriminating evidence. Additional benefits included clearing cases, recovering a body or a missing person, recovering stolen property, and the like.

Interrogation "outside *Miranda*" was ruled unconstitutional by the Ninth Circuit Court of Appeals in 1999.[41] The fear of liability may have caused police trainers in California to no longer recommend this practice.[42] *Chavez v. Martinez* (2003) then held that a direct violation of *Miranda* is not a constitutional violation for which a person can sue the police, thus in effect overruling the Ninth Circuit. The logical consequence of the *Chavez* plurality opinion will allow police throughout the nation to blatantly disregard those *Miranda* provisions that order police to cease questioning when a suspect invokes the right to silence or requests an attorney. *Chavez v. Martinez* has thus forced the Court to confront questions about *Miranda* exceptions left unanswered by *Dickerson*. If the Court opens the door to unrestricted interrogation "outside *Miranda*," it will create a paradigm shift in confessions law that will partially overrule *Miranda* and will expose the Court to blatant hypocrisy.[43]

There may be a way for the Court to soften this possibility in its forthcoming cases. In *United States v. Patane*[44] an officer negligently failed to complete his recitation of *Miranda* warnings to a man arrested outside his home. The officer asked about a gun and obtained both an incriminating statement and the gun. The Tenth Circuit Court held the statement and the gun inadmissible on what appears to be an erroneous reading of *Dickerson*. The Supreme Court could affirm the Circuit Court and thus entirely dismantle the rule of *Michigan v. Tucker* (1974) by applying the fruit of the poisonous tree rule to any *Miranda* violation. Such a liberal ruling seems unlikely. The way lies open, however, for the Court to find that *Miranda* exceptions exist where the violations of police are inadvertent or negligent.

In the other case before the Supreme Court, *Missouri v. Seibert*,[45] a police officer deliberately questioned a murder suspect for a half-hour in the police station at about 4:00 A.M. without reading *Miranda* warnings. When Ms. Seibert made incriminating admissions, the officer allowed a twenty-minute break. He then read *Miranda* warnings, obtained a waiver, and procured a confession from Ms. Seibert during the second interrogation. The Missouri Supreme Court suppressed both statements. The United States Supreme Court might affirm this decision on the ground that a *deliberate* violation of *Miranda* not only excludes the initial statement but renders subsequent "cured" statements inadmissible. It may decide that under the particular facts of this case the second confession was involuntary, or it might more broadly rule that the *Oregon v. Elstad* (1985) exception only applies to inadvertent violations. In this way, the Supreme Court might tone down the police use of interrogation "outside *Miranda*" while not entirely eliminating the *Miranda* exceptions. Much depends on whether five justices will see interrogation "outside *Miranda*" as the kind of threat to the core right of the privilege against self-incrimination that requires protective rules.[46]

INTERPRETING *MIRANDA*

Miranda v. Arizona (1966) spawned scores of cases that interpreted each particular rule that together make up the decision. For the most part, the rulings have provided sufficient flexibility to the police to ensure that the rules do not unduly hamper interrogations. In some areas, however, the Court has strengthened protections for suspects being interrogated.

Adequacy of Warnings

Police officers need not use the *precise words* found in *Miranda,* or any rigid formula, when reciting the four warnings to a suspect prior to interrogation. They must, however, adequately convey the *substance* of each warning (*California v. Prysock,* 1981). Randall Prysock, a minor, was arrested for murder and declined to talk to his interrogator, Police Sergeant Byrd. His parents spoke with Randall at the Sheriff's office and he agreed to talk. In a taped interrogation, Sergeant Byrd informed Randall and his parents of Randall's right to silence, that incriminating evidence would be used against him, to have a lawyer present before and during questioning, and as a juvenile, to have his parents present. Sergeant Byrd stated the right to have counsel provided for an indigent person with these words: "You all, uh,—if,—you have the right to have a lawyer appointed to represent you at no cost to yourself." The Supreme Court majority found that "[i]t is clear that the police in this case fully conveyed to respondent his rights as required by *Miranda.*" Justice Stevens dissented because, as the California courts found, the warning failed to inform Prysock "that the services of a free attorney were available *prior* to the impending questioning." It was more likely that Prysock would have decided not to talk until he had a lawyer had the warning been clearer.

The Court again, in *Duckworth v. Eagan* (1989), refused (5–4) to find somewhat "nonstandard" language in the warnings given to a defendant to be inadequate. Eagan was told, as part of otherwise complete *Miranda* warnings, that:

> You have a right to talk to a lawyer for advice before we ask you any questions, and to have him with you during questioning. You have this right to the advice and presence of a lawyer even if you cannot afford to hire one. *We have no way of giving you a lawyer, but one will be appointed for you, if you wish, if and when you go to court.* If you wish to answer questions now without a lawyer present, you have the right to stop answering questions at any time. You also have the right to stop answering at any time until you've talked to a lawyer. (*Duckworth v. Eagan*, 1989, emphasis added)

Chief Justice Rehnquist, for the majority, noted that the warnings as a whole "touched all of the bases required by *Miranda*." The additional phrase that a lawyer will be appointed "if and when you go to court" merely informs the suspect of the normal routine of how lawyers are appointed. He also noted that, under *Miranda*, lawyers need not be producible on call, nor do police stations need to have attorneys on the premises at all times to advise suspects.

Justice Marshall, for the dissenters, thought the warnings given here would mislead the average suspect into believing that only suspects who could *afford* lawyers could have one immediately; others "not so fortunate" must wait. Also, "a warning qualified by an 'if and when' caveat still fails to give a suspect any indication of when he will be taken to court. Upon hearing the warnings given in this case, a suspect would likely conclude that no lawyer would be provided until trial" (*Duckworth v. Eagan*, 1989, Marshall, J., dissenting). The dissents in *Prysock* and *Eagan* aimed at making *Miranda* protections clear and unambiguous to defendants, even to the point of *expanding* the content of the required warnings. The majority opinions adhere more closely to the contours of *Miranda* on this issue.

The Supreme Court has not added new warnings or *additional information* to the four basic warnings (*Colorado v. Spring,* 1987). Spring was questioned twice while in jail, about three months apart, first by federal agents and a second time by Colorado officers. Complete *Miranda* warnings were administered both times, and Spring signed waiver forms. The federal agents questioned Spring about a firearms violation. They knew he was a homicide suspect and asked him, during the questioning, if he had ever shot anyone. "Spring admitted that he had 'shot [a] guy once.'" This statement was later used in evidence against him in his Colorado murder trial. The Supreme Court held it was not necessary, under *Miranda,* for the federal officers to tell Spring that they knew he was a murder suspect or that he would later be approached by Colorado officers about that crime. "The Constitution does not require that a criminal suspect know and understand every possible consequence of a waiver of the Fifth Amendment privilege. . . . Here, the additional information could affect only the wisdom of a *Miranda* waiver, not its essential voluntary and knowing nature." Justice Marshall, dissenting, saw this as a psychological ploy designed to undermine Spring's will to remain silent. Under these circumstances, he argued, a failure to give the suspect additional information nullified the voluntary, knowing, and intelligent nature of the waiver of rights, making the confession unconstitutional.

Waiver of Rights

Miranda v. Arizona (1966) held that if a confession is obtained, "a *heavy burden* rests on the Government to demonstrate that the defendant *knowingly* and *intelligently* waived his privilege against self-incrimination and his right to retained or appointed counsel." The Court allowed an *oral* waiver but stated that "a valid waiver will not be presumed simply from the silence of the accused after warnings are given or simply from the fact that a confession was in fact eventually obtained."

The "heavy burden" of proving a voluntary waiver was met in **North Carolina v. Butler** (1979). Butler was read his rights and refused to sign a waiver form. The officer told him that he did not have to speak or sign the form but that he wanted to talk to Butler. Butler replied, "I will talk to you but I am not signing any form." Justice Stewart ruled this a valid waiver:

> An express written or oral statement of waiver of the right to remain silent or of the right to counsel is usually strong proof of the validity of that waiver, but is not inevitably either necessary or sufficient to establish waiver. The question is not one of form, but rather whether the defendant *in fact* knowingly and voluntarily waived the rights delineated in the *Miranda* case. As was unequivocally said in *Miranda* mere silence is not enough. That does not mean that the defendant's silence, coupled with an understanding of his rights and a course of conduct indicating waiver, may never support a conclusion that a defendant has waived his rights. (*North Carolina v. Butler*, 1979, emphasis added)

The majority found, after examining the facts and circumstances, that the defendant had knowingly and voluntarily waived his rights. The minority view, expressed by Justice Brennan for three dissenting justices, interpreted *Miranda* to require an *affirmative waiver*. They therefore considered Butler's confession invalid. While an affirmative waiver, such as signing a *Miranda* form, is the normal practice today, *Butler* indicates that where the state meets its heavy burden of proving a voluntary waiver, a verbal agreement to speak can constitute a waiver of rights. *Butler* is an example of the Court's reluctance to strictly enforce the rules of *Miranda*.

The "heavy burden" was not met in **Tague v. Louisiana** (1980), where the state produced no evidence to show that the defendant knowingly or voluntarily waived his rights. In *Butler* the *record* indicated that the full complement of warnings was read and that the defendant understood them. In *Tague* the arresting officer who testified at the hearing to suppress the confession could not recall whether the defendant understood his rights. Without a record, it was an error to *presume* that the suspect understood the warnings.

Connecticut v. Barrett (1987) held that a suspect can *partially waive Miranda* rights. After warnings were read to him, Barrett said he was willing to talk to the police but would not sign a statement without a lawyer present. As a general rule, questioning should have ceased. In this case, however, Barrett was very clear that he was willing to talk about the crime but wanted a lawyer's advice as to whether he should *sign* a statement. He repeated this at his trial. The Supreme Court held his incriminating statements admissible. Here, his "affirmative announcements of his willingness to speak with the authorities" overrode his limited request for a lawyer. This is an exceptional case and the general rule is that a request for a lawyer ends a confession session.

Termination and Resumption of Questioning

> Once warnings have been given, the subsequent procedure is clear. If the individual indicates in any manner, at any time prior to or during questioning, that he wishes to remain silent, the interrogation must cease. At this point he has shown that he intends to exercise his Fifth Amendment privilege; any statement taken after the person invokes his privilege cannot be other than the product of compulsion, subtle or otherwise. Without the right to cut off questioning, the setting of in-custody interrogation operates on the individual to overcome free choice in producing a statement after the privilege has been once invoked. (*Miranda v. Arizona*, pp. 473–74)

Chief Justice Warren, an experienced former prosecutor, knew it was quite common for interrogating officers to badger suspects—to continue questioning them even after they invoke their right to remain silent. Although the passage may seem clear on its face, the Supreme Court later thought that it is ambiguous:

> This passage . . . does not state under what circumstances, if any, a resumption of questioning is permissible. The passage could be literally read to mean that a person who has invoked his "right to silence" can never again be subjected to custodial interrogation by any police officer at any time or place on any subject. Another possible construction of the passage would characterize "any statement taken after the person has invoked his privilege" as "the product of compulsion" and would therefore mandate its exclusion from evidence, even if it were volunteered by the person in custody without any further interrogation whatever. Or the passage could be interpreted to require only the immediate cessation of questioning, and to permit a resumption of interrogation after a momentary respite. (**Michigan v. Mosley,** 1975, pp. 101–02)

Richard Mosley was arrested for a robbery. During questioning at Detroit police headquarters, after having been read his rights, Mosley said he did not want to talk about the case, whereupon questioning ceased. A few hours later, Mosley was taken from his fourth-floor cell to the homicide division on the fifth floor of the same building. He was read his rights, agreed to talk, and made an incriminating statement that led to evidence that was used to convict him of a homicide. The Supreme Court ruled that Mosley's second statement was admissible at trial. Justice Stewart fashioned a facts-and-circumstances rule

TERMINATION AND RESUMPTION IN THE STATES

TENNESSEE   Melvin Crump, an escapee from a Department of Corrections work detail was arrested for a murder at about 1:00 P.M. He was handcuffed, placed in the backseat of a patrol car, *Mirandized,* and asked if he wished to talk. He said that he did not. The officer terminated questioning and told Crump that he was wanted for murder. Other officers arrived and were informed that Crump, after hearing warnings, refused to talk. For the next few hours, Crump was taken "on a ride through north Nashville to retrace his escape route, with the hope of 'learning something that deals with the homicide.'" At the location of a car robbery connected to the homicide, officers asked Crump if he had taken anything from the car. He admitted to doing so. The officers told Crump that this connected him to the homicide. At this point his emotions changed, and he looked upset. When they returned to the police station,

Crump made a confession. The "trial court found that Crump's right to cut off questioning and remain silent was not 'scrupulously honored,'" under *Mosley.*

The Tennessee Supreme Court agreed. "Thirty minutes after responding to Miranda warnings with 'I don't have anything to say,' he was taken on a 30 to 45-minute drive and questioned while retracing the route of his escape. This clearly constituted an impermissible resumption of in-custodial interrogation, which caused the admissions made by Crump during the drive to be inadmissible." Noting that the Tennessee constitutional self-incrimination provision is "more protective of individual rights than the test of voluntariness under the Fifth Amendment," the Tennessee court distinguished *Mosley* and ruled that the violation in this case was of constitutional magnitude and the confession was suppressed. (*State v. Crump*, 1992)[48]

that allows the police to question a defendant who has invoked his rights about an entirely *different crime* after a *lapse of time.* Mosley's statement was admissible in evidence because he was properly warned and *never requested a lawyer.* Also, when he asked that questioning cease, his request was immediately honored. The mere fact that he once terminated the interrogation, however, did not bar requestioning for a different criminal act.

The *Mosley* test is treated as a "totality of the circumstances" test. Lower courts have identified five *Mosley* factors that support the use of a statement after a suspect has invoked her right of silence: (1) initial *Miranda* warnings were given; (2) police immediately ceased interrogation when the suspect invoked silence; (3) a significant time period elapsed between the two interrogations; (4) a fresh *Miranda* warning was given before the second interrogation; and (5) the second interrogation was for a different crime than that investigated in the first interrogation or was triggered by new circumstances (e.g., a confession by a confederate).[47]

Invoking the Right to Counsel

[A]n individual held for interrogation must be clearly informed that he has the right to consult with a lawyer and to have the lawyer with him during interrogation. . . . This warning is an absolute prerequisite to interrogation. No amount of circumstantial evidence that the person may have been aware of this right will suffice to stand in its stead. (*Miranda v. Arizona,* pp. 471–72)

Once a defendant claims a desire to see an attorney, questioning must stop. The Supreme Court has, with a few exceptions, interpreted this requirement favorably for suspects.

For example, in *Smith v. Illinois* (1984), an eighteen-year-old robbery suspect, while in custody, was read the required *Miranda* warnings. Told he had a right to consult with a lawyer

and have a lawyer present while being questioned, he replied, "*Uh, yeah. I'd like to do that.*" The officer did not stop, but continued to advise Smith of his rights and asked, "Do you wish to talk to me at this time without a lawyer being present?" Smith replied, "*Yeah and no, uh, I don't know what's what really.*" To this, the officer said, "*Well. You either have [to agree] to talk to me this time without a lawyer being present* and if you do agree . . . you can stop at any time you want to." Smith replied, "All right. I'll talk to you then," and subsequently confessed.

The Court found that Smith *invoked his right to counsel* by his first statement in a clear and unambiguous way. While the statements made after the first request for counsel may have been ambiguous, the Court held that "[w]here nothing about the request for counsel or the circumstances leading up to the request would render it ambiguous, all questioning must cease" (*Smith v. Illinois*, 1984). The Court also ruled that "an accused's postrequest responses to further interrogation may not be used to cast retrospective doubt on the clarity of the initial request itself. Such subsequent statements are relevant only to the distinct question of waiver." Justice Rehnquist, writing for three dissenters, believed that the interrogation had not yet begun but that police were still in the process of giving Smith his warnings. He noted that Smith had not been badgered. Justice Rehnquist felt that the *Miranda* warning process should be examined in its totality. The holding of *Smith v. Illinois*, however, demonstrates that invocation of the right to counsel is defined strictly by the Supreme Court.

NONLEGAL ADVISORS   The Court's strict posture regarding requests for *counsel* is not extended to requests for help from other individuals or officials. In *Fare v. Michael C.* (1979) a juvenile in custody asked to see his probation officer during a murder interrogation. Justice Blackmun held that a request for a probation officer was not equivalent to a *Miranda* request for an attorney. "The *per se* aspect of *Miranda* [was] based on the unique role the lawyer plays in the adversarial system of criminal justice. . . ." A probation officer is a state employee who is a peace officer and does not act unequivocally on behalf of the suspect. Justice Marshall dissented (joined by Justices Brennan and Stevens), reinterpreting *Miranda* to say that questioning should stop whenever a juvenile requests an adult who is obligated to represent his or her interests. He suggested that it is unrealistic to expect a juvenile to call for a lawyer; it is more likely for a youth to turn to parents or another adult, such as a welfare worker, as the only means of securing legal counsel. However reasonable this point is, the Court was not willing to *expand Miranda* rights.

THIRD-PARTY INVOLVEMENT   What happens if third parties—such as parents, friends, or relatives—request an attorney for suspects being held by the police, even though the accused themselves have not invoked their *Miranda* rights? The Court has ruled that this is not an invocation of Fifth Amendment rights by the suspect personally, and any confession made while an attorney is trying to contact the suspect does not violate the *Miranda* rule.

In *Moran v. Burbine* (1986) Brian Burbine was arrested for breaking and entering and was suspected of an earlier murder. After his arrest, his sister called the public defender's office to obtain an attorney's assistance. Allegra Munson, a staff attorney, called the police department. Advised that Burbine was in custody, she told the police, over the telephone, that she was representing him in the event he was questioned or placed in a lineup. The unidentified officer told Munson that Burbine would not be questioned that night. An hour later, however, police did *Mirandize* and question Burbine, who waived his rights and ultimately made incriminating statements.

Burbine raised issues of waiver and the right to counsel. Regarding waiver, Justice O'Connor, for the majority, held that "[e]vents occurring outside of the presence of the suspect and entirely unknown to him surely can have no bearing on the capacity to comprehend and knowingly relinquish a constitutional right." Even the officer's deception of attorney Munson, whether inadvertent or not, unethical or not, does not change the fact that Burbine knowingly and intelligently waived his rights. The Court refused to add a requirement to *Miranda* that the police must inform a defendant of attempts of an attorney to reach him, citing practical problems that such a requirement would raise.

That someone had procured counsel for Burbine before he was questioned did not change the complexion of his rights. Justice O'Connor stated:

> the suggestion that the existence of an attorney-client relationship itself triggers the protections of the Sixth Amendment misconceives the underlying purposes of the right to counsel. The Sixth Amendment's intended function is not to wrap a protective cloak around the attorney-client relationship for its own sake any more than it is to protect a suspect from the consequences of his own candor. Its purpose, rather, is to assure that in any "criminal prosecutio[n]" the accused shall not be left to his own devices in facing the "prosecutorial forces of organized society." (*Moran v. Burbine*, p. 430, internal quotations eliminated)

Also, since Burbine had not yet been charged by a grand jury or by information, the Sixth Amendment right to an attorney did not yet apply. The majority refused to apply *Escobedo v. Illinois*, which had come to be reinterpreted as a case concerned more with the right against self-incrimination than the right to counsel. In effect, the *Escobedo* ruling became a dead letter.

Justice Stevens wrote a scathing dissent. "Until today, incommunicado questioning has been viewed with the strictest scrutiny by this Court; today, incommunicado questioning is embraced as a societal goal of the highest order that justifies police deception of the shabbiest kind" (*Moran v. Burbine*, pp. 438–39). He noted that the rulings of many state courts and the standards of the American Bar Association find that statements taken after deception of a client's attorney should be excluded from evidence. He noted that police "interference with communications between an attorney and his client is a recurrent problem" and was concerned that the ruling in *Moran* would do nothing to curb this kind of improper behavior.

TERMINATION AND RESUMPTION OF QUESTIONING   The Supreme Court protects the rights of suspects who invoke the right to counsel more strictly than those who terminate questioning without asking for the assistance of counsel. In *Edwards v. Arizona* (1981) Robert Edwards was arrested for robbery, burglary, and murder. Questioned at the police station after being given proper *Miranda* warnings, he told the officers that he wanted to "make a deal," but the police terminated the discussion when he said, "I want an attorney before making a deal." The next day, detectives came to the lockup and reinterrogated him. After playing him a taped statement of an alleged accomplice, Edwards agreed to talk as long as it was not tape-recorded, and he implicated himself in the crime. The Supreme Court reversed his conviction. Although a person may validly waive rights, Justice White, for the majority, held:

> when an accused has invoked his right to have counsel present during custodial interrogation, a valid waiver of that right cannot be established by showing only that he responded to further police-initiated custodial interrogation even if he has been advised of his rights. We further *hold* that an accused, such as Edwards, having expressed his desire to deal with the police only through counsel, is not subject to further interrogation by the authorities until *counsel has been made available* to him, *unless the accused himself initiates* further communication, exchanges, or conversations with the police. (*Edwards v. Arizona*, 1981, emphasis added)

Oregon v. Bradshaw (1983) dealt with the question of the suspect initiating further questioning. In this case, interrogation ceased after Bradshaw requested counsel. The Court held that it was properly initiated by Bradshaw's question made during the trip between the police station and jail, "*Well, what is going to happen to me now?*" Bradshaw was again read his rights, and in a "general conversation," he agreed to take a lie detector test. The next day, Bradshaw took a lie detector test, preceded by *Miranda* warnings, that resulted in an incriminating admission. A four-justice plurality said that Bradshaw's question, although ambiguous, "evinced a willingness and a desire for a generalized discussion about the investigation." A four-justice dissent, written by Justice Marshall, found this interpretation placed on Bradshaw's words by the plurality to be preposterous:

> If respondent's question had been posed by Jean-Paul Sartre before a class of philosophy students, it might well have evinced a desire for a "generalized" discussion. But under the circumstances of this case, it is plain that respondent's only "desire" was to find out where the police were going to take him. (*Oregon v. Bradshaw*, p. 1055)

The Supreme Court, in **Davis v. United States** (1995), held that in order to invoke the protection of *Edwards*, the request for counsel must be made *clearly*. Naval investigators suspected that Robert L. Davis beat another sailor to death with a pool cue. Davis was arrested, advised of his rights under military law, and waived his right to remain silent. An hour and a half into the interview, Davis said, "*Maybe I should talk to a lawyer.*" A Navy investigator testified:

> We made it very clear that we're not here to violate his rights, that if he wants a lawyer, then we will stop any kind of questioning with him, that we weren't going to pursue the matter unless we have it clarified is he asking for a lawyer or is he just making a comment about a lawyer, and he said, "No, I'm not asking for a lawyer," and then he continued on, and said, "No, I don't want a lawyer." (*Davis v. United States*, p. 455)

The investigators took a short break and then reminded Davis of his rights to remain silent and to counsel. They continued the interview for another hour, and at that point Davis said, "I think I want a lawyer before I say anything else." Questioning then ceased. An incriminating statement was made after Davis said "Maybe I should talk to a lawyer." The Court held that the statement was admissible and that Davis's rights under *Edwards* were not violated.

Analytically, there are three possible options to determine if a suspect's mention of a lawyer invoked the right to counsel: (1) any mention of counsel, however ambiguous, invokes counsel; (2) the *Edwards* protection is invoked if the suspect's request meets a "threshold" standard of clarity; or (3) whenever a suspect mentions a lawyer, questioning must cease, but interrogators may ask "narrow questions designed to clarify the earlier statement and the [suspect's] desires respecting counsel." The Court selected the second option.

Noting that *Edwards*'s prohibition on questioning is not itself a constitutional right but, like the *Miranda* rule, a protection for the Fifth Amendment, Justice O'Connor, writing for the Court, held that "after a knowing and voluntary waiver of the *Miranda* rights, law enforcement officers may continue questioning until and unless the suspect clearly requests an attorney." Justice O'Connor said that asking "clarifying questions" (option number three), while good police practice, is not required. *Davis* upholds the bright-line rule of *Edwards* by not forcing interrogating officers "to make difficult judgment calls about whether the suspect in fact wants a lawyer even though he hasn't said so, with the threat of suppression if they guess wrong."

Although the *Bradshaw* plurality strained in order to rule in favor of the state, and *Davis* burdens a suspect's rights under *Edwards*, the following cases show that for the most part the Supreme Court has interpreted the *Edwards* "bright-line rule" in favor of suspects.

For example, **Michigan v. Jackson** (1986) held that a suspect invokes the right to counsel for interrogation purposes when, at a formal arraignment, the suspect tells a judge that he wants a lawyer. Police officers present at Jackson's arraignment were bound by the *Edwards* rule and could not lawfully interrogate him simply by reading him his *Miranda* warnings. In **Arizona v. Roberson** (1988) the Court held that once a suspect asked to see a lawyer before speaking, this knowledge applied not only to the officer who first *Mirandized* the suspect, but to every officer in the same agency. This is a necessary corollary to the *Edwards* rule since it would be too easy for police officers to sidestep the *Edwards* rule by claiming ignorance of an invocation of rights by the suspect. Justice Stewart noted that "[C]ustodial interrogation must be conducted pursuant to established procedures, and those procedures in turn must enable an officer who proposes to initiate an interrogation to determine whether the suspect has previously requested counsel." In a well-run police department, an officer who questions a suspect should know which other officers had previously questioned him and be apprised of any request for counsel.

Support for the *Edwards* rule continued in **Minnick v. Mississippi** (1990). A suspect invoked the right to counsel during an interrogation, was allowed to consult with a lawyer, and was thereafter interrogated without counsel present. He made an admission during the second interrogation. The Court held, in an opinion by Justice Kennedy, that simply allowing the suspect to confer with counsel does not satisfy *Edwards*. A suspect who asks to speak to a lawyer is demanding a right to have a lawyer *present during interrogation*. Unless a subsequent uncounseled conversation is *initiated* by the suspect, as required by *Edwards*, the police cannot reinterrogate. The Court emphasized that a different standard would dilute the clarity of *Edwards*'s bright-line rule; it could create confusion whereby a suspect would gain *Edwards* protection at several points during custody by invoking the right to counsel, and then lose it after conferring with an attorney.

Justice Kennedy listed several benefits of maintaining the *Edwards* rule. It prevents the police from badgering suspects; it conserves judicial resources that would be expended in making factually complex voluntariness determinations; it avoids the burden on officials to determine when a prior consultation with counsel is sufficient to create a waiver; and it avoids counsel delaying meetings with clients so as to preserve their *Edwards* protections.

Justice Scalia dissented, joined by Chief Justice Rehnquist. He stressed that both *Miranda* and *Edwards* were prophylactic and not constitutional rules, and that *Edwards* sets a higher standard for waiver of rights than that of *Johnson v. Zerbst* (1938). He believed that the Court in *Minnick* established an irrebuttable presumption (i.e., virtually a firm rule) against waiving the right to counsel. Instead, he would allow the state to prove—after an invocation of the right to counsel and after counsel has been provided—that a confession was made knowingly and voluntarily.

Defining Custody

> By custodial interrogation, we mean questioning initiated by law enforcement officers after a person has been taken into custody or deprived of his freedom of action in any significant way. (*Miranda v. Arizona*, p. 444)

The Supreme Court has expanded *Miranda*'s definition of *police custody* beyond the station house. The basic question is: does the setting in which a confession is given create the compulsion contemplated by the Fifth Amendment privilege that brings the *Miranda* requirement and its exclusionary rule into play? That is, is the interrogation setting coercive? This eliminates the Sixth Amendment "focus" or "target" test of *Escobedo* and of grand jury procedure that forbids questioning the *target* of an investigation. This is appropriate because the Fifth Amendment does not forbid interrogation, but looks instead to see whether the questioning is accompanied by compulsion.

HOME   Thus, for example, being questioned in one's own *home* may be custodial depending upon the facts. There was custody in **Orozco v. Texas** (1969) when police entered the defendant's house at 4:00 A.M. and questioned him while he was under arrest, not free to leave, and surrounded by police officers. On the other hand, in **Beckwith v. United States** (1975), although Beckwith was the target of a criminal tax investigation, the IRS agents came to his home, politely requested admittance during the daytime, and gave him time to finish dressing. The interview was conducted in a friendly and relaxed manner at Beckwith's diningroom table. He was not pressed to answer questions and was told at the beginning of the interview that he had a right to refuse to answer questions. On these facts, the interview was held not custodial and *Miranda* warnings did not have to be given. This was so even though Beckwith, as a target of an investigation, could have legally refused to answer questions had he been subpoenaed.

PRISON   **Mathis v. United States** (1968) seems to hold that *all* interrogation of inmates that occur in *prison* must be preceded by *Miranda* warnings. IRS agents interviewed Mathis in *prison*, without issuing *Miranda* warnings, about tax issues *unrelated* to his prison conviction. Based on his *custody status*, the Supreme Court found a *Miranda* violation and overturned his conviction. Justice White, dissenting, believed that the underlying rationale of *Miranda* "rested not on the mere fact of physical restriction but on a conclusion that coercion—pressure to answer questions—usually flows from a certain type of custody, police station interrogation," of a suspect. Since Mathis was in familiar surroundings when questioned, even though confined, Justice White felt he was under no pressure to talk.

POLICE STATION   Interrogation in a police station does not become custodial merely because of the location—it depends instead on the circumstances of the interrogation atmosphere.

The majority in **Oregon v. Mathiason** (1977) found no custody or significant curtailment of freedom of action when a suspect voluntarily complied with a police request that he come to the station house for an interview. Carl Mathiason, a parolee, was identified as a probable burglar. A police officer left a card at Mathiason's residence asking him to call. At Mathiason's convenience, a meeting was held at a police station. The officer shook Mathiason's hand when he came to the station, and they met in a closed office with the officer sitting across a desk. The officer falsely told Mathiason that his fingerprints were found, whereupon he confessed. *Miranda* warnings were then read and another confession was taken. The Court concluded that Mathiason was not in custody before he confessed, so no *Miranda* warnings had to be read. The Court said that "Any interview of one suspected of a crime by a police officer will have coercive aspects to it, simply by virtue of the fact that the police officer is part of a law enforcement system which may ultimately cause the suspect to be charged with a crime." One can think of this kind of pressure as analogous to "background radiation" that attaches to police officers and is different from the heightened compulsion that occurs when a person is taken into custody. Justice Marshall dissented. He felt that Mathiason's freedom of movement was curtailed in a true sense, and that he was in custody even though not formally placed under arrest. The Court reached the same result in *California v. Behler* (1983) on similar facts, except the defendant was not a parolee, and he went voluntarily to the police station to tell the police that he was at the scene of a homicide.

The test of custody is an *objective* determination of whether the suspect was deprived of freedom in any significant way. In **Stansbury v. California** (1994) a police detective investigating the abduction and rape-murder of a ten-year-old girl questioned Robert Stansbury, one of two ice cream truck drivers to whom the girl had spoken on the day she was killed. Stansbury was not read *Miranda* warnings because the detective thought the other driver was the likely suspect. During the interview, Stansbury described a borrowed car he drove on the night of the murder that was similar to a description of the car given by a witness. This aroused the officer's suspicion and in his mind he *focused* on Stansbury as a suspect. Stansbury had no way of reading the officer's mind. The officer did not, by word or deed, convey to Stansbury that he was not free to leave. Under the objective standard, therefore, Stansbury was not yet in custody, and his incriminating statements about the car were admissible. As the questioning continued, Stansbury said he had prior convictions for rape, kidnapping, and child molestation. At this point the officer terminated the interview and another officer read Stansbury his *Miranda* warnings. The Court ruled that "an officer's subjective and undisclosed view concerning whether the person being interrogated is a suspect is irrelevant to the assessment whether the person is in custody."

PROBATION INTERVIEW   The Supreme Court held in **Minnesota v. Murphy** (1984) that a *probation interview* is not custody for *Miranda* purposes, even though a probationer is *legally* required to attend probation interviews and a condition of probation is that he answer all questions truthfully. The probationer, Marshall Murphy, was not under arrest nor was his freedom of movement seriously restrained. In this case, Murphy's probation officer planned in advance to ask him about previous crimes designed to elicit incriminating information. She gave Murphy no prior warning of such questions. He admitted to previously committing a rape and murder, and the statement to the probation officer was admissible in his first-degree murder trial.

The reason Murphy's statement was not compelled is that, except for the *Miranda* situation, the Fifth Amendment privilege against self-incrimination is *not self-executing*. Incriminating statements are not automatically excluded simply because a person makes them to a listener. With the exception of a police custodial interrogation situation, in which a person must be informed of his rights, a person must *claim* the privilege in order to rely on it. Once a person utters an incriminating statement, it is presumed voluntary, and the listener can tell what he or she heard to prosecutorial authorities (or anyone else) and may testify in court as to what was heard.

Murphy claimed that the probation condition that required truthful answers to the probation officer's questions amounted to compulsion. The Court disagreed. The probationer is in a similar situation as a witness subpoenaed before a grand jury. Both are legally compelled to attend, to answer truthfully, and they are not granted immunity. The probation conditions did not deprive Murphy of his Fifth Amendment rights. He could have refused to answer the questions that could have incriminated him. Murphy claimed that he feared revocation of probation if he did not answer. There was no proof, however, that Minnesota law or practice punished a probationer who claimed the protection of the Fifth Amendment.

TRAFFIC STOPS   A motorist stopped for a moving violation, whether a misdemeanor or felony, such as speeding or operating under the influence of drugs or alcohol, is detained for the time it takes to write a ticket or proceed to an arrest. Writing for a nearly unanimous Court in **Berkemer v. McCarty** (1984), Justice Marshall held that "persons temporarily detained pursuant to" police roadside stops of vehicles for traffic violations "are not 'in custody' for the purposes of *Miranda*." Such stops do not significantly restrain the freedom of movement of persons to such an extent as to deprive them of their will as contemplated by *Miranda*, for two simple reasons. First, "detention of a motorist pursuant to a traffic stop is presumptively temporary and brief." Second, the stop occurs in public so that the motorist does not feel completely at the mercy of the police. Thus, although the motorist is detained, these factors "mitigate the danger that a person questioned will be induced 'to speak where he would not otherwise do so freely'" (*Berkemer v. McCarty*, quoting *Miranda*). The stopped motorist is far less likely, under this reasoning, to be coerced into giving up Fifth Amendment rights.

McCarty was stopped by a trooper who saw his car weaving in traffic. After he failed a field sobriety test, he was told he would be taken into custody. Asked if he had taken any in-

toxicants, McCarty said that "he had consumed two beers and had smoked several joints of marijuana a short time before." At the jail, McCarty was again asked questions and gave incriminating answers. At no time were *Miranda* warnings read. McCarty's roadside statements were admitted into evidence.

Berkemer v. McCarty, however, did hold that once a motorist has been arrested or taken into custody on traffic felony or misdemeanor charges, *Miranda* warnings must be read prior to interrogation. The Court equated traffic misdemeanors with felonies in order to uphold the "simplicity and clarity of the holding of *Miranda*." An exception from warnings for traffic misdemeanors would create confusion and the potential for endless litigation. For example, some crimes escalate from misdemeanors to felonies depending on the number of prior DUI convictions, and it is not clear at the time of the vehicle stop whether a driving offense is a misdemeanor or felony. Thus, admissions made by McCarty on the roadside were admissible, but those made at the police station were inadmissible.

Pennsylvania v. Muniz (1990) further clarified the application of *Miranda* when a driver is stopped for driving under the influence (DUI) and is ordered to undergo a field sobriety test. (1) The Supreme Court held that *Miranda* warnings were not required simply for stopping a driver for DUI. The fact that the driver's *speech is slurred*, however incriminating, does not come under *Miranda* because physical inability to articulate words is not testimonial evidence. (2) Similarly, ordering a driver to perform and videotaping standard physical sobriety tests—the horizontal-gaze-nystagmus test, the walk-and-turn test, and the one-leg-stand test—are not testimonial. An officer orders a DUI suspect to perform the tests in "carefully scripted instructions as to how the tests were to be performed. These instructions were not likely to be perceived as calling for any verbal response and therefore were not 'words or actions' constituting custodial interrogation." As a result, *Miranda* warnings are not required. (3) Furthermore, an officer can ask a driver's name, address, height, weight, eye color, date of birth, and current age. The Court held that answers to these questions are admissible under a "*routine booking question*" exception to *Miranda*. Biographical data that is needed to complete booking or pretrial services and is requested for record-keeping purposes only is reasonably related to police administrative concerns. (4) In this case, Muniz made unsolicited, incriminating statements that he had been drinking while the officer read him another carefully prepared script concerning the nature of Pennsylvania's implied consent law and a request to submit to a Breathalyzer test. The only questions asked of Muniz were whether he understood the instructions and whether he wished to submit to the test. "These limited and focused" questions were a part of legitimate police procedure and were not designed or likely to be perceived as calling for an incriminating response." Therefore, Muniz's statements that he had been drinking were admissible.

The Court held that *Miranda* warnings were required only as to one question posed by the officer: "Do you know what the date was of your sixth birthday?" This was held to be testimonial interrogation. Muniz gave an incoherent response, which implied that he was intoxicated, which was not admissible because the question was asked before *Miranda* warnings were administered. Justice Brennan, for the majority, reasoned that the *content* of the answer allowed the police officer to infer that the driver's mental state was confused. This was not physical evidence—the physical status of Muniz's brain merely described the way in which the inference from the answer was incriminating. Because the incriminating inference was drawn from a testimonial act rather than a physical fact, the question confronted the suspect with the classic "trilemma" of self-incrimination, perjury, or contempt. Chief Justice Rehnquist disagreed on this point, claiming that Justice Brennan's assumption about human behavior was wrong. Given the nature of the question to Muniz, which was basically to check how well he could add the number six to his date of birth, there was no real incentive for Muniz to lie and commit perjury. In this view, the question was closer to the physical tests and the "booking questions" that did not violate the Fifth Amendment in this case.

The Nature of Interrogation

Miranda v. Arizona (1966) applies to custodial interrogation. **Rhode Island v. Innis** (1980) ruled that:

> *Miranda* safeguards come into play whenever a person in custody is subjected to either *express questioning* or its *functional equivalent*. That is to say, the term "interrogation" under *Miranda* refers not only to express questioning, but also to any words or actions on the part of the police (other than normally attendant to arrest and custody) that the police should know are reasonably likely to elicit an incriminating response from the suspect. (*Rhode Island v. Innis*, emphasis added)

The functional equivalent of express interrogation can be discovered from the facts and circumstances of cases.

Police arrested Innis at 4:30 A.M. on suspicion of murdering a taxicab driver with a shotgun. They advised him of his rights. He said he wanted to speak with a lawyer, terminating any interrogation. Innis was placed in the back of a patrol car and driven to the station. On the way to the station, Officer Gleckman spoke to Officer McKenna about the shotgun, saying there was a school for handicapped children in the area "and God forbid one of them might find a weapon with shells and they might hurt themselves." McKenna agreed and suggested that they should continue to search for the shotgun. At that point, Innis interrupted the conversation, stating that he could lead the officers to the gun, which he did. This incriminating statement and the shotgun were admitted into evidence to convict him.

Was this exchange the functional equivalent of interrogation? Justice Stewart, writing for the majority, said "no." He characterized the comments as only a few offhand remarks that the police could not have known would suddenly move Innis to make a self-incriminating response. A lengthy and more pointed "harangue" might become interrogation, but not the conversation here. The Court suggested that an example of a functional equivalent of interrogation is a "reverse lineup" where the police plant a "witness" in the lineup room to vocally accuse the suspect of a fictitious crime in order to induce him to confess to the actual crime. The Court added an important embellishment to its "functional equivalent" rule:

> But, since the police surely cannot be held accountable for the unforeseeable results of their words or actions, the definition of interrogation can extend only to words or actions on the part of police officers that they *should have known* were reasonably likely to elicit an incriminating response. (*Rhode Island v. Innis*)

To go further, police knowledge includes not only the likely effect of words on a hypothetical person, but also on a suspect with *known weaknesses or susceptibilities*.

Justice Marshall concurred with the definition of "interrogation" but dissented from its application to the facts in this case. He noted that appeals to the decency and the honor of the suspect are classic interrogation ploys and that "[o]ne can scarcely imagine a stronger appeal to the conscience of a suspect." Justice Stevens, also dissenting, suggested a different definition of interrogation: "any statement that would normally be understood by the average listener as calling for a response is the functional equivalent of a direct question, whether or not it is punctuated by a question mark." This definition focuses on the intention of the officers to some degree. The majority's rule, however, "focuses primarily upon the perceptions of the suspect, rather than the intent of the police."

The *Innis* definition was applied in **Arizona v. Mauro** (1987). William Mauro was arrested for the murder of his son after turning himself in at a local K-Mart store. He refused to make statements without a lawyer present and he was not questioned. Police interviewed Mrs. Mauro at the station. She insisted on speaking with her husband and was allowed to after some resistance on the part of the police. She was told that an officer would be present, and a tape recorder was placed prominently on the table. Mr. Mauro told his wife not to answer questions until a lawyer was present. At trial, the taped conversation was admitted into evidence to refute Mauro's insanity defense.

The Court held (5–4), in an opinion by Justice Powell, that the recording of the conversation was not the functional equivalent of interrogation under *Miranda* or *Innis*. The police did not send Mrs. Mauro in to speak with her husband, and the presence of the officer during their conversation was not improper. The mere possibility that a suspect in custody will incriminate himself under these circumstances does not amount to interrogation. "[T]he actions in this case were far less questionable than the 'subtle compulsion' that we held *not* to be interrogation in *Innis*. . . . Officers do not interrogate a suspect simply by hoping that he will incriminate himself."

Justice Stevens, for the dissenters, reasoned that the police used a "powerful psychological ploy" when they allowed Mrs. Mauro to speak to her husband—it was bound to generate some discussion after he had manifested a clear desire to remain silent. The legitimacy of the police presence is irrelevant to this finding, for on the witness stand, the police captain admitted that one reason for allowing the meeting was to obtain statements that could "shed light on our case." Also, a police detective testified that a standard police technique used to get juveniles to talk is to bring their parents into the police station. It is noteworthy that in both the *Innis* and the *Mauro* cases, the state supreme courts believed that interrogation, or its functional equivalent under *Miranda*, had occurred.

Colorado v. Connelly (1986) is an example of noninterrogation. Francis Connelly, a chronic schizophrenic, traveled from Boston to Denver because the "voice of God" commanded him to do so. He approached a police officer on a downtown Denver street "and, *without any prompting,* stated that he had murdered someone and wanted to talk about it." Connelly was immediately informed of his rights, but he insisted he wanted to speak. He gave a confession on the street, after two additional *Miranda* warnings, and appeared at that point to be mentally normal. Connelly's confession was held valid because it was a *purely voluntary statement* not barred by the Fifth Amendment. Justice Brennan dissented, joined by Justice Marshall, finding the admission of a statement by a person diagnosed with chronic paranoid schizophrenia to be a due process violation. "Today the Court denies Mr. Connelly his fundamental right to make a vital choice with a sane mind, involving a determination that could allow the State to deprive him of liberty or even life. This holding is unprecedented" (*Colorado v. Connelly*, p. 174).

The Use of Deception

The defendant in *Frazier v. Cupp* (1969) was arrested for a murder and interrogated by the police. After a time, an officer told the defendant that his cousin, who was also a suspect, had confessed. This was a lie. "Petitioner (Frazier) still was reluctant to talk, but after the officer sympathetically suggested that the victim had started a fight by making homosexual advances, petitioner began to spill out his story" (*Frazier v. Cupp*, pp. 737–38). The fact that the police officer told a flat lie in order to induce Frazier to confess was not even raised as an issue in the case. This is taken as precedent for the proposition that oral lies told by the police during interrogation do not violate due process or self-incrimination rights of a suspect.

Police are allowed to employ deception during interrogation, and the literature reports frequent instances of police deceitfully telling suspects that a confederate lied or that a fingerprint or blood test put them at the crime scene when that is not the case. The idea is that a truly guilty party may at that point confess, while a truly innocent person will deny such charges. A risk is that police lying, combined with forceful and prolonged interrogation, has also led innocent people to confess (see *Law in Society*).[49] Deception should not extend to express lies about the law.

Illinois v. Perkins (1990) upheld the use of a jail "plant"—an undercover agent—to obtain an incriminating statement from a suspect. Charlton, a state prisoner, told the police that Perkins admitted to committing a murder. Shortly after this, Perkins was transferred to a jail on an aggravated battery charge unrelated to the murder. An undercover agent, posing as an escaped convict, was admitted to the jail and placed in the same cell as Charlton and Perkins. The undercover officer won Perkins's confidence by suggesting they escape from the jail together, and he *initiated* Perkins's narration of the crime by asking him whether he had ever "done someone." Perkins then recounted the events of the murder in detail. Perkins was later charged with the murder and the agent testified at his murder trial to what Perkins said while in the jail cell. As Justice Kennedy dryly noted, the officer did not give Perkins *Miranda* warnings before the conversation in the jail cell. The Illinois courts held that because Perkins was *in correctional custody*, and the agent's statement was *indirect interrogation* under *Rhode Island v. Innis,* the rule of *Mathis v. United States* (1968) required that *Miranda* warnings be given.

The Supreme Court (8–1) disagreed. It held that the conversation was *not* interrogation because the essential *Miranda* ingredients of a "police-dominated atmosphere" and compulsion were missing. Perkins had no idea he was speaking to a police officer, and "[c]oercion is determined from the perspective of the suspect." The Court reasoned that for the purposes of *Miranda*, Perkins was not in custody. "We reject the argument that *Miranda* warnings are required whenever a suspect is in custody in a technical sense and converses with someone who happens to be a government agent. . . . [W]here a suspect does not know that he is conversing with a government agent, [mutually reinforcing psychological pressures that weaken a suspect's will] are not present."

Finally, Justice Kennedy noted that a certain amount of deception by law enforcement officers is allowed under *Miranda* as long as the deception does not become coercive. "Ploys to mislead a suspect or lull him into a false sense of security that do not rise to the level of compulsion or coercion to speak are not within *Miranda*'s concerns." The Court distinguished *Mathis* by noting that in that case, the defendant knew he was questioned by law enforcement officers. The majority opinion distinguished *Perkins* from *United States v. Henry* (1980) and *Maine v. Moulton* (1985) (discussed later) which were decided under the *Massiah* Sixth Amendment right to counsel rule. Those cases involved undercover agent–suspect interactions *after* the suspects had been *formally charged* and had attorneys. In *Perkins* no charges had been filed on the subject of the interrogation, so the Sixth Amendment did not come into play. *Perkins* allows the use of a valuable investigation tool, although law enforcement should be especially vigilant because inmate snitches have led to the conviction of many innocent persons.[50]

INTERROGATION IN A TIME OF TERROR

After 9/11 the propriety of using torture to elicit information from would-be terrorists became a lively topic. Harvard Law Professor Alan Dershowitz stoked controversy by suggesting that "torture warrants" would be appropriate in some cases, provoking a torrent of criticism.[51] The question is not entirely theoretical for detainees captured during the war in Afghanistan, held in overseas bases including Camp X-Ray in the American military base at Guantanamo, Cuba. An in-depth *Washington Post* story late in 2002 reported on Al Qaeda and Taliban commanders held at the U.S.-occupied Bagram air base in Afghanistan:

> Those who refuse to cooperate inside this secret CIA interrogation center are sometimes kept standing or kneeling for hours, in black hoods or spray-painted goggles, according to intelligence specialists familiar with CIA interrogation methods. At times they are held in awkward, painful positions and deprived of sleep with a 24-hour bombardment of lights—subject to what are known as "stress and duress" techniques.[52]

Officials are obviously not entirely forthcoming about practices in the tightly controlled and off-limits areas under military control outside of United States territory. A spokesman for the National Security Council stated that enemy combatants are treated humanely and "in a manner consistent with the principles of the Third Geneva Convention of 1949. . . . Other U.S. government officials, speaking on condition of anonymity, acknowledged that interrogators deprive some captives of sleep, a practice with ambiguous status in international law."[53] This report also indicated that after typically violent arrests, Al Qaeda suspects are handled by "take-down teams," including military special forces, FBI agents, CIA case officers, and local allies. Their goal is to disorient and intimidate the suspects on the way to detention facilities.

> According to Americans with direct knowledge and others who have witnessed the treatment, captives are often "softened up" by MPs and U.S. Army Special Forces troops who beat them up and confine them in tiny rooms. The alleged terrorists are commonly blindfolded and thrown into walls, bound in painful positions, subjected to loud noises and deprived of sleep. The tone of intimidation and fear is the beginning, they said, of a process of piercing a prisoner's resistance.
>
> The take-down teams often "package" prisoners for transport, fitting them with hoods and gags, and binding them to stretchers with duct tape.[54]

Are these techniques legal? Are they effective? In international law, torture is distinguished from "other cruel, inhuman or degrading treatment or punishment," or, in short, "inhuman treatment."[55] The line between torture and inhuman treatment is not exact. A decision of the European Court of Human Rights, *Ireland v. United Kingdom* (1980) stated that the "difference between torture and inhuman treatment 'derives principally from a difference in the intensity of the suffering inflicted.'"[56] Torture is absolutely prohibited for all reasons. The International Convention Against Torture states that "No exceptional circumstances whatsoever, whether a state of war or threat of war, internal political instability or any other public emergency, may be invoked as a justification of torture." The Convention enjoins states that sign the convention to "undertake to prevent" inhuman treatment but omits the "no exceptional circumstances" statement that applies to torture.[57] The United States is a signatory to the antitorture Convention, but the Senate's ratification has softened the international definition by providing that torture includes the *intent* to inflict

severe physical or mental pain and by narrowing the definition of mental pain. Commenting on the news reports of treatment of Al Qaeda prisoners at Bagram air base, Prof. John Parry concludes that if true, they "reveal that the United States is involved or implicated in a range of interrogation practices that are illegal under domestic and international law."[58] He nevertheless admits that in light of the secrecy and partial knowledge of the conditions of interrogation, any conclusions must be tentative.

Somewhat surprisingly, Prof. Parry argues that under the most limited circumstances torture or inhuman treatment, although illegal, might be justified, not for uncovering those responsible for past attacks or in order to destroy terrorist organizations, but to prevent imminent future attacks.[59] The commentator Christopher Hitchens makes the wise point that the "favourite experimental scenario—the man knows where the bomb is, put the hooks into him swiftly—is actually a contingency almost impossible to visualise. I certainly know of no such real-life case."[60] Further, he argues that the examples of North Ireland and Israel indicate that the political goals behind torture have not been successful. Knowledge of the use of torture in many countries demonstrates that the hideous and degrading practices—both to the torturers as well as the victims—has always come at the cost of deeply scarring societies that allow it. Prof. Parry suggests that the use of torture or at least of inhuman treatment in the post-9/11 questioning of captured combatants is an "open secret" in America—a "policy" adopted in secret by the executive and military branches, without the kind of judicial and legislative airing that is possible in a democracy, and was indeed conducted in Israel and led to the banning of such techniques.[61]

To condemn torture as illegal, immoral, and ineffective is not to say in the least that a program of interrogation of Al Qaeda and other likely terror suspects is unwarranted. On the contrary, CIA director George J. Tenet noted that overseas interrogations yielded significant information that led to the capture or killing of about one-third of the Al Qaeda leadership. "Many of these successes have come as a result of information gained during interrogations." Most significant, "Time, rather than technique, has produced the most helpful information," according to several national security and intelligence officials. "Using its global computer database, the CIA is able to quickly check leads from captives in one country with information divulged by captives in another." The United States now has information about the personalities of terrorist leaders, "how the networks are established, what they think are important targets, how they think we will react," said retired Army general Wayne Downing, a former deputy national security adviser for combating terrorism.[62] The conclusion is that intelligent, patient, and professionally directed interrogation is an important tool in the fight against terrorism. The use of torture and inhuman treatment may (or may not) assist the short-term goals of interrogation, but in the long run may prove self-defeating.

These issues are not entirely removed from courts in this country. Mohamed Rashed Daoud Al-'Owhali, a member of

Al Qaeda, was prosecuted in 2001 in a New York federal court for the 1998 bombing of the United States embassy in Nairobi, Kenya. He raised a self-incrimination claim to exclude statements made during his interrogation in Kenya by an FBI special agent and an assistant U.S. attorney who interrogated Al-'Owhali in Kenya. Federal Judge Leonard Sand ruled, in a case of first impression, that U.S. law enforcement personnel interrogating suspects abroad with the consent of the host country for purposes of prosecuting the suspects in United States courts must abide by *Miranda:*

> [A] principled, but realistic application of *Miranda*'s familiar warning/waiver framework, in the absence of a constitutionally-adequate alternative, is both necessary and appropriate under the Fifth Amendment. Only by doing so can courts meaningfully safeguard from governmental incursion the privilege against self-incrimination afforded to all criminal defendants in this country—wherever in the world they might initially be apprehended—while at the same time imposing manageable costs on the transnational investigatory capabilities of America's law enforcement personnel. . . .
>
> We therefore hold that a defendant's statements, if extracted by U.S. agents acting abroad, should be admitted as evidence at trial only if the Government demonstrates that the defendant was first advised of his rights and that he validly waived those rights.[63]

Judge Sand noted that under prior case law, the involvement of U.S. agents in questioning by foreign police personnel imposed a warnings requirement. He specifically held that on foreign soil, a suspect must be warned of the right to silence. "He must also be told that anything he does say may be used against him in a court in the United States or elsewhere. This much is un-controversial."[64] However, the need to warn a suspect that he has a right to the presence of counsel depends on whether that is a right that exists under the law of the host country.

> *Miranda* does not require law enforcement to promise that which they cannot guarantee or that which is in fact impossible to fulfill. No constitutional purpose is served by compelling law enforcement personnel to lie or mislead subjects of interrogation. Nor does *Miranda* mandate that U.S. agents compel a foreign sovereign to accept blind allegiance to American criminal procedure, at least when U.S. involvement in the foreign investigation is limited to mutual cooperation.[65]

Judge Sand rejected the prosecution's argument that giving the warnings, with modifications if necessary, would impose intolerable costs to international investigations with cooperating nations or America's ability to deter transnational crime. Indeed, the federal agents did read extensive warnings to Al-'Owhali. Relying on an "Overseas FBI Advice of Rights Form," Judge Sand held that the form was facially deficient because it only informed the suspect that he would have a right to counsel if he were in the United States, creating the impression that no such right was available in the country in which the interrogation occurred. Indeed, Kenyan law raised the possibility that counsel might be available at interrogation. As a result, five days of interrogation of Al-'Owhali was suppressed. Al-'Owhali indicated he wished to inculpate himself

in exchange for a guarantee that he be tried in the United States and statements taken on that day were admissible because they were preceded by an oral statement by a U.S. attorney that he could have an attorney present. Al-'Owhali got his wish. He and three others were found guilty of the embassy bombing in United States federal courts, just weeks after the 9/11 attacks. They were sentenced to life in prison without any chance of release.[66]

It is worth noting that this decision in *Bin Laden* accords with the theory put forth in *Chavez v. Martinez* (2003)—that *Miranda* rights and the right against self-incrimination are essentially exclusionary rules, violations of which occur at the time and place of introducing compelled statements. Therefore, the requirement of *Miranda* rights in Kenya is designed to protect a suspect's privilege against self-incrimination in New York.

QUESTIONING AFTER FORMAL CHARGING: THE SIXTH AMENDMENT

Pre-indictment interrogation of a suspect in police custody is limited by rules developed under the Due Process and the Self-Incrimination Clauses. Once the suspect is *formally charged*, whether by grand jury indictment, a prosecutor's information, or a magistrate's bindover after a preliminary examination, the legal picture changes. At this point, the criminal *prosecution* has begun and the Sixth Amendment right to counsel "attaches." Once charged, different and *more stringent constraints* on police questioning and eavesdropping apply. Post-indictment statements obtained by the police surreptitiously, or in disregard of the defendant's right to counsel, are excluded from the trial.

This rule was established in ***Massiah v. United States*** (1964). Winston Massiah, a crew member on a ship from South America, was charged in New York with transporting cocaine into the United States, *indicted,* and released on bail. While on bail, Massiah's codefendant, one Colson, agreed to cooperate with the government. A listening device was placed in Colson's car and transmitted evidence of Massiah making incriminating statements. A government agent testified to the incriminating statements at Massiah's trial. The Supreme Court held that introducing the testimony violated Massiah's *Sixth Amendment* right to counsel. The Court said that counsel has long been considered essential during the pretrial stages and held that secretly obtaining incriminating statements from an indicted defendant interfered with his right to legal representation.

Justice Stewart's majority opinion repeated his views in *Spano v. New York* (1959), a pre-*Miranda* confession case decided under the voluntariness test. He noted that obtaining a confession from an indicted defendant without notifying an attorney "might deny a defendant 'effective assistance of counsel at the only stage when legal aid and advice would help him'" (*Massiah*, quoting *Spano*). That is, secretly taping incriminating statements virtually convicts the defendant, in effect creating a critical stage where counsel has to be present. The same goes for open interviews between police or prosecutors and the defendant. If a plea arrangement is desired, the defendant's lawyer must be present.

Justice White, dissenting, believed there was no interference with Massiah's right to counsel. Unlike the Canon of Professional Ethics that prevents an *attorney* from interviewing an opposing party, he argued there is no ethical restriction on *investigators* contacting a defendant. "Law enforcement may have the elements of a contest about it, but it is not a game" (*Massiah v. United States*, p. 213, White, J., dissenting). Justice White's view failed to acknowledge that once the investigator speaks to or overhears a suspect and gets incriminating statements, the value of a lawyer's advice is nullified.

The *Massiah* area of law deals with similar functional issues to those that arise under *Miranda*, including the definition of interrogation and the validity of a waiver. Such questions arose in the notorious "Christian Burial Speech" case of *Brewer v. Williams* (1977). Williams, incidentally, was retried and found guilty. The Supreme Court upheld the second conviction under the doctrine of inevitable discovery in *Nix v. Williams* (1984) (*Williams II*, see Chapter 2).

—*Brewer v. Williams* Case & Comments —

• CASE & COMMENTS •

Brewer v. Williams
430 U.S. 387, 97 S.Ct. 1232, 51 L.Ed.2d 424 (1977)

MR. JUSTICE STEWART delivered the opinion of the Court.

I

* * * [Robert Williams, a mental hospital escapee, turned himself in to Davenport, Iowa, police for the murder of a ten-year-old girl at a Des Moines YMCA on December 26, 1968. **[a]** He was arrested, formally arraigned (charged) for the crime, and advised of his rights by the judge, who noted that Williams was represented by attorney McKnight in Des Moines and attorney Kelly in Davenport. McKnight spoke to Williams on the phone, in the presence of Des Moines police detective Leaming. He informed Williams that Des Moines officers would drive to Davenport, pick him up, and they would not interrogate him or mistreat him. He warned Williams not to talk to the officers about the crime. When Detective Leaming picked up Williams, Kelly, the Davenport lawyer, was denied a request to ride back to Des Moines with them. Kelly repeated to Detective Leaming that Williams was not to be questioned on the ride back.

On the 160-mile ride to Des Moines, Williams expressed no desire to be interrogated without his lawyer present; he said he would tell the whole story at the end of the trip. Leaming knew Williams was a deeply religious former mental patient and engaged him in a general discussion. Soon after the trip began, Leaming delivered the so-called] "Christian burial speech." Addressing Williams as "Reverend," the detective said: **[b]**

> "I want to give you something to think about while we're traveling down the road. . . . Number one, I want you to observe the weather conditions, it's raining, it's sleeting, it's freezing, driving is very treacherous, visibility is poor, it's going to be dark early this evening. They are predicting several inches of snow for tonight, and I feel that you yourself are the only person that knows where this little girl's body is, that you yourself have only been there once, and if you get a snow on top of it you yourself may be unable to find it. And, since we will be going right past the area on the way into Des Moines, I feel that we could stop and locate the body, that the parents of this little girl should be entitled to a Christian burial for the little girl who was snatched away from them on Christmas [E]ve and murdered. And I feel we should stop and locate it on the way in rather than waiting until morning and trying to come back out after a snow storm and possibly not being able to find it at all."

Williams asked Detective Leaming why he thought their route to Des Moines would be taking them past the girl's body, and Leaming responded that he knew the body was in the area of Mitchellville—a town they would be passing on the way to Des Moines. Leaming then stated: "I do not want you to answer me. I don't want to discuss it any further. Just think about it as we're riding down the road." **[c]**

As the car approached Grinnell, a town approximately 100 miles west of Davenport, Williams asked whether the police had found the victim's shoes. When Detective Leaming replied that he was unsure, Williams directed the officers to a service station where he said he had left the shoes; a search for them proved unsuccessful. As they continued towards Des Moines, Williams asked whether the police had found the blanket, and directed the officers to a rest area where he said he had disposed of the blanket. Nothing was found. The car continued towards Des Moines, and as it approached Mitchellville, Williams said that he would show the officers where the body was. He then directed the police to the body of Pamela Powers.

[a] Numerous facts are stated. Which are essential to the holding of the case?

[b] Do you think Detective Leaming made the speech deliberately to elicit incriminating evidence or just to pass the time?

[c] The call for silence at this point allowed Leaming's speech to work on Williams's mind.

• CASE & COMMENTS •

* * *

[This evidence was introduced and used to convict Williams of murder. The Iowa courts ruled that Williams waived his right to counsel, but the lower federal courts, on a writ of habeas corpus, ruled the evidence inadmissible on the alternative grounds of denial of assistance of counsel, a *Miranda* violation, and that his statements were involuntary.]

II

B

* * * [*Miranda v. Arizona* does not apply to this case.] For it is clear that the judgment before us must in any event be affirmed upon the ground that Williams was deprived of a different constitutional right—the right to the assistance of counsel. **[d]**

This right, guaranteed by the Sixth and Fourteenth amendments, is indispensable to the fair administration of our adversary system of criminal justice. [It is a] vital need at the pretrial stage. * * *

* * * Whatever else it may mean, the right to counsel granted by the Sixth and Fourteenth amendments means at least that a person is entitled to the help of a lawyer at or after the time that judicial proceedings have been initiated against him—"whether by way of formal charge, preliminary hearing, indictment, information, or arraignment." * * *

There can be no doubt in the present case that judicial proceedings [by arraignment] had been initiated against Williams before the start of the automobile ride from Davenport to Des Moines. * * *

There can be no serious doubt, either, that Detective Leaming deliberately and designedly set out to elicit information from Williams just as surely as—and perhaps more effectively than—if he had formally interrogated him. **[e]** Detective Leaming was fully aware before departing for Des Moines that Williams was being represented in Davenport by Kelly and in Des Moines by McKnight. Yet he purposely sought during Williams' isolation from his lawyers to obtain as much incriminating information as possible. Indeed, Detective Leaming conceded as much when he testified at Williams' trial. * * *

The circumstances of this case are thus constitutionally indistinguishable from those presented in *Massiah v. United States.* * * * **[f]**

That the incriminating statements were elicited surreptitiously in the *Massiah* case, and otherwise here, is constitutionally irrelevant. * * * Rather, the clear rule of *Massiah* is that once adversary proceedings have commenced against an individual, he has a right to legal representation when the government interrogates him. * * *

III

The Iowa courts recognized that Williams had been denied the constitutional right to the assistance of counsel. **[g]** They held, however, that he had waived that right during the course of the automobile trip from Davenport to Des Moines. * * *

[The Iowa courts applied a "totality of circumstances" test to ascertain whether Williams waived his right to counsel. The federal courts held that this was the wrong standard under the constitutional guarantee to counsel: There must be an affirmative waiver.]

* * *

The [lower federal courts] were also correct in their understanding of the proper standard to be applied in determining the question of waiver as a matter of federal constitutional law—that it was incumbent upon the State to prove "an intentional relinquishment or abandonment of a known right or privilege." * * * **[h]** We have said that the right to counsel does not depend upon a request by the defendant, * * * and that courts indulge in every reasonable presumption against waiver. * * * This strict standard applies equally to an alleged waiver of the right to counsel whether at trial or at a critical stage of pretrial proceedings. * * *

We conclude, finally, that the Court of Appeals was correct in holding that, judged by these standards, the record in this case falls far short of sustaining petitioner's burden. It is true that Williams had been informed of and appeared to understand his right to counsel. **[i]** But waiver requires not merely comprehension but relinquishment, and Williams' consistent reliance upon the advice of counsel in dealing with the authorities refutes any suggestion that he waived that right. [He spoke to both the Des Moines and Davenport attorneys numerous times before the trip.] Throughout, Williams was advised not to make any statements before seeing McKnight in Des Moines, and was assured that the police had agreed not to question him. His statements while in the car that he would tell the whole story *after*

[d] As noted in Chapter 6, the right to counsel attaches pretrial at *critical stages. Hamilton v. Alabama* (1961) required counsel at arraignment.

[e] Is this obvious? If so, is there any logic in Justice Blackmun's dissent? Should the Supreme Court allow blatant violations of rights if the crime is horrible?

[f] This clarifies the *Massiah* ruling. It is, essentially, a right to counsel case, and is not limited to cases where government agents eavesdrop.

[g] Part III deals with whether Williams properly waived his right to counsel.

[h] This is the test of *Johnson v. Zerbst* (1938), which is the test for waiver of counsel at trial.

[i] The state had the burden of proof that Williams voluntarily waived his right to counsel. The majority thinks the burden was not met. Compare this to Justice White's dissent. Should Det. Leaming have informed Williams of his right to counsel, and given him the chance to waive that right?

seeing McKnight in Des Moines were the clearest expressions by Williams himself that he desired the presence of an attorney before any interrogation took place. But even before making these statements, Williams had effectively asserted his right to counsel by having secured attorneys at both ends of the automobile trip, both of whom, acting as his agents, had made clear to the police that no interrogation was to occur during the journey. Williams knew of that agreement and, particularly in view of his consistent reliance on counsel, there is no basis for concluding that he disavowed it.

Detective Leaming proceeded to elicit incriminating statements from Williams. Leaming did not preface this effort by telling Williams that he had a right to the presence of a lawyer, and made no effort at all to ascertain whether Williams wished to relinquish that right. The circumstances of record in this case thus provide no reasonable basis for finding that Williams waived his right to the assistance of counsel.

The Court of Appeals did not hold, nor do we, that under the circumstances of this case Williams *could not,* without notice to counsel, have waived his rights under the Sixth and Fourteenth amendments. It only held, as do we, that he did not.

IV

The crime of which Williams was convicted was senseless and brutal, calling for swift and energetic action by the police to apprehend the perpetrator and gather evidence with which he could be convicted. **[j]** No mission of law enforcement officials is more important. Yet, "[d]isinterested zeal for the public good does not assure either wisdom or right in the methods it pursues." * * * Although we do not lightly affirm the issuance of a writ of habeas corpus in this case, so clear a violation of the Sixth and Fourteenth amendments as here occurred cannot be condoned. The pressures on state executive and judicial officers charged with the administration of the criminal law are great, especially when the crime is murder and the victim a small child. But it is precisely the predictability of those pressures that makes imperative a resolute loyalty to the guarantees that the Constitution extends to us all.

The judgment of the Court of Appeals is affirmed.

It is so ordered.

[Justices Marshall, Powell, and Stevens concurred in separate opinions.]

MR. CHIEF JUSTICE BURGER, dissenting.

The result in this case ought to be intolerable in any society which purports to call itself an organized society. **[k]** It continues the Court—by the narrowest margin—on the much-criticized course of punishing the public for the mistakes and misdeeds of law enforcement officers, instead of punishing the officer directly, if in fact he is guilty of wrongdoing. It mechanically and blindly keeps reliable evidence from juries whether the claimed constitutional violation involves gross police misconduct or honest human error.

* * *

[Further in his opinion the CHIEF JUSTICE argued that the exclusionary rule should not apply to non-egregious police conduct.]

MR. JUSTICE WHITE, with whom MR. JUSTICE BLACKMUN and MR. JUSTICE REHN-QUIST join, dissenting.

* * *

Respondent relinquished his right not to talk to the police about his crime when the car approached the place where he had hidden the victim's clothes. Men usually intend to do what they do, and there is nothing in the record to support the proposition that respondent's decision to talk was anything but an exercise of his own free will. **[l]** Apparently, without any prodding from the officers, respondent—who had earlier said that he would tell the whole story when he arrived in Des Moines—spontaneously changed his mind about the timing of his disclosures when the car approached the places where he had hidden the evidence. However, even if his statements were influenced by Detective Leaming's above-quoted statement, respondent's decision to talk in the absence of counsel can hardly be viewed as the product of an overborne will. The statement by Leaming was not coercive; it was accompanied by a request that respondent not respond to it; and it was delivered hours before respondent decided to make any statement. Respondent's waiver was thus knowing and intentional.

* * *

[j] The majority refuses to "bend the rules" of constitutional rights to gain a conviction in a terrible crime. Compare the remarks of Chief Justice Burger.

[k] This is political "tough on crime" rhetoric. Does it belong in a Supreme Court opinion? Do suspects have too many rights? Can this rhetoric lead to the permanent loss of rights?

[l] What is Justice White's logic? Can this logic make legal any incriminating statement except those obtained by torture? Was Williams's admission spontaneous?

• CASE & COMMENTS •

MR. JUSTICE BLACKMUN, with whom MR. JUSTICE WHITE and MR. JUSTICE REHN-QUIST join, dissenting.

* * *

What the Court chooses to do here, and with which I disagree, is to hold that respondent Williams' situation was in the mold of *Massiah v. United States,* that is, that it was dominated by a denial to Williams of his Sixth Amendment right to counsel after criminal proceedings had been instituted against him. **[m]** The Court rules that the Sixth Amendment was violated because Detective Leaming "purposely sought during Williams' isolation from his lawyers to obtain as much incriminating information as possible." I cannot regard that as unconstitutional *per se.*

First, the police did not deliberately seek to isolate Williams from his lawyers so as to deprive him of the assistance of counsel. **[n]** * * * The isolation in this case was a necessary incident of transporting Williams to the county where the crime was committed.

Second, Leaming's purpose was not solely to obtain incriminating evidence. The victim had been missing for only two days, and the police could not be certain that she was dead. Leaming, of course, and in accord with his duty, was "hoping to find out where that little girl was," * * * but such motivation does not equate with an intention to evade the Sixth Amendment. * * *

Third, not every attempt to elicit information should be regarded as "tantamount to interrogation." * * * **[o]** I am not persuaded that Leaming's observations and comments, made as the police car traversed the snowy and slippery miles between Davenport and Des Moines that winter afternoon, were an interrogation, direct or subtle, of Williams. * * * In summary, it seems to me that the Court is holding that *Massiah* is violated whenever police engage in any conduct, in the absence of counsel, with the subjective desire to obtain information from a suspect after arraignment. Such a rule is far too broad. Persons in custody frequently volunteer statements in response to stimuli other than interrogation. * * * When there is no interrogation, such statements should be admissible as long as they are truly voluntary. * * *

* * *

[m] A question not settled by this case is whether it is ever possible for police to interview a suspect without his or her lawyer present after formal charges.

[n] Do the first two points made by Justice Blackmun pass the "giggle test"?

[o] Like *Rhode Island v. Innis* and *Arizona v. Mauro* the case is also about the functional equivalent of interrogation. If Det. Leaming's speech is not the functional equivalent, what is?

THE *MASSIAH* RIGHT AFTER *BREWER V. WILLIAMS*
The Supreme Court found in favor of the defendants in **Michigan v. Jackson** (1986) A defendant who requests a lawyer at arraignment has invoked his right to counsel, and police may not initiate interrogation until counsel has been made available to the suspect. This seemed to extend the rule of *Edwards v. Arizona* (1981) to the Sixth Amendment (a questioned suspect who asks for a lawyer under *Miranda* cannot be interrogated without counsel present). However, the Court shrunk this extension of a defendant's Sixth Amendment rights in the following cases.

Patterson v. Illinois (1988) resolved an issue not completely answered in *Brewer v. Williams*. It held that an indicted defendant who is read *Miranda* warnings may validly waive his right to counsel. Under some circumstances, then, a charged defendant can speak to police without an attorney present, as long as there is an *express* waiver of the right to counsel. Dissenters in *Patterson* wanted the Court to impose additional warnings to the four required by *Miranda* for suspects who have been formally charged, but the majority refused to do so. Justice Stevens, dissenting in *Patterson*, raised a different point: that it is *unethical* for investigators or prosecutors during trial preparation to go behind the backs of their adversaries and communicate with a defendant. In his view,

since it is a breach of professional ethics for an *attorney* to communicate with an opposing party without the knowledge of opposing counsel, the *Massiah* rule also "suggest[s] that law enforcement personnel may not bypass counsel in favor of direct communications with an accused." The majority did not accede to this view.

The Court further limited *Massiah* rights in **McNeil v. Wisconsin** (1991). A defendant who invokes the right to counsel for one crime (and cannot be questioned about it) is not automatically protected against police questioning for another crime. The Court held that the Sixth Amendment right to counsel is *offense-specific*, unlike the right to counsel created by the Supreme Court in *Miranda* to protect Fifth Amendment rights. The reason for this distinction is that the purpose of the Sixth Amendment right to counsel is to protect the unaided layperson at a critical confrontation. The purpose of the *Miranda-Edwards* rule is to protect a suspect's desire to deal with police only through counsel.

A strong example of Rehnquist Court activist-conservative reasoning is found in **Michigan v. Harvey** (1990), which held that a statement taken in violation of one's *Massiah* rights under *Michigan v. Jackson* can be used at a trial to *impeach* the defendant should he or she choose to testify. Since a violation of *Jackson* seems to be a direct violation of a suspect's Sixth

Amendment rights, it is difficult to see how a statement gotten by a blatant violation of *Massiah* and *Jackson* could be used in any proceeding. Chief Justice Rehnquist, writing for the majority, achieved this goal by muddying the clear distinction between Fifth and Sixth amendment rights, which Justice Potter Stewart had worked to achieve in cases like *Spano, Massiah,* and *Brewer v. Williams*. Rehnquist's opinion minimized the difference between *Miranda* and *Massiah*, arguing that although *Michigan v. Jackson* "is based on the Sixth Amendment" . . . its roots lie in this Court's decisions in *Miranda v. Arizona* and succeeding cases." It is difficult to comprehend the cause and effect since *Massiah* (1964) *preceded Miranda* (1966) by two years. The Court reasoned that *Michigan v. Jackson* borrowed its bright-line rule from *Edwards v. Arizona,* a *Miranda* case. By this reasoning, the Court held that the rights announced in *Michigan v. Jackson* were mere *prophylactic rules* and so could be used to impeach the defendant.

Justice Stevens dissented (joined by Justices Brennan, Marshall, and Blackmun). He stated that the right to counsel is much *more pervasive* than other rights "because it affects the ability of the accused to assert any other rights he may have." Because of this, rules for waiving counsel are extremely stringent. Further, he said that the majority argument was a ploy to confuse the true basis of a *Massiah* right. In this case, Harvey's right to see his lawyer was violated by a police officer who told a confused Harvey that he didn't have to see his lawyer. Stevens virtually accused the majority's recharacterization of the facts of this case as one "involving nothing more than the violation of a 'prophylactic' rule" as a smokescreen that undermined the rule of *Massiah* and a suspect's primary right to counsel.

Justice Stevens added a practical reason for excluding all use of evidence obtained in violation of *Massiah* rights:

> The police would have everything to gain and nothing to lose by repeatedly visiting with the defendant and seeking to elicit as many comments as possible about the pending trial. Knowledge that such conversations could not be used affirmatively would not detract from the State's interest in obtaining them for their value as impeachment evidence.

Michigan v. Harvey is an example of judicial decision making that reflects the Crime Control over the Due Process Model of criminal justice (discussed in Chapter 1).

The Court may be considering the creation of another *Miranda*-type exception in the *Massiah* area (***Fellers v. United States,*** 2004). Police armed with an arrest warrant came to the home of John J. Fellers, who had been *indicted* for a drug-dealing conspiracy. In a discussion during the arrest police deliberately elicited incriminating statements. Later, at the station house, Fellers was read his rights under *Miranda* and *Patterson v. Illinois*. The lower courts erroneously treated the case as coming under *Miranda*. The Court of Appeals said that *Patterson* was not applicable, because Fellers was not interrogated in his home. The Supreme Court made it clear that under *Massiah* the applicable standard was not whether police interrogated a suspect but whether they *deliberately elicited* a statement. Because Fellers had been indicted, the police behavior

violated his right to counsel under the Sixth Amendment and the in-home statement had to be suppressed. The Court of Appeals further applied the *Elstad* exception to this case, ruling that his waiver of counsel at the station house "cured" any *Miranda* violation in the home. The Court reversed and remanded the case, requesting that the Circuit Court examine the issue of "whether the rationale of *Elstad* applies when a suspect makes incriminating statements after a knowing and voluntary waiver of his right to counsel notwithstanding earlier police questioning in violation of Sixth Amendment standards." Any future ruling in *Fellers* may depend in part on the decision that the Court will make in regard to an *Elstad* issue currently before it in *Missouri v. Seibert* (discussed above).

Undercover Policing and the Right to Counsel

In *Illinois v. Perkins* (1990), discussed earlier, the Court allowed undercover policing to proceed without warning individuals that they were suspects, because incriminating statements made to false friends, even in jail, are not compelled. This kind of deception is not a substitute for coercion. *Massiah,* on the other hand, seems to rule out this kind of deception once a person has been formally charged and is clothed with the right to counsel. The Court has maintained, but softened, the *Massiah* rule to some degree when agents or informants are planted in a suspect's jail cell to listen for incriminating statements.

JAIL CELL CASES   An incriminating statement made by a suspect in a jail cell to an informant in ***United States v. Henry*** (1980) was ruled inadmissible as a *Massiah* violation because the informant "*deliberately elicited*" the statement from Henry by engaging in conversations that resulted in the incriminating statement. On the other hand, in ***Kuhlman v. Wilson*** (1986) a jail informant placed in a cell with Wilson did not deliberately elicit the incriminating evidence. The informant did not initiate any conversations about the crime but "only listened" to Wilson and took notes later. The rule, then, is that the police can place a *passive listener* in a cell who acts like a *listening device,* which is allowable in a jail setting, as long as the cellmate does not start conversations that are likely to lead the suspect to incriminate himself. This ruling, favorable to the prosecution, does not take into account the human tendency of an inmate to talk to a cellmate, increasing the likelihood of making incriminating statements.

UNDERCOVER INFORMANT   *Maine v. Moulton* (1985) is factually similar to *Massiah* and restates the jail case rules in the context of undercover policing. Colson, a codefendant of Moulton, agreed to obtain information for the police in return for the state dropping charges against him.[67] Both Moulton and Colson, out on bail, got together to *plan trial strategy* during which Moulton made incriminating statements. The Supreme Court held that the statements were barred by the *Massiah* rule:

> The Sixth Amendment guarantees the accused, at least after the initiation of formal charges, the right to rely on counsel as a

'medium' between him and the State. . . . [T]his guarantee includes the State's affirmative obligation not to act in a manner that circumvents the protections accorded the accused by invoking this right. . . . Thus, the Sixth Amendment is not violated whenever—by luck or happenstance—the State obtains incriminating statements from the accused after the right to counsel has attached. . . . However, *knowing exploitation* by the State of an opportunity to confront the accused without counsel being present is as much a breach of the State's obligation not to circumvent the right to the assistance of counsel as the intentional creation of such an opportunity. (*Maine v. Moulton,* 1985, emphasis added)

The majority agreed that handing up an indictment does not prevent the police from continuing to investigate a case or from investigating the defendant for other crimes. However, they must not obtain evidence surreptitiously from an indicted defendant in a way that cuts the defendant off from the defense lawyer. Therefore, the majority made it clear that if the police are investigating a suspect for Crime B, and the suspect has already been indicted for Crime A, an undercover agent may investigate the suspect for Crime B for which the suspect has not been charged. Evidence obtained by the undercover agent pertaining to Crime A may not be admitted. Only evidence for the new crime (Crime B) is admissible.

LAW IN SOCIETY

THE SOCIAL REALITY OF CONFESSIONS

THE ACCEPTANCE OF *MIRANDA*

Despite its bitter reception by police and others in 1966, the ruling has since been accepted by the legal and law enforcement communities. Chief Justice Warren Burger stated in 1980, "The meaning of *Miranda* has become reasonably clear and law enforcement practices have adjusted to its strictures; I would neither overrule *Miranda,* disparage it, nor extend it at this late date" (*Rhode Island v. Innis,* 1980). This signaled that *Miranda*'s opponents could now live with it, in part because the case did not undermine effective policing. Chief Justice Burger also wanted to avoid another round of appeals designed to clarify a major legal revolution in established and well-known confessions rules.

Many police see *Miranda,* and the study of constitutional law in general, as enhancing the professional status of policing. Some officers accept that without legal strictures, their crime-fighting behavior could turn to lawlessness. Others have internalized the *Miranda* rules and are happy to apply them to the extent that they accord with what the officers believe is "fair and decent" behavior.[68] In this light, it is important to be clear that "*Miranda* has not failed to achieve its limited goals"—which was *not* to eliminate interrogation and confessions, or completely equalize the power relationship between a suspect and the police, or lower confession rates. *Miranda* was designed to reduce the *compulsion* of the interrogation process. Understanding this, police are happy to follow the let-

ter of the *Miranda* decision if the goals of law enforcement can be generally realized.[69] This has resulted in police *adaptation* to the *Miranda* requirements.

POLICE INTERROGATION TODAY: ADAPTING TO *MIRANDA*

What do we know about how custodial interrogation is conducted? "During the first few years after *Miranda,* empirical studies suggested that *Miranda*'s impact was minimal."[70] Few studies of *Miranda*'s effect appeared for some time, but since 1996, several have enlarged our understanding of *Miranda* and some have generated a lively debate over the "costs" to law enforcement of the need to warn interrogated suspects of their rights.

HOW ARE INTERROGATIONS CONDUCTED? As a routine practice, "third degree" tactics—the use and threats of beatings—have disappeared as police interrogation techniques. Police today use sophisticated psychological techniques to "persuade" recalcitrant defendants to admit their guilt. A study by Richard Leo of 182 interrogations observed in three California police departments in 1992 and 1993 provided a picture of contemporary interrogation. Most of the suspects were young working-class African American males. Seventy percent of the primary detectives conducting the questioning were white and 90 percent were males. In 69 percent of the cases, interrogation was conducted by one officer; and in 31 percent, two officers interrogated. Forty-three percent of the cases were for robberies; 24 percent were for assault; 12 percent were for homicide; and the other 21 percent were for burglaries, thefts, and other crimes.

Only 21 percent of the suspects invoked their *Miranda* rights after they were read. Suspects with prior felony records invoked their rights more often (30 percent) than those with no record (8 percent) or prior misdemeanor involvement (11 percent) in the criminal justice system. Thirty-six percent of the suspects made no incriminating statement; 22 percent made an incriminating statement; 18 percent made a partial admission; and 24 percent made a full confession. Thirty-five percent of the interrogations lasted less than thirty minutes; 36 percent lasted thirty to sixty minutes; 21 percent lasted for one to two hours; and 8 percent lasted more than two hours.[71] Leo concluded that under legal criteria, only four out of 182 cases, or 2 percent, "rose to the level of 'coercion.'"[72]

Professor Leo provides six in-depth vignettes from the cases he observed. In each, the officers use a variety of *psychological ploys* to get confessions. A suspect accused of smashing in a car window and stealing its contents was told that several witnesses saw him do this. "The detective was, of course, fabricating evidence against the suspect, but the suspect did not know this."[73] The interrogation lasted more than an hour; the suspect admitted breaking into the car and, on a plea bargain, received a one-year sentence. Another suspect, a twenty-one-year-old Hispanic male, was accused of kidnapping a fourteen-year-old girl from a party and brutally raping and anally and orally sodomizing her before returning the girl to the party with a warning that he would shoot her if she spoke. The victim immediately told a friend, who called the police. A swift medical examination confirmed severe physical injury. During the interrogation, the detective, a Hispanic female, "went from somewhat formal language (which it appeared he didn't understand) to slang, crude even profane language to ask him questions about the sexual acts." He appeared nervous, but "she quickly put her hand on his in a friendly gesture, smiled, and told him to trust her, that she wouldn't be embarrassed by anything he told her. . . ." The suspect invoked counsel, ending the interrogation after thirty-four minutes. He pled guilty to statutory rape and received a one-month sentence plus four years of "formal probation."[74] This indicates that failure to obtain confessions in some cases may allow guilty parties to go free or receive less than adequate punishment.

WHY DO SUSPECTS WAIVE THEIR MIRANDA RIGHTS?
Observations of police interrogation practices show that a variety of psychological methods are used to get suspects to talk. If the police follow the spirit of Miranda, then they would at least deliver the warnings in a neutral way at the beginning of an interrogation session. Some do. But many others de-emphasize the importance of Miranda waivers in several ways. They may indicate that the waiver is an unimportant bureaucratic detail (a mere formality) or build rapport and engage in small talk before mentioning Miranda. Another "selling" technique is to stress the importance of the suspect "telling his side of the story."[75] A more insidious technique is to weave the warnings into questions and answers over a long period of time so that the suspect waives rights, and after this is read the warnings in a block—a method dubbed "participating Miranda" by Professors Peter Lewis and Harry Allen.[76]

Leo describes the process by characterizing police interrogation as a "confidence game." Like a "con man," or perhaps any good salesperson, the police interrogator must psychologically "size up" and figure out how to manipulate the suspect. This requires knowledge of the crime, the victim, and the suspect. Unlike a true confidence man, a police interrogator cannot select or "qualify" the "mark." The officer "cultivates" the suspect by projecting a friendly and sincere image, offering coffee, and engaging in light banter. Simultaneously, the barren interrogation room, the thick case folder with the suspect's name prominently attached, and various interrogation techniques, such as pitting the suspect against a shadowy but fearsome prosecutor or judge and jury, are designed to raise the suspect's anxiety. The police frame their questions with admonitions about telling the truth; telling the truth will "make it go better" for the suspect and make him feel better. To elicit a confession, the police draw on various techniques of persuasion, deception, and neutralization: contradicting false statements, minimizing the immoral nature of what was done, posing false statements, and many more. Finally, the officers, knowing that the confessions will be attacked once defense lawyers come into the

case, "cool the mark" by complimenting the suspect for the honesty and cooperation and maintaining a neutral tone and positive reaction to the defendant to the end.[77]

INTERROGATION/CONFESSIONS "OUTSIDE" MIRANDA
As noted in the body of this chapter, a troubling interrogation practice, known as interrogation "outside Miranda," has become prevalent in some places, whereby police deliberately violate a suspect's Miranda rights in order to gain the collateral use of evidence. The Supreme Court's decisions will help determine the extent of the practice. The existence of this practice reveals the need for vigilance in protecting individual rights.[78]

THE BENEFITS OF MIRANDA
Professor Leo asserts that Miranda has had four positive long-range social effects. In his view, conservative critics of the 1980s were wrong to contend that Miranda has undermined effective law enforcement, and liberals have been shortsighted in saying that Miranda's effects have been more symbolic than real. (1) "Miranda has exercised a civilizing influence on police behavior inside the interrogation room" by accelerating a process that was in place in 1966. This has helped to make the police more professional by establishing objective and written standards of police behavior. As a result, "American police in the last thirty years have, by necessity, become more solicitous of suspects' rights, more respectful of their dignity, and more concerned with their welfare inside the interrogation room." (2) Miranda "has transformed the culture—the shared norms, values and attitudes—of police . . . by fundamentally re-framing how police talk and think about the process of custodial interrogation." (3) Miranda has increased public awareness of constitutional rights. (4) "Miranda has inspired police to develop more specialized, more sophisticated and seemingly more effective interrogation techniques with which to elicit inculpatory statements from custodial suspects." Thus, Miranda is part of a larger and longer term trend in Western society in which government power is "more controlling of its subjects" but at the same time "more subject to control itself legal institutions, professional standards, and social norms."[79]

IMPROVING MIRANDA: VIDEOTAPING
This does not mean that police interrogation is without its problems. As will be explored later, numerous false confessions raise concerns about how interrogation is conducted. To ensure that interrogation becomes more professional and effective, Professor Leo, borrowing from a 1993 Department of Justice study, has urged that courts mandate the videotaping of interrogations as a matter of due process.[80] There are many good reasons for videotaping interrogations: (1) It creates an "objective, reviewable record of custodial questioning that protects [police] against false accusations—accusations such as "softening up" a suspect prior to Miranda, failing to correctly read the Miranda warnings, or eliciting a confession through improper inducements.'

(2) It is "likely to improve the quality of police work and thus contribute to more professional and more effective interrogation practices. Officers and detectives who know they will be videotaped are more likely to prepare their strategies beforehand and to be more self-conscious about their conduct during questioning." (3) Tapes can be used for training. (4) Videotaping can increase law enforcement effectiveness, for it "facilitates the identification, prosecution, and conviction of guilty offenders." For example, it "preserves the details of a suspect's statement that may not have been initially recorded in a detective's notes but may subsequently become important." (5) Videotapes are believed to have helped prosecutors negotiate a higher percentage of guilty pleas and obtain longer sentences because they provide "a more complete record with which to better assess the state's case against the accused" including "the demeanor and sophistication of the suspect." As a result, some defense attorneys oppose videotaping confessions because it makes it more difficult to challenge the stories of detectives, although high-caseload public defenders appreciate videotapes because they help them to more quickly cut through clients' lies so as to produce accurate guilty pleas more quickly.

WHY DO INNOCENT PEOPLE CONFESS?

The English common law harbors a traditional distrust of confessions (found in the rule that uncorroborated confessions are inadmissible in court) out of fear that psychological manipulation would induce innocent persons to confess. Although it seems improbable that police get innocent parties to confess without using force, recent research indicates that this happens *frequently* through the use of modern "psychological interrogation." The Innocence Project reports that false confessions were present in 22 percent of their first seventy-four exonerations.[81] A classic study of 350 miscarriages of justice in capital cases concluded that 14 percent resulted from false confessions.[82] A recent study by Professors Drizin and Leo review in detail one-hundred and twenty-five *proven* false confessions since 1970, with most occurring in the 1990s.[83] As no official records are kept, it is likely that more such cases have occurred.

HOW INNOCENT PEOPLE CONFESS Recent scholarship by Professors Richard Ofshe and Richard Leo, drawing on prior scholarship regarding false confessions and on their own inquiry, has explored many cases of false confessions. In one article, they review sixty cases of allegedly false confessions, and after examining available court and news media records, classify them into (1) thirty-four confessions that were proven false, (2) eighteen highly probable false confessions, and (3) eight probable false confessions.[84] In other writings, Ofshe and Leo acknowledge that the actual number of false confessions cannot be known because (a) police do not keep complete records of interrogations, making it difficult to evaluate the reliability of the interrogation or whether there was any undue pressure; (b) no criminal justice agency keeps records or collects statistics on the number or frequency of interrogations, and (c) many cases of false confession are not reported.[85] Nevertheless, there are so many documented cases just in the past decade that false confessions must be seen as an important policy area to be addressed.[86]

Ofshe and Leo have intensively explored false confessions in a lengthy article, which relies heavily on field data—transcripts of both true and false confessions—to display how certain processes lead to false confessions by the innocent.[87] They classify four types of false confessions. (1) *Stress-Compliant False Confessions*. The modern psychological interrogation is stressful by design and for some individuals—especially those with an abnormal reactivity to stress, who may be phobic, or with intellectual limitations who cope by becoming submissive—the pressure requires alleviation by saying, "I did it." (2) *Coerced-Compliant False Confessions*. This often results from the familiar "accident scenario technique," or "maximization/minimization." This is a subtle promise and threat (traditionally outlawed in England) by which the police convince the suspect that what he did was not all that serious, because there is a legal excuse or mitigation and that by confessing, he will receive lenient treatment. (3) and (4) *Voluntary and Involuntary Persuaded False Confessions*. These are instances where, after a good deal of interviewing and subtle or not-so-subtle badgering, the innocent person becomes so confused that confidence in his own memory is shattered. He reports that despite no overt memory of committing the crime, he agrees that the interrogators' recitation of events and (fabricated) "facts" must mean he is guilty.[88]

Ofshe and Leo do not suggest that confessions be abolished. They recommend safeguards because the process by which the innocent confess is very close to the process by which investigators obtain confessions from guilty persons. The steps by which confessions are obtained in the era of psychological interrogation show why this is so. Detectives have two categories of suspects, "likely suspects, for whom there exists solid evidence suggesting their guilt; and possible suspects, which includes everyone whose name comes up during an investigation." Interrogation is superficially the same for both types. The detective may begin with an interview rather than interrogation format, especially for a possible suspect, to gain rapport and lull the interviewee into forgetting the adversarial nature of the encounter. Once *Miranda* warnings are read, neither "an innocent nor a guilty party is likely to appreciate the full significance of the . . . warnings." The innocent person thinks that he or she has nothing to hide. At that point, the tone and content of the interaction become confrontational and demanding. To get the suspect to say, "I did it," an investigator must strongly reject denials and insist that objective evidence points to guilt. At this point, a truly innocent person "is likely to experience considerable shock and disorientation . . . because he is wholly unprepared for the confrontation and accusations that are the core of the process, and will not understand how an investigator could possibly suspect him." The tragedy of wrongful confessions occurs because the response to questioning by the guilty and the innocent "are often indistinguishable to an investigator." The investigator must now convince the suspect that his arrest is imminent and get the suspect to make an admission—get him to say, "I did it." Once this watershed is crossed, the investigator then moves the process toward obtaining a full confession.[89]

AN EXAMPLE OF A FALSE CONFESSION In 1986 Thomas F. Sawyer, a thirty-six-year-old groundskeeper, was charged with the murder of his next-door neighbor, a single twenty-five-year-old woman, in Clearwater, Florida, on the basis of a confession. Janet Staschak was found strangled, nude, facedown on her bed with wire and tape marks on her ankles. Sawyer, a recovering alcoholic, was extremely shy, suffered from bouts of anxiety, and often turned red and sweated profusely in ordinary social situations. When Sawyer was initially questioned by police officers, they noted his odd mannerisms and targeted him as a suspect. However, hair and blood samples obtained from Sawyer before his interrogation did not match samples found on the dead woman.

Although there was no corroborating evidence, two Clearwater detectives, John Dean and Peter Fire, obtained a confession from Sawyer. Before, during, and after the interrogation, Sawyer maintained his innocence. Then, how or why would an innocent person confess?[90]

Understanding Sawyer's confession in this case is aided by the transcript of what occurred during the entire taped sixteen-hour interrogation session, which stretched from 4:00 P.M. to 8:00 A.M., with time out for a ninety-minute nap. After several hours of questioning, the detectives asked Sawyer to pretend he was a police officer and to suggest methods and motives for the crime. Later during the questioning, they would take his statements and say that he knew too much about the crime to have guessed about the state of the room and the way in which the crime was carried out. Yet police officers had for some time before the questioning been back and forth between Sawyer's and Staschak's apartments, and he may have heard a good deal about the crime; furthermore, the transcript, at this point, included a good deal of prompting by the detectives.

At about 8:00 P.M., four hours after the questioning began in a small room at the police station, the officers warned Sawyer of his rights, an example of "participating *Miranda*":

DEAN: All right. We got this squared away. Now Tom, because this is a criminal investigation, obviously, what we've been doing—There's a new phase we have to enter into now. And before I do that, I have to read you your rights. You watch television. You know. So just let me read you these. You have the right to remain silent. Do you understand that?

SAWYER: Uh-huh.

DEAN: Anything you say can and will be used against you in a court of law. Do you understand that? *[Sawyer nods.]*

FIRE: You got to go, "yes."

SAWYER: Yes.

FIRE: Okay.

DEAN: You have the right to talk to a lawyer—

FIRE: No, wait a minute. You don't *have* to say yes. You answer the way you want to answer, but we have to hear you. I know you're saying yes with your nod, okay? You nodded yes, but—Okay?

SAWYER: Yeah. Okay.

DEAN: You have the right to talk to a lawyer. Have him present with you while you are being questioned. Do you understand that?

SAWYER: Yes.

DEAN: If you can't afford to hire a lawyer, one will be appointed to represent you before any questioning if you wish. Do you understand that?

SAWYER: Say it again. I wasn't—

DEAN: Okay. If you cannot afford to hire a lawyer, one will be appointed to represent you before any questioning if you wish. Do you understand that?

SAWYER: Yes.

DEAN: Okay. You can decide at any time to exercise your rights and not answer any questions or make any statements. Do you understand that?

SAWYER: Yes.

DEAN: Okay.

FIRE: Okay. So you understand everything. Okay. Listen, Tom. John and I—we've been talking to you all evening about this. Right? Okay? So why don't you tell us what happened. Tell us what happened.

          [This was followed by continuous denials by Sawyer and insistent statements by Dean and Fire that Sawyer was guilty.]

SAWYER: I didn't do it.

FIRE: Tommy, it's not the truth.

SAWYER: Yes, it is.

FIRE: No it's not. Tom. Tell me the truth. Tell me what happened. It was an accident, Tom. I know it was. I know it was an accident. I need for you to tell me what happened.

SAWYER: I was never there. I never did it.

FIRE: Tom.

SAWYER: I'll look you in the eye and say that all night.

FIRE: I know, we got all night.

Throughout the session, Sawyer believed that his hair samples matched those found on Janet Staschak, and that a polygraph test indicated he was lying.[91] Playing on this, the detectives suggested to Sawyer that he had "blacked out" during the crime and committed it, although he did not remember anything. Throughout the session, Dean and Fire told Sawyer that he was an intelligent and good person; that the crime was not premeditated; that he would feel a great sense of relief if he confessed. Worn down, Sawyer finally confessed not only to a murder, but also to having raped Janet Staschak when in fact there was no physical evidence of sexual penetration. Many of the facts he admitted to were stated only after several false starts with persistent prompting by Fire and Dean. He made his confession conditional on the physical evidence: "The only reason I believe I did it is if my hairs were in her car and on her body and in her apartment."

At the preliminary examination, the trial court, lacking corroborating physical evidence, threw out the confession in a detailed decision. By fastening onto the closest possible suspect, the police failed to diligently follow up possible leads. Staschak had taken in roommates to help pay her rent; at first a heterosexual couple who were dealing drugs and later a homosexual couple. Both pairs had been evicted by her, and both had left her in some fear. By fastening on Sawyer, the Clearwater officers likely let the real culprits escape. The trial judge described the interrogation session as an intellectual wrestling match. The Florida Court of Appeals agreed and upheld the suppression of the confession.

PREVENTING FALSE CONFESSIONS As noted above, Ofshe and Leo do not recommend abolishing police interrogation. They do have recommendations to lessen the possibility of false confessions. One recommendation, discussed earlier, is that custodial interrogations be videotaped. A lengthy interrogation contains so many subtle, forward-moving points of persuasion-threat-coercion, such as maximization-minimization techniques that "it is beyond human ability to remember just what happened." Since interrogators are zealous in achieving their goals of obtaining confession, they are naturally biased and simply will not see that they did anything that might induce a false confession.

Ofshe and Leo's central point is that false confessions come about when commonplace interrogation methods (including the verbal fabrication of "evidence") are used improperly, inappropriately, or ineptly.[92] Therefore, police training is critical to avoiding false confessions. Police need to be educated in the facts of false confessions and to understand that they do occur. Since there is a subtle difference between the proper and improper use of the psychological interrogation, the most important factor is for police to be aware that when they have a possible suspect, as opposed to a likely suspect, they should seek corroborating evidence. "If police and prosecutors recognized that the mere admission 'I did it' is not necessarily a true statement, they would be far less likely to arrest and prosecute suspects who give false confessions."[93]

The last recommendation is that trial judges "should evaluate the reliability of confession statements," as they do hearsay statements, to determine whether they should be allowed into evidence. "Oddly, the constitutional law of criminal procedure has no substantive safeguards in place to specifically prevent the admission of even demonstrably false confessions." The constitutional rules for confessions under the Fifth and Sixth amendments are designed to ensure procedural regularity but not reliability, and the same has become true under the due process voluntariness test. Given this constitutional vacuum, it is critically important for judges to perform this task. The stakes for fairness are high: "It has been shown that placing a confession before a jury is tantamount to an instruction to convict, even when the confession fails to accurately describe the crime, fails to produce corroboration, and is contradicted by considerable evidence pointing to a suspect's innocence." Therefore, judges should demand that confessions display a minimal level of reliability. This can be done without

any change in statutes or court rules. Judges routinely rule on admissibility and would, for example, not allow a jury to see a photograph that had been doctored. "A false confession is analogous to a doctored photograph. The mechanism for creating it is the ancient technology of human influence carried forward into the interrogation room."

A short decade ago, there was at best a vague awareness that false confessions were a rare and tragic human failing. Recent scholarship has brought the problem to the forefront. Judges, prosecutors, leaders of the bar, and police officials have no reason to claim ignorance. It remains to be seen if the legal world will respond to this challenge.

SUMMARY

The Constitution protects against abusive interrogation by the due process exclusionary rule of involuntary confessions, the Fifth Amendment privilege against self-incrimination for suspects who have not yet been indicted, and the Sixth Amendment right to counsel for persons who have been formally charged. The privilege against self-incrimination allows natural persons who are sworn to testify in formal proceedings to claim the privilege if their testimony would tend to incriminate them. The privilege does not bar the taking and use of physical evidence, including a person's appearance and evidence from his body (e.g., hair, blood, DNA), to convict a suspect. The privilege prevents a person from having to face the "cruel trilemma" of self-accusation, perjury, or contempt. When applicable, the privilege against self-incrimination is an absolute bar against the use of compelled testimony taken from natural persons. The privilege may not be claimed to protect against civil commitment, as under Sexually Dangerous Person Acts.

Under the Due Process Clause, state or federal confessions or admissions are inadmissible if they are not made voluntarily. Statements obtained by threats, promises, the use of force or undue psychological pressure are involuntary and inadmissible as due process violations. The Court gave various purposes of the voluntariness rule: to ensure accurate confessions, to prevent egregious police behavior, and to assure that a confession is the product of a free and rational choice. Judicial displeasure with the subjectivity of the voluntariness test led the Supreme Court to seek a more concrete rule. In 1963 and 1964, the Supreme Court incorporated the Sixth Amendment right to the assistance counsel and the privilege against self-incrimination.

Miranda v. Arizona (1966) held that custodial interrogation by police is inherently coercive, requiring that police inform suspects of their rights in order to dispel the coercive atmosphere of police custody. Four warnings must be given: that the suspect has a right to remain silent; that any statement may be used as evidence against him; that he has a right to the presence of an attorney; and that if he cannot afford an attorney, one will be appointed. A defendant may waive these rights if the waiver is made voluntarily, knowingly, and intelligently.

Following the *Miranda* decision, a more conservative Supreme Court declared that *Miranda* warnings were not themselves constitutional rights but prophylactic rules designed to protect the underlying Fifth Amendment right against self-incrimination. As a result, statements taken in violation of *Miranda* could be used to impeach the defendant and as leads to other evidence. It also allowed the use of warned confessions taken after a violation of the *Miranda* rule. A public safety exception was created under this theory, allowing the admission into evidence of unwarned statements made in answers to questions designed to protect the safety of arresting officers and other persons in the immediate area (*New York v. Quarles*, 1984).

Despite this, *Dickerson v. United States* (2000) held that the *Miranda* warnings were constitutional rules that could not be overridden by a congressional statute purporting to reinstate the voluntariness test as the sole measure of the constitutionality of confessions in federal cases. The Supreme Court recognized that *Miranda* had become so widely accepted that the concerns of precedent *(stare decisis)* compelled a recognition of the rule as being constitutional. But the effect of *Dickerson* has been put into question by *Chavez v. Martinez* (2003), which held that a simple failure to read *Miranda* warnings is not a violation of any right. A plurality of the Court held that the privilege and the *Miranda* warnings operate only as exclusionary rules, so that violations occur only when compelled evidence is sought to be introduced.

The Fourteenth Amendment due process voluntariness test exists as a backstop to, and not a replacement for, the *Miranda* rule.

Numerous cases clarify the meaning of *Miranda*. Warnings need not be given in the precise language found in *Miranda* as long as the correct understanding of the warnings is conveyed. Police do not have to add anything to the warnings such as the consequences of confessing or their knowledge that the suspect may have committed crimes that are not the immediate subject of the questioning. The prosecution has the burden of proving that a waiver is made voluntarily. A waiver is not presumed from silence, and an oral waiver is allowable as long as it was made expressly and is shown on the record. Written waivers are the common form of proving that the rights to silence and counsel were waived voluntarily.

Police must cease questioning a suspect who has waived his or her rights and indicates during interrogation the wish to terminate the interrogation. However, police may resume questioning at a later time if the resumption is reasonable. Police must cease questioning a suspect who personally and clearly invokes a desire to see an attorney and not another kind of counselor. The police may not thereafter resume questioning unless it is initiated by the suspect. This rule is violated if an officer in a department reinterrogates a suspect who invoked counsel in ignorance of his prior request for an attorney. Simple consultation with a lawyer does not dispel *Edwards* protection; a defendant has a right, after invoking counsel, to be questioned by police or prosecutors only with counsel present.

A person is in *Miranda* custody if the circumstances or surroundings are objectively coercive. Depending upon the circumstances, interviews in one's home, at a police station, or by a probation officer may not be coercive. Interrogation in prison, even for a crime unrelated to the original crime, require *Miranda* warnings. Questioning by a patrol officer after a routine traffic stop is generally not custodial because this kind of common detention is in public and lacks the coercive atmosphere of the police station. Questions designed to produce an incriminating answer or questions asked after a person has been arrested at the roadside constitute custodial interrogation.

Interrogation consists of express questioning or its functional equivalent: Words or actions on the part of the police (other than normally attendant to arrest and custody) that the police should know are reasonably likely to elicit an incriminating response from the suspect. Deception by police interrogators is allowed. Undercover agents, in or out of jail, are not required to give *Miranda* warnings when they ask incriminating questions because the interrogation is not conducted in a coercive atmosphere.

The war on terrorism has raised concerns about the use of excessive force by American agents seeking background information from suspects. A federal court has ruled that U.S. agents must read *Miranda* warnings to suspects interrogated overseas in order for their statements to be admissible in American courts.

Once a person is formally arraigned, the police may not question or eavesdrop on her without a lawyer present. A defendant may waive this Sixth Amendment right after being read *Miranda* warnings. This rule was violated in *Brewer v. Williams* (1977) when an officer made the functional equivalent of an interrogation designed to elicit a response by delivering a "Christian Burial" speech to an isolated mental patient. Undercover agents who investigate a person who has been formally charged must not ask any questions or initiate conversations likely to generate incriminating statements. They may, however, listen for such statements, which are then admissible.

LEGAL PUZZLES

HOW HAVE COURTS DECIDED THESE CASES?

WAIVER; INVOKING COUNSEL

7–1. Terry Mincey and two other men robbed a Mini Food Store. Mincey shot two bystanders and killed one of them. Mincey was arrested the next day. As he was being driven to jail, Officer Boren read Mincey his *Miranda* rights in full. Mincey stated that he understood his rights. Mincey claims that he told the officers to "go ahead and run the lawyers." When asked by his attorney what he meant by that, Mincey replied, "I needed lawyers because, you know, on this case I knew I needed one."

At the jail Mincey was again advised of his rights. He read the *Miranda* form for three minutes, but refused to sign it, saying, "I'm not going to sign anything. I signed the last time. I'm not going to sign anything this time. I did time the las time. . . . You had me for armed robbery before. . . . Man I'm looking at two murders this time. I'm not signing anything." Mincey had been convicted of robbery five years earlier. During this session, Mincey asked that certain of the rights on the waiver form be deleted, but he still refused to sign. At one point, he asked that certain provisions of the waiver form be deleted but still refused to sign.

After refusing to sign the waiver form, Mincey told Officer Spires about the Mini Food Store robbery and shootings. When asked at a suppression hearing why he spoke, Mincey said, "I don't know, I just saw that I wasn't going to get a lawyer so I figured I had better talk to him because I knew him. And I didn't too much want to talk to Boren because he was playing, you know, the rough side of it." He admitted that he spoke to the officers of his own free will. This session took twenty minutes.

Mincey was then taken to a conference room, and over the next forty-five minutes, was interviewed by Boren, Spires, and a deputy sheriff. Mincey, again read his rights, responded, "I know my rights." Mincey acknowledged that he had been to the store with the two other men and admitted shooting one of the victims. He again refused to sign a waiver statement, saying, "I'm not going to sign anything, I'm not going to give you anything, nothing written. . . . I need forty-five lawyers to get out of this [expletive]." After Mincey made this statement, the officers ceased their questioning.

The two other robbers pled guilty. Mincey was put on trial for murder.

1. Did Mincey waive his right to counsel under *Miranda?*
2. Did he invoke the right to counsel?

HELD: (1) Yes; (2) No

7–1. (1) Mincey was read his rights fully, and he read the waiver form carefully. He said that he understood them. He was knowledgeable of his rights due to his past contacts with the law enforcement process, i.e., he understood that he had a right to the presence of counsel before the officers questioned him, or at any time during the interview, and that (with or without counsel) he had the right to remain silent. Mincey's request that certain portions of the waiver of rights form be deleted and his subsequent refusal to sign the form, was not a request for counsel or an invocation of the right to remain silent; rather, it demonstrated that Mincey was "toying with" the officer. Mincey "knew that it would be easier to deny his statements if they were not in writing and that is why he refused to sign the waiver form."

There is no evidence that Mincey was bullied or tricked into answering questions, or that any promises were made.

Although a refusal to sign a waiver of rights form may indicate that the suspect is invoking his right to counsel, it is not conclusive proof that he has invoked the right (*North Carolina v. Butler*). In light of all the circumstances, Mincey waived his rights to silence and to the presence of counsel.

(2) Mincey's statements, "go ahead and run the lawyers," and that "it would take forty-five lawyers to get out of this

[expletive]" were not unequivocal requests for a lawyer (*Davis v. United States*, 1995). In any event, the officers ceased questioning Mincey after the latter statement.

Mincey v. Head, 206 F.3d 1106 (11th Cir. 2000)

PUBLIC SAFETY EXCEPTION

7–2. Delbert Mobley was arrested at his apartment at 8:30 A.M. by eight FBI agents, armed with arrest and search warrants, on suspicion of being involved in a conspiracy to distribute crack cocaine. Mobley opened the door to a knock and announcement of police presence and was immediately secured against a wall while agents performed a protective sweep. He was naked when arrested. He was advised that he was under arrest, dressed under surveillance and was read *Miranda* rights. Mobley said he wished to speak with an attorney and questioning ceased. An agent told Mobley that his apartment would be searched. The agent asked him if there was anything in the apartment, and specifically if any weapons were in the apartment that could be of danger to the agents who would be remaining at the apartment to conduct the search warrant. In response to the question, Mobley stated that there was a weapon in the bedroom closet on one of the shelves, and he led the agents to it.

1. Does the "public safety exception" of *New York v. Quarles* (1984) apply *after Miranda* warnings have been read to an arrested person who is asked about the presence of a gun?
2. Do the facts of this case raise such a concern about public safety to bring Mobley's admission within the *Quarles* exception?

Holding available from instructor

INTERROGATION

7–3. A confidential informant told Agent Mino, working on undercover drug investigations, that Montez Jackson was engaged in narcotics distribution. Mino had Sergeant Latham arrange two narcotics purchases from Jackson, who was not arrested. Jackson was later arrested for an unrelated traffic violation, and an inventory search of his car disclosed crack cocaine. The following day, Jackson was removed from his cell and advised of his *Miranda* rights for the purpose of getting a statement. Jackson told the officer that he would not make a statement unless a lawyer was present, and Jackson was returned to his cell. The next day, Mino visited the Police Department and noticed Jackson's name on the previous day's arrest sheet. Agent Mino was told that when Jackson was stopped for a traffic violation cocaine was found in his car. Mino got permission to speak with Jackson about Mino's ongoing investigation stemming from the two earlier drug sales. Jackson was brought to an interview room where Mino was waiting. Prior to the interview, Jackson signed a *Miranda* waiver form.

Mino identified himself as a drug task force narcotics agent and explained to Jackson that he was not concerned with any of the details of Jackson's traffic arrest. Mino advised Jackson that he was the subject of an ongoing drug investigation and that he (Mino) had knowledge that Jackson had sold crack cocaine on two separate occasions to an undercover officer. Mino told Jackson that he was not interested in obtaining any statement from him and that he was a "little fish" who could help the police catch his supplier. Mino told Jackson he was interested in seeing if Jackson would assist in different avenues of investigation. Mino gave Jackson his pager number and told him to call if he was interested in cooperating after his release from jail. Mino's conversation with Jackson lasted approximately twenty minutes. As Officer Berry escorted the defendant back to his cell, Jackson mentioned to Berry that after speaking to Mino, he realized that he was in a lot of trouble and said he wanted to clear up an earlier matter of the traffic stop. Jackson proceeded to make incriminating statements about his drug involvement.

Jackson argues that the conversation with Agent Mino was an interrogation initiated by the police, which violated his right to be interrogated only in the presence of an attorney following his request for an attorney.

Was the conversation between Agent Mino and Jackson an interrogation?

Holding available from instructor

CUSTODY

7–4. A jury found Mesa Rith guilty of unlawful possession of an unregistered sawed-off shotgun. Officer Mikkel Roe was informed that Sam Rith and his wife, Mesa's parents, were concerned about firearms they had seen their son carry into their home and hide in a garbage can. Fearful of guns and afraid that their son was involved in a gang, the Riths requested that Officer Roe check the home and ascertain if the guns were stolen. Sam Rith gave permission to Officer Roe and Detective Terry Chen to search his home for the guns. Fearing confrontation with his son, Sam Rith declined to accompany the officers during the search. Instead, he gave the officers a house key so that no damage would be done to the house in the event they were not otherwise allowed entry. Sam Rith told the officers that Mesa Rith was eighteen years of age and was not paying rent.

At the Rith home, Mesa allowed the officers to enter when they showed him the house key. Detective Chen spoke with Rith in the kitchen, told him again that they knew he had brought illegal guns into the house, and asked Rith where the guns were hidden. Rith told the officers that he only had one gun and that it was in his bedroom, downstairs, under the mattress. A loaded sawed-off shotgun was retrieved from underneath Rith's mattress. Detective Chen returned to the kitchen and confronted Rith with the shotgun. Rith stated that he knew it was illegal to possess a sawed-off shotgun and that the gun was probably stolen by the person who had given it to him. Officer Roe, who had gone outside and found a rifle in the garbage can, returned to the kitchen and read Rith his *Miranda*

rights. After Officer Roe confirmed that Rith understood his rights, Rith repeated that he knew it was illegal to possess a sawed-off shotgun and that the guns were probably stolen. The officers then arrested Rith for possession of stolen property and illegal weapons.

Was Mesa Rith in custody when the officers first asked him about the location of guns, before any were retrieved?

Holding available from instructor

ADMISSION TO CELLMATE AFTER COUNSEL APPOINTED

7–5. Justin Sincock, a transitional resident inmate at a community correctional center in Casper, Wyoming, was required to maintain employment. He was hired by Dan Horkan to work as a laborer for his floor-covering business. On a day that Horkan was scheduled to work out of town, he had Sincock do some painting of his house, where Horkan's wife, Becky, and the Horkans' two children were present. Becky dropped the children off at her mother's house, and planned to deliver lunch to Sincock. Becky did not reappear. Her body was discovered that afternoon lying facedown in the upstairs bathtub of her home, shot in the head at close range. Sincock was arrested in Columbia, Missouri, where his family lived, having the Horkans' car, credit cards, and checks in his possession. He was charged with first-degree premeditated murder and other crimes.

Byron Burke was an acquaintance of Justin Sincock who was an inmate at the community correctional center while Sincock was there. On the day Becky was murdered, Burke was at the Horkan residence briefly at Sincock's request. By chance, Burke was also an inmate at the detention center at the same time Sincock was incarcerated and awaiting trial for Becky's murder. In August of 1998, because of disciplinary problems, Burke was transferred to the part of the detention center where Sincock was being held. When Sincock saw Burke, he told Burke he needed to talk to him about what happened on the day of the murder because they needed to get their stories straight. Burke contacted a police detective. Burke told the detective that if he were moved to Sincock's cell, he could try to get information from him about the murder. The detective informed Burke that would make him an informant and an agent of the state, and as such, he would be required to advise Sincock of his rights before attempting to get information from him. The detective did not seem interested in having Burke act as an informant nor did he ask Burke to be an informant, do anything to get information from Sincock, or move into Sincock's cell. Burke then filled out a written request asking to be placed in Sincock's cell. He stated in the request: "I was supposed to testify against him in court about that murder, and the detectives want me in there to find out as much as possible since we still get along." In fact, no one from the police department asked Burke to move into Sincock's cell. Burke testified that he made the request because he thought if he obtained information from Sincock helpful to the police, he might not have to go to prison. Some time after the written request, Burke was moved into Sincock's cell and Sincock made incriminating statements to him.

Was Sincock's Sixth Amendment right to counsel violated by the way in which Burke obtained incriminating statements, requiring their suppression?

Holding available from instructor

FURTHER READING

R. H. Helmholz, et al., *The Privilege Against Self-Incrimination: Its Origins and Development* (Chicago: University of Chicago Press, 1997).

Liva Baker, Miranda: *Crime, Law and Politics* (New York: Atheneum, 1985).

Richard A. Leo and George C. Thomas III, *The Miranda Debate: Law, Justice and Policing* (Boston: Northeastern University Press, 1998).

ENDNOTES

1. See, e.g., George Scibel, *Enlightened Police Questioning: Interviewing, Interrogation & Investigation* (Mesilla, NM: Prairie Avenue Press, 2003); Charles E. O'Hara and Gregory O'Hara, *Fundamentals of Criminal Investigation*, 5th ed. (Springfield, IL: Charles C. Thomas, 1988).

2. Human Rights Watch, *Shielded from Justice: Police Brutality and Accountability in the United States* (New York: Human Rights Watch, 1998); Malcolm Holmes, "Minority Threat and Police Brutality: Determinants of Civil Rights Criminal Complaints in U.S. Municipalities," *Criminology* 38 (2) (2000): 343–67.

3. See Steven A. Drizin and Richard A. Leo, "The Problem of False Confessions in the Post-DNA World," *North Carolina Law Review* 82 (2004): 891; *Law in Society* section, this chapter.

4. *Dickerson v. United States* (2000); *Chavez v. Martinez* (2003).

5. *Missouri v. Seibert*, 93 S.W.3d 700 (Mo. 2002), cert. granted, 123 S. Ct. 2091 (2003); *United States v. Patane*, 304 F.3d 1013 (10th Cir. 2002), cert. granted, 123 S. Ct. 1788 (2003).

6. Stacey M. Studnicki and John P. Apol, "Witness Detention and Intimidation: The History and Future of Material Witness Law," *St. John's Law Review* 76 (2002): 483–533.

7. Amanda H. Frost, "Updating the Marital Privileges: A Witness-Centered Rationale," *Wisconsin Women's Law Journal* 14 (1999): 1–44.

8. R. H. Helmholz, Introduction in *The Privilege Against Self-Incrimination: Its Origins and Development* by R. H. Helmholz, et al. (Chicago: University of Chicago Press, 1997), 1.

9. John H. Langbein, *Torture and the Law of Proof: Europe and England in the Ancien Régime* (Chicago: University of Chicago Press, 1977); Edward Peters, *Torture* (Oxford: Basil Blackwell, 1985).

10. Richard S. Frase, Review Essay: The Search for the Whole Truth about American and European Criminal Justice—*Trials without Truth: Why Our System of Criminal Trials Has Become an Expensive Failure and What We Need to Do to Rebuild It* (New York: New York University Press, 1999) by William T. Pizzi, *Buffalo Criminal Law Review* 3 (2000): 785–849.

11. Project, "Twenty-Fifth Annual Review of Criminal Procedure," *Georgetown Law Journal* 84 (1996): 641, 1212–13 (footnotes omitted).

12. Steven D. Clymer, "Are Police Free to Disregard Miranda?" *Yale Law Journal* 112: 447–552 (2002) pp. 468–69 (footnotes omitted).

13. Charles H. Whitebread and Christopher Slobogin, *Criminal Procedure: An Analysis of Cases and Concepts*, 4th ed. (New York: Foundation Press, 2000), 379.

14. Laura Mansnerus, "Questions Rise over Imprisoning Sex Offenders Past Their Terms," *New York Times*, November 17, 2003.

15. Project, "Twenty-Ninth Annual Review of Criminal Procedure," *Georgetown Law Journal* 88 (2000): 879, 1431–32 (footnotes omitted, emphasis added).

16. P. W. Valentine, "Woman, Jailed for Contempt, Freed After 7 Years; Md. Mother Failed to Reveal Son's Location," *Washington Post*, November 1, 1995; Associated Press, "Mother Ends 7-Year Jail Stay, Still Silent about Missing Child," *New York Times,* November 2, 1995.

17. Delmar Karlen, *Anglo-American Criminal Justice* (New York: Oxford University Press, 1967), 121; David J. Bodenhamer, *Fair Trial: Rights of the Accused in American History* (New York: Oxford University Press, 1992), 53–4. More recent scholarship suggests that the "due process" rule excluding the admission of coerced confessions at trial may have had an organic connection with the privilege against self-incrimination. See Lawrence Herman, "The Unexplored Relationship Between the Privilege Against Compulsory Self-Incrimination and the Involuntary Confession Rule," *Ohio State Law Journal* 53 (1992): 101–209, 497–553.

18. Karlen, *Anglo-American Criminal Justice*, 122.

19. See Samuel Walker, *Popular Justice: A History of American Criminal Justice* (New York: Oxford University Press, 1980), 173–75, 189, 231. Richard Leo, "Police Interrogation in America: A Study of Violence, Civility, and Social Change" (Ph.D. diss., University of California at Berkeley, 1995), 12–66, examined the third degree and suggested that the practice declined because of increasing police professionalism, changing attitudes, and changes in legal doctrine.

20. Bodenhamer, *Fair Trial*, 101.

21. Richard C. Cortner, *The Supreme Court and the Second Bill of Rights* (Madison: University of Wisconsin Press, 1981), 150.

22. Note, "Developments in the Law of Confessions," *Harvard Law Review* 79 (1966): 935, 964 (emphases added).

23. Fred P. Graham, *The Due Process Revolution: The Warren Court's Impact on Criminal Law* (New York: Hayden Book Co., 1970), 154.

24. Ibid., 155.

25. Ibid., 153–93; Liva Baker, *Miranda: Crime, Law and Politics* (New York: Atheneum, 1985).

26. Baker, *Miranda*, 191–94, 408–09.

27. Herman, "The Unexplored Relationship," 101–209, 497–553.

28. The liberal majority that decided *Miranda* was roundly criticized by politicians and police personnel. In the 1968 presidential campaign, Richard Nixon denounced *Miranda* and the liberal Warren Court. As president, he was able to appoint conservative justices. Thus, upon the retirement of Justices Warren, Black, Harlan, and Fortas, President Nixon nominated Chief Justice Burger, and Justices Blackmun, Powell, and Rehnquist by 1972.

This created a pro-prosecution, centrist-to-conservative Court. Baker, *Miranda*, 221–324; A. L. Galub, *The Burger Court 1968–1984: The Supreme Court in American Life*, vol. 9 (Millwood, NY: Associated Faculty Press, 1986); Charles M. Lamb and Stephen C. Halpern, eds., *The Burger Court: Political and Judicial Profiles* (Urbana: University of Illinois Press, 1991).

29. Baker, *Miranda*, 346.

30. See Joseph D. Grano, *Confessions, Truth and the Law* (Ann Arbor: University of Michigan Press, 1993), 173–222, quote at 197–98. Professor Grano lays out the argument for overruling at pp. 199–222. The articles of a leading supporter of *Miranda* are collected in Yale Kamisar, *Police Interrogation and Confessions: Essays in Law and Policy* (Ann Arbor: University of Michigan Press, 1980). For a more recent compilation of essays: Richard A. Leo and George C. Thomas III, eds., *The Miranda Debate: Law, Justice and Policing* (Boston: Northeastern University Press, 1998).

31. The interrogation occurred before *Miranda* was decided, but the trial took place after the *Miranda* decision. Therefore, the *Miranda* ruling applied to this case.

32. 428 N.W.2d 406 (Minn. App. 1988).

33. The moving force behind the appeal invoking §3501, which federal prosecutors had studiously avoided for three decades, was probably due to the passionate advocacy of Paul Cassell, then a law professor who expended great energy on a crusade to overturn *Miranda*. See George C. Thomas and Richard Leo, "The Effects of *Miranda v. Arizona*: 'Embedded' in Our National Culture?" *Crime and Justice: A Review of Research* 29 (2002): 203–71. See Roger Parloff, "*Miranda* on the Hot Seat," *New York Times Magazine*, September 26, 1999. Prof. Cassell, described as "an indefatigable, ideologically driven young law professor at the University of Utah" has made a career of trying to get the courts to use §3501 to overrule *Miranda*. "For seven years, Cassell filed such briefs in one or two cases a year, primarily in the District of Utah or in the Fourth Circuit. These were his current and former stomping grounds and two of the most inviting venues legally, based on controlling Federal precedents in those regions."

34. Richard Harris, *The Fear of Crime* (New York: Praeger, 1969), 58.

35. Susan R. Klein, "Identifying and Reformulating Prophylactic Rules, Safe Harbors, and Incidental Rights in Constitutional Criminal Procedure," *Michigan Law Review* 99 (2001): 1031, 1071.

36. Stephen J. Schulhofer, "*Miranda, Dickerson*, and the Puzzling Persistence of Fifth Amendment Exceptionalism," *Michigan Law Review* 99 (2001): 941.

37. Arnold H. Loewy, "Police-Obtained Evidence and the Constitution: Distinguishing Unconstitutionally Obtained Evidence from Unconstitutionally Used Evidence," *Michigan Law Review* 87 (1989): 907–39.

38. The cases are *United States v. Patane,* 304 F.3d 1013 (10th Cir. 2002), cert. granted, 123 S. Ct. 1788 (2003); *Missouri v. Seibert*, 93 S.W.3d 700 (Mo. 2002), cert. granted, 123 S. Ct. 2091 (2003).

39. Charles D. Weisselberg, "Saving *Miranda*," *Cornell Law Review* 84 (1998): 109–92, citing Devallis Rutledge, "Questioning 'Outside Miranda,' Did You Know . . ." (California Dist. Attorney's Assn., Sacramento, Cal., June 1995), 133.

40. Ibid.

41. *Cal. Att'ys for Crim. Justice v. Butts*, 195 F.3d 1039 (9th Cir. 1999).

42. Charles D. Weisselberg, "Deterring Police from Deliberately Violating *Miranda*: In the Stationhouse after *Dickerson*," *Michigan Law Review* 99 (2001): 1121–67.

43. See Marvin Zalman, "The Coming Paradigm Shift on *Miranda*: The Impact of *Chavez v. Martinez*," *Criminal Law Bulletin* 39 (2003): 334–52.

44. 304 F.3d 1013 (10th Cir. 2002), cert. granted, 123 S. Ct. 1788 (2003).

45. 93 S.W.3d 700 (Mo. 2002), cert. granted, 123 S. Ct. 2091 (2003).

46. This issue is discussed at length in Marvin Zalman, "Reading the Tea Leaves of *Chavez v. Martinez*: The Future of *Miranda*," *Criminal Law Bulletin* 40 (2004) [forthcoming].

47. *Weeks v. Angelone*, 176 F.3d 249 (4th Cir. 1999).

48. 834 S.W.2d 265 (Tenn. 1992).

49. See *Gauger v. Hendle*, 2002 U.S. Dist. LEXIS 18002 (U.S. Dist. Ct. N.D. Ill. 2002).

50. See Clifford S. Zimmerman, "Toward a New Vision of Informants: A History of Abuses and Suggestions for Reform," *Hastings Constitutional Law Quarterly* 22 (1994): 81–178; Barry Scheck, Peter Neufeld, and Jim Dwyer, *Actual Innocence: When Justice Goes Wrong and How to Make It Right* (New York: Signet, 2001); Edward Humes, *Mean Justice* (New York: Simon & Schuster, 1999).

51. Alan M. Dershowitz, "Is There a Torturous Road to Justice?" *Los Angeles Times*, November 8, 2001; Christopher Hitchens, "In Case Anyone's Forgotten: Torture Doesn't Work," *The Guardian* (London), November 14, 2001.

52. Dana Priest and Barton Gellman, "U.S. Decries Abuse but Defends Interrogations; 'Stress and Duress' Tactics Used on Terrorism Suspects Held in Secret Overseas Facilities," *Washington Post*, December 26, 2002.

53. Ibid.

54. Ibid.

55. John T. Parry, "What Is Torture, Are We Doing It, and What If We Are?" *University of Pittsburgh Law Review* 64 (2003): 237–262.

56. Ibid., 2, n. 25. The citation for the case is *Ireland v. United Kingdom*, App. No. 5310/71, 2 Eur. H.R. Rep. 25 (1980) (Eur. Ct. of H.R.).

57. See Parry, "Torture," 243, n. 10; United Nations General Assembly, "Convention Against Torture and Other Cruel, Inhuman or Degrading Treatment or Punishment," United Nations, http://www.un.org/documents/ga/res/39/a39r046.htm, reprinted in Nigel S. Rodley, The Treatment of Prisoners Under International Law, annex 2a, at 391 (2d ed. 1999).

58. Parry, "Torture," 249–50.

59. Parry, "Torture," 258–60.

60. Hitchens, "In Case Anyone's Forgotten."

61. Parry, "Torture," 26–62.

62. Priest and Gellman, "U.S. Decries."

63. *United States v. Usama Bin Laden*, 132 F. Supp. 2d 168, 185–86, 187 (S.D.N.Y. 2001)

64. Ibid., 188.

65. Ibid.

66. Benjamin Weiser, "4 Are Sentenced to Life in Prison in 1998 U.S. Embassy Bombing," *New York Times*, October 19, 2001. The jury had voted 9–3 for the death sentence. Execution required a unanimous verdict of death.

67. Not the same Colson in the *Massiah* case.

68. T. Jacoby, "Fighting Crime by the Rules," *Newsweek*, July 18, 1988, 53, reviewing *Tempered Zeal* by R. Uviller.

69. Leo, *Police Interrogation*, 335–42.

70. Richard A. Leo and Welsh S. White, "Adapting to *Miranda*: Modern Interrogators' Strategies for Dealing with the Obstacles Posed by *Miranda*," *Minnesota Law Review* 84 (1999): 397–472, 402, n. 18 lists some of the early studies.

71. Leo, *Police Interrogation*, 258–68, 276–77. Leo's dissertation has been published in several articles: "Inside the Interrogation Room," *Journal of Criminal Law and Criminology* 86 (1996): 266–303; Richard A. Leo, "*Miranda*'s Revenge: Police Interrogation as a Confidence Game," *Law & Society Review* 30 (1996): 259–88.

72. Leo, 271.

73. Leo, 191.

74. Leo, 212–20.

75. Leo and White, "Adapting to *Miranda*," 431–47.

76. P. W. Lewis and H. E. Allen, "'Participating *Miranda*': An Attempt to Subvert Certain Constitutional Safeguards," *Crime and Delinquency* 23 (1) (1977): 75–80.

77. See Leo, 230–51; D. Simon, *Homicide: A Year on the Killing Streets* (Boston: Houghton Mifflin, 1991).

78. Weisselberg, "Saving *Miranda*,"; Leo and White, "Adapting to *Miranda*," 447–50.

79. Leo, 354, 357–63, 416.

80. Richard Leo, "The Impact of *Miranda* Revisited," *Journal of Criminal Law & Criminology* 86 (1996): 621–692, relying on William A. Geller, U.S. Department of Justice, *Videotaping Interrogations and Confessions* (March 1993).

81. Barry Scheck, Peter Neufeld, and Jim Dwyer, *Actual Innocence: When Justice Goes Wrong and How to Make It Right* (New York: Signet, 2001), 120, 361.

82. Hugo Adam Bedau and Michael L. Radelet, "Miscarriages of Justice in Potentially Capital Cases," *Stanford Law Review* 40 (1987): 21, 58.

83. Steven A. Drizin and Richard A. Leo, "The Problem of False Confessions in the Post-DNA World," *North Carolina Law Review* 82 (2004): 891.

84. Richard A. Leo and Richard J. Ofshe, "The Consequences of False Confessions: Deprivations of Liberty and Miscarriages of Justice in the Age of Psychological Interrogation," *Journal of Criminal Law and Criminology* 88 (1998): 429–96.

85. Richard A. Leo and Richard J. Ofshe, "Missing the Forest for the Trees: A Response to Paul Cassell's 'Balanced Approach' to the False Confession Problem," *Denver University Law Review* 74 (1997): 1135.

86. Jim Dwyer, Peter Neufeld, and Barry Scheck, *Actual Innocence* (New York: Doubleday, 2000), 78–106. The law professors who operate the "innocence project" list false confessions as one of several problems that contribute to what DNA testing has disclosed to be a major problem of convicting the innocent.

87. Richard J. Ofshe and Richard A. Leo, "The Decision to Confess Falsely: Rational Choice and Irrational Action," *Denver University Law Review* 74 (1997): 979–1122.

88. Ibid., 997–1000.

89. Ibid., 986–94.

90. The information on the Sawyer case is derived from a 292-page transcript of the police interrogation. The secondary sources used that reprinted parts of the transcript are found in: "Readings: [Transcript] True Confession?," *Harper's*, (October 1989), 17–201 and Philip Weiss, "Untrue Confessions," *Mother Jones* (September 1989), 18–24+.

91. The lie detector examination was given during the evening when he was under great stress. A later polygraph examination indicated that Sawyer's denial of the murder was truthful.

92. Leo and Ofshe, "Missing the Forest," n. 49.

93. Ofshe and Leo, "The Decision to Confess," 1119–1120, n. 51.

JUSTICES OF THE SUPREME COURT

Enduring Liberals
Brennan—Marshall

When William Brennan was appointed by President Eisenhower and Thurgood Marshall by President Johnson, the Supreme Court was representative of the ascendant liberal ideology of the day. Their backgrounds, experiences, and beliefs about the Court's role well suited them to play a role in expanding the rights of society's outcasts. As justices with long tenures, their careers coincided with a long swing of the political pendulum, from liberal to conservative, that has marked American politics since the 1960s. The careers of Justices Brennan and Marshall exemplify an important institutional aspect of the Supreme Court. Presidents nominate individuals who represent the political aspirations of the day, but with life tenure, justices who sit for several decades can extend their philosophies over time. This places the Court somewhat above the political passions of the period and offers a form of stability. The disadvantage is that at times it makes the Court unresponsive to the needs and demands of the polity.

The resignation of Justices Goldberg, Fortas, and Warren between 1965 and 1970 led to a change in the Court's composition that reflect and possibly accelerated a shift toward a conservative mood in some issues. This has persisted since 1970 as ten nominees of Republican Presidents Nixon, Ford, Reagan, and Bush have moved the Court progressively to the right. Democratic President Carter had no opportunity to nominate a justice, and President Clinton has carefully selected moderate rather than liberal justices.

Thus, for two decades, Justices Brennan and Marshall, the enduring liberals, penned more than a normal share of dissents in many criminal procedure cases. At times, their dissents expressed outrage and dire warnings that conservative justices were subverting constitutional rights. Less frequently, they joined with at least three moderate justices to rule in favor of the defendant. For the most part, their dissents after 1970 were written not so much for the present, but for the future, in the hope that a new generation of justices will be more open to defendants' claims.

William J. Brennan, Jr.

New Jersey 1906–1997

Democrat

Appointed by
Dwight Eisenhower

Years of Service:
1956–1990

Collection of the Supreme Court of the United States. Photographer: Robert Oakes

Life and Career The son of an Irish immigrant who became a political leader in Newark, New Jersey, noted for integrity and efficiency, William Brennan grew up in comfortable circumstances. He graduated from the Wharton School of the University of Pennsylvania with honors and was in the top 10 percent of his class at Harvard Law School in 1931. He practiced law with a prestigious Newark firm specializing in labor issues for corporate clients. During World War II, he was a labor productivity troubleshooter for the undersecretary of war, rising to the

rank of colonel. After the war, he became associated with the judicial reform efforts of New Jersey's renowned Chief Justice Arthur Vanderbilt and as a result was appointed a trial judge. He rose to become an associate justice of the New Jersey Supreme Court and came to the attention of U.S. Attorney General Brownell at a conference on judicial administration, where he sat in for Vanderbilt. The next year when a vacancy appeared on the Court, Brennan fit the requirements of being a Catholic, an Easterner, and a nominal Democrat acceptable to Republicans. The only senator to vote against his confirmation to the Supreme Court was Joseph McCarthy, the demagogic Communist-hunter who may have been angered by Brennan's earlier public criticism of "McCarthyism."

Contribution to Criminal Procedure Justice Brennan wrote few criminal procedure majority opinions in the 1960s, although he consistently voted for incorporation and defendants' rights. Under a more conservative Court, he authored many criminal procedure dissents, as in *Leon* (1984) (good faith exception to exclusionary rule), *Gates* (1983) (abolishing the *Spinelli* two-pronged test for reliability of informant), *Calandra* (1974) (use of illegally obtained evidence in grand jury is constitutional), *Florida v. Riley* (1989) (helicopter overflights not a search subject to Fourth Amendment warrant requirement), *Hampton* (1976) (no entrapment if government agent supplies illegal drug), *Mosley* (1975) (reinterrogation allowed after a suspect claims right to silence), *Ash* (1973) (*Wade* lineup rule does not apply to photographic identification), *Kuhlman v. Wilson* (1986) (passive jail informant does not violate a suspect's right to counsel under the *Massiah* doctrine), and other cases.

In many dissents, he was outspokenly critical of the majority, often accusing it of ignoring facts or twisting precedent simply to arrive at a desired outcome—the same charge of result-oriented jurisprudence that was hurled at the activist Warren Court during the 1960s. In reaction to the curtailment of defendants' rights, Justice Brennan called on state court judges to apply their own state constitutions to afford more rights to suspects than were granted under the current reading of the Bill of Rights. This indeed has been a growing trend and is an ironic twist for a justice who championed federal rights in the 1960s.

SIGNATURE OPINION Dissenting opinion in *Illinois v. Gates* (1983). In this *tour de force,* Justice Brennan directly attacked the ideological basis of the conservative Court's criminal procedure rulings as "code words for an overly permissive attitude toward police practices in derogation of the rights secured by the Fourth Amendment."

ASSESSMENT He was called "a towering figure in modern law who embodied the liberal vision of the Constitution as an engine of social and political change" and many commentators referred to the Warren Court as the "Brennan Court," so great was the influence of his prolific opinions and his ability to gain majorities for his opinions. He strongly influenced all the major areas of the Warren Court's liberal agenda, including free speech, free press, separation of church and state, voting apportionment, school busing, and criminal procedure.

FURTHER READING

Kim Isaac Eisler, *Justice for All: William J. Brennan, Jr., and the Decisions That Transformed America* (New York: Simon and Schuster, 1993).

THURGOOD MARSHALL

New York 1908–1991

Democrat

Appointed by
Lyndon Johnson

Years of Service:
1967–1991

Collection of the Supreme Court of the United States. Photographer: Joseph Lavenburg

LIFE AND CAREER Thurgood Marshall had one of the most distinguished and significant legal careers in American constitutional history. Born in Baltimore into a middle-class family, the great-grandson of a slave graduated from Lincoln University (Chester, Pennsylvania) and was first in his class at Howard University Law School. From 1933 to 1938, he was the counsel for the National Association for the Advancement of Colored People (NAACP) in Baltimore; and from 1938 to 1960, he was the chief counsel of the Legal Defense Fund, the legal organization spun off from the NAACP to defend the civil rights of African Americans in a then legally segregated society. As such, he led the legal battle to overturn segregation laws and thus played a central role in the Civil Rights movement. He appeared before the Supreme Court thirty-two times and won thirteen of the sixteen cases in which he was the principal attorney. His most significant victories were *Shelly v. Kramer* (1948), which declared restrictive covenants on real estate deeds unenforceable in the courts, and *Brown v. Board of Education* (1954), the most important case of the twentieth century, which overturned the "separate but equal doctrine" and outlawed school segregation. In 1961 President Kennedy named Marshall to the Court of Appeals for the Second Circuit; and in 1965 President Johnson named him as the solicitor general, the chief federal attorney to argue cases before the Supreme Court.

CONTRIBUTION TO CRIMINAL PROCEDURE As the Court moved steadily to the right after 1970, Marshall, along with Brennan and on occasion Blackmun and Stevens, dissented in most criminal procedure cases. His opinions were often trenchant and eloquent denunciations of what he saw as the Court's conservative majority's oppressive misreading of the Bill of Rights and seeking to dismantle constitutional protections. In *Schneckloth v. Bustamonte* (1973) (knowledge of rights not required to give valid consent to search), for example, he stated, "I have difficulty in comprehending how a decision made without knowledge of available alternatives can be treated as a choice at all."

Along with Justice Brennan, he held that the death penalty is a flat violation of the cruel and unusual punishment clause of the Eighth Amendment and voted to overturn each capital punishment case, a position adopted by Blackmun a few months before his retirement. On occasion, he wrote a majority opinion for a unanimous Court as in the ruling that a brief roadside stop of a motorist for a traffic violation does not constitute the kind of custodial interrogation that triggers the need for *Miranda* warnings (*Berkemer v. McCarty*, 1984).

SIGNATURE OPINION Concurring opinion in *Batson v. Kentucky* (1986). Although the Court's majority issued a "liberal" decision, that the exclusion of a juror on account of race in a single trial could be challenged, Marshall moved beyond the

(Continued)

frontiers of the decision and argued that use of peremptory challenges during voir dire perpetuates the potential for discrimination and should be eliminated altogether.

Assessment Marshall was a staunch supporter of civil rights. He consistently voted throughout the Burger Court era and into the Rehnquist Court era to uphold liberal positions that were staked out during the 1960s. He dissented powerfully in cases that limited the scope of school integration orders to districts that had practiced deliberate discrimination. Marshall was often an engaging, blunt, and humorous speaker, but issued critical dissents. He was sharply critical of his successor on the bench, Clarence Thomas. Nevertheless, Thurgood Marshall exuded great warmth and when he retired, he was praised by his colleagues. Even those who did not agree with him respected his convictions, accomplishments, and fierce candor.

Further Reading

Michael E. Davis and Hunter R. Clark, *Thurgood Marshall: Warrior at the Bar, Rebel on the Bench*, updated and rev. ed. (New York: Citadel Press, 1994).

IDENTIFICATION OF SUSPECTS: LINEUPS AND SHOWUPS

Law enforcement may have the elements of a contest about it, but it is not a game.

—Justice Byron White, dissenting in *Massiah v. United States*,
377 U.S. 201, 213 (1964)

CHAPTER OUTLINE

KEY TERMS AND PHRASES

Cross-examination

Eyewitness identification

Lineup

Showup

Suggestibility

Testimonial evidence

Introduction: The Persistence of Mistaken Identification

Eyewitness identification is the most important source of truth in most criminal cases and, ironically, the leading source of error that results in the conviction of innocent persons. The use of eyewitnesses at every stage of the criminal process is self-evident. A street mugging victim sits in a police car and is asked whether a suspect matches her description. A store clerk at a police station **lineup** is asked whether each person in a lineup is or is not the armed robber. At a trial, a householder sitting in the witness box is asked to identify the burglar; she raises her arm, points to the person sitting next to the defense lawyer, and says, "That's the man; I'd know him anywhere."

Honestly mistaken identification is part of commonsense psychology. An attorney conducting a **cross-examination** of an eyewitness in a criminal trial asks commonsense questions to cast doubt on the accuracy of the witness's perception. For how long did the witness observe the perpetrator? Was the witness wearing eyeglasses? What were the lighting conditions? The legal system places great faith in the ability of cross-examination to ferret out the truth. A century ago, Dean Henry Wigmore (1863–1943) of Northwestern University Law School called cross-examination "the greatest legal engine ever invented for the discovery of truth." The Supreme Court said that "cross-examination is the principal means by which the believability of a witness and the truth of his testimony are tested" (*Davis v. Alaska*, 1974).[1]

Nevertheless, it has been known for a century that human identification is fraught with error. Classroom experiments by psychologist Hugo Münsterberg were published in 1908 and dramatically demonstrated that human recall of recent events is filled with errors.[2] In 1932 Yale Law Professor Edwin Borchard published *Convicting the Innocent: Sixty-five Actual Errors of Criminal Justice,* which details cases of individuals who were found guilty of felonies and were later proven to be completely innocent.[3] Most miscarriages of justice were caused by mistaken eyewitness identification. In some cases, there was prosecutorial misconduct. The released individuals were sometimes given monetary compensation by special acts of state legislatures. A similar book appeared in 1957 by the jurist Jerome Frank and Barbara Frank, with thirty-four documented instances of innocents convicted in American courts.[4] An estimate by Huff, Rattner, and Sagarin, put the number of wrongful convictions at almost ten thousand annually—based on responses by Ohio judges and criminal justice officials, of whom 94 percent said that wrongful convictions sometimes occur.[5] Another estimate is that "more than 4,250 Americans per year are wrongfully convicted due to sincere, yet woefully inaccurate eyewitness identifications."[6] Bedeau and Radelet's exhaustive and systematic study of innocent persons convicted of capital or potentially capital cases found 350 such

wrongful convictions between 1900 and 1985 in American jurisdictions, with no indication that the justice system is becoming progressively more accurate.[7]

News accounts of the exoneration of the innocent occur with astonishing regularity.[8] A New York assistant prosecutor charged with attempted rape in 1985 was released when a look-alike confessed.[9] In a 1974 New York case, a person was held for a year for armed robbery based on a photo identification but no voice identification. When the victim discovered a year later that the suspect had a thick West Indian accent, the innocent suspect was released.[10] "Freedom for Another Dallas Prisoner," a newspaper story, reported that five innocent persons convicted in Dallas within a few years had been freed.[11] A Roman Catholic priest, Father Bernard Pagano, was mistaken for the "gentleman robber" in Delaware.[12] Lenel Geter, a young African American engineer, was convicted of a fast-food franchise robbery, although coworkers testified he was at work, fifty miles from the robbery site, and he bore little resemblance to the robber's description. There was "intense national publicity, including a feature story on CBS's *60 Minutes*" before Geter was released.[13] Randall Dale Adams, convicted of the murder of Dallas police officer Robert Wood in 1977, had his case brought to light by a riveting documentary film, *The Thin Blue Line,* produced by Errol Morris. The film exposed a combination of prosecutorial overzealousness and witness incompetence that generated the conviction and elicited a virtual confession from David Harris, who appears to have been the actual killer.[14] Recent books have detailed the nationally famous convictions, later shown to be false, of Sam Sheppard and Rubin "Hurricane" Carter.[15]

A cursory review of news stories over a three-month period in 2000 disclosed that:

- In Houston, Texas, DNA tests cleared two men who were wrongfully convicted of rape on the basis of faulty eyewitness testimony.

- In Orange County, California, eighteen-year-old Arthur Carmona spent two years in prison for a robbery that he did not commit; his conviction was based on eyewitnesses who later recanted their testimonies.

- In Norfolk, Virginia, a judge threw out a drug prosecution of a man identified by an undercover informant as a drug seller who was in jail on the day of the alleged sale, leading state authorities to drop thirty-seven other cases based on the informer's identification.

- A Boston, Massachusetts, man was freed on the basis of DNA tests after spending ten years in prison for a rape he did not commit.

- In another Boston case, Marlon Passley was released after prosecutors admitted that his murder conviction had been obtained on the basis of mistaken eyewitness identification—Passley had just lost an appeal after spending four years in prison.

• Also in Orange County, California, three other men were released from prison for serious crimes, two after decades.[16]

In June 2000 Jennifer Thompson, a rape victim, wrote a moving article detailing her experience of positively identifying the wrong man, after making efforts to recall her assailant. DNA tests identified another man who later confessed to the crime. Thompson wrote, "If anything good can come out of what Ronald Cotton suffered because of my limitations as a human being, let it be an awareness of the fact that eyewitnesses can and do make mistakes."[17] Thompson urged Texas to halt the execution of Gary Graham. Graham was convicted of murder largely on the testimony of a single witness who said she saw him from thirty to forty feet away through her car windshield. No physical evidence linked Graham to the crime. Tests showed the gun he was carrying was not the murder weapon. Two witnesses who were never called to testify said they had seen the killer—and it was not Graham. He was represented by a court-appointed lawyer who failed to mount a meaningful defense. Despite these substantial indications of doubt, the Texas governor refused to intervene in the pardon process, asserting that "there has not been one innocent person executed since I've been governor" in the 135 executions he had presided over. Gary Graham was executed on June 22, 2000.[18]

The number of wrongful convictions can be reduced by administrative and legal means. Administrative changes in how the police investigate cases, interview witnesses, and conduct lineups logically would have greater effect than legal measures. The ability of cross-examination to correct errors of mistaken eyewitness testimony, for example, is limited. By the 1960s, problems with eyewitness identification were sufficiently known to be a concern among criminal justice professionals and lawyers. Nevertheless, very little action had been taken by courts or police departments to systematically investigate wrongful convictions and take appropriate action.

Motivated by this problem, the Warren Court established novel constitutional rules to remedy deficiencies in the identification process. The Court explored three areas: (1) the Sixth Amendment right to counsel during a lineup; (2) the Fifth Amendment right against self-incrimination of a suspect during a lineup or **showup**; and (3) the Fifth and Fourteenth amendment due process rights of lineup and showup participants. In truth, refined legal procedures, such as providing an attorney at lineups, are marginally helpful in reducing mistaken eyewitness identification. These procedures do not get at the heart of the problem—the psychology of perception—that mostly leads to the misidentification of defendants. On the other hand, given the lack of action on the part of the criminal justice system, the Supreme Court's involvement raised the visibility of this issue.

As of the late 1990s, serious attention has been paid to changing police identification procedures to improve accuracy and decrease errors. In 1999, at the urging of Attorney General Janet Reno, a National Institute of Justice report, *Eyewitness Evidence: A Guide for Law Enforcement,* suggested specific guidelines for the conduct of: initial reports, the composition of mug books, witness interviews, field identifications procedures (showups), and lineups. This report was stimulated by (1) substantial psychological research adding to the store of knowledge about identification procedures, and (2) the stunning revelations of wrongful convictions generated by forensic DNA testing. The Innocence Project, run by Professors Barry Scheck and Peter Neufeld at Cardozo Law School,[19] the exoneration of half of Illinois's death row inmates,[20] and the publication of *Convicted by Juries, Exonerated by Science* by the National Institute of Justice detailing DNA exonerations, have brought home to the criminal justice system its responsibility to improve the process of identification.[21] This theme is continued in the Law in Society section.

IDENTIFICATION AND THE RIGHT TO COUNSEL

The Supreme Court turned its attention to lineup identification in 1967, just four years after *Gideon v. Wainwright* and one year after *Miranda v. Arizona.* The tide of the Court's Due Process Revolution was still riding high, and the lineup cases were a logical sequel. Yet, these cases startled the legal community because the issue lacked precedents. Unlike search and seizure, confessions, and the right to appointed counsel, which had been the subject of litigation for decades and which rested on ancient legal principles, the lineup rules were created by imaginative lawyers who, imbued with the innovative spirit of the Due Process Revolution, suggested ways of expanding the frontiers of the Bill of Rights. This annoyed conservative jurists. United States Court of Appeals Judge Warren Burger said in 1965, four years prior to his elevation to chief justice of the United States, "Such 'Disneyland' contentions as that absence of counsel at the police line-up voids a conviction are becoming commonplace."[22]

The Right to Counsel at Postindictment Lineups

In 1967 the Court decided *United States v. Wade,* and its companion case, *Gilbert v. California,* holding that a *postindictment* lineup is a *critical stage* requiring that counsel be present. In addition, *Stovall v. Denno* applied due process fairness principles to lineups. Stovall also ruled that the lineup right to counsel was not to be applied retroactively to earlier cases in which lineups were conducted without counsel.

—*United States v. Wade* Case & Comments —

United States v. Wade
388 U.S. 218, 87 S.Ct. 1926, 18 L.Ed.2d 1149 (1967)

MR. JUSTICE BRENNAN delivered the opinion of the Court.

The question here is whether courtroom identifications of an accused at trial are to be excluded from evidence because the accused was exhibited to the witnesses before trial at a postindictment lineup conducted for identification purposes without notice to and in the absence of the accused's appointed counsel. **[a]**

[In September 1964 a bank was robbed by a man with a small strip of tape on each side of his face. He forced a teller and bank officer, at gunpoint, to fill a pillowcase with money. He escaped with an accomplice waiting in a stolen car. In March 1965 Wade and two others were indicted for conspiracy and bank robbery.] **[b]** Wade was arrested on April 2, and counsel was appointed to represent him on April 26. Fifteen days later an FBI agent, without notice to Wade's lawyer, arranged to have the two bank employees observe a lineup made up of Wade and five or six other prisoners and conducted in a courtroom of the local county courthouse. **[c]** Each person in the line wore strips of tape such as allegedly worn by the robber and upon direction each said something like "put the money in the bag," the words allegedly uttered by the robber. Both bank employees identified Wade in the lineup as the bank robber.

At trial, the two employees, when asked on direct examination if the robber was in the courtroom, pointed to Wade. The prior lineup identification was then elicited from both employees on cross-examination. **[d]** At the close of testimony, Wade's counsel moved for a judgment of acquittal or, alternatively, to strike the bank officials' courtroom identifications on the ground that conduct of the lineup, without notice to and in the absence of his appointed counsel, violated his Fifth Amendment privilege against self-incrimination and his Sixth Amendment right to the assistance of counsel. The motion was denied, and Wade was convicted. The Court of Appeals for the Fifth Circuit reversed the conviction and ordered a new trial at which the in-court identification evidence was to be excluded, holding that, though the lineup did not violate Wade's Fifth Amendment rights, "the lineup, held as it was, in the absence of counsel, already chosen to represent appellant, was a violation of his Sixth Amendment rights. . . ." **[e]** * * * We reverse the judgment of the Court of Appeals and remand to that court with direction to enter a new judgment vacating the conviction and remanding the case to the District Court for further proceedings consistent with this opinion.

I

[The Court ruled that no Fifth Amendment violation occurred by requiring Wade to participate in the lineup, or by placing strips of tape on his face or by repeating what was said at the robbery. Providing physical evidence of one's identity is not the kind of **"testimonial evidence"** protected by the privilege against self-incrimination.]

II

[This part reviewed the Sixth Amendment right to counsel, deemed indispensable to protect the right to a fair trial. Dissenters said that lawyers had never participated in lineups and had no proper role to play at lineups. In Part II Justice Brennan replied: "The Framers of the Bill of Rights envisaged a broader role for counsel than under the practice then prevailing in England of merely advising his client in 'matters of law,' and eschewing any responsibility for 'matters of fact.'" The Sixth Amendment requires counsel at any critical stage of the criminal proceedings, which can include a lineup if it potentially and substantially prejudices a defendant's rights.]

III

The Government characterizes the lineup as a mere preparatory step in the gathering of the prosecution's evidence, not different—for Sixth Amendment purposes—from various other preparatory steps, such as systematized or scientific analyzing of the accused's fingerprints, blood sample, clothing, hair, and the like. **[f]** We think there are differences which preclude such stages being characterized as critical stages at which the accused has the right to the presence of his counsel. Knowledge of the techniques of science and technology is sufficiently available, and the variables in techniques few enough, that the accused has the opportunity for a meaningful confrontation of the Government's case at trial through the ordinary processes of cross-examination of the Government's expert witnesses and the presentation of the evidence of his own experts. The denial of a right to have his counsel present at such

[a] This narrow statement of the issue is linked to the "remedy" in Part V of the opinion. There are other legal issues in the case.

[b] Wade's indictment prior to the lineup seems like a minor detail. It became an important factor in determining the scope of the right to counsel in later cases.

[c] Additional facts are found in Part IV. Case facts are sometimes scattered through an opinion, making them difficult to read.

[d] Note the *two* identifications—in the courtroom and at the lineup.

[e] The court of appeals, believing that the witnesses might not have identified Wade if they had not participated in the lineup, simply eliminated their in-court identification. Compare the Supreme Court's remedy in Part V.

[f] Taking and analyzing physical evidence is clear cut and errors can be ascertained by cross-examination—it is *not* a *critical stage*. To the contrary, improper suggestions at the lineup can take many forms and cannot be reconstructed by cross-examination.

• CASE & COMMENTS •

analyses does not therefore violate the Sixth Amendment; they are not critical stages since there is minimal risk that his counsel's absence at such stages might derogate from his right to a fair trial.

IV

But the confrontation compelled by the State between the accused and the victim or witnesses to a crime to elicit identification evidence is peculiarly riddled with innumerable dangers and variable factors which might seriously, even crucially, derogate from a fair trial. **[g]** The vagaries of eyewitness identification are well-known; the annals of criminal law are rife with instances of mistaken identification. * * * A major factor contributing to the high incidence of miscarriage of justice from mistaken identification has been the degree of suggestion inherent in the manner in which the prosecution presents the suspect to witnesses for pretrial identification. A commentator has observed that "[t]he influence of improper suggestion upon identifying witnesses probably accounts for more miscarriages of justice than any other single factor—perhaps it is responsible for more such errors than all other factors combined." **[h]** * * * Suggestion can be created intentionally or unintentionally in many subtle ways. And the dangers for the suspect are particularly grave when the witness' opportunity for observation was insubstantial, and thus his susceptibility to suggestion the greatest.

Moreover, "[i]t is a matter of common experience that, once a witness has picked out the accused at the line-up, he is not likely to go back on his word later on, so that in practice the issue of identity may (in the absence of other relevant evidence) for all practical purposes be determined there and then, before the trial." **[i]**

The pretrial confrontation for purpose of identification may take the form of a lineup, also known as an "identification parade" or "showup," as in the present case, or presentation of the suspect alone to the witness. * * * It is obvious that risks of suggestion attend either form of confrontation and increase the dangers inhering in eyewitness identification. But as is the case with secret interrogations, there is serious difficulty in depicting what transpires at lineups and other forms of identification confrontations. * * * For the same reasons, the defense can seldom reconstruct the manner and mode of lineup identification for judge or jury at trial. Those participating in a lineup with the accused may often be police officers; in any event, the participants' names are rarely recorded or divulged at trial. The impediments to an objective observation are increased when the victim is the witness. Lineups are prevalent in rape and robbery prosecutions and present a particular hazard that a victim's understandable outrage may excite vengeful or spiteful motives. * * * [T]he accused's inability effectively to reconstruct at trial any unfairness that occurred at the lineup may deprive him of his only opportunity meaningfully to attack the credibility of the witness' courtroom identification.

* * *

The potential for improper influence is illustrated by the circumstances, insofar as they appear, surrounding the prior identifications in the three cases we decide today. In the present case, the testimony of the identifying witnesses elicited on cross-examination revealed that those witnesses were taken to the courthouse and seated in the courtroom to await assembly of the lineup. **[j]** The courtroom faced on a hallway observable to the witnesses through an open door. The cashier testified that she saw Wade "standing in the hall" within sight of an FBI agent. Five or six other prisoners later appeared in the hall. The vice president testified that he saw a person in the hall in the custody of the agent who "resembled the person that we identified as the one that had entered the bank."

The lineup in *Gilbert* [a companion case], was conducted in an auditorium in which some 100 witnesses to several alleged state and federal robberies charged to Gilbert made wholesale identifications of Gilbert as the robber in each other's presence, a procedure said to be fraught with dangers of suggestion. And the vice of suggestion created by the identification in *Stovall* was the presentation to the witness of the suspect alone handcuffed to police officers. **[k]** It is hard to imagine a situation more clearly conveying the suggestion to the witness that the one presented is believed guilty by the police. * * *

The few cases that have surfaced therefore reveal the existence of a process attended with hazards of serious unfairness to the criminal accused. * * * We do not assume that these risks are the result of police procedures intentionally designed to prejudice an accused. Rather we assume they derive from the dangers inherent in eyewitness identification and the **suggestibility** inherent in the context of the pretrial identification. * * * **[l]** "[T]he fact that the police themselves have, in a given case, little or no doubt that the man put up for identification has committed the offense, and that their chief pre-occupation is with the problem of getting sufficient proof, because he has not 'come clean,'

[g] Should the Court intervene if the problem of misidentification results only from human failings?

[h] "Suggestion" is not simply a human failing. It is something done by the police, thus providing the "state action" necessary for the Court to intervene.

[i] This is a virtual definition of a "critical stage"; the lineup determines the outcome of the trial.

[j] This is a "showup" and is highly suggestive of guilt.

[k] The "contagion" effect in *Gilbert* is clear. *Stovall* is also a showup.

[l] Suggestibility is so well known in medical trials that "double blind" procedures require the person dispensing drugs or placebo not know which is which.

• CASE & COMMENTS •

involves a danger that this persuasion may communicate itself even in a doubtful case to the witness in some way. . . ." * * *

* * * [E]ven though cross-examination is a precious safeguard to a fair trial, it cannot be viewed as an absolute assurance of accuracy and reliability. Thus in the present context, where so many variables and pitfalls exist, the first line of defense must be the prevention of unfairness and the lessening of the hazards of eyewitness identification at the lineup itself. The trial which might determine the accused's fate may well not be that in the courtroom but that at the pretrial confrontation, with the State aligned against the accused, the witness the sole jury, and the accused unprotected against the overreaching, intentional or unintentional, and with little or no effective appeal from the judgment there rendered by the witness—"that's the man."

* * * [T]here can be little doubt that for Wade the postindictment lineup was a critical stage of the prosecution at which he was "as much entitled to such aid [of counsel] . . . as at the trial itself." * * * Thus both Wade and his counsel should have been notified of the impending lineup, and counsel's presence should have been a requisite to conduct of the lineup, absent an "intelligent waiver." **[m]** * * * No substantial countervailing policy considerations have been advanced against the requirement of the presence of counsel. Concern is expressed that the requirement will forestall prompt identifications and result in obstruction of the confrontations. As for the first, we note that in the two cases in which the right to counsel is today held to apply, counsel had already been appointed and no argument is made in either case that notice to counsel would have prejudicially delayed the confrontations. [Substitute counsel might also reduce delay.] And to refuse to recognize the right to counsel for fear that counsel will obstruct the course of justice is contrary to the basic assumptions upon which this Court has operated in Sixth Amendment cases. * * * In our view counsel can hardly impede legitimate law enforcement; on the contrary, for the reasons expressed, law enforcement may be assisted by preventing the infiltration of taint in the prosecution's identification evidence. That result cannot help the guilty avoid conviction but can only help assure that the right man has been brought to justice. **[n]**

Legislative or other regulations, such as those of local police departments, which eliminate the risks of abuse and unintentional suggestion at lineup proceedings and the impediments to meaningful confrontation at trial may also remove the basis for regarding the stage as "critical." But neither Congress nor the federal authorities have seen fit to provide a solution. What we hold today "in no way creates a constitutional straitjacket which will handicap sound efforts at reform, nor is it intended to have this effect." * * *

V

We come now to the question whether the denial of Wade's motion to strike the courtroom identification by the bank witnesses at trial because of the absence of his counsel at the lineup required, as the Court of Appeals held, the grant of a new trial at which such evidence is to be excluded. **[o]** We do not think this disposition can be justified without first giving the Government the opportunity to establish by clear and convincing evidence that the in-court identifications were based upon observations of the suspect other than the lineup identification. * * * Where, as here, the admissibility of evidence of the lineup identification itself is not involved, a *per se* rule of exclusion of courtroom identification would be unjustified. * * * A rule limited solely to the exclusion of testimony concerning identification at the lineup itself, without regard to admissibility of the courtroom identification, would render the right to counsel an empty one. **[p]** The lineup is most often used, as in the present case, to crystallize the witnesses' identification of the defendant for future reference. We have already noted that the lineup identification will have that effect. The State may then rest upon the witnesses' unequivocal courtroom identification, and not mention the pretrial identification as part of the State's case at trial. Counsel is then in the predicament in which Wade's counsel found himself—realizing that possible unfairness at the lineup may be the sole means of attack upon the unequivocal courtroom identification, and having to probe in the dark in an attempt to discover and reveal unfairness, while bolstering the government witness' courtroom identification by bringing out and dwelling upon his prior identification. Since counsel's presence at the lineup would equip him to attack not only the lineup identification but the courtroom identification as well, limiting the impact of violation of the right to counsel to exclusion of evidence only of identification at the lineup itself disregards a critical element of that right.

We think it follows that the proper test to be applied in these situations is that quoted in *Wong Sun v. United States* [1963], "[W]hether, granting establishment of the primary illegality, the evidence to which instant objection is made has been come at by exploitation of that illegality or instead by means

[m] The substantive rule of the case is stated here, as well as a reply to the dissents.

[n] Justice Brennan is three decades ahead of his time. The prosecution is helped by defense counsel who prevent the conviction of innocent persons. Legislation is finally beginning to address the conduct of lineups.

[o] This Part concerns the remedy. How does it differ from that of the Court of Appeals?

[p] The courtroom identification is linked to whether the witness is recalling the defendant from the crime or from the lineup.

sufficiently distinguishable to be purged of the primary taint.' * * *" **[q]** Application of this test in the present context requires consideration of various factors; for example, the prior opportunity to observe the alleged criminal act, the existence of any discrepancy between any pre-lineup description and the defendant's actual description, any identification prior to lineup of another person, the identification by picture of the defendant prior to the lineup, failure to identify the defendant on a prior occasion, and the lapse of time between the alleged act and the lineup identification. **[r]** It is also relevant to consider those facts which, despite the absence of counsel, are disclosed concerning the conduct of the lineup.

We doubt that the Court of Appeals applied the proper test for exclusion of the in-court identification of the two witnesses. * * * [The judgment of the Court of Appeals was vacated and the case remanded for further proceedings].

[Chief Justice Warren and Justices Black, Douglas, and Fortas concurred, but believed that compelling Wade to wear tape and speak at the lineup violated his Fifth Amendment privilege against self-incrimination. Justice Clark concurred in the majority opinion.]

MR. JUSTICE BLACK, dissenting in part and concurring in part.
[Justice Black agreed that a lineup is a critical stage at which counsel is required. However, he found fault with the Court's remedy (in Part V) on both practical and constitutional grounds. He would have allowed the witness to identify the defendant at the trial and voted to uphold the conviction.] **[s]**

In the first place, even if this Court has power to establish such a rule of evidence, I think the rule fashioned by the Court is unsound. The "tainted fruit" determination required by the Court involves more than considerable difficulty. I think it is practically impossible. How is a witness capable of probing the recesses of his mind to draw a sharp line between a courtroom identification due exclusively to an earlier lineup and a courtroom identification due to memory not based on the lineup? What kind of "clear and convincing evidence" can the prosecution offer to prove upon what particular events memories resulting in an in-court identification rest? How long will trials be delayed while judges turn psychologists to probe the subconscious minds of witnesses? All these questions are posed but not answered by the Court's opinion. * * *

MR. JUSTICE WHITE, whom MR. JUSTICE HARLAN and MR. JUSTICE STEWART join, dissenting in part and concurring in part.
* * *
I share the Court's view that the criminal trial, at the very least, should aim at truthful factfinding, including accurate eyewitness identifications. I doubt, however, on the basis of our present information, that the tragic mistakes which have occurred in criminal trials are as much the product of improper police conduct as they are the consequence of the difficulties inherent in eyewitness testimony and in resolving evidentiary conflicts by court or jury. **[t]** I doubt that the Court's new rule will obviate these difficulties, or that the situation will be measurably improved by inserting defense counsel into the investigative processes of police departments everywhere.

But, it may be asked, what possible state interest militates against requiring the presence of defense counsel at lineups? After all, the argument goes, he *may* do some good, he *may* upgrade the quality of identification evidence in state courts and he can scarcely do any harm. Even if true, this is a feeble foundation for fastening an ironclad constitutional rule upon state criminal procedures. Absent some reliably established constitutional violation, the processes by which the States enforce their criminal laws are their own prerogative. * * *
* * *

[q] What is the "primary illegality" in the lineup situation? What is the "exploitation of that illegality"?

[r] What are these factors designed to do?

[s] Justice Black also attacked the majority for exercising what he believed was unconstitutional power under the Due Process Clause to make new law.

[t] Justice White argues, in contrast to Justice Brennan, that the problem is not suggestibility but the fallibility of human memory. Thus, there is no "state action" and no basis for the jurisdiction of federal courts. This argument displays a belief in federalism.

Did *Wade* require that a lawyer be present when police apprehend a suspect immediately after a crime, based on a victim's or witness's description, and show the stopped suspect to the victim or witness? This standard practice has the dual benefit of immediately exonerating innocent look-alikes and presenting an identification opportunity to a witness when recall is the strongest. To delay such a showup until a lawyer can be secured can multiply injustices for both the victim and the defendant.[23] Faced with the unpalatable possibility of extending the right to counsel rule to on-the-street situations, the liberal United States Court of Appeals for the District of Columbia Circuit in 1969 carved out an exception to the right to counsel for immediate postarrest showups.[24] The need for such an exception became unnecessary after the Supreme Court dealt with the timing of the right to counsel at lineups in *Kirby v. Illinois* (1972).

When Does the Right to Counsel at Lineups Attach?

The lineup in *Wade* occurred *after* Wade had been indicted. The issue in *Kirby v. Illinois* (1972) was whether the right to counsel applied to a lineup that was conducted *before* a suspect was indicted. There is little doubt that had the same Court that decided *Wade* decided this issue, the right to counsel would have been extended to preindictment lineups. A *holding* of a case is the rule of the case that is controlled by its essential facts. Was the timing of the lineup (postindictment) an essential fact of Wade? Justice Brennan, who wrote the majority opinion in *Wade* and dissented in *Kirby,* said "No." The majority in *Kirby* disagreed. What had changed between the years 1967 and 1972 was the composition of the Court. A more conservative Supreme Court, bent on reversing or limiting the individual rights advanced by the Warren Court, set to work in *Kirby* and like cases to limit, if not overrule, expansive Warren Court rulings.

The facts of *Kirby* were simple. Willie Shard, a robbery victim, was asked to identify two suspects who were detained in a police station two days after the incident. The victim immediately identified the suspects, Thomas Kirby and Ralph Bean, who had been found with the victim's traveler's checks and Social Security card. No lawyer was present during the identification. The suspects did not ask for a lawyer, nor were they advised of any right to the presence of counsel. Six weeks later, the suspects were indicted for the robbery. At trial, Shard identified Kirby and Bean and testified to his police station identifications. The Illinois Supreme Court upheld the legality of this identification process. Kirby argued that the benefits of counsel to dispel or record suggestive action by police officers is equally important in a preindictment lineup as in a postindictment lineup. The Supreme Court upheld Kirby's conviction.

Justice Stewart, who dissented in *Wade,* wrote the majority opinion in *Kirby.* The *Wade-Gilbert* right to counsel was based on the Sixth Amendment, not the Fifth Amendment privilege against self-incrimination. All previous Sixth Amendment cases held that the right to counsel "attaches at the time of arraignment" or the "initiation of judicial criminal proceedings." The right to counsel in *Miranda,* by contrast, was based on vindicating the privilege against self-incrimination. Therefore, reasoned the Court, the Sixth Amendment right to counsel does not apply to preindictment lineups but only to lineups and showups "at or after the time that adversary judicial proceedings have been initiated against him."

To justify the decision, Justice Stewart noted that:

> The initiation of judicial criminal proceedings is far from a mere formalism. It is the starting point of our whole system of adversary criminal justice. For it is only then that the government has committed itself to prosecute, and only then that the adverse positions of government and defendant have solidified. It is then that a defendant finds himself faced with the prosecutorial forces of organized society, and immersed in the intricacies of substantive and procedural criminal law. (*Kirby v. Illinois,* pp. 689–90)

If any abuses were alleged to occur during a preindictment lineup or showup, the defendant could urge a court to apply the due process rule, which was announced in *Stovall v. Denno* (discussed later in this chapter). The majority opinion was joined by each of the justices who were appointed by President Nixon: Chief Justice Burger and Justices Blackmun, Powell, and Rehnquist.

Justice Brennan's dissent in *Kirby,* like his majority opinion in *Wade,* argued that the right to counsel is designed to ensure a fair trial. Having a lawyer present at a police station showup is necessary to prevent the suggestibility that influences a witness and thus is crucial to a fair trial. The essence of the *Wade-Gilbert* rule is that an attorney be present at a *pretrial* identification confrontation, for the unfairness of suggestibility can equally infect a preindictment or a postindictment showup or lineup. In this regard, "an abstract consideration of the words 'criminal prosecutions' in the Sixth Amendment" should not limit the extension of the right to counsel at all stationhouse-identification procedures. Justice Brennan virtually accused the majority of willfully misconstruing the real meaning of the *Wade* and *Gilbert* cases by inflating the importance of the fortuitous circumstance that the lineups in those cases occurred after indictments. Indeed, "every United States Court of Appeals that has confronted the question has applied *Wade* and *Gilbert* to preindictment confrontations," as did the appellate courts of thirteen states. Against this, only five states at that time ruled, as did Illinois, that the *Wade* rule applied only to postindictment lineups. Justice Brennan was joined not only by liberal Justices Douglas and Marshall but also by Justice Byron White, who had dissented in *Wade.* Justice White confirmed Justice Brennan's hint that the *Kirby* majority was motivated by conservative ideological activism. He expressed the "judicial conservatism" of *stare decisis* by noting that *Wade* and *Gilbert* "govern this case and compel reversal of the judgment below."

Kirby revealed the Burger Court's discontent with the *Wade* rule by limiting it, but also an unwillingness or inability to completely overturn it. The Court nevertheless stood by the *Kirby* rule in *Moore v. Illinois* (1977). A rape victim gave the police a description of the rapist. She examined two sets of photographs in the week following the crime, and whittled possible suspects down to two or three from two hundred photographs. One of these was of Moore. He was arrested and presented at a preliminary examination the next day to determine whether he should be formally charged by the grand jury. The police accompanied the victim to the preliminary examination, during which she was to view Moore and to "identify him if she could." She positively identified him. The detectives had her sign a complaint that named Moore as her assailant. Moore, unrepresented by a lawyer at this point, was bound over.

Moore challenged the introduction of the identification, arguing that the preliminary hearing "marked the initiation of adversary judicial criminal proceedings against him. Hence, under *Wade, Gilbert,* and *Kirby,* he was entitled to the presence of counsel at that confrontation." The Supreme Court agreed with Moore. *Kirby* applied the *Wade* counsel rule not only after *indictment,* but "at or after the initiation of adversary judicial criminal proceedings," including proceedings instituted "by way of formal charge [or] *preliminary hearing.*" Thus, not only did the showup in the *Moore* case fall within the direct rule of *Kirby,* it was obviously a *critical stage:* Moore faced a state prosecutor at the hearing; it was a hearing where the charges could have been dismissed; the state had to produce evidence against the defendant at that point or drop the case; and, of course, the defendant was identified at that proceeding.

In addition, the Court made it absolutely clear that the *Wade-Gilbert-Kirby* rules apply to a *showup* of one suspect, as well as to a *lineup* of several look-alikes:

> Although *Wade* and *Gilbert* both involved lineups, *Wade* clearly contemplated that counsel would be required in both situations. * * * Indeed, a one-on-one confrontation generally is thought to present greater risks of mistaken identification than a lineup. . . . There is no reason, then, to hold that a one-on-one identification procedure is not subject to the same requirements as a lineup.
> (*Moore v. Illinois,* p. 229)

Finally, the prosecution argued that the victim's identification testimony should be automatically introduced at trial because there was an "independent source" for it. That is, the victim said she thought she had seen Moore at a neighborhood bar. The Supreme Court rejected this argument. It ruled that the prosecution cannot violate the *Wade-Gilbert* rules, and then simply allow the defendant to be identified in the case-in-chief based on the theory that the identification was based on the crime or other encounter. The case was remanded to determine if the victim's memory was based on the incident or the showup. Justice Rehnquist grudgingly concurred, noting that he would prefer that *Wade-Gilbert*'s *per se* exclusionary rule of the lineup/showup identification be replaced with a "totality of the circumstances" approach. In conclusion, although the Supreme Court erected a somewhat artificial distinction in *Kirby,* it maintained the doctrinal integrity of the *Kirby* rule in *Moore v. Illinois.*

Does the Right to Counsel Apply to Photographic Identification?

A year after *Kirby,* the Supreme Court faced the issue of whether an attorney was required to be present at a postindictment "photographic lineup." Victims and witnesses are sometimes shown single photos of a suspect, in a photographic counterpart of a showup. Photo lineups can be in the form of an array of six photos of similar-looking individuals (a "six-pack"), or the witness can leaf through a stack of head shots or page through photos in "mugbooks."

In **United States v. Ash** (1973) the Supreme Court rejected the *Wade-Kirby* Sixth Amendment approach to photographic identification and held that under the Sixth Amendment a lawyer is *never* required when photographs that include the suspect's likeness are shown to a witness. Instead, the admissibility of photographs depends on whether the showing violated due process fairness.

An informant told FBI agents that Charles J. Ash, Jr., had been involved in a bank robbery. Prior to pressing formal charges, the agents "showed five black-and-white mug shots of Negro males of generally the same age, height, and weight, one of which was of Ash, to four witnesses. All four made uncertain identifications of Ash's picture." Prior to trial, after Ash had been formally charged, the prosecutor "decided to use a photographic display to determine whether the witnesses he planned to call would be able to make in-court identifications. Shortly before the trial, an FBI agent and the prosecutor showed five color photographs to the four witnesses who previously had tentatively identified the black-and-white photograph of Ash. Three of the witnesses selected the picture of Ash, but one was unable to make any selection." Ash claimed that this process violated his right to counsel at a *critical stage* of the prosecution. The trial judge denied this claim. At trial, the three witnesses who had been inside the bank identified Ash as the gunman, but they were unwilling to state that they were certain of their identifications. The trial judge ruled that all five color photographs would be admitted into evidence. The jury convicted Ash. The Court of Appeals applied the *Wade-Gilbert* rule and held that Ash's right to counsel was violated when his attorney was not given the opportunity to be present at the postindictment, pretrial photographic displays.

The Supreme Court, by a 6–3 vote, reversed. Several reasons for the decision can be discerned in Justice Blackmun's lengthy and murky majority opinion. One reason is that the suspect is not physically present at a photo lineup, and therefore "no possibility arises that the accused might be misled by his lack of familiarity with the law or overpowered by his professional adversary" (*Ash,* p. 317). Because a suspect is not subjected to testimonial questioning at a lineup, this point refers to a scenario in which police have the suspect say more or do more at a live lineup that makes him stand out to the witnesses. This however, falls logically under the category of suggestibility that can also affect a photo identification, if, for example, an officer pauses at greater length at the suspect's photo.

Related to this reason is the point that "the counsel guarantee would not be used to produce equality in a trial-like adversary confrontation" where "the function of the lawyer has remained essentially the same as his function at trial" (*Ash,* pp. 312, 317). This means that the Supreme Court is reluctant to extend the right to counsel to settings that do not have some of the attributes of a trial where the lawyer's forensic skill is used: questioning witnesses, cross-examining, and projecting and analyzing legal arguments. The Court, however, had indeed extended the right to counsel in non-trial-like settings for postindictment lineups (*Wade*), but, illogically, drew the line at preindictment lineups (*Kirby*). The Court clearly did not desire to further expand the right to counsel beyond arraignments, pretrial examinations, and the like, where counsel acts "as a spokesman for, or advisor to, the accused" (*Ash,* p. 312).

Another point was that although the use of photography in criminal investigation was relatively new, witnesses had been questioned by magistrates and police for hundreds of years without the presence of defense counsel. The Court clearly was concerned that a ruling in Ash's favor could lead to pressure to bring police interviewing under the Sixth Amendment, however remote the possibility.

The Court's weakest argument was that photo identification is less suggestive than live lineups and can be more easily cured by cross-examination at trial. This point was prominently made by Justice Stewart, concurring, as well as by Justice Blackmun.

> A photographic identification is quite different from a lineup, for there are substantially fewer possibilities of impermissible suggestion when photographs are used, and those unfair influences can be readily reconstructed at trial. It is true that the defendant's photograph may be markedly different from the others displayed, but this unfairness can be demonstrated at trial from an actual comparison of the photographs used or from the witness' description of the display. Similarly, it is possible that the photographs could be arranged in a suggestive manner, or that by comment or gesture the prosecuting authorities might single out the defendant's picture. But these are the kinds of overt influence that a witness can easily recount and that would serve to impeach the identification testimony. In short, there are few possibilities for unfair suggestiveness—and those rather blatant and easily reconstructed. Accordingly, an accused would not be foreclosed from an effective cross-examination of an identification witness simply because his counsel was not present at the photographic display. For this reason, a photographic display cannot fairly be considered a "critical stage" of the prosecution. (*United States v. Ash*, Stewart, J., concurring, pp. 324–25)

It seems, however, that Justice Brennan dissenting with Justices Douglas and Marshall, had the better argument on this point. In a photo identification, "as in the lineup situation, the possibilities for impermissible suggestion in the context of a photographic display are manifold" (*Ash*, p. 333). Indeed, Justice Stewart suggested some of the ways in which a police officer, even inadvertently, could suggest that a certain photo is that of the suspect. Without an attorney present to observe the showing, how would it be possible for the defense lawyer to form cross-examination questions that are on the mark? As a matter of logic and experience, Justice Stewart's views on the ability of cross-examination to detect suggestibility is not very convincing except in the most outrageous examples. He limits his examples only to overt suggestibility and says nothing about other factors discussed by Justice Brennan, including "the manner in which the photographs are displayed to the witness" by, for example, emphasizing the suspect's photograph by leaving it out longer, arraying it in a way to point it out, and so forth, and by "gestures or comments of the prosecutor at the time of the display [that] may lead an otherwise uncertain witness to select the 'correct' photograph." In this regard, Justice Brennan touched on the powerful psychological effect that is conveyed even by unintentional cues: "More subtly, the prosecutor's inflection, facial expressions, physical motions, and myriad other almost imperceptible means of communication might tend, intentionally or unintentionally, to compromise the witness' objectivity" (*Ash*, Brennan, J., dissenting, pp. 333–34). In these situations, reconstruction of the suggestion is next to impossible.

Justice Brennan concluded that the Court's logic was "a triumph of form over substance" (*Ash*, p. 338) because in past instances where the Court found that a critical stage existed, requiring the presence of counsel, the essential point was that the stage of the criminal process was one in which unfairness would undermine the fairness of the trial itself. Since, in the view of the dissenters, the uncorrectable suggestibility of the photographic identification would taint the trial, it was a critical stage.

United States v. Ash (1973), similarly to *Kirby v. Illinois* (1972), is a clear example of the conservative Burger Court limiting expansive Warren Court rulings, not by overruling them, but trimming them back or preventing any expansion. The goals of the Court now clearly marked the "Crime Control Model" over the "Due Process Model" of constitutional analysis specified by Professor Herbert Packer.[25] The majority was concerned with creating rules that might interfere with the work of police and prosecutors as the "war on crime" became a seemingly permanent feature of American political and social life. The dissenters displayed greater concern with the overall fairness of the process and were willing to make the investigation process less efficient for the purpose of reducing the possibility of wrongful convictions. Indeed, as later research and analysis indicated, numerous miscarriages of justice resulted from improper photo identification.[26]

IDENTIFICATION AND THE FIFTH AMENDMENT

United States v. Wade held that "Neither the lineup itself nor anything shown by this record that Wade was required to do in the lineup violated his privilege against self-incrimination." This holding can be divided into two rules. The first, unanimously supported by the Court, is that the simple display of a person at trial or at a lineup so that he can be identified as a suspect does not violate the Fifth Amendment privilege against self-incrimination. The Fifth Amendment prohibits only the *compulsion* of *testimonial evidence*.

> We have no doubt that compelling the accused merely to exhibit his person for observation by a prosecution witness prior to trial involves no compulsion of the accused to give evidence having testimonial significance. It is compulsion of the accused to exhibit his physical characteristics, not compulsion to disclose any knowledge he might have. (*United States v. Wade*, p. 222).

Wade raised another argument that was accepted by four dissenting justices: Justice Black in a separate dissent, and Justice Fortas in a dissent joined by Chief Justice Warren and Justice Douglas. Wade, along with other lineup participants, was required to wear strips of tape on each side of his face, as had the robber, and to speak words that were spoken by the robber. The second self-incrimination ruling by the *Wade* majority is that this kind of compelled behavior, which goes beyond the simple display of a suspect's face, also does not violate the privilege.

Justice Brennan's dissent relied on the precedent of ***Schmerber v. California*** (1966). Blood was drawn from Schmerber by medical personnel on the order of a police officer after he was arrested for a drunk driving fatality. The Supreme Court held that the self-incrimination principle was designed to protect individuals from divulging information "of a *communicative* nature." This means that the Fifth Amendment privilege prohibits the state from forcing a person to admit guilt by *spoken words*, *actions that convey meaning*, or *writings that convey a sense of guilt*. The state, however, in enforcing the law, may have access to any *physical evidence* that is probative and that may be obtained without violating due process or Fourth Amendment protections.

The *Schmerber* principle has allowed the use of different kinds of physical evidence, including blood samples; handwriting exemplars to show that the handwriting of the defendant matched that of an incriminating note;[27] voice exemplars;[28] and body evidence such as fingerprints, photographs, hair samples, and cell scrapings from which DNA tracers can be identified; and one's name.[29]

The dissenters thought that what Wade was required to do "is more than passive, mute assistance to the eyes of the victim or of witnesses. It is the kind of volitional act—the kind of forced cooperation by the accused—which is within the historical perimeter of the privilege against compelled self-incrimination." Nevertheless, as Justice Brennan pointed out for the majority, the precedent of *Holt v. United States* (1910), authored by Justice Holmes, upheld the right of the state to require a suspect at a lineup to wear an article of clothing that was worn at the crime.

DUE PROCESS AND EYEWITNESS IDENTIFICATION

The Supreme Court, in *Stovall v. Denno* (1967) ruled that the suggestiveness of a lineup or showup must be guided by the Fifth or Fourteenth amendments' Due Process Clauses, because unnecessarily suggestive pretrial identification procedures are *fundamentally unfair*. Fairness is a *flexible* test that requires a court to examine the *totality of the circumstances*. A due process rule, therefore, is more a *general standard* than a clear-cut or *bright-line* rule. As a result, in due process litigation, the Court frequently is faced with finely differentiated fact situations that require careful examination.

Stovall v. Denno (1967) demonstrates that the requirement of non-suggestive identification procedures is not absolute. The necessities of law enforcement may override the purity of the identification process. In this case a physician, Dr. Behrendt, was stabbed to death in the kitchen of his home at midnight of August 23. His wife, also a physician, entered the kitchen and jumped at the assailant. He knocked her to the floor and stabbed her eleven times. Physical clues led the police to Stovall, and he was arrested on the afternoon of August 24. The wife was hospitalized for major surgery to save her life that same day.

> The police, without affording [Stovall] time to retain counsel, arranged with her surgeon to permit them to bring petitioner to her hospital room about noon of August 25, the day after the surgery. Petitioner was handcuffed to one of five police officers who, with two members of the staff of the District Attorney, brought him to the hospital room. [Stovall] was the only Negro in the room. Mrs. Behrendt identified him from her hospital bed after being asked by an officer whether he "was the man" and

after petitioner repeated at the direction of an officer a "few words for voice identification." None of the witnesses could recall the words that were used. Mrs. Behrendt and the officers testified at the trial to her identification of the petitioner in the hospital room, and she also made an in-court identification of petitioner in the courtroom. (*Stovall v. Denno*, p. 295).

A federal appellate court, on a habeas corpus petition, reversed the state conviction on the ground that the eyewitness identification violated Stovall's right to counsel. The Supreme Court, in a majority opinion by Justice Brennan, reversed this part of the holding and decided in *Stovall* that the *Wade-Gilbert* rule did not apply retroactively, concerned "that retroactive application of *Wade* and *Gilbert* 'would seriously disrupt the administration of our criminal laws.'" The remaining issue was whether the conviction should be overturned because the identification procedure "was so unnecessarily suggestive and conducive to irreparable mistaken identification that he was denied due process of law" (*Stovall*, p. 302).

Justice Brennan, noting that the "practice of showing suspects singly to persons for the purpose of identification, and not as part of a lineup, has been widely condemned," nevertheless ruled against Stovall, without specifically evaluating whether the showup was suggestive. Instead, the Court held that the totality of circumstances included the law enforcement exigency that without the showup the only evidence of the crime might be lost, quoting from the Court of Appeals opinion:

> "Here was the only person in the world who could possibly exonerate Stovall. Her words, and only her words, 'He is not the man' could have resulted in freedom for Stovall. The hospital was not far distant from the courthouse and jail. No one knew how long Mrs. Behrendt might live. Faced with the responsibility of identifying the attacker, with the need for immediate action and with the knowledge that Mrs. Behrendt could not visit the jail, the police followed the only feasible procedure and took Stovall to the hospital room. Under these circumstances, the usual police station line-up, which Stovall now argues he should have had, was out of the question."
> (*Stovall v. Denno*, p. 302, quoting the Court of Appeals decision)

Although the showup in *Stovall* surely *was* suggestive under the circumstances—which included the reasonable possibility that the only eyewitness to the serious crime might soon die, the impossibility to construct a lineup, and the fact that the suspect was not chosen at random but was tied to the crime scene by physical evidence—the choice was between a suggestive identification procedure or none at all. These circumstances resulted in the conclusion that the showup in this case was not fundamentally unfair.

A clear example of a lineup that violated due process was *Foster v. California* (1969). Foster, a thin, six-foot-tall robbery suspect, wearing a leather jacket similar to the robber's, was placed in a lineup with two other men who were approximately five-foot-five and were not wearing leather jackets. Despite these discrepancies, the witness could not identify Foster, so he was brought into a room with the witness and made to speak. "Even after this one-to-one confrontation [the witness] still was uncertain whether petitioner was one of the robbers: 'Truthfully—I was not sure,' he testified at trial." In a second lineup a week later, Foster was the only individual from the first lineup. At this point, the witness was convinced. Justice Fortas's opinion, finding that due process was violated, relied on the element of *reliability:* "The suggestive elements in this identification procedure made it all but inevitable that [the witness] would identify [Foster] whether or not he was in fact 'the man.' In effect, the police repeatedly said to the witness, 'This is the man.' . . . This procedure so undermined the reliability of the eyewitness identification as to violate due process" (*Foster v. California,* p. 443).

The Supreme Court refused to hold that the showing of a suspect's photograph to crime victims during the investigation of a crime, while the suspect was still at large, violated due process (**Simmons v. United States,** 1968). Although such a procedure is necessarily suggestive, "this procedure has been used widely and effectively in criminal law enforcement, from the standpoint both of apprehending offenders and of sparing innocent suspects the ignominy of arrest by allowing eyewitnesses to exonerate them through scrutiny of photographs" (*Simmons,* p. 384). Any risk of misidentification can be corrected at trial through cross-examination.

The Supreme Court has substantially reduced the protection offered by the due process test in the previous two due process cases decided by the Supreme Court. These cases no longer allow the use of showups only when there is a real exigency, as in *Stovall v. Denno,* and have established the rule that identification resulting from a suggestive showup may be allowed into evidence if the suggestibility is offset by strong indicia of reliability.

Neil v. Biggers (1972) concerned a rape conviction based on evidence consisting in part of the victim's visual and voice identification of Biggers at a stationhouse showup seven months after the crime. The victim had been in her assailant's presence for fifteen minutes to a half hour and had directly observed him indoors and under a full moon outdoors. She gave the police a description of the assailant. Over a period of seven months the victim viewed suspects in her home or at the police station, some in lineups and others in showups, and was shown between thirty and forty photographs, but did not identify any of these. The police called her to identify the suspect, who was being held on another charge, at the police station. They could not locate individuals at the city jail or the city juvenile home fitting Biggers's unusual physical description, so they conducted a showup instead. The victim testified that she had "no doubt" that Biggers was her assailant.

On federal habeas corpus, the lower federal courts held that the confrontation was so suggestive as to violate due process. The Supreme Court reversed and held that the evidence had properly been allowed to go to the jury. The Court in *Biggers* summed up earlier cases to establish *general guidelines* concerning the due process rules concerning identification.

> It is, first of all, apparent that the primary evil to be avoided is "a very substantial likelihood of irreparable misidentification." [*Simmons*] While the phrase was coined as a standard for determining whether an in-court identification would be admissible in the wake of a suggestive out-of-court

identification, with the deletion of "irreparable" it serves equally well as a standard for the admissibility of testimony concerning the out-of-court identification itself. It is the likelihood of misidentification which violates a defendant's right to due process, and it is this which was the basis of the exclusion of evidence in *Foster.* Suggestive confrontations are disapproved because they increase the likelihood of misidentification, and unnecessarily suggestive ones are condemned for the further reason that the increased chance of misidentification is gratuitous. But as *Stovall* makes clear, the admission of evidence of a showup without more does not violate due process.

> What is less clear from our cases is whether, as intimated by the district court, unnecessary suggestiveness alone requires the exclusion of evidence. While we are inclined to agree with the courts below that the police did not exhaust all possibilities in seeking persons physically comparable to respondent, we do not think that the evidence must therefore be excluded. The purpose of a strict rule barring evidence of unnecessarily suggestive confrontations would be to deter the police from using a less reliable procedure where a more reliable one may be available, and would not be based on the assumption that in every instance the admission of evidence of such a confrontation offends due process. (*Neil v. Biggers,* pp. 198–99)

With this in mind the Court turned to evaluating the totality of circumstances in *Biggers* to determine whether his due process rights to fundamentally fair procedures had been followed.

> [T]he factors to be considered in evaluating the likelihood of misidentification include the opportunity of the witness to view the criminal at the time of the crime, the witness' degree of attention, the accuracy of the witness' prior description of the criminal, the level of certainty demonstrated by the witness at the confrontation, and the length of time between the crime and the confrontation. (*Neil v. Biggers,* pp. 199–200)

On one hand, the procedure was suggestive; the police were not fully diligent in searching for lineup participants, and seven months elapsed between the crime and the positive identification. On the other hand, the victim had ample opportunity to observe her assailant under good light; she was a practical nurse by profession, which implies that she was trained to make accurate observations; her description to the police was complete, including the assailant's approximate age, height, weight, complexion, skin texture, build, and voice; and over the seven-month lapse she had "made no previous identification at any of the showups, lineups, or photographic showings" indicating that her "record for reliability was . . . a good one, as she had previously resisted whatever suggestiveness inheres in a showup." On balance, the identification did not violate Biggers's right to due process in an identification.

The final case in this series, **Manson v. Brathwaite** (1977), generated somewhat more specific criteria for evaluating the *Biggers* factors. The facts in *Manson* were that Glover, a narcotics undercover police officer, and Brown, an informant, went to a suspected apartment building in Hartford, Connecticut, during daylight, to make a controlled narcotics buy. Glover and Brown were observed by backup Officers D'Onofrio and Gaffey. Glover and Brown knocked on a third-floor door in an area illuminated by natural light from a window in the hallway. A man opened the door. Brown asked for "two things" of narcotics. Glover handed over a ten-dollar bill and observed the man in the apartment. The door closed; a moment later, the man opened the door and handed Glover two glassine bags of heroin. Glover was within two feet of the seller and observed his face.

At headquarters, Glover, who is African American, described the seller to D'Onofrio as "a colored man, approximately five feet eleven inches tall, dark complexion, black hair, short Afro style, and having high cheekbones, and of heavy build. He was wearing at the time blue pants and a plaid shirt." D'Onofrio thought that Brathwaite might be the seller and left a photograph of him at Glover's office. Two days later, Glover viewed the photograph for the first time and identified Brathwaite as the seller. At the trial, eight months after the sale, the identification photograph was received in evidence without defense objection. Glover said he had no doubt that the person in the photograph was the seller, and he made an in-court identification. No explanation was offered by the prosecution for the failure to utilize a photographic array or to conduct a lineup.

The Connecticut Supreme Court upheld Brathwaite's conviction, saying that no "substantial injustice resulted from the admission of this evidence." On a habeas corpus petition appeal, the federal Court of Appeals ruled that the photograph should have been excluded, regardless of reliability, because the examination of the single photograph was unnecessary, suggestive, and possibly unreliable. The Supreme Court reversed.

In this case the viewing of the single photograph left for Glover was suggestive and unnecessary, since D'Onofrio could have prepared a photographic array. The Court noted that the showup in *Biggers* also had been suggestive and unnecessary, but maintained the rule that this alone did not require the *per se* exclusion of such identifications. The Court did recognize, indeed, that a *per se* exclusionary rule would tend to make identification more reliable and lessen the opportunity of mistaken identification. The more lenient "*totality of circumstances*" *approach*, while possibly allowing more instances of injustice, was instead upheld. The Supreme Court acknowledged that the *per se* approach was more likely to deter improper police procedures. On the other hand, it said that the totality rule also guards against impropriety, since a suggestive showup or lineup might be excluded. Finally, the *per se* approach made it more likely that a guilty party would go free. On balance, the Court continued to uphold the due process totality of circumstances approach in evaluating the admissibility of suggestive identification procedures, again indicating a preference for the Crime Control Model over the Due Process Model of criminal justice.

The Court then analyzed each of the *Biggers* factors and found that the "indicators of Glover's ability to make an accurate identification are hardly outweighed by the corrupting effect of the challenged identification itself."

1. The opportunity to view. The facts indicated that Glover had natural lighting and two to three minutes to observe Brathwaite from two feet away.

2. The degree of attention. Glover was a trained, on-duty police officer specializing in narcotics enforcement, was an African American and could be expected "to pay scrupulous attention to detail, for he knew that subsequently he would have to find and arrest his vendor" and testify about this in court.

3. The accuracy of the description. Glover's description was given to D'Onofrio within minutes after the transaction and included the vendor's race, height, build, the color and style of his hair, and the high-cheekbone facial feature. It also included clothing the vendor wore. D'Onofrio reacted positively, and two days later, when Glover was alone, he viewed the photograph and identified its subject as the narcotics seller.

4. The witness's level of certainty. Glover, in response to a question whether the photograph was that of the seller, testified: "There is no question whatsoever."

5. The time between the crime and the confrontation-identification was very short. The Court concluded that "we cannot say that under all the circumstances of this case there is 'a very substantial likelihood of irreparable misidentification.'"

LAW IN SOCIETY

REDUCING THE ERROR OF EYEWITNESS IDENTIFICATION

The obligation that police, prosecutors, judges, and juries have to detect, prosecute, and convict the guilty carries an obligation not to convict innocent persons. Studies persistently show that eyewitnesses are frequently mistaken in their identifications of suspects and half of the wrongfully convicted are victims of mistaken eyewitness identification.[30] The criminal justice system has perennially accepted wrongful convictions based on misidentification as the inevitable failing of a human system. Lawyers believed, with some justification, that properly conducted criminal trials kept mistaken identification to a minimum. An experienced defense attorney with sufficient time and resources to investigate a case prior to trial, and skillful in cross-examining witnesses, was sufficient to ferret out the truth. This faith might have been justified up to the beginning of the twentieth century. The growing findings of modern scientific psychological research, however, demonstrate the variability of human memory and legal scholars have become more aware that an alarming number of completely innocent people are wrongfully convicted.[31]

By the 1960s, this knowledge led the Warren Court to augment the legal protections of the common law jury trial with constitutional rules meant to prevent wrongful conviction. This effort had limited success as the more conservative Burger Court restricted the right to counsel at identification procedures (*Kirby v. Illinois,* 1972; *United States v. Ash,* 1973; *Manson v. Brathwaite,* 1977). Of greater significance, the right to counsel during identification procedures and due process rules concerning suggestiveness are crude tools to prevent and correct misidentification.

Since the 1960s, several factors have laid a foundation for a major breakthrough in the problem of wrongful conviction. First, extensive research by psychologists has led to better explanations of human identification and misidentification, establishing a scientific foundation for improvements. They have also designed studies to find out which kinds of questioning and identification procedures are more likely to provide accurate identification. This research has been disseminated to the legal community, making it more aware of its shortcomings, although prosecutors believe in the accuracy of eyewitnesses far more than do defense lawyers.[32] At the same time, celebrated cases of wrongful conviction, such as those of Rubin "Hurricane" Carter, Dr. Sam Shepard, or Randall Adams, and the dramatic moratorium on executions by Illinois governor George Ryan after half of those on death row were exonerated, have sensitized the wider public to the fact that misidentification is a persistent problem.

The factor that has made the greatest impression since 1990 has been DNA testing. It has revealed that the worst fears of critics have been justified: An unacceptably high proportion of people who are charged with crimes and convicted are innocent. The DNA breakthrough is not a prescription for complacency. The authors of *Actual Innocence,* who run the Innocence Project at Cardozo Law School, write:

> Most of the lessons of the DNA era have nothing to do with high-tech gizmos or biotechnical wizardry. "Jurors should get innocence training," says Kevin Green, [a wrongly convicted man]. They need to be told: "'You're doing this because we have to find the truth. The police haven't necessarily found the truth. The district attorney hasn't found the truth. Only you can.'"[33]

The authors note that England established "an official Criminal Case Review Commission that investigates claims of innocence."[34] Barry Scheck and Peter Neufeld, attorneys who have done as much as anyone to force authorities to allow inmates with credible claims to have DNA tests, warn that these tests are not a panacea for correcting wrongful convictions:

> In a few years, the era of DNA exonerations will come to an end. The population of prisoners who can be helped by DNA testing is shrinking, because the technology has been used widely since the early 1990s, clearing thousands of innocent suspects before trial. Yet blameless people will remain in prison, stranded because their cases don't involve biological evidence. . . .
>
> From Borchard's review of cases stretching back to the dawn of the American republic, all the way to the dawn of the twenty-first century, the causes of wrongful conviction remain the same. Clarity is manufactured about moments of inherent confusion. Witnesses swear they can identify the man who held the gun or knife. Police officers then coax or force confessions from suspects they believe guilty. Prosecutors bury exculpatory evidence and defense lawyers sleep on the job. . . .[35]

Thus, steps can and should be taken to improve the accuracy of identification throughout the investigation and trial process. Before a sound program of accurate identification can be put in place, a foundation of scientific knowledge about the nature of memory and recall is required.

UNDERSTANDING MEMORY AND RECALL

Research has generated a better understanding of human perception, memory, and recall than "common sense," even if an integrated theory of perception has not been fully developed.[36] This information helps us better understand eyewitness testimony.

An important starting point is the wide agreement in perception research that eyewitness testimony is often unreliable. This contradicts the beliefs of many people and the experience of jurors: Under experimental conditions such as a staged crime before a class "witnesses have been proven to be remarkably inaccurate."[37, 38] An experiment by Buckhout had a New York television news program run a staged robbery for twelve seconds. A six-man lineup was then shown, and viewers were invited to call in to pick out the perpetrator. More than two thousand viewers called in and only 14.1 percent picked the correct man, a result that was no better than a random guess.[39] Because psychological experiments can modify the elements of perception and recall, the percent of accurate recall in various experiments has varied from no better than chance to 90 percent.[40]

A field experiment by Brigham and colleagues assessed the accuracy of facial recall in a real-life setting.[41] Two men, one white and one African American, entered seventy-three convenience food stores within five minutes of one another, posing as customers. One paid for a pack of cigarettes entirely with pennies and asked for directions. The other asked for directions after fumbling around for change. Two hours later two men pretending to be law interns asked the clerk to identify each "customer" from two photo arrays, one of six whites and one of six African Americans. The overall rate of accurate identifications was 34.2 percent, which increased to 46.8 percent when instances of "no identification" were omitted. This is significantly higher than the 16.7 percent rate (one out of six) that would be expected by random guessing, but it also confirms a large number of incorrect identifications. The correct recall of convenience store clerks fell to chance when the "law interns" presented the photo arrays more than twenty-four hours after the "customers" left the store.

This study also found, in accord with other research, that identification accuracy of a person of *one's own race* is higher and that the ability of white clerks to identify the African American "customer" was significantly related to the amount of cross-racial experience of the white clerk. The African American clerks in this study had higher accuracy rates than the white clerks: They were 13 percent more accurate in identifying the white "customer" and 23 percent more accurate in identifying the African American "customer." As expected, recognition was higher for the "customers" who were more attractive or distinctive and from lineups using larger pictures.

Elizabeth Loftus's summary of research findings first notes that the memory process is *selective.* Humans do not simply record events like a videotape recorder but *process* information at the *acquisition* stage when the event is perceived, during the *retention* stage, and again at the *retrieval* stage during which a person recalls stored information.[42] A complex event consists of a vast amount of information; an individual's sensory mechanism selects only certain aspects of the visual stimulus. People are therefore much better at remembering salient facts of an event than peripheral details.[43]

Acquisition is affected by *event factors:* retention time and frequency (the longer or more frequently something is viewed, the more information is stored) and the type of fact observed (people have great difficulty in assessing speed and time; violent and emotional events produce lower accuracy of memory).[44] "Studies also show that the amount of time perceived as going by is overestimated under conditions of danger and that the overestimation tends to increase as the stress increases."[45] *Witness factors* also affect observation. The "role that stress plays at the time a witness is perceiving a complex event is captured in the Yerkes-Dodson Law[:] . . . that strong motivational states such as stress or other emotional arousal facilitate learning and performance up to a point, after which there is a decrement."[46] Much social-psychological research demonstrates that individual bias affects perception, whether the bias is a result of situational expectations, personal or cultural prejudice, or expectations from past experience.[47]

The *retention stage* is affected by the time lapse between the event and recall. More unnerving, the memory of an event can *change.* "Postevent information can not only enhance existing memories but also change a witness's memory and even cause nonexistent details to become incorporated into a previously acquired memory."[48] This underlines the danger of suggestibility, so prominent in the *Wade-Gilbert-Stovall* trilogy of cases. Studies have shown that: (1) the *likelihood of recall* of an event is enhanced simply by mentioning it; (2) *postevent suggestion* can cause the memory to compromise between what was originally seen and what is reported; and (3) mentioning a *nonexistent object* to a witness can cause the witness to later report having seen it. Not only simple facts, but also subjective recollections about the violence of an event can be modified by postevent suggestion.

Verbal cues subtly influence retention. Subjects shown a filmed traffic accident were asked if they saw broken glass, although there was none. Seven percent of those asked about cars that "hit" reported broken glass compared to 16 percent of those asked about cars that "smashed" into each other. Both *original* information and *external* information acquired *after the event* become merged into one memory. Labeling a situation influences memory as does the practice of witnesses guessing at information if they are not sure of their original memory. The dangers of inaccuracy during memory retention are worsened by a *freezing effect:* A person who makes a statement about an event, tends to more strongly remember the *statement* at a later time; and this applies to objectively true elements of the original event as well as false information.[49]

Similar memory modification occurs during the *retrieval stage.* Accuracy of recall is increased when a person relays it in a familiar and comfortable setting and in a narrative form rather than answering controlled questions. Increased status of the questioner enhances the quantity and accuracy of responses. The wording of questions influences responses. An experiment demonstrated that more witnesses asked to describe "the" event said they saw something not present in a film compared to those asked about "an" event.[50]

TOWARD MORE ACCURATE IDENTIFICATION

It is utopian to believe that wrongful convictions can be entirely eliminated. Nevertheless, practical knowledge exists that can be applied by police agencies to substantially reduce this injustice. As noted earlier, the National Institute of Justice issued a 1999 report, *Eyewitness Evidence: A Guide for Law Enforcement.* This forty-four page booklet was compiled by a group of law enforcement personnel, defense lawyers, and psychologists. It does not provide the background research but, rather, lists precise procedural suggestions for law enforcement agencies. The *Guide* goes a long way toward establishing national criteria, although it has some weaknesses. Professor Donald Judges's thorough review of the *Guide,* states that it is "the most faithful to research findings in its recommendations to avoid instruction bias."[51] On the other hand, he faults it for not recommending double-blind and sequential lineup procedures.[52]

The *Guide* offers recommendations to police in five areas: taking the *initial report* of a crime; preparing *mug books* and composites and instructing witnesses who view them, procedures for *follow-up interviews* of witnesses, field identification *(showup)* procedure, and *lineup* procedures for eyewitness identification of suspects. Under *lineups,* procedures are recommended for composing photo and live lineups, instructing witnesses prior to lineups, and conducting identification procedures. The *Guide* indicates that the NIJ is planning a second phase of the eyewitness project to produce training criteria for these procedures. It notes that no validation studies have been authorized and that changes may be recommended in the future.

In general terms, the *Guide's* recommendations are designed to improve the accuracy of police interviewing and identification. In regard to the initial interviews and follow-up interviews with witnesses, the *Guide* adopts many research findings of what is known as the cognitive interview.[53] Police are instructed to ask open-ended questions and augment answers with closed-ended questions, to avoid asking suggestive or leading questions, to separate witnesses, to instruct witnesses to avoid discussing details of the incident with other witnesses, to encourage the witnesses to volunteer information without prompting, to encourage the witnesses to report all details—even if they seem trivial, to caution the witnesses not to guess, to avoid interrupting the witnesses, and so forth. According to Professor Judges, the *Guide* misses some points.

> For example, in its statements of principle or policy, the Guide does not explicitly state the concepts underlying the components of the cognitive interview, including the witness-centered control of information. Other specific recommendations from CI [Cognitive Interview] are either lacking or only obliquely referred to, such as inviting narrative presentation, witness-compatible questioning (i.e., tailoring questions to witnesses' mental representation of the event, such as a witness who viewed the perpetrator from the side or rear only),

and the varied-retrieval method (e.g., having the witness recall the event in reverse chronological order).[54]

In the remainder of this section, some methods experts have proposed to improve lineups are reviewed.

IMPROVING LINEUPS

Establish Double-Blind Procedures

The dangers of suggestibility or contamination of witnesses by even subtle or unintended emphasis is very well established and uniformly supported by psychological research.[55] Professor Judges urges that "eyewitness identification procedures should be conducted only by persons who are ignorant of which lineup member is the suspect. . . . Use of 'double-blind' procedures—which has long been standard practice in human-subject research—would preclude the possibility of contamination even from inadvertent or subtle feedback cues from the investigator."[56]

Conduct Lineups in a Sequential Manner, Not Simultaneously

The problem with the more typical simultaneous lineup, where all the individuals are viewed while standing together is that it forces the witness to engage in relative (comparative) judgment ("does this person look more like the suspect than that person"), instead of absolute judgment ("that is the man"). A review of research found that "critical tests of this hypothesis have consistently shown that a sequential procedure produces fewer false identifications than does a simultaneous procedure with little or no decrease in rates of accurate identification." This manipulation, because it directly addresses the cognitive source of the problem, is an especially important component of the set of recommendations advanced by researchers in this area for reducing the risk of false identifications.[57]

Use "Lineup Context Cues"

"Lineup context cues" improve the accuracy of lineup identifications. Cutler and Penrod recommend:

> that lineup procedures should ensure the use of voice samples and should show the lineup members from three-quarter poses and, whenever possible and appropriate, allow the witness to watch the lineup members walking in and out of the observation room. Such cues should also be taken into consideration when photographs are taken for the purpose of mug books.[58]

Construct Lineups Fairly

This seems to be axiomatic, but police in the past have been tempted to construct the lineup so that the suspect stands out. The *Guide* urges fairness. Lindsay and Wells note that as non-suspects ("foils") in a lineup come to resemble the suspect more, more witnesses can be expected to erroneously identify the foils, suggesting a trade-off between a high probability of selecting the suspect in unfair (low-similarity) lineups and a high probability of selecting an innocent person in high-similarity lineups. Using experimental lineups with a "criminal" present and a "criminal" absent, Lindsay and Wells found that the choice of a "guilty" suspect fell from 71 percent in unfair lineups to 58 percent in fair ones in the criminal-present mode. However, choosing the "innocent suspect" (a look-alike to the "criminal") fell from 70 percent to 31 percent in the criminal-absent mode. Lindsay and Wells developed diagnosticity ratios that indicated mathematically that the fair lineups improve the relative quality of both identifications and no identifications over the unfair lineups. The practical value of this experiment is to dissuade police from setting up unfair lineups in the hope of highlighting suspects who they are "certain" are guilty.[59] After all, since the selection and conviction of an innocent person leaves the real criminal at large, law enforcement and prosecution have as real a desire to make lineups more fair as do defendants.

The Officer Who Constructs a Lineup Should Be the Same Race as the Suspect

Research shows that same-race identification tends to be more accurate than recognition of other-race faces. If other-race faces tend to look similar, there is a risk that, for example, a white officer who constructs a lineup of a black suspect and black foils for black witnesses may construct a lineup of faces that look alike to him but will appear dissimilar to the witnesses.[60] This point is conjectural and has not yet been subject to rigorous research.

Use Expert Witnesses or Closing Arguments to Rebut Errors about Eyewitness Identification

Using expert witnesses on closing arguments to rebut errors about eyewitness identification has been strenuously resisted by prosecutors for fear that experts would undermine juror confidence in eyewitnesses. Courts and scholars are split on whether to allow experts to testify. Huff, Rattner, and Sagarin would always allow expert witnesses on the issue of reliability, while Donald Judges is skeptical of its value.[61] Attorneys could use closing statements to inform jurors about known information about eyewitness identification. For example, an area in which research contradicts common sense is witness certainty and accuracy of a prior description. Many studies show little or no correlation between the confidence that witnesses express in their certainty and the accuracy of their observations, while others do.[62] The common finding of no confidence-accuracy correlation is counterintuitive; in fact, the Supreme Court in *Neil v. Biggers* (1972) and *Manson v. Brathwaite* (1977) relied on confidence as one of five indicia of certainty, thus possibly injecting an element of factual injustice into some cases. An expert could be useful in bringing this to the attention of a jury, as well as alerting them to other possibly relevant issues.

This list does not exhaust all of the ways in which identification procedures can be made more accurate. The *Guide* is only a first step, and it has flaws. It is probably the case that very few law enforcement departments conduct lineups in a double-blind fashion, and given the disruption of routine, it is not expected that many will change rapidly. It is worth keeping in mind that research will continue to refine knowledge in the area of witness perception. The hopeful sign is that, for the first time, serious national attention has been given to the issue. Time will tell whether real advances will be made in making the identification process more accurate or whether these efforts will be soon forgotten.

SUMMARY

Eyewitness identification is an important source of truth in the justice process but is often mistaken and leads to the unwarranted conviction of innocent persons. Legal rules are less important in preventing mistaken eyewitness identification than proper police procedures. Identification can be made by identifying one suspect—known as a showup. A lineup—live or photographic—is a police identification procedure in which a witness views a suspect to the crime along with others with similar physical characteristics.

The Supreme Court has established rules for the admissibility of eyewitness identification. *United States v. Wade* (1967) held, under the Sixth Amendment, that a suspect is entitled to counsel during a postindictment police lineup. Counsel's role at lineup is to prevent suggestiveness, or to detect and record it. A witness may not identify a defendant in a trial after viewing the suspect in an uncounseled postindictment lineup unless the government can show by clear and convincing evidence that witness's memory is based on observations made at the time of the crime. The *Wade* rule is based on the potential suggestibility by police at a lineup.

In *Kirby v. Illinois* (1972) the Court limited this right to counsel only to postindictment lineups. A lawyer is not required at a preindictment lineup. The Court held that suspects are entitled to counsel only after an adversary judicial proceeding has been directed against them. Counsel is required at a lineup held after a defendant has been processed at a preliminary examination.

There is no right to counsel at photographic identification procedure, whether held before or after indictment. A photo array is determined not to present the same dangers of suggestibility as a lineup, any suggestive behavior can be cured by cross-examination at trial, and the defendant is not present at a photo identification, eliminating the need for counsel to protect the defendant's rights.

The Fifth Amendment protects against compelled testimonial evidence and, therefore, does not prevent the state from exhibiting the defendant at a lineup or trial for identification purposes. Further, the suspect may be required to wear distinctive clothing or to speak words to improve his or her identification.

Due process requires that identification procedures be conducted fairly. The due process rule is a "totality of the circumstances" test; the Court has rejected a narrower *per se* rule. In deciding whether a defendant's due process rights have been violated, the necessity to conduct a showup may be taken into account. A showup is justified if a witness may die, or if

any suggestibility is offset by procedures that ensure reliability. Pictures of a lone suspect may be shown to witnesses prior to arrest to aid in apprehension. Identification after a grossly unfair lineup in which the suspect is made to stand out violates due process and results in the suppression of the identification.

Five factors may be taken into account in determining whether a suggestive showup has been offset by indicia of reliability: (1) the witness's opportunity to view the suspect at the scene of the crime, (2) the witness's degree of attention, (3) the accuracy of the witness's original description, (4) the witness's level of certainty, and (5) the time elapsed between the crime and the identification procedure.

LEGAL PUZZLES

HOW HAVE COURTS DECIDED THESE CASES?

SHOWUP; DUE PROCESS TEST

8–1. Bank tellers Rodriguez and Quesnot were robbed at gunpoint. The robber passed a note to Rodriguez and showed a gun handle. Rodriguez and Quesnot took cash from the vault and put a cash drawer on the counter in front of the robber for him to take what he wanted. Rodriguez was two feet from the robber while Quesnot was five feet away. Both had a good opportunity to observe his face. Shortly after, Rodriguez and Quesnot gave police separate descriptions of the robber, describing the robber as a white man, thirty to forty years old, with a medium build, wearing a T-shirt and a dark jacket. Both said the robber wore a long white bandana with lettering or a design on it around his head.

Wayne Burbridge was soon arrested and discarded clothing linked by forensic evidence to Burbridge's clothing when he was arrested matched the bank tellers' descriptions of the robber's garb, including a white bandana with pinkish lettering. Rodriguez and Quesnot each separately and positively identified Burbridge as the bank robber within two hours of the robbery at separate showups. Five months later, Quesnot and Rodriguez again separately identified Burbridge as the bank robber in a six-person photographic lineup. They also identified Burbridge in court as the robber during his criminal trial. Rodriguez testified that his in-court identification was based on Burbridge's distinct facial features.

Did the showups violate Burbridge's due process rights?

HELD: No

A pretrial identification that is so impermissibly suggestive as to give rise to a substantial likelihood of irreparable misidentification cannot be used. Admissibility requires a two-step analysis: (1) whether the identification procedure was impermissibly suggestive; and if it was, (2) whether, under the totality of the circumstances, the suggestiveness led to a substantial likelihood of irreparable misidentification.

Even if the showups were suggestive, under the totality of the circumstances irreparable misidentification did not result. Five factors determine whether irreparable misidentification resulted: opportunity of the witness to view the criminal during the crime, witness's degree of attention, accuracy of the witness's prior description of the criminal, level of certainty demonstrated at the confrontation, and time between the crime and the confrontation. Rodriguez and Quesnot had ample opportunity to view the robber as he stood facing them a few feet away for at least fifteen seconds with his face unmasked. Rodriguez and Quesnot said they closely observed Burbridge's face during the crime. Because Burbridge committed an open armed robbery, they were very attentive to him. Both Rodriguez and Quesnot were certain that Burbridge was the perpetrator when they saw him at the showups. Finally, less than two hours had passed between the robbery and the showups, and the witnesses' memories were still fresh at the time they made their positive identifications. Under these circumstances, the district court did not err in admitting the identification evidence. *United States v. Burbridge*, 252 F.3d 775 (5th Cir. 2001)

LIVE LINEUP; DUE PROCESS TEST

8–2. Randy Downs was charged with bank robbery. The teller at the bank, Denise Brown, observed the robber's face carefully for about a minute and gave the police a description that matched that given by another teller: a white male wearing sunglasses and a blue hat. Teller Brown said that she paid close attention to his mouth and lower face, because she was concerned that the robber might become agitated if she had difficulty understanding him. In the fifty-some seconds she had to observe him, she also formed the impression that he was lightly unshaven, between 5'6" and 5'8" tall, about 150 pounds, and between thirty-five and forty-five years old.

An informant indicated that Downs might be the robber. Teller Brown could not identify Downs from a photo array. Teller Brown suggested that it would be more helpful to see people wearing hats and sunglasses. A few days later, Downs was placed in a sequential lineup with four other men. He was the only member of the lineup without a moustache. Each man stepped in, walked around, and said "No, put the money in the envelope, hurry." Downs was the second to walk in. Teller Brown positively identified the defendant as soon as he appeared—he was the second person to be shown. Brown then viewed the last three lineup participants, and at the end reiterated that she was "positive" the robber was Downs, based on "the lower half of his face" and his "stocky upper body." The other four lineup participants all sported heavy moustaches; only Downs had no facial hair at all. Otherwise they were similar in body build.

1. Was the lineup suggestive?
2. Did the lineup violate Downs' due process rights?

Holding available from instructor

WITNESS PRESSURE; DUE PROCESS TEST

8–3. In the early morning hours, two men approached Adam Harding, Trineka English, and Otis Taylor while standing on a street corner. The two men were known as "Juice" and "Black." After asking to speak to Harding, "Juice" unexpectedly grabbed Harding around the neck, placing him in a headlock, and "Black" pointed a gun at Harding's head and demanded his keys and wallet. After complying with "Black's" demands, Harding was dragged into a nearby alley by both assailants and was then shot in the head by "Black." Harding, although severely injured, survived.

At a suppression hearing and trial, the defendant, Tremaine Conyers, moved to suppress identification evidence on the ground that the identification procedure had been impermissibly suggestive.

Ms. English testified that she had been shown two photo array cards, each containing six photographs. She was asked, "Do you see anyone who looks familiar in these pictures?" Ms. English pointed to Conyers's photograph and stated that he looked familiar. Detective Mitchell asked what she meant by "he looks familiar." She stated that "he looks like the other guy." Detective Mitchell testified that he said, "The second guy who was with Juice? She said yes. I asked her, are you sure it's him? And this whole thing took about 15 seconds. And she stated, I'm sure. And then as I'm writing this, she wrote, I never forget a face." Ms. English testified at the suppression hearing that no one ever suggested to her which photograph to pick and that the photograph she ultimately picked was that of Conyers. The trial judge ruled that the extrajudicial identification was untainted.

Defendant argues that Ms. English was pressured or prodded into making her extrajudicial identification "under suggestive conditions, in light of the fact that she stood accused of being criminally involved in the incident at the time she was shown the photo arrays." He refers to the fact that "she was forcefully brought into the police station by Detective Mitchell." He claims that she "made her identification under the shadow of police accusations that she was personally involved in the shooting and robbery."

Does this last contention, if true, render the identification impermissibly suggestive and a due process violation?

Holding available from instructor

PHOTO LINEUP; DUE PROCESS

8–4. On February 22, 1998, Narcotics Agent Marshall Pack made an arranged drug purchase in a Dairy Queen parking lot. It was set up by Tabitha Spann, an informant, who was tape-recorded by agents arranging the buy with Clarence Honer, one of four Honer brothers—suspected drug dealers. Agent Pack had previously seen photographs of the Honer brothers. Spann believed from her conversation with Clarence that "Clarence's brother" or someone named Earl would meet her at the Dairy Queen to consummate the sale. The transaction was monitored by a surveillance team. At the Dairy Queen, Spann got out of the car and went inside. A "box Chevy" with two persons inside parked next to Agent Pack's vehicle. The driver motioned for Agent Pack to roll down his window and then asked about Spann. Agent Pack responded that she was inside, but that he had the cash and could make the buy without Spann. Agent Pack got into the backseat of the Chevy and conversed with the driver while he and an unidentified passenger broke up the cocaine base, which was cooked into "crack." Agent Pack paid $1,275, which he counted out in cash, in exchange for one and a half ounces of crack. When Spann emerged from the restaurant, she briefly conversed with the driver of the Chevy, and they all departed.

During a post–drug purchase meeting at headquarters the next day, Agent Melvin presented Agent Pack and Spann with a photo lineup containing several pictures. All of the pictures were of young to middle-aged black males with skin tones from brown to dark brown and similar hair styles. Agent Pack and Spann independently identified Jackie Honer as the person who sold the drugs. Agent Pack described Honer as being approximately six feet tall and 185 pounds, and having had gold teeth.

Jackie Honer was arrested in December 1998, was indicted for drug sale, and was identified by Agent Pack at the time of his arrest. During discovery and at trial, the Government could not produce the photographs of the other subjects used in the pretrial identification photo array. The district court denied the motion to exclude the identification on the grounds that Spann and Pack would identify Honer based on their personal encounters with him. Jackie Honer is actually 5'11" in height and 170 pounds, and at trial had no gold teeth. At trial Agent Pack identified Honer, but Spann was unable to identify Honer. On cross-examination she said that her interaction with the driver only lasted "a second." As for Spann's having identified Honer's picture out of the lineup the day after the purchase, she could only testify that the photograph she picked out "by glancing at him that night [] looked like the same person." The single photo Spann identified of Jackie Honer was admitted into evidence. Jackie Honer was convicted and sentenced for the sale of drugs.

Honer moved to suppress any evidence of the out-of-court, pretrial identifications by Agent Pack and Spann, and the in-court identification by Pack, on the grounds that the absence of the photo array made the identification process inherently unreliable.

1. Were the pretrial identifications in February impermissibly suggestive?
2. Should Pack's identifications be declared inadmissible?
3. Should Spann's pretrial identification be declared inadmissible?

Holding available from instructor

FURTHER READING

Elizabeth Loftus, *Eyewitness Testimony* (Cambridge: Harvard University Press, 1979).

C. Ronald Huff, Arye Rattner, and Edward Sagarin, *Convicted but Innocent: Wrongful Conviction and Public Policy* (Thousand Oaks, CA: Sage, 1996).

Edward Connors, Thomas Lundregan, Neal Miller, and Tom McEwen, *Convicted by Juries, Exonerated by Science: Case Studies in the Use of DNA Evidence to Establish Innocence after Trial* (National Institute of Justice, June 1996, NCJ 161258).

ENDNOTES

1. John H. Wigmore, *Evidence in Trials at Common Law* §1367 Vol. 5 (John H. Chadbourn rev. ed. 1974).

2. Noted in James Marshall, *Law and Psychology in Conflict* (Indianapolis: Bobbs-Merrill, 1966).

3. Edwin M. Borchard, *Convicting the Innocent: Sixty-five Actual Errors of Criminal Justice* (New York: Garden City Publishing Company, 1932).

4. Jerome Frank and Barbara Frank, *Not Guilty* (Garden City, N.Y.: Doubleday, 1957).

5. C. R. Huff, A. Rattner, and E. Sagarin, *Convicted but Innocent: Wrongful Conviction and Public Policy* (Thousand Oaks, CA: Sage, 1996).

6. Andre A. Moenssens, et al., *Scientific Evidence in Civil and Criminal Cases,* 4th ed §9.15, 1171–72 (Mineola, N.Y.: Foundation Press, 1995), cited in Laurie L. Levenson, "Eyewitness IDs," *The National Law Journal*, July 10, 2000, A20.

7. Hugo A. Bedau and Michael L. Radelet, "Miscarriages of Justice in Potentially Capital Cases," *Stanford Law Review* 40 (1987): 21, 31–36. The authors define a "miscarriage of justice," as cases where "the defendant was legally or physically uninvolved in the case" (p. 38). Of these 350 cases, 116 resulted in death sentences, and 23 innocent persons were actually convicted. For an updated account of this research see Michael Radelet, Hugo Bedau, and Constance Putnam, *In Spite of Innocence* (Boston: Northeastern University Press, 1992).

8. See Scott Christianson, *Innocent: Inside Wrongful Conviction Cases* (New York: NYU Press, 2004).

9. S. Raab, "Man Wrongfully Imprisoned by New York to Get $600,000," *New York Times,* January 18, 1985, 1.

10. R. Hermann, "The Case of the Jamaican Accent," *New York Times Magazine,* December 1, 1974, 30.

11. *New York Times,* February 16, 1990, (nat. ed.).

12. Mentioned in E. Loftus, "Trials of an Expert Witness," *Newsweek,* June 29, 1987, 10.

13. C. R. Huff, A. Rattner, and E. Sagarin, "Guilty Until Proven Innocent: Wrongful Conviction and Public Policy," *Crime and Delinquency* 32 (4) (1986): 518–44.

14. P. Applebome, "Overturned Murder Conviction Spotlights Dallas-Style Justice," *New York Times,* March 7, 1989, 11 (nat. ed.); R. D. Adams, with W. Hoffer and M. M. Hoffer, *Adams v. Texas* (New York: St. Martin's, 1991).

15. Cynthia L. Cooper and Sam Reese Sheppard, *Mockery of Justice* (Boston: Northeastern University Press, 1995); James Neff, *The Wrong Man: The Final Verdict on the Dr. Sam Sheppard Murder Case* (New York: Random House, 2002); James S. Hirsch, *Hurricane* (Boston: Houghton Mifflin, 2000).

16. Lisa Teachey and Amy Raskin, "DNA Tests Clear 2 of Rape; New Questions Raised about Eyewitness Testimony," *Houston Chronicle,* September 30, 2000; Stuart Pfeifer, Jack Leonard, and Jeff Gottlieb, "Youth to Be Freed as Judge Voids Conviction," *Los Angeles Times,* August 22, 2000; Matthew Bruun,

"More Rely on Miracle of DNA Test; Power to Convict, Exonerate," *Sunday Telegram* (Worcester, MA.), July 16, 2000; Sacha Pfeiffer, "After Serving 4 Years, Man Is Exonerated in '95 Slaying," *Boston Globe,* September 14, 2000; Hector Becerra, "Yet Another Reversal with a Witness Issue," *Los Angeles Times,* August 22, 2000.

17. Jennifer Thompson, "I Was Certain, but I Was Wrong," *New York Times,* June 18, 2000.

18. Editorial, "Irreversible Error in Texas," *New York Times,* June 23, 2000; Jim Yardley, "In Death Row Dispute, a Witness Stands Firm," *New York Times,* June 16, 2000.

19. Barry Scheck, Peter Neufeld, and Jim Dwyer, *Actual Innocence* (New York: Doubleday, 2000).

20. Dirk Johnson, "Illinois, Citing Faulty Verdicts, Bars Executions," *New York Times,* February 1, 2000 (noted that "13 men had been sentenced to death in Illinois since 1977 for crimes they did not commit, before ultimately being exonerated and freed by the courts").

21. Edward Connors, Thomas Lundregan, Neal Miller, and Tom McEwen, *Convicted by Juries, Exonerated by Science: Case Studies in the Use of DNA Evidence to Establish Innocence After Trial* (National Institute of Justice, June 1996, NCJ 161258).

22. *Williams v. United States,* 345 F.2d 733, 736 (D.C. Cir. 1965), quoted in Fred P. Graham, *The Due Process Revolution* (New York: Hayden Books Co., 1970) (originally *The Self-Inflicted Wound*), 223.

23. Fred Graham, *Due Process,* 236–37, referring to the unreported case of *United States v. Beasley.*

24. *Russell v. United States,* 408 F.2d 1280 (D.C. Cir. 1969); see comments on this case in Graham, *Due Process,* 238.

25. Herbert L. Packer, "Two Models of the Criminal Process," *University of Pennsylvania Law Review* 113 (1964): 1–68, discussed in Chapter 1.

26. Connie Mayer, "Due Process Challenges to Eyewitness Identification Based on Pretrial Photographic Arrays," *Pace Law Review* 13 (1994): 815-861.

27. *Gilbert v. California* (1967); *United States v. Mara* (1973).

28. *United States v. Dionisio* (1973).

29. *California v. Byers* (1971), upholding a law that required drivers involved in an accident to stop and leave their names; such activity does not provide testimonial or communicative evidence.

30. Jennifer L. Devenport, Steven D. Penrod, and Brian Cutler, "Eyewitness Identification Evidence: Evaluating Commonsense Evaluations," *Psychology, Public Policy and Law* 3 (1997): 338–58.

31. Donald P. Judges, "Two Cheers for the Department of Justice's Eyewitness Evidence: A Guide for Law Enforcement," *Arkansas Law Review* 53 (2000): 231–97.

32. J. C. Brigham and M. P. Wolfskiel, "Opinions of Attorneys and Law Enforcement Personnel on the Accuracy of Eyewitness Identifications," *Law and Human Behavior* 7 (1983): 337–39.

33. Scheck, et al., *Actual Innocence,* 245, n. 19.

34. Scheck, et al., *Actual Innocence,* 246, n. 19 see Lissa Griffin, "The Correction of Wrongful Convictions: A Comparative Perspective," *American University International Law Review* 16 (2001): 1241–1308. The Web site of England's Criminal Cases Review Commission is http://www.ccrc.gov.uk/.

35. Scheck, et al., *Actual Innocence,* 250, n. 19.

36. See, for example, E. F. Loftus, *Eyewitness Testimony* (Cambridge, MA: Harvard University Press, 1979); A. D. Yarmey, *The Psychology of Eyewitness Testimony* (New York: The Free Press, 1979); John C. Yuille, "A Critical Examination of the Psychological and Practical Implications of Eyewitness Research," *Law and Human Behavior* 4 (4) (1980): 335–45.

37. Loftus, *Eyewitness,* 19, n. 36.

38. Yuille, "Critical Examination," 336, n. 36.

39. R. Buckhout, "Nearly 2,000 Witnesses Can Be Wrong," quoted in Loftus, *Eyewitness,* 135–36, n. 36.

40. Woodhead, et al., (n.d.), recounted in Loftus, *Eyewitness,* 166–70, n. 36.

41. J. Brigham, A. Maass, L. Snyder, and K. Spaulding, "Accuracy of Eyewitness Identifications in a Field Setting," *Journal of Personality and Social Psychology* 42 (4) (1982): 673–81.

42. Loftus, *Eyewitness,* 21, n. 36 (citations omitted).

43. Ibid., 21, 25–27.

44. Ibid., 23–32.

45. Yarmey, *Psychology,* 52.

46. Loftus, *Eyewitness,* 33, n. 36.

47. Ibid., 32–51.

48. Ibid., 55.

49. Ibid., 52–87.

50. Ibid., 88–104.

51. Judges, "Two Cheers," 277, n. 31.

52. Ibid., 238–39, 253, 262–63, 270, n. 31.

53. Warren E. Leary, "Novel Methods Unlock Witnesses' Memories," *New York Times,* November 15, 1988; Ronald P. Fisher, "Interviewing Victims and Witnesses of Crime," *Psychology, Public Policy and Law* 1 (4) (1995): 732–764.

54. Judges, "Two Cheers," 274, n. 31.

55. Gary L. Wells and Eric P. Seelau, "Eyewitness Identification: Psychological Research and Legal Policy on Lineups," *Psychology, Public Policy and Law* 1 (1995): 765; other sources noted in Judges, "Two Cheers," footnote 31.

56. Judges, "Two Cheers," 270, n. 31.

57. Ibid., 263, n. 31, citing Wells and Seelau, "Eyewitness Identification," n. 55.

58. Brian Cutler and Steven Penrod, "Improving the Reliability of Eyewitness Identification: Lineup Construction and Presentation," *Journal of Applied Psychology* 72 (2) (1988): 281–90.

59. Ibid.

60. John C. Brigham, "Perspectives on the Impact of Lineup Composition, Race, and Witness Confidence on Identification Accuracy," *Law and Human Behavior* 4 (4) (1980): 315–21; Christian A. Meissner and John C. Brigham, "Thirty Years of Investigating the Own-Race Bias in Memory for Faces: A Meta-Analytic Review," *Psychology, Public Policy and Law* 7 (2001): 3–35.

61. Huff, et al., *Convicted but Innocent,* 151, n. 5; Judges, "Two Cheers," 289–90, n. 31.

62. Yarmey, *Psychology,* 150–51, 156, n. 36; Loftus, *Eyewitness,* 100–101, n. 36; Brigham et al., "Accuracy," n. 39.

JUSTICES OF THE SUPREME COURT

NIXON'S CONSERVATIVES
BURGER—REHNQUIST

President Nixon had the good political fortune to name four justices during his first term in office and thus was able to significantly mold the Court's direction. He attacked the Warren Court as a campaign issue in 1968, and was only too happy to fill retiring Chief Justice Warren's seat with Warren Burger, an outspoken critic of the Warren Court's criminal procedure rulings. Justice Rehnquist, appointed in 1972 from a position in the Justice Department, was the most consistently conservative justice over the next three decades.

The Burger Court's output, while more conservative than that of the Warren Court, did not achieve a radical conservative counterrevolution contemplated by the extreme right. Thus, the Burger Court supported gender equality, was moderately supportive of prisoner's rights, and did not significantly inhibit freedom of expression. Indeed, the Court's 1973

abortion rights decision has been a constant lightning rod for criticism from conservatives. Its criminal procedure cases were generally conservative; they halted the expansion of suspects' rights without overruling Warren Court decisions. On the whole, the Supreme Court probably reflects a nation that may be better described as moderate (or perhaps vacillating), rather than strictly conservative, in social issues.

Justice Rehnquist was elevated to Chief Justice in 1986, upon Warren Burger's retirement, only the third sitting associate justice to have been so promoted. (The other two were Edward D. White and Harlan Fisk Stone. Charles Evans Hughes, a retired associate justice, was later named chief justice). Although a chief justice has only one vote among nine, when in the majority he appoints the writer of the opinion, and thus has an additional opportunity to shape the emphasis of American constitutional law.

WARREN EARL BURGER

Virginia 1907–1995

Republican

Appointed by Richard Nixon as Chief Justice

Years of Service: 1969–1987

Collection of the Supreme Court of the United States. Photographer: Robert S. Oakes

LIFE AND CAREER Burger, a Minnesota native, was graduated *magna cum laude* from the St. Paul College of Law, and practiced with a substantial St. Paul law firm from 1931 to 1956. Active in political affairs, he supported governor Harold Stassen's bid for the presidential nomination on the Republican ticket in 1948. At the 1952 nominating convention, Burger played a key role in swinging Stassen's delegates to Eisenhower, ensuring his nomination over Ohio's Senator Taft. Thereafter, President Eisenhower's attorney general, Herbert Brownell, brought Burger to the Justice Department as an assistant attorney general. He was appointed to the U.S. Court of Appeals for the District of Columbia in 1956, where he gained recognition as a highly competent jurist who was outspoken in criticizing the Warren Court's expansion of the rights of criminal suspects. This reputation was an important factor in Burger's nomination by Richard Nixon, whose 1968 presidential campaign included sharp criticism of the liberal Supreme Court's criminal decisions.

CONTRIBUTION TO CRIMINAL PROCEDURE He was quite conservative, calling for abolition of the exclusionary rule and limiting its scope wherever possible (e.g., noncoerced statements obtained in violation of *Miranda* could be used to impeach a witness; the exclusionary rule is not a constitutional right but merely a Court-created police deterrent). On the other hand, in *Chadwick* (1977) he upheld the plain text of the Fourth Amendment by ruling that a warrant was required to search a footlocker.

SIGNATURE OPINION Dissent in *Bivens v. Six Unknown Named Agents* (1971). The Court, in an opinion by Justice Brennan, held, for the first time, that a person whose Fourth Amendment rights are violated by federal law enforcement officers may bring a civil, tort lawsuit in federal court against such officers. Chief Justice Burger dissented, arguing that the Fourth Amendment itself created no such lawsuit and that under the separation of powers, the Court should not authorize such a suit but wait for Congress to establish a federal civil remedy. In his opinion, he wrote broadly on the exclusionary rule, trying to narrow its scope by characterizing it as resting only "on the deterrent rationale—the hope that law enforcement officials would be deterred from unlawful searches and seizures" if the products of such searches were suppressed.

ASSESSMENT In other areas, the Chief Justice was often moderate to conservative and pragmatic. In First Amendment law, he broadened the scope of what is considered obscenity but struck down a gag order on the press in criminal trials. In civil rights, he upheld busing to integrate deliberately segregated school systems but not where segregation was not intended; he upheld the denial of federal tax credits to schools that discriminate but voted against holding that inequitable school taxes

(Continued)

violated the Equal Protection Clause. He concurred in *Roe v. Wade* (1973) (abortion rights) and in *United States v. Nixon* (1974) wrote for a unanimous Court that President Nixon's claim of executive privilege did not override a court order to turn over tapes of his Watergate conversations. He was not known as an especially effective leader as chief justice, and during his tenure Justices Brennan, Rehnquist, and Powell were more influential with their fellow justices. In 1987 Burger stepped down to head the national celebration of the bicentennial of the Constitution, a fitting role after eighteen years of service as chief justice of the United States.

FURTHER READING

Charles M. Lamb, "Chief Justice Warren E. Burger: A Conservative Chief for Conservative Times," in *The Burger Court: Political and Judicial Profiles,* Charles M. Lamb and Stephen C. Halpern, eds., 129–162 (Urbana: University of Illinois Press, 1991).

WILLIAM H. REHNQUIST

Arizona 1924–

Republican

Appointed by
Richard Nixon and Ronald Reagan

Years of Service: Associate Justice: 1972–1986; Chief Justice: 1986–

Collection of the Supreme Court of the United States. Photographer: Dane Penland.

LIFE AND CAREER   Rehnquist was born in Milwaukee, Wisconsin, and attended Stanford University after service during World War II. His very conservative views were formed early in his life. He received a master's degree in political science and graduated first in his class from Stanford Law School. He clerked for Justice Robert Jackson; practiced law in Phoenix, Arizona, from 1953 to 1969; was active in conservative Republican politics; and in 1969 became an assistant attorney general in the Nixon administration. He was appointed to the Court at the relatively young age of forty-seven and, at that time, was the most conservative member of the Court. He faced strong opposition in his initial appointment, and again in 1986 when President Reagan nominated Rehnquist to the position of chief justice.

CONTRIBUTION TO CRIMINAL PROCEDURE   Justice Rehnquist has been a prolific opinion writer in criminal procedure cases and has helped to shape a very conservative view of Fourth Amendment rights. His majority opinions have restricted Fourth Amendment standing to those with property-like interests, replaced the two-pronged rule for accepting the hearsay

of a secret informant to obtain a search warrant, with the more lenient "totality of the circumstances" test, held that *Miranda* warnings were only protective devices and not themselves constitutionally protected rights, created a "public safety exception" to the *Miranda* rule, expanded *Terry* stops to crimes of possession based on hearsay, limited the right to counsel on second appeals, and held that drug courier profiles constituted reasonable suspicion for a stop. More recently, he has held that prosecuting a higher proportion of African Americans for possession of crack cocaine, which carries a heavier penalty than powdered cocaine, is not selective prosecution; that a law that allows the forfeiture of a wife's interest in her car, which her husband used for a tryst with a prostitute, does not violate due process; and that a lawyer's failure to object to an aggravating factor at a death penalty trial does not prejudice the defendant.

SIGNATURE OPINION   *Dickerson v. United States* (2000). Chief Justice Rehnquist, for a 7–2 majority, upheld the *Miranda* ruling, calling it "a constitutional rule that Congress may not supersede legislatively." His adroit opinion seemed to go against his many earlier opinions that established the rule that "The prophylactic *Miranda* warnings therefore are not themselves rights protected by the Constitution but are instead measures to insure that the right against compulsory self-incrimination is protected"—Rehnquist's own words in the majority opinions of *Michigan v. Tucker* (1974) and *New York v. Quarles* (1984). Indeed, *Dickerson*'s reasoning, while plausible in some respects, did not easily square with the earlier pronouncements of the Chief Justice and the Court. How can this be explained? The answer seems to be that Rehnquist saw the institutional role of the Supreme Court as outweighing doctrinal purity in this case. The nation had come to rely on *Miranda* warnings to such an extent that they "have become part of our national culture." As such, the dictates of *stare decisis,* a doctrine that Rehnquist never thought was paramount in constitutional adjudication, nevertheless carried the day here.

ASSESSMENT   Justice Rehnquist's judicial philosophy dictates the outcome of many of his cases. He believes that American federalism requires the Court to play a small role in the affairs of the states and of other branches of government. He disfavored the incorporation doctrine and would prefer that the states make their own decisions in regard to defendants' rights. He has written that the Supreme Court does not have a special position as the ultimate guardian of individual rights because that was not a role intended by the framers of the Constitution. Rehnquist's constitutional philosophy of strict federalism and deference to the elected branches of government can be seen as democratic in giving the majority a greater voice, while reducing the Court's role as a "guardian" of minorities.

FURTHER READING

Sue Davis, *Justice Rehnquist and the Constitution* (Princeton, NJ: Princeton University Press, 1989).

CHAPTER
9

ENTRAPMENT

"Fidelity" to the commands of the Constitution suggests balanced judgment rather than exhortation. The highest "fidelity" is not achieved by the judge who instinctively goes furthest in upholding even the most bizarre claim of individual constitutional rights, any more than it is achieved by a judge who instinctively goes furthest in accepting the most restrictive claims of governmental authorities. The task of this Court, as of other courts, is to "hold the balance true."

—Justice William H. Rehnquist in *Illinois v. Gates,*
462 U.S. 213, 241 (1986)

CHAPTER OUTLINE

KEY TERMS AND PHRASES

Agent provocateur

Covert facilitation

Criminal law approach

Criminal procedure approach

Decoy

Due process defense

Encouragement

Entrapment

Hypothetical person test

Inducement

Objective test

Outrageous conduct test

Predisposition

Subjective test

Supervisory power

Introduction

Entrapment is a complete defense to a crime; if a court or jury concludes that a defendant was entrapped, the indictment is dismissed or the defendant is acquitted. It seems a strange rule, because the absolved defendant did indeed "commit" the crime charged. Nevertheless, the defendant is released under the law when it appears to judge or jury that police used tactics that planted the idea of the crime in the defendant's mind. The rule is not based on the Constitution. Therefore, each state is free to adopt its own entrapment rule or to have no entrapment rule. It is fair to say that, although the defense of entrapment is not based directly on the Due Process Clauses of the Fifth or Fourteenth amendments, it originated in a sense of fairness and limits on government power that underlies due process. The entrapment defense announces that there is a limit to what the police will be allowed to do in order to ferret out crime.

Classification and Origins of the Entrapment Defense

Entrapment differs from other criminal procedure doctrines, because it is classified as a rule of substantive criminal law (as a defense to crime) *and* as a rule of criminal procedure.[1] How can this be? Entrapment was created as a criminal law defense by state supreme court decisions in the late nineteenth and early twentieth centuries. They interpreted criminal statutes to declare that the legislature intended to criminalize only persons whose criminal intent was not conceived by the police. As this criminal law defense is clearly concerned with restraining excessive police action, it is also properly a subject of criminal procedure. Entrapment is a uniquely American rule that is not the product of the English common law and has had no counterpart in Roman/civil law (e.g., the German or French legal systems), although this may be changing.[2]

As a criminal law defense, lawyers argued that where police overreached their responsibility and drew the defendant into crime, courts should "condemn excessive police encouragement [and] completely absolve any individuals who commit the encouraged acts."[3] Some sympathetic courts at first simply condemned police manipulation that led weak persons into crime, but upheld the convictions. Earlier courts felt that a defendant who gave in to temptation—even if manufactured by the police—should not have a criminal defense.[4] By 1878, as seen in the Michigan case of *Saunders v. State,* courts began to recognize, in dictum, that an entrapment defense should exist.[5] A lawyer improperly asked a police officer to leave a courtroom unlocked so that he could have access to records. The officer, instead of refusing, laid a trap and arrested the attorney. The court held that this was not entrapment, but rather only furnished an opportunity to commit the crime. Nonetheless, it ruled that evidence of the "entrapment context of the crime ought to be available to the jury."[6] In a proper case, therefore, a jury could acquit a person, because government officers caused the defendant to commit a crime. A concurring justice in *Saunders* noted that "human nature is frail enough at best, and requires no encouragement in wrong-doing."[7] Over time, state supreme courts went from condemning extreme police encouragement to adopting entrapment as a defense. In the century after *Saunders,* every state had adopted a form of entrapment defense either by court ruling or by statute.

A brilliant analysis by Rebecca Roiphe links the emergence of the entrapment defense in the late nineteenth and early twentieth centuries to the growth of the state, and specifically to the expansion and bureaucratization of local, state, and federal police forces. "Entrapment caught the attention of judges and academics in the context of this rapidly transforming system of law enforcement. It gradually took hold amidst the increasingly interrelated and invasive tactics of both federal and local police."[8] In the mid-1800s courts praised law enforcement tactics involving trickery and deceit to catch criminals, at a time when police forces were in a nascent state and most relations between the individual and the state were still personalized. By the late 1870s and 1880s the courts began to denounce "the involvement of the state in their overzealous pursuit of undercover investigations and prosecutions."[9] By 1900, courts came to understand entrapment "as a way of ascertaining voluntariness in the context of a prevalent and powerful state using increasingly sophisticated law enforcement techniques."[10] Thus, from the outset, whether courts clearly articulated this component of entrapment, the defense was concerned with the basic function of constitutional criminal procedure: to maintain a balance between effective law enforcement and basic individual liberties.

The distinction between entrapment as a criminal law rule or criminal procedure rule (or both) is important, because it suggests different *theories of entrapment.* Under the **criminal law approach,** the main purpose of entrapment is to protect the essentially innocent person. This "subjective" theory, or **subjective test,** emphasizes whether the defendant had a **predisposition** to commit the crime in the first place, and whether the defendant was *induced* into the commission of the crime by police acts. To those who favor the **criminal procedure approach,** the essence of entrapment lies in the *control of excessive police activity.* This "objective" theory (or **objective test**) requires courts to determine when police participation goes too far, whatever the defendant's predisposition. The debate is not entirely theoretical; different approaches can result in more or fewer entrapment acquittals or dismissals for different sorts of defendants.

An important limit on the entrapment defense is that it "is unavailable when causing or threatening bodily injury is an element of the offense."[11] Entrapment is most often claimed as a defense in vice crimes (e.g., drug dealing and manufacture, prostitution, loan sharking, liquor bootlegging); bribery and various forms of corrupt practices (e.g., prison guards smuggling contraband, kickbacks in awarding government contracts); political subversion cases; buying or selling stolen property; extortion; counterfeiting; many white collar crimes; money laundering; and the like. No cases appear to involve crimes of violence.

Before continuing to explore the entrapment defense, we briefly review police encouragement tactics, and whether police undercover investigation, out of which entrapment claims arise, is constitutional.

Covert Policing: Encouragement and Undercover Agents

Encouragement and undercover investigation are lawful and necessary police functions. Because they involve deception, however, they are prone to abuses. Entrapment, for example, occurs when police undercover agents or informants go too far in using techniques of encouragement. Covert techniques are most useful in enforcing such crimes as drug dealing or bribery, where the perpetrator and victim are willing participants in an illicit business transaction that they conceal from public scrutiny. It may be impossible to penetrate organized or white-collar crime without covert policing techniques.

"Encouragement," also called **covert facilitation,** is:

[T]he activity of the police officer or police agent (a) who acts as a victim; (b) who intends, by his actions, to encourage a suspect to commit a crime; (c) who actually communicates this encouragement to the suspect; and (d) who has thereby some influence upon the commission of the crime. Encouragement does not usually consist of a single act but a series of acts, part of the normal interplay between victim and suspect.[12]

A police **decoy** poses as a "street person" or a taxicab driver, and makes an arrest when attacked by a mugger or a cab robber. He plays the role of a potential victim and only provides the *opportunity* for a crime, but provides no or little encouragement. An undercover officer who poses as a prostitute, who buys drugs from a dealer, or who offers a bribe to a public official, goes further to *encourage* a targeted suspect to commit a specific crime. The undercover officer communicates to the target that the officer is a willing participant in an illicit transaction and thus influences the target to engage in the illegal act. Undercover officers engage in a double lie about their identities and the true motives of their transactions. But this alone is not entrapment.

Encouragement, though lawful and necessary to make arrests in secretive crimes, is inherently unethical conduct that can only be justified by a concept of the "greater good." Some officers who regularly engage in deceit may lie about the specifics of the suspect's behavior in borderline cases in order to make questionable arrests "stick" (see *Law in Society* section, Chapter 3). Courts, therefore, become suspicious of overzealous police officers who convince suspects to commit crimes they would not have otherwise initiated. At this point, encouragement slips over to entrapment: The criminal intent is implanted in the mind of an otherwise law-abiding citizen.

Consider, for example, the common scenario of a female police officer dressed as a "lady of the evening." She pretends to be a consenting participant in the "victimless" crime of prostitution. If a potential "customer" approaches her, and she accepts an illicit offer, her behavior is lawful encouragement because it only provides the opportunity. On the other hand, if the officer actively solicits males walking by and arrests one who accepts her advances, the officer's actions might be considered entrapment by a judge or jury, because it cannot be shown that the passerby *otherwise* would have agreed to engage in sex for hire had he not been approached. It is true that the "John"

made the illegal offer, but it may be that he had no prior intention to do the illegal act until he was tempted by the officer's active solicitation. The real danger is that police entrapment *manufactures* crime. Entrapment also results when the police use *civilian* undercover informers to play the role of criminal participants in return for money, nonprosecution, or other benefits.

UNDERCOVER AGENTS AND INFORMERS *Hoffa v. United States* (1966) held that the simple use of undercover agents violates no provision of the Constitution. Jimmy Hoffa, national Teamsters Union president, was on trial in Nashville, Tennessee, on federal charges related to union matters. During the trial, Edward Partin, a local Teamsters official in criminal trouble with the federal government, spent time at Hoffa's Nashville apartment with the knowledge and support of federal agents. During this espionage, Partin learned that Hoffa was engaged in jury tampering. In exchange for leniency in his own case and payments to his wife, Partin divulged jury tampering information to federal agents. In a subsequent criminal prosecution against Hoffa for jury tampering, Hoffa claimed that this use of an undercover agent violated his Fourth, Fifth, Sixth, and Fourteenth Amendment rights, and that Partin's evidence should therefore be excluded.

The Supreme Court, in an opinion by Justice Potter Stewart, held that the entry of an undercover agent into a home does not violate the search and seizure amendment. Applying the pre-*Katz* (1967) "constitutionally protected area" doctrine, it found that no interest protected by the amendment was violated. "Neither this Court nor any member of it has ever expressed the view that the Fourth Amendment protects a wrongdoer's misplaced belief that a person to whom he voluntarily confides his wrongdoing will not reveal it." Clearly, even under the *Katz* "expectation of privacy" doctrine, the misplaced confidence in a *false friend* does not violate the right to be free from illegal search and seizure.

Nor does an undercover agent violate the right to be free from *compelled self-incrimination.* The Fifth Amendment prohibits the government from *compelling* a person to testify. The statements in *Hoffa* were *wholly voluntary.* The deception maintained by undercover agents is not a substitute for Fifth Amendment compulsion. Neither was Hoffa's Sixth Amendment *right to counsel* violated, because Hoffa could not prove that Partin heard privileged statements between Hoffa and his lawyer. The right to counsel does include "the right of a defendant and his counsel to prepare for trial without intrusion upon their confidential relationship by an agent of the Government, the defendant's trial adversary." However, Partin's mere presence in the apartment while Hoffa conferred with his lawyers did not violate the Constitution. The Court also ruled that the government has no obligation to arrest a person as soon as it has enough evidence to support probable cause, so as to protect the right to counsel. "There is no constitutional right to be arrested." An investigation may continue after the police have probable cause to arrest so as to gather more convincing evidence for use at a trial.

Finally, the Court rejected Hoffa's claims that using an undercover agent violated his due process right to fundamental fairness because the use of informers is an odious practice and given Partin's motives, there was a high probability that he would commit perjury. Quoting Learned Hand, a renowned federal judge, the Court said, "Courts have countenanced the use of informers from time immemorial; in cases of conspiracy, or in other cases when the crime consists of preparing for another crime, it is usually necessary to rely upon them or upon accomplices because the criminals will almost certainly proceed covertly. . . ."[13] As for the second point, any possible perjury by Partin could be uncovered through cross-examination. Informers are bound by the legal and constitutional restrictions that apply to all witnesses and governmental agents. But "the use of secret informers is not *per se* unconstitutional."

Chief Justice Earl Warren, perhaps disturbed by Attorney General Robert Kennedy's personal vendetta to indict Hoffa, dissented.[14] He did not seek an absolute ban on undercover police work. He thought the conviction should be reversed under a flexible rule allowing a court to throw out evidence obtained by an undercover agent in specific cases "in order to insure that the protections of the Constitution are respected and to maintain the integrity of federal law enforcement." The Chief Justice argued that the Court should use its **supervisory power** over federal criminal justice to exclude evidence or order new trials in flagrant circumstances. No other justice joined him in this view.

THE SUBJECTIVE AND OBJECTIVE TESTS OF ENTRAPMENT
Development of Federal Entrapment Law

Parallel with the development of the entrapment defense in the states, an 1878 federal case stated *in dictum* that a court should not "lend its countenance to a violation of positive law, or to contrivances for inducing a person to commit a crime."[15] For the first time, in 1915, a federal appeals court reversed a conviction on the grounds that it was obtained by entrapment. In *Woo Wai v. United States,* federal undercover agents, who had no reason to believe that Woo Wai was smuggling aliens into the United States, nevertheless spent several months pressuring him to assist them in bringing Chinese aliens into the United States from Mexico. He continually resisted their pleas, saying that to do so was illegal. He finally relented and was convicted. The Ninth Circuit Court of Appeals overturned the conviction. "We are of the opinion that it is against public policy to sustain a conviction obtained" in this way "and a sound public policy can be upheld only by denying the criminality of those who are thus induced to commit acts which infringe the letter of the law."[16]

The Supreme Court first adopted the entrapment defense in *Sorrells v. United States* (1932), whose majority and concurring opinions clearly enunciated the subjective and objective theories that continue to frame legal analysis of entrapment. The subjective, or **inducement,** theory was explained by Chief Justice Charles Evans Hughes writing for the majority: a defendant *not predisposed* to commit a crime may claim entrapment as a defense if the idea for the crime was *implanted* by the police. An undercover Prohibition agent, pre-

tending to be an out of town businessman, was introduced to Sorrells by a third person. They visited at Sorrells's home for an hour and a half, sharing their mutual war experiences. The agent, four or five times, said he would like to bring home some whiskey. Sorrells said he "did not fool with whiskey." After repeated requests, however, Sorrells left his home and returned a half hour later with a half-gallon of liquor, which he sold to the "businessman." There was no evidence that Sorrells was a professional "rum runner."

Chief Justice Hughes ruled that although the National Prohibition Law contained no statutory defense of entrapment, it was within the authority of the Court to *interpret the statute* to find such a defense. To read the statute literally would produce a clear injustice. "We are unable to conclude that it was the intention of Congress in enacting this statute that its processes of detection and enforcement should be abused by the instigation by government officials of an act on the part of persons otherwise innocent in order to lure them to its commission and to punish them." Merely using an "artifice or stratagem" to catch criminals by enabling law enforcement to "reveal the criminal design" is legal and often necessary. However, "[a] different question is presented when *the criminal design originates with the officials* of the Government, and they implant in the mind of an innocent person the disposition to commit the alleged offense and induce its commission in order that they may prosecute" (emphasis added). In such case, the defendant may raise to the jury the defense that she was entrapped and be acquitted on that ground.

Justice Owen Roberts, joined by Justices Brandeis and Stone, concurred in finding entrapment, but argued for a different theory as the basis for entrapment. He criticized the majority's reasoning that Congress intended to create an entrapment defense in a Prohibition statute that was silent on the subject. "This seems a strained and unwarranted construction of the statute; and amounts, in fact, to judicial amendment. It is not merely broad construction, but addition of an element not contained in the legislation." He then proposed, as the true basis of entrapment, a judicial policy of fair law enforcement:

> The doctrine rests, rather, on a fundamental rule of public policy. The protection of its own functions and the preservation of the purity of its own temple belongs only to the courts. It is the province of the court and of the court alone to protect itself and the government from such prostitution of the criminal law. The violation of the principles of justice by the entrapment of the unwary into crime should be dealt with by the court no matter by whom or at what stage of the proceedings. . . . Proof of entrapment, at any stage of the case, requires the court to stop the prosecution, direct that the indictment be quashed, and the defendant set at liberty. If in doubt as to the facts it may submit the issue of entrapment to a jury for advice. But whatever may be the finding upon such submission the power and the duty to act remain with the court and not with the jury. (*Sorrells v. United States,* p. 457)

Twenty-five years later, the Court clarified and continued the *Sorrells* doctrine in *Sherman v. United States* (1956), in which a majority of the Court again upheld the entrapment defense based on the subjective theory, while a concurring minority urged the objective theory as the rationale for entrapment. Although the facts of the cases differ somewhat, there are strong similarities between *Sorrells* and *Sherman*. Sherman was a heroin addict who was visiting a physician for treatment. He was befriended in the doctor's office by a government informer, one Kalchinian, in August 1951, who was also a heroin addict. After spending a period of time and several meetings in getting to know Sherman, Kalchinian asked if he knew of a good source of narcotics, claiming that he was not responding to treatment. Sherman avoided the issue, but Kalchinian repeatedly asked Sherman for a source when they met. Sherman finally gave in and obtained a personal amount of drugs, which he shared with Kalchinian for cost. After several such sales, Kalchinian informed Bureau of Narcotics agents that he had another seller for them. On three occasions during November 1951, the agents observed Sherman sell narcotics to Kalchinian with money supplied by the government. Sherman was convicted by a jury, which was presented with the entrapment defense, and sentenced to ten years in prison.

The majority held that as a matter of law, entrapment was made out in this case under the rule of *Sorrells*. The Court gave several reasons to show that Sherman was not predisposed to sell drugs when he first met Kalchinian and that he was induced to sell by Kalchinian. The idea of selling drugs originated with Kalchinian, who was an active informer. He had recently led narcotics agents to two other prosecutions before entrapping Sherman. Although Kalchinian was not paid money, in 1951 he was under criminal charges for illegally selling narcotics and had not yet been sentenced. The federal agent in charge of the case never bothered to question Kalchinian about the way in which he made contact with Sherman. It appeared that Kalchinian was seeking a sentence reduction and the government was interested in getting convictions.

There was no evidence Sherman was a dealer. Two prior convictions for narcotics possession in 1942 and 1946 were not evidence of being in the business of selling drugs. A search of his house produced no narcotics. He made no profit from the sales. The multiple sales were not evidence that Sherman was predisposed, because each was induced by Kalchinian's pleas for help—they were "the product of the inducement." This was not a case where Sherman was offered an opportunity to deal and he quickly accepted it. Kalchinian had to repeatedly ask Sherman for a source of drugs before he agreed to find one. As in *Sorrells,* the facts here showed that the government was manufacturing of crime; that the criminal conduct was "the product of the *creative* activity" of law enforcement officials. Entrapment was established, because the government crossed the line "drawn between the trap for the unwary innocent and the trap for the unwary criminal." The government played on the weaknesses of an innocent party and beguiled him into committing crimes that he otherwise would not have attempted. "Law enforcement does not require methods such as this."

Four justices—liberal (Douglas and Brennan) and conservative (Frankfurter and Harlan)—concurred. The concurring opinion by Justice Frankfurter argued that entrapment in this case should be based not on the theory that the drug statute included a "silent" defense based on the defendant's lack of predisposition—it is a legal fiction that Congress never approved such a defense. When Sherman sold drugs to Kalchinian, he knew what he was doing and committed the act of the crime with the requisite criminal intent. "If [the defendant] is to be relieved from the usual punitive consequences, it is on no account because he is innocent of the offense described. In these circumstances, conduct is not less criminal because the result of temptation, whether the tempter is a private person or a government agent or informer."

In place of the subjective theory, Justice Frankfurter argued that "The courts refuse to convict an entrapped defendant, not because his conduct falls outside the proscription of the statute, but because, even if his guilt be admitted, the methods employed on behalf of the Government to bring about conviction cannot be countenanced." This "objective" theory, then, blocks a prosecution from going forward because the judge in the case deems the actions of the law enforcement officers excessive. The legal basis for federal courts to impose this restriction on federal law enforcement officers is the supervisory authority of the courts, not any constitutional provision.

Justice Frankfurter acknowledged that the "lower courts have continued gropingly to express the feeling of outrage at conduct of law enforcers that brought recognition of the defense in the first instance, but without the formulated basis in reason that it is the first duty of courts to construct for justifying and guiding emotion and instinct." A weakness in Justice Frankfurter's opinion, however, was an inability to define precisely which police action brought about entrapment. He referred to "lawless means or means that violate rationally vindicated standards of justice"—hardly a clear guide to trial judges. It seems that Justice Frankfurter recognized that the so-called objective test really was not clear cut: "The crucial question, not easy of answer, to which the court must direct itself is whether the police conduct revealed in the particular case falls below standards, to which common feelings respond, for the proper use of governmental power." In effect, this left it to the judges to intuit what police tactics were excessive, based on their view of what was "commonly felt" (by whom it was not said) to be too extreme.

His opinion was more effective in pointing out problems with the subjective test, aside from the "fictional" character of the defense. For example, to prove its case against an entrapment defense, the government has to dig up evidence of the defendant's personal past, which can prejudice a jury. He felt that this allowed the police to use excessive tactics against people with past criminal records, and deflected the attention of courts away from what the police were doing.

The Entrapment Tests in Action

The subjective and objective tests overlap. Both are concerned with police conduct and both seek "to determine whether the government's involvement is the principal cause of the crime."[17] This meshing of concerns is observed in *Jacobson v. United States* (1992), the most recent Supreme Court entrapment case.

— *Jacobson v. United States* **Case & Comments** —

• CASE & COMMENTS •

Jacobson v. United States
503 U.S. 540, 112 S.Ct. 1535; 118 L.Ed.2d 174 (1992)

JUSTICE WHITE delivered the opinion of the Court.

On September 24, 1987, petitioner Keith Jacobson was indicted for violating a provision of the Child Protection Act of 1984 which criminalizes the knowing receipt through the mails of a "visual depiction [that] involves the use of a minor engaging in sexually explicit conduct. . . ." Petitioner defended on the ground that the Government entrapped him into committing the crime through a series of communications from undercover agents that spanned the 26 months preceding his arrest. Petitioner was found guilty after a jury trial. The Court of Appeals affirmed his conviction, holding that the Government had carried its burden of proving beyond reasonable doubt that petitioner was predisposed to break the law and hence was not entrapped. **[a]**

Because the Government overstepped the line between setting a trap for the "unwary innocent" and the "unwary criminal," *Sherman v. United States* (1958), and as a matter of law failed to establish that petitioner was independently predisposed to commit the crime for which he was arrested, we reverse the Court of Appeals' judgment affirming his conviction.

I

In February 1984, petitioner, a 56-year-old veteran-turned-farmer who supported his elderly father in Nebraska, ordered two magazines and a brochure from a California adult bookstore. The magazines, entitled Bare Boys I and Bare Boys II, contained photographs of nude preteen and teenage boys. [Jacobson] testified that he had expected to receive photographs of "young men 18 years or older." * * * The young men depicted in the magazines were not engaged in sexual activity, and petitioner's receipt of the magazines was legal under both federal and Nebraska law. Within three months, the law with respect to child pornography changed; Congress passed the Act illegalizing the receipt through the mails of sexually explicit depictions of children. In the very month that the new provision became law, postal inspectors found petitioner's name on the mailing list of the California bookstore that had mailed him Bare Boys I and II. There followed over the next 2½ years repeated efforts by two Government agencies, through five fictitious organizations and a bogus pen pal, to explore petitioner's willingness to break the new law by ordering sexually explicit photographs of children through the mail.

[In January 1985 Postal Service agents targeted Jacobson, and others, with mailings not directly offering child pornography for sale. Instead, "prohibited mailing specialists" sent mailings from sham organizations that blended civil liberties and free speech messages with hints at sexual interests. The first came from the "American Hedonist Society," advocating the "right to read what we desire, . . . discuss similar interests with those who share our philosophy, and finally . . . to seek pleasure without restrictions being placed on us by outdated puritan morality." This anodyne message included a membership application and a "sex survey. " Jacobson checked a box labeled "enjoy" to indicate that preteen sex gave him pleasure, but indicated that he was opposed to pedophilia.

A May 1986 mailing from "Midlands Data Research" extolled the "joys of sex and the complete awareness of those lusty and youthful lads and lasses" without specifying whether it referred to minors or young adults. Jacobson responded, expressing an interest in teenage sexuality and requesting "Please keep my name confidential." A similar solicitation, from another fictitious organization, "Heartland Institute for a New Tomorrow" (HINT), promoted "sexual freedom and freedom of choice." Jacobson indicated that his interest in "preteen sex-homosexual" material was above average, but not high. An agent then sent personal letters, under a pseudonym. He "mirrored" Jacobson's interests and asked for letters indicating Jacobson's sexual interests. In reply Jacobson wrote, "As far as my likes are concerned, I like good looking young guys (in their late teens and early 20's) doing their thing together," but made no reference to child pornography. Jacobson stopped writing after two letters.] **[b]**

By March 1987, 34 months had passed since the Government obtained petitioner's name from the mailing list of the California bookstore, and 26 months had passed since the Postal Service had commenced its mailings to petitioner. Although petitioner had responded to surveys and letters, the Government had no evidence that petitioner had ever intentionally possessed or been exposed to child pornography. The Postal Service had not checked petitioner's mail to determine whether he was receiving questionable mailings from persons—other than the Government—involved in the child pornography industry.

[a] The government concedes that it induced Jacobson, or at least offered him child pornography. The case turns on the question of whether Jacobson was predisposed to make the purchase. Notice that the Supreme Court majority drew a different conclusion from the same facts available to the Court of Appeals. The dissenters in this case agree with the way in which the Court of Appeals interpreted Jacobson's state of mind.

[b] Do these efforts seem to be an efficient way of discovering child pornography rings? Should the government play on specific individuals' "weaknesses" or predilections in this way?

• CASE & COMMENTS •

[This was followed by a Customs Service solicitation from its own child pornography sting, to which Jacobson responded but an order for materials was never filled. Finally, another Postal Service solicitation from another fictitious government-front organization, the "Far Eastern Trading Company Ltd," was made. Jacobson sent for a catalog, from which he] ordered Boys Who Love Boys, a pornographic magazine depicting young boys engaged in various sexual activities. Petitioner was arrested after a controlled delivery of a photocopy of the magazine.

When petitioner was asked at trial why he placed such an order, he explained that the Government had succeeded in piquing his curiosity:

"Well, the statement was made of all the trouble and the hysteria over pornography and I wanted to see what the material was. It didn't describe the—I didn't know for sure what kind of sexual action they were referring to in the Canadian letter."

In petitioner's home, the Government found the Bare Boys magazines and materials that the Government had sent to him in the course of its protracted investigation, but no other materials that would indicate that petitioner collected, or was actively interested in, child pornography. [c] * * *

II

There can be no dispute about the evils of child pornography or the difficulties that laws and law enforcement have encountered in eliminating it. * * * Likewise, there can be no dispute that the Government may use undercover agents to enforce the law. * * *

In their zeal to enforce the law, however, Government agents may not originate a criminal design, implant in an innocent person's mind the disposition to commit a criminal act, and then induce commission of the crime so that the Government may prosecute. Where the Government has induced an individual to break the law and the defense of entrapment is at issue, as it was in this case, the prosecution must prove beyond reasonable doubt that the defendant was disposed to commit the criminal act prior to first being approached by Government agents. [d]

Thus, an agent deployed to stop the traffic in illegal drugs may offer the opportunity to buy or sell drugs and, if the offer is accepted, make an arrest on the spot or later. In such a typical case, or in a more elaborate "sting" operation involving government-sponsored fencing where the defendant is simply provided with the opportunity to commit a crime, the entrapment defense is of little use because the ready commission of the criminal act amply demonstrates the defendant's predisposition. Had the agents in this case simply offered petitioner the opportunity to order child pornography through the mails, and petitioner—who must be presumed to know the law—had promptly availed himself of this criminal opportunity, it is unlikely that his entrapment defense would have warranted a jury instruction. [e]

But that is not what happened here. By the time petitioner finally placed his order, he had already been the target of 26 months of repeated mailings and communications from Government agents and fictitious organizations. Therefore, although he had become predisposed to break the law by May 1987, it is our view that the Government did not prove that this predisposition was independent and not the product of the attention that the Government had directed at petitioner since January 1985.

* * * The sole piece of preinvestigation evidence is petitioner's 1984 order and receipt of the Bare Boys magazines. But this is scant if any proof of petitioner's predisposition to commit an illegal act, the criminal character of which a defendant is presumed to know. It may indicate a predisposition to view sexually oriented photographs that are responsive to his sexual tastes; but evidence that merely indicates a generic inclination to act within a broad range, not all of which is criminal, is of little probative value in establishing predisposition.

Furthermore, petitioner was acting within the law at the time he received these magazines. * * * Evidence of predisposition to do what once was lawful is not, by itself, sufficient to show predisposition to do what is now illegal, for there is a common understanding that most people obey the law even when they disapprove of it. [f] This obedience may reflect a generalized respect for legality or the fear of prosecution, but for whatever reason, the law's prohibitions are matters of consequence. Hence, the fact that petitioner legally ordered and received the Bare Boys magazines does little to further the Government's burden of proving that petitioner was predisposed to commit a criminal act. This is particularly true given petitioner's unchallenged testimony that he did not know until they arrived that the magazines would depict minors.

[Justice White reviewed Jacobson's responses to the questions asked in the numerous solicitations by undercover agents posing behind front organizations. He concluded they did not prove that

[c] How significant is the lack of child pornography, other than the mailing sent by the government, in Jacobson's home?

[d] This statement announces a rule that is significant to the outcome in this case. The government must prove that Jacobson's predisposition, if any, existed in February 1984, when his name first came to the attention of the Postal Service, and not after years of "working on" him.

[e] The Court makes it clear that its ruling is not designed to disrupt typical undercover law enforcement.

[f] The Court here adds another element of the federal entrapment defense—prior *legal* acts cannot be used to prove current illegal activity.

• CASE & COMMENTS •

Jacobson was predisposed to purchasing child pornography. The responses] were at most indicative of certain personal inclinations, including a predisposition to view photographs of preteen sex and a willingness to promote a given agenda by supporting lobbying organizations. Even so, petitioner's responses hardly support an inference that he would commit the crime of receiving child pornography through the mails. Furthermore, a person's inclinations and "fantasies . . . are his own and beyond the reach of government. . . ."

On the other hand, the strong arguable inference is that, by waving the banner of individual rights and disparaging the legitimacy and constitutionality of efforts to restrict the availability of sexually explicit materials, the Government not only excited petitioner's interest in sexually explicit materials banned by law but also exerted substantial pressure on petitioner to obtain and read such material as part of a fight against censorship and the infringement of individual rights. * * * **[g]**

Petitioner's ready response to these solicitations cannot be enough to establish beyond reasonable doubt that he was predisposed, prior to the Government acts intended to create predisposition, to commit the crime of receiving child pornography through the mails. The evidence that petitioner was ready and willing to commit the offense came only after the Government had devoted 2½ years to convincing him that he had or should have the right to engage in the very behavior proscribed by law. Rational jurors could not say beyond a reasonable doubt that petitioner possessed the requisite predisposition prior to the Government's investigation and that it existed independent of the Government's many and varied approaches to petitioner. As was explained in *Sherman,* where entrapment was found as a matter of law, "the Government [may not] play on the weaknesses of an innocent party and beguile him into committing crimes which he otherwise would not have attempted."

Law enforcement officials go too far when they "implant in the mind of an innocent person the *disposition* to commit the alleged offense and induce its commission in order that they may prosecute." (*Sorrells,* emphasis added). * * * When the Government's quest for convictions leads to the apprehension of an otherwise law-abiding citizen who, if left to his own devices, likely would have never run afoul of the law, the courts should intervene.

Because we conclude that this is such a case and that the prosecution failed, as a matter of law, to adduce evidence to support the jury verdict that petitioner was predisposed, independent of the Government's acts and beyond a reasonable doubt, to violate the law by receiving child pornography through the mails, we reverse the Court of Appeals' judgment affirming the conviction of Keith Jacobson.

JUSTICE O'CONNOR, with whom THE CHIEF JUSTICE and JUSTICE KENNEDY join, and with whom JUSTICE SCALIA joins except as to Part II, dissenting.

Keith Jacobson was offered only two opportunities to buy child pornography through the mail. Both times, he ordered. Both times, he asked for opportunities to buy more. He needed no Government agent to coax, threaten, or persuade him; no one played on his sympathies, friendship, or suggested that his committing the crime would further a greater good. **[h]** In fact, no Government agent even contacted him face to face. The Government contends that from the enthusiasm with which Mr. Jacobson responded to the chance to commit a crime, a reasonable jury could permissibly infer beyond a reasonable doubt that he was predisposed to commit the crime. I agree.

* * *

I

* * *

Today, the Court holds that Government conduct may be considered to create a predisposition to commit a crime, even before any Government action to induce the commission of the crime. In my view, this holding changes entrapment doctrine. Generally, the inquiry is whether a suspect is predisposed before the Government induces the commission of the crime, not before the Government makes initial contact with him. **[i]** There is no dispute here that the Government's questionnaires and letters were not sufficient to establish inducement; they did not even suggest that Mr. Jacobson should engage in any illegal activity. If all the Government had done was to send these materials, Mr. Jacobson's entrapment defense would fail. Yet the Court holds that the Government must prove not only that a suspect was predisposed to commit the crime before the opportunity to commit it arose, but also before the Government came on the scene.

[g] Suppose a person targeted by the Postal Service with these materials was taking a college class and was doing research on the First Amendment freedom of speech for a term paper. Sexually explicit Web sites are now common. Should law enforcement officers be allowed to access the names of all who access such sites for targeting?

[h] Do you find Justice White's or Justice O'Connor's depiction of what went on in Keith Jacobson's mind more persuasive?

[i] Under this view, the question is whether a defendant is predisposed to commit a crime after government agents worked on a person's predilections for several years. Is this fair?

Keith Jacobson was entrapped in one of a number of investigations run by the U.S. Postal Service investigating obscenity and child pornography, named Project Looking Glass. Many of these projects are aimed at commercial child pornography dealers. The Postal Service claims that one-third of the suspects arrested for child pornography offenses have also sexually abused children. Project Looking Glass resulted in 165 convictions.[18] "There were also four suicides, including another Nebraska farmer and a Wisconsin man who left a note saying he had been 'cursed with a demon for a sexual preference.'"[19] This suggests that this particular sting, unlike the interception of active and ongoing "kiddy-porn" groups, may have cast its net too widely. There seems to be a big difference between an investigation based on substantial evidence that nets a child pornography buyer who possesses thousands of videotapes and an operation that trawls for and badgers individuals against whom little evidence exists, a prescription for entrapping innocent people.[20]

Although *Jacobson* reaffirms the subjective test, the case shows a preoccupation with the heavy-handed practices of law enforcement. "[W]hat is new in *Jacobson* is the extent to which the Court was willing to take its disapproval of police methods as authorization to immunize the defendant."[21] In the case, Justice White dwelled on the facts of government excess—twenty-six months of repeated mailings; phony front organizations; and appeals to genuine First Amendment rights to snag a person who, despite his sexual inclinations, was not otherwise a purchaser of child pornography.

PROOF OF PREDISPOSITION A major preoccupation with the subjective test is *proving* predisposition. Some courts have tended to rule that it is not necessary to prove that the defendant intended to commit the *specific* crime charged at a specific time and place. These courts say that the defendant's *general intent* or purpose to commit *a* crime when the opportunity was provided is sufficient; that is, "if the defendant is of a frame of mind such that once his attention is called to the criminal opportunity, his decision to commit the crime is the product of his own preference and not the product of government persuasion." Other courts have ruled that the predisposition must be to commit *the specific* crime charged.[22]

The kind of evidence needed to prove predisposition generally falls into six categories: (1) the defendant's character or reputation, including any prior criminal record; (2) whether the government agent was the first to suggest criminal activity; (3) whether the defendant was engaged in the criminal activity for profit; (4) whether the defendant showed reluctance to commit the offense, overcome only by repeated government inducement or persuasion; (5) the nature of the inducement or persuasion supplied by the police; and (6) whether the defendant has the ability to carry out the crime.[23]

These factors are not mechanically applied. For example, in *United States v. Sherman* (1956) Sherman's two drug convictions were several years old, showing only that he was an addict and not a drug dealer. Also, in *Jacobson* (1992) the Supreme Court made it clear that the relevant inquiry is to

prior *crimes*, not to prior *acts*. The kind of crime makes a difference. Prosecutors could not introduce an expressed willingness to deal in *stolen property* in a firearms case because the two kinds of dealing are quite different.[24] Sophistication about how to commit a crime is a good sign of predisposition, but the inability to carry out a crime does not necessarily mean a lack of predisposition.[25]

THE OBJECTIVE AND SUBJECTIVE TESTS IN PRACTICE The Florida case of ***Cruz v. State*** exemplifies the objective test.[26] A police decoy, smelling of alcohol and posing as a drunken "skid row bum," had $150 sticking out of a pocket. Cruz passed by and noticed the money. He returned after fifteen minutes, took the cash, and was arrested. His conviction was reversed. Although the decoy was placed in a high-crime Tampa neighborhood, there was no specific problem with drunks being "rolled" there. The amount of money protruding from the decoy's pocket was said by the Florida Supreme Court to be *too tempting*. It was large enough to create a substantial risk that an ordinary (hypothetical) person, who would not usually seek to rob drunks, would be tempted to take the money.

Both the subjective and objective tests of entrapment have weaknesses. The legislative intent basis of the subjective test is a legal fiction, that is "extraordinarily tenuous considering that the defendant has, in fact, engaged in legislatively proscribed conduct."[27] More important, a criminal law–subjective approach does not rest logically on the concept of moral blameworthiness, a bedrock principle of substantive criminal law. Entrapment is not a defense when a nonpredisposed person is induced to commit a crime by a *private* person. Yet the identical inducement by an undercover police agent does constitute a defense. This clearly indicates that even the subjective test is mainly concerned with improper government action.[28]

The objective test focuses on how egregious is the conduct of the police. As Justice Frankfurter's concurring opinion in *Sherman* honestly noted, this cannot be determined with scientific exactitude: "The crucial question, not easy of answer, to which the court must direct itself is whether the police conduct revealed in the particular case falls below standards, to which common feelings respond, for the proper use of governmental power."

The objective test was adopted by the *Model Penal Code* in this formulation:

> A public law enforcement official or a person acting in cooperation with such an official perpetrates an entrapment if for the purpose of obtaining evidence of the commission of an offense, he induces or encourages another person to engage in conduct constituting such offense by either:
> (a) making knowingly false representations designed to induce the belief that such conduct is not prohibited; or
> (b) employing methods of persuasion or inducement that create substantial risk that such an offense will be committed by persons other than those who are ready to commit it.[29]

Part (b) establishes the **hypothetical person test**. Justice Frankfurter stated in *Sherman* that police encouragement should be of such a nature "as is likely to induce to the commission of crime only these persons [who are ready and willing to commit the crime] and not others who would normally avoid crime and through self-struggle resist ordinary temptations." Otherwise, the government has the resources to offer such lavish temptations that morally weaker persons—who were not bent on crime—would succumb. The objective test, by focusing on a "hypothetical" or "average" person, avoids the problem of having to introduce potentially prejudicial evidence about the defendant's past crimes to the jury in order to prove predisposition.

The objective test, though, has some flaws. First, police actions may be declared objectively to be such that would entrap a hypothetical person, and lead to the acquittal of defendants who are clearly predisposed—ready, willing, and able to commit crimes. Next, trying to determine whether particular police encouragement would entrap a "hypothetical person" is highly speculative and may depend more on the judge's predilections than on any objective standard. The Court's focus on police operations in most cases tends to show that "separation of the objective and subjective approaches is unworkable. Inducement cannot be considered in isolation from predisposition."[30] This points the way to the consideration of other approaches to entrapment.

OTHER TESTS: DUE PROCESS AND OUTRAGEOUS CONDUCT

Federal and state courts have begun to consider alternatives to the subjective and objective tests. In 1971 a federal court for the first time threw out the conviction of *predisposed* whiskey bootleggers because a government agent was their *business collaborator* for two and a half years and the government was their only buyer! Although entrapment as such did not exist, the court was offended by outrageous governmental conduct that violated its sense of justice.[31]

The Supreme Court twice considered whether an **outrageous conduct test** existed as a matter of due process. In both cases, the Court (1) applied the subjective test and found the defendants were predisposed, and (2) announced that a **due process defense** was *theoretically* possible in cases of outrageous governmental conduct, but did not apply an outrageous conduct or due process defense.

In *United States v. Russell* (1973) a federal undercover narcotics agent, Joe Shapiro, got to know three men operating a methamphetamine laboratory. Shapiro supplied them with the chemical phenyl-2-propanone—a legal but hard-to-get essential ingredient in manufacturing methamphetamine—in return for one-half of the drug produced. Shapiro visited the laboratory and watched the drug being produced. The defendants were convicted.

The Ninth Circuit Court of Appeals overturned the conviction on grounds of "an intolerable degree of governmental participation in the criminal enterprise." The decision was based on two theories. First, that entrapment existed whenever the government *furnished contraband* to a suspect. The second

rationale was an outrageous government conduct test: "because a government investigator was so enmeshed in the criminal activity . . . the prosecution of the defendants was . . . repugnant to the American criminal justice system."[32] The Circuit Court said that both rationales "are premised on fundamental concepts of due process and evince the reluctance of the judiciary to countenance overzealous law enforcement."[33]

Justice Rehnquist, writing for five justices, reversed and upheld the *Sherman* predisposition test. In this case, the chemical could have been obtained from other sources and, therefore, the government was not an exclusive supplier (a fact disputed in Justice Stewart's dissent). His opinion disapproved of the discretion that the due process rule would place in the hands of judges:

> [T]he defense of entrapment * * * was not intended to give the federal judiciary a "chancellor's foot" veto over law enforcement practices of which it did not approve. The execution of the federal laws under our Constitution is confided primarily to the Executive Branch of the Government, *subject to applicable constitutional and statutory limitations* and to judicially fashioned rules to enforce those limitations. We think that the decision of the Court of Appeals in this case quite unnecessarily introduces an unmanageably subjective standard which is contrary to the holdings of this Court in *Sorrells* and *Sherman.* (*United States v. Russell,* 1973, p. 435, emphasis added)

The majority opinion, however, also stated, "While we may *some day* be presented with a situation in which the conduct of law enforcement agents is so outrageous that due process principles would absolutely bar the government from invoking judicial processes to obtain a conviction, . . . the instant case is distinctly not of that breed" (*United States v. Russell,* 1973, pp. 431–32, emphasis added). "This 'some day' dicta, as the passage has come to be known, has been so widely cited in connection with the outrageous government conduct defense that it has effectively become a battle cry for the defense's proponents."[34] Subsequently, Justice Rehnquist tried, but failed, to kill the possibility of the Court ever adopting a due process entrapment defense.

In *Hampton v. United States* (1976) the Court once again refused to apply a due process theory of entrapment. Hampton was convicted of selling heroin to two Drug Enforcement Administration (DEA) agents. The sale was set up by DEA informant Hutton, who was an acquaintance of Hampton. The two were shooting pool when Hampton noticed "track" (needle) marks on Hutton's arms. Hampton said that he needed money and knew where he could get some heroin. Hutton said he could find a buyer and Hampton suggested that he "get in touch with those people." Hutton then called a DEA officer and arranged a sale. Hampton made two sales—for $145 and $500—to DEA agents posing as dealers. The government claimed that Hampton obtained the drugs on his own. Hampton claimed that Hutton introduced him to a pharmacist who manufactured a legal counterfeit drug; that he and Hutton were supplied with this supposedly counterfeit drug; and that they sold this to another person before selling it to the DEA agents.

That is, he claimed that the government *sold and purchased* illicit drugs. Hampton was convicted by a jury. The trial judge refused to instruct the jury that they must acquit whenever the government supplies drugs to a suspect before arresting him.

The Supreme Court upheld the conviction. The voting lineup kept alive the existence of a due process–outrageous conduct entrapment test. There was no majority opinion in *Hampton.* Justice Rehnquist, writing the plurality opinion for himself, Chief Justice Burger and Justice White, stated that in *Russell,* "We ruled out the possibility that the defense of entrapment could ever be based upon governmental misconduct in a case, such as this one, where the predisposition of the defendant to commit the crime was established." That is, Justice Rehnquist tried to reverse the meaning of the "some day" dicta in *Russell.* He asserted that the difference between *Hampton* and *Russell* was only one of degree, despite the fact that the government supplied Hampton with *illegal* drugs, which was the essence of the crime, while the substance supplied to Russell was a *legal* chemical. To Justice Rehnquist, this difference did not matter because both defendants were predisposed and therefore not entrapped. The idea of engaging in a drug sale to raise money was not implanted in Hampton's mind by the government agent. Justice Rehnquist urged that a due process defense could operate only when the actions of a government undercover agent violated some other constitutional right as well. If taken seriously, this would mean that no matter how outrageous the police conduct, a defendant could *never* claim a due process violation based only on excessive undercover involvement in the crime.

This attempt to close off the due process defense failed because a total of five justices of the eight who participated in the case disagreed on this last point. Justice Powell, joined by Justice Blackmun, concurred in upholding the conviction, and agreed that in this case the government conduct was not outrageous. But he felt that *Russell* did not foreclose the Court's use of its supervisory power in future cases "to bar conviction of a predisposed defendant because of outrageous police conduct." Three dissenting justices (Brennan, Stewart, and Marshall) would have (1) adopted the objective theory of entrapment, (2) found that Hampton was entrapped under the subjective approach, (3) agreed with Justice Powell that the Court can exercise its supervisory power or rely on due process to dismiss convictions of predisposed defendants "where the conduct of law enforcement authorities is sufficiently offensive," and (4) found that the police activity was outrageous in this case because the police supplied contraband and because the government action was a setup and the government itself was too heavily involved in the case.

After *Hampton,* the due process approach has been successfully used on rare occasions by lower federal courts, although it has been rejected in principle by some circuits.[35] *United States v. Twigg* (1978) is an example of the application of the due process test.[36] In this case, Robert Kubica, a convicted methamphetamine manufacturer, agreed to apprehend illegal drug dealers for the DEA in order to have a four-year prison sentence reduced. Kubica contacted an old friend, Henry Neville, to discuss setting up a "speed" laboratory and over a period of months drew Neville into the scheme. They worked together to set up a lab, and Kubica's contributions were funded by the government, including two and a half gallons of phenyl-2-propanone costing $475. Seven months later, Neville introduced Kubica to William Twigg, who got involved in the operation to repay a debt to Neville. Twigg played a minor role in the process, often running errands for groceries or coffee. He was present in the lab while Kubica actually produced six pounds of methamphetamine hydrochloride during the one week that the lab was in operation. Twigg was convicted for the manufacture of illegal drugs.

A federal Court of Appeals reversed the convictions. "The nature and extent of police involvement in this crime was so overreaching as to bar prosecution of the defendants as a matter of due process of law. Although no Supreme Court decision has reversed a conviction on this basis, the police conduct in this case went far beyond the behavior found permissible in previous cases" (*Twigg,* p. 377). Essentially, the government set up a criminal enterprise, actively worked at it, and then prosecuted its collaborators (*Twigg,* p. 379). Significantly, the criminal scheme was *initiated* by the government through a convicted felon seeking to reduce the severity of his sentence. A major factor in the case was that the government supplied a substantial amount of the funds and materials for the laboratory when it was not clear that the parties had the means to obtain the chemicals on their own. Indeed, the DEA made arrangements with chemical suppliers to circumvent regulations needed to get controlled chemicals. "Neither defendant had the know-how with which to actually manufacture methamphetamine. The assistance they provided was minimal and then at the specific direction of Kubica" (*Twigg,* p. 381).

Although Neville and Twigg were predisposed, they would not have gotten into the drug manufacturing business if Kubica had not proposed the scheme. "This egregious conduct on the part of government agents *generated new crimes* by the defendant merely for the sake of pressing criminal charges against him when, as far as the record reveals, he was lawfully and peacefully minding his own affairs. Fundamental fairness does not permit us to countenance such actions by law enforcement officials and prosecution for a crime so fomented by them will be barred" (*Twigg,* p. 381).

THE ENTRAPMENT DEFENSE IN THE STATES

Selecting the Subjective and Objective Tests

Because the entrapment defense is not based on the Constitution, the states are free to develop their own rules. Most states have kept the subjective theory; a minority have adopted the objective standard of entrapment, and a few combine both approaches into various *hybrid* tests.

The **Ohio** Supreme Court gave three reasons for affirmatively selecting the subjective test in *State v. Doran* (1983).[37] First, the objective test can result in convicting "otherwise innocent" people if the police activity is not objectively outrageous, although it actually induces the criminal acts. Second, "real" (predisposed) criminals, who regularly engage in crime, can be released under the objective test. Third, in practice, the objective test can lead to difficulties of proof and "swearing contests" as to what the police actually did, because the acts that led to claims of entrapment usually occurred in private. Although the subjective test posed fewer problems, the Ohio court did express concern about the use of reputation evidence, standing alone, as proof of predisposition.

Alaska was the first jurisdiction to adopt the objective test in *Grossman v. State* (1969), in the phrasing of the Model Penal Code: inducement by a law enforcement official, "which would be effective to persuade an average person other than the one who is ready and willing, to commit such an offense."[38] Examples of objective entrapment include "extreme pleas of desperate illness, appeals based primarily on sympathy, pity or close personal friendship, and offers of inordinate amounts of money." The Alaska Supreme Court, nevertheless, included a concern that is part of the subjective approach: "[W]e do not intend that entrapment should become a ready escape hatch for those who are engaged in a course of criminal enterprise. But, under standards of civilized justice, there must be some control on the kind of police conduct which can be permitted in the manufacturing of crime."

Michigan, in *People v. Turner* (1973), also adopted the objective approach.[39] In 1967 Partridge, a part-time sheriff's deputy and truck driver, befriended Turner, an antiques dealer. Turner had no adult criminal record. Six months later, Turner sold Partridge legal caffeine pills. The two maintained a casual friendship for three years. Partridge told the state police he suspected Turner of selling drugs and an undercover agent, Ewers, posing as a truck driver, joined Partridge in 1969 in his meetings with Turner. Partridge asked Turner to sell him drugs several times. Turner said he did not know anything about them and lectured Partridge on the harmful effects of marijuana and heroin. Partridge then invented a story about a good-looking girlfriend who was a heroin addict and would leave Partridge if he did not get some heroin for her. Turner ultimately obtained twenty dollars' worth of heroin from a friend in Detroit who had become an addict. Turner sold it to Partridge at cost, but refused further requests to purchase drugs for Partridge. At Partridge's urging, he drove Partridge and Ewers to Detroit and introduced them to his addict friend, from whom they purchased heroin. Turner was convicted of these two sales and received a minimum prison sentence of twenty years. A majority of the Michigan court held that this was entrapment as a matter of law and adopted the objective formulation of the concurring justices in *Sorrells* and *Sherman*. "This is the type of overreaching by the police condemned by our Court in *Saunders v. People* (1878). . . ."

Mississippi relies on the subjective test, except for one situation, where one state agent furnishes drugs to a defendant and another buys the drugs from the defendant. *Epps v. State* (1982) held that this is repugnant and *per se* entrapment in Mississippi law.[40] This ruling, which drew on similar New Jersey and Illinois cases, echoes Justice Brennan's dissent in *Hampton* (1976)—that the "Government is doing nothing less than buying contraband from itself through an intermediary and jailing the intermediary."[41] *Epps* is interesting because it shows that a state supreme court can create *situation-specific entrapment rules* to deal with persistent problems of police overreaching.

Some states that adopt the objective rule by statute do not establish clear rules. By statute, **Pennsylvania** defined entrapment as does the Model Penal Code as police activity that would draw a hypothetical person into crime.[42] Nevertheless, Pennsylvania courts interpreted the statute inconsistently, with some cases following a subjective test and others the objective test.[43] To make matters worse, another section of the Pennsylvania code on the burden needed to prove entrapment injects a subjective element. The defendant has the burden to show that his or her behavior was *actually* caused by the inducement, making the lack of predisposition important.[44] This level of confusion concerning the entrapment test is not unique to Pennsylvania.[45]

Because the subjective and objective tests have some drawbacks, several states have tried to improve their entrapment rules by combining both tests into hybrid rules.

The Hybrid Approach

A state can combine the subjective and objective tests into a *composite* hybrid approach, where a defendant has to prove entrapment both under the subjective *and* the objective approaches, or into a *discrete* hybrid approach, where a defendant has to prove entrapment either under the subjective *or* the objective approach in order to be released.[46] The composite hybrid approach is unfair because it forces a genuinely non-predisposed defendant to show that the nature of the police inducement would also lead a hypothetical person into crime. The benefit of the objective test in disallowing prejudicial evidence of the defendant's past is negated by the composite approach, because past crimes are still allowed into evidence.[47] This was the result of the **New Jersey** Supreme Court's interpretation of a statute intended to prevent governmental misconduct in *State v. Rockholt*.[48] Thus, instead of benefitting the defendant, as New Jersey had intended, the hybrid elements of its entrapment defense favor the state unfairly.[49]

The *discrete hybrid approach* "gives a defendant greater latitude to assert an entrapment defense while reducing the burden of persuasion. It provides the non-predisposed defendant with a defense against the government's overwhelming power to coerce, and also gives the non-predisposed defendant a defense against egregious police conduct."[50] **Florida** adopted the discrete hybrid approach in *Cruz v. State* (the decoy case discussed previously) to describe an example of the objective approach.[51] The Florida court improved on the two tests by adding two policy issues into a determination of whether entrapment existed as a matter of law:

1. Is the police activity aimed at interrupting *specific ongoing criminal activity?*
2. Have the police used *means reasonably tailored* to apprehend those involved in ongoing criminal activity?

If the answer to either of these questions is negative, the effect of the undercover work is to *create crimes* where none of that type had been occurring. The state also must provide some evidence of the likelihood of predisposition.

Conclusion

A 1993 article estimated that every state had adopted an entrapment test with the majority favoring the subjective approach.[52] According to this count, twenty states had adopted the subjective approach by case decisions and another thirteen by statute. A more recent count by Kenneth Lord notes that the majority of the states follow the subjective test; that twelve states currently follow the objective test; while six states have adopted hybrid tests of entrapment, with three adopting a composite ("and") hybrid approach and three the discrete ("or") hybrid test.[53]

It appears that in practice the subjective (predisposition) and objective (nature of the inducement) factors often become intertwined, as confirmed by Kenneth Lord's study.[54] Lord recommends that a two-step entrapment approach, similar to the discrete hybrid approach, is preferable. The court would first explore whether the government's acts are outrageous or would induce a typical person to commit a crime. "If this inquiry fails, the jury can then proceed with a subjective inquiry to determine whether the defendant was an unwary innocent induced into committing a crime by the government. . . . [U]sing an objective approach as a backstop allows courts to provide explicit guidance to police agencies concerning the appropriateness of their actions in undercover operations."[55] Roiphe, critical of scholars who have supported strictly objective approaches, sees wisdom in the adherence of most courts to the subjective approach:

> While both the objective and subjective tests are sloppy, the idea of predisposition involved in the subjective test is the most reasonable way for courts to determine how much control the defendant had over his own actions and thus, whether he ought to be held responsible. This may require the fact finder to resort to his own experience writ large, to what sort of inducements seem unfair, and to some approximation of what kind of inducements would lead most normal people to commit crimes. Judges and juries do this anyway. . . . Asking whether the government created the criminal and whether the accused was predisposed to commit the crime integrates into the law a general notion that the government's monopoly over intelligence and information can undermine free will, and that it is the court's role to preserve and protect it.[56]

LAW IN SOCIETY

UNDERCOVER POLICING AND ITS CONTROL

Undercover police work is fascinating and varied. It includes dangerous tactics by courageous officers to uncover major crimes, sleazy and routine vice enforcement, and questionable tactics where the police manufacture crime. Undercover work often includes encouragement (also called covert facilitation) but may involve spying as the officer or informant gathers information about crime.[57] Undercover policing is an essential tool of law enforcement for detecting covert consensual forms of crime (e.g., vice, white-collar crime) or organized crime. Yet it poses so many undesirable side effects that it must be carefully monitored by police agencies.

THE NATURE AND GROWTH OF UNDERCOVER POLICING

According to Professor Gary Marx's comprehensive study, undercover policing has three major functions: intelligence, prevention, and facilitation. "*Intelligence* operations use covert and deceptive tactics to gather information about crimes that" have occurred, might be planned, or are in progress. An example is a police agent befriending a suspect in order to gather more information and get a confession.[58] This happened in *Arizona v. Fulminante* (1991) when Anthony Sarivola—an ex-cop prisoner—played a "mobster" in prison and befriended Fulminante to gain a confession to the murder of Fulminante's stepdaughter (see Chapter 7). This was not entrapment, but the confession was coerced because of the implied threats to Fulminante's life. Intelligence gathering includes police putting snitches in jail cells. *Prevention* occurs when police infiltrate an organization, such as an extremist political group, and convince its members to refrain from acts of violence. The classical counterpoint to this is the **agent provocateur** who tries to stir up violent protest in order to arrest members of the organization. *Facilitation* is encouragement and the form of undercover policing most likely to result in entrapment. In using facilitative techniques, agents can pose either as victims (e.g., decoys) or as coconspirators.[59]

Prior to 1975, most undercover activity focused on vice: public solicitation for prostitution, operating after-hours bars, selling drugs, and the like, although FBI monitoring and infiltration of radical political organizations occurred.[60] Since the 1970s, undercover police activity has expanded to many new areas. Decoy officers dress and act as potential victims, such as "skid row bums" or elderly people who are prey to muggers. In New York City decoy officers drove taxicabs after a rash of cabdriver robbery-murders. Sting operations became popular. Police set up fictitious criminal enterprises to do business with criminals such as burglars or car thieves. Police have posed as major drug dealers, selling to or buying from wholesale drug traffickers. Undercover operations develop in response to a changing society. The rapid growth of Internet use has spawned computer crime. A particularly odious form—sexual predation of minors by pedophiles—has been met by police officers going online and posing as young teens on sexually oriented chat lines. According to a news account, between 1998 and 2000 the "number of Illinois law enforcement agencies dedicating an officer or unit to investigate computer sex crimes has jumped from six to 50 [and] arrests and convictions of cyber pedophiles have nearly doubled."[61]

Since the 1970s, undercover work has grown enormously and has shifted in focus to target white-collar crime, organized crime, and political corruption.[62] Justice Department appropriations for undercover activities increased from one million dollars in 1977 to twelve million dollars in 1984.[63] Professor Marx estimated that in 1982 "the proportion of all police arrests involving undercover work has roughly doubled in the last 15 years."[64] The number of federal undercover operations investigating political corruption in the United States jumped from fifty in the late 1970s to 463 in 1981.[65] This trend has continued. Between 1985 and 1995, federal spending on informers alone increased from twenty-five million dollars to about one hundred million dollars a year—a figure that does not include local law enforcement expenditures.[66]

Organized crime, long thought immune from infiltration, has been penetrated by government agents, including the famous seven-year undercover operation of FBI Agent Joseph Pistone who as "Donnie Brasco" infiltrated the leadership of the Bonanno crime family.[67] Undercover work can be part of a larger strategy to disrupt organized crime by intelligence gathering, electronic surveillance, and coordinated police and prosecution strategies.[68] A 1990 FBI operation known as Catcom (for catch communications), for example, put a dent in cocaine importation. For three years, federal agents infiltrated a Miami communications shop used as a meeting point for drug dealers. Hidden video cameras gathered evidence that led to the breakup of the drug importation ring, the arrest of sixty-eight suspects, the seizure of several millions of dollars in cash and property, and the seizure of drugs worth several hundreds of millions of dollars. The operation, which generated eight hundred reports, gave federal authorities a better picture of Colombian cocaine trafficking patterns.[69]

Since the Watergate scandal in the early 1970s, federal investigation of local government corruption has become routine. Rumors of judicial corruption in Chicago, for example, led to an astonishing investigation: "Operation Greylord." A downstate Illinois judge was transferred to Chicago and "wired" to record incriminating statements of corrupt fellow judges. This resulted in the conviction of nine local Chicago judges, thirty-seven attorneys, and nineteen court officers and clerks by mid-1988.[70] Integrity testing is also important in police and correctional agencies to ensure that police and correctional officers do not succumb to the temptations that regularly come their way. The Detroit Police Department recently inaugurated integrity testing, after officers were found guilty of selling the drugs that they took during raids. The tests include police supervisors leaving cash and drugs in drug houses to see if officers sent there turn them in. Such integrity testing has been used in cities such as New York; Washington, D.C.; and New Orleans, and it seems to have had positive effects.[71]

The most extensive corruption probe was *Abscam* (short for Abdul scam—1978 to 1980). It began when an informant, during a stolen art sting, told investigators that the mayor of Camden, New Jersey, was taking bribes. The FBI set up a fictitious company, "Abdul Enterprises, Ltd.," furnished with offices and a yacht, that played on the then-popular theme of oil-rich Arabian sheiks with vast wealth seeking to buy favors. The "sheik" (FBI agent Anthony Amoroso) worked with

Melvin Weinberg, a convicted con man, who made connections with politicians. The FBI allowed Weinberg to design what, in effect, became a major integrity-testing program. The Abscam players, in the course of discussing supposedly legitimate investment and immigration matters, offered huge sums of money to political figures and operatives. Camden's mayor, for example, was videotaped receiving $125,000 in return for promising to help get permission for "Abdul Ltd." to open a casino in Atlantic City. The sting operation snowballed. Congressmen were to be paid $50,000 to introduce private bills to allow fictitious "sheiks" refugee status. Abscam middlemen spread tales about huge sums of money available for returning favors. "The operation was finally forced to shut down due to the large number of minor politicians seeking bribe money from the sheik." By 1980, "six United States congressmen, one United States senator, a United States Immigration Service official, three members of the Philadelphia City Council, the mayor of Camden, New Jersey, and assorted bagmen, middlemen, and corrupt lawyers" were exposed by Abscam, convicted, and sent to prison. Was Abscam entrapment? The courts said no, and upheld the convictions of the politicians and middlemen. Some appellate judges expressed concern that the huge sums offered, "in excess of real-world opportunities," might have created crimes. Most judges, however, saw this as creating a grapevine to which corrupt and greedy politicians responded.[72]

White-collar crime milks billions of dollars from consumers and honest business firms, creates dangers that cause injuries and deaths, and undermines public confidence in business. Past violations were treated as administrative errors, and even after prosecution, penalties were light.[73] After the Watergate scandal, which included revelations of illegal business payoffs to politicians, local and federal prosecutors began to prosecute white-collar crimes with greater vigor—judicial sentences included prison terms for corporate executives. In this climate of opinion, the government has used undercover agents in some unusual areas.

For example, an elaborate FBI operation to investigate corruption in the Chicago Board of Trade (the "Merc") ran from 1987 to 1989.[74] Suspicion arose that traders were overcharging customers, not paying full proceeds of sales, and using knowledge of customers' orders to first trade for themselves. Archer-Daniels-Midland Company, a large agricultural concern, complained about abuses and aided the FBI sting by "hiring" two agents to work for the company's trading subsidiary. Getting information was difficult because Merc traders formed tight-knit cliques where much depended on mutual trust. Over a two-year period, four undercover agents lived the fast-paced lives of Chicago futures traders with false identities, fabricated college degrees (verified by cooperating universities), expensive apartments and cars, memberships in trendy health clubs, and seats on the Merc so they could work regularly as traders. They infiltrated the trader culture so as to win other traders' confidence. "Once into the sting operation, the agents tape recorded traders in restaurants, at parties, in health clubs and on the noisy floors of the exchanges themselves." At the conclusion of the operation, the agents had sufficient incriminating evidence to subpoena fifty traders and others for various securities violations and frauds.

White-collar sting operations can be expensive to run and can involve immense stakes. At times, they expose links between big business and political corruption. Some investigations have international repercussions, and prosecution plans may become entangled with conflicting policies of the State Department, the Commerce Department, and even the White House.[75] In other white-collar stings, big business mixes with ordinary crime. The flamboyant automobile entrepreneur, John Z. DeLorean, desperately needed ten million dollars to finance a sinking enterprise to build sports cars in Ireland. He was approached by a former neighbor—a narcotics dealer and FBI informant—with the prospect of raising money through a cocaine deal. When DeLorean could not raise the cash for the drug deal, the agent proposed that he sign over his company as collateral. DeLorean may have been convicted if the subjective test of entrapment had been adhered to strictly, but he was acquitted. The jury apparently disapproved of the government's unrelenting tactics and the singling out of the defendant because of his high visibility.[76]

PROBLEMS WITH COVERT POLICING

Undercover work is subject to abuses and unintended consequences, aside from entrapment. First, despite the heroic TV and movie images of undercover work, some officers are *psychologically or physically damaged* by the high-stress effort required to play a negative role, thus raising moral dilemmas that often go unresolved. In extreme cases, agents cannot return to normal work; some turn criminal. Covert work puts greater than ordinary strains on officers' family lives. Undercover police are sometimes mistaken for real criminals and mistreated by uniformed officers. In an extreme example, a Detroit robbery decoy unit set up in the late 1960s resulted in three officers and sixteen civilians being killed before the unit was disbanded.[77] Recently, New York City was rocked by the killing of a completely innocent man in a reverse sting. Patrick Dorismond, twenty-six, father of two, and an off-duty security guard was hailing a cab outside a midtown Manhattan bar when he was rushed by an undercover police officer who wanted to buy marijuana. Dorismond, offended, brushed him off. They argued, scuffled, and the undercover detective called for backup. In a moment, Dorismond, who was African American, was shot and killed.[78]

Higher rates of entrapment can be expected, for example, when police use notoriously unreliable drug informants to make unobserved buys.[79] Informants may be motivated by revenge and are sometimes paid for their work. Police recruits may be selected because they are not known to local criminals. To ensure their credibility and the lack of a "police attitude," they are put on the street before entering the academy with virtually no training or briefing. Since these agents may remain on the street for many months, making hundreds of buys before terminating their covers, the dangers of lost evidence and misidentification are multiplied.[80] Unfortunately, undercover officers have been known to falsify drug purchase reports by not including information that could clear a defendant; since they work in secret, this form of perjury is hard to detect. Some studies show that officers' *reports* adhere to the letter of the law even if their *actions* do not.[81]

Overuse of sting operations, such as a fictitious business buying stolen goods from burglars, raises serious *cost-benefit questions* beyond issues of entrapment. These operations are costly, and there should be an administrative determination of whether the total costs of running the operation are worth it in terms of the amount of property recovered. Another issue, which is difficult to measure, is whether a sting operation increases the quantity of crime. A new sting operation might stimulate people with no record as burglars to commit crimes when they hear that there is money to be made at this "new outlet."[82]

Undercover work poses risks to citizens as a result of administrative bungling. A chilling example was documented by R. E. Payne, a Covington, Louisiana, newspaper reporter.[83] Payne went to the FBI with a tip about an organized crime murder of a tow-truck operator and agreed to go undercover to detect a political corruption connection. He met with a businessman, K. T. Fogg, who was a local official and requested a bribe for silence about incriminating information. Payne was not wired for sound; what he did not know was that Fogg had become an undercover operative for a *separate* FBI political corruption unit and was wearing a recording device. As a result of their conversation, Payne was indicted for conspiracy, and his FBI handler refused to acknowledge that Payne was working undercover! Payne was saved from conviction when his attorney obtained a memorandum proving his undercover status. As undercover work expands, more *administrative mismanagement*, leading to botched cases and gross injustice, can occur. Close administrative supervision is essential in any espionage work, whether it involves national security or civilian criminal justice.

Covert policing carries political risks to democratic government. For most of the twentieth century, the FBI has used informers not only to infiltrate foreign espionage cells, but also to spy on citizens' groups with extremist political views. In the turbulent days of the late 1960s, FBI *agent provocateurs*, often criminals, infiltrated groups of war protesters to provoke violent incidents that would lead to arrests. The worst case involved an informer in the Chicago Black Panther Party who provided a diagram of the Panthers' apartment, indicating where everyone slept. The FBI passed it to a Chicago police unit and persuaded it to make the 1969 predawn raid in which Fred Hampton, the local leader, was killed in his bed by a hail of police bullets. The FBI role was not discovered for several years.[84]

Despite the risks of abuse, poorly defined benefits, and dangers of generating crime and entrapment, undercover policing is necessary. It would be impossible or outrageously expensive to police criminal behavior that is secret and where victims do not come forward to complain. The question, then, is how to appropriately control abuses.

JUDICIAL AND ADMINISTRATIVE CONTROL OF UNDERCOVER POLICING

There are limits to the judicial control of undercover work. The entrapment defense, useful in marking the outer limits of covert facilitation, does not provide appropriate guidance of undercover policing. Some scholars advocate further legal and judicial control of undercover work: that police not engage in covert facilitation unless reasonable suspicion or probable cause exists to believe that known or unknown suspects are engaged in the crime targeted by the covert facilitation and that a judge has approved the covert facilitation "for only one integrity test."[85] These suggestions are misplaced. Undercover policing is not a search, so warrants are not constitutionally required.[86] Even if created by statute, undercover probable cause warrants would go beyond traditional judicial case-by-case reasoning. Judges would have to enter into administrative oversight and pass on the wisdom of police work, a task for which they are not trained. Courts have assumed administrative control of prisons and other executive agencies only in extreme cases to preserve the constitutional rights of inmates. The quasi-administrative role of supervising undercover work could tarnish the judicial role. Conversely, judicial involvement can hamper proper undercover work: some judges might unnecessarily restrict creative policing while others would rubber-stamp unwise stings. Judge shopping can cause even greater inconsistencies.

Undercover policies and operations are best directed by police agencies that should adopt administrative standards and guidelines for encouragement techniques. General standards can be mandated by law, but operations should be planned at high levels in police departments and the reason for each general undercover program should be well thought out. For example, Irvin Nathan, the Abscam coordinator, suggested guidelines for federal agencies before they undertake corruption stings: "(A) the corrupt nature of the activity is reasonably clear to potential subjects; (B) there is reasonable indication that the undercover operation will reveal illegal activities; and (C) the nature of any inducement is not unjustifiable in view of the character of the illegal transaction in which the individual is invited to engage." Before commencing, anticorruption stings would be approved by an agency review board.[87]

The effective use of guidelines ensures that law enforcement controls an essential function, assures the public that abuses will be kept to a minimum, and avoids overreliance on the entrapment defense, which is not well suited to the routine guidance of police undercover work.

SUMMARY

Entrapment is a complete defense to crime based on the concept that the idea for the crime was implanted in the defendant's mind by police. It is both a criminal law defense and a doctrine of criminal procedure. It is not a constitutional defense, but is a judge-made doctrine of statutory interpretation. The defense is not applied to crimes of violence.

Covert police work—encouragement and undercover policing—involves the lawful use of deception. Undercover police pretend to be victims (decoys) or participants in crime. They may or may not use the technique of encouragement. Encouragement is police activity in which an undercover agent pretends to be a participant in crimes and furnishes an opportunity for a person to engage in crime. Undercover work does not, in itself, violate any provision of the Constitution.

There are two theories of entrapment. The subjective test—favored by a majority of states and the federal courts—views entrapment as occurring when a law enforcement officer implants a criminal idea into the mind of a person who otherwise would not have engaged in an illegal act. A person predisposed to commit a crime cannot claim entrapment under the subjective test. Proof of entrapment allows the introduction into evidence such prejudicial facts as prior criminal acts. The objective test—favored by some Supreme Court justices in the past and a few states—holds that entrapment occurs when government agents perform acts that would tend to draw average persons into crime. Both the subjective and objective tests are concerned with predisposition and excessive police behavior.

Under the subjective test, the defendant must establish that the government has induced an individual to break the law and the defense of entrapment is at issue. The prosecution must then prove beyond reasonable doubt that the defendant was disposed to commit the criminal act prior to first being approached and induced by government agents.

Another test, suggested by the United States Supreme Court and applied by a few courts, is that particularly outrageous law enforcement action used to draw a person into crime violates the defendant's due process rights. Some state rules declare that outrageous conduct occurs when government agents sell drugs to a suspect and then buy them back from him. The Supreme Court has held this not to be entrapment if the defendant is predisposed to commit the crime.

Most states follow the subjective test. Several have adopted hybrid tests that combine the subjective and objective tests. A composite hybrid approach requires a defendant to prove that entrapment occurred under both the subjective and the objective approaches; the discrete hybrid approach allows the defense where a defendant proves entrapment under either the subjective or the objective approach.

The subjective and objective tests overlap in their goal of limiting excessive police actions that draw essentially innocent persons into crime.

LEGAL PUZZLES

HOW HAVE COURTS DECIDED THESE CASES?

9–1. Barbara, Susan's supervisor at McDonald's, knew that Susan was taking hydrocodone, a prescribed pain medicine for fibromyalgia. Barbara told Susan that she had a very sick friend who needed additional pain medication. Susan offered to give the friend some of her medicine, but Barbara insisted that her friend could pay for it, reminding Susan that she needed money. Barbara set the price at $5 per tablet and arranged a meeting at a bar where Susan sold the pills to Silverman. Barbara continued pressuring Susan at work until she agreed to meet with Silverman again. Barbara arranged subsequent meetings for the purchase and sale of hydrocodone.

Silverman was a sheriff's deputy. Barbara was trying to reduce her own sentence on a criminal conviction by providing substantial assistance to the St. Lucie County (Florida) Sheriff's Office. In exchange for leniency on her sentence, Barbara was arranging drug buys for Silverman. Silverman did not supervise Barbara. He was never present when Barbara spoke to Susan about any of the transactions, nor did he record any such conversations. Barbara was left to her own devices as to how to provide substantial assistance to the sheriff's office.

1. Did Barbara entrap Susan into committing a crime of selling a controlled substance?
2. If so, which theory of entrapment applied?

HELD: (1) Yes; (2) Due Process.

The government's actions violated Susan's due process rights. Florida law recognizes both a subjective entrapment defense based on a defendant's predisposition to commit the offense and an objective entrapment defense based on whether police conduct offends due process under the Florida constitution. The Florida Supreme Court said that convictions brought about by methods that offend one's sense of justice are barred.

This case is similar to other Florida cases where "hooked" criminals are working with law enforcement to reduce their sentences. Barbara was not given guidance or limitations about with whom to negotiate drug deals or how to avoid entrapment. Her conversations with Susan were not monitored. Furthermore, Barbara exploited her position as a work supervisor to create a crime where none existed. When Susan offered to let Barbara's sick friend have some of her medicine, Barbara insisted that Susan needed the money and her friend was able to pay. Barbara repeatedly urged the appellant to follow through with the "drug deal." As in other cases, Susan had no criminal record and there was no evidence she was suspected of criminal activity before Barbara brought her into this scheme. Barbara's conduct in this case offended due process under Florida's constitution and constituted entrapment as a matter of law. Susan's conviction was reversed on appeal and a motion for a judgment of acquittal was entered.

Dial v. State, 799 So. 2d 407 (Fla. App. 4th Dist. 2001)

9–2. Detective Sandino was working undercover attempting to purchase narcotics in areas about which the police department had received complaints. As he was driving in a vehicle equipped with audio and video recording devices, he saw Rogers walking along the street. Det. Sandino stopped his vehicle near Rogers, rolled down the window, and asked where he could get "two twenties"—street slang for two $20 rocks of crack cocaine. Rogers instructed Det. Sandino to drive around

the corner, after which Rogers entered the passenger's side of Det. Sandino's vehicle. He gave Det. Sandino directions to a house. Rogers told the detective to pull over and was given $40 to buy crack cocaine. Rogers gave Det. Sandino a crack pipe to hold as "collateral." Rogers exited the car and told Sandino to drive around the block. When he returned, Rogers leaned into the car and spit out two off-white rock-like objects. The video- and audio-taped recordings of these events were entered into evidence at trial. The off-white rock-like objects tested positive for cocaine and weighed .3 grams in total.

1. Did Det. Sandino entrap Rogers into selling cocaine?
2. If so, under which theory?

Holding available from instructor

9–3. A police detective placed an advertisement in a "swingers" magazine in May 1995 that included the following: "female, 31; Single mom, two girls, one boy, seeks male as partner and mentor, seeks fun, enjoys travel and photography." More than one hundred responses were made to this ad and the detective responded to the ninety-seven individuals who sent addresses. The detective, pretending to be a woman named "Frances," maintained a correspondence with Paul, who lived in another state, from October 1995 to January 1996. Paul and Frances exchanged about ten letters. Paul had no criminal record. In his early letters, Paul expressed an interest in having sexual relations with Frances and a willingness to go fishing and camping with her children and his son. Early in the correspondence Frances wrote to Paul suggesting that by a "mentor" she meant an adult male who would provide "sex training" to children aged twelve, ten, and eight. By the fifth letter, Paul stated, after being told by Frances that she participated "during sex training with [her] children," that he would be willing to engage in sex acts with the children. He also stated that he wanted to establish a family situation.

A meeting was ultimately arranged. Frances suggested that Paul bring video equipment, but he indicated that he had no experience with such equipment. Paul was arrested. A search of his vehicle disclosed bags of snacks, soft drinks and a bottle of wine, a vibrator, a Polaroid camera loaded with film, ten extra cartridges of film, nine condoms, a tube of lubricating jelly, a partially used tube of jelly, and a number of items conflictingly described as "small condoms" by the detective and as "finger cots" by Paul, who testified at trial that they are used to protect injured fingers. Several of these latter items were also found in appellant's pockets, within a plastic bag which also contained jelly and adult condoms. A search of his home produced no evidence that Paul was interested in, or had a history of, the exploitation of children or child pornography. Paul was convicted of the federal offense of travelling in interstate commerce for the purpose of engaging in an illegal "sexual act" with minors. The trial judge refused to charge the jury with a defense of entrapment.

Should the jury have been given instructions on the defense of entrapment on the facts of this case?

Holding available from instructor

9–4. A paid informant for the government, Horcasitas, testified that three weeks after he moved into the trailer next door to Garcia, Garcia suggested to Horcasitas that he should sell cocaine. At trial, Garcia's sole defense was that Horcasitas entrapped him. The jury returned a guilty verdict.

In conversations with Horcasitas about drugs, Garcia used phrases like "animals," "bundles," and "papers," and Garcia understood Horcasitas's use of slang. In one conversation Garcia said he wanted to look "at the papers to see if I like them, to see if they work on the roof." A police officer testified that such code is used by people "familiar with dealing in drugs." The amount of cocaine involved in the transaction was 2.987 kilograms. Garcia refused to transport the cocaine from Las Cruces, New Mexico, to Hatch, New Mexico. Garcia insisted that the drug deal occur near his home area and be completed quickly at the time Garcia, not the buyers, demanded. He suggested that the locations for the drug deal frequently change. Garcia maintained a cool, calm, and collected businesslike demeanor throughout the entire drug transaction.

Was there sufficient evidence to show that Garcia was predisposed to committing the crime of drug dealing?

Holding available from instructor

FURTHER READING

Gary Marx, *Undercover: Police Surveillance in America* (Berkeley: University of California Press, 1988).

David Wise, *The American Police State: The Government Against the People* (New York: Random House, 1976).

Scott Turow, *Personal Injuries* (Toronto: HarperCollins, 1999).

ENDNOTES

1. The subject is found in criminal law and criminal procedure textbooks: W. LaFave and A. W. Scott, Jr., *Handbook on Criminal Law* (St. Paul: West Publishing, 1972), 369–74; C. Whitebread and C. Slobogin, *Criminal Procedure,* 4th ed. (New York: Foundation Press, 2000), 503–20.

2. Paul Marcus, "The Development of Entrapment Law," *Wayne Law Review* 33 (1986): 5–37; Comment, C. Robton Perelli-Minetti, "Causation and Intention in the Entrapment Defense," *UCLA Law Review* 28 (1981): 859–905; George Fletcher, *Rethinking Criminal Law* (Boston: Little, Brown, 1978), 541; Mark M. Stavsky, "The 'Sting' Reconsidered: Organized Crime, Corruption and Entrapment," *Rutgers Law Journal* 16 (1985): 937–89, notes that in New Zealand entrapment may result in the exclusion of evidence, and Canadian dictum indicates that entrapment is a legitimate defense.

3. Stavsky, "The 'Sting,'" 949.

4. *Board of Commissioners v. Backus,* 29 How. Pr. 33, 42 (New York, 1864), quoted in Marcus, "Development," 9; Rebecca Roiphe, "The Serpent Beguiled Me: A History of the Entrapment Defense," *Seton Hall Law Review* 33 (2003): 257–302. A

sophisticated analysis of the nineteenth-century cases demonstrates that the entrapment defense arose out of contract notions of consent as a defense to crime.

5. 38 Mich. 218 (1878), commented on by Marcus, "Development." The Michigan Supreme Court was one of the most highly respected state supreme courts in the mid- to late-nineteenth century, under Chief Justice Thomas M. Cooley, a leading legal scholar.

6. Marcus, "Development," 10.

7. Justice Marston in *Saunders v. Michigan,* 38 Mich. 218 (1878), commented on by Marcus, "Development."

8. Roiphe, "History of Entrapment," 270.

9. Ibid., 274.

10. Ibid., 275.

11. Model Penal Code sec. 2.13(3).

12. Lawrence P. Tiffany, Donald M. McIntyre, Jr., and Daniel L. Rotenberg, *Detection of Crime* (Boston: Little, Brown, 1967), Part III, Encouragement and Entrapment, 207–82, quotation at p. 210. In this text, illegal *entrapment* is distinguished from lawful *encouragement.* The Model Penal Code and some state statutes, however, use these terms synonymously.

13. *Hoffa v. United States* (1966), quoting from *United States v. Dennis,* 183 F.2d 201, 224 (2d Cir. 1949) (prosecution of leaders of the American Communist Party).

14. See Victor Navasky, *Kennedy Justice* (New York: Atheneum, 1971).

15. *United States v. Whittier,* 28 F. Cas. 591 (C.C.E.D. Mo. 1878) (No. 16,688), discussed in Marcus, "Development," 12.

16. 223 F. 412 (9th Cir. 1915), reported in Marcus, "Development," 12–13.

17. Kenneth Lord, "Entrapment and Due Process: Moving Toward a Dual System of Defenses," *Florida State University Law Review* 25 (1998): 463–517.

18. Lawrence Maxwell, Testimony Before the Senate Judiciary Committee (Federal Document Clearing House Congressional Testimony, October 15, 2003).

19. Ruth Marcus, "Fair Sting or Foul Trap?; Child Pornography Investigation Challenged," *Washington Post,* November 6, 1991.

20. John Holliman, "Postal Service Delivers Child Pornography Ring," CNN NEWS, May 9, 1996, Transcript #1221-1.

21. Nancy Y. T. Hanewicz, Comment, "*Jacobson v. United States*: The Entrapment Defense and Judicial Supervision of the Criminal Justice System," *Wisconsin Law Review* (1993): 1163–93.

22. Lord, "Entrapment and Due Process," 475–76; general intent: see *State v. Houpt,* 504 P.2d 570 (Kan. 1972); *United States v. Williams,* 705 F.2d 603, (2d Cir. 1983); specific intent: *United States v. Ortiz,* 804 F.2d 1161 (10th Cir. 1986); *United States v. Perez-Leon,* 757 F.2d 866 (7th Cir. 1985); *Jacobson v. United States* (1992).

23. Lord, "Entrapment and Due Process," 478, 489–90, citing *United States v. Kaminski,* 703 F.2d 1004 (7th Cir. 1983).

24. Lord, "Entrapment and Due Process," 479–80, citing *United States v. Swiatek,* 819 F.2d 721 (7th Cir. 1987).

25. Lord, "Entrapment and Due Process," 489–90, citing *Gossmeyer v. State,* 482 N.E.2d 239 (Ind. 1985); *United States v. Aikens,* 64 F.3d 372 (8th Cir. 1995) (defendant predisposed—demonstrated selling crack cocaine to undercover officer); *United States v. Hernandez,* 31 F.3d 354 (6th Cir. 1994) (sophisticated advice to

undercover officer about cocaine trafficking, shows defendant not innocent dupe); *Collins v. State,* 520 N.E.2d 1258 (Ind. 1988); *United States v. Hollingsworth,* 27 F.3d 1196 (7th Cir. 1994) (en banc).

26. 465 So.2d 516 (Fla. 1985); see Kelly M. Haynes, Casenote, "Criminal Law—Florida Adopts a Dual Approach to Entrapment—*Cruz v. State,* 465 So. 2d 516 (Fla. 1985)," *Florida State University Law Review* 13 (1996): 1171–89.

27. Lord, "Entrapment and Due Process," 490.

28. Lord, "Entrapment and Due Process," 465, 489–90.

29. American Law Institute, *Model Penal Code,* sec. 2.13 (Philadelphia, 1985).

30. Hanewicz, "The Entrapment Defense," 1182.

31. *Greene v. United States,* 454 F.2d 783 (9th Cir. 1971); Lord, "Entrapment and Due Process," 504–05.

32. Quoted in *United States v. Russell,* 428.

33. Ibid., internal quotation marks eliminated.

34. Lord, "Entrapment and Due Process," 509.

35. *United States v. Tucker,* 28 F.3d 1420 (6th Cir. 1994).

36. 588 F.2d 373 (3rd Cir. 1978).

37. 5 Ohio St. 3d 187, 449 N.E.2d 1295 (1983), commented on in Margaret Baker, Comment, "Criminal Law: Entrapment in Ohio," *Akron Law Review* 17 (1984): 709–15.

38. 457 P.2d 226 (Alaska 1969) (remanded to determine whether entrapment made out under facts).

39. 390 Mich. 7, 210 N.W.2d 336 (1973).

40. See John S. Knowles, III, Casenote, "Criminal Procedure— Entrapment as a Matter of Law: Contraband Supplied to Defendants by Government Agents—*Epps v. State,* 417 So. 2d 543 (Miss. 1982)," *Mississippi College Law Review* 4 (1983): 99–111.

41. *Ibid.;* New Jersey: *State v. Talbot,* 71 N.J. 160, 364 A.2d 9 (1976); Illinois: *People v. Strong,* 21 Ill. 2d 320, 172 N.E.2d 765 (1961).

42. Brian Victor, Comment, "The Citizen and the Serpent: *State v. Rockholt* and Entrapment in New Jersey," *Rutgers Law Review* 38 (1984): 589–617.

43. Paul F. George, "Comment: Entrapment, The Myth of the Model Penal Code in Pennsylvania," *Dickenson Law Review* 86 (1981): 115–36, 121–24.

44. *Pennsylvania Crimes Code,* sec. 313(b), reprinted in ibid., 120.

45. George, "Entrapment," 130–31.

46. Lord, "Entrapment and Due Process," 498–504.

47. Ibid, 498–501.

48. 96 N.J. 570, 476 A.2d 1236 (1984); see Victor, "The Citizen," 589.

49. Victor, "The Citizen," 611–16.

50. Lord, "Entrapment and Due Process," 502.

51. 465 So.2d 516 (Fla. 1985); see Kelly M. Haynes, Casenote, "Criminal Law—Florida Adopts a Dual Approach to Entrapment—*Cruz v. State,* 465 So. 2d 516 (Fla. 1985)," *Florida State University Law Review* 13 (1986): 1171–89.

52. The summary of the state entrapment tests is found in Erich Weyand, Comment, "Entrapment: From Sorrells to Jacobson— The Development Continues," *Ohio Northern University Law Review* 20 (1993): 293–317.

53. Lord, "Entrapment and Due Process," 496, 498, 502. The states following the objective test are Alaska, Arkansas, Colorado, Hawaii, Iowa, Kansas, Michigan, New York, Pennsylvania, Texas, Utah, and Vermont. North Dakota had adopted the objective test, but its legislature added a subjective element in 1993, creating a hybrid approach.

54. Lord, "Entrapment and Due Process," 516.

55. Ibid.

56. Roiphe, "The Serpent," 297–98.

57. John Braithwaite, Brent Fisse, and Gilbert Geis, "Covert Facilitation and Crime: Restoring Balance to the Entrapment Debate," *Journal of Social Issues,* 43 (1987): 5–41.

58. Gary Marx, *Undercover: Police Surveillance in America* (Berkeley: University of California Press, 1988), 61.

59. Ibid., 60–65.

60. Tiffany, et al., *Detection of Crime.* The data for this study were collected in Detroit, Milwaukee, and Topeka in the 1950s. For FBI infiltration of the Communist Party or the Ku Klux Klan under J. Edgar Hoover see Richard Gid Powers, *Secrecy and Power: The Life of J. Edgar Hoover* (New York: Free Press, 1987).

61. F. Main, A. Pallasch, and D. Rozek, "Stings Netting Online Deviants; Arrests, Convictions of Pedophiles Soar," *Chicago Sun-Times,* February 27, 2000.

62. Stavsky, "The 'Sting,'" 955. White-collar crimes include tax evasion, bribery, embezzlement of pension funds, and some forms of political corruption; much organized crime includes intimidation-type crimes such as protection rackets, loan-sharking, blackmail, or simple extortion, which are often "invisible crimes" because victims are reluctant to come forward. This new focus was due in large measure to the FBI's changed priorities after the death of J. Edgar Hoover in 1972; see Powers, *Secrecy and Power.*

63. Maura F. J. Whelan, "Lead Us Not into (Unwarranted) Temptation: A Proposal to Replace the Entrapment Defense with a Reasonable-Suspicion Requirement," *University of Pennsylvania Law Review* 133 (1985): 1193–1230, 1194, n. 6, citing a 1984 congressional subcommittee report.

64. See Gary T. Marx, "Who Really Gets Stung? Some Issues Raised by the New Police Undercover Work," in *ABSCAM Ethics: Moral Issues and Deception in Law Enforcement,* Gerald M. Caplan, ed. (Washington, D.C.: Police Foundation, 1983), 65–99.

65. Stavsky, "The 'Sting,'" 956; David Katz, "The Paradoxical Role of Informers within the Criminal Justice System. A Unique Perspective," *University of Dayton Law Review* 7 (1981): 51–71, reports that in the late 1970s the FBI engaged 2,800 "operators" and paid nearly $1.5 million to informants, resulting in 2,600 arrests. James B. Stewart, *The Prosecutors: Inside the Offices of the Government's Most Powerful Lawyers* (New York: Simon and Schuster/Touchstone, 1987), 91.

66. Stephen Labaton, "The Nation; The Price Can Be High for Talk That's Cheap," *New York Times,* April 2, 1995.

67. Howard Abadinsky, *Organized Crime,* 2nd ed. (Chicago: Nelson-Hall, 1988), 295; Robert P. Rhodes, *Organized Crime: Crime Control vs. Civil Liberties* (New York: Random House, 1984); Arnold H. Lubasch, "F.B.I. Infiltrator Says Mob Chief Told of Slayings," *New York Times,* August 4, 1982.

68. Ralph Blumenthal, "New Technology Helps in Effort to Fight Mafia," *New York Times,* November 24, 1986.

69. Jeff Gerth, "A Covert and Major Victory Is Reported in the Drug War," *New York Times,* April 23, 1990.

70. James Tuohy and Rob Warden, *Greylord: Justice, Chicago Style* (New York: Putnam, 1989).

71. Darren A. Nichols, "Cops Divided on Sting Testing: They React to Plan to Test Honesty of Detroit Force," *The Detroit News,* February 3, 2000.

72. Whelan, "Lead Us Not," 1200–1203; Stavsky, "The 'Sting,'" 956–61, 957; *United States v. Kelly,* 707 F.2d 1460 (D.C. Cir. 1983), by then Judge Ruth Bader Ginsburg; *United States v. Kelly,* 707 F.2d 1460 (D.C. Cir. 1983), by Judge MacKinnon. A spirited defense of the Abscam operation is presented by its Justice Department coordinator: Irvin B. Nathan, "ABSCAM: A Fair and Effective Method for Fighting Public Corruption," in *ABSCAM Ethics,* Caplan, ed., 1–16.

73. Gilbert Geis, *White-Collar Criminal: The Offender in Business and the Professions* (New York: Atherton Press, 1968).

74. Eric N. Berg, with assistance of Kurt Eichenwald and Julia Flynn Siler, "F.B.I. Commodities 'Sting': Fast Money, Secret Lives," *New York Times,* January 30, 1989.

75. Stewart, *The Prosecutors,* 92, discussing a sting of corporate executives of Hitachi, Ltd., a major Japanese manufacturer, who were attempting to illegally purchase IBM secrets regarding the design of new computers.

76. Whelan, "Lead Us Not," 1197–1200.

77. Marx, *Undercover,* 159–79.

78. Editorial, "The Patrick Dorismond Case," *New York Times,* March 21, 2000.

79. Stavsky, "The 'Sting,'" 953.

80. George I. Miller, "Observations on Police Undercover Work," *Criminology* 25 (1987): 27–46.

81. Ibid., 39–40; the other studies referred to are Jerome Skolnick, *Justice without Trial* (New York: Wiley, 1975) and Peter K. Manning, "Police Lying," *Urban Life and Culture* 3 (1974): 283–306.

82. See Marx, "Who Really Gets Stung?"

83. Andrew Radolf, "Lesson Learned: Working Undercover for the FBI Nearly Lands a Louisiana Reporter in Jail; Articles by a Columnist for Another Paper Help Him Beat Extortion Rap," *Editor and Publisher,* September 24, 1988.

84. Nelson Blackstock, *Cointelpro: The FBI's Secret War on Political Freedom* (New York: Vintage Books, 1975), 12–13; John Kifner, "The Nation—Informers: A Tale in Itself," *New York Times,* January 22, 1995.

85. Braithwaite, et al., "Covert Facilitation," 9–10; Whelan, "Lead Us Not," 1216–1218.

86. Lawrence W. Sherman, "Reinventing Probable Cause: Target Selection in Proactive Investigations," *Journal of Social Issues* 43 (1987): 87–94.

87. Nathan, "ABSCAM," 15.

JUSTICES OF THE SUPREME COURT

THE NIXON-FORD MODERATES
BLACKMUN—POWELL—STEVENS

To a significant degree, these moderate justices really defined the agenda of the Burger Court. With staunch liberal (Douglas, Brennan, and Marshall) and conservative (Burger and Rehnquist) wings, and with Justice White joining various alignments depending upon the issue, Blackmun, Powell, and Stevens were often the "swing" votes that determined the outcome of cases in the 1970s and 1980s. At the beginning of his career on the Supreme Court, it appeared that Justice Blackmun would be a clone of Chief Justice Burger (they were irreverently dubbed "the Minnesota twins"). But in the late 1970s, his voting patterns began to shift away from the Court's conservative wing, and he often voted with Brennan and Marshall, but not so consistently to have been labeled a liberal. Roe v. Wade, his abortion rights opinion in 1973, blocking state laws from prohibiting first trimester abortions, was by far the most controversial liberal decision in the past decades.

In civil liberties areas including obscenity, school prayer, public religious displays, and free press, the Burger Court did not decide cases in ways favored by the extreme Right. In these and in civil rights cases, Justices Blackmun, Powell, and Stevens took moderate or liberal positions. On the other hand, Justice Powell tended generally to rule for the prosecution in criminal cases, with Blackmun and Stevens voting for defendants more often than Powell but not as often as Brennan and Marshall. In the affirmative action decisions, the Court was so evenly balanced that Justice Powell's compromise opinions became the law of the land.

This kaleidoscope of opinions should make it abundantly clear that it is a gross oversimplification to label the Supreme Court at a particular time as liberal or conservative in general. Even in specific areas of law, it is more meaningful to pay close attention to the reasoning of the Justices in order to obtain a better understanding of the Court's work.

HARRY A. BLACKMUN

Minnesota 1908–1999

Republican

Appointed by
Richard Nixon

Years of Service:
1970–1994

Collection of the Supreme Court of the United States. Photographer: Joseph D Lavenburg

LIFE AND CAREER A lifelong friend of Warren Burger, Harry Blackmun graduated *summa cum laude* as a mathematics major from Harvard University and from Harvard Law School in 1931. He clerked for a federal judge and practiced estate and tax law from 1934 to 1950 with a Minneapolis firm. He also engaged in public service and taught law. He was resident counsel for the Mayo Clinic in Rochester, Minnesota, during the 1950s, an association that may have influenced his famous *Roe v. Wade* (1973) abortion rights decision. Appointed to the U.S. Court of Appeals for the Eighth Circuit (Missouri, Minnesota, Arkansas, Iowa, Nebraska, South Dakota, and North Dakota) in 1959, he developed a reputation as a conservative but not inflexible judge, usually denying a criminal defendant's claims but holding that whipping inmates was cruel and unusual punishment. In the turbulent Vietnam War era, he ex-

pressed dismay at the militant antiestablishment views of many young people.

CONTRIBUTION TO CRIMINAL PROCEDURE It is difficult to characterize Blackmun's position because, although he was at first a moderate-conservative on criminal procedure issues, after 1988 he began to shift to the left, and by 1992 his votes put him on the liberal wing of a Court that was growing progressively more conservative. On the conservative side, he joined Chief Justice Burger's campaign to overturn the exclusionary rule, holding that illegally seized evidence need not be excluded from civil proceedings (*United States v. Janis*, 1976); ruled that the right to counsel does not extend to photographic identification procedures after a defendant was formally charged (*United States v. Ash*, 1973); ruled against a juvenile defendant's right to a jury trial (*McKeiver v. Pennsylvania*, 1971); and dissented in the "Christian Burial Speech" case, claiming that police could interrogate a formally charged suspect without his lawyers being present.

He began to diverge from a solidly conservative position by joining the dissenters in three cases that upheld aerial surveillance by fixed-wing aircraft and helicopters. His decisions regarding confessions were mixed, agreeing that a confession made while an attorney was trying to contact her client is admissible (*Moran v. Burbine*, 1986) but joining the dissent in *Arizona v. Mauro* (1987) (taped conversation between husband-suspect and wife after the murder of their child constituted an interrogation). He wrote the dissent protesting the

(Continued)

decision that upheld the law allowing the confiscation of funds used for the payment of attorney fees. Shortly before his retirement, his growing concern over the application of the death penalty led him to hold that it was not possible to apply the death penalty in a constitutional manner, and he would henceforth vote against every application of capital punishment (*Callins v. Collins,* 1994).

SIGNATURE OPINION *California v. Acevedo* (1991). For a 6–3 majority, Blackmun ruled that police having probable cause could search a container in an automobile without a warrant. Although Blackmun generally upheld an individual's Fourth Amendment right of privacy in the home, he ruled in such a way as to defer to the needs of police in automobile searches, giving them a bright-line rule that allowed the opening of containers whether probable cause extended to the entire car or to the specific container.

ASSESSMENT Despite his pro-prosecution rulings in the 1970s, a generally conservative stance in free speech and obscenity cases, and inconsistent positions in equal protection cases, Justice Blackmun produced several major surprises. He authored three opinions that upset the older "commercial speech" doctrine, which said that First Amendment protections do not apply to commercial speech. He was the author of *Roe v. Wade* (1973), the abortion rights decision, the most controversial opinion of the Burger Court and an issue that has continued to spark public, political, and legal contention.

FURTHER READING

Stephen L. Wasby, "Justice Blackmun and Criminal Justice: A Modest Overview," *Akron Law Review* 28 (1995): 125–186.

LEWIS F. POWELL, JR.

Virginia 1907–1998

Democrat

Appointed by Richard Nixon

Years of Service: 1972–1987

Collection of the Supreme Court of the United States. Photographer: Joseph Bailey

LIFE AND CAREER Lewis Powell, from a well-to-do background in Norfolk, Virginia, graduated first in his class at Washington and Lee College where he was class president; completed a three-year law program at Washington and Lee in

two years, again graduating first; and after studying law at Harvard University for a year, entered the private practice of law in Richmond, Virginia. His practice was primarily in corporate law, representing some of the nation's largest businesses. During World War II, he served as an Air Force intelligence officer in North Africa. Powell was always involved in substantial public and professional service activities. While serving as president of the Richmond School Board from 1952 to 1961, his moderation and leadership fostered the peaceful racial integration of the public schools. He served as president of the American Bar Association, the American College of Trial Lawyers, the Virginia State Board of Education, and was a member of President Johnson's Crime Commission in the late 1960s.

CONTRIBUTION TO CRIMINAL PROCEDURE Justice Powell generally voted in favor of the state. In *Stone v. Powell* (1976) he ruled that federal habeas corpus should not be open to state defendants who argued the issues before state courts, thus cutting off access of a large group of cases to the Supreme Court. He ruled against an absolute right to counsel at probation revocation hearings but allowed for a due process "totality of circumstances" rule that would require counsel if special circumstances existed (*Gagnon v. Scarpelli,* 1973). If core values of the Bill of Rights were attacked, he would rule against the government; he ruled that the president cannot issue electronic eavesdropping orders without a warrant (*United States v. U.S. District Court,* 1972).

SIGNATURE OPINION In *United States v. Calandra* (1974), Justice Powell raised the theory that the purpose of the exclusionary rule is primarily to deter police misconduct. While this arguably misread the intent of *Mapp v. Ohio* (1961), it was a potent approach that gave the Burger and Rehnquist Courts the intellectual ammunition to curtail the scope of the exclusionary rule, which paved the way to the *Leon* exception, which allowed illegally seized evidence to be introduced into evidence if it was seized by police relying in good faith on a bad search warrant.

ASSESSMENT At the time he retired, Justice Powell was called the most powerful man in America because he often provided the deciding vote in important Supreme Court cases. Outside of his generally conservative stance in criminal procedure, he tended to be a nondoctrinaire judge. Under the Equal Protection Clause, he voted against gender inequality or laws that imposed extra fiscal burdens on indigents. He precisely analyzed competing interests in cases. In a First Amendment case, for example, he ruled that a shopping mall did not have to allow the distribution of leaflets because, unlike in a company town, the leaflet distributors could find other places to make their views known.

His greatest "balancing act" was in the *Bakke* (1978) medical school admissions affirmative action case. Affirmative action programs posed an explosive issue for the Court. If racial quotas were upheld, a white backlash could wipe out the programs, while a finding of unconstitutionality could produce resentment and even violence in parts of the minority community. In *Bakke* eight justices split in each of these liberal and conservative directions. Justice Powell's opinion split the difference by ruling that numeric quotas were unconstitutional but that race could legitimately be taken into account in admissions decisions in order to achieve the laudable goals of affirmative action. This statesmanlike decision legitimated affirmative action programs in a way designed to be most acceptable to the entire society.

FURTHER READING

John C. Jeffries, Jr., *Justice Lewis F. Powell, Jr.* (New York: Charles Scribner's Sons, 1994).

JOHN PAUL STEVENS

Illinois 1920–

Republican

Appointed by
Gerald Ford

Years of Service:
1975–

Collection of the Supreme Court of the United States. Photographer: Joseph Bailey

LIFE AND CAREER Born into a wealthy Chicago household, Stevens graduated Phi Beta Kappa from the University of Chicago, served as a naval officer during World War II, graduated first in his class from Northwestern University Law School, clerked for Supreme Court Justice Wiley Rutledge, and practiced law in Chicago from 1948 to 1970. His expertise in antitrust law led to his service as an advisor on antitrust reform to Congress and the U.S. Attorney General. He published several articles on antitrust law and taught courses at the University of Chicago and Northwestern University Law Schools. Appointed to the United States Court of Appeals for the Seventh Circuit in 1970, he gained a reputation as one of the best appellate judges in the country. His first written opinion—a dissent urging that a legislature could not use its contempt power to summarily imprison one who disrupted a legislative session—was adopted by the Supreme Court, which held that due process required a hearing before imprisonment. One reason that President Ford nominated Stevens was the correct perception that he was centrist; after the resignation of President Nixon, Ford was not in a political position to appoint a sharply conservative person to the Court.

CONTRIBUTION TO CRIMINAL PROCEDURE By joining with liberal and moderate justices, Stevens prevented the dismantling of the major features of the due process revolution: the Fourth Amendment exclusionary rule and the *Miranda* rule. Compared to a staunch liberal such as Justice Brennan, Stevens would be considered a moderate, but in recent years has been viewed as liberal on criminal procedure issues. During the Burger Court era, he voted for the prosecution in 44 percent of criminal cases. These included his majority opinion extending the automobile search exception to closed containers where the police have probable cause to search the entire vehicle (*United States v. Ross,* 1982); allowing police to detain the owner of premises while executing a search warrant (*Michigan v. Summers,* 1981); and holding that in cases of multiple representation, the Sixth Amendment does not require a trial judge to inquire into the possibility of a conflict of interest (*Burger v. Kemp,* 1987).

However, Justice Stevens has often written or voted in favor of the defendant in dissent: ambiguous *Miranda* (1966) warnings violate a suspect's rights (*California v. Prysock,* 1981); the "public safety" exception to *Miranda* violates a suspect's rights (*New York v. Quarles,* 1984); police should not be able to stop a person on the basis of a barely corroborated anonymous telephone call (*Alabama v. White,* 1990). His dissent in *Moran v. Burbine* (1986), arguing that confessions taken after an attorney attempts to contact a suspect should be inadmissible, is a masterful essay on the fundamental attributes of our adversarial system of justice.

SIGNATURE OPINION *Payton v. New York* (1979) held that an arrest warrant is a prerequisite to a lawful entry of a person's home in order to arrest him. "In this case . . . neither history nor this Nation's experience requires us to disregard the overriding respect for the sanctity of the home that has been embedded in our traditions since the origins of the Republic."

ASSESSMENT Justice Stevens has hewed an independent course not easily identified as either liberal or conservative. He often writes separate concurring opinions to clearly state his position and seems more interested in staking out an independent position than in modifying his views to build coalitions. In First Amendment religion cases he was a reliable liberal but less so in freedom of expression cases. In cases concerning protection for underprivileged or vulnerable groups, such as aliens, illegitimate children, or prisoners, he tends to find in favor of the rights of the underdog.

FURTHER READING

Bradley G. Canon, "Justice John Paul Stevens: The Lone Ranger in a Black Robe," in *The Burger Court: Political and Judicial Profiles,* Charles M. Lamb and Stephen C. Halpern, eds., 343–374 (Urbana: University of Illinois Press, 1991).

CHAPTER
10

THE PRETRIAL PROCESS

The [prosecutor] is the representative not of an ordinary party to a controversy, but of a sovereignty whose obligation to govern impartially is as compelling as its obligation to govern at all; and whose interest, therefore, in a criminal prosecution is not that it shall win a case, but that justice shall be done. As such, he is in a peculiar and very definite sense the servant of the law, the twofold aim of which is that guilt shall not escape or innocence suffer. He may prosecute with earnestness and vigor—indeed, he should do so. But, while he may strike hard blows, he is not at liberty to strike foul ones. It is as much his duty to refrain from improper methods calculated to produce a wrongful conviction as it is to use every legitimate means to bring about a just one.

—Justice George Sutherland, *Berger v. United States*,
295 U.S. 78, 88 (1935)

CHAPTER OUTLINE

KEY TERMS AND PHRASES *(CONTINUES ON NEXT PAGE)*

Absolute immunity

Adversary system

Arraignment

Bail

Bail bond

Bail bondsman

Bind over

Charging

Deposit bond

Discovery

Facial attack

Formal charges

Grand jury

Immunity

Indictment

Information

Initial appearance

Motions

Preliminary examination

Prima facie case

Preventive detention

Qualified immunity	Subpoena	Use immunity
Release on recognizance	Subpoena power	Venue
Screening	Transactional immunity	Vindictive prosecution
Selective prosecution	Trial *de novo*	
Separation of powers doctrine	True bill	

INTRODUCTION: PRETRIAL JUSTICE

The pretrial process is the most important part of the judicial process for most persons arrested for committing crimes. The most important reason for this observation is that only a tiny fraction of those who are arrested ever reach a full trial. The overwhelming proportion of criminal cases either are *dismissed* at the pretrial stage or are adjudicated by *guilty plea*. A small proportion of cases result in other dispositions, such as diversion. In 2001 federal prosecutors declined to prosecute 27 percent of the 121,818 suspects investigated for possible federal crimes.[1] The U.S. district courts terminated cases involving 77,145 defendants, and 89 percent of them were convicted. "Almost all (95%) of those convicted pleaded guilty or no contest."[2]

Similarly, most state felony defendants either had their cases dismissed or pled guilty. A Bureau of Justice Statistics report on felony case processing in the nation's seventy-five largest counties found that for all felony cases filed in May 2000, the total conviction rate was 64 percent. The felony conviction rate was 52 percent, of which 49 percent were convicted by plea and 3 percent at trial. Of the 12 percent of felony charges that resulted in misdemeanor convictions, 12 percent were adjudicated by plea and a negligible number by trial.[3] "In most cases where the defendant was not convicted, it was because the charges against the defendant were dismissed. An estimated 26 percent of all cases ended in this way." Another 9 percent of cases were diverted or placed on deferred adjudication. Only about 1 percent overall were acquitted.[4]

It is worth considering that for the prosecution and the defense the most important happenings during the pretrial process are not legal or procedural matters, but the *factual investigation* of the case. A prosecutor's decision whether to dismiss a case or press charges, and which specific crimes to charge, depends in large measure on the *facts* that have been discovered and reported by the police. The prosecutor reads the police report and should question the officers to determine if there are weaknesses in the evidence or case factors that would caution against proceeding with the case. American Bar Association standards state that a prosecutor should not institute criminal charges that are not supported by probable cause or without "sufficient admissible evidence to support a conviction."[5] In major cases the prosecutor may be part of the investigative team, and will suggest what kinds of legally obtained evidence must be found in order to gain a conviction under a crime's legal definition.[6]

A defense attorney's first step in any case is to interview his client to find out what happened. Depending upon the mental capacities of the client and her willingness or ability to be entirely truthful, this task may be far from easy.[7] Again depending on the client's resources and the seriousness of the charges or potential charges, the attorney may hire a trained investigator. The attorney himself typically questions witnesses to investigate the case. A client free on pretrial release is often the best person to find alibi or other witnesses, but the attorney brings fact-finding knowledge of the substantive criminal law. This knowledge helps him direct the search for facts relevant to a defense or to establish reasonable doubt. Leading *legal* scholars indicate "that interviewing and fact investigation are probably the most important skills that a good defense lawyer can offer her client."[8]

Despite the overriding importance of fact investigation, the pretrial process involves a large number of legal procedures. These procedures are likely to be utterly bewildering to the defendant and yet critically important to his ability to receive substantial justice and a fair trial. Pretrial release, by bail or personal recognizance, will determine whether the defendant sits in jail or goes free before trial. An attorney can facilitate pretrial release, and if it is refused, can continue to press for it. Defense counsel can make pretrial motions that challenge the admissibility of unconstitutionally obtained evidence. A lawyer can work for a dismissal throughout the pretrial period. This requires the skills that a good attorney brings to bear in preparing for a satisfactory negotiated plea, or to prepare for trial: thorough knowledge of the substantive criminal law, a careful analysis of the evidence, a sober weighing of the strengths and weaknesses of the case, and a willingness to use this information to fight for the client's interests.

At the same time the prosecutor uses the same skills to decide whether to dismiss, to adequately negotiate a plea, or to determine which are the proper charges. The prosecutor's preparation is required to present an adequate case before a grand jury in those jurisdictions that require an **indictment.** Similarly, although a judge decides whether to **bind over** a felony case for trial after a preliminary hearing, it is up to the prosecutor to establish a **prima facie case** at that point, or it will be dismissed. A defense lawyer plays an important role at the **preliminary examination.** She must cross-examine prosecution witnesses or potentially lose that opportunity if the witness fails to appear at trial. Also, by probing the prosecutor's case, the defendant's lawyer prepares for a favorable plea agreement based on a better understanding of the strength of the case.

Some critics say that the decline in the number of trials and the heavy reliance on pretrial settlement by guilty plea has made our justice system less fair than in the past and has undermined the **adversary system.**[9] But as this brief introduction indicates, the pretrial process in America has become a lengthy and complex process. Many cases are quickly dismissed, but a typical felony case takes on average from six months to a year from arrest to adjudication, although only half of all murder cases are resolved within one year.[10] In contrast to the view that adjudication by plea undermines justice and adversariness, Professor Malcolm Feeley suggests that despite the decline in the number of trials, the expanded use of pretrial procedures actually *strengthens* the adversary system:

> Probable cause hearings, bills of particulars, motions to suppress evidence, and the like, all shape the criminal process prior to trial and formal adjudication of guilt or innocence. In many cases, pretrial hearings—or for that matter negotiations in the shadow of the law—can become mini-trials. Whether the early review of the evidence reveals a strong or weak case or whether the testimony of a particular witness or the introduction of a specific piece of evidence will or will not be admitted into the record can make or break a case, and depending on the conclusion reached, charges may be dropped, reduced, or the accused may plead guilty or take his case to trial. So, while we have witnessed the demise of the trial, we have at the same time experienced an increase in pretrial opportunities to review in adversarial context some of the same types of issues that once were *less* carefully considered by the jury at trial.[11]

The modern pretrial process thus provides a defendant with fair treatment. An attorney is provided early in the process. Weaker cases are removed, by dismissal or plea, leaving trials for closely contested cases or more serious crimes.

As suggested, the pretrial process is complex and filled with many important legal steps. This chapter closely examines a few of these processes: pretrial release or bail, the prosecutor's **charging** decision, **discovery,** and the **screening** institutions of the grand jury and preliminary examination. The felony pretrial process includes other critical steps. Misdemeanors are typically handled in a more perfunctory way, although as statistics cited above indicate, about 12 percent of cases initially charged as felonies result in misdemeanor convictions. Some of these processes include:

• Initial Appearance   A suspect is brought before a magistrate within twenty-four to forty-eight hours of arrest and is informed of the charges and constitutional rights including the right to remain silent. At the **initial appearance** a defendant may have his retained lawyer; indigents are provided an assigned counsel or a public defender. Bail or other mode of pretrial release is arranged or denied.

• Suppression Hearings   Defendants may challenge the introduction of confessions, physical or eyewitness evidence, lineups, electronic eavesdropping evidence, and the like under constitutional or statutory exclusionary rules in special suppression hearings conducted before a judge to determine whether such evidence was obtained illegally.

• Pretrial Motions   **Motions** are formal written requests to a judge to obtain a ruling or order. There are standard pretrial motions, but a motion may be uniquely tailored to the case. Judges may grant or deny motions summarily or may order that hearings be held during which attorneys make extended arguments to support or oppose the motions. Suppression hearings, for example, are initiated by motion. Motion hearings are open to the public (*Waller v. Georgia,* 1984). Motion practice is extremely important to the fairness in the trial process. Motions for a change of **venue,** for example, may play a vital role in avoiding local prejudice. Common motions include those to obtain continuances (adjournments); to request psychiatric services; to lower the amount of bail; to waive filing fees on the ground of indigence; for a competency hearing; to be tried by jury; to strike redundant counts of an indictment; to join or sever codefendants or charges in the same or separate trials, and so forth.

• Discovery   Very few processes are as critical in major cases. Unlike pretrial rules in civil cases that expedite the exchange of factual information between the parties before a trial, criminal procedural rules have been less open. The imbalance between the state's police resources to investigate crimes and the limited resources of most indigent defendants has led the Supreme Court to mandate a level of sharing (*Brady v. Maryland,* 1963), although in recent years it has limited full disclosure. It is incumbent on competent defense lawyers to use all legal means to gain access to factual information gathered by the state.

• Prosecutor-Defense Conferences   In many jurisdictions today, plea arrangements or arrangements for the conduct of a trial are worked out between the prosecutor and the defense lawyer. They allow for rationalized discovery, an exchange of information such as the defendant notifying the prosecutor of an alibi or insanity defense, and a calm atmosphere in which to discuss the strengths and weaknesses of a case. Conferences improve court efficiency and the rational handling of cases.

• Arraignment   The **arraignment** is a brief procedure where the charges are read to the defendant, who is then given the opportunity to plead guilty, not guilty, *nolo contendere,* or to remain mute. The practice is a mere formality in most courts, and is often the arena for the taking of pleas after plea bargaining.

THE BAIL DECISION: PRETRIAL RELEASE

The Eighth Amendment states: "Excessive bail shall not be required. . . ." This does not guarantee pretrial release in every case, but reflects a policy favoring the pretrial freedom of a criminal suspect. It supports the presumption of innocence. The bail provision reflects the traditional method of balancing individual freedom with the state's need to ensure that defendants will return to court to stand trial. **Bail** is the release of a defendant before trial based on that defendant's promise to return. The promise is *secured* by some form of collateral, such as money, that the defendant agrees to transfer to the court if he or she does not show up for the trial. However, appellate courts have held that in extreme circumstances, where it appears that no amount of bail will be sufficient to compel a defendant to return to court for trial, bail may be refused.[12]

This legal device has become a business. A **bail bondsman** receives a portion of the bail amount from the defendant, usually 10 percent, and in return posts a **bail bond** with the court, promising to pay the full bail amount if the defendant does not show. This results in pretrial freedom for the defendant, an income for the bail bondsman, and some assurance to the court that the defendant will show up. Some bail bondsmen employ bounty hunters to search for absconding defendants, itself a controversial practice.[13] If the defendant defaults by "skipping town," the bail bondsman must pay the full amount of the bail to the court and then find and sue the defendant for that money. Courts have the power to forgive part or all of the forfeited amount. Whereas this discretion may be fair in some instances, it is also an obvious source of corruption.

A defendant has a real interest in pretrial freedom. While released the defendant can continue to work, earn money, and maintain family relations. A person jailed for longer than a few days may lose a job and find it hard to get a new one. The defendant can play a more active role in finding witnesses and gathering evidence. He can also confer more freely with the defense attorney. Of course, the defendant, although presumed to be innocent, avoids the unpleasant reality of living under often squalid jail conditions.

The public may have different interests, for freedom makes it possible for a defendant to hide and avoid the trial process. Witness intimidation and killing is a possibility. A *New York Times* investigation suggests that "At least 19 witnesses have been killed in New York City since 1980. Around the state in the last seven years, local district attorneys have charged at least 14 people with killing witnesses."[14] The report admitted that "[n]o one knows how many criminal cases evaporate because witnesses are threatened or assaulted. . . . Some prosecutors acknowledge that fear among witnesses is a staple of their work lives."[15] The problem of witness intimidation may be especially pervasive in areas infested with criminal gangs. A 1996 National Institute of Justice Report noted that a sample of prosecutors indicated that witness intimidation was a major problem for half of the prosecutors in large jurisdictions and 43 percent of prosecutors in small jurisdictions.[16] This is a matter of national concern. At the end of 2003, Congress was moving toward passing a law to provide $90 million a year to state and local prosecutors for local witness protection programs.[17]

The Eighth Amendment and the Right to Bail

The Eighth Amendment does not absolutely guarantee pretrial release. Under English common law and American criminal procedure, bail is the presumed position in noncapital cases. Under common law, capital crimes punishable by death were not bailable. The modern approach to bail in capital cases is to establish a *presumption* against bail where "the proof is evident or the presumption of guilt is great." Thus, even a capital suspect may obtain bail if a magistrate determines that the prosecutor's case has weaknesses. If the prosecutor can show that a defendant had attempted to destroy evidence or intimidate witnesses, bail can be denied.

The leading case of **Stack v. Boyle** (1951) overturned the high bail set for twelve Communist Party leaders who were charged with advocating the violent overthrow of the American government under the Smith Act. The bail amount for each was set at fifty thousand dollars. The Supreme Court found little evidence that the defendants had a history or intention of fleeing prosecution and no support that the defendants would "jump bail" because they were involved in a conspiracy with worldwide Communist powers. The typical bail amount for persons charged with crimes carrying a maximum penalty of five years imprisonment and a ten thousand–dollar fine was usually much lower than fifty thousand dollars. The Supreme Court held that the high bail amount was arbitrary, excessive, and a violation of the Eighth Amendment. Chief Justice Fred Vinson said, "Unless this right to bail before trial is preserved, the presumption of innocence, secured only after centuries of struggle, would lose its meaning."

Modern Forms of Pretrial Release

Bail practice was for many years criticized as discriminatory, confining persons who were otherwise good risks to return for trial, simply because they lacked sufficient funds. Since the 1960s, most states and the federal government have established release mechanisms designed to release suspects who are likely to return for trial proceedings.

RELEASE ON RECOGNIZANCE (ROR) A court officer interviews the defendant to determine whether personal characteristics make him a good prospect to return to court for additional hearings or trial. Objective characteristics include home stability, living with a family member, having a job or attending school, and prior history of escapes. If the suspect receives a high score, indicating a likelihood of returning, eligibility is established for **release on recognizance (ROR)** without posting any kind of security, but by making a formal promise to return to court when summoned.

CONDITIONS OF RELEASE Modern laws allow a judge to place restrictions on a suspect released before trial, in addition to bail or as part of ROR, to ensure the suspect's return to court for further proceedings. The Federal Bail Reform Act of 1984, which applies only to federal courts, includes that the defendant follow these conditions:

1. Report to a police, pretrial release, or probation officer or other court agency on a regular basis.
2. Stay away from certain people (e.g., victim or witnesses) or places (e.g., airports, bars).
3. Be under the custody or care of a specific individual or treatment program that can ensure the defendant will appear and not endanger the community.
4. Maintain employment or schooling.
5. Comply with a curfew.
6. Do not possess a deadly weapon.
7. Refrain from alcohol or drug use.
8. Undergo medical, psychiatric, or drug treatment.
9. Agree to forfeit property or money on failure to appear.
10. Execute a bail bond.
11. Be jailed in the evening and on weekends.

These conditions must be reasonably related to facilitating the defendant's return and be tailored to the defendant's circumstances.

DEPOSIT BOND   A few states, to end the unsavory business of bail bondsmen, and to ensure equal treatment for indigents, have created the **deposit bond,** also known as an appearance bond, as a bail bond substitute. If a judge believes that ROR is not appropriate, a bail amount is set and the defendant must raise 10 percent of the bail amount to be released. The 10 percent is paid not to a bail bondsman but to the court. If the defendant fails to appear, he or she becomes liable for the entire amount. Defendants who return to court, on the other hand, receive the deposit amount less a 1 percent retention fee.

The Illinois deposit bond law was challenged as a due process and equal protection violation but was upheld in *Schilb v. Kuebel* (1971), which referred to bail bondsmen in harsh terms. The Supreme Court rejected the argument that the 1 percent fee ultimately retained by the courts was discriminatory against indigents. The Court said the fee was reasonable; also, the statute had an ROR provision that the judge could use as a release mechanism for indigent defendants who were good risks, thus avoiding any discrimination. The *Schilb* decision, in addition to upholding the deposit bond system, displays faith in the nation's trial court judges to fairly administer pretrial release.

PREVENTIVE DETENTION   One theory of bail—a pro-defendant, Due Process Model approach—is that the *only* reason to detain a suspect before trial is to ensure the *integrity of the trial process*. Under this theory, bail amounts should be set with only this purpose in mind, i.e., to ensure the return of the defendant, or to revoke bail to those who have attempted to destroy evidence or intimidate witnesses while on bail. An alternate theory—a pro-prosecution, Crime Control Model view—is that bail also serves other functions. It was widely known that in fact judges often set high bail to detain a suspect feared *likely* to commit crimes while awaiting trial. Denying bail for this reason is called **preventive detention.** Congress, believing that preventive detention can be constitutional when accompanied by procedural safeguards, authorized its use in the Bail Reform Act of 1984 (18 *U.S.C.* §§3141–3150). The constitutionality of the act was upheld in *United States v. Salerno* (1987).

—United States v. Salerno **Case & Comments—**

• CASE & COMMENTS •

United States v. Salerno
481 U.S. 739, 107 S.Ct. 2095, 95 L.Ed.2d 697 (1987)

CHIEF JUSTICE REHNQUIST delivered the opinion of the Court.

The Bail Reform Act of 1984 (Act) allows a federal court to detain an arrestee pending trial if the Government demonstrates by clear and convincing evidence after an adversary hearing that no release conditions "will reasonably assure . . . the safety of any other person and the community." **[a]** * * * We granted certiorari because of a conflict among the Courts of Appeals regarding the validity of the Act. We hold that, as against the facial attack mounted by these respondents, the Act fully comports with constitutional requirements. **[b]** * * *

I.

[The Act is a response to "the alarming problem of crimes committed by persons on release." It gives a "judicial officer" discretion to order the pretrial detention of an arrestee if the judge "finds that no condition[s] will reasonably assure the appearance of the person as required and the safety of any other person and the community." **[c]** The law includes procedural safeguards: the rights to the presence of counsel, to testify, to present witnesses and evidence, and to cross-examine other witnesses. If the judge finds that no release conditions "can reasonably assure the safety of other persons and the community," the findings of fact must be stated in writing, supported by "clear and convincing evidence."]

The judicial officer is not given unbridled discretion in making the detention determination, [but must consider several statutory factors: **[d]** (1) the nature and seriousness of the charges, (2) the substantiality of the government's evidence against the arrestee, (3) the arrestee's background and characteristics, and (4) the nature and seriousness of the danger posed by the suspect's release. If pretrial detention is ordered,] the detainee is entitled to expedited appellate review of the detention order.

[Anthony Salerno was charged in a twenty-nine-count indictment with racketeering. Facts were presented to show that Salerno was a high-ranking "boss" in an organized crime "family." In the preventive detention hearing, the government submitted evidence from court-ordered wiretaps and offered to produce testimony of two trial witnesses who would assert that Salerno personally participated in two of the murder conspiracies charged against him. Salerno presented character witnesses. The district court, believing the government's allegations and that Salerno would intimidate witnesses if released, denied release before his trial.] **[e]**

[a] Clear and convincing is a very high standard of proof. See Table 3-1.

[b] A **facial attack** means that the statute is unconstitutional under all circumstances, and not just as applied in this case.

[c] Congress decided that crimes committed by persons on bail is such a serious problem that judges should *predict* whether a defendant will commit a crime while on bail.

[d] Which of these factors seem predictive of future behavior?

[e] Do you agree with the decision of the district court or the Court of Appeals?

• CASE & COMMENTS •

[The Court of Appeals reversed, concluding that detaining persons because they were thought to present a future danger to the community violates due process.] It reasoned that our criminal law system holds persons accountable for past actions, not anticipated future actions. Although a court could detain an arrestee who threatened to flee before trial, such detention would be permissible because it would serve the basic objective of a criminal system—bringing the accused to trial. * * *

II.

* * * Respondents present two grounds for invalidating the Bail Reform Act's provisions permitting pretrial detention on the basis of future dangerousness. First, they rely upon the Court of Appeals' conclusion that the Act exceeds the limitations placed upon the Federal Government by the Due Process Clause of the Fifth Amendment. Second, they contend that the Act contravenes the Eighth Amendment's proscription against excessive bail. We treat these contentions in turn.

A

* * * Respondents first argue that the Act violates substantive due process because the pretrial detention it authorizes constitutes impermissible punishment before trial. * * * The Court of Appeals assumed that pretrial detention under the Bail Reform Act is regulatory, not penal, and we agree that it is. **[f]**

As an initial matter, the mere fact that a person is detained does not inexorably lead to the conclusion that the government has imposed punishment. * * * To determine whether a restriction on liberty constitutes impermissible punishment or permissible regulation, we first look to legislative intent. * * * Unless Congress expressly intended to impose punitive restrictions, the punitive/regulatory distinction turns on "'whether an alternative purpose to which [the restriction] may rationally be connected is assignable for it, and whether it appears excessive in relation to the alternative purpose assigned [to it].'" * * *

We conclude that the detention imposed by the Act falls on the regulatory side of the dichotomy. The legislative history of the Bail Reform Act clearly indicates that Congress did not formulate the pretrial detention provisions as punishment for dangerous individuals. * * * Congress instead perceived pretrial detention as a potential solution to a pressing societal problem. * * * There is no doubt that preventing danger to the community is a legitimate regulatory goal.

Nor are the incidents of pretrial detention excessive in relation to the regulatory goal Congress sought to achieve. **[g]** The Bail Reform Act [is] carefully limit[ed] * * * to the most serious of crimes[:] * * * crimes of violence, offenses for which the sentence is life imprisonment or death, serious drug offenses, or certain repeat offenders. The arrestee is entitled to a prompt detention hearing, * * * and the maximum length of pretrial detention is limited by the stringent time limitations of the Speedy Trial Act. * * * Moreover, * * * the conditions of confinement envisioned by the Act "appear to reflect the regulatory purposes relied upon by the" Government [requiring] that detainees be housed in a "facility separate, to the extent practicable, from persons awaiting or serving sentences or being held in custody pending appeal." * * * We conclude, therefore, that the pretrial detention contemplated by the Bail Reform Act is regulatory in nature, and does not constitute punishment before trial in violation of the Due Process Clause.

[Other kinds of regulatory detention, upheld by the Supreme Court as not violating due process, include: **[h]** wartime detention of persons believed to be dangerous, potentially dangerous resident aliens pending deportation proceedings, mentally unstable individuals who present a danger to the public, dangerous defendants who become incompetent to stand trial, dangerous arrested juveniles before trial, and defendants who present risks of flight or dangers to witnesses.]

* * * The Bail Reform Act * * * narrowly focuses on a particularly acute problem in which the Government interests are overwhelming. **[i]** The Act operates only on individuals who have been arrested for a specific category of extremely serious offenses. * * * Congress specifically found that these individuals are far more likely to be responsible for dangerous acts in the community after arrest. * * *

[Chief Justice Rehnquist recognized the individual's strong interest in liberty, but held that given the carefully delineated law, individual liberty must be "subordinated to the greater needs of society." He concluded this section by holding that the procedures of the Bail Reform Act were] "adequate to authorize the pretrial detention of at least some [persons] charged with crimes," * * * As we stated in *Schall* [*v. Martin* (1984)], "there is nothing inherently unattainable about a prediction of future criminal conduct." * * * **[j]**

B

* * * We think that the Act survives a challenge founded upon the Eighth Amendment.

The Eighth Amendment addresses pretrial release by providing merely that "[e]xcessive bail shall not be required." This clause, of course, says nothing about whether bail shall be available at all. Respondents nevertheless contend that this Clause grants them a right to bail calculated solely upon

[f] Part II A addresses the due process challenge to the statute. What is the distinction that determines whether the detention ordered by the statute violates Salerno's due process liberty interests?

[g] Notice the two "punishment" arguments: first, whether preventive detention *is* punishment, and second, whether preventive detention is so excessive a means to achieve the regulatory purpose of preventing crime by those released on bail as to violate due process.

[h] Are these examples similar to preventive detention or can they be "distinguished" as a matter of law?

[i] Does this mean that *all* defendants charged with extremely serious crimes can always be denied pretrial freedom?

[j] *Schall* upheld preventive detention for juvenile defendants.

• **CASE & COMMENTS** •

considerations of flight. They rely on *Stack v. Boyle.* * * * In respondents' view, since the Bail Reform Act allows a court essentially to set bail at an infinite amount for reasons not related to the risk of flight, it violates the Excessive Bail Clause. **[k]** Respondents concede that the right to bail they have discovered in the Eighth Amendment is not absolute. A court may, for example, refuse bail in capital cases. And, as the Court of Appeals noted and respondents admit, a court may refuse bail when the defendant presents a threat to the judicial process by intimidating witnesses. Respondents characterize these exceptions as consistent with what they claim to be the sole purpose of bail—to ensure the integrity of the judicial process. **[l]**

    * * * [W]e reject the proposition that the Eighth Amendment categorically prohibits the government from pursuing other admittedly compelling interests through regulation of pretrial release. * * *

    * * * Nothing in the text of the Bail Clause limits permissible government considerations solely to questions of flight. The only arguable substantive limitation of the Bail Clause is that the government's proposed conditions of release or detention not be "excessive" in light of the perceived evil. Of course, to determine whether the government's response is excessive, we must compare that response against the interest the government seeks to protect by means of that response. Thus, when the government has admitted that its only interest is in preventing flight, bail must be set by a court at a sum designed to ensure that goal, and no more. * * * We believe that when Congress has mandated detention on the basis of a compelling interest other than prevention of flight, as it has here, the Eighth Amendment does not require release on bail.

* * *

JUSTICE MARSHALL, with whom JUSTICE BRENNAN joins, dissenting.

    This case brings before the Court for the first time a statute in which Congress declares that a person innocent of any crime may be jailed indefinitely, pending the trial of allegations which are legally presumed to be untrue, if the Government shows to the satisfaction of a judge that the accused is likely to commit crimes, unrelated to the pending charges, at anytime in the future. **[m]** Such statutes, consistent with the usages of tyranny and the excesses of what bitter experience teaches us to call the police state, have long been thought incompatible with the fundamental human rights protected by our Constitution. Today a majority of this Court holds otherwise. Its decision disregards basic principles of justice established centuries ago and enshrined beyond the reach of governmental interference in the Bill of Rights. * * *

II.

* * * Let us apply the majority's reasoning to a similar, hypothetical case. After investigation, Congress determines (not unrealistically) that a large proportion of violent crime is perpetrated by persons who are unemployed. It also determines, equally reasonably, that much violent crime is committed at night. From amongst the panoply of "potential solutions," Congress chooses a statute which permits, after judicial proceedings, the imposition of a dusk-to-dawn curfew on anyone who is unemployed. Since this is not a measure enacted for the purpose of punishing the unemployed, and since the majority finds that preventing danger to the community is a legitimate regulatory goal, the curfew statute would, according to the majority's analysis, be a mere "regulatory" detention statute, entirely compatible with the substantive components of the Due Process Clause. **[n]**

    [Justice Marshall claims that the majority simply redefined punishment as regulation, and so allows a clear violation of the due process rights of detainees.] * * *

III.

The essence of this case may be found, ironically enough, in [another] provision of the Act to which the majority does not refer, [p]rovid[ing] that "[n]othing in this section shall be construed as modifying or limiting the presumption of innocence." But the very pith and purpose of this statute is an abhorrent limitation of the presumption of innocence. The majority's untenable conclusion that the present Act is constitutional arises from a specious denial of the role of the Bail Clause and the Due Process Clause in protecting the invaluable guarantee afforded by the presumption of innocence.

* * *

[Justice Stevens dissented].

---

[k] Part II B discusses the Eighth Amendment challenge. Is the denial of bail the same as imposing excessive bail?

[l] The integrity of the judicial process is undermined when a defendant flees from the trial, but not when he commits a crime while on bail.

[m] Do you agree that the law is inconsistent with the presumption of innocence?

[n] Does Justice Marshall's shocking hypothesis apply to the majority's reasoning? On the one hand, the Act applies only to *arrested* persons; on the other hand, it applies to persons presumed to be innocent. Which factor best fits Marshall's hypothetical?

PRETRIAL DETENTION IN A TIME OF TERROR

"In the two months following September 11, approximately 1,200 foreign nationals living in the United States were arrested and detained by federal law enforcement agencies."[18] More than half had been detained on immigration charges. By August 2002, 81 remained in custody, about two dozen material witnesses, and the other detainees held on various state and federal criminal charges.[19] The precise number of the detainees has not been released by the government. According to the press account, "Michael J. Creppy, the nation's chief immigration judge, quietly issued sweeping instructions to hundreds of judges for what would turn out to be more than 600 "special interest" immigration cases."[20] These cases were tried under strict secrecy, not entered into regular files, and immigration judges were not to admit or deny any information about them.

> The government has never formally explained how it decided which visa violators would be singled out for this extraordinary process, and it has insisted that the designations could not be reviewed by the courts.
>
> But as it turns out, most of these cases involved Arab and Muslim men who were detained in fairly haphazard ways, for example at traffic stops or through tips from suspicious neighbors. Law enforcement officials have acknowledged that only a few of these detainees had any significant information about possible terrorists.[21]

A report issued in the summer of 2003 by the inspector general of the Department of Justice concluded that this "roundup of hundreds of illegal immigrants in the months after the Sept. 11 attacks was plagued with 'significant problems' that forced many people with no connection to terrorism to languish in jails in unduly harsh conditions."[22]

The secrecy policy of the Justice Department had the effect of keeping the mistakes made by the government hidden from the public. One such case of secret deportation hearings was challenged by the *Detroit Free Press*. The case involved Rabih Haddad, suspected but not formally charged with sponsoring a charity that channeled funds to terrorists. The Court of Appeals for the Sixth Circuit overruled the Creppy order and held that the hearings had to be open to the public, and that the government could apply to the judge to exclude any classified materials that threatened national security. The government argued that seemingly innocuous bits and pieces of information that came out at a deportation hearing could fit into a mosaic that would expose the government's antiterrorism investigation. The court found that the government admitted that this was *not* the situation in Haddad's case. There was no indication that the government had carefully reviewed the more than seven hundred cases of secret detentions, and that there was no limit to what the government could justify under this reasoning.[23] Although secrecy is necessary in terrorism investigations, including decisions about detentions, the "Bush administration has put a much tighter lid than recent presidents on government proceedings and the public release of information, exhibiting a penchant for secrecy that has been striking to historians, legal

experts and lawmakers of both parties."[24] This general policy raises suspicions that in an administration that seems to favor secrecy for political advantage, detentions on national security grounds may go unchecked. Haddad and his family were deported in mid-2003.[25]

A basic question underlying the sweeping detention of aliens is whether they have any right to be free of detention on the authority of executive branch officers without judicial oversight. In the case of citizens charged with crime, pretrial detention is a question regulated by Eighth Amendment policy that generally favors pretrial freedom, that prohibits excessive bail, but that does not absolutely guarantee release before trial (*United States v. Salerno,* 1987). Does the Eighth Amendment or any other constitutional guideline apply to aliens? Many constitutional provisions do not apply to the deportation of aliens, because deportation is held not to be a punishment, but an administrative measure.[26] The Fifth Amendment, however, protects every *person* from deprivation of life, liberty, or property by the government without due process of law. In *Zadvydas v. Davis* (2001), decided a few months before 9/11, an alien who had been ordered deported was held in custody because no nation would take him. Facing the prospect of indefinite confinement under the statute, he brought a habeas corpus challenge. The Supreme Court held that he was protected from detention for a period longer than is "reasonably necessary to bring about [his] removal from the United States. It does not permit indefinite detention. . . . Freedom from imprisonment—from government custody, detention, or other forms of physical restraint—lies at the heart of the liberty that Clause protects" (*Zadvydas v. Davis,* 2001, p. 690).

Under the Due Process Clause, therefore, an alien has a "liberty interest" in remaining out of custody pending deportation hearings. In 1996 Congress passed a law that required that aliens pending removal, who had certain criminal convictions, be held in custody without bail.[27] Several Courts of Appeal have found this mandatory provision to be an unconstitutional violation of the due process rights of aliens pending deportation. The Supreme Court has not yet reviewed this question, but the gist of the appellate court cases, consistent with *Salerno*, is that preventive detention before a hearing to determine a person's rights, must be based on an individualized procedure, and not on a wholesale basis.

Section 412 of the USA PATRIOT Act states that immigrants who are "certified" as threats to national security must be held in government custody without bond pending deportation proceedings and removal from the country. Does this blanket denial of bail in §412 violate due process of persons who are protected by the Fifth Amendment? Certification of aliens as threats to national security includes "not just individuals who plot or undertake acts of terrorism, but also individuals who are more remotely affiliated with proscribed organizations."[28] This includes individuals who have provided material support, such as making a donation, to a group designated by the Attorney General as a terrorist organization. The standards for designation are low under §411 of the PATRIOT Act and include "organizations that engage both in lawful conduct (for instance, political struggle and social work) and in violent activities."[29] Thus, an alien who had donated to a terrorist organization like Hamas, can be "certified" as a threat and held without bail for seven days. Within that time, the person must be charged with a crime, put on a list for deportation action, or released. Preventive detention is automatic and does not depend on the person's criminal history or actual suspicion as a terrorist.

Under established Fifth Amendment law, a person whose liberty interests are threatened is guaranteed notice and a hearing if there is a "risk of an erroneous deprivation of such interest through the procedures used."[30] Given the high level of inaccuracy in the roundup of the twelve hundred persons after the 9/11 attack, it would seem that §412 raises a serious possibility of a due process violation. A "certified alien" has a habeas corpus appeal under §412, but if the proceedings remain secret, he "would be in the precarious position of proving he was not a terrorist in the face of undisclosed charges."[31] The argument for the government is that "the elimination of mandatory detention might lead to the release of some aliens on bond who are threats to the public or who may not subsequently appear for deportation."[32] The reply to this argument is that "[a]dditional procedures do not block the government from detaining aliens who are genuine threats; it merely provides for a level of review where the individual herself has an opportunity to present her side." One commentator concludes that the procedures of notice and hearing for preventive detention for possible terrorists would not unduly burden the government before depriving a person of liberty "for months or years. . . . [F]ears of terrorism should not trump constitutional integrity."[33]

PROSECUTORIAL CHARGING

Prosecutors have nearly unlimited discretion in deciding whether to *formally charge* (accuse) a person with a crime, as long as there is probable cause to support the accusation, or *dismiss* charges filed by the police. This discretion includes deciding *which crimes* to charge (*Ball v. United States,* 1985), whether or not to *plea-bargain, when* to bring charges (*United States v. Lovasco,* 1977), and whether to grant **immunity** to one or more defendants in a case.[34] Courts do not normally oversee this decision nor do they review the prosecutor's decision to charge with a more or less serious case on the same facts, or in a murder case, whether to seek the death penalty in states that allow that sentence.

Formal charges drafted by the prosecutor are either indictments or informations. In federal prosecutions and approximately one-third of the states, formal charges are drawn up by the prosecutor and approved by a citizen's **grand jury.**[35] This body hears witnesses and reviews relevant evidence *in secret.* It votes on the charges and hands up (approves) an *indictment* by *majority* vote. In states that do not require a grand jury indictment, a prosecutor initiates the prosecution by filing an **information** against the defendant, after a preliminary examination has been held and a prima facie case established, or has been waived by the defendant. Both indictments and informa-

tions are formal charging instruments (documents) that list the specific crimes the prosecutor must prove and the defendant must oppose. They state a few facts sufficient to establish a basis—either probable cause or a prima facie case—for the prosecutor to go forward with the case.

In practice, the prosecutor has almost as much control over charges by indictment as by information, for grand juries almost always follow the prosecutor's lead. Formal charges are important because they tell the defendant that he or she will stand trial only on the crimes charged. If new facts come to light, the prosecutor can charge a defendant with additional "counts" (specific crimes) in an *amended* indictment approved by the grand jury or an amended information approved by a judge.

Discretion and the Separation of Powers Doctrine

A prime reason for prosecutorial discretion is the **separation of powers doctrine.** The prosecutor is an *executive branch* officer and is typically an elected county official. Federal prosecutors are appointed by the president. Judges, whether elected or appointed, are responsible for "the Judiciary," a separate branch of government, and do not exercise direct control over prosecutors. This is so even though prosecutors are "officers of the court," as are all lawyers. An example of the separation of powers doctrine arose in the civil rights–era Court of Appeals decision in **United States v. Cox** (1965). A federal judge in Mississippi believed that African American defendants lied in testifying that a local registrar refused to give them voting registration applications. He referred their case to a grand jury, which proceeded to hand up indictments for perjury. The United States attorney (i.e., the federal prosecutor) in that district, on orders of the Attorney General of the United States, refused to sign the indictment, thus blocking a prosecution. The federal district court judge then held the United States attorney in contempt and threatened to hold the Attorney General in contempt. The case was quickly appealed to the Court of Appeals, which reversed the trial court:

> The discretionary power of the attorney for the United States in determining whether a prosecution shall be commenced or maintained may well depend upon matters of policy wholly apart from any question of probable cause. Although as a member of the bar, the attorney for the United States is an officer of the court, he is nevertheless an executive officer of the Government, and it is as an officer of the executive department that he exercises a discretion as to whether or not there shall be a prosecution in a particular case. It follows, as an incident of the constitutional separation of powers, that the courts are not to interfere with the free exercise of the discretionary powers of the attorneys of the United States in their control over criminal prosecutions. (*United States v. Cox,* 5th Cir. 1965).[36]

The basic rule, therefore, is one of *prosecutorial autonomy* from judicial control in the charging function (*Town of Newton v. Rumery,* 1987; *United States v. Armstrong,* 1996).

Many reasons explain why discretion is necessary in the charging process. One is that the same behavior can often be charged under different sections of the penal code, carrying higher or lower maximum penalties. The forcible taking of property can be charged as a robbery with a potential life sentence or as a theft from the person, which carries a lower maximum sentence. Or a single criminal incident can generate a variety of separate charges. A robber or rapist who drives a victim some distance, for example, can also be charged with kidnapping in jurisdictions in which a ransom demand is not part of the crime definition. Or a prosecutor can decline to charge separate crimes for reasons of efficiency. A burglar may be charged with one offense if he admits to numerous others, thus helping the police to clear a number of crimes. He can still be sentenced, under various sentencing systems, to a sufficiently severe penalty for the single crime to achieve public condemnation and deterrence. Prosecutors can charge all individuals involved in a crime, or can dismiss charges against a minor participant. The prosecutor can offer a grant immunity to a lesser actor to insure testimony against other codefendants. The charging power gives the prosecutor substantial leverage in positioning a case to the state's advantage at trial or in plea bargaining. There is no rule that requires the prosecutor to charge the maximum in all of these examples. To do so may create unnecessary oppression. The "right" level of charging requires a judgment.

There are morally difficult decisions where the prosecutor does not seek a maximum penalty for other policy reasons. In the case of Gary L. Ridgway, the "Green River killer"—perhaps the worst serial killer in American history—the prosecutor agreed to not seek the death penalty so that Ridgway would identify his victims and bring closure to the victims' families. DNA linked Ridgway to seven victims, but under his plea arrangement, he admitted to killing at least forty-eight women. The King County (Seattle) prosecutor, Norm Maleng, "said it had been excruciating to decide whether to prosecute Mr. Ridgway for the seven murders and pursue the death penalty or spare him the death penalty in exchange for information on the killings."[37]

As an elected or appointed official, a charging prosecutor's decisions cannot be entirely divorced from politics. Most decisions follow legal standards (e.g., evidence inadequate to convict) and legitimate policy factors (e.g., negligible harm caused by crime; restitution), but the suspicion often lingers that political factors, such as reelection, may weigh in the charging decision. The positive side of elected prosecutors is that their policies and practices are more open to public input; on occasion a prosecutor who pursues an unpopular course may be removed by the ballot box. This was the case with a Michigan prosecutor who was seen as overly zealous in his failed attempts to convict Dr. Jack Kevorkian of attempted suicide.[38] The negative side is that political consideration may warp the decision to charge, which ideally is made evenhandedly according to legal criteria. Even if political considerations are not visible, critics accuse prosecutors of using their discretion to routinely *overcharge* defendants so that they will be forced into disadvantageous plea bargains. Prosecutors reply that they frame charges by fitting the facts to the definitions of the penal law. In rebuttal, defense-oriented critics maintain that statutory criminal penalties are unrealistically harsh.

Constitutional Limits: Selective and Vindictive Prosecution

Selective prosecution occurs when a defendant is singled out for charging on impermissible grounds, such as race, religion, political beliefs, or for exercising constitutional rights. It is very difficult for a defendant to succeed in proving selective prosecution. The discrimination has to be blatant, where, for example, after a fatal robbery, a prosecutor charges an African American defendant with capital murder while charging white coconspirators with second-degree murder, unless a rational factor distinguished the codefendants. The classic case of selective prosecution, which violates the *equal protection of the law* under the Fourteenth Amendment, was *Yick Wo v. Hopkins* (1886). A San Francisco ordinance required laundries to operate in brick or stone buildings, unless the board of supervisors granted a waiver. The board granted permits to operate laundries in wooden buildings to all white applicants except one, but it denied such permits to two hundred Chinese applicants. This blatant racial discrimination in the enforcement of a law, which was essentially fair if it had been applied uniformly, was held to violate the Equal Protection Clause.

In *Oyler v. Boles* (1962) the Supreme Court held that some prosecutor selectivity in deciding to prosecute some offenders under a habitual offender statute does not violate the Equal Protection Clause unless the "selection was deliberately based upon an unjustifiable standard such as race, religion, or other arbitrary classification." In *Wayte v. United States* (1985) the Supreme Court found no selective prosecution where only sixteen men were indicted for failing to register for the draft out of about 674,000 who had failed to register. Wayte claims that he was singled out for prosecution because he wrote letters to the government stating he would not register on grounds of conscience, i.e., for exercising his right to free speech under the First Amendment. The facts showed that 8.3 million out of 9 million men required to register did so. The Selective Service System (SSS) adopted a policy of "passive enforcement." That is, it decided to not actively investigate and prosecute nonregistrants unless they advised the SSS they were not registering. Instead, the SSS wrote to *known* violators, requested that they comply with their duty to register or explain why not, and warned that a violation could result in criminal prosecution. After a year of this, the SSS sent the names of 134 young men, including Wayte, to the Department of Justice (DOJ) for investigation and potential prosecution. Further names were screened out, and FBI agents were sent to interview nonregistrants to persuade them to change their minds—this was known as the "beg" policy. After six months, the DOJ instructed United States attorneys not to initiate prosecutions. Instead, the president announced a grace period to give nonregistrants a further opportunity to register without penalty. Wayte still did not register and was finally prosecuted. Those not indicted were exempt from the draft, could not be found, or were still under investigation.

The Supreme Court held that there was no selective prosecution. Wayte was prosecuted essentially for failing to register and not because he protested his reasons for nonregistration vocally. It was true that "the Government was aware that the passive enforcement policy would result in prosecution of vocal objectors. . . ." Discriminatory purpose, however, implies more than awareness of consequences. "It implies that the decisionmaker . . . selected . . . a particular course of action at least in part 'because of,' not merely 'in spite of,' its adverse effects upon an identifiable group." This could not be shown in the present case. The selective prosecution doctrine under the Equal Protection Clause requires a showing of both *discriminatory effect* and *discriminatory purpose*. Under the passive enforcement program, some, but not all, of those who exercised their First Amendment rights to protest draft registration were prosecuted. Some men who had *not* protested were indicted. Wayte "has not shown that the enforcement policy selected nonregistrants for prosecution on the basis of their speech. . . . The Government treated all reported nonregistrants similarly. It did not subject vocal nonregistrants to any special burden. Indeed, those prosecuted in effect selected themselves for prosecution by refusing to register after being reported and warned by the Government." Therefore, the Court found no discriminatory effect.

—*United States v. Armstrong* **Case & Comments**—

• CASE & COMMENTS •

United States v. Armstrong
517 U.S. 456, 116 S.Ct. 1480, 134 L.Ed.2d 687 (1996)

CHIEF JUSTICE REHNQUIST delivered the opinion of the Court.

[Christopher Lee Armstrong and other African American men ("respondents") were indicted in Los Angeles federal court for possession with intent to distribute more than fifty grams of crack cocaine, and for federal firearms charges. A federal-state drug task force investigation established that they were regular dealers. The respondents filed a motion to dismiss the indictment alleging that they were selected for federal prosecution because they are black. They also requested discovery of the prosecutor's files to ascertain whether racial bias existed. The Supreme Court denied the discovery motion. Discovery allows defendants access only to factual material in response to specific charges, and not to the Government's "work product." The Supreme Court also noted that discovery to locate evidence of selective prosecution requires prosecutors to comb their files looking for documents "which might corroborate or refute the defendant's claim," thus diverting prosecutors' resources and possibly disclosing the Government's prosecutorial strategy.]

In this case, we consider the showing necessary for a defendant to be entitled to discovery on a claim that the prosecuting attorney singled him out for prosecution on the basis of his race. We conclude that respondents failed to satisfy the threshold showing: They failed to show that the Government declined to prosecute similarly situated suspects of other races. * * *

[In support of their motion, respondents] offered only an affidavit by a "Paralegal Specialist," employed by the Office of the Federal Public Defender representing one of the respondents. The only allegation in the affidavit was that, in every one of the 24 [crack cocaine] cases closed by the office during 1991, the defendant was black. Accompanying the affidavit was a "study" listing the 24 defendants, their race, whether they were prosecuted for dealing cocaine as well as crack, and the status of each case. * * *

The Government * * * submitted affidavits and other evidence to explain why it had chosen to prosecute respondents. * * * The federal and local agents * * * alleged in affidavits that race played no role in their investigation. An Assistant United States Attorney explained in an affidavit that the decision to prosecute met the general criteria for prosecution, because [of the large quantity of cocaine involved, the multiple sales, the firearms violations connected to the sales, and the criminal histories of the defendants]. The Government also submitted sections of a published 1989 Drug Enforcement Administration report which concluded that "large-scale, interstate trafficking networks controlled by Jamaicans, Haitians and Black street gangs dominate the manufacture and distribution of crack." [a]

In response, one of respondents' attorneys submitted an affidavit alleging that an intake coordinator at a drug treatment center had told her that there are "an equal number of caucasian users and dealers to minority users and dealers." Respondents also submitted an affidavit from a criminal defense attorney alleging that in his experience many nonblacks are prosecuted in state court for crack offenses, and a newspaper article reporting that federal "crack criminals . . . are being punished far

[a] What are the sources of the evidence put forward by the prosecution and the defense? Which seems stronger?

more severely than if they had been caught with powder cocaine, and almost every single one of them is black." * * *

A selective-prosecution claim is not a defense on the merits to the criminal charge itself, but an independent assertion that the prosecutor has brought the charge for reasons forbidden by the Constitution. Our cases delineating the necessary elements to prove a claim of selective prosecution have taken great pains to explain that the standard is a demanding one. **[b]** These cases afford a "background presumption," that the showing necessary to obtain discovery should itself be a significant barrier to the litigation of insubstantial claims.

A selective-prosecution claim asks a court to exercise judicial power over a "special province" of the Executive. The Attorney General and United States Attorneys retain "'broad discretion'" to enforce the Nation's criminal laws. *Wayte v. United States* (1985). They have this latitude because they are designated by statute as the President's delegates to help him discharge his constitutional responsibility to "take Care that the Laws be faithfully executed." U.S. Const., Art. II, §3. As a result, "the presumption of regularity supports" their prosecutorial decisions and, "in the absence of clear evidence to the contrary, courts presume that they have properly discharged their official duties." **[c]** In the ordinary case, "so long as the prosecutor has probable cause to believe that the accused committed an offense defined by statute, the decision whether or not to prosecute, and what charge to file or bring before a grand jury, generally rests entirely in his discretion."

Of course, a prosecutor's discretion is "subject to constitutional constraints." One of these constraints, imposed by the equal protection component of the Due Process Clause of the Fifth Amendment, is that the decision whether to prosecute may not be based on "an unjustifiable standard such as race, religion, or other arbitrary classification." **[d]** A defendant may demonstrate that the administration of a criminal law is "directed so exclusively against a particular class of persons . . . with a mind so unequal and oppressive" that the system of prosecution amounts to "a practical denial" of equal protection of the law. *Yick Wo v. Hopkins* (1886).

In order to dispel the presumption that a prosecutor has not violated equal protection, a criminal defendant must present "clear evidence to the contrary." We explained in *Wayte* why courts are "properly hesitant to examine the decision whether to prosecute." Judicial deference to the decisions of these executive officers rests in part on an assessment of the relative competence of prosecutors and courts. "Such factors as the strength of the case, the prosecution's general deterrence value, the Government's enforcement priorities, and the case's relationship to the Government's overall enforcement plan are not readily susceptible to the kind of analysis the courts are competent to undertake." **[e]** It also stems from a concern not to unnecessarily impair the performance of a core executive constitutional function. "Examining the basis of a prosecution delays the criminal proceeding, threatens to chill law enforcement by subjecting the prosecutor's motives and decisionmaking to outside inquiry, and may undermine prosecutorial effectiveness by revealing the Government's enforcement policy."

The requirements for a selective-prosecution claim draw on "ordinary equal protection standards." The claimant must demonstrate that the federal prosecutorial policy "had a discriminatory effect and that it was motivated by a discriminatory purpose." **[f]** To establish a discriminatory effect in a race case, the claimant must show that similarly situated individuals of a different race were not prosecuted. This requirement has been [long] established in our case law. * * *

The similarly situated requirement does not make a selective-prosecution claim impossible to prove. * * * [W]e invalidated an ordinance, also adopted by San Francisco, that prohibited the operation of laundries in wooden buildings. *Yick Wo.* The plaintiff in error successfully demonstrated that the ordinance was applied against Chinese nationals but not against other laundry-shop operators. The authorities had denied the applications of 200 Chinese subjects for permits to operate shops in wooden buildings, but granted the applications of 80 individuals who were not Chinese subjects to operate laundries in wooden buildings "under similar conditions." *Ibid.* * * *

[The Supreme Court restated the rule that the respondents had to show not only that black defendants were prosecuted, but that white defendants were *not* prosecuted for crack cocaine offenses. It is not relevant, as did the Circuit Court, to simply start] "with the presumption that people of *all* races commit *all* types of crimes—not with the premise that any type of crime is the exclusive province of any particular racial or ethnic group." It cited no authority for this proposition, which seems contradicted by the most recent statistics of the United States Sentencing Commission. Those statistics show: More than 90% of the persons sentenced in 1994 for crack cocaine trafficking were black, 93.4% of convicted LSD dealers were white, and 91% of those convicted for pornography or prostitution were white. Presumptions at war with presumably reliable statistics have no proper place in the analysis of this issue.

[b] The defendant in a selective prosecution challenge is handicapped at the outset. Is this a reasonable starting point?

[c] An evidentiary standard is provided—a defendant must show selective prosecution by "clear evidence."

[d] The Fifth Amendment (1791) has a Due Process Clause but no Equal Protection Clause, as does the Fourteenth Amendment (1868). In *Bolling v. Sharpe* (1954), a companion case to *Brown v. Board*, the Court held that the Fifth Amendment Due Process Clause includes an equal protection principle. Discrimination forbidden to the states is also forbidden to the federal government.

[e] Two reasons are given: the competence of the executive in juggling a number of policy considerations, and a desire not to weaken effective prosecution.

[f] The rule has two prongs, making it more difficult for a defendant to prove.

• CASE & COMMENTS •

* * * In the present case, if the claim of selective prosecution were well founded, it should not have been an insuperable task to prove that persons of other races were being treated differently than respondents. For instance, respondents could have investigated whether similarly situated persons of other races were prosecuted by the State of California and were known to federal law enforcement officers, but were not prosecuted in federal court. We think the required threshold—a credible showing of different treatment of similarly situated persons—adequately balances the Government's interest in vigorous prosecution and the defendant's interest in avoiding selective prosecution.

In the case before us, respondents' "study" did not constitute "some evidence tending to show the existence of the essential elements of" a selective-prosecution claim. The study failed to identify individuals who were not black and could have been prosecuted for the offenses for which respondents were charged, but were not so prosecuted. This omission was not remedied by respondents' evidence in opposition to the Government's motion for reconsideration. The newspaper article, which discussed the discriminatory effect of federal drug sentencing laws, was not relevant to an allegation of discrimination in decisions to prosecute. **[g]** Respondents' affidavits, which recounted one attorney's conversation with a drug treatment center employee and the experience of another attorney defending drug prosecutions in state court, recounted hearsay and reported personal conclusions based on anecdotal evidence. The judgment of the Court of Appeals is therefore reversed, and the case is remanded for proceedings consistent with this opinion.

It is so ordered.

[Justices Souter, Ginsburg, and Breyer concurred in the judgment as to selective prosecution, but expressed reservations or dissent as to its ruling on the issue of discovery.]

JUSTICE STEVENS, dissenting.

Federal prosecutors are respected members of a respected profession. Despite an occasional misstep, the excellence of their work abundantly justifies the presumption that "they have properly discharged their official duties." Nevertheless, the possibility that political or racial animosity may infect a decision to institute criminal proceedings cannot be ignored. For that reason, it has long been settled that the prosecutor's broad discretion to determine when criminal charges should be filed is not completely unbridled. As the Court notes, however, the scope of judicial review of particular exercises of that discretion is not fully defined.

The United States Attorney for the Central District of California is a member and an officer of the bar of that District Court. As such, she has a duty to the judges of that Court to maintain the standards of the profession in the performance of her official functions. If a District Judge has reason to suspect that she, or a member of her staff, has singled out particular defendants for prosecution on the basis of their race, it is surely appropriate for the judge to determine whether there is a factual basis for such a concern. * * *

The Court correctly concludes that in this case the facts presented to the District Court in support of respondents' claim that they had been singled out for prosecution because of their race were not sufficient to prove that defense. [Justice Stevens, nevertheless, argued that the discovery ordered by the district judge should have gone forward for the following three reasons.] * * * **[h]**

* * * First, the Anti-Drug Abuse Act of 1986 and subsequent legislation established a regime of extremely high penalties for the possession and distribution of so-called "crack" cocaine. Those provisions treat one gram of crack as the equivalent of 100 grams of powder cocaine. The distribution of 50 grams of crack is thus punishable by the same mandatory minimum sentence of 10 years in prison that applies to the distribution of 5,000 grams of powder cocaine. * * *

Second, the disparity between the treatment of crack cocaine and powder cocaine is matched by the disparity between the severity of the punishment imposed by federal law and that imposed by state law for the same conduct. * * * [T]erms of imprisonment for drug offenses tend to be substantially lower in state systems than in the federal system.

Finally, it is undisputed that the brunt of the elevated federal penalties falls heavily on blacks. While 65% of the persons who have used crack are white, in 1993 they represented only 4% of the federal offenders convicted of trafficking in crack. Eighty-eight percent of such defendants were black. During the first 18 months of full guideline implementation, the sentencing disparity between black and white defendants grew from preguideline levels: Blacks on average received sentences over 40% longer than whites. * * * Those figures represent a major threat to the integrity of federal sentencing reform, whose main purpose was the elimination of disparity (especially racial) in sentencing. The Sentencing

[g] Constitutional challenges claiming discrimination often have to amass considerable evidence collected by expert social scientists to prove a claim and to thwart doubts about the conclusion.

[h] If Justice Stevens agreed that the defendants did not amass proof of selective prosecution by the federal prosecutor based on race, how can he support the conduct of a hearing on the issue by the trial judge? The answer that unfolds depends on the federal nature of American government and the growing phenomenon that the same crime may be prosecuted under federal or state law.

Commission acknowledges that the heightened crack penalties are a "primary cause of the growing disparity between sentences for Black and White federal defendants." **[i]**

The extraordinary severity of the imposed penalties and the troubling racial patterns of enforcement give rise to a special concern about the fairness of charging practices for crack offenses. Evidence tending to prove that black defendants charged with distribution of crack in the Central District of California are prosecuted in federal court, whereas members of other races charged with similar offenses are prosecuted in state court, warrants close scrutiny by the federal judges in that district. * * *

* * *

In sum, I agree with the Sentencing Commission that "while the exercise of discretion by prosecutors and investigators has an impact on sentences in almost all cases to some extent, because of the 100-to-1 quantity ratio and federal mandatory minimum penalties, discretionary decisions in cocaine cases often have dramatic effects." The severity of the penalty heightens both the danger of arbitrary enforcement and the need for careful scrutiny of any colorable claim of discriminatory enforcement. * * * I therefore respectfully dissent.

* * *

[i] Justice Stevens shows, by relying on official statistics, that prosecutions against African Americans for crack cocaine possession in federal courts result in much longer sentences than comparable prosecutions in state courts. He would allow the district court judge to hold a hearing to establish this racial disproportionality in order to create a foundation for Armstrong's constitutional challenge to his conviction.

Vindictive prosecution occurs when new and more serious charges are brought simply because a defendant has exercised her statutory or constitutional rights. For example, if a defendant wins a new trial after appealing a conviction for breaking and entering, it is illegally vindictive behavior for a prosecutor to recharge the more serious crime of burglary. Increasing the charge might be interpreted as the prosecutor "getting even" with the defendant for exercising the legal right to appeal. ***North Carolina v. Pearce*** (1969) dealt with a situation where a defendant successfully overturns a conviction on appeal (whether for constitutional or nonconstitutional errors), is retried, reconvicted, and resentenced for the same crime. The Supreme Court ruled that vindictiveness must play no part in the resentencing. The concern was that a harsher sentence after the successful appeal was seen to punish defendants for exercising their constitutional rights to appeal. This would "chill" the right to appeal, i.e., cause prisoners to not pursue their rights. In practice, this meant that the second sentencing could not be harsher than the first, unless new facts came to the attention of the sentencing judge.

The *Pearce* nonvindictiveness principle, based on due process fairness concepts, was applied to cases where a prosecutor has an opportunity to charge a defendant a second time. In ***Blackledge v. Perry*** (1974) Perry was found guilty of a *misdemeanor* and sentenced to six month's incarceration. Under North Carolina's two-tiered trial system, instead of appealing, he was granted a **trial** *de novo* in the superior court, where "the slate is wiped clean, the prior conviction annulled, and the prosecution and defense begin anew." The prosecutor then charged Perry with the *felony* of assault with a deadly weapon. He was convicted and sentenced to a term of five to seven years in prison. On appeal to the Supreme Court, Justice Stewart held that the prosecutor's enhancement of the charges constituted a due process violation for "vindictiveness." It was not necessary to show that the prosecutor was motivated by ill will or bad faith, only that the

harsher charge was in response to the defendant's exercise of a *legal* right. The basis of the vindictiveness rule is "the fear that such vindictiveness may unconstitutionally deter a defendant's exercise of the right to appeal his first conviction. . . ." Due process requires that "a defendant be freed of the apprehension of such a retaliatory motivation" on the part of the prosecutor. In this instance, "[a] person convicted of an offense is entitled to pursue his statutory right to a trial *de novo* without apprehension that the State will retaliate by substituting a more serious charge for the original one thus subjecting him to a significantly increased potential period of incarceration."

In ***United States v. Goodwin*** (1982) Goodwin was stopped for speeding by a federal park police officer in Maryland; he was ordered back into his car by the officer and asked to raise the front seat armrest so the officer could see what was in a clear plastic bag. Instead, Goodwin drove off, knocking the officer down. The officer filed a complaint against Goodwin in the federal district court, charging him with misdemeanor assault. The case was set for trial, but Goodwin fled the jurisdiction. He was found in custody in Virginia three years later and returned to federal custody in Maryland. His misdemeanor charges were to be tried before a federal magistrate. Goodwin then requested a jury trial. The case was transferred from the magistrate's court, which had no authority to try felonies, to a felony-level court. The United States attorney obtained a felony assault indictment for forcibly assaulting a federal officer. After conviction, Goodwin claimed that the enhanced charge amounted to vindictiveness under the rule of *Blackledge*. The Court disagreed and found no vindictiveness.

There is good reason to be cautious before adopting an inflexible presumption of prosecutorial vindictiveness in a pretrial setting. In the course of preparing a case for trial, the prosecutor may uncover additional information that suggests a basis for further prosecution or he simply may come to realize that information possessed by the State has a broader significance. At this stage of the proceedings, the prosecutor's assessment of the proper extent of prosecution may not have crystallized. In contrast, once a trial begins—and certainly by the time a conviction has been obtained—it is much more likely that the State has discovered and assessed all of the information against an accused and has made a determination, on the basis of that information, of the extent to which he should be prosecuted. Thus, a change in the charging decision made after an initial trial is completed is much more likely to be improperly motivated than is a pretrial decision.

Therefore, a defendant's request for a jury over a bench trial, before trial, does not trigger a presumption of vindictiveness when charges are thereafter increased.

In *Thigpen v. Roberts* (1984) Barry Joe Roberts lost control of his car and collided with a pickup truck, killing a passenger in the truck. He was convicted of four misdemeanor driving offenses in a Mississippi justice of the peace court. The charges were brought by a county prosecutor who had responsibility only for misdemeanors. Roberts sought a trial *de novo* in the circuit court and the District Attorney, who could seek a felony indictment, brought felony charges against Roberts. After conviction, he appealed. The Supreme Court held that the case was governed by the rule of *Blackledge v. Perry* and held that the felony prosecution violated his due process rights. The fact that two different prosecutors were involved did not eliminate the possibility of *institutional vindictiveness*.

SCREENING: THE GRAND JURY AND PRELIMINARY EXAMINATION

An essential function at the pretrial stage of the judicial process is screening—eliminating cases that should not go to trial. The value of quickly screening out innocent suspects eliminates "easy" cases from trial dockets and relieves innocent suspects from further expense, inconvenience, and fear. As noted above, most cases are screened out of the judicial process by prosecutors declining to prosecute persons arrested by the police. Prosecutors may exercise their discretion to dismiss even when probable cause to convict exists. The discretionary dismissal may depend on a host of factors: the harm caused is trivial, satisfactory restitution has been made, a key witness refuses to testify, an informant is being rewarded, the defendant has been granted immunity, a jury is highly unlikely to convict although probable cause exists, and so forth.

Two screening institutions—the grand jury and the preliminary examination—have roots in the common law era. The formal function of each is the same: to decide whether the state can present probable cause to support a prosecution.

It is axiomatic that the prosecutor at the preliminary examination needs to present proofs for each element of the crime. An exception to this rule concerns the charge of open murder, through which the prosecutor does not specify whether the crime is first-degree murder or second-degree murder.[39]

If the prosecutor cannot establish probable cause, the prosecution must be dismissed. In fact, neither of these institutions screens out very many cases today, although they play other useful functions in the pretrial process. The grand jury (or the "jury of presentment") is a panel of citizens that dates back to the origin of trial by jury in the thirteenth century. The preliminary examination, created by statute in the sixteenth century, was designed to secure information of the crime immediately after an arrest.[40] The modern preliminary examination culminates with the magistrate either binding over a case for trial or dismissing, depending on whether the prosecutor established probable cause.

The Grand Jury

During the seventeenth-century, grand juries in England gained popular respect by refusing to indict popular political opponents of the crown. This resistance to British authority made the grand jury popular in the American colonies. Each new American state and the federal government required that criminal prosecutions be initiated by grand jury, and federal grand juries were guaranteed in the Fifth Amendment of the Bill of Rights (1791).

In the mid-nineteenth century, more than half the states eliminated the grand jury indictment requirement as costly and cumbersome. With the expansion of the right to vote, it was believed that elected prosecutors would charge defendants fairly by information. A defendant in California argued that his prosecution by information violated his right to a grand jury indictment under the Fifth Amendment. The Supreme Court ruled in *Hurtado v. California* (1884) that the Bill of Rights did not apply to the states, i.e., it did not "incorporate" this provision (see Chapter 1). Further, it ruled that the requirement that "[n]o person shall be held to answer for a capital, or otherwise infamous crime, unless on a presentment or indictment of a Grand Jury" is not so fundamental to liberty and justice as to be an element of due process under the Fourteenth Amendment. States that dropped the indictment requirement as a routine way of formally charging still retain grand juries and allow them to be called by a prosecutor in special cases. These tend to be complex, white-collar, organized crime, or government corruption cases where grand jury secrecy and its **subpoena** powers prove useful. The grand jury therefore continues to play an important role in American criminal justice.

Depending on a state's law, citizen grand juries number between twelve and twenty-three persons. They determine whether there is probable cause to hold a suspect for trial by majority vote, and issue either a **"true bill"** or a "no bill" of indictment. The prosecutor must sign the bill of indictment for it to become the formal charge against a defendant. The grand jury may rely on hearsay evidence in coming to its decision, such as summarizations of testimony by government agents rather than the direct testimony of witnesses (*Costello v. United States,* 1956). As noted in Chapter 2, *United States v. Calandra* (1974) held that grand jury questions may be based on *illegally seized evidence*. The *Calandra* rule makes it considerably easier for prosecutors to gain indictments.

Grand jurors "investigate" crimes mainly by listening to witnesses. In theory, they could issue subpoenas on their own, but rarely do. The prosecutor presents cases to the grand jury and generally guides its activities. The court is responsible for deciding evidentiary questions that may arise during grand jury proceedings. As a citizens' body, the grand jury is not administratively or legally within any of the three branches of government.

The term of a federal grand jury is eighteen months with six-month extensions. In practice, federal grand jury service lasts for a month. Then, although the grand jurors no longer meet, the grand jury retains its "legal" existence. This is important because a person who is granted immunity in order to testify before a grand jury, but refuses to do so, can be held in contempt and jailed during the entire life of the grand jury, even if the jury is not actively sitting.

Racial bias in the *selection* of members of a grand jury results in the automatic reversal of the indictment (*Ex Parte Virginia*, 1880; *Cassell v. Texas*, 1950). Legal objections to a grand jury's racial composition ordinarily must be brought before the case goes to trial. If an objection was not possible before the trial began, however, it is still possible for the indictment to be reversed even though the defendant was found guilty by an unbiased petit jury. In **Vasquez v. Hillary** (1986) the appellant's conviction occurred *twenty-four years* prior to the appeal being filed. Justice Marshall, writing for the majority, pointed out that a conviction does not erase all the damage inflicted by a biased grand jury. Even if there was probable cause, the grand jury might have charged the defendant with a lesser crime, on fewer counts, or on a noncapital rather than a capital charge. "Once having found discrimination in the selection of a grand jury, we simply cannot know that the need to indict would have been assessed in the same way by a grand jury properly constituted." As Justice Blackmun forcefully noted in *Rose v. Mitchell* (1979):

> Selection of members of a grand jury because they are of one race and not another destroys the appearance of justice and thereby casts doubt on the integrity of the judicial process. The exclusion from grand jury service of Negroes, or any group otherwise qualified to serve, impairs the confidence of the public in the administration of justice. As this Court repeatedly has emphasized, such discrimination "not only violates our Constitution and the laws enacted under it but is at war with our basic concepts of a democratic society and a representative government."

Grand Jury Functions and Powers

Aside from the grand jury's function as a "*shield*," to *screen* cases brought by the prosecutor, the grand jury has several powers that make it an effective "*sword*," to *investigate* crime. These powers are in truth, used by the prosecutor, with the agreement of the majority of a grand jury, and include the power to subpoena witnesses and documents and to provide grants of immunity.

SUBPOENA   The grand jury has, under the court's authority, **subpoena power** to require individuals to testify (subpoena *ad testificandum*) or to bring papers and evidence (subpoena *duces tecum*) in an effort to further a criminal investigation. There is a general obligation to obey grand jury subpoenas. In *Branzburg v. Hayes* (1972) the Supreme Court held that a news reporter does not have a First Amendment privilege to withhold information or to avoid testifying before a grand jury when the reporter promised not to reveal sources who may have been involved in criminal activity. Failure to obey a subpoena can be punished with a contempt of court citation (charge). Testimony before the grand jury is under oath, so false or contradictory statements can be used later to impeach the witness or be used as a basis for a perjury prosecution. Courts may overrule a subpoena if (1) the requested evidence is not relevant to the investigation, or (2) the request for documents is too vague or unreasonable.[41]

IMMUNITY   A related power is the grant of immunity to witnesses who refuse to testify on Fifth Amendment self-incrimination grounds (see Chapter 7). Immunity granted by a *state* court at a prosecutor's request also prohibits *federal* prosecution, and federal immunity prevents state prosecution (*Murphy v. Waterfront Commission*, 1964). The *scope* of immunity may be either narrow or broad. Prosecutors in **Counselman v. Hitchcock** (1892) granted a limited form of **use immunity** to grand jury witnesses. This prevents the use and derivative use of testimony in future prosecutions, but does not bar future prosecutions of the defendant if evidence is obtained from an *independent source*. The Supreme Court held in 1892 that such immunity was not sufficient to protect the witness's privilege against self-incrimination. In response to *Counselman*, Congress adopted a **transactional immunity** statute that provided that a witness required to testify was granted broad immunity "for or on account of any transaction, matter, or thing concerning which he may testify or produce evidence." The Court began to shift its ground in *Murphy v. Waterfront Commission* (1964), leading Congress to again narrow its immunity statute. The Supreme Court upheld the constitutionality of the narrower use immunity in **Kastigar v. United States** (1972). This narrowing of the privilege against self-incrimination is another indication of the Burger Court's Crime Control Model approach to criminal justice.

SECRECY   The grand jury meets in *secrecy*. Lawyers of witnesses and suspects are barred, as is the general public. The Supreme Court gives five reasons for grand jury secrecy:

1. To prevent the escape of indicted persons.
2. To ensure great freedom of deliberation for grand jurors.
3. To prevent witness tampering.
4. To encourage the free testimony of persons with information about the crime.
5. To protect the identity of an innocent suspect who is exonerated (*United States v. Procter & Gamble Co.*, 1958).

Under the Federal Rules of Criminal Procedure, grand jury information (except for the jury deliberations and vote of specific grand jurors) may be released automatically to other prosecutors or law enforcement personnel to assist them in their official duties.[42] Otherwise, grand jury information may be released only upon a court order, with or without a request by the defendant.

Misuse of the Grand Jury and the Calls for Reform

Abuses have led to a call for the abolition or reform of the grand jury, which, indeed, was abolished in England in 1933 on the grounds that it was a cumbersome institution that did little to protect defendants from improper prosecution. One perennial criticism is that the grand jury is not an independent citizen's body anymore; it has become a rubber stamp for the prosecutor, who values it only for its secrecy and enormous powers of compelling testimony. Another is that it has been used to intimidate witnesses.[43]

The worst abuses in recent history occurred during the Nixon administration (1969–1974), when the Justice Department's Internal Security Division used federal grand juries to harass and intimidate antiwar activists and peaceful dissidents. Using its national jurisdiction, these prosecutors would subpoena witnesses on short notice, fly them across the nation to a place they had never been, and grill them for days to gain information.[44] These politically motivated abuses went a long way to limiting federal prosecutorial authority that in the early twenty-first century is deemed necessary in the campaign to deal with terrorism. The excesses of the past are a reminder that the grand jury's powers can be used for oppressive purposes.

Abuses led some to propose eliminating the grand jury.[45] One reform proposal is to allow witnesses' attorneys be allowed in the grand jury room during testimony to advise their clients on the legality of questions, but not be allowed to offer substantive challenges. This would be fair and efficient, eliminating the need for delays as witnesses leave the grand jury room to confer with counsel. Today, about fifteen states allow counsel to be brought into their grand jury hearings.[46] Another reform allows the "target" of the grand jury investigation to testify voluntarily and present evidence before the grand jury. Although this makes a grand jury hearing resemble a trial or preliminary hearing, about ten states now require evidence standards approaching the requirements imposed at trial.[47]

In opposition to reforms, some experienced lawyers concede that the federal grand jury is a tool of the prosecutor, but oppose these reforms. They argue that (1) its power is not usually abused, and (2) it is an important cog in the government's investigatory machinery. Without the grand jury, prosecutorial charging followed by preliminary examinations in complex white-collar crime cases could lead to hearings occupying weeks of judicial time. Also, questions asked by grand jurors often help the prosecutor to sharpen the focus of the indictment or decide to terminate further investigation.[48] As the movement for grand jury abolition has waned, the strengthening of the grand jury and instituting some procedural reform seems the appropriate course for the federal and state governments.

The Preliminary Examination

The preliminary examination is a trial-like adversary hearing. It is not guaranteed by the Constitution but is a statutory right in every jurisdiction.[49] Under the Federal Rules of Criminal Procedure, the preliminary examination must be held within ten days after the initial appearance if the defendant is in custody or within twenty days if the defendant had been released.[50]

The screening function of the preliminary examination overlaps with that of the grand jury. In jurisdictions that initiate prosecutions by a grand jury indictment, the general rule is that once the indictment is handed up, the defendant no longer has a right to a preliminary examination. This rule was inserted into the Federal Rules of Criminal Procedure in 1972. Defense attorneys have objected to "quick indictments" by prosecutors because the defendants lose access to the other valuable functions of the preliminary examination. The effect of this rule has been to virtually eliminate the preliminary examination in some federal district courts. In states where formal charges are brought by information, courts have held that a defendant is entitled to a preliminary hearing even after a grand jury indictment.[51] Although this may appear to be needless duplication, it provides an independent determination of probable cause and acknowledges the existence of important informal functions of the preliminary examination.

A defendant may waive his or her right to a preliminary examination. This is often inadvisable, especially if a defendant waives the examination at the initial hearing, before consulting with an attorney. If counsel believes a preliminary examination favors the prosecutor, a waiver may be a wise course. For example, defense counsel may want to avoid giving prosecution witnesses an opportunity to become practiced and at ease in the courtroom. Prosecutors in many jurisdictions can insist upon a preliminary examination even if the defendant waives it.

Preliminary Examination Procedures

A preliminary examination is conducted much like a trial—it is open to the public and held in a courtroom before a magistrate or judge; witnesses may be called and cross-examined; and a transcript is made of the proceedings. The defendant must be present and be represented by an attorney. The preliminary examination is noticeably different than the grand jury, which operates in strict secrecy. Defendants rarely present witnesses at the preliminary examination, but tend to probe prosecution witnesses to develop a sense of the strength of the prosecutor's case.

The goal of the preliminary examination—to determine whether probable cause exists—means that the testimony elicited by the prosecutor is more limited than that presented at trial, where the prosecutor seeks to prove a defendant guilty beyond a reasonable doubt. The magistrate may restrict the scope of the questioning or the cross-examination if, for example, he believes that the cross-examination goes beyond an attempt to undermine probable cause and becomes a quest for discovery.[52] Also, in most states, evidence may be admitted in a preliminary examination that is not admissible at the trial.

As with a trial, a preliminary examination must be *open to the public*. ***Press Enterprise Co. v. Superior Court*** (1986) involved a forty-one-day preliminary examination where the defendant was charged with murdering twelve people by administering a heart drug. The magistrate refused to release the transcript of the hearing to a news organization, on the grounds that it would prejudice the defendant's right to a fair trial. The Supreme Court reversed. The news organization's First Amendment right guaranteed access to the preliminary examination. Further, "public access plays a significant positive role in the functioning" of the preliminary examination, which is often the only public airing of a criminal prosecution. In the absence of a jury, the presence of the public helps prevent corrupt or overzealous prosecution, or compliant, biased, or eccentric judges. A magistrate can legally bar the public from a preliminary examination if he or she makes a specific, on-the-record finding that demonstrates that closure is essential to preserve "higher values," such as the fairness of the trial, and is narrowly tailored to serve that interest.

The preliminary examination is a critical stage of the criminal prosecution under the Sixth Amendment, requiring that a defendant be represented by counsel, unless waived. Counsel must be provided by the state for indigent defendants. In *Coleman v. Alabama* (1970) the Supreme Court reasoned that lack of counsel at the preliminary examination would *undermine* the defendant's right to a *fair trial*.

> First, the lawyer's skilled examination and cross-examination of witnesses may expose fatal weaknesses in the State's case that may lead the magistrate to refuse to bind the accused over. Second, in any event, the skilled interrogation of witnesses by an experienced lawyer can fashion a vital impeachment tool for use in cross-examination of the State's witnesses at the trial, or preserve testimony favorable to the accused of a witness who does not appear at the trial. Third, retained counsel can more effectively discover the case the State has against his client and make possible the preparation of a proper defense to meet that case at the trial. Fourth, counsel can also be influential at the preliminary hearing in making effective arguments for the accused on such matters as the necessity for early psychiatric examination or bail. The inability of the indigent accused on his own to realize these advantages of a lawyer's assistance compels the conclusion that the Alabama preliminary hearing is a "critical stage" of the State's criminal process at which the accused is 'as much entitled to such aid [of counsel] . . . as at the trial itself.' *Powell v. Alabama*. (*Coleman v. Alabama*, 1970)

Coleman demonstrated that having counsel at the preliminary examination was as crucial to a defendant's interests in a fair defense as it was at the actual trial.

The Functions of the Preliminary Examination

Aside from its screening purpose, the preliminary examination serves other useful functions that are not explicitly recognized by statutes. These have lower legitimacy in the eyes of many judges. The least controversial "covert" function is to *preserve testimony* in the transcript of the examination. Because witnesses are under oath and subject to cross-examination, the transcripts may be used to *impeach* the testimony of a witness during trial. The inconsistencies of a witness who testifies differently at the preliminary examination and at trial can be used to discredit him or her.

The transcript of a preliminary examination may be introduced into evidence if a witness is *unavailable* for trial due to death, disability, or disappearance. This is a recognized hearsay rule exception. In ***California v. Green*** (1970) the defendant was charged with furnishing marijuana to Porter, a minor. On the witness stand, Porter became evasive and uncooperative and claimed a lapse of memory when asked about receiving marijuana from Green. The prosecutor then introduced the preliminary hearing transcript to prove that Porter had received illegal substances from Green. The Supreme Court upheld this practice. It ruled that the Sixth Amendment Confrontation Clause was not violated by the introduction of testimony made during a prior hearing because the witness was *subject* to cross-examination, even if he had *not actually* been cross-examined. The fact that preliminary examination questioning is not usually as intense as cross-examination at trial does not alter the rule. Although the witness was physically present, he was unavailable for *constitutional* purposes. The state did its best to question Porter, and when he "clammed up" nothing in the Confrontation Clause prohibited the State from also relying on his prior testimony to prove its case against Green (*California v. Green*, 1970).

More controversial is the defense use of the preliminary examination as a *discovery device* to gather information and assess the strength of the prosecution's case. This purpose is less important in jurisdictions where prosecutors fully and promptly share factual information with the defense. On the other hand, prosecutors who keep information from the defense for tactical reasons (e.g., obtaining a favorable guilty plea despite weak evidence) encourage this covert use of the preliminary examination by opposing counsel. Most judges believe that discovery is subordinate to the primary bind-over function and may limit cross-examination by the defense if it appears to be aimed at only discovering information in the hands of the prosecutor rather than probing the existence of probable cause.

The preliminary examination plays a role in plea bargaining by clarifying the prosecutor's case and disclosing whether it is strong or weak. This may expedite a willingness to enter a plea agreement by the party with the weaker hand. If a case does go to trial, the prosecution may benefit by having given witnesses an "audition," so they become more familiar with the courtroom setting and with their "lines." They are less apt to show nervousness when they testify at trial and will be more believable.

LAW IN SOCIETY

PROSECUTORIAL MISCONDUCT AND CONVICTING THE INNOCENT

THE PROSECUTOR'S POWER, MISCONDUCT, AND ETHICS

The prosecutor is the most powerful actor in the criminal justice system, with virtually unreviewable power to charge crimes or to dismiss arrests and to investigate crimes, especially using the grand jury's subpoena power.[53] Prosecutors use "hardball" tactics like surprise subpoenas to get parties to testify before a grand jury and subpoenaing family members to shake information loose about a suspect.[54] The Supreme Court has deliberately limited judicial control on these executive branch functions to enable the government to vigorously investigate cases and prosecute crimes. Judicial controls would give defendants with large resources (e.g., white-collar criminals) the ability to tie up prosecutors in preliminary challenges.[55] Judicial control over vindictive and selective prosecution, as noted in the text, is quite limited. Civil remedies against prosecutorial misconduct are extremely limited because prosecutors enjoy **absolute immunity** against civil lawsuits that challenge such core functions as charging, appearing in pretrial hearings, and trying a case, even if the prosecutor presented false information, not knowing that it is false (*Imbler v. Pachtman*, 1976; *Burns v. Reed*, 1991). **Qualified immunity,** opening the prosecutor to civil suit, applies only when misconduct occurs in noncore professional activity, e.g., appearing at a press conference or swearing to the truth of facts in an affidavit to support a charge (*Kalina v. Fletcher*, 1997).

The Supreme Court has drawn the line at cases in which prosecutors fabricate evidence or knowingly allow perjured evidence to be used against a defendant. In such cases, the defendant's right to due process has been violated and the conviction must be reversed. In *Mooney v. Holohan* (1935) the Supreme Court noted in dictum that "a deliberate deception of court and jury by the presentation of testimony known to be perjured" would violate the defendant's due process rights. The Court denied relief on procedural grounds. This case arose out of the conviction of a well-known labor radical, Tom Mooney, for setting off a bomb during a pro-military parade in San Francisco in 1916 that killed ten people and seriously injured forty. There was strong exonerating evidence, but it was a period of antiradical hysteria and the prosecutor relied on "eyewitnesses" who were known liars. Mooney was pardoned soon after the Supreme Court's ruling.[56] Other post-*Mooney* cases have reversed convictions when prosecutors have knowingly elicited materially misleading facts from a witness (*Alcorta v. Texas*, 1957), knowingly letting a witness lie about being paid or being given a lenient sentence in return for testimony (*Napue v. Illinois*, 1959), or deliberately mischaracterizing innocent evidence to make it appear incriminating (*Miller v. Pate*, 1967).

Prosecutorial misconduct takes many forms because errors and violations can be made at every stage of the pretrial and trial process.[57] Common forms include appealing to the passions and fears of jurors by inflammatory language, making innuendoes of guilt unsupported by evidence, announcing that the defendant or witnesses took a polygraph test, and the like.[58] Even when courts find that a prosecutor violated a rule of legal ethics or due process, a case will not be reversed on appeal if the error was harmless, that is, unless the error caused the verdict.[59] This section focuses on examples of misconduct that can lead to the conviction of innocent persons.

Given the lack of external controls on prosecutorial misconduct, the adherence to standards of ethics by prosecutors is profoundly important. In a 1940 address, Robert Jackson stated that "the spirit of fair play and decency . . . should animate the federal prosecutor." He admonished federal prosecutors "that while you are being diligent, strict, and vigorous in law enforcement you can also afford to be just. Although the government technically loses its case, it has really won if justice be done."[60] The problem is that such moral exhortations, while followed by many prosecutors, are not binding. If only a few rogue prosecutors decide to not play by the rules, they can significantly increase the convictions of innocent persons.

PROSECUTION ERROR AND WRONGFUL CONVICTION

Various studies of wrongful conviction list prosecution misconduct as one of the major causes of sending innocent men and women to prison, including death row.

- The Innocence Project (2001) reviewed seventy-four cases of actual innocence established by DNA. Twelve factors causing the wrongful convictions were present in one or more cases. Prosecutorial misconduct was the fourth most common error, appearing in thirty-three (45 percent) of the cases.[61]
- Liebman et al. (2000) found that the overall error rate in capital convictions from 1973 to 1995 was 68 percent (7 percent were completely exonerated) and that of the total cases, "prosecutorial suppression of evidence that the defendant is innocent or does not deserve the death penalty" accounted for 16 percent of state postconviction reversals.[62]
- Huff et al. (1996) estimated that of 205 wrongful convictions they identified, nineteen resulted from negligence by criminal justice officials and five from perjury by criminal justice officials.[63]
- Borchard (1932), the first systematic study of sixty-five wrongful convictions in the United States, found that in sixteen cases prosecutorial "fault, carelessness, or overzealousness" was present.[64]
- The Web site for the Innocence Project finds that the kinds of prosecutorial misconduct connected with cases of falsely convicted persons include: suppression of exculpatory evidence (37 percent), knowing use of false testimony (25 percent), coerced witness (11 percent), improper closing arguments (9 percent), false statements to jury (9 percent), evidence fabrications (5 percent), and other misconduct (4 percent).[65]

It should be kept in mind that rarely is one kind of error alone the cause of a wrongful conviction. Castelle and Loftus (2001) identify the "cross-contamination of evidence: when one piece of misinformation contaminates other information in a case and ultimately results in the conviction of the innocent."[66] An initial misidentification by a witness may cause the police to form a rigid idea that the correct suspect has been apprehended, and the initial error may be compounded by a failure of the prosecutor to expose the error. As Prof. Brian Forst suggests, however, this is a weak excuse for prosecutors.

PROSECUTION POLICY AND THE CONVICTION OF INNOCENTS

Prof. Brian Forst notes that prosecutors typically measure success by such criteria as conviction rates and success in being reelected. These criteria do not probe the more vital and more difficult-to-measure goals of reducing crime, pursuing justice, evenhandedness, and enhancing the legitimacy of government, although such goals are probably part of prosecutors' unarticulated motives in deciding whether to charge a defendant and at which level of severity. Prosecutors rarely consider whether their policies are aimed at reducing the incidence of wrongful convictions. In fact, as Forst indicates, prosecutors are in a very good position to *control* "errors of justice."[67] Prosecutors can

> ferret out errors made by the police by screening arrests more carefully, directing postarrest investigations to resolve conflicting sources of evidence, working more diligently with victims and witnesses to establish, precisely and accurately, pertinent events that preceded and followed the episode in question, and directing the forensic processing of key items of physical evidence to resolve ambiguities involving both incriminating and exculpatory evidence."[68]

The failure of prosecutors to more often pursue such ends exposes systemic flaws in the criminal justice system.

EXAMPLES OF EGREGIOUS PROSECUTORIAL MISCONDUCT

- Erick Jackson was convicted in 1980 for felony murder stemming from the setting of a fire in a Brooklyn, New York, supermarket in which six firefighters were killed. He supposedly confessed to having been paid to set a fire on the roof of the market. But a court, years later, found that the confession was uncorroborated and confused his statements about a different fire with the fatal blaze. After a decade in prison, Jackson won release when an appellate court ruled that the prosecutor deliberately withheld evidence that could have exonerated Jackson at trial. An investigator conducted experiments and concluded that the cause of the fire was not arson but faulty wiring. A civil attorney hired to represent the firefighters' widows later disclosed a report of the investigator that showed that in addition to the initial accidental fire, firefighters deliberately set additional fires in the building in order to aid the families of the deceased firefighters. Citing another judge in a recent case,

the trial judge who dismissed the case and released Jackson said "It is truly a scandal which reflects unfavorably on all participants in the criminal justice system."[69]

- The Dallas District Attorney's office under DA Henry Wade from the 1950s to 1986 had a reputation for getting convictions at any cost. In two nationally known cases, it appeared that truth was of no consequence. Lenell Geter, a black electronics engineer was convicted of a 1982 armed robbery committed in a Dallas suburb. The prosecution relied on "a photo identification by a victim, and ignored testimony from Geter's coworkers at E-Systems that he was at work the entire time the robbery was taking place" sixty miles away. Outraged coworkers convinced CBS-TV's *60 Minutes* to air a segment on this miscarriage of justice. That segment "established the guilt of another man and the likelihood that prosecutors knew Geter was innocent."[70]

  Another notorious Dallas case was that of Randall Dale Adams, sentenced to death in 1977 for the murder of a police officer. His case came to national attention with the release of the 1988 film, "The Thin Blue Line." The film not only exposed the real killer (in prison for another crime), demonstrated Adams complete innocence, and revealed what should have been fatal weaknesses in the evidence against Adams, but "suggests that the prosecutors *knew*" Adams did not kill the officer. Even as the case against Adams unravelled in postappeal procedures, the prosecutor's office resisted releasing Adams.[71]

- Dr. Sam Sheppard was convicted of killing his wife in 1956, in a Cleveland trial that took place in a "circus atmosphere" created by the news media which convicted Sheppard in the headlines well before trial. The police conducted a sloppy investigation and broadcast their evidence to the public. The trial judge utterly failed to control the situation. At the heart of the wrongs in the case, however, was the prosecutorial suppression of evidence contradictory to its case. A defense demand for files and records was ignored. A forensic examination of the crime scene brought out evidence favorable to Sheppard, which the prosecutor ignored. In 1966 the Supreme Court reversed the case (*Sheppard v. Maxwell*, 1966), and in a retrial with a more vigorous and focused defense counsel, F. Lee Bailey, Sheppard was acquitted on a powerful presentation of forensic evidence.[72]

- Pulitzer Prize–winning author Edward Humes recounts in detail the rise of Edward Jagels, a law and order prosecutor in Bakersfield, California, in the 1980s, based on political "dirty tricks" involving the filching of a confidential file from a court. An exemplar of overly aggressive prosecution, the combative Jagels actually reveled in his frequent chastisement by appellate courts for misconduct, knowing that it made him popular with the public. With his active assistance, the criminal justice system in Kern County began one of the first of the extravagant and nightmarish witch hunts of the 1980s that rounded up hundreds of innocent persons accused of child molestation. In total, Kern County authorities investigated more than ten child-molestation "rings," investigating more than two hundred persons, charging eighty-three and convicting forty. Some of the charges involved "over the top" allegations of satanic ritual abuse, a widely believed and never-proved phenomenon in the 1980s. Of these forty convictions, most were overturned and only six remained in prison, three from the only ring "in which a majority of the accused appear to be genuinely guilty. . . . Uniquely, all but one were members of the same household, preying upon their own child relatives." This witch hunt inflicted an enormous amount of human suffering and the disruption of lives.[73]

- The convictions of Rolando Cruz and Alejandro Hernandez in 1983, for the abduction, rape, and murder of ten-year-old Jeanine Nicarico, were so riddled with prosecutorial error that the prosecutors themselves were later charged criminally with misfeasance, a virtually unheard-of turn of events. At three trials of Cruz, DuPage County, Illinois, prosecutors presented evidence that Cruz told police about the crime from a dream that he had, although the detectives had no written report of this account. The police tried to link a boot-print found outside Jeanine's home to Cruz and Hernandez. An evidence technician told the prosecutors that analysis by the Nike shoe company verified that the prints came from a woman's shoe or one that was too small for either Cruz or Hernandez. "The prosecutor put the technician on the witness stand and carefully avoided any mention of shoe size or likely gender. In fact, the defense was not told about the Nike analysis." Even worse, after the first trial, which was overturned on appeal, the real killer, Brian Dugan, a pedophile, came forward and volunteered to this and other murders to avoid the death penalty. Later DNA tests confirmed that Dugan was the killer and showed no evidence that Cruz or Hernandez participated. The prosecutors nevertheless pressed on and obtained a second conviction, which was again overturned. At a third trial before a judge, the various lies of police and prosecutors were exposed, and the case was thrown out after twelve years.

This was followed by an astonishing circumstance. The state assigned a special prosecutor to investigate the prosecution. As a result, three prosecutors and four sheriff's investigators were indicted for perjury and obstruction of justice. Charges against two of the prosecutors were dismissed and the remaining defendants were acquitted. Scheck et al. suggest the reason for the acquittal was the "thin" recollection of grand jurors in the original prosecution of Cruz and Hernandez that there was some testimony about Cruz's "dream" and the suggestion to the jury that if the investigators and prosecutors were convicted, the county would be sued for astronomical sums.[74]

CORRECTING PROSECUTORIAL MISCONDUCT

The prospects for radical change in the way in which prosecutors pursue justice are limited. The elective nature of most prosecutor's offices and the very nature of the adversary system, which relies on the competitiveness of attorneys, will

continue to breed attitudes that stress winning. Even prosecutors who understand the emptiness of conviction rates as a measure of success will do little to downplay this, for to do otherwise would leave the prosecutor vulnerable to electoral defeat. The wider public is not likely to be impressed with internal reforms that allow closer case monitoring. Also, prosecutors who decide to look more closely into the arrests brought to them for charging might antagonize police forces, creating interagency friction and potential political antagonism.

In many of the exonerations that have become common in recent years, prosecutors typically refuse to admit that an error was made. After one such exoneration, the prosecutor said: "'I am not saying loud and clear Rudolph Holton is innocent,' Hillsborough County State Atty. Mark Ober said at a news conference. 'I am saying we cannot prove his guilt beyond a reasonable doubt.'"[75] It is psychologically difficult and professionally costly for prosecutors to admit to incompetence or worse. A prosecutor, who helped to exonerate defendants in their fifth trial as a witness in a neighboring county, was well-positioned to comment on the prosecutorial mind-set. "'As a prosecutor, I knew they'd invested too much in [their] theory to start over,' he said. 'There's a mind-set. The theory fits as well as anything; we're going to stick with it no matter what happens.'"[76] It is easier to hide behind the "not proven" tack, rather than to open up the case and seek the actual culprit. As a result, a double injustice often occurs.

It is highly unlikely, and perhaps unwise, for courts to exercise oversight of the prosecutor's discretionary powers. Appellate courts have exercised a useful if limited role in reversing convictions. Courts, however, have no authority to explore the factual basis of convictions and can only review for legal error. There is no place in the common law system of the United States for a factual review of possibly erroneous verdicts, although commissions to review doubtful convictions have been established in Canada and the United Kingdom.[77]

Prosecutorial misconduct seems to be a real problem that the justice system does not appear to be adequately dealing with at the present time. It is time for prosecutors to take to heart a judge's charge to a jury: "The government always wins when justice is done, regardless of whether the verdict be guilty or not guilty."[78]

SUMMARY

The pretrial process contains numerous steps, involves important constitutional rights, and adds substantial complexity and due process to the prosecution of crimes. The trade-off for this complexity is that cases are thoroughly screened so that, ideally, only those that are based on solid evidence and are deserving of prosecution go forward to trial. Consequently, the government is able to give more formal attention to serious and important cases.

The important processes that occur before trial include: initial appearance, bail hearings, prosecutorial charging, discovery, plea negotiations, grand jury and/or preliminary hearings, and pretrial motion hearings. The decisions rendered at each of these stages can influence prosecutorial discretion to bring a case forward or to forgo further criminal prosecution.

Pretrial release, or bail, is a critical pretrial process. *Stack v. Boyle* held that defendants are entitled to "reasonable" bail that is not out of line with current practices. Disparity in who gets released has led some jurisdictions to develop such reform programs as release on recognizance for indigents who are good risks, and court-run deposit bond systems designed to lower the cost of bonds and eliminate the need for bail bondsmen. At the same time, the federal government passed a preventive detention statute under which suspects may be held without bail prior to trial if they are considered to be a danger to society. In *United States v. Salerno* (1987) the Supreme Court upheld the legality of such measures if there are hearings and proper procedural guidelines to maintain the due process rights of persons held without bail on the prediction that they may commit crimes while on pretrial release.

Following 9/11 more than twelve hundred aliens were apprehended and held in secrecy, often for months. None were involved in terroristic activity. The Supreme Court has held that aliens have some due process protections prior to deportation and cannot be held indefinitely. The USA PATRIOT Act's automatic preventive detention provision, however, seems to contradict this ruling.

Prosecutors have great discretion in bringing criminal charges. As a general rule, courts cannot dismiss charges that they think are unwise, but can dismiss where there is selective or vindictive prosecution. Selective prosecution occurs when a defendant is prosecuted on impermissible grounds, such as race, religion, political beliefs, or for exercising constitutional rights, where the prosecutor's intent is discriminatory. For a dismissal on vindictive prosecution grounds, discriminatory intent need not be proven. It occurs when more serious charges are preferred against a defendant who exercised his or her constitutional rights.

The grand jury is a citizens' institution originated in the common law. It meets in secret to investigate charges and decide whether to indict suspects. It may issue subpoenas to compel persons to testify or supply evidence and request immunity for witnesses who plead the privilege against self-incrimination. Grand juries are criticized for meeting in secret and for being the prosecutor's rubber stamp. The federal constitutional guarantee of prosecution only on indictment by grand jury is not applicable to the states. Proposals for the reform of grand jury procedures include the right of counsel to attend as witnesses' advisors and the right of a target of investigation to attend and voluntarily address the grand jury.

The preliminary examination consists of the presentation of prosecution witnesses before a lower court judge to determine if probable cause exists to bind the defendant over for trial. Preliminary hearings are open to the public; prosecution witnesses can be cross-examined; and defendants have a right to counsel. The preliminary hearing preserves testimony for trial if a witness should become unavailable and may be a way for the defense to discover the strengths and weaknesses of the prosecutor's case as well as factual information.

LEGAL PUZZLES

HOW HAVE COURTS DECIDED THESE CASES?

PREVENTIVE DETENTION

10–1. Jack Ferranti was charged in federal court with an arson resulting in death. He allegedly set fire to a residential building at 11:00 P.M. in which he owned a ground-floor clothing boutique. A firefighter was killed in the fire. The government moved for preventive detention; the hearing, at which witnesses' testimony was proffered, lasted five hours. The following evidence was found to be true. Ferranti lied to the police about his whereabouts on the night of the fire. He was under indictment in another federal court for being a felon in possession of a weapon (a fully loaded, but possibly disabled, .22-caliber revolver). Ferranti directed relatives to intimidate tenants in the numerous buildings that he owned, using a large dog to physically evict tenants. He directed his brother, Mario, to intimidate a mortgagee, Robert Cohen, when Ferranti fell behind on mortgage payments; Cohen threatened to foreclose; shortly thereafter, Cohen was shot in the neck at his home by unidentified men; he promptly sold the mortgages back to Ferranti at a loss. Jack Ferranti ordered Mario Ferranti to terrorize and kill Bruce Bailey, a tenants' rights activist, who was found murdered and his body dismembered.

Does this evidence show, by clear and convincing evidence, that, under the preventive detention act, "no condition or combination of conditions will reasonably assure . . . the safety . . . of the community"?

HELD: Yes

10–1. The fact that the weapon that he was charged with possessing was disabled does not detract from the effect it would have on others; Ferranti's possession of a loaded weapon in a public place at the very least suggests his willingness to use it as a tool for intimidation. The cumulative effect of these acts, established by clear and convincing evidence, was obvious threats to community safety. It is not necessary that the defendant had carried out all of the acts personally; having others carry out his orders still constitutes danger to the community. *United States v. Ferranti*, 66 F.3d 540 (2d Cir 1995)

PREVENTIVE DETENTION

10–2. El-Hage, arrested in 1998 in the United States, was charged with participating in conspiracies to kill U.S. citizens and destroy U.S. property abroad as a key participant in Al Qaeda (the Base). He was also charged with twenty counts of perjury before a grand jury. El-Hage, a native of Lebanon, is a U.S. citizen, residing in Texas with his wife and seven children, who appeared for both of his grand jury hearings. He was one of Osama Bin-Laden's trusted associates, privy to Al Qaeda's secrets and plans.

The indictment alleged acts of training for guerilla warfare and military and intelligence training involving assassination, kidnapping, and the acquisition of weapons and explosives.

The acts were linked to the killing of eighteen American military men in Mogadishu, Somalia, in 1993 and the bombing of U.S. embassies in Nairobi, Kenya, and Dar es Salaam, Tanzania, causing hundreds of deaths.

El-Hage was denied bail by a federal district judge on the ground of risk of flight, without reaching the issue of dangerousness, relying on his foreign ties and extensive foreign travel, a failure to appear on a minor bad check charge in Texas, the perjury charges, and the gravity of the then-unindicted accusations against him. El-Hage has been a frequent traveler to Afghanistan, Pakistan, Sudan, Kenya, the United States, and other countries. He has demonstrated access to false travel documents.

His pretrial confinement will be for thirty to thirty-three months from arrest to the expected trial date. The first fifteen months were spent in solitary confinement. He is permitted three calls a month to his family. The underlying case is exceptionally complex; discovery and trial preparation are of necessity extremely time consuming for both sides. The district court did not find any delay attributable to the government. El-Hage declares that, despite reams of exhibits, there is not a single witness who can state directly that the defendant was a member of Al Qaeda.

1. Are El-Hage's due process rights denied because he has been denied the right to participate in the preparation of his defense?
2. Is his pretrial confinement so long that it has become punishment?

Holding available from instructor

SELECTIVE PROSECUTION

10–3. Frank Smith and Connie Tyree were convicted of multiple counts of voting more than once in a federal election and casting fraudulent absentee ballots in the names of voters without the voters' knowledge and consent. They claim to be victims of selective prosecution, in that they were prosecuted because they are black *and* belong to the Alabama New South Coalition (ANSC), which is predominantly made up of black voters. They claim that members of a rival political faction, the Citizens for a Better Greene County (CBGC), black and white, committed similar acts but were not prosecuted because CBGC represented the predominantly white power elite. The evidence indicated that Tyree had fraudulently applied for and cast absentee ballots in the names of seven named voters and that Smith had done so for three voters. The defendants point to two white individuals affiliated with CBGC who harassed voters and handled absentee ballots at the post office.

There is some evidence (not necessarily clear) in the FBI reports that absentee ballots, other than those involved in the Smith and Tyree cases, were voted in the name of someone who said that he did not cast it. In four of these instances, single individuals witnessed two ballots, and the voters in whose names the ballots were cast told the FBI that they did not vote. Another eight individuals witnessed one ballot each in the name of a voter who stated that he did not vote. Those individuals may have committed the same type of crimes as the defendants.

Did Smith and Tyree establish selective prosecution?

Holding available from instructor

VINDICTIVE PROSECUTION

10–4. Henry Peterson pled *nolo contendere* in a Rhode Island state court to possession with intent to distribute controlled substances, namely five grams of crack cocaine and some marijuana. He also pled to firearm possession after conviction for a crime of violence, and possession of stolen goods. He received a ten-year sentence, seven years of which were suspended.

Federal prosecutors, apparently dissatisfied with the length of the state sentence, then sought indictment under federal narcotics and firearms law. At trial, the defense rested without offering evidence. Peterson was ultimately convicted on all five counts, including two counts of being a felon in possession of a firearm. Based on three prior state convictions for breaking and entering, he was sentenced as an armed career criminal, which provides for a fifteen-year minimum sentence.

Peterson claims that the federal prosecutor engaged in vindictive prosecution. [Note: under the dual sovereignty doctrine, the federal prosecution for drug possession after a state conviction for the same acts does not violate the Fifth Amendment Double Jeopardy Clause.]

Did the federal prosecutor engage in vindictive prosecution?

Holding available from instructor

FURTHER READING

Milton Heumann, *Plea Bargaining: The Experience of Prosecutors, Judges, and Defense Attorneys* (Chicago: University of Chicago Press, 1979).

Jim McGee and Brian Duffy, *Main Justice: The Men and Women Who Enforce the Nation's Criminal Laws and Guard Its Civil Liberties* (New York: Simon and Schuster, 1996).

H. Richard Uviller, *Virtual Justice: The Flawed Prosecution of Crime in America* (New Haven: Yale University Press, 1996).

ENDNOTES

1. U.S. Department of Justice, Bureau of Justice Statistics, *Federal Criminal Case Processing, 2001: With Trends 1982–2001* (NCJ 197104, January 2002), 1. The prosecutor's decision to dismiss a case is complex. See Frank W. Miller, *Prosecution: The Decisions to Charge a Suspect with a Crime* (Boston: Little, Brown, 1969).
2. Ibid.
3. Gerard Rainville and Brian A. Reaves, *Felony Defendants in Large Urban Counties, 2000* (U.S. Department of Justice, Bureau of Justice Statistics; NCJ 202021, December 2003), 24, Table 23.
4. Ibid., 24.

5. American Bar Association, *Standards for Criminal Justice: The Prosecution Function*, 3rd ed., Standard 3(a) (1993).

6. Peter J. Henning, "Prosecutorial Misconduct in Grand Jury Investigations," *South Carolina Law Review* 51 (1999): 1–61.

7. Joshua Dressler and George C. Thomas, III, *Criminal Procedure: Principles, Policies and Perspectives*, 2nd ed. (West Group, 2003), 820.

8. Ibid.

9. Albert W. Alschuler, "Implementing the Criminal Defendant's Right to Trial: Alternatives to the Plea Bargaining System," *University of Chicago Law Review* 50 (1983): 931–1050.

10. "A fourth of defendants had their case adjudicated within 1 month of arrest, and half within 3 months. At the end of the one year study period 86% of all cases had been adjudicated." *Felony Defendants* by Rainville and Reaves, iv. See p. 23 for details.

11. Malcolm M. Feeley, "Plea Bargaining and the Structure of the Criminal Process," *Justice System Journal* 7 (1982): 338–55.

12. *United States v. Abrahams*, 575 F.2d 3 (1st Cir. 1978).

13. Jonathan Drimmer, "When Man Hunts Man: The Rights and Duties of Bounty Hunters in the American Criminal Justice System," *Houston Law Review* 33 (1996): 731–93.

14. William Glaberson, "'Lie or Die'—Aftermath of a Murder; Justice, Safety and the System: A Witness Is Slain in Brooklyn," *New York Times*, July 6, 2003.

15. Ibid.

16. Peter Finn and Kerry Murphy Healy, *Preventing Gang- and Drug-Related Witness Intimidation* (U.S. DOJ, National Institute of Justice, NCJ 163067, November 1996), 5.

17. William Glaberson, "Bill to Bolster Protection of Witnesses Gets Backing," *New York Times*, December 13, 2003.

18. Stephen J. Schulhofer, *The Enemy Within: Intelligence Gathering, Law Enforcement, and Civil Liberties in the Wake of September 11* (New York: Century Foundation Press, 2000), 11.

19. Adam Liptak, Neil A. Lewis, and Benjamin Weiser, "After Sept. 11, a Legal Battle on the Limits of Civil Liberty," *New York Times*, August 4, 2002.

20. Ibid.

21. Ibid.

22. Eric Lichtblau, "U.S. Report Faults the Roundup of Illegal Immigrants after 9/11," *New York Times*, June 3, 2003.

23. *Detroit Free Press v. Ashcroft*, 303 F.3d 681 (6th Cir. 2002).

24. Adam Clymer, "Government Openness at Issue as Bush Holds on to Records, " *New York Times*, January 3, 2003.

25. Rachel L. Swarns, "U.S. Deports Charity Leader in Visa Dispute," *New York Times*, July 16, 2003.

26. See *Immigration and Naturalization Service v. Lopez-Mendoza* (1984).

27. The Illegal Immigration Reform and Immigrant Responsibility Act of 1996. See Shirin Sinnar, "Note: Patriotic or Unconstitutional? The Mandatory Detention of Aliens under the USA PATRIOT Act," *Stanford Law Review* 55 (2003): 1419–1456.

28. Sinnar, "Patriotic or Unconstitutional?" 1422.

29. Sinnar, "Patriotic or Unconstitutional?" 1423.

30. *Matthews v. Eldridge* (1976), cited in Sinnar, "Patriotic or Unconstitutional?" 1437–38.

31. Sinnar, "Patriotic or Unconstitutional?" 1439.

32. Sinnar, "Patriotic or Unconstitutional?" 1442.

33. Sinnar, "Patriotic or Unconstitutional?" 1441, 1454.

34. *United States v. Williams*, 47 F.3d 658 (4th Cir. 1995) (plea bargaining); *United States v. Schweihs*, 971 F.2d 1302 (7th Cir. 1992) (immunity grant).

35. Deborah Emerson, *Grand Jury Reform: A Review of Key Issues* (Washington, D.C.: Dept. of Justice, National Institute of Justice, 1983).

36. 342 F.2d 167 (5th Cir. 1965).

37. Sarah Kershaw, "In Plea Deal That Spares His Life, Man Admits Killing 48 Women," *New York Times*, November 6, 2003.

38. L. L. Brasier and Alison Young, "Verdict Is In: Thompson Is Out Attorney Gorcyca, and Kevorkian, Beat Prosecutor," *Detroit Free Press*, August 7, 1996.

39. Steven Kaplan, "District Courts: Preliminary Examination Issues" *Michigan Bar Journal* 75 (February 1996): 144.

40. John H. Langbein, "The Criminal Trial Before the Lawyers," *University of Chicago Law Review* 45 (1978): 263–316.

41. *United States v. Gurule*, 437 F.2d 239 (10th Cir. 1970).

42. Federal Rules of Criminal Procedure 6(e)(3).

43. Marvin E. Frankel and Gary P. Naftalis, *The Grand Jury: An Institution on Trial* (New York: Hill & Wang, 1977).

44. Barry Winograd and Martin Fassler, "The Political Question," *Trial Magazine*, January/February 1973, 16–20.

45. William J. Campbell, "Eliminate the Grand Jury," *Journal of Criminal Law and Criminology* 64 (1973): 174.

46. Bureau of Justice Statistics, *Report to the Nation on Crime and Justice*, 2d ed. (Washington, D.C.: U.S. Department of Justice, 1988), 72.

47. Ibid., 72.

48. Thomas P. Sullivan and Robert D. Nachman, "If It Ain't Broke, Don't Fix It: Why the Grand Jury's Accusatory Function Should Not Be Changed," *Journal of Criminal Law and Criminology* 75 (1984): 1047–69.

49. See Federal Magistrate's Act, 18 U.S.C. §3060; Rules 5 and 5.1 of the Federal Rules of Criminal Procedure.

50. Rule 5(d). The conduct of the preliminary examination is guided by Rule 5.1.

51. Federal Rules of Criminal Procedure 5(d). See *Sciortino v. Zampano*, 385 F.2d 132 (2d Cir. 1967); *United States v. Quinn*, 357 F. Supp. 1348 (N.D. Ga. 1973), holding that if an indictment is obtained *during* the conduct of a preliminary examination, the examination must be terminated; Yale Kamisar, Wayne R. LaFave, and Jerold H. Israel, *Modern Criminal Procedure*, 6th ed. (St. Paul: West Publishing, 1986), 944; *People v. Duncan*, 201 N.W.2d 629 (Mich. 1972).

52. *Coleman v. Burnett*, 477 F.2d 1187 (D.C. Cir. 1973).

53. Robert Jackson, "The Federal Prosecutor," *Journal of the American Institute of Criminal Law and Criminology* 31 (1940): 3–6; Lyn Morton, "Seeking the Elusive Remedy for Prosecutorial Misconduct: Suppression, Dismissal, or Discipline?" *Georgetown Journal of Legal Ethics* 7 (1994): 1083–1116.

54. Rory K. Little, "Proportionality as an Ethical Precept for Prosecutors in Their Investigative Role," *Fordham Law Review* 68 (1999): 723–770.

55. Henning, "Prosecutorial Misconduct in Grand Jury Investigations."

56. Richard H. Frost, *The Mooney Case* (Stanford: Stanford University Press, 1968).

57. "Given the assortment of interactions between prosecutors, defendants, and defense counsel, it should not be surprising that the term 'prosecutorial misconduct' does not describe any particular type of act or category of violation." "Prosecutorial Misconduct and Constitutional Remedies," by Peter J. Henning, *Washington University Law Quarterly* 77 (1999): 713–833.

58. See Bennett L. Gershman, *Prosecutorial Misconduct* (Deerfield, IL: Clark Boardman Callaghan, 1995).

59. Henning, "Prosecutorial Misconduct and Constitutional Remedies," 721–22.

60. Jackson, "Federal Prosecutor," 4.

61. Barry Scheck, Peter Neufeld, and Jim Dwyer, *Actual Innocence: When Justice Goes Wrong and How to Make It Right* (New York: Signet, 2001), 361.

62. James S. Liebman, Jeffrey Fagan, Valerie West, and Jonathan Lloyd, "Capital Attrition: Error Rates in Capital Cases, 1973–1995," *Texas Law Review* 78 (2000): 1839–1865.

63. C. Ronald Huff, Arye Rattner, and Edward Sagarin, Convicted but Innocent: Wrongful Conviction and Public Policy (Thousand Oaks, CA: Sage, 1996), 64, 70–73.

64. Edwin Borchard, *Convicting the Innocent; Sixty-five Actual Errors of Criminal Justice* (Garden City, NY: Garden City Pub. Co., 1932), xv.

65. Innocence Project, http://www.innocenceproject.org/ (accessed January 6, 2004).

66. George Castelle and Elizabeth Loftus, "Misinformation and Wrongful Convictions" in *Wrongly Convicted: Perspectives on Failed Justice* by Saundra D. Westervelt and John A. Humphrey (New Brunswick, NJ: Rutgers University Press, 2001), 18.

67. Brian Forst, *Errors of Justice: Nature, Sources and Remedies* (Cambridge University Press, 2004), 3–6. Forst defines errors of justice as *both* the conviction of innocent parties and sanctions against the guilty that are less than optimal, including failures to prosecute guilty parties whose cases are not properly dismissed on the grounds of justice, e.g., trivial offenses.

68. Forst, *Errors of Justice*, 112.

69. Scott Christianson, *Innocent: Inside Wrongful Conviction Cases* (New York: New York University Press, 2004), 144–47; *People v. Jackson*, 154 Misc.2d 718, 593 N.Y.S.2d 410 (Sup. Ct. Kings. Co. 1992).

70. Richard L. Fricker, "Crime and Punishment in Dallas," *American Bar Association Journal* 75 (July 1989): 52.

71. Ibid.; Randall Dale Adams, William Hoffer, Marilyn Mona Hoffer, *Adams v. Texas* (New York: St. Martin's Press, 1991).

72. James Neff, *The Wrong Man: The Final Verdict on the Dr. Sam Sheppard Murder Case* (New York: Random House, 2001).

73. Edward Humes, *Mean Justice* (New York: Simon & Schuster, 1999), 451 (see pp. 128–140, 205, 228, 361–380).

74. Barry Scheck, Peter Neufeld, and Jim Dwyer, *Actual Innocence: When Justice Goes Wrong and How to Make It Right* (New York: Signet, 2001), 226–232.

75. Steve Mills and Maurice Possley, "Officials Often Insist Ex-inmates Are Guilty: Authorities Often Slow to Admit Mistakes," *Chicago Tribune*, October 27, 2003.

76. Ibid.

77. David Horan, "The Innocence Commission: An Independent Review Board for Wrongful Convictions," *Northern Illinois University Law Review* 20 (2000): 9–189.

78. Kenneth Bresler, "'I Never Lost a Trial': When Prosecutors Keep Score of Criminal Convictions," *Georgetown Journal of Legal Ethics* 9 (1996): 537–46.

JUSTICES OF THE SUPREME COURT

REAGAN'S CONSERVATIVE LEGACY
O'CONNOR—SCALIA—KENNEDY

Ronald Reagan's presidency capped off a dramatic political shift whereby the conservative wing of the Republican Party became dominant and sought to transform American politics as deeply as had President Roosevelt in the 1930s. Although the Senate was controlled by Republicans at the onset of the Reagan years, the Congress reverted to Democratic hands, and the sweep of the Reagan revolution was not complete. The greatest Reagan victories were in economic deregulation and a military buildup. The ideologically far-right social agenda of some conservatives has never been fully achieved. Still, the shift to the right has been felt in the Supreme Court to which Reagan appointed three justices—including the first female justice, Sandra Day O'Connor.

President Reagan's three successful Supreme Court nominees joined the Burger Court, which was better de-

scribed as moderate than conservative. Justice Antonin Scalia was a brilliant academic and judicial supporter of conservative economic theories before being named to the Court. Justice Anthony Kennedy was a low-keyed and popular nominee after President Reagan's tumultuous failed attempts to have Judge Robert Bork and then Judge Douglas Ginsberg named to the Court.

Justices O'Connor, Scalia, and Kennedy are highly rated for their judicial craft and acuity. While each has voted for the prosecution far more often than for the defense, they do not vote in lockstep, and each has displayed independence in evaluating the facts and doctrines of criminal procedure cases, leading each to decide specific cases for the individual on the basis of carefully reasoned criteria.

SANDRA DAY O'CONNOR

Arizona 1930–

Republican

Appointed by
Ronald Reagan

Years of Service:
1981–

Collection of the Supreme Court of the United States. Photographer: Dane Penland

LIFE AND CAREER Justice O'Connor holds the distinction of being the first woman appointed to the Supreme Court. She graduated *magna cum laude* from Stanford University and was third in the 1952 Stanford Law School class in which William Rehnquist graduated first. Despite her academic attainments, she received no offers from private firms because of the gender bias of that era. She worked as a county attorney in San Mateo, California; as a civilian attorney for the Army while her husband served; and in private practice while raising a family in Phoenix, Arizona. Active in civic and political activities—and described as a "mainstream pragmatic Republican"—O'Connor served as assistant attorney general of Arizona from 1965 to 1969. She was appointed and then elected twice to the Arizona Senate, rising to Senate majority leader before becoming judge of the Maricopa County Superior Court in 1974 and judge of the Arizona Intermediate Court of Appeals in 1979.

CONTRIBUTION TO CRIMINAL PROCEDURE Her position is generally conservative. In right-to-counsel cases, she found no constitutional violation by the forfeiture of funds to pay for counsel (*Caplin & Drysdale v. United States*, 1989). Her opinion in *Moran v. Burbine* held that the fact that an attorney has been retained and is attempting to reach a suspect does not affect the voluntariness of a confession given after *Miranda* warnings have been read and the suspect has waived the right to remain silent.

In *Illinois v. Krull* (1987) O'Connor dissented from a ruling that evidence of an illegal search based on the good-faith reliance on a statute is admissible. Although she joined the conservative majority in *Leon* (1984), holding illegal evidence seized in a good-faith reliance on a bad warrant is admissible, her experience as a legislator led her to distinguish a warrant from a statute. A legislature's "unreasonable authorization may affect thousands or millions," while a magistrate's error only affects the individual involved, and legislators are more subject to "political pressures that may threaten Fourth Amendment values" than are judges.

SIGNATURE OPINION *Strickland v. Washington* (1984). While holding that a defendant's Sixth Amendment right to counsel can be violated by the ineffective assistance of counsel, she formulated a weak standard which requires a defendant to show a serious deficiency in an attorney's performance and also requires that this performance was responsible for the verdict or sentence.

ASSESSMENT She came to the Supreme Court with a moderate to conservative record, supporting the death penalty, having a mixed position on abortion, and in favor of the Equal Rights Amendment and other proposals to equalize the legal

(Continued)

position of women. In general, these policies have characterized her votes as a justice. Her judicial philosophy downplays broad ideological positions. As a *judicial* conservative, she seeks to avoid constitutional issues where possible and changes the law in incremental steps. This lawyer-like approach has anchored the law in precedent and to the facts of cases and prevented a radical conservative legal revolution that Justices Scalia and Thomas would be willing to lead. O'Connor often influences the law through concurring opinions, by joining the conservative majority in high-visibility areas such as abortion, the death penalty, and church-state relations, but preventing it from establishing sweeping doctrines. For example, she has voted to allow the states to place some restrictions on abortions but has voted against overturning *Roe v. Wade* (1973). In the church-state area, her concept that Christmas season displays that are predominantly secular are permissible under the First Amendment has become the Court's position.

FURTHER READING

Nancy Maveety, *Justice Sandra Day O'Connor: Strategist on the Supreme Court* (Lanham, MD: Rowman & Littlefield, 1996).

ANTONIN SCALIA

New Jersey 1936–

Republican

Appointed by Ronald Reagan

Years of Service: 1986–

Collection of the Supreme Court of the United States. Photographer: Joseph Lavenburg

LIFE AND CAREER Antonin Scalia, the son of a Sicilian immigrant and professor of romance languages at Brooklyn College, was a superb student, graduating first in his class from Xavier High School and Georgetown University. He was an editor on the *Harvard Law Review* and received his law degree from Harvard Law School in 1960. His strong conservative beliefs were pronounced even as a schoolboy. He practiced corporate law; taught at the University of Virginia Law School; and from 1971 to 1977, held several key appointments on legal advisory staffs to Presidents Nixon and Ford, including assistant attorney general in charge of the Justice Department's Office of Legal Counsel. He spent a year as scholar-in-residence at the American Enterprise Institute, a conservative think tank; four years as law professor at the University of Chicago; and

was appointed to the U.S. Court of Appeals for the District of Columbia in 1982.

Scalia was a leading conservative spokesperson on issues of law and economics, asserting the power of the executive branch, favoring judicial restraint, and backing deregulation of the marketplace; he blasted judicially supported affirmative action programs. These positions were evident in many of his opinions on the Court of Appeals. His opinions were forceful, and when he was appointed to replace Justice Rehnquist (who was elevated to the office of Chief Justice) it was thought that his charm and powers of persuasion would solidify a conservative court that would overturn *Roe v. Wade*. His nomination sailed through the Senate and he was confirmed by a 98-to-0 vote.

CONTRIBUTION TO CRIMINAL PROCEDURE His position in criminal procedure has proven to be something of a surprise. While hardly a liberal—most of his criminal law votes favor the prosecution—he has, on several occasions, taken positions where the logic of the law lead him to support the defendant. These include his opinion in *Arizona v. Hicks* (1987) (a slight movement of property to view a serial number constitutes a search) and dissenting opinions in *Nat'l Treasury Emp. Union v. Von Raab* (1989) (automatic drug testing of every customs officer is not based on a real need but on political motivations and violates the Fourth Amendment) and *Maryland v. Craig* (1990) (placing a screen between a defendant and an accuser who is a minor violates the Sixth Amendment confrontation clause).

His many pro-prosecution opinions include *Wyoming v. Houghton* (1999) (police can search handbag of passenger of stopped car, where probable cause to search car exists, despite lack of suspicion against the passenger); *Whren v. United States* (1996) (pretext search of automobile upheld); and *Vernonia School District 47J v. Acton* (1995) (special needs allows drug testing of every public high school student athlete).

SIGNATURE OPINION *California v. Hodari D.* (1991). A youth fleeing from the police threw away drugs before being tackled. For the Court, Scalia wrote that there was no stop or arrest before the youth was physically seized; the drugs were, therefore, abandoned and admissible into evidence. To reach this result, he set aside the existing rule that a person is seized when she reasonably believes she is not free to leave and replaced it with the physical restraint standard.

ASSESSMENT Scalia is a leading intellectual on the Court and has been instrumental in the Court reviving the rights of property owners against government regulation. His votes are generally conservative in First Amendment and other civil rights areas, although less so than Rehnquist and Thomas. He is known for his opinions and writings that argue that the plain text of statutes should be the leading principle as to their interpretation and wary of legislative history as a guide to statutory interpretation. He has been a lone dissenter on the question of the separation of powers where he believes that sharp lines must be drawn between the branches of government and thus voted against the constitutionality of the U.S. Sentencing Commission on which judges and executive appointees join to set policy.

FURTHER READING

David A. Schultz and Christopher E. Smith, *The Jurisprudential Vision of Justice Antonin Scalia* (Lanham, MD: Rowman & Littlefield, 1996).

ANTHONY KENNEDY

California 1936–

Republican

Appointed by Ronald Reagan

Years of Service: 1988–

Collection of the Supreme Court of the United States. Photographer: Joseph Bailey

LIFE AND CAREER   A Sacramento, California, native, Kennedy graduated from Stanford University (member of Phi Beta Kappa) and graduated *cum laude* from Harvard Law School in 1961. He practiced law in San Francisco and took over his father's Sacramento law and lobbying practice in 1963. His approach to law practice was scholarly, and for twenty-three years he taught law part-time at the McGeorge School of Law. He came to Governor Reagan's attention in 1971 by drafting a tax-limitation amendment that was the forerunner of California's famous Proposition 13. On Reagan's recommendation, he was appointed to the Ninth Circuit Court of Appeals in 1975 by President Ford.

Kennedy was a respected federal judge, who upheld precedent, carefully considered all sides of a case before rendering a decision, and in civil rights cases generally did not find in favor of women, minorities, or homosexuals. His decision declaring the "legislative veto" unconstitutional (i.e., Congress delegates power to administrative agencies to over-rule agency rules) was upheld by the Supreme Court.

He was quickly confirmed as associate justice after the monumental battle that blocked President Reagan's nomina-tion of Robert Bork to the Supreme Court and the failed attempt to have a second nominee, Judge Douglas Ginsburg, approved.

CONTRIBUTION TO CRIMINAL PROCEDURE   In most cases, Kennedy votes for the government and against the individual. He has voted to uphold the drug courier profile as a basis for a *Terry* stop, to find that ambiguity in a *Miranda* warning does not void a confession, that a judge can deny a defendant's free choice of attorney on grounds of conflict of interest over the defendant's objections, and that a helicopter overflight of a residential backyard is not a search. In *Skinner v. Railway Labor Executives' Association* (1989) and *National Treasury Employees Union v. Von Raab* (1989) he upheld drug testing on the basis of the special needs doctrine.

SIGNATURE OPINION   *Powers v. Ohio* (1991). A prosecutor used peremptory challenges to keep seven blacks off the jury in a murder trial. For the majority, Justice Kennedy held that a white defendant could object. He wrote, "Jury service is an exercise of responsible citizenship by all members of the community, including those who otherwise might not have the opportunity to contribute to our civic life."

ASSESSMENT   Aside from criminal procedure cases, Justice Kennedy is a conservative moderate who is often aligned with O'Connor and Souter and not with the most conservative wing of the Court (Rehnquist, Scalia, and Thomas). In a pivotal abortion case, he wrote a joint opinion with O'Connor and Souter upholding a woman's right to choose based on the concept of precedent. He held that the burning of the American flag during a protest was protected speech and could not be criminal because the result was compelled by the Constitution. In a case involving the solicitation of funds and distribution of leaflets by members of Hare Krishna at an airport, he joined the moderates on the Court holding that while the solicitation could be banned, the leafleting was protected by the First Amendment. And in *Romer v. Evans* (1996) he wrote for a majority that struck down a state referendum that specifically stated that homosexual orientation could not be a basis for heightened antidiscrimination protection. Kennedy viewed this law as violating the Equal Protection Clause because it singled out a certain class of citizens for disfavored legal status or general hardships.

FURTHER READING

Akhil Reed Amar, "Justice Kennedy and the Ideal of Equality," *Pacific Law Journal* 28 (1997): 515–32.

CHAPTER
11

THE TRIAL PROCESS

[T]here are principles of liberty and justice, lying at the foundation of our civil and political institutions, which no State can violate consistently with that due process of law required by the Fourteenth Amendment in proceedings involving life, liberty, or property.

—Justice John Marshall Harlan I, dissenting, *Hurtado v. California*, 110 U.S. 516, 546 (1884)

CHAPTER OUTLINE

KEY TERMS AND PHRASES

Abuse of discretion

Accusatorial trial system

Adversarial trial system

Adverse comment

Bench trial

Challenge for cause

Common law justice system

Compulsory process

Confrontation Clause

Cross-examination

Expert witness

Hearsay evidence

In camera

Inquisitorial justice system

Inquisitorial trial

Invidious discrimination

Jury deliberation

Jury pool

Jury trial

"Key Man" method

Master jury list

Peremptory challenges

Petty crime

Presumption of innocence

Reasonable doubt

Representative cross-section

Subpoena

Venire

Verdict

Voir dire

Waiver trial

THE IDEAL OF THE FAIR TRIAL

All cultures develop some kind of trial process to ascertain the guilt of those accused of committing crimes. Even when offenders are caught "red handed," there seems to be a human tendency to conduct a formal process by which guilt can be formally declared. The trial, therefore, has two functions. The first is to ascertain the guilt of a suspect in a practical and efficient manner. The second is to provide a formal setting that solemnizes the conclusion that *this* person is guilty and must be punished. In the Anglo-American legal tradition, this institution is the **jury trial.**[1] Trial by jury was not legislated into being all at once as the best way to resolve criminal cases. Rather, it evolved over centuries in England. Because of this, many have argued that it is not the most efficient or effective method of separating the guilty from the innocent. Nevertheless, it is solidly embedded in American culture and is guaranteed by Article III and by the Sixth and Seventh amendments of the United States Constitution, as well as by the constitution of every state.

Unlike the English jury trial, the mode of trial used in continental European countries is quite different. These differences began after the Roman Catholic Church, at the Fourth Lateran Council of 1215, forbade priests from participating in trials by ordeal. Ordeals were superstitious appeals to God to decide cases in which evidence pointed to a suspect, but there was no certain proof of guilt. In England the nascent jury used to settle land claims was used in doubtful criminal trials, while on the continent judges modified a method for the inquisition of heretics promulgated by the Church at the Fourth Lateran Council.

Both trial by jury and the **inquisitorial trial** were advances over the superstitious and brutal methods of trial by ordeal. After the seventeenth century, the common law criminal jury trial was extolled as a guarantor of British liberty because in politicized trials citizens resisted authoritarian government pressure and acquitted political opponents of the state.[2] On the other hand, the jury trial has been criticized as inefficient and error prone.[3] Professor John Langbein notes that the conduct of English criminal trials before lawyers regularly defended suspects (about 1750) left much to be desired. The defendant had to defend himself and the jury sat through as many as twenty trials a day, each typically lasting about half an hour. Decisions were made on groups of cases in open court. The judge dominated the jury and could openly influence its **verdict.**[4]

Although these earlier trials were inferior to modern standards of due process, a sense of fair play prevailed. The English maxim—*it is better that twenty guilty go free than one innocent be convicted*—sums up the common law attitude to criminal justice. As a result, English common law trials did not use torture, unlike continental inquisitorial trials prior to the eighteenth century. At the core of the **adversarial trial system** is the idea of a fair fight, one in which the defendant is given a full opportunity to challenge the prosecution, to present witnesses, to confront the accusers, to cross-examine them, and to present the case to an impartial group of legal equals. The prosecutor, further, has a very high burden of proof—proof beyond a reasonable doubt. In the forum of the trial court, the prosecutor is simply another party before an impartial judge and has no special status. Despite its glorious history and high repute, unpopular verdicts and the knowledge that many innocent persons have been convicted has raised serious doubts about the ability of the jury trial to achieve fair verdicts.

Barton Ingraham notes that in the **common law justice system** and the **inquisitorial justice system,** trials are generally *open to the public* and play an expressive as well as a functional role:

> Legal systems to determine guilt are fundamentally different from administrative methods of determining facts, which can be carried out secretly, but with accuracy and impartiality, by police or other investigators. Legal proceedings, however, must give the appearance of being fair and accurate, and the best way—perhaps the only way—to give that appearance is by allowing the community either to witness the process through which the decision is made or to participate in some way. This lends the proceeding legitimacy, avoids suspicion and rumor of official prejudice and arbitrariness, and gives the public a feeling of security. In the second place, public adjudication proceedings perform an important function in the administration of criminal justice which cannot be achieved by administrative fact-finding: they dramatize moral issues and inform the public of the sad consequences which attend violation of the law. Through their public ceremonies adjudication proceedings condemn, educate, and deter.[5]

A brief comparison of the two trial systems will sharpen an understanding of the jury trial.

COMPARING ADVERSARIAL AND INQUISITORIAL TRIALS Jury trials in the United States, England, and former English colonies are central to the "common law" system of justice. As noted in Chapter 1, judge-made law is a central feature of the common law. European criminal trials, typically conducted before professional judges, derive from the "civil" or "Roman" system of justice, in which law derives from a code promulgated by the state. Common law trials are accusatorial or adversarial, while civil law trials, which are the norm in most countries of the world except for those colonized by England, are said to be inquisitorial.[6]

The most obvious difference is that (1) in the common law trial, a group of *ordinary citizens,* the jury, chosen to hear one or a few cases, makes the key determination as to what happened, and then disperse back into the population. They are the sole triers of fact. In the inquisitorial mode of trial, both the law and the facts are decided by trained *professional judges,* although in recent times European countries have allowed citizens to participate in assisting judges in fact finding. (2) Another difference is that English and American judges are drawn from the ranks of *practicing lawyers,* while inquisitorial judges are highly trained, lifelong *career professionals.* (3) Common law trials are based primarily on *oral testimony* that, ideally, should be heard in a continuous process. Written or physical evidence has to be introduced with testimony as to its authenticity. Inquisitorial trials allow the introduction of written or documentary evidence to a greater extent. The investigation file, or *dossier,* is the focus of the inquisitorial trial. Minor cases in the inquisitorial system can be tried largely upon documentary evidence. (4) The *judge* is the central actor in the inquisitorial trial. The judge "runs" the trial, conducts most of the questioning, and shapes the introduction of evidence. The common law judge, by contrast, is more of a *referee,* who decides whether the lawyers are in error and occasionally supplements the questions of attorneys with his or her own. (5) The *privilege against self-incrimination* exists in both systems. In practice, defendants usually participate and testify in inquisitorial trials. In American jury trials, defendants often do not testify. Negative inferences may not be drawn from this silence in American trials but are now allowed to be made in England. (6) Today the burden of proof is on the prosecution in both systems and in both the defendant is presumed innocent.

An important distinction between the systems is the centrality of the *search for the truth.* In the modern inquisitorial system, the search for the truth is paramount, while the adversarial trial is multipurposed. Professor Ingraham notes that the adversary system is unique in "the degree to which the question of guilt or innocence is left to the game-playing skills of two adversary lawyers."[7] Because the adversarial jury system supports goals other than the truth of the case, (e.g., suppressing illegally seized evidence in order to deter police and prosecutorial misconduct) it is a better counterweight to political oppression. Whether one system or the other produces more accurate verdicts and is less likely to convict innocent persons is subject to debate.

Steps in the Jury Trial

JURY SELECTION   The two phases of jury selection are selecting the jury pool and **voir dire.** First, the court or a jury commission creates a **master jury list** of all eligible jurors, by methods that produce a statistically accurate cross-section of the community. **Jury pools** are drawn randomly from this list and summoned to serve. At the courthouse, smaller **venires** are chosen and assigned to courtrooms. Second, this venire, which may number from forty prospective jurors to many more in a major case, is seated. The process of voir dire allows the judge, attorneys, or both to question jurors to determine if they are biased. An unlimited number of **challenges for cause** are permitted to eliminate those individuals shown to be biased. A limited number of **peremptory challenges** are granted to each side that allows the attorneys to eliminate jurors for any or no reason, except for the deliberate elimination of jurors on the grounds of race or gender.

OPENING STATEMENTS   Each lawyer outlines the main points of the case to the jury, putting the best interpretation on the case. Both in voir dire and in opening statements, lawyers also try to make good personal impressions on jurors.

PROSECUTOR'S CASE-IN-CHIEF   The heart of the case is the presentation of witnesses who testify as to their personal observations. **Expert witnesses,** on the other hand, are allowed to offer opinions in the areas of their expertise. A witness may also introduce documents or physical evidence. After each witness testifies, the defense may cross-examine the witness in an attempt to discredit the testimony or credibility with the jury. The prosecutor may then ask questions on redirect that are limited to clarifying or rehabilitating the witness on the points specifically raised by **cross-examination.** The job of the prosecutor is to establish guilt at the end of the case. The defense may make a motion at the conclusion of the prosecutor's case-in-chief to dismiss the case on the grounds that proof of guilt has not been established. The motion is typically denied, but may succeed if the prosecutor has not offered proof as to an essential element of the crime. The job of the defense attorney is to raise a **reasonable doubt** as to guilt, and if the defense believes that this has been established through its cross-examination, it may rest its case without calling any witnesses.

DEFENSE CASE-IN-CHIEF   Like the prosecutor, the defense calls witnesses, including expert witnesses. Another type of witness, who may give opinion evidence, is a character witness who may relate the defendant's general reputation for good character. The prosecutor may cross-examine each witness, and redirect is available to the defense.

PROSECUTION REBUTTAL   The prosecutor may offer evidence to refute or contradict evidence that is initially presented by the defendant, most typically evidence of an alibi or insanity.

CLOSING STATEMENTS   The defense attorney first addresses the jury, followed by the prosecutor. The prosecutor has the last word because of the heavy burden of proof. The attorneys bring together the various pieces of testimony and evidence, weaving it together in a coherent and convincing narrative. The prosecutor explains why the evidence indicates that the defendant is guilty beyond a reasonable doubt, while the defense explains why the evidence points to reasonable doubt. Perhaps the most pithy and famous example of reasonable doubt is Johnnie Cochran's exhortation to the jury in the O. J. Simpson murder trial—if the glove doesn't fit, you must acquit.

JURY INSTRUCTIONS   Following the presentation of evidence and closing statements, the judge instructs the jurors on the law by defining and explaining the definitions of the crime's charges, the rules of evidence, and the possible verdicts that are allowed.

JURY DELIBERATIONS   Jurors are sworn to follow the law as instructed by the judge and deliberate in private to review and vote on the case.

VERDICT   The result of deliberations is the jury's verdict. For each count of the indictment, the jury must enter a verdict of either "guilty" or "not guilty." The verdict must be unanimous, except in states that allow a verdict based on a supermajority vote such as 11–1. If a jury is deadlocked, and the vote is lopsided, the judge will admonish holdout jurors not to be rigid, and to reasonably review the evidence as viewed by the majority. If further deliberations do not change the vote, the court declares a hung jury and the case may be retried.

POSTVERDICT MOTIONS   The defense can submit a motion notwithstanding the verdict or motion in arrest of judgment, arguing that the jury could not have reasonably convicted the defendant based on the evidence presented. The defense can also file a motion for a new trial based on the judge's errors in admitting evidence. Such motions are rarely successful.

An actual trial involves more complex preparation, strategy analysis, psychological penetration, and dramatic human action than this list can show.[8]

TRIAL IN A TIME OF TERROR

The United States has upheld the rule of law by trying terrorists in civilian courts under standard rules of criminal procedure. The first jury trial of terrorists to result in verdicts, held in a federal court in Detroit, concluded in June 2003, with the conviction of two defendants of providing material assistance to terrorists, the conviction of another on document fraud charges, and the acquittal of a fourth. Three of the four were arrested six days after the 9/11 attack in a raid on a Dearborn, Michigan, apartment. The men, who were employed at the Detroit Metropolitan Airport, had a cache of forged passports and identification papers, and the sketches of potential terror targets. The fourth defendant, believed to be the leader of the group, Abdel-Ilah Elmardoudi, a Moroccan, was carrying $83,000 when arrested in North Carolina. After the trial, a juror said, "We totally separated 9/11, the war on terrorism. From what we were doing. . . . We were focused on what we had in front of us."[9] These cases are among thirty being prosecuted as of mid-2003.[10] In the Detroit case, Attorney General John Ashcroft twice at press conferences linked the defendants to the 9/11 attack, a link never made by the prosecutors, and thereby violated a gag order laid down by Judge Gerald Rosen. After the trial, Judge Rosen considered holding the Attorney General in contempt, which could have led to his disbarment. Instead, he issued a public, written admonishment to Mr. Ashcroft after the trial. Because his remarks were inadvertent, Ashcroft apologized to the court in writing, and Judge Rosen determined that Ashcroft's violation did not influence the outcome of the trial. In an editorial applauding the judge, the Detroit News wrote:

> [T]he admonishment is fair warning to Ashcroft and the Justice Department. Terrorism is a serious charge and carries serious penalties. Those charged with the offense have every right to expect they will receive a fair trial and all the due process protections afforded them by the Constitution.
>
> Violations of the gag order could have easily led to a mistrial, certainly not an outcome the government desired.
>
> And while Ashcroft has an obligation to keep the public informed, boastful press conferences designed for political hay-making are inappropriate while a trial is ongoing.[11]

This episode points to the risks to the rights of defendants and of overly politicizing highly charged terror trials.

President George W. Bush's authorization of military tribunals has been far more controversial. On November 13, 2001, under his authority as commander in chief of the armed forces, he promulgated a military order establishing military commissions to try noncitizens "for any and all offenses triable by military commission" of persons who engage in or prepare for terrorism, or persons who harbor terrorists. The military commission can use any evidence it deems probative, no matter how it is obtained; can keep classified materials secret; and can convict and sentence defendants to death on a two-thirds vote of the commission members. It appears that civilian defense lawyers can be barred from representing defendants in these tribunals.[12] This order eliminated "whatever jurisdiction federal courts might have by statute and den[ied] federal court access to individuals prosecuted or detained for terrorism."[13] Before 9/11, international and alien terrorists responsible for such acts as the 1993 truck bombing of the World Trade Center or the bombings of U.S. embassies in Africa were tried and convicted in civilian courts in the United States. The Afghan and Iraq wars have shifted the paradigm of response from the criminal model to the war model. Some experts believe that military tribunals are sanctioned by international law and are a lawful and proper way to try captured enemy combatants who have committed war crimes, which might include acts defined as terrorism.[14]

Nevertheless, the government seems to have overreached by its attempt to try a citizen arrested in the United States as an enemy combatant. "On May 8, 2002, Jose Padilla, also known as Abdullah al-Muhajir, was arrested at Chicago O'Hare International Airport. The government suspects that Padilla, a U.S. citizen, was plotting a 'dirty bomb' attack on the United States. On June 9, 2002, the government transferred Padilla to detention at a military base in Virginia pursuant to an order by the President. Padilla was neither charged with a crime nor allowed access to a lawyer."[15] The basis for his detention under military rather than civilian authority was the determination by the president that Padilla was an enemy combatant under his military order. The "central issue" confronting a federal District Court in New York in a habeas corpus challenge by Padilla was "whether the President has the authority to designate as an unlawful combatant an American citizen, captured on American soil, and to detain him without trial."[16] Resolving this issue places two Supreme Court precedents in opposition. *Ex Parte Milligan* (1866) dealt with the detention of a civilian during the Civil War who was

> tried before a military commission on a charge of conspiring against the United States by planning to seize weapons, free Confederate prisoners, and kidnap the governor of Indiana. Convicted and sentenced to death, he filed a habeas corpus petition challenging the jurisdiction of the military commission to try him. The Court set aside the conviction, declaring that the "[laws of war] can never be applied to citizens in states which have upheld the authority of the government, and where the courts are open and their process unobstructed." The Court found that the military commission had unlawfully usurped the judicial function, reasoning that although the President had the

power to suspend the writ of habeas corpus during the Civil War, all other rights remained intact, even in wartime. The Framers, the Court found, "limited the [power of] suspension to one great right [i.e., the right to petition for habeas corpus], and left the rest to remain forever inviolable."[17]

Pitted against *Milligan* is *Ex Parte Quirin* (1942) in which German military men, including a United States citizen, came ashore in the United States and while dressed in civilian clothes undertook to commit acts of sabotage. President Roosevelt established a miliary commission which tried the saboteurs. The Supreme Court upheld the military commission

> Because the *Quirin* Court found that the German saboteurs were not only attempting to harm the United States during an armed conflict but doing so as persons associated with an enemy's armed forces, the Court concluded that the saboteurs, unlike Milligan, could be treated as unlawful combatants. Padilla, like the saboteurs, is alleged to be in active association with an enemy with whom the United States is at war.[18]

The federal district court, giving deference to the political branches of government, found that Padilla's situation was more like Quirin's and has upheld the president's declaration. The court also held that. The case is presently pending appeal.[19]

Unlike the support for the use of military commissions to try persons captured on the battlefields of Afghanistan or Iraq for any war crimes they may have committed, there has been scant support for the government's actions against Padilla. For one thing, declaring him an illegal enemy combatant is in sharp contrast to its treatment of others. Richard Reid, the "shoebomber,"—a British citizen who was caught attempting do blow up a jet liner—was tried and pled guilty in a civilian federal court. His act of attempted terrorism was more immediate than Padilla's, and as an alien, he has less of a claim to be tried in a civilian court. John Walker Lindh, the "American Taliban," is a United States citizen who was captured in Afghanistan by Northern Alliance and American forces, after having had military training in an Al Qaeda camp and having fought on the front lines against the United States. *Ex Parte Quirin* is clear authority for the power of the United States to try him in a military commission, but he, too, was tried in a civilian court and pled guilty. In contrast, Yasser Esam Hamdi, also an American citizen, was captured by American-led forces in a zone of active combat in Afghanistan, and has been remitted to the custody of the military. Zacarias Moussaoui, the "twentieth hijacker," is a French national. He trained with Al Qaeda in Afghanistan, entered the United States with a visa to attend flight school, and was arrested on immigration charges before 9/11. He, too, has been charged in a federal civilian court with conspiracy to commit acts of terrorism.[20]

The fact that World War II was a declared war is not a good basis for distinguishing Padilla's case from that of Quirin, for there were congressional declarations of support for the Afghan and Iraq military actions. Unlike Quirin, who was clearly in the German military and who entered the country secretly, it is not clear that Padilla had. "There is no proof that Padilla has participated in al-Qaeda training camps or actively armed himself in alliance with the Taliban against American troops in the war in Afghanistan."[21] The Courts of the United States are open and have successfully conducted numerous trials of terrorists in the past decade. Although the nation is at risk of attack, "[i]t would be a stretch, in light of precedent, to suggest that all of America is under immediate danger in such a way that any person could be detained indefinitely without constitutional protection."[22]

Commentators, including conservatives, have been deeply concerned that the government had taken the power to declare a citizen subject to secret military trials and continues to press for the denial of counsel to Padilla.[23]

> Surely it's not true that an American citizen can be plucked off the street of his home town and "disappeared" by the government. Can bureaucrats like Attorney General John Ashcroft simply take you off to break rocks indefinitely without ever charging you with a crime, or presenting real evidence against you? Without ever letting you appear before a judge? Without letting you talk to anyone else, ever again?
>
> Nah. That's the kind of thing that happens in the old Soviet Russia—not in America. Right? Well, consider U.S. citizen Jose Padilla: arrested by the FBI in Chicago in May 2002, declared by Ashcroft at a June 2002 press conference in Moscow to be an "enemy combatant," and hauled off to a Pentagon brig in South Carolina. Padilla has an ugly criminal record, but the basis for his indefinite detention without trial is a mere six-page statement by a Pentagon official."[24]

The military spokesperson admitted, however, that one source of information against Padilla subsequently recanted, while another was being treated with drugs, and that their information may have been an attempt to mislead interrogators. It may be more than worrisome that the administration is so strenuously seeking to try a citizen by military commission using such flimsy evidence. In a major series of editorial comments, the conservative *Detroit News* warned in a headline that "assault on procedural rights threatens the safeguards that keep America from becoming a police state."[25] The point is that the government can virtually designate anyone connected with terrorism, including legitimate suspects and defendants, to military tribunals. To disconnect military tribunals from their accepted use creates a dangerous precedent that threatens the liberty of future generations of Americans.

By the beginning of 2004, the Supreme Court has decided to hear the cases of Hamdi and the Guantanamo prisoners, and the Second Circuit Court of Appeals ruled that the government lacked authority to hold Padilla in military custody.[26] The issue of terrorism in our time is headed for a historic resolution in the nation's highest court. Whatever its decision, it will provide a landmark for the limits of government power vis-à-vis personal rights in the United States for some time to come.

IMPORTANT CONSTITUTIONAL TRIAL RIGHTS

The trial is guided by many complex rules of criminal procedure and evidence law. This section presents an overview of some important constitutional trial rights.

The Right to Be Present

A defendant's right to be present at the trial is based on the **Confrontation Clause** of the Sixth Amendment (*Diaz v. United States*, 1912) and on *due process*. A defendant has the right to accompany the jury if it leaves the courtroom briefly to view the scene of the crime. However, in **United States v. Gagnon** (1985) the Court held there was no Sixth Amendment violation when a judge met with a juror and the defense attorney (out of the defendant's presence) in regard to a juror's nervousness caused by the fact that the defendant drew sketches of the jurors during the trial. The defendant's presence at the meeting was not required to ensure fundamental fairness or a reasonable opportunity to conduct the defense. The *Gagnon* rule applies to cases where the defendant is excluded from pretrial evidence suppression hearings.

Secret trials ("kangaroo courts," "star chamber proceedings") are anathema to the **accusatorial trial system** and have been eliminated from United States jurisprudence. The celebrated 1989 trial of Col. Oliver North—for lying to Congress regarding the illegal secret sale of arms to Iran and covert support of the Nicaraguan Contras with the sales proceeds in the 1980s—involved a law designed to avoid secret trials. The *Classified Information Procedures Act* of 1980 balances the open trial guarantee with the need to protect government secrets in prosecutions where classified information is vital evidence. Under the law, the defense may use classified material, but it must notify the prosecutor in advance as to which secrets will be used. The government is then given the opportunity to submit edited statements in place of the disputed documents. If the judge is not satisfied that these statements are fair to the defense, the prosecution is then given the option of allowing the documents to be made public or to drop the charges that bring the secrets to light in the courtroom.[27]

DISRUPTIVE DEFENDANTS   A defendant who behaves in a loud, obnoxious, and disruptive manner cannot force the state to delay or dismiss a case. In **Illinois v. Allen** (1970), Justice Black stated:

> It is essential to the proper administration of criminal justice that dignity, order, and decorum be the hallmarks of all court proceedings in our country. The flagrant disregard in the courtroom of elementary standards of proper conduct should not and cannot be tolerated. We believe trial judges confronted with disruptive, contumacious, stubbornly defiant defendants must be given sufficient discretion to meet the circumstances of each case. No one formula for maintaining the appropriate courtroom atmosphere will be best in all situations. We think there are at least three constitutionally permissible ways for a trial judge to handle an obstreperous defendant like Allen: (1) bind and gag him, thereby keeping him present; (2) cite him for contempt; (3) take him out of the courtroom until he promises to conduct himself properly. (*Illinois v. Allen*, 1970)

A trial judge must first be patient with and admonish a disruptive defendant, explaining that obstructionist tactics will not work, before taking the drastic steps of binding or removal. As communications technology improves, defendants forcibly removed from the courtroom are able to view the trial and communicate with their lawyers from a jail cell by interactive video links.

ABSCONDING DEFENDANTS   A defendant who skips out in the middle of a trial forfeits the right to be present, and the trial may continue in his or her absence. The Supreme Court rejected the argument that for the trial to continue *in absentia,* the judge had to have explicitly warned the defendant about a right to be present. This would add a meaningless formality. Defendants don't have to be told that they are required to be present and that if they abscond, the trial, "where judge, jury, witnesses and lawyers are present and ready to continue," will continue in their absence (*Taylor v. United States,* 1973).

The Right to Compulsory Process

The Sixth Amendment guarantee "to have **compulsory process** for obtaining witnesses in his favor"—the **subpoena** right—is meant to eliminate barriers to relevant testimony that the defendant wishes to offer. A trial would be grossly unfair if only the state, and not the defense, had such power. The right was *incorporated* into the Fourteenth Amendment Due Process Clause in **Washington v. Texas** (1967). Washington was charged with murder for a killing that occurred during an argument. His defense was that he was trying to persuade Fuller, the actual killer, to leave and was not in the room when the gun went off. Fuller had been convicted and was willing to testify in Washington's defense. The state blocked his testimony by relying on a Texas law that forbade an accomplice to testify for another. The Supreme Court held that this law violated the Compulsory Process Clause. A state may prevent some defense testimony under ordinary rules of evidence (e.g., on the grounds that the testimony is irrelevant or incompetent), but may not disallow relevant evidence.

In **Webb v. Texas** (1972) the defendant's only witness was subpoenaed from prison where he was serving a sentence. The trial judge threatened the witness with heavy-handed warnings against committing perjury and said that lying would extend the witness's prison term and be counted against him by the parole board. This so terrified the witness that he refused to testify. The Supreme Court ruled that the trial judge's unnecessarily emphatic warning "drove the witness off the stand." This *due process* violation tended to undermine the subpoena right. In recent years, the Supreme Court has weakened the right to compulsory process.

In **United States v. Valenzuela-Bernal** (1982) the Supreme Court held that the government could deport illegal immigrants before a trial in which they might be called as defense witnesses concerning their being smuggled into the United States. The defense attorney did not even have an opportunity to interview them. The Court felt that the government's legal obligation to swiftly deport aliens, the financial costs of prolonged detention, and the human costs to the detainees were more important than a defendant's Sixth Amendment right to subpoena witnesses.

In **Pennsylvania v. Ritchie** (1987) a father charged with incest sought to subpoena records from Children and Youth

Services (CYS), a protective service agency, claiming that the records were necessary for the defense to cross-examine witnesses. Pennsylvania courts granted the defense request to fully examine the contents of CYS confidential files on the basis of the defendant's confrontation and compulsory process rights. The United States Supreme Court reversed, noting that the Confrontation Clause "does not include the power to require the pretrial disclosure of any and all information that might be useful in contradicting unfavorable testimony." Since the defense counsel was able to cross-examine all prosecution witnesses fully, there was no violation of the Confrontation Clause. Justice Powell, writing for the majority, also noted that Pennsylvania law allowed a court to disclose parts of a youth's record. The Court agreed that Ritchie was entitled to have a trial judge, but not the defense lawyer, review the CYS records to determine which were material. In this way, the defendant's compulsory process right was balanced with "the Commonwealth's compelling interest in protecting its child abuse information." The *Ritchie* rule places much discretion and trust in the judge's hands, but undermines the adversary system of justice that is premised on the understanding that the lawyers are better able to detect favorable facts in a record because they are motivated to do so.

Prosecutorial Misconduct and False Evidence

As noted in Chapter 10, a defendant's right to due process and a fair trial is violated if a prosecutor deliberately introduces *perjured testimony* (*Mooney v. Holohan,* 1935). Post-*Mooney* cases highlight the importance to the fairness of the adversary system of honest prosecutors who check their facts. Prosecutors must have an evenhanded attitude and a desire to achieve the truth rather than to get a conviction at any price. The cases show that cross-examination is effective as a truth-getting device only if trials are conducted honestly.

MISLEADING TESTIMONY   The *Mooney* principle was applied in **Alcorta v. Texas** (1957), which held that due process is violated by introducing evidence that creates a *false impression* regarding a *material fact*, if it was *elicited by the prosecutor with knowledge of its inaccuracy.* *Alcorta* was a prosecution of a jealous husband for murdering his cheating wife. Before the trial, the wife's lover told the prosecutor that he and Alcorta's wife had been sexually intimate. The prosecutor told him not to volunteer such evidence but to answer questions put to him at trial truthfully. At trial, the lover testified that he had not kissed the deceased woman on the night she died, and that he only had a casual affair with her. The truth was disclosed after the defendant was convicted of first-degree murder. This violated Alcorta's due process right to a fair and meaningful trial, even though the prosecutor's actions were not as deliberate as those in *Mooney* and affected the *level* of guilt and punishment rather than a determination of guilt or innocence.

WITNESS CREDIBILITY   In **Napue v. Illinois** (1959) a prosecution witness testified on direct examination that he received no promise of consideration for his testimony. The prosecutor knew this was false and made no effort to correct the falsehood. The lie was not directly material to the issue of guilt, but it undermined the ability of the defense to properly cross-examine by impeaching the witness's credibility. This violated due process.

MISCHARACTERIZING EVIDENCE   In **Miller v. Pate** (1967) an innocent taxi driver was convicted of the rape and murder of a young girl on the basis of red-stained underpants found near the murder scene and a confession that was obtained under duress. At trial, the prosecutor held up the garment and referred to it as "bloody shorts." Only after a lengthy appeal process, during which Miller spent years on Illinois's death row, did forensic tests by the defense disclose that the red stains were paint and not blood. Miller was freed from his decade-long ordeal by a Supreme Court finding that the prosecutor's trial oratory violated due process. The prosecutor must be accurate and check facts.

The rule against the prosecutor injecting false or misleading evidence is strengthened by the pretrial discovery rule of **Brady v. Maryland** (1963), which requires the prosecution to turn over material factual evidence that is favorable to the defendant, although the *Brady* rule has also been watered down by the Supreme Court in recent years.

Due Process and the Preservation of Evidence

Closely related to the *Brady* rule is what may be called the "constitutionally guaranteed access to evidence" (*United States v. Valenzuela-Bernal,* 1982). In two cases, the Supreme Court has ruled against defendants seeking to make the *preservation of evidence* by police a due process requirement. More specifically, the Court has held that Breathalyzer and semen evidence that has not been physically preserved may nevertheless be introduced into evidence against a defendant. In neither case was there any evidence of bad faith on the part of the police in trying to evade the rule that requires the prosecution to turn over factual evidence to the defendant. At the worst, the police were negligent in failing to preserve the evidence.

In **California v. Trombetta** (1984) defendants convicted on evidence of breath alcohol readings challenged their convictions on the ground that their pretrial requests for preserved samples of their breath (which is technically feasible) was denied. The police departments replied that they do not ordinarily preserve breath samples, and made no effort to do so. Trombetta argued that if he had a sample of the test, he could impeach the accuracy of the test. The Court ruled that the introduction of the results of the Breathalyzer tests did not violate a defendant's due process right to a fair trial. An important factor for the holding is that "the chances are extremely low that preserved samples would have been exculpatory." The Breathalyzer test is relatively routine, and if administered properly, there is a low probability that it is inaccurate. Prior cases held that a defendant's due process rights were not violated when evidence was admitted based on preliminary field notes taken by FBI agents (used to prepare a formal report) that were inadvertently destroyed (*Killian v. United States,* 1961). The

YOUNGBLOOD IN THE STATES

Vermont: The state constitution guarantees that a defendant can call for evidence in his or her favor. Under it, the Vermont Supreme Court has rejected the *Youngblood* standard. It is too narrow because it limits due process violations only to instances of bad faith; it is too broad because it imposes sanctions on the prosecution even though the defendant shows no prejudice to his case. The Vermont approach allows the courts to more closely examine the evidence in the case to see whether the defendant's ability to make a defense is substantially undermined. The state's test balances (1) the degree of negligence or bad faith on the part of the government, (2) the importance of the evidence lost, and (3) other evidence of guilt adduced at trial. *State v. Bailey;*[28] *State v. Gibney.*[29]

Court noted that the accuracy of Breathalyzer tests can be generally challenged by defendant counsel. There was a hint that for the Court to impose an administrative requirement on all police departments bordered on the Court exercising its supervisory power.

A more difficult case arose in ***Arizona v. Youngblood*** (1988). Youngblood was identified by the victim in a photo lineup nine days after the abduction and anal sodomy of a 10-year-old boy. Shortly after the assault, a physical at a hospital collected evidence using a "sexual assault kit," including samples of the boy's saliva, blood, and hair, and swabs from the boy's rectum and mouth. Microscopic slides of the samples were made but not examined at any time. The police placed the kit in a secure refrigerator at the police station. At the hospital, the police also collected the boy's underwear and T-shirt. This clothing was not refrigerated or frozen. Ten days after the attack, a state criminalist examined the kit, but not the clothing, to determine that sexual contact had occurred; as a matter of routine, he did not perform any other tests, including a blood group test. Prior to Youngblood's trial, examination of the materials in the kit indicated that the samples were insufficient to supply a saliva comparison or to detect any blood group substances. Approximately fourteen months later, the boy's clothing was examined and two semen stains were found. Because the clothing had not been refrigerated, the semen stains could not yield information as to the blood type of the semen depositor under tests that were available at that time. At his trial, Youngblood argued that the victim's identification was inaccurate, and that he could have proven his innocence if the clothing had been properly refrigerated.

As in *Trombetta*, the state courts in *Youngblood* found that "when identity is an issue at trial and the police permit the destruction of evidence that could eliminate the defendant as the perpetrator, such loss is material to the defense and is a denial of due process." The United States Supreme Court reversed. Again, there was no bad faith attempt by the police to hide evidence from the defendant in order to get around his *Brady* right to disclosure. Although the semen evidence, if properly preserved, might have exonerated Youngblood, the majority noted that the Court had in the past been reluctant to say that the fundamental fairness idea of due process imposed on the police an undifferentiated and absolute duty to retain and to preserve all material that might be of conceivable evidentiary significance in a particular prosecution" (citing *Lisenba v. California*, 1941). Justice Stevens concurred. Because the police had no reason to hide accurate information of the crime, their actions were negligent and not deliberate. The jury was instructed that they could take the missing evidence into account, but they still found Youngblood guilty.

Justice Blackmun dissented, joined by Justices Brennan and Marshall. The main points of his dissent were that (1) the *Brady* line of cases did *not* rest on a prosecutor's bad faith—i.e., any failure to provide evidence was a constitutional wrong, whether done maliciously or negligently; (2) the real test of whether a trial is *fundamentally unfair* is whether the unavailable evidence was "*constitutionally material*"; (3) the *Trombetta* decision relied on the high accuracy level of Breathalyzer tests, so that the breath samples were not constitutionally material; (4) a preserved semen stain could have identified a blood type marker that could clearly have exonerated Youngblood if his semen blood type marker did not match that of the semen on the victim's clothing; therefore, (5) semen evidence is constitutionally material. Justice Blackmun noted that due process must take the burdens on law enforcement into account. In a case such as this, the state could have had the proper and available tests conducted in a timely fashion or could notify the defense that it intends to discard the original evidence and thus, given the defense time to have the evidence tested.

The Youngblood case underscores the vital importance of proper police procedures in preserving evidence. In the 1990s DNA testing became available, allowing tests on small samples of dry body evidence. A DNA test on the preserved semen stain on the unrefrigerated clothing in the Youngblood case showed that he could not have been the attacker of the ten-year-old boy. Youngblood was released from custody in August 2000. One journalist speculated that social prejudice may have played a role in the initial conviction of a "black, one-eyed, homosexual rapist who claimed it was a case of mistaken identity. P.S.: He also walked with a limp." Jane Siegel Greene, executive director of the Innocence Project at the Cardozo School of Law, commenting on the *Youngblood* case noted: "What the case says is that the state has no duty to preserve evidence, and they've based that law, now, on somebody who is actually innocent. So now he's freed, but how many other people like him—because of case law just like Arizona vs. Youngblood—have no access to their evidence."[30]

Right to Silence

The Fifth Amendment right to not "be compelled in any criminal case to be a witness against himself" was held to mean in **Griffin v. California** (1965) (overruling *Adamson v. California,* 1947) that if a defendant in a state trial chooses not to testify, the Constitution strictly forbids the judge or prosecutor from making a comment that allows a jury to draw an adverse inference. This was the federal rule (*Wilson v. United States,* 1893). **Adverse comment** on silence "is a penalty imposed by our courts for exercising a constitutional privilege. It cuts down on the privilege by making its assertion costly. . . . What the jury may infer given no help from the court is one thing. What they may infer when the court solemnizes the silence of the accused into evidence against him is quite another." Further, a prosecutor cannot introduce evidence that a defendant remained silent after being read *Miranda* warnings, to impeach him (**Doyle v. Ohio,** 1976). This due process violation is inconsistent with the implied guarantee that silence in response to the *Miranda* warnings will carry no penalty.

Carter v. Kentucky (1978) ruled, however, that a trial judge, when *requested* by the *defense, must* instruct the jury that the defendant's silence does not lead to a negative inference. Justice Potter Stewart noted in *Carter* that a trial judge has "an affirmative constitutional obligation" to instruct the jury: "No judge can prevent jurors from speculating about why a defendant stands mute in the face of a criminal accusation, but a judge can, and must, if requested to do so, use the unique power of the jury instruction to reduce that speculation to a minimum." On the other hand, **Lakeside v. Oregon** (1978) held that the trial judge can constitutionally give such a protective instruction, *over the objection* of the defense, if he or she believes that to not do so would lead to an *unfair trial*. This ruling places great faith in the ability of trial judges to control their courtrooms and to ensure fair trials.

Confrontation, Hearsay, and Cross-examination

INCORPORATION   The Confrontation Clause was incorporated into the Due Process Clause of the Fourteenth Amendment in **Pointer v. Texas** (1965). *Pointer* held that a witness's statement taken at a preliminary hearing, at which there was *no adequate opportunity for cross-examination* (because the defendant had no lawyer at that point), could not be introduced in the trial. To do so violated Pointer's Sixth Amendment rights. The right to confront witnesses means, among other things, that the defendant must have an opportunity to meaningfully *challenge* the witnesses' assertions, whenever they are made, through the time-honored method of cross-examination.

The confrontation right is fulfilled when the *opportunity* to cross-examine exists. If a defense attorney decides not to cross-examine at a preliminary hearing for tactical reasons, the right is fulfilled. In such case, evidence obtained from a witness who is later unavailable is admissible at trial (**Ohio v. Roberts,** 1980). Also, there is no confrontation violation if the defense

attorney failed to counter a hearsay statement at the preliminary examination by not calling the speaker of the statement to the witness stand at the examination (*Dutton v. Evans,* 1970).

CONFRONTATION, HEARSAY, AND CROSS-EXAMINATION   *Pointer* demonstrates the strong relationship between the confrontation guarantee, the evidentiary rule against **hearsay evidence,** and the chief common law device of ascertaining the truth: cross-examination. The primary reason for the common law rule excluding hearsay evidence (where a witness testifies to something that the witness did not personally observe) from the trial is not its inherent unreliability but the problem that the opposing counsel cannot subject the original witness to cross-examination—the defendant cannot therefore meaningfully confront the one who made the damaging statement.

THE PURPOSE OF CROSS-EXAMINATION   The heart of the adversarial truth-seeking method is cross-examination:

> The purpose of cross-examination is to weaken the testimony the witness has given, or, at best, negate it, or, less spectacularly but highly useful, to do no more than clarify ambiguous responses. The cross-examiner seeks to show inadequacy of observation, confusion, bias, inconsistency, even contradiction. The dramatic interest, of course, arises mainly from the contest between the witness bent on maintaining his position and a lawyer bent on destroying it. The audience, at a real trial or a fictional one, loves the plangent clash and wants to see the witness bleed, or the lawyer bleed, or, even better, both. The contest can be good-humored, or at least courteous, but it is often drenched in hostility. The cross-examined witness is typically a cross examined witness.
>
> The fight is fine; it suits the adversary system. But it should stay cool, and its function kept in mind. Petty triumph is not the goal. . . . The lawyer should do nothing whose aim is personal gratification.[31]

SECRET WITNESSES   *Rovario v. United States* (1957) held that the government may *not* conceal the *identity* of an informer who testifies at a trial. The police testified exclusively about what agent "John Doe" did but did not want to produce him at trial. John Doe was Rovario's one material witness. His opportunity to cross-examine the police officer "was hardly a substitute for an opportunity to examine the man who had been nearest to him and took part in the transaction. Doe had helped to set up the criminal occurrence and had played a prominent part in it. His testimony might have disclosed an entrapment. He might have thrown doubt upon petitioner's identity or on the identity of the package. . . . The desirability of calling John Doe as a witness, or at least interviewing him in preparation for trial, was a matter for the accused rather than the Government to decide." *Rovario* was decided on the basis of the Court's supervisory power over federal cases. Nevertheless, the "*Rovario* rule" stands for the proposition that confrontation includes the right to *know the identity of one's accusers*. The rule forces prosecutors, in cases involving undercover police agents or informants, to lift the agent's "cover" in order to bring a prosecution. If the prosecutor believes it is more important to preserve the informant's anonymity, the prosecution must be dropped. This creates tough choices for prosecutors, but a different rule is not compatible with the unconstitutionality of secret trials.

A similar Confrontation Clause issue arises when the trial court or the prosecutor, for one reason or another, *withholds information* from the defense that may be of value in the cross-examination. When this has occurred, the Supreme Court has required that the information be made available. For example, the refusal of an undercover narcotics officer to give his *real name* at trial violates the defendant's constitutional rights because it does not give the defense a full opportunity to gather information that might cast a shadow on the witness's credibility (*Smith v. Illinois,* 1968). In another case, the Court said that withholding the fact that a witness was on probation for juvenile delinquency, when that fact was relevant to the witness's possible bias, unconstitutionally weakened the defendant's ability to cross-examine the witness (*Davis v. Alaska,* 1974).

Confrontation in Child Sex-Abuse Cases

One of the most difficult and sensitive tasks confronting prosecutors and defense counsel is the examination of child witnesses in sexual abuse cases. The onslaught of sex-abuse cases has made this a major area of social and legal concern, raising four legal issues: (1) the competence of children as witnesses, (2) their credibility, (3) the rights of children, and (4) the rights of defendants.[32] This section focuses on Supreme Court cases dealing with confrontation rights in sex-abuse cases.

The reliance on cross-examination as the underpinning of the Confrontation Clause was underscored in **Kentucky v. Stincer** (1987). Stincer, charged with child sexual abuse against children eight, seven, and five years of age, was excluded from **in camera** (in chambers) proceedings where the judge questioned the children to determine if the two younger children were competent to testify. Stincer's lawyer was present. The Supreme Court held that Stincer's Sixth Amendment Confrontation Clause was not violated because his exclusion did not preclude effective cross-examination by defense counsel. Any background questions relevant to the trial could be repeated on direct examination of the child witnesses in court. "[T]he critical tool of cross-examination was available to counsel as a means of establishing that the witnesses were not competent to testify, as well as a means of undermining the credibility of their testimony" (*Stincer,* 1987). Justice Marshall, dissenting (joined by Justices Blackmun and Stevens), wrote, "Although cross-examination may be a primary means for ensuring the reliability of testimony from adverse witnesses, we have never held that standing alone it will suffice in every case. . . . Physical presence of the defendant enhances the reliability of the factfinding process" (*Stincer* 1987).

Stincer must be distinguished from the issue of *face-to-face confrontation* at the *trial* itself. More recent cases deal with attempts by state legislatures to shield child witnesses from the direct gaze of defendants in order to make it more likely for them to testify. The state's argument is that actual face-to-face confrontation may undermine the entire prosecution by mak-

ing the child witness unable to testify due to psychological pressure. The defendant's argument is that this is a basic purpose of confronting one's witnesses. Indeed, among the real cases of child sexual abuse there has been a wave of improbable prosecutions against totally innocent people who worked in day care centers, which are based on public hysteria reminiscent of the Salem witch trials of 1692.[33] In just such cases, shielding the testifying child from the defendant's view may cause profound injustices. Trial procedure has evolved over the centuries to create a sober courtroom atmosphere to search for the truth, removed from prejudice and popular hysteria. When procedures to protect the defendant—presumed to be innocent—are weakened, the worst injustices can occur.

In **Coy v. Iowa** (1988) the Supreme Court struck down a state rule that allowed two fifteen-year-old sexual abuse victims to testify from behind a *screen* so as to avoid eye-to-eye contact with the defendant. This violated the Confrontation Clause. The majority did not go so far as to say that eye-to-eye contact was absolutely required by the Sixth Amendment. It held that the legislature could not presume that every child sex-abuse case caused such trauma to the alleged victim that the child could not testify in the presence of the accused. Instead, the trial court had to make "individualized findings that these particular witnesses needed special protection. . . ." Otherwise, a legislative presumption would override a constitutional right. Justice O'Connor, concurring, noted that while only Iowa provided for a screen in the courtroom in sensitive cases, by 1988, half the states had trial rules that allowed the presentation of testimony in child sex-abuse cases by one- or two-way closed-circuit television. She suggested that the *Coy* ruling did not prevent the use of such devices. Justice Blackmun, dissenting, asserted that the requirements of live testimony and cross-examination were fulfilled in this case and that, therefore, there was no violation of the Confrontation Clause.

The issue left open in *Coy* was resolved in **Maryland v. Craig** (1990), which upheld (5–4) the use of *one-way closed-circuit television* to transmit the testimony of a child witness where *procedural safeguards* were in place. Under Maryland law, closed-circuit testimony is used only where absolutely necessary and only on a case-by-case basis. The trial court had to establish that the *specific witness*, in this case a six-year-old allegedly victimized by the owner of a child care center, would suffer serious *emotional distress* such that she could *not reasonably communicate* in a face-to-face confrontation. The closed-circuit television hookup had to allow the defendant to observe the demeanor of the witness during examination and cross-examination, and the defendant was in electronic communication with her defense counsel at all times. Counsel retained the right to object to any questions.

Justice O'Connor, for the majority, held that the Sixth Amendment does *not* guarantee an *absolute* right to a face-to-face meeting at the trial. Instead, "[t]he central concern of the Confrontation Clause is to ensure the reliability of the evidence against a criminal defendant by subjecting it to rigorous testing in the context of an adversary proceeding before the trier of fact. The word 'confront,' after all, also means a clashing of forces or ideas, thus carrying with it the notion of adversariness" (*Maryland v. Craig*, 1990). She noted that while face-to-face confrontation is an important aspect of the right, there are other protections found in the Maryland practice: (1) the witness must testify under *oath,* to impress on her the seriousness of the procedure and to establish the perjury penalty for lying; (2) *cross-examination,* the "greatest legal engine ever invented for the discovery of truth" is allowed; and (3) that the jury observes the witness's demeanor so as to assess her credibility. It is these factors together that satisfy the right of confrontation. The defendant's rights had to be balanced against the important state interest of protecting minor victim-witnesses from further trauma and psychological harm.

Justice Scalia wrote for four dissenters:

> Seldom has the Court failed so conspicuously to sustain a *categorical* guarantee of the Constitution against the tide of prevailing current opinion. . . . The purpose of enshrining [the Confrontation Clause] protection in the Constitution was to assure that none of the many policy interests from time to time pursued by statutory law could overcome a defendant's right to face his or her accusers in court. . . .
>
> . . . [The Court's] reasoning abstracts from the right to its purposes, and then eliminates the right. It is wrong because the Confrontation Clause does not guarantee reliable evidence; it guarantees specific trial procedures that were thought to *assure* reliable evidence, undeniably among which was "face-to-face" confrontation. Whatever else it may mean in addition, the defendant's constitutional right "to be confronted with the witnesses against him" means, always and everywhere, at least what it explicitly says: the "right to meet face to face all those who appear and give evidence at trial." (*Maryland v. Craig*, 1990, emphasis added)

On the day the Court decided *Maryland v. Craig*, it held in **Idaho v. Wright** (1990) (5–4) that the hearsay testimony of a pediatrician about what child sex-abuse victims said, did *not* have "circumstantial guarantees of trustworthiness" and was therefore inadmissible as a Confrontation Clause violation. A physician interviewed victimized children, aged two-and-one-half and five-and-one-half at the time of the crimes charged, but failed to keep a picture that he drew during the interview and did not keep detailed notes recording changes in the children's affects or attitudes. The Idaho Supreme Court ruled that the admission of the pediatrician's hearsay violated the Sixth Amendment because the testimony did not fall within a recognized hearsay exception, which provides a traditional standard of trustworthiness, and the interview lacked procedural safeguards. Unlike standard hearsay exceptions, such as the business-records exception that inherently provides an index of trustworthiness, the physician's statements were admitted under a "residual hearsay exception." In affirming the state court, Justice O'Connor expressed the concern that were the Court to say that statements under the residual hearsay exception were automatically admissible, this would grant every statutory hearsay exception "constitutional stature, a step this Court has repeatedly declined to take."

Maryland v. Craig and *Idaho v. Wright,* taken together, indicate a willingness on the part of the Court to allow state law to water down the traditional Sixth Amendment rule of face-to-face confrontation for a child witness in sex-abuse cases, as long as this expansion of prosecutorial power is used only where necessary and is limited by procedural safeguards.

Presumption of Innocence and Proof Beyond a Reasonable Doubt

Two fundamental and closely linked rules are central to a fair trial: (1) a defendant is clothed with the **presumption of innocence,** and (2) the state must prove the defendant guilty of every element of the crime charged by proof *beyond a reasonable doubt.* The text of the Constitution includes neither rule. They are so fundamental that they were assumed to be part of the trial by jury guarantee. The Supreme Court first confronted them in 1970, and held in *In re Winship,* a juvenile delinquency adjudication, that the reasonable doubt standard is essential to due process.

Reasonable doubt is an elusive concept. It is allowed for a judge to instruct a jury that they must not convict a defendant if they have a reasonable doubt about guilt without defining the term. If a judge does define it, no special form or words are required, but "taken as a whole, the instructions [must] correctly convey the *concept* of reasonable doubt to the jury" (*Holland v. United States*, 1954). The danger to the defendant's due process right is that a judge might define the term in a way that makes the defendant's task of establishing a reasonable doubt more difficult than what the Constitution requires.

In *Cage v. Louisiana* (1990) the Court held that a judge's instruction violates due process for this reason. The judge in *Cage* gave the jury the following instruction:

> "'[A reasonable doubt] is one that is founded upon a real tangible substantial basis and not upon mere caprice and conjecture. *It must be such doubt as would give rise to a grave uncertainty*, raised in your mind by reasons of the unsatisfactory character of the evidence or lack thereof. A reasonable doubt is not a mere possible doubt. *It is an actual substantial doubt*. It is a doubt that a reasonable man can seriously entertain. What is required is not an absolute or mathematical certainty, but a *moral certainty*.'" (*Cage v. Louisiana*, emphasis in original)

Cage's rights were violated because the words, "substantial" and "grave," as they are commonly understood, suggest a *higher* degree of *doubt* than is required for acquittal under the reasonable doubt standard. A judge's instruction that tends to make a juror think that the defendant must raise an almost certain doubt lowers the prosecutor's burden of proof. The test of whether a judge's definition of reasonable doubt violates due process is not whether the jury "could have" applied it in an unconstitutional manner, but whether there is a *reasonable likelihood* that the jury *did* so apply the instruction (*Estelle v. McGuire*, 1991).

The archaic words, "moral certainty" have tended to confuse jurors. Nevertheless, the Supreme Court in **Victor v. Nebraska** (1994) upheld a jury instruction using it in defining reasonable doubt:

"It is *not a mere possible doubt;* because everything relating to human affairs, and *depending on moral evidence,* is open to some possible or imaginary doubt. It is that state of the case which, after the entire comparison and consideration of all the evidence, leaves the minds of the jurors in that condition that they cannot say they feel an abiding conviction, *to a moral certainty,* of the truth of the charge."

The use of the term "moral certainty" did not violate the defendant's due process right to a fair trial because, although the term is rarely used, it means "highly probable"—which is permissible. Courts would be well advised to drop such no-longer-used words in charging juries in the serious task of evaluating trial evidence.

A second issue in *Victor* was the use of "substantial doubt" to define reasonable doubt in the instruction in a companion case. These words might convey a sense of near certainty, thus overstating the degree of doubt necessary for acquittal. Alternatively, the term could simply mean "that [doubt] specified to a large degree." The Court ruled that taken in the context of the entire charge to the jury, the term did not mislead the jury into thinking that they had to expel virtually all doubt. The court told the jurors that a substantial doubt does not mean an imaginary doubt or a fanciful conjecture.

It is likely that the justices in *Victor* were not happy with the instructions in these cases, but decided not to interfere with them, in part, because they did not want to impose a rigid rule on the states. In a useful concurrence, Justice Ginsburg suggested a better instruction drafted by the Federal Judicial Center:

Proof beyond a reasonable doubt is proof that leaves you firmly convinced of the defendant's guilt. There are very few things in this world that we know with absolute certainty, and in criminal cases the law does not require proof that overcomes every possible doubt. If, based on your consideration of the evidence, you are firmly convinced that the defendant is guilty of the crime charged, you must find him guilty. If on the other hand, you think there is a real possibility that he is not guilty, you must give him the benefit of the doubt and find him not guilty (*Victor v. Nebraska,* 1994, Ginsburg, J., concurring).

THE JURY

In all criminal prosecutions, the accused shall enjoy the right to a speedy and public trial, by an impartial jury of the State and district wherein the crime shall have been committed, which district shall have been previously ascertained by law, and to be informed of the nature and cause of the accusation; to be confronted with the witnesses against him; to have compulsory process for obtaining witnesses in his favor, and to have the Assistance of Counsel for his defence.

—Sixth Amendment, United States Constitution

Constitutional Requirements

CONSTITUTIONAL FOUNDATION   Trial by jury is guaranteed by Article III of the Constitution (1789) (in criminal cases) and by the Sixth (criminal) and Seventh (civil) amendments of the Bill of Rights (1791). In 1968 the Supreme Court

incorporated the Sixth Amendment right to a jury trial in criminal cases into Fourteenth Amendment due process, giving the Supreme Court the constitutional authority to establish the constitutional parameters of state jury trials:

Because we believe that trial by jury in criminal cases is fundamental to the American scheme of justice, we hold that the Fourteenth Amendment guarantees a right of jury trial in all criminal cases which—were they to be tried in federal court—would come within the Sixth Amendment guarantee. (*Duncan v. Louisiana,* 1968)

Duncan held that a person actually sentenced to less than six months imprisonment is entitled to a jury trial if the crime carries a potential penalty of two years.

The Court, however, has ruled that under the Sixth Amendment, federal jury requirements can differ from those imposed on the states. Federal juries adhere to the traditional common law requirements of twelve persons who render verdicts of "guilty" or "not guilty" by unanimous decisions. State criminal juries, on the other hand, have been held by the Supreme Court to differ in several regards, thus weakening the idea that incorporation (see Chapter 1) establishes identical rights for state and federal defendants. The Seventh Amendment right to a federal jury in civil cases has not been incorporated.

THE PETTY CRIME–SERIOUS CRIME DISTINCTION
The Court in *Duncan* feared that requiring a jury in "all crimes" would saddle the states with added expense and delay if jury trials were demanded in **petty crimes.** *Duncan* reaffirmed the long-established view that so-called "petty offenses" may be tried without a jury. What this meant was tested in ***Baldwin v. New York*** (1970), which held that "no offense can be deemed 'petty' for purposes of the right to trial by jury where imprisonment for *more than six months* is authorized." A New York City ordinance that disallowed juries in crimes with penalties up to *one year* in prison was held unconstitutional. Justices Black and Douglas disagreed with this part of the case: They felt that the Sixth Amendment, by its terms, guaranteed a jury trial in "*all* criminal prosecutions." The prime criterion of distinguishing a serious from a petty crime, then, is the *length of the maximum penalty,* with the dividing line at six months.

In ***Blanton v. City of North Las Vegas*** (1989) the Court held that a crime punishable by up to six months incarceration is still "petty" even though it carries *additional penalties* such as a minimum jail stay and community service. *Blanton,* however, left open the possibility that additional statutory penalties could be so severe that a crime carrying a maximum jail sentence of less than six months might still require a jury trial. (The likelihood of the Court following the hint in *Blanton* appears slim.) ***Lewis v. United States*** (1996) held that a defendant who is prosecuted in a single trial for *multiple petty crimes* and whose total punishment could amount to more than six months of imprisonment is not entitled to a jury trial. The Court adhered strictly to the notion that a petty crime depends on the *legislative judgment* in setting the authorized maximum penalty for the offense. The actual term of imprisonment meted out is *not* the criterion by which the petty-serious distinction is judged. The one exception to this rule is that the actual aggregate jail term for a *criminal contempt of court,* where the maximum is not fixed by the legislature, determines whether a jury is legally required (***Codispoti v. Pennsylvania,*** 1973).

Four justices disagreed with the majority in *Lewis.* Justice Kennedy, concurring, wrote that the "holding both in its doctrinal formulation and in its practical effect is one of the most serious incursions on the right to jury trial in the Court's history, and it cannot be squared with our precedents." He pointed out that the "primary purpose of the jury in our legal system is to stand between the accused and the powers of the State. Among the most ominous of those is the power to imprison." In summary, then, the concurring and the dissenting justices (Stevens and Ginsburg) were profoundly disturbed by a policy that allows the state to imprison a person for years without the protection afforded by a citizens' jury.

THE SIZE OF THE JURY   ***Williams v. Florida*** (1970) held that a *six-person felony jury* did not violate the Sixth Amendment, reversing an eight-hundred-year common law tradition requiring twelve jurors. Justice White relied on *functional analysis* to support this decision:

> The purpose of the jury trial . . . is to prevent oppression by the Government. . . . Given this purpose, the essential feature of a jury obviously lies in the interposition between the accused and his accuser of the common-sense judgment of a group of laymen, and in the community participation and shared responsibility which results from this group's determination of guilt or innocence. The performance of this role is not a function of the particular number of the body which makes up the jury. To be sure, the number should probably be large enough to promote group deliberation, free from outside attempts at intimidation, and to provide a fair possibility for obtaining a representative cross section of the community. But we find little reason to think that these goals are in any meaningful sense less likely to be achieved when the jury numbers six, than when it numbers 12—particularly if the requirement of unanimity is retained. And, certainly the reliability of the jury as a fact-finder hardly seems likely to be a function of its size. . . .
>
> Similarly, while in theory the number of viewpoints represented on a randomly selected jury ought to increase as the size of the jury increases, in practice the difference between the 12-man and the six-man jury in terms of the cross section of the community represented seems likely to be negligible. (*Williams v. Florida,* 1970)

Justice White based these views on a handful of social science studies then available that supported his conclusions.

The Court drew the line on the constitutionally permissible size of a felony jury by striking down a five-person jury in ***Ballew v. Georgia*** (1978) as a violation of the Sixth Amendment; henceforth, juries must contain at least six members. *Ballew* contained a subtle admission that the functional analysis of *Williams* was premature. Justice Blackmun's opinion noted that (1) recent studies cast doubt on the accuracy of small-jury verdicts, (2) the defense seems to be hurt by small juries, (3) minority group representation decreases in smaller juries, and (4) there are no significant gains in cost or effi-

ciency in a five-person jury. Nevertheless, the *Williams* rule still stands. Only a dozen states still require twelve-person juries in felony trials.

THE VOTING REQUIREMENT: MAJORITY VERSUS UNANIMITY   The common law requires a *unanimous* jury verdict. A single holdout juror can cause a "hung jury," blocking a verdict of either guilt or acquittal. The government may order a retrial after a hung jury. Several states authorize felony verdicts based on less than unanimous votes. The Supreme Court has upheld such laws under the Sixth Amendment if they require a *super-majority* vote for a guilty verdict, allowing guilty verdicts by votes of eleven-to-one and ten-to-two in ***Apodaca v. Oregon*** (1972). In ***Johnson v. Louisiana*** (1972) the Court approved a law authorizing a nine-to-three verdict under the Fourteenth Amendment Equal Protection Clause. Justice White, in *Apodaca,* again relied on functional analysis: a "requirement of unanimity . . . does not materially contribute to the exercise of [the] commonsense judgment" of a group of laymen. "Requiring unanimity would obviously produce hung juries in some situations where nonunanimous juries will convict or acquit. But in either case, the interest of the defendant in having the judgment of his peers interposed between himself and the officers of the State who prosecute and judge him is equally well served." Such majority verdicts were held to not undermine the proof beyond a reasonable doubt standard.

Justice Douglas, dissenting in *Johnson* and *Apodaca,* expressed strong misgivings. "The diminution of verdict reliability flows from the fact that nonunanimous juries need not debate and deliberate as fully as must unanimous juries. As soon as the requisite majority is attained, further consideration is not required . . . even though the dissident jurors might, if given the chance, be able to convince the majority." Justice Douglas cited an empirical study to show that such reversals by persuasion occurred in 10 percent of all **jury deliberations.**[34] Additionally, deadlocks usually occur because one, two, or three jurors hold out. Since the majority favors the prosecutions in most deadlocked cases, the majority vote rule upsets a traditional common law protection of defendants.

Concern for this point led the Court to prohibit nonunanimous verdicts in six-person misdemeanor juries. A law allowing guilty verdicts by five out of six jurors in crimes carrying less than six months of imprisonment was declared unconstitutional by a unanimous Supreme Court in ***Burch v. Louisiana*** (1979). Justice Rehnquist reasoned that "lines must be drawn somewhere if the substance of the jury trial right is to be preserved." Only two states at that time allowed majority verdicts in six-person juries, thus indicating the national view favored unanimity.

WAIVER OF THE RIGHT TO A JURY   Defendants may have strategic reasons to waive a jury trial and opt for a **"bench trial"** or **"waiver trial"** with a judge as the sole trier of fact. They may believe that a jury would be prejudiced and unlikely to render a fair decision, or that a trained judge is better able to find reasonable doubt than a lay jury. A defendant's waiver to surrender the right to a jury trial must be express and intelligent (*Patton v. United States,* 1930). Under federal law, the jury trial is considered the standard mode of adjudication, and waiver requires *agreement of the judge and prosecutor* as well as the defendant.[35] The Supreme Court ruled, in an opinion by Chief Justice Warren, that "[a] defendant's only constitutional right concerning the method of trial is to an impartial trial by jury. . . . The Constitution recognizes an adversary system as the proper method of determining guilt, and the Government, as a litigant, has a legitimate interest in seeing that cases in which it believes a conviction is warranted are tried before the tribunal which the Constitution regards as most likely to produce a fair result" (***Singer v. United States,*** 1965). Thus, a jury trial in federal court can be had at the behest of the prosecutor, over the defendant's objection. Some states, on the other hand, view the jury primarily as a protection to the defendant, and the defendant has the last word as to whether the trial will be held before a judge or a jury.

THE JURY RIGHT IN JUVENILE DELINQUENCY HEARINGS   The Supreme Court has ruled, in **McKeiver v. Pennsylvania** (1971), that a jury trial is *not* constitutionally required in juvenile delinquency proceedings. The decision surprised juvenile justice experts because it halted a trend of decisions between 1966 and 1971 granting juvenile offenders legal rights equal to adults under due process in delinquency adjudications. *Kent v. United States* (1966) imposed the due process requirements of *notice* and *counsel* if a juvenile was to be transferred to the adult court system for a criminal trial. The Supreme Court in *In re Gault* (1967), noting that a delinquency determination could result in state confinement much like a criminal conviction, held that the essentials of due process and fair treatment in juvenile delinquency adjudications included *notice* of charges, the right to *trial, confrontation* of witnesses and *cross-examination*, and the right against *self-incrimination*. And *In re Winship* (1970) held that "the constitutional safeguard of proof beyond a *reasonable doubt* is as much required during the adjudicatory stage of a delinquency proceeding as are those constitutional safeguards applied in *Gault*."

Nevertheless, the Court (5–3) refused to extend the jury right to juvenile delinquency adjudication proceedings. The Court noted in *McKeiver* that, although juvenile delinquency trials are due process hearings requiring procedural safeguards, they are not Sixth Amendment criminal prosecutions where the jury right would automatically apply. Relying on a more flexible, policy-oriented approach under the Due Process Clause, Justice Blackmun noted that despite criticisms of the juvenile court system, its existence represented the view that juveniles should be processed less formally than adults, in special proceedings that allow consideration of social factors not related to factual guilt. A jury requirement would be the final blow to this concept, bringing formality, legalism, and delay, which are incompatible with the ideals of the juvenile court. *McKeiver* also supported federalism, deferring to the needs of the states. Justice Blackmun expressed a desire not to impose a single national standard but to allow the states to experiment with advisory juries, if they wished, in juvenile adjudication.

Selecting an Unbiased Jury

Selecting an unbiased, impartial jury takes two steps. First, a jury pool is selected from among eligible jurors in the citizenry that reflects a **representative cross-section.** Second, the actual jurors in a case are selected in a process known as voir dire to weed out jurors with actual or potential biases. The mechanics of jury selection requires a unit of government, typically a county, to compile a master jury list (also called a jury wheel or master wheel) of eligible jurors from among the citizenry. From this list, a jury pool is selected and summoned to appear for jury service. (The term *venire* is often interchanged with *jury pool*.) At the courthouse, jury panels are drawn from the entire venire. The panel then undergoes voir dire and the twelve or six jurors, plus alternates, are selected.

Prior to the *Federal Jury Selection Act* of 1968, methods used to select the master jury list did not guarantee a representative cross-section. Indeed, some methods were designed to select an elite. Since the passage of the act, the more egalitarian ideal that the jury master list and venire be a representative cross-section of eligible jurors is attained, first, by supplementing voter lists as a source of eligible jurors with drivers' licenses lists, city or telephone directories, and the like. Next, rigorous statistical methods are applied to ensure unbiased selection.[36] The Supreme Court has ruled on various challenges to laws and practices which in the past have fostered racial and gender discrimination in the makeup of juries under two distinct constitutional provisions.

THE EQUAL PROTECTION CASES   The Fourteenth Amendment (1868) was designed to promote basic rights and political equality of African Americans. Jury service, along with voting, is a primary method by which American citizens express their sovereign political influence. Preventing groups of citizens from serving on juries or voting was meant to cripple their political participation and influence. The Equal Protection Clause declares: "No State shall . . . deny to any person within its jurisdiction the equal protection of the laws." Relying on this clause, the Supreme Court, in **Strauder v. West Virginia** (1880), held that a statute that *explicitly* excluded African Americans from jury service was unconstitutional. The following year, the Court held that a *practice* that excluded African Americans from juries under a neutral statute was unconstitutional (**Neal v. Delaware,** 1881).

The malign power of Jim Crow segregation made a mockery of these rulings in the South. For example, facially race-neutral laws requiring jury members be property holders eliminated minorities from juries. In fact, blacks were denied the right to serve on juries (and to vote) in the South for a century after the Civil War. These rights were gained after the struggles of the civil rights movement of the 1950s to the 1970s. In 1935 the Court in **Norris v. Alabama,** one of the "Scottsboro" cases, at last recognized that virtual *exclusion* of African Americans from grand juries violated equal protection. Despite *Norris,* blacks continued to be underrepresented on juries. The *Norris* rule was weak, and under it a bare showing that African Americans made up nearly 7 percent of grand jury panels in a Texas county where they comprised more than 15 percent of the population was held *not* to be discrimination *per se* (*Cassell v. Texas*, 1950). In *Avery v. Georgia* (1953) the fact that *not one* African American was selected for a jury panel of sixty people, where 5 percent of the jury list was African American, was held in itself *not* sufficient to establish discrimination. On the other hand, *Avery* held there was an equal protection violation only because color-coded jury ballots demonstrated *intentional* discrimination, normally very hard to prove.

In the 1960s the Supreme Court was slow to extend the social insights of its desegregation rulings to jury selection. ***Swain v. Alabama*** (1965) held that the exclusion of a prospective juror *on account of race* violated the defendant's equal protection rights. However, the *Swain* Court found *no* equal protection violation where, for more than a decade, only 10 to 15 percent of jurors were black in a county where African Americans were 26 percent of the eligible voters. The Court was blind to the fact that this statistical pattern was nearly impossible in a fair selection system.[37] Instead, noting that Alabama did not totally exclude African Americans from jury venire panels, and that a defendant is not entitled to a petit jury or a panel on which a proportionate number of her race sit, Justice White stated that "[n]either the jury roll nor the venire need be a perfect mirror of the community or accurately reflect the proportionate strength of every identifiable group."

After *Swain*, the Supreme Court seemed to realize its error and finally began to recognize that a *statistically significant imbalance* had to be the product of **invidious discrimination.** The Court seemed to reflect the political gains achieved by the civil rights movement.

- *Whitus v. Georgia* (1967): There is a prima facie case of purposeful discrimination where three of thirty-three prospective grand jurors and seven of ninety in the petit jury venire were African Americans in a county where 43 percent of males over twenty-one years old were black.
- *Turner v. Fouche* (1970): There is prima facie discrimination where, in a county with 60 percent black population, 37 percent of the grand jury list was African American and 171 of the 178 persons disqualified for lack of "intelligence" or "uprightness" were African American.
- *Alexander v. Louisiana* (1972): A prima facie case of discrimination existed where there was less than 7 percent African American representation on grand jury panels, although nearly 14 percent of grand jury questionnaires were submitted by blacks, and the county was 21 percent African American.

Casteneda v. Partida (1977), involving underrepresentation of Hispanics on grand juries, specified a three-step process for deciding an equal protection claim. (1) The underrepresented group must be a recognizable, *distinct class*. (2) The *degree* of underrepresentation must be proved by *comparing* the proportion of the group in the total population to the proportion of the group called to serve as grand jurors over a *significant period of time*. (3) "A *selection procedure* that is *susceptible to abuse* or not racially neutral supports the pre-

sumption of discrimination." Once a prima facie case is made, the burden shifts to the government to rebut discrimination. In *Casteneda* a prima facie case was made by showing that, in a county that was 79 percent Mexican American, between 39 and 50 percent of the grand jurors had Spanish surnames and that the **"key man" method** of selection (whereby the district judge selects three to five jury commissioners who in turn select fifteen to twenty persons known to them in the county) was not neutral. The prima facie case was not rebutted by the district judge's bare assertion that there were no prejudicial motives in the selection process. Nor was the prima facie discrimination rebutted by the theory that discrimination is impossible where the recognizable group constitutes a "governing majority" in the jurisdiction. The methods announced in *Casteneda* would be applied to juries less than a decade later in *Batson v. Kentucky* (1986).

THE SIXTH AMENDMENT: AN IMPARTIAL JURY
A Sixth Amendment challenge claiming that a jury is not impartial is far broader than an equal protection challenge. Under the Equal Protection Clause, a defendant can claim that a jury was selected to discriminate against *that person's* ethnic or racial group or gender. *Every* defendant, on the other hand, has a right to an impartial jury. Once the impartial jury provision was incorporated in *Parker v. Gladden* (1966), the way was clear for application in jury selection.[38]

Thus, a *white male* defendant is entitled to a jury system that does not systematically exclude *blacks* (***Peters v. Kiff,*** 1972), and a *male* defendant is entitled to a jury drawn from a selection process that does not suppress the number of *females* who might otherwise serve (***Taylor v. Louisiana,*** 1975). These cases constitutionalized the right "to a jury drawn from a venire constituting a fair cross section of the community" (*Taylor,* 1975). Justice White, in *Taylor v. Louisiana,* explained that:

> The purpose of a jury is to guard against the exercise of arbitrary power—to make available the common sense judgment of the community as a hedge against the overzealous or mistaken prosecutor and in preference to the professional or perhaps overconditioned or biased response of a judge. This prophylactic vehicle is not provided if the jury pool is made up of only special segments of the populace or if large, distinctive groups are excluded from the pool. Community participation in the administration of the criminal law, moreover, is not only consistent with our democratic heritage but is also critical to public confidence in the fairness of the criminal justice system. Restricting jury service to only special groups or excluding identifiable segments playing major roles in the community cannot be squared with the constitutional concept of jury trial.

Taylor eliminated a practice whereby a woman who wanted to serve on a jury had to file a written declaration of her desire. Incidentally, women constitute a distinctive segment of the population for purposes of jury service (a federal rule: *Ballard v. United States,* 1946), even though they do not respond to issues as a class any more than do men. The Court rejected the argument of Louisiana that women play a distinctive role in society that is deterred by jury service. The Victorian notion that women have to be "protected" from jury service is simply passé in an era when women have almost reached numerical parity with men in the legal profession.

The Court expanded the *Taylor* rule in **Duren v. Missouri** (1979), holding that the gross underrepresentation of women on jury venires (15 percent out of 54 percent of the population) as a result of rules that made it very easy for women to decline jury service (for example by not showing up) constituted a prima facie violation of the Sixth Amendment rule that juries constitute a fair cross-section of the population. *Duren* ruled that a prima facie case of discrimination requires a showing that: (1) the excluded group is "distinctive" in the community; (2) the group is statistically underrepresented in venires; and (3) the underrepresentation is due to systematic exclusion of the group in the jury selection process.

Aside from minority groups and women, federal courts have *not* upheld claims that various subgroups of the population constitute "distinctive groups" under *Duren:* blue-collar workers, college students, less-educated people, young adults, rural inhabitants, persons who chose not to register to vote, jurors with last names beginning with M to Z, persons over the age of seventy, and jurors with absolute scruples against imposing the death penalty.[39] Several lower courts have held that absolute disparities of *more than 10 percent* constitutes unfair representation and have refused to accept smaller disparities as discrimination.[40] Lower courts have also ruled that the systematic-exclusion prong of the *Duren* rule was held not to apply to rules that allow certain professionals such as doctors, lawyers, and sole proprietors, to be excluded from jury service upon request. This was seen as a rational accommodation to the community's needs.[41] In recent years, the laws and rules of many states have disallowed such exclusion as the one-day, one-trial practice has become common.

Voir Dire and Fairness

Voir dire involves questioning prospective jurors for bias. Each side has an unlimited number of challenges for cause. All jurors who say they cannot be fair or are shown to be biased must be excused by the judge as a matter of fundamental fairness and the impartial jury requirement of the Sixth Amendment.

An important issue regarding the conduct of voir dire is whether the trial judge asks all the questions or allows the lawyers to conduct voir dire. Lawyers believe that judge-conducted voir dire fails to probe sufficiently to elicit bias. Judge-conducted voir dire purports to conserve time or to prevent attorneys to "spin" a case before the jury. Attorneys can submit questions to judges who conduct voir dire, but the judges are not obligated to ask them. An attorney can appeal a judge's refusal to ask or allow a question, but to win, the attorney must meet the high legal standard of whether the denial amounts to an **abuse of discretion.**

In **Ham v. South Carolina** (1973) the Supreme Court ruled that a judge who disallowed questions about *racial prejudice* in a prosecution of a bearded, African American, civil rights worker for possession of marijuana violated his right to due process. No violation occurred, however, in **Ristaino v. Ross** (1976). The judge refused to allow ques-

tions about prejudice regarding the defendant's beard in a robbery case where the defendant was black and the victim white. In this case, the possible prejudice regarding the defendant's beard was tenuous. More important, *Ristaino* held that the Constitution does not require such questions whenever the defendant is black and the victim white. There were no factors of racial tension or animosity in *Ristaino* that raised a real need for a special instruction.

An exception to *Ristaino* is made in death penalty cases. "[A] capital defendant accused of an interracial crime is entitled to have prospective jurors informed of the race of the victim and questioned on the issue of racial bias" (**Turner v. Murray,** 1986). Justice White's rationale for the decision was that because the jury has *greater discretion* in the sentencing phase of a capital case than in the guilt-finding phase, the death sentence should not stand where the *voir dire* did not inquire into race prejudice. The Supreme Court also held in **Morgan v. Illinois** (1992) (6–3) that in a death penalty case a requested voir dire question about a juror's propensity to automatically impose the death penalty even if mitigating factors existed, had to be asked.

Mu'Min v. Virginia (1991) was a murder case with substantial pretrial publicity. The judge on voir dire questioned prospective jurors about whether they had read or heard about the case and whether they had formed an opinion based on outside information. The judge, however, refused to question prospective jurors about the *content* of their information, as requested by the defense. The Supreme Court held this did *not* violate due process. Justice Marshall, dissenting, argued it is constitutionally unfair to not allow attorneys to ask content questions because they (1) determine whether the type and extent of pretrial publicity would disqualify the juror as a matter of law, (2) give "legal depth" to the trial court's finding of impartiality, and (3) facilitate accurate trial court fact finding.

PEREMPTORY CHALLENGES   In addition to unlimited challenges for cause, both sides in a criminal prosecution have a *limited* number of peremptory challenges, whereby a juror is excused without a stated cause or reason. These are often based on an attorney's "hunch" that the individual will prove unsympathetic to a client's cause. Where several defendants are tried together, each is entitled to peremptory challenges while the prosecutor may be limited to a smaller number.

In the 1980s defendants protested that the use of peremptories by prosecutors to deliberately produce racially unbalanced juries is unconstitutional. In 1986 the Supreme Court responded positively to this claim, making an important change in the law regarding peremptory challenges. In *Batson v. Kentucky* (1986) the Supreme Court drew on and modified the procedures for determining bias in jury selection that was first set out in *Casteneda v. Partida* (1977). Given the two lines of cases on fair jury selection, one under the Equal Protection Clause and the other under the Sixth Amendment impartial jury requirement, *Batson* made his claim on both. The Court decided the case on the basis of the Fourteenth Amendment.

—Batson v. Kentucky **Case & Comments—**

• CASE & COMMENTS •

Batson v. Kentucky
476 U.S. 79, 106 S.Ct. 1712, 90 L.Ed.2d 69 (1986)

JUSTICE POWELL delivered the opinion of the Court.

This case requires us to reexamine that portion of *Swain v. Alabama* (1965), concerning the evidentiary burden placed on a criminal defendant who claims that he has been denied equal protection through the State's use of peremptory challenges to exclude members of his race from the petit jury. **[a]**

I

Petitioner, a black man, was indicted in Kentucky on charges of second-degree burglary and receipt of stolen goods. [At the trial,] the judge conducted *voir dire* examination of the venire, excused certain jurors for cause, and permitted the parties to exercise peremptory challenges. The prosecutor used his peremptory challenges to strike all four black persons on the venire, and a jury composed only of white persons was selected. [Counsel claimed] that the prosecutor's removal of the black veniremen violated petitioner's rights under the Sixth and Fourteenth Amendments to a jury drawn from a cross section of the community, and under the Fourteenth Amendment to equal protection of the laws. [The judge denied the motion, observing] that the parties were entitled to use their peremptory challenges to "strike anybody they want to." * * * **[b]**

[Batson's conviction was upheld by the Kentucky Supreme Court, which relied on *Swain*:] a defendant alleging lack of a fair cross section must demonstrate systematic exclusion of a group of jurors from the venire. * * * We granted certiorari and now reverse.

II

In *Swain v. Alabama*, this Court recognized that a "State's purposeful or deliberate denial to Negroes on account of race of participation as jurors in the administration of justice violates the Equal Protection Clause." **[c]** * * * This principle has been "consistently and repeatedly" reaffirmed, * * * in numerous decisions of this Court both preceding and following *Swain*. We reaffirm the principle today.

A

* * * In holding that racial discrimination in jury selection offends the Equal Protection Clause, the Court in *Strauder* recognized, however, that a defendant has no right to a "petit jury composed in whole or in part of persons of his own race." * * * "The number of our races and nationalities stands in the way of evolution of such a conception" of the demand of equal protection. * * * **[d]** But the defendant does have the right to be tried by a jury whose members are selected pursuant to non-discriminatory criteria. * * * The Equal Protection Clause guarantees the defendant that the State will not exclude members of his race from the jury venire on account of race, * * * or on the false assumption that members of his race as a group are not qualified to serve as jurors.

Purposeful racial discrimination in selection of the venire violates a defendant's right to equal protection because it denies him the protection that a trial by jury is intended to secure. "The very idea of a jury is a body . . . composed of the peers or equals of the person whose rights it is selected or summoned to determine; that is, of his neighbors, fellows, associates, persons having the same legal status in society as that which he holds." **[e]** The petit jury has occupied a central position in our system of justice by safeguarding a person accused of crime against the arbitrary exercise of power by prosecutor or judge. * * * Those on the venire must be "indifferently chosen," to secure the defendant's right under the Fourteenth Amendment to "protection of life and liberty against race or color prejudice." * * *

* * *

The harm from discriminatory jury selection extends beyond that inflicted on the defendant and the excluded juror to touch the entire community. **[f]** Selection procedures that purposefully exclude black persons from juries undermine public confidence in the fairness of our system of justice. Discrimination within the judicial system is most pernicious because it is "a stimulant to that race prejudice which is an impediment to securing to [African Americans] that equal justice which the law aims to secure to all others."

B

[In this part the Court ruled that the Equal Protection Clause applies to the prosecutor's exercise of peremptory challenges.] Although a prosecutor ordinarily is entitled to exercise permitted peremptory

---

[a] *Swain* held that race could not be a basis for excluding a juror, but made it nearly impossible to prove. The issue in *Batson* is whether a defendant can prove racial bias in excluding jurors based on what happened in *this case*.

[b] Batson raised a Sixth Amendment (impartial jury) as well as a Fourteenth Amendment (equal protection) challenge, because he was not sure he could win on equal protection grounds. This case is decided exclusively on Fourteenth Amendment, equal protection grounds.

[c] The substantive *Swain* rule of equality means little if it is almost impossible for a defendant to prove a racially biased exercise of the prosecutor's peremptories.

[d] This remains the rule. A fair selection process cannot guarantee that a six- or twelve-person jury will include a member of one's own race or a cross-section of the community.

[e] "Peers" are said to be persons with the same *legal* status, i.e., any eligible jurors, *not* people who match the defendant in terms of race, age, or social class. Do you think an all-white jury will usually be as fair to a black defendant as a racially mixed jury?

[f] This in effect says the *jurors* have rights, as well as the defendant. The Supreme Court confirmed this position in later peremptory challenge cases.

• CASE & COMMENTS •

challenges "for any reason at all, as long as that reason is related to his view concerning the outcome" of the case to be tried, * * * the Equal Protection Clause forbids the prosecutor to challenge potential jurors solely on account of their race or on the assumption that black jurors as a group will be unable impartially to consider the State's case against a black defendant.

III

* * * A recurring question in [the jury selection] cases, as in any case alleging a violation of the Equal Protection Clause, was whether the defendant had met his burden of proving purposeful discrimination on the part of the State. * * * That question also was at the heart of the portion of *Swain v. Alabama* we reexamine today.

A

[In this section the Court noted that in practice the *Swain* rule made it virtually impossible for a defendant to ever challenge a prosecutor's use of peremptory challenges to excuse African American jurors.]

B

[In this section the Court reviewed the equal protection cases regarding discrimination in selecting the jury *pool* or *venire*. Those cases placed the burden of proof on the defendant to show that the state had a racially discriminatory purpose in its selection procedures. **[g]** Once the defendant established a prima facie case of discrimination, the state has to explain why racial disparities in the larger jury pool were not caused by racial discrimination. Courts could examine direct and circumstantial evidence in deciding whether jury pool selection was racially biased. Further, a defendant may make a prima facie showing of purposeful racial discrimination in selection of the venire by relying solely on the facts concerning its selection *in his case.*

[g] Rules regarding the nondiscriminatory selection of the jury pool are transferred below to the selection of the petit jury.

C

* * * [A] defendant may establish a prima facie case of purposeful discrimination in selection of the petit jury solely on evidence concerning the prosecutor's exercise of peremptory challenges at the defendant's trial. To establish such a case, the defendant first must show that he is a member of a cognizable racial group * * * and that the prosecutor has exercised peremptory challenges to remove from the venire members of the defendant's race. Second, the defendant is entitled to rely on the fact, as to which there can be no dispute, that peremptory challenges constitute a jury selection practice that permits "those to discriminate who are of a mind to discriminate." **[h]** * * * Finally, the defendant must show that these facts and any other relevant circumstances raise an inference that the prosecutor used that practice to exclude the veniremen from the petit jury on account of their race. This combination of factors in the empaneling of the petit jury, as in the selection of the venire, raises the necessary inference of purposeful discrimination.

[h] The Court here establishes the *first* three-step procedure by which lower courts can determine whether a *prima facie* case or *inference* of discrimination in exercising the peremptory challenge has been established.

In deciding whether the defendant has made the requisite showing, the trial court should consider all relevant circumstances. For example, a "pattern" of strikes against black jurors included in the particular venire might give rise to an inference of discrimination. Similarly, the prosecutor's questions and statements during *voir dire* examination and in exercising his challenges may support or refute an inference of discriminatory purpose. These examples are merely illustrative. We have confidence that trial judges, experienced in supervising *voir dire*, will be able to decide if the circumstances concerning the prosecutor's use of peremptory challenges creates a prima facie case of discrimination against black jurors.

Once the defendant makes a prima facie showing, the burden shifts to the State to come forward with a neutral explanation for challenging black jurors. **[i]** Though this requirement imposes a limitation in some cases on the full peremptory character of the historic challenge, we emphasize that the prosecutor's explanation need not rise to the level justifying exercise of a challenge for cause. * * * But the prosecutor may not rebut the defendant's prima facie case of discrimination by stating merely that he challenged jurors of the defendant's race on the assumption—or his intuitive judgment—that they would be partial to the defendant because of their shared race. * * * Just as the Equal Protection Clause forbids the States to exclude black persons from the venire on the assumption that blacks as a group are unqualified to serve as jurors, * * * so it forbids the States to strike black veniremen on the assumption that they will be biased in a particular case simply because the defendant is black. **[j]** The core guarantee of equal protection, ensuring citizens that their State will not discriminate on account

[i] The defendant's prima facie showing does not end the matter—it raises an *inference* of discrimination. Another set of procedures follow.

[j] Blanket assumptions that persons of a certain class, age, religion, ethnicity, etc., think only in one way cannot be used to justify strikes.

• CASE & COMMENTS •

of race, would be meaningless were we to approve the exclusion of jurors on the basis of such assumptions, which arise solely from the jurors' race. Nor may the prosecutor rebut the defendant's case merely by denying that he had a discriminatory motive or "affirm[ing] [his] good faith in making individual selections." * * * If these general assertions were accepted as rebutting a defendant's prima facie case, the Equal Protection Clause "would be but a vain and illusory requirement." * * * The prosecutor therefore must articulate a neutral explanation related to the particular case to be tried. The trial court then will have the duty to determine if the defendant has established purposeful discrimination.

IV

The State * * * argues that the privilege of unfettered exercise of the challenge is of vital importance to the criminal justice system. **[k]**

> While we recognize, of course, that the peremptory challenge occupies an important position in our trial procedures, we do not agree that our decision today will undermine the contribution the challenge generally makes to the administration of justice. The reality of practice, amply reflected in many state- and federal-court opinions, shows that the challenge may be, and unfortunately at times has been, used to discriminate against black jurors. By requiring trial courts to be sensitive to the racially discriminatory use of peremptory challenges, our decision enforces the mandate of equal protection and furthers the ends of justice. In view of the heterogeneous population of our Nation, public respect for our criminal justice system and the rule of law will be strengthened if we ensure that no citizen is disqualified from jury service because of his race. * * *

[The case was remanded.]

JUSTICE MARSHALL, concurring.

I join JUSTICE POWELL's eloquent opinion for the Court, which takes a historic step toward eliminating the shameful practice of racial discrimination in the selection of juries. * * * I nonetheless write separately to express my views. The decision today will not end the racial discrimination that peremptories inject into the jury-selection process. That goal can be accomplished only by eliminating peremptory challenges entirely.

I

* * *

Misuse of the peremptory challenge to exclude black jurors has become both common and flagrant. * * *

II

* * * Cases . . . illustrate the limitations of the [Court's] approach. First, defendants cannot attack the discriminatory use of peremptory challenges at all unless the challenges are so flagrant as to establish a prima facie case. This means, in those States, that where only one or two black jurors survive the challenges for cause, the prosecutor need have no compunction about striking them from the jury because of their race. * * * Prosecutors are left free to discriminate against blacks in jury selection provided that they hold that discrimination to an "acceptable" level.

> Second, when a defendant can establish a prima facie case, trial courts face the difficult burden of assessing prosecutors' motives. * * * Any prosecutor can easily assert facially neutral reasons for striking a juror, and trial courts are ill equipped to second-guess those reasons. **[l]** * * *

> Nor is outright prevarication by prosecutors the only danger here. "[I]t is even possible that an attorney may lie to himself in an effort to convince himself that his motives are legal." * * * A prosecutor's own conscious or unconscious racism may lead him easily to the conclusion that a prospective black juror is "sullen," or "distant," a characterization that would not have come to his mind if a white juror had acted identically. . . .

* * *

CHIEF JUSTICE BURGER, joined by JUSTICE REHNQUIST, dissenting.

[Chief Justice Burger's dissent raised several points: (1) the peremptory challenge helps select juries that will decide cases on the basis of the evidence; (2) unlike the *Strauder* rule, which properly applies equal protection violation to *classes* of persons excluded from the venire, this case applies to

[k] The majority wishes to keep the peremptory challenge alive, but to modify it so that it will not perpetuate the known use of racial discrimination by prosecutors.

[l] Justice Marshall's concerns have been borne out in later cases that demonstrate that prosecutors' race-neutral explanations are easy to make.

discrete decisions about specific individuals; (3) the majority's rule applies only to race and not to such other groupings as sex, religion, political affiliation, mental capacity, or profession; and (4) as an equal protection rule, the *Batson* principle must also be applied to *defendants,* denying them the ability to strike classes of jurors believed to be racially biased.

[Further, the *Batson* procedures, especially the need for a prosecutor to give a race-neutral explanation, will destroy the peremptory nature of the challenge. In addition, the rule will be impossible to apply.]

* * * I am at a loss to discern the governing principles here. A "clear and reasonably specific" explanation of "legitimate reasons" for exercising the challenge will be difficult to distinguish from a challenge for cause. . . . Apparently the Court envisions permissible challenges short of a challenge for cause that are just a little bit arbitrary—but not too much. While our trial judges are "experienced in supervising *voir dire,*" * * * they have no experience in administering rules like this.

* * *

Batson's **Aftermath**

Batson set in motion a series of challenges that widened the application of the Fourteenth Amendment Equal Protection Clause to voir dire in many situations. An interesting aspect of the following cases is that the Court grafted onto the equal protection doctrine the impartial jury notion that a defendant could claim that the other party's use of a peremptory challenge was discriminatory, even though the discrimination was not against that party's ethnic group or gender. The Court did this by expanding the category of the parties, so to speak. In each claim of bias in the exercise of a peremptory, the Court ruled that the equal protection right of the *jurors* were at stake as well as that of the party.

The Equal Protection Clause rule of *Batson* was applied to the use of peremptory challenges to other categories of cases.

- *White Defendant*—A white defendant has *third-party standing* to challenge a *prosecutor's peremptory challenge* to remove an African American from the jury (*Powers v. Ohio,* 1991). "A prosecutor's discriminatory use of peremptory challenges harms the excluded jurors and the community at large."
- *Civil Lawsuits*—The *Batson* rule applies to all parties in civil lawsuits; the necessary *state action* predicate for an equal protection violation lies in the *judge's* action of dismissing a challenged juror on a party's request (*Edmonson v. Leesville Concrete Co.,* 1991).
- *Hispanic Jurors*—The *Batson* rule extends to the exclusion of Hispanic jurors on account of their ethnicity. Under *Batson* this is akin to "a cognizable racial group" (*Hernandez v. New York,* 1991).
- *Criminal Defendant's Peremptory*—The prosecutor is now allowed to challenge the discriminatory exercise of a peremptory *by the defendant,* as was predicted by the dissent in *Batson.* "A criminal defendant's exercise of peremptory

challenges in a racially discriminatory manner inflicts the harms addressed by *Batson.*" It erodes *public confidence* in a fair and impartial jury (*Georgia v. McCollum,* 1992).

- *Gender*—Neither male nor female jurors can be stricken by use of peremptory challenges solely on the basis of their sex. The equal protection violation lay in the assumption that men and women "hold particular views simply because of their gender," and this stereotype reflects and reinforces patterns of historical discrimination (*J.E.B. v. Alabama,* 1994).

Prosecutors' *race-neutral explanations* for exercising peremptory challenges against *Batson* categories have been readily accepted:

- A prosecutor's exclusion of Latino jurors, on the grounds that there was some reason to believe specific Spanish-speaking jury panel members would not automatically accept that the official translator's version of testimony given in Spanish, was deemed race-neutral by the Supreme Court (*Hernandez v. New York,* 1991).
- The Court also held in *Hernandez* that a state court's finding of the absence of discriminatory intent by the party exercising a peremptory is "a pure issue of fact" that is accorded significant deference and will not be overturned on appeal unless clearly erroneous.
- A prosecutor eliminated two African American jurors, and when challenged under *Batson* said they were excluded not because of their race, but because each had long unkempt hair, a mustache, and a goatee. The Supreme Court remanded to consider whether this was a race-neutral reason (*Purkett v. Elem,* 1995).
- The Supreme Court thus tilted procedures to favor prosecutors' race-neutral explanations. *Purkett v. Elem* (1995) held that *any* race-neutral explanation for striking a juror must at first be accepted by a trial judge. Then, the burden shifts to the opponent of the peremptory strike to *prove* that the proffered

explanation is an *implausible* or *fantastic justification* that is a *pretext* or cover for purposeful discrimination. In *Purkett* the Court said the lower court acted too quickly in rejecting the peremptory challenge.

• Despite this deference, the court ruled that even under new federal laws that make it very difficult for a state defendant to bring a federal habeas corpus appeal, federal appellate courts should review a case in which a prosecutor struck ten out of eleven African American jurors remaining after challenges for cause. That is, the prosecutor struck 91 percent of the eligible black jurors by peremptory strikes, compared to just 13 percent (four out of thirty-one) of the eligible non-black prospective jurors. On its face, such action demonstrates "a substantial showing of the denial of a constitutional right" (*Miller-el v. Cockrell*, 2003).

Professor Charles J. Ogletree, reviewing the application of *Batson* in lower courts, concluded that "trial judges' acceptance of prosecutors' facially neutral explanations for peremptory strikes have undermined the protection *Batson* was meant to offer against discriminatory peremptory strikes."[42] This has led many scholars to call for the complete elimination of peremptory challenges. Others have suggested, as correctives, (1) requiring that some minority jurors be seated in the trial of a minority defendant, (2) race-conscious change-of-venue statutes, (3) increasing the number of minorities on the jury venire, (4) seating minority jurors who are struck by peremptories, and (5) reducing the number of prosecutors' peremptory challenges.[43] Professor Ogletree adds: (1) dismissing a prosecution where a prosecutor violates *Batson*, or (2) eliminate prosecution, but not defense, use of peremptory challenges. This last seemingly unbalanced proposal is based on a concern that a total elimination of peremptories would empower trial judges to seat biased jurors. It is unlikely that the current Supreme Court or state legislatures would adopt any of these extremely pro-defendant or racially based rules. These suggestions, however, point to serious problems with the administration of the *Batson* rule.

LAW IN SOCIETY

JURY TRIALS AND WRONGFUL CONVICTIONS

CONVICTING THE INNOCENT

Since 1989, the Innocence Project reported 140 persons convicted of serious crimes have been exonerated after DNA testing proved that they could not have been involved.[44] Not included were many more cleared of guilt who did not involve DNA testing. For example the notorious case of grossly unprofessional and blatantly racist police work by undercover officer Thomas Coleman in the small town of Tulia, Texas, led to the convictions in 1999 of thirty-five persons, almost all African American, for major drug sales. After thorough reinvestigations of the circumstances of the case, in 2003 Governor Rick Perry "pardoned 35 people, 31 of them black." Thompson was indicted on perjury charges.[45] Stories of the wrongly convicted seem to appear in the news every week, like the Christmas Eve 2003 release of Darryl Hunt, after serving nineteen years for a rape-murder committed by another in Winston-Salem, North Carolina.[46] Most news accounts of wrongfully convicted persons involve the most serious crimes and involve persons who served many years behind bars for crimes they did not commit. Many were on death row.

This issue has become a national concern and has affected the administration of the death penalty. Thus far two death penalty states, Illinois and Maryland, have placed moratoria on executions. The Pennsylvania Supreme Court recommended a death penalty moratorium. At the end of his term in January 2003, Gov. George Ryan of Illinois pardoned four condemned men on death row and commuted the sentences of another 167 death-row inmates to life imprisonment, "the largest such emptying of death row in history." In taking this action, Gov. Ryan said, "Our capital system is haunted by the demon of error: error in determining guilt and error in determining who among the guilty deserves to die." In the face of these news stories, juries are beginning to balk at imposing the death sentence, and as of mid-2003 "[f]ederal prosecutors failed to persuade juries to impose the death penalty in 15 of the last 16 trials in which they sought it."[47]

There are many causes of wrongful conviction including eyewitness misidentification,[48] false testimony by state forensic experts,[49] substandard DNA labs that misidentify parties,[50] misconduct by police and prosecutors (see Chapter 10), perjury by snitches, false confessions (see Chapter 7), community pressure, ineffective assistance of counsel (see Chapter 6), and more. A widely quoted study based on responses by criminal justice officials in one state estimates that one-half of 1 percent of all convictions are erroneous. If so, that would have resulted in the conviction of nearly ten-thousand innocent persons in 1990.[51] Prof. Daniel Givelber, reviewing two major studies of criminal jury trials, one in the United States and one in England, suggested higher rates in jury trials.[52] These studies, by Kalven and Zeisel (U.S.) and Baldwin and McConville (U.K.), looked at the agreement between jury verdicts in actual cases and the opinions of judges (U.S.)[53] and courtroom observers (U.K.). These disagreements do not necessarily mean that jury convictions were erroneous. Yet, after careful review,

> Baldwin and McConville found that 5.2% of trials ended in the conviction of an arguably innocent person. The Kalven and Zeisel data suggest a figure of about 3%. These numbers represent the percentage of all trials: because only about two-thirds of studied trials ended in convictions, the percentage of convictions involving innocent defendants is higher—7.9% in the English study and 5% in the Kalven and Zeisel study.[54]

When we consider the devastating consequences of convicting the innocent, these figures ought to be unacceptable. Not only does an innocent person pay for another person's crime, the guilty party remains free to inflict harm on others. Ultimately, justice is not done, and the families of victims are put through unnecessary trauma. For the public at large, the very legitimacy of the criminal justice system is weakened.

WHY TRIALS DO NOT STOP WRONGFUL CONVICTIONS

The question here is whether the jury trial can catch errors made earlier in the criminal justice process. The evidence is not encouraging.

- The prosecutor has enormous leverage to get defendants to plead guilty. Penalties in American jurisdictions are bizarrely harsh by European standards. The promise of months in jail instead of years in prison; of years versus decades in prison; of decades versus death, is likely to make some innocent defendants plead guilty.[55]

- Juries are biased toward conviction. There is an operative assumption of guilt at work in every criminal trial. "The state's decision to charge the defendant with the crime has considerable evidentiary weight regardless of the presumption of innocence or any other platitude. . . . By prosecuting a case, the state does more than simply provide the jury with two conflicting stories—it suggests that the victim's story is believable."[56]

- This factor is much stronger in capital cases, because to be selected for the jury, a prospective juror must not have "scruples" against imposing the death penalty if the defendant is found guilty. "Many studies have shown that these exclusions [of "scrupled" jurors] make the jury more likely to convict.[57]

- Prosecutors are reluctant to back down after charging a defendant with a crime. But the charge is based in most cases on the police report and "the police are more interested in closing the case than obtaining convictions."[58] Thus, the police report will provide sufficient information to make out a prima facie case, but may not be sufficiently strong for a conviction. To make matters worse, careful study of police reports indicates that many are shoddy and filled with misinformation, which the prosecutor is in no position to correct.[59] If the defense presents very strong evidence of innocence, the prosecutor may dismiss, although that decision may be sharply criticized by police and victims.[60] In other cases the prosecutor is likely to push on.

> Having made this decision [to prosecute], the prosecutor will not retreat easily from it without securing something in return, such as a plea, even to a lesser offense. The prosecutor's ability to charge the defendant with the most serious crime supported by the facts will enable the prosecutor to offer significant discounts in return for the plea. If, despite the offer, the defendant refuses to plead guilty, the prosecutor may well prefer to risk a jury verdict of not guilty than to concede that the charge was erroneous, particularly if the victim or the police are committed to the proposition that the defendant is guilty.[61]

- Another reason trials do not stop the conviction of innocent parties is the great imbalance of investigation resources, except in the case of extremely wealthy defendants. In many instances of wrongful conviction, it turns out that exculpatory evidence was buried in police or prosecutorial files. There is no general rule of discovery in criminal cases.

There is "no constitutional requirement that the prosecution make a complete and detailed accounting to the defense of all police investigatory work on a case" (*Moore v. Illinois*, 1972). The rule of *Brady v. Maryland* (1963), although a great advance, only provides that due process requires the prosecutor to turn over material factual evidence that is *favorable* to the defendant. It is the prosecutor, a partisan, who decides what is helpful or favorable to the defendant.

> [I]f the prosecutor believes in the defendant's guilt, the prosecutor probably views the helpful information as a "red herring" with which defense counsel may make mischief, possibly leading to the guilty defendant's acquittal. If the material were truly exculpatory, arguably, the prosecutor would not have brought the case in the first instance.[62]

- Some prosecutors have voluntarily adopted open files policies, but the Supreme Court has not made this better practice a requirement.[63]

- Professor Forst has noted a litany of reasons lay juries make mistakes, each of which has been the subject of an enormous amount of scholarship: juries may not be representative of the people in the community and thus lose the distinctive insight of excluded members; jurors who are not allowed to take notes may fail to recall essential elements of the case in deliberations; some jurors may be genuinely incompetent; jurors are swayed in favor of the prosecution by their sympathy for the victim in particularly gruesome crimes; judges' instructions delivered in "legalese" may be very difficult to understand and may independently lead to mistaken verdicts.[64]

- The Supreme Court has allowed states to have six-person felony juries and has allowed twelve-person juries to reach nonunanimous verdicts by "super-majorities." In the few states that allow this, studies have shown such juries to be more prone to prosecution. Significantly, all capital juries are twelve-person juries that must reach verdicts of guilt and of the penalty by unanimous vote.[65]

IS THE CIVIL LAW TRIAL SYSTEM BETTER?

> In the end, a statement made by an eminent comparative law scholar, after long and careful study, is instructive: he said that if he were innocent, he would prefer to be tried by a civil law court, but that if he were guilty, he would prefer to be tried by a common law court. This is, in effect, a judgment that criminal proceedings in the civil law world are more likely to distinguish accurately between the guilty and the innocent.[66]

Part of the problem is that in the American trial system, the triers of fact are passive and simply receive evidence without any ability to probe what may be clear deficiencies. In the adversary system, to paraphrase Givelber, courts are unconcerned with the obligations of the police or prosecutor to conduct a thorough investigation, "to maintain comprehensive records, or even to choose wisely which potential defendants to charge. These matters—the very essence of a system concerned with actual innocence—are extra-constitutional."[67]

A detailed description of a murder investigation and trial in France provides a graphic example of how the civil law trial can be beneficial to the defendant. In such a trial, the defendant typically is actively involved in the case and although protected by a presumption of innocence, tends to speak and explain his role in the crime. The really important part of the French case is the investigation, which is directed by an investigating magistrate, who, although a member of the judicial arm of government, can direct the police to investigate a case. Perhaps most significantly, the defense counsel can request the government to carry out specific types of investigation.[68]

However attractive this may seem for the plight of the innocent accused, any wholesale modification of our constitutionally entrenched adversary system is fanciful. An argument has been made in a detailed exploration of an extremely colorful British murder case in which an innocent man was acquitted, that under the civil trial system a conviction might have been more likely.[69] Prof. Chrisje Brants, a Dutch-English legal scholar, noting that errors of justice and the conviction of innocent persons has occurred in Europe, suggests that it is not helpful to think of one system or the other as "best." In the modern civil law trial, one version of the truth is developed in the case file or dossier. The trial is not a clash of opposing views of the truth but rather is a verification or refutation of the dossier. The "defence role is limited to an attempt to undermine what is essentially the prosecution case, among other things by prompting the judge to ask relevant questions."[70] The ability of the civil law system to reach the truth depends, much as it does in the adversary system, on the adequacy of the state's investigatory resources and on the probity and competence of police and prosecutors.

Although there is much to be learned from a comparative study of the civil law system, the best that can be expected in the short run are piecemeal and incremental modifications to the adversary trial system that reduce the opportunities for miscarriages of justice. Much of this will of necessity have to be detailed suggestions by practitioners within each state system. Of course, awareness and acknowledgment of the problem of wrongful conviction will be a step toward stimulating state bar associations, prosecutors groups, and the judiciary to explore needed reforms. Beyond this, Professor Givelber suggests that regulating investigation (e.g., a rule requiring police to preserve evidence), supplying defendants with exculpatory information, eliminating incentives for jailhouse informants, and stopping punishing defendants for claiming innocence would go a long way to making trials less hazardous to innocent defendants.[71] Each of these reforms are, of course, subject to debate. Until the judicial and criminal justice systems come to grips with the problem, we can expect to see a steady stream of news stories about the release from prison or death row of wrongly convicted defendants.

SUMMARY

The common law jury trial is a central legal institution in America that has great symbolic and functional importance to support and ensure justice in the processing of criminal suspects. Unlike the trial practices of civil law nations, the common law trial is marked by the unique power of the citizen jury to be the final arbiter of the facts of the case and by the extent to which the trial is conducted by attorneys rather than by the judge.

In the current terrorism crisis, the government has tried some terror suspects in civilian courts under the due process rights afforded to every person charged with crime, thereby upholding the Rule of Law. In other cases, however, the government has taken several shortcuts to the right to trial for persons declared enemy aliens, and even several citizens. These actions do not fit into the constitutional framework for trials in times of national danger that have been worked out by the Supreme Court when the existence of the nation was in greater peril. The Supreme Court has decided to hear these cases and will, for better or worse, issue historic rulings that may affect the liberties for which many are now fighting for the long-run future.

The jury trial of a felony consists of many steps and involves numerous rights enumerated in the Sixth Amendment. After jury selection, the prosecutor and defense counsel may make opening statements. The prosecution enters evidence that is subject to cross-examination by the defense. The defense may then introduce evidence that is subject to the prosecutor's cross-examination, or it may rest without introducing evidence. A defendant has a constitutional right to be present at all phases of the trial unless the defendant voluntarily absents himself or acts disruptively. This right does not include every conference between the judge and the attorneys, in-camera competence hearings, or brief meetings with witnesses or jurors where the meetings are not unfair and the defense attorney is on hand. It does include such aspects of the trial as a visit to the scene of the crime. Compulsory process to subpoena witnesses is another important right that supports a fair trial.

The Fifth Amendment right against self-incrimination requires that the prosecutor and the judge refrain from commenting on the defendant's absolute right not to testify, unless so requested by the defendant. If the prosecutor makes prejudicial statements in closing arguments, they may be the basis for a reversal of the conviction. A mistrial or reversal must be ordered if the prosecutor knowingly allows false evidence to be introduced into the trial. The prosecution may conceal the identity of an informant before a trial, but if the informant testifies, his or her identity must be disclosed to the defense. There is no due process right that the police preserve evidence, as long as evidence is not destroyed in bad faith.

Confrontation is central to the common law trial because it affords the defendant the opportunity to cross-examine the prosecution's witnesses. Cross-examination is the central method used in the trial to elicit the truth; in cross-examination, the lawyer tests the credibility of the witness and the strength of the testimony. A defense attorney seeks to establish a reasonable doubt by cross-examination. The elimination of eye-to-eye contact in the trial itself has been held to be a violation of the Confrontation Clause, unless special circumstances are proven.

Proof of guilt must be beyond a reasonable doubt, a standard of evidence inherent in due process. No specific constitutional definition of reasonable doubt exists; a judge's instruction to the jury on reasonable doubt is constitutional if, taken as a whole, it correctly conveys the idea of reasonable doubt. An instruction that defines it as a "doubt as would give rise to a *grave uncertainty*," standing alone, violates due process because it suggests a higher degree of doubt than is required for acquittal under the reasonable doubt standard. On the other hand, an instruction to the jury that "A reasonable doubt is an *actual and substantial doubt* arising from the evidence, . . . as distinguished from a doubt arising from mere possibility, from bare imagination, or from fanciful conjecture" does not violate due process because it is tied to real facts. A jury instruction using the archaic phrase "moral certainty" does not automatically violate due process.

The jury is guaranteed by the Sixth Amendment in the criminal trial of all but petty crimes and is not required in juvenile delinquency hearings. Some constitutional variations are allowed between the federal common law jury, which requires twelve members and a unanimous verdict, and state juries, some of which consist of fewer than twelve persons and allow verdicts by a "super-majority" (e.g., nine to three).

A fair jury is required under (1) the Equal Protection Clause of the Fourteenth Amendment—persons cannot be excluded from the jury because they share the race, ethnicity or gender of the defendant, or (2) the Sixth Amendment requirement of an impartial jury—any jury must be selected from a panel that reflects a fair cross-section of the community, whatever the relation between the defendant's race, etc. and the characteristics of jury pool members.

The jury itself, because of its small size, need not reflect a fair cross-section of the community, but if the prosecutor uses peremptory challenges to excuse prospective jurors because of their race, ethnicity, or gender, *Batson v. Kentucky* (1986) holds that the Equal Protection Clause requires that the conviction be reversed, unless a race-neutral explanation of the peremptory is accepted. Post-*Batson* cases have extended its rule to civil trials and criminal defendants, and to the categories of gender and ethnicity. The Court has been lenient in accepting race-neutral explanations for striking minorities from juries.

LEGAL PUZZLES

HOW HAVE COURTS DECIDED THESE CASES?

RIGHT TO BE PRESENT

11–1. Rodney Gillam was charged with murdering his wife in 1998. He is paralyzed from the waist down as the result of a prior injury. Some time after his injury he developed a severe vascular disease and in 1996 both of his legs were amputated. Severe complications followed the amputations. Gillam was hospitalized twice in the months before the killing for infections that became severe and required additional surgery. Gillam went to trial in December 1999.

As the trial began, the district court was informed that Gillam was not taking pain medication, limiting the amount of time he could sit upright in his wheelchair. The court accommodated his needs, shortening the workday to six hours and lengthening the breaks so Gillam could return to the jail to lie

down. Three days later, Gillam's medical condition deteriorated further. The jail physician recommended that Gillam spend no more than four hours per day in his wheelchair—any longer would worsen his leg lesions and infections. The physician testified that Gillam would collapse unless he used a bed allowing him to adjust his position to relieve the pressure on his lesions; that use of his wheelchair kept constant pressure on his infected lesions; and that if a continuance were granted, it could take six months to several years before Gillam's lesions healed enough to allow for a regular trial schedule. The court ordered a hospital bed to be available and ordered Gillam to use it either in the courtroom or in an adjacent room where interactive video equipment was connected to the courtroom.

Gillam refused to use the bed in either location, and he warned the deputies that if they tried to put him in the bed, he would throw his urine bag at them. The court then ordered that Gillam be returned to the jail and not allowed to return to court until he agreed to use the bed. After several days of jury selection, Gillam returned to the courtroom. He requested to be allowed to sit in his wheelchair, but the judge refused, whereupon Gillam cursed the court with obscene language and made obscene gestures at everyone present. He was then excluded from the court, and jury selection continued in his absence. Gillam was permitted to return to the courtroom for the first day of trial. At the conclusion of the state's opening argument, Gillam began stating very loudly that he wanted to speak, but the court told him "no." In the midst of Gillam's protests, the court told him that if he kept talking, he would be excluded from the courtroom. Gillam asked again, telling the court that he wanted to represent himself, and he wanted his turn to speak to the jury. He told the court, "I haven't killed anybody." When Gillam refused to stop talking, the court ordered the jury out of the courtroom and called a recess over Gillam's protests. When court was reconvened, the court ordered Gillam excluded from the courtroom for the remainder of the trial.

Did the judge's exclusion order violate Gillam's right to be present during his trial?

HELD: No

11–1. Gillam did not voluntarily absent himself from the trial. He was removed for his conduct. Gillam argues that in *Illinois v. Allen* (1970) the Supreme Court focused on the steps the lower court took to continually inform Allen after his exclusion that he could return to the courtroom if his conduct improved. Gillam suggests that in this case the district court violated his constitutional rights because he was not invited back into the courtroom. However, in *Allen,* the Supreme Court held that a defendant could reclaim his right to be present only when he is willing to behave with the appropriate decorum and respect. *Allen* does not appear to stand for the proposition that courts are to continually question an obstreperous defendant to determine whether that defendant is ready to behave. Instead, *Allen* indicates that the defendant has the burden to inform the court when he is ready to physically return and conform his conduct to the requirements of the court.

In the instant case, Gillam has presented some evidence that he requested that he be permitted to return to the courtroom, the record indicates that there is no evidence indicating that Gillam would have curtailed his disruptive behavior upon his return to the courtroom. Rather, the record indicates that Gillam intended from the beginning to do whatever was necessary to prevent his trial from proceeding. Gillam's unwillingness to take pain medication; multiple dismissals of his court-appointed attorney, followed by requests for continuances; repeated requests for a substitute attorney; threats of throwing his urine bag; ongoing verbal abuse of the judge and others present in the courtroom; and his refusal to sit in a hospital bed rather than in his wheelchair were all designed to interrupt and delay the proceedings. The record reflects that while the district court was concerned about moving the process along, it also was concerned about the possibility of having to stop midtrial and having a delay of several months to more than one year.

The district court did not abuse its discretion in denying Gillam his right to be present during jury selection and during trial because Gillam's conduct warranted his exclusion. *State v. Gillam*, 629 N.W.2d 440 (Minn. 2001)

PRESERVATION OF EVIDENCE

11–2. Patrick Rivers was charged with one count of DUI with serious bodily injury following a motorcycle crash involving Rivers and his friend, Morrie Yedor. After the accident, law enforcement took an oral statement from Yedor, which was later transcribed. The officer who took the statement reviewed the transcript and said it was an accurate transcription of Yedor's statement. The bulk of Yedor's statement refers to Rivers as the driver of the motorcycle and Yedor as the passenger. However, at the end of his statement, Yedor said: "I made a left turn and lost control of the motorcycle." The audiotape of Yedor's statement was subsequently lost, but the transcript was not. Because Yedor's last statement would appear to exonerate Rivers, Rivers argued that the loss of the audiotape of Yedor's statement violated Rivers's right to due process.

Did the loss of the audiotape require the dismissal of charges against Rivers?

Holding available from instructor

CONFRONTATION

11–3. Defendant was convicted by a jury of first-degree sexual conduct against his daughter when she was five years old. She initially named someone else of committing sexually abusive acts, but eventually accused her father. He denied the charges. At defendant's preliminary examination, it became clear that the complainant likely would be unable to testify in court at trial. Her preliminary examination testimony was obtained on videotape in closed chambers with only the judge, a social worker, and the attorneys present. At trial, over the defendant's objection, the judge removed the defendant from the courtroom and allowed the child to testify in his absence. The court-

room was closed to everyone but the jury, a social worker, the attorneys, a law enforcement officer, and the court's staff. The defendant was allowed to watch the child's testimony on closed-circuit television and to confer with counsel during the single recess that was called. To assist with this, the defendant was permitted to take notes with a pencil and paper. The judge gave a brief explanation of the defendant's absence from the courtroom to the jury, indicating that he would be able to view the testimony from another room. The complainant told the jury of one incident where the defendant encouraged her to kiss his privates and of a second where he penetrated her digitally.

A Michigan statute, dating back to 1846, reads: "No person indicted for a felony shall be tried unless personally present during the trial. . . ."

1. Was the statute violated?
2. If so, was this grounds to reverse the conviction and order a new trial?

Holding available from instructor

PEREMPTORY CHALLENGE

11–4. Vincent Roundtree was convicted in the Gwinett County (Georgia) Superior Court of shoplifting. The trial court allowed the State to strike juror Troy Marshall, who is African American, with a peremptory challenge. Marshall was the only member of Roundtree's race on the jury panel. The State conceded that Roundtree made out a prima facie inference of racial discrimination, but asserted that it also met its burden of providing race-neutral reasons to explain the strike. In response to the *Batson* challenge, the prosecutor explained that he struck juror Marshall because he had a prior bad experience with a white police officer, and all the prosecution witnesses in the case, including the police officer who arrested Roundtree, were white. Marshall explained that while riding in Jackson, Mississippi, in his father's car, he was pulled over by a white police officer who ran a check to determine if the car had been stolen. Marshall believed that he was pulled over only because he was an African American man driving a nice car. The prosecutor also cited Marshall's ongoing work with a prison ministry, which the prosecutor felt, in combination with his prior negative experience with police, would affect the juror's ability to be fair and impartial. The trial court denied the *Batson* challenge, noting that he understood the prosecution's strike to be based, in part, upon a concern that the juror may have racial animus himself.

Was the prosecutor's explanation for striking the juror race neutral?

Holding available from instructor

FURTHER READING

Jeffrey Abramson, *We, the Jury: The Jury System and the Ideal of Democracy* (New York: Basic Books, 1994).

George P. Fletcher, *With Justice for Some: Victims' Rights in Criminal Trials* (Reading, MA: Addison-Wesley, 1995).

Barry Scheck, Peter Neufeld, and Jim Dwyer, *Actual Innocence: Five Days to Execution, and Other Dispatches from the Wrongly Convicted* (New York: Doubleday, 2000).

ENDNOTES

1. See Charles Rembar, *The Law of the Land: The Evolution of Our Legal System* (New York: Touchstone Books, 1980).

2. William Blackstone, *Commentaries on the Laws of England, Vol. 4, of Public Wrongs* (1769 facsimile, Chicago: University of Chicago Press, 1979), 342–43.

3. See Jerome Frank, *Courts on Trial: Myth and Reality in American Justice* (1949; repr., New York: Atheneum, 1963); Stephen J. Adler, *The Jury: Disorder in the Courts* (New York: Doubleday, 1994).

4. John H. Langbein, "The Criminal Trial before the Lawyers," *University of Chicago Law Review* 45 (1978): 263–316; Malcolm M. Feeley, "Plea Bargaining and the Structure of the Criminal Process," in *Criminal Justice: Law and Politics*, 5th ed., George F. Cole, ed. (Pacific Grove, CA: Brooks/Cole, 1988), 467–82.

5. Barton L. Ingraham, *The Structure of Criminal Procedure: Law and Practice of France, the Soviet Union, China, and the United States* (New York: Greenwood Press, 1987), 86.

6. See Rene David and John E. C. Brierly, *Major Legal Systems in the World Today*, 3d ed. (London: Stephens & Sons, 1985); Rene David and Henry P. de Vries, *The French Legal System: An Introduction to Civil Law Systems* (New York: Oceana Publications, 1958); Richard J. Terrill, *World Criminal Justice Systems: A Survey, Fifth Edition* (Cincinnati: Anderson, 2003).

7. Ingraham, *Criminal Procedure*, 85.

8. From among a vast and fascinating literature, see Stephen Phillips, *No Heroes, No Villains* (New York: Random House, 1977); Marshall Houts, *King's X: Common Law and the Death of Sir Harry Oaks* (New York: Morrow, 1972); Paul and Shirley Eberle, *The Abuse of Innocence: The McMartin Preschool Trial* (Buffalo, NY: Prometheus Books, 1993).

9. Danny Hakim, "Threats and Responses: The Detroit Trial; 2 Arabs Convicted and 2 Cleared of Terrorist Plot against the U.S.," *New York Times*, June 4, 2003; Hearing of the Senate Finance Committee, "The Alias Among Us: The Homeland Security and Terrorism Threat from Document Fraud, Identity Theft and Social Security Number Misuse," *Federal News Service*, September 9, 2003 (testimony of Richard Convertino, Assistant U.S. Attorney, Eastern District of Michigan, Department of Justice and Yousseff Hmimssa, federal prisoner testifying on the Detroit terrorist sleeper cell case; Lexis: News File).

10. Siobhan Roth, "Material Support Law: Weapon in War on Terror the United States Has Charged More Than 30 People with Aiding Terrorists; A Roundup of Where the Cases Stand," *Legal Times*, May 5, 2003.

11. Editorial, "Ashcroft Earned Admonishment by Bragging Too Much," *Detroit News*, December 14, 2003.

12. President of the United States, Military Order of November 13, 2001, "Detention, Treatment, and Trial of Certain Non-Citizens in the War Against Terrorism," 66 Federal Register 57,833 (November 16, 2001).

13. A. Christopher Bryant and Carl Tobias, "Civil Liberties in a Time of Terror: Article: *Quirin* Revisited," *Wisconsin Law Review* 2003 (2003): 309–364.

14. Kenneth Anderson, "The Military Tribunal Order: What to Do with Bin Laden and Al Qaeda Terrorists: A Qualified Defense of Military Commissions and United States Policy on Detainees at Guantanamo Naval Base," *Harvard Journal of Law & Public Policy* 25(2002): 591–634; Ruth Wedgewood, "Al Qaeda, Terrorism and Military Commissions," *American Journal of International Law* 96(2002): 328–337.

15. Samantha A. Pitts-Kiefer, "Note: Jose Padilla: Enemy Combatant or Common Criminal?" *Villanova Law Review* 48 (2003): 875–910, 882 (footnotes omitted).

16. *Padilla v. Rumsfeld*, 233 F.Supp.2d 564, 593 (S.D.N.Y., 2002).

17. 233 F.Supp.2d at 593–94.

18. 233 F.Supp.2d at 594.

19. *Padilla v. Rumsfeld*, 256 F.Supp.2d 218 (S.D.N.Y. 2003).

20. See Alejandra Rodriguez, "Comment: Is the War on Terrorism Compromising Civil Liberties? A Discussion of *Hamdi* and *Padilla*," *California Western Law Review* 39 (2003): 379–394.

21. Pitts-Kiefer, "Jose Padilla," 900–901.

22. Ibid., 903.

23. Benjamin Weiser, "Judge Affirms Terror Suspect Must Meet with Lawyers," *New York Times*, March 12, 2003.

24. Matt Bivens, "Kafkaesque Justice," *The St. Petersburg* (FL.) *Times*, September 16, 2003.

25. Editorial, "Key Legal Shields Forfeited in War on Terrorism; Assault on Procedural Rights Threatens the Safeguards That Keep America from Becoming a Police State," *Detroit News*, September 14, 2003.

26. Linda Greenhouse, "Justices to Hear Case of Citizen Held as Enemy," *New York Times*, January 10, 2004.

27. S. Engleberg, "At Storm's Eye, a Law about Secrets," *New York Times*, February 13, 1989.

28. 144 Vt. 86; 475 A.2d 1045 (1984).

29. 2003 Vt. 26; 825 A.2d 32 (2003).

30. Tim O'Brien, "Reasonable Doubt and DNA," *Washington Post*, September 7, 2000; Associated Press, "Innocence Proved; Case Was Source of Adverse Evidence Preservation Ruling," *Associated Press State & Local Wire*, August 10, 2000.

31. Charles Rembar, *The Law of the Land: The Evolution of Our Legal System* (New York: Touchstone Books, 1980), 337.

32. Nancy Walker Perry and Lawrence S. Wrightsman, *The Child Witness: Legal Issues and Dilemmas* (Newbury Park, CA: Sage, 1991).

33. See Dorothy Rabinowitz, *No Crueler Tyrannies: Accusation, False Witness and Other Terrors of Our Times* (Wall Street Journal Book, 2003).

34. Harry Kalven and Hans Zeisel, *The American Jury* (Boston: Little, Brown, 1966), 490.

35. Federal Rules of Criminal Procedure 23(a).

36. See Hiroshi Fukurai, Edgar W. Butler, and Richard Krooth, *Race and the Jury* (New York: Plenum Press, 1993).

37. Michael Finkelstein, "The Application of Statistical Decision Theory to the Jury Discrimination Cases," *Harvard Law Review* 80(1966): 338.

38. See Henry J. Abraham, *Freedom and the Court: Civil Rights and Liberties in the United States*, 4th ed. (New York: Oxford University Press, 1982), 76.

39. Cases collected in "Project: Twenty-Fifth Annual Review of Criminal Procedure," *Georgetown Law Journal* 76(1996): 713–1530, 1145, n. 1714.

40. *United States v. Hafen,* 726 F.2d 21 (1st Cir. 1984); *United States v. Rodriguez,* 776 F.2d 1509 (11th Cir. 1985); *United States v. Pepe,* 747 F.2d 632 (11th Cir. 1984); *State v. McCarthy,* 496 A.2d 513 (Conn. 1985).

41. *United States v. Arnett,* 342 F. Supp. 1255 (D. Mass. 1970).

42. Charles J. Ogletree, "Just Say No!: A Proposal to Eliminate Racially Discriminatory Uses of Peremptory Challenges," *American Criminal Law Review* 31 (1994): 1099–151.

43. Ibid., 1113–16.

44. Innocence Project, http://www.innocenceproject.org/index.php, (accessed January 11, 2004).

45. Adam Liptak, "Texas Governor Pardons 35 Arrested in Tainted Sting," *New York Times,* August 23, 2003.

46. Bob Herbert, "Justice Takes Its Time," *New York Times,* January 2, 2004; Bob Herbert, "Getting Away With . . ." *New York Times,* January 5, 2004.

47. Adam Liptak, "Suspension of Executions Is Urged for Pennsylvania," *New York Times* March 5, 2003; Jodi Wilgoren, "Citing Issue of Fairness, Governor Clears out Death Row in Illinois," *New York Times*, January 12, 2003; Alex Kotlowitz, "In the Face of Death," *New York Times Magazine,* July 6, 2003. Sec. 6, pp. 32 et seq; Adam Liptak, "Juries Reject Death Penalty in Nearly All Federal Trials," *New York Times*, June 15, 2003.

48. See Barry Scheck, Peter Neufeld, and Jim Dwyer, *Actual Innocence: When Justice Goes Wrong and How to Make It Right* (New York: Signet, 2001), ch. 3.

49. Francis X. Clines, "Work by Expert Witness Is Now on Trial," *New York Times,* September 5, 2001 (regarding Fred Zain); Jim Yardley, "Flaws in Chemist's Findings Free Man at Center of Inquiry," *New York Times*, May 8, 2001 (regarding Joyce Gilchrist).

50. Adam Liptak, "Houston DNA Review Clears Convicted Rapist, and Ripples in Texas Could Be Vast," *New York Times*, March 11, 2003.

51. C. Ronald Huff, Arye Rattner, and Edward Sagarin, *Convicted but Innocent: Wrongful Conviction and Public Policy* (Thousand Oaks, CA: Sage, 1996), 53–62.

52. Daniel Givelber, "Meaningless Acquittals, Meaningful Convictions: Do We Reliably Acquit the Innocent?" *Rutgers Law Review* 49 (1997): 1317–1396.

53. Harry Kalven, Jr. and Hans Zeisel, *The American Jury* (Boston: Little, Brown, 1966); John Baldwin and Michael McConville, *Jury Trials* (1979)

54. Givelber, "Meaningless Acquittals," 1343.

55. See Samuel R. Gross, "The Risks of Death: Why Erroneous Convictions Are Common in Capital Cases," *Buffalo Law Review* 44 (1996): 469–500.

56. Givelber, "Meaningless Acquittals," 1372.

57. Gross, "Risks of Death," 494–95.

58. Givelber, "Meaningless Acquittals," 1361.

59. Stanley Z. Fisher, "Just the Facts, Ma'am: Lying and the Omission of Exculpatory Evidence in Police Reports," *New England Law Review* 28(1993): 1–62.

60. See Gross, "Risks of Death," 490–91.

61. Givelber, "Meaningless Acquittals," 1363 (footnotes omitted).

62. Givelber, "Meaningless Acquittals," 1375 (footnotes omitted).

63. H. Lee Sarokin and William Zuckerman, "Presumed Innocent? Restrictions on Criminal Discovery in Federal Court Belie This Presumption," *Rutgers Law Review* 43(1991): 1089.

64. Brian Forst, *Errors of Justice* (Cambridge University Press, 2004), 137–38.

65. Ibid., 140–45.

66. Givelber, "Meaningless Acquittals," 1317, quoting John H. Merryman, *The Civil Law Tradition* 132 (2d ed. 1985).

67. Givelber, "Meaningless Acquittals," 1371 (footnotes omitted). Givelber was referring specifically to Supreme Court cases, but his point refers to the role of trial judges as well.

68. Bron McKillop, "Anatomy of a French Murder Case," *American Journal of Comparative Law,* 45(1997): 527–583.

69. See Marshall Houts, *Kings X: Common Law and the Death of Sir Harry Oakes* (New York: William Morrow, 1972).

70. Chrisjie Brants, "Miscarriages of Justice and Comparative Research: Pitfalls and Potential," Paper presented at the Annual Conference of the American Society of Criminology, Denver, CO, November 2003.

71. Givelber, "Meaningless Acquittals," 1381–1394.

JUSTICES OF THE SUPREME COURT

THE TWENTY-FIRST CENTURY COURT
SOUTER—THOMAS—GINSBURG—BREYER

Each of these justices previously served as federal judges, although David Souter, a New Hampshire supreme court judge, had barely taken his federal appointment to the First Circuit Court of Appeals before his elevation to the Supreme Court, and Clarence Thomas had only one year of judicial experience. These appointments of President George Bush replaced the most enduring liberals on the Court—Brennan and Marshall. Many thought that these appointments would mark the end of the politically inflammatory abortion rights decision, Roe v. Wade. *This was not to be. In the criminal procedure area, however, the new appointments did not change the generally pro-prosecution cast of the Court. What was lost with the retirement of Brennan and Marshall was a strong liberal voice, even if in dissent. Justice Souter aligned with the moderate-conservative center of the court and Justice Thomas joined the extreme conservatives on these issues.*

President Bill Clinton, appointing the first Democrats to the Court since 1967 (Thurgood Marshall), disappointed some supporters by not naming liberals to offset the distinctive conservatism of Justices Scalia and Thomas. Justices Ginsburg and Breyer both had reputations as extremely competent and moderate federal judges. Ruth Bader Ginsburg had been a leading litigator in womens' rights cases before the Supreme Court in the 1970s and was viewed as liberal on some issues. Justice Breyer had a national reputation as an original thinker on issues of economic regula-tion and as a member of the federal Sentencing Commission. Neither of them, replacing Justices Blackmun and White, were expected to modify the Court's position on criminal procedure. Indeed, they have proven to be centrists. This reflects the national mood and President Clinton's position as moderately conservative on crime issues.

Oddly, then, the only sitting justice who might fairly be called a criminal procedure liberal is Justice Stevens, who migrated to the position from a centrist posture. The Court at the outset of the twenty-first century can best be described as moderate to conservative on criminal procedure issues. The general framework of incorporation, a legacy of the Warren Court's "due process revolution," has endured; but it has been weakened by decisions that block access to federal courts (i.e., standing and habeas corpus) and by decisions that interpret such categories as due process, reasonable suspicion, probable cause, and cruel and unusual punishment in ways that are favorable to the state. Defendants have been able to prevail on issues associated with property rights (e.g., asset forfeiture) or race discrimination (peremptory challenges to remove jurors). Recent decisions holding that auto checkpoints for crime control purposes violate the Fourth Amendment or that a bare anonymous tip does not sustain reasonable suspicion may indicate that even a very conservative Supreme Court has reached a point beyond which individual rights under the Constitution cannot be denied without eroding the fabric of American liberty.

DAVID H. SOUTER

New Hampshire 1939–

Republican

Appointed by
George Bush

Years of Service.
1990–

*Collection of the Supreme Court of the United States.
Photographer: Joseph Bailey*

LIFE AND CAREER   Souter's pre-Court record was so obscure that he was dubbed the "stealth" candidate, after the radar-avoiding airplane. This politically prudent choice by President Bush put a candidate with no known views on the abortion issue before the Senate, which had blocked Judge Robert Bork's 1987 appointment because of his outspoken and radically conservative views. Justice Souter's smooth nomination proved the wisdom of this choice.

A native of New Hampshire, Souter attended Harvard College, spent two years at Oxford University as a Rhodes Scholar, and after graduating from Harvard Law School practiced law for two years in Concord, New Hampshire. He served as deputy state attorney general under Warren Rudman and was then appointed state attorney general. In 1978 he became a trial judge, and in 1983 Governor John Sununu, on the recommendation of Senator Warren Rudman, named Souter to the New Hampshire Supreme Court. In 1990 Souter was appointed to the federal Circuit Court of Appeals but was soon

(Continued)

after nominated to the Supreme Court, clearly on the recommendation of President Bush's White House chief of staff, John Sununu.

CONTRIBUTION TO CRIMINAL PROCEDURE By replacing Justice Brennan, the most liberal justice on the Court, Souter at first swung the Court's criminal procedure jurisprudence generally in favor of the state. In his first year on the Court, he voted with the majority in every case, almost always for the prosecution argument. By 1995, he began to shift to a more moderate stance, in his majority opinion holding that a state appellate court on collateral review must grant a new trial to the defendant if a prosecutor withheld relevant evidence (*Kyles v. Whitely*, 1995). Although he still votes more often for the prosecution, in some cases he has joined what passes for a liberal bloc, for example, in joining Justice Stevens's dissent in *Illinois v. Wardlow* (2000) (flight from police constitutes reasonable suspicion), along with Ginsburg and Breyer.

SIGNATURE OPINION Dissenting opinion in *Pennsylvania Board of Probation and Parole v. Scott* (1998). In a formulaic opinion by Justice Thomas, the Court's majority held that evidence seized in violation of a parolee's Fourth Amendment rights (parole agents entered his home without a warrant or exigent circumstances) is not excluded under the exclusionary rule. Souter's dissent (joined by Stevens, Ginsburg, and Breyer) relied on a functional analysis of the work of parole officers to demonstrate that they are subject to similar motives as police and that the deterrent rationale of the exclusionary rule should therefore apply to them.

ASSESSMENT Souter is a part of the moderate-conservative center of the Court. In *Planned Parenthood v. Casey* (1992) he joined with O'Connor and Kennedy, in upholding *Roe v. Wade* (by a narrow 5–4 vote) on the basis of *stare decisis*. *Casey* signaled that the most extreme conservative interpretations of the Constitution, espoused by Chief Justice Rehnquist and Justices Scalia and Thomas, would not become the law of the land. In today's world of extremely partisan politics, Souter has become a lightening rod for conservative ire. "No more Souters!" had become a slogan of conservatives frustrated that the Reagan-Bush appointees on the Supreme Court have not been able to overturn a woman's right to choose abortion, *Miranda*, and the ban on school prayer under the First Amendment.

FURTHER READING

David Garrow, "Justice Souter Emerges," *The New York Times Magazine*, September 25, 1994.

CLARENCE THOMAS

Virginia 1948–

Republican

Appointed by George Bush

Years of Service: 1991–

Collection of the Supreme Court of the United States. Photographer: Joseph Bailey

LIFE AND CAREER Thomas was born into a poor family in segregated Savannah, Georgia. He was raised by his grandparents, who instilled in him a sense of pride and discipline, self-reliance and hard work, commitment to black solidarity through the NAACP, and a determination that education was the key to a better life. He attended Catholic school and experienced blatant racism of fellow students in a Missouri seminary. He graduated from Holy Cross College and Yale Law School, where he developed a dislike for affirmative action. After graduation in 1974, he worked as an assistant attorney-general in Missouri, as a corporate lawyer, and as legislative assistant to Senator Danforth of Missouri in Washington.

As one of few African American conservatives during the Reagan administration, he became chairman of the Equal Employment Opportunity Commission (EEOC), an agency to which the administration was hostile. Thomas handled this difficult assignment by ultimately abandoning the agency's affirmative action agenda and class-action suits and focusing instead on individual discrimination cases. Many criticized his EEOC leadership as failing to effectively support claims of minorities, women, and the elderly. He was nominated to the U.S. Court of Appeals for the Washington, D.C., Circuit in 1989, an appointment that was viewed as a stepping stone to the Supreme Court.

Thomas's confirmation process, when nominated by President Bush to the Supreme Court to replace retiring Justice Thurgood Marshall, was extremely controversial. He was lambasted for his conservatism, his lack of high judicial qualifications, and his opposition to *Roe v. Wade*. Many thought that George Bush cynically manipulated the "black seat" on the Court to make it difficult for African Americans to oppose a black candidate. And this was *before* the sensational story broke that he had sexually harassed Anita Hill, a former employee and a law professor. The hearings on Professor Hill's testimony and Judge Thomas's impassioned defense were televised and were the scandal of the hour. Thomas denied the allegations and called the ordeal "a high-tech lynching for uppity blacks." His nomination was affirmed by a 52-to-48 vote of the Senate.

CONTRIBUTION TO CRIMINAL PROCEDURE From 1991 to 1995, Thomas was second only to Chief Justice Rehnquist in conservative voting in criminal procedure cases, supporting individuals in only 19 percent of cases. Although he is a solid conservative on a conservative court, he has little influence because he is not given opportunities to write majority opinions for the Court in important cases, but typically writes majority opinions only when the justices share a strong consensus, as was the case in holding that the "knock-and-announce" rule of search warrant execution is a constitutional rule (*Wilson v. Arkansas,* 1995). He is the most conservative justice in death penalty, habeas corpus, and Eighth Amendment cases.

SIGNATURE OPINION Dissenting opinion in *Hudson v. McMillan* (1992). The court held that excessive force by a prison guard (the beating alleged was deliberate and resulted in minor bruises, facial swelling, loosened teeth, and a cracked dental plate) may constitute cruel and unusual punishment even though the inmate does not suffer serious injury. Justice Thomas said, "In my view, a use of force that causes only insignificant harm to a prisoner may be immoral, it may be tortious, it may be criminal, and it may even be remediable under other provisions of the Federal Constitution, but it is not 'cruel and unusual punishment.'"

ASSESSMENT He applied the theory of originalism more rigidly than Justice Scalia, and although he expresses confidently that he knows the intent of the framers of the Constitution, it was noted that he "has shown little familiarity with the most recent scholarship about" the origin of the Fourteenth Amendment, where he seems to have mistakenly asserted that its framers intended to create a "color-blind" Constitution, a position that supports his votes.

FURTHER READING

Christopher E. Smith, "Clarence Thomas: A Distinctive Justice," *Seton Hall Law Review* 28 (1997): 1–28.

RUTH BADER GINSBURG

New York 1933 –

Democrat

Appointed by William Clinton

Years of Service: 1993–

Collection of the Supreme Court of the United States. Photographer: Richard Strauss

LIFE AND CAREER Ruth Bader grew up in Brooklyn, New York, in a Jewish, lower-middle-class family. An excellent student, she won a scholarship to Cornell University, and decided to pursue a career in the law with her husband, Martin Ginsburg. Following Martin's army service and the birth of their first child, she entered Harvard Law School a year after Martin did. She was one of only nine women in a class of five hundred students. Martin was diagnosed with cancer and underwent radiation therapy while Ruth took notes in his classes as well as her own, and typed his third-year paper while caring for their child. Martin recovered, obtained a position with a New York law firm, and Ruth transferred to Columbia Law School. Justice Ginsburg was the first woman to have served on two law reviews.

After graduation, sexism prevented her from being hired by a law firm. She clerked for a state judge. She joined the Rutgers Law School faculty in 1963; in 1972 she became the first tenured woman law professor at Columbia Law School. Between 1972 and 1978 Ginsburg argued six and won five gender-equality cases before the Supreme Court, on the basis that sex-role stereotypes violated the Equal Protection Clause. Some have called her "the Thurgood Marshall of womens' rights." In 1980 she was appointed to the U.S. Court of Appeals for the District of Columbia, where she developed an excellent reputation as a leading centrist judge.

CONTRIBUTION TO CRIMINAL PROCEDURE Ginsburg's votes in criminal cases are liberal to moderate. She has been described as pragmatic. She has sided with the government in upholding drug testing of school athletes, pretext searches, gaining consent to search cars without informing drivers of their rights, the forfeiture of a wife's interest in a car that was confiscated after her husband was found guilty of soliciting prostitution, and ordering nonsuspicious passengers out of stopped cars.

However, she has joined with liberal and moderate justices to support individual rights in dissent where fleeing from an officer has been held to constitute reasonable suspicion, where a car was seized for forfeiture without a warrant, where parole officers entered a parolee's home without a warrant, and where police searched the handbag of a nonsuspicious automobile passenger. She, along with Justice Stevens, has attacked the way in which *Michigan v. Long* (1983) has applied the adequate and independent state grounds doctrine, arguing in *Arizona v. Evans* (1995) that the Court should not overturn state court decisions that expand defendants constitutional rights.

SIGNATURE OPINION *Florida v. J.L.* (2000). For a unanimous Court, Ginsburg held that an anonymous phone call "that a young black male standing at a particular bus stop and wearing a plaid shirt was carrying a gun" does not in itself establish reasonable suspicion to conduct a *Terry* stop if all that the police know is that a person at the described place fits the description given by the caller. The ruling indicates that the

(Continued)

Court has become wary of extending the reach of police powers that clearly go beyond constitutional protections: "an automatic firearm exception to our established reliability analysis would rove too far."

ASSESSMENT   She is a moderate liberal and takes a dynamic approach to the complex issues of legal process. The major themes of her writings include the ideal of a person's day in court; court efficiency; and judicial integrity, including *stare decisis* and procedural regularity. In *United States v. Virginia* (1996) she wrote the majority opinion holding that the Virginia Military Institute could not lawfully exclude women students.

FURTHER READING

Elijah Yip and Eric K. Yamamoto, "Justice Ruth Bader Ginsburg's Jurisprudence of Process and Procedure," *Hawaii Law Review* 20 (1998): 647–698.

STEPHEN G. BREYER

Massachusetts 1938 –

Democrat

Appointed by
William Clinton

Years of Service:
1994–

*Collection of the Supreme Court of
the United States.*
Photographer: Richard Strauss

LIFE AND CAREER   Raised in San Francisco, Breyer's father, a lawyer, brought him to a voting booth when he was young and helped to impart "a love for the possibilities of democracy." His mother was active in local Democratic politics and the League of Women Voters and instilled in Stephen a sense that intellectual activity had to be balanced by an ability to work with and help people. He was Boy Scout, worked as a delivery boy, and dug ditches for a local utility company. He graduated from Stanford University with highest honors; earned another degree at Oxford University in philosophy, politics, and economics; and was graduated *magna cum laude* from Harvard Law School in 1964.

After law school, Breyer clerked for Justice Goldberg. He thereafter was an antitrust lawyer in the Justice Department and a Harvard Law School professor. He developed a sophisticated but pragmatic theory of the regulatory state and believes that economic regulation should maximize competition and not burden the private sector with unnecessary government restraints. He also served as an assistant on the Watergate Special Prosecution force that helped to topple President Nixon, and as counsel to the Senate Judiciary Committee. In 1980 he was appointed to the First Circuit Court of Appeals. He was a coalition builder on that court. In 1985 Judge Breyer was appointed to the United States Sentencing Commission, which was designed to rationalize federal sentencing practices.

CONTRIBUTION TO CRIMINAL PROCEDURE   As an expert in economic regulation, Breyer has written few major opinions in the criminal procedure area. His voting pattern is middle-of-the-road. He voted for the government in *United States v. Armstrong* (1996) (not selective prosecution to charge a disproportionate percentage of African Americans for crack cocaine offenses); *Carlisle v. United States* (1996) (motion for judgment of acquittal cannot be granted if filed one day beyond time limit); *Lewis v. Casey* (1996) (no violation of rights from inadequate law library unless actual injury shown); *Wyoming v. Houghton* (1999) (police can search handbag of a nonsuspicious automobile passenger); and *Bond v. United States* (2000) (traveler has no expectation of privacy "that strangers will not push, pull, prod, squeeze, or otherwise manipulate his luggage" on an intercity bus). He has, on occasion, joined liberal and moderate justices: in dissent where fleeing from an officer has been held to constitute reasonable suspicion, in dissent where parole officers entered a parolee's home without a warrant, and in dissent where a wife's interest in a car was forfeited for her husband's crime.

SIGNATURE OPINION   Dissenting opinion in *Apprendi v. New Jersey* (2000). The majority held that a factual element of the crime used to enhance a sentence must be submitted to a jury and proved beyond a reasonable doubt. Breyer, dissenting, stated that "the real world of criminal justice cannot hope to meet" the ideal that "juries, not judges, determin[e] the existence of those facts upon which increased punishment turns." "It can function only with the help of procedural compromises, particularly in respect to sentencing."

ASSESSMENT   In *United States v. Lopez* (1995) the Court struck down a federal law based on the commerce clause—making it a federal crime to possess a weapon within one hundred feet of a local school—for the first time since the 1930s. Breyer wrote a sharp and detailed dissent, joined by Justices Stevens, Souter, and Ginsburg, defending federal authority to pass such a law.

FURTHER READING

Walter E. Joyce, "The Early Constitutional Jurisprudence of Justice Stephen G. Breyer: A Study of the Justice's First Year on the United States Supreme Court," *Seton Hall Constitutional Law Journal* 7(1996): 149–163.

*Selected Provisions of the
Constitution of the United States*

We the People of the United States, in Order to form a more perfect Union, establish Justice, insure domestic Tranquility, provide for the common defence, promote the general Welfare, and secure the Blessings of Liberty to ourselves and our Posterity, do ordain and establish this Constitution for the United States of America.

Article I

Section 1. All legislative Powers herein granted shall be vested in a Congress of the United States, which shall consist of a Senate and House of Representatives.

Section 2. The House of Representatives shall be composed of Members chosen every second Year by the People of the several States, and the Electors in each State shall have the Qualifications requisite for Electors of the most numerous Branch of the State Legislature.

No Person shall be a Representative who shall not have attained to the Age of twenty five Years, and been seven Years a Citizen of the United States, and who shall not, when elected, be an Inhabitant of that State in which he shall be chosen.

[Representatives and direct Taxes shall be apportioned among the several States which maybe included within this Union, according to their respective Numbers, which shall be determined by adding to the whole Number of free Persons, including those bound to Service for a Term of Years, and excluding Indians not taxed, three fifths of all other Persons.][1] The actual Enumeration shall be made within three Years after the first Meeting of the Congress of the United States, and within every subsequent Term of ten Years, in such Manner as they shall by Law direct. The number of Representatives shall not exceed one for every thirty Thousand, but each State shall have at Least one Representative; and until such enumeration shall be made, the State of New Hampshire shall be entitled to chuse three, Massachusetts eight, Rhode Island and Providence Plantations one, Connecticut five, New York six, New Jersey four, Pennsylvania eight, Delaware one, Maryland six, Virginia ten, North Carolina five, South Carolina five, and Georgia three.

When vacancies happen in the Representation from any State, the Executive Authority thereof shall issue Writs of Election to fill such Vacancies.

The House of Representatives shall chuse their Speaker and other Officers; and shall have the sole Power of Impeachment

Section 3. The Senate of the United States shall be composed of two Senators from each State, [chosen by the Legislature thereof,][2] for six Years; and each Senator shall have one Vote.

Immediately after they shall be assembled in Consequence of the first Election, they shall be divided as equally as may be into three Classes. The Seats of the Senators of the first Class shall be vacated at the Expiration of the second Year, of the second Class at the Expiration of the fourth Year, and of the third Class at the Expiration of the sixth Year, so that one third may be chosen every second Year; [and if Vacancies happen by Resignation, or otherwise, during the Recess of the Legislature of any State, the Executive thereof may make temporary Appointments until the next Meeting of the Legislature, which shall then fill such Vacancies.][3]

No Person shall be a Senator who shall not have attained to the Age of thirty Years, and been nine Years a Citizen of the United States, and who shall not, when elected, be an Inhabitant of that State for which he shall be chosen.

The Vice President of the United States shall be President of the Senate, but shall have no Vote, unless they be equally divided.

The Senate shall chuse their other Officers, and also a President pro tempore, in the Absence of the Vice President, or when he shall exercise the Office of President of the United States.

The Senate shall have the sole Power to try all Impeachments. When sitting for that Purpose, they shall be on Oath or Affirmation. When the President of the United States is tried, the Chief Justice shall preside: And no Person shall be convicted without the Concurrence of two thirds of the Members present.

---

[1] Changed by section 2 of the Fourteenth Amendment.
[2] Changed by the Seventeenth Amendment to allow popular election of Senators.
[3] Changed by the Seventeenth Amendment.

Judgment in Cases of Impeachment shall not extend further than to removal from Office, and disqualification to hold and enjoy any Office of honor, Trust or Profit under the United States: but the Party convicted shall nevertheless be liable and subject to Indictment, Trial, Judgment and Punishment, according to Law.

Section 4. The Times, Places and Manner of holding Elections for Senators and Representatives, shall be prescribed in each State by the Legislature thereof; but the Congress may at any time by Law make or alter such Regulations, except as to the Places of chusing Senators.

The Congress shall assemble at least once in every Year, and such Meeting shall be [on the first Monday in December,][4] unless they shall by Law appoint a different Day.

Section 5. Each House shall be the Judge of the Elections, Returns and Qualifications of its own Members, and a Majority of each shall constitute a Quorum to do Business; but a smaller Number may adjourn from day to day, and may be authorized to compel the Attendance of absent Members, in such Manner, and under such Penalties as each House may provide.

Each House may determine the Rules of its Proceedings, punish its Members for disorderly Behaviour, and, with the Concurrence of two thirds, expel a Member.

Each House shall keep a Journal of its Proceedings, and from time to time publish the same, excepting such Parts as may in their Judgment require Secrecy; and the Yeas and Nays of the Members of either House on any question shall, at the Desire of one fifth of those Present, be entered on the Journal.

Neither House, during the Session of Congress, shall, without the Consent of the other, adjourn for more than three days, nor to any other Place than that in which the two Houses shall be sitting.

Section 6. The Senators and Representatives shall receive a Compensation for their Services, to be ascertained by Law, and paid out of the Treasury of the United States. They shall in all Cases, except Treason, Felony and Breach of the Peace, be privileged from Arrest during their Attendance at the Session of their respective Houses, and in going to and returning from the same; and for any Speech or Debate in either House, they shall not be questioned in any other Place.

No Senator or Representative shall, during the Time for which he was elected, be appointed to any civil Office under the Authority of the United States, which shall have been created, or the Emoluments whereof shall have been encreased during such time; and no Person holding any Office under the United States, shall be a Member of either House during his Continuance in Office.

Section 7. All Bills for raising Revenue shall originate in the House of Representatives; but the Senate may propose or concur with Amendments as on other Bills.

Every Bill which shall have passed the House of Representatives and the Senate, shall, before it becomes a Law, be presented to the President of the United States; If he approve he shall sign it, but if not he shall return it, with his Objections to that House in which it shall have originated, who shall enter the Objections at large on their Journal, and proceed to reconsider it. If after such Reconsideration two thirds of that House shall agree to pass the Bill, it shall be sent, together with the Objections, to the other House, by which it shall likewise be reconsidered, and if approved by two thirds of that House, it shall become a Law. But in all such Cases the Votes of both Houses shall be determined by Yeas and Nays, and the Names of the Persons voting for and against the Bill shall be entered on the Journal of each House respectively. If any Bill shall not be returned by the President within ten Days (Sundays excepted) after it shall have been presented to him, the Same shall be a Law, in like Manner as if he had signed it, unless the Congress by their Adjournment prevent its Return, in which Case it shall not be a Law.

Every Order, Resolution, or Vote to which the Concurrence of the Senate and House of Representatives may be necessary (except on a question of Adjournment) shall be presented to the President of the United States; and before the Same shall take Effect, shall be approved by him, or being disapproved by him, shall be repassed by two thirds of the Senate and House of Representatives, according to the Rules and Limitations prescribed in the Case of a Bill.

Section 8. The Congress shall have Power To lay and collect Taxes, Duties, Imposts and Excises, to pay the Debts and provide for the common Defence and general Welfare of the United States; but all Duties, Imposts and Excises shall be uniform throughout the United States;

To borrow Money on the credit of the United States;

To regulate Commerce with foreign Nations, and among the several States, and with the Indian Tribes;

---

[4] Changed by section 2 of the Twentieth Amendment.

• CONSTITUTION OF THE UNITED STATES •

To establish an uniform Rule of Naturalization, and uniform Laws on the subject of Bankruptcies throughout the United States;

To coin Money, regulate the Value thereof, and of foreign Coin, and fix the Standard of Weights and Measures;

To provide for the Punishment of counterfeiting the Securities and current Coin of the United States;

To establish Post Offices and post Roads;

To promote the Progress of Science and useful Arts, by securing for limited Times to Authors and Inventors the exclusive Right to their respective Writings and Discoveries;

To constitute Tribunals inferior to the supreme Court;

To define and punish Piracies and Felonies committed on the high Seas, and Offenses against the Law of Nations;

To declare War, grant Letters of Marque and Reprisal, and make Rules concerning Captures on Land and Water;

To raise and support Armies, but no Appropriation of Money to that Use shall be for a longer Term than two Years;

To provide and maintain a Navy;

To make Rules for the Government and Regulation of the land and naval Forces;

To provide for calling forth the Militia to execute the Laws of the Union, suppress Insurrections and repel Invasions;

To provide for organizing, arming, and disciplining, the Militia, and for governing such Part of them as may be employed in the Service of the United States, reserving to the States respectively, the Appointment of the Officers, and the Authority of training the Militia according to the discipline prescribed by Congress;

To exercise exclusive Legislation in all Cases whatsoever, over such District (not exceeding ten Miles square) as may, by Cession of particular States, and the Acceptance of Congress, become the Seat of the Government of the United States, and to exercise like Authority over an Places purchased by the Consent of the Legislature of the State in which the Same shall be, for the Erection of Forts, Magazines, Arsenals, dock-Yards and other needful Buildings;—And

To make all Laws which shall be necessary and proper for carrying into Execution the foregoing Powers, and all other Powers vested by this Constitution in the Government of the United States or in any Department or Officer thereof.

Section 9. The Migration or Importation of such Persons as any of the States now existing shall think proper to admit, shall not be prohibited by the Congress prior to the Year one thousand eight hundred and eight, but a Tax or duty may be imposed on such Importation, not exceeding ten dollars for each Person.

The Privilege of the Writ of Habeas Corpus shall not be suspended, unless when in Cases of Rebellion or Invasion the public Safety may require it.

No Bill of Attainder or ex post facto Law shall be passed.

No Capitation, or other direct, Tax shall be laid, unless in Proportion to the Census or Enumeration herein before directed to be taken.[5]

No Tax or Duty shall be laid on Articles exported from any State.

No Preference shall be given by any Regulation of Commerce or Revenue to the Ports of one State over those of another; nor shall Vessels bound to, or from, one State, be obliged to enter, clear, or pay Duties in another.

No Money shall be drawn from the Treasury, but in Consequence of Appropriations made by Law, and a regular Statement and Account of the Receipts and Expenditures of all public Money shall be published from time to time.

No Title of Nobility shall be granted by the United States: And no Person holding any Office of Profit or Trust under them, shall, without the Consent of the Congress, accept of any present, Emolument, Office, or Title, of any kind whatever, from any King, Prince, or foreign State.

Section 10. No State shall enter into any Treaty, Alliance, or Confederation; grant Letters of Marque and Reprisal; coin Money; emit Bills of Credit; make any Thing but gold and silver Coin a Tender in Payment of Debts; pass any Bill of Attainder, ex post facto Law, or Law impairing the Obligation of Contracts, or grant any Title of Nobility.

---

[5] Sixteenth Amendment to allow for an income tax.

• CONSTITUTION OF THE UNITED STATES •

No State shall, without the Consent of the Congress, lay any Imposts or Duties on Imports or Exports, except what may be absolutely necessary for executing it's inspection Laws: and the net Produce of all Duties and Imposts, laid by any State on Imports or Exports, shall be for the Use of the Treasury of the United States; and all such Laws shall be subject to the Revision and Controul of the Congress.

No State shall, without the Consent of Congress, lay any Duty of Tonnage, keep Troops, or Ships of War in time of Peace, enter into any Agreement or Compact with another State, or with a foreign Power, or engage in War, unless actually invaded, or in such imminent Danger as will not admit of delay.

Article II

Section 1. The executive Power shall be vested in a President of the United States of America. He shall hold his Office during the Term of four Years, and, together with the Vice President, chosen for the same Term, be elected, as follows

Each State shall appoint, in such Manner as the Legislature thereof may direct, a Number of Electors, equal to the whole Number of Senators and Representatives to which the State may be entitled in the Congress: but no Senator or Representative, or Person holding an Office of Trust or Profit under the United States, shall be appointed an Elector.

[Sections on electoral college and amendments omitted.]

The Congress may determine the Time of chusing the Electors, and the Day on which they shall give their Votes; which Day shall be the same throughout the United States. No Person except a natural born Citizen, or a Citizen of the United States, at the time of the Adoption of this Constitution, shall be eligible to the Office of President; neither shall any person be eligible to that Office who shall not have attained to the Age of thirty five Years, and been fourteen Years a Resident within the United States.

[In Case of the Removal of the President from Office, or of his Death, Resignation, or Inability to discharge the Powers and Duties of the said Office, the Same shall devolve on the Vice President, and the Congress may by Law provide for the Case of Removal, Death, Resignation or Inability, both of the President and Vice President, declaring what Officer shall then act as President, and such Officer shall act accordingly, until the Disability be removed, or a President shall be elected.][6]

The President shall, at stated Times, receive for his Services, a Compensation, which shall neither be increased nor diminished during the Period for which he shall have been elected, and he shall not receive within that Period any other Emolument from the United States, or any of them.

Before he enter on the Execution of his Office, he shall take the following Oath or Affirmation:— "I do solemnly swear (or affirm) that I will faithfully execute the Office of President of the United States, and will to the best of my Ability, preserve, protect and defend the Constitution of the United States."

Section 2. The President shall be Commander in Chief of the Army and Navy of the United States, and of the Militia of the several States, when called into the actual Service of the United States; he may require the Opinion, in writing, of the principal Officer in each of the executive Departments, upon any Subject relating to the Duties of their respective Offices, and he shall have Power to grant Reprieves and Pardons for Offenses against the United States, except in Cases of Impeachment.

He shall have Power, by and with the Advice and Consent of the Senate, to make Treaties, provided two thirds of the Senators present concur; and he shall nominate, and by and with the Advice and Consent of the Senate, shall appoint Ambassadors, other public Ministers and Consuls, Judges of the supreme Court, and all other Officers of the United States, whose Appointments are not herein otherwise provided for, and which shall be established by Law: but the Congress may by Law vest the Appointment of such inferior Officers, as they think proper, in the President alone, in the Courts of Law, or in the Heads of Departments.

The President shall have Power to fill up all Vacancies that may happen during the Recess of the Senate, by granting Commissions which shall expire at the End of their next Session.

Section 3. He shall from time to time give to the Congress Information of the State of the Union, and recommend to their Consideration such Measures as he shall judge necessary and expedient; he may, on extraordinary Occasions, convene both Houses, or either of them, and in Case of Disagreement between them, with Respect to the Time of Adjournment, he may adjourn them to such Time as he shall

---

[6] Changed by the Twenty-Fifth Amendment.

• CONSTITUTION OF THE UNITED STATES •

think proper; he shall receive Ambassadors and other public Ministers; he shall take Care that the Laws be faithfully executed, and shall Commission all the Officers of the United States.

Section 4. The President, Vice President and all civil Officers of the United States, shall be removed from Office on Impeachment for, and Conviction of, Treason, Bribery, or other high Crimes and Misdemeanors.

Article III

Section 1. The judicial Power of the United States, shall be vested in one supreme Court, and in such inferior Courts as the Congress may from time to time ordain and establish. The Judges, both of the supreme and inferior Courts, shall hold their Offices during good Behaviour, and shall, at stated Times, receive for their Services, a Compensation, which shall not be diminished during their Continuance in Office.

Section 2. The judicial Power shall extend to all Cases, in Law and Equity, arising under this Constitution, the Laws of the United States, and Treaties made, or which shall be made, under their Authority;—to all Cases affecting Ambassadors, other public Ministers and Consuls;—to all Cases of admiralty and maritime Jurisdiction;—to Controversies to which the United States shall be a Party; to Controversies between two or more States;—[between a State and Citizens of another State;—] between Citizens of different States,—between Citizens of the same State claiming Lands under Grants of different States, [and between a State, or the Citizens thereof, and foreign States, Citizens or Subjects.][7]

In all Cases affecting Ambassadors, other public Ministers and Consuls, and those in which a State shall be Party, the supreme Court shall have original Jurisdiction. In all the other Cases before mentioned, the supreme Court shall have appellate Jurisdiction, both as to Law and Fact, with such Exceptions, and under such Regulations as the Congress shall make.

The Trial of all Crimes, except in Cases of Impeachment; shall be by Jury; and such Trial shall be held in the State where the said Crimes shall have been committed; but when not committed within any State, the Trial shall be at such Place or Places as the Congress may by Law have directed.

Section 3. Treason against the United States, shall consist only in levying War against them, or in adhering to their Enemies, giving them Aid and Comfort. No Person shall be convicted of Treason unless on the Testimony of two Witnesses to the same overt Act, or on Confession in open Court.

The Congress shall have Power to declare the Punishment of Treason, but no Attainder of Treason shall work Corruption of Blood, or Forfeiture except during the Life of the Person attainted.

Article IV

Section 1. Full Faith and Credit shall be given in each State to the public Acts, Records, and judicial Proceedings of every other State; And the Congress may by general Laws prescribe the Manner in which such Acts, Records and Proceedings shall be proved, and the Effect thereof.

Section 2. The Citizens of each State shall be entitled to all Privileges and Immunities of Citizens in the several States.

A Person charged in any State with Treason, Felony, or other Crime, who shall flee from Justice, and be found in another State, shall on Demand of the executive Authority of the State from which he fled, be delivered up, to be removed to the State having Jurisdiction of the Crime.

[No Person held to Service or Labour in one State, under the Laws thereof, escaping into another, shall, in Consequence of any Law or Regulation therein, be discharged from such Service or Labour, but shall be delivered up on Claim of the Party to whom such Service or Labour may be due.][8]

Section 3. New States may be admitted by the Congress into this Union; but no new State shall be formed or erected within the Jurisdiction of any other State; nor any State be formed by the Junction of two or more States, or Parts of States, without the Consent of the Legislatures of the States concerned as well as of the Congress.

The Congress shall have Power to dispose of and make all needful Rules and Regulations respecting the Territory or other Property belonging to the United States; and nothing in this Constitution shall be so construed as to Prejudice any Claims of the United States, or of any particular State.

---

[7] Changed by the Eleventh Amendment to prohibit suits against state governments without their consent.
[8] Changed by the Thirteenth Amendment.

• CONSTITUTION OF THE UNITED STATES •

Section 4. The United States shall guarantee to every State in this Union a Republican Form of Government, and shall protect each of them against Invasion; and on Application of the Legislature, or of the Executive (when the Legislature cannot be convened) against domestic Violence.

Article V

The Congress, whenever two thirds of both Houses shall deem it necessary, shall propose Amendments to this Constitution, or, on the Application of the Legislatures of two thirds of the several States, shall call a Convention for proposing Amendments, which, in either Case, shall be valid to all Intents and Purposes, as Part of this Constitution, when ratified by the Legislatures of three fourths of the several States, or by Conventions in three fourths thereof, as the one or the other Mode of Ratification may be proposed by the Congress; Provided that no Amendment which may be made prior to the Year One thousand eight hundred and eight shall in any Manner affect the first and fourth Clauses in the Ninth Section of the first Article; and that no State, without its Consent, shall be deprived of it's equal Suffrage in the Senate.

Article VI

All Debts contracted and Engagements entered into, before the Adoption of this Constitution, shall be as valid against the United States under this Constitution, as under the Confederation.

This Constitution, and the Laws of the United States which shall be made in Pursuance thereof; and all Treaties made, or which shall be made, under the Authority of the United States, shall be the supreme Law of the Land; and the Judges in every State shall be bound thereby, any Thing in the Constitution or Laws of any State to the Contrary notwithstanding.

The Senators and Representatives before mentioned, and the Members of the several State Legislatures and all executive and judicial Officers, both of the United States and of the several States, shall be bound by Oath or Affirmation, to support this Constitution; but no religious Test shall ever be required as a Qualification to any Office or public Trust under the United States.

Article VII

The Ratification of the Conventions of nine States, shall be sufficient for the Establishment of this Constitution between the States so ratifying the Same.

Done in Convention by the Unanimous Consent of the States present the Seventeenth Day of September in the Year of our Lord one thousand seven hundred and Eighty seven and of the Independence of the United States of America the Twelfth In Witness whereof We have hereunto subscribed our Names, [signers omitted].

• CONSTITUTION OF THE UNITED STATES •

Amendments to the Constitution of the United States of America

Amendment I[9]

Congress shall make no law respecting an establishment of religion, or prohibiting the free exercise thereof; or abridging the freedom of speech, or of the press, or the right of the people peaceably to assemble, and to petition the Government for a redress of grievances.

Amendment II

A well regulated Militia, being necessary to the security of a free State, the right of the people to keep and bear Arms, shall not be infringed.

Amendment III

No Soldier shall, in time of peace be quartered in any house, without the consent of the Owner, nor in time of war, but in a manner to be prescribed by law.

Amendment IV

The right of the people to be secure in their persons, houses, papers, and effects, against unreasonable searches and seizures, shall not be violated, and no Warrants shall issue, but upon probable cause, supported by Oath or affirmation, and particularly describing the place to be searched, and the persons or things to be seized.

Amendment V

No person shall be held to answer for a capital, or otherwise infamous crime, unless on a presentment or indictment of a Grand Jury, except in cases arising in the land or naval forces, or in the Militia, when in actual service in time of War or public danger; nor shall any person be subject for the same offense to be twice put in jeopardy of life or limb, nor shall be compelled in any criminal case to be a witness against himself, nor be deprived of life, liberty, or property, without due process of law; nor shall private property be taken for public use without just compensation.

Amendment VI

In all criminal prosecutions, the accused shall enjoy the right to a speedy and public trial, by an impartial jury of the State and district wherein the crime shall have been committed; which district shall have been previously ascertained by law, and to be informed of the nature and cause of the accusation; to be confronted with the witnesses against him; to have compulsory process for obtaining witnesses in his favor, and to have the assistance of counsel for his defence.

Amendment VII

In Suits at common law, where the value in controversy shall exceed twenty dollars, the right of trial by jury shall be preserved, and no fact tried by a jury shall be otherwise reexamined in any Court of the United States, than according to the rules of the common law.

Amendment VIII

Excessive bail shall not be required, nor excessive fines imposed, nor cruel and unusual punishments inflicted.

Amendment IX

The enumeration in the Constitution of certain rights shall not be construed to deny or disparage others retained by the people.

Amendment X

The powers not delegated to the United States by the Constitution, nor prohibited by it to the States, are reserved to the States respectively, or to the people.

---

[9] The first ten Amendments (Bill of Rights) were ratified effective December 15, 1791.

• CONSTITUTION OF THE UNITED STATES •

Amendment XI[10]

The Judicial power of the United States shall not be construed to extend to any suit in law or equity, commenced or prosecuted against one of the United States by Citizens of another State, or by Citizens or Subjects of any Foreign State.

Amendment XII

[Amends procedures for selection of the President, superseded by the Twentieth Amendment]

Amendment XIII[11]

Section 1. Neither slavery nor involuntary servitude, except as a punishment for crime whereof the party shall have been duly convicted, shall exist within the United States, or any place subject to their jurisdiction.

Section 2. Congress shall have power to enforce this article by appropriate legislation.

Amendment XIV[12]

Section 1. All persons born or naturalized in the United States and subject to the jurisdiction thereof, are citizens of the United States and of the State wherein they reside. No State shall make or enforce any law which shall abridge the privileges or immunities of citizens of the United States; nor shall any State deprive any person of life, liberty, or property, without due process of law; nor deny to any person within its jurisdiction the equal protection of the laws.

Section 2. Representatives shall be apportioned among the several States according to their respective numbers, counting the whole number of persons in each State, excluding Indians not taxed. But when the right to vote at any election for the choice of electors for President and Vice President of the United States, Representatives in Congress, the Executive and Judicial officers of a State, or the members of the Legislature thereof, is denied to any of the male inhabitants of such State, being twenty-one years of age, and citizens of the United States, or in any way abridged, except for participation in rebellion, or other crime, the basis of representation therein shall be reduced in the proportion which the number of such male citizens shall bear to the whole number of male citizens twenty-one years of age in such State.

Section 3. No person shall be a Senator or Representative in Congress, or elector of President and Vice President, or hold any office, civil or military, under the United States, or under any State, who, having previously taken an oath, as a member of Congress, or as an officer of the United States, or as a member of any State legislature, or as an executive or judicial officer of any State, to support the Constitution of the United States, shall have engaged in insurrection or rebellion against the same, or given aid or comfort to the enemies thereof. But Congress may by a vote of two-thirds of each House, remove such disability.

Section 4. The validity of the public debt of the United States, authorized by law, including debts incurred for payment of pensions and bounties for services in suppressing insurrection or rebellion, shall not be questioned. But neither the United States nor any State shall assume or pay any debt or obligation incurred in aid of insurrection or rebellion against the United States, or any claim for the loss or emancipation of any slave; but all such debts, obligations and claims shall be held illegal and void.

Section 5. The Congress shall have power to enforce, by appropriate legislation, the provisions of this article.

Amendment XV[13]

Section 1. The right of citizens of the United States to vote shall not be denied or abridged by the United States or by any State on account of race, color, or previous condition of servitude.

Section 2. The Congress shall have power to enforce this article by appropriate legislation.

[Amendments 16 to 27 omitted]

---

[10] The Eleventh Amendment was ratified February 7, 1795.

[11] The Thirteenth Amendment was ratified December 6, 1865.

[12] The Fourteenth Amendment was ratified July 9, 1868.

[13] The Fifteenth Amendment was ratified February 3, 1870.

SUMMARY INFORMATION ABOUT SELECTED SUPREME COURT JUSTICES

JUSTICE	PRESIDENT APPOINTING	YEARS OF SERVICE	POLITICAL PARTY	POSITIONS AND NOTED ACTION IN CRIMINAL PROCEDURE
John M. Harlan (I)	Hayes	1877–1911	Rep.	Championed total incorporation of Bill of Rights to apply to the states.
Oliver W. Holmes	Roosevelt, T.	1902–1932	Rep.	*Moore v. Dempsey*—apply due process to state errors; *Olmstead* dissent.
Louis Brandeis	Wilson	1916–1939	Rep.	*Olmstead* dissent—classic statement of Rule of Law.
William H. Taft, CJ	Harding	1921–1930	Rep.	Conservative. *Olmstead*—wiretapping not covered by Fourth Amendment.
George Sutherland	Harding	1922–1938	Rep.	*Powell v. Alabama*—Scottsboro case: due process violated by lack of counsel.
Harlan Fiske Stone	Coolidge	1925–1941	Rep.	Moderate. *Carolene Products* (1938) footnote 4 pointed to a civil rights agenda.
Edward Sanford	Harding	1923–1930	Rep.	Wrote opinions incorporating First Amendment rights, advanced incorporation.
Benjamin Cardozo	Hoover	1932–1938	Dem.	Blocked advance of incorporation in *Palko* (1937).
Hugo Black	Roosevelt, F.	1937–1971	Dem.	Championed incorporation, dissent in *Adamson*; right to counsel—*Gideon* (1963).
Stanley Reed	Roosevelt, F.	1938–1957	Dem.	Opposed incorporation; majority opinion in *Adamson v. California* (1947).
Felix Frankfurter	Roosevelt, F.	1939–1962	Ind.	Conservative-moderate. Opposed incorporation; favored due process approach.
William Douglas	Roosevelt, F.	1939–1975	Dem.	Liberal. Favored incorporation.
Frank Murphy	Roosevelt, F.	1940–1949	Dem.	Liberal. Favored incorporation.
Harlan Fiske Stone	Roosevelt, F.	1941–1946	Rep.	Moderate-liberal; championed freedom of belief in flag-salute cases.
Robert Jackson	Roosevelt, F.	1941–1954	Dem.	New Deal liberal—close to Frankfurter in criminal procedure.
Wiley Rutledge	Roosevelt, F.	1943–1949	Dem.	Liberal. Favored incorporation. Classic definition of probable cause in *Brinegar* (1949).
Harold Burton	Truman	1945–1958	Rep.	Stalwart conservative.
Fred Vinson, CJ	Truman	1946–1953	Dem.	Stalwart conservative.
Tom Clark	Truman	1949–1967	Dem.	Conservative-moderate; wrote majority in *Mapp v. Ohio* (1961).
Sherman Minton	Truman	1949–1956	Dem.	Stalwart conservative.
Earl Warren, CJ	Eisenhower	1953–1969	Rep.	Liberal. Authored *Miranda*, *Terry*.

SUMMARY INFORMATION ABOUT SELECTED SUPREME COURT JUSTICES

JUSTICE	PRESIDENT APPOINTING	YEARS OF SERVICE	POLITICAL PARTY	POSITIONS AND NOTED ACTION IN CRIMINAL PROCEDURE
John Harlan (II)	Eisenhower	1954–1971	Rep.	Conservative-moderate. Opposed incorporation.
William Brennan	Eisenhower	1956–1990	Dem.	Liberal. Active writing liberal dissents in Burger & Rehnquist Court eras.
Charles Whittaker	Eisenhower	1957–1962	Rep.	Stalwart conservative.
Potter Stewart	Eisenhower	1958–1981	Rep.	Moderate-conservative. Wrote many criminal procedure opinions.
Byron White	Kennedy	1962–1993	Dem.	Mixed. Wrote many criminal procedure opinions.
Arthur Goldberg	Kennedy	1962–1965	Dem.	Liberal. Opinion in *U.S. v. Ventresca* (1965)—preference for search warrant.
Abe Fortas	Johnson, L.	1965–1969	Dem.	Liberal. Major opinions for juvenile rights: *In re Gault* (1967).
Thurgood Marshall	Johnson, L.	1967–1991	Dem.	Liberal. Active writing liberal dissents in Burger & Rehnquist Court eras.
Warren Burger, CJ	Nixon	1969–1986	Rep.	Conservative. Initially opposed the exclusionary rule.
Harry Blackmun	Nixon	1970–1994	Rep.	Changed from conservative to liberal over time.
Lewis Powell	Nixon	1972–1987	Dem.	Conservative. Opinions limited access to courts on 4th Amend. issues.
William Rehnquist	Nixon	1972–1986	Rep.	Conservative. Wrote many criminal procedure opinions.
John Paul Stevens	Ford	1975–	Rep.	Moderate; has swung to liberal in criminal procedure.
Sandra Day O'Connor	Reagan	1981–	Rep.	Conservative; can join moderate, pro-defendant decisions.
Antonin Scalia	Reagan	1986–	Rep.	Conservative; originalist. Favors defendant regarding Confrontation Clause.
William Rehnquist, CJ	Reagan	1986–	Rep.	Conservative. Continues to write many criminal procedure opinions.
Anthony Kennedy	Reagan	1988–	Rep.	Conservative. Can join moderate, pro-defendant decisions.
William Souter	Bush	1990–	Rep.	Moderate-conservative. Appears to be moving to more liberal position.
Clarence Thomas	Bush	1991–	Rep.	Conservative; originalist.
Ruth Bader Ginsburg	Clinton	1993–	Dem.	Moderate-liberal.
Steven Breyer	Clinton	1994–	Dem.	Moderate-liberal; takes conservative position in some cases.

GLOSSARY

Abuse of discretion   A high standard for an appellate court to reverse the decision of a lower court where the trial court was lawfully invested with discretion. It does not imply an intentional wrong or bad faith, but the exercise of discretion was clearly against logic.

Accusatorial trial system   The Anglo-American or common law system of adjudication. Its key elements include: judge is an impartial referee; lawyers control the presentation of evidence; witnesses are cross-examined; innocence is presumed; prosecutor must prove guilt beyond a reasonable doubt; privilege against self-incrimination protects the defendant from testifying; facts are conclusively determined by a citizen jury.

Actual border   For purposes of border search cases, stops that are made at or very near the actual border between the United States and a neighboring nation; border searches may also take place farther inland either at fixed checkpoints or by roving patrols.

Actual mobility   The automobile exception to the search warrant requirement applies to vehicles that are actually capable of being driven.

Actual imprisonment rule   Counsel is an absolute Sixth Amendment requirement for the trial of a misdemeanor only if the defendant has been actually imprisoned after conviction.

Adequate and independent state grounds   A state court ruling concerning the rights of a suspect that is based exclusively on state constitutional grounds cannot be disturbed by a federal court as long as the state constitutional ruling does not fall below the minimum standards of the Fourteenth Amendment Due Process Clause. To determine if a state ruling is based on state or federal grounds, where the ruling discussed both federal and state law, the Supreme Court examines it to determine if the holding is based on adequate and independent state grounds. See *judicial federalism.*

Ad hoc   "For this"; for a special purpose without application to a general purpose; for example, an *ad hoc* rule is intended to apply to only the particular circumstances at hand and is not intended to be a general rule.

Adjudicate   To judge a case; to resolve an issue in the exercise of judicial authority.

Administrative search   The entry and search of premises by a governmental officer who is enforcing a governmental regulation regarding public health or safety, rather than a police search for persons or items in relation to the enforcement of the criminal law.

Admission   Statements made by a party that acknowledge the existence of certain facts. See *confession.*

Adversary or Adversarial [trial] system   Same as *accusatorial [trial] system.*

Adverse comment   A comment by the judge or prosecutor to a jury in a criminal case, pointing out that the defendant did not take the witness stand.

Advisory opinion   An *opinion* issued by a court at the request of the government or a party indicating how it would rule on an issue were it to arise in litigation. Some state supreme courts issue advisory opinions. The United States Supreme Court does not issue such opinions because its jurisdiction is limited in Article III, Section 2, of the Constitution to "cases and controversies."

Affiant   The person who makes and subscribes an affidavit.

Affidavit   A written declaration or statement of facts made voluntarily and confirmed by oath before a person with the authority to take such an oath.

Affirm   An appellate court that upholds the ruling of a lower court is said to affirm the ruling.

Anticipatory warrants   Search warrants authorized by the Federal Rules of Criminal Procedure that may be issued on probable cause that evidence will be located in a particular place on the date of execution. See *controlled delivery.*

Antifederalists   Those opposed to the ratification of the Constitution in 1788 on the grounds that it created too much central power.

Appearance bond   See *bail bond.*

Appellate decision   The outcome of an appellate court; an appellate court may affirm, modify, reverse, and/or remand the decisions of the lower court.

Appellate opinion   See *opinion.*

Appointed counsel   A lawyer for an indigent defendant may be appointed by the court on an informal basis, through organized lists established by a local bar association, or by the court; the lawyer is paid by the county according to a fee schedule for work performed. Same as *assigned counsel.*

Arraignment   The procedure whereby a defendant is brought before a court to plead to a criminal charge.

Arrest   To deprive a person of liberty by legal authority; an arrest occurs in law when a person is taken into custody by government officers, even if the purpose is for investigation or harassment. It is not necessary for a booking to occur for an arrest to be made. An arrest may be made with or without a warrant.

Arrest warrant   Judicial warrant concluding that probable cause exists supporting the belief that a crime has been committed and that the named person has committed it, and authorizing law enforcement to take the suspect into custody; the warrant is required, except for an exigency, if officers must enter the home of the person to be arrested.

Asset forfeiture   Laws that authorize the forfeiture of noncontraband assets used in and moneys derived from the commission of certain crimes. The assets may be seized as of the time the crime was committed and thus be denied to lawyers representing defendants whose assets are forfeited.

Assigned counsel   See *appointed counsel.*

Assize   A name for general trial courts in England and France.

Attenuation rule   An exception to the "fruit-of-the-poisonous-tree doctrine." It comes into play when the link between the initial illegality and the evidence sought to be introduced has become so weak or tenuous that the "fruit" has become "untainted."

Authorized imprisonment rule   A position that counsel should be absolutely guaranteed by the Sixth Amendment in all misdemeanor trials where the statutory penalty allows for imprisonment; this rule was rejected by the Supreme Court.

Automobile search   An exception to the requirement that a search of an effect be authorized in advance by a judicial search warrant, based on the exigency of a mobile vehicle and on the lower expectation of privacy accorded to automobiles, as long as the officer has probable cause to believe there is contraband in the automobile. Also known as the vehicle exception.

Bail   To procure the release of a person charged with a crime by ensuring his or her further attendance in court; this is done by having the person pledge or deposit something of value that will be returned when he or she appears in court and/or by having a third party agree to be responsible for the return of the person.

Bail bond   A bond (an "instrument" or writing promising to pay money) that is executed by a third party promising to forfeit money to the court if the defendant who is released on bail does not appear for further criminal proceedings; also known as an appearance bond.

Bail bondsman   A businessperson who receives a portion of the bail amount from a defendant, usually 10 percent, and posts a bail bond with the court promising to pay the full bail amount if the defendant does not show; is responsible for ensuring the appearance of the defendant in court.

Balancing of interests   See *balancing test.*

Balancing test   A widely used phrase in criminal procedure, especially in Fourth Amendment adjudication, referring to appellate courts attempting to balance the needs of effective law enforcement against the privacy rights of individuals.

Bench   In law, a term for the court or the judge. For an appellate court, the bench consists of all the judges on the court or who are sitting on a panel of the court.

Bench trial   A trial without a jury; the judge (who sits on the "bench") is the trier of both the facts and the law. In a jury trial, the judge is the finder only of legal issues and the jury finds the facts. See *waiver trial.*

Beeper   An electronic device that emits a signal indicating its location; it may be used by agents to track the movement of a vehicle or object.

Bill of attainder   A special act of a legislature passing the death penalty or other penalty on a person without recourse to standard judicial proceedings; in England, attainder led to the entire estate of a person convicted of a felony or treason being forfeited to the crown. The United States Constitution (Art. I, Secs. 9 and 10) forbids the federal government and the states from passing bills of attainder.

Bill of particulars   A form of discovery in which the prosecution sets forth the time, place, manner, and means of the commission of the crime as alleged in the complaint or indictment.

Bill of Rights   A designation for the first ten amendments to the United States Constitution.

Bind-over decision   The decision of the judge, at the conclusion of the preliminary examination, as to whether there is sufficient evidence to establish probable cause that the defendant committed the crime and "bind the defendant over," that is, require him or her to go to trial.

Bivens **suit**   A federal tort suit by a person against federal officers alleged to have violated the person's Fourth Amendment rights; created in *Bivens v. Six Unknown Agents* (1971).

Body cavity search   Procedure whereby authorized law enforcement or correctional personnel conduct a visual inspection of oral, genital, or anal areas for contraband. Also called *strip search.*

Booking   An administrative process conducted by police officials that typically follows an arrest and includes the taking of the suspect's name and identifying information, photographing, fingerprinting, searching, and inventorying of personal property.

Border   The international boundary of a nation; for purposes of law, immigration, and customs searches, the border includes international airports, inland ports, and fixed checkpoints remote from the actual boundary.

Border search   A search at the national border by immigration officers for illegal immigrants and by customs officers for contraband, criminals, fugitives, and terrorists.

Brevity requirement   Rule under *Terry v. Ohio* (1968) that a "stop and frisk" be concluded quickly, or in just enough time for an officer to confirm or dispel whether the officer's reasonable suspicion constitutes probable cause; strictly interpreted by the Supreme Court.

Brief   A brief is a written argument presented to a trial or appellate court by a lawyer to support the attorney's position on legal issues. Briefs can be as long as one hundred pages. Appellate briefs are accompanied with the record on appeal and may include the trial transcript.

Briefing a case   This refers to notes taken by law students that abstract the essential points of an *opinion,* especially the facts, legal issues, holding, and reasons for the holding.

Bright-line rule   A clear-cut and easy-to-apply standard established by a court to distinguish legal categories.

Bug   An electronic listening device that is placed surreptitiously to overhear conversations.

Burger Court   The Supreme Court during the period that Warren Burger was Chief Justice of the United States (1969 to 1986); a moderately conservative period in criminal procedure.

Capital crime   In common law, a crime punishable with death; today, in some states, it includes crimes punishable with life imprisonment. Under the laws of some states, bail may be denied to persons charged with capital crimes.

Case of first impression   A law case in which the issue to be decided has never been resolved by an appellate court.

Case law   See *common law.*

Caveat   A warning to be careful.

Certiorari   A writ used by the United States Supreme Court to determine in its discretion which filed cases it will hear and decide.

Challenge for cause   In the *voir dire,* the ability of one of the sides to request the judge to dismiss a prospective juror because the juror has indicated a bias; the number of challenges for cause are unlimited.

Chancery   English court established under the king's chancellor to do equity or to decide cases according to rules of justice rather than under formal writs of common law courts of Common Pleas and King's Bench. Over time, chancery courts became part of the common law court system. Common law courts render money judgments as legal remedies whereas equity or chancery courts grant "equitable relief," i.e., orders requiring that a party perform or cease some activity. Most American states merged courts of law and equity; a few still have separate chancery or equity courts. See *equity.*

Charging   The process by which the prosecutor decides which offenses to formally prefer or "charge" against a suspect, either in a prosecutor's information or an indictment.

Checks and balances   A political and constitutional doctrine for maintaining balanced government by giving different branches of government the power to limit the authority of other branches in specified ways; closely related to the separation of powers doctrine.

Citizen's arrest   An arrest made by a person who is not a law enforcement officer; if the arrest is in error (i.e., no crime was committed or the wrong person was arrested), the citizen who made the arrest is subject to a civil suit for false arrest even if probable cause existed.

Civil law system   The legal system of the nations of Europe, Latin America, Africa, and Asia (except for England and former British colonies) that is found primarily in codes; civil law trials follow the inquisitorial model; it is contrasted to the common law system.

Civil rights function   Criminal-procedure law has two broad functions: to facilitate prosecution and, simultaneously, to protect the civil rights of suspects and defendants.

Civil War amendments   The Thirteenth, Fourteenth, and Fifteenth Amendments, ratified in 1866, 1868, and 1870, respectively. Also called the *Reconstruction amendments.*

Collateral proceeding   Not a direct appeal from a conviction on a point of law, but instead a second "appeal," not of right; habeas corpus proceedings are collateral proceedings.

Common law   In England, America, and other common law countries (e.g., Australia, Canada, India), law is created by judges through appellate court *opinions.* Also called *case law* or *precedent,* because the rule established in one case becomes a binding precedent on later courts. The term arose because the law created by royal judges was common to all of England. Common law is subordinate to legislation.

Common law trial system   Same as *accusatorial trial system.*

Companion case   A case decided along with another case. *Sibron v. New York* (1967) and *Peters v. New York* (1967) were companion cases to *Terry v. Ohio* (1967). Companion cases may be consolidated into one case; *Miranda v. Arizona* (1966) also decided the companion cases of *Vignera v. New York* (1996), *Westover v. United States* (1966), and *California v. Stewart* (1966).

Compulsion   A person is protected by the Fifth Amendment against being "compelled in any criminal case to be a witness against himself." The Fifth Amendment applies only if evidence is obtained by compulsion, as by a court order or grand jury subpoena. Fifth Amendment compulsion in law of confessions, under *Miranda,* supplied by in-custody police interrogation, which is inherently compelling. See *self-incrimination rule.*

Compulsory process   A subpoena to produce witnesses or real evidence; a right guaranteed to defendants by the Sixth Amendment.

Confession   A statement made by one person to another admitting guilt of an offense and disclosing facts about the crime and the suspect's role in it; may include inculpatory or exculpatory statements. See *admission.*

Conflict of interest   In regard to the right to counsel, a conflict of interest most typically arises when, as a result of multiple representation, an attorney must sacrifice a defense technique for one defendant in order to better defend another defendant. See *multiple representation.*

Confrontation Clause   The provision of the Sixth Amendment that in all criminal prosecutions, "the accused shall enjoy the right . . . to be confronted with the witnesses against him."

Consent   The voluntary agreement of one person who has the capacity to make an agreement of free will to do an act proposed by another. In the administration of criminal justice, a suspect or defendant can consent to cooperate with police or prosecutors. More specifically, a person can consent to a search or seizure of an area over which a person has an expectation of privacy. See *waiver.*

Consent search A search made by a police officer after a person has given consent to the search; consent to search validates a warrantless search or a search made without probable cause.

Constitutionalism A political theory of balanced government; modern constitutionalism includes the concepts of civil rights and the rule of law.

Contempt of court An act that is calculated to embarrass, hinder, or obstruct a court in the administration of justice; may be punished by a judge with fine or imprisonment.

Continuance A delay in legal proceedings granted by the judge.

Contraband Any property that is illegal either to produce or possess, such as controlled substances or untaxed, smuggled goods.

Controlled delivery A law enforcement technique by which contraband is intercepted and then delivered to the suspected criminal party under police surveillance. "Anticipatory warrants" may be issued in cases where controlled deliveries are set up.

Counsel, right to This word is used interchangeably with "lawyer," "attorney," and "attorney-at-law."

Court of general jurisdiction A trial court with jurisdiction to try all matters, including felonies; typically called a superior or circuit court.

Court of limited jurisdiction A trial court whose jurisdiction is limited by statute to certain matters; usually to civil cases where the amount in dispute is below a certain amount (e.g., $10,000), to the dispositions of misdemeanors, and to conducting the preliminary phases of a felony case before binding over the case to a court of general jurisdiction for trial.

Covert facilitation Same as *encouragement.*

Crime Control Model A theory developed by Herbert Packer that suggests that within a constitutional system of criminal justice there are two general attitudes; the Crime Control Model stresses crime control, efficiency, a "presumption of guilt, and finality." See *Due Process Model.*

Crime scene investigation exception The Supreme Court has refused to create a Fourth Amendment exception to allow police, without a warrant, to remain beyond the time of the exigency, on the premises where a crime has been committed, for purposes of conducting an investigation of the premises.

Criminal law approach In the law of entrapment, the majority rule, known also as the *subjective test.* Based on legal fiction that legislature did not intend statute to apply to persons who were not predisposed to commit the crime but were induced by police.

Critical stage The point in criminal proceedings when counsel is constitutionally required because, at that point, rights may be lost, defenses waived, or privileges claimed or waived that can affect the outcome of the case.

Cross-examination The examination of a witness at a trial or hearing by the party opposed to the side that produced the witness, after direct examination, to test the truth of the witness, to further develop the evidence, or for other purposes.

Cruel trilemma A witness who is asked a question that may prove to be incriminating faces three negative consequences: self-accusation, perjury, or the risk of being held in contempt of court for refusing to testify.

Curtilage Area protected by Fourth Amendment under eaves of the main house; various small structures that are near the main house, such as a garage, shed, or smokehouse, and the fenced-in area around a house. See *open fields.*

Custodial arrest When a police officer arrests a person for a crime that authorizes the officer to take the suspect into custody, the officer may perform a complete search incident to arrest.

Custody The keeping, guarding, care, watch, inspection, preservation, or security of a thing or person. The custody of a person is a prerequisite for a Fourth Amendment seizure under *California v. Hodari D.* (1991).

Damages Monetary compensation awarded by a court in a civil case to compensate a party for losses.

Decoy In entrapment law and practice, an officer who poses as a potential victim (usually of a crime of violence such as street robbery) waiting to be attacked, in order to arrest a perpetrator.

Deficient performance The first prong of the rule that the ineffective assistance of counsel in a criminal trial violates the Sixth Amendment rights of the defendant. Deficient performance of an attorney is an objective standard determined by what constitutes reasonably effective assistance according to prevailing norms of legal practice.

De minimis Shorthand for *de minimis non curat lex:* the law does not take notice of very small or trifling matters; i.e., a technical violation of a law that results in trifling or purely theoretical injury may not recognized by a court.

Democracy A political philosophy that emphasizes the participation of all citizens in government decisions on an equal basis either directly or by representation; it is a value that underlies constitutional criminal procedure.

De novo **review** A rehearing of an issue that does not take into consideration findings made at an earlier hearing.

De novo **trial (or trial *de novo*)** A second or new trial that is held as if no decision had been previously rendered. A trial *de novo* is not an appeal because the facts are relitigated.

Deposit bond A bail bond that is executed by the defendant; under the laws of several states, the defendant puts up 10 percent of the bail amount, which is returned, except for a 1 percent fee, when the defendant returns to court for the trial.

Derivative evidence In the Fourth and Fifth Amendment context, evidence that police obtain on the basis of illegally seized evidence; under the "fruit-of-the-poisonous-tree doctrine," such derivative evidence must be excluded from a trial to prove the guilt of a defendant.

Dictum An abbreviated form of *obiter dictum,* a "remark by the way," that is, a remark by a judge in an *opinion,* commenting on the legal rule of the case, that is not essential to the determination of the holding or decision and, therefore, does not have weight as precedent.

Discovery A set of practices in both civil and criminal trial procedure that allows both sides to obtain factual evidence in the possession of the other side; it is designed to encourage settlements or prevent surprises at the trial so as to avoid delays.

Disgorgement The theory of jurisprudence that a person who has wrongfully obtained goods should be made to give them up.

Disseised To be dispossessed of one's land, in English medieval land law. See *novel disseisin.*

Diversity of citizenship jurisdiction Article III of the Constitution allows federal courts to hear cases between "citizens" of different states.

Domestic tranquillity A phrase in the Preamble to the Constitution of the United States; it recognizes that maintaining public safety is a fundamental purpose of government.

Dossier A bundle of papers (French); a report on an individual.

Drug courier profile A set of behavioral characteristics developed by the Drug Enforcement Agency (DEA) to determine whether a person fits the model of a person surreptitiously transporting illegal drugs, the profile itself, even if it consists entirely of innocent actions, constitutes a basis for finding that reasonable suspicion exists.

Due process approach In constitutional criminal procedure, this term designates a philosophy on the part of Supreme Court justices that errors in state criminal procedure that constitute grossly unfair and unjust proceedings can be reviewed by the federal courts under the Due Process Clause of the Fourteenth Amendment. The term also conveys the idea that a decision made under this approach does not necessarily produce bright-line rules, because every case is decided on the totality of its facts and circumstances.

Due Process Clause The Fifth Amendment and the Fourteenth Amendment include such clauses, the first applying against the federal government and the second against state governments, saying that no person shall be deprived of life, liberty, or property without due process of law.

Due process defense In entrapment law, the theory that entrapment may be established by police conduct that was so outrageous as to violate the Due Process Clause.

Due Process Model A theory developed by Herbert Packer suggests that within a constitutional system of criminal justice there are two general attitudes; the due process model stresses an insistence on formal, adjudicative, adversary fact finding, the prevention and elimination of mistakes, a stress on legal (as opposed to actual) guilt, and viewing the presumption of innocence to mean that every suspect must be treated as if he were innocent. See *Crime Control Model.*

Due Process Revolution The period from 1961 to 1969 when most of the criminal provisions of the Bill of Rights were incorporated. See *incorporation doctrine.*

Egalitarianism A political theory that supports the eradication of legal and social distinctions between citizens; it is an ideal of American republicanism and has been a force behind the expansion of rights such as the right of all citizens to serve on juries; it is a value that underlies constitutional criminal procedure. See *equality.*

En banc An appellate case heard and decided by the entire appellate bench rather than by a panel of judges drawn from the entire bench.

Encouragement A term describing a range of police investigatory activity designed to create a criminal opportunity for offenders who commit crimes that are difficult to detect, but without inducing them to commit the crimes. See *entrapment.*

Enhancement device Mechanism that is used to enhance the natural senses of a law enforcement officer to detect contraband; may include flashlights, binoculars, and sophisticated electronic listening and thermal-detection devices.

Entrapment Act of police officers or government agents inducing a person to commit a crime for the purpose of arresting and prosecuting the person; a defense to conviction. See *encouragement.*

Equality See *egalitarianism.*

Equal Protection Clause Section 1 of the Fourteenth Amendment guarantees that "No state shall . . . deny to any person within its jurisdiction the equal protection of the laws." This right can be enforced by federal courts and by congressional legislation.

Equity See *chancery.*

Exclusionary rule A legal rule that illegally obtained evidence may not be used in legal proceedings; may be created by common law (e.g., as to coerced confessions), constitutional adjudication (e.g., the Fourth Amendment exclusionary rule established in *Weeks v. United States,* 1914), or by statute (e.g., the exclusionary rule for illegal electronic eavesdropping).

Exculpatory statement A statement that tends to justify, excuse, or clear the defendant from alleged fault or guilt.

Exigency exception Generally, an emergency requiring immediate action; pressing; urgent. In Fourth Amendment law, an exigency is an emergency that gives rise to an exception to the warrant requirement.

Ex parte On one side only. A judicial hearing is *ex parte* when it occurs at the request of one party without the other party being present.

Expectation of privacy The basis for determining the existence of Fourth Amendment rights under *Katz v. United States* (1967).

Expert witness A witness who, by reason of specialized education or experience, possesses superior knowledge regarding a subject about which persons having no particular training are incapable of forming an accurate opinion; a witness who is qualified as an expert is allowed to assist the jury in understanding complicated or technical subjects and may be allowed to answer hypothetical questions.

Ex post facto law A criminal law passed after the occurrence of an act that retrospectively changes the legal consequences by making an innocent act criminal, by increasing the penalty for an act, or by changing rules of evidence that make it easier to obtain a conviction; United States Constitution, Art. I, §§9 and 10 prohibits the federal and state governments from creating such laws.

Extraterritorial Beyond the physical and juridical boundaries of a particular state or nation; laws may have extraterritorial effect.

Eyewitness One who saw the act, fact, or transaction to which one testifies. It may be distinguished from an ear-witness (*auritus*); but, for purposes of the law of identification, similar rules apply.

Facial attack A legal challenge to the constitutionality of a statute is either (1) a facial attack, which means that the statute is challenged "on its face" or in every way in which it may be applied, or (2) "as applied," a narrower attack that is unconstitutional only if applied in a certain way.

Facilitating function Criminal-procedure law has two broad functions: to facilitate prosecution and, simultaneously, to protect the civil rights of suspects and defendants.

Fair cross-section See *representative cross-section.*

False arrest An arrest that is not based upon probable cause; evidence seized as the result of a false arrest is inadmissible. A false arrest is a basis for a civil action against a peace officer who made the arrest.

Federalism The division and relationship of power between the state and federal governments.

Federalists Those favoring the ratification of the Constitution in 1788. This group emerged as the political party of Presidents George Washington and John Adams; those favoring a strong federal government; Chief Justice John Marshall was a prominent Federalist.

Field interrogation Police practice of ordering persons to briefly stop and answer questions in regard to suspicious behavior.

Fixed checkpoint In border search law, a search of automobiles at a fixed checkpoint on a road within one hundred miles from the U.S. border for illegal aliens; an investigative stop of a car slowed at such a point must be based on reasonable suspicion.

"Fleeing felon" rule A common law rule that allows a police officer to shoot to kill any fleeing felon, whether or not the felon had used deadly force. The rule was brought under the Fourth Amendment by *Tennessee v. Garner* (1985)—an officer may now lawfully shoot at a fleeing felon only if the suspect is reasonably believed to be armed and dangerous.

Formal charge rule The right to counsel at a lineup or showup attaches only after the defendant has been formally charged with a crime. In these procedures the Supreme Court has not applied the *critical stage* rule.

Formal charges A suspect is informally charged with an offense by a police officer's report or arrest warrant or other initial charging document issued by the magistrate after an initial appearance; formal charges are the charges upon which the state intends to prosecute the defendant and typically are the prosecutor's information that has been found by a magistrate to establish probable cause in a bind-over proceeding, or an indictment that has been voted on by a grand jury. Formal charges can only be amended with the approval of a court.

Formal rights In the history of the incorporation doctrine, prior to 1961 the designation of rights located in the Bill of Rights as "formal" (as opposed to fundamental) meant that they were not incorporated into the Fourteenth Amendment Due Process Clause.

Framers Term used collectively to include the men involved in the drafting of the United States Constitution and Bill of Rights; narrower term than "founders," which refers to individuals who led the rebellion from England and the founding of the federal republic of the United States.

Frisk A colloquial term used to describe a police search of a person who is stopped; it consists of a "pat down" of the outer clothing to determine if the person stopped has a weapon.

Fruit-of-the-poisonous-tree doctrine A Fourth Amendment doctrine that states that evidence derived from illegally seized evidence cannot be used by the prosecution; it applies to confessions if an otherwise valid confession is obtained from a suspect who is illegally detained.

Fundamental fairness A meaning attached to due process, i.e., a procedure violates due process if the procedure is deemed by a court to be fundamentally unfair. Another way of stating the "due process approach," so that for a court to decide if a procedure is fundamentally unfair, it must examine the totality of the circumstances.

Fundamental rights test The test by which it is decided whether a right located in the Bill of Rights is to be incorporated into the Due Process Clause of the Fourteenth Amendment by a process of *selective incorporation* and made applicable to the states; a right that is "fundamental" must be incorporated, but one deemed "formal" is not.

General-reasonableness construction In Fourth Amendment jurisprudence, a conservative doctrine that emphasized the idea that the constitutionality of a search and seizure is to be decided by whether it is reasonable.

General warrant A search warrant without limit; a general warrant violates the particularity requirement of the Fourth Amendment. The term was used at the time of the Revolution by Americans to describe the writs of assistance issued by colonial governors.

Grand jury A jury summoned to hear charges against persons accused of crime to determine whether there is enough evidence for the persons to stand trial; the common law grand jury (i.e., the "large" jury) consists of twenty-three persons and decides whether to indict by a majority vote.

Habeas corpus, writ of A judicial writ requiring that a person claiming illegal detention be brought to court forthwith to determine the legality of detention.

Hearsay evidence A statement, other than one made by the declarant while testifying at the trial or hearing, offered in evidence to prove the truth of the matter asserted. In ordinary affairs, hearsay evidence may be reliable, but a hearsay statement cannot be subject to cross-examination. The general rule of evidence is that hearsay statements are not admissible, but there are numerous exceptions to the hearsay evidence rule.

Hierarchy of courts Courts may be ranked by their authority to declare precedent, with a Supreme Court establishing common law rules, which must be followed by all courts "below" it, and an intermediate appellate court having such authority over trial courts.

Hierarchy of law The relative authority of law derives from the body that creates it; thus constitutional law is superior to legislation, which may in turn abolish or modify court-made common law.

Hierarchy of rights The Burger Court's rulings in criminal procedure have tended to be more supportive of Fifth and Sixth Amendment rights in comparison to the Fourth Amendment, especially the Fourth Amendment exclusionary rule, which is treated as a right of lesser status.

Holding The legal principle to be drawn from the opinion or decision; in an appellate case the holding includes the rule and the facts on which the decision rests.

Hot pursuit A common law right of a police officer to follow a felon across jurisdictional lines or to enter a house or other area protected by a Fourth Amendment expectation of privacy to make an arrest if the officer is in hot pursuit, that is, closely following the felon.

Human rights A special class of rights held by a person simply by virtue of being human; moral rights grounded in the equal moral dignity of each person, that can and should be made legally binding in national, regional, or international law.

Hypothetical person test In entrapment law, an element of the "objective test"—where the inducement offered by the government agent is so great as to persuade persons other than those who are ready and willing to commit the crime.

Identification parade British terminology for a lineup.

Illegal arrest An arrest that is made by an officer who has no legal authority or jurisdiction to make such an arrest, e.g., where an officer arrests a person in a foreign state. Where a suspect is brought into the jurisdiction of a court on the basis of an illegal arrest, the court does not thereby lose jurisdiction to try the case.

Immunity In criminal law, this refers to a person being immune from prosecution for a crime as a result of a binding promise by the government, allowed by statute, to not prosecute in return for the person's testimony in another prosecution; it is granted to override the person's privilege against self incrimination. See *transactional immunity* and *use immunity*.

Impanel a jury A process whereby the clerk of court makes up a list of the jurors selected for a particular trial.

Impeach To impeach a witness is to challenge the truthfulness of the witness by presenting evidence that tends to contradict the testimony or to show that for some other reason the witness might have lied.

Impound To seize and take an item, such as an automobile, into lawful custody of a court or law enforcement agency. An impoundment is a prelude to an inventory search, and the rules of many police departments require an inventory search following an impoundment.

In camera Hearings held in the judge's chamber, away from the public and the jury.

Incompetent evidence Evidence that is relevant to prove an issue but is not allowed to be used in the trial because of other policy considerations; examples are hearsay or unconstitutionally seized evidence; generally, inadmissible evidence.

Incorporation by reference The method of making one document of any kind become a part of separate document by referring to the former in the latter.

Incorporation doctrine The constitutional doctrine by which provisions of the Bill of Rights become "incorporated" (in a rough analogy to the legal concept of *incorporation by reference*) into the Fourteenth Amendment and thus made applicable to the states.

Incorporation plus The incorporation doctrine plus the ability of courts to apply the due process approach where a specific right in the Bill of Rights does not apply.

Inculpatory statement A statement that tends to establish guilt or incriminate.

Independent source rule An exception to the "fruit-of-the-poisonous-tree doctrine." It comes into play when the evidence in question also was obtained in a lawful manner via an independent source.

Index crime Eight felonies counted by the FBI to construct a "crime index." They include murder or non-negligent manslaughter, rape, robbery, aggravated assault, burglary, automobile theft, larceny, and arson.

Indictment A formal, written criminal accusation voted on by a grand jury setting out the charges (crimes) for which the defendant must stand trial.

Indigent Needy; poor; an indigent defendant is a person without funds to hire a lawyer for the defense and is entitled to appointed counsel by operation of the Sixth and Fourteenth Amendments.

Inducement In entrapment law, the benefits offered to commit a crime that is posed by the undercover agent.

Inevitable discovery rule A Fourth Amendment doctrine that overlooks unconstitutional police acts so as not to exclude evidence if the evidence would have been discovered in any event.

Inferior courts Lower courts; for example, trial courts, which are "below" appellate courts in the judicial hierarchy.

Information A formal, written, criminal accusation drawn up by a prosecutor setting out the charges (crimes) for which the defendant must stand trial; this replaces the indictment in many states and often follows the bind-over decision.

In loco parentis The doctrine that a school teacher stands in the place of a parent and may exercise parental authority; the Supreme Court has ruled that this is *not* a basis for a search of a public school student under the Fourth Amendment.

Initial appearance The hearing before a magistrate that occurs typically within twenty-four hours after a defendant's arrest; the purposes of the hearing are to inform the defendant of the charges, take an initial plea, set bail, and determine whether a defendant has an attorney; known as the "arraignment on the [arrest] warrant" in some states.

Injunction A court order requiring that a party perform some act or refrain from some act; a remedy in an action in a court of equity or in a court with equitable powers.

***In personam* jurisdiction** The jurisdiction a court has over a person in its custody; a court does not lose *in personam* jurisdiction if a defendant was brought into the court's custody as the result of an illegal arrest.

In presence rule In the law of arrest, the general common law rule is that a police officer can arrest a person for a misdemeanor only if the crime was committed in the officer's presence; exceptions for traffic violations and domestic violence have been created by statute.

Inquisitorial trial system European system of adjudication based on Roman law in civil law countries. Distinguishing features include: cases are developed by civil service prosecutors operating under judicial instruction; defendants are under a general obligation to answer some questions in the preliminary stages but need not answer at trial; defendants' silence may be used against them; the judge plays an active role in the trial by questioning witnesses, there is no independent jury; and jurors may advise the professional judges.

Internal passport In some countries, residents must carry official personal identification at all times; under the Fourth Amendment there can be no general obligation to carry an internal passport or to provide identification without an arrest or stop.

Interrogation Generally, to interrogate is to question; in criminal procedure, it refers more specifically to the process of questions posed by the police to a suspect or a witness in an effort to solve a crime. Interrogation may also include the functional equivalent of questioning whereby actions by the police are designed to elicit incriminating statements from a suspect.

Inventory and return A sworn document prepared by law enforcement officers who have been issued and have executed a search warrant, indicating the execution and itemizing the items seized.

Inventory search A search made for the purpose of making an inventory, that is, a detailed list of articles of property.

Investigative stop Same as a *Terry* stop; forceful stopping of a person for field questioning when reasonable suspicion exists to believe the person is involved in criminal activity.

Invidious discrimination The kind of distinction based on race, gender, or other irrational factor that allows a court to determine that a distinction caused by law violates the rights of a person to the "equal protection of the laws" under the Fourteenth Amendment; not every legal distinction between persons is invidious.

Ipse dixit He himself said it; a bare assertion resting on the authority of the individual.

Irrelevant evidence Evidence that does not logically pertain to the issue to be decided.

Judicial craftsmanship The quality of a judge's *opinions*, based on the intensity of the judge's legal scholarship, the judge's understanding of issues, and the caliber of the judge's writing style.

Judicial federalism In constitutional criminal procedure, the interaction between federal and state constitutional rights; the Fourteenth Amendment establishes a "constitutional floor" of minimum standards of rights that cannot be violated by a state; above this "floor" a state may grant additional rights under its own constitution or statutes. See *adequate and independent state grounds.*

Judicial independence The right and the actual ability of a court to decide cases on the basis of the facts and its interpretation of law without interference from other branches of the government; a vital aspect of the rule of law. Judicial independence is made more certain by the appointment of judges for good behavior and by the provision of Article III that the compensation of federal judges shall not be diminished.

Judicial philosophy An aspect of *judicial statesmanship*—whether a judge favors judicial restraint or judicial activism.

Judicial policy An aspect of *judicial statesmanship*—what particular policy views a judge may hold on any issue. For example, in criminal procedure, some justices are identified by their voting patterns as being "pro-prosecution," others as "pro-defense," and others as "middle of the road."

Judicial restraint A philosophy of the judicial function that holds that judges should not make broad rulings that have legislative effect.

Judicial review The authority of a court to review a statute and declare it null and void if the statute is in conflict with a provision of the state or federal constitution.

Judicial statesmanship The ability of Supreme Court justices to write *opinions* that properly guide the nation.

Jurisdiction Legal power or authority.

Jurisprudence The philosophy of law; also used to indicate a body of rules in a subfield of law, e.g., "criminal jurisprudence."

Jury deliberation In deciding on a verdict, a jury is supposed to discuss the evidence and not simply take a vote.

Jury independence The right of a jury to determine the facts of a case independently without judicial interference; this right was held to be a part of the common law jury process in *Bushell's* case (1670).

Jury nullification The idea that a jury may disregard the legal instruction of the judge and render a verdict purely on the basis of conscience or feelings; although this happens, it is not usually authorized by legal doctrine.

Jury panel The group of prospective jurors called to the courthouse from which juries are chosen.

Jury trial The trial of a matter before a jury as opposed to a judge (or bench) trial; guaranteed by the United States Constitution Art. III, §2, and by the Sixth and Seventh Amendments.

Jury wheel A physical device or electronic system for the storage and random selection of the names or identifying numbers of prospective jurors.

Just Compensation Clause The Fifth Amendment states: "nor shall private property be taken for public use without just compensation." This provision was in effect incorporated as a due process right that federal courts applied against state takings (*Chicago, Burlington & Quincy Rr. Co. v. Chicago,* 1897) in an era when personal rights were not incorporated, thus creating a double standard.

Justice The term used for a judge of the Supreme Court; generally interchangeable with judge.

"Key man" method A method of selecting members of petit or grand juries whereby a judge picks a small number of jury commissioners known to him personally, and the commissioners in turn select persons known to them for the grand jury; this method, which dates back to the nineteenth century and tends to perpetuate established power relationships in county government while keeping minorities or new residents from jury service, is no longer used.

Knock and announce rule The common law rule that before an officer may open or break in the door to a premises to execute a search warrant, the officer must announce the presence of police and demand entry; declared to be a constitutional rule in *Wilson v. Arkansas* (1995). See *no-knock* warrant.

Law A body of written rules issued by legitimate sources of order in a state (e.g., the legislature, appellate courts) and designed to guide and control the actions of citizens. Law also derives from the text of a written constitution and, in common law jurisdictions, from the *opinions* of appellate judges.

Law of the land A phrase in the Magna Carta, indicating that no peer could be punished except by "the law of the land"; believed to express the concept of due process.

Least intrusive means When a constitutional liberty collides with a state action required to maintain order, courts at times require that the state's intrusion be done in a manner that intrudes the least on individual privacy. Such a rule has not been applied to arrest or stop under the Fourth Amendment.

Legal doctrine The common law process of case interpretation results in the development of rules that arise from the decisions of numerous similar, but not identical, cases. The rules in a related body of law are formed into legal doctrines. Over time, the rationales for such doctrines often change or erode. Thus, many legal doctrines of the common law often have a life cycle of birth, a period of growth and utility, change, and decline.

Legal fiction A legal doctrine or assumption that may not be true but that is adopted in order to achieve a beneficial end. The idea that entrapment is a defense to a crime that is inferred by the legislature is a legal fiction adopted by judges who first announced the doctrine.

Legal reasoning The mental process of ratiocination by a judge, by which the rules of an earlier case are discerned and applied to a case at hand; legal reasoning is not a mechanical process and is considered a branch of jurisprudence or legal philosophy. See *precedent.*

Legislative history The background and events, including committee reports, hearings, and floor debates, leading up to the enactment of a law (including constitutional provisions). Such history is important to courts when they are required to determine the legislative intent of a particular statute.

Liberty A political theory that undergirds criminal procedure; it connotes that the purpose of government is to allow individuals maximum freedom to pursue their individual and collective goals within the rule of law.

Lineup A police identification procedure by which the suspect in a crime is exhibited before the victim or witness to determine if he committed the offense. In a lineup, the suspect is lined up with other individuals for purposes of identification.

Magistrate The term can apply to (1) an inferior (i.e., lower) judicial officer, (2) any judge, or (3) any public civil officer with executive or judicial authority.

Magna Carta (1215) A charter of liberties sworn by King John of England to his barons; its *law of the land* clause is believed to be the forerunner of due process.

Mandamus, writ of A judicial writ ordering a government officer to perform some "ministerial act," that is, an act required by law over which the officer has no discretion to not carry out.

Master jury list Also called a jury wheel; the master list compiled by a county or district jury commission from the most widely available lists of eligible voters, including voting registration lists, driver's license and state identification lists, and city directories. Jury venires are drawn from the master jury list.

Material witness A person who can give testimony that no one else, or very few persons, can give; a material witness may be held by the state against his or her will to ensure testimony.

Media ride-along A practice of some police departments to invite news reporters and/or photo or video journalists to accompany the police during the execution of warrants; held to violate the Fourth Amendment rights of householders in *Wilson v. Layne* (1999).

Merchant's privilege   A statutory right enacted in most states that allows security personnel to conduct brief investigatory detentions of suspected shoppers that would be tortious or criminal if carried out by ordinary citizens.

Missouri Compromise   A compromise measure adopted by Congress in 1820 declaring that slavery could not be introduced into new states north of the southern boundary of Missouri. The compromise paired the admission of new free and slave states into the union as a way of maintaining parity between the North and the South. It was designed to preserve the Union and prevent sectional conflicts from erupting into disunion or civil war. An 1850 extension was declared unconstitutional in *Scott v. Sandford* (1857), hastening the Civil War.

Mistaken arrest   An arrest that is based on probable cause but results in the arrest of a person who is not, in fact, the suspect. A police officer who makes such an arrest is protected against civil liability; a private person who makes a mistaken citizen's arrest, is subject to a tort action for false imprisonment. A statutory exception exists, see *merchant's privilege.*

Mixed question of law and fact   A question depending for solution on questions of both law and fact, but is really a question of either law or fact to be decided by either judge or jury.

Motion   An application made to a court to obtain an order requiring some act to be done in the favor of the applicant.

Multiple-district prosecution   A practice of federal prosecutors whereby an enterprise is simultaneously prosecuted in several districts in which the enterprise does business; generally viewed as an unfair prosecution tactic.

Multiple representation   A situation where one attorney represents two or more defendants in the same matter; the defendants may be tried in the same or in different (severed) trials. See *conflict of interest.*

Neutral and detached magistrate   Phrase from *Johnson v. United States* (1948) explaining rationale for Fourth Amendment search warrant—that a judicial officer is less partisan than a police officer in deciding whether probable cause exists on the basis of the institutional role and traditions of the judicial officer.

No-knock warrant   A warrant that explicitly authorizes police to enter a premises without knocking and announcing their presence, based on probable cause to believe that the occupants are likely to immediately destroy contraband or pose a threat of deadly violence to police executing the warrant. See *knock and announce rule.*

Nonincorporation era   A period designated in this text as falling between the ratification of the Bill of Rights in 1791 to the ratification of the Civil War amendments in 1870, when it was clear doctrine that the Bill of Rights was not intended to be applied to the states; thereafter, the issue became contested.

Notice   The due process requirement that a defendant be informed in writing of the precise crimes charged and the facts on which those charges are based; the defendant can be tried only on those charges.

Novel disseisin   A medieval English writ that set up an efficient procedure to determine the rightful possession of land taken by force; it utilized a precursor to the modern jury to determine facts.

Objective test   In entrapment law, the view held by a minority of Supreme Court justices and a minority of the states, that entrapment should be based on whether the conduct of the police fell to such a level as would induce a hypothetical person to engage in the criminal behavior.

Open fields   Private land not protected against police trespass under the Fourth Amendment. See *curtilage.*

Opinion   An appellate court's opinion is the essay written by the majority, expounding the law that applies to the case, and giving the reasons for its decision. A signed majority opinion is primarily written by the named judge but the judges in the majority may have suggested that certain points be included or excluded. Individual judges may write concurring or dissenting opinions. See *Per curiam opinion.*

Order   When contrasted to liberty, it implies the lawful limits placed on the freedom of individuals necessary to maintain the "domestic tranquillity" that is a necessary function of government; the contrast cannot be absolute because public order is necessary for individuals and groups to enjoy their liberty.

Ordered liberty   Resonant phrase found in *Palko v. Connecticut* (1938) and other cases, that encapsulates the tension between two fundamental aspects of American governance.

Originalism   A theory of constitutional interpretation that holds that judges must apply the Constitution in accordance with the true intent of the framers. The theory is based on the principle of separation of powers and the idea that judges should not "make" law. Opponents argue that the true intent of the framers cannot be known with certainty in regard to broad constitutional rights (e.g., due process) and that changing conditions require justices to interpret provisions to meet contemporary needs.

Outrageous conduct test   In entrapment law, same as *due process defense.*

Overrule   When an appellate court finds that one of its prior decisions was incorrect or unsound, it may overrule the prior case and replace it with a different ruling; thus, strictly speaking, an appellate court is not bound by its own precedent. See *reverse.*

Parallel right   Prior to the incorporation of the Bill of Rights, the Supreme Court established certain rights under the Due Process Clause that were parallel to rights found in the Bill of Rights, but not applied with the same level of certainty. An example is the Sixth Amendment rule stating that counsel was automatically required in every federal felony trial, unless waived, whereas due process held states to provide counsel for indigents only if special circumstances existed.

Parliamentary supremacy   The English system in which the statute (a declaration of the legislature) is superior to any written or unwritten constitutional provision or custom.

Particularity requirement   The requirement, drawn from the Fourth Amendment, that search warrants "particularly describe[e] the place to be searched, and the persons or things to be seized." The opposite are *general warrants* that the Fourth Amendment was designed to abolish.

Pattern and practice suit   A review of a local police department by the U.S. Justice Department for discriminatory patterns and practices; under the law passed in 1994, a special master can be appointed to oversee modifications in the training and supervision provided by the local police department.

Peer   In England, a member of the nobility; originally, "jury of peers" meant that non-nobles could not sit on juries to judge the guilt of peers. In modern usage, the term refers to equals. A "jury of peers" in America is composed of fellow citizens, without regard to class, gender, race/ethnicity, economic status, or other irrelevant attribute.

Pen register   A device that electronically registers the telephone numbers from or to which a particular telephone makes calls, without recording the contents of the conversations.

Per curiam opinion   An unsigned *opinion* written by the entire appellate court.

Peremptory challenge   In the voir dire, each side has a limited number of challenges that may be used to excuse a prospective juror even though the person has not exhibited any clear bias; recently, the Supreme Court has limited the ability of parties to exercise peremptory challenges in ways that are based primarily on race or gender. See *voir dire.*

Persuasive authority   When an appellate court follows the reasoning of another court, even though the other court has no power to set binding precedent for the appellate court, the *opinion* followed is called "persuasive authority."

Pervasively regulated industry   In the law of administrative searches, an administrative warrant is *not* required to search the place of a "pervasively regulated" industry.

Petit jury   The common law, twelve-person trial jury that has the authority to determine the facts and render a verdict in criminal trials; *"petit"* is the French word for "small" and refers to the size of the jury in contrast to the twenty-three-person grand jury.

Petty crime   The designation of a crime as "petty" carries the constitutional consequence that it may be tried without a jury.

"Plain feel" rule   The concept that evidence seized in plain view includes evidence lawfully felt by police and that is immediately apparent as contraband.

Plain statement   The United States Supreme Court will not disturb a state court criminal procedure ruling if the state *opinion* includes a plain statement that the ruling is based on adequate and independent state grounds.

Plain view doctrine   Contraband that is located in a public place or in a private place where an officer has a right to be present may be seized "in plain view" without a search warrant.

Plurality opinion   A decision of the Supreme Court (or any appellate court) that is based on a vote of less than a majority; this occurs when there are concurring opinions but fewer than five justices (if nine justices participate) agree on the reason for a rule. Plurality opinions represent the law but do not have the same authority as majority opinions and are more easily subject to being overruled.

Police officer expertise   In *Terry v. Ohio* (1968) the traditional rule that a Fourth Amendment seizure of a person may be based only on probable cause was eased to allow a temporary stop on the basis of reasonable suspicion in part on the fact that the on-the-street situation was evaluated by a police officer applying his or her special expertise. This element of *Terry* was dropped when the Court decided that reasonable suspicion could be based on the hearsay statement of an informant.

Police power   A concept of constitutional law that state governments have plenary or general authority to pass laws for the health, safety, morals, general welfare, and good ordering of the people.

Precedent   In law, an adjudged case or decision of a court that furnishes authority for an identical or similar case that arises afterward on a similar question of law. See *legal reasoning*.

Predisposition   In entrapment law, a defendant's state of mind that is inclined toward the commission of the crime in question prior to the police "encouragement" activity.

Prejudice   This commonly means bias. In appellate procedure, it means that an error that occurred at the trial or pretrial stage was the likely cause of the guilty verdict; in some instances, a conviction will not be overturned unless the appellate court finds prejudice in this sense.

Prejudice the case   The second prong of the rule stating that the ineffective assistance of counsel in a criminal trial violates the Sixth Amendment rights of the defendant. Prejudice in this sense is made out by a reasonable probability that, absent the errors, the factfinder would have had a reasonable doubt respecting guilt.

Preliminary examination or hearing   A hearing before a magistrate to determine whether the prosecution can present sufficient evidence to establish probable cause to show that the defendant committed a crime; if so, the judge binds the defendant over for trial.

Presentment   Instead of an indictment, a formal accusation based on the personal knowledge of the grand jurors themselves; this is rare or nonexistent today. An accusation initiated by the grand jury; an instruction to the prosecutor to prepare an indictment.

Presumption of innocence   A feature of the common law trial that is guaranteed by the Due Process Clause; it requires that the burden of proof of guilt of every element of a crime is placed on the prosecution and that the burden is proof beyond a reasonable doubt.

Pretext search   *Whren v. United States* (1996) held that a search of an automobile made by an officer who stopped the car on the objectively correct basis of a traffic violation is valid even if the traffic stop was made for the real purpose of searching the automobile for drugs.

Preventive detention   Confinement of a defendant before trial; the formal denial of bail on the grounds that the defendant is likely to commit a crime while awaiting trial.

Prima facie case   Sufficient evidence to require a criminal defendant to proceed with his case; evidence to sustain an indictment; if uncontradicted, evidence sufficient to establish a guilty verdict.

Private law   Involves the rights and disputes of private individuals, groups, and corporations; subject matter areas include contracts, property, torts (the law of injuries), commercial law, and civil procedure; in contrast to public law.

Privilege   In law, a particular benefit or a right or immunity against or beyond the course of law. Thus, the privilege against self-incrimination allows a person to refuse to testify despite the general legal obligation that a person has to testify when summoned to a court.

Privileges or Immunities Clause   Clause in Section 1 of the Fourteenth Amendment, stating that "No state shall make or enforce any law which shall abridge the privileges or immunities of citizens of the United States. . . ." This clause was thought to be the basis of the idea of "total incorporation." The clause was interpreted in such a manner as to render it a virtual nullity by the *Slaughter-house Cases* (1873).

Probable cause   A standard to determine whether sufficient evidence exists that allows a prudent person to conclude that other facts exist; the standard for the validity of an arrest, a lawful search, and the holding of a person for trial.

Pro bono publico   For the good of the public; attorneys take a certain number of cases without fee to represent indigents *pro bono*.

Procedural law   Prescribes the methods of enforcing rights that are breached and includes rules of jurisdiction and the serving of legal process (e.g., a summons) and rules that guide the conduct of a trial.

Pro forma   As a matter of form; a decision made *pro forma* is made not because it is right but merely to facilitate further proceedings.

Property theory   In Fourth Amendment jurisprudence, the concept that Fourth Amendment rights are based on an individual's legal claims over private property; this theory has been superseded by the *expectation of privacy* concept.

Pro se defense   Self-representation, Latin meaning, "for himself."

Prosecutor's information   Formal document charging a defendant with crimes on which the defendant must stand trial; replaces the grand jury indictment in states that allow informations; used in jurisdictions with grand juries in cases in which the defendant waives the grand jury.

Protective sweep   "A quick and limited search of a premises, incident to an arrest and conducted to protect the safety of police officers or others. It is narrowly confined to a cursory visual inspection of those places in which a person might be hiding" *Maryland v. Buie* (1990).

Public defender   A full time, paid position as a defense attorney for indigent defendants. Caseloads of public defenders tend to be high.

Public law   Law that concerns the powers of governmental bodies and involves disputes between governmental departments or between private persons and government. Public law includes such subjects as constitutional law, administrative law, tax law, substantive criminal law, and criminal procedure.

Quash   To annul, make void; e.g., to quash an indictment.

Radical Republicans   The ascendant wing of the Republican Party which, in the aftermath of the Civil War, pushed for legislation that supported the full civil rights of African Americans and imposed punitive measures on the South.

Radio bulletin   Information transmitted by radio from one police department to others notifying them that a specified individual is wanted for a crime; evidence seized in a search incident to an arrest made on the basis of such a report is admissible even if there was no probable cause for the initial report; it has the effect of a mistaken arrest.

Real evidence   Physical evidence.

Reasonable doubt   The standard of evidence sufficiency for a verdict of guilt in a criminal case; a doubt that would cause a prudent person to hesitate before acting in a matter of personal importance; not a fanciful doubt.

Reasonable force   Police may use reasonable force to make an arrest, as determined by all the facts and circumstances.

Reasonableness clause   The first part of the Fourth Amendment that prohibits "unreasonable searches and seizures." It is the basis of the *general-reasonableness construction*.

Reconstruction amendments   See *Civil War amendments*.

Recoupment   The process by which the state or unit of local government later recovers the cost of providing assistance of counsel to a formerly indigent defendant.

Rehnquist Court   The Supreme Court during the period that William Rehnquist has been Chief Justice of the United States, from 1986 to the present. A conservative period in criminal procedure.

Release on recognizance   Pretrial release of a defendant without the posting of a bail bond or other security but only on the promise of the defendant to return to court for trial or further proceedings.

Remand   An action of an appellate court sending all or part of a case back to the lower court without overturning the lower court's ruling but with instructions for further proceedings that may range from conducting a new trial to entering a proper judgment.

Remedial law   Law that determines the actual benefits or remedies that a successful party to a lawsuit will receive. In criminal law the "remedy" is the punishment meted out. In constitutional criminal procedure, the exclusion of evidence after a court has decided that evidence has been seized in violation of a person's constitutional protections is deemed a "remedy."

Reparation Repayment; remedy designed to restore the injured party to his or her position before the injury occurred.

Representative cross-section In jury selection, the larger groups of prospective jurors on the jury master list or jury wheel, or the venire must be selected in a manner to be most likely to statistically represent the larger community under federal law and constitutional standards of equal protection. The particular jury panel (or venire) from which the petit jury is selected, and the jury itself, need not be a representative sample. See *fair cross-section*.

Republicanism Political theory that government is instituted for benefit of all the people; formal classes, nobility, or monarchy inconsistent with republicanism. As a result, for example, jury of peers means a jury of citizens.

Retained counsel A lawyer hired by and paid for by the defendant.

Reverse An appellate court is said to reverse the decision of a lower court when it disagrees with the decision and orders the lower court to change it to be in conformity with the appellate court ruling. See *overrule*.

Roadblock An automobile that crashes into a police roadblock effectively arrests the driver; injuries that result from such a crash may be the basis of police liability for effecting the arrest with excessive force if the placement of the roadblock was unreasonable.

Roving patrol Refers to a stop of a vehicle being driven on the highway by border patrol agents within one hundred air miles of the U.S. border; distinguished from a fixed checkpoint stop.

Rule application A major function of trial courts—to decide cases in accord with the law; contrasted with *rule making*.

Rule of Law The political and legal principle that the government must act in accordance with established law and that governmental officers must not exceed their authority; also known as the "principle of legality."

Rule making A process of interpretation of prior cases, statutes or constitutional provisions by appellate courts by which rules of common law are developed. See *legal reasoning* and *precedent*.

Scope of search incident to arrest Police may search the area within an arrested person's immediate control to ensure officer safety and to secure evidence from destruction; the scope may include an area to which the arrested person may reach, but does not authorize the search of an entire premises.

Screening device The preliminary hearing and grand jury are pretrial screening devices. They screen out cases where probable cause cannot be established in order to prevent hasty or oppressive prosecutions.

Search incident to arrest A search of an individual and the arrested person's immediate surroundings that takes place immediately upon or after the arrest; the search is a part of the arrest process. The search is for weapons (to protect the arresting officer and others) and for incriminating evidence.

Secret informant A person who supplies evidence of probable cause to obtain a search warrant but whose identity is not divulged to the magistrate in order to maintain the security of an investigation; may be an undercover police agent or a paid "snitch."

Section 1983 suit A civil lawsuit in federal court against a state officer or municipality who has violated the federal or constitutional rights of an individual; established under 42 U.S.C. §1983. Enacted in 1871 as a civil rights act designed to curb the terrorism of the Ku Klux Klan. Also called a "constitutional tort" suit.

Sectional conflict Political, economic, or social friction between different sections of the nation; specifically, the conflict between the North and the South before the Civil War.

Seditious libel A writing that has the intent of inciting the people to overthrow the government by force. It was long a political crime in Great Britain.

Seizure of the person An arrest or stop constitutes a seizure under the Fourth Amendment.

Selective incorporation The concept that individual provisions of the Bill of Rights may become incorporated into the Fourteenth Amendment due process doctrine if the Supreme Court finds that such provisions are fundamental to our system of ordered liberty. See *total incorporation*.

Selective prosecution Occurs when a defendant is singled out for charging on impermissible grounds, such as race, religion, political beliefs, or for exercising constitutional rights.

Self-incrimination rule The constitutional doctrine that a criminal defendant is privileged to remain silent in the face of an accusation, whether made in court or before; the right extends to all persons questioned in official hearings where what they say may "incriminate" them. The right is based on the constitutional provision in the Fifth Amendment that "No person . . . shall be compelled in any criminal case to be a witness against himself. . . ." See *compulsion*.

Self-representation A situation where a defendant waives the right to appointed counsel and conducts his or her own defense.

Separation of powers A political and constitutional doctrine that states that the essential functions of one branch of government are not to be exercised by another.

Sequester a jury Require a jury to be removed from the community during the period of a trial so as to avoid the contaminating influences of news accounts or discussions with friends, relatives, and strangers about a crime; it was required in the early common law and is now infrequent.

"Shocks the conscience" test Formula for the due process test to determine when police action is so egregious during arrest and/or search activity to violate the Due Process Clause; it excludes the notions of the application of the Fourth Amendment and its exclusionary rule.

Showup One-to-one confrontation between the suspect and a witness to a crime. It is a form of pretrial identification procedure in which the suspect is confronted by or exposed to the victim or witness to a crime.

Silver platter doctrine Rules established by the United States Supreme Court under its supervisory power prior to *Mapp v. Ohio* (1961) that forbade federal officers from supplying state officers with illegally seized evidence, and then testifying as to the evidence in state court, or from receiving illegally seized evidence from state officers.

Sobriety checklane A roadblock set up by police for the purpose of determining whether drivers are under the influence of intoxicants is not a stop for a criminal investigation, and, therefore, such a temporary detention without individualized suspicion does not violate the Fourth Amendment.

Source city An element of the drug courier profile is that the place from which the stopped person has traveled from is a "source city" for drugs.

Source of law Law is made by a specific human institution: courts develop rules of common law; legislatures and governors fashion legislation; and constitutions are made by "the people" in special constitutional conventions or by special rules for amending constitutions.

Sovereign immunity Legal doctrine that prevents a party from suing a government unless the government by law allows itself to be sued.

Special circumstances rule Rule of *Powell v. Alabama* (1932) that due process requires a state to pay for a lawyer for an indigent defendant only if special circumstances exist.

"Special needs" doctrine A doctrine developed by Supreme Court constitutional adjudication, which allows government agents to search without a warrant, and possibly without individualized suspicion where searches are conducted for "special needs beyond the normal need for law enforcement," such as the search of the bags of public school students suspected of carrying items banned under school rules.

Standby counsel Counsel appointed at the discretion of the trial judge to advise a *pro se* defendant and to ensure that the defendant's rights are not undermined.

Standing A plaintiff has standing to sue in a court when there is an actual case or controversy between the plaintiff and a defendant that a court may hear and decide; the party must have a real stake in the outcome of the case.

Stare decisis Doctrine of precedent.

Status quo ante The existing state of things before a given time.

Stop The temporary restraint of a person's mobility by a police officer where the officer has reasonable suspicion to believe that the person stopped has just committed, is committing, or is about to commit a crime; practice declared constitutional in *Terry v. Ohio* (1968).

Stop and frisk The colloquial term for a *Terry* stop. Also called an *investigative stop*.

Strip search See *body cavity search*.

Subjective test or theory The majority rule of entrapment law. The theory that entrapment exists when police activity plants the idea of the crime in a person who is otherwise not predisposed to commit it.

Subpoena A command of a court to a witness to appear at a certain time and place to give testimony; a grand jury also has subpoena power. If the subpoena is not obeyed, the person refusing to appear may be held in contempt of court and fined or jailed until she agrees to cooperate with the legal process. The word derives from the Latin, meaning under (*sub*) the penalty (*poena*) of law.

Subpoena *ad testificandum* A subpoena to testify.

Subpoena *duces tecum* A subpoena to produce documents, books, papers, and other matters for inspection in a case.

Sub rosa Confidential, secret.

Substantive due process The concept that the Due Process Clause includes substantive rights that limit the power of government to legislate. Applied to property rights by the Supreme Court before the New Deal. The right to privacy that supports the abortion rights case, *Roe v. Wade* (1973), is a substantive due process concept. Contrast to procedural due process.

Substantive law Establishes, defines, and governs rights, powers, obligations, and freedoms. Rules of substantive law, for example, establish contractual obligations, property rights, or the right to recovery for personal injuries (torts). Substantive criminal law defines crimes such as homicide and theft and defenses such as insanity.

Suggestibility A term for the human process by which the subtle reactions of one person can influence the thinking of another; in *U.S. v. Wade* (1967) it was the legal basis for the Supreme Court to determine that state action existed as the basis for its holding.

Sui generis Of its own kind or class, i.e., unique, the only one of its kind.

Sumptuary law A law designed to regulate habits primarily on moral or religious grounds but justified for the health or welfare of the community; *sumptuary crimes* is synonymous with "vice" or "victimless crimes."

Supervisory authority The power of higher courts to require lower courts to act within their jurisdiction; the power is sometimes used by the United States Supreme Court as a way of enforcing appropriate standards on federal law enforcement agencies.

Supremacy Clause Article VI, Paragraph 2, of the United States Constitution, which declares that the Constitution, laws, and treaties of the federal government are the "Supreme Law of the Land"; that is, they supersede state laws when there is a conflict between state and federal law.

Telephonic warrant A search warrant allowed by the Federal Rules of Criminal Procedure and the laws of some states, that allows a magistrate to receive an affidavit from an officer by telephonic means.

Terry **stop** See *stop* and *stop and frisk.*

Testimonial evidence Evidence elicited from a witness to prove a fact, as opposed to documentary evidence or real (i.e., tangible) evidence.

Thermal imaging An advanced technology used by law enforcement to detect whether an unusually high amount of heat is emanating from a premises; may indicate the presence of the commercial growing of marijuana indoors.

Third degree The process of securing a confession of information from a suspect or prisoner by prolonged questioning, the use of threats, or actual violence.

Tort A private or civil wrong or injury, other than breach of contract, for which the court will provide a remedy in the form of an action for damages.

Total incorporation The concept that the privileges and immunities clause or the Due Process Clause of the Fourteenth Amendment intended to make the first eight amendments of the Bill of Rights applicable to the states upon ratification in 1868. See *selective incorporation.*

Totality of circumstances See *due process approach.*

Transactional immunity A blanket immunity against prosecution for the crimes about which the immunized witness is testifying; broader protection than use immunity.

Treason Clause Provisions of United States Constitution, Art. 3, Sec. 3 that limit the definition and punishment of treason against the United States; such limitation implies that republican government intended to be liberal and restrained and operate within the Rule of Law.

Trespass A common law tort; the wrongful interference with property rights.

Trial *de novo* Same as *de novo trial.*

True bill An indictment that has not yet been signed by the prosecuting attorney; when the grand jury votes to indict an accused person, it issues a "true bill"; when it votes against indicting an accused, it votes a "no bill."

Two-pronged test In Fourth Amendment law, a test to be applied by a magistrate on whether or not to issue a warrant where information has been supplied by a secret informant; the test requires that the affidavit indicate the basis of the informant's knowledge and a basis for accepting the informant's veracity. The test has been supplanted by a "totality of the circumstances" test.

Undercover agent A police officer who lies about his or her identity in order to pose as a victim or criminal for the purposes of law enforcement investigation.

Unenumerated Rights Clause The Ninth Amendment to the constitution: "The enumeration in the Constitution of certain rights shall not be construed to deny or disparage others retained by the people." The Supreme Court has yet to decide a case that declares an unenumerated right to be protected by the Court.

Unindicted coconspirator A person so named by a grand jury is one against whom there may be a *prima facie* case of guilt, but for some reason is not indicted.

Use immunity This form of immunity prohibits the witness's compelled testimony or its fruits from being used in any way to prosecute the witness; however, the witness may be prosecuted on the basis of independently obtained evidence; narrower protection than transactional immunity.

Universal Declaration of Human Rights A formal document promulgated by the United Nations in 1948, which attempts to codify all human rights; many provisions are borrowed from or parallel to provisions of the Bill of Rights—the first ten amendments to the United States Constitution.

Vagrancy statute A law making it a crime to loiter; older vagrancy statutes prior to *Papachristou v. City of Jacksonville* (1972) were quite vague and gave police discretion to arrest whom they would; modern vagrancy statutes are closely tailored to describe particular types of vagrancy such as house prowling or streetwalking prostitution.

Venire In jury practice, the list of jurors summoned to serve during a particular court term; from the Latin word meaning "to come"; to appear in court.

Venue The locality or place where a trial is to be held; the usual rule is that it is to be held in the locality (often the county) where the crime was committed; it may be changed if there is so much publicity in the locality as to make it impossible to select an unbiased jury.

Verdict The decision of a jury or judge as finder of fact in a criminal case: guilty or not guilty of the charges.

Vindictive prosecution Occurs when new and more serious charges are brought simply because a defendant has exercised statutory or constitutional rights.

Voir dire The process of jury selection involving the questioning of prospective jurors in order to determine biases; after questioning, the juror is either selected or dismissed for cause or for no reason under the peremptory challenge. See *challenges for cause* and *peremptory challenge.*

Voluntariness test A common law rule developed in the eighteenth and nineteenth centuries claiming that any confession obtained by violence, threats, or promises is involuntary and is excluded from evidence; the rule was adopted as a due process rule that the Supreme Court applied to state cases. The rule still exists as a backup to the *Miranda* rule.

Waiver The waiver of a Fifth or Sixth Amendment right must be an "intelligent relinquishment or abandonment of a known right or privilege." See *consent.*

Waiver of counsel A defendant can waive the right to the assistance of counsel if the decision is made with full knowledge of the right; a trial judge cannot require that a defendant be represented by counsel if the defendant can do a minimally competent job of defending himself or herself.

Waiver trial Same as a *bench trial;* the defendant waives the right to a jury and opts to be tried by a sole judge.

Warrant Generally, the command of an authority; in criminal procedure, it refers to a written order issued by a judge or magistrate. A search warrant authorizes police officers to search a premises where there is probable cause to believe contraband is hidden. An arrest warrant authorizes officers to arrest a named person where there is probable cause to believe that the person committed a crime.

Warrant clause   The second clause of the Fourth Amendment specifying rules concerning a search warrant.

Warrantless search   A search conducted by an officer without having obtained a search or arrest warrant.

Warrant-preference construction   A liberal construction of Fourth Amendment rights that holds that a search is presumptively unreasonable if it is not accompanied by a search warrant unless there exists a narrowly drawn exception to the warrant requirement.

Warren Court   The Supreme Court during the period that Earl Warren was Chief Justice of the United States (1953 to 1969); a liberal period in criminal procedure.

Whig party   Political party in the United States in the first half of the nineteenth century; it was absorbed by the Republican Party in the 1850s.

Wiretap (Tap)   A means of listening in on telephone conversations by electronically intercepting the conversations at some point outside the place where the telephone is located.

Writs of assistance   General search warrants issued by British colonial governors in America to enforce the hated Stamp Act; these writs and their enforcement became political issues that helped to ignite the American Revolution.

TABLE OF CASES

INDEX

Note: Pages in italic indicate a table is on that page.

A